Lifespan Development

Helen Bee

Lifespan Development

2nd edition

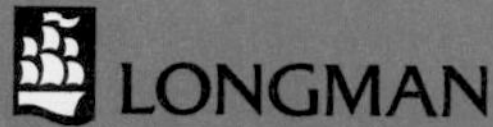

An imprint of Addison Wesley Longman, Inc.

New York • Reading, Massachusetts • Menlo Park, California • Harlow, England
Don Mills, Ontario • Sydney • Mexico City • Madrid • Amsterdam

Executive Editor: Rebecca Dudley
Developmental Editor: Rebecca Kohn
Supplements Editor: Cyndy Taylor
Marketing Manager: Jay O'Callaghan
Project Editor: Susan Goldfarb
Text and Cover Designer: Mary Archondes
Cover Photo: Keith Tishkan
Art Studio: Academy Artworks Inc.
Photo Researcher: Rosemary Hunter
Production Manager: Alexandra Odulak
Desktop Coordinator: Joanne Del Ben
Manufacturing Manager: Hilda Koparanian
Electronic Page Makeup: Americomp
Printer and Binder: RR Donnelley & Sons Company
Cover Printer: The Lehigh Press

Library of Congress Cataloging-in-Publication Data

Bee, Helen L., 1939–
Lifespan development / Helen Bee.—2nd ed.
p. cm.
Includes bibliographical references and indexes.
ISBN 0–321–01121-X (hardcover)
1. Developmental psychology. I. Title.
BF713.B435 1997
155—dc21 97–5362
CIP

ISBN 0-321-01121-X

Please visit our website at **http://longman.awl.com**

12345678910—DOW—00999897

To Carl—husband, friend, teacher

Brief Contents

Detailed Contents

To the Student

To my admittedly prejudiced view, the study of human development is one of the most fascinating of all subjects. Because humans are astonishingly complex, understanding comes slowly and with great effort. But the process of trying to achieve understanding is full of wonderful puzzles and questions, blind alleys, theoretical leaps forward. There is an added element of intrigue because it is *ourselves* we are studying. One of my great hopes in writing this book is that I can draw you into the excitement and fascination.

I have used every strategy I know to lure you. I have written the book in the first person so that it sounds like a live person talking to you. In the process, I have told you my opinions, shared some of my concerns, and said clearly when we do not know or cannot answer some question. I have also talked about how to apply the research and theory to your own life, both in extended discussions in "Real World" boxes and in the text itself.

I have also tried to entice you into thinking more deeply and critically about what you are reading by the use of critical thinking questions in the margin. Each time you encounter such a question, I hope you will pause and consider, mull over the dilemma posed, think about your feelings on the issue under discussion, or try to figure out some way of testing a specific hypothesis. Critical thinking is a skill that can be practiced and learned. It involves active processes, such as analyzing data for value and content, synthesizing information, resisting overgeneralization, being open-minded about divergent views, distinguishing fact from opinion, and applying knowledge to new situations. It also involves observing your own thinking process, or going back later and trying to figure out how you reached a particular conclusion. In your adult life, you will find the ability to think critically to be a vital skill. Here's a chance to practice it.

In the final analysis, I hope that the greatest attraction of this text is the science itself—the enormous amount of research by skillful people who are attempting to understand human development more and more fully. My wish is that your journey through this book will be intriguing and full of learning, just as I hope your everyday life over the years is fascinating and full of opportunities for growth.

Helen Bee

To the Instructor

Second editions are particularly nice books to write. The original tough decisions about how to organize the book, what major topics to include or exclude, and what tone to take have all been dealt with in the first edition. The second time around one can fine-tune and update. The challenge with subsequent editions is to avoid letting the book get longer and longer—a great temptation in the face of requests from reviewers to expand old topics or add new ones. In this edition I have worked very hard to keep this expansion to a minimum, although with the concurrence of the majority of reviewers, I have added a total of about 25 pages. Still, this remains one of the briefest lifespan texts available. Your students will not be shortchanged because of this relative brevity; I have covered all the major theories and topics. But I have also aimed to make the text manageable for students in a one-quarter course.

Goals

This second edition of *Lifespan Development* maintains the four basic goals of the first:

1. To find that difficult but essential balance between theory, research, and practical application;
2. To make the study of child development relevant not just for psychologists but also for students in the many other fields in which this information is needed, including nursing, medicine, social work, education, and home economics;
3. To keep all discussions as current as humanly possible, so that students can encounter the very latest thinking and the most recent research;
4. To write to the student in as direct a way as possible, so that the book is more like a conversation than a traditional text. Such a personal style need not clash either with theoretical clarity or with rigor of research, both of which I continue to work hard to achieve.

What's New in the Second Edition

In addition to updating everything, I have added material or increased the emphasis in several areas.

Increased Biological Emphasis. I have strengthened and expanded discussions of the biological aspects of development throughout, since this is a burgeoning and highly fruitful current area of research and theorizing. You will see this new emphasis in a considerably expanded discussion of behavior genetics (Chapter 1); in an expanded discussion of synaptogenesis, dendrite formation, and pruning and of the development of the nervous system in childhood and in late adulthood (Chapters 4 and 17); in the discussion of the latest behavior genetic research on temperament and personality (e.g., Chapters 6 and 14); and in a fully updated discussion of theories of aging (Chapter 17).

Strengthened Emphasis on Culture. In the first edition, one of my primary goals was to infuse the entire book with a multicultural or cross-cultural flavor—to search for those basic developmental processes that are the same across cultures, and to try to understand the ways in which culture and subculture shape an individual child's development. In this edition, I have tried to further this process, for example, by introducing the contrast between cultural *individualism* and cultural *collectivism*. I have presented this distinction in Chapter 1, in an expanded introduction to the concept of culture, and have then carried the concept throughout the text.

I have also struggled, as do all social scientists, with the problem of terminology and labels for various cultural and ethnic groups. Should one use *black* or *African-American*? Should one say *Hispanic* or *Latino*? And how should one label the dominant white cultural group: *white*, *Caucasian*, *Anglo*, or *Euro-American*? Some authors have resolved the dilemma by choosing one label from each set and then using those labels consistently. I have rejected that solution because there just seems to me to be still too much flux, too much variability of usage by members of these groups as well as by social scientists and other writers. I have opted instead for a less elegant solution that I think better reflects current usage: I have used all of the alternative terms at various times, as the occasion seemed to demand. For example, when I report results from the Census Bureau's wide-ranging research, I typically use the terms *white* and *black*, because these are the labels the Census Bureau uses; when I talk about studies of Hispanic children, I have generally used the word *Anglo* to refer to the contrasting white culture, because this is the term most often used by Hispanics themselves. And when I need to emphasize the European origin of the dominant white culture in the United States, I have used the term *Euro-American*, especially in conjunction with other hyphenated groups descriptors such as African-American and Asian-American. Sometimes, I confess, I have used the briefer terms simply because the repeated use of hyphenated labels becomes cumbersome.

New and Expanded Topics

Naturally, the entire book has been updated to reflect current research and theories. I have also added coverage of a number of topics and theories that did not appear in the first edition, and significantly expanded the coverage of many subjects, including

- Vygotsky's theory (Chapters 2 and 7)
- The importance of folic acid (Chapter 3)
- Surfactant therapy for low-birth-weight infants (Chapter 3)
- Dendritic development and pruning (Chapter 4)
- Discrimination of faces by sight at birth; intersensory integration and cross-modal transfer (Chapter 5)
- Links between models of temperament and personality (Chapter 6)
- Day care and its effects (Chapter 6)
- The importance of reading to the child (Chapter 7)
- Cross-cultural research on the appearance–reality distinction in preschoolers (Chapter 7)
- The effect of single-parent families and other family structures on child development (Chapter 8)
- Sports for children (Chapter 9)
- The child as witness (Chapter 9)
- Factors that affect the child's adjustment to school (Chapter 9) and level of achievement (Chapter 11)
- Learning disabilities (Chapter 9)
- Sibling relationships in middle childhood (Chapter 10)
- The impact of poverty, particularly inner-city poverty (Chapter 10)
- Teen pregnancy: who gets pregnant and who does not (Chapter 11)
- Risky behavior in adolescence, including drug and alcohol use and risky sexual practices (Chapter 11)

- Social structures in junior high schools and high schools: crowds and cliques, and their effects on adolescent behavior (Chapter 12)
- Delinquency, including delinquency among girls (Chapter 12)
- Alternative pathways through adolescence: deviant and nondeviant (Chapter 12)
- Sternberg's model of love (Chapter 14)
- Types of good and bad marriages, based on Gottman's work (Chapter 14)
- Hormone replacement therapy, links between weight and longevity, and exercise and health (Chapters 13 and 15)
- Sexual activity and impotence in midlife (Chapter 15)
- The midlife role of caring for an aging parent (Chapter 16)
- The Baltes model of "selective optimization with compensation" (Chapter 16)
- The genetics of Alzheimer's disease and depression in late adulthood (Chapter 17)
- Balance, dexterity, and stamina in old age (Chapter 17)
- Cross-linking and free radicals as explanations of aging (Chapter 17)
- Cross-cultural comparison of pension systems in the United States and Germany (Chapter 18)
- Disengagement theory and activity theory contrasted (Chapter 18)
- Euthanasia and physician-assisted suicide (Chapter 19)

Special Features

The book has several special features, designed to further my basic goals.

1. **Critical Thinking questions,** which appear in the margins of every chapter, are designed to encourage the students to ponder, analyze, and think more creatively. Sometimes these questions ask students to pause and consider a particular point before going on, or to consider how the material may apply to their own lives. In other cases, they ask students to think about how one could design a piece of research to answer a particular question. Sometimes they ask theoretical questions; sometimes they ask students to analyze their own point of view or feelings on the subject at issue. These questions may be useful for provoking class discussion; it is also my hope that they will make the reading process more active and thus make learning deeper. They may also help students to gain greater skill in the important process of critical thinking—learning how to think about and evaluate their own feelings, thoughts, and behavior so as to clarify and improve them.

2. A second special feature are the **Interludes** that cap each section. Many chronological texts are mere catalogues of behavior changes at each age, without a focus on the key underlying processes. The Interludes are designed to fill that gap by providing a brief review and analysis of the age period covered in that section. They may also provide a good study tool for the students as they review the material in the book and in the course.

3. Each chapter also contains a number of **boxes**—a common feature of current texts—that allow excursions into interesting side channels or practical applications. In this book there are four types of boxes:

- **Cultures and Contexts,** which focus on two aspects of cross-cultural or cross-ethnic group research: evidence showing that basic developmental processes are the *same* in children or adults of every culture, and research cataloging the variations in life experience or developmental patterns as a function of culture or subcultural differences. An example of the first type is a box in Chapter 7 on common patterns of early language development around the world; an example of the second type is a box in Chapter 14 on adult kin relationships in African-American and Hispanic-American families.

- **Research Reports,** which provide more detailed descriptions of individual research projects or highly specific research areas, such as Anne Streissguth's studies of fetal alcohol exposure (Chapter 3), studies of ethnic differences in styles of parenting (Chapter 8), or alternative explanations of the greater longevity of women compared with that of men (Chapter 15).
- **The Real World,** which explore some practical application of research or theory, such as how much weight a woman should gain in pregnancy (Chapter 3), how to choose a toy for a child (Chapter 7), the effects of cohabitation on subsequent marital success (Chapter 14), or the pros and cons of hormone replacement therapy after menopause (Chapter 15).
- **Across Development,** which touch on links between child and adult development. For example, in the chapter on early attachment (Chapter 6), there is a box discussing the connections between the adult's internal model of attachment and the security of the infant's attachment. And in the chapter on peer relationships among school-age children (Chapter 10), there is a box on the links between early unpopularity or aggressiveness with peers and later juvenile delinquency or adult deviance. Boxes of this type are not as common as the others, since we lack good long-term longitudinal information in many cases. But I thought it important to remind the students, whenever possible, that there is continuity as well as change operating across the life span.

4. **Other Pedagogical Aids** Other useful pedagogical aids include

- *Chapter Summaries*, which highlight the key points and provide the students with a focus for their reviews
- *Key Terms*, boldfaced in the text, and defined in a glossary
- *Suggested Readings* for each chapter, annotated, to direct students to the next level of scientific discussion or practical application

Projects

Those of you who have used any of my other texts on child development or lifespan development may know that I used to include student projects in the text itself. Each project laid out a plan for the student to observe a child or adult, to collect some data, or to investigate programs available for children or adults in their community. In recent editions of all my books I have changed that strategy and put the projects in the Instructor's Manual. The main purpose of the change is to give instructors more control over the process of obtaining informed consent for such endeavors. The Instructor's Manual includes three types of projects:

- Twenty *Research Projects*, each of which involves students' observing or testing one or more individual subjects of some age, for instance, listening to the language of a 2-year-old or asking adults of various ages about their personal social networks.
- Six *At-Home Projects*, each of which involves some analysis that can be done at home without having to locate individual subjects or obtain any informed consent. Examples include analyzing aggression or sex roles on TV programs, analyzing one's own diet and comparing it with lists of risk factors for cancer and heart disease, and estimating one's own likely longevity.
- Four *Investigative Projects*, each of which is designed for a single student or a small group of students, to determine the availability of certain kinds of services within your own community, such as day-care options, birth options, and the like.

These projects are available from the publisher on a computer disk for those instructors who wish to adapt them for their own individual use.

Supplements

There are a variety of supplements available to the instructor and the student.

For the Instructor

- **Instructor's Manual.** Written by Karen Saenz of Houston Community College, each chapter of the manual includes an overview of materials, a chapter preview, learning goals, a teaching outline, and key terms.
- **Test Bank.** Prepared by Pat Lefler of Lexington Community College, the Test Bank is composed of approximately 2000 fully referenced questions, written in the multiple-choice, true-false, short answer, matching, and essay formats. This supplement is also available in a computerized version, both for Macintosh and Windows.
- **Video.** A new custom video is available with brief "lecture launcher" segments highlighting important concepts across the life span.
- **Transparencies.** An extensive set of four-color transparencies is available through your Longman representative.

For the Student

- **Study Guide.** Written by Randall Osborne and William Brown of Indiana University, the Study Guide includes study aids such as chapter outlines, review questions, summaries, glossary terms, essay questions, and matching and true-false questions. It features a large selection of multiple-choice questions provided by the Test Bank author.
- **SuperShell.** Created by Pam Griesler, this interactive software allows students to test their knowledge. It is avalable for both Macintosh and IBM compatibles and includes a detailed outline; multiple-choice, true-false, and short-answer questions for each chapter; and a complete textbook glossary.

Some Bouquets

No book is an independent project, even one written by a single author. I need lots of help. Happily for me, my publisher figured out several years ago that if they assign the same development editor and the same photo researcher to each subsequent edition of a book, the whole process is made far easier. Becky Kohn has been my development editor for five years and is truly a wonder. She is reliable, clever, helpful and frank. What more could an author want! During the same years, Rosemary Hunter has been a fine photo researcher, wide-ranging in her searches and exceptionally careful about all the details. To say "Thank you" to them both in this public fashion is a great pleasure, though it is hardly sufficient to convey my deep gratitude.

Two acquisitions editors have been involved in this project. Jill Lectka planned the book in her usual enthusiastic way; Becky Dudley has seen it through to completion. I thank them both for their efficiency and their continuing support of my work.

Equally critical for any text are comments, criticisms, and suggestions from the many colleagues who serve as reviewers at various stages of manuscript preparation. Twenty-two different faculty members have provided this kind of assistance for this book—16 who reviewed the first edition and 6 who looked at early revision drafts. I greatly appreciated the thought and care given to the text by each of these individuals:

Mark Alcorn, University of Northern Colorado

Judith Anderson, Clark State Community College

Jeffrey Arnett, University of Missouri

Frank Asbury, Valdosta State University

Mel Ciena, University of San Francisco

Mary Gauvain, University of California, Riverside

William Fisk, Clemson University

Thomas Frangicetto, Northampton Community College

Cathy Furlong, Tulsa Junior College–SEC

Gordon Greenwood, University of Florida

Susan Kerwin-Boudreau, Champlain Regional College

Harriett Light, North Dakota State University

Anthony Marcattilio, St. Cloud State University

John Mastenbrook, DelMar College

Michael McMullen, Glendale Community College

Fayneese Miller, Brown University

Robin Montvilo, Rhode Island College

Karen Nelson, Austin College

Sherri Addis Palmer, NE Missouri State University

Don Stanley, North Harris College

Granville Sydnor, San Jacinto College North

Bruce Tallon, Niagara College

Finally, I need to express my thanks to my husband, Carl de Boor, and to the friends and family who form my own personal "convoy," without whom an intensive effort like this could not be undertaken, let alone completed on schedule.

Helen Bee

Lifespan Development

Setting the Stage: Basic Concepts and Methods

I

Each summer, I spend several months at an unusual camp in the state of Washington, where adults of all ages as well as families with young children live for short periods as a temporary community. Because many of the same people come back year after year, bringing their children (and often later their grandchildren), I see these growing children in once-a-year snapshots. When a family arrives, I am quite naturally struck by how much the children have changed, and I find myself saying to the kids, "Good grief, you've grown a foot," or, "Last time I saw you, you were only this big." (I say these things, remembering full well how much I hated it when people said these things to me at the same age. *Of course* I had grown. And because I was always taller than anyone my age, I didn't like to be reminded of this peculiarity.)

But when I see the returning adults, I am much less struck by the changes. I am more likely to say something like "You look great" or "You haven't changed a bit." If I notice change it is more likely to be something peripheral like a new hairdo or loss of weight. Some of this may be flattery. We assume that adults don't like to be reminded that they're getting older, so we may lie a little when we say someone hasn't changed. But there is a basic difference in our reaction to a child and to an adult. We *expect* a child to change; we expect an adult to remain the same. Yet children also show continuity, and adults also change—albeit over longer periods. The shy 2-year-old is still likely to be more shy than average at 8 or 12 (or 25). And the 40-year-old not only looks different from the 20-year-old, he is also likely to have different attitudes, different values, and a different pattern of daily life. In fact, as adults most of us feel as if we are changing, growing, and learning. Many of us resent assumptions by family or friends that we are just the same as we always were, much as those of you who are 19 or 20 resent people treating you as if you were 15 and not recognizing your new maturity.

CRITICAL THINKING

Think of yourself as you are now and as you were when you were 10 or 12. In what ways are you the same, and in what ways have you changed? Do you think the people around you have really acknowledged those changes, or do they still treat you as "a kid"?

To understand development, then, we must look at both change and continuity across the entire age range from conception to death. What kinds of changes do we see, and at what ages? We also need to understand which of those changes (or continuities) are shared by individuals in all cultures and which are unique to a given culture, to a group within a culture, or to a particular individual. For example, most of us assume that mental abilities decline as we move into old age. Certainly that is true on average, but is it true for everyone?

Understanding development also means that we need to figure out the origins of both the changes and the continuities. This issue is often framed in terms of biology *versus* environment—nature versus nurture—as if the explanation had to be one or the other. But of course nature and nurture are *both* involved in almost every developmental pattern we see. For example, we have lots of evidence that adults become slower in their thinking processes as they get older. A biological explanation of this change might emphasize fundamental age-linked changes in the nervous system; an environmental explanation might focus on the fact that older adults simply practice complex thinking less often than do younger adults. But we do not have to choose between these two alternatives; very likely the two influences interact with one another so that those adults who remain the most mentally active show the slowest physiological decline. (I certainly hope that is true! I'm counting on it!) We will need to look for similar interactions between nature and nurture in each facet of development, at each age.

Although we will soon be looking at each age period individually, we need to begin our journey through development by exploring some of the basic concepts and theories about continuity and change, so that you can begin to be familiar with the terminology and the key issues and arguments. Let me start with the question of change with age and what might cause it.

Explaining Change over the Life Span

Psychologists and sociologists who study development talk about three basic categories of change with age:

1. Shared changes, common to every individual in a species and linked to specific ages;

2. Less universal changes that are shared by a particular subgroup growing up together—either a particular culture, or a particular generation within a given culture;
3. Individual changes resulting from unique, nonshared events.

Basic maturational changes in the physical body are so regular and predictable that a computer could be programmed to take the baby in the upper photo and generate an accurate prediction of the facial features of the same child as a teenager (in the lower photo), even though the shape of his head, nose, teeth, and chin have all changed.

Shared Changes Linked to Age

When most of us think about "developmental change," we're thinking about just this type of change that is basic to human behavior, inevitable for all of us, and linked to age. At least three factors or processes might produce such age-linked changes.

Biologically Influenced Changes. Some of the changes we see are shared because we are all biological organisms involved in a natural, genetically programmed maturing process. The infant who shifts from crawling to walking, the teenage girl who develops breasts and begins to menstruate, and the older adult whose skin becomes progressively more wrinkled all seem to be following a ground plan laid down in the physical body, most likely in the genetic code itself. Many years ago, Arnold Gesell (1925; Thelen & Adolph, 1992) suggested the term **maturation** to describe such genetically programmed sequential patterns of change. Changes in body size and shape, changes in hormones at puberty, changes in muscles and bones, and changes in the circulatory system in middle and old age all may be programmed in this way, a kind of **biological clock,** ticking away in the background.

Gesell thought that maturationally determined development occurred regardless of practice, training, or effort. You don't have to practice growing pubic hair or be taught how to walk; you do not intentionally slow down your reaction time as you get older. Despite these obvious examples, modern researchers and theorists are convinced that no "pure" maturational effects actually exist. The environment always has some effect. Even powerful, apparently automatic maturational patterns such as brain growth in the first year of life require at least some minimal environmental support (Greenough, 1991). The baby whose environment is severely impoverished is not going to develop the same density of neural connections in the brain as will an infant who grows in a complex environment. And at the other end of the age spectrum, regular exercise may help slow down the compression of the spine, and good diet may reduce loss of elasticity in the skin.

I should point out that the term *maturation* does not mean the same thing as *growth*, although the two terms are sometimes used as if they were synonyms. *Maturation* describes any systematic physical change that is grounded in some basic, genetically programmed physiological process. *Growth* refers to some kind of step-by-step change in quantity, as in size, that might occur either with or without an underlying maturational process. For example, a child's body could grow because she is getting older (a maturationally based change) or because her diet has significantly improved, which would reflect growth without any maturational change. To put it another way, the term *growth* is a *description* of change, while the concept of maturation is one *explanation* of change.

Keeping physically active and fit, like this 97-year-old gardener, will not allow you to evade the inevitable maturational decline of old age. But it may significantly retard the process.

Shared Experiences. The biological clock is not the only one ticking. A **social clock** also shapes all (or most) lives into shared patterns of change (Helson, Mitchell, & Moane, 1984). In each culture, the social clock defines a sequence of normal life experiences, such as the right time for children to start school, the appropriate timing of marriage and childbearing, and the expected time of retirement.

In adulthood the social clock is particularly noisy. Sociologist Matilda White Riley (Riley, 1976, 1986) points out that virtually every society is organized into **age strata**—periods in the life span that have common tasks, common expectations, and common societal norms. Across cultures, there are many common themes in the

Critical Thinking

Think for a minute about the characteristics of each major adult age stratum in our culture. How do our expectations of 20-year-olds differ from our expectations of 70-year-olds?

ways such age strata are defined. In almost every culture around the world, children are expected to start school between ages 5 and 7, young adults are expected to form families, and those in their middle and later years are typically granted increased power and authority. But the expectations for a given age group may also differ across cultures.

In American culture, for example, older adults are very often described or perceived as uncertain, infirm, cranky, childlike, senile, or useless. These views have changed somewhat in recent years, as health and vigor among the older groups have improved, but the predominant attitude is still quite negative, a form of what gerontologists call **ageism**—analogous to sexism or racism (Palmore, 1990). In sharp contrast are many Asian cultures, in which older adults are by tradition afforded the status of *elder* and treated with *more* respect than other age groups—a form of positive ageism (Maeda, 1993).

Such collections of attitudes about and expectations for each age constitute the **age norms** for a given culture or subculture. Over the life span, each individual passes through a sequence of such age norms, and this shared pathway tends to shape all adult lives—in a given culture, at a given time of history—into common trajectories.

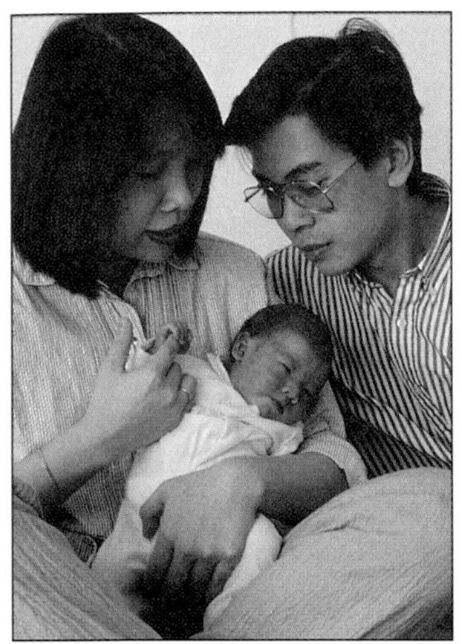

The biological clock obviously constrains the social clock to at least some extent. Virtually every culture emphasizes family formation in early adulthood because that is, in fact, the optimum biological time for childbearing.

Shared Psychological Changes. The social clock defines what we do, how we spend our days, and what roles we may occupy. But both the biological and the social clocks can also shape our inner psychological experiences, such as our personality or self-esteem. For example, when a baby learns to walk (a maturational change), her increased physical independence may also stimulate a shift toward greater psychological independence or confidence.

A second example comes from early adulthood: In every culture that I know of, young adults are required to learn and perform a complex set of roles—marrying and forming a family, bearing and rearing children, working. By middle adulthood, though, these roles are less confining, partly because at this point they are well learned, and partly because children are mostly grown and demand less attention. This shift in the social clock seems to be accompanied by—and may indeed trigger—a deeper psychological change, marked by a movement toward a greater sense of autonomy, assertiveness, and self-confidence. Figure 1.1 shows the results from one study illustrating this change. In this study, the same individuals were interviewed repeatedly from early childhood through late midlife. You can see that in their late 30s these subjects experienced a sharp rise in self-confidence. These results alone do not tell us that such a shift is universal or even common, nor do they reveal the cause. But the results do illustrate a psychological change that *may* be triggered by common social tasks or biological maturation.

Cultures and Cohorts

Development is also shaped by less universally shared experiences, including both cultural variations and variations in the historical experiences of generations with each culture.

Cultural Effects. The term **culture** has no commonly agreed-upon definition, but in essence it describes some *system of meanings and customs*, including values, attitudes, goals, laws, beliefs, morals, and physical artifacts of various kinds, such as tools, forms of dwellings, and the like. Furthermore, to be called a culture, this system of meanings and customs must be *shared by some identifiable group*, whether that group is a subsection of some population or a larger unit, and *transmitted from one generation of that group to the next* (Betancourt & Lopez, 1993; Cole, 1992).

My awareness of the power of even quite small cultural variations was greatly enhanced by a recent year spent in Germany. My goal had been to learn German,

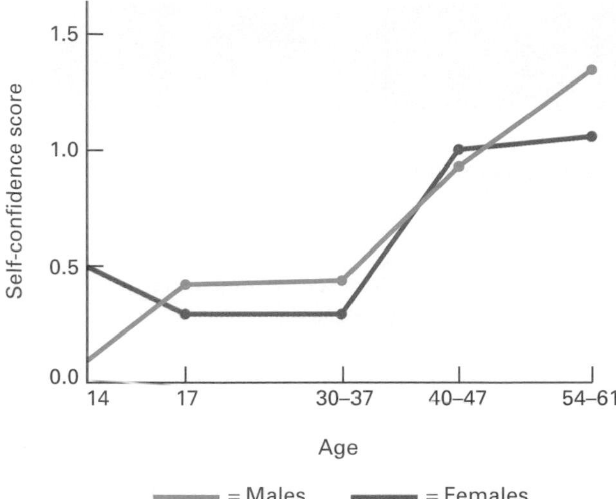

FIGURE 1.1 These results are from a famous study in Berkeley and Oakland, California, of a group of subjects born either in 1920 or in 1928. They were tested frequently in childhood and adolescence, as well as three times in adulthood. Here you can see the sharp rise in self-confidence that occurred for both men and women in this group in their 30s—a pattern that *may* reflect a shared personality change, triggered by the common experiences of the social clock. (*Source:* Haan, Millsap, & Hartka, 1986, Figure 1, p. 228.)

which is my husband's native tongue, but I learned as much about culture as about language. The two cultures—German and American—are outwardly quite similar. But even quite small variations often left me feeling dislocated and uncertain. One fairly trivial example: I found that strangers in Germany almost never speak to one another in casual situations. So if I smiled or said hello to someone I met while out walking, they would not reply, would not look at me, or would even turn their heads away. I experienced these behaviors as coldness and rejection of my friendliness and felt increasingly isolated, even when my logical mind told me these were merely cultural differences and not anything personal. Experiences like this convinced me that Sapir was right when he said: "The worlds in which different societies live are distinct worlds, not merely the same world with different words attached" (1929, p. 209).

Anthropologists point out that a key dimension on which cultural worlds differ from one another is that of **individualism** versus **collectivism** (e.g., Kim et al., 1994). Cultures with an individualistic emphasis assume that the world is made up of independent individuals whose achievement and responsibility is individual rather than collective. Most European cultures are based on such individualistic assumptions, as is the Euro-American culture. But Patricia Greenfield (1994) points out that roughly 70 percent of the world's population operates with a collectivist belief system, in which the emphasis is on collective rather than individual identity, on group solidarity, sharing, duties and obligations, and group decision making. A person living in such a system is integrated into a strong, cohesive group that protects and nourishes that individual throughout life. Collectivism is the dominant theme in most Asian countries, as well as in many African and Latin American cultures. Among minority groups in the United States, collectivism is central to the cultural beliefs of most Native Americans, African Americans, Mexican Americans, and Asian Americans.

An example of the impact of individualism and collectivism: Aggression between preschoolers, like what we see here between Laura and Megan, turns out to be more common among Euro-American children, whose family culture is rooted in individualism, than among Asian-American children, whose family culture emphasizes cooperation and collectivism (Farver, Kim, & Lee, 1995).

This distinction between individualism and collectivism can give us a useful conceptual framework for understanding cultural differences and cultural effects. But

Research Report

Children and Adolescents in the Great Depression of the 1930s: An Example of a Cohort Effect

Research by Glen Elder on children and adolescents who grew up during the Great Depression illustrates exceptionally clearly that the same historical event can have very different effects on adjacent cohorts (Elder, 1974; 1978; Elder, Liker, & Cross, 1984). Elder used information from one of the most famous long-term studies in the psychological literature, the Berkeley/Oakland Growth study. The several hundred subjects who were involved in this study had been born either in 1920 or in 1928. All have been studied in detail over the succeeding years, with the most recent assessments completed when they were in their 50s. Those in the 1920 group were in their teens during the Depression; those born in 1928 were still young children during the worst economic times.

In each of these two adjacent cohorts, Elder compared the experiences of children whose families had lost more than 35 percent of their pre-Depression income with those whose economic condition was better. In the most general terms, he found that the economic hardship was largely beneficial to the cohort born in 1920, who were teenagers when the Depression struck full force, while the experience was generally detrimental to the cohort born in 1928.

Most of the teenagers whose families experienced the worst economic hardship were pushed into prematurely adult responsibilities. Many worked at odd jobs, earning money that was vitally important to the family's welfare. They felt, and were, needed by their families. As adults, they have had a strong work ethic and a strong commitment to family.

Those who were born in 1928 had a very different Depression experience. These children were quite young during the hardest years and so spent a larger proportion of their early years under conditions of hardship. Because of the economic stress, their families frequently experienced a loss of cohesion and warmth. Their parents had little time to meet the emotional needs of their younger children. The consequences were generally negative for the children, especially the boys. These youngsters were less hopeful and less confident than their less economically stressed peers; in adolescence they did less well in school, completed fewer years of education, and were less ambitious and less successful as adults.

These two cohorts were only 8 years apart, yet their experiences were strikingly different because of the timing of a key environmental event in their lives.

the more basic point is that we must be very careful not to assume that patterns of development we see in white, middle-class American children or adults are necessarily going to occur in other subcultures within our own society, or in widely different cultures. Fortunately, our store of cross-cultural research is growing steadily. In a few areas, such as the study of children's language, moral development, and attachment, we already have a fair amount of information about developmental patterns in myriad cultures. In many other areas, though, our research is still highly Eurocentric and thus highly individualistic in emphasis.

Cohort Effects. An equally important source of variation in life experience comes from historical forces that affect each generation somewhat differently. Social scientists use the word **cohort** to describe groups of individuals born within some fairly narrow band of years who share the same historical experiences at the same times in their lives. Within any given culture, successive cohorts may have quite different life experiences. For example, my father, born in 1914, was a teenager when the Great Depression hit in the United States. He and all his cohort were profoundly affected by that experience.

An example that may be closer to home is that of the Baby Boom—the major increase in birth rate that occurred in the United States as well as in many other industrialized countries right after World War II, peaking between 1955 and 1965. The unusual size of this cohort has had widespread effects. If you are part of this cohort, you went to crowded schools, had a harder time getting into college because the competition for each space was greater, and have competed with more people for jobs. Those of us in the much smaller cohort born right before the Baby Boom (as I am, born in 1939) have had much less competition at many stages of our lives. Thus, the timing of one's birth may have long-term consequences for the experiences and attitudes we will have, and the way in which we will develop.

These examples show that the concept of a cohort can help us in two ways. It can help to explain why people in a given age group are similar to one another, and it can help to explain why groups close in age may have very different developmental trajectories.

The concept of a cohort becomes particularly important as we try to interpret studies of adults. A great deal of research on adulthood involves comparisons of sets of people from different age groups—a strategy called a *cross-sectional study*. We test or measure some variable in each age group, such as work satisfaction, loneliness, depression, or cognitive skill, and then compare the average scores for each age, looking for patterns of similarity or change across ages. But when we compare those averages, we are comparing cohorts as well as age groups, which makes the results very difficult to interpret.

For instance, not long ago, *Newsweek* magazine (February 17, 1992, p. 50) reported on results from a Gallup poll that included a question about whether the person would feel bad if he (or she) was unable to pay his bills. Fifty-one percent of the 18- to 29-year-olds in this survey said they would feel bad, compared with 57 percent of those between 38 and 40, and 80 percent of those over 50. How would you interpret age differences like this? Do they show a basic developmental shift toward more self-criticism as we get older, or do they show only a cohort difference? Perhaps the cohorts now over 50 grew up at a time when there were different cultural values, including a greater emphasis on personal responsibility. Nothing in the statistics themselves permits us to choose between these possibilities.

It is important to keep these cohort-specific variations in mind as we go along. They make the job of sorting out shared, basic developmental patterns much more difficult. But at the same time they can be immensely informative and interesting. To understand human development we need to do more than merely identify those patterns of change with age that occur regardless of environmental variation. We also need to understand how specific experiences can shift whole groups of people into different pathways. Cohort comparisons can shine an enormous amount of light on just such questions.

CRITICAL THINKING

Another example: Those adults now in their 50s represent the leading edge of a cohort that experienced a massive increase in women's labor force participation and in divorce rates. What effects do you think these demographic characteristics might have on the aging experiences of this cohort, compared with the cohorts now in old age? More single older women? Fewer poor elders?

Unique, Nonshared Events

In the same vein, we have to try to understand the ways in which individual or nonshared experiences shape the lives of children and adults. What is the impact of a divorce on a child? Does the child's age at the time of the divorce make a difference? What about a man being laid off work in his early 30s, or a couple delaying childbirth until their 40s? And what of those chance encounters with a single individual—a remarkable teacher, a rapist, a mentoring boss—that may alter an individual's life path (Bandura, 1982a, 1989)? Each individual's development is shaped by a unique combination of specific events. While we cannot study every individual, we can look for basic processes or rules that seem to govern how individual experiences will affect an individual's developmental pathway.

Timing of Experience. Many psychologists have concluded that one of the key aspects of individual experiences is their *timing*. Timing effects have been central in studies of both children and adults, but the issue is phrased differently in the two cases.

In theories of child development, the significant concept is that of a **critical period.** The basic idea is that there may be specific periods in development when an organism is especially sensitive to the presence (or absence) of some particular kind of experience; the same experience at a later or earlier time has little or no effect. In baby ducks, the period about 15 hours after hatching is a critical period for the development of an attachment and following response. They will follow any duck or any other quacking, moving object that happens to be around them at that critical time. If nothing is moving or quacking at that critical point, they don't develop any attachment or following response at all (Hess, 1972).

We can see similar critical periods in the action of various **teratogens** in prenatal development. A teratogen is some outside agent, such as a disease organism or chemical, that, if present during prenatal development, adversely affects the developmental process. While some teratogens can have negative consequences at any time in gestation, most have effects only during some critical period. For example, if a mother contracts the disease rubella (commonly called German measles) during a narrow range of days in the first three months of pregnancy, some damage or deformity occurs in the fetus. Infection with the same virus after the third month of pregnancy has no such effect.

In the months after birth, too, there seem to be critical periods in brain development—specific weeks or months during which the child needs to encounter certain types of stimulation or experience for the nervous system to develop normally and fully (Hirsch & Tieman, 1987).

The broader and somewhat looser concept of a **sensitive period** has also been widely used. A sensitive period is a span of months or years during which a child may be particularly responsive to specific forms of experience, or particularly influenced by their absence. For example, the period from 6 to 12 months of age may be a sensitive period for the formation of a core attachment to the parents.

Critical Thinking

Does this idea about the effects of on-timeness and off-timeness make sense to you? Can you think of examples in your own life, or in the lives of your friends or family members?

In studies of adults, the central timing concept has been the contrast between *on-time* and *off-time* events (Neugarten, 1979). The basic idea is that any experience occurring at the normal, expectable time for that culture (or that cohort) will pose far fewer difficulties for the adult's adaptation than will any off-time experience. Thus, being widowed at 30 or laid off work at 40 is far more likely to produce serious life disruption or forms of pathology such as depression than would being widowed at 70 or ending your work life at 65.

It may seem at first glance that the concept of critical or sensitive periods and the concept of on-timeness are quite different notions. But there is an underlying similarity. In both cases the basic idea is that the normal trajectory of development rests on a foundation of common experiences occurring in a particular sequence at particular times. Any individual—child or adult—whose life experiences deviate from that normal sequence or timing may be thrown off track in some way.

Explaining Continuity over the Life Span

Because this is a book about *development* over the life span, you will not be surprised that we will spend most of our time looking at changes that occur with age. But we can't ignore the continuities, either. We have a number of alternative approaches to choose from in describing and explaining such continuities.

Biological Explanations of Consistency: Behavior Genetics

The concept of maturation assumes that all members of a given species share basic genetic codes that shape the patterns of normal development. But our genetic heritage is individual as well as collective. The study of genetic contributions to individual behavior, called **behavior genetics,** has become a particularly vibrant and influential research area in recent years and has contributed greatly to a renewed interest in the biological roots of behavior.

Research Report

How Do Behavior Geneticists Identify Genetic Effects?

Investigators can search for a genetic influence on a trait in either of two primary ways: They can study identical and fraternal twins, or they can study adopted children. Identical twins share exactly the same genetic patterning because they develop from the same fertilized ovum. Fraternal twins each develop from a separate ovum, separately fertilized. They are therefore no more alike than are any other pair of siblings, except that they have shared the same prenatal environment and grow up in the same sequential niche within the family. If identical twins turn out to be more like one another on any given trait than do fraternal twins, that would be evidence for the influence of heredity on that trait.

A powerful variant of the twin strategy is to study twins who have been reared apart. If identical twins are still more like one another on some dimension, despite having grown up in different environments, we have even clearer evidence of a genetic contribution for that trait.

In the case of adopted children, the strategy is to compare the degree of similarity between the adopted child and her birth parents (with whom she shares genes but not environment) with the degree of similarity between the adopted child and her adoptive parents (with whom she shares environment but not genes). If the child should turn out to be more similar to her birth parents than to her adoptive parents, or if her behavior or skill is better predicted by the characteristics of her birth parents than by characteristics of her adoptive parents, that would again demonstrate the influence of heredity.

Let me give you two examples, both from studies of IQ. Bouchard and McGue (1981, p. 1056, Fig. 1) have combined the results of dozens of twin studies on the heritability of IQ scores, with the following results:

Identical twins reared together	.85
Identical twins reared apart	.67
Fraternal twins reared together	.58
Siblings (including fraternal twins) reared apart	.24

The numbers here are correlations—a statistic I'll explain more fully later in this chapter. For now you need to know only that a correlation can range from 0 to +1.00 or −1.00. The closer it is to 1.00, the stronger the relationship it describes. In this case, the number reflects how similar the IQs are of the two members of a twin pair. You can see that identical twins reared together have IQs that are highly similar, much more similar than what occurs for fraternal twins reared together. You can also see, though, that environment plays a role, since identical twins reared apart are less similar than are those reared together.

The same conclusion comes from two well-known studies of adopted children, the Texas Adoption Project (Loehlin, Horn, & Willerman, 1994) and the Minnesota Transracial Adoption Study (Scarr, Weinberg, & Waldman, 1993). In both studies, the adopted children were recently given IQ tests at roughly age 18. Their scores on this test were then correlated with the earlier-measured IQ scores of their natural mothers and of their adoptive mothers and fathers:

Correlation	**Texas**	**Minnesota**
With the natural mother's IQ	.44	.29
With the adoptive mother's IQ	.03	.14
With the adoptive father's IQ	.06	.08

In both cases, the children's IQs were at least somewhat predicted by their natural mothers' IQs, but *not* by the IQs of their adoptive parents, with whom they had spent their entire childhood. Thus, the adoption studies, like the twin studies of IQ, tell us that there is indeed a substantial genetic component in what we measure with an IQ test.

Using two primary research techniques—the study of identical and fraternal twins and the study of adopted children, described in the Research Report above—behavior geneticists have shown that specific heredity affects a remarkably broad range of behaviors. Included in the list are not only obvious physical differences such as height, body shape, or a tendency to skinniness or obesity, but also cognitive abilities such as general intelligence (about which I will have a great deal more to say in Chapter 7), spatial visualization ability, or reading disability (Rose, 1995). Newer research is also showing that many aspects of pathological behavior are genetically influenced, including alcoholism, schizophrenia, excessive aggressiveness or antisocial behavior, even anorexia (Gottesman & Goldsmith, 1994; McGue, 1994). Finally, and importantly, behavior geneticists have found a significant genetic influence on children's temperament and adults' personality, including such dimensions as emotionality (the tendency to get distressed or upset easily), activity (the tendency toward vigorous, rapid behavior), and sociability (the tendency to prefer the presence of others to being alone) (Plomin et al., 1993)—a point I'll come back to in Chapter 6.

None of these characteristics is completely fixed by a person's genetic heritage or entirely consistent over a person's lifetime. The particular behavior an individual shows will *always* be a joint product of the genetic pattern and the environment the individual has grown up in or exists in as an adult. Still, it is clear that we are born with certain response patterns that shape our reactions to the world. And because we carry those same response patterns with us through our lives, these inherited characteristics create a base of continuity over time.

Environmental Sources of Continuity

Continuity is also fostered by the environment and by our own behavior (Caspi, Bem, & Elder, 1989). For example, we tend to choose environments that fit our characteristics, creating a unique niche for ourselves within our family, among our peers, in our workplace (Scarr, 1992). As children, we choose activities we think we might be good at, and avoid those we think we can't do. (Being somewhat gawky and uncoordinated, I always avoided competitive sports; I was afraid I would be embarrassed by my klutziness or that I would let down the team.) As adults, we choose jobs that match our skills and personality. This protects us from experiences that might force change and thus helps to create continuity in behavior. Continuity is also created by the fact that as we are growing up, we learn particular behaviors, or strategies for solving problems, that are successful for us. Faced with some new situation, we try what we know.

At the same time, our habitual patterns trigger reactions from others that are likely to perpetuate those patterns. For instance, someone who complains a lot—about his work, his life, his friends—is far more likely to be met with negative reactions than is a more positive, sunny-dispositioned person. Such negative reactions, in turn, reinforce the complaining behavior by giving the complainer yet more things to complain about, thus generating continuity over time.

A wonderful illustration of how all these various pressures toward continuity can operate jointly comes from research by Avshalom Caspi and his colleagues (Caspi & Elder, 1988; Caspi, Elder, & Bem, 1987, 1988). Caspi has studied the life histories of 284 children born in the 1920s—the same group of subjects, by the way, that Elder studied in his research on the effects of the Great Depression, described in the Research Report on page 6. Among these subjects was a group who had been rated "ill-tempered" as children. Caspi wanted to know what happened to these children as they moved into adulthood.

It turned out that men who had been ill-tempered boys had life pathways very different from those of their more even-tempered peers. They completed fewer years of school, had lower-status jobs, achieved lower rank when they served in the military, and were twice as likely to be divorced by age 40. They also changed jobs more often, but as you can see in Figure 1.2, that was true only for those in low-status jobs. Ill-tempered boys who were able to move into jobs with higher status had stable job careers. Why the difference? Caspi suggests that the difficulty for these ill-tempered men is that they react badly to any kind of authority figure. Higher-status jobs are likely to involve less supervision and thus have less chance of eliciting the pattern of ill-temper. Ill-tempered men in low-status jobs are likely to have many more contacts with authority figures, so their habitual reaction is triggered more often, eliciting displeasure from the supervisor.

All the various types of pressures for continuity are at work here. Heredity no doubt helps to create the initial ill-temperedness. For most, the ill-tempered behav-

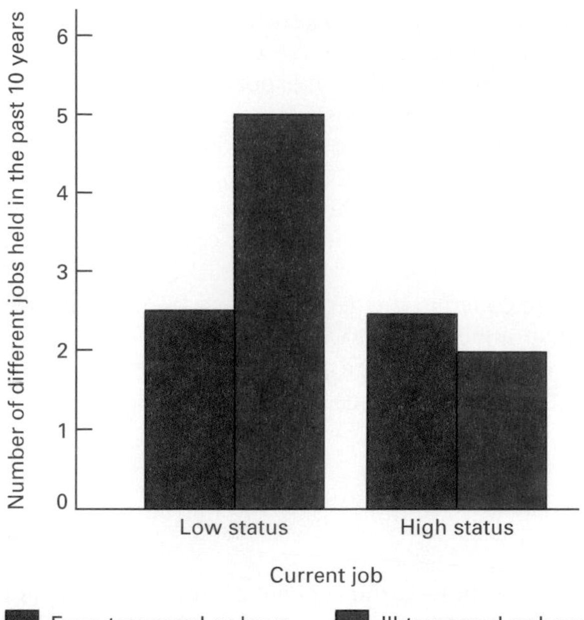

FIGURE 1.2 In this study, based on the same sample shown in Figure 1.1, men who had been ill-tempered as boys changed jobs more often in adult life than did those who had been more even-tempered—but only if the men were in low-status, low-autonomy jobs. (*Source:* Caspi & Elder, 1988, Figure 6.3, p. 128.)

ior persists through childhood and into adulthood because of the choices the individual makes and because of environmental forces toward continuity. But in those rarer cases when the environment does *not* sustain the initial pattern, change can and does occur.

Nature and Nurture

Even this very brief foray into the questions of change and continuity over age highlights the fundamental tension between nature and nurture, between biology and environment. Genetic patterns play a major role in both common change over time and in individual continuity; they form each person's unique heritage, and thus set each of us on a slightly different trajectory. At the same time, the environment both shapes our individuality and pushes us into common paths. The problem has been to figure out the relative impact of these two forces on any given aspect of human development, and to conceptualize the ways in which each force—nature and nurture—operates to influence us. In struggling with these questions, psychologists have been moving away from simple dichotomous approaches in which nature and nurture are contrasted as opposites, and toward more subtle ways of looking at the ways the two factors interact with one another. Let me give you some examples.

Inborn Biases: A Modern "Nature" Formulation

One of the newer ways to think and talk about the nature half of the traditional dichotomy rests on the concept of **inborn biases.** The basic idea is that children are born with tendencies to respond in certain ways. In computer language, we could say that infants are born with certain "default options"; the system is *already* programmed or "biased."

Some of these inborn biases are shared by virtually all children. For instance, from the earliest days of life babies seem to listen more to the beginnings and ends of sentences than to the middle (Slobin, 1985a), and they respond visually to motion and to shifts from dark to light (Haith, 1980). Babies also come equipped with a set of apparently instinctive behaviors that entice others to care for them, including crying, snuggling, and—very soon after birth—smiling. Other inborn biases may vary from one individual to another. For example, we can think of variations from one infant to the next in such temperamental qualities as crankiness or sociability as kinds of inborn biases.

Whether these inborn patterns are coded in the genes in some fashion, are created by variations in the prenatal environment, or through some combination of the two, the basic point is that the baby is not a blank slate at birth. She starts out life already prepared to seek out and react to particular kinds of experiences.

Two Modern "Nurture" Concepts

We can find subtler and more complex ways of thinking on the nurture side of the equation as well.

Internal Models of Experience. One of these is the concept of internal models of experience. There are two key elements to this concept. The first is the idea that the effect of some experience lies not in any objective properties of the experience but rather in the individual's *interpretation* of it, the *meaning* the individual puts on that experience. If you think about it, you can come up with lots of everyday examples of this principle. For instance, suppose a friend says to you: "Your new haircut looks great; it's a lot nicer when it's short like that." Your friend intends it as a compliment, but you also hear an implied criticism ("Your hair *used* to look awful . . ."), so your reactions, your feelings, and even your relationship with your friend are affected by how you read the comment, not by what your friend meant or by any objective qualities of his remark.

Furthermore, according to this theory, our interpretations of experience are not random or governed by temporary moods but rather are organized into *models*, which we might think of as organized sets of assumptions or expectations about oneself or others. For example, if you regularly hear criticism in other people's comments, we might infer that you have an internal model with a basic assumption similar to this: "I usually do things wrong, so other people criticize me."

This second-grader at a Texas track meet may have done quite well in the long jump. But if the concept of internal models is correct, then what matters is not his absolute success but rather how he interpreted it and how that interpretation fits into his network of assumptions and expectations.

Some theorists argue that each child creates several such internal models, through which all subsequent experience is filtered (Epstein, 1991). John Bowlby expressed this idea when he talked about the child's "internal working model" of attachment (1969, 1980). A child with a "secure" model of attachment assumes that affection and attention are reliably available. A child with a less secure model may assume that affection is contingent on "being good," or that adults are generally angry and hostile and are not reliable sources of support. Of course these expectations are based at least partially on actual experiences, but once formed into an internal model they generalize beyond the original experience and affect the way the child interprets future experiences. A child who expects adults to be reliable and affectionate will be more likely to interpret the behavior of new adults in this way, and will recreate friendly and affectionate relationships with others outside the family; a child who expects hostility will read hostility into otherwise fairly neutral encounters.

A child's self-concept seems to operate in much the same way, as an internal working model of "who I am" (Bretherton, 1991). This self-model is based on experience, but it also shapes future experience.

The concept of internal models, which originated in studies of infants and young children, has now begun to appear in studies of adults as well. For example, Deborah Cohn and her colleagues (Cohn et al., 1991) have found that adult couples in which both partners have insecure working models of attachment report more conflict and less positive interaction than do other couples.

Research on stress and social support sends us a similar message. Again and again researchers have found that the objective amount of stress an adult experiences or the number of friends or family members she may have in her support network is not what matters; the crucial factor is how the adult *perceives* the stress and the support. If she perceives her support as inadequate, no matter how much objective support there may appear to be, her risk of illness, depression, or another dysfunction goes up (Cohen & Wills, 1985; Krause, Liang, & Yatomi, 1989).

The concept of internal models obviously also helps us account for continuity of behavior over time. The models we create in childhood are not unchangeable, but they do tend to be carried forward and they continue to shape and define our experiences as adults.

Critical Thinking

See if you can identify some of your own basic assumptions, your own internal models. Do you assume that other people are basically trustworthy and reliable? Do you assume that you are lovable, or are you surprised when people like you? Think about it.

The Ecological Perspective. Another important facet of current thinking about environmental influences is a growing emphasis on the importance of looking beyond the child's immediate family for explanations of development. In this view, we must understand the *ecology* or *context* in which the child is growing: his neighborhood and school, the occupations of his parents and their level of satisfaction in these occupations, the relationships his parents have with each other and their own families, and so on and on (e.g., Bronfenbrenner, 1979, 1989; Pence, 1988). A child growing up in a poverty-stricken inner-city neighborhood, where drugs and violence are a part of everyday life, is coping with a set of problems radically different from those of a suburban child in a safe neighborhood. Similarly, when parents are overwhelmed with the problems in their own lives and are isolated from family or friends who might provide help, they are likely to create a more stressful family environment than will parents whose lives are more stable and supported.

Critical Thinking

How would you describe the "ecology" of your own childhood? What sort of family, neighborhood, and school did you have? What other significant people were in your life? What significant events affected your parents' lives?

A particularly nice example of research that examines such a larger system of influences is Gerald Patterson's work on the origins of antisocial (highly aggressive) behavior in children (Patterson, Capaldi, & Bank, 1991; Patterson, DeBarsyshe, & Ramsey, 1989). His studies show that parents who use poor discipline techniques and poor monitoring are more likely to have noncompliant or antisocial children. Once established, such an antisocial behavior pattern has repercussions in other areas of the child's life, leading both to rejection by peers and to academic difficulty. These problems, in turn, are likely to push the young person toward a deviant peer group and still further delinquency (Dishion et al., 1991; Vuchinich, Bank, & Patterson, 1992). So a pattern that began in the family is maintained and exacerbated by interactions with peers and with the school system.

Patterson also argues that the family's good or poor disciplinary techniques are not random events but are shaped by the larger context in which the family exists. He finds that those parents who were themselves poorly disciplined are more likely to use those same poor strategies with their children. But he also finds that even parents who possess good basic child-management skills may fall into poor patterns when the stresses in their own lives are increased. A recent divorce or period of unemployment increases the likelihood that parents will use poor disciplinary practices and thus increases the likelihood that the child will develop a pattern of antisocial behavior. Figure 1.3 shows Patterson's conception of how these various components fit together. Clearly, by taking into account the larger social ecology in which the family is embedded, our understanding of the process is greatly enhanced.

The Interaction of Nature and Nurture

Patterson's model and the many others like it take us a long way toward a more complete look at development. What he has omitted in this model, though, is any mention of the influence of "nature." What happens if we add that to the system?

It's not such a big step. In the case of Patterson's model, we need only assume that children begin life with different initial temperaments. Some are cranky and hard to handle; others are sunny-dispositioned and easy to care for. A parent with a

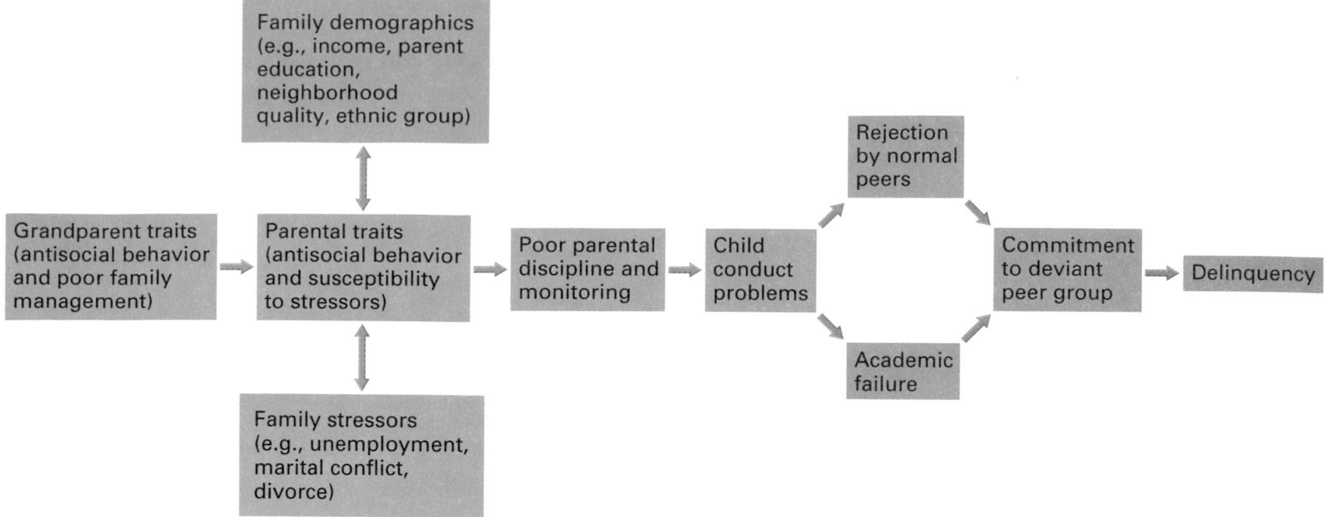

FIGURE 1.3 Patterson expands the definition of "nurture" in this model of the many factors that influence the development of delinquency. In his view, the core of the process is the interaction between the child and the parent. But the parents' ability to handle the child effectively is, in turn, affected by their own histories, and by their current support and life satisfaction. (*Source:* Patterson, DeBarsyshe, & Ramsey, 1989, Figures 1 and 2, pp. 331 and 333.)

cranky or difficult baby will need more skill to avoid spiraling into a pattern that ends up reinforcing the child's defiance. Thus, the qualities that the child brings to the interaction create a bias in the system to which the parents and others in the environment must respond.

A similarly interactionist model is implicit in the ideas of **vulnerability** and **resilience** (Garmezy, 1993; Garmezy & Rutter, 1983; Masten, Best, & Garmezy, 1990; Moen & Erickson, 1995; Rutter, 1987; Werner, 1995). According to this view, each child is born with certain vulnerabilities, such as a difficult temperament, a physical abnormality, allergies, a genetic tendency toward alcoholism, or whatever. Each child is also born with some *protective factors*, such as high intelligence, good coordination, an easy temperament, or a lovely smile, that tend to make her more resilient in the face of stress.

These vulnerabilities and protective factors then interact with the child's environment so that the *same* environment can have quite different effects, depending on the qualities the child brings to the interaction. In particular, as Frances Horowitz has argued (Horowitz, 1987, 1990), the combination of a highly vulnerable child and a poor or unsupportive environment produces by far the most negative outcomes. Either of these two negative conditions alone—a vulnerable child or a poor environment—can be overcome. A resilient child in a poor environment may do quite well since she can find and take advantage of all the stimulation and opportunities available; similarly, a vulnerable child may do quite well in a highly facilitative environment in which supportive parents help the child overcome or cope with her vulnerabilities. According to Horowitz, it is only the double whammy—the vulnerable child in a poor environment—that leads to really poor outcomes for the child.

As you will see throughout the book, a growing body of research shows precisely this pattern. For example, very low IQ scores are most common among children who had a low birth weight *and* were reared in poverty-level families, while low-birth-weight children reared in middle-class families have essentially normal IQs, as do normal-weight infants reared in poverty-level families (Werner, 1986). Other researchers find that even among low-birth-weight children reared in poverty-level families, those whose families show "protective" factors (such as greater residential stability, less crowded living conditions, more acceptance, more stimulation, and more learning materials) turn out better than do equivalently low-birth-weight children reared in the least optimum poverty conditions (Bradley et al., 1994). The key point here is that neither the quality of the environment nor the child's inborn vulnerabilities alone cause specific outcomes, but rather the unique combination of the two.

What Is the Nature of Developmental Change?

The nature/nurture controversy is not the only "big question" in developmental psychology. An equally central dispute concerns the nature of developmental change itself. Does a child simply get better and better at things, such as walking, running, or reading? That is, are the *processes* the same and only the efficiency or the speed different, or are there different processes at different ages? Does an older adult use different strategies to solve problems, or does he simply use the same strategies somewhat more slowly? Concisely stated: Is developmental change *quantitative* or *qualitative*? This question is particularly central in discussions of cognitive development over the life span, but it is also relevant to the various arguments about personality change over adulthood.

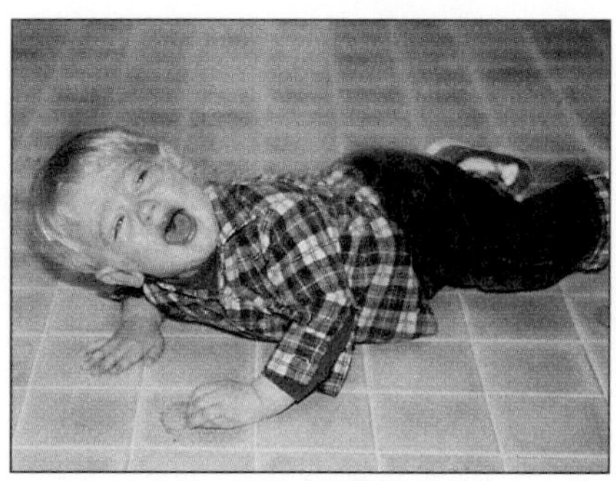

You might explain this little boy's tantrummy behavior by saying he was in the "terrible twos." Stage concepts like this are common in everyday language and in developmental theory.

Stages and Sequences. An important related question concerns the presence or absence of *stages* in the course of development. If development consists only of additions (quantitative change), then the concept of stages is not needed. But if development involves reorganization of old skills or the emergence of wholly new strategies or skills (qualitative change), then the notion of stages may become attractive. Certainly we hear a great deal of "stagelike" language in everyday conversation, such as references to the "terrible twos" or the "midlife crisis."

But to what extent does development across the life span really progress in clear stages? I think we have persuasive evidence for qualitative and not just quantitative change from one age to the next, particularly during childhood and adolescence. Twelve-year-olds really don't think like 3-year-olds; adult relationships seem to me to be qualitatively different from those we see in 6-year-olds. But the notion of stages goes beyond this and requires not only fixed sequences of changes, but some kind of reorganization, some kind of new structure or understanding in each stage. Stage models of development are appealing (and I have been greatly drawn to them) because of the clarity and order they offer. But as you will see as we go along, in many areas the evidence doesn't lend a great deal of support to the idea that development proceeds in fixed stages, particularly in adulthood. Still, many influential stage theories remain and the whole issue of the existence of stages is still very much an open question.

Finding the Answers: Research on Development

I've asked an enormous number of questions already in this chapter. But before you can understand the answers, you need to have some familiarity with the methods researchers use when they explore questions about development. The easiest way to do that is to look at some specific questions and the alternative ways we might answer them.

For example, older adults frequently complain that they have more trouble remembering people's names or phone numbers than they did when they were younger. Suppose I wanted to find out whether memory really declines as we age. How would I go about answering this question? I would face a number of decisions:

- Should I compare groups of different ages to see whether the older groups have lower memory scores? Or should I start with a group of middle-aged adults and follow them over time to see whether every individual shows some loss of memory? This is a question of *research design*.

- How will I measure memory? Can I merely ask people to tell me how much trouble they have remembering, or do I need a standardized assessment? These are questions of *research methodology*.
- How will I interpret the results? Is it enough to know that older adults do or do not show a decline in memory skill? What other analyses might I do that would make the results clearer? These are questions of *research analysis*.

Research Design

Choosing a research design is crucial for any research, but especially so when the subject matter you are trying to study is change (or continuity) with age. You have basically three choices: (1) Study different groups of people of different ages, called a **cross-sectional design;** (2) study the *same* people over a period of time, called a **longitudinal design;** (3) combine cross-sectional and longitudinal designs in some fashion in a **sequential design** (Schaie, 1983a, 1994). And if you want to know whether the same patterns hold across different cultures or contexts, you will need to do some kind of **cross-cultural research,** in which equivalent or parallel methods are used in more than one context.

Cross-Sectional Designs

The key feature of cross-sectional studies is that they include *separate* groups of subjects of *different* ages, with each subject tested only once. To study memory cross-sectionally I might select groups of subjects at each of a series of ages, such as groups of 25-, 35-, 45-, 55-, 65-, 75-, and 85-year-olds. I'd test each person with my measure of memory skill and then see whether the scores go down steadily with age. Figure 1.4 shows the results of just such a study, in which adults of different ages listened to a list of letters being read to them one letter per second and then had to

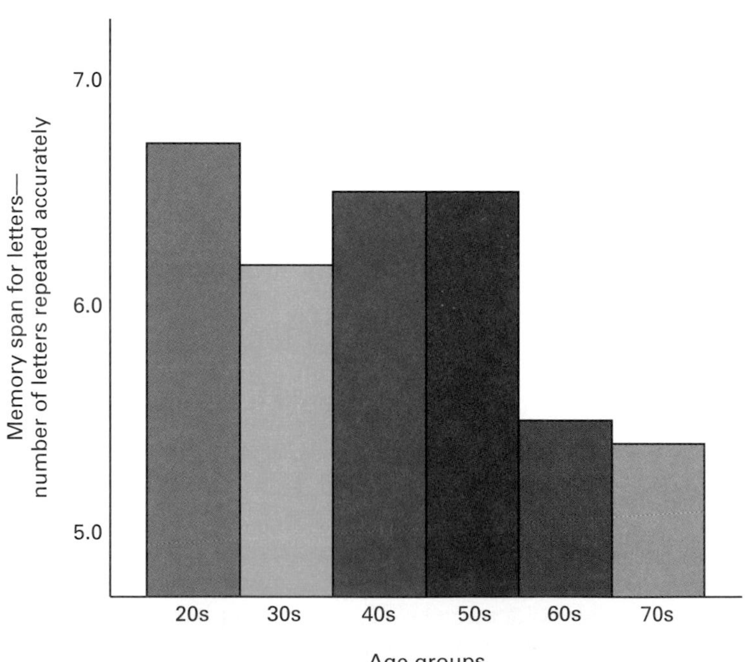

FIGURE 1.4 In this study, adults of various ages listened to an experimenter reading a series of letters, one letter per second. The subject's task was to try to repeat back the list in the order it had been read. The scores shown here are the average number of letters each age group could repeat back. (The apparent drop among 30-year-olds, by the way, is not statistically significant and thus is presumed to be chance variation.) Can we legitimately interpret these results as meaning that memory ability *declines* with age? (*Source:* Botwinick & Storandt, 1974.)

repeat the letters back in the order given—a task not unlike what you have to do when you try to remember a phone number someone has read to you. You can see that there was a sharply lower performance among the 60- and 70-year-olds—a pattern found in a great many studies (Salthouse, 1991).

Because these findings fit our hypothesis, it is tempting to conclude that memory ability *declines* with age. But this is precisely what we cannot say with cross-sectional data, since these adults differ not only in age, but in cohort. Among other things, we know that in most industrialized cultures today, older cohorts have had fewer years of education than younger cohorts. So the differences in memory might reflect education differences (or some other cohort difference) and not changes actually linked to age or development.

Cross-sectional research is often enormously useful. It is relatively quick to do and can give us a glimpse of possible age differences or age changes. But in any cross-sectional study, age and cohort are entirely *confounded*—that is, they vary simultaneously, so we cannot sort out their differential effect. Furthermore, cross-sectional studies cannot tell us anything about sequences of change over age, or about the consistency of individual behavior over time, because each subject is tested only once. So if you want to know whether the adults with good memories at 40 are still likely to have good memories at 60 or 80, a cross-sectional study won't help.

Critical Thinking

Suppose a cross-sectional study of sex-role attitudes reveals that adults between ages 20 and 50 have the most egalitarian attitudes, while teenagers and those over 50 have more traditional attitudes. How could you interpret these results?

Longitudinal Designs

Longitudinal designs seem to solve these problems because they follow the *same* individuals over a period of time. They allow us to look at sequences of change and at individual consistency or inconsistency over time. And because they compare performances by the same people at different ages, they get around the obvious cohort problem.

Short-term longitudinal studies, in which groups of children or adults are studied for a period of several years, have become common in recent years. A few famous long-term longitudinal studies have followed groups of children into adulthood, or groups of adults from early to late adult life.

The Berkeley/Oakland Growth Study, which I've already talked about several times (see Figures 1.1 and 1.2), is one of the most famous of these long-term studies (Eichorn et al., 1981). The Grant study of Harvard men is perhaps equally famous (Vaillant, 1977). In this study, several hundred men were studied from age 18 until they were in their 60s.

Sounds perfect, doesn't it? In fact, though, longitudinal designs have several major difficulties.

Practice Effects. One problem is that longitudinal designs typically involve giving each subject the same tests over and over again. Over time, people learn how to take the tests. Such practice effects may distort the measurement of any underlying developmental changes.

Selective Attrition and Dropout. Another significant problem is that not everyone sticks with the program. You can imagine that it might become quite intrusive to have researchers coming back year after year to ask you endless questions. Some subjects just say no after a while. Others move and can't be located. Some die. As a general rule, the healthiest and best educated are most likely to stick it out, and that fact biases the results, particularly if the study covers the final decades of life. Each succeeding testing includes proportionately more and more healthy adults, which may make it look as if there is less change, or less decline, than actually exists.

Time of Measurement Effects. Longitudinal studies also don't really get around the cohort problem. For example, the Grant study and the Oakland Growth Study both observed and tested subjects born in the same decade (1918–1928). Even if both studies showed the same pattern of change with age, we wouldn't know whether the pattern was unique to that cohort or reflected more basic developmental changes that would be observed in other cultures and other cohorts. This is referred to as a *time of measurement effect* because the time at which a particular group is studied affects the results you obtain.

Sequential Designs

One way to avoid this problem is to use a sequential design. Sequential designs are essentially combinations of longitudinal and cross-sectional designs. They all involve studying more than one cohort over time, but there are a number of alternatives, illustrated in Figure 1.5. (I know this figure is complicated, but a bit of time spent trying to understand it will repay you in the end.) On the top of the figure are years of birth of each cohort; on the left are the years in which we might measure some behavior in a set of individuals. Entered in the table are the *ages* of each cohort at the time of measurement. Within this matrix, you can see that a cross-sectional study involves a comparison across any one row in the table, while a longitudinal study involves part of any single column. Sequential designs involve combinations of these two. There are a number of possibilities.

1. *Time-lag design*: The simplest of the sequential designs involves studying several cohorts at the *same ages*, and thus involves comparisons along one of the diagonals, such as the circled entries in the figure. When we compare the SAT scores of high school seniors over the years from 1970 to 1995, or compare the drug use of today's college students with those of 10 years ago, we are using a time-lag design. In each case we are looking directly at cohort differences without the confounding of age.

2. *Time-sequential design*: A more complex possibility is to do a set of cross-sectional studies several years apart. In Figure 1.5, this would involve studying parts of any two or more rows. If the researchers who did the study of memory shown in Figure 1.4 were to repeat the very same study today, obtaining the same results, they could be more confident that the pattern of decline in the 60s and 70s was related to age, and not just to cohort effects.

Year in which measurement was obtained	Year of birth of each cohort							
	1905	1915	1925	1935	1945	1955	1965	1975
1920	15							
1930	25	15						
1940	35	25	15					
1950	45	35	25	15				
1960	55	45	35	25	15			
1970	65	55	45	35	25	15		
1980	75	65	55	45	35	25	15	
1990	85	75	65	55	45	35	25	15
2000	95	85	75	65	55	45	35	25
2010		95	85	75	65	55	45	35
2020			95	85	75	65	55	45

FIGURE 1.5 Each entry in the table is the age of some group of individuals, born in a particular cohort, at some particular time of measurement. So the top number *15* means that an individual or group born in 1905 would be age 15 when tested in 1920. The same group would be age 25 when tested in 1930, and so on. Cross-sectional studies involve studies of parts of any one row; longitudinal studies, any one column. Sequential studies involve combinations of these, of which the most complex is a cohort-sequential design, which would involve both multiple cross-sectional and multiple longitudinal studies, such as the set of cells in the shaded rectangle.

3. *Cohort sequential design*: The next logical possibility is to do two or more longitudinal studies, each with a different cohort. In the figure, this would mean studying two or more columns. If the Grant study investigators, studying a group of men who were Harvard freshmen in 1937, had later identified and followed another group, perhaps those who were freshmen in 1960, they would have a cohort sequential design.

4. *Cross-sequential design*: The most complex of the sequential designs involves studying multiple rows *and* multiple columns, such as the box outlined in the figure. The researcher would begin with several age groups and then follow *each* group longitudinally. A good example of this is one of the Duke Longitudinal Studies of Aging (Palmore, 1981). The investigators started by testing a sample from each of five age groups: 45, 50, 55, 60, and 65. They then retested all the subjects every two years for six years.

Sociologists frequently use a variant of the cross-sequential design called a *panel study* (Jackson & Antonucci, 1994). They select a large (often nationally representative) sample that covers a wide age range, then follow every subject over a period of years, sometimes decades. One particularly rich example is the Michigan Panel Study of Income Dynamics (Duncan & Morgan, 1985), which started in 1968 with a nationally representative sample of 5000 families. Each year since then, one member of each family has been interviewed at length about the entire family.

Sequential designs are becoming much more prevalent as researchers struggle to find ways to uncover basic developmental patterns.

Cross-Cultural or Cross-Context Designs

Also increasingly common are studies specifically designed to compare cultures or contexts, a task that researchers have approached in several ways.

One strategy involves what anthropologists call an **ethnography**—a detailed description of a single culture or context, based on extensive observation. Often the observer lives within the culture for a period of time, perhaps as long as several years. Each of these descriptions is intended to stand alone, although it is sometimes possible to combine information from several different ethnographies to see whether similar developmental patterns exist in varying contexts (Whiting & Edwards, 1988). For example, are girls and boys given different tasks in every culture, and are those gender assignments similar from one context, one culture, to the next?

Alternatively, investigators may attempt to compare two or more cultures directly, by studying or testing samples of children or adults in each of several cultures or contexts, using the same or comparable instruments or measures. Sometimes this involves comparing across different countries, as in the example of research described in the Cultures and Contexts box on page 20. Sometimes the comparisons are between subcultures within the same country, such as the increasingly common research in the United States involving comparisons of children or adults living in different ethnic groups or communities, such as African Americans, Hispanic Americans, Asian Americans and Euro-Americans. You'll see many examples of this kind of work as we go along.

Such cross-cultural or cross-context comparisons are immensely difficult to do well. One of the troublesome difficulties is the problem of equivalence of measurement. Is it enough just to translate some test into another language? Will the same measure or assessment technique be equally valid in all cultures? Do behaviors have the same *meaning* in other contexts, other cultures? For example, Anne-Marie Ambert (1994) makes the point that when Western researchers study parent behavior, they begin with the assumption that the mother is the most central figure in a child's upbringing. But in many cultures in the world, multiple mothering is the rule and the biological mother may do relatively little nurturing. If we then try to measure the "quality" of the mother's caregiving behavior by counting the number of her nurturing acts or the frequency of her smiles or verbal interactions, we may come to quite erroneous conclusions.

Cultures and Contexts

An Example of a Cross-Cultural Comparison Study

Mark Bornstein and his colleagues (Bornstein, Tal, & Tamis-LeMonda, 1991; Bornstein et al., 1992) videotaped 24 mothers in each of three countries—Japan, France, and the United States—interacting in their homes with their 5-month-old infants. They noted that the *babies* behaved very similarly, which suggests that any differences in the mothers' behavior can't be attributed to varying signals or responses from the babies. The mothers also behaved very similarly in some ways. In particular, they all showed similar rates of nurturance toward their infants and similar levels of imitation. Nonetheless, there were some intriguing differences.

First of all, American mothers simply provided much more stimulation to their babies than did either Japanese or French mothers. They pointed, named, described, touched, and positioned their babies more. Furthermore, mothers in these three cultures gave different weight to various types of stimulation. American mothers and French mothers focused more attention on getting their babies to interact with objects and less attention on getting their babies to interact with Mom. Japanese mothers focused about equally on each of these elements. A third difference was that American mothers were a lot more likely to use a special, high-pitched sort of speech toward their infants—a form of speech sometimes called "motherese." Both the French and Japanese mothers used motherese much less often than the American mothers. French and Japanese mothers were more likely to talk to their babies using ordinary adult conversational tones. Such a finding does not—or does not necessarily—mean that the *process* of development is different in these different cultures. Babies in every culture may respond similarly to motherese, for example. Rather, these results suggest some of the subtle but significant ways that babies may be shaped into the cultural pattern in which they are growing.

Experimental Designs

Most of the research designs I have described so far represent alternative ways to look at changes with age. But if we are interested in examining a basic process—such as learning or memory—or in *explaining* any observed phenomena, we may do **experiments.**

An experiment is normally designed to test a specific hypothesis, a particular causal explanation. Suppose, for example, that I think the observed age differences in memory span are a function of how often adults of various ages actually use their memories. I could test this hypothesis by providing special memory practice to some older adults and no such training to another group the same age. If the trained adults can remember more letters or numbers than they did before training and the no-training group shows no change, this would be consistent with my hypothesis.

A key feature of an experiment, then, is that subjects are assigned *randomly* to participate in one of several groups. Subjects in the **experimental group** receive the treatment the experimenter thinks will produce an identified effect, while those in the **control group** receive either no special treatment or a neutral treatment. The presumed causal element in the experiment is called the **independent variable** (in this case the memory training), and any behavior on which the independent variable is expected to show its impact is called a **dependent variable** (in this case, a score on the memory test).

Problems with Experiments in Studying Development. Experiments like this are essential for our understanding of many aspects of development. But two special problems in studying child or adult development limit the use of experimental designs.

First, many of the questions we want to answer have to do with the effects of particular unpleasant or stressful experiences on individuals—abuse, prenatal influences such as alcohol or tobacco, low birth weight, poverty, unemployment, widowhood. For obvious ethical reasons, we cannot manipulate these variables. We cannot ask one set of pregnant women to have two alcoholic drinks a day and others to have none; we cannot randomly assign adults to become unemployed. To study the effects of such experiences we must rely on nonexperimental designs, including longitudinal and sequential studies.

Second, the independent variable we are often most interested in is age itself, and *we cannot assign subjects randomly to age groups.* We can compare 4-year-olds and 6-year-olds in their approach to some particular task, such as searching for a lost object, but the children differ in a host of ways other than their ages. Older children have had more and different experiences. Thus, unlike psychologists studying other aspects of behavior, developmental psychologists *cannot* systematically manipulate many of the variables we are most interested in.

To get around this problem, we can use any one of a series of strategies, sometimes called *quasi experiments,* in which we compare groups without assigning the subjects randomly. Cross-sectional comparisons are a form of quasi experiment. So are studies in which we select naturally occurring groups that differ in some dimension of interest, such as children whose parents choose to place them in day-care programs compared with children whose parents rear them at home, or adults who have been laid off from work compared with those who are still employed in the same industry.

Such comparisons have built-in problems, because groups that differ in one way are likely to be different in other ways as well. Families who place their children in day care, compared with those who rear them at home, are also likely to be poorer,

Research Report

Ethical Issues in Research on Development

Any time we try to understand human behavior by observing, testing, or asking questions, we are probing into personal lives. If we go into a person's home to observe the way she interacts with her children, we are invading her privacy. We may even inadvertently give the impression that there must be something wrong with the way she is raising her family. If we give adults or children laboratory tests, such as those illustrated in Figure 1.4 measuring memory span, some subjects will do very well and others will not. How will the less-successful subject interpret this experience? What is the risk that some subject will become depressed over what he perceives as a poor performance?

Any research on human behavior involves some risks and raises some ethical questions. Because of this, psychologists and other social and biological scientists have established clear procedures and guidelines that must be followed before any observation can be undertaken, any test given. In every school or college—the settings in which most such research is done—there is a committee of peers who must approve any research plan involving human subjects. The most basic guideline is that subjects must always be protected from any potential mental or physical harm. More specific principles include the following:

- *Informed Consent.* Each adult subject must give written consent to participate. In the case of research on children, **informed consent** must be obtained from the parent or guardian, and the child's *assent* (willingness) must also be clear before any procedure can go forward. In every case, the procedure and its possible consequences must be explained in detail. If there are potential risks, these must be described. For example, if you were studying patterns of problem solving in married couples, you might want to observe each couple while they talked about some unresolved issue between them. As part of your informed consent request, you would have to explain to each couple that while such discussions often lead to greater clarity, they also occasionally increase tension between the pair. And you would need to provide support and debriefing at the end of the procedure to assist any couple who found the task stressful or destabilizing.
- *Right of Privacy.* Subjects must be assured that highly personal information they may provide will be kept entirely private—including information about income, attitudes, or illegal behavior like drug taking. Researchers can use the information *collectively,* but they cannot report it individually in any way that will associate a subject's name with some piece of data—unless the subject has specifically given permission for such use. In virtually all cases, it is also considered unethical to observe through a one-way mirror without the subject's knowledge, or to secretly record behavior.
- *Testing Children.* The above principles are important for any research, but particularly so for research on children. Any child who balks at being tested or observed must *not* be tested or observed; any child who becomes distressed must be comforted; any risk to the child's self-esteem must be avoided.

are more likely to have only a single parent, and may have different values or religious backgrounds. If we find that the two groups of children differ in some fashion, is it because they have spent their daytime hours in different places or because of these other differences in their families? We can make such comparisons a bit cleaner if we select our comparison groups initially so that they are matched on those variables we think might matter, such as income, marital status, or religion. But a quasi experiment, by its very nature, will always yield more ambiguous results than will a fully controlled experiment.

Research Methods

Choosing a research design is only the first crucial decision an investigator must make. Equally important is to decide what subjects to study, and how one will study them.

Choosing the Subjects. Because we would like to uncover basic developmental patterns that are true for all children, all adolescents, or all adults, the ideal strategy would be to select a random sample of all people in the world to study. This is clearly impractical, so some kind of compromise is necessary. One compromise, more and more common in today's research, is to select large samples that are representative of some subgroup in a particular country or city or neighborhood, such as black adults across the United States, older adults living in Florida, high school seniors, all sixth-grade children in Dallas, or whatever. This is a widely used strategy in sociology and epidemiology, and it can be very fruitful in psychology as well. But because it is difficult to collect highly detailed information from or about large numbers of subjects, this strategy frequently requires trading off depth for breadth.

The other alternative, very common in psychological research on children and in many longitudinal studies of adults, is to study a smaller (and less representative) group of subjects in greater depth and detail, in an attempt to uncover very basic processes. For instance, Alan Sroufe and his colleagues (Sroufe, 1989; Sroufe, Egeland, & Kreutzer, 1990) have studied a group of 267 children and families, beginning before the birth of the child. Families were deliberately chosen from among those thought to be at high risk for later caregiving problems, such as low-education single mothers with unplanned pregnancies. The children have now been repeatedly studied, each time in considerable detail. The sample is not representative of the population as a whole, but the results are enormously informative nonetheless and may tell us more about the process of emotional and social development than we could glean from larger samples studied more broadly.

Neither strategy is better than the other; both are useful. In either case, we need to remember that the conclusions we can draw will be limited by the sample we studied and by the type of information we could obtain.

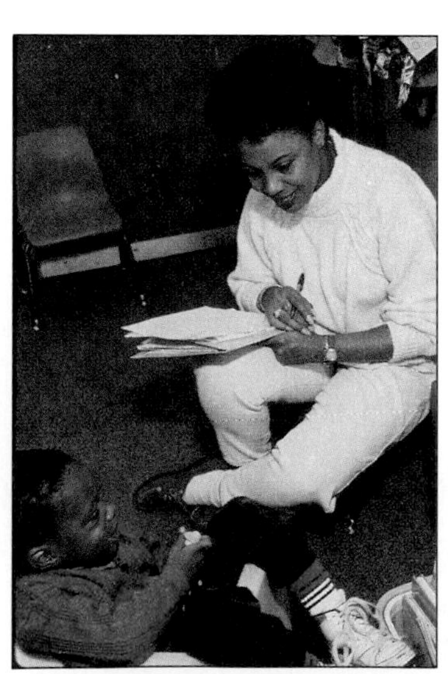

One way to collect information is by direct observation, as this student is doing in a nursery school.

Collecting the Information from Your Subjects. Having chosen your basic design and the subjects you wish to study, you then need to decide how to assess them. The options are usually grouped into two subsets, *naturalistic* and *laboratory* research, but in fact there are many shadings in between. On the far end of the naturalistic category are completely unstructured observations in natural settings, such as watching children on playgrounds or observing elderly adults in a nursing home. At the opposite end of the continuum would be highly structured tasks given to subjects in controlled laboratory settings. In between lie many semistructured test situations, often used in studies of children, as well as a vast array of interviews, questionnaires, and pencil-and-paper tests widely used in studies of adults.

Each of these alternatives has costs and benefits. Structured laboratory tests give the experimenter excellent control over the situation, so that each subject is confronted with the same task under the same conditions. But because they are artificial, such tests may not give us an accurate portrayal of how individuals behave in the more complex natural environment. Interviews, especially very open-ended ones in which the subject is only guided toward general topics, may give a rich picture of an individual's thoughts and feelings, but how do you reduce the answers to comparable scores? Questionnaires solve some of this problem, but the trade-off may be the richness and individuality of replies. Often the best strategy—although one not always possible because of cost in time or money—is to collect many different kinds of information from each subject.

Research Analysis

Finally, you need to analyze the results of your research. In studies of development, there are two broad forms of analysis.

First, we can compare different age groups by simply calculating the average score of each group on some measure, just as in Figure 1.4. You will see *many* examples of exactly this kind of analysis as you go through the book.

A second strategy allows us to look at relationships between two separate variables, using a statistic called a **correlation,** which I mentioned in the box on behavior genetics (p. 9). A correlation is simply a number ranging from −1.00 to +1.00 that describes the strength of a relationship between two variables. A zero correlation indicates that there is no linear relationship between those variables. For instance, you might expect to find a zero or near-zero correlation between the length of big toes and IQ. People with toes of all sizes have high IQs, and those with toes of all sizes have low IQs. The closer a correlation comes to −1.00 or +1.00, the stronger the relationship being described. If the correlation is positive, it indicates that high scores on the two dimensions tend to go together, and low scores tend to go together, such as length of big toes and shoe size, for example, or height and weight.

If the correlation is negative, it means that high scores on one variable are associated with low scores on the other. For example, we find a negative correlation between the amount of disorder and chaos in a family and the child's later IQ: High chaos is associated with lower IQ, and low chaos with higher IQ.

Perfect correlations (−1.00 or +1.00) do not happen in the real world, but correlations of .80 or .70 do occur and correlations of .50 are common in psychological research, indicating a relationship of moderate strength.

Correlations are an enormously useful descriptive tool. If I want to know whether shy 4-year-olds are still shy at 20, and I have a suitable set of longitudinal data, I would use a correlation to look at the degree of consistency. If I want to know whether better-educated mothers are more likely to have children with larger vocabularies, I would use a correlation.

CRITICAL THINKING

Researchers have found a positive correlation between a mother's age at the birth of her child and the child's later IQ: Very young mothers have children with lower IQs. How many different explanations of this correlation can you think of?

Useful as they are, though, correlations have a major limitation: They do not tell us about *causal* relationships. For example, several researchers have found a moderate positive correlation between the "difficultness" of a child's temperament and the amount of punishment the child receives from her parents: The more difficult the temperament the more often the child is punished. But which way does the causality run? Do difficult children *elicit* more punishment? Or do children become more difficult because they have been punished more often? Or is there some third factor that may cause both, such as perhaps some genetic contribution both to the child's difficultness and to the parent's tendency to punish? The correlation alone does not allow us to choose among these alternatives. Indeed, no correlation, standing alone, can prove causality. A correlation may point in a particular direction or suggest possible causal links, but to discover the causes we must explore the possibilities with other techniques, including experiments.

A Final Word

It is not only professional researchers who find such details about research design to be of interest and value. You, too, will find this knowledge helpful, even if you never conduct such research yourself. Let me give you just one practical example. In 1991,

Time magazine published an article about a system for providing stimulation for the unborn baby. In this system, the pregnant woman wears a belt full of audio equipment, on which tapes of various complex patterns of heartbeat sounds are played. The article reported that the maker of this gadget had done some "research" to demonstrate that this procedure produces smarter, faster-developing babies. To quote *Time*: "Last year 50 of the youngsters [whose mothers had worn the belt], ranging in age from six months to 34 months, were given standardized language, social and motor-skills tests. Their overall score was 25 percent above the national norm" (September 30, 1991, p. 76).

I hope you would not go out and buy this apparatus on the basis of that finding! After reading what I've said about research design, you should immediately be able to see that self-selection is a major problem here. What kind of mothers will buy such a gadget? How are they likely to differ from mothers who would not buy it? In fact, this reported "research" tells us nothing. It isn't even a quasi experiment because no comparison group was included. Equivalent reports of research on children, adolescents, and adults appear in the newspapers and popular magazines every day. Obviously, I want you to be critical analysts of the research I'll talk about in this book. But if nothing else, I want you to become very critical consumers of popularly presented research information. Some of it is very good. A lot of it is bunk, or at the very least inconclusive. I hope you are now in a better position to tell the difference.

Summary

1. In studying development over the life span, we need to understand both change and continuity, shared and individual patterns of development, and the relative influences of nature and nurture.
2. One major type of change consists of shared changes linked to age, which might be the product of maturation (biological clock), common social prescriptions (social clock), or inner changes triggered by either the biological or social clock.
3. Cultures affect the definition of the social clock as well as many other features of individual life. One important dimension along which cultures vary widely is individualism versus collectivism. Most Western cultures emphasize individualism, while Asian, Latin, and African cultures are more likely to emphasize collectivism.
4. Experiences unique to particular cohorts—such as the Great Depression or the women's movement—also shape the social clock, which can alter the underlying pattern of development. Awareness of such cohort differences is especially crucial in studies of adults, in which comparisons of different age groups are inevitably confounded with cohort effects.
5. Individual life pathways are also affected by unique, nonshared experiences. The timing of such individual experiences may be especially important in shaping an individual's developmental pattern.
6. Consistency over time can also be explained in biological terms. Using studies of twins and adopted children, behavior geneticists have found significant genetic influence on a wide range of behavior.
7. Consistency in behavior over time may also be fostered because of the cumulative effects of early behaviors, and because children and adults tend to select niches in which their basic behaviors fit well.
8. Historically, psychologists and philosophers have argued about nature *versus* nurture, but we now know that every behavior, every developmental change, is a product of both.
9. Babies appear to be born with a wide variety of inborn biases in their ways of responding to the stimulation around them.
10. Each child and each adult also creates internal models of meaning to interpret past experience and to understand new experience.
11. In studying nurture, it is important to look well beyond the immediate family and consider the larger cultural influences and the impact of the entire environmental system.
12. Inborn or acquired vulnerabilities and resilience resources interact with the richness of the environment in nonadditive ways. The most seriously detrimental combination appears to be a high level of vulnerability combined with a poor environment.
13. Researchers and theorists differ about whether development should be conceived as purely quantitative or as qualitative. Similarly, theorists disagree about whether there are distinct, qualitatively different stages of development over the life span.
14. In studying any aspect of development, three main types of research design are possible: cross-sectional, in which separate age groups are each tested once; longitudinal, in which the same individuals are tested repeatedly over time; and sequential, which offers combinations of the first two.
15. Longitudinal or sequential research is required to study sequences of development or consistency over time.

16. To test specific hypotheses, experimental designs are also possible in which subjects are assigned randomly to treatment or control groups. However, there are limitations in the use of experimental designs in studies of development.
17. The choice of subjects may have a major effect on the generalizability of results from any one study.
18. Correlational research, common in studies of development, can be informative, but correlations do not describe causal relationships, so care is needed in interpretation.
19. A basic understanding of research design will help you be a cautious and critical consumer of popularly presented descriptions of research.
20. Any individual who participates in psychological research must give informed consent, and the privacy of any personal information provided must be guarded.

Key Terms

ageism
age norms
age strata
behavior genetics
biological clock
cohort
collectivism
control group
correlation
critical period
cross-cultural research
cross-sectional design
culture
dependent variable
ethnography
experiment
experimental group
inborn biases
independent variable
individualism
informed consent
longitudinal design
maturation
resilience
sensitive period
sequential design
social clock
teratogen
vulnerability

Suggested Readings

Bornstein, M. H. (Ed.) (1987). *Sensitive periods in development: Interdisciplinary perspectives.* Hillsdale, NJ: Erlbaum.

Bornstein's own paper in this collection is an excellent introduction to the concept of sensitive periods. There are also several other excellent papers analyzing the evidence for critical or sensitive periods in a number of areas of development, including language and social relations.

Cole, M. (1992). Culture in development. In M. H. Bornstein & M. E. Lamb (Eds.), *Developmental psychology: An advanced textbook* (3rd ed.) (pp. 731–738). Hillsdale, NJ: Erlbaum.

Not at all easy reading, but one of the best analyses I have yet seen of this very complicated subject.

Neugarten, B. L., & Neugarten, D. A. (1987). The changing meanings of age. *Psychology Today*, 21 (5), 29–33.

In this brief paper, Neugarten argues that age strata in our culture are shifting rather rapidly, with new strata created, such as "middle-aged," which was not a recognizable stratum until a few decades ago.

Plomin, R., & McClearn, G. E. (Eds.). (1993). *Nature, nurture and psychology.* Washington, DC: American Psychological Association.

If you think the "great debate" about nature and nurture is an outmoded issue, this book will quickly persuade you otherwise. The controversy is alive and well, although the papers in this book reflect the efforts of many people to recast it in more useful terms.

Rowe, J. W., Wang, S. Y., & Elahi, D. (1990). Design, conduct, and analysis of human aging research. In E. R. Schneider & J. W. Rowe (Eds.), *Handbook of the biology of aging* (3rd ed.) (pp. 63–71). San Diego, CA: Academic Press.

Included in this paper is a particularly good—albeit high-level—discussion of the pros and cons of longitudinal research designs in studies of adulthood and aging.

Seitz, V. (1988). Methodology. In M. H. Bornstein & M. E. Lamb (Eds.), *Developmental psychology: An advanced textbook* (2nd ed.) (pp. 51–84). Hillsdale, NJ: Erlbaum.

A well-organized, clearly written review of many of the methodological issues I have talked about in this chapter.

Wright, L. (1995). Double mystery. *The New Yorker*, August 7, 1995, pp. 45–62.

An utterly fascinating, clearly written article about twins, about the study of twins in behavior genetic research, and about what it means to grow up as a twin.

2 Theories of Development

Students often tell me that they hate reading about theories. What they want are the facts. But I hope I can persuade you that theories are not only essential, they are part of your everyday life. No fact stands alone without any explanation or framework; instead, we all interpret and create theories about each fact that comes our way.

Suppose your best friend frowns at you. That's a "fact." But how do you *interpret* that fact? What theory do you have to explain it? If you think about it for a minute, you'll realize that the theory or explanation you apply to this frown makes a huge difference in the way you react. If your theory is that your friend is tired, your response might be sympathy; if your theory is that your friend is annoyed with you, your response might be defensiveness or irritation. In these terms, the internal models of experience I talked about in Chapter 1 are simply more general types of personal theories that we each tend to apply to a wide variety of situations.

Scientists operate this way too. Naturally we try to collect facts. But both the collection of the facts and the interpretation of them are guided by theory. For example, here's a fact: Virtually all children show some negative effects when their parents divorce, but boys show a greater increase in aggression and other behavior problems, and their school performance deteriorates more than is true for girls (e.g., Hetherington, 1989; Kline et al., 1989).

When parents divorce, boys are more likely to show disturbed behavior or poorer school performance than are girls. But why? We need theories to help us explain facts like these.

This fact is extremely interesting in and of itself, but it makes a big difference how we explain it. Do mothers treat their sons and daughters differently after a divorce? When the mother has custody, do boys suffer more from the absence of the father? Or perhaps boys are somehow inherently less able to handle stress of any kind. Each of these alternative explanations is derived from a different theory, and each suggests different types of additional research we might do to check on the validity of the explanation. If differential treatment of sons and daughters is the answer, then we ought to study family interactions in recently divorced families in some detail. If the absence of the father in the son's life is the crucial factor, then we ought to study boys and girls living with their fathers after divorce. If response to stress is involved, we would want to look at other stressful occurrences in family life, such as unexpected parental unemployment, the death of a family member, or a major move, and see whether in these cases, too, boys show more extreme responses. The point is that the creation of models or theories is a natural and necessary process if we are to make sense out of our personal experience, or out of scientific facts.

My primary goal in this chapter is to introduce you to four major families of theories that have been centrally influential in the study of human development: psychoanalytic, humanistic, cognitive-developmental, and learning theories. I'll also talk about two theories that do not fit neatly into the traditional category scheme but that have influenced our thinking about adult development.

A second goal is to make clear just how real and important the differences among these various models can be. Learning theories, for example, emphasize the vital role of experience in *shaping* the individual. Cognitive-developmental theorists like Piaget, on the other hand, argue that the child uses experiences to *construct* her own reality, her own understanding. Not only do these two views lead to very different kinds of research, they also have quite different practical applications. For example, a teacher who believes that children are shaped by their specific experiences would want to create a highly structured classroom environment in which the child's learning is guided and reinforced very carefully. A teacher who is convinced that children construct their own understanding of the world would want to create a much more open, exploratory type of classroom in which children can experiment on their own.

I'll come back to the issue of the contrasts among these various theories at the end of the chapter. But as you go along, keep in mind that theories shape the way we think about facts, the questions we ask, and the educational programs we create.

Psychoanalytic Theories

The family of theorists called psychoanalytic includes Sigmund Freud, Carl Jung, Alfred Adler, Erik Erikson, Jane Loevinger, and many others. All have been interested in explaining human behavior by understanding the underlying processes of the *psyche*, a Greek term meaning soul, spirit, or mind. Sigmund Freud (1905, 1920) is usually credited with originating the psychoanalytic approach, and his terminology and many of his concepts have become part of our intellectual culture, even while his explicit influence on developmental psychology has waned.

Freud's Theory of Psychosexual Development

One of Freud's most distinctive theoretical contributions is the idea that behavior is governed not only by conscious but by *unconscious* processes. The most basic of these unconscious processes, according to Freud, is an instinctual sexual drive he called the **libido,** present at birth and forming the motive force behind virtually all our behavior. Further unconscious material is also created over time through the functioning of the various **defense mechanisms**—those automatic, normal, unconscious strategies for reducing anxiety that we all use on a daily basis, such as repression, denial, or projection.

Freud also argued that personality has a structure that develops over time. Freud proposed three parts, the **id,** in which the libido is centered; the **ego,** a much more conscious element that serves as the executive of the personality; and the **superego,** the center of conscience and morality, incorporating the norms and moral strictures of the family and society. In Freud's theory, these three parts are not all present at birth. The infant or toddler is all id, all instinct, all desire, without the

The Real World

We All Use Defense Mechanisms Every Day

I suspect that when many of you hear the phrase "defense mechanisms," you think of some kind of abnormal or deviant behavior. It is important for you to understand, though, that Freud conceived of defense mechanisms not only as unconscious but also as entirely normal. Their primary purpose is to help us protect ourselves against anxiety. Since we all feel anxious some of the time, we all use some form of defense.

Suppose I send a paper to a professional journal and it comes back with a rejection letter. To deal with the anxiety I naturally feel after such a rejection, I resort (unconsciously) to some kind of defense mechanism.

All defense mechanisms distort reality to some extent, but they vary in the amount of distortion involved. At one extreme end is *denial.* I might deny that I had ever submitted the paper or that it had ever been rejected. A notch less distorting are mechanisms like *projection,* in which I push my feelings onto someone else. ("Those people who rejected this paper are really stupid! They don't know what they're doing.") In this way, I ascribe to others the qualities I fear may be true for me—in this instance, stupidity. I might also *repress* my feelings, insisting that I really don't mind at all that my paper is rejected; later, I might simply forget that I had ever submitted that paper. Or I could use *intellectualization,* in which I consider, in emotionally very bland terms, all the reasons why the paper was rejected. Intellectualization sounds quite rational and open, as if there were no defense involved. But what has been pushed away is the emotion.

Among the least distorting defenses is *suppression,* in which I allow myself to be aware of my distress but still shove it away for a while by saying, à la Scarlett O'Hara, "I'll think about it tomorrow." So I push it away, but not so firmly into the unconscious as is true for repression.

Not long ago I was reminded very forcibly of just how powerful these defensive processes can be. I received a phone call at noon one day from a friend who told me that a man who was very dear to me had died from AIDS. I said all the right things at the time, finished my lunch, and went back to work, pressing to meet a deadline. At dinner that evening, I had this vague feeling that there was some important news I meant to tell my husband, but I *couldn't remember what it was.* I went to a choir rehearsal that evening and was unbearably grumpy and irritable but couldn't figure out why. As I got into my car to drive home, the memory of my friend's death suddenly returned, and I burst into tears in the parking lot. This is a perfect example of repression. I couldn't deal with the news when it first arrived, so I pushed it out of my conscious memory long enough to get me through the day.

Can you think of equivalent examples in your own life? When was the last time something uncomfortable happened to you? How did you handle it? Bear in mind that these defenses are entirely normal.

Table 2.1 Freud's Stages of Psychosexual Development

Stage	Age	Erogenous Zones	Major Developmental Task (Potential Source of Conflict)	Some Adult Characteristics of People Who Have Been Fixated at This Stage
Oral	0–1	Mouth, lips, tongue	Weaning	Oral behavior, such as smoking and overeating; passivity and gullibility.
Anal	2–3	Anus	Toilet training	Orderliness, parsimoniousness, obstinacy, or the opposite.
Phallic	4–5	Genitals	Oedipus complex	Vanity, recklessness, and the opposite.
Latency*	6–12	No specific area	Development of defense mechanisms	None: fixation does not normally occur at this stage.
Genital	13–18	Genitals	Mature sexual intimacy	Adults who have successfully integrated earlier stages should emerge with sincere interest in others and mature sexuality.

*The latency period, strictly speaking, is not a psychosexual stage because Freud thought that libido was not invested in the body during this period; sexual energy is quiescent in this period.

restraining influence of the ego or the superego. The ego begins to develop in the years from 2 to about 4 or 5 as the child learns to adapt his instant-gratification strategies. Finally, the superego begins to develop just before school age, as the child incorporates the parents' values and cultural mores.

Freud also proposed a series of **psychosexual stages** (summarized in Table 2.1) through which the child moves in a fixed sequence strongly influenced by maturation. In each, the libido is invested in that part of the body that is most sensitive at that age. In a newborn, the mouth is the most sensitive part of the body, so libidinal energy is focused there. The stage is therefore called the *oral* stage. As neurological development progresses, the infant develops more sensation in the anus (hence the *anal* stage), and later in the genitalia (the *phallic* and eventually the *genital* stages).

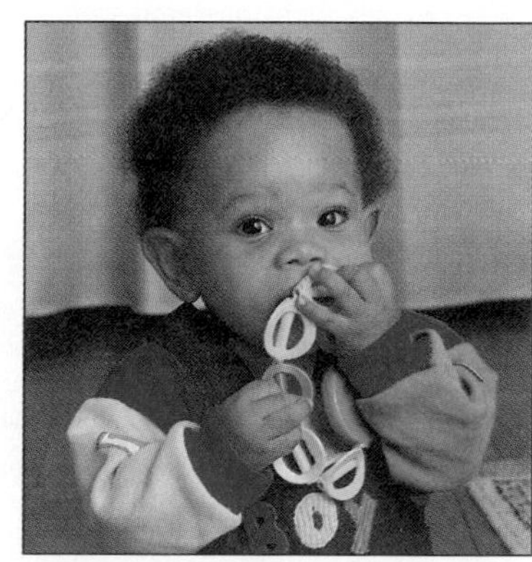

Freud thought that babies like 6-month-old Christopher put things into their mouths because that is where they have the most pleasurable sensations. If babies don't get enough oral stimulation, he argued, they may become fixated at the oral stage.

The most famous of these stages is probably the phallic, since it is here that the *Oedipus conflict* is said to occur. This stage begins at about age 3 or 4, when the genitals increase in sensitivity. Freud proposed that during this stage, the boy "rather naively wishes to use his new-found source of pleasure, his penis, to please his oldest source of pleasure, his mother" (Schaeffer, 1971, p. 12). He becomes envious of his father, who has access to the mother's body in a way that the boy does not. The boy also sees his father as a powerful and threatening figure who has the ultimate power—the power to castrate. The boy is caught between desire for his mother and fear of his father's power.

Most of these feelings and the resultant conflict are unconscious. The boy does not have overt sexual feelings or behavior toward his mother. But unconscious or not, the result of this conflict is anxiety. How can the little boy handle this anxiety? In Freud's view, the boy responds with a defensive process called **identification:** The boy "incorporates" his image of his father and attempts to match his own behavior to that image. By trying to make himself as much like his father as possible, the boy not only reduces the chance of an attack from the father, he takes on some of the father's power as well. Furthermore, it is the "inner father," with his values and moral judgments, that serves as the core of the child's superego.

Critical Thinking

How do you think Freud might explain the higher incidence of problem behavior among boys in divorced families? In Freud's theory, would it make a difference how old the boy or girl was when the divorce occurred?

A parallel process is supposed to occur in girls. The girl experiences the same kind of "sexual" attraction to her father as the boy does toward his mother, sees her mother as a rival for her father's sexual attentions, and has some fear of her mother. Like the boy, she resolves the problem by identifying with the same-sex parent.

Optimum development, according to Freud, requires an environment that will satisfy the unique needs of each period. The baby needs sufficient opportunity for oral stimulation; the 4-year-old boy needs a father present with whom to identify and a mother who is not too seductive. An inadequate early environment will leave a residue of unresolved problems and unmet needs, which are then carried forward to subsequent stages.

This emphasis on the formative role of early experience, particularly early family experience, is a hallmark of psychoanalytic theories. In this view, the first five or six years of life are a kind of sensitive period for the creation of the individual personality.

Erikson's Theory of Psychosocial Stages

Apart from Freud, the psychoanalytic theorist who has had the greatest influence on the study of development has been Erik Erikson (Erikson, 1950, 1959, 1980b, 1982; Erikson, Erikson, & Kivnick, 1986; Evans, 1969). Erikson shared most of Freud's basic assumptions but differed from him on several key points. Unlike Freud, who placed central emphasis on inner instincts, Erikson thought development resulted from the interaction between inner instincts and outer cultural and social demands; hence the name **psychosocial stages** rather than *psychosexual*. Furthermore, Erikson thought that development continued through the entire life span, as the child and then the adult developed a sense of ever-changing **identity.** To develop a complete, stable identity, the individual must move through and successfully resolve eight "crises" or "dilemmas" over the course of the lifetime, summarized in Table 2.2. Each

Table 2.2 Erikson's Stages of Psychosocial Development

Approximate Age	Ego Quality to Be Developed	Potential Strength to Be Gained	Some Tasks and Activities of the Stage
0–1	Basic trust versus mistrust	Hope	Trust in mother or central caregiver and in one's own ability to make things happen. A key element in an early secure attachment.
2–3	Autonomy versus shame, doubt	Will	New physical skills lead to free choice; toilet training occurs; child learns control but may develop shame if not handled properly.
4–5	Initiative versus guilt	Purpose	Organize activities around some goal; become more assertive and aggressive; Oedipus conflict with parent of same sex may lead to guilt.
6–12	Industry versus inferiority	Competence	Absorb all the basic cultural skills and norms, including school skills and tool use.
13–18	Identity versus role confusion	Fidelity	Adapt sense of self to pubertal changes, make occupational choice, achieve adultlike sexual identity, and search for new values.
19–25	Intimacy versus isolation	Love	Form one or more intimate relationships that go beyond adolescent love; form family groups.
26–65	Generativity versus self-absorbtion and stagnation	Care	Bear and rear children, focus on occupational achievement or creativity, and train the next generation; turn outward from the self toward others.
65+	Ego integrity versus despair	Wisdom	Integrate earlier stages and come to terms with basic identity. Accept self.

dilemma emerges as the child or adult is challenged by new relationships, new tasks, or new demands. The fourth stage of "industry versus inferiority," for example, begins when the child starts school and is challenged by the demand to learn to read and write and absorb great chunks of new information.

Each dilemma or stage is defined by a pair of opposing possibilities, such as trust versus mistrust, or integrity versus despair. A healthy resolution of each dilemma results in the development of a particular strength, such as the quality of hope that may emerge from the dilemma of trust versus mistrust. A "healthy resolution" of each dilemma, however, does not mean moving totally to the apparently positive end of any one of the continua Erikson describes. For example, an infant needs to have experienced some mistrust in order to learn to trust discerningly; too much industriousness can lead to narrow virtuosity; too much identity cohesion in adolescence can result in fanaticism. But healthy development requires a favorable ratio of positive to negative.

Of the eight stages described in Table 2.2, four have been the focus of the greatest amount of theorizing and research: trust in infancy, identity in adolescence, intimacy in early adulthood, and generativity in middle adulthood.

Basic Trust Versus Mistrust. Erikson believed that the behavior of the major caregiver (usually the mother) is critical to the child's establishing a sense of basic trust. For a successful resolution of this task, the parent must be consistently loving and respond predictably and reliably to the child. Those infants whose early care has been erratic or harsh may develop *mis*trust. In either case, the child carries this aspect of basic identity through development, affecting the resolution of later tasks.

Identity Versus Role Confusion. Erikson's description of the central adolescent dilemma has been particularly influential. He argued that every adolescent, in order to arrive at a mature sexual and occupational identity, must reexamine his identity and the roles he must occupy. He must achieve a reintegrated sense of self, of what he wants to do and be, and of his appropriate sexual role. The risk is that of confusion, arising from the profusion of roles opening up to the child at this age.

Intimacy Versus Isolation. In the first of the three adult stages, the young adult builds upon the identity established in adolescence. Erikson defined intimacy as "the ability to fuse your identity with someone else's without fear that you're going to lose something yourself" (Erikson, in Evans, 1969). Many young people, Erikson thought, make the mistake of thinking they will find their identity in a relationship, but in his view it is only those who have already formed (or are well on the way to forming) a clear identity who can successfully enter this fusion of identities that he calls intimacy. For those whose identities are weak or unformed, relationships will remain shallow and the young person will experience a sense of isolation or loneliness.

Generativity can be expressed in many ways, including teaching or being a Big Brother.

Generativity Versus Self-Absorption and Stagnation. The key task of middle adulthood is generativity, which "is primarily the concern in establishing and guiding the next generation" (Erikson, 1963, p. 267). The rearing of children is the most obvious way to achieve such a sense of generativity, but it is not the only way. Creative work, service to organizations or society, serving as mentor to younger colleagues—all these can help the midlife adult achieve a sense of generativity. Failing that, the self-absorbed, nongenerative adult may feel a sense of stagnation.

A key idea to take away with you from this very brief presentation of Erikson's theory is that each new task, each dilemma, is thrust upon the developing person because of changes in social demands. We might rephrase this idea in Matilda Riley's terms by saying that each age stratum has its own central psychological task. Because age marches along willy-nilly, the developing person is confronted with new tasks whether or not she has successfully resolved earlier dilemmas. You can't stay a

20-year-old until you get it right! You are, instead, pushed forward, carrying the unresolved issues with you as excess baggage. The very earliest tasks are thus especially important because they set the stage for everything that follows.

Other Psychoanalytic Theorists

A number of other theorists who have had an important influence on current thinking about development have been strongly influenced by psychoanalytic theory.

John Bowlby's Model of Attachment. John Bowlby's theory of the development of attachment, which I mentioned briefly in Chapter 1 (1969, 1973, 1980), is well grounded in psychoanalytic thought. Like Freud and Erikson, Bowlby assumed that the root of human personality lies in the earliest childhood relationships. Significant failure or trauma in those relationships will permanently shape the child's development. Bowlby focused his attention on the child's first attachment to the mother because it is usually the earliest, and is arguably the most central.

To describe how that attachment comes about, Bowlby introduced several concepts from *ethological theory*, which brings evolutionary concepts to bear on the study of behavior. Human evolution, Bowlby suggested, has resulted in the child being born with a repertoire of instinctive behaviors that elicit caregiving from others—behaviors like crying, smiling, or making eye contact. Similarly, the mother (or other caregiving adult) is equipped with various instinctive behaviors toward the infant, such as responding to a cry or speaking in a higher voice. Together these instinctive patterns bring mother and infant together in an intricate chain of stimulus and response that causes the child to form a specific attachment to that one adult—a process I'll be talking about in some detail in Chapter 6.

Although Bowlby's theory is not a full-fledged stage theory of development in the manner of Freud or Erikson, it is nonetheless based on many of the underlying psychoanalytic assumptions. It has also stimulated and profoundly influenced the large body of current research on attachment, including a growing interest in attachment during adulthood.

Jane Loevinger's Theory of Ego Development. Jane Loevinger (1976) has focused on the development of one part of Freud's personality structure, namely the ego. She proposes a series of ten stages or steps from childhood through adulthood, but unlike Freud or Erikson, Loevinger does not think these stages are tied to age. She argues instead that people move through a *sequence* of steps in the same order, but not all individuals will progress to the same level or move at the same speed. In her view, each new step or stage—if it is achieved at all—represents a new perspective, a new way of understanding oneself and one's relationship to the world.

One particular stage shift Loevinger describes, from the *conformist* to the *conscientious* stage, turns out to be especially helpful in talking about some of the changes in adult personality. The conformist stage is typically (but not invariably) reached in late adolescence or early adulthood. An individual in this stage identifies her own welfare with that of some group—family, work group, religious group, or whatever. She *defines herself* in terms of membership in that group or subgroup, and tends to define others as either being one of "us" or one of "them." Inwardly, she understands her own emotions in parallel ways, such as either happy or sad, good or bad, but without many gradations in between.

After passing through a transitional phase Loevinger calls the self-aware level, the adult *may* eventually move out of the conformist stance and arrive at the *conscientious stage*. A radical change is involved in this transition. In the conformist stage, authority is external to the self; in the conscientious stage, authority is taken inward. The person now creates her own rules and attempts to live by them. She has a much richer inner life with many more shadings of feeling, and perceives others in more subtle and individualistic terms as well.

According to Loevinger, not all adults actually make this shift. But for those who do, it represents a fundamental change in the person's basic "theory" about the world and her place in it.

Critique of Psychoanalytic Theories

Psychoanalytic theories like Freud's or Erikson's have several great attractions. Most centrally, they highlight the importance of the emotional quality of the child's earliest relationship with the caregivers. Furthermore, they suggest that the child's needs or "tasks" change with age, so that the parents must constantly adapt to the changing child. One of the implications of this is that we should not think of "good parenting" as if it were a global quality. Some of us may be very good at meeting the needs of an infant but quite awful at dealing with teenagers' identity struggles; others of us may have the opposite pattern. The child's eventual personality, and her overall "health" thus depend on the interaction or transaction that develops in the particular family. This is an extremely attractive element of these theories because more and more of the research within developmental psychology is moving us toward just such a transactional conception of the process.

Psychoanalytic theory has also given us a number of helpful concepts—such as the unconscious, defense mechanisms, and identification—that have been so widely adopted that they have become a part of everyday language as well as theory. The concept of unconscious motivations, in particular, has been a profoundly important idea whose traces we can certainly see in current theories emphasizing internal models.

A third strength has been the emphasis on continued development during adulthood. Psychoanalytic theorists like Erikson, Loevinger, and Bowlby have described basic psychological processes such as identity development, ego development, and attachment that have their roots in childhood but continue throughout life. These ideas have provided a framework for a great deal of new research and theorizing about adult development.

The great weakness of all the psychoanalytic approaches is the fuzziness of many of the concepts. Identification may be an intriguing theoretical notion, but how do we measure it? How do we detect the presence of specific defense mechanisms? Without more precise operational definitions it is impossible to disconfirm the theory. Those areas in which the general concepts of psychoanalytic theory have been most fruitfully applied to our understanding of development have nearly always been areas in which other theorists or researchers have offered more precise definitions or clearer methods for measuring some Freudian or Eriksonian construct, such as Bowlby's concept of security of attachment. Psychoanalytic theory may thus sometimes offer a provocative framework for our thinking, but it has not been a highly testable theory of development.

Humanistic Theories

Some psychologists with roots in the psychoanalytic tradition took issue with the emphasis on pathology that often pervades psychoanalytic theory and practice. They began, instead, with the highly optimistic assumption that each individual is fundamentally motivated to achieve his full potential. The key figure in this *humanistic* tradition is Abraham Maslow (1968, 1970a, 1970b, 1971), who used the term *self-actualization* to describe this ultimate goal of human life.

Maslow's greatest interest was in the development of motives or needs, which he divided into two subsets, **deficiency motives** and **being motives.** Deficiency motives involve drives to maintain physical or emotional homeostasis (inner balance), such as the drive to get enough to eat or drink, the sexual drive, or even a drive to obtain sufficient love or respect from others. Being motives involve the desire to understand, to give to others, and to grow. In general, the satisfaction of deficiency motives prevents or cures illness or re-creates homeostasis. In contrast, the satisfaction of being motives produces positive health. The distinction is like the "difference between fending off threat or attack, and positive triumph and achievement" (Maslow, 1968, p. 32).

Critical Thinking

Do you know anyone you would think of as "self-actualized?" What are that person's qualities or characteristics?

Maslow described these various needs or motives in his famous *needs hierarchy*, shown in Figure 2.1. He argued that the various needs must be met from the bottom up. Only when the physiological needs are met do safety needs come to the fore; only when love and esteem needs are met can the need for self-actualization become dominant. For that reason, Maslow thought that being needs were likely to be significant only in adulthood, and only in those individuals who had found stable ways to satisfy both love and esteem needs—needs that sound very similar to Erikson's stages of intimacy and generativity.

Critique of Humanistic Theories

One of the strongest attractions of the humanistic theories is their deep-seated optimism. Carl Rogers, a psychotherapist who contributed greatly to the body of writings in the humanistic tradition, talked about the capacity each of us has to become a "fully functioning" person—without guilt or seriously distorting defenses (Rogers, 1961). In this idea, as in Maslow's concept of self-actualization, we see an assumption that it is never too late; that adults not only *can* overcome early conditioning or the residue of unresolved dilemmas, but that people are motivated to try to do just that.

Another strength of Maslow's model, to my way of thinking, is his emphasis on the *sequence* of emergent needs, rather than on stages. He did not say that everyone achieves self-actualization, so we shouldn't expect all adults to do so. Instead, like Loevinger, he tells us about the path we must travel to get there.

But as is true of psychoanalytic theories, humanistic models like Maslow's are stated in broad, rather imprecise terms. They have appealed to a great many people because they seem to resonate with some aspects of everyday experience. But they are difficult to test empirically because the propositions are not stated clearly enough.

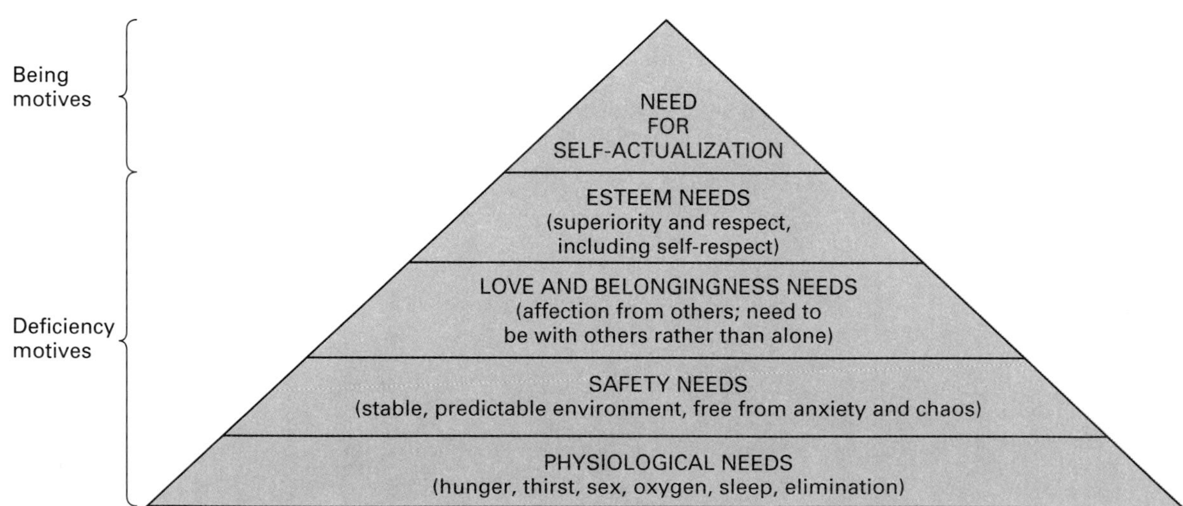

FIGURE 2.1 In Maslow's view, needs operate from the bottom up in this needs hierarchy. Until physiological needs are met, no other need will be prominent; until love needs are met, esteem needs will not emerge; and so on. Similarly, there is a developmental aspect: A baby is primarily dominated by physiological needs, a toddler by safety needs, and so forth. Only in adulthood may the need for self-actualization become central. (*Sources:* Maslow, 1968, 1970b.)

Cognitive-Developmental Theories

In contrast, cognitive-developmental theories have been extremely influential not only because many of the ideas are inherently intriguing, but also because Piaget and others stated those ideas with precision, which made it possible for other researchers to test specific hypotheses derived from the theory.

Piaget's Theory

The central figure in cognitive-developmental theory has been Jean Piaget (Piaget, 1952, 1970, 1977; Piaget & Inhelder, 1969), a Swiss scientist whose theories have shaped the thinking of several generations of developmental psychologists. Piaget described himself as a "genetic epistemologist" rather than a psychologist; for him the central and only question of interest was "How does thinking develop?" As he began to try to answer that question, he was struck by the fact that all children seem to go through the same kinds of sequential discoveries about their world, making the same sorts of mistakes and arriving at the same solutions. For example, 3- and 4-year-olds all seem to think that if you pour water from a short, fat glass into a tall, thin one, there is now more water, because the water level is higher in the thin glass than it was in the fat glass. But most 7-year-olds realize that the amount of water has not changed.

Piaget's detailed observations of children's thinking led him to several conclusions, the most central of which is that it is the nature of the human organism to *adapt* to its environment. This is an active process. Piaget does not think that the environment *shapes* the child but that the child (like the adult) actively seeks to understand her environment. In the process, she explores, manipulates, and examines the objects and people in her world.

The Concept of Scheme. A pivotal concept in Piaget's model—and one of the hardest to grasp—is that of a **scheme** (sometimes written *schema*). This term is often used as roughly analogous to the word *concept* or the phrases "mental category" or "complex of ideas." But Piaget used it even more broadly than that to describe mental or physical *actions*. Thus, a scheme is not really a category but the *action of categorizing* in some particular fashion. Some purely physical or sensory actions are also schemes. If you pick up and look at a ball, you are using your "looking scheme," your "picking-up scheme," and your "holding scheme." Piaget proposed that each baby begins life with a small repertoire of simple sensory or motor schemes, such as looking, tasting, touching, hearing, and reaching. For the baby, an object *is* a thing that tastes a certain way, feels a certain way when it is touched, or has a particular color. Later, the toddler and child develops mental schemes as well, such as categorizing or comparing one object to another. Over development, the child gradually adds extremely complex mental schemes, such as deductive analysis or systematic reasoning.

Using Piaget's language, we would say that 9-month-old Jesse is assimilating this spoon to his grasping scheme. As he adapts his way of grasping, he is also accommodating the grasping scheme.

But how does the child get from the simple, built-in sensorimotor schemes to the more internalized, increasingly complex mental schemes we see in later childhood? Piaget proposed three basic processes to account for the emergence of new skills: **assimilation, accommodation,** and **equilibration.**

Assimilation. Assimilation is the process of *taking in*, of absorbing some event or experience to some scheme. When a baby looks at and then reaches for a mobile above his crib, Piaget would say that the baby had assimilated the mobile to his looking and reaching schemes; when an older child sees a dog and labels it "dog," she is assimilating that animal to her dog category or scheme. When you read this paragraph you are assimilating the information, hooking the concept onto whatever other concept (scheme) you have that may be similar.

The key here is that assimilation is an *active* process. For one thing, we assimilate selectively. When I was living in Germany and struggling to learn German, I could assimilate only a portion of what my German teacher said—the parts for which I already had schemes. And I could imitate or use only the parts that I had assimilated. In addition, the very act of assimilating changes the information that is assimilated, because each assimilated event or experience takes on some of the characteristics of the scheme to which it was assimilated. If I label your new sweater as green (that is, if I assimilate it to my green scheme) even though it is really chartreuse, I will remember it as more green and less yellow than it really is.

Accommodation. The complementary process is accommodation, which involves *changing the scheme* as a result of some new information you have taken in by assimilation. As I assimilated new German words and grammar, I gradually changed (accommodated) my concepts and categories, so that I had mental categories for several forms of past tense instead of only one, or mental groupings of words with a given prefix. The baby who sees and grasps a square object for the first time will accommodate his grasping scheme, so that next time he reaches for a square object his hand will be more appropriately bent to grasp it. Thus, in Piaget's theory, the process of accommodation is the key to developmental change. Through accommodation, we reorganize our thoughts, improve our skills, change our strategies

Critical Thinking

See if you can think of three or four more examples of assimilation and accommodation in your everyday life.

Equilibration. The third aspect of adaptation is equilibration. Piaget assumed that in the process of adaptation, the child is always striving for coherence, to stay "in balance," to have an understanding of the world that makes overall sense. This is not unlike what a scientist does when she develops a theory—just what I am talking about in this chapter. She wants a theory that will make sense out of every observation and that has internal coherence. When new research findings come along, she assimilates them to her existing theory; if they don't fit perfectly, she might simply set aside the deviant data or she may make minor modifications in her theory. But if enough nonconfirming evidence accumulates, she may have to throw out her theory altogether and start over or she may need to change some basic theoretical assumptions, either of which would be a kind of equilibration.

Piaget thought that a child operated in a similar way, as a "little scientist," creating coherent, more or less internally consistent models or theories. Because the infant starts with a very limited repertoire of schemes, his early "theories" or structures are inevitably primitive and imperfect, which forces him to make periodic major changes in his internal structure.

Piaget saw three particularly significant reorganizations or equilibration points, each ushering in a new stage of development. The first is between roughly 18 and 24 months of age, when the toddler shifts from the dominance of simple sensory and motor schemes to the first really internal representations. The second happens at roughly age 6 or 7, when the child adds a whole new set of powerful schemes Piaget calls **operations.** These are far more abstract and general mental actions, such as mental addition or subtraction.

The third major equilibration occurs at adolescence, when the child figures out how to "operate on" (to think about, analyze, reorganize, compare) ideas as well as events or objects. These three major equilibrations create four stages:

- The **sensorimotor stage,** from birth to 18 months
- The **preoperational stage,** from 18 months to about age 6
- The **concrete operational stage** from 6 to about 12
- The **formal operational stage,** from age 12 onward

Table 2.3 expands somewhat more fully on these stages, each of which I will describe in greater detail in the appropriate age-based chapters. The key for now is to understand that in Piaget's view, each stage grows out of the one that precedes it, and, as

Table 2.3 Piaget's Stages of Cognitive Development

Approximate Age	Stage	Description
0–2	Sensorimotor	The baby understands the world in terms of her senses and her motor actions. A mobile is how it feels to grasp, how it looks, how it tastes in the mouth.
2–6	Preoperational	By 18 to 24 months, the child can use symbols to represent objects to himself internally; be able to take others' perspectives, to classify objects, and to use simple logic.
7–11	Concrete operations	The child's logic takes a great leap forward with the development of powerful new internal mental operations, such as addition, subtraction, and class inclusion. The child is still tied to specific experience but can do mental as well as physical manipulations with known objects.
12+	Formal operations	The child becomes able to manipulate ideas as well as known objects or events. She can imagine and think about things she has never seen or that have not yet happened; she can organize ideas or objects systematically and think deductively.

with Loevinger's stages of ego development, each involves a major restructuring of the child's way of thinking. Also like Loevinger, Piaget did not conceive of progress through all these stages as inevitable. He thought the sequence was fixed, so that if the child made cognitive progress it would be in this order, but not all children would necessarily reach the same end point or move at the same speed. So the ages are approximate but the sequence is fixed. Piaget thought that virtually all children would move to at least preoperational thought, that the vast majority would achieve concrete operations, but that not all would necessarily achieve formal operations in adolescence or even in adulthood.

Vygotsky's Theory

Russian psychologist Lev Vygotsky (1978), who was born the same year as Piaget but died at the early age of 38, is normally thought of as belonging to the cognitive-developmental camp, but he placed the emphasis somewhat differently (Duncan, 1995). In particular, he was convinced that complex forms of thinking have their origins in *social* interactions rather than in the child's private explorations. According to Vygotsky, children's learning of new cognitive skills is guided by an adult (or a more skilled child, such as an older sibling), who models and structures the child's learning experience, a process he called *scaffolding*. Such new learning, Vygotsky suggested, is best achieved in what he called the **zone of proximal development**—that range of tasks that are too hard for the child to do alone but that he can manage with guidance. As the child becomes more skilled, the zone of proximal development steadily shifts upward, including ever-harder tasks.

Creating an appropriate scaffold for the child's learning is no simple matter for parents. To be optimally effective, the parent must gain and keep the child's attention, model the best strategy or solution, and adapt the whole process carefully to the child's level of skill and understanding (Landry et al., 1996; Rogoff, 1990). Vygotsky thought that the key was the language the adult used to describe or frame the task. Later, the child uses this same language to guide his independent attempts to do the same kinds of tasks.

Vygotsky's ideas have some obvious educational applications. As with Piaget's theory, Vygotsky's suggests the importance of opportunities for exploration and active participation. But some form of *assisted discovery* would play a greater role in a Vygotskian than in a Piagetian classroom; the teacher would provide the scaffolding for the children's discovery, through questions, demonstrations, and explanations (Tharp & Gallimore, 1988). To be effective, such assisted discovery processes would have to lie within the zone of proximal development of each child, a condition that would be hard to meet in a highly heterogenous classroom.

Critique of Cognitive-Developmental Theories

It would be difficult to overstate the impact Piaget's ideas have had on the study and understanding of children's development. His work has been controversial precisely because it has called into question so many earlier, more simplistic views. Piaget also devised a number of remarkably creative techniques for exploring children's thinking—techniques that often showed unexpected and counterintuitive responses from children, as you can see in the Research Report on page 39. So not only did he offer us a theory that forced us to think about children and their development in a new way, he provided a set of empirical facts that were impossible to ignore and difficult to explain.

By being quite explicit about many hypotheses and predictions, Piaget also enabled others to test his theory. When those tests have been done, Piaget has sometimes turned out to be wrong about the specific ages at which children develop particular skills. As you will see in later chapters, researchers have consistently found evidence of complex concepts at much earlier ages than Piaget proposed, although the *sequences* Piaget proposed have very often been substantiated. More importantly, Piaget was probably wrong about the breadth and generality of the stages themselves. Most 8-year-olds, for example, show "concrete operational" thinking on some tasks but not on others, and they are much more likely to show complex thinking on a task with which they are very familiar than one with which they have little experience. The whole process is a great deal less stagelike than Piaget proposed and more influenced by specific experiences than Piaget had thought. Nevertheless, a number of aspects of his theory remain strongly influential, including the following:

- *Constructivism*. The most pervasively influential idea to come from Piaget's theory is that the child is *constructing* his understanding of the world. He is not passive; he actively seeks to understand. A majority of developmentalists have accepted this proposition as a starting point (Flavell, 1992).
- *Qualitative change*. Piaget's emphasis on qualitative change has also been highly significant. Virtually all developmental psychologists would agree that a 15-year-old approaches problems and tasks in a way that is not just faster but qualitatively different from the way a 3-year-old approaches the same tasks.
- *Other specific concepts and terms*. Finally, of course, Piaget has left us with a legacy of terminology and concepts that are widely used. These include *scheme, assimilation, accommodation, egocentrism, conservation*, and the *object concept*. In addition, Piaget's division of childhood into four stages has shaped the very way we talk about childhood and the way we organize our textbooks.

Thus, even though Piaget's ideas have not always proven to be correct in their specifics, his theory truly revolutionized the field of developmental psychology. He changed the way we thought and the questions we asked.

Learning Theories

Learning theories represent a very different theoretical tradition, one in which the emphasis is much more on the way the environment *shapes* the child than on how the child understands his experiences. Although learning theorists disagree a good deal

Research Report

Piaget's Clever Research

Piaget had an enormous impact on developmental psychologists not only because he proposed a novel and provocative theory, but because of the creative strategies he devised for testing children's understanding. These strategies often showed children doing or saying very unexpected things—results that other theorists found hard to assimilate into their models.

The most famous of all Piaget's clever techniques is probably his method for studying *conservation*. Piaget would begin with two equal balls of clay, show them to the child, and let the child hold and manipulate the clay until she agreed that they had the same amount. Then in full view of the child, Piaget would squish one of the balls into a pancake, or roll it into a sausage. Then he'd ask the child whether there was still the same amount, or whether the pancake or the ball had more. Children of 4 and 5 consistently said that the ball had more; children of 6 and 7 consistently said that they were still the same.

Or Piaget would start with two equal-size water glasses, each containing exactly the same amount of liquid. The child would agree that there was the same amount of water or juice in each one. Then, in full view of the child, he'd pour the water from one glass into a shorter, fatter glass, so that the water level in the new glass was lower than the water level in the original. Then he'd ask again whether there was the same amount of water in both. Four- and 5-year-olds thought the amounts were now different, while 6- and 7-year-olds knew that there was still the same amount no matter what size glass the liquid was poured into. Thus, the older child has acquired the concept of conservation; she understands that the quantity of water or clay is *conserved* even though it is changed in some other dimension.

In another study, Piaget explored the concept of *class inclusion*—the understanding that a given object can belong simultaneously to more than one category. Fido is *both* a dog and an animal; a high chair is both a chair and furniture. Piaget usually studied this by having children first create their own classes and subclasses, and then asking them questions about these. One 5½-year-old child, for example, had been playing with a set of flowers and had made two heaps, one large group of primroses and a smaller group of other mixed flowers. Piaget then had this conversation with the child:

> *Piaget:* "If I make a bouquet of all the primroses and you make one of all the flowers, which will be bigger?"
> *Child:* "Yours."
> *Piaget:* "If I gather all the primroses in a meadow will any flowers remain?"
> *Child:* "Yes." (Piaget & Inhelder, 1959, p. 108)

The child understood that there are other flowers than primroses, but did *not* yet understand that all primroses are flowers—that the smaller, subordinate class is *included in* the larger class.

In these conversations with children, Piaget was always trying to understand how the child thought, rather than whether the child could come up with the right answer or not. So he used a "clinical method" in which he followed the child's lead, asking probing questions or creating special exploratory tests to try to discover the child's logic. In the early days of Piaget's work, many American researchers were critical of this method, since Piaget did not ask precisely the same questions of each child. Still, the results were so striking, and often so surprising, that they couldn't be ignored. And when stricter research techniques were devised, more often than not the investigators discovered that Piaget's observations were accurate.

on the particulars, all would agree with Albert Bandura when he says that "human nature is characterized by a vast potentiality that can be fashioned by direct and vicarious experience into a variety of forms within biological limits" (1989, p. 51).

No learning theorist is arguing that genetics or built-in biases are unimportant. But theorists of this group see human behavior as enormously plastic, shaped by predictable processes of learning. The most central of these processes are classical conditioning and operant conditioning. If you have encountered these concepts in earlier courses, you can skim the next section. But for those of you who lack such a background, a brief description is needed.

Classical Conditioning

This type of learning, made famous by Pavlov's experiments with his salivating dog, involves the acquisition of new signals for existing responses. If you touch a baby on the cheek, he will turn toward the touch and begin to suck. In the technical terminology of **classical conditioning,** the touch on the cheek is the **unconditional stimulus;**

the turning and sucking are **unconditioned responses.** The baby is already programmed to do all that; these are automatic reflexes. Learning occurs when some *new* stimulus is hooked into the system. The general model is that other stimuli that are present just before or at the same time as the unconditional stimulus will eventually trigger the same responses. In the typical home situation, for example, a number of stimuli occur at about the same time as the touch on the baby's cheek before feeding. There is the sound of the mother's footsteps approaching, the kinesthetic cues of being picked up, and the tactile cues of being held in the mother's arms. All these stimuli may eventually become **conditional stimuli** and may trigger the infant's response of turning and sucking, even without any touch on the cheek.

Classical conditioning is of special interest in our study of human development because of the role it plays in the development of emotional responses. For example, things or people present when you feel good will become conditional stimuli for that same sense of goodwill, while those previously associated with some uncomfortable feeling may become conditional stimuli for a sense of unease or anxiety. This is especially important in infancy, since a child's mother or father is present so often when nice things happen—when the child feels warm, comfortable, and cuddled. In this way mother and father usually come to be a conditional stimulus for pleasant feelings, a fact that makes it possible for the parents' mere presence to reinforce other behaviors as well. But a tormenting older sibling might come to be a conditional stimulus for angry feelings, even after the sibling has long since stopped the tormenting. Such conditioned emotional reactions are formed in adulthood as well. I feel a surge of embarrassment every time I drive by a town in which I gave a particularly poor lecture; I feel peaceful each time I visit, or even imagine visiting, a particular beach. These classically conditioned emotional responses profoundly affect each individual's emotional experiences.

Operant Conditioning

The second major type of learning is most often called **operant conditioning,** a term coined by B. F. Skinner, the most famous modern proponent of this theory (Skinner, 1953, 1980). Unlike classical conditioning, which involves attaching an old response to a new stimulus, operant conditioning involves attaching a new response to an old stimulus, achieved by the application of appropriate principles of reinforcement. Any behavior that is reinforced will be more likely to occur again in the same or a similar situation. There are two types of reinforcements. A **positive reinforcement** is any event that, following some behavior, increases the chances that the behavior will occur again in that situation. Certain classes of pleasant consequences, such as praise, a smile, food, a hug, or attention, serve as reinforcers for most people most of the time. But strictly speaking, a reinforcement is defined by its effect; we don't know something is reinforcing unless we see that its presence increases the probability of some behavior.

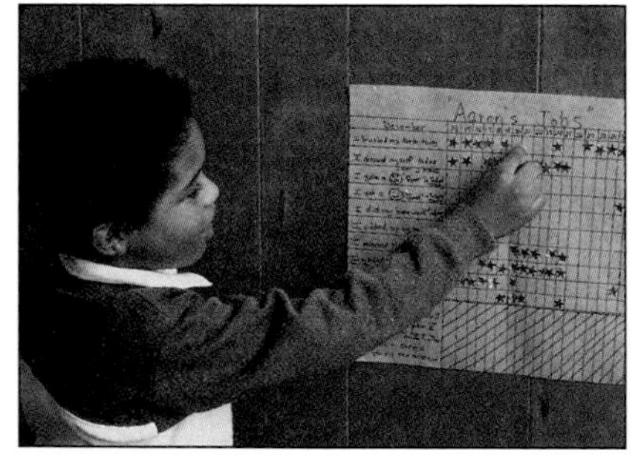

Aaron, like many children, finds this daily achievement chart highly reinforcing.

The second major type is a **negative reinforcement,** which occurs when something an individual finds *unpleasant* is *stopped* or avoided. Suppose your little boy is whining and begging you to pick him up. At first you ignore him but finally you do pick him up. What happens? He stops whining. So your picking-up behavior has been *negatively reinforced* by the cessation of his whining, and you will be *more* likely to pick him up the next time he whines. At the same time, his whining has probably been *positively reinforced* by your attention, so he will be more likely to whine on similar occasions.

Both positive and negative reinforcements strengthen behavior. **Punishment,** in contrast, is intended to weaken some undesired behavior. Sometimes punishments involve eliminating nice things (like "grounding" a child, or taking away TV privileges, or sending her to her room); often they involve administering unpleasant things such as a scolding or a spanking. This use of the word *punishment* fits with the common understanding of the term and shouldn't be too confusing. What *is* confusing is

Critical Thinking

Think of examples in your everyday life in which your behavior is affected by classical or operant conditioning, or in which you use these principles to affect others' behavior.

the fact that such punishments don't always do what they are intended to do: They do not always suppress the undesired behavior. If your child has thrown his glass of milk at you to get your attention, spanking him may be a positive reinforcement instead of the punishment you had intended.

The reverse process is **extinction,** which is a decrease in the likelihood of some response after repeated *non*reinforcements. If you stopped reinforcing whining behavior in your child, eventually the child would stop whining, not only on this occasion but on subsequent occasions.

In laboratory settings, experimenters can control the situation so that a particular behavior is reinforced every time it occurs, or stop reinforcement completely and so cause extinction of the response. But in the real world, consistency of reinforcement is the exception rather than the rule. Much more common is a pattern of **partial reinforcement,** in which a behavior is reinforced on some occasions but not others. Studies of partial reinforcement show that children and adults take longer to learn a new behavior under partial reinforcement conditions, but once established, such behaviors are much more resistant to extinction. If you smile at your daughter only every fifth or sixth time she brings a picture to show you (and if she finds your smile reinforcing), she'll keep on bringing pictures for a very long stretch, even if you were to quit smiling altogether.

The same principle might help us understand why some marriages endure even when little apparent vitality or affection remains. The reinforcement rate may be very low—few smiles, few hugs or other affection—but it may nonetheless be sufficient to sustain "staying behavior," making it remarkably resistant to extinction.

The Real World

Learning Principles in Real Family Life

It is a lot harder than you may think to apply basic learning principles consistently and correctly with children at home or in schools. Virtually all parents do try to reinforce some behaviors in their children by praising them or by giving them attention or treats. And most of us do our best to discourage unpleasant behavior through punishment. But it is easy to misapply the principles or to create unintended consequences because we have not fully understood all the mechanisms involved.

For example, suppose your favorite armchair is being systematically ruined by the dirt and pressure of little feet climbing on it. You want the children to *stop* climbing up the chair. So you scold them. After a while you may even stoop to nagging. If you are really conscientious and knowledgeable, you may carefully try to time your scolding so that it operates as a negative reinforcer, by stopping your scolding when they stop climbing. But nothing works. They keep on leaving those muddy footprints on your favorite chair. Why? It could be because the children *enjoy* climbing up the chair. So the climbing is intrinsically reinforcing to the children, and that effect is clearly stronger than your negative reinforcement or punishment. One way to deal with this might be to provide something *else* for them to climb on.

Another example: Suppose your 3-year-old son repeatedly demands your attention while you are fixing dinner (a common state of affairs, as any parent of a 3-year-old can tell you). Because you don't want to reinforce this behavior, you ignore him the first six or eight times he says "Daddy" or tugs at your clothes. But after the ninth or tenth repetition, with his voice getting louder and whinier each time, you can't stand it any longer and finally say something like "All right! What do you want?" Since you have ignored most of his demands, you might well be convinced that you have not been reinforcing his demanding behavior. But what you have actually done is to create a partial reinforcement schedule; you have rewarded only every tenth demand or whine. And we know that this pattern of reinforcement helps to create behavior that is *very* hard to extinguish. So your son may continue to be demanding and whining for a very long time, even if you succeed in ignoring it completely.

If such situations are familiar to you, it may pay to keep careful records for a while, noting each incident and your response, and then see whether you can figure out which principles are really at work and how you might change the pattern.

Bandura's Social Cognitive Theory

Bandura (1977a, 1982a, 1989), whose variation of learning theory is by far the most influential among developmental psychologists today, has built upon the base of these traditional learning concepts but has added several other key ideas. First, he argues that learning does not always require direct reinforcement. Learning may also occur merely as a result of watching someone else perform some action. Learning of this type, called **observational learning** or **modeling,** is involved in a wide range of behaviors. Children learn ways of hitting from watching other people in real life and on TV. They learn how to be generous by watching others donate money or goods. Adults learn job skills by observing or being shown by others.

Bandura also calls attention to another class of reinforcements called **intrinsic reinforcements** or *intrinsic rewards*. These are reinforcements internal to the individual, such as the pleasure a child feels when she finally figures out how to draw a star, or the sense of satisfaction you may experience after strenuous exercise. Pride, discovery, and that "aha" experience are all powerful intrinsic rewards, and all have the same power to strengthen behavior as do extrinsic reinforcements such as praise or attention.

Third, and perhaps most important, Bandura has gone far toward bridging the gap between learning theory and cognitive-developmental theory by emphasizing important *cognitive* (mental) elements in learning. Indeed he now calls his theory "social cognitive theory" rather than "social learning theory," as it was originally labeled (1986, 1989). For example, Bandura now stresses the fact that modeling can be the vehicle for the learning of abstract as well as concrete skills or information. In this *abstract modeling*, the observer extracts a rule that may be the basis of the model's behavior, and learns the rule as well as the specific behavior. So if a child sees his parents volunteering one day a month at a food bank and taking Christmas baskets to homeless families, he may extract a rule about the importance of "helping others," even if the parents never articulate this rule specifically. In such a fashion, a child or adult acquires attitudes, values, ways of solving problems, and even standards of self-evaluation through modeling. Furthermore, what a person learns from observing someone else is influenced by other cognitive processes, such as what we pay attention to, our ability to make sense out of and remember what we saw, and our actual capacity to repeat the observed action. (I will never become an expert tennis player merely by watching Steffi Graf play!) To my ear, all this sounds a great deal like Piaget's concept of assimilation.

Children learn a wide variety of skills and behaviors through modeling.

Bandura introduces other cognitive components as well. In learning situations, children and adults *set goals*, *create expectations* about what kinds of consequences are likely, and *judge* their own performance. Collectively, these additions to traditional learning theory make the system far more flexible and powerful.

Critique of Learning Theories

Several implications of learning theories are worth emphasizing. First of all, learning theorists can handle either consistency or change in child or adult behavior. If a child is friendly and smiling both at home and at school, this could be explained by saying that the child is being reinforced for that behavior in both settings rather than by assuming that the child has a "gregarious temperament." But it is equally possible to explain how an adult can be friendly and helpful in a work setting and unhelpful and frowning at home. We need only assume that the reinforcement contingencies are different in the two settings. To be sure, individuals tend to choose settings that maintain their accustomed behavior, and a person's behavior will tend to *elicit* similar responses (reinforcements) from others in many settings, which creates a bias toward consistency. But learning theorists have less trouble accounting for normal "situational variability" in behavior than do other theorists.

A related implication is that learning theorists tend to be optimistic about the possibility of change. Children's behavior can change if the reinforcement system, or their beliefs about themselves, change. So "problem behavior" can be modified.

The great strength of this view of social behavior is that it seems to give an accurate picture of the way in which many behaviors are learned. It is perfectly clear that children do learn through modeling; and it is equally clear that children and adults will continue to perform behaviors that "pay off" for them. The addition of the cognitive elements to Bandura's theory adds further strength, since it offers a beginning integration of learning models and cognitive-developmental approaches.

On the debit side of the ledger, from my view, is the fact that this approach is really not developmental. That is, it doesn't tell us much about change *with age*, either in childhood or adulthood. Even Bandura's variation on learning theory does not tell us whether there are any changes with age in what a child can or will learn from modeling. Thus, learning models can help us understand human *behavior* more fully than they can help us understand human *development*.

Two Theories of Adult Development

Finally, I want to describe two theories that don't fit neatly into any of the four primary traditions, but that have been influential in our thinking about adulthood. One of these, a model of life course transitions, emerges from sociology; the other, Levinson's model, is rooted in psychology.

Life Course Transitions: A Sociological Perspective

Sociologists, who for many years thought about adult life changes in terms of specific shifts in family roles, have been struggling toward a more general model of adulthood, based on several key notions.

Role Theory. One of the most important ingredients is the concept of a **role.** Any social system can be thought of as being made up of a series of interlocking *positions* (also called *statuses*), such as "employer," "worker," "supervisor," "teacher," "student," "retired person," or "widow." A role is the *content* of a social position—the behaviors and char-

The role of "grandmother" may be defined somewhat differently for this Katmandu grandma than it is in Western cultures.

CRITICAL THINKING

What roles do you now occupy? What role conflict, or role strain, do you experience?

acteristics expected of a person filling that position (Marshall, 1996). Thus, a role is a kind of job description. A teacher, for example, is expected to be knowledgeable, able to communicate, be a good "role model" for others, prepared, well organized, clear, and so forth. This set of expected behaviors or qualities defines the *role* of teacher.

Several aspects of the concept of roles are important for our understanding of development. First, roles are at least partially culture- and cohort-specific. "Teacher" may be a different role (a different set of expected behaviors) in one culture than another, or in the same culture from one time to another. A hundred years ago in the United States, women teachers were generally expected to be unmarried and celibate. Nowadays it is illegal even to ask a prospective teacher whether she (or he) is married.

Second, occupying the multiple roles each of us fills at any one moment inevitably involves frictions of various kinds. I am a psychologist, wife, mother, stepmother, grandmother, daughter, sister, sister-in-law, aunt, niece, friend, author, board member, singer, and volunteer, and there are certainly times when these roles don't fit together tidily! Sociologists use the term **role conflict** to describe any situation in which two or more roles are at least partially incompatible, either because they call for different behaviors or because their separate demands add up to more hours than there are in the day. At the moment, for example, I am in conflict over my inability to find time for several valued friendships because the demands of my work role are especially intense.

Role strain occurs when an individual's own qualities or skills do not measure up to the demands of some role. A parent who feels incompetent because she just can't figure out how to keep her 3-year-old from drawing on the walls is experiencing role strain. A newly minted Ph.D. in her first professional job who feels anxious about her ability to do high-quality research is also experiencing role strain. (I remember both of these!)

The concept of roles can also help us understand *changes* in adult life because certain roles shift predictably with age. As I pointed out in Chapter 1, each age stratum has accompanying roles. Even more conspicuously, family roles change in predictable ways, and one could argue that adult life marches to the rhythm of just such shifts in family roles.

Family Life Stages. Evelyn Duvall (1962) described a sequence of eight such family life stages, listed in Table 2.4. Each stage involves either adding or deleting some role, or changing the content of a central role.

This conceptualization served as an organizing model for a great deal of sociological research on adulthood. Instead of comparing adults of different ages, re-

Table 2.4 Duvall's Family Life Cycle Stages

Stage	Description
1	Adult is newly married, no children; spousal role is added.
2	First child is born; role of parent is added.
3	Oldest child is between 2 and 6; role of parent has changed.
4	Oldest child is between 6 and 12; parent role has changed again as child enters school.
5	Oldest child is an adolescent; role of parent changes again.
6	Oldest child has left home; sometimes called the *launching center* phase, as parents assist children to become independent.
7	All children have left home; dramatic change in parental role; sometimes called the *empty nest* or *postparental* stage.
8	One or both spouses has retired; sometimes called "aging families."

Source: Duvall, 1962.

searchers have compared adults in different life-cycle stages, creating a variant of the cross-sectional design. The basic idea, obviously, is that an individual's behavior and attitudes are shaped by the roles he occupies. And since these roles change with age in systematic and predictable ways, adults will also change systematically and predictably. Knowing that a person has a new infant tells you something about his life. If you knew that another person's youngest child had just gone off to college, you would quite correctly infer very different things about her daily existence.

But the conceptualization of family life stages reflected in Table 2.4, helpful as it has been, has become far less influential because of two major flaws. First, a number of important roles are totally omitted from the model, such as the role of grandparent or that of caregiver to one's own aging parents. The model also contains no subdivision of the years past 65, as if no further changes in roles or life patterns occur past retirement. Yet it is increasingly clear that substantial variations in life patterns and roles exist among those over 60. Indeed, gerontologists today customarily divide adults in these later years into three periods: the **young old** (60 to about 75), the **old old** (from 75 to about 85), and the **oldest old** (those over 85).

An even more telling problem with Duvall's simple model of family life cycle stages is that in today's industrialized societies a great many people simply don't move through this sequence of roles in the listed order. Increasing numbers of today's adults do not marry or do not have children; many divorce and move through complex combinations of family roles. To use myself as an example again, I did not marry until I was 32, then became the instant mother of two stepchildren (aged 3 and 11) with whom I lived for seven years. Then I was alone for four years after a divorce, lived for one year with my newly adult stepson, and then remarried, becoming stepmother to four more children, all more or less grown and flown. I cannot find my life in Duvall's model, and neither can a growing number of adults.

Current Reconceptualizations. Yet the concept of the family life cycle, or *family careers*, as Joan Aldous labels it (1996), has important elements that both sociologists and psychologists would like to retain. Although the sequence and timing may vary, the particular family life cycle an individual experiences clearly has an important effect on his or her life pattern. And in any given culture or cohort, some role shifts are likely to be shared, such as retirement in one's 60s in most industrialized countries. Sociologist Linda George (1993) suggests that we think of each life course as containing a number of *transitions*, defined as "changes in status that are discrete and bounded in duration" (George, 1993, p. 358), such as shifting from being single to being married, or from working to being retired. Transitions that are highly predictable and widely shared in any given culture or cohort she calls *life course markers*. In recent cohorts in industrialized countries, many of the family life transitions that are concentrated in early adulthood—such as marriage and first parenthood—have become less predictable, with highly variable timing and sequence. At the same time, some transitions in middle and late adulthood have become more prevalent and predictable, such as the death of a parent while one is in middle age, or voluntary retirement in one's 60s.

What George and other sociologists are saying (e.g., Caspi & Elder, 1988) is that some aspects of the basic theoretical perspective remain useful despite the fact that family life stages are not precisely the same for all adults. The specific sequence of roles, or the timing of those roles, may change from one cohort to the next, from one culture to the next, or even for different subgroups within a given culture, but dealing with *some* normative sequence of roles is the very stuff of adult life.

Levinson's Model of Seasons of Adulthood

Psychologist Daniel Levinson also talked about adult life in terms of rhythms and shared patterns (1978, 1980, 1986, 1990, 1996). His central concept is that of the **life structure,** which is the "underlying pattern or design of a person's life at a given time" (1986, p. 6). The life structure obviously includes roles and the balance among roles each individual creates, but it also includes the quality and pattern of the relationships one has, all filtered through one's personality or temperament. Life structures are not permanent. Precisely because roles and relationships change, life structures must change too. In fact, Levinson proposed that each adult creates a series of life structures, at specific ages, with transitional periods in between when the old life structure is either given up or reexamined and changed. You can see his model more precisely in Figure 2.2.

Levinson divided the life span into a series of broad *eras*, each lasting perhaps 25 years, with a major transition between each era. Within each era, he proposed three periods: The creation of an initial or entry life structure, described as a *novice phase*; a mid-era transition in which the person reassesses that novice life structure; and then a *culminating phase*, in which the individual creates an improved life structure.

He also proposed that each phase, transition, or era has a particular content—a particular set of issues or tasks. For example, the midlife transition, between 40 and 45, is centered around the growing awareness of one's own mortality and the realization that the dreams of one's youth may never be realized.

CRITICAL THINKING

Levinson proposes that everyone, in every culture, goes through some kind of transition between age 40 and 45. How could you test this hypothesis?

Of course Levinson did not mean that all adult lives are exactly alike. That is clearly nonsense. Nor did he say that each new life structure is in any way better or more integrated or elegant than the one that went before. He *did* say that adult life is made up of a basic alternation between stable life structures and transition periods. And he proposed that this orderly pattern, including the basic tasks or issues associated with each era and age, is shared by *all* people in all cultures.

Critique of Duvall and Levinson

I find it difficult to accept Levinson's hypothesis that all adults, in every culture and every cohort, move through eras and transitions at precisely the same ages, such as one at 30 and another between 40 and 45. Research evidence offers either very lukewarm support for or frank contradiction of this aspect of his theory (e.g., Dunn & Merriam, 1995; Harris, Ellicott, & Holmes, 1986; Reinke, Holmes, & Harris, 1985). At the same time, I find much that is appealing about Levinson's model or a family life stage view of human development, particularly the idea of a basic rhythm to adult

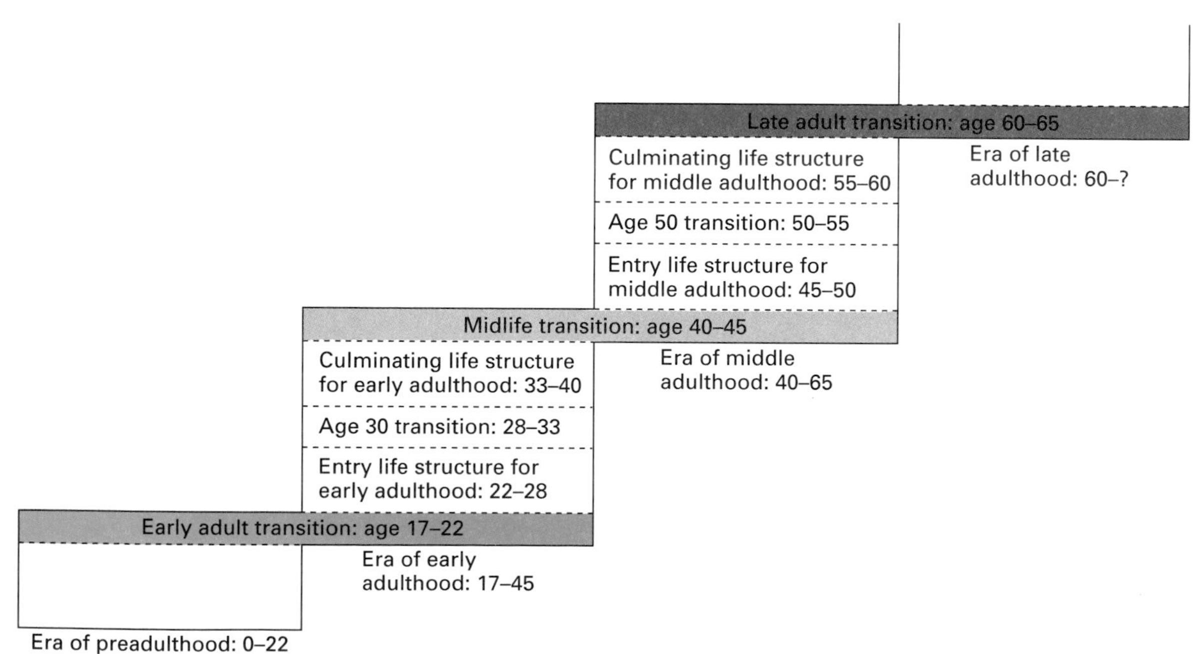

FIGURE 2.2 Levinson's model of adult development. Each stable life structure is followed by a period of transition in which that structure is reexamined. (*Source:* Levinson, 1986, adapted from Levinson 1978. Copyright © 1978 by Daniel J. Levinson. Reprinted by permission of Alfred A. Knopf, Inc.)

life, and perhaps to childhood and adolescence as well. Certainly we can see a biological rhythm, marked by such changes as motor development in infancy, puberty at adolescence, and the climacteric in middle adulthood.

We might think of the social clock, too, as having a basic rhythm. If we look at role changes in very general terms, I think a very good case can be made that virtually all adults move through a shared series of changes. In early adulthood we *acquire* a whole range of new roles, whether or not we marry or have children. These include new work roles, new definitions of friendship, and a new role as an independent person. In middle adulthood we *redefine* our roles. We may have more authority in work; our children may be grown and gone so that parenthood changes definition. In late adulthood, we *shed* roles. The specifics may not follow the particular role sequence Duvall proposed, but I think a particular pattern of role change is characteristic of nearly all our lives.

Thus, what I find most useful from theories like Levinson's or Duvall's are not the specific stages proposed—though they can be helpful in understanding some groups—but the idea of a basic shared alternation between stable life structures and transition, and the notion of a basic pattern of acquisition and elimination of roles.

Combining and Contrasting the Theories

As I have gone along, I've pointed out some of the similarities and differences among these various theories. But it may help to lay out some of the contrasts more formally. A particularly clear contrast pops out when we compare the various theories simultaneously on two dimensions: (1) whether or not they propose stages, and (2) whether they emphasize that change with age involves movement in some specific direction or instead is merely change without any clear goal or direction. For example, Levinson argued for systematic stagelike change, but he was quite adamant that each successive stage was not in any sense "higher" or "more developed" than the last, merely that it included a different set of tasks. In contrast, Piaget clearly proposed that each successive stage of cognitive development was a shift in the direction of more mature and more complex thinking.

In Figure 2.3 I have laid out these two dimensions on a grid so that you can see where the various theories lie. Clearly, every possible combination of positions is represented by at least one theory. On these dimensions, psychoanalytic and cognitive-developmental theory are quite a lot alike and both contrast most sharply with learning theories. On other dimensions we would find different configurations. For example, if we compare the theories on the degree to which they see the child or adult as an *active participant* in the developmental process rather than a more *passive recipient* of influences, we would find Piaget out on one end of the continuum along with perhaps Levinson, while Erikson and Freud would be more in the middle.

CRITICAL THINKING

Compare the various theories on their views on the relative influence of nature and nurture.

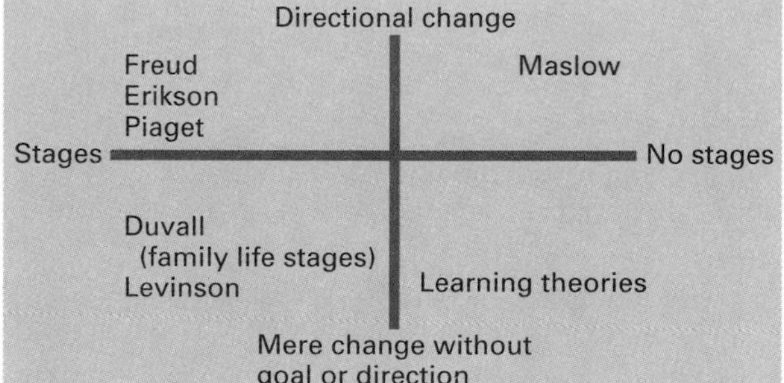

FIGURE 2.3 The dozens of theories of human development can be organized along many possible dimensions. On the two dimensions shown here, there is at least one theory in every quadrant.

An Afterword

I wouldn't be surprised if you are a bit bleary-eyed after all these theories. Even with simplified contrasts like the one shown in Figure 2.3 it is hard to make the theoretical issues real to you before you have delved into the data. I have nonetheless chosen to describe the alternative theories in this early chapter because I think it is almost impossible to assimilate and integrate all the data you will be reading about without having some theoretical models to hook them onto. At this stage, I want to make only a couple of final points.

First, let me reemphasize something I said at the beginning of the chapter: These are real disagreements with potentially important differences in implication and application. It makes a huge practical difference whether one posits that nature and not nurture is the most critical influence; it makes a difference whether you believe that stages are strongly linked to age or only sequential. If they are linked to age, then we shouldn't waste our time trying to teach something before the child or adult is "ready" for that change.

Similarly, those who study adulthood ask very different questions, and interpret results very differently, depending on their theoretical persuasion or even the academic discipline from which they begin. Sociologist Dale Dannefer (1984a, 1984b, 1988) has rather scathingly pointed out that psychologists, in the face of anything that looks like an age-linked pattern, are likely to jump immediately to the conclusion that they have uncovered a basic developmental process. Presented with the same set of data, a sociologist is likely to look for the social forces that might have shaped the responses of different cohorts. To psychologists, cohort differences are "noise" in the system, distorting their attempt to uncover basic human patterns. To sociologists, cohort differences are the very stuff of interest, since they tell us about how the individual and the society interact.

A second key point is that we do not have to make firm or final choices among these different models. In fact, most psychologists (and sociologists) are highly eclectic in their theoretical approach, borrowing a few ideas from each of several different models or trying to synthesize several theories into a new perspective. My own thinking is very much in this more eclectic tradition, as you can see from the evaluative comments I have made about each theory. I find useful ideas in all these approaches.

Still, I think it is very helpful to keep the contrasting models in mind as you move through the rest of the text. I will come back to them again and again, trying to show not only how the data we've collected have been shaped by the theoretical assumptions researchers have made, but also how the different theoretical perspectives can help us to understand the information that has accumulated. So hang in there. These ideas will turn out to be useful, helping you (and me) to create some order out of the vast array of facts.

Summary

1. Facts alone will not explain any phenomenon, including development. Theory is also required.
2. Several families of theories have been prominent in discussions of development: psychoanalytic, humanistic, cognitive-developmental, and learning.
3. Freud, the "father" of psychoanalytic theory, emphasized that behavior is governed by unconscious as well as conscious motives, and that the personality develops in steps: first the id, then the ego, then the superego.
4. Freud also proposed a set of five psychosexual stages: oral, anal, phallic, latency, and genital. The Oedipal crisis occurs in the phallic stage.
5. Erikson emphasized social forces, more than unconscious drives, as motives for development. The key concept is the development of identity, said to occur in eight psychosocial stages over the course of the life span: trust, autonomy, initiative, industry, identity, intimacy, generativity, and ego integrity.

6. Another psychoanalytically oriented theorist is Loevinger, who proposes a set of ten stages that are achieved in a given sequence, but not at specific ages and not by everyone.
7. Bowlby's theory of attachment also has its roots strongly in psychoanalytic thought, but adds elements from ethological theory.
8. The primary humanistic theorist, Abraham Maslow, argued that each individual is motivated not only by "deficiency drives," but also by a drive toward self-actualization.
9. Piaget focused on the development of thinking rather than personality. A key concept is that of adaptation, made up of the subprocesses of assimilation, accommodation, and equilibration.
10. The result of several major equilibrations is a set of four cognitive stages, each of which Piaget thought resulted in a coherent cognitive system: sensorimotor, preoperational, concrete operations, and formal operations.
11. Learning theorists emphasize the key importance of basic principles—such as classical conditioning, operant conditioning, and modeling—in the acquisition and maintenance of many behaviors.
12. Bandura's social cognitive variation of learning theory includes many more cognitive elements, with a more active role for the individual.
13. Sociological theorists, who initially emphasized a lockstep sequence of family life cycle stages, have moved toward a more flexible model of transitions and shared life course markers.
14. A key concept in sociological models of adulthood is that of a role, which is a job description for a specific position or status within a culture, such as the role of teacher or even a sex role. Roles change systematically with age, especially in adulthood.
15. Levinson proposes a set of fixed stages in adulthood, reflecting an ebb and flow between stable life structures and transition periods.
16. The theories can be contrasted along many dimensions, such as whether or not they propose stages, or whether or not they believe development moves toward some higher, better, or more mature state.
17. No one of these theories can adequately account for all the available evidence on human development, but each offers useful concepts and each may provide a framework within which we can examine bodies of research data.

Key Terms

accommodation
assimilation
being motives
classical conditioning
concrete operational stage
conditional stimulus
defense mechanisms
deficiency motives
ego
equilibration
extinction
formal operational stage
id
identification
identity
intrinsic reinforcements
libido
life structure
modeling
negative reinforcement
observational learning
old old
oldest old
operant conditioning
operations
partial reinforcement
positive reinforcement
preoperational stage
psychosexual stages
psychosocial stages
punishment
role
role conflict
role strain
scheme
sensorimotor stage
superego
unconditioned response
unconditional stimulus
young old
zone of proximal development

Suggested Readings

Aldous, J. (1996). *Family careers. Rethinking the developmental perspective.* Thousand Oaks, CA: Sage.

Sociologist Joan Aldous gives us a careful reanalysis of many of the older ideas about family life cycles, looking at the various types of families that now exist.

Erikson, E. H. (1980). *Identity and the life cycle.* New York: W. W. Norton (originally published 1959).

The middle section of this book, "Growth and Crises of the Healthy Personality," is the best description I have found of Erikson's model of the psychosocial stages of development.

Grusec, J. E. (1992). Social learning theory and developmental psychology: The legacies of Robert Sears and Albert Bandura. *Developmental Psychology*, 28, 776–786.

One of a series of papers to mark the centennial of the American Psychological Association, *describing and celebrating the work of key theorists.*

Lerner, R. M. (1986). *Concepts and theories of human development* (2nd ed.). New York: Random House.

A very good discussion of most of the major theoretical approaches I have described here.

Smelser, N. J., & Erikson, E. H. (1980). *Themes of work and love in adulthood*. Cambridge, MA: Harvard University Press.

It would be hard to find a better collection of papers by leading theorists on adult life. Levinson has a paper here, as do several other prominent thinkers. The articles are not overly technical.

Thomas, R. M. (Ed.) (1990). *The encyclopedia of human development and education: Theory, research, and studies.* Oxford: Pergamon Press.

A very useful volume that includes brief descriptions of virtually all the theories I have described in this chapter as well as a helpful chapter on the concept of stages. Each chapter is quite brief but covers many of the critical issues.

Prenatal Development and Birth

3

Like any good story, human development has a beginning, a middle, and an end. So let us start the story at the beginning—with conception and with the months of prenatal development. What does normal prenatal development look like? What forces shape it and what forces can deflect it from its normal path? For example, how much can the mother's health or her health practices help or hinder the process? These questions have great practical importance for those of you who expect to bear (or father) children in the future. But they are also important basic issues as we begin the study of lifespan development. The heredity passed on to the new individual at the moment of conception and the neurological and other physical developments in these first months set the stage for all that is to follow.

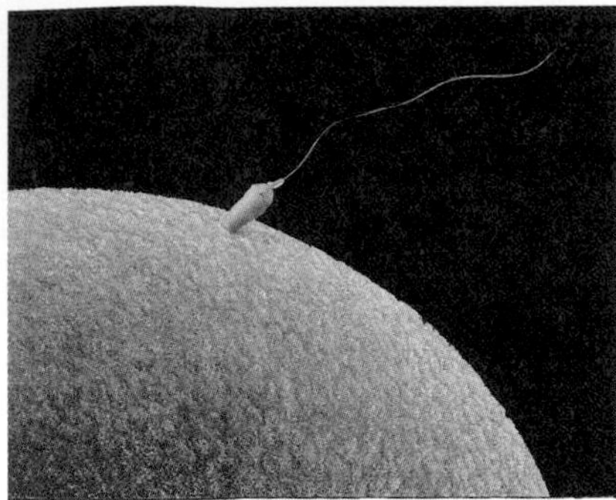

FIGURE 3.1 The moment of conception, when a single sperm has pierced the shell of the ovum.

Conception

The first step in the development of a single human being is that moment of conception when a single sperm cell from the male pierces the wall of the ovum of the female—a moment captured in the photo in Figure 3.1. Ordinarily, a woman produces one **ovum** (egg cell) per month from one of her two ovaries. This occurs roughly midway between two menstrual periods. If the ovum is not fertilized, it travels from the ovary down the **fallopian tube** toward the **uterus,** where it gradually disintegrates and is expelled as part of the next menstruation.

But if a couple has intercourse during the crucial few days when the ovum is in the fallopian tube, one of the millions of sperm ejaculated as part of each male orgasm may travel the full distance through the woman's vagina, cervix, uterus, and fallopian tube, and penetrate the wall of the ovum. A child is conceived. Interestingly (and perhaps surprising to many of us) only about half of such conceptuses are likely to survive to birth. About a quarter are lost in the first few days after conception, often because of a flaw in the genetic material. Another quarter are spontaneously aborted ("miscarried") at a later point in the pregnancy (Wilcox et al., 1988).

The Basic Genetics of Conception

It is hard to overestimate the importance of the genetic events accompanying conception. The combination of genes from the father in the sperm and from the mother in the ovum creates a unique genetic blueprint—the **genotype**—that characterizes that specific individual. To explain how this occurs, I need to back up a few steps.

Except in individuals with particular types of genetic abnormality, the nucleus of each cell in the body contains a set of 46 **chromosomes**, arranged in 23 pairs. These chromosomes include all the genetic information for that individual, including not only genetic information controlling highly individual characteristics like hair color, height, body shape, temperament, and aspects of intelligence, but also all those characteristics shared by all members of our species, such as patterns of physical development and "built-in biases" of various kinds.

The only cells that do *not* contain 46 chromosomes are the sperm and the ovum, collectively called **gametes** or germ cells. In the early stages of development, gametes divide as all other cells do (a process called *mitosis*), with each set of 23 chromosome pairs unzipping and duplicating itself. But gamete division includes a final step, called *meiosis*, in which each new cell receives only one chromosome from each original pair. Thus, each gamete has only 23 chromosomes, instead of 23 *pairs*. When a child is conceived, the 23 chromosomes in the ovum and the 23 in the sperm combine to form the 23 *pairs* that will be part of each cell in the newly developing body.

The chromosomes, in turn, are composed of long strings of molecules of a chemical called **deoxyribonucleic acid** (DNA), in the shape of a *double helix*, a kind of twisted ladder. The remarkable feature of this ladder is that the rungs are made up in such a way that the whole thing can unzip and then each half can guide the duplication of the missing part, thus allowing multiplication of cells so that each new cell contains the full set of genetic information.

The string of DNA that makes up each chromosome can be further subdivided into segments, called **genes,** each of which controls or influences a particular feature or a portion of some developmental pattern. A gene controlling some specific characteristic, such as your blood type or your hair color, always appears in the same place (the *locus*) on the same chromosome in every individual of the same species. The locus of the gene that determines whether you have type A, B, or O blood is on chromosome 9; the locus of the gene that determines whether you have the Rh factor in your blood is on chromosome 1; and so forth. Geneticists have made remarkable strides in recent years in mapping the loci for a great many features or characteristics—a scientific achievement that has allowed similarly giant strides in our ability to diagnose various genetic defects or inherited diseases before a child is born.

Dominant and Recessive Genes

Because each individual inherits *two* of each chromosome (one from each parent), the genetic instructions at any given locus may be either the same (*homozygous*) or different (*heterozygous*). If you receive a gene for blue eyes from both parents, your inheritance is homozygous and you will have blue eyes. But what if you receive heterozygous information, such as a gene for blue eyes from one parent and a brown-eye gene from the other?

Heterozygosity is resolved in several different ways, depending on the particular genes involved. Sometimes the two signals appear to blend, resulting in some intermediate characteristic. For example, the children of one tall parent and one short parent most often have height that falls in between. A rarer type of outcome is for the child to express *both* characteristics. For example, type AB blood results from the inheritance of a type A gene from one parent and a type B gene from the other. A third type of resolution of heterozygosity is that one of the two genes is *dominant* over the other, and only the dominant gene is actually expressed. The nondominant gene, called a *recessive* gene, has no visible effect on the individual's behavior, but it continues to be part of the genotype and can be passed on to offspring through meiosis.

A large number of inherited diseases appear to be transmitted through the operation of dominant and recessive genes, such as Tay-Sachs disease, sickle-cell anemia, and cystic fibrosis. Figure 3.2 shows how this might work in the case of sickle-cell anemia, which is caused by a *recessive* gene. For an individual to have this disease, she or he must inherit the disease gene from *both* parents. A "carrier" is someone who inherits the disease gene from only one parent. Such a person does not actually have the disease, but can pass the disease gene on to his or her children. If two carriers have children together (example III in the figure), or if a carrier and someone with the disease have children (example IV in the figure), their offspring may inherit disease genes from both parents and thus have the disease.

CRITICAL THINKING

The inheritance pattern for eye color is that brown is dominant over blue. Can you figure out what your parents' genotype for eye color has to be, based on the color of your eyes, your siblings' eyes, and that of your grandparents?

Unlike this simple example, most human characteristics are *polygenic*, that is, they are affected by many more than one gene. Temperament, intelligence, rate of growth, and even apparently simple characteristics such as eye color all involve the interaction of multiple genes. Very exciting new genetic research has also pointed toward totally unexpected additional complexities. For example, researchers studying muscular dystrophy, a recessive gene disease, have observed that this disease often becomes more severe from one generation to the next, apparently through some kind of multiplication of the DNA in the section of the chromosome that signals the disease (Fu et al., 1992). Research like this is beginning to unlock the secrets of genetic transmission, but our understanding is still far from complete.

Males and Females

Still another complexity comes from the fact that there are actually two types of chromosomes. In 22 of the chromosome pairs, called *autosomes*, the members of the pair look alike and contain exactly matching genetic loci. The twenty-third pair, however, operates differently. The chromosomes of this pair, which determine the child's sex and are therefore called the *sex chromosomes*, come in two varieties, referred to by convention as the X and the Y chromosomes. A normal human female has two X chromosomes on this twenty-third pair (an XX pattern), while the normal human male has one X and one Y (an XY pattern). The X chromosome is considerably larger than the Y and contains many genetic loci not matched on the Y.

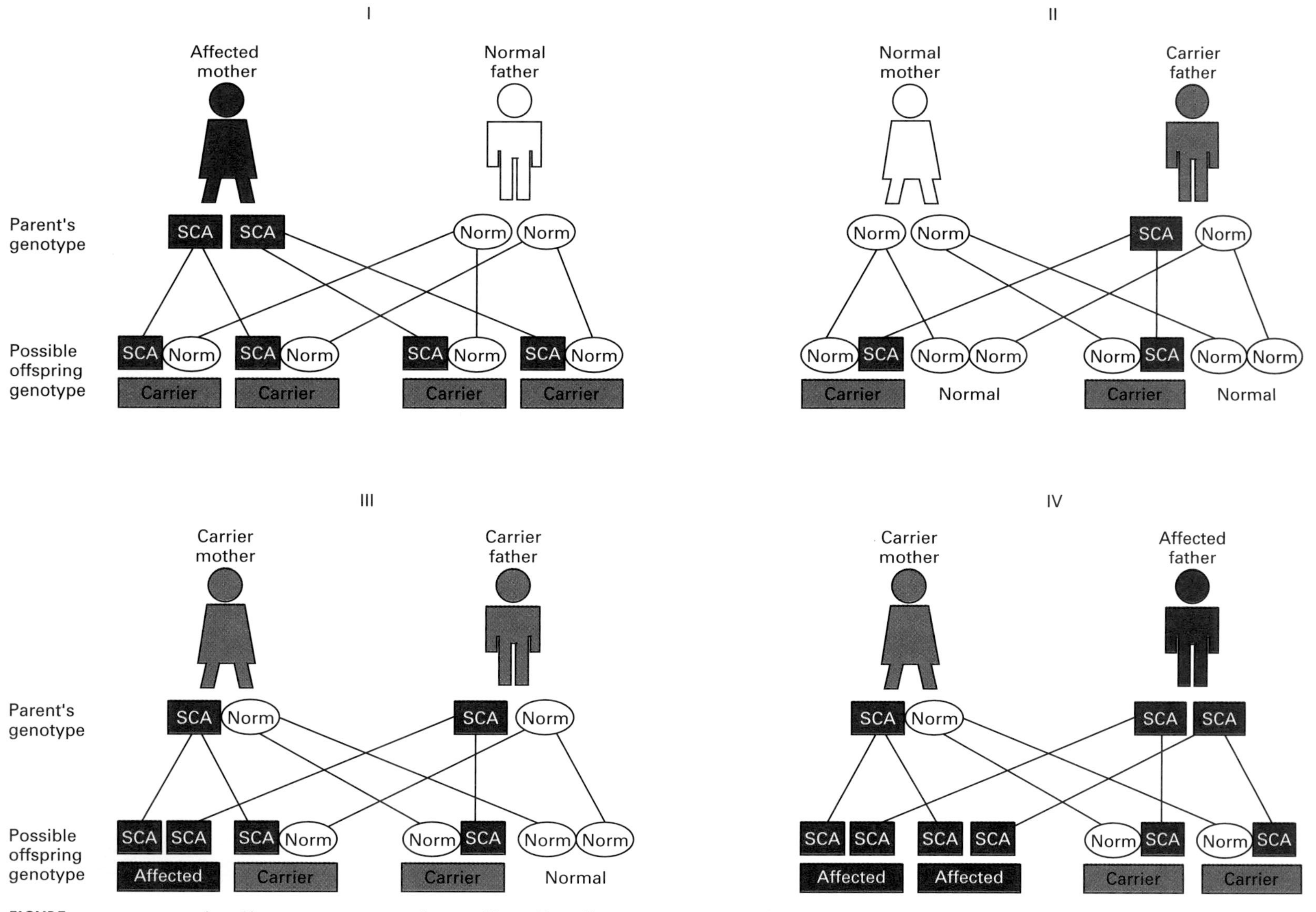

FIGURE 3.2 Some examples of how a recessive gene disease, like sickle-cell anemia, is transmitted. In section I, a mother who has the disease passes her sickle-cell disease gene to all her children, but since her partner is normal, none of the children actually express the disease. In section II, a normal mother and a carrier father have no children with the disease, but each of their children has a 50/50 chance of carrying the SCA gene. The child can inherit the actual disease either of two ways: with two affected parents (section III) or with one carrier parent and one affected parent (section IV).

Note that the sex of the child is determined by the sex chromosome it receives from the sperm. Because the mother has *only* X chromosomes, every ovum carries an X. But the father has both X and Y chromosomes. When the father's gametes divide, half the sperm will carry an X, half a Y. If the sperm that fertilizes the ovum carries an X, then the child inherits an XX pattern and will be a girl. If the fertilizing sperm carries a Y, then the combination is XY, and the infant will be a boy.

Geneticists have now discovered that only one very small section of the Y chromosome actually determines maleness—a segment referred to as TDF, or *testis-determining factor* (Page et al., 1987). Fertilized ova that are genetically XY but that lack the TDF develop physically as female. Preliminary results from several new studies also point to the possibility that there may be a "femaleness" gene or genes (Arn et al., 1994; Bardoni et al., 1994). As in so many areas of science, the more we discover, the more complex we see the process really is.

One important consequence of the difference between X and Y chromosomes is that a boy inherits many genes from his mother on his X chromosome that are not matched or counteracted by equivalent genetic material on the smaller Y chromosome. Among other things, this means that recessive diseases or other characteristics that have their loci on the nonmatched parts of the X chromosome may be inherited by a boy directly from his mother, a pattern called *sex-linked* transmission, illustrated in Figure 3.3. As examples, both hemophilia and muscular dystrophy are transmitted in this way.

You can see from the figure that, as with other recessive-gene characteristics, a girl can inherit a sex-linked disease such as hemophilia only if she inherits the recessive gene from both parents. But a male will inherit the disease by receiving the recessive gene only from his mother. Since his Y chromosome from his father contains no parallel loci for this characteristic, there are no counteracting instructions and the recessive mother's gene dominates. Each of the sons of women who carry such recessive disease genes will have a 50 percent chance of having the disease, and the daughters will have a 50 percent chance of being carriers. The sons of those carrier daughters, in turn, will have a 50/50 chance of inheriting the gene for the disease.

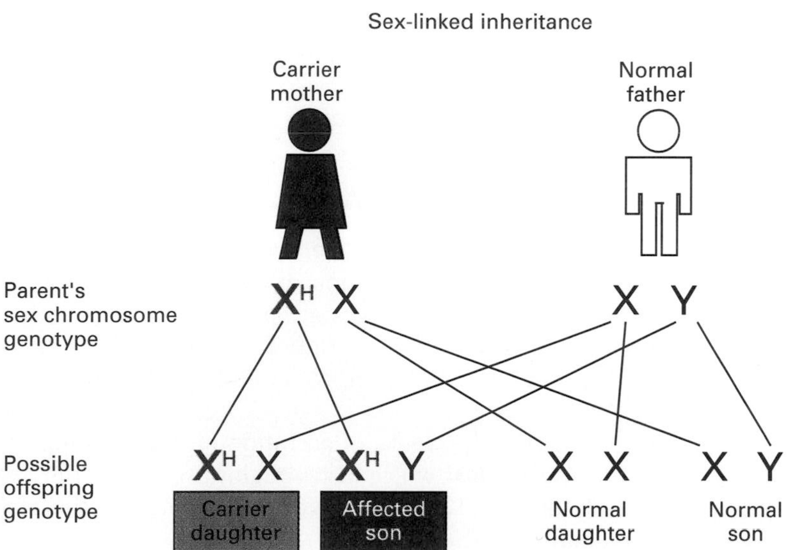

FIGURE 3.3 Compare this pattern of sex-linked transmission of a recessive disease (hemophilia) with the pattern already shown in Figure 3.2. In a sex-linked inheritance, a carrier mother can pass on the disease to half her sons (on average) because there is no offsetting gene on the Y chromosome. Daughters of carrier mothers have a 50 percent chance of becoming carriers themselves, but cannot inherit the disease itself unless the father actually has the disease and the mother is a carrier.

Twins and Siblings

In the great majority of cases, babies are conceived and born one at a time. But roughly one out of each hundred births is a multiple birth. The great majority of these are twins; triplets occur only about once in every 6,400 births, quadruplets only about once in 512,000 births. Roughly two-thirds of twins are *fraternal twins*, when more than one ovum has been produced and both have been fertilized, each by a separate sperm. Such twins, also called *dizygotic* twins, are no more alike genetically than any other pair of siblings, and need not even be of the same sex. The remaining one-third of twins are *identical* (*monozygotic*). In such cases, a single fertilized ovum apparently initially divides in the normal way, but then for unknown reasons separates into two parts, usually just before implantation, with each developing into a separate individual. Because identical twins develop from precisely the same original fertilized ovum, they have identical genetic heritages. You'll remember from Chapter 1 that comparisons of the degree of similarity of these two types of twins is one of the major research strategies in the important field of behavior genetics.

Genotypes and Phenotypes

Using data from twin and adoption studies, behavior geneticists have made great strides in identifying those skills, characteristics, or traits that are influenced by heredity. But no geneticist proposes that an inherited combination of genes fully *determines* any outcome for a given individual. Geneticists (and psychologists) make an important distinction between the genotype, which is the specific set of "instructions" contained in a given individual's genes, and the **phenotype,** which is the actual observed characteristics of the individual. The phenotype is a product of three things: the genotype, environmental influences from the time of conception onward, and the interaction between the environment and the genotype. A child might have a genotype associated with high IQ, but if his mother drinks too much alcohol during the pregnancy there may be damage to the nervous system, resulting in mild retardation. Another child might have a genotype for a "difficult" temperament but have parents who are particularly sensitive and thoughtful, so that the child learns other ways to handle himself.

CRITICAL THINKING

Can you think of other examples where the phenotype would be different from the genotype?

The distinction between genotype and phenotype is an important one. Genetic codes are not irrevocable signals for this or that pattern of development, or this or that disease. The eventual developmental outcome is also affected by the specific experiences the individual has from conception onward.

Development from Conception to Birth

If we assume that conception takes place two weeks after a menstrual period, when ovulation normally occurs, then the period of gestation of the human infant is 38 weeks (about 265 days). Most physicians calculate gestation as 40 weeks, counting from the last menstrual period. However, all the specifications of weeks of gestation I've given here are based on the 38-week calculation, counting from the presumed time of conception.

Biologists and embryologists divide the weeks of gestation into three subperiods of unequal length. These are: the *germinal*, which lasts roughly two weeks; the *embryonic*, which continues until about 8 to 12 weeks after conception; and the *fetal* stage, which makes up the remaining 24–28 weeks.

The Germinal Stage: From Conception to Implantation

Sometime during the first 24 to 36 hours after conception, cell division begins; within two to three days there are several dozen cells and the whole mass is about the size of a pinhead. This mass of cells is undifferentiated until about four days after conception. At that point the organism, now called a *blastocyst,* begins to subdivide, forming a hollow sphere with two layers of cells. The outer cells will form the various structures that will support the developing organism, while the inner mass will form the **embryo** itself. When it touches the wall of the uterus, the outer shell of cells breaks down at the point of contact. Small tendrils develop and attach the cell mass to the uterine wall, a process called *implantation.* When implantation is complete, normally ten days to two weeks after conception, there are perhaps 150 cells in the blastocyst (Tanner, 1978). You can see the sequence schematically in Figure 3.4.

The Embryonic Stage

The embryonic stage begins when implantation is complete and continues until the various support structures are fully formed and all the major organ systems have been laid down in at least rudimentary form, a process that normally takes another six to ten weeks.

Development of Support Structures. The outer layer of cells itself specializes further into two layers. An inner membrane, called the **amnion,** creates a sac or bag, filled with liquid (*amniotic fluid*), in which the baby floats. From the outer layer, called the **chorion,** two further organs develop, the **placenta** and the **umbilical cord.** The placenta, which is fully developed by about four weeks of gestation, is a platelike mass of cells that lies against the wall of the uterus. It serves as liver, lungs, and kidneys for the embryo and fetus, and is connected to the embryo's circulatory system via the umbilical cord. Thus, the placenta lies between the mother's circulatory system and the embryo's, and can serve as a sort of filter. Nutrients such as oxygen, proteins, sugars, and vitamins from the maternal blood can pass through to the embryo or fetus, while digestive wastes and carbon dioxide from the infant's blood pass back through to the mother, whose own body can eliminate them (Rosenblith, 1992). At the same time, many (but not all) harmful substances, such as viruses the mother may carry or the mother's hormones, are filtered out because they are too large to

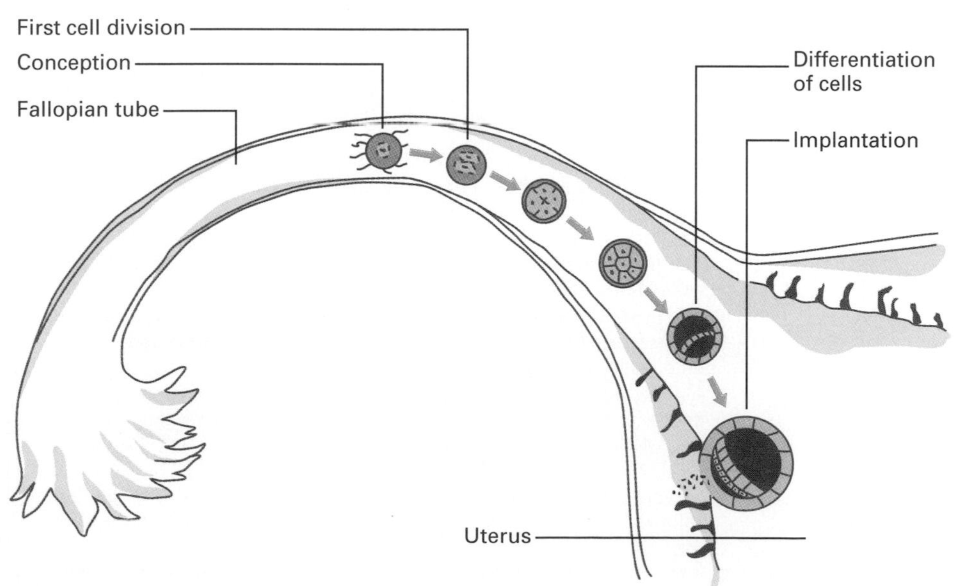

FIGURE 3.4 In this schematic drawing, you can see the sequence of changes during the germinal stage, with the first cell division and the first differentiation of cell function normally occurring in the fallopian tube.

pass through the various membranes in the placenta. Most drugs and anesthetics, however, do pass through the placenta, as do some disease organisms.

Development of the Embryo. At the same time, the mass of cells that will form the embryo is itself differentiating further into several types of cells that form the rudiments of skin, sense receptors, nerve cells, muscles, circulatory system, and internal organs. A heartbeat can be detected roughly four weeks after conception; the beginnings of lungs and limbs also are apparent at this time. By the end of the embryonic period, rudimentary fingers and toes, eyes, eyelids, nose, mouth, and external ears are all present, as are the basic parts of the nervous system (spinal cord, midbrain, forebrain, etc.) (Allen, 1996). When this *organogenesis* is complete, a new stage, that of the **fetus,** begins.

The Fetal Stage

The seven months of the fetal stage involve primarily a process of refining all the primitive organ systems already in place, much like what happens in constructing a house: The framework is created quickly, but the finishing work is lengthy. Table 3.1 summarizes some of the changes. The two photos in Figure 3.5, one from the beginning of the fetal period and one at about 28 weeks, give you a more graphic view.

Development of the Nervous System. One organ system that develops almost entirely during the fetal period is the nervous system, which exists in only the most rudimentary form at the end of the embryonic period. Two basic types of cells are involved, **neurons** and **glial cells.** The glial cells are the glue that holds the whole nervous system together, providing firmness and structure to the brain, helping to remove debris after neuronal death or injury, and segregating neurons from one

Table 3.1 Major Milestones of Fetal Development

Gestational Age	Major New Developments
12 weeks	Sex of child can be determined; muscles are developed more extensively; eyelids and lips are present; by 14 weeks the genitalia are fully differentiated; the head is about half the total size of the fetus at this stage.
16 weeks	First fetal movement is usually felt by the mother; bones begin to develop; fairly complete ear is formed.
20 weeks	Hair growth begins; fetus is very human looking at this age, although the head is still comparatively large (about 1/3 the total body); and thumb sucking may be seen.
24 weeks	Eyes are completely formed (but closed); fingernails, sweat glands, and taste buds are all formed; some fat deposit beneath skin. The fetus is capable of breathing if born prematurely at this stage, but survival rate is still low for those born this small.
28 weeks	Nervous system, blood, and breathing systems are all well enough developed to support life, although prematures born at this stage have poor sleep/wake cycles and irregular breathing.
29–40 weeks	Interconnections between individual nerve cells (neurons) develop rapidly; weight is added; general "finishing" of body systems takes place.

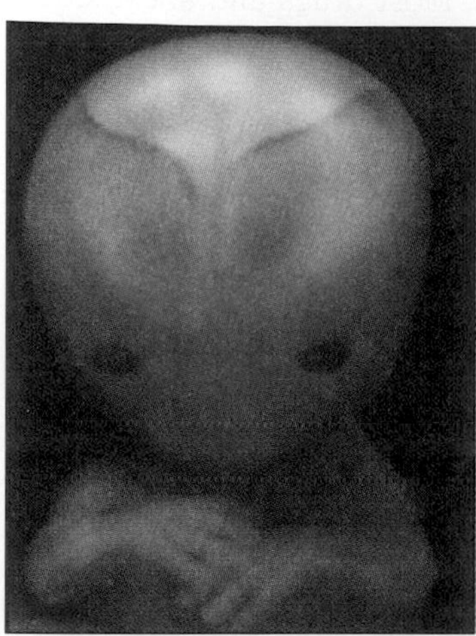

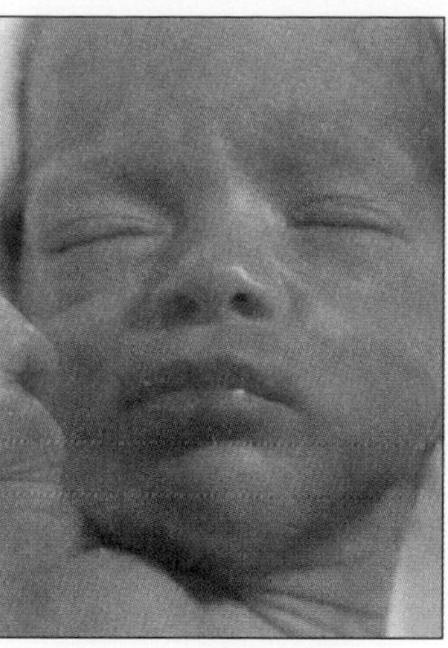

FIGURE 3.5 The photo on the left shows a fetus of 10–12 weeks gestation. The sex of the child can be determined; muscles, eyelids, and lips are present; feet have toes and hands have fingers. The photo at the right shows a fetus about 15 weeks older (about 28 weeks' gestation). At this stage the eyes are formed (but closed), as are hair, fingernails, sweat glands, and tastebuds. Many infants born at 28 weeks survive. (*Sources:* Lennart Nilsson, *A Child Is Born*, 1990, p. 106; Petit Forman/Nesle/Science Source/Photo Researchers.)

another. It is the neurons that do the job of receiving and sending messages from one part of the brain to another, or from one part of the body to another.

Neurons have four main parts, shown schematically in Figure 3.6: (1) a cell body; (2) branchlike extensions of the cell body called **dendrites** that are the major *receptors* of nerve impulses; (3) a tubular extension of the cell body called the **axon,** which can extend as far as 1 meter in length in humans (about 3 feet); and (4) branchlike terminal fibers at the end of the axon, which form the primary *transmitting* apparatus of the nervous system. Because of the branchlike appearance of dendrites, physiologists often use botanical terms to describe them, speaking of the "dendritic arbor" or of "pruning" the dendrites.

The point at which two neurons connect, where the axon's transmitting fibers come into close contact with another neuron's dendrites, is called a **synapse.** Synapses can also be formed between neurons and other kinds of cells, such as muscle cells, and the communication itself is accomplished with chemical *neurotransmitters*. The number of such synapses is vast. A single cell in the part of the brain that controls vision, for instance, may have as many as 10,000 to 30,000 synaptic inputs to its dendrites (Greenough, Black, & Wallace, 1987).

Glial cells begin to develop at about 13 weeks after conception and continue to be added until perhaps two years after birth. The great majority of neurons are formed between 10 and 18 weeks of gestation (Huttenlocher, 1994; Todd et al., 1995), and—with rare exceptions—these are all the neurons the individual will ever have. Neurons lost later are not replaced.

CRITICAL THINKING

Can you think of any practical consequences of the fact that all the neurons one is ever going to have are present by about 28 weeks of gestation?

In these early weeks of the fetal period, neurons are very simple. They consist largely of the cell body with short axons and little dendritic development. It is in the last two months before birth and in the first few years after birth that the lengthening of the axons and the major growth of the "dendritic arbor" occurs. Indeed, as the dendrites first develop in the eighth and ninth months of gestation, they appear to be sent out in a kind of exploratory system; many of these early dendrites are later reabsorbed, with only the useful expansions remaining. In these final fetal months,

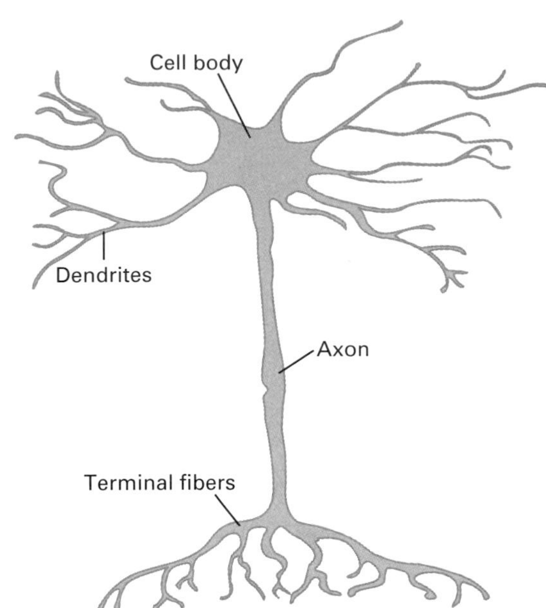

FIGURE 3.6 The structure of a single developed neuron. The cell bodies are the first to be developed, primarily between weeks 12 and 24. Axons and dendrites develop later, especially during the final 12 weeks, and continue to increase in size and complexity for several years after birth.

however, synapse formation is much slower; most synapses are formed after birth. For example, in the part of the brain involved in vision, babies have about ten times the number of synapses at 6 months as they had at birth (Huttenlocher, 1994).

Development of Length and Weight. Similarly, the major growth in fetal size occurs late in the fetal period. The fetus is about half her birth length by about 20 weeks gestation, but she does not reach half her birth weight until nearly three months later, at about 32 weeks.

An Overview of Prenatal Development

One of the most important points about the child's prenatal development is how remarkably regular and predictable it is. If the embryo has survived the early, risky period (roughly the first 12 weeks), development usually proceeds smoothly, with the various changes occurring in what is apparently a fixed order, at fixed time intervals, following a clear maturational ground plan.

This sequence of development is not immune to modification or outside influence, as you'll soon see in detail. Indeed, as psychologists and biologists have looked more carefully at various kinds of teratogens, it has become clear that the sequence is more vulnerable than had earlier appeared. But before I begin talking about the various things that can go wrong, I want to make sure to state clearly that the maturational system is really quite robust. Normal prenatal development requires an adequate environment, but "adequate" seems to cover a fairly broad range. *Most* children are quite normal. The list of things that *can* go wrong is long, and getting longer as our knowledge expands. Yet many of these possibilities are quite rare, many are partially or wholly preventable, and many need not have permanent consequences for the child. Keep this in mind as you read through the next few pages.

The potential problems fall into two large classes: genetic errors and those damaging environmental events called *teratogens*. Genetic errors occur at the moment of conception and cannot be altered (although new technology may change that eventually); teratogens may affect development any time from conception onward.

This Down syndrome boy, triumphant in the Special Olympics, shows the distinctive facial features of this disorder.

Genetic Errors

In perhaps 3 to 8 percent of all fertilized ova, the genetic material itself contains errors because either the sperm or the ovum has failed to divide correctly, so that there are either too many or too few chromosomes. Current estimates are that perhaps 90 percent of these abnormal conceptuses are spontaneously aborted. Only about 1 percent of live newborns have such abnormalities.

Over 50 different types of chromosomal anomaly have been identified, many of them very rare. The most common is **Down syndrome** (also called *mongolism* and *trisomy* 21), in which the child has three copies of chromosome 21 rather than the normal two. Roughly 1 in every 800 or 1000 infants is born with this abnormality (Nightingale & Goodman, 1990). These children have distinctive facial features (as you can see in the photo), reduced total brain size (Haier et al., 1995), and often other physical abnormalities such as heart defects. They are typically retarded.

The risk of bearing a child with this deviant pattern is greatest for mothers over 35. Among women aged 35–39, the incidence of Down syndrome is about 1 in 280 births; among those over 45 it is as high as 1 in 50 births (D'Alton & DeCherney, 1993). Research by epidemiologists is also revealing a link between exposure to environmental toxins of various kinds and the risk of offspring with Down syndrome. For example, one large study in Canada shows that men who work as mechanics, farm laborers, or sawmill workers, all of whom are regularly exposed to solvents, oils, lead, and pesticides, are at higher risk for fathering Down syndrome children than are men who work in cleaner environments (Olshan, Baird, & Teschke, 1989). Findings like this suggest that chromosomal anomalies may not be purely random events, but may themselves be a response to various teratogens.

Sex-Chromosome Anomalies. A second class of anomalies is associated with an incomplete or incorrect division of either sex chromosome, which occurs in roughly 1 out of every 400 births (Berch & Bender, 1987). The most common is an XXY pattern, called Klinefelter's syndrome, which occurs in 1 or 2 out of every 1000 males. Affected boys most often look quite normal, although they have underdeveloped testes and, as adults, a sparsity of sperm. Most are not mentally retarded, but language and learning disabilities are common. Somewhat rarer is an XYY pattern. These children also develop as boys, are typically unusually tall, with mild retardation. A single-X pattern (XO), called Turner's syndrome, and a triple-X pattern (XXX) may also occur, and in both cases the child develops as a girl. Girls with Turner's syndrome show stunted growth and are usually sterile. Without hormone therapy, they do not menstruate or develop breasts at puberty. These girls also show an interesting imbalance in their cognitive skills: They often perform particularly poorly on tests that measure spatial ability but usually perform at or above normal levels on tests of verbal skill (Golombok & Fivush, 1994). Girls with an XXX pattern are of normal size but are slow in physical development. In contrast to Turner's syndrome girls, they have markedly *poor* verbal abilities, overall low IQ, and do particularly poorly in school compared with other groups with sex chromosome anomalies (Bender et al., 1995; Rovet & Netley, 1983).

Fragile X Syndrome. A quite different type of genetic anomaly is referred to as a "fragile X." The full syndrome occurs in about 1 out of every 1300 males (Adesman, 1996; Rose, 1995) and involves not an improper number of chromosomes, but rather an abnormal, fragile section of DNA at a specific location on the X chromosome (Dykens, Hodapp, & Leckman, 1994). This is an *inherited* disorder, following the sex-linked inheritance pattern illustrated earlier in Figure 3.3. Thus, both boys and girls may inherit a fragile X (ordinarily from a carrier mother), but boys, lacking the potentially overriding influence of a normal X, are much more susceptible to the negative intellectual or behavioral consequences. Almost all affected boys have at least some degree of mental retardation; very often they show a drop in IQ of perhaps 10 points between toddlerhood and adolescence, a decline that often shifts them from a level of mild retardation to one of moderate retardation (Adesman, 1996). Current estimates are that among males, 5 to 7 percent of all retardation is caused by this syndrome (Zigler & Hodapp, 1991).

Single Gene Defects. As I have already indicated, problems can also occur at conception if the child inherits a gene for a specific disease. In a few cases, such diseases may be caused by a dominant gene. The best-known example is Huntington's disease, a severe neurological disorder resulting in rapid loss of both mental and physical functioning, with symptoms usually appearing only at midlife. Lethal dominant gene diseases are relatively rare because the affected parent would almost always know that he or she was suffering from the disorder and might be unable or unwilling to reproduce. Far more common are recessive-gene diseases. I've listed a few examples in Table 3.2, but this list cannot really convey the diversity of such disorders. Among known causes of mental retardation are 141 diseases or disorders with known genetic loci and 361 more whose locus has not yet been identified (Wahlström, 1990).

Table 3.2 Some of the Major Inherited Diseases

- **Phenylketonuria.** A metabolic disorder that prevents metabolism of a common amino acid (phenylalanine). Treatment consists of a special phenylalanine-free diet. The child is not allowed many types of food, including milk. If not placed on the special diet shortly after birth, the child usually becomes very retarded. Affects only 1 in 8000 children. Diagnostic tests for this disorder are now routinely given at birth; cannot be diagnosed prenatally.
- **Tay-Sachs Disease.** An invariably fatal degenerative disease of the nervous system; virtually all victims die within the first three to four years. This gene is most common among Jews of Eastern European origin, among whom it occurs in approximately 1 in 3500 births. Can be diagnosed prenatally with amniocentesis or chorionic villus sampling.
- **Sickle-Cell Anemia.** A sometimes fatal blood disease, with joint pain, increased susceptibility to infection, and other symptoms. The gene for this disease is carried by about 2 million Americans, most often blacks. Can now be diagnosed prenatally through amniocentesis or chorionic villus sampling.
- **Cystic Fibrosis.** A fatal disease affecting the lungs and intestinal tract. Many children with CF now live into their 20s. The gene is carried by over 10 million Americans, most often whites. Carriers cannot be identified before pregnancy, and affected children cannot be diagnosed prenatally. If a couple has had one CF child, however, they know that their chances of having another are 1 in 4.
- **Muscular Dystrophy.** A fatal muscle-wasting disease, carried on the X chromosome and thus found almost exclusively among boys. The gene for the most common type of MD, Duchenne's, has just been located, so prenatal diagnosis may soon be available.

Geneticists estimate that the average adult carries genes for four different recessive diseases or abnormalities (Scarr & Kidd, 1983), but for any one disease the distribution of genes is not random. For example, sickle cell genes are more common among blacks; Tay-Sachs is most common among Jews of Eastern European origin.

The Real World

Prenatal Diagnosis of Genetic Errors

Not so many years ago, when a child was conceived, that child was born with whatever deformities, diseases, or anomalies happened to come along. The parents had no choices. That is no longer true. Parents today may have access to genetic testing, genetic counseling, and any one of several prenatal diagnostic tests that can detect fetal abnormalities.

Prepregnancy Genetic Testing

Before conceiving, you and your spouse can have blood tests done that will tell you whether you are carriers of genes for those specific diseases for which the loci are known, such as Tay-Sachs or sickle cell anemia. Because the locations of genes for all genetic diseases have not yet been located, carriers of many diseases (such as cystic fibrosis) cannot yet be identified in this way. But blood testing may still be an important step if you and your spouse belong to a subgroup known to be likely to carry particular recessive genes.

Prenatal Diagnosis

Four prenatal diagnostic strategies are now available. Two of these, the **alpha-fetoprotein test** (AFP) and **ultrasound,** are primarily used to detect problems in the formation of the *neural tube,* the structure that becomes the brain and spinal cord. If the tube fails to close at the bottom end, a disability called *spina bifida* occurs. Children with this defect are often partially paralyzed, and many (but not all) are retarded.

Alpha-fetoprotein is a substance produced by the fetus and is detectable in the mother's blood. If the levels are abnormally high, it suggests that there may be some problem with the spinal cord or brain. The blood test is normally not done until the second trimester. If the AFP value is high, it does not mean a problem definitely exists; it means that there is a higher *risk* of problems and that further tests are usually indicated.

One such further test is ultrasound, which involves the use of sound waves to provide an actual "moving picture" of the fetus. It is frequently possible to detect, or rule out, neural tube defects—or other physical abnormalities—with this method. The procedure is not painful and gives parents an often delightful chance to see their unborn child moving, and very often it can show whether the fetus is a boy or a girl. But ultrasound cannot provide information about the presence of chromosomal anomalies or inherited diseases.

If you want the latter information, you have two choices: **amniocentesis** or **chorionic villus sampling** (CVS). In both cases, a needle is inserted and cells are taken from the developing embryo. In CVS, the sample is taken from what will become the placenta; in amniocentesis, the sample is from the amniotic fluid.

Both CVS and amniocentesis will provide information about any of the chromosomal anomalies, and about the presence of genes for many of the major genetic diseases. Each technique has its own advantages and disadvantages. Amniocentesis was developed earlier and is the more widely used of the two. Its major drawback is that because the amniotic sac must be large enough to allow a sample of fluid to be taken with very little danger to the fetus, the test cannot be done until the sixteenth week of gestation and the results are typically not available for several more weeks. If the test reveals an abnormality, and if the parents decide to abort, it is quite late for an abortion to be performed. Chorionic villus sampling, in contrast, is done between the ninth and eleventh weeks of gestation. Early studies suggested that CVS was somewhat riskier than amniocentesis, with higher rates of miscarriage caused by the procedure. More recent research, however, suggests that the risks are about the same for the two procedures (Nightingale & Goodman, 1990).

By the time you are facing this choice, there may be still newer options using maternal blood samples. Experimental evidence already indicates that such a technique may be suitable for diagnosing Down syndrome or even the sex of the fetus (Lo et al., 1989; Wald et al., 1988). But no matter what technique you select, the moral and ethical choices you may have to make are far from easy.

For example, consider the case of diseases that can occur in mild or moderate as well as severe forms, such as sickle-cell anemia. Prenatal tests can tell you whether the child will inherit the disease, but they cannot tell you how severely the child will be affected. An equally difficult decision faces parents when a chromosomal anomaly is detected, but one so rare that little information about outcome may be available. Genetic counselors may play a very helpful role, but ultimately each couple has to make its own decisions.

Teratogens: Diseases and Drugs

Deviant prenatal development can also result from variations in the environment in which the embryo and fetus is nurtured. I pointed out in Chapter 1 that the effect of most teratogens seems to depend heavily on their *timing*, an example of *critical periods*. The general rule is that each organ system is most vulnerable to disruption at the time when it is developing most rapidly (Moore & Persaud, 1993). At that point it is most sensitive to outside interference, whether from a disease organism that passes through the placental barrier, inappropriate hormones, drugs, or whatever. Because most organ systems develop most rapidly during the first 12 weeks of gestation, this is the period of greatest risk for most teratogens. Of the many teratogens, the most critical are probably drugs the mother may take and diseases she may have or may contract during the pregnancy.

Diseases of the Mother

A disease in the mother can affect the embryo or fetus by any one of three mechanisms. Some diseases, particularly viruses, can attack the placenta, reducing the nutrients available to the embryo. Some others have molecules small enough to pass through the placental filters and attack the embryo or fetus directly. Examples of this type include rubella and rubeola (both forms of measles), cytomegalovirus (CMV), syphilis, diphtheria, influenza, typhoid, serum hepatitis, and chicken pox. The third possibility is that disease organisms present in the mucus membranes of the birth canal may infect the infant during birth itself. Genital herpes, for example, is transmitted this way. So far as researchers now know, AIDS is transmitted both directly through the placenta and during delivery, as well as through breast milk after birth (Van de Perre et al., 1991). Of all these diseases, probably the riskiest for the child are rubella, AIDS, and CMV.

Rubella. **Rubella** (also called *German measles*) is most risky during the first few weeks of gestation. Most infants exposed in the first four to five weeks show some abnormality, compared with only about 10 percent among those exposed in the final six months of the pregnancy (Moore & Persaud, 1993). Deafness, cataracts, and heart defects are the most common abnormalities.

Fortunately, rubella is preventable. Vaccination is available and should be given to all children as part of a regular immunization program. Adult women who were not vaccinated as children can be vaccinated later, but it must be done at least three months before a pregnancy to provide complete immunity.

Critical Thinking

Women readers: Have you been vaccinated for rubella? If you don't know, find out; if you have not been, arrange for such a vaccination—but only if you are sure you are not pregnant!

AIDS. Worldwide, an estimated 3 million women are infected with HIV, the virus that causes AIDS, and the number of infected women of childbearing age is rising everywhere. In the United States in 1993, approximately 6500 infants were born to mothers infected with HIV (Davis et al., 1995). In areas with a high population of drug users, as many as 3 to 5 percent of all pregnant women are now HIV-infected, and roughly one-half of 1 percent of babies test positive for the AIDS virus at birth (Heagarty, 1991).

These are grim numbers, but there are several bits of good news amid all this depressing information. First, the numbers of HIV-infected women giving birth has been declining in recent years, although researchers do not yet know why (Davis et al., 1995). Even more encouraging is the now well-established conclusion that only about a quarter of infants born to HIV-infected mothers themselves become infected (Abrams et al., 1995; Annunziato & Frenkel, 1993). Transmission appears to be more likely when the mother has AIDS than when she is HIV positive but is not yet experiencing symptoms of AIDS (Abrams et al., 1995), but beyond that, physicians have not been able to predict the likelihood of infection with any accuracy (Peckham, 1994).

The Real World

Rh Factor: Another Type of Genetic Problem

Rh factor incompatibility is neither a genetic defect nor an inherited disease, but rather an incompatibility between the mother's genes and the baby's. One of the many factors in the blood is the presence or absence of a red cell antigen called the Rh factor because rhesus monkeys have it. Humans who have this factor are called Rh+ (Rh positive), while those who lack it are Rh– (Rh negative). Only about 15 percent of whites and 5 percent of blacks in the United States are Rh–; it is quite rare among Asians and Native Americans.

Problems arise if the mother is Rh– and the baby is Rh+. Because Rh+ is dominant, a baby with an Rh+ father could inherit an Rh+ gene from him, even though the mother is Rh–. If the mother's and fetus's blood mix in the uterus, the mother's body considers the baby's Rh+ factor to be a foreign substance and her immune system tries to fight it off by producing antibodies. These antibodies cross the placenta and attack the baby's blood, producing a chemical substance in the baby called bilirubin. Babies with high levels of bilirubin look quite yellow; if untreated, brain damage can occur.

The risk of damage to the fetus increases with each succeeding pregnancy in which an Rh– mother carries an Rh+ baby. Normally, the placenta keeps the two blood systems separate, but during birth some mixing usually occurs. So after the first baby, the mother produces some antibodies. With a second incompatible baby, these antibodies attack the infant's blood, producing negative effects.

This problem used to be treated with rather heroic measures, such as complete exchange of the infant's blood shortly after birth to remove all the antibodies. Fortunately, scientists have now discovered a much simpler and safer treatment. Within 3 days of the birth of her first child, an Rh– mother can be injected with a substance called RhoGam, which prevents the buildup of antibodies, and thus protects subsequent infants, even if they are also Rh+.

The third piece of good news is that mothers who are treated with the drug AZT during their pregnancy have a markedly lowered risk of transmitting the disease to their children—as low as 8 percent (Centers for Disease Control, 1994b).

CMV. A much less well-known, but remarkably widespread and potentially serious disease is cytomegalovirus (CMV), a virus in the herpes group. It is now thought to be the single most important known infectious cause of both congenital mental retardation and deafness.

As many as 60 percent of *all* women have antibodies to CMV, but most have no recognized symptoms. Of babies whose mothers have CMV antibodies, 1–2 percent become infected prenatally. When the mother's disease is in an active phase, the transmission rate is more like 40–50 percent (Blackman, 1990). As with AIDS, researchers have not yet uncovered all the details of the mechanisms of transmission. Nor have they understood why only about 5 to 10 percent of babies infected prenatally show clear symptoms of the disease at birth. But the 2500 babies born each year in the United States who do display symptoms of the disease have a variety of serious problems, often including deafness and widespread damage to the central nervous system. Most are mentally retarded (Blackman, 1990).

I am aware, by the way, that what I have just said about CMV is potentially fairly alarming, given the high rate of silent infection. However, keep the statistics correctly in mind: If the mother's disease is not active, only 1 to 2 percent of babies become infected, and of this number, only at most 10 percent show symptoms of the disease—which means that at most 2 out of every 1000 infants whose mothers carry an inactive antibody will show any effect.

Critical Thinking

Given these new findings, should all pregnant women be required to be tested for HIV infection so that they can be given the appropriate drug? Medical ethicists have offered strong arguments on both sides of this question. What do you think?

Drugs Taken by the Mother

There is now a huge literature on the effects of prenatal drugs, involving everything from aspirin to antibiotics to alcohol and cocaine. Sorting out their effects has proven to be an immensely challenging task, not only because it is clearly not possible to assign women randomly to various drug groups, but also because in the real world, many women take multiple drugs during their pregnancy. For example, women who drink alcohol are also more likely to smoke; those who use cocaine are also likely to take other illegal drugs, or to smoke or drink to excess. What's more, the effects of drugs may be subtle, visible only many years after birth in the form of minor learning disabilities or increased risk of behavior problems. Still, we are creeping toward some fairly clear conclusions in several areas. Let me give you some examples.

Smoking. One of the most extensive bodies of research describes the effect of smoking. One consistent result stands out: Infants of mothers who smoke are on average about half a pound lighter at birth than are infants of nonsmoking mothers, and such lowered birth weight has a variety of potential negative consequences I'll talk about later (Floyd et al., 1993). This does not mean that every mother who smokes has a very small baby. It does mean that the risk of such an outcome is higher for mothers who smoke.

The primary mechanism seems to work this way: Nicotine constricts the blood vessels, reducing blood flow to the placenta and in turn reducing nutrition to the fetus. In the long term, such nutritional deprivation seems to increase slightly the risk of learning problems or poor attention span at school age. There are also some signs of higher rates of behavior problems among children whose mothers smoked heavily during pregnancy (Fergusson, Horwood, & Lynskey, 1993).

Although research on the effects of smoking is not always easy to interpret, because women who smoke are likely to differ in other ways from those who do not, the moral seems clear: The safest plan is not to smoke during pregnancy. If you are a smoker, quit as soon as you learn you are pregnant: Smokers who quit smoking early in their pregnancy have the same rates of preterm or low-birth-weight infants as do those who did not smoke at all (Ahlsten, Cnattingius, & Lindmark, 1993). The research also shows a relationship between the "dose" (the amount of nicotine you are taking in) and the severity of consequences for the child. So if you cannot quit entirely, at least cut back.

Drinking. Recent work on the effects of maternal drinking on prenatal and postnatal development also carries a clear message: To be safe, don't drink during pregnancy.

The effects of alcohol on the developing fetus range from mild to severe. At the extreme end of the continuum are children who exhibit a syndrome called **fetal alcohol syndrome (FAS).** These children, whose mothers were usually heavy drinkers or alcoholics, are generally smaller than normal, with smaller brains. They frequently have heart defects, and their faces are distinctively different (as you can see in Figure 3.7), with a somewhat flattened nose and nose bridge, and often an unusually long space between nose and mouth. As children, adolescents, and adults, they continue to be shorter than normal, have smaller heads, and achieve IQ scores in the range of mild mental retardation. Indeed, FAS is the leading known cause of retardation in the United States, exceeding even Down syndrome (Streissguth et al., 1991).

But the effects of alcohol during pregnancy are not confined to cases in which the mother is clearly an alcoholic or a very heavy drinker. Recent evidence also points to milder effects of moderate or "social" drinking, such as two glasses of wine a day. Children of mothers who drank at this level during pregnancy are more likely to have IQs below 85 and show poorer attention span. I've given some details about one of the best studies in the Research Report on page 67 so you can get some feeling for how investigators have gone about studying this problem.

We do not yet know whether there is any safe level of alcohol consumption during pregnancy, although most of those who work in this field are convinced that there is a linear relationship between the amount of alcohol ingested and the risk for

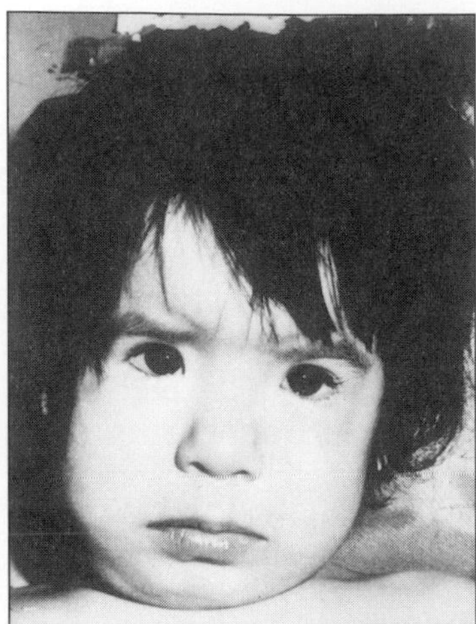
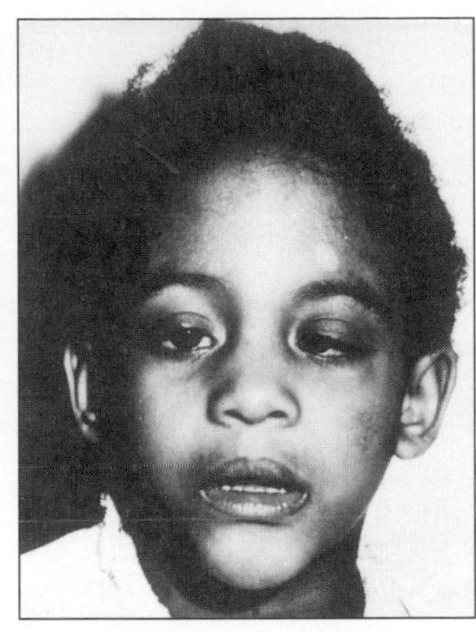
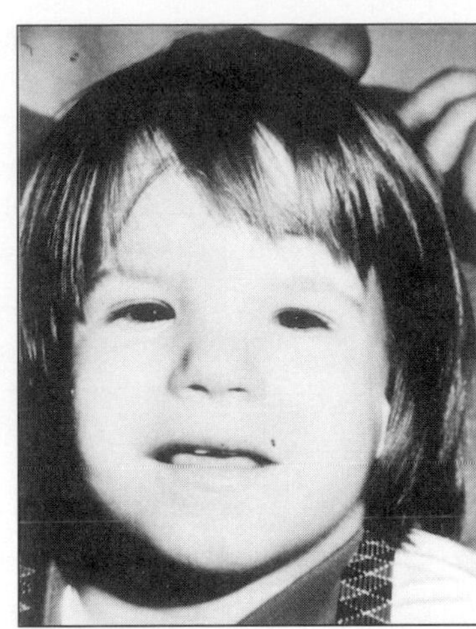

FIGURE 3.7 Fetal alcohol syndrome children, like Down syndrome children, have distinctive features, whatever their familial racial heritage. (*Source:* Streissguth et al., *Science, 209* [July 18, 1980): Figure 2, p. 355. Copyright © 1980 by the American Association for the Advancement of Science.)

Research Report

Streissguth's Study of Prenatal Alcohol Exposure

The best single study of the consequences of prenatal alcohol exposure has been done by Ann Streissguth and her colleagues (Olson et al., 1992; Streissguth, Barr, & Sampson, 1990; Streissguth et al., 1989, 1995, 1980, 1984, 1981), who have followed a group of over 500 women and children beginning early in the woman's pregnancy. Because the study was begun before there were widespread warnings about the possible impact of alcohol during pregnancy, the sample includes many well-educated middle-class women with good diets who did not use many other recreational drugs but who did drink alcohol in moderate or even fairly heavy amounts while pregnant—a set of conditions that would be impossible to duplicate today, at least in the United States or other countries in which the risks of alcohol in pregnancy are well advertised.

Streissguth tested the children repeatedly, beginning immediately after birth, again later in infancy, at age 4, at school age, and again at ages 11 and 14. She found that the mother's alcohol consumption in pregnancy was associated with sluggishness and weaker sucking in infancy, lower scores on a test of infant intelligence at 8 months, lower IQ at 4 and 7 years, and problems with attention and vigilance at 4, 7, 11, and 14. Teachers also rated the 11-year-olds on overall school performance and on various behavior problems, and on both measures those whose mothers had consumed the most alcohol during pregnancy were rated significantly worse.

Streissguth also was careful to obtain information about other drug use in pregnancy, including smoking, and asked mothers about their diet, education, and life habits. She found that the links between alcohol consumption and poor outcomes for the child held up even when all these other variables were controlled statistically.

Setting aside those cases in which the child was diagnosed with the full fetal alcohol syndrome, the effects of moderate levels of alcohol use during pregnancy are not large in absolute terms, but they have significant practical consequences. For example, the difference in IQ scores at age 7 between children of abstainers and children of women who drank 1 ounce or more of alcohol per day during their pregnancy (roughly equivalent to two ounces of hard liquor or one 8-ounce glass of wine) was only about 6 points in Streissguth's sample (Streissguth et al., 1990). But this relatively small absolute difference means that three times as many alcohol-exposed children have IQs below 85 than is true among children of abstainers. Alcohol-exposed children are thus greatly overrepresented in special classes in schools and probably also appear in overlarge numbers among high school dropouts and the underemployed in adulthood—although those links remain for longer-term longitudinal studies to confirm.

the infant. This means that even at low dosage there is *some* increased risk. It probably also matters when in the pregnancy the drinking occurs, and it clearly matters how many drinks the mother has on any one occasion. Binge drinking (usually defined as five or more drinks on any one occasion) is significantly riskier than regular smaller doses (Olson et al., 1992; Streissguth et al., 1990). In the face of our remaining ignorance, the *safest* course is not to drink at all.

Cocaine. Significant numbers of pregnant women in the United States (and presumably elsewhere in the world) also take various illegal drugs, most notably cocaine, although it is of course difficult to know exactly how prevalent the problem is, because many women are understandably reluctant to reveal such information to researchers or physicians. The best current estimates are that roughly 3 percent of all babies born in the United States have been prenatally exposed to cocaine. Among babies born to poor, inner-city mothers, the rate may be as high as 20 or 30 percent (Hawley & Disney, 1992).

Cocaine appears to cross the placental barrier quite readily, but unlike alcohol, it creates no regular or recognizable syndrome of abnormalities. About a third of all cocaine-exposed babies are born prematurely, and among those born after a normal gestation period, many more have lower than normal birth weight—a pattern that is very similar to what we see with smoking during pregnancy. In addition, they are three times as likely to have a very small head circumference. Some cocaine-exposed babies also show significant drug withdrawal symptoms after birth, such as irritability, restlessness, shrill crying, and tremors. Whether any long-term consequences can be ascribed clearly to prenatal cocaine exposure, however, is not yet clear. Some studies show long-term effects; others do not (Griffith, Azuma, & Chasnoff, 1994; Richardson & Day, 1994). My sense is that we will eventually find, as with alcohol exposure, that the effects of cocaine are subtle and long-lasting, but that remains to be definitively shown.

Critical Thinking

A question of medical ethics for you to ponder: There are now several cases of pregnant women being held in custody to prevent them from excessive drinking or drug taking, on the grounds that the court has the responsibility to prevent harm to the fetus. What do you think about this?

Other Teratogens

There are a great many other teratogens—including excess amounts of vitamin A, methylmercury, and lead—and many drugs or chemicals suspected of being teratogens about which we have insufficient information. The latter category includes anticonvulsant medication taken by epileptics, polychlorinated biphenyls (PCBs, compounds widely used in electrical transformers and paint), radiation at high doses, aspirin, some antidepressants, some artificial hormones, and some pesticides (Vorhees & Mollnow, 1987). I don't have room to go into detail about what we know (or don't know) in each case, but let me say just a word about several of the items that have clear practical significance.

Diethylstilbestrol (DES). Diethylstilbestrol is a synthetic estrogen that at one time was commonly given to pregnant women to prevent miscarriages. The daughters of such women have been found to have higher rates of some kinds of cancers; sons have higher rates of congenital malformations of the genitalia. Some—but not all—research suggests that the sons also have higher rates of infertility (Rosenblith, 1992; Wilcox et al., 1995).

Vitamin A. Vitamin A in small doses is essential for the development of the embryo, but when taken in very large doses (10,000 International Units—IU—or more per day) during the first two months of pregnancy, it is linked to significantly increased risk of birth defects, particularly malformations of the head, face, heart, and nervous system (e.g., Rothman et al., 1995). The recommended daily allowance of Vitamin A is 2,700 IU. Most multivitamin pills of the type normally recommended for pregnant women contain 4,000 to 5,000 units, but some brands contain as much as 10,000, and straight Vitamin A capsules can contain as much as 25,000 units. Because relatively few women take doses as high as 10,000 units per day, this problem is relatively rare; it is also easy to prevent by checking ingredients—not only of multivitamin capsules, but also vitamin-A enriched cereals.

Aspirin. One of the most widely used drugs, aspirin, is teratogenic in animals when given in high doses. Humans rarely take high enough doses to produce such effects directly, but it turns out that aspirin in moderate amounts can have negative effects on the human fetus if it is ingested along with benzoic acid, a chemical widely used as a preservative in such foods as ketchup. This combination, especially in the first trimester, seems to increase the risk of physical malformations in the embryo/fetus.

Lead. In most industrialized countries, adults are exposed to fairly high dosages of lead, although the introduction of unleaded gasoline has had a significant impact on dosages, as has the elimination of lead-based paint. We have known for some time that high exposure to lead, as from lead-based paints in old houses, has highly negative consequences for children, lowering their IQ, increasing their distractibility, and possibly increasing their level of aggressiveness (Needleman et al., 1996). A newer set of studies shows that even quite low levels of lead in the blood of newborns or toddlers—levels previously classified as "safe" by U.S. federal guidelines and found in children who live in houses without lead-based paint—are associated with slightly lower IQ scores at later ages than we see in children with still lower lead levels (Tesman & Hills, 1994). Several longitudinal studies show that the effects are still detectable at ages 7 to 10 (Bellinger, Stiles, & Needleman, 1992). Because of this new evidence, the Centers for Disease Control have changed their guidelines so that much lower blood lead levels are defined as dangerous.

As the study of teratogens expands, psychologists have realized that prenatal development is less insulated, less fully protected than we had first thought. In particular, many chemicals associated with modern industrial societies may have unforeseen effects on the fetus.

Other Influences on Prenatal Development

Diet. Another risk for the fetus is poor maternal nutrition. Some specific nutrients are vital, such as a sufficient level of folic acid, a B vitamin found in beans, spinach, orange juice, wheat germ, and other foods. Inadequate amounts of this nutrient have been clearly linked to the risk of neural tube defects, such as spina bifida (Daly et al., 1995). The potential negative effects of insufficient folic acid occur in the very earliest weeks of pregnancy, before a woman may even know she is pregnant. So it is important for women who plan a pregnancy to maintain at least the minimum level of this vitamin, 400 micrograms daily. Such a level can be achieved either by careful choice of foods, or by taking supplementary vitamins.

It is also obviously important for the mother to have sufficient overall calories and protein to prevent malnutrition. When a woman experiences severe malnutrition during pregnancy, particularly during the final three months, she has a greatly increased risk of stillbirths, low birth weight, and infant death during the first year of life (Stein et al., 1975). The impact appears to be greatest on the developing nervous system—a pattern found in studies of both humans and other mammals. For example, rats whose caloric intake has been substantially restricted during the fetal and early postnatal periods show a pattern described as *brain stunting*, with both the weight and volume of the brain reduced. They also show less dendritic development and less rich synaptic formation (Pollitt & Gorman, 1994).

In human studies of cases in which prenatal malnutrition has been severe enough to cause the death of the fetus or newborn, effects very similar to the rat studies have been observed. These infants have smaller brains and fewer and smaller brain cells (Georgieff, 1994).

Critical Thinking

What kind of study would you have to do to figure out whether it is okay for pregnant women to maintain high levels of exercise, such as running 30 miles a week?

But whether similarly lasting effects on brain development occur in cases of prenatal *sub*nutrition, such as the chronic protein-energy malnutrition common in many populations around the world, is simply not clear. For one thing, such children are highly likely to encounter mal- or subnutrition after birth as well as prenatally, frequently accompanied by lower levels of stimulation in the home. This makes it extremely difficult to sort out the effects of the *pre*natal nutrition from the effects of *post*natal insufficiencies. At the moment, most experts in this area have abandoned the idea that typical levels of prenatal subnutrition have some direct, irremediable, negative effect on the developing brain (Ricciuti, 1993). Instead, what seems to happen is some variation of the interaction pattern I described in Chapter 1 (recall Figure 1.4): Prenatal subnutrition may make the infant more "vulnerable," perhaps because it makes him less energetic or responsive, or less able to learn from his experiences. In a nonstimulating environment such a vulnerable child is likely to do poorly. But a stimulating environment can overcome the vulnerability.

The Mother's Age. One of the particularly intriguing trends in modern family life in the United States and many other industrialized countries is the increasing likelihood that women will postpone their first pregnancy into their late 20s or early 30s. In 1992, 23.5 percent of first births in the United States were to women over 30, more than double the rate in 1970 (U.S. Bureau of the Census, 1995). Of course women have many reasons for such delayed childbearing, chief among them the increased need for second incomes in families and the desire of many young women to complete job training and early career steps before bearing children. I'm not going to debate all the pros and cons of such a choice. But I do want to explore the question

The Real World

How Much Weight Should You Gain in Pregnancy?

As recently as 1950, the standard advice to pregnant women in the United States was to gain no more than 20 pounds over the 9 months. In the 1970s, however, new data accumulated showing that weight gains in that range were associated with increased risk of low birth weight and neurological impairment in the infant. This prompted a new recommendation from the American College of Obstetricians and Gynecologists and the American Academy of Pediatrics for a gain of between 22 and 27 pounds. In 1990, the National Institute of Medicine issued still newer guidelines that base the recommended gain on a woman's prepregnancy weight-for-height (Taffel, Keppel, & Jones, 1993):

- A woman whose weight is normal for her height should gain between 25 and 35 pounds;
- A woman who is unusually lightweight for her height should gain 28 to 40 pounds;
- A woman who is heavy for her height should gain 15 to 25 pounds, and an obese woman should gain no less than 15 pounds.

Unfortunately, the very women who are otherwise at highest risk for various kinds of problems, including bearing a low-birth-weight infant, are also most likely to gain an insufficient amount: those who are lightweight for their height before pregnancy, women older than 35, and those with low education (Centers for Disease Control, 1992).

Interestingly, it begins to look as if variations in maternal weight gain during pregnancy may be one contributor to the large difference between African-American and U.S. whites in neonatal mortality—a pattern I'll talk about in Chapter 4. The connective chain goes like this: Black women in the United States are, on average, heavier than white women of comparable social class, and more likely to be obese. Because of this, they are more likely to be (badly) advised, or they themselves choose, to restrict their weight gain during pregnancy, which in turn increases the likelihood of low birth weight in the infant (Kempe et al., 1992; Luke & Murtaugh, 1993). In fact, it looks as if for black women, even more than for white women, the optimum weight gain is one that is at the *upper* end of the range appropriate for their prepregnancy weight (Hickey et al., 1993).

that is relevant for the subject of this chapter—namely, the impact of maternal age on the mother's experience of pregnancy and on the developing fetus.

Current research suggests that for the woman, the optimum time for childbearing is in her early 20s. Mothers over 30 (particularly those over 35) are at increased risk for several kinds of problems, including miscarriage (McFalls, 1990), complications of pregnancy such as high blood pressure or bleeding (Berkowitz et al., 1990), and death during pregnancy or delivery (Buehler et al., 1986). For example, in one large study of nearly 4000 women in New York, all of whom had received adequate prenatal care, Gertrud Berkowitz and her colleagues (1990) found that women 35 and older during their first pregnancies were almost twice as likely as women in their 20s to suffer some pregnancy complication. These effects of age seem to be exacerbated if the mother has not had adequate prenatal care or has poor health habits. For example, the negative effects of maternal smoking on birth weight is considerably *greater* among women over 35 than among young women (Wen et al., 1990).

Whether the infants born to these older mothers also have higher risk of problems is not so clear. The evidence is conflicting. Infants born to older mothers appear to be only slightly more likely to have low birth weight (Berkowitz et al., 1990; Cnattingius, Berendes, & Forman, 1993), and are probably not more likely to have birth defects—aside from the well-established risk of chromosomal anomalies such as Down syndrome (Baird, Sadovnick, & Yee, 1991). However, researchers in Sweden, where mothers of all ages receive remarkably comprehensive prenatal care, have recently reported higher rates of late-pregnancy miscarriage and heightened infant mortality for infants born to older mothers, especially for first births to mothers over 35 (Cnattingius et al., 1993). Given these varying results, the experts have been unable to reach a clear conclusion about risks for babies born to older mothers.

At the other end of the age continuum—very young mothers—there is also disagreement about how to interpret the findings. If we simply compare the rates of problems of pregnancy seen in teenage mothers compared with mothers in their 20s, almost all researchers find higher levels of problems among the teens. But how do we account for this difference? Because teen mothers are also more likely to be poor and less likely to receive adequate prenatal care, it is very hard to sort out the causal factors. A number of researchers have found that when poverty and prenatal care are taken into account, the differences in rates of problems between teen and older mothers disappears (e.g., McCarthy & Hardy, 1993; Osofsky, Hann, & Peebles, 1993). But an unusually well-designed new study calls this somewhat optimistic conclusion into question.

Alison Fraser and her colleagues studied 135,088 white girls and women, aged 13 to 24, who gave birth in the state of Utah between 1970 and 1990 (Fraser, Brockert, & Ward, 1995). This is an unusual sample for studies on this subject: Almost two-thirds of the teenage mothers in this group were married and most had adequate prenatal care; 95 percent remained in school. These special conditions have enabled Fraser to disentangle the effects of ethnicity, poverty, marital status, and the mother's age—all of which are normally confounded in studies of teenage childbearing. Overall, Fraser found higher rates of adverse pregnancy outcomes among mothers age 17 and younger than among the mothers in their 20s. The rate of preterm births was twice as high; the incidence of low birth weight was almost twice as high. And these differences were found even when Fraser looked only at teenage mothers who were married, remained in school, and had adequate prenatal care. Outcomes were riskier still among teenage mothers who lacked adequate prenatal care, but good care alone did not eliminate the heightened risk of problems linked to teenage birth. Just why such a heightened risk should exist is not entirely clear. The most likely possibility is that there is some biological consequence of pregnancy in a girl whose own growth is not complete. But whatever the underlying reason, these new results raise a variety of red flags.

The Mother's Emotional State. Finally, the mother's state of mind during the pregnancy may be significant, although the research findings here, too, are decidedly mixed (Istvan, 1986). Results from infrahuman studies are clear: Exposure of the pregnant female to stressors such as heat, light, noise, shock, or crowding significantly increases the risk of low birth weight as well as later problems in the offspring (Schneider, 1992). Studies of humans, however, have not pointed to such a clear conclusion, in part because researchers have not agreed on how one ought to measure stress or anxiety. The most reasonable hypothesis at the moment seems to be that long-term, chronic stressors have little direct impact on a specific pregnancy, while substantial *increases* in anxiety or stress during a pregnancy may have more deleterious effects. For example, in a major longitudinal study in Hawaii, Emmy Werner (1986) found that among middle-class women, those who had negative feelings about their pregnancy or who experienced some psychological trauma during the pregnancy had more birth complications and more infants with low birth weight than did those with lower stress or anxiety. But these same patterns did not hold among poor women in this study, many of whom lived in states of chronic stress or disorganization.

Folklore in virtually all cultures certainly assumes a causal link between the mother's emotional experiences during her pregnancy and the outcome for the child. But at the moment the best I can say is that the hypothesis is still plausible but not clearly substantiated.

Critical Thinking

What three pieces of advice would you want to give a pregnant friend, based on this chapter? Why those three?

Sex Differences in Prenatal Development

Because nearly all prenatal development is controlled by maturational codes that are the same for all members of our species, male and female alike, there aren't very many sex differences in prenatal development. But there are a few, and they set the stage for some of the physical differences we'll see at later ages.

- Sometime between four and eight weeks after conception, the male embryo begins to secrete the male hormone *testosterone* from the rudimentary testes. If this hormone is not secreted or is secreted in inadequate amounts, the embryo will be "demasculinized," even to the extent of developing female genitalia. Female embryos do not appear to secrete any equivalent hormone prenatally. However, the accidental presence of male hormone at the critical time (as from some drug the mother may take, or from a genetic disease called *congenital adrenal hyperplasia*) acts to "defeminize" or masculinize the female fetus, sometimes resulting in malelike genitalia, frequently resulting in masculinization of later behavior, such as more rough-and-tumble play (Collaer & Hines, 1995).
- The several hormones that affect the development of genitalia prenatally (particularly testosterone in males) also appear to affect the pattern of brain development, resulting in subtle brain differences between males and females affecting patterns of growth-hormone secretions in adolescence, levels of physical aggression, and the relative dominance of the right and left hemispheres of the brain (Todd et al., 1995). The research evidence in this area is still fairly sketchy; it is clear that whatever role such prenatal hormones play in brain architecture and functioning is highly complex. But the early research has raised some very intriguing questions.
- Girls are a bit faster in some aspects of prenatal development, particularly skeletal development. They are about 1–2 weeks ahead in bone development at birth (Tanner, 1978).
- Despite the more rapid development of girls, boys are heavier and longer at birth (Tanner, 1978).
- Boys are considerably more vulnerable to all kinds of prenatal problems. Many more boys than girls are conceived—on the order of about 120 to 150 male embryos to every 100 female—but more of the males are sponta-

neously aborted. At birth, there are about 105 boys for every 100 girls. Boys are also more likely to experience injuries at birth (perhaps because they are larger), and they have more congenital malformations (Zaslow & Hayes, 1986).

The striking sex difference in vulnerability is particularly intriguing, especially since it seems to persist throughout the life span. Older boys are more prone to problems as well, as are adult men. Males have shorter life expectancy, higher rates of behavior problems, more learning disabilities, and usually more negative responses to major stresses, such as divorce. One possible explanation for at least some of this sex difference may lie in the basic genetic difference. The XX combination affords the girl more protection against the fragile-X syndrome and against any "bad" genes that may be carried on the X chromosome. For instance, geneticists have found that a gene affecting susceptibility to infectious disease is carried on the X chromosome (Brooks-Gunn & Matthews, 1979). Because boys have only one X chromosome, such a gene is much more likely to be expressed phenotypically in a boy.

Birth

Once the 38 weeks of gestation are over, the fetus must be born into the world—an event that holds some pain as well as a good deal of joy for most parents. In the normal process, labor progresses through three stages of unequal length.

The First Stage of Labor. Stage 1 covers the period during which two important processes occur: dilation and effacement. The cervix (the opening at the bottom of the uterus) must open up like the lens of a camera (*dilation*) and also flatten out (*effacement*). At the time of actual delivery, the cervix must normally be dilated to about 10 centimeters (about 4 inches). This part of labor has been likened to putting on a sweater with a neck that is too tight. You have to pull and stretch the neck of the sweater with your head in order to get it on. Eventually the neck is stretched wide enough so that the widest part of your head can pass through.

Customarily, stage 1 is itself divided into phases. In the *early* (or *latent*) phase, contractions are relatively far apart and are typically not too uncomfortable. In the *active* phase, which begins when the cervix is 3 to 4 cm dilated and continues until dilation has reached 8 cm, contractions are closer together and more intense. The last 2 centimeters of dilation are achieved during a period usually called *transition*. It is this period, when contractions are closely spaced and strong, that women typically find the most painful. Fortunately, transition is also ordinarily the shortest phase.

Figure 3.8 shows the typical length of these various phases of labor for first births and later births. What the figure does not convey is the wide individual variability that exists. Among women delivering a first child, stage 1 may last as few as 3 hours or as many as 20 (Biswas & Craigo, 1994; Kilpatrick & Laros, 1989).

Second Stage of Labor. At the end of the transition phase, the mother will normally have the urge to help the infant out by "pushing." When the birth attendant (physician or midwife) is sure the cervix is fully dilated, she or he will encourage this pushing, and the second stage of labor—the actual delivery—begins. The baby's head moves past the stretched cervix, into the birth canal, and finally out of the mother's body. Most women find this part of labor markedly less distressing than the transition phase because it is here that they can assist the delivery process by pushing. It typically lasts less than an hour and rarely takes longer than two hours.

Most infants are delivered head first, facing toward the mother's spine; 3 to 4 percent, however, are oriented differently, either feet first or bottom first (called *breech* presentations) (Brown, Karrison, & Cibils, 1994). In the United States today,

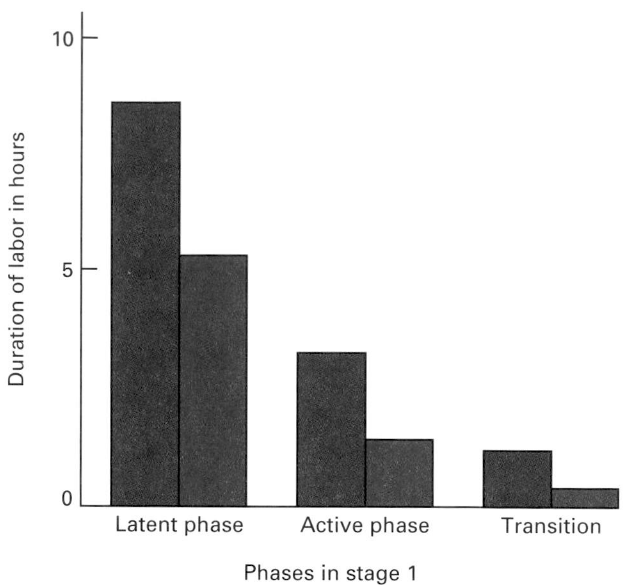

FIGURE 3.8 Typical pattern of timing of the phases of labor for first births and subsequent births. The relatively long latent phase shown here counts from zero centimeters dilation. (*Source*: Based on Biswas & Craigo, 1994, from Figures 10-16, p. 216, and 10-17, p. 217).

infants in breech positions are nearly all delivered through an abdominal incision (a **cesarean section**) rather than vaginally.

In most delivery situations in the United States, once the baby has emerged he is placed immediately on the mother's abdomen or given to her (and the father) to hold after the cord has been cut and the baby is cleaned up a bit—a matter of a few minutes. For most parents, this first greeting of the baby is a time for remarkable delight, as they stroke the baby's skin, count the fingers, look at the baby's eyes, talk to the infant.

The Third Stage of Labor. Stage 3, typically quite brief, is the delivery of the placenta (also called the "afterbirth") and other material from the uterus.

Birth Choices

What I am going to say here about birth choices is necessarily specific to options and experiences in industrialized countries. In many other cultures there are no decisions to be made about such questions as where the delivery will occur, whether the father should be present, or whether the mother should be given drugs to ease her pain. Custom dictates the answers. But in many Western industrialized countries, patterns and customs in this area continue to change rapidly, which leaves individual parents with decisions to make—decisions that may affect the child's health or the mother's satisfaction with the delivery. Because many of you will face these choices at some point in the future, I want to give you the best current information I have.

Drugs During Delivery. One key decision concerns the use of drugs during delivery. Three types of drugs are commonly used:

1. A*nalgesics* (such as the common drug Demerol) that are given during stage 1 of labor to reduce pain;

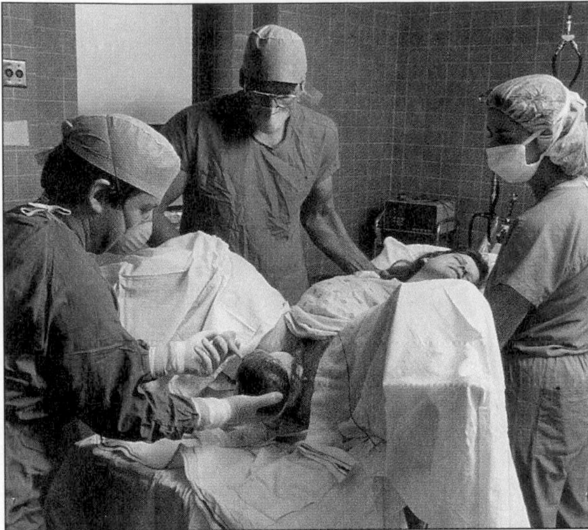

In the United States, the most common delivery setting is still in a hospital, assisted by a physician, as shown in the photo on the left; in Europe, home deliveries assisted by a midwife are much more common, as in the French birth shown in the photo on the right. But note that in both settings the father is present—now the norm in Western countries.

2. *Sedatives* or *tranquilizers* (such as Nembutol, Valium, or Thorazine) given during stage 1 labor to reduce anxiety; and
3. *Anesthesia*, given during transition or the second stage of labor to block pain either totally (general anesthesia) or in portions of the body (local anesthesia).

Of the three, anesthesia is the least often used in the United States, although the use of one form of local anesthesia, the epidural block, has been increasing in frequency, with a current rate of up to 16 percent of all labors (Fields & Wall, 1993).

Studying the causal links between such drug use and the baby's later behavior or development has proven to be monumentally difficult. Controlled experiments are obviously not possible, since women cannot be randomly assigned to specific drug regimens. And drugs are given in myriad different combinations. But a few reasonably clear conclusions are emerging.

First, it's clear that nearly all drugs given during labor pass through the placenta, enter the fetal bloodstream, and may remain there for several days. Not surprisingly, then, infants whose mothers have received any type of drug are typically slightly more sluggish, gain a little less weight, and spend more time sleeping in the first few weeks than do infants of nondrugged moms (Maurer & Maurer, 1988). These differences are quite small but have been observed repeatedly.

Second, beyond the first few days there are no consistently observed effects from analgesics and tranquilizers, and only hints from a few studies of long-term effects of anesthesia (Rosenblith, 1992). Given such contradictory findings, only one specific piece of advice seems warranted: If you have received medication, you need to bear in mind that your baby is also drugged, and that this will affect her behavior in the first few days. If you allow for this effect and realize that it will wear off, your long-term relationship with your child is likely to be unaffected.

The Location of Birth. A second choice parents must make is *where* the baby is to be born. Today in the U.S. there are typically four alternatives

1. A traditional hospital maternity unit;
2. A hospital-based birth center or birthing room, located within a hospital but providing a more homelike setting, with labor and delivery both completed in the same room and family members often present throughout;

3. A free-standing birth center, like a hospital birth center except that it is located apart from the hospital, with delivery typically attended by a midwife rather than (or in addition to) a physician; and
4. Home delivery.

At the turn of the century, only about 5 percent of babies in the United States were born in hospitals; today the figure is 98.3 percent (U.S. Bureau of the Census, 1994). About 1.0 percent are born at home, and the remainder in birthing centers—a choice that is particularly common among Mexican-American mothers, especially in Texas. Because home deliveries are so uncommon in the United States, much of what we know about them comes from research in Europe, where such deliveries are thought to be both more natural and less expensive for the medical care system. For example, in the Netherlands, a third of all deliveries occur at home (Eskes, 1992). Such deliveries are encouraged for uncomplicated pregnancies in which the woman has received good prenatal care. When these conditions are met, with a trained birth attendant present at delivery, the rate of delivery complications or infant problems is no higher than in hospital deliveries (Rooks et al., 1989; Tew, 1985). In contrast, studies in the United States show that infant mortality rates are significantly higher in *unplanned* home deliveries, those without trained attendants, or those in which the mother had experienced some complication of pregnancy (Schramm, Barnes, & Bakewell, 1987).

Incidentally, we have no evidence that babies born at home or in birthing centers are in any way better or worse off in the long run than are babies born in more traditional hospital settings. Assuming appropriate safety precautions are in place, then, the choice should be based on what is most comfortable for the individual woman or couple.

CRITICAL THINKING

Which birthing location do you think you would choose, and why?

The Presence of Fathers at Delivery. A third important decision is whether the father should be present at delivery. In the United States today this hardly seems like a "decision." As recently as 1972 only about a quarter of U.S. hospitals permitted the father to be present in the delivery room; by 1980, four-fifths of them did (Parke & Tinsley, 1984), and today the father's presence has become absolutely the norm.

There have been several compelling arguments offered in favor of such a norm: The father's presence may lessen the mother's anxiety and give her psychological support; by coaching her in breathing and other techniques he may help her control her pain; and he may become more strongly attached to the infant by being present at the birth. At least some evidence supports the first two of these arguments, but—perhaps unexpectedly for some of you—the third argument has little support.

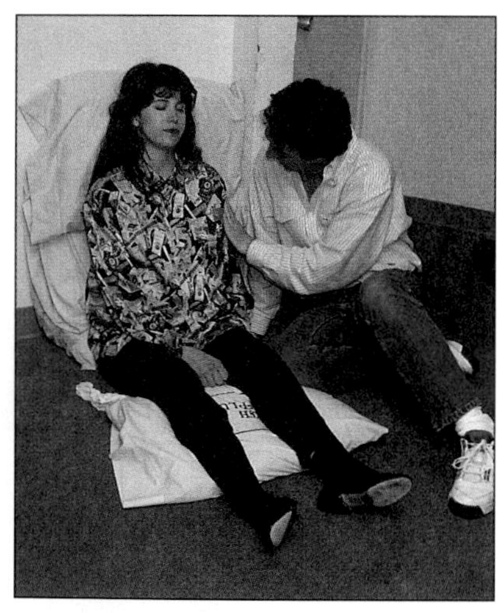

More and more fathers are taking special prenatal classes like this one so that they can provide support and coaching to their wives during labor. Here a Dad is learning how to help his wife with her breathing.

When fathers are present during labor and delivery, mothers report lower levels of pain and receive less medication (Henneborn & Cogan, 1975). And when the mother has a coach (the father or someone else), the incidence of problems of labor and delivery goes down, as does the duration of labor (Sosa et al., 1980). Furthermore, at least one study shows that women are more likely to report that the birth was a "peak" experience if the father was present (Entwisle & Doering, 1981). But presence at the delivery does not seem to have any magical effect on the father's emotional bond to the baby (Palkovitz, 1985). A father who sees his child for the first time in the newborn nursery, or days later at home, may nonetheless become as strongly attached to the infant as are those fathers who were present at the birth.

This statement is not in any way intended as an argument against fathers' participation in the delivery process. The fact that the father's presence seems to help the mother control pain, seems to reduce medication and labor duration, and may enhance the husband-wife relationship all seem to me to be compelling reasons for encouraging continued high levels of paternal participation. In addition, of course, most fathers report powerful feelings of delight at being present at the birth of their children—reason enough.

Problems at Birth

As with prenatal development, there are some things that can alter the normal pattern I have been describing. One of the most common problems is that the delivery itself may not proceed normally, leading to a surgical delivery through an abdominal incision, called a cesarean section (usually abbreviated C-section). A second common problem is that the infant may be born too early.

Cesarean-section Delivery. Cesarean section deliveries occur for a variety of reasons, of which the most common are a breech position of the fetus, some sign of fetal distress, or a mother who has had a previous C-section. Cesarean section deliveries are also more common among older mothers in the United States—a group that makes up an increasingly large proportion of all pregnancies (Adashek et al., 1993).

The frequency of C-sections has risen rapidly in many industrialized countries in the past few decades, including Australia, Canada, Britain, Norway, and other European countries (e.g., Notzon et al., 1994). In the United States the increase has been particularly striking, more than quadrupling between 1970 and 1985, to a rate of roughly one in every four births (U.S. Bureau of the Census, 1994). The rate has now dropped somewhat (to 21.8 percent in 1993) (U.S. Bureau of the Census, 1995), amid growing agreement that the current rate is substantially higher than is medically necessary. The Centers for Disease Control, in fact, list the reduction of this rate to something closer to 12 to 15 percent as a significant health objective for the year 2000 (Centers for Disease Control, 1993a). Evidence from studies in a number of European countries, such as Sweden, suggests that such a reduction in the rate of C-sections need not be accompanied by any increase in infant or maternal mortality (Notzon et al., 1994).

Low Birth Weight. In talking about various teratogens I have often mentioned low birth weight as one of the clearest negative outcomes. Babies who weigh too little are simply at much higher risk for a whole range of problems, including death during infancy and later learning problems.

Several different labels are used to describe infants with less than optimal weight. All babies below 2500 grams (about 5.5 pounds) are described with the most general term of **low birth weight (LBW).** Those below 1500 grams (about 3.3 pounds) are usually called *very low birth weight*, while those below 1000 grams are called *extremely low birth weight*. The incidence of low birth weight has declined in the United States in the past decade, but it is still high: In 1992, 7.1 percent of all newborns were below 2500 grams—a total of about 290,000 infants each year (U.S. Bureau of the Census, 1995). About 15 percent of those babies weighed less than 1500 grams. Low birth weight is considerably more common among blacks than among either Anglos or Hispanics in the United States. In 1991, the respective rates were 13.6 percent, 5.8 percent, and 6.1 percent. (Interestingly, this black/white difference in low birth weight apparently does *not* exist in Cuba [Hogue & Hargraves, 1993]).

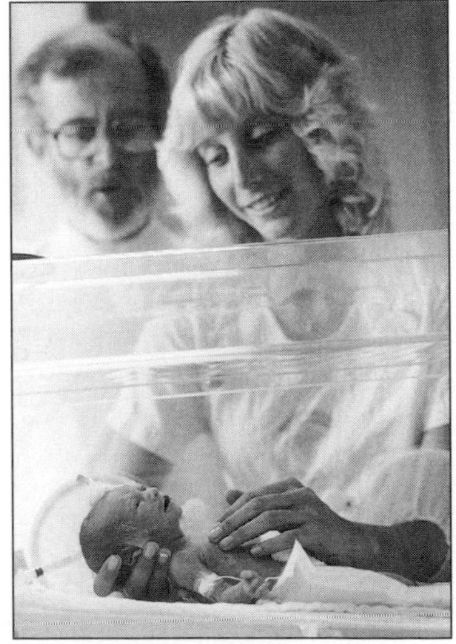

Low-birth-weight infants are kept in special isolettes, like this one, so that the temperature can be controlled. These babies are not only small, they are also more wrinkled and skinny because the layer of fat under the skin has not fully developed.

There are a variety of reasons for low birth weight, of which the most common is that the infant is born before the full 38 weeks of gestation. Any baby born before 38 weeks of gestation is labeled *preterm*. It is also possible for an infant to have completed the full 38-week gestational period but still weigh less than 2500 grams, or to weigh less than would be expected for the number of weeks of gestation completed, however long that may have been. Such an infant is called *small for date*. Infants in this group appear to have suffered from prenatal malnutrition, such as might occur with constriction of blood flow caused by the mother's smoking or from other significant problems prenatally. As a group, they have poorer prognoses than do equivalent-weight infants who weigh an appropriate amount for their gestational age.

All low-birth-weight infants share some characteristics, including markedly lower levels of responsiveness at birth and in the early months of life. Those born more than 6 weeks before term also often suffer from *respiratory distress syndrome* (also

The Real World

Postpartum Depression

An added difficulty for many women after the birth of a child is a period of depressed mood, often called the "maternity blues" or "postpartum blues." Estimates vary, but Western studies suggest that something between half and three-quarters of all women go through a brief period of frequent crying and feeling unexpectedly low in mood (Hopkins, Marcus, & Campbell, 1984). Most women pass through this depression in a few days and then return to a more positive and stable mood state. But somewhere between 10 and 25 percent of women appear to experience a longer-lasting and more severe postpartum mood disturbance, commonly called a **postpartum depression**—a pattern found in studies in Australia, China, Sweden, and Scotland as well as in the United States (Campbell et al., 1992; Guo, 1993; Lundh & Gyllang, 1993; Webster et al., 1994).

Clinicians use the term *depression* or the phrase *clinical depression* to describe more than just the blues, although sadness or persisting low mood is one of the critical ingredients. To be diagnosed as suffering from a clinical depression, including postpartum depression, a person must also show at least half of the following additional symptoms: poor appetite, sleep disturbances (inability to sleep, or excessive sleep), loss of pleasure in everyday activities, feelings of worthlessness, complaints of diminished ability to think or concentrate, or recurrent thoughts of death or suicide.

You can see from this description that such a depressive episode is not a trivial experience. So the fact that as many as two women out of every ten experience such feelings after the birth of a child is striking. Fortunately, a postpartum depression is normally of briefer duration than other forms of clinical depression, lasting typically six to eight weeks, after which the woman gradually recovers her normal mood. But for perhaps 1 or 2 percent of women, the depression persists for a year or longer.

The origins of these depressive episodes are not totally clear, although new research points to the likelihood that hormone patterns play a key role. Specifically, it looks as if women who have unusually high levels of steroid hormones in the late stage of their pregnancies are more likely to experience depression, apparently as a kind of withdrawal symptom from the rapid decline in hormones (Harris et al., 1994). Postpartum depression is also more common in women who did not plan their pregnancy, in those who were high in anxiety during the pregnancy, and in those whose partner is not supportive of them or is displeased with the arrival of the child (Campbell et al., 1992; O'Hara et al., 1992). When a woman has experienced high levels of life changes during the pregnancy and immediately after the birth—changes such as moving, the death of someone close, the loss of a job, or the like—her risk of depression also rises.

Understandably, mothers who are in the midst of a significant postpartum depression interact differently with their infants than do mothers whose mood is more normal. For example, Alison Fleming and her colleagues (1988) found that depressed mothers stroked and touched their infants with affection less frequently in the first three months after delivery than did nondepressed mothers. However, these differences did *not* persist after the mother's depression lifted; at 16 months, Fleming could find no differences in mother-child interaction between the mothers who had been depressed and those who had not.

I think it is quite common in our society to pass off a woman's postpartum depression as if it were a minor event, "just the blues." And of course for many women, it is. But for a minority, the arrival of a child ushers in a much more significant depressive episode, requiring at the very least a sympathetic and supportive environment, if not clinical intervention.

referred to as *hyaline membrane disease*). Their poorly developed lungs lack an important chemical, called *surfactant*, that enables the air sacs to remain inflated; some of the sacs collapse, resulting in serious breathing difficulties. Beginning in 1990, neonatologists began treating this problem by administering a synthetic or an animal-derived version of surfactant, a therapy that has reduced the rate of death among very low-birth-weight infants by about 30 percent (Corbet et al., 1995; Schwartz et al., 1994).

About 80 percent of all low-birth-weight infants now survive long enough to leave the hospital, but the lower the birth weight the greater the risk of neonatal death. The limit of viability is about 500–600 grams, or about 23 weeks gestation. Babies born before 23 weeks rarely survive, even with aggressive neonatal care; those born at 23 weeks have at least a small chance of survival, while those born at 24 weeks have better than a 50 percent survival rate (e.g., Allen, Donohue, & Dusman,

1993). To put it in terms of birth weight: In current cohorts of preterms receiving top-notch neonatal care, those weighing less than 500 grams rarely survive while those between 500 and 600 grams survive about a quarter of the time. The survival rate rises to about 50 percent for those 600–700 grams, and to over 60 percent for those between 700 and 800 grams (La Pine, Jackson, & Bennett, 1995).

You might think that virtually all these very tiny babies who do survive will have major developmental problems. But that is not the case. The long-term outcomes depend not only on the quality of care available to the infant, but on just how small the baby was and what kind of family he or she grows up in (Bendersky & Lewis, 1994). The great majority of those above 1500 grams who are not small for date catch up to their normal peers within the first few years of life. But those below 1500 grams, especially those below 1000, have significantly higher rates of long-term problems, including neurological impairment, lower IQs, smaller size, and greater problems in school (Breslau et al., 1994; Hack et al., 1994). In fact, 40–50 percent of such babies show some kind of significant later problem. But of course this means that half of these very small babies show little or no lasting problem. So it is not the case that *all* LBW children are *somewhat* affected, but rather that *some* LBW children are significantly affected while others appear to develop normally. Unfortunately, physicians and researchers have not yet found reliable ways to predict which babies are likely to have later difficulties, beyond the general correlation with birth weight itself. We do know that those babies who experience intraventricular hemorrhage (hemorrhage in the brain) in the weeks immediately after birth are more likely to have later problems (e.g., Bendersky & Lewis, 1994), but even in this group, significant deficits at school age are not universal. Our ignorance means that parents of LBW infants may be left in suspense for many years.

A Final Word: A More Optimistic View of Risks and Long-Term Consequences of Prenatal and Birth Problems

Each time I write this chapter, I am aware that the list of things that can go wrong seems to get longer and longer and scarier and scarier. Physicians, biologists, and psychologists keep learning more about prenatal and birth risks, so the number of warnings to pregnant women seems to increase yearly, if not monthly. One of the ironies of this is that too much worry about such potential consequences can make a woman more anxious, and anxiety is on the list of warnings for pregnant women! So before you begin worrying too much, let me try to put this information into perspective.

First, remember again that *most* pregnancies are normal and largely uneventful, and most babies are healthy and normal at birth. Second, there are specific preventive steps that any woman can take to reduce the risks for herself and her unborn child. She can be properly immunized; she can stop smoking and drinking; she can watch her diet and make sure her weight gain is sufficient; and she can get early and regular prenatal care. Many studies show that mothers who receive adequate prenatal care reduce the risks to themselves and their infants. Just one example: Jann Murray and Merton Bernfield (1988), in a study of over 30,000 births, found that the risk of giving birth to a low-birth-weight infant was more than three times as great among women who had received inadequate prenatal care as among those receiving adequate care, and this pattern held among both blacks and whites. Unfortunately, inadequate care remains common in the United States. In 1993, 21 percent of all mothers did not begin their prenatal care until at least the second trimester, and 5 percent either had no care at all or saw a health care provider only in the final few months (Guyer et al., 1995). Inadequate care was twice as common among black mothers as among whites (9.9 and 4.2 percent, respectively), and in both groups inadequate care was more common among mothers living in poverty and among teenage mothers.

A third point to be made about prenatal problems is that if something does go wrong, chances are good that the negative consequences will not be permanent. Of course some negative outcomes *are* permanent and have long-term consequences for the child. Chromosomal anomalies are clearly permanent and are nearly always associated with lasting mental retardation or school difficulties. Some teratogens or diseases also have permanent effects, such as fetal alcohol syndrome, deafness resulting from rubella, or AIDS. And a significant fraction of very low-birth-weight infants experience lasting problems.

But many of the negative outcomes I have talked about in this chapter may be detectable only for the first few years of the child's life, and then only in some families. In fact, the relationship between prenatal or birth problems and long-term outcomes illustrates the very pattern of interaction between nature and nurture I talked about in Chapter 1: A biological problem may be amplified by an unstimulating environment but greatly reduced by a supportive one. For example, numerous studies show that low-birth-weight infants, those with poor prenatal nutrition, or those with equivalent difficulties are likely to show persisting problems if they are reared in unstimulating or unsupportive environments, but develop much more normally if reared in more intellectually and emotionally nurturing families (Beckwith & Rodning, 1991; Breitmayer & Ramey, 1986; Kopp, 1990). So it is not the prenatal or birth problem alone that is the cause of the child's later problem; rather, a nonoptimal prenatal environment may make the infant more vulnerable to later environmental inadequacy. Such children may require a better family environment to develop normally, but in many cases normal development *is* possible. So don't despair when you read the long list of cautions and potential problems. The story isn't as gloomy as it first seems.

Summary

1. At conception, the 23 chromosomes from the sperm join with 23 from the ovum to make up the set of 46 that will be reproduced in each cell of the new child's body. Each chromosome consists of a long string of deoxyribonucleic acid (DNA), divisible into specific segments, called genes.
2. The child's sex is determined by the twenty-third pair of chromosomes, a pattern of XX for a girl and XY for a boy.
3. Geneticists distinguish between the genotype, which is the pattern of inherited characteristics, and the phenotype, which is the result of the interaction of genotype and environment.
4. During the first days after conception, called the germinal stage of development, the initial cell divides, travels down the fallopian tube, and is implanted in the wall of the uterus.
5. The second stage, the period of the embryo, includes the development of the various structures that support fetal development, such as the placenta, as well as primitive forms of all organ systems.
6. The final 30 weeks of gestation, called the fetal period, is devoted primarily to enlargement and refinements in all the organ systems.
7. All the neurons an individual will ever have are developed between 10 and 20 weeks gestation, but the development of the axon and dendrites on each neuron occurs primarily in the final two months of gestation and in the first few years after birth.
8. Normal prenatal development seems heavily determined by maturation—a "road map" contained in the genes. Disruptions in this sequence can occur; the timing of the disruption determines the nature and severity of the effect.
9. Deviations from the normal pattern can be caused at conception by any of a variety of chromosomal anomalies, such as Down syndrome, or by the transmission of genes for specific diseases.
10. Prior to conception, it is possible to test the parents for the presence of genes for many inherited diseases. After conception, several diagnostic techniques exist that identify chromosomal anomalies or recessive-gene diseases in the fetus.
11. Some diseases contracted by the mother may affect the child, including rubella, AIDS, and CMV. Any of these may result in disease or physical abnormalities in the child.

12. Drugs such as alcohol and nicotine appear to have significantly harmful effects on the developing fetus; the greater the dose, the larger the potential effect appears to be.
13. The mother's diet is also important. If she is severely malnourished there are increased risks of stillbirth, low birth weight, and infant death during the first year of life. Long-term consequences of milder subnutrition, however, have been more difficult to establish.
14. Older mothers and very young mothers also run increased risks, as do their infants.
15. High levels of anxiety or stress in the mother may also increase the risk of complications of pregnancy or difficulties in the infant, although the research findings here are mixed.
16. During the embryonic period, the XY embryo secretes the hormone testosterone, which stimulates the growth of male genitalia and shifts the brain into a "male" pattern. Without that hormone, the embryo develops as a girl, as do normal XX embryos.
17. Other sex differences in prenatal development are few in number. Boys are slower to develop, bigger at birth, and more vulnerable to most forms of prenatal stress.
18. The normal birth process has three parts: dilation, delivery, and placental delivery.
19. Most drugs given to the mother during delivery pass through to the infant's bloodstream and have short-term effects on infant responsiveness and feeding patterns. There may be some longer-term effects, but this is in dispute.
20. In uncomplicated low-risk pregnancies, delivery at home or in a birthing center is as safe as hospital delivery.
21. The presence of the father during delivery has a variety of positive consequences, including reduced pain experience for the mother, but does not appear to affect the father's attachment to the infant.
22. Nearly one-fourth of all deliveries in the United States are now by cesarean section—a statistic that has been the cause of considerable debate.
23. Infants born weighing less than 2500 grams are designated as low birth weight, those below 1500 grams are very low birth weight, those below 1000 are extremely low birth weight. The lower the weight, the greater the risk of significant lasting problems, such as low IQ or learning disabilities.
24. Some prenatal or birth difficulties can produce permanent disabilities or deformities, but many disorders associated with prenatal life or with birth can be overcome if the child is reared in a supportive and stimulating environment.

Key Terms

alpha-fetoprotein test
amniocentesis
amnion
axon
cesarean section
chorion
chorionic villus sampling
chromosomes
dendrites
deoxyribonucleic acid
Down syndrome
embryo
fallopian tube
fetal alcohol syndrome (FAS)
fetus
gametes
gene
genotype
glial cells
low birth weight (LBW)
neurons
ovum
phenotype
placenta
postpartum depression
rubella
synapse
ultrasound
umbilical cord
uterus

Suggested Readings

The Boston Women's Health Collective (1992). *The new our bodies, ourselves: A book by and for women*. New York: Simon & Schuster.

This recent revision of a popular book is really focused on the adult female's body, rather than on prenatal development, but it has an excellent discussion of health during pregnancy. This is a strongly feminist book; some of you may not be entirely in sympathy with all the political views included. But it is nonetheless a very good compact source of information on all facets of pregnancy and childbirth.

Moore, K. L., & Persaud, T. V. N. (1993). *The developing human: Clinically oriented embryology* (5th ed.). Philadelphia: W. B. Saunders.

A highly technical book aimed at medical students that may give more detail than you want, but I guarantee it will tell you anything you might want to know about prenatal development—and then some!

Nightingale, E. O., & Goodman, M. (1990). *Before birth: Prenatal testing for genetic disease.* Cambridge, MA: Harvard University Press.

This is an extremely informative, clearly written, helpful small book.

Nilsson, L. (1990). *A child is born.* New York: Delacorte Press.

This is a remarkable book, full of the most stunning photographs of all phases of conception, prenatal development, and birth.

Rosenblith, J. F. (1992). *In the beginning: Development in the first two years of life* (2nd ed.). Newbury Park, CA: Sage.

A first-rate text covering prenatal development and infancy. Much less technical than the Moore *and* Persaud *book listed above, it would be an excellent next step in your reading if you are interested in this area.*

Physical Development in Infancy

4

I spoke recently with a friend whose first baby was just about 6 months old. When I asked her how it was going she said three very typical things: "No one told me how much fun it would be"; "No one told me how much work it would be"; and "I didn't expect it to be this fascinating. She's changing every day. Now she seems like a real person, sitting up, crawling, beginning to make wonderful noises."

I suspect that someone had indeed told her all those things, but she hadn't heard them. Only when you are with a child every day, care for the child, and love the child does the reality of the whole amazing process come home to you. I'll do my best to convey that amazement to you, but some of what I am going to say may not be "real" unless and until you help to rear a child yourself. Let me begin by describing the child's physical development during the first 18–24 months, starting with a snapshot of the newborn.

The Newborn

Assessing the Newborn

It has become customary in most hospitals to evaluate an infant's status immediately after birth, and then again five minutes later, to detect any problems that may require special care. The most frequently used assessment system is something called an **Apgar score,** developed by a physician, Virginia Apgar (1953). The newborn is given a score of 0, 1, or 2 on each of five criteria, listed in Table 4.1. A maximum score of 10 is fairly unusual immediately after birth, because most infants are still somewhat blue in the fingers and toes at that stage. At the five-minute assessment, however, 85 to 90 percent of infants are scored as 9 or 10, meaning that they are getting off to a good start. Any score of 7 or better indicates that the baby is in no danger. A score of 4, 5, or 6 usually means that the baby needs help establishing normal breathing patterns; a score of 3 or below indicates a baby in critical condition, although babies with such low Apgar scores can and do often survive, and, given a sufficiently supportive environment, most develop normally (Breitmayer & Ramey, 1986).

Another test used to assess newborns, widely used by researchers, is the *Brazelton Neonatal Behavioral Assessment Scale* (Brazelton, 1984). Over a period of about 30 minutes, a skilled examiner checks out the neonate's responses to a variety of stimuli, the baby's reflexes and muscle tone, her alertness and cuddliness, and her ability to quiet or soothe herself after being upset. Scores on this test can be helpful in identifying children who may have significant neurological problems. More interestingly, several investigators have found that teaching *parents* how to administer this scale to their own infant turns out to have beneficial effects on the parent-infant interaction, apparently because it heightens the parent's awareness of all the subtle cues the baby provides (Francis, Self, & Horowitz, 1987).

Table 4.1 Evaluation Method for Apgar Score

	Score Assigned		
Aspect of Infant Observed	**0**	**1**	**2**
Heart rate	Absent	<100/min.	>100/min.
Respiratory rate	No breathing	Weak cry and shallow breathing	Good strong cry and regular breathing
Muscle tone	Flaccid	Some flexion of extremities	Well flexed
Response to stimulation of feet	None	Some motion	Cry
Color	Blue; pale	Body pink, extremities blue	Completely pink

Source: Francis, Self, & Horowitz, 1987, pp. 731–732

Reflexes

Infants are born with a large collection of **reflexes,** which are physical responses triggered involuntarily by specific stimuli. Many of these reflexes are still present in adults—for example, your knee jerking when the doctor taps it, your automatic eyeblink when a puff of air hits your eye, or the involuntary narrowing of the pupil of your eye when you're in a bright light.

The newborn's reflexes can be roughly grouped into two categories. First, infants have many *adaptive reflexes* that help them survive. Sucking and swallowing reflexes are prominent in this category, as is the rooting reflex—the automatic turn of the head toward any touch on the cheek, a reflex that helps the baby get the nipple into his mouth during nursing. These reflexes are no longer present in older children or adults, but are clearly highly adaptive for the newborn.

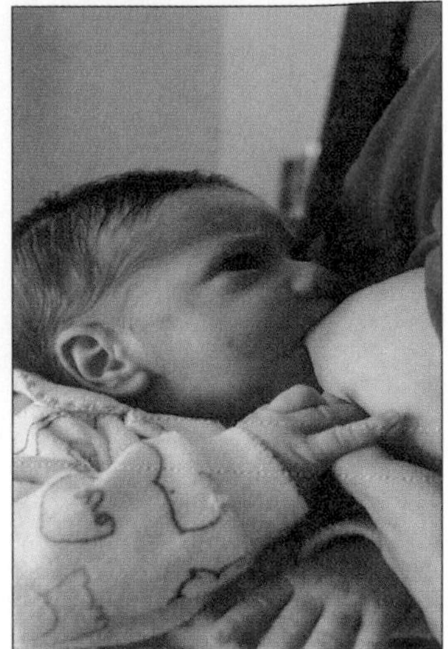

This 4-week-old baby is using two inborn reflexes: sucking and grasping.

Other adaptive reflexes persist over the whole life span, including a withdrawal reaction from a painful stimulus, the opening and closing of the pupil of the eye to variations in brightness, and many others. Finally, some reflexes that were adaptive in evolutionary history are still present in newborn humans, even though they are no longer needed. The grasping reflex is one clear example. If you place your finger across a newborn baby's palm, he will reflexively close his fist tightly around your finger. If you do this with both palms, the baby's grasp is strong enough so that you can lift him up by his hands. This reflex is also seen in monkeys and apes, for whom it is highly useful, since the infant primate must be able to cling to the mother's body while she moves about, or to a tree branch or vine. Most observers assume that this reflex in humans is merely one residual from our evolutionary past.

A second category includes the *primitive reflexes,* so called because they are controlled by the more primitive parts of the brain, the medulla and the midbrain, both of which are close to being fully developed at birth. For example, if you make a loud noise or startle a baby in some other way, you'll see her throw her arms outward and arch her back, a pattern that is part of the *Moro* or *startle* reflex. Stroke the bottom of her foot and she will splay out her toes and then curl them in, a reaction called the *Babinski* reflex.

CRITICAL THINKING

What would be different about development, and about adult-baby interactions, if babies were born *without* any reflexes, but instead had to learn every behavior?

By about 6 months of age these primitive reflexes begin to disappear, apparently superseded by the action of the cortex, which by this age is much more fully developed. In fact, when such reflexes persist past about 6 months, it may signal the existence of some kind of neurological problem.

These two categories of reflexes obviously overlap. Many adaptive reflexes—including the sucking and rooting reflexes—begin to fade late in the first year of life, indicating that they are controlled by the more primitive parts of the brain. But I think it is still helpful to distinguish between those reflexes that continue to have daily usefulness for the baby and those that more purely reflect the status of the nervous system, without other adaptive functions.

Initial Perceptual Skills: What the Newborn Sees, Hears, and Feels

Babies also come equipped with a surprisingly mature set of perceptual skills. I'll be describing the development of those skills in the next chapter, but I do want you to have some sense of the starting point. The newborn can

Newborns are pretty nearsighted, but they can focus very well at about 8 to 10 inches—just about the distance this dad has chosen, and about the distance between a parent's face and the baby's eyes when the baby is held for feeding.

- Focus both eyes on the same spot, with 8 to 10 inches being roughly the best focal distance. Within a few weeks the baby can at least roughly follow a moving object with his eyes, and he can discriminate Mom's face from other faces almost immediately.
- Easily hear sounds within the pitch and loudness range of the human voice; roughly locate objects by their sounds, and discriminate some individual voices, particularly the mother's voice.

- Taste the four basic tastes (sweet, sour, bitter, and salty) and identify familiar body odors, including discriminating Mom's smell from the smell of a strange woman.

Brief as this summary is, several points nonetheless stand out. First of all, newborns' perceptual skills are a great deal better than most parents believe—and better than most psychologists or physicians believed until a few years ago. The better our research techniques have become, the more we have discovered just how skillful the new baby is.

It's also clear from this brief list that the baby's perceptual skills are especially well adapted for interacting with the people in his world. He hears best in the range of the human voice; he can discriminate his mother (or other regular caregiver) from others on the basis of smell, sight, and sound almost immediately; the distance at which he can focus his eyes best is roughly the distance between his eyes and the face of an adult holding him during feeding.

Initial Motor Skills: Moving Around

But while the new baby's perceptual skills may be unexpectedly impressive, her motor skills certainly are not. She can't reach for things she's looking at; she can't hold up her head, roll over, or sit up. These skills emerge only gradually in the early weeks. By 1 month the baby can hold her chin up off the floor or mattress. By 2 months, she is beginning to use her hands to swipe at objects near her. But babies start their progress in motor development at a much lower level than they start the development of sophisticated perceptual skills.

Critical Thinking

Calves, foals, lambs, and newborns of virtually all mammals besides humans can stand and walk within a few hours after birth. Can you think of any useful evolutionary function for the greater motor helplessness of the human newborn?

A Day in the Life of a Baby

What is it like to live with a newborn? How is the infant's day organized? What sort of natural rhythms occur in the daily cycles? What can you expect from the baby, as you struggle to adapt to and care for this new person in your life?

Researchers who have studied newborns have described five different states of sleep and wakefulness in infants, referred to as **states of consciousness,** summarized in Table 4.2. In the newborn, the least common of these five states are the two types of awakeness. On average, newborns are awake and not fussing only about two to three hours each day.

***Table 4.2* The Basic States of Infant Sleep and Wakefulness**

State	Characteristics
Deep sleep	Eyes closed, regular breathing, no movement except occasional startles
Active sleep	Eyes closed, irregular breathing, small twitches, no gross body movement
Quiet awake	Eyes open, no major body movement, regular breathing
Active awake	Eyes open, with movements of the head, limbs, and trunk; irregular breathing
Crying and fussing	Eyes may be partly or entirely closed, vigorous diffuse movement with crying or fussing sounds

Source: Based on the work of Hutt, Lenard, & Prechtl, 1969; Parmelee, Wenner, & Schulz, 1964; Prechtl & Beintema, 1964.

The five main states tend to occur in cycles, just as your own states occur in a daily rhythm. In the newborn, the basic period in the cycle is about $1\frac{1}{2}$ to 2 hours. Most infants move through the states from deep sleep to lighter sleep to fussing and hunger and then to alert wakefulness. After they are fed, they become drowsy and drop back into deep sleep. This cycle then repeats itself about every two hours: sleep, cry, eat, look; sleep, cry, eat, look. Because the first three parts of this repeating pattern—sleeping, crying, and eating—are so crucial for parents, let me say just a word more about each.

Sleeping

Newborns sleep as much as 90 percent of the time, as much in the daytime as at night (Whitney & Thoman, 1994). By 6 or 8 weeks of age, the total amount of sleep per day has dropped somewhat and we see signs of day/night sleep rhythms (called *circadian rhythms*)—at least among infants in Western countries, where regular sleep/wake cycles are more highly valued. Babies this age begin to string two or three 2-hour cycles together without coming to full wakefulness, at which point we say that the baby can "sleep through the night." By 6 months, babies are still sleeping a bit over 14 hours per day, but the regularity and predictability of the baby's sleep is even more noticeable—at least in Western samples. Not only do most 6-month-olds have clear nighttime sleep patterns, they also begin to nap during the day at more predictable times.

I've given you the average figures, but of course babies vary a lot around these norms. Of the 6-week-old babies in one study, there was one who slept 22 hours per day and another who slept only 8.8 hours per day (Bamford, et al., 1990). (Now there must be one tired set of parents!) And some babies, even in Western cultures, do not develop a long nighttime sleep period until late in the first year of life.

All these aspects of the baby's sleep pattern have implications for the emerging parent-infant interaction. Psychologists have also been interested in sleep patterns because marked irregularity of sleep cycles may be a symptom of some disorder or problem. For example, some babies born to mothers who used cocaine during pregnancy have difficulty establishing a regular pattern of sleeping and waking. Brain-damaged infants often have the same kind of difficulties, so any time an infant fails to develop clear sleep-waking regularity, it *may* be a sign of trouble.

Crying

Newborns actually cry less than you might think. One researcher, studying normal newborns, found that the figure ranged from 2 to 11 percent of the time (Korner et al., 1981). This percentage typically increases over the first few weeks, peaking at about 6 weeks and then dropping off. Such a peak in crying at 6 weeks has been observed in infants from a number of different cultures, including cultures in which mothers have almost constant body contact with the infant (St. James-Roberts et al., 1994), suggesting that this crying pattern is not unique to U.S. or Western cultures. Initially, infants cry most in the evening; later their most intense crying occurs just before feedings.

The basic function of the child's cry, obviously, is to signal need. Because babies can't move *to* someone, they have to *bring* someone to them, and crying is the main way they have to attract attention. In fact, infants have a whole repertoire of cry sounds, with different cries for pain, anger, or hunger. The basic cry, which often signals hunger, is usually a rhythmical pattern: cry, silence, breath, cry, silence, breath, with a kind of whistling sound often accompanying the in-breath. An anger cry is typically louder and more intense, and the pain cry normally has a very abrupt onset—unlike the more basic kinds of cries, which usually begin with whimpering or moaning. However, not all infants cry in precisely the same way, so each parent must learn the specific sounds of his or her own baby. Alan Wiesenfeld and his colleagues

Critical Thinking

The obvious explanation of the mother's greater ability to discriminate among the different cries of her baby is that she spends more time in caregiving than does the father. What kind of study could you design to test this hypothesis?

(Wiesenfeld, Malatesta, & DeLoach, 1981) found that mothers (but not fathers) of 5-month-olds could discriminate between taped episodes of anger and pain cries in their own babies, while neither parent could reliably make the same discrimination with the taped cries of another baby.

In all this, as with the nature of the cries themselves, we see wide individual differences. For instance, 15 to 20 percent of infants develop a pattern called *colic*, which involves intense daily bouts of crying, totaling 3 or more hours a day. The crying is generally worst in late afternoon or early evening—a particularly inopportune time for parents, of course, because that is just the time when they are tired and needing time with one another. Colic typically appears at about 2 weeks of age and then disappears spontaneously at 3 or 4 months of age. Neither psychologists nor physicians know why colic begins, or why it stops without any intervention. It is a difficult pattern to live with, but the good news is that it *does* go away.

One of the enduring practical questions for parents about a baby's crying is how they should respond to it. If they pick up the baby right away, every time he cries, will that simply reinforce the baby's crying so that he will cry more? Or will such an immediate response reassure the child, building the child's expectation that the world is a safe and reliable place?

Ten years ago I was confident that I knew the answer to this question: Always respond immediately. Results from early studies gave no indication that such immediate responding increased the child's crying, and there was a lot of evidence that predictable responding was one ingredient in the development of a secure attachment to the parent. More recent studies, though, make the answer less clear-cut. It now looks as if the parents' response should depend on the type of crying the child is doing. Intense crying, such as when the infant is very hungry, very wet, or very uncomfortable, should be responded to immediately. But whimpering and milder crying, such as what a baby may do when she is put down for a nap, is another matter. When

Research Report

Variations in Children's Cries

Parents have always known that some babies had cries that were particularly penetrating or grating; other babies seem to make much less noxious crying sounds. Researchers have confirmed this parental observation in a wide range of studies.

Many groups of babies with known medical abnormalities have different-sounding cries, including those with Down syndrome, encephalitis, meningitis, and many types of brain damage. Barry Lester has extended this observation to babies who appear physically normal but are at risk for later problems because of some perinatal problem, such as preterm or small-for-date babies (Lester, 1987; Lester & Dreher, 1989). Such babies typically make crying sounds that are acoustically distinguishable from what you hear in a normal low-risk baby. In particular, the cry of such higher-risk babies has a more grating, piercing quality. Interestingly, the cries of babies with colic also have some of these same qualities (Lester et al., 1992).

On the assumption that the baby's cry may reflect some basic aspect of neurological integrity, Lester also wondered whether one could use the quality of the cry as a *diagnostic* test. Among a group of high-risk babies, for example, could one predict later intellectual functioning from a measure of the gratingness or pitch of the baby's cry? The answer seems to be yes. Lester found that among preterms, those with higher-pitched cries in the first days of life had lower scores on an IQ test at age 5 years (Lester, 1987). The same kind of connection has also been found among both normal babies and those exposed to methadone prenatally. In all these groups, the higher the pitch and more grating the cry, the lower the child's later IQ or motor development (Huntington, Hans, & Zeskind, 1990).

Eventually, it may be possible for physicians to use the presence of such a grating or piercing cry as a signal that there may be some underlying physical problem with the infant, or to make better guesses about the long-term outcomes for individual babies at high risk of later problems, such as low-birth-weight babies.

a parent responds immediately to all these milder cries, babies seem to learn to cry more often (Hubbard & van IJzendoorn, 1987). Thus, both reassurance and reinforcement seem to be involved, and it takes real sensitivity on the part of the parent to sort it out.

Eating

Eating is not a "state," but it is certainly something that newborn babies do frequently! Given that the baby's natural cycle seems to be about two hours long, a newborn may eat as many as ten times a day. By 1 month the average number is down to about five and a half feedings, with a very gradual decline from that number over the first year. Both breast-fed and bottle-fed babies eat at about the same frequency, but these two forms of feeding do differ in other important ways.

Breast- Versus Bottle-Feeding. After several decades of extensive research in many countries, physicians and epidemiologists have reached clear agreement that breast-feeding is substantially superior nutritionally to bottle-feeding. Breast milk provides important antibodies for the infant against many kinds of diseases, especially gastrointestinal and upper respiratory infections (Cunningham, Jelliffe, & Jelliffe, 1991). Human breast milk also appears to promote the growth of the nerves and intestinal tract, to contribute to more rapid weight and size gain (Prentice, 1994), and possibly to stimulate better immune system function over the long term. On the down side is the fact that some viruses (including HIV) can be transmitted through breast milk.

Those women who find breast-feeding logistically difficult because of work or other demands may take some comfort from the fact that babies seem to derive some protection from as little as one breast-feeding per day. There is also comfort in the observation that the *social* interactions between mother and child seem to be unaffected by the type of feeding. Bottle-fed babies are held and cuddled in the same ways as are breast-fed babies, and their mothers appear to be just as sensitive and responsive to their babies, just as bonded to their babies, as are mothers of breast-fed infants (Field, 1977).

Still, although babies can and do thrive on formula, it is clear that *if* you have a choice, breast-feeding at least part of the time is healthier for the infant.

Critical Thinking

What specific changes in policies or practices do you think would increase the rate of breast-feeding in your country?

Other Feeding Issues. Some parents begin giving their infants solid food, such as cereal, as early as 2 months, apparently in the mistaken belief that it will help the baby sleep through the night. It doesn't work, and in fact it interferes with the baby's nutritional needs. Up until about 4 to 6 months, babies need only breast milk or formula. After that, they benefit from a mixture of milk and solid food, with a broader and broader range of solid foods added throughout the first year of life (American Academy of Pediatrics Committee on Nutrition, 1986)

Another poor feeding practice is to give a baby or toddler a bottle of juice at naptime or bedtime. Most juice is very high in sugar; when the baby falls asleep with juice in his mouth, the sugar attacks the emerging teeth and can have long-term negative effects on the child's dental health.

Physical Changes

As my friend with the 6-month-old observed, one of the remarkable things about babies is just how fast they change. If I need any further reminder of this fact, I need only look in my wallet, where I carry several pictures of my now 5-year-old grandson, Sam, taken at different stages of his infancy. The newborn pictures were (of course!) charming, but the 4-month pictures show a remarkably different child. He was beginning to sit up with a little help; he was reaching for things and smiling more often. The 11-month photos show him already walking.

Cultures and Contexts

Cultural and Social Class Differences in Patterns of Breast-Feeding, and Their Consequences

If you look at the incidence of breast-feeding in countries around the world over the past 40 or 50 years, you'll find some very curious patterns. In the 1950s and 1960s, breast-feeding declined dramatically in most Western countries, including the United States. By 1971, only 25 percent of U.S. women breast-fed even for a few weeks. At the same time, breast-feeding continued to be the normative method of infant feeding in non-Western countries, including virtually all Third World countries (World Health Organization, 1981).

In the succeeding two decades, these two trends reversed. Breast-feeding rose in many industrialized countries as evidence of its importance came to light; by 1984, 60 percent of U.S. women breast-fed for at least a few weeks (Ryan et al., 1991). In the same years an opposite trend occurred in most Third World and developing countries: Breast-feeding remained the most common mode of infant feeding but rates and durations of breast-feeding began to drop in many countries, particularly among those living in urban settings (Amador, Silva, & Valdes-Lazo, 1994; Perez-Escamilla, 1994).

One contributor to the decline of breast-feeding in less-industrialized countries appears to have been the marketing of infant formula. Manufacturers of formula often gave free samples or free feeding bottles to new mothers and assured them that formula was as good or better for babies, while frequently failing to provide adequate instruction on how formula should be used. Some women, knowing no better and faced with extreme economic hardship, diluted their infant's formula with water in order to make it stretch farther. Sterilization procedures were also not well explained; for many women, proper sterilization was simply not feasible. Worldwide, the concern aroused by this change in normal feeding practices was sufficient to cause the World Health Organization to issue an "International Code of Marketing of Breast-milk Substitutes" in 1981. Marketing practices have since been modified. Yet the decline in breast-feeding has continued (Stewart et al., 1991).

Such a decline is cause for real concern, because bottle-fed babies in developing or Third World countries are at far higher risk of serious disease or death. In Bangladesh, for example, the risk of death from diarrhea is three times higher among bottle-fed than among breast-fed babies; in Brazil, the risk of death from various kinds of infections ranges from 2½ to 14 times higher among the bottle-fed. In all these studies, the risk associated with bottle-feeding is far higher where the sanitary conditions are poorest (Cunningham et al., 1991). Breast-feeding is thus better for two reasons: It provides the baby with needed antibodies against infection, and it is likely to expose the baby to less infection in the first place.

Patterns in the United States. In view of such findings, it is disturbing to find that in the United States the trend line is again downward. Between 1984 and 1989 the percentage of women beginning breast-feeding dropped from 60 to 52 percent (Ryan et al., 1991). At both time points, it was the same subgroups that were more likely to breast-feed: older, well-educated, or higher-income mothers. Whites are also more likely than either blacks or Hispanics to breast-feed. In 1989, the respective rates in the first weeks of the baby's life were 58, 23, and 48 percent (Ryan et al., 1991). In all three groups, however, better-educated mothers are more likely to breast-feed, while the less-educated and the poor are least likely to do so (MacGowan et al., 1991). This pattern is of special concern because rates of mortality and illness are already higher among infants born to poor mothers.

A mother's work status also makes some difference in her decision about breast- or bottle-feeding, but it is *not* the deciding factor in many cases. The majority of women who do *not* work also do not breast-feed, while many working women find creative ways to combine employment (especially part-time work) and breast-feeding (Lindberg, 1996; Ryan et al., 1991). If we had societal supports for such a combination, it could be made still easier.

Overall, it is clear that a large public health task still remains, not only in the United States but around the world, to educate women still further about the importance of breast-feeding and to create the cultural and practical supports needed to make breast-feeding easier.

Basic Patterns

These very obvious physical changes in the early months follow two broad patterns: Development proceeds from the head downward, called **cephalocaudal,** and from the trunk outward, called **proximodistal**—patterns originally identified by Gesell. We see the operation of these two principles in visible behavior, such as the baby's

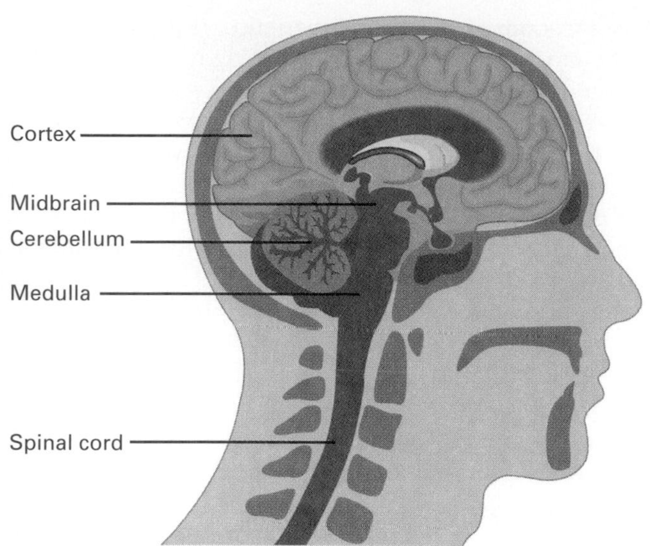

FIGURE 4.1 The medulla and the midbrain are largely developed at birth. In the first two years after birth it is primarily the cortex that develops, with each neuron going through an enormous growth of dendrites and a vast increase in synapses.

being able to hold up his head before he can sit, and sit before he can crawl. We can also document the same patterns in the development of the nervous system.

The Nervous System

Figure 4.1 shows the main structures of the brain. At birth, the midbrain and the medulla are the most fully developed. These two parts, both in the lower part of the skull and connecting to the spinal cord, regulate such basic tasks as attention and habituation, sleeping, waking, elimination, and movement of the head and neck (but not movement of the trunk or limbs)—all tasks a newborn can perform at least moderately well. The least-developed part of the brain at birth is the **cortex,** the convoluted gray matter that wraps around the midbrain and is involved in perception, body movement, and all complex thinking and language.

Recall from Chapter 3 that all these brain structures are composed of two basic types of cells, *neurons* and *glial cells*. Virtually all of both types of cells are already present at birth. The developmental process after birth is primarily the creation of synapses, which involves enormous growth of both the dendritic arbor and the axons and their terminal fibers in the neurons. Most of that dendritic growth occurs in the cortex, primarily during the first year or two after birth, resulting in a tripling of the overall weight of the brain during those years (Nowakowski, 1987).

This remarkable brain development is not entirely smooth and continuous. Neurophysiologists have identified an initial burst of synapse formation in the first year or so after birth, followed by a "pruning" of synapses in each area of the brain, as redundant pathways and connections are eliminated and the "wiring diagram" is cleaned up (Huttenlocher, 1994).

For example, early in development each skeletal muscle cell seems to develop synaptic connections with several motor neurons in the spinal cord. But after the pruning process has occurred, each muscle fiber is connected to only one neuron. Some neurophysiologists, such as William Greenough (Greenough et al., 1987), have suggested that the initial surge of development of the dendritic arbor and synaptic formation follows a built-in pattern; the organism is programmed to create certain kinds of neural connections and does so in abundance, creating redundant pathways. According to this argument, the pruning that then takes place beginning at around 18 months or 2 years is a response to specific experience, resulting in selective retention of the used, or the most efficient pathways. Putting it briefly, "Experience does not create tracings on a blank tablet; rather, experience erases some of them" (Bertenthal & Campos, 1987).

Greenough does not think that all synaptic development is governed by such built-in programming. He suggests that other synapses are formed entirely as a result of specific experience, and go on being created throughout our lives as we learn new skills. But basic motor and sensory processes may initially follow built-in patterns, with pruning then based on experience.

Interestingly, pruning does not occur at the same time in all parts of the brain. For example, the maximum density of synapses in the portions of the brain that have to do with language comprehension and production occurs at about age 3 years, while the part of the cortex devoted to vision is maximally dense at 4 *months* of age, with rapid pruning thereafter (Huttenlocher, 1994).

One of the most intriguing points about all this is that the combination of the early surge of synaptic growth and then pruning means that the 1-year-old actually has a *denser* set of dendrites and synapses than an adult does—a piece of information that has surprised many psychologists. Pruning also continues throughout childhood and adolescence. Even at age 4, when the early burst of pruning has occurred in all areas of the brain, synaptic density is about twice what we see in an adult's brain.

We can draw several important implications from all this new information about neurological development. First, we can see that a kind of "programmed plasticity" is built into the human organism. The brain has a remarkable ability to reorganize itself, to make the wiring diagram more efficient, and to find compensatory pathways following some injury. But this plasticity is greater in infancy than it is later. Perhaps paradoxically, the period of greatest plasticity is also the period in which the child may be most vulnerable to major deficits. Just as the time of most rapid growth of any body system prenatally is the time when the fetus is most vulnerable to teratogens, so the young infant needs sufficient stimulation and order in his environment to maximize the early period of rapid growth and plasticity (de Haan et al., 1994). A really inadequate diet or a serious lack of stimulation in the early months may thus have subtle but long-range effects on the child's later cognitive progress.

Critical Thinking

Someone might argue, based on this information, that programs like Head Start—designed to alleviate the negative effects of poverty—begin too late. Perhaps we ought to aim any supplementary stimulation programs at infants. What do you think?

At the same time, the new information about the continuation of the pruning process throughout childhood and adolescence has forced developmental psychologists to change their ideas about the links between brain development and behavior. If the brain is pretty much complete by age 2, as most of us believed until recently, it seemed logical to assume that whatever developments occurred after that age were largely the product of specific experience. But now we know that the brain changes significantly throughout childhood, which reopens all the questions about brain-behavior connections. Is there a language spurt between ages 2 and 3 because that is when the relevant portion of the brain is undergoing significant reorganization? Or is the reverse true? Similarly, are the changes in thinking that we see at age 4, or at age 7, or at adolescence, linked in some causal way to further changes in the brain? We do not yet have the data to answer such questions, but the theoretical climate has definitely shifted toward a far greater interest in the neurological underpinnings of development in childhood and adolescence.

Myelinization. Another crucial process in neuronal development is the development of sheaths around individual axons, which electrically insulate them from one another and improve the conductivity of the nerve. This sheath is made up of a substance called **myelin;** the process of developing the sheath is called **myelinization.**

The sequence with which nerves are myelinized follows both cephalocaudal and proximodistal patterns. Thus, nerves serving muscle cells in the arms and hands are myelinized earlier than those serving the lower trunk and the legs. Myelinization is

Because motor development is both cephalocaudal and proximodistal, both 7-month-old Helen and 5-month-old Laura are better at reaching and grasping than they are at crawling.

most rapid during the first two years after birth, but it continues at a slower pace throughout childhood and adolescence. For example, the parts of the brain that govern motor movements are not fully myelinized until perhaps age 6 (Todd et al., 1995).

To understand the importance of myelin, it may help you to know that *multiple sclerosis* is a disease in which the myelin begins to break down. An individual with this disease gradually loses motor control, with the specific symptoms depending on the portion of the nervous system in which the myelin is affected.

Bones and Muscles

These changes in the nervous system are paralleled by changes in other body structures, including bones and muscles, although here the changes occur fairly gradually from infancy through adolescence, rather than in the remarkable early spurt we see in the nervous system.

Bones. The hand, wrist, ankle, and foot all have fewer bones at birth than they will have at full maturity. For example, an adult has nine separate bones in her wrist; a 1-year-old has only three. The remaining six develop over the period of childhood, with complete growth by adolescence.

One set of bones, though, fuses rather than differentiating. The skull of a newborn is made up of several bones separated by spaces called **fontanels.** Fontanels allow the head to be compressed without injury during the birth process, and they also give the brain room to grow. In most children, the fontanels are filled in by bone by 12 to 18 months, creating a single connected skull bone.

All the infant's bones are also softer, with a higher water content, than adults' bones. The process of bone hardening, called **ossification,** occurs steadily from birth through puberty, with bones in different parts of the body hardening in a sequence that follows the typical proximodistal and cephalocaudal patterns. So, for example, bones of the hand and wrist harden before those in the feet.

Bone hardening has some fairly direct practical relevance. Soft bones are clearly needed if the fetus is going to have enough flexibility to fit into the cramped space of the uterus. But that very flexibility contributes to a newborn human's relative floppiness and motor immaturity. As the bones stiffen, the baby is able to manipulate his body more surely, which increases the range of exploration he can enjoy and makes him much more independent.

Muscles. In contrast to bones, muscle fibers are virtually all present at birth (Tanner, 1978). But like the infant's bones, muscle fibers are initially small and watery, becoming longer, thicker, and firmer at a fairly steady rate until adolescence. The sequence is again both proximodistal and cephalocaudal. So the baby gains muscle strength in the neck fairly early, but does not have enough muscle strength in the legs to support walking until some months later.

Size and Shape

All these internal changes obviously affect the baby's size and shape. Babies grow very rapidly in the first months, adding 10 to 12 inches in length and tripling their body weight in the first year. By age 2 for girls, and about age 2½ for boys, the toddler is *half as tall as she or he will be as an adult*—a fact I put in italics because it is so surprising to most of us. We are deceived in part by the fact that the baby's body proportions are quite different from those of an adult. In particular, babies have proportionately much larger heads than do adults—obviously needed to hold that nearly full-sized brain.

Motor Development

All these physical changes form the substrate on which the child's rapidly improving motor skills are constructed. And of course it is precisely those new physical abilities that are so striking and remarkable to parents (and grandparents!).

Robert Malina (1982) suggests that we divide the wide range of motor skills into three rough groups: *locomotor* patterns, such as walking, running, jumping, hopping and skipping; *nonlocomotor* patterns, such as pushing, pulling, and bending; and *manipulative* skills, such as grasping, throwing, catching, kicking, and other actions involving receiving and moving objects. In Table 4.3 I've summarized the developments in each of these three areas over the first 18 months, based primarily on two large studies, one in the United States and one in the Netherlands. The U.S. study (Capute et al., 1984) involved 381 babies tested by their pediatricians at regular visits through the first two years; the Dutch study (Den Ouden et al., 1991) included 555 babies who had been tested repeatedly for their first five years. The milestones described in these two studies are highly similar in sequence, as were the ages at which babies passed each test.

In these early months of life, babies seem pleased to repeat their limited repertoire of motor skills again and again. They kick, rock, wave, bounce, bang, rub, scratch, or sway repeatedly and rhythmically. Such repeated patterns become particularly prominent at about 6 or 7 months of age, although you can see some such behavior even in the first weeks, particularly in finger movements and leg kicking. These repeated movements do not seem to be totally voluntary or coordinated, but they also do not appear to be random. For instance, Esther Thelen (1981) has observed that kicking movements peak just before the baby begins to crawl, as if the rhythmic kicking were a part of the preparation for crawling.

Thelen's observation reminds us that the baby's new motor skills do not spring forth full blown. Each emerges from the coordination of a wide range of component abilities, perceptual as well as motor (Thelen, 1989; Thelen & Ulrich, 1991). Using a spoon to feed yourself, for example, requires development of muscles in the hand and wrist, bone development in the wrist, eye-hand coordination skills that allow you to readjust the aim of the spoon as you move it toward your mouth, and coordination of all these with properly timed mouth opening (Connolly & Dalgleish, 1989).

Table 4.3 **Milestones of Motor Development in the First Two Years**

Age in Months	Locomotor Skills	Nonlocomotor Skills	Manipulative Skills
1	Stepping reflex	Lifts head slightly; follows slowly moving objects with eyes.	Holds object if placed in hand.
2–3		Lifts head up to 90 degrees when lying on stomach.	Begins to swipe at objects in sight.
4–6	Rolls over; sits with some support; moves on hands and knees ("creeps").	Holds head erect in sitting position	Reaches for and grasps objects.
7–9	Sits without support; crawls.		Transfers objects from one hand to the other.
10–12	Pulls himself to standing; walks grasping furniture ("cruising"); then walks without help.	Squats and stoops.	Some signs of hand preference; grasps a spoon across palm but has poor aim of food to mouth.
13–18	Walks backward and sideways; runs (14–20 mo).	Rolls ball to adult.	Stacks two blocks; puts object into small containers and dumps them.

Sources: Capute et al., 1986, and Den Ouden et al., 1991.

Most of us are unaware of this complex of developmental processes when we watch an infant. What we are struck with is the daily change in the baby's behavior and skill.

Explaining Early Physical Development

When we search for explanations for the series of physical changes I've been describing, there are some obvious candidates: maturation, heredity, and various environmental factors, including both diet and practice.

Maturation and Heredity

Maturational sequences seem necessarily to be part of the explanation, especially for such central patterns as neuronal changes and changes in muscles and bones. In all these areas, while the *rate* of development varies from one child to the next, the *sequence* is virtually the same for all children, even those with marked physical or mental handicaps. Mentally retarded children, for example, typically move through the various motor milestones more slowly than do normal children, but they follow the same sequence. Whenever we find such robust sequences, maturation of some kind seems an obvious explanation—although the maturational process itself is immensely complex, involving interlocking changes in muscles, bones, perception, and thinking (Thelen, 1995).

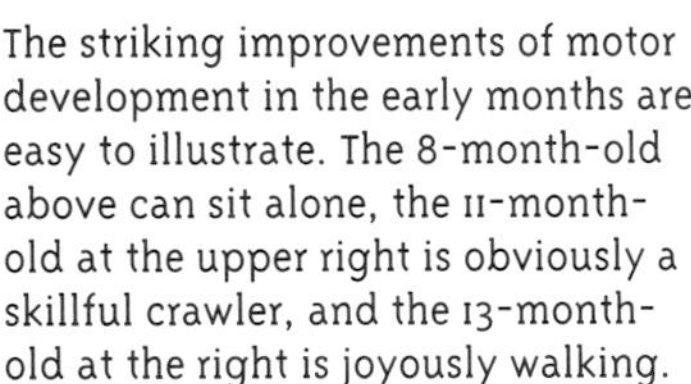

The striking improvements of motor development in the early months are easy to illustrate. The 8-month-old above can sit alone, the 11-month-old at the upper right is obviously a skillful crawler, and the 13-month-old at the right is joyously walking.

At the same time, our genetic heritage is individual as well as species-specific. In addition to being programmed for many basic sequences of physical development, each of us also receives instructions for unique growth tendencies. Parents and children are similar not only in such obvious characteristics as height, but also in hip width, arm length, and short or long trunk (some ancestor certainly passed on a gene for long arms to me!).

Rate or tempo of growth, as well as final shape or size, seems to be an inherited pattern as well. Parents who were themselves early developers, as measured by such things as bone ossification, tend to have children who are faster developers too (Garn, 1980).

Environmental Effects

Diet. I mentioned in the last chapter that mothers who are malnourished during pregnancy are more likely to have stillborn infants, or infants who die in the first year. It seems logical to assume that the baby's diet after birth would also make a difference in many aspects of physical development, perhaps especially neurological development. But this hypothesis has been very difficult to test clearly, in large part because most babies who are undernourished are also growing up in environments that are low in other types of stimulation as well.

What we do know is that poorly nourished children grow more slowly and don't end up as large (Malina, 1982). If their diet later improves, such children may show some catch-up in height or growth rate, but they are typically shorter and slower than their peers. In addition, malnourished or undernourished children have less energy, which in turn can affect the nature of the interactions the child has with both the objects and the people around him. For example, in a recent study of toddlers in Kenya, Egypt, Mexico, and the United States, Marian Sigman and her colleagues (Sigman, 1995; Wachs & Sigman, 1995) found that children who are chronically undernourished (but not clinically *mal*nourished) are less alert, less advanced in their forms of play, and less skilled in social interactions with other children than are their better nourished peers.

Similarly, Michael Espinosa and his colleagues (Espinosa et al., 1992), studying school-age children in Kenya, observed that undernourished kids were more solitary and less active on the playground than their well-nourished peers. Like the youngsters in Sigman's studies, the children in Espinosa's study were not severely malnourished. They were taking in about 1500 calories per day (including adequate protein), which is enough to sustain the child but not enough to provide the energy needed for play or perhaps for concentration in school over long periods.

It may seem obvious that a baby who gets to practice climbing stairs a lot would become a skillful stair-climber more quickly, but in fact researchers are not sure whether that is true.

Practice. We can also think of environmental influences on physical development in terms of the child's own opportunities to practice various physical activities. Does a baby who spends a lot of time in a toy called an infant walker, which holds up the baby while she moves around, learn independent walking any sooner than a baby who never has that practice? Does a toddler who has a chance to try to climb stairs learn to climb them sooner, or more skillfully, than a toddler who is rarely exposed to stairs?

The answer, as usual, is fairly complicated. Two conclusions are reasonably clear. First, the development of such universal basic skills as crawling or walking requires some minimum amount of practice just to keep the system working as it should. Children who are deprived of such normal practice develop motor skills much more slowly, and not in the normal sequence. A classic early study by Wayne Dennis of children raised in Iranian orphanages is a good illustration (1960). The babies in one of the institutions were routinely placed on their backs in cribs with very lumpy mattresses. They had little or no experience of lying or moving on their stomachs as a normal baby would, and even had difficulty rolling over because of the hollows in the mattresses. These babies almost never went through the normal sequence of learning to walk—presumably because they didn't have enough opportunity to practice all the on-the-stomach parts of the skill. They did learn to walk eventually, but they were about a year late.

We also know that the development of really smooth, coordinated skill in virtually all complex motor tasks requires practice. The strength and coordination required to throw a basketball high enough to reach the basket may develop in predictable ways over the early years, assuming the environment is sufficiently rich to provide needed maintenance. But to develop the skill needed to get the ball through the hoop with regularity, from different angles and distances, requires endless practice.

Where we are still uncertain is about the role of practice in the acquisition of the basic component skills, such as sitting, walking up stairs, climbing, or catching objects. Early studies seemed to show that extra practice in such basic skills didn't speed up their development at all, perhaps because virtually all children have enough opportunity for minimal practice in their ordinary lives. But some recent studies contradict this conclusion, including one showing that very young babies who are given more practice sitting are able to sit upright longer than those without such practice (Zelazo et al., 1993). The jury is still out on this one.

Health

Illnesses in the First Two Years

Virtually all babies get sick, most of them repeatedly. In the United States, the average baby has seven respiratory illnesses in the first year of life. (That's a lot of nose-wipes!) Interestingly, research in a number of countries shows that babies in day-care centers have about twice as many infections as do those reared entirely at home, with those in small-group day care falling somewhere in between, presumably because babies in group care settings are exposed to a wider range of germs and viruses (Collet et al., 1994; Hurwitz et al., 1991). In general, the more different people a baby is exposed to, the more often she is likely to be sick. But this is not the unmitigated negative that it may appear to be. First of all, the heightened risk of infection among infants in day care drops after the first few months, while those reared entirely at home have very high rates of illness when they first attend school. Attendance at day care simply means that the baby is exposed earlier to the various microorganisms typically carried by children.

Infant Mortality

For a small minority of babies, though, the issue is not a few sniffles but the possibility of death. Provisional 1994 data suggest that in the United States, 7.9 babies out of every 1000 died before age 1 (Guyer et al., 1995). This *infant mortality rate* has been declining steadily for the past few decades (down from 20.0 per 1000 in 1970), but it still places the United States twenty-second in the world. Almost two-thirds of these infant deaths occurred in the first month of life and were directly linked either

Cultures and Contexts

Immunizations

Most of the killer diseases of childhood are entirely preventable when appropriate types of vaccination are given in the first few years of life, and therein lies a wonderfully optimistic tale. Twenty years ago, only about 5 percent of the children in developing countries were fully vaccinated against tetanus, polio, measles, whooping cough, tuberculosis, and diphtheria. By 1987 this figure had risen to 50 percent in developing countries; by 1993, roughly 80 percent of all infants and young children worldwide had been immunized against measles, polio, and diphtheria, with tetanus lagging somewhat behind. Astonishingly, many countries—including China, Egypt, Vietnam, Bangladesh, and Algeria—have brought their coverage to over 90 percent (World Health Organization, 1994). In some parts of the world, some of these diseases have been eradicated altogether. As just one example, not a single polio case has been reported in all of the Americas since 1991.

This enormous change is the result of a massive effort by the World Health Organization (WHO) and all its member nations. Some nations reached the goal of 80 percent immunization by mass media campaigns; others have tried to build immunization programs into their primary health care system. Both these strategies have been successful in the short term, although sustained high levels of immunization appear to be more likely when immunization has been made part of an expanded primary care system—as in Burkina Faso, Indonesia, China, and India, to name only a few.

Millions of children have been saved as a result of this effort, as have millions of dollars in health care costs. The Centers for Disease Control estimate that for every dollar spent on the measles-mumps-rubella vaccine, $21 is saved in costs to society. An added benefit, particularly in developing countries, is a decrease in the birthrate. More complete immunizations mean that fewer children die in childhood; parents become more confident that children will survive and be able to take on the roles the family needs filled, so fewer children are conceived and born.

Successful as this WHO effort has been, we should not be too sanguine. There is more to be accomplished. In the United States as recently as 1992, only 55 percent of children had received the full set of immunizations—a schedule that includes 3 hepatitis, 4 diphtheria/tetanus/pertussis, 3 influenza, 3 polio, 1 measles/rubella, and 1 varicella zoster virus vaccines (Committee on Infectious Diseases, 1996). By 1995, after intensive efforts, this rate was raised to 75 percent (Pear, 1996), an admirable improvement but still short of the goal of 90 percent; more than a million children in the United States are not fully immunized. There is also an object lesson in the experience of the newly independent states of the former USSR, where the incidence of diphtheria skyrocketed in the somewhat chaotic years immediately after the dissolution of the USSR. Between 1989 and 1994, the rate went from 0.4 to 26.6 per 100,000 population. Clearly, constant vigilance is needed to reach and maintain a sufficiently high rate of immunization to prevent the spread of these killer diseases.

to congenital anomalies or to low birth weight. Only about 3 deaths per 1000 births occurred in the remainder of the first year, and nearly half of those were cases of **sudden infant death syndrome (SIDS),** in which an apparently healthy infant dies suddenly and unexpectedly. In 1994, 4180 babies in the United States died of SIDS (Guyer et al., 1995).

Sudden infant death syndrome is certainly not unique to the United States. It occurs worldwide, although for unexplained reasons, the rate varies quite a lot from country to country. For example, SIDS rates are particularly high in Australia and New Zealand, and particularly low in Japan and Sweden (Hoffman & Hillman, 1992).

Physicians have not yet uncovered the basic cause of these deaths. But they have learned a fair amount about the groups that are at higher risk: babies born preterm or with low birth weight, males, African Americans, and those with young mothers (e.g., Malloy & Hoffman, 1995). It is also more common in the wintertime and more likely among babies who sleep on their stomachs (Hoffman & Hillman, 1992; Ponsonby et al., 1993), especially if the baby is sleeping on a soft or fluffy mattress, pillow, or comforter.

The growing evidence on the role of sleeping position in the risk of SIDS has persuaded pediatricians in many countries to change their standard advice to hospitals and families about the best sleeping position for babies. The American Academy of Pediatrics, for example, has been recommending since 1992 that when healthy infants are put down to sleep, they should be positioned on their sides or backs. This change in policy has been followed by a 12 percent drop in SIDS cases nationwide, with even more dramatic declines of as much as 50 percent in areas where the new recommendation has been widely publicized (Spiers & Guntheroth, 1994). In England, Wales, New Zealand and Sweden, major campaigns to discourage parents from placing their babies in the prone position have all been followed by sharp drops in SIDS rates (Gilman et al., 1995). Still, sleeping position cannot be the full explanation, because of course *most* babies who sleep on their stomachs do not die of SIDS.

Another important contributor is smoking, by the mother during pregnancy or by anyone in the home after the child's birth. Babies exposed to such smoke are about four times as likely to die of SIDS as are babies with no smoking exposure (Klonoff-Cohen et al., 1995; Schoendorf & Kiely, 1992; Taylor & Danderson, 1995). One more powerful reason not to smoke.

The higher risk of SIDS for African-American infants is part of a persistent pattern. Infant mortality in general is more than twice as high among blacks as among white infants in the United States (16.3 and 6.8, respectively, in 1992). A somewhat heightened risk also exists for Native American infants, although *not* for Hispanic-American babies, a set of findings that raises a whole host of questions (Singh & Yu, 1995). The black/white difference has existed at least since record keeping began (in 1915) and has *not* been declining. It is found even when researchers compare only infants born to college-educated mothers (Schoendorf et al., 1992). Physicians and physiologists do not yet understand all the reasons for this discrepancy, although it is clear that one significant factor is that infants born to African-American mothers are much more likely to be born before the full gestational period is completed, and thus have low birth weight. When only full-term, normal-weight babies are compared, infant mortality is about the same in the two groups. But saying that only pushes the explanation back one step. We still need to know why African-American mothers have more preterm, low-birth-weight babies, and the answer to this question is still unclear.

Critical Thinking

Can you generate any reasonable hypotheses to explain the finding that infant mortality is not elevated among Hispanic Americans, while it is among African Americans, even though both groups experience significant poverty? What kind of information would you need to check out your hypotheses?

Individual Differences

I've already touched on several kinds of differences among babies that affect their physical development in the first few years: diet, feeding experience, and opportunities for motor practice. Let me sketch several others.

Table 4.4 Comparison of Developmental Milestones in Preterm and Normal-Term Babies in the First Two Years

	Age at Which 50% of Babies Passed	
Developmental Milestone	**Preterm (< 32 weeks)**	**Normal Term**
Lifts head slightly	10 weeks	6 weeks
Transfers object hand to hand	36 weeks	23 weeks
Rolls over	37 weeks	24 weeks
Crawls	51 weeks	36 weeks
Pulls to standing position	51 weeks	42 weeks

Source: Den Ouden et al., 1991, from Table V, p. 402.

Preterm babies. Preterm or low-birth-weight babies move more slowly through all the developmental milestones I listed in Table 4.3. You can get some sense of the degree of difference from Table 4.4, which gives several comparisons. The data here are from the same Dutch study I cited in Table 4.3. In addition to studying 555 normal infants, Den Ouden and her colleagues also tested 555 preterm babies—all the otherwise physically normal preterms born at less than 32 weeks gestation in the Netherlands in 1983. You can see in the table that the preterms are about 10 to 15 weeks behind their full-term peers on most physical skills. This is entirely what we would expect, of course, because the preterm baby is, in fact, maturationally younger than the full-term baby. If you correct for the baby's "gestational age," most (but not all) of the difference in physical development disappears. Parents of preterms need to keep this in mind when they compare their baby's progress with that of a full-term baby. By age 2 or 3, the physically normal preterm will catch up to his peers, but in the early months he is definitely behind.

Boys and Girls. When you hear that a friend or family member has had a new baby, what is your first question? Probably "Is it a boy or a girl?" A new child's gender is obviously highly salient to all of us. You might assume that such a preoccupation exists because boy and girl babies are really very different from one another. But in fact they are not. There are remarkably few sex differences in physical development in young infants. As was true at birth, girls continue to be ahead in some aspects of physical maturity, such as the development of bone density, although boys have more muscle tissue and are heavier and taller than girls. Boys continue to be more vulnerable, with higher infant mortality rates. More mixed are the findings on activity level. When researchers observe a difference it is likely to be infant boys who are found to be slightly more active (Campbell & Eaton, 1995), but many investigators report no difference at all (Cossette, Malcuit, & Pomerleau, 1991). There are actually bigger differences between babies from different ethnic groups—described in the box on page 101—than there are between boys and girls.

The physical development of infants is probably more clearly governed by built-in sequences and timetables, and more similar from one baby to another, than any other aspect of development we'll be looking at. What is striking to the observer is not "boyness" or "girlness," or blackness or whiteness, but "babyness."

Cultures and Contexts

Differences in Early Physical Development

The sequence of physical changes I've been describing in this chapter does seem to hold true for babies in all cultures. But there are nonetheless interesting differences.

Black babies—whether born in Africa or elsewhere—develop somewhat faster, both prenatally and after birth. In fact, the gestational period for the black fetus seems actually to be slightly shorter than for the white fetus (Smith, 1978). Black babies also show somewhat faster development of motor skills such as walking, and are slightly taller than their white counterparts, with longer legs, more muscle, and heavier bones (Tanner, 1978).

In contrast, Asian infants are somewhat slower to achieve many early motor milestones. This could reflect simply differences in rate of maturation, or it could reflect some ethnic differences in the baby's level of activity or placidity, a possibility suggested by Daniel Freedman's research (1979).

Freedman observed newborn babies from four different cultures: Caucasian, Chinese, Navaho, and Japanese. Of the four, he found that the Caucasian babies were the most active and irritable and the hardest to console. Both the Chinese and the Navaho infants he observed were relatively placid, while the Japanese infants responded vigorously but were easier to quiet than the Caucasian infants.

One specific illustration: When Freedman tested each baby for the Moro reflex, he found that the Caucasian babies showed the typical pattern in which they reflexively extended both arms, cried vigorously and persistently, and moved their bodies in an agitated way. Navaho babies, on the other hand, showed quite a different pattern. Instead of thrusting their limbs outward they retracted their arms and legs, rarely cried, and showed little or very brief agitation.

Jerome Kagan and his colleagues (1994) have replicated part of these results in their recent comparison of Chinese, Irish, and Euro-American 4-month-olds. They found that the Chinese infants were significantly less active, less irritable, and less vocal than were babies in the other two groups. The white American infants showed the strongest reactions to new sights, sounds, and smells. Similarly, Chisholm has replicated some of Freedman's observations, finding Navaho babies to be significantly less irritable, less excitable, and more able to quiet themselves than Euro-American babies (1989).

Because such differences are visible in newborns, they cannot be the result of systematic shaping by the parents. But the parents, too, bring their cultural training to the interaction. Freedman and other researchers have observed that both Japanese and Chinese mothers talk much less to their infants than do Caucasian mothers. These differences in mothers' behavior were present from their first encounters with their infants after delivery, so the pattern is not a response to the baby's quieter behavior. But such similarity of temperamental pattern between mother and child may strengthen the pattern in the child, which would tend to make the cultural differences larger over time.

One of the key points from this research is that our notions of what is "normal" behavior for an infant may be strongly influenced by our own cultural patterns and assumptions.

Summary

1. Newborns are typically assessed using the Apgar score, which is a rating on five dimensions.
2. Infants have both adaptive and primitive reflexes. The former group includes such essential reflexes as sucking and rooting; primitive reflexes include the Moro and Babinski, which disappear within a few months.
3. At birth the baby has a far wider array of perceptual skills than psychologists had supposed. In particular, she can see and hear well enough for most social encounters.
4. Babies move through a series of "states of consciousness," from quiet sleep to active sleep to fussing to eating to quiet wakefulness, in a cycle that lasts roughly 1½ to 2 hours.
5. Persisting irregularity of sleep patterns or a particularly high-pitched or grating cry may indicate some neurological problem.
6. Breast-feeding has been shown repeatedly to be better for the baby nutritionally, providing needed antibodies and reducing the risk of various infections.
7. Changes in the nervous system are extremely rapid in the first two years. In most parts of the brain, dendritic and synaptic development reaches its peak between 12 and 24 months, after which there is a "pruning" of synapses. Myelinization of nerve fibers also occurs rapidly in the early years.
8. Bones increase in number and density; muscle fibers become larger and less watery.

9. Babies triple their body weight in the first year and add 12 to 15 inches in length before age 2.
10. Rapid improvement in locomotor and manipulative skills occurs in the first two years, as the baby moves from creeping to crawling to walking to running, and from poor to good ability to grasp objects.
11. These virtually universal sequences of development are clearly influenced strongly by common maturational patterns. But individual heredity also makes a difference, as does diet. The role of practice is less clear.
12. On average, babies have 7 to 8 respiratory illnesses in each of the first two years. This rate is higher among infants in day care.
13. Most infant deaths in the first weeks are due to congenital anomalies or low birth weight; past the first weeks, sudden infant death syndrome is the most common cause of death in the first year.
14. Infant mortality rates are roughly twice as high among African Americans as among Caucasian Americans, a difference that is not entirely explainable by differences in poverty.
15. Preterm infants are behind their full-term peers in achieving the milestones of development, but they normally catch up within a few years.
16. There are relatively few differences between boys and girls in early physical development. Ethnic differences do exist, however. Black infants develop somewhat more rapidly; Asian infants somewhat more slowly.

Key Terms

Apgar score
cephalocaudal
cortex
fontanels
myelin
myelinization
ossification
proximodistal
reflexes
states of consciousness
sudden infant death syndrome (SIDS)

Suggested Readings

Field, T. (1990). *Infancy*. Cambridge, MA: Harvard University Press.

Field reviews what we know about infancy in an engaging and clear style.

Rosenblith, J. F. (1992). *In the beginning: Development in the first two years of life*, 2nd ed. Newbury Park, CA: Sage.

A fine basic text on infant development.

Slater, A. M., & Bremner, J. G. (Eds.) (1989). *Infant development*. Hillsdale, NJ: Lawrence Erlbaum Associates.

A good summary, written by scientists and based on research, but aimed at the lay reader.

Perceptual and Cognitive Development in Infancy

5

Three years ago, my husband and I lived in Germany for eight months. Because he was born in Germany and has many relatives there who speak no English, it seemed like a good idea for me to learn enough German to be able to speak to his family. So I took intensive German classes and struggled to learn new vocabulary and complex grammar. The entire process turned out to be a lot harder than I had expected, but it certainly gave me a chance to observe the ways I go about learning, remembering, and using new information. I had, throughout, an almost physical sense of my brain at work, struggling to create order and sense out of a bombardment of new information. (Periodically my brain would simply go on strike and refuse to take in anything more—a sensation I suspect most of you have had at one time or another!)

In our everyday lives, each of us faces myriad tasks that call for the same kinds of skills I used in my efforts to learn this new language. We study for exams, try to remember what to buy at the grocery store, balance the checkbook, remember phone numbers, use a map. Not all of us do these things equally well or equally quickly. But all of us perform such activities every day of our lives.

These activities are all part of what psychologists call *cognitive functioning*. What I will be exploring here, and in the parallel chapters on cognition for each age period throughout the book, is how we all acquire and maintain the ability to do these things. One-year-olds cannot use maps or balance a checkbook. How do they eventually come to be able to do so? And how do psychologists explain the fact that not all children learn these things at the same rate, or become as skilled?

Theoretical Perspectives

Our ability to answer questions like these has been complicated by the fact that psychologists have developed three distinctly different views of cognition, each of which has led to a separate body of research and commentary.

Historically, the first approach to studying cognitive development focused on individual differences. It is inescapably true that people differ in their intellectual skill, their ability to remember things, the speed with which they solve problems, and their ability to analyze complex situations. When we say someone is "bright" or "very intelligent," it is just such skills we mean; one typical psychologist's definition of the term *intelligence*, for example, is "the aggregate or global capacity of the individual to act purposefully, to think rationally and to deal effectively with his environment" (Wechsler, 1939, p. 3). When most of us use the term *intelligence*, we also assume that we can rank-order people in their degree of intelligence, an assumption that lies directly behind the development of intelligence tests, which were designed simply to give us a way of measuring individual differences in intellectual power.

Critical Thinking

When you say someone is "bright" or "intelligent," do you mean some kind of overall intellectual "power?" What else do you mean by these terms?

This "power" definition of intelligence, also referred to as a psychometric approach, held sway for many years. But it has one great weakness: It does not deal with the equally compelling fact that intelligence develops. As children grow, their thinking becomes more and more abstract and complex. If you give a 5-year-old a mental list of things to remember to buy at the grocery store, she will have trouble remembering more than a few items. She is also very unlikely to use good strategies to aid her memory, such as rehearsing the list or organizing the items into groups in her mind. An 8-year-old would remember more things, and probably would rehearse the list under his breath, or in his head, as he was walking to the store. Or he might remember that there were three vegetables on the list, a strategy that makes it more likely that he will remember to buy all three.

The fact that intelligence develops in this way forms the foundation of the second great tradition in the study of cognitive development, the cognitive developmental approach of Jean Piaget and his many followers. Piaget focused on the development of cognitive structures rather than intellectual power, on patterns of development that are common to all children rather than on individual differences.

These two traditions have lived side by side for some years now, like polite but not very friendly neighbors. In the past few years, though, the two have developed a mutual friend—a third view, called the **information processing** approach, that partially integrates power and structure approaches. Proponents of this third view argue that "intelligence is not a faculty or trait of the mind. Intelligence is not mental content. Intelligence is processing" (Fagan, 1992, p. 82). According to this view, if we are to understand intelligence we need to uncover and find ways to measure the basic processes that make up cognitive activity. Once we have identified such basic processes, we can then ask *both* developmental and individual-differences questions: Do these basic processes change with age? Do people differ in their speed or skill in using the basic processes?

These three themes will appear again and again as we look at cognitive development over the life span. But the research in each tradition is not equally distributed across the several age strata. In particular, Piaget's theory has been the most clearly dominant in research on infant intelligence—perhaps because he was really the first theorist to think of the infant's behavior in terms of intelligence. Thus, much of what I will be talking about in this chapter has been cast in a Piagetian framework rather than a cognitive power or information processing frame, although you will see elements of both cognitive power and information processing approaches entering into the overall theoretical fabric.

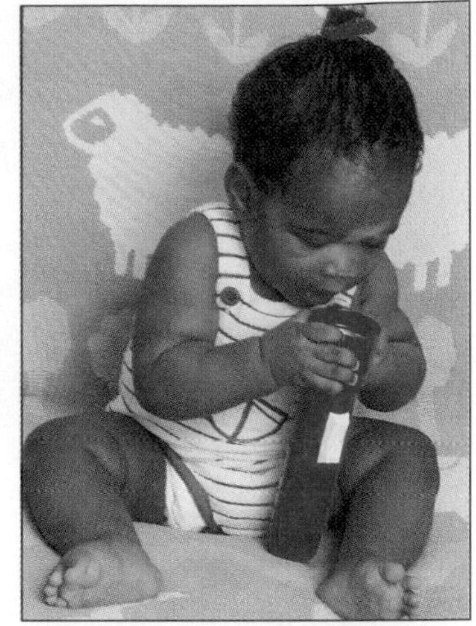

This baby may look as if she is merely "playing," but she is also engaged in an important cognitive activity—trying to understand the world around her.

Piaget's View of the Sensorimotor Period

Recall from Chapter 2 that Piaget assumes the baby is engaged in an *adaptive* process, trying to make sense out of the world around her. She assimilates incoming information to the limited array of schemes she is born with—looking, listening, sucking, grasping—and accommodates those schemes based on her experiences. According to Piaget, this is the starting point for the entire process of cognitive development. He called this primitive form of thinking *sensorimotor intelligence*, and the entire stage he called the *sensorimotor period*.

Basic Features of Sensorimotor Intelligence. In Piaget's view, the baby comes equipped only with reflexes and simple sensory and motor schemes. In the beginning, she is entirely tied to the immediate present, responding to whatever stimuli are available. She does not remember events or things from one encounter to the next, and does not appear to plan or intend. This gradually changes during the first 18 months as the baby comes to understand that objects continue to exist even when they are out of sight, and becomes able to remember objects, actions, and individuals over periods of time. But Piaget insisted that the sensorimotor infant is as yet unable to *manipulate* these early mental images or memories, nor does she use *symbols* to stand for objects or events. It is the new ability to manipulate internal symbols, such as words or images, that marks the beginning of the next stage, *preoperational thought*, at roughly 18–24 months of age. John Flavell (1985) summarizes all this very nicely:

> [The infant] exhibits a wholly practical, perceiving-and-doing, action-bound kind of intellectual functioning; she does not exhibit the more contemplative, reflective, symbol-manipulating kind we usually think of in connection with cognition. The infant "knows" in the sense of recognizing or anticipating familiar, recurring objects and happenings, and "thinks" in the sense of behaving toward them with mouth, hand, eye, and other sensory-motor instruments in predictable, organized, and often adaptive ways. . . . It is the kind of noncontemplative intelligence that your dog relies on to make its way in the world. (p. 13)

The change from the limited repertoire of schemes available to the newborn to the ability to use symbols beginning at roughly 18 months is gradual, although Piaget identified six substages, summarized in Table 5.1.

Each substage represents some specific advance over the one that came before. Substage 2 is marked especially by the beginning of those important coordinations between looking and listening, reaching and looking, and reaching and sucking that are such central features of the 2-month-old's means of exploring the world. The term *primary circular reactions* refers to the many simple repetitive actions we see at this time, each organized around the infant's own body. The baby accidentally sucks

Table 5.1 Substages of the Sensorimotor Period According to Piaget

Substage	Age in Months	Piaget's Label	Characteristics
1	0–1	Reflexes	Practice of built-in schemes or reflexes such as sucking or looking. Primitive schemes begin to change through very small steps of accommodation. No imitation; no ability to integrate information from several senses.
2	1–4	Primary circular reactions	Further accommodation of basic schemes, as the baby practices them endlessly—grasping, looking, sucking. Beginning coordination of schemes from different senses, so that the baby now looks toward a sound and sucks on anything he can reach and bring to his mouth. But the baby does not yet link his body actions to some result outside his body.
3	4–8	Secondary circular reactions	The baby becomes much more aware of events outside his own body and makes them happen again in a kind of trial-and-error learning. Not clear that there is understanding of the causal links yet, however. Imitation may occur, but only of schemes already in the baby's repertoire. Beginning understanding of the "object concept" also detected in this period.
4	8–12	Coordination of secondary schemes	Clear intentional means-ends behavior. The baby not only goes after what she wants, she may combine two schemes to do so, such as knocking a pillow away to reach a toy. Imitation of novel behaviors occurs, as does transfer of information from one sense to the other (cross-modal transfer).
5	12–18	Tertiary circular reactions	"Experimentation" begins, in which the infant tries out new ways of playing with or manipulating objects. Very active, very purposeful trial-and-error exploration.
6	18–24	Beginning of representational thought	Development of use of symbols to represent object or events. The child understands that the symbol is separate from the object. Deferred imitation occurs first here, because it requires ability to represent internally the event to be imitated.

his thumb one day, finds it pleasurable, and repeats the action. *Secondary circular reactions*, in substage 3, differ only in that the baby is now repeating some action in order to trigger a reaction outside his own body. The baby coos and Mom smiles, so the baby coos again, apparently in order to get Mom to smile again. These initial connections between body actions and external consequences are pretty automatic, very like a kind of operant conditioning. Only in substage 4 do we see the beginnings of real understanding of causal connections, and at this point the baby really moves into exploratory high gear.

In substage 5 this becomes even more marked with the emergence of what Piaget calls *tertiary circular reactions*. In this pattern the baby is not content merely to repeat the original behavior but tries out variations. The baby in substage 5 might try out many other sounds or facial expressions to see if they will trigger Mom's smile, or try dropping a toy from several heights to see if it makes different sounds or lands in different places. At this stage the baby's behavior has a purposeful, experimental quality. Nonetheless, Piaget thought that even in substage 5 the baby does not have internal *symbols* to stand for objects. The development of such symbols is the mark of substage 6.

Piaget's descriptions of this sequence of development, largely based on remarkably detailed observations of his own three children, have provoked a very rich array of research, some of which confirms the general outlines of his proposals and some of which does not. Let me illustrate the current findings by focusing on several specific lines of research: early learning and memory, early perceptual skills such as the ability to combine data from more than one sense, imitation, and the object concept. Not all this research has been done within an explicitly Piagetian framework, but it nonetheless helps us to get a sense of what the baby can do, as well as to evaluate aspects of Piaget's theory.

Learning and Habituation

Most of the work on learning in infancy has been stimulated not by Piaget's theory but by the broader nature/nurture controversy. Those who argue that a child's behaviors and characteristics are a product of experience, rather than being genetically patterned, have attempted to demonstrate that an infant can indeed learn from such experience.

The question of whether very young infants learn from experience is also important from a practical point of view, if only because the answer affects the sort of advice parents may be given about suitable stimulation for their child. For example, if a child's perceptual abilities develop largely through maturation rather than learning, experts would be less likely to advise parents to buy mobiles to hang above the baby's crib. But if learning is possible from the earliest days of life, then various kinds of enrichment would be beneficial.

What does the evidence tell us?

Classical Conditioning. The bulk of the research suggests that the newborn can be classically conditioned, although it is difficult; by 3 or 4 weeks of age classical conditioning occurs easily. In particular, this means that the conditioned emotional responses I talked about in Chapter 2 may begin to develop as early as the first week of life. Thus, the mere presence of Mom or Dad or another favored person may trigger the sense of "feeling good," a pattern that may contribute to what we see as the child's attachment to the parent.

Critical Thinking

Can you think of other examples of classically conditioned emotional responses that might develop in early infancy? What about negative emotions?

Operant Conditioning. Newborns also clearly learn by operant conditioning. Both the sucking response and head turning have been successfully increased by the use of reinforcements such as sweet-tasting liquids or the sound of the mother's voice or heartbeat (Moon & Fifer, 1990). At the least, the fact that conditioning of this kind can take place means that whatever neurological wiring is needed for learning is present at birth. Results like this also tell us something about the sorts of reinforcements that are effective with very young children; it is surely highly significant for the whole process of mother-infant interaction that the mother's voice is an effective reinforcer for virtually all babies.

Schematic Learning. The fact that babies can recognize voices and heartbeats in the first days of life is also important because it suggests that another kind of learning is going on as well. This third type of learning, sometimes referred to as *schematic learning*, draws both its name and many of its conceptual roots from Piaget's theory. The basic idea is that from the beginning the baby organizes her experiences into expectancies, or "known" combinations. These expectancies, often called *schemas*, are built up over many exposures to particular experiences. Once formed, they help the baby to distinguish between the familiar and the unfamiliar. Carolyn Rovee-Collier (1986) has suggested that we might think of classical conditioning in infants as being a variety of schematic learning. When a baby begins to move her head as if to search for the nipple as soon as she hears her mom's footsteps coming into the room, in classical conditioning terms she is indeed displaying a conditioned response, but we could also think of this behavior as the beginning of the development of expectancies. From the earliest weeks, the baby seems to begin to make connections between events in her world, such as the link between the sound of her mother's footsteps and the feeling of being picked up, or between the touch of the breast and the feeling of a full stomach. Thus, early classical conditioning may be the beginnings of the process of cognitive development.

Habituation. A related concept is that of **habituation.** Habituation is the automatic reduction in the strength or vigor of a response to a repeated stimulus. For example, suppose you live on a fairly noisy street. The sound of cars going by is repeated over and over during each day. But after a while, you not only don't react to the sound, you quite literally *do not perceive it as being as loud*. The ability to do this—to dampen down the intensity of a physical response to some repeated stimulus—is obviously vital in our everyday lives. If we reacted constantly to every sight and sound and smell that came along, we'd spend all our time responding to these repeated events and not have energy or attention left over for things that are new and deserve attention.

The ability to *dishabituate* is equally important. When a habituated stimulus changes in some way, such as a sudden extra-loud screech of tires on the busy street by your house, you again respond fully. Thus, the reemergence of the original response strength is a sign that the perceiver—infant, child, or adult—notices some significant change.

The ability both to habituate and to dishabituate is already present in rudimentary form in a newborn and is well developed by 10 weeks of age. An infant will stop looking at something you keep putting in front of her face; she will stop showing a startle reaction (Moro reflex) to loud sounds after the first few presentations, but will again show a startle response if the sound is changed. Such habituation itself is not a voluntary process; it is entirely automatic. But in order for it to work, the newborn must be equipped with the capacity to "recognize" familiar experiences. That is, she must have, or must develop, schemas of some kind.

CRITICAL THINKING

Try to imagine a baby who was unable to habituate. What might be the consequences of such a lack?

The existence of these processes in the newborn has an added benefit for researchers: It has enabled them to figure out what an infant responds to as "the same" or "different." If a baby is habituated to some stimulus, such as a sound or a specific picture, the experimenter can then present slight variations on the original stimulus to see the point at which dishabituation occurs. In this way, researchers have begun to get a picture of how the newborn baby or young infant experiences the world around him.

Results of research of this type tell us that Piaget underestimated the very young infant. Newborns have a good deal to work with besides just primitive schemes applied one at a time. From the earliest weeks of life, they can learn connections

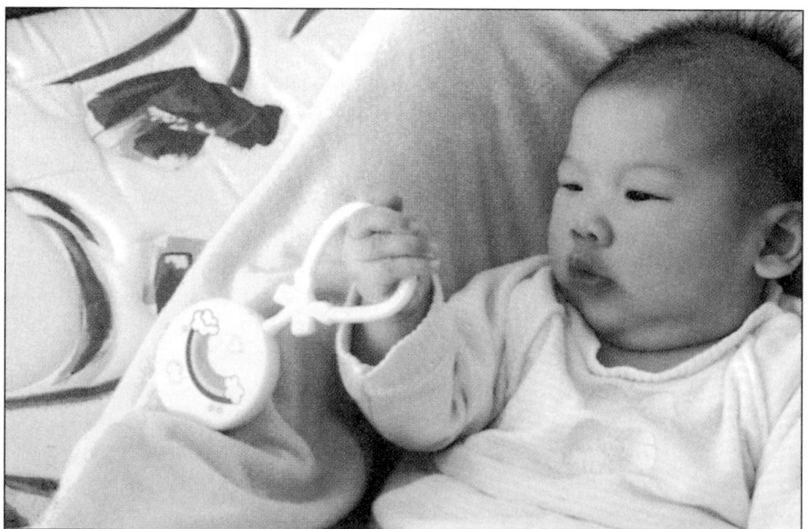

Three-month-old Andrea may be showing a secondary circular reaction here, shaking her hand repeatedly to hear the sound of the rattle. But she is probably also habituating to the sound it makes.

between their own actions and environmental results, they can create expectancies about which events go together, and they have some ability—however automatic—to store information about previously occurring events so that habituation and dishabituation are possible.

Memory

Such an ability to store information is also obviously part of the baby's emerging memory skills, shown very cleverly in Carolyn Rovee-Collier's studies (Bhatt & Rovee-Collier, 1996; Hayne & Rovee-Collier, 1995; Rovee-Collier, 1993). She has used an ingenious variation of an operant conditioning procedure to demonstrate that babies as young as 3 months of age can remember specific objects, and their own actions with those objects, over periods of as long as a week.

Rovee-Collier first hangs an attractive mobile over the baby's crib and watches to see how the baby responds. In particular, she is interested in how often the baby normally kicks his legs while looking at the mobile. After three minutes of this "baseline" observation, she attaches a string from the mobile to the baby's leg, as you can see in Figure 5.1, so that each time the baby kicks his leg, the mobile moves. Babies quickly learn to kick repeatedly in order to make this interesting new thing happen (what Piaget would call a secondary circular reaction). Within three to six minutes, 3-month-olds double or triple their kick rates, showing that learning has clearly occurred. Rovee-Collier then tests the baby's memory of this learning by coming back some days later, hanging the same mobile over the crib but *not* attaching the string to his foot. The crucial issue is whether the baby will kick at the mere sight of the mobile. If the baby remembers the previous occasion, he should kick at a higher rate than he did when he first saw the mobile, which is precisely what 3-month-old babies do, even after a delay of as long as a week.

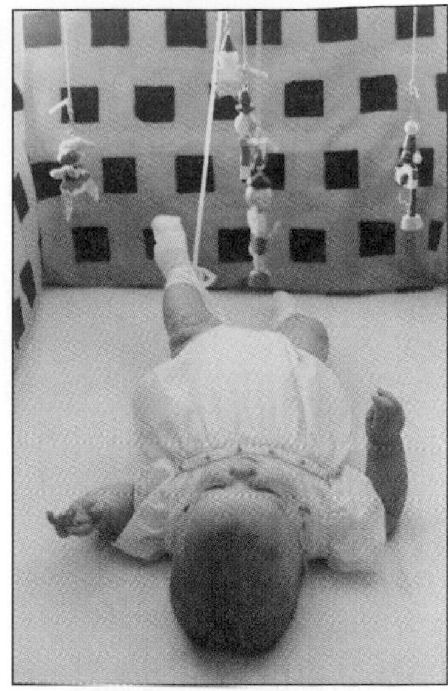

FIGURE 5.1 This 3-month-old baby in one of Rovee-Collier's memory experiments will quickly learn to kick her foot in order to make the mobile move. And she will remember this connection between kicking and the mobile several days later. (*Source:* Rovee-Collier, 1993, page 131.)

In some experiments, Rovee-Collier also "reminds" the baby of the original learning by coming back some time after the first training, hanging the mobile over the crib, and tugging on the string herself at the same rate that the baby had learned to kick. So the baby sees the mobile moving in a rhythmic pattern, but has no chance to move the mobile himself. Then the experimenter comes back a third time and merely hangs the mobile over the crib, watching the rate of the baby's kicks. With the reminder in between, babies as young as 3 months old remember the original learned connection between kicking and the mobile over several weeks.

Why is this so interesting? Primarily because it shows us that the young infant is cognitively a whole lot more sophisticated than we (and Piaget) had supposed. At the same time, Rovee-Collier's work also offers some kind of support for Piaget's views, since she observes systematic gains over the months of infancy in the baby's ability to remember. Two-month-olds can remember their kicking action for only one day; 3-month-olds can remember over a week, and by 6 months the baby can remember over two weeks. Similarly, reminders work better and better as the baby gets older. But all these early infant memories are *strongly* tied to the specific context in which the original experience occurred. Even 6-month-olds do not recognize or remember the mobile if you change the context even slightly, such as hanging a different cloth around the playpen in which the child was originally tested. Thus, babies do remember—far more than Piaget believed—but their memories are highly specific. With age, their memories become less and less tied to specific cues or contexts.

Early Perceptual Development

Much the same story emerges from the very rich array of research on early perceptual skills: Babies have many more skills than we had thought. You already know from Chapter 4 that at birth, or in the early weeks of life, the baby can focus his eyes, follow a moving object at least roughly, taste the major tastes, and hear most pitches.

These are obviously important skills. They enable the baby to enter into key interactions with caregivers and to react to objects around him. Far more interesting, though, is the recent evidence that very young infants can make remarkably fine discriminations among sounds, sights, and feelings, and that they pay attention to and respond to *patterns*, not just to individual events. I have room here only to sample this fascinating new body of research, but a few examples will give you the flavor.

Discriminating Mom from Other People

For years I have been telling my friends and relatives that there was clear research showing that babies can't recognize their mothers' faces until at least 1 or 2 months of age. None of my friends or relatives believed me; they all said, "I don't care what the research says; I know my baby could recognize my face right away." Well, it looks as if they were right, and the older research—and I—were wrong.

CRITICAL THINKING

How many hypotheses can you think of to explain the fact that newborns can discriminate between Mom's voice and a stranger's, but not between Dad's voice and a stranger's?

We have known for some time that newborns can distinguish between one person and another, particularly between Mom and other people, by using their hearing. DeCasper and Fifer (1980) found that newborns could tell their mother's voice from another female voice (but not their father's voice from another male voice) and preferred the mother's, possibly because the baby has become familiar with the mother's voice while still in utero. By 6 months, babies can even match voices with faces. If you put an infant of this age in a situation where she can see both her father and mother and can hear a tape-recorded voice of one of them, she will look toward the parent whose voice she hears (Spelke & Owsley, 1979).

The ability to discriminate by smell also seems to be part of the baby's very early repertoire. Babies as young as a week old can tell the difference between their mother's smell and the smell of a stranger, although this seems to be true only for babies who are being breastfed and thus spend quite a lot of time with their noses against the mother's bare skin (Cernoch & Porter, 1985).

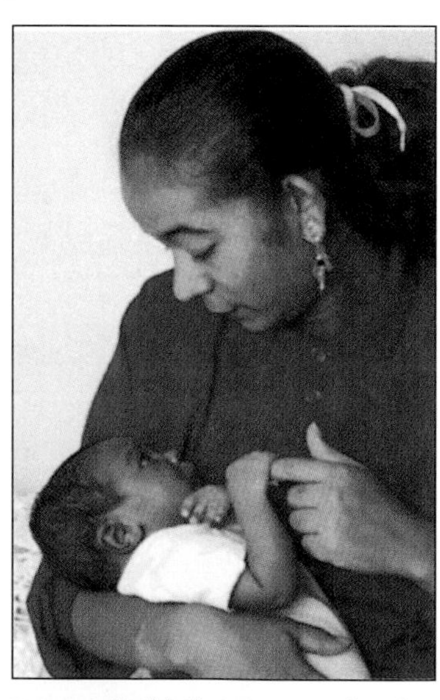

Two-week-old Christian can already discriminate his mom's face from the face of another woman, and can recognize his mom's voice and smell.

What has been most surprising is the discovery that newborns can also recognize their mothers by sight. Several new studies show this, but the clearest and cleanest is one by Gail Walton (Walton, Bower, & Bower, 1992). Walton videotaped the faces of 12 mothers of newborns, and then matched each of these videos with a video of another woman whose hair color, eye color, complexion, and hairstyle were the same as the mom's. Each baby was then given a chance to look at the videos of her mother and of the matched woman's face. These babies, who were only a day or two old at the time of the testing, looked longer at the video of Mom, which shows not only that they could tell the difference between the two faces, but that they preferred the mother's face. Walton also has some preliminary information that babies do *not* discriminate, or do not prefer, their fathers' faces as early as this.

This is a fascinating result. A baby can learn the sound of the mother's voice in utero, but obviously has to learn the details of the mother's features after birth. Walton's study tells us that babies achieve such learning within hours of birth. But how is this possible? Is there some kind of imprinting going on here to the first face the baby sees after it is born? If so, then the process should be affected by birth practices, or by the amount of contact the baby has had with various individuals. As is often the case, this one study seems to settle one question but raises many more.

Beyond the question of preference, there is also the issue of just what it is that babies are looking at when they scan a face. Before about 2 months of age, babies seem to look mostly at the edges of the faces (the hairline and the chin); after 2 months they seem to look more at the internal features, particularly the eyes.

What Babies Look At

This change at about 2 months in the way babies look at faces is part of a more general shift at about that age in the ways babies look at all objects. From the first days of life babies scan the world around themselves—not very smoothly or skillfully, to

Research Report

Langlois's Studies of Babies' Preferences for Attractive Faces

So many of the current studies on infant perception seem to point toward the conclusion that many more abilities and preferences are built in than we had supposed. Among all this new work, Judith Langlois's studies of infant preferences for attractive faces rank as some of the most surprising and intriguing. Langlois has found that babies as young as 2 months old will look longer at a face that adults rate as attractive than at one adults judge to be less attractive.

In the first study in this series, Langlois and her colleagues (Langlois et al., 1987) tested 2- to 3-month-olds and 6- to 8-month-olds. Each baby, while seated on Mom's lap, was shown pairs of color slides of 16 adult Caucasian women, half rated by adult judges as attractive, half rated as unattractive. On each trial, the baby saw two slides simultaneously shown on a screen, with each face approximately life-size, while the experimenter peeked through a hole in the screen to count the number of seconds the baby looked at each picture. Each baby saw some attractive/attractive pairs, some unattractive/unattractive pairs, and some mixed pairs. With mixed pairs, even the 2- and 3-month-old babies consistently looked longer at the attractive faces.

One of the nice features of this study is that the experimenters used a variety of attractive and unattractive faces. In a later study (Langlois et al., 1991), Langlois added even more variability by using pictures of men and women, African-American women's faces, and baby faces. Again she found that for all types of face pairs, babies looked longer at the faces that had been rated by adults as more attractive.

In another exploration of this same issue, Langlois, Roggman, and Rieser-Danner (1990) observed 1-year-old babies interacting with an adult wearing either an attractive or an unattractive mask. They found that the toddlers showed more positive affective tone, less withdrawal, and more play involvement with the stranger in the attractive mask. These 1-year-olds also played more with an attractive than an unattractive doll.

It is hard to imagine what sort of learning experiences could account for such a preference in a 2-month-old. Instead, these findings raise the possibility that there is some inborn template for the "correct" or "most desired" shape and configuration for members of our species, and that we simply prefer those who match this template better. Indeed, in support of this possibility, Langlois has found that the faces babies (and adults) find most attractive and prefer to look at most are those that represent the mathematical average of human faces (Langlois & Roggman, 1990; Langlois, Roggman, & Musselman, 1994). These preferences have real implications for the ways parents interact with their infants. For example, Langlois has found (1995) that mothers of infants that judges rate as more attractive show more affection and playfulness toward their newborns than do mothers of infants rated as less attractive. All in all, Langlois's results raise a whole host of fascinating, and highly practical, questions.

be sure, but nonetheless regularly, even in the dark (Haith, 1980). They will keep moving their eyes until they come to a sharp light/dark contrast, which typically signals the edge of some object. Having found such an edge, the baby stops searching and moves his eyes back and forth across and around the edge. These strategies (which Haith [1980] calls "rules babies look by") seem to change at about 2 months, perhaps because the cortex has then developed more fully, or perhaps because of experience, or both. Whatever the cause, at about this time the baby's attention seems to shift from *where* an object is to *what* an object is. Put another way, the baby seems to move from a scanning strategy designed primarily to *find things* to a strategy designed primarily to *identify* things.

Discriminating Emotional Expressions

At about the same time—2 to 3 months of age—babies begin to respond differently to various emotional expressions as well as to facial features. For example, Haviland and Lelwica (1987) found that when mothers expressed happiness, 10-week-old babies looked happy and interested and gazed at the mother; when the mother expressed sadness, babies showed increased mouth movements or looked away; when the mother expressed anger, some babies cried vigorously, while others showed a kind of still or "frozen" look. These responses did not seem to be merely imitation, but rather responses to the parent's specific emotions.

By 5 or 6 months, babies respond differently to strangers' faces displaying different emotions (Balaban, 1995), as well as to voices speaking with varying emotional tones. They can tell the difference between happy and sad voices, and between happy, surprised, and fearful faces (Nelson, 1987; Walker-Andrews & Lennon, 1991). By roughly 10 to 12 months, infants may use such emotional cues to help them figure out what to do in novel situations, such as when a stranger comes to visit, or in the doctor's office, or even when a new toy is put in front of them. Babies this age will first look at Mom's or Dad's face to check for the adult's emotional expression. If Mom looks pleased or happy the baby is likely to explore the new toy with more ease, or to accept the stranger with less fuss. If Mom looks concerned or frightened, the baby responds to those cues and reacts to the novel situation with equivalent fear or concern. Researchers have described this as a process of **social referencing** (Walden, 1991).

CRITICAL THINKING

How might a parent use knowledge of the process of social referencing?

Responding to Patterns

To me, the most surprising discovery to come out of the surge of new research on perception is that babies as young as 3 or 4 months old pay attention to *relationships* among objects, or among features of objects. For example, suppose you show babies a series of drawings, one at a time, each of which shows a small object above a larger object of the same shape—something like the ones in the top row of Figure 5.2. After seeing a series of such pictures, babies will habituate. That is, they will look for shorter and shorter periods of time until they are barely glancing at a new version of the figure before looking away. "Ho hum, another one of those." Once habituation is established, you can then throw in a test picture that illustrates the opposite pattern (in this case, big-over-small), like the one shown at the bottom of Figure 5.2. What you are likely to find is that babies of 3 and 4 months will show renewed interest in

FIGURE 5.2 In Caron and Caron's study, babies were first habituated to a series of pictures, each of which displayed the same pattern, like those in the upper row. Then they were tested either on more of the same, or on one with a reverse pattern, like the one on the bottom. Three- and 4-month-old babies show renewed interest in the test stimulus, which indicates that they noticed the pattern and saw that it had changed.

this different pattern; this tells us that the baby's original habituation had not been to the *specific* stimuli but to a *pattern* (Caron & Caron, 1981).

Using auditory stimuli, you can find the same awareness of pattern in even younger babies. A study by DeCasper (DeCasper & Spence, 1986) is a particularly striking example. He had pregnant women read a children's story like Dr. Seuss's *The Cat in the Hat* out loud each day for the final six weeks of their pregnancy. After the infants were born, he tested each baby using a procedure based on operant conditioning. He found that these babies would learn to suck on a pacifier in a particular way in order to listen to a recording of the familiar story, but did not increase their sucking in order to listen to an unfamiliar story. That is, the familiar story was reinforcing, while the unfamiliar story was not, showing that the babies preferred the sound of the story they had heard *in utero*. In a more recent study (DeCasper et al., 1994), done in France, DeCasper had pregnant women recite a short children's rhyme out loud each day between weeks 33 and 37 of their pregnancy. In week 38 he played a recording of either the same rhyme the mother had been reading or of another rhyme and measured the fetal heart rate. He found that fetal heart rates dropped during the recording of the familiar rhyme, but not during the unfamiliar rhyme. So even in the last weeks of gestation the fetus is already paying attention to and discriminating among complex patterns of sounds. I find this amazing.

Cross-Modal Transfer

If you think about the way you receive and use perceptual information, you'll realize quickly that you rarely have information from only one sense at one time. Ordinarily you have some complex combination of sound, sight, touch, and smell. Psychologists have been interested in knowing how early an infant can combine such information. For example, how early can an infant integrate information from several senses, such as knowing which mouth movements go with which sounds? Even more complex, how early can a baby learn something via one sense and transfer that information to another sense? For example, at what age can a child recognize solely by feel a toy he has seen but never felt before? The first of these two skills is usually called *intersensory integration*, while the latter is called **cross-modal** (or intermodal) **transfer.**

Piaget believed that both these skills were simply not present until quite late in the first year of life, after the infant had accumulated many experiences with specific objects and how they simultaneously looked, sounded, and felt. Other theorists, including James and Eleanor Gibson, have argued that some intersensory integration or even transfer is built in from birth. The baby then builds on that inborn set of skills with specific experience with objects. Research favors the Gibsonian view: Empirical findings show that cross-modal transfer is possible as early as 1 month and becomes common by 6 months (Rose & Ruff, 1987).

Eight-month-old Ruth may not be looking at this toy while she is chewing on it, but she is nonetheless learning something about how it *ought* to look, just from the way it feels in her mouth and in her hands.

For example, if you attach a nubby sphere to a pacifier and let a baby suck on it, you can test for cross-modal transfer by showing the baby pictures of a nubby sphere and a smooth sphere. If the baby looks longer at the nubby sphere, that would suggest cross-modal transfer. In one recent study of this type, Kaye and Bower have demonstrated such transfer in infants 12 *hours* old (1994), a result that provides a strong argument for the "nature" side of the ancient dispute.

In older infants, intersensory integration and transfer can be readily demonstrated, not only between touch and sight, but between other modalities such as sound and sight. For instance, in one study, Jeffery Pickens (1994) showed 5-month-old babies two films side by side, each displaying a train moving along a track. Then out of a loudspeaker, he played recordings of engine sounds of various types. In one recording, the engine sounds got gradually louder (as if the engine were coming closer), while in the other the engine sounds got gradually fainter (as if the engine were moving away). The babies in this experiment looked longer at the film of a train whose movement matched the pattern of engine sounds. That is, they appeared to have some understanding of the link between the pattern of sound and the pattern of movement—knowledge that not only demonstrates intersensory integration, but also suggests surprisingly sophisticated understanding of the accompaniments of motion.

Equally remarkable is a study in which the researchers showed 7-month-olds pairs of faces displaying happy and angry expressions. Simultaneously, the baby heard a recording of words spoken either in a happy or angry voice. The babies looked longer at the face that matched the *emotion* in the speaking voice—a finding that again points to remarkable sophistication of intermodal integration by age 7 or 8 months (Soken & Pick, 1992).

I do not want to leave you with the impression that intermodal integration or transfer is a completely automatic process in young infants. It isn't. In 4- and 5-month-olds, it often doesn't occur at all, or only under special circumstances (Lewkowicz, 1994). But it is clear that young infants have at least some ability to link simultaneous information from several senses.

All in all, Piaget seems to have been wrong not only about the specific ages at which many of these cognitive and perceptual skills develop, but perhaps even in whether they need to "develop" at all. It begins to look as if a great deal of basic understanding about the events in the world is already "built in" at birth—a conclusion further buttressed by recent studies of the object concept.

Development of the Object Concept

One of Piaget's most striking observations of infants was that they seemed not to have a grasp of certain basic properties of objects that adults take completely for granted. You and I know that objects exist outside of our own actions on them. My computer exists independent of my looking at it and I know that it continues to sit here in my office even if I am somewhere else—an understanding that Piaget called **object permanence.** Piaget thought that babies did not initially know any of these things about objects and acquired this understanding only gradually during the sensorimotor period.

According to his observations, replicated frequently by later researchers, the first sign that the baby is developing object permanence comes at about 2 months of age (in substage 2). Suppose you show a toy to a child of this age, then put a screen in front of the toy and remove the toy. When you then remove the screen, the baby shows some indication of surprise, as if she knew that something should still be there. The child thus seems to have a rudimentary schema or expectation about the permanence of an object. But infants of this age show no signs of searching for a toy they may have dropped over the edge of the crib or that has disappeared beneath a blanket or behind a screen.

In substage 3, however (at about age 6 or 8 months), babies *will* look over the edge of the crib for the dropped toys, or for food that was spilled. (In fact, babies of this age may drive their parents nuts playing "dropsy" in the high chair.) Infants this age will also search for partially hidden objects. If you put a favorite toy under a cloth but leave part of it sticking out, the infant will reach for the toy, which indicates that in some sense the infant "recognizes" that the whole object is there even though she can see only part of it. But if you cover the toy completely with the cloth or put it behind a screen, the infant will stop looking at it and will not reach for it, even if she has seen you put the cloth over it—a pattern shown clearly in the photos in Figure 5.3.

This changes again somewhere between 8 and 12 months, in substage 4. Infants this age will reach for or search for a toy that has been covered completely by a cloth

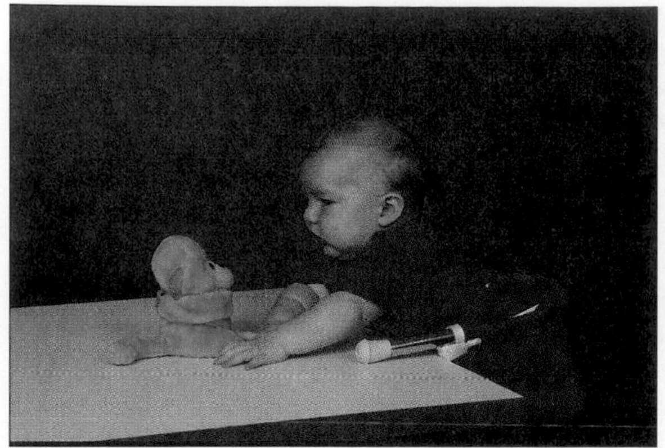

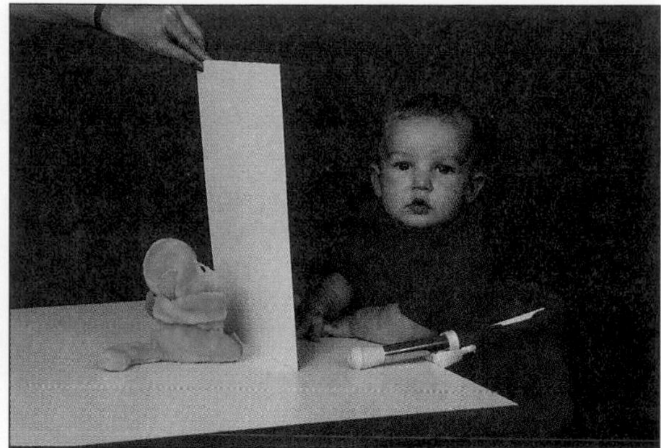

FIGURE 5.3 A baby in stage 3 of the development of object constancy. The infant stops reaching as soon as the screen is put in front of the toy, and shows no sign of knowing that the toy is still there. (As an aside: The type of hook-on-the-table seat shown in these photos is nowadays thought to be too dangerous by many pediatricians and is no longer recommended.)

or hidden by a screen. Thus, by 12 months, most infants appear to grasp the basic fact that objects continue to exist even when they are no longer visible.

This sequence of development has been so compelling, so interesting, and so surprising to many researchers that it has been the subject of reams of research. Until recently, most researchers had concluded that Piaget's description of the sequence of development of the object concept was correct. Certainly, if you follow Piaget's procedures, you will see essentially the same results among children in all cultures.

Newer research, though, points to the possibility that very young babies have far more understanding than Piaget supposed of the properties of objects, including their permanence. For example, Renée Baillargeon (1987; 1994; Baillargeon & DeVos, 1991; Baillargeon, Spelke, & Wasserman, 1985), in a series of clever studies, has shown that babies as young as $3\frac{1}{2}$ or 4 months show clear signs of object permanence if you use a *visual* response rather than a reaching response to test it. Similarly, in a whole series of experiments, Elizabeth Spelke (1991) has shown that young infants respond to objects in a far less transitory and ephemeral way than Piaget thought. In particular, 2- and 3-month-olds are remarkably aware of what kinds of movements objects are capable of—even when they are out of sight. They expect objects to continue to move on their initial trajectories, and show surprise if the object appears somewhere else. They also seem to have some awareness that solid objects cannot pass through other solid objects.

In one experiment in this series, Spelke used the procedure shown schematically in Figure 5.4. Two-month-old babies were repeatedly shown a series of events like that in the "familiarization" section of the figure: A ball starting on the left-hand side

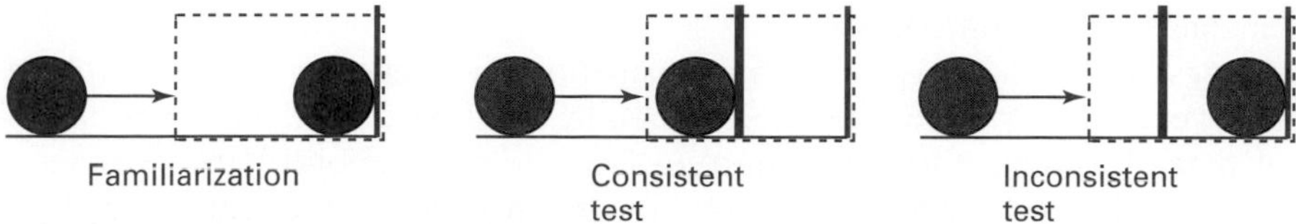

FIGURE 5.4 This shows you, in schematic form, the three conditions Spelke used. She found that babies stopped looking at the ball and screen after a number of familiarization trials, but showed renewed interest in the inconsistent version—a sign that the babies saw this as somehow different or surprising. (*Source*: Spelke, 1991, Figure 5.3.)

Cultures and Contexts

Object Permanence in Zambian Infants

Piaget believed that the emergence of the child's understanding of object permanence followed a universal sequence. One way to test this assumption, of course, is to observe or test children in non-Western societies, particularly infants or children whose early experiences are different from what we see in the United States or Europe. Susan Goldberg's longitudinal study of 38 Zambian infants (1972) gives us one such cross-cultural look.

Goldberg's two years of observations in Zambia made clear that the typical experience of a Zambian baby was quite different in a number of respects from that of most Western infants. From shortly after birth, Zambian babies are carried about in a sling on their mother's back. They spend very little time on the floor or in any position in which they have much chance of independent movement until they are able to sit up at about 6 months. At that point they are usually placed on a mat in the yard of the house. From this vantage the baby can watch all the activity around the house and in the neighborhood, but he has few objects to play with. Goldberg reported that the Zambian mothers did not see it as their task to provide play objects for their infants, nor to structure the child's play in any way. Indeed, Goldberg says she rarely saw the babies playing with objects, even those that might have been available in the yards.

Yet despite this very limited experience manipulating objects, tests of object permanence showed that the Zambian babies were *ahead* of the American averages on a measure of the object concept at 6 months of age. At 9 and 12 months of age, the Zambian babies were slightly behind the U.S. norms, but Goldberg believes this difference is due not to any cognitive failure but to the fact that at these ages the Zambian babies were quite unresponsive and passive toward objects, and thus very difficult to test. One possible explanation of this is that in Zambian culture, at least as Goldberg observed it, obedience is a highly valued quality in a child. The babies are trained from very early on to be particularly obedient to prohibitions of various kinds. When the baby plays with some object that he is forbidden to touch, the object is taken away. Perhaps, then, the infants learn that when an object is removed, it means "don't play with that" and he makes no further move to reach for the toy during the object permanence test. This does not necessarily mean that the baby has not understood these later stages of object permanence; it could also mean that our traditional ways of measuring this understanding would need to be modified for these children.

Goldberg's observations thus illustrate both the robustness of some basic developmental patterns *and* the impact of culture on the ways those patterns are displayed by children. Babies in Zambia appear to develop the early steps of the understanding of object permanence even though they have little chance to manipulate objects. But their response to objects is also affected by their training and experience.

Critical Thinking

I find it astonishing that a 2-month-old baby can have enough understanding of the physical world to "know" in some fashion that it is unexpected for the ball to be on the other side of the middle wall in this experiment. Are you also astonished by this result?

was rolled to the right and disappeared behind a screen. The screen was then taken away and the baby could see that the ball was stopped against the wall on the right. After the baby got bored looking at this sequence (habituated), he or she was tested with two variations, one "consistent" and one "inconsistent." In the consistent variation, a second wall was placed behind the screen and the sequence run as before, except that now when the screen was removed, the ball could be seen resting up against the nearer wall. In the inconsistent variation, the ball was surreptitiously placed on the *far* side of the new wall. When the screen was removed the ball was visible in this new and presumably impossible place. Babies in this experiment were quite uninterested in the consistent condition, but showed sharply renewed interest in the inconsistent condition.

Findings like this have reopened the debate about Piaget's description of the development of object permanence. More generally, they have sparked a new discussion of that old friend, the nature/nurture issue (e.g., Diamond, 1991; Fischer & Bidell, 1991; Karmiloff-Smith, 1991). Just how much is built in at birth? Piaget, of course, never said that *nothing* was built in. He assumed that the baby came equipped with a repertoire of sensorimotor schemes. But his most fundamental theoretical proposal was that the child *constructed* his understanding of the world, based on experience. On the other side of this new argument are those who see the baby as being endowed not only with specific knowledge about the world, but also with built-in constraints in the ways he processes information.

Spelke's own conclusion is that the development of the understanding of objects is more a process of elaboration than discovery. Newborn or very young babies may have considerable awareness of objects as separate entities that follow certain rules. Certainly all the research on the perception of patterns suggests that babies pay far more attention to relationships between events than Piaget's model had led us to suppose. Indeed, the research on babies' preferences for attractive faces, which I talked about in the box on page 111, suggests that there may be built-in preferences for particular patterns. Still, even Spelke would not argue that the baby comes equipped with a full-fledged knowledge of objects or a well-developed ability to experiment with the world. It remains to be seen just how much of Piaget's view will need to be changed because of work of this type, but it has raised a whole host of new questions.

Imitation

As a final example of research on infant cognition that has flowed from Piaget's theory, let me say just a word about studies of imitation. If you go back and look at Table 5.1 again, you'll see that Piaget thought that as early as the first few months of life, infants could imitate actions they could see themselves make, such as hand gestures. But he thought they could *not* imitate other people's facial gestures until about substage 4 (8–12 months). This second form of imitation seems to require some kind of cross-modal transfer, combining the visual cues from seeing the other's face with the kinesthetic cues from one's own facial movements. Piaget also argued that imitation of any action that wasn't already in the child's repertoire did not occur until about 1 year, and that *deferred* imitation, in which a child sees some action and then imitates it at a later point, was possible only at substage 6, since deferred imitation requires some kind of internal representation.

In broad terms Piaget's proposed sequence has been supported. Imitation of someone else's hand movements or their actions with objects seems to improve steadily during the months of infancy, starting at 1 or 2 months of age; imitation of two-part actions develops much later, perhaps at 15 to 18 months (Poulson, Nunes, & Warren, 1989). Yet there are also two important exceptions to this general confirmation of Piaget's theory: Infants imitate some facial gestures in the first weeks of life, and deferred imitation seems to occur earlier than Piaget proposed.

Several researchers have found that newborn babies will imitate certain facial gestures, particularly tongue protrusion (Anisfeld, 1991). This seems to work only if the model sits there with his tongue out looking at the baby for a fairly long period of time, perhaps as long as a minute. But the fact that newborns imitate at all is striking—although it is entirely consistent with the observation that quite young babies are capable of tactual/visual cross-modal transfer.

Studies of deferred imitation are not so strikingly discordant with Piaget's description, but at least one study (Meltzoff, 1988) shows that babies as young as 9 months can defer their imitation over as long as 24 hours. By 14 months, toddlers can recall and later imitate someone's actions over periods of 2 days (Hanna & Meltzoff, 1993).

These findings are significant for several reasons. First of all, they make it clear that children of this age can and do learn specific behaviors through modeling, even when they have no chance to imitate the behavior immediately. In addition, these results, like so many I have been describing to you in this chapter, suggest that babies may be more skillful than Piaget thought, and that there may be more abilities than he suggested built in from the beginning. But they leave open the deeper question of

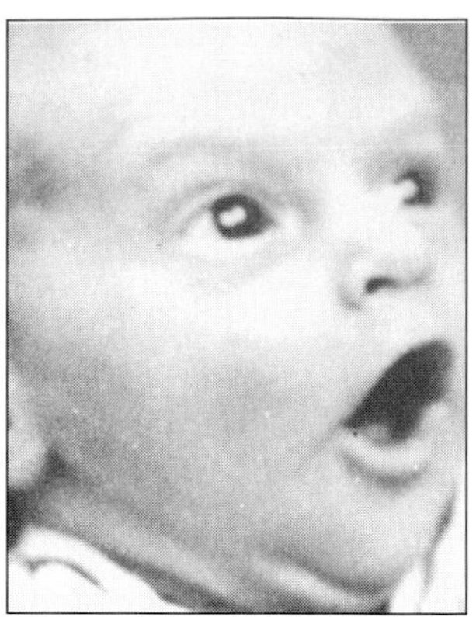
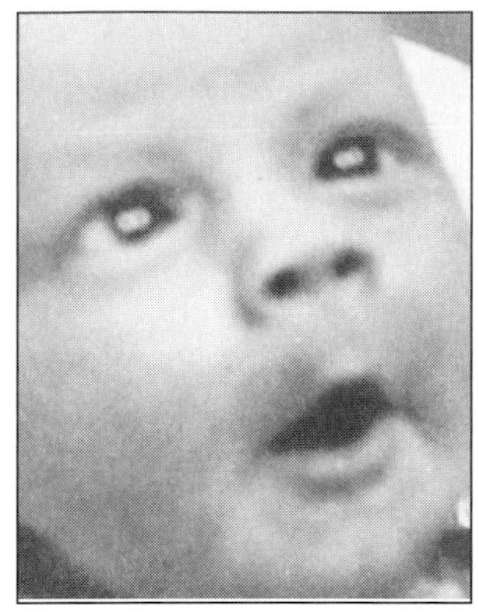

FIGURE 5.5 This mom was asked to model an exaggerated "surprise" expression to her newborn—an expression the baby imitated, providing further evidence that at least some kinds of complex imitation occur in the first days of life. (*Source*: T. M. Field, Social perception and responsivity in early infancy. In T. M. Field, A. Huston, H. C. Quay, L. Troll, & G. E. Finley, eds., *Review of human development.* Copyright 1982 by John Wiley & Sons, New York, p. 26.)

whether the baby is *constructing* her understanding of the world through her experience, or whether both her understanding and her experience are *constrained* by powerful built-in biases—issues that arise yet again when we look at the early stages of the development of language in these same months.

The Precursors of Language

Most of us think of "language" as beginning when the baby uses her first words, which happens (to the delight of most parents) at about 12 months of age. But all sorts of important developments precede the first words.

Perception of Speech Sounds

Let's start with the basic perceptual skills. A baby cannot learn language until he can hear the individual sounds as distinct. Just how early can he do that? If you hadn't just read the rest of this chapter you might be surprised by the answer. But by now, you know how this song goes. The answer is, "Remarkably early."

As early as 1 month, babies can discriminate between speech sounds like *pa* and *ba* (Trehub & Rabinovitch, 1972). By perhaps 6 months of age, they can discriminate between two-syllable "words" like *bada* and *baga* and can even respond to a syllable that is hidden inside a string of other syllables (like ti*ba*ti or ko*ba*ko) (Fernald & Kuhl, 1987; Goodsitt et al., 1984; Morse & Cowan, 1982). Even more remarkable, it doesn't even seem to matter what voice quality the sound is said in. By 2 or 3 months of age, babies respond to individual sounds as the same whether they are spoken by male or female voices, or a child versus adult voices (Marean, Werner, & Kuhl, 1992).

Even more striking is the finding that babies are actually better at discriminating some kinds of speech sounds than adults are. Each language uses only a subset of all possible speech sounds. Japanese, for example, does not use the *l* sound that appears in English; Spanish makes a different distinction between the *d* and *t* sound than occurs in English. It turns out that up to about 6 months of age, babies can accurately discriminate all sound contrasts that appear in *any* language, including sounds they do not hear in the language spoken to them. At about 6 months of age, they begin to lose the ability to distinguish pairs of vowels that do not occur in the language they are hearing; by age 1, the ability to discriminate nonheard consonant contrasts begins to fade (Polka & Werker, 1994).

Some of the best evidence on this point comes from the work of Janet Werker and her colleagues (Werker & Desjardins, 1995; Werker & Tees, 1984). They have

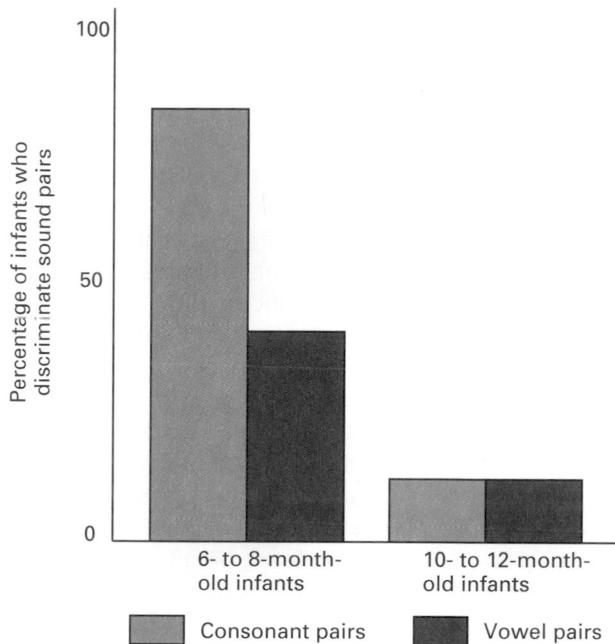

FIGURE 5.6 These data from Werker's studies are for babies growing up in English-language families, but she has similar results from Hindi-languge and Salish-language infants. In every case, 6-month-olds can still "hear" the distinctions between consonant pairs that do not occur in their family's language, but by 12 months that ability has largely disappeared. (*Source:* Werker & Desjardins, 1995, from Figure 2, p. 80.)

tested 6- and 10-month-old infants on various consonant pairs, including one pair that is meaningful in English (*ba* versus *da*); a pair that occurs in a North American Indian language, Salish (*ki* versus *qi*); and one from Hindi, a language from the Indian subcontinent (*ṭa* versus *ta*). Other infants were tested with both English and German vowel contrasts. Figure 5.6 shows the results for babies growing up in English-speaking families on contrasts that do not occur in English. You can see that at 6 months, these babies could still readily hear the differences between pairs of foreign consonants but were already losing the ability to discriminate vowels. Ten- and 12-month-old infants could not hear either type of contrast. Similarly, 12-month-old Hindi infants can easily discriminate a Hindi contrast but not an English contrast. So each group of infants loses only the ability to distinguish pairs that do not appear in the language they are hearing.

It seems to me that these findings are consistent with what we now know about the pattern of rapid, apparently preprogrammed growth of synapses in the early months of life, followed by synaptic pruning. Many connections are initially created, permitting discriminations along all possible sound continua. But only those pathways that are actually used in the language the child hears are strengthened or retained.

Early Sounds and Gestures

The early ability to discriminate among sounds is not matched right away by much skill in producing sounds. From birth to about 1 month of age, the most common sound an infant makes is a cry, although you can also hear other fussing, gurgling, and satisfied sounds. This sound repertoire expands at about 1 or 2 months, when we begin to hear some laughing and **cooing** vowel sounds, like *uuuuuu*. Sounds like this are usually signals of pleasure in babies, and may show quite a lot of variation in tone, running up and down in volume or pitch.

such promptings as "How does the doggie go?" or "What's that?" Typically, this early word learning is very slow, requiring many repetitions for each word. In the first six months of word usage, children may learn as few as 30 words. Most linguists have concluded that in this earliest word-use phase, the child learns each word as something connected to a set of specific contexts. What the toddler has apparently not yet grasped is that words are *symbolic*—that they refer to objects or events.

In this early period, toddlers often combine a single word with a gesture to create a "two-word meaning" before they actually use two words together in their speech. Elizabeth Bates (Bates et al., 1987) suggests an example: The infant may point to Daddy's shoe and say "Daddy," as if to convey "Daddy's shoe." Or she may say "Cookie!" while simultaneously reaching out her hand and opening and closing her fingers, as if to say "Give cookie!" In both cases a sentencelike meaning is conveyed by the use of gesture and body language combined with a word. Linguists call these word-and-gesture combinations **holophrases,** and they are common between the ages of 12 and 18 months.

The Naming Explosion. Somewhere between 16 and 24 months, after the early period of very slow word learning, most children begin to add new words rapidly, as if they had figured out that "things have names." According to Fenson's very large cross-sectional study, based on mothers' reports, the average 16-month-old has a speaking vocabulary of about 50 words; by 24 months this has multiplied more than sixfold, to about 320 (Fenson et al., 1994). In this new phase, children seem to learn new words with very few repetitions, and they generalize these new words to many more situations.

For most children, this naming explosion is not a steady, gradual process; instead, vocabulary "spurts" beginning right about the time that the child has acquired 50 words. You can see this pattern in Figure 5.7, which shows the vocabulary growth curves of six children studied longitudinally by Goldfield and Reznick (1990)—a pattern found by other researchers as well (e.g., Bloom, 1993).

Not all children show precisely this pattern. In Goldfield and Reznick's study, for example, 13 children showed a vocabulary spurt; 11 other children in the study followed varying growth patterns, including several who showed no spurt at all but only gradual acquisition of vocabulary. But a rapid increase over a period of a few months is the most common pattern.

During this early period of rapid vocabulary growth, most observers agree that the bulk of new words are names for things or people, like *ball, car, milk, doggie, he,* or

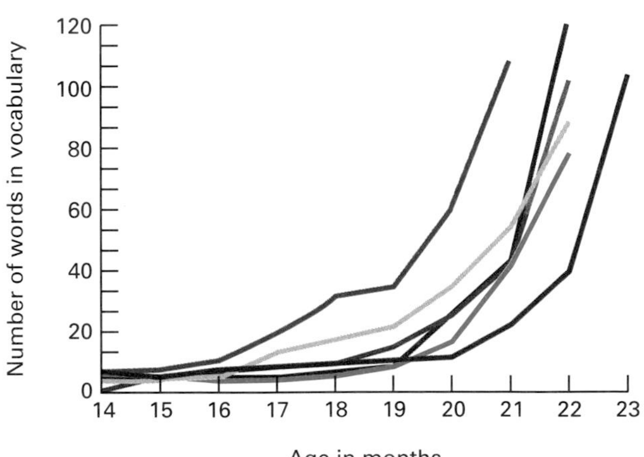

FIGURE 5.7 Each of the lines in this figure represents the vocabulary growth of one of the children studied longitudinally by Goldfield and Reznick. The six children shown here each acquired new words in the most common pattern: slow initial growth followed by a fairly rapid spurt. (*Source*: Goldfield & Reznick, 1990, Figure 3, p. 177.)

that. Verblike words tend to develop later, perhaps because they label *relationships* between objects rather than just a single object (Gleitman & Gleitman, 1992). For example, over half the first 50 words of the eight children Katherine Nelson studied were nounlike words, while only 13 percent were action words (Nelson, 1973). And in Fenson's large cross-sectional study (1994), 63 percent of the words mothers said their children knew by age 2 were nouns, while only 8.5 percent were verbs. Studies of children learning other languages show very similar patterns, as you can see in the Cultures and Contexts box.

However, this noun-before-verb pattern does not hold for all children. Katherine Nelson (1973) first noticed that some toddlers use what she called an **expressive style.** For them, most early words are linked to social relationships rather than to objects. They often learn pronouns (you, me) early, and use many more of what Nelson calls "personal-social" words, such as "no," "yes," "want," or "please." Their early vocabulary may also include some multiword strings, like *love you* or *do it* or *go away*. This is in sharp contrast to children who use what Nelson calls a **referential style,** whose early vocabulary is made up predominantly of nounlike words. Later researchers

Critical Thinking

It seems reasonable to guess that referential- and expressive-style babies would differ from each other in other ways as well. Can you make any guesses about just what those differences might be?

Cultures and Contexts

Early Words by Children in Many Cultures

Cross-cultural studies of children's early language support the generalization that in their earliest word learning, children learn words for people or things before they learn words for actions or other parts of speech. Here are some (translated) samples from the very early vocabularies of one child from each of four cultures, all studied by Dedre Gentner (1982).

It is impressive how very similar these early vocabularies are. Of course there are some variations, but all these children had names for Mommy and Daddy, for some other relative, for other live creatures, and for food. All but the Chinese child had words for toys or clothes. All four had also learned more naming words than any other type, with very similar proportions. They don't know the *same* words, but the pattern is remarkably similar.

	German Boy	English Girl	Turkish Girl	Chinese Girl
Some of the words for people or things	Mommy	Mommy	Mama	Momma
	Papa	Daddy	Daddy	Papa
	Gaga	babar	Aba	grandmother
	baby	baby	baby	horse
	dog	dog	food	chicken
	bird	dolly	apple	uncooked rice
	cat	kitty	banana	cooked rice
	milk	juice	bread	noodles
	ball	book	ball	flower
	nose	eye	pencil	wall clock
	moon	moon	towel	lamp
Some of the nonnaming words	cry	run	cry	go
	come	all gone	come	come
	eat	more	put on	pick up
	sleep	bye-bye	went pooh	not want
	want	want	want	afraid
	no	no	hello	thank you
Total percentage of naming words	67%	69%	57%	59%

have confirmed the existence of these two different styles (Shore, 1995; Thal & Bates, 1990), a set of observations that should remind us that we need to search not just for common developmental pathways, but also to note and try to understand individual variations.

Individual Differences

Discussions of individual differences in cognitive skill are nearly always cast in "cognitive power" terms. We ask whether there are differences in *rate* of development, and whether such differences in rate are consistent over time. Questions of this kind about infant development have an important practical implication: If we could accurately measure differences in infants' rates (or patterns) of development in the early months of life, then we might be able to identify infants who are later going to have problems learning to read or to perform in school in other ways. It might then be possible to intervene very early, perhaps thereby averting or at least ameliorating the problem.

Salma, at 21 months, would clearly pass the 17-month item on the Bayley Scales of Infant Development that calls for the child to build a tower of three blocks.

Just such a hope that test scores could be used to help identify infants with current or prospective problems was one of the motivations behind the development of the various infant IQ tests. Most such tests, such as the widely used **Bayley Scales of Infant Development** (Bayley, 1969, revised 1993), have been constructed rather like IQ tests for older children in that they include a series of items of increasing difficulty. But instead of testing schoollike skills—skills an infant does not yet have—infant IQ tests measure primarily sensory and motor skills, such as reaching for a dangling ring (an item for a typical 3-month-old), putting cubes in a cup on request (9 months), or building a tower of three cubes (17 months). Some more clearly cognitive items are also included, such as uncovering a toy hidden by a cloth, an item used with 8-month-old infants to measure an aspect of object permanence.

Bayley's test and others like it have proven to be helpful in identifying infants and toddlers with serious developmental delays (Lewis & Sullivan, 1985). But as a more general predictive tool to forecast later IQ or school performance, such tests have not been nearly as useful as many had hoped. For example, the typical correlation between a 12-month Bayley test score and a 4-year-old IQ score is only about .20 to .30 (e.g., Bee et al., 1982)—statistically significant, but not robust. On the whole it looks as if what is being measured on typical infant tests is not the same as what is tapped by the common childhood or adult intelligence tests (Colombo, 1993). But recent work emerging from an information processing framework has pointed us in a new direction in our efforts to find links between infant skills and later intellectual abilities.

The most extensive body of such information-processing research has dealt with variations in "recognition memory" among infants—the ability to recognize that one has seen or experienced some object or person before. One way to measure this is with a standard habituation test. If we show a baby an object or a picture, over and over, how many exposures does it take before the infant stops showing interest? That is, how quickly does the baby "recognize" the object or picture? The speed with which such habituation/recognition takes place may tell us something about the efficiency of the perceptual/cognitive system and its neurological underpinnings. And if such efficiency lies behind some of the characteristics we normally call "intelligence," then individual differences in rate of habituation in the early months of life may predict later intelligence test scores.

That is exactly what researchers have found in studies over the past 15 years. Babies who habituate quickly (that is, who rapidly become uninterested when shown the same object repeatedly) when they are 4 or 5 months old are likely to have higher IQs at later ages, while slower infant habituation is associated with subsequent lower IQ and poorer language. The average correlation in studies in both the United States and England is in the range of .45 to .50 (Rose & Feldman, 1995; Slater, 1995). This is certainly not perfect, but it is remarkably high, given the difficulties involved in measuring habituation rate in babies.

Certainly these correlations do not prove that intelligence, as we measure it on an IQ test, is *only* a reflection of some kind of "speed of basic processing." But results like these underline the potential importance of looking at the underlying components of information processing if we want to understand individual differences in cognitive skills in early infancy.

Cognitive Development in Infancy: An Overall Look

In a number of important respects, Piaget seems to have underestimated the ability of infants to store, remember, and organize sensory and motor information. Very young babies pay much more attention to patterns, sequence, and prototypical features than Piaget thought, and can apparently remember them over at least short intervals. Many current theorists have taken this evidence to mean that the baby comes equipped with a wide range of built-in knowledge or inborn constraints on his ways of understanding the world around him.

On the other side of the argument, however, is the obvious fact that newborns, despite their remarkable perceptual and cognitive abilities, are *not* as skilled as 6- or 12-month-olds. Newborns do not use gestures to communicate, they do not talk, they do not show deferred imitation. Six-month-olds do not combine several strategies to achieve some goal and do not seem to experiment with objects in the same way as we see later. Even at 12 months toddlers do not seem to use symbols to stand for things in any general way. They use a few words, but don't yet show pretend play, for example. So despite all the new and fascinating evidence that casts doubt on many of Piaget's specific observations, it still appears to be correct to describe the infant as *sensorimotor* rather than *symbolic* in her thinking. Over the first 18 to 24 months the baby seems to be building toward such symbol use, a shift that John Flavell correctly sees as remarkable:

> "A cognitive system that uses symbols just seems . . . to be radically, drastically, qualitatively different from one that [does] not. So great is the difference that the transformation of one system into the other during the first 2 years of life still seems nothing short of miraculous to me, no matter how much we learn about it." (1985, p. 82)

Summary

1. Three distinct theoretical emphases exist in the study of intelligence and cognition: intellectual power, intellectual structure, and information processing.
2. Studies of infant cognition have been most strongly influenced by Piaget's structural view of intelligence.
3. Piaget described the sensorimotor infant as beginning with a small repertoire of basic schemes, from which she moves toward symbolic representation in a series of six substages.
4. Substage 1 is essentially automatic pilot; substage 2 includes coordination of different modalities; in substage 3 the baby focuses more on the outside world; in substage 4 causal connections are understood and the object concept is grasped in a preliminary way; in substage 5, the baby begins to experiment more fully; and in substage 6, we see first signs of symbol usage.
5. Babies are able to learn by both classical and operant conditioning within the first few weeks of life, earlier than Piaget thought.
6. Newborns are also able to habituate to repeated stimuli, indicating that they have the ability to "recognize" that something has been experienced before.
7. In the first weeks of life, infants appear to be intent on locating objects; after about 2 months, they seem intent on identifying objects, so their method of scanning changes.
8. Three- and 4-month-old infants show signs of remembering specific experiences over periods of as long as a few days or a week, a sign that they must have some form of internal representation well before Piaget supposed.
9. Newborns can discriminate Mom from other people by sight, sound, and smell. By 3 months they respond differently to varying emotional expressions.
10. From the earliest weeks, babies respond to the patterns of stimuli or to relationships among stimuli, such as "big over small" or the sound of a particular story or melody. They also prefer to look at attractive rather than at less attractive faces.

11. Babies also show cross-modal transfer as early as a few weeks of age, far earlier than Piaget supposed.

12. Piaget described a sequence of development in the child's understanding of the concept of object permanence—that objects continue to exist when they are out of sight or not being acted on by the child. In Piaget's experiments, babies began to show real comprehension of this only at about 8 months.

13. Newer research suggests that babies may have far more elaborate understanding of the properties of objects—including their permanence—at much earlier ages than Piaget supposed.

14. Babies are able to imitate some facial expressions in the first days of life. But they do not show deferred imitation until much later.

15. Babies can discriminate among speech sounds in the first weeks. Until about 10 months, in fact, they can make discriminations that adults can no longer make.

16. Babies' earliest sounds are cries, followed at about 2 months by cooing, then by babbling at about 6 months. At 9 months babies typically use meaningful gestures and can understand a small vocabulary of spoken words.

17. The first spoken word typically occurs at about 1 year, after which toddlers add words slowly for a few months and then rapidly. Most have a vocabulary of about 50 words by 18 months.

18. The earliest words are more often names for people or objects than they are words to describe actions.

19. Attempts to measure individual differences in sensorimotor development by constructing IQ-like tests have not been as successful as hoped; such tests are not strongly related to later measures of IQ.

20. Much more predictive are measures of more basic information processing skills in infancy, such as rate of habituation at 4 months, which is correlated with later IQ.

21. On the whole, Piaget seems to have underestimated the infant; it may also be that far more is built in at birth than Piaget supposed. But all would agree that progressive development occurs, built upon the base with which the baby begins. The early development culminates in the emergence of the ability to use symbols in play and in thought, at about 18 to 24 months of age.

Key Terms

babbling

Bayley Scales of Infant Development

cooing

cross-modal transfer

expressive language

expressive style

habituation

holophrase

information processing

object permanence

receptive language

referential style

social referencing

Suggested Readings

Aslin, R. N. (1987b). Visual and auditory development in infancy. In J. D. Osofsky (Ed.), *Handbook of infant development*, 2nd ed. New York: Wiley-Interscience.

Aslin has written a number of summaries and reviews of the research on early perceptual development, of which this is perhaps the most easily understood by a nonexpert. Even so, it is quite technical and considerably more detailed than I have been in this chapter.

Baillargeon, R. (1994). How do infants learn about the physical world? *Current Directions in Psychological Science*, 3, 133–140.

This is a wonderful brief paper describing some of Baillargeon's fascinating work on young infants' understanding of objects and the physical world. The paper was written for a general audience of fellow psychologists, rather than for experts in perception, so with a little effort it should be comprehensible to an undergraduate student.

Field, T. (1990). *Infancy*. Cambridge, MA: Harvard University Press.

One of an excellent series of books on topics in child development, written by experts but intended for lay readers. Field covers many of the topics I have discussed in this chapter and in Chapter 6.

Flavell, J. H. (1985). *Cognitive development*, 2nd ed. Englewood Cliffs, NJ: Prentice-Hall.

This is a first-rate basic text in the field, written by one of the major current figures in cognitive developmental theory. The introductory chapter and the chapter on infancy may be especially helpful if you find Piaget's theory somewhat hard to grasp.

Haith, M. M. (1990). Progress in the understanding of sensory and perceptual processes in early infancy. *Merrill-Palmer Quarterly*, 36, 1–26.

In this relatively brief paper Haith looks back on the last 25 years of research on perceptual development. He comments not only on the knowledge gained but on the processes by which scientific progress has been made and the tasks still facing the field. Very interesting reading.

Social and Personality Development in Infancy

6

Not long ago, as I had lunch in a restaurant with a friend, we were happily distracted by the sight of an adorable baby at the next table. The infant, perhaps 4 or 5 months old, was sitting on her mom's lap, facing outward, and gazing with delight at an older woman sitting across from her—perhaps her grandmother. As the older woman talked to the baby in a high and lilting voice, smiled, and tickled the baby's tummy, the infant responded with one huge smile after another. My friend and I stopped talking as we watched, and could hardly restrain ourselves from

Jane's mom has obviously learned just what it takes to coax a smile or a giggle from her 4-month-old.

trying to join in the whole process. I had my "talking-with-baby voice" all warmed up and ready to go, and found myself smiling as if to try to entice an answering smile from the infant—although the baby didn't look our way at all.

But even as I was personally drawn into this small scene, the psychologist in me was also aware of many aspects of the interaction. In particular, I could see the separate contributions of the baby and the adult to this charming exchange. The infant brought her inborn and emerging physical and cognitive skills, including smiling and a general ability to entice; the adult contributed her own instinctive responses to babies, as well as specific knowledge of what would please or attract this particular infant. Just as dance partners need to learn each other's moves in order to dance smoothly, so babies and the adults who care for them adapt to one another's style and rhythm, and become more and more skilled at reading one another's cues. To understand infants, we need to look at the development of these earliest relationships. We also need to look at the individual styles of behavior that each baby brings to the interaction with her caregivers.

Attachment Theory

The strongest theoretical influence in modern-day studies of infant-parent relationships is attachment theory, particularly the work of John Bowlby (1969, 1973, 1980, 1988a, 1988b), whose approach I described briefly in Chapter 2. Bowlby argued that "the propensity to make strong emotional bonds to particular individuals [is] a basic component of human nature, already present in germinal form in the neonate" (1988a, p. 3). Such relationships have *survival* value, because they bring nurturance to the infant. They are built and maintained by an interlocking repertoire of instinctive behaviors that create and sustain proximity between parent and child, or between other bonded pairs.

In Bowlby's writings, and in the equally influential writings of Mary Ainsworth (1972, 1982, 1989; Ainsworth et al., 1978), the key concepts are those of an affectional bond, an attachment, and attachment behaviors.

Ainsworth defines an **affectional bond** as "a relatively long-enduring tie in which the partner is important as a unique individual and is interchangeable with none other. In an affectional bond, there is a desire to maintain closeness to the partner" (1989, p. 711). An **attachment** is a subvariety of emotional bond in which a person's sense of security is bound up in the relationship. When you are attached, you feel (or hope to feel) a special sense of security and comfort in the presence of the other, and you can use the other as a "safe base" from which to explore the rest of the world.

Critical Thinking

Think about your own relationships. In Bowlby's and Ainsworth's terms, which are attachments and which are affectional bonds?

In these terms, the child's relationship with the parent is an attachment, but the parents' relationship with the child is not. The parent presumably does not feel an enhanced sense of security in the presence of the infant, or use the infant as a safe base. In contrast, an adult's relationship with her or his spouse or partner, or with a very close friend, typically is an attachment in the sense Ainsworth and Bowlby mean the term.

Because affectional bonds and attachments are internal states, we cannot see them directly. Instead we deduce their existence by observing **attachment behaviors,** which are all those behaviors that allow a child or adult to achieve and retain proximity to someone else to whom he is attached. This could include smiling, making eye contact, calling out to the other person across a room, touching, clinging, and crying.

Critical Thinking

Pick one of your attachment relationships and make a list of all the attachment behaviors you show toward that person. Are any of these the same as the kind of attachment behaviors we see in an infant?

It is important to make clear that the number of different attachment behaviors a child (or adult) shows on any one occasion is not necessarily a good measure of the strength of the child's underlying attachment. The attachment is an enduring underlying state, while attachment behaviors are elicited primarily when the individual feels the need for care, support, or comfort. An infant is in such a needy state a good deal of the time, so he shows attachment behaviors frequently. An older child, or an adult, will be likely to show attachment behaviors only when she is frightened, tired, or otherwise under stress. It is the *pattern* of these behaviors, not the frequency, that tells us something about the strength or quality of the attachment or the affectional bond.

To understand the early relationship between parent and infant, we need to look at both sides of the equation—at the development both of the parents' bond to the child and of the child's attachment to the parent.

The Parents' Bond to the Infant

The Initial Bond

If you read the popular press, I am sure you have come across articles proclaiming that mothers (or fathers) must have immediate contact with their newborn infant if they are to become properly bonded with the baby. This belief has been based primarily on the work of two pediatricians, Marshall Klaus and John Kennell (1976), who proposed the hypothesis that the first few hours after an infant's birth is a "critical period" for the development of a mother's bond to her infant. Mothers who are denied early contact, Klaus and Kennell thought, are likely to form weaker bonds and thus be at higher risk for a range of disorders of parenting.

Their proposal was one of many factors leading to significant changes in birth practices, including the now-normal presence of fathers at delivery. Although I would certainly not want to turn back the clock on such changes, it now looks as if Klaus and Kennell's hypothesis is essentially incorrect. Immediate contact does not appear to be either necessary or sufficient for the formation of a stable long-term affectional bond between either mother or father and child (Myers, 1987).

A few studies show some short-term beneficial effects of very early contact. In the first few days after delivery, mothers with such contact may show more tender fondling or more gazing at the baby than is true of mothers who first held their babies some hours after birth (e.g., de Chateau, 1980). But there is little indication of a lasting effect. Two or three months after delivery, mothers who have had immediate contact with their newborns do not smile at them more or hold them differently than do mothers who had delayed contact. Only among mothers who are otherwise at higher risk for problems with parenting—such as first-time mothers, mothers living in poverty, or very young mothers—are there a few signs that early contact may make a difference. Among such mothers, extended or early contact with the infant in the first days of life seems to help lower the risk of later problems, such as abuse or neglect (O'Connor et al., 1980). But for the majority of mothers, neither early nor extended contact appears to be an essential ingredient in forming a strong affectional bond.

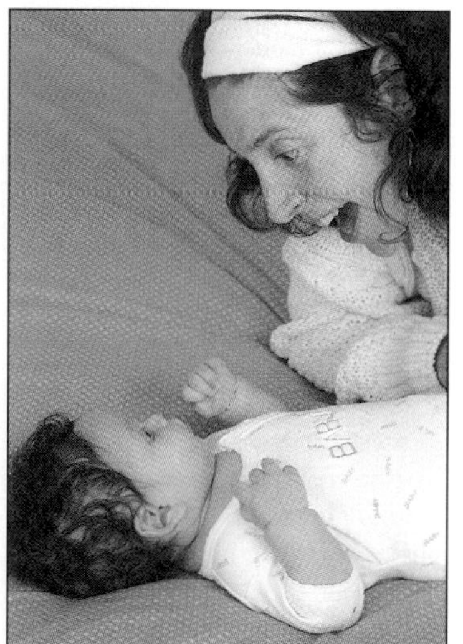

Adults all over the world show this same "mock surprise" expression when they are talking to or playing with a baby. The mouth is open and turned up at the corners, the eyebrows are raised, the eyes are wide, and the forehead is wrinkled.

The Development of Synchrony

What *is* essential in the formation of that bond is the opportunity for the parent and infant to develop a mutual, interlocking pattern of attachment behaviors, a smooth "dance" of interaction. The baby signals his needs by crying or smiling; he responds to being held by quieting or snuggling; he looks at the parents when they look at him. The parents (or grandparents), in their turn, enter into this two-person dance with their own repertoire of caregiving behaviors. They pick the baby up when he cries, wait for and respond to his signals of hunger or other need, smile at him when he smiles, and gaze into his eyes when he looks at them. Some researchers and theorists have described this as the development of *synchrony* (Isabella, Belsky, & von Eye, 1989).

One of the most intriguing things about this process is that we all seem to know how to do this particular dance and we do it in very similar ways. In the presence of a young infant, most adults will automatically display a distinctive pattern of interactive behaviors, including smiling, raised eyebrows, and very wide-open eyes. And we all seem to use our voices in special ways with babies as well. Parents all over the world use a characteristic high-pitched and lilting voice when speaking to an infant, and use similar intonation patterns to signal different meanings. For example, Hanus and Mechthild Papousek (1991) found that Chinese, German, and U.S. mothers all tend to use a rising voice inflection when they want their baby to "take a turn" in the interaction, and a falling intonation when they want to soothe their baby.

Critical Thinking

Watch yourself next time you interact with a baby. Does your facial expression match the "mock surprise" in the photo? Do you speak in a higher, lilting voice? Do your intonation patterns match the ones in the Papousek study?

But while we can perform all these attachment *behaviors* with many infants, we do not form a bond with every baby we coo at in a restaurant or the grocery store. For an adult, the critical ingredient for the formation of a bond seems to be the opportunity to develop real synchrony—to practice the dance until the partners follow one another's lead smoothly and pleasurably. This takes time and many rehearsals, and some parents (and infants) become more skillful at it than others. In general, the smoother and more predictable the process becomes, the more satisfying it seems to be to the parents and the stronger their bond to the infant becomes.

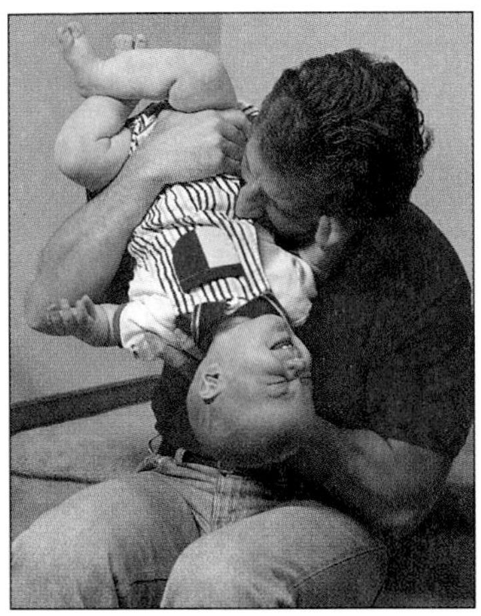

Holding a baby upside down or tossing him in the air is something that dads do much more often than moms.

This second step appears to be *far* more important than the initial contact at birth in establishing a strong parental bond to the child. But this second process, too, can fail. I've explored some of the possible reasons for such a failure in the Real World box on page 132.

Father-Child Bonds

Most of the research I have talked about so far has involved studies of mothers. Still, many of the same principles seem to hold for fathers as well. The father's bond, like the mother's, seems to depend more on the development of mutuality than on contact immediately after birth. Aiding the development of such mutuality is the fact that fathers seem to have the same repertoire of attachment behaviors as do mothers. In the early weeks of the baby's life, Dads touch, talk to, and cuddle their babies in the same ways that mothers do (Parke & Tinsley, 1981).

Past these first weeks of life, however, we see signs of a kind of specialization of parental behaviors with infants and toddlers. Dads spend more time playing with the baby, with more physical roughhousing. Moms spend more time in routine caregiving, and also talk and smile more at the baby (Walker et al., 1992). This does not mean that fathers have a weaker affectional bond with the infant; it does mean that the attachment behaviors they show toward the infant are typically somewhat different from those mothers show.

One obvious question is whether such sex differences in parenting behaviors reflect culturally based role definitions or whether they might be instinctive, built-in differences. One crucial test would be to study families in which the father is the primary caregiver. So far we have only pale imitations of this crucial test—studies of families in which the father has been the primary caregiver, or an equal caregiver, for a few months of the child's early life. Unfortunately, the few studies of this type, done in Sweden, the United States, and Australia, have yielded totally contradictory results (Field, 1978; Lamb et al., 1982; Russell, 1982), which leaves the question still open.

Critical Thinking

Can you think of any other way a researcher might try to figure out whether the differences between moms and dads in their typical way of interacting with babies are cultural or built-in?

The Baby's Attachment to the Parents

Like the parent's bond to the baby, the baby's attachment emerges gradually. Bowlby (1969) suggested three phases in the development of the infant's attachment, sketched schematically in Figure 6.1.

Phase 1: Nonfocused Orienting and Signaling. Bowlby thought that the baby begins life with a set of innate behavior patterns that orient him toward others and signal his needs. Mary Ainsworth describes these as "proximity promoting" behaviors—they

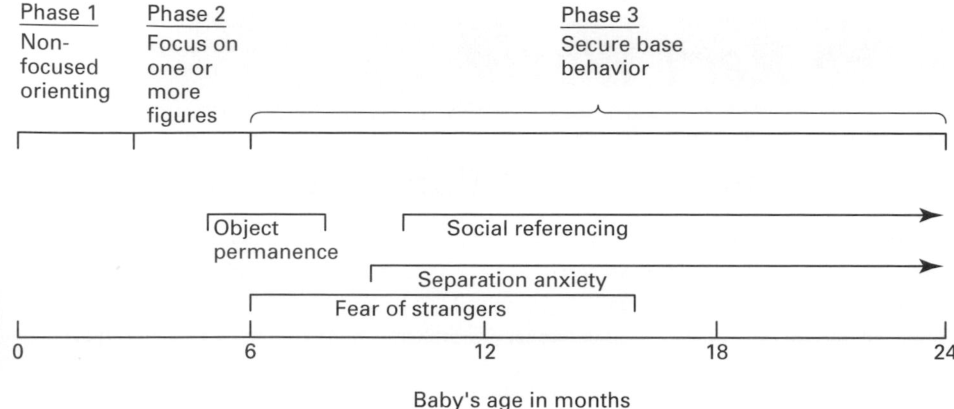

FIGURE 6.1 This schematic may help you see how the various threads of the development of attachment are woven together.

bring people closer. In the newborn's repertoire, these include crying, making eye contact, clinging, cuddling, and responding to caregiving efforts by being soothed.

At this stage there is little evidence of an attachment. As Ainsworth says, "These attachment behaviors are simply emitted, rather than being directed toward any specific person" (1989, p. 710). Nonetheless, the roots of attachment are to be found in this phase. The baby is building up expectancies, schemas, and the ability to discriminate Mom and Dad from others.

Phase 2: Focus on One or More Figure(s). By 3 months of age, the baby begins to aim her attachment behaviors somewhat more narrowly. She may smile more to the people who regularly take care of her, and may not smile readily to a stranger. Yet despite the change, Bowlby and Ainsworth have argued that the infant does not yet have a full-blown attachment. The child still favors a number of people with her "proximity promoting" behaviors and no one person has yet become the "safe base." Children in this phase show no special anxiety at being separated from their parent, and no fear of strangers.

Phase 3: Secure Base Behavior. Bowlby thought that the baby forms a genuine attachment only at about 6 months of age. At roughly that same age, the dominant mode of the baby's attachment behavior changes. Because the 6- to 7-month-old begins to be able to move about the world more freely by creeping and crawling, she can move *toward* the caregiver as well as enticing the caregiver to come to her. Her attachment behaviors therefore shift from mostly "come here" signals (proximity promoting) to what Ainsworth calls "proximity seeking," which we might think of as "go there" behaviors. We also see a child of this age using the "most important person" as a safe base from which to explore the world around her—one of the key signs that an attachment exists.

I should note that not all infants have a *single* attachment figure, even at this stage. Some may show strong attachment to both parents, or to a parent and another caregiver, such as a baby-sitter or a grandparent. But even these babies, when under stress, usually show a preference for one of their favored persons over the others.

Once the child has developed a clear attachment, at about 6 to 8 months, several related behaviors also appear. One of these is social referencing, which I talked about in the last chapter. The 10-month-old uses his new abilities to discriminate among various facial expressions to guide his safe-base behavior. He begins to check out Mom's or Dad's expression before deciding whether to venture forth into some novel situation. At about the same age, babies also typically show both fear of strangers and separation protest.

The Real World

Child Abuse and Other Consequences of Failure of Bonding

In any given year, children's protective services in the United States investigate roughly one million cases of neglect, physical abuse, and sexual abuse (U.S. Bureau of the Census, 1995). Most such abuse is inflicted on older children; the average age of children in cases reported to child protective services is 7. But in many cases the origins of later abuse or neglect may lie in a failure of the parent to form a strong affectional bond to the baby in the first months of life. Such a failure can occur if either the baby or the parents lack the skills to enter into the "dance" of interaction fully. Of the two, the more serious problems seem to arise if it is the parent who lacks skills, but problems can also arise when the baby is handicapped in some way, or otherwise lacks the full repertoire of attachment behaviors (van IJzendoorn et al., 1992).

For example, blind babies smile less and do not show mutual gaze, and preterm infants are typically very unresponsive in the early weeks and months (Fraiberg, 1974, 1975). Most parents of handicapped or premature infants form a strong bond to the child despite the baby's problems, but the rate of abuse is higher among preterm than term infants, and higher among families whose babies are sick a lot in the first few months (Belsky, 1993).

On the other side of the interaction, a parent might lack "attachment skill" because she (or he) did not form a secure attachment with her own parents, perhaps because of abuse (Crittenden, Partridge, & Claussen, 1991). The majority of parents who abuse their children were themselves abused as children—although it is important to emphasize that the reverse is not the case: The majority of adults who experienced abuse in childhood manage to break the cycle of violence and refrain from abusing their children (Zigler & Hall, 1989). Still, there appears to be a significant "intergenerational transmission" of such violence (Belsky, 1993). Those who are unable to break this cycle are typically those who lack other social skills, who have no adequate social support, or who are living under high levels of stress.

Another serious problem on the parents' side of the equation is depression, which not only disrupts the parents' nurturing behavior but affects the child's response as well. Babies interacting with depressed mothers, or even with mothers who have been told to look depressed or "blank-faced," smile less, show more sad and angry facial expressions, and are more disorganized and distressed. Depressed mothers, for their part, look at, touch, or talk to their babies less often, and are less affectionate toward their infants than are nondepressed moms (Field, 1995). These deficiencies in the mother's behavior with the infant even persist after the mother is no longer depressed, and they generalize beyond the mother-infant dyad; babies with depressed mothers show similar distressed or nonsynchronous behaviors when they interact with a nondepressed adult (Field et al., 1988). Such children are less likely to form a secure attachment with the mother, and are at higher risk for later behavior problems, including either heightened aggression or withdrawal (Cummings & Davies, 1994; Teti et al., 1995).

One common theme in all these findings is that a parent, regardless of depression or history of abuse, is more likely to abuse a child when her current life conditions are highly stressful. So abuse is more likely in families in which at least one parent is alcoholic (Famularo et al., 1986), in large families, in single-parent households, and in families living in poverty or in extremely crowded conditions (Garbarino & Sherman, 1980; Pianta, Egeland, & Erickson, 1989; Sack, Mason, & Higgins, 1985). Even these adverse conditions can be surmounted, though, if the parents have adequate emotional support, either from one another or from others outside the family.

Fear of Strangers and Separation Protest. Both these forms of distress are rare before 5 or 6 months, rise in frequency until about 12 to 16 months, and then decline. The research findings are not altogether consistent, but it looks as though fear of strangers normally appears first. Separation anxiety starts a bit later but continues to be visible for a longer period, a pattern I've indicated in Figure 6.1.

Such an increase in fear and anxiety has been observed in children from a number of different cultures, and in both home-reared and day-care-reared children in the United States, all of which makes it look as if some basic cognitive or other age-related developmental timetable underlies this pattern (Kagan, Kearsley, & Zelazo, 1978). But while the general timing of these two phenomena may be common to virtually all children, the intensity of the fearful reaction is not. Children differ widely in

Cultures and Contexts

Attachment in a Very Different Cultural System

Is the sequence of phases Bowlby and Ainsworth describe universal? Do all babies go through this same sequence, no matter what kind of family or culture they live in? Maybe yes, maybe no. Ainsworth herself observed the same basic three phases in forming a clear attachment among children in Uganda, although these children showed a more intense fear of strangers than is usually found in American samples. But among the Ganda, as in American and other Western families, the mother is the primary caregiver. What would we find in a culture in which the child's early care is much more communal?

Edward Tronick and his colleagues (Tronick, Morelli, & Ivey, 1992) have studied just such a culture, a pygmy group called the Efe, who forage in the forests of Zaire. They live in small groups of perhaps twenty individuals in camps, each consisting of several extended families, often brothers and their wives.

Infants in these communities are cared for communally in the early months and years of life. They are carried and held by all the adult women, and interact regularly with many different adults. If they have needs, they are tended by whichever adult or older child is nearby; they may even be nursed by women other than the mother, although they normally sleep with the mother.

Tronick and his colleagues report two things of particular interest about early attachment in this group. First, Efe infants seem to use virtually any adult or older child in their world as a safe base, which suggests that they may have no single central attachment. But at the same time, beginning at about 6 months, the Efe infants nonetheless seem to insist on being with their mother more and to prefer her over other women, although other women continue to help care for the child.

Thus, even in an extremely communal rearing arrangement, we can still see some sign of a central attachment, albeit perhaps less dominant. At the same time, it is clear, as Inge Bretherton says, that "attachment behavior is never purely instinctive, but is heavily overlain with cultural prescriptions" (1992b, p. 150).

how much fear they show toward strangers or toward novel situations. Some of this difference may reflect basic temperamental variations (Kagan, 1994), a subject I'll take up in a moment. Heightened fearfulness may also be a response to some upheaval or stress in the child's life, such as a recent move or a parent changing jobs. Whatever the origin of such variations in fearfulness, the pattern does eventually disappear in most toddlers, typically by the middle of the second year.

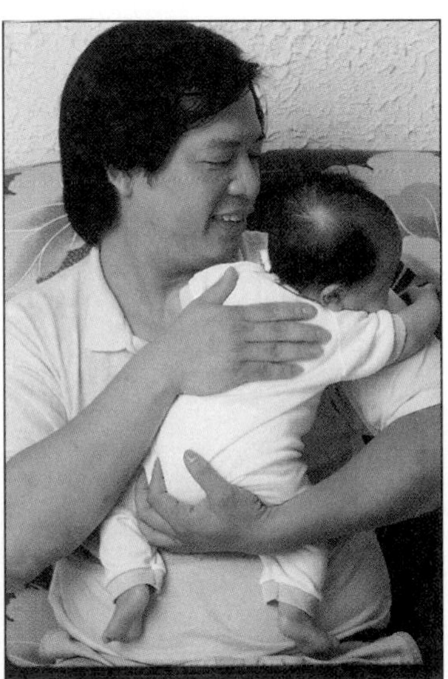
Dads like this one, who get involved with the day-to-day care of their babies, seem to reap the reward in a stronger attachment from their babies.

Attachments to Mothers and Fathers

I pointed out earlier that both fathers and mothers appear to form strong bonds to their infants, although their behavior with infants varies somewhat. But what about the child's half of this relationship? Are infants and children equally attached to their fathers and mothers?

In general, yes. From the age of 7 to 8 months, when strong attachments are first seen, infants prefer *either* the father or the mother to a stranger. And when both the father and the mother are available, an infant will smile at or approach either or both, *except* when he is frightened or under stress. When that happens, especially between 8 and 24 months of age, the child typically turns to the mother rather than the father (Lamb, 1981).

Logically enough, the strength of the baby's attachment to the father is linked to the amount of time the dad actually spends in caregiving (e.g., Ross et al., 1975). Quite possibly, if the father were the full-time caregiver, the infant would turn to Dad instead of to Mom when under stress, although we do not yet have any research to test that possibility.

Variations in the Quality of Infants' Attachments

Virtually all babies seem to go through the sequence I've described from preattachment to attachment. But the *quality* of the attachments they form differs from one infant to the next. In Bowlby's terminology, infants create different **internal working models** of their relationship with parents and key others. This internal working model of attachment relationships includes such elements as the child's confidence (or lack of it) that the attachment figure will be available or reliable, the child's expectation of rebuff or affection, and the child's sense of assurance that the other is really a safe base for exploration.

The internal model begins to be formed late in the child's first year of life and becomes increasingly elaborated and firm through the first four or five years. By age 5, most children have clear internal models of the mother (or other caregiver), a self model, and a model of relationships. Once formed, such models shape and explain experiences and affect memory and attention. We notice and remember experiences that fit our models, and miss or forget experiences that don't match. Using Piaget's language, we could say that a child more readily assimilates data that fit the model. More importantly, the model affects the child's behavior: The child tends to re-create, in each new relationship, the pattern with which he is familiar. Alan Sroufe gives a nice example:

> What is rejection to one child is benign to another. What is warmth to a second child is confusing or ambiguous to another. For example, a child approaches another and asks to play. Turned down, the child goes off and sulks in a corner. A second child receiving the same negative reaction skips on to another partner and successfully engages him in play. Their experiences of rejection are vastly different. Each receives confirmation of quite different inner working models. (1988, p. 23)

CRITICAL THINKING

If internal working models tend to persist and to affect later relationships, is this the same as saying that the first few years of life are a critical period for the creation of patterns of relationships? How else could we conceptualize it?

Secure and Insecure Attachments

All the theorists in this tradition share the assumption that the first attachment relationship is the most influential ingredient in the creation of the child's working model. Variations in that first attachment relationship are now almost universally described using Mary Ainsworth's category system (Ainsworth et al., 1978). She distinguishes between **secure attachment** and two types of **insecure attachment,** which she has assessed using a procedure called the **Strange Situation.**

The Strange Situation consists of a series of eight episodes in a laboratory setting, typically used when the child is between 12 and 18 months of age. The child is first with the mother, then with the mother and a stranger, alone with the stranger, completely alone for a few minutes, reunited with the mother, left alone again, and then reunited first with the stranger, and then the mother. Ainsworth suggested that children's reactions to this situation—particularly to the reunion episodes—could be classified into three types: *securely attached*, *insecure/avoidant*, and *insecure/ambivalent* (also sometimes called resistant). Mary Main (Main & Solomon, 1990) has suggested a fourth group, which she calls *insecure/disorganized/disoriented*. I have listed some of the characteristics of the different types in Table 6.1. As you read the descriptions, note that whether the child cries when he is separated from his mother is *not* a helpful indicator of the security of his attachment. Some securely attached infants cry then, others do not, as is true of insecurely attached infants as well. It is the entire pattern of the child's response to the Strange Situation that is critical, not any one response.

These attachment types have been observed in studies in many different countries, and in every country secure attachment is the most common pattern—as you can see from the information in the Cultures and Contexts box on page 136.

This category system and the theory that lies behind it have prompted an enormous amount of research and new theory, much of it fascinating and much of it with

Table 6.1 Categorization of Secure and Insecure Attachment in Ainsworth's Strange Situation

- **Securely Attached.** Child readily separates from the caregiver and easily becomes absorbed in exploration; when threatened or frightened, child actively seeks contact and is readily consoled, and does not avoid or resist contact if mother initiates it. When reunited with mother after absence, child greets her positively, or is easily soothed if upset. Clearly prefers mother to stranger.
- **Insecurely Attached: Detached/Avoidant.** Child avoids contact with mother, especially at reunion after an absence. Does not resist mother's efforts to make contact, but does not seek much contact. Shows no preference of mother over the stranger.
- **Insecurely Attached: Resistant/Ambivalent.** Child shows little exploration and is wary of the stranger. Greatly upset when separated from mother, but not reassured by mother's return or her efforts at comforting. Child both seeks and avoids contact at different times. May show anger toward mother at reunion, and resists both comfort from and contact with stranger.
- **Insecurely Attached: Disorganized/Disoriented.** Dazed behavior, confusion, or apprehension. Child may show contradictory behavior patterns simultaneously, such as moving toward mother while keeping gaze averted.

Source: Ainsworth et al., 1978; Carlson & Sroufe, 1995; Main & Solomon, 1990.

practical ramifications. So let me take some time to explore a few of the issues and implications.

Stability of Attachment Classification. One of the key questions is whether security of attachment is stable over time. Does a child who is securely or insecurely attached to his mother at 12 months still show the same quality of attachment at 24 or 36 months, or at school age? This is a particularly important question for those researchers and therapists who are concerned about the possible permanence of effects of early abuse, neglect, or other sources of insecure attachment. Can children recover from such early treatment? Conversely, is a child who is securely attached at 1 year of age forever buffered from the effects of later difficult life circumstances?

The answer, perhaps not surprisingly, is that both consistency and inconsistency occur, depending on the circumstances. When the child's family environment or life circumstances are reasonably consistent, the security or insecurity of attachment also seems to remain consistent, even over many years. For example, Claire Hamilton assessed current attachment security/insecurity in a small group of adolescents whose security had also been assessed when they were infants (Hamilton, 1995). Sixteen of the 18 adolescents who had been rated as insecurely attached at 12 months of age were still rated as insecurely attached at age 17, while 7 of the 11 teens who had been classed as securely attached as infants were still rated as securely attached at 17. Similarly, in a shorter-term study in Germany (Wartner et al., 1994), 82 percent of a group of youngsters from stable middle-class families were rated in the same category of attachment security at age 6 as they had been at age 1.

But when the child's circumstances change in some major way—such as when she starts going to day care or nursery school, or grandma comes to live with the family, or the parents divorce or move—the security of the child's attachment may change as well, either from secure to insecure, or the reverse. For example, Everett Waters and his colleagues (1995) followed one group of middle-class white children from age 1 to age 21, measuring their adult attachment using a new method called

Cultures and Contexts

Secure and Insecure Attachments in Different Cultures

Studies in a variety of countries support Mary Ainsworth's contention that some form of "secure base behavior" occurs in every child, in every culture (e.g., Posada et al., 1995). But we also have some evidence suggesting that secure attachments may be more likely in certain cultures than others. The most thorough analyses have come from a Dutch psychologist, Marinus van IJzendoorn, who has examined the results of 32 separate studies in eight different countries. You can see the percentage of babies classified in each category for each country in the table below (van IJzendoorn & Kroonenberg, 1988).

We need to be cautious about overinterpreting the information in this table, because in most cases we have only one or two studies from a given country, normally with quite small samples. The single study from China, for example, included only 36 babies. Still, the findings are thought provoking.

The most striking thing about these data is actually their consistency. In each of the eight countries, a secure attachment is the most common pattern, found in more than half of all babies studied; in six of the eight, an avoidant pattern is the more common of the two forms of insecure attachment. Only in Israel and Japan is this pattern significantly reversed. How can we explain such differences?

One possibility is that the Strange Situation is simply not an appropriate measure of attachment security in all cultures. For example, because Japanese babies are rarely separated from their mothers in the first year of life, being left totally alone in the midst of the Strange Situation may be far more stressful for them, which might result in more intense, inconsolable crying and hence a classification of ambivalent attachment. Yet when we look directly at the toddlers' actual behavior in the Strange Situation, we see few cultural differences in such things as proximity seeking or avoidance of Mom, all of which gives us more confidence that the Strange Situation is tapping similar processes among children in many cultures (Sagi, van IJzendoorn, & Koren-Karie, 1991).

It is also possible that the *meaning* of a "secure" or "avoidant" pattern is different in different cultures, even if the percentages of each category are similar. German researchers, for example, have suggested that an insecure-avoidant classification in their culture may reflect not indifference by mothers, but explicit training toward greater independence in the baby (Grossmann et al., 1985).

On the other hand, research in Israel (Sagi, 1990) shows that the Strange Situation attachment classification predicts the baby's later social skills in much the same way as is found in U.S. samples, which suggests that the classification system is valid in both cultures.

At the moment the most plausible hypothesis is that the same factors in mother-infant interaction contribute to secure and insecure attachments in all cultures, and that these patterns reflect similar internal models. But it will take more research like the Israeli work, in which the long-term outcomes of the various categories are studied, before we can be sure whether this is correct.

Cross-Cultural Comparisons of Secure and Insecure Attachments

Country	Number of Studies	Secure	Avoidant	Ambivalent
West Germany	3	56.6%	35.3%	8.1%
Great Britain	1	75.0%	22.2%	2.8%
Netherlands	4	67.3%	26.3%	6.4%
Sweden	1	74.5%	21.6%	3.9%
Israel	2	64.4%	6.8%	28.8%
Japan	2	67.7%	5.2%	25.0%
China	1	50.0%	25.0%	25.0%
United States	18	64.8%	21.1%	14.1%
Overall Average		65.0%	21.3%	13.7%

Source: Based on Table 1 of van IJzendoorn & Kroonenberg, 1988, pp. 150–151.

the Adult Attachment Interview. Those whose attachment classification changed over this long interval had nearly all experienced some major upheaval, such as the death of a parent, physical or sexual abuse, or a serious illness.

The very fact that a child's security can change from one time to the next does not refute the notion of attachment as an internal working model. Bowlby suggested that for the first two or three years, the particular pattern of attachment a child shows is in some sense a property of each specific *relationship*. For example, studies of toddlers' attachments to mothers and fathers show that about 30 percent of the time the child is securely attached to one parent and insecurely attached to the other, with both possible combinations equally represented (Fox, Kimmerly, & Schafer, 1991). It is the quality of each relationship that determines the child's security with that specific adult. If that relationship changes markedly, the security of the baby's attachment to that individual may change, too. But Bowlby argued that by age 4 or 5, the internal working model becomes more a property of the *child*, more generalized across relationships, and thus more resistant to change. At that point, the child tends to impose it upon new relationships, including relationships with teachers or peers.

Thus, a child may "recover" from an initially insecure attachment, or lose a secure one. But consistency over time is more typical, both because children's relationships tend to be reasonably stable for the first few years, and because once the internal model is clearly formed, it tends to perpetuate itself.

Origins of Secure and Insecure Attachments. Where do these differences come from? We know that insecurely attached infants are more likely to be found in poverty-level families, in families with a history of abuse, or in families in which the mother is diagnosed as seriously depressed (Cicchetti & Barnett, 1991; Spieker & Booth, 1988). But such a catalog doesn't tell us what is actually happening between parents and children that may foster secure or insecure attachments. Studies of actual parent-child interactions suggest that the crucial ingredients for a secure attachment are acceptance of the infant by the parents and *contingent responsiveness* from the parents toward the infant (Isabella, 1995; Pederson & Moran, 1995; Pederson et al., 1990; Seifer et al., 1996). Contingent responsiveness does not just mean that the parents love the baby or take care of the baby well, but rather that in their caregiving and other behavior toward the child they are *sensitive* to the child's own cues and respond appropriately. They smile when the baby smiles, talk to the baby when he vocalizes, pick him up when he cries, and so on (Ainsworth & Marvin, 1995).

Our certainty that this type of responsiveness is a key ingredient in a secure attachment has been greatly strengthened by an experimental demonstration of the effect by Dymphna van den Boom (1994). Van den Boom identified 100 lower-class Dutch mothers whose infants had all been rated as high in irritability shortly after birth. Half the mothers were then assigned randomly to participate in a set of three relatively brief training sessions aimed at helping them improve their responsiveness to their infant. The other half of the mothers received no such help. When the babies were 12 months old, van den Boom observed the mothers interacting with their infants at home, and also observed the baby and mother in the standard Strange Situation. The effects were quite clear: The trained mothers had indeed become more responsive to their babies, and their babies were more likely to be securely attached, as you can see from the results in Table 6.2—a difference that van den Boom later found persisted to at least age 18 months (van den Boom, 1995).

A low level of responsiveness thus appears to be an ingredient in any type of insecure attachment. But each of the several subvarieties of insecure attachment have additional distinct antecedents. For example, a disorganized/disoriented pattern seems especially likely when the child has been abused, and in families in which either parent had some unresolved trauma in his or her own childhood, such as either abuse or a parent's early death (Cassidy & Berlin, 1994; Main & Hesse, 1990). An

Table 6.2 The Effect of Mothers' Responsiveness Training on Infants' Attachment Security

	Attachment Classification at 12 Months	
	Number Secure	Number Insecure
Training	31	19
No training	11	39

Source: van den Boom, 1994, from Table 5, p. 1472.

ambivalent pattern is more common when the mother is inconsistently or unreliably available to the child. Mothers may show such unavailability or periodic neglect for a variety of reasons, but a common ingredient is depression in the mother—a phenomenon I talked about briefly in the Real World box on page 132 (Teti et al., 1995). When the mother rejects the infant or regularly (rather than intermittently) withdraws from contact with the infant, the infant is more likely to show an avoidant pattern of attachment, although avoidance also seems to occur when the mother is *overly* intrusive or overly stimulating of the infant (Isabella, 1995).

Long-Term Consequences of Secure and Insecure Attachment. Ainsworth's classification system has proven to be extremely helpful in predicting a remarkably wide range of other behaviors in children, both as toddlers and in later childhood and adolescence. Dozens of studies show that children rated as securely attached to their mothers in infancy are later more sociable, more positive in their behavior toward friends and siblings, less clinging and dependent on teachers, less aggressive and disruptive, more empathetic, and more emotionally mature in their approach to school and other nonhome settings (e.g., Carlson & Sroufe, 1995; Leve & Fagor, 1995).

At adolescence, those who were rated as securely attached in infancy or who are classed as secure on the basis of interviews in adolescence are also more socially skilled, have more intimate friendships, are more likely to be rated as leaders, and have higher self-esteem (Black & McCartney, 1995; Lieberman, Doyle, & Markiewicz, 1995; Ostoja et al., 1995). Those with insecure attachments—particularly those with avoidant attachments—not only have less positive and supportive friendships in adolescence, they are also more likely to become sexually active early and practice riskier sex (O'Beirne & Moore, 1995).

One particularly clear demonstration of some of these links comes from a longitudinal study by Alan Sroufe and his co-workers (Sroufe, Carlson, & Schulman, 1993; Urban et al., 1991), who have followed a group of youngsters from infancy through early adolescence. Among other things, they observed their subjects at a specially designed summer camp when the children were 11. The counselors rated each child on a range of characteristics, and observers noted how often children spent time together or with the counselors. Naturally, neither the counselors nor the observers knew what the children's initial attachment classification had been. The findings are clear: Those with histories of secure attachment in infancy were rated as more self-confident and as having more social competence. They complied more readily with counselor requests, expressed more positive emotions, and had a greater sense of their ability to accomplish things, a quality Sroufe calls *agency*. They created more friendships, especially with other securely attached youngsters, and engaged in more complex activities when playing in groups. In contrast, the majority of those with histories of insecure attachment showed some kind of deviant behavior pattern at age 11, such as

The Real World

Promoting Secure Attachments with Infant Carriers

In many parts of the world, particularly in the Third World, mothers carry their babies with them most of the time, using some kind of sling or wrap that keeps the child against the mother's body—as the Masai mother is doing in the photo. In the United States in recent years, variations on such a system have become a fairly common sight as well. Moms or dads are seen with a young infant snuggled against them, held by some kind of soft baby carrier. This not only allows moms or dads to have hands free to work or move while keeping the baby nearby, it also seems to foster a more secure attachment. Mary Ainsworth observed such a link in her studies in Uganda (Ainsworth, 1967). Now we have experimental data from the United States demonstrating the same effect.

Elizabeth Anisfeld and her colleagues (Anisfeld et al., 1990) gave each of a group of low-income mothers a gift right after the birth of her baby. Half were given a soft baby carrier, and the other half received a plastic infant seat. Both groups were encouraged to use the item daily, and most did use the item at least some of the time. When the infants were tested in the Strange Situation at 13 months, Anisfeld found that 87 percent of the babies carried in the soft carrier were securely attached, compared with only 38 percent of the children whose mothers received the infant seat. Because the mothers had been assigned randomly to these two conditions, we can be more confident of the causal link between the expanded physical contact fostered by the baby carrier and the child's secure attachment.

The application to everyday life seems straightforward: More physical contact between baby and parents is beneficial, and a baby carrier is a particularly good way to achieve such contact. It is also a pleasure!

isolation from peers, bizarre behavior, passivity, hyperactivity, or aggressiveness. Only a few of the originally securely attached children showed any of these patterns.

Collectively the findings point to potentially long-term consequences of attachment patterns or internal working models of relationships constructed in the first year of life. But fluidity and change also occur, and we need to know much more about the factors that tend to maintain, or alter, the earliest models.

The Development of the Sense of Self

During the same months that the baby is developing an attachment to Mom or Dad and creating an initial, primitive internal working model of attachment, she is also developing a parallel internal model of *self*.

Our thinking about infants' emerging sense of self has been strongly influenced by both Freud and Piaget, each of whom assumed that the baby began life with no sense of separateness. Freud emphasized what he called the *symbiotic* relationship between the mother and young infant in which the two are joined together as if they are one. He believed that the infant did not understand himself to be separate from the mother. Piaget emphasized that the infant's understanding of the basic concept of object permanence was a necessary precursor for the child's attaining *self-*

Across Development

Links to Adult Attachments

Researchers who study attachment have begun to ask a new set of questions about the long-term consequences of early attachment patterns: Do adults' internal models of attachment—presumably a product of their own early history—affect the way they behave with their children, and thus shape the child's emerging attachment patterns? That is, is there some kind of intergenerational transmission of secure, or insecure, attachment?

Mary Main and her colleagues have devised an interview that allows them to classify the security or insecurity of an adult's attachment to his or her own parents (Main & Hesse, 1990; Main, Kaplan, & Cassidy, 1985), so we are now able to explore such questions. In this interview, adults are asked about their childhood experiences and their current relationship with their parents. In one question, the adult is asked to choose five adjectives to describe her relationship with each parent, and to say why she chose each adjective. She is also asked whether she ever felt rejected in childhood, and how she feels about her parents currently. On the basis of the interview, the adult's internal working model of attachment is classified as being in one of three categories:

- *Secure/Autonomous/Balanced.* These individuals value attachment relations and see their early experiences as influential, but are objective in describing both good and bad qualities. The subject speaks coherently about her early experiences and has thought about what motivated her parents' behavior.
- *Dismissing or Detached.* The adult minimizes the importance or the effects of his early experience. He may idealize his parents, perhaps even denying the existence of any negative experiences. He emphasizes his own personal strengths.
- *Preoccupied or Enmeshed.* The adult often talks about inconsistent or role-reversed parenting. These individuals are still engrossed with their relationship with their parents, still actively struggling to please them or very angry at them. They are confused and ambivalent, but still engaged.

When these adult models are linked to the security of attachment displayed by the *children* of those adults, the expected pattern emerges strongly: Adults with secure models of attachment to their own parents are much more likely to have infants or toddlers with secure attachments. Those with dismissing models are more likely to have infants with avoidant attachments, while adults with preoccupied attachments are more likely to have infants with ambivalent attachment. Across 20 studies, the typical finding is that three-quarters of the mother-infant pairs share the same attachment category (van IJzendoorn, 1995). Diane Benoit (Benoit & Parker, 1994) has even found marked consistency across *three* generations: grandmothers, young mothers, and infants.

This is not a genetic transmission—at least not directly. Rather, the link across generations appears to lie in the mother's own behavior toward her child, which varies as a function of her own internal working model of attachment. Mothers who are themselves securely attached are more responsive and sensitive in their behavior toward their infants or young children (van IJzendoorn, 1995). For example, Judith Crowell and Shirley Feldman (1988) observed moms with their preschoolers in a free-play setting. In the middle of the play period, the mother left the child alone for several minutes and then returned. Mothers who were themselves classed as secure in their attachment model were more likely to prepare the child ahead of time for the impending separation, had less difficulty themselves with the separation, and were most physically responsive to the child during reunion. Preoccupied moms were themselves more anxious about separating from the child, and prepared the child less. Dismissing mothers also prepared the child very little, but left without difficulty and remained physically distant from their children after returning to the playroom.

Crowell and Feldman also noted that mothers with dismissing or preoccupied internal models interpreted the child's behavior very differently than did the secure moms.

> One mother observed her crying child through the observation window and said, "See, she isn't upset about being left." At reunion, she said to the child, "Why are you crying? I didn't leave." (1991, p. 604)

Thus, not only does the mother's own internal model affect her actual behavior, it affects the meaning she ascribes to the child's behavior, both of which will affect the child's developing model of attachment.

permanence—a sense of himself as a stable, continuing entity. Both of these aspects of early self-development reappear in current descriptions of the emergence of the sense of self. Michael Lewis, for example (1990, 1991), divides the process into two main steps or tasks.

The Subjective Self

Lewis argues that the child's first task is to figure out that he is separate from others and that this separate self endures over time and space. He calls this aspect of the self-concept the **subjective self,** or sometimes the *existential self* because the key awareness seems to be that "I exist." Lewis places the germs of this existential understanding in the first two or three months of life, when the baby grasps the basic distinction between self and everything else. In Lewis's view, the roots of this understanding lie in the myriad everyday interactions the baby has with the objects and people in his world that lead the baby to understand that he can have effects on things. When the child touches the mobile, it moves; when he cries, someone responds; when he smiles, his mother smiles back. By this process the baby separates out self from everything else and a sense of "I" begins to emerge.

But it is not until the baby has constructed a fairly complete understanding of object permanence, at about 8 to 12 months, that we can say that a subjective self has fully emerged. Just as he is figuring out that Mom and Dad continue to exist when they are out of sight, he is figuring out—at least in some preliminary way—that *he* exists separately and has some permanence.

The Objective Self

The second major step, according to Lewis, is for the toddler to come to understand that she is also an *object* in the world. Just as a ball has properties—roundness, the ability to roll, a certain feel in the hand—so the "self" also has qualities or properties, such as gender, size, a name, or qualities like shyness or boldness, coordination or clumsiness. It is this *self-awareness* that is the hallmark of the second phase of identity development. Lewis refers to this as the **objective self,** or sometimes the *categorical self,* because once the child achieves self-awareness the process of defining the self involves placing oneself in a whole series of categories.

It has not been easy to determine just when a child has developed the initial self-awareness that defines the beginning of the objective self. The most commonly used procedure involves a mirror. First the baby is placed in front of a mirror, just to see how she behaves. Most infants of about 9–12 months will look at their own images, make faces, or try to interact with the baby-in-the-mirror in some way. After allowing this free exploration for a time, the experimenter, while pretending to wipe the baby's face with a cloth, puts a spot of rouge on the baby's nose, and then again lets the baby look in the mirror. The crucial test of self-recognition, and thus of awareness of the self, is whether the baby reaches for the spot on her *own* nose, rather than the nose on the face in the mirror.

The result from one of Lewis's studies using this procedure are in Figure 6.2. As you can see, none of the 9- to 12-month-old children in this study touched their noses, but by 21 months, three-quarters of the children showed that level of self-recognition, a result confirmed in a variety of other research, including studies in Europe (e.g., Asendorpf, Warkentin, & Baudonnière, 1996). The figure also shows the rate at which children refer to themselves by name when they are shown a picture of themselves, which is another commonly used measure of self-awareness. You can see that this development occurs at almost exactly the same time as self-recognition in a mirror. Both are present by about the middle of the second year of life, a finding confirmed by other investigators (Bullock & Lütkenhaus, 1990).

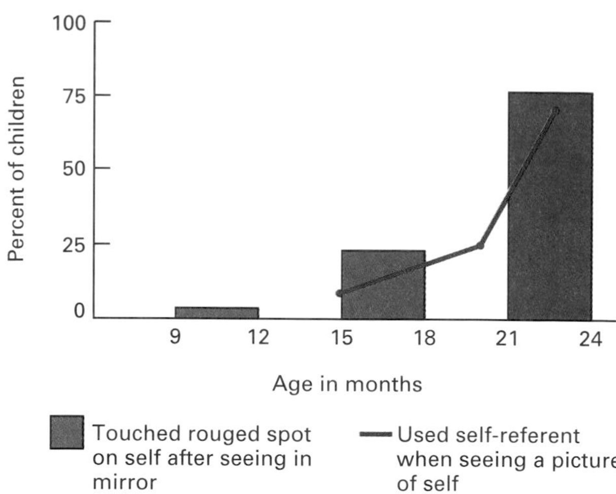

FIGURE 6.2 Mirror recognition and self-naming develop at almost exactly the same time. (*Source*: Lewis & Brooks, 1978, pp. 214–215.)

We can see signs of this new self-awareness in a whole range of other behaviors. It is only at this point in toddlerhood, for example, that toddlers begin to insist on doing things for themselves and show a newly proprietary attitude toward toys or other treasured objects ("Mine!"). Looked at this way, much of the legendary "terrible twos" can be understood as an outgrowth of self-awareness.

At 10 months, Rosa's emotional reaction here is best described as joy or delight rather than pride; she does not yet have a well-enough developed sense of self to feel pride.

The Emergence of Emotional Expression. These developmental shifts in the child's understanding of self are matched by parallel progressions in the baby's expression of emotions. You already know from Chapter 5 that babies are able to read others' emotions to at least some extent. They respond differently to their mothers' happy or sad expressions, and by 10 months show social referencing. During these same months of infancy, babies also develop an expanding repertoire of their own emotional expressions.

At birth, infants have different facial expressions for interest, pain, and disgust; an expression that conveys enjoyment develops very quickly. By the time the baby is 2 to 3 months old, adult observers can also distinguish expressions of anger and sadness, with expressions of fear appearing by 6 or 7 months (Izard et al., 1995; Izard & Harris, 1995). But it is only early in the second year of life, at about the same time that a child shows self-recognition in the mirror, that we see the emergence of such self-conscious emotional expressions as embarrassment, pride, or shame, all of which involve some aspect of self-evaluation (Lewis, Allesandri, & Sullivan, 1992; Lewis et al., 1989; Mascolo & Fischer, 1995).

Early Self-Definitions. Having achieved an initial self-awareness, the preschool child begins to define "who I am" by learning about her own qualities and her social roles. One of the earliest dimensions of such self-definition is gender. Two-year-olds can label themselves accurately as boys or girls, and their behavior begins to diverge in clear ways at about this age. For example, if you observe children while they play in a room stocked with a wide range of attractive toys, 2- and 3-year-old girls are more likely to play with dolls or at various housekeeping games, including sewing, stringing beads, or cooking. Boys the same age will more often choose to play with guns, toy trucks, fire engines, or carpentry tools (O'Brien, 1992). By age 3, children begin to show a preference for same-sex playmates and are much more sociable with playmates of the same sex (Maccoby, 1988, 1990; Maccoby & Jacklin, 1987)—a pattern that gets progressively stronger through the preschool and early elementary school years.

Toddlers also categorize themselves on other simple dichotomous dimensions, such as big versus little, smart versus dumb, good versus bad. At this early stage, they see themselves as one or the other, not both at different times.

In Bowlby's language, what seems to be happening here is that the child is creating an internal working model of self, just as he creates an internal model of relationships. He first learns that he exists separately and that he has effects on the world. Then he begins to understand that he is also an object in the world, with properties including size and gender. The internal model of self, or the self-scheme as it is often labeled, is not developed fully at this early age. But the toddler is already building up an image of himself, his qualities, and his abilities. Like the internal model of attachment, this self-model or self-scheme affects the choices the toddler makes—such as choosing to play with other children of the same gender—as well as influencing the way the toddler will interpret experiences. In this way the internal model is not only strengthened but tends to carry forward.

Individual Differences: Personality and Temperament

In developing both their self-scheme and their internal model of attachment, babies do not begin with a blank slate. Each baby starts life with certain built-in qualities, patterns of response, and styles of interacting. These built-in patterns affect the way others respond to each infant as well as shaping the way each baby is likely to understand or interpret her experiences.

Psychologists normally use the word **personality** to describe these differences in the way children and adults go about relating to the people and objects in the world around themselves. Like the concept of intelligence, the concept of personality is designed to describe *enduring individual differences* in behavior. Whether we are gregarious or shy, independent or dependent, confident or uncertain; whether we plunge into new things or hold back—all these (and many more) are usually thought of as elements of personality.

Personality differences appear to rest on a very basic *emotional substrate,* usually referred to as **temperament.** These core qualities or response patterns are visible in infancy and reflected in such things as typical activity level, irritability or emotionality, soothability, fearfulness, and sociability (Hartup & van Lieshout, 1995, p. 658). According to this way of thinking, temperament is "the matrix from which later child and adult personality develops" (Ahadi & Rothbart, 1994, p. 190).

This distinction between temperament and personality is a little like the difference between a genotype and a phenotype. The genotype sets the basic pattern but the eventual outcome is the result of that basic pattern affected by specific experience. Thus, temperament may represent the basic pattern; what we measure as personality later in childhood or adulthood reflects the basic pattern affected by myriad life experiences. I'll be talking about personality variations in later chapters. But here I want to focus on temperament, not only because it is thought to represent the initial substrate, most clearly visible in infancy, but because *all* the research on personal or style differences in infancy has been couched in the language of temperament. Psychologists simply don't talk about infant "personality." They talk about variations in infant temperament.

Dimensions of Temperament. Unfortunately, the psychologists who have studied infant temperament have not yet agreed on a basic set of temperament dimensions. One influential early theory, proposed by Thomas and Chess (1977), included a list of nine dimensions: activity level, rhythmicity, approach/withdrawal, adaptability to new experience, threshold of responsiveness, intensity of reaction, quality of mood

Table 6.3 Thomas and Chess's Typology of Temperament

- **The Easy Child.** The easy child is regular in biological functioning, with good sleeping and eating cycles; he is usually happy and adjusts easily to change or new experiences.
- **The Difficult Child.** The difficult child is less regular in body functioning and is slow to develop regular sleeping and eating cycles. He reacts vigorously and negatively to new things, is more irritable, and cries more. His cries also have a more "spoiled," grating sound than do the cries of "easy" babies (Boukydis & Burgess, 1982).
- **The Slow-to-Warm-Up Child.** The slow-to-warm-up infant shows few intense reactions, either positive or negative. To new experiences, he may show a kind of passive resistance, such as drooling out unwanted new foods rather than spitting them out or crying. Once he has adapted to something new, however, his reaction is usually fairly positive.

Source: Thomas & Chess, 1977

(positive or negative), distractibility, and persistence. Thomas and Chess further proposed that variations in these nine qualities tended to cluster into three types—which they called the *easy child*, the *difficult child*, and the *slow-to-warm-up child*—described in Table 6.3. The concept of "difficultness" has been especially influential in early research on infant temperament.

In contrast, Buss and Plomin (Buss, 1989; Buss & Plomin, 1984, 1986) have argued for three basic dimensions: activity level, emotionality, and sociability. The questionnaire they devised to measure these three qualities has been widely used by researchers studying infants, children, and adults—including some of the research described in the Research Report on page 146.

But neither of these two models has quite won the day. Temperament researchers are still struggling to define the key dimensions and have not reached a clear agreement. However, a few key dimensions are now appearing in the lists of dimensions described by many of the key researchers (Ahadi & Rothbart, 1994; Belsky, Hsieh, & Crnic, 1996; Kagan, 1994; Martin, Wisenbaker, & Huttunen, 1994), so agreement may be close at hand:

Of course we can't judge this toddler's temperament from one picture, but if this kind of behavior is typical, we would rate her as high in "negative emotionality."

- *Activity Level.* A tendency to move often and vigorously, rather than to remain passive or immobile.
- *Approach/Positive Emotionality.* A tendency to move toward rather than away from people, new things, or objects, usually accompanied by positive emotion. This is similar to what Buss and Plomin call sociability.
- *Inhibition.* The flip side of approach is a tendency to respond with fear or withdrawal to new people, new situations, new objects. This dimension has been intensely studied by Jerome Kagan and his colleagues (e.g., 1994; Kagan, Reznick, & Snidman, 1990), who see this as the precursor to what is called shyness in everyday language.
- *Negative Emotionality.* A tendency to respond with anger, fussing, loudness, or irritability; a low threshold of frustration. This appears to be what Thomas and Chess are tapping with their concept of the "difficult" child, and what Buss and Plomin call emotionality.
- *Effortful Control/Task Persistence.* An ability to stay focused, to manage attention and effort.

This is obviously not a final list; temperament researchers are still working their way toward common ground. But this set of traits or qualities is probably fairly close to the list we will all eventually agree on. Still, reaching even this degree of consensus leaves us with several huge questions to answer, including the issue of where these differences come from and whether they persist into childhood and adulthood.

The Inheritance of Temperament

Virtually every researcher who studies temperament shares the assumption that temperamental qualities are *inborn*, carried in the genes. The idea here is not so very different from the notion of "inborn biases" or "constraints" I talked about in earlier chapters, except that here we are talking about *individual* rather than shared behavioral dispositions.

Clear, strong evidence supports such an assertion (Goldsmith, Buss, & Lemery, 1995; Rose, 1995), both in studies of adult personality (discussed in the Research Report on page 146) and in studies of children's temperament. Studies of twins in many countries show that identical twins are quite a lot more alike in their temperament or personality than are fraternal twins (Rose, 1995). One fairly typical set of results comes from a study by Robert Plomin, Robert Emde, and their many collaborators (Emde et al., 1992; Plomin et al., 1993). They have studied 100 pairs of identical and 100 pairs of fraternal twins at both 14 and 20 months. At each age, the toddlers' temperaments were rated by their mothers using the Buss and Plomin categories. In addition, each child's level of behavioral inhibition was measured by observing how she reacted to a strange adult and strange toys in a special laboratory playroom. Did the child approach the novel toys quickly and eagerly, or did she hang back or seem fearful? Did she approach the strange adult, or did she remain close to Mom? You can see in Table 6.4 that the correlations between temperament scores on all four of these dimensions were consistently higher for identical than for fraternal twins, indicating a strong genetic effect.

Many (but not all) temperament theorists take the argument a step further and trace the basic differences in behavior to variations in underlying physiological patterns (e.g., Gunnar, 1994; Rothbart, Derryberry, & Posner, 1994). For example, Jerome Kagan has suggested that differences in behavioral inhibition are based on differing

Table 6.4 Similarity of Identical and Fraternal Twin Toddlers

	14-Month Correlations		20-Month Correlations	
Temperament Scale	**Identical**	**Fraternal**	**Identical**	**Fraternal**
Rated by Parents				
Emotionality	.35*	−.02	.51*	−.05
Activity	.50*	−.25	.59*	−.24
Sociability	.35*	.03	.51*	.11
Observed				
Behavioral inhibition	.57*	.26*	.45*	.17

* indicates that the correlation is statistically significant.

Source: Plomin et al., 1993, from Table 2, p. 1364.

Research Report

The Inheritance of Personality Patterns: Evidence from Adults

In the past decade, a number of methodologically careful new studies of adult twins have repeatedly demonstrated that identical twins are more like one another than are fraternal twins on measures of key personality traits, as well as on measures of temperament using Buss and Plomin's categories (Loehlin, 1992).

For example, a group of researchers including Nancy Pedersen and Robert Plomin (Bergeman et al., 1993; Pedersen et al., 1988) have taken advantage of the existence of an amazingly extensive and up-to-date twin registry in Sweden that includes 25,000 pairs of twins born between 1886 and 1958. From this set, they were able to identify 99 pairs of identical twins and 229 pairs of fraternal twins reared apart, and could then compare these with similar groups of twins reared together. On measures of emotionality, activity, and sociability, identical twins were more similar than were fraternal twins. The degree of similarity was less for identical twins reared apart, but these pairs were nonetheless significantly more alike than were fraternal twins reared apart.

A smaller but much more famous study in the United States is the Minnesota Twin Study (Bouchard, 1984; Lykken et al., 1992; Tellegen et al., 1988)—a study that has been the subject of a great many articles in the popular press. These researchers have been particularly interested in identical twins reared apart, frequently arranging for them to meet one another for the first time. On standard personality tests they find the now-familiar pattern: Identical twins are simply much more like one another than are fraternal twins, even when the identical twins did not grow up together. This was true on measures such as positive and negative emotionality (which may be similar to Buss and Plomin's dimension of emotionality), but also on less-obvious measures, such as a sense of "social potency" or a sense of well-being. Even a measure of "traditionalism"—an affinity for traditional values and a strong allegiance to established authority—shows slightly higher correlations among identical than among fraternal twins.

What has intrigued the popular press much more, though, are the less-precise but far more striking descriptions of the similarities in clothing preferences, interests, posture and body language, speed and tempo of talking, favorite jokes, and hobbies in pairs of identical twins reared apart:

> One male pair who had never previously met arrived in England sporting identical beards, haircuts, wire-rimmed glasses and shirts. . . . One pair had practically the same items in their toilet cases, including the same brand of cologne and a Swedish brand of toothpaste. . . . [One pair] had the same fears and phobias. Both were afraid of water and had adopted the same coping strategy: backing into the ocean up to their knees (Holden, 1987, p. 18).

It is difficult to imagine what sort of genetic process could account for similar preferences in hairstyles or for a particular brand of toothpaste. But we can't merely dismiss the results because they are hard to explain. At the very least, these findings certainly point to strong genetic components in many of the elements of personal style and emotional responsiveness that temperament researchers are trying to identify and track in children.

thresholds for arousal in those parts of the brain that control responses to uncertainty—the amygdala and the hypothalamus (1994; Kagan et al., 1990; Kagan, Snidman, & Arcus, 1993). Arousal of these parts of the brain leads to increases in muscle tension and heart rate. Shy or inhibited children are thought to have a *low* threshold for such a reaction. That is, they more readily become tense and alert in the presence of uncertainty, perhaps even interpreting a wider range of situations as uncertain. What we inherit, then, is not "shyness" or some equivalent, but a tendency for the brain to react in particular ways.

Consistency of Temperament over Time

Most of those who study temperament in infants also assume that such dispositions persist through childhood and into adulthood. No one is proposing that initial temperamental dispositions remain unchanged by experience—a point I'll come back to in a moment. But if temperament patterns create a kind of "bias" in the system toward particular behaviors, we ought to see a fair amount of stability of temperament over time. Such stability ought to show itself in the form of at least modest correlations between measures of a given temperamental dimension from one age to another.

Although the research evidence is somewhat mixed, we have growing evidence of consistency in temperamental ratings over rather long periods of infancy and childhood. For example, Australian researchers studying a group of 450 children found that mothers' reports of children's irritability, cooperation/manageability, inflexibility, rhythmicity, persistence, and tendency to approach (rather than avoid) contact were all quite consistent from infancy through age 8 (Pedlow et al., 1993). Similarly, in an American longitudinal study covering the years from age 1 to age 12, Diana Guerin and Allen Gottfried (1994a, 1994b) have found strong consistency in parent reports of their children's overall "difficultness" as well as approach versus withdrawal, positive versus negative mood, and activity level.

Kagan has also found considerable consistency over the same age range in his measure of inhibition, which is based on direct observation of the child's behavior rather than on the mother's ratings of the child's temperament. He reports that half of the children in his longitudinal study who had shown high levels of crying and motor activity in response to a novel situation when they were 4 months old were still classified as highly inhibited at age 8, while three-fourths of those rated as *un*inhibited at 4 months remained in that category eight years later (Kagan et al., 1993).

Thus, babies who approach the world around them with some eagerness and with a positive attitude continue to be more positive as young teenagers, while babies who show a high level of behavioral inhibition are quite likely to continue to show such "shyness" at later ages. Similarly, cranky, temperamentally difficult babies continue to show many of the same temperamental qualities ten years later.

Temperament and Environment

Clearly, however, temperament does not inevitably determine personality. The child's experiences play a crucial role as well.

A number of temperament/environment interactions tend to strengthen built-in qualities. For one thing, each of us (including young children) *chooses* our experiences, a process Sandra Scarr refers to as *niche-picking* (Scarr & McCartney, 1983). Highly sociable children seek out contact with others; children low on the activity dimension are more likely to choose sedentary activities like puzzles or board games than baseball. Similarly, temperament may affect the way in which a child *interprets* a given experience—a factor that helps to account for the fact that two children in the same family may experience the family pattern of interaction quite differently.

Imagine, for example, a family that moves often, such as a military family. If one child in this family has a strong built-in pattern of behavioral inhibition, the myriad changes and new experiences will trigger fear responses over and over. This child comes to anticipate each new move with dread and is likely to interpret his family life as highly stressful. A second child in the same family, with a more strongly approach-oriented temperament, finds the many moves stimulating and energizing, and is likely to think of his childhood in a much more positive light.

A third environmental factor that tends to reinforce built-in temperamental patterns is the tendency of parents (and others in the child's world) to respond quite differently to children with varying temperaments. The sociable child, who may smile often, is likely to elicit more smiles and more positive interactions with parents, simply because she has reinforced their behavior by her positive temperament. Buss and Plomin (1984) have proposed the general argument that children in the middle range on temperament dimensions typically adapt *to* their environment, while those children whose temperament is extreme—like extremely difficult children—force their environment to adapt to them. Parents of difficult children, for example, adapt to the children's negativity by punishing them more and providing them with less

Critical Thinking

The statement that difficult babies are more often punished is open to several possible interpretations. What are they?

support and stimulation than do parents of more adaptable children (Luster, Boger, & Hannan, 1993; Rutter, 1978).

But Buss and Plomin's proposal, while accurate, doesn't convey the additional complexities of the process. First of all, sensitive and responsive parents can moderate the more extreme forms of infant or child temperament. A particularly nice example comes from the work of Megan Gunnar and her colleagues (Gunnar, 1994), who have studied a group of highly inhibited toddlers who differed in the security of their attachment to their mothers. In a series of studies (Colton et al., 1992; Nachmias, 1993), they have found that *in*securely attached inhibited toddlers showed the usual physiological responses to challenging or novel situations. But *securely* attached temperamentally inhibited toddlers showed no such indications of physiological arousal in the face of novelty or challenge. Thus, the secure attachment appears to have modified a basic physiological/temperamental response. Over time, this may shift the child's personality pattern away from extreme inhibition or shyness.

Thus, while many forces within the environment tend to reinforce the child's basic temperament and thus create stability and consistency of temperament/personality over time, environmental forces can also push a child toward new patterns or aid a child in controlling extreme forms of basic physiological reactions.

Beyond the Family: The Effects of Day Care

In virtually every industrialized country in the world, in the past two decades, women have gone into the workforce in great numbers. In the United States the change has been particularly rapid and massive: In 1970, only 18 percent of married women with children under age 6 were in the labor force; by 1994, 61.7 percent of such women (and more than half of women with children under age 1) were working outside the home at least part time, a rate that appears to be higher than in any other country in the world (Cherlin, 1992b; U.S. Bureau of the Census, 1995). It is now typical for infants as well as school-age children to spend a significant amount of time being cared for by someone other than a parent. Similar changes have occurred in other countries to a lesser degree, but in the discussion to follow I'm going to be talking almost exclusively about day care as it exists in the United States—although the fundamental questions to be addressed would be similar in any country.

The key question for psychologists is what effect such nonparental care may have on infants and young children. As you can easily imagine, this is *not* a simple question to answer, for a whole host of reasons:

- An enormous variety of different care arrangements are all lumped under the general title of "day care."
- Children enter these care arrangements at different ages, and remain in them for varying lengths of time.
- Some children have the same alternate caregiver over many years; others shift often from one care setting to another.
- Day care varies hugely in quality.
- Families who place their children in day care are undoubtedly different in a whole host of ways from those who care for their children primarily at home. How can we be sure that effects attributed to day care are not the result of these other family differences instead?
- Mothers also differ in their attitudes toward the care arrangements they have made. Among mothers with children in day care are some who would far rather be at home taking care of their children and others who are happy to be working; similarly, among mothers who are at home full time are some who would rather be working and some who are delighted to be at home. Research tells us that children show more positive effects when the mother is satisfied with her situation, whether she is working or at home (e.g., DeMeis, Hock, & McBride, 1986; Greenberger & Goldberg, 1989), but in most

studies of the effects of day care, we have no information at all about the mother's satisfaction or dissatisfaction.

Most of the research we have to draw on does not really take these complexities into account. Researchers have frequently compared children "in day care" with those "reared at home," and assumed that any differences between the two groups were attributable to the day-care experience. Recent studies are often better, but we are still a long way from having clear or good answers to even the most basic questions about the impact of day care on children's development. Nonetheless, because the question is so critical, you need to be aware of what we know, as well as what we do not yet know.

Who Is Taking Care of the Children?

Let me begin at the descriptive level. Just who is taking care of all those children while their parents work? In some countries, such as France or Belgium, child care is organized and subsidized by the government and free to all parents. In the United States we have no such governmental system, and each family must make its own arrangements as best it can.

Figure 6.3 summarizes the solutions working parents have found. I'll bet these numbers surprise you. When most people think of "day care," they think of a day-care center or perhaps someone caring for a group of children in her own home (called **family day care**). But in fact, the most common pattern in the United States today—especially for infants and toddlers—is for a child to be cared for in his *own* home, by the father, by another relative, or by someone employed for that purpose. Family day care is a close second, while day-care centers are actually one of the least common arrangements (U.S. Bureau of the Census, 1995).

But even the wide variability in the type of care illustrated in the figure does not begin to convey the enormous variety of solutions parents arrive at in seeking alternative care for their children (Clarke-Stewart, Gruber, & Fitzgerald, 1994). For example, in one recent national survey, between a quarter and a third of employed mothers reported that their children were in some type of *combined* care, such as family day care some of the time and care by a relative part of the time (Folk & Yi, 1994).

High-quality care is possible in any of these settings, although they do differ from one another in systematic ways. For example, center care typically provides the most cognitive enrichment, while family day-care homes typically provide the least;

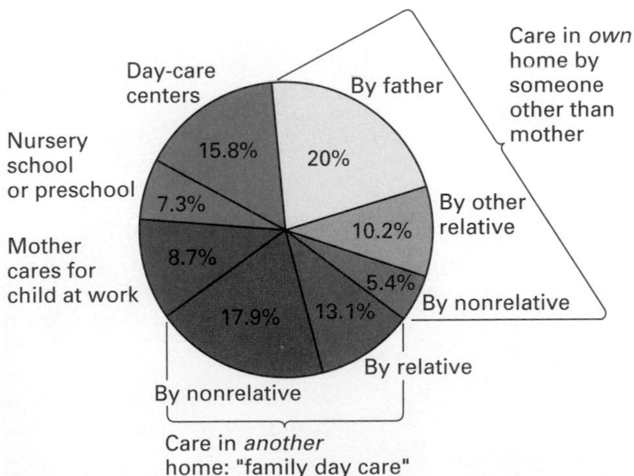

FIGURE 6.3 Child care arrangements for children 5 and under in the United States in 1991. The most common arrangement is care in the child's own home by someone other than the mother. (*Source*: U.S. Bureau of the Census, 1995, Table 615.)

both center care and family day care give the child an opportunity to play with same-age peers, while at-home care normally does not. Such variations make it very difficult to talk about global effects of day care. Furthermore, the majority of researchers have studied only children in center care, and we cannot be sure that these findings will generalize to children in family day care or with at-home care by someone other than a parent (let alone to some other culture altogether!). Still, let me tell you what the current evidence suggests.

Effects on Cognitive Development

We have a good deal of evidence that high-quality, cognitively enriched day care has beneficial effects on many children's overall cognitive development. This effect is particularly vivid for infants and children from poor families, who show significant and lasting gains in IQ and later school performance after attending highly enriched day care throughout infancy and early childhood (Campbell & Ramey, 1994; Ramey, 1993; Ramey & Campbell, 1987). Even middle-class children show some cognitive benefit when they are in good care (e.g., Peisner-Feinberg, 1995). For example, Alison Clarke-Stewart (Clarke-Stewart et al., 1994) found that regardless of the economic situation of the child's parents, the more cognitively enriched the child's daytime experience, the higher the child's later cognitive performance. Children who are read to, talked to, and explicitly taught show greater cognitive gains than do children who spend their days in less stimulating environments—and this was true whether they were cared for entirely at home or in some other care setting. Studies in Sweden confirm such a positive effect of high-quality day care: Among 13-year-olds, those who had spent the most time in Sweden's very good-quality day-care centers had better school performance throughout elementary school than did children who had been totally home-reared or those with only minimal day-care experience (Andersson, 1992).

But the picture is not entirely rosy. For example, several studies in the United States point to possible negative effects of day-care experience on cognitive development in some children, perhaps particularly middle-class children. For example, in one large study of over one thousand 3- and 4-year-olds, Baydar (Baydar and Brooks-Gunn, 1991) found that white children—but *not* black children—who began some kind of alternative care in the first year of life had the lowest vocabulary scores

The majority of infants in the United States now experience at least some nonparental care, some of them in group settings like this one.

later in preschool, whether they were from advantaged or poverty-level families. No negative effects were found for those who entered day care after age 1. In a similar large study of 5- and 6-year-olds (Caughy, DiPietro, & Strobino, 1994), researchers found that children from poor families who began day care before age 1 had *higher* reading and math scores at the start of school, while those from middle-class families who entered day care in infancy had *poorer* scores.

How can we reconcile these conflicting findings? One fairly straightforward possibility is that the crucial issue is the discrepancy between the level of stimulation the child would receive at home and the quality of the child care. When the particular day-care setting for a given child provides *more* enrichment than the child would have received at home, then we see some beneficial cognitive effects of day care attendance; when day care is less stimulating than full-time home care would have been for that child, then day care has negative effects. Most (but not all) of the results I've described are consistent with this hypothesis, but we don't yet have enough good large studies to be confident that this is the right way to conceptualize the process.

CRITICAL THINKING

Do you buy this argument? What other explanation(s) can you come up with?

Effects on Personality

When we look at the impact of day care on children's personality, we find yet another confusing story. A number of investigators have found that children in day care are more sociable, more popular, and have better peer-play skills than do those reared primarily at home. Andersson found this in his longitudinal study in Sweden (1989, 1992), as have researchers in the United States (Scarr & Eisenberg, 1993). But this is by no means the universal finding. Many other researchers find day-care attendance linked to subsequently heightened aggression with peers and lower compliance with teachers and parents. For example, in one very well designed large study, John Bates and his colleagues (Bates et al., 1994) found that kindergarten children who had spent the most time in day care—in infancy, toddlerhood, or preschool years—were more aggressive and less popular with their peers at school age than were children who had been reared entirely at home or who had spent fewer years in day care. Bates did not find that those who had entered day care early in infancy were worse off; the critical variable was the total length of time in nonhome care, not the timing of that care. These negative effects are fairly small. A child's level of aggressiveness in elementary school is influenced by a whole variety of things, including temperament and the effectiveness of the parents' disciplinary techniques. But the fact that day care is implicated in this equation certainly raises a cautionary note.

Confusing, isn't it? By some measures day-care children seem to be *more* socially competent; by other measures, they seem less so. One possible resolution is again to look at the relative quality of care at home or in day care. Consistent with this argument is a finding by Tiffany Field (1991) that the beneficial effects of day-care experience on the child's social competence holds only for *good-quality* care. Similarly, Alison Clarke-Stewart, in a study comparing various types of day care (Clarke-Stewart et al., 1994), finds that what is critical for the child's level of aggression is whether the child was spending his daytime hours in an organized, well-structured situation, or in a messy, unstimulating one—whether the unstructured and messy setting was at home or in day care. If this argument holds, then it is not day care per se that is at issue, but the child's actual experiences on a day-to-day basis. But even if this turns out to be the best explanation of the observed negative effects, it is hardly cause for cheering. The children in Bates's study, for example, were in ordinary, everyday types of day-care situations. And if such run-of-the-mill care is of such poor quality that it has even small negative effects on children's later behavior, we need to be concerned. Some psychologists, perhaps most notably Jay Belsky, take this pessimism a step further and argue that these hints of behavioral maladjustment among children who have been in day care may reflect more basic difficulties in the child, such as problems with attachment.

Effects on Children's Attachment to Parents

Can an infant or toddler develop a secure attachment to her mother or father if she is repeatedly separated from them? This question has been at the center of a hot debate. We know that the majority of infants develop secure attachments to their fathers, even though the father typically goes away every day to work, so it is clear that such regular separations do not *preclude* secure attachment. Still, perhaps separation from both parents on a daily basis adversely affects the security of the child's attachment.

We can narrow the window of uncertainty a good deal if we consider the child's age at the time she or he first enters day care. All parties to the current dispute agree that children who enter day care after the first year of life show *no* consistent loss of security of attachment to their parents. But the effects on infants who enter day care before 12 months of age are still hotly disputed.

Until about a decade ago, most psychologists reading the relevant research had concluded that there was no negative effect of infant day care. But then Belsky, in a series of papers and in testimony before a congressional committee, sounded an alarm (Belsky, 1985, 1992; Belsky & Rovine, 1988). Combining data from several studies, he concluded that there was a heightened risk of an insecure attachment among infants who enter day care before their first birthday. Controversy erupted. Since that time, a number of other researchers have analyzed the combined results from larger numbers of studies and confirmed Belsky's original conclusion.

Summing across the findings from 13 different studies involving 897 infants, Michael Lamb (Lamb, Sternberg, & Prodromidis, 1992) reports that 35 percent of infants who had experienced at least 5 hours per week of nonmaternal care were insecurely attached, compared to 29 percent of the infants with exclusively maternal care. He also found that the risk of an insecure attachment did *not* rise as the number of hours of the mother's employment increased. That is, babies whose mothers worked 40 hours a week or 20 hours a week were not more likely to be insecurely attached than those whose mothers worked 5 hours a week.

The difference between 35 and 29 percent is clearly not huge, although it is statistically significant. The present controversy swirls around how to interpret or explain this difference.

Belsky has his supporters. Alan Sroufe, one of the major figures in studies of early attachment, points out that we know that security of attachment is fostered both by the child's sense of the responsiveness of care, and by the opportunity for parent and child to fine-tune their interactive dance. Both of these may be disrupted by placing the child in day care, although clearly in the majority of cases, parents find ways to counteract such disruptions, because the majority of children in day care are nonetheless securely attached (Sroufe, 1990).

On the other side of the argument is ranged a group of researchers who either don't believe a serious problem exists, or argue that there are so many confounding variables that it is impossible to draw any clear conclusion (e.g., Roggman et al., 1994). For one thing, a significant problem of self-selection is involved in any comparison of day-care and parent-reared infants. Mothers who work are different in other ways from mothers who do not. More are single mothers, more prefer to work or find child care onerous. So how can we be sure that any heightened probability of insecure attachment is due to the day-care experience, and not to other factors?

Critical Thinking

What other differences might you expect to find between working and nonworking mothers of infants? How might those differences affect the likelihood that a child would be securely or insecurely attached?

For these and other reasons, Alison Clarke-Stewart (1990) concluded that "at the present time . . . it is not appropriate to interpret the difference, as Belsky appears to, as suggesting that these children are emotionally insecure" (p. 69). Others have concluded that there may indeed be a link between some aspect of day care and security of attachment, but that we simply don't yet know what the link might be (Lamb et al., 1992).

One can also argue that Belsky is asking the wrong question. For the vast majority of families, the question is not "Should I put my child in day care?" but rather

Table 6.5 Ideal Characteristics of a Day Care Setting

- *A low teacher/child ratio.* For children younger than 2, the ratio should be no higher than 1:4; for 2- to 3-year-olds, ratios between 1:4 and 1:10 appear to be okay.
- *A small group size.* The smaller the number of children cared for together—whether in one room in a day-care center or in a home—the better for the child. For infants, a maximum of 6 to 8 per group appears best; for 1- to 2-year-olds, between 6 and 12 per group; for older children, groups as large as 15 or 20 appear to be okay.
- *A clean, colorful space, adapted to child play.* Lots of expensive toys are not critical, but there must be a variety of activities that children will find engaging, organized in a way that encourages play.
- *A daily plan with at least some structure,* some specific teaching, some supervised activities. Too much regimentation is not ideal, but children are better off with *some* structure.
- *A caregiver who is positive, involved, and responsive to the child, not merely custodial.*
- *A caregiver with some knowledge of child development.*

Sources: Clarke-Stewart, 1992; Howes, Phillips & Whitebook, 1992; Scarr & Eisenberg, 1993.

"Given that I have to work to help support my family, how do I find good-quality, affordable care for my child?"

Everything I have already said underlines the importance of the quality of the child's care. Good-quality care is generally linked with positive or neutral outcomes, while inconsistent or poor-quality custodial care can be actively detrimental to the child. In Table 6.5 I've listed the characteristics of good-quality programs, a list that might serve as a starting point in your evaluation of alternatives if and when you face this choice with your own children. Beyond that, all I can tell you at this point is that the debate about the effects of day care on children is still very much ongoing.

Summary

1. It is important to distinguish between an affectional bond (an enduring tie to a uniquely viewed partner) and an attachment, which involves the element of security and a safe base.
2. An attachment is deduced from the existence of attachment behaviors.
3. For the parents to form a strong bond to the infant, what is most crucial is the learning and repetition of mutually reinforcing and interlocking attachment behaviors, and not immediate contact at birth.
4. A failure by parents to form a bond to the infant can occur either because the infant lacks the needed enticing skills, or the parent lacks skills. In either case the consequence may be neglect or abuse.
5. Fathers as well as mothers form strong bonds to their infants, but fathers show more physically playful behaviors with their children than do mothers.
6. Bowlby proposed that the child's attachment to the caregiver develops through a series of steps, beginning with rather indiscriminate aiming of attachment behaviors toward anyone within reach, through a focus on one or more figures, and finally "secure base behavior," beginning at about 6 months of age, which signals the presence of a clear attachment.
7. In the second half of the first year, babies also typically show fear of strangers and protest at separation from their favored person.
8. Children typically develop strong attachments to both father and mother.
9. Children differ in the security of their first attachments, and thus in the internal working model that they develop. The secure infant uses the parent as a safe base for exploration and can be readily consoled by the parent.
10. Studies in many countries suggest that a secure attachment is the most common pattern everywhere, but cultures differ in the frequency of different types of insecure attachment.

11. The security of the initial attachment is reasonably stable and is fostered by contingent responsiveness and acceptance by the parent.
12. Securely attached children appear to be more socially skillful, more curious and persistent in approaching new tasks, and more mature.
13. In the same months the infant is also beginning to develop a sense of self, including the awareness of a separate self and the understanding of self-permanence (which may be collectively called the subjective self) and awareness of herself as an object in the world (the objective self).
14. The subjective self develops in the first year of life; we see real self-awareness and the emergence of the objective self in the second year, when the toddler begins to place herself in specific categories, including gender.
15. Researchers studying individual differences in infants' style of responding have focused on the study of temperament, which is best thought of as the built-in patterns that form the emotional substrate of personality.
16. There remain sizable differences among temperament theorists on just how best to characterize the basic dimensions of temperament among children, but reasonable agreement exists on the following: activity level, approach/positive emotionality, inhibition, negative emotionality, and effortful control/task persistence.
17. Other formulations that remain influential are Thomas and Chess's easy, difficult, and slow-to-warm-up temperaments, and Buss and Plomin's three-way category system of emotionality, activity, and sociability.
18. There is strong evidence that temperamental differences have a genetic component, and that they are at least somewhat stable over infancy and childhood.
19. Temperament is not totally determined by heredity or ongoing physiological processes, although the child's built-in temperament does shape the child's interactions with the world and affect others' responses to the child.
20. The majority of children in the United States now spend some part of their infancy or preschool years in some form of nonparental care. The currently most common forms of such care are care in the child's own home by someone other than the mother, and family day care.
21. Day care often has positive effects on the cognitive development of less advantaged children, but it may have negative effects on advantaged children if the discrepancy between the home environment and the level of stimulation in day care is large.
22. The impact of day care on children's personality is unclear. Some studies show children with a history of day care to be more aggressive; others show them to be more socially skillful.
23. Numerous studies show a small difference in security of attachment between children in day care and those reared at home. Interpreting this difference has proven difficult and contentious.
24. The quality of care appears to be a highly significant element. Good-quality care involves small groups of children, in clean spaces designed for children's play, with responsive caregivers trained in child development.

Key Terms

affectional bond	family day care	objective self	Strange Situation
attachment	insecure attachment	personality	subjective self
attachment behaviors	internal working model	secure attachment	temperament

Suggested Readings

Booth, A. (Ed.) (1992). *Child care in the 1990s: Trends and consequences.* Hillsdale, NJ: Erlbaum

If you want to get the day-care debate from the horses' mouths, this is an excellent source. It includes a summary of the effects of day care on children by Alison Clarke-Stewart, along with a reply by Belsky and others. If nothing else, this book will persuade you that academic arguments are not always dry and dull; there is plenty of heat here!

Bowlby, J. (1988b). *A secure base.* New York: Basic Books.

This splendid small book, Bowlby's last before his death, includes a number of his most important early papers as well as new chapters that bring his theory up to date. See particularly Chapters 7 and 9.

Bretherton, I. (1992a). The origins of attachment theory: John Bowlby and Mary Ainsworth. *Developmental Psychology, 28,* 759–775.

A clear, current, thoughtful review of both Bowlby's and Ainsworth's ideas, including new data from anthropology and other cross-cultural analyses.

Kagan, J. (1994). *Galen's prophecy.* New York: Basic Books.

A detailed presentation, for the lay reader, of Kagan's ideas about the biological bases of temperament, particularly the aspect of temperament he calls behavioral inhibition.

Karen, R. (1994). *Becoming attached.* New York: Warner Books.

In this fine book, Robert Karen, who is both a psychologist and a journalist, tells the story of the early research on attachment, focusing on the central players in the scientific drama. Written for the lay reader, this book will tell you a lot about both attachment and the process of science.

Interlude 1

Summing Up Infant Development

Why Interludes?

This is the first of these "interludes," so let me say a word about their purpose. Because this book is organized chronologically, with a set of chapters describing each age period, you might think that you will automatically gain a sense of the basic characteristics of each era. But psychological research tends to focus on only one system at a time, such as attachment, perceptual skills, or language, and my descriptions tend to follow the same pattern. In these interludes, I want to try to put the baby (or child or adult) back together, to look at all the threads at once.

A second purpose is to examine, albeit briefly, some of the external influences on the basic processes. In particular, I want to be sure that we keep coming back to the effects of the larger social system in which the child/adult is developing.

In each interlude, then, I will ask the same three questions: What are the *basic characteristics* of development in that period? What are the *central processes* that seem to be shaping those developmental patterns? What other forces affect or *influence* those processes?

Basic Characteristics of Infancy

The table on page 156 summarizes the various developmental patterns I've described in the past three chapters. The rows in the table correspond to the various threads of development; what we need to do now is read up and down the table in addition to looking across the rows.

The overriding impression one gets of the newborn—despite her remarkable skills and capacities—is that she is very much on automatic pilot. There seem to be built-in rules or schemas that govern the way the infant looks, listens, explores the world, and relates to others.

One of the really remarkable things about these rules is how well designed they are to lead both the child and the caregivers into the "dance" of interaction and attachment. Think of an infant being breast-fed. The baby has the needed rooting, sucking, and swallowing reflexes to take in the milk; in this position, the mother's face is at just about the optimum distance from the baby's eyes for the infant's best focusing; the mother's facial features, particularly her eyes and mouth, are just the sort of visual stimuli that the baby is most likely to look at; the baby is particularly sensitive to the range of sounds of the human voice, particularly the upper register, so the higher-pitched, lilting voice most mothers use is easily heard by the infant. And during breast-feeding the release of a hormone called *cortisol* in the mother has the effect of relaxing her and making her more alert to the baby's signals. Both the adult and the infant are thus primed to interact with one another.

Sometime around 6 to 8 weeks there seems to be a change, with these automatic, reflexive responses giving way to behavior that looks more volitional.

The child now looks at objects differently, apparently trying to identify what an object is rather than merely where it is; at this age she also smiles more, may sleep through the night, and generally becomes a more responsive creature.

Because of these changes in the baby, and also because it takes most mothers six to eight weeks to recover physically from the delivery (and for the mother and father jointly to begin to adjust to the immense change in their routine), we also see big changes in mother-infant interaction patterns at this time. The need for routine caretaking continues, of course (ah, the joys of diapers!), but as the child stays awake for longer periods and smiles and makes eye contact more, exchanges between parent and child become more playful and smoother-paced.

Once this transition has occurred there seems to be a brief period of consolidation lasting perhaps 5 or 6 months. Of course change continues during this consolidation period. Neurological change, in particular, is rapid, with the motor and perceptual areas of the cortex continuing to develop. The child's perceptual skills also show major changes during these months, with depth perception, clear cross-modal transfer, and identification of patterns of sounds and

A Summary of the Threads of Infant Development

Aspect of Development	Age in Months 0	2	4	6	8	10	12	14	16	18	20	22
Physical development		Increase in cortical involvement	Reaches for objects	Sits	Stands; crawls		Walks alone			Dendritic and synaptic "pruning"		
Perceptual development	Many perceptual skills present at birth; visually discriminates Mom from stranger	Scans to identify object	Discriminates patterns of sounds and sights; cross-modal transfer	Discriminates facial expressions								
Cognitive development	Possibly imitation of some facial gestures		Beginning of object permanence; specific memories over 1 week		Object permanence quite well established; coordinates actions to solve problems			Deferred imitation; finds *new* solutions to problems			Beginning internal manipulation of symbols	
Language development		Coos		Babbles	Meaningful gestures; understands a few words		First word			Vocabulary of 3–50 words		
Social/personality development		Spontaneous social smiling	Early signs of attachment; self/other differentiation		Clear attachment	Stranger fear and anxiety			Plays with peers	Clear evidence of self-awareness		

sights all emerging. But despite all these changes, a kind of equilibrium nonetheless exists in this period—an equilibrium that is altered by a series of changes that occur between about 7 and 9 months, when (1) the baby forms a strong central attachment, followed a few months later by separation anxiety and fear of strangers; (2) the infant begins to move around independently (albeit very slowly and haltingly at first); (3) communication between infant and parents changes substantially, as the baby begins to use meaningful gestures and to comprehend individual words; and (4) object permanence is grasped at a new level, with the baby now understanding that objects and people can continue to exist even when they are out of sight. At the very least, these changes profoundly alter the parent-child interactive system, requiring

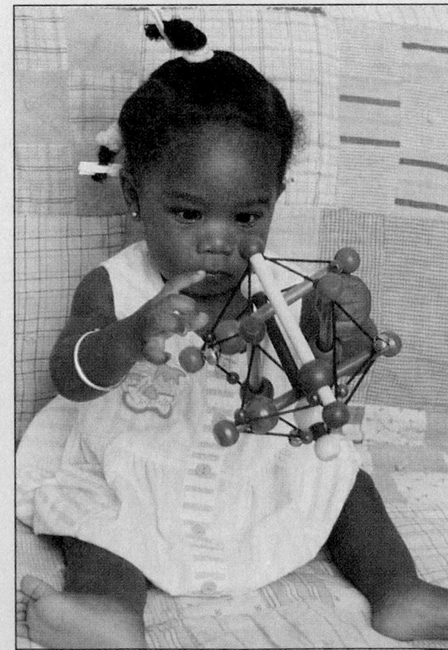

the establishment of a new equilibrium, a new consolidation, a new system.

The baby continues to build gradually on this set of new skills—learning a few spoken words, learning to walk, consolidating the basic attachment—until 18 or 20 months of age, at which point the child's language and cognitive development appear to take another major leap forward—a set of changes I'll be talking about in chapters yet to come.

Central Processes

So what is causing all these changes? Any short list of such causes is inevitably going to be a gross oversimplification. Still, undaunted, let me suggest four key processes that seem to me to be shaping the patterns shown in the summary table.

Physical Maturation. First and most obviously, the biological clock is ticking very loudly indeed during these early few months. Only at adolescence, and again in old age, do we see such an obvious maturational pattern at work. In infancy, it is the prepatterned growth of neural dendrites and synapses that appears to be the key. The shift in behavior we see at 2 months, for example, seems to be governed by just such built-in changes, as synapses in the cortex develop sufficiently to control behavior more fully.

Important as this built-in program is, it nonetheless *depends on* the presence of a minimum "expectable" environment (Greenough et al., 1987). The brain may be wired to create certain synapses, but the process has to be triggered by exposure to particular kinds of experience. Because such a minimum environment exists for virtually all infants, the perceptual, motor, and cognitive developments we see are virtually identical from one baby to the next. But that does not mean that the environment is unimportant.

The Child's Explorations. A second key process is the child's own exploration of the world around her. She is born *ready* to explore and to learn from her experience, but she still has to learn the specific connections between seeing and hearing, to tell the differences between Mom's face and someone else's, to pay attention to the sounds emphasized in the language she is hearing, to discover that her actions have consequences, and so on and on.

Clearly, physiological maturation and the child's own exploration are intimately linked in a kind of perpetual feedback loop. The rapid changes in the nervous system, bones, and muscles permit more and more exploration, which in turn affects the child's perceptual and cognitive skills, which in turn affects the architecture of the brain. For example, we now have a good deal of evidence that the ability to crawl—a skill that rests on a whole host of maturationally based physical changes—profoundly affects the baby's understanding of the world. Before the baby can move independently, he seems to locate objects only in relation to his own body; after he can crawl, he begins to locate objects with reference to fixed landmarks (Bertenthal, Campos, & Kermoian, 1994). This shift, in turn, probably contributes to the infant's growing understanding of himself as an object in space.

Attachment. A third key process seems obviously to be the relationship between the infant and the caregiver(s). I am convinced that Bowlby is right about the built-in *readiness* of all infants to create an attachment. But in this domain, the quality of the specific experience the child encounters seems to have a more formative effect than is true for other aspects of development. A wide range of environments are "good enough" to support physical, perceptual, and cognitive growth in these early months. But for the establishment of a secure central attachment, the acceptable range seems to be narrower.

Still, attachment does not develop along an independent track. Its emergence is linked both to maturational change and to the child's own exploration. For example, the child's understanding of object permanence may be a necessary precondition for the development of a basic attachment. As John Flavell puts it, "How ever could a child persistently yearn and search for a specific other person if the child were still cognitively incapable of mentally representing that person in the person's absence?" (1985, p. 135).

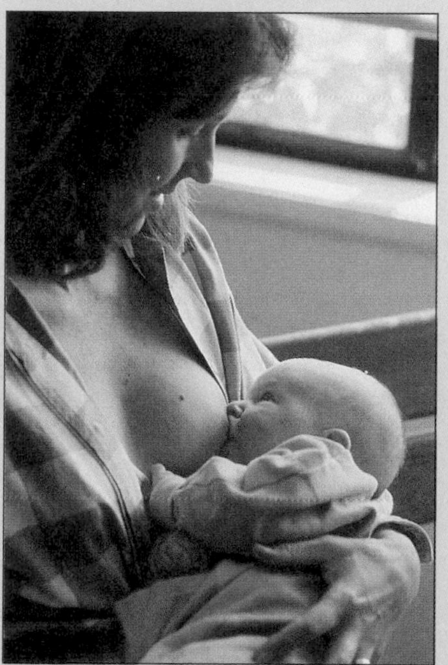

We might also turn this hypothesis on its head and argue that the process of establishing a clear attachment may cause, or at least affect, the child's cognitive development. For example, securely attached youngsters appear to persist longer in their play and develop the object concept more rapidly (e.g., Bates et al., 1982). Such a connection might exist because the securely attached child is simply more comfortable exploring the world around him from the safe base of his secure person. He thus has a richer and more varied set of experiences, which may stimulate more rapid cognitive (and neurological) development.

Internal Working Models. We could also think of attachment as being a subcategory of a broader process, namely the creation of internal working models. Seymour Epstein (1991) proposes that what the baby is doing is nothing less than beginning to create a "theory of reality." In Epstein's view, such a theory includes at least four elements:

- A belief about the degree to which the world is a place of pleasure or pain;
- A belief about the extent to which the world is meaningful—predictable, controllable, and just versus capricious, chaotic, or uncontrollable;
- A belief about whether people are desirable to relate to or threatening;
- A belief about the worthiness or unworthiness of the self.

The roots of this theory of reality, so Epstein and others argue (e.g., Bretherton, 1991), lie in the experiences of infancy, particularly the experiences with caregivers and other humans. Indeed, Epstein suggests that the beliefs created in infancy are likely to be the most basic and therefore the most durable and resistant to change at later ages. Not all psychologists would agree with Epstein about the broadness of the infant's "theory" of reality. But virtually all would now agree that the baby begins to create at least two significant internal models—one of the self and one of relationships with others (attachment). Of the two, the attachment model seems to be the most fully developed at 18 or 24 months; the model of the self undergoes many elaborations in the years that follow. It is only at about age 6 or 7 that the child seems to have a sense of his *global* worth—a characteristic we usually call self-esteem (Harter, 1987; 1990).

Influences on the Basic Processes

These four basic processes are quite robust (Masten et al., 1990). Nonetheless, infants can be deflected from the common trajectory by several kinds of influences.

Organic Damage. The most obvious potential influence is some kind of damage to the physical organism, either from genetic anomalies, inherited disease, or teratogenic effects in utero. But even here, we see an interaction between nature and nurture. Recall from Chapter 3 that the long-term consequences of such damage may be more or less severe, depending on the richness and supportiveness of the environment the baby grows up in.

Family Environment. The specific family environment in which the child is reared also affects the trajectory. On one end of the continuum we can see beneficial effects from an optimal environment that includes a variety of objects for the baby to investigate, at least some free opportunity to explore, and loving, responsive, and sensitive adults who talk to the infant often and respond to the infant's cues (Bradley et al., 1989). On the other end of the continuum, some environments can be so poor that they fall outside the "good enough" range, and thus fail to support the child's most basic development. Severe neglect or abuse would fall into this category, as might deep or lasting depression in a parent or persisting upheaval or stress in family life. In between these extremes are many variations in enrichment, responsiveness, and loving support, all of which seem to have at least some impact on the child's pattern of attachment, his motivation, the content of his self-concept, and his willingness to explore, as well as his specific knowledge. We see the consequences of such differences further down the developmental road, when the child is facing the challenging tasks of school and the demands of relating to other children.

Influences on the Family. I've made the point before, but let me make it again: The baby is embedded in the family, but the family is part of a larger economic, social, and cultural system, all of which can have both direct and indirect effects on the infant. Let me give you just two examples.

The most obvious point is that the parents' overall economic circumstances may have a very wide-ranging impact on the baby's life experience. Poor families are less able to provide a safe and secure environment. Their infants are more likely to be exposed to environmental toxins such as lead; less likely to have regular health care, including immunizations; and more likely to have nutritionally inadequate diets. If poor families place their infant in day care, they may be unable to afford good-quality care, and they are more likely to have to shift their baby from one care arrangement to another. Collectively, these are large differences. We do not see the effects immediately; babies reared in poverty-level families do not look much different from babies reared in more affluent circumstances. But the differences begin to be obvious at age 2 or 3 or 4.

Another example, one that cuts across all social classes, is the effect of the parents' own social support on the infant's development. Parents who have access to adequate emotional and physical support—from each other, or from friends and family—are able to respond to their children more warmly, more consistently, and with better control (Crnic et al., 1983; Taylor, Casten, & Flickinger, 1993). Their children, in turn, look better on a variety of measures (Melson, Ladd, & Hsu, 1993). For example, children whose parents have access to more assistance from friends complete more years of school than do children whose parents have less support of this type (Hofferth, Boisjoly, & Duncan, 1995).

The effect of social support on parents is particularly evident when they are experiencing stress of some kind, such as job loss, chronic poverty, teenage childbirth, a temperamentally difficult or handicapped infant, divorce, or even just fatigue. One example comes from a study by Susan Crockenberg (1981), who found that temperamentally irritable infants were likely to end up with an insecure attachment to their mothers only when the mother *lacked* adequate social support. When the mother felt that she had enough support, similarly irritable children were later securely attached.

This "buffering" effect of social support can even be demonstrated experimentally. Jacobson and Frye (1991) randomly assigned 46 poverty-level mothers either to a control group or to participate in an experimental support group that met both prenatally and for the first year after delivery. When Jacobson and Frye evaluated the infants' attachment at 14 months, they found that the babies whose moms had been in the support group were more securely attached than those whose moms had had no such special help.

One Last Word. One of the strongest impressions one gets from so much of the current research on babies is that they are far more capable than we had thought. They appear to be born with many more skills, many more templates for handling their experiences. But they are not 6-year-olds and we need to be careful not to get too carried away with our statements about how much the baby can do. As you will see in the next two chapters, the preschooler makes huge strides in every area.

Physical and Cognitive Development from 2 to 6

7

Watch an 18-month-old playing near his mom or dad and you'll notice that he doesn't go too far away. He may also glance at his parent regularly, as if checking to make sure the safe base is still there. Watch the same child a few years later and he is probably playing in a separate room, maybe with a chum. He may call out to Mom or Dad once in a while, asking them to come and see something he has created. Or he may wander past Mom or Dad periodically, but he is comfortable being further away. Changes like this may be less dramatic and obvious than the physical and cognitive changes in infancy, but they are nonetheless profound. In the years from 2 to 6, the child changes from being a dependent toddler, able to communicate only in very primitive ways, to being a remarkably competent, communicative, social creature, ready to begin school.

Physical Changes

In Chapter 4, I chronicled the many rapid changes in the infant's body. When we look at physical changes between ages 2 and 6, the story is much briefer. In the nervous system, new synapses are still formed as the child explores the world more fully, and some myelinization still continues. But the rate of change is vastly slower than what occurs in the early months of life.

Similarly, changes in height and weight are far slower in these toddler and preschool years than in infancy. Each year from about age 2 to adolescence, children add about 2 to 3 inches in height and about 6 pounds in weight.

Motor Development

These more gradual changes nonetheless combine to enable the child to make steady progress in motor development. The changes are not so dramatic as the beginning of walking, but they enable the toddler and preschooler to acquire skills that markedly increase his independence and exploratory ability.

Table 7.1, which parallels Table 4.3, shows the major locomotor, nonlocomotor, and manipulative skills that emerge in these preschool years. What is most striking are the impressive gains the child makes in large muscle skills. By age 5 or 6, children are running, jumping, hopping, galloping, climbing, and skipping. They can ride a trike; some can ride a two-wheeled bike. The degree of confidence with which the 5-year-old uses her body for these movements is impressive, particularly in contrast to the somewhat unsteady movements of the 18-month-old.

Small-muscle or "fine motor" abilities also improve in these preschool years, but not to the same level of confident skill. Three-year-olds can indeed pick up Cheerios, and by 5 they can thread beads on a string. But even at age 5 or 6, children are not highly skilled at such fine motor tasks as using a pencil or crayon, or cutting accu-

Table 7.1 Milestones of Motor Development from 2 to 6

Age	Locomotor Skills	Nonlocomotor Skills	Manipulative Skills
18–24 mo	Runs (20 mo); walks well (24 mo); climbs stairs with both feet on each step	Pushes and pulls boxes or wheeled toys; unscrews lid on a jar	Shows clear hand preference; stacks 4 to 6 blocks; turns pages one at a time; picks things up without overbalancing
2–3 yr	Runs easily; climbs up and down furniture unaided	Hauls and shoves big toys around obstacles	Picks up small objects (e.g., Cheerios); throws small ball forward while standing
3–4 yr	Walks upstairs one foot per step; skips on both feet; walks on tiptoe	Pedals and steers a tricycle; walks in any direction pulling a big toy	Catches large ball between outstretched arms; cuts paper with scissors; holds pencil between thumb and first two fingers
4–5 yr	Walks up *and* downstairs one foot per step; stands, runs, and walks well on tiptoe		Strikes ball with bat; kicks and catches ball; threads beads but not needle; grasps pencil maturely
5–6 yr	Skips on alternate feet; walks a thin line; slides, swings		Plays ball games quite well; threads needle and sews stitches

Sources: Connolly & Dalgliesh, 1989; The Diagram Group, 1977; Fagard & Jaquet, 1989; Mathew & Cook, 1990; Thomas, 1990a.

rately with scissors. When they use a crayon or a pencil, their whole body is still involved—the tongue moving and the whole arm and back involved in the writing or drawing motion. This is important for teachers to understand; it is the rare kindergartner who is really skilled at such fine motor tasks.

Health in the Preschool Years

Physicians distinguish between *acute* and *chronic* illnesses. The former are all those illnesses lasting less than 3 months, such as colds and flu. The latter are illnesses lasting longer than 3 months, such as diabetes, muscular dystrophy, or asthma.

Acute illnesses are common among young children, just as they are among infants. In the United States, the average preschooler has four to six brief bouts of sickness each year, most often colds or the flu (Parmelee, 1986). In contrast, only one in ten preschoolers has any kind of chronic illness. The most common types are allergies, asthma, chronic bronchitis, and diabetes (Starfield, 1991).

At every age, children who are experiencing high levels of stress or family upheaval are more likely to become ill. For example, a large nationwide study in the United States shows that children living in mother-only families have more asthma, more headaches, and a generally higher vulnerability to illnesses of many types than do those living with both biological parents (Dawson, 1991). Figure 7.1 shows one comparison from this study, using a "health vulnerability score" that is the sum of nine questions answered by parents about their child's health. You can see in the figure that the average score is only about 1.0 out of a possible 9, which implies that most children are quite healthy. But it is clear that children living in more stressful family structures have higher health vulnerability—and this is true even when such other differences between the families as race, income, and mother's level of education are factored out.

Another danger for children is accidents. In any given year, about a quarter of all children under 5 in the United States have at least one accident that requires some kind of medical attention, and accidents are the major cause of death in preschool and school-age children (Starfield, 1991; U.S. Bureau of the Census, 1995). At every age, accidents are more common among boys than among girls, presumably because of their more active and daring styles of play. The majority of accidents among kids in this age range occur at home—falls, cuts, accidental poisonings, and the like. Automobile accidents are the second leading source of injuries among preschoolers, although happily the rate of serious injury and death from auto accidents has been dropping dramatically in recent years because of new laws mandating the use of restraint devices for infants and toddlers traveling in cars (Christophersen, 1989).

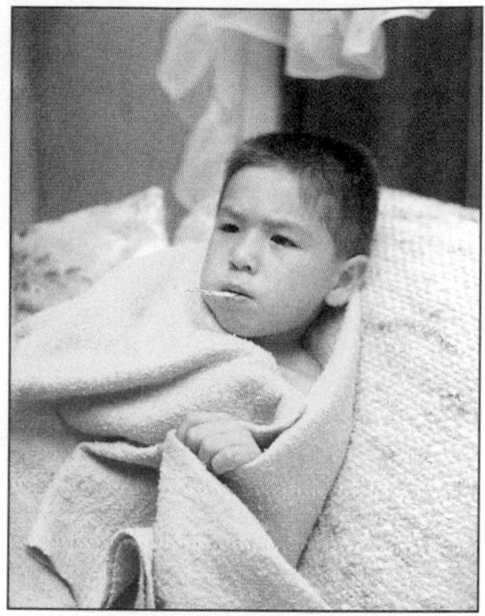

The average preschooler is sick like this, with an "acute" illness, about six times a year.

Critical Thinking

Children who are sick a lot early in life have a higher risk of having health problems in adolescence or adulthood. How many different explanations can you think of for such a link between childhood illness and adult health?

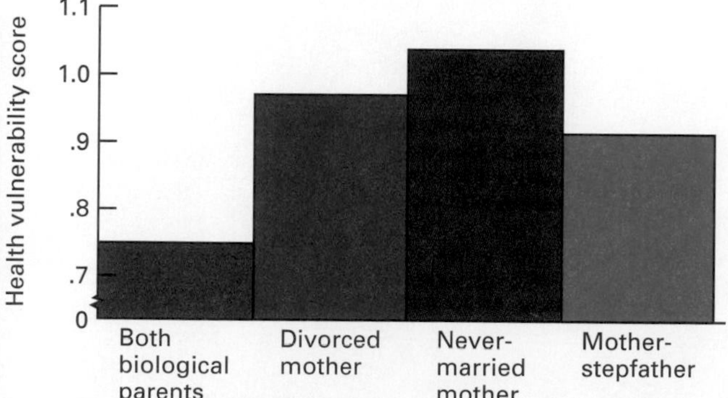

FIGURE 7.1 If we assume that single-parent and stepparent families are higher in stress for children (an assumption supported by research), then these results are yet another illustration of the link between higher stress and increased rates of illness. (*Source:* Dawson, 1991, from Table 3, p. 577.)

Talking in Sentences: The Next Steps in Language Development

When we left the infant in Chapter 5, he was just beginning to use a few individual words. This is no small accomplishment, but what happens to language in the following few years is even more remarkable. By age $2\frac{1}{2}$, the average child has a vocabulary of about 600 words; by age 5 or 6, that number has risen to roughly fifteen *thousand* words (Pinker, 1994). The toddler also moves with amazing rapidity from single words to simple and then complex sentences. By age 3, most children have acquired all the basic tools needed to form sentences and make conversation (Bloom, 1991).

First Sentences: 18 to 27 Months

The first two-word sentences usually appear between 18 and 24 months. This is not a random or independent event. Recent research, such as Fenson's large cross-sectional study (Fenson et al., 1994), suggests that sentences appear only when a child has reached a threshold vocabulary of around 100 to 200 words. So children with slower early vocabulary growth also begin to speak in sentences somewhat later.

The first sentences have several distinguishing features: They are *short*—generally two or three words—and they are *simple*. Nouns, verbs, and adjectives are usually included, but virtually all the purely grammatical markers (which linguists call **inflections**) are missing. At the beginning, for example, children learning English do not normally use the *s* for plurals or put the *ed* ending on verbs to make the past tense, nor do they use the *'s* of the possessive or auxiliary verbs like *am* or *do*.

It is also clear that even at this earliest stage children create sentences following rules—not adult rules, to be sure, but rules nonetheless. They focus on certain types of words, and put them together in particular orders. They also manage to convey a variety of different meanings with their simple sentences.

For example, young children frequently use a sentence made up of two nouns, such as *Mommy sock* or *sweater chair* (Bloom, 1973). We might conclude from this that a "two noun" form is a basic grammatical characteristic of early child language. But that misses the complexity. For instance, the child in Lois Bloom's study who said *Mommy sock* said it on two different occasions. The first time was when she picked up

Katherine, at 16 months, probably uses only a few words, but within a year she is likely to have a vocabulary of over 600 words and to be creating a variety of simple sentences. Here she is responding to a question from her mother: "Where are Daddy's teeth?"

her mother's sock and the second was when the mother put the child's own sock on the child's foot. In the first case, *Mommy sock* seems to mean Mommy's sock (a possessive relationship). But in the second instance the child seems to convey "Mommy is putting a sock on me," which is an *agent* (Mommy)–*object* (sock) relationship.

Grammar Explosion: 27 to 36 Months

Just as a vocabulary explosion follows an early, slow beginning, so a grammar explosion follows several months of simple sentences. Beginning sometime in the third year, most children rather quickly add many of the inflections and function words. Within a few months, they use plurals, past tenses, auxiliary verbs such as *is* or *does*, prepositions, and the like. They also begin to create negative sentences and to ask questions with the auxiliary verb in the correct order. You can get some feeling for the sound of the change from Table 7.2, which lists some of the sentences of a little boy named Daniel, recorded by David Ingram (1981). The left-hand column lists some of Daniel's sentences at about 21 months of age, when he was still using the simplest forms; the right-hand column lists some of his sentences only 2½ months later (age 23 to 24 months), when he had shifted into higher gear.

Adding Inflections. Daniel obviously did not add all the inflections at once. In the sample of his speech shown in the table's right-hand column, he uses only a few, such as the *s* for plural, although the beginning of a negative construction is apparent in "no book" and the beginning of a question form shows in "Where going?" Within each language community, children seem to add inflections and more complex word orders in fairly predictable sequences. In a classic early study, Roger Brown (1973) found that the earliest inflection among children learning English is most often the *ing* added onto a verb, such as in I *playing* or *doggie running*. Then come (in order) prepositions like *on* and *in*, the plural *s* on nouns, irregular past tenses (such as *broke* or *ran*), possessives, articles (*a* and *the* in English), the *s* that we add to third-person verbs such as *he wants*, regular past tenses like *played* and *wanted*, and the various forms of the auxiliary verb, as in I *am going*.

Table 7.2 **Examples of Daniel's Stage I and Stage II Sentences**

Early Simple Sentences: Age 21 Months	More Complex Sentences: Age 23 Months
A bottle	A little boat
Broke-it	Doggies here
Here bottle	Give you the book
Hi Daddy	It's a boy
Horse doggie	It's a robot
What that?	Little box there
Kitty cat	No book
Poor Daddy	Oh cars
That monkey	That flowers
Want bottle	Where going?

Source: Reprinted by permission of the publisher. D. Ingram, Early patterns of grammatical development, in R. E. Stark (Ed.), *Language behavior in infancy and early childhood,* Tables 6 and 7, pp. 344–345. Copyright © 1981 by Elsevier Science Publishing Co., Inc.

Questions and Negatives. We also hear predictable sequences in the child's developing use of questions and negatives. In each case, the child seems to go through periods when he creates types of sentences that he has not heard adults use, but that are consistent with the particular set of rules he is using. For example, in the development of questions there is a point at which the child gets a *wh* word (who, what, when, where, why) at the front end of a sentence, but doesn't yet have the auxiliary verb put in the right place, such as: *Why it is resting now?* Similarly, in the development of negatives, we hear a stage in which the *not* or *n't* or *no* is put in, but the auxiliary verb is omitted, as in I *not crying*, or *there no squirrels*.

Overregularization. Another intriguing phenomenon of this second phase of sentence construction is **overregularization** or overgeneralization. No language is perfectly regular; every language includes some irregularly conjugated verbs or unusual forms of plurals. What children this age do is to apply the basic rule to all these irregular instances, thus making the language more regular than it really is. In English, this is especially clear in children's creation of past tenses like *wented*, *blowed*, *sitted*, or in plurals like *teeths* or *blockses* (Fenson et al., 1994; Kuczaj, 1977, 1978). Stan Kuczaj pointed out that young children initially learn a small number of irregular past tenses and use them correctly for a short time. But then rather suddenly the child seems to discover the rule of adding *ed* and overgeneralizes this rule to all verbs. He then relearns the exceptions one at a time. Even among preschoolers this type of "error" is not hugely common (only about 2 to 3 percent of all past tenses in English according to one recent study [Marcus et al., 1992]). But these overregularizations stand out because they are so distinctive, and because they illustrate yet again that children create forms that they have not heard but that are logical within their current grammar.

Complex Sentences: 36 to 48 Months

After children have figured out the inflections and basic sentence forms like negation and questions, they soon begin to create remarkably complex sentences, using conjunctions like *and* or *but* to combine two ideas or using embedded clauses. Here are some examples from de Villiers and de Villiers from children aged 30 to 48 months old (1992, p. 379):

> I didn't catch it but Teddy did!
>
> I'm gonna sit on the one you're sitting on.
>
> Where did you say you put my doll?
>
> Those are punk rockers, aren't they?

When you remember that only about 18 months earlier the child had been saying sentences little more complex than S*ee doggie*, you can appreciate how far he has come in a short time.

The Development of Word Meaning

To understand language development, it is not enough to know how children learn to string words together to form sentences. We also have to understand how the words in those sentences come to have meaning. Linguists are still searching for good ways to describe (or explain) children's emerging word meaning. So far, several sets of questions have dominated the research.

Which Comes First, the Meaning or the Word? The most fundamental question is whether the child learns a word to describe a category or class he has *already* created

The Real World

Bilingual Children

What I've said so far about early language development describes what happens when a child learns a *single* language. But what about children who are exposed to two or more languages from the beginning? How confusing is this for a child? And how can parents ease the process? At least two important practical questions surround this issue of bilingualism:

- Should parents who speak different native languages try to expose their children to both, or will that only confuse the child and make any kind of language learning harder? What's the best way to do this?
- If a child arrives at school age without speaking the dominant language of schooling, what is the best way for the child to acquire that second language?

Learning Two Languages at the Same Time

Parents should have no fears about exposing their child to two or more languages from the very beginning. Such simultaneous exposure does seem to result in slightly slower early steps in word learning and sentence construction, and the child will initially "mix" words or grammar from the two languages in individual sentences (Genesee, 1993). But bilingual children catch up rapidly to their monolingual peers and by age 2 or 3 can switch readily from one language to the other.

The experts agree that the best way to help a child to learn two languages fluently is to speak both languages to the child from the beginning, *especially* if the two languages come at the child from different sources. For example, if Mom's native language is English and Dad's is Italian, Mom should speak only English to the infant/toddler and Dad should speak only Italian. If both parents speak both languages to the child, or mix them up in their own speech, this is a much more difficult situation for the child and language learning will be delayed (McLaughlin, 1984). It will also work if one language is always spoken at home and the other in a day-care center, or with playmates, or in some other outside situation.

Bilingual Education

For many children, the need to be bilingual does not begin in the home but only at school age. In the United States today, there are 2.5 million school-age children for whom English is not the primary language of the home (Hakuta & Garcia, 1989). Many of those children arrive at school with little or no facility in English. For educators, then, the question is, What is the best way to teach children a second language at the same time as the child is also being taught basic subject matter such as reading and mathematics? Should the child be immediately immersed in the new language? Should the child learn basic academic skills in his native language and only later learn English as a second language? Or is there some combination of the two that will work?

The research findings are messy. Still, one thread does run through it all: Neither full immersion nor English-as-a-second-language programs are as effective as truly bilingual programs in which the child is given at least some of her basic instruction in subject matter in her native language in the first year or two of school, but is also exposed to the second language in the same classroom (Padilla et al., 1991; Willig, 1985). After several years of such combined instruction, the child then makes a rapid transition to full use of the second language for all instruction. Interestingly, in her analysis of this research, Ann Willig has found that the ideal arrangement is very much like what works best at home with toddlers: If some subjects are always taught in one language and other subjects in the other language, children learn the second language most easily. But if each sentence is translated, children do not learn the new language as quickly or as well.

Note, though, that even such ideal bilingual education programs will not be effective for children who come to school without good spoken language in their native tongue. Learning to read, in any language, requires that the child have a fairly extensive awareness of the structure of language—a point I will explore in Chapter 9. Any child who lacks such awareness—because she has been exposed to relatively little language, or was not read to or talked to much in infancy and preschool years—will have difficulty learning to read, whether the instruction is given in the native language or in English.

through his manipulations of the world around him, or whether the existence of a word forces the child to create new cognitive categories. This may seem like a highly abstract argument, but it touches on the fundamental issue of the relationship between language and thought. Does the child learn to represent objects to himself *because* he now has language, or does language simply come along at about this point and make the representations easier?

Not surprisingly, the answer seems to be both (Clark, 1983; Cromer, 1991; Greenberg & Kuczaj, 1982). On the cognitive side of the argument are several pieces of evidence I described in Chapter 5, such as the fact that young babies are able to remember and imitate objects and actions over periods of time, long before they have language to assist them.

Further evidence of cognitive primacy comes from the study of the child's use of various prepositions like *in*, *between*, or *in front of*, each of which seems to be used spontaneously in language only after the child has understood the concept (Johnston, 1985).

The naming explosion may also rest on new cognitive understandings. Vygotsky noted many years ago (1962) that there seems to be a point somewhere in the child's second year when she "discovers" that objects have names and begins to ask for the names of objects all around her. In part, this new discovery seems to rest on another new cognitive ability, the ability to categorize things. In several studies, Alison Gopnik and Andrew Meltzoff (1987, 1992) have found that the naming explosion typically occurs just after, or at the same time as, children first show spontaneous categorization of mixed sets of objects, such as putting balls into one group and blocks into another. Having discovered "categories," the child may now rapidly learn the names for categories she already knows.

Extending the Class. But what kind of categories does the child create? Suppose your 2-year-old, on catching sight of the family tabby, says *See kitty*. No doubt you will be pleased that the child has the right word applied to the animal. But what does the word *kitty* mean to the child? Does he think it is a name only for that particular fuzzy beast? Or does he think it applies to all furry creatures, or all things with four legs, or things with pointed ears, or what?

One way to figure out the kind of class or category the child has created is to see what other creatures or things he also calls *kitty*. That is, we can ask how the class is *extended* in the child's language. If the child has a kitty category based on furriness, then many dogs and perhaps sheep would also be called kitty. Or perhaps the child uses the word *kitty* only for the family cat. This would imply a very narrow category indeed. The general question for researchers has been whether children tend to use words narrowly or broadly, overextending or underextending them.

Our current information tells us that underextension is most common at the earliest stages, particularly before the naming explosion (Harris, 1992), which suggests that most children initially think of words as belonging to only one thing, not as names for categories. Once the naming explosion starts, however, the child appears to grasp the idea that words go with categories, and overextension becomes more common. At that stage, we're more likely to hear the word *cat* applied to dogs or guinea pigs than we are to hear it used for just one animal (Clark, 1983). All children seem to show overextensions, but the particular classes the child creates are unique to each child. One child Eve Clark observed used the word *ball* to refer to toy balls, radishes, and stone spheres at park entrances, while another child used the word *ball* to refer to apples, grapes, eggs, squash, and a bell clapper (Clark, 1975).

Chances are this toddler has a word for *ball*, and chances are also good that he uses the word *ball* to refer to a variety of other round things, thus showing overextension.

Constraints on Word Learning. Another of the fundamental questions about word meanings, and the subject of hot debate among linguists in recent years, is just how a child figures out which part of some scene a word may refer to. The classic example: A child sees a brown dog running across the grass with a bone in its mouth. An adult points and says "doggie." From such an encounter the toddler is somehow supposed to figure out that *doggie* refers to the animal, and not to running, bone, dog-plus-bone, brownness, ears, grass, or any other combination of elements in the whole scene.

Many linguists have proposed that a child could cope with this monumentally complex task only if he operated with some built-in biases or *constraints* (e.g., Bald-

If Dad says "goose" while he and his toddler are looking at this scene, how does the boy know that "goose" means the animal, and not "white," or "dirt" or "honk, honk" or some other feature? In fact, in this case as in most instances, the child first *points* and then the father labels, which greatly simplifies the problem.

win, 1995; Golinkoff, Mervis, & Hirsh-Pasek, 1994; Markman, 1992; Waxman & Kosowski, 1990). For example, the child may have a built-in assumption that words refer to objects *or* events but not both, or an assumption that words refer to whole objects and not to their parts or attributes.

Another possible built-in constraint is the *principle of contrast*, which is the assumption that every word has a different meaning, so if a new word is used, it must refer to some different object or a different aspect of an object (Clark, 1990). For example, in a widely quoted early study, Carey and Bartlett (1978) interrupted a play session with 2- and 3-year-old children by pointing to two trays and saying, "Bring me the chromium tray, not the red one, the chromium one." These children already knew the word *red* but did not know the word *chromium*. Nonetheless, most of the children were able to follow the instruction by bringing the nonred tray. Furthermore, a week later about half of the children remembered that the word *chromium* referred to some color, and that the color was "not red." Thus, they learned the meaning by contrast.

Early proponents of constraints argued that the constraints are innate—built into the brain in some fashion. Another alternative is that the child learns the various principles over time. For example, Carolyn Mervis and Jacquelyn Bertrand (1994) have found that not all children between 16 and 20 months use the principle of contrast to learn the name of a new unknown object. In their sample, those children who did use this principle also had larger vocabularies and were more likely to be good at sorting objects into sets. Thus, the use of the principle of contrast may be a reflection of the child's general level of language or cognitive skill, rather than something that is built in to all children.

This whole dispute obviously brings us back to the broader nature/nurture argument. You've already seen from the research on early perceptual development that quite a lot seems to be built in at birth. To what extent may this also be true of language? Is a baby born already programmed in some fashion to acquire language? Or does the child construct language based on specific experience?

Explaining Language Development

Explaining how a child learns language has proven to be one of the most compelling, and one of the most difficult, challenges within developmental psychology. This may surprise you. I suspect that most of you just take for granted that a child learns to talk by listening to the language she hears. What is magical or complicated about that? Well, the more you think about it, the more amazing and mysterious it becomes. For one thing, as Steven Pinker (1987) points out, there is a veritable chasm between what the child hears as language input and the language the child must eventually speak. The input consists of some set of sentences spoken to the child, with intonation, stress, and timing. They are spoken in the presence of objects and events, and the words are given in a particular order. All that may be helpful, even essential. But what the child must acquire from such input is nothing less than a set of rules for *creating* sentences. And the rules are not directly given in the sentences she hears. How does the child accomplish this feat? Theories abound. Let me start on the nurture end of the theoretical continuum.

Imitation and Reinforcement. The earliest theories of language were based either on learning theory or on the commonsense idea that language is learned by imitation. Imitation obviously has to play some part; children imitate sentences they hear and they learn to speak with the accent of their parents. And those toddlers who most readily imitate an adult when the adult speaks a new word are also the ones who show the most rapid vocabulary growth in the first year or two of the language explosion (Masur, 1995). Still, imitation alone can't explain all language acquisition because it cannot account for the creative quality of the child's language. In particular, children consistently create types of sentences and forms of words that they have never heard—words like *goed* or *beated*.

Reinforcement theories such as Skinner's (1957) fare no better. Skinner argued that, in addition to the role of imitation, parents shape language through systematic reinforcements, gradually rewarding better and better approximations of adult speech. But in fact parents don't seem to do anything like this. Instead, parents are remarkably forgiving of all sorts of peculiar constructions (Brown & Hanlon, 1970; Hirsh-Pasek, Trieman, & Schneiderman, 1984); they reinforce children's sentences on the basis of whether the sentence is true rather than on whether it is grammatically correct. In addition, children learn many grammatical forms, such as plurals in English, with relatively few errors, so some process other than shaping has to be involved.

Newer Environmental Theories: Talking to the Child. Still, it seems obvious that what is said to the child has to play *some* role in the process. At the simplest level, we know that children whose parents talk to them often, read to them regularly, and use a wide range of words in their speech begin to talk sooner, develop larger vocabularies, and learn to read more readily when they reach school age (Hart & Risley, 1995; Huttenlocher, 1995). Furthermore, the children who are exposed to less (and less varied) language in their earliest years don't seem to catch up later in vocabulary. Instead, the gap continues to widen, all of which tells us that the richness and variety of the language a child hears has a significant long-term impact on at least this aspect of language learning.

Still, the child's learning of grammar might nonetheless require—or at least be assisted by—certain forms of speech to the child. In particular, we know that adults talk to children in a special kind of very simple language, originally called **motherese** by many linguists, now more scientifically described as **infant-directed speech.** This simple language is spoken in a higher-pitched voice and at a slower pace than is talk between adults. The sentences are short, with simple, concrete vocabulary, and they are grammatically simple. When speaking to children, parents also repeat a lot,

Research Report

The Importance of Reading to the Child

One intriguing piece of evidence showing the importance of the child's environment in early language learning comes from a series of studies by G. J. Whitehurst and his colleagues. In their first study (Whitehurst et al., 1988), they trained some parents to read picture books to their toddlers and to interact with them in a special way during the reading, using a style Whitehurst calls *dialogic* reading. Specifically, they were trained to use questions that could not be answered just by pointing. So a mother reading a story about Winnie the Pooh might say, "There's Eeyore. What's happening to him?" Or the parent might ask, pointing to some object shown in a book, "What's the name of that?" or ask a question about some character in a story, such as "Do you think the kitty will get into trouble?" Other parents were encouraged to read to the child, but were given no special instructions about how to read. After a month, the children in the experimental group showed a larger gain in vocabulary than did the children in the comparison group.

Whitehurst has now replicated this study in day-care centers for poor children in both Mexico and New York City (Valdez-Menchaca & Whitehurst, 1992; Whitehurst et al., 1994) and in a large number of Head Start classrooms (Whitehurst et al., 1995). In the Mexican study, one teacher in a day-care center was trained in dialogic reading. She then spent 10 minutes each day for 6 to 7 weeks reading with each of ten 2-year-olds. A comparison group of children in the same day-care center spent an equivalent amount of time with the same teacher each day, but were given arts and crafts instruction rather than reading. At the end of the intervention, the children who had been read to had higher vocabulary scores on a variety of standardized tests, and used more complex grammar when talking in a special test conversation with another adult.

In Whitehurst's U.S. day-care and Head Start studies, children were read to in this special way either by their teacher or by both their mother and the teacher, while control group children experienced normal interactions with day-care workers or teachers. In both studies, the children who had participated in dialogic reading gained in vocabulary significantly more than did the control group children, and the effect appears to last.

Similarly, Catherine Crain-Thoreson and Philip Dale (1995) found that they could significantly increase language skills in language-delayed children by teaching either parents or teachers to read to them in this special way.

The fact that we now have evidence of the same types of effects in two different cultures—with two different languages, with both teachers and parents, with both poor and middle-class children, and with language-delayed children—strengthens the argument that richer interactive language between adult and child is one important ingredient in fostering the child's language growth.

introducing minor variations ("Where is the ball? Can you see the ball? Where is the ball? There is the ball!"). They may also repeat the child's own sentences but in slightly longer, more grammatically correct forms—a pattern referred to as an *expansion* or a *recasting*.

Parents don't talk this way to children in order to teach them language. They do so with the hope that they will communicate better by using simpler language. But infant-directed speech may nonetheless be very useful, even necessary, for the child's language acquisition. We know, for example, that babies as young as a few days old can discriminate between motherese and adult-directed speech and that *they prefer to listen to motherese* (Cooper & Aslin, 1994; Pegg, Werker, & McLeod, 1992; Werker, Pegg, & McLeod, 1994). The quality of motherese that seems to be particularly attractive to babies is its higher pitch. Once the child's attention is drawn by this special tone, the very simplicity and repetitiveness of the adult's speech may help the child to pick out repeating grammatical forms.

Children's attention also seems to be drawn to recast sentences. For example, Farrar (1992) found that a 2-year-old was twice or three times as likely to imitate a correct grammatical form after he had heard his mother recast his own sentences than he was when the mother used that same correct grammatical form in her own normal conversation. Experimental studies confirm this effect of recastings. Children who are deliberately exposed to higher rates of specific types of recast sentences seem to learn those grammatical forms more quickly (Nelson, 1977).

Sounds good, doesn't it? But environmental theories of language acquisition nontheless have holes. For one thing, recasts are actually relatively rare in normal parent-toddler conversations. Yet virtually all children nevertheless acquire a complex grammar, which suggests that the kind of feedback provided by recastings is unlikely to be a major source of grammatical information for most children (Morgan, Bonamo, & Travis, 1995). And while motherese does seem to occur in the vast majority of cultures and contexts, it does not occur in *all*. For example, Pye (1986) could find no sign of motherese in one Mayan culture, and studies in the United States show it is greatly reduced among depressed mothers (Bettes, 1988). Children of these mothers nonetheless learn language. Thus, while motherese may be helpful, it cannot be *necessary* for language.

Innateness Theories. On the other side of the theoretical spectrum we have the innateness theorists, who argue that much of what the child needs for learning language is built into the organism. Early innateness theorists like Noam Chomsky (1965, 1975, 1986, 1988) were especially struck by two phenomena: the extreme complexity of the task the child must accomplish and the apparent similarities in the steps and stages of children's early language. Newer cross-language comparisons now make it clear that more variability exists than first appeared—a set of findings I've described in the Cultures and Contexts box on page 171. Nonetheless, innateness theories are alive and well and increasingly accepted.

One particularly influential innateness theorist is Dan Slobin (1985a, 1985b), who assumes that every child is born with a basic language-making capacity made up of a set of fundamental *operating principles*. Just as the newborn infant seems to come programmed with "rules to look by," so Slobin is arguing that infants and children are programmed with "rules to listen by."

You've already encountered a good deal of evidence in Chapter 5 that is consistent with this proposal. We know that from earliest infancy, babies focus on individual sounds and on syllables in the stream of sounds they hear, that they pay attention to sound rhythm, and that they prefer speech of a particular pattern, namely motherese. Babies also seem to be preprogrammed to pay attention to the beginnings and endings of strings of sounds, and to stressed sounds (Morgan, 1994). Together, these operating principles would help to explain some of the features of children's early grammars. In English, for example, the stressed words in a sentence are normally the verb and the noun—precisely the words that English-speaking children use in their earliest sentences. In Turkish, on the other hand, prefixes are stressed, and Turkish-speaking children learn prefixes very early. Both these patterns make sense if we assume that what is built in is not "verbness" or "nounness" or "prefixness" but "pay attention to stressed sounds."

The fact that this innateness model is consistent with the growing information about apparently built-in perceptual skills and processing biases is certainly a strong argument in its favor. But other compelling theoretical alternatives have also been proposed. In particular, some theorists argue that what is important is not the built-in biases, but the child's *construction* of language as part of the broader process of cognitive development. In this view, the child is a "little linguist," applying her emerging cognitive understanding to the problem of language, searching for regularities and patterns.

Constructivist Theories of Language. Melissa Bowerman (1985) is one proponent of this view. She puts the proposition this way: "When language starts to come in, it does not introduce new meanings to the child. Rather, it is used to express only those meanings the child has already formulated independently of language" (1985, p. 372). In a similar vein, Lois Bloom suggests that "words a child hears from others

Cultures and Contexts

Universals and Variations in Early Language

In the early years of research on children's language development, linguists and psychologists were strongly impressed by the apparent similarities across languages in children's early language. You've already seen some of the evidence that supports this impression in an earlier Cultures and Contexts box (p. 123), illustrating large similarities in early vocabularies. Studies in a wide variety of language communities, including Turkish, Serbo-Croatian, Hungarian, Hebrew, Japanese, a New Guinean language called Kaluli, German, and Italian have revealed other important similarities in early language:

- The prelinguistic phase seems to be identical in all language communities. All babies coo, then babble; all babies understand language before they can speak it; babies in all cultures begin to use their first words at about 12 months.
- In all language communities studied so far, a one-word phase precedes the two-word phase, with the latter beginning at about 18 months.
- In all languages studied so far, prepositions describing locations are added in essentially the same order. Words for *in, on, under,* and *beside* are learned first. Then the child learns the words for *front* and *back* (Slobin, 1985a).
- Children seem to pay more attention to the ends of words than the beginnings, so they learn suffixes before they learn prefixes.

At the same time, cross-linguistic comparisons show that children's beginning sentences are not nearly so similar as the early innateness theorists had supposed. For example:

- The specific word order that a child uses in early sentences is not the same for all children in all languages. In some languages a noun/verb sequence is fairly common, in others a verb/noun sequence may be heard.
- Particular inflections are learned in highly varying orders from one language to another. Japanese children, for example, begin very early to use a special kind of marker, called a *pragmatic* marker, that tells something about the feeling or the context. For instance, in Japanese, the word *yo* is used at the end of a sentence when the speaker is experiencing some resistance from the listener; the word *ne* is used when the speaker expects approval or agreement. Japanese children begin to use these markers very early, much earlier than other inflections appear in most languages.
- Most strikingly, in some languages there seems to be no simple two-word sentence stage in which the sentences contain no inflections. Children learning Turkish, for example, use essentially the full set of noun and verb inflections by age 2 and never go through a stage of using uninflected words. Their language is simple but it is rarely ungrammatical from the adult's point of view (Aksu-Koc & Slobin, 1985).

Obviously any theory of language acquisition must account for both the common ground and the wide variations from one language to the next.

will be learned if they connect with what the child is thinking and feeling" (1993, p. 247).

If this is true, then we should observe clear links between achievements in language development and the child's broader cognitive development. And, in fact, we do. For example, symbolic play, such as drinking from an empty cup, and imitation of sounds and gestures both appear at about the same time as the child's first words, suggesting some broad "symbolic" understanding that is reflected in a number of behaviors. In children whose language is significantly delayed, both symbolic play and imitation are normally delayed, too (Bates et al., 1987; Ungerer & Sigman, 1984).

A second example occurs later: At about the time when two-word sentences appear we can also see children begin to combine several gestures into a sequence in their pretend play, such as pouring imaginary liquid, drinking, then wiping the mouth. Those children who are the first to show this sequencing in their play are also the first to show two- or three-word sentences in their speech (e.g., McCune, 1995; Shore, 1986).

These apparent linkages between language and cognition are impressive, but an interesting bit of counterevidence comes from recent studies of children with Williams syndrome, a genetic disorder linked to mental retardation. Williams syndrome children and adults, like those with Down syndrome, have general deficiencies in most aspects of cognitive functioning. But unlike Down syndrome children, Williams syndrome children develop excellent language skills—large vocabularies and complex grammar. Their language is delayed in the early years, just as is the language of Down syndrome children, but their eventual language skill—both comprehension and production—is close to normal (Mervis et al., 1995; Pober, 1996). In these children, then, we see no linkage between overall cognitive development and language development, a result that obviously poses problems for Bowerman's model.

My own view is that at this stage we should not choose between Slobin's and Bowerman's approaches. Both may be true. The child may begin with built-in operating principles that aim the child's attention at crucial features of the language input. The child then processes that information according to her initial (perhaps built-in) strategies or schemes. But then she modifies those strategies or rules as she receives new information, such as by deducing some of the constraints about word meanings. The result is a series of rules for understanding and creating language. The strong similarities we see among children in their early language constructions come about both because all children share the same initial processing rules and because most children are exposed to very similar input from the people around them. But because the input is not identical, because languages differ, language development follows less and less common pathways as the child progresses.

As these brief descriptions of theory make clear, linguists and psychologists who have studied language have made progress. But we have not yet cracked the code. The fact that children learn complex and varied use of their native tongue within a few years remains both miraculous and largely mysterious.

The broader changes in the child's cognitive skills over the same years seem less mysterious, but we continue to learn more about the remarkable cognitive accomplishments of the preschool child, as well as the limitations on her thinking.

Changes in Thinking

Let me begin, as I did in Chapter 5, with a look at Piaget's view of the cognitive changes during these years, because his thinking has formed the framework of so much of our research on this age period.

Piaget's View of the Preoperational Period

According to Piaget, at about age 2 the child begins to use *symbols*—images or words or actions that *stand for* something else. Children this age begin to pretend in their play, for example (a development I've talked about in the Real World box on page 173). At age 2 or 3 or 4 a broom may become a horsie, or a block may become a train. We can also see such symbol use in the emergence of language or in the preschooler's primitive ability to understand scale models or simple maps (DeLoache, 1995). And we see the child's improving ability to manipulate these symbols internally in such things as her improving memory, or in her ability to search more systematically for lost or hidden objects.

Beyond the accomplishment of symbol use, Piaget focused mostly on all the things the preschool-age child still *cannot* do, which gives an oddly negative tone to his description of this period. Even the term he used to describe this stage conveys some of this tone: It is *pre*operational.

For example, Piaget described the preoperational child as one who looks at things entirely from her own perspective or frame of reference, a characteristic Piaget

The Real World

Young Children's Play

If you watch young children during their unstructured time you'll see them building towers out of blocks, talking to or feeding their dolls, making "tea" with the tea set, racing toy trucks across the floor, and dressing up in grown-up clothes. They are, in a word, *playing.* This is not trivial or empty activity; it is the stuff of which much of cognitive development seems to be built.

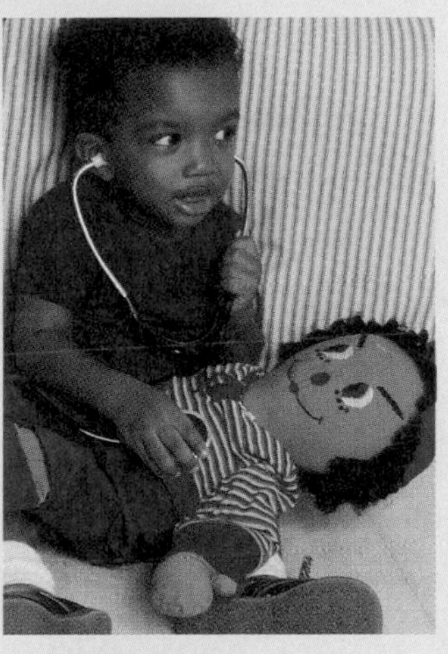

Early pretend play

Constructive play

The form of this play changes in very obvious ways during the years from 1 to 6, following a sequence that matches Piaget's stages rather well (Rubin, Fein, & Vandenberg, 1983):

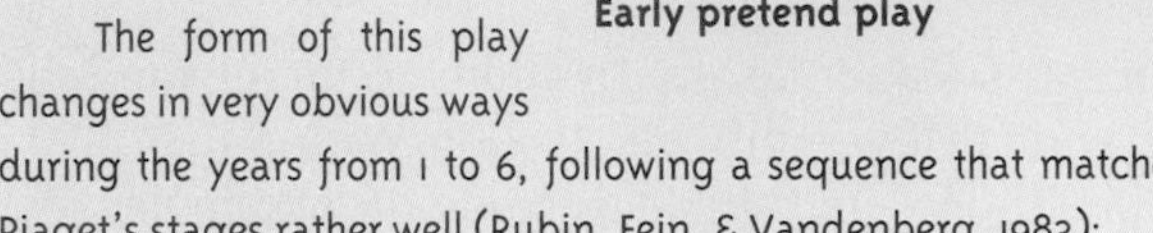

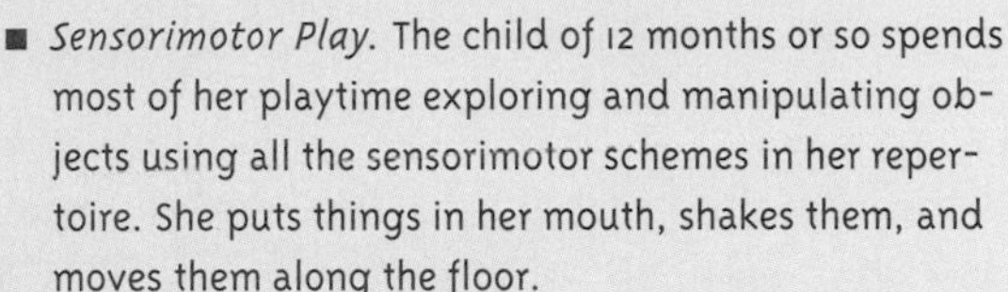

- *Sensorimotor Play.* The child of 12 months or so spends most of her playtime exploring and manipulating objects using all the sensorimotor schemes in her repertoire. She puts things in her mouth, shakes them, and moves them along the floor.
- *Constructive Play.* Such exploratory play with objects does continue past 12 months, especially with some totally new object, but by age 2 or so children also begin to use objects to build or construct things—creating a block tower, putting together a puzzle, making something out of clay or with Tinkertoys—a form of play that makes up nearly half the play of children aged 3 to 6.
- *First Pretend Play.* Pretend play also begins at about the same time. The first sign of such pretending is usually something like a child using a toy spoon to "feed" himself, or a toy comb to comb his hair. The toys are still used for their actual or typical purposes (spoon for feeding), and the actions are still oriented to the *self,* but some pretending is involved. This shifts between 15 and 21 months: The recipient of the pretend action now becomes another person or a toy, most often a doll. The child is still using objects for their usual purposes (such as drinking from a cup), but now she is using the toy cup with a doll instead of herself. Dolls are especially good toys for this kind of pretending, because it is not a very large leap from doing things to yourself to doing things with a doll. So children feed dolls imaginary food, comb their hair, and soothe them.
- *Substitute Pretend Play.* Between 2 and 3 years of age children begin to use objects to stand for something altogether different. They may comb the doll's hair with a baby bottle while saying that it is a comb, or use a broom to be a horsie, or make "trucks" out of blocks. By age 4 or 5, children spend as much as 20 percent of their playtime in this new, complicated kind of pretending (Field, De Stefano, & Koewler, 1982).
- *Sociodramatic Play.* Somewhere in the preschool years children also begin to play parts or take roles. This is really still a form of pretending, except that now several children create a mutual pretense. They play "daddy and mommy," "cowboys and Indians," "doctor and patient," and the like. At first children simply take up these roles; later they name the roles to one another, and may give each other explicit instructions about the right way to pretend a particular role. You can begin to see this form of play in some 2-year-olds; by age 4 virtually all children engage in some play of this type (Howes & Matheson, 1992). Interestingly, at about the same ages a great many children seem to create imaginary companions (Taylor, Cartwright, & Carlson, 1993). For many years psychologists believed that the existence of such an imaginary companion was a sign of disturbance in a child; now it is clear that such a creation is a normal part of the development of pretense in many children.

Children clearly get great delight from all these often elaborate fantasies. Equally important, by playing roles and pretending to be someone else, they also become more and more aware of how things may look or feel to someone else, and their egocentric approach to the world declines.

Critical Thinking

Can you think of any examples of egocentrism in your own behavior? What about buying someone else the gift you were hoping to receive yourself? Other examples?

FIGURE 7.2 This kind of experimental situation is similar to one Piaget used to study egocentrism in children. The child is asked to pick out the picture that shows how the two mountains look to him, and then to pick out the picture that shows how the mountains look to the little clay man.

The 3-year-old on the right is able to adapt her speech and her play to the needs of her blind friend, one of many indications that preschoolers are less egocentric than Piaget thought.

called **egocentrism** (Piaget, 1954). The child is not being selfish; rather she simply assumes that everyone sees the world as she does. Figure 7.2 is a photo of a classic experiment illustrating this kind of egocentrism. The child is shown a three-dimensional scene with mountains of different sizes and colors. From a set of drawings, he picks out the one that shows the scene the way he sees it. Most preschoolers can do this without much difficulty. Then the examiner asks the child to pick out the drawing that shows how someone *else* sees the scene, such as the little clay man or the examiner. At this point preschool children have difficulty. Most often they again pick the drawing that shows their *own* view of the mountains (Flavell et al., 1981; Gzesh & Surber, 1985).

Piaget also pointed out that the preschool-age child was captured by the appearance of objects—a theme that still dominates the research on children of this age. In Piaget's work, this theme is evident in some of the most famous of his studies, those on **conservation,** which I described in a Research Report in Chapter 2 (page 39). Children rarely show any type of conservation before age 5. They think that spreading out a row of pennies means that there are now more pennies, or that pouring water from a fat glass into a taller, thinner glass means there is now more water because the water has risen higher in the thinner glass. Piaget took such responses as a sign that preschoolers were still captured by the *appearance* of change, and did not focus on the underlying, unchanging aspect.

Newer Views of the Preoperational Child

These same two themes—egocentrism and the child's ability to understand the distinction between appearance and reality—continue to dominate much of the research on the thinking of the preschool-age child. A rich and intriguing new body of evidence suggests that preschoolers are a great deal less egocentric than Piaget thought, but that they do indeed struggle with the problem of distinguishing between appearance and reality.

Perspective Taking. Research on the child's ability to take others' perspectives shows that children as young as 2 and 3 have at least *some* ability to understand that another person sees things or experiences things differently from the way they do. For example, children this age will adapt their speech or their play to the demands of their companion. They play differently with older or younger playmates, and talk differently to a younger or a handicapped child (Brownell, 1990; Guralnick & Paul-Brown, 1984).

But such understanding is clearly not perfect at this young age. John Flavell has proposed two levels of perspective-taking ability. At level 1, the child knows *that* some other person experiences something differently. At level 2, the child develops a whole series of complex rules for figuring out precisely *what* the other person sees or experiences (Flavell, Green, & Flavell, 1990). Two- and 3-year-olds have level 1 knowledge but not level 2. We begin to see some Level 2 knowledge in 4- and 5-year-olds.

Appearance and Reality. This shift seems to be part of a much broader change in the child's understanding of appearance and reality. Flavell has studied this in a variety of ways, such as by showing objects under colored lights to change the apparent color, or putting masks on animals to make them look like another animal. He finds that 2- and 3-year-olds consistently judge things by their appearance; by age 5, the child begins to be able to separate the appearance from the underlying reality and knows that some object isn't "really" red even though it looks red under a red-colored light, or that a cat with a dog mask is still "really" a cat (Flavell, Green, & Flavell, 1989; Flavell et al., 1987).

In the most famous Flavell procedure, the experimenter shows the child a sponge that has been painted to look like a rock. Three-year-olds, faced with this odd object, will either say that the object looks like a sponge and is a sponge or that it looks like a rock and is a rock. But 4- and 5-year-olds can distinguish the two; they realize that it looks like a rock but *is* a sponge (Flavell, 1986). Thus, the older child now understands that the same object can be represented differently, depending on one's point of view.

Using the same type of materials, investigators have also asked whether a child can grasp the principle of a *false belief*. For example, after the child has felt the sponge/rock and has answered questions about what it looks like and what it "really" is, you can ask something like this: "John [a playmate of the subject's] hasn't touched this, he hasn't squeezed it. If John just sees it over here like this, what will he think it is? Will he think it's a rock or will he think that it's a sponge?" (Gopnik & Astington, 1988, p. 35). By and large, 3-year-olds think that John will believe it is a sponge, while 4- and 5-year-olds realize that because John hasn't felt the sponge, he will have a false belief that it is a rock. Thus, the child of 4 or 5 understands that someone else can believe something that isn't true *and will act on that belief.*

Theories of Mind. Evidence like this has led a number of theorists (e.g., Astington & Gopnik, 1991; Gopnik & Wellman, 1994; Harris, 1989) to propose that the 4- or 5-year-old has developed a new and quite sophisticated **theory of mind.** The child this age has begun to understand that you cannot predict what other people will do

Cultures and Contexts

Understanding of Appearance and Reality in Other Cultures

A number of studies from widely different cultures suggest that the shift at about age 4 in children's understanding of appearance and reality and of false belief may well be a universal developmental pattern.

Jeremy Avis and Paul Harris (1991) adapted the traditional false-belief testing procedure for use with a tribe called the Baka, who live in Cameroon. The Baka are a hunter-gatherer people who live together in camps. Each child was tested in his or her own hut, using materials with which they were completely familiar. They watched one adult, named Mopfana (a member of the tribe), put some mango kernels into a bowl with a lid. Mopfana then left the hut, and a second adult (also a tribe member) told the child they were going to play a game with Mopfana: They were going to hide the kernels in a cooking pot. Then he asked the child what Mopfana was going to do when he came back. Would he look for the kernels in the bowl, or in the pot? The second adult also asked the child whether Mopfana's heart would feel good or bad before he lifted the lid of the bowl, and after he lifted the lid. Younger children—2-, 3-, and early 4-year-olds—were likely to say that Mopfana would look for the seeds in the pot or that he would be sad before he looked in the bowl, while older 4- and 5-year-olds were nearly always right on all three questions.

Similarly, when Flavell used his sponge/rock task with children in mainland China, he found that Chinese 3-year-olds were just as confused about this task as are American or British 3-year-olds, whereas 5-year-old Chinese children had no difficulty with the problem (Flavell et al., 1983).

Using a somewhat different kind of problem, but one that still touches on the difference between appearance and reality, Paul Harris and his colleagues (Harris, 1989) have asked children in several cultures how characters in a story *really* feel and what emotion *appears* on their faces. For example:

> Diana is playing a game with her friend. At the end of the game Diana wins and her friend loses. Diana tries to hide how she feels because otherwise her friend won't play any more. (Harris, 1989, p. 134)

Four-year-old children in Britain and the United States, faced with such stories, have no trouble saying how the character will really feel, but more trouble saying how the character would look, while by 5 or 6, the child grasps the possible difference. Harris has found that the same age shift occurs in Japan (Gardner et al., 1988), and Joshi and MacLean (1994) found a similar shift in India, despite the fact that both the Japanese and Indian cultures put far more emphasis on the disguising of emotions than is true in British or American culture.

In these very different cultures, then, something similar seems to be occurring between age 3 and age 5. In these years, all children seem to understand something general about the difference between appearance and reality—they seem to develop a certain type of theory of mind.

The relatively late development of the child's understanding of conservation makes sense if we think of conservation tasks as a particularly sophisticated form of the problem of appearance and reality. When I pour juice from a short fat glass into a tall thin glass, the amount of juice appears to increase (rises higher in the glass) even though in reality it remains the same. Thus, conservation cannot be grasped until after the child has made considerable progress in understanding the distinction between appearance and reality, typically by age 5 or so.

Overview of the Preschool Child's Thinking

How can we add up the bits and pieces of information about the preschool child's thinking? At the least, we can say that preschool children are capable of forms of logic that Piaget thought impossible at this stage. In particular, by age 4, and certainly by age 5, they not only can take others' perspectives, they understand at least in a preliminary way that other people's behavior rests on inner beliefs and feelings.

Of course it might be that Piaget was right about the basic sequences but simply got the ages wrong, that the transition he saw at 6 or 7 really happens at around age 4 or 5. Certainly the various understandings that children seem to come to at about that age—about false belief, about appearance and reality, about other people's physical perspective, and about the meanings of emotional expressions—are remarkably stagelike in that they all tend to appear at about the same time.

Or it might be that the newer research exaggerates the preschooler's abilities to at least some degree. Preschoolers can indeed do some sophisticated-looking things, but their understanding remains specific rather than general. It is still tied heavily to specific situations and can be displayed only with a good deal of support. Studies of both conservation and children's logic show that sophisticated performances can be *elicited* in 2-, 3-, and 4-year-old children, but preschoolers do not typically show such skills spontaneously. In order for the preschool child to demonstrate these relatively advanced forms of thinking, you have to make the task quite simple, eliminate distractions, or give special clues. The fact that children this age can solve these problems at all is striking, but Piaget was clearly correct in pointing out that preschool children think differently from older children. The very fact that they can perform certain tasks *only* when the tasks are made very simple or undistracting is evidence for such a difference.

More broadly, preschoolers do not seem to experience the world or think about it with as general a set of rules or principles as we see in older children, and thus they do not easily generalize something they have learned in one context to a similar but not identical situation. It is precisely such a switch to general rules that Piaget thought characterized the thinking of the school-age child—a subject I'll take up in Chapter 9.

Individual Differences

The descriptions of the sequences and patterns of language and cognitive development I've given tell you something about the average or normative pattern, but any such average is at least partially misleading. Children vary in important ways, particularly in their relative ability to perform intellectual tasks. We see such differences not only in the speed of the child's language development, but in measures of cognitive power such as IQ tests.

Differences in Rate of Language Development

Some children begin using individual words at 8 months, others not until 18 months; some do not use two-word sentences until 3 years or even later. This high degree of variability has been found not only by those who have followed children longitudinally (e.g., Blake, 1994; Bloom, 1991; Brown, 1973), but also in Fenson's very large cross-sectional study of more than a thousand toddlers whose language was described by their parents. In this group, the earliest age at which parents reported that their child used predominantly complex (inflected) sentences was about 22 months, with an average of about 27 months. Yet as many as a quarter of children had not reached this point by 30 months (Fenson et al., 1994).

I should point out that most children who talk late catch up later, and earliness or lateness of complex speech is *not* predictive of later IQ or later reading ability, *except* for those few late talkers who also have poor *receptive* language. This group appears to remain behind in language development and perhaps in cognitive development more generally (Bates, 1993).

Such variations in speed of early language acquisition seem to have at least some genetic basis (Mather & Black, 1984; Plomin & DeFries, 1985), but they are also at least partly a response to differences in the richness of the language environment, as I noted earlier.

Differences in Intelligence Among Preschoolers

In Chapter 5, I mentioned that so-called infant IQ tests were not strongly related to later measures of IQ. But I did not give you a full description of such later measures, nor did I define IQ. It is now time to do both.

Remember from Chapter 5 that the study of intelligence is part of the "cognitive power" tradition. Those who approached the study of thinking in this way were struck by the obvious variations among individuals in their ability to think, analyze, solve problems, and learn new material. These researchers sought ways to measure and understand those differences.

The First IQ Tests. The first modern intelligence test was published in 1905 by two Frenchmen, Alfred Binet and Theodore Simon (Binet & Simon, 1905). From the beginning, the test had a practical purpose—namely, to identify children who might have difficulty in school. For this reason, the tests Binet and Simon devised were very much like some school tasks, including measures of vocabulary, comprehension of facts and relationships, and mathematical and verbal reasoning. For example, can the child describe the difference between wood and glass? Can the young child touch his nose, his ear, his head? Can he tell which of two weights is heavier?

Lewis Terman and his associates at Stanford University (Terman, 1916; Terman & Merrill, 1937) modified and extended many of Binet's original tests when they translated and revised the test for use in the United States. The several Terman revisions, called the **Stanford-Binet,** consist of a series of six individual tests for children of each age. A child taking the test is given the age tests beginning below his actual age, then those for his age, then those for each successively older age until the child reaches a level at which he fails all six tests.

Terman initially described a child's performance in terms of a score called an **intelligence quotient,** later shortened to IQ. This score was computed by comparing the child's chronological age (in years and months) with his *mental age*, defined as the level of questions he could answer correctly. For example, a child who could solve the problems for a 6-year-old but not those for a 7-year-old would have a mental age of 6. The formula used to calculate the IQ was

$$\frac{\text{Mental age}}{\text{Chronological age}} \times 100 = \text{IQ}$$

This formula results in an IQ above 100 for children whose mental age is higher than their chronological age and an IQ below 100 for children whose mental age is below their chronological age.

This old system for calculating the IQ is not used any longer, even in the modern revisions of the Stanford-Binet. Instead, IQ score calculations are now based on a direct comparison of a child's performance with the average performance of a large group of other children his own age. But the scoring is arranged so that an IQ of 100 is still average. Two-thirds of all children achieve scores between 85 and 115; roughly 95 percent of scores fall between 70 and 130. Children who score above 130 are often called *gifted*; those who score below 70 are normally referred to as *retarded*, although such a label should not be applied unless the child also has problems with "adaptive behavior," such as an inability to dress or eat alone, a problem getting along with others, or a significant problem adapting to the demands of a regular school classroom. Some children with IQ scores in this low range are nonetheless able to function in a regular schoolroom, and are not properly labeled as retarded.

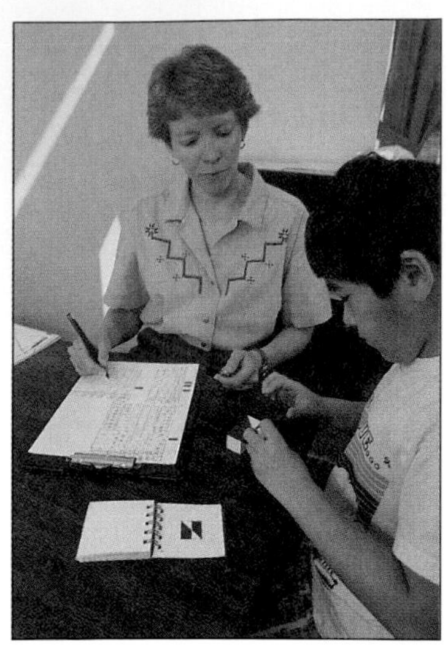

This second-grader is working on one of the subtests of the WISC in which he must use a set of blocks to try to copy the design shown in the book.

Modern IQ Tests. The tests used most frequently by psychologists today are the Revised Stanford-Binet and the third revision of the Wechsler Intelligence Scales for Children, called the **WISC-III,** a test originally developed by David Wechsler (1974). On all the WISC tests, the child is tested with ten different types of problems, each ranging from very easy to very hard. The ten tests are divided into two subgroups, one relying strongly on verbal skills (e.g., vocabulary, describing similarities between objects, general information) and the other involving less-verbal types of thinking, collectively called *performance* tests, such as arranging pictures in an order that tells a story or copying a pattern using a set of colored blocks. Many psychologists find this distinction between verbal and performance tests helpful, because significant unevenness in a child's test skill may indicate particular kinds of learning problems.

Stability and Predictive Value of IQ Tests. Because these tests were originally designed to predict a child's ability to perform in school, it is obviously crucial to know whether they do this job well. The research findings on this point are quite consistent: The correlation between a child's test score and her current or future grades in school is about .50 to .60 (Brody, 1992; Carver, 1990; Neisser et al., 1996). This is a strong but by no means perfect correlation. It tells us that on the whole, children with top IQ scores will also be among the high achievers in school, and those who score low will be among the low achievers. But success in school also depends on many other factors than IQ, including motivation, interest, and persistence. Because of this, some children with high IQ scores don't shine in school while some lower-IQ children do.

It is important to point out that this relationship between school performance and IQ scores holds *within* each social class and racial group in the United States, as well as in other countries and cultures. Among the poor as well as among the middle class, and among African Americans and Hispanics as well as among Anglos, those children with higher IQ are most likely to get good grades, complete high school, and go on to college (Brody, 1992). Such findings have led a number of theorists to argue that intelligence adds to the child's *resilience*—a concept I talked about in Chapter 1. Numerous studies now show that poor children, be they white, Hispanic, African-American, or from another minority group, are far more likely to develop the kind of self-confidence and personal competence it takes to move out of poverty if they have higher IQ (Luthar & Zigler, 1992; Werner & Smith, 1992).

Critical Thinking

How or why do you think having a higher IQ makes the child more resilient? For example, in what specific ways might the life of a brighter child living in a slum be different from the life of a less-bright child in the same environment?

At the other end of the scale, low intelligence is associated with a number of negative long-term outcomes, including adult illiteracy, delinquency in adolescence, and criminal behavior in adulthood (Baydar, Brooks-Gunn, & Furstenberg, 1993; Stattin & Klackenberg-Larsson, 1993). This is not to say that all lower-IQ individuals are illiterate or criminals. That is clearly not the case. But low IQ makes a child more vulnerable, just as high IQ increases the child's resilience.

IQ scores are also quite stable. If two tests are given a few months or a few years apart, the scores are likely to be very similar. The correlations between adjacent-year IQ scores in middle childhood, for example, are typically in the range of .80 (Honzik, 1986). Yet this high level of predictability masks an interesting fact: Many children show quite wide fluctuations in their scores. Robert McCall, analyzing several longitudinal studies in which children had been given IQ tests repeatedly over many years, concludes that about half of all children show noticeable changes from one test to another and over time (McCall, 1993). Some show steadily rising scores, some declining; some show a peak in middle childhood and then a decline in adolescence. In rare cases, the shifts may cover a range as large as 40 points.

Such wide fluctuations are more common in young children. The general rule of thumb is that the older the child, the more stable the IQ score becomes, although even in older children, scores may still show fluctuations in response to major stresses such as parental divorce, changing schools, or the birth of a sibling.

Limitations of IQ Tests. Before I move on to the question of the possible origins of differences in IQ, it is important to emphasize a few key limitations of such tests or the scores derived from them.

IQ tests do not measure underlying competence. An IQ score cannot tell you (or a teacher, or anyone else) that your child has some specific, fixed, underlying capacity. Traditional IQ tests also do not measure a whole host of skills that are likely to be highly significant for getting along in the world. Originally, IQ tests were designed to measure only the specific range of skills that are needed for success in school. This they do quite well. What they do not tell us is how good a particular person may be at other cognitive tasks requiring skills, such as creativity, insight, street-smarts, reading social cues, or understanding spatial relationships (Gardner, 1983; Sternberg & Wagner, 1993).

Critical Thinking

Given what I have said so far about IQ tests, do you think it would be worthwhile to have every preschool child tested? How would you use such scores? What would be the drawbacks of such universal testing?

Explaining Differences in IQ

You will not be surprised to discover that the arguments about the origins of differences in IQ nearly always boil down to a dispute about nature versus nurture. When Binet and Simon wrote the first IQ test, they did not assume that intelligence as measured on an IQ was fixed or inborn. But many of the American psychologists who revised and promoted the use of the tests *did* believe that intellectual capacity is inherited and largely fixed at birth. Those who share this view have been arguing for at least 60 years with those who believe that the environment is crucial in shaping a child's intellectual performance.

Evidence for the Importance of Heredity. Both twin studies and studies of adopted children show strong hereditary influences on IQ, as you already know from the Research Report in Chapter 1 (page 9). Identical twins are more like one another in IQ than are fraternal twins, and the IQs of adopted children are better predicted from the IQs of their natural parents than from those of their adoptive parents (Brody, 1992; Loehlin et al., 1994; Scarr et al., 1993). These are precisely the findings we would expect if a strong genetic element were at work.

Evidence for the Importance of Environment. Adoption studies also provide some strong support for an environmental influence on IQ scores because the actual *level* of the IQ scores of adopted children is clearly affected by the environment in which they have grown up. The clearest evidence for this comes from a French study by Christiane Capron and Michel Duyme (1989), who studied a group of 38 French children, all adopted in infancy. Roughly half the children had been born to better educated/higher-social-class parents, while the other half had been born to working-class or poverty-level parents. Some of the children in each group had then been adopted by higher-social-class parents, while the others grew up in poorer families. Table 7.3 shows the children's IQ scores in adolescence. If you compare the two columns in the table, you can see the effect of rearing conditions: The children reared in upper-class homes have IQs that are 11 or 12 points higher than do those reared in lower-class families, regardless of the social class level or education of the birth parents. At the same time, you can see a genetic effect if you compare the two

Table 7.3 IQ Scores at Adolescence for Capron and Duyme's Adopted Children*

	Social Class of Adoptive Parents	
Social Class of Biological Parents	**High**	**Low**
High	119.60	107.50
Low	103.60	92.40

*The numbers in each cell represent the average IQ score for that group of children.
Source: Capron & Duyme, 1989, Table 2, p. 553.

rows in the table: The children *born to* upper-class parents have higher IQs than do those from lower-class families, no matter what kind of rearing environment they encountered.

Combining the Information. Virtually all psychologists would now agree that heredity is a highly important influence on IQ scores. Studies around the world consistently yield estimates that roughly half the variation in IQ within the population is due to heredity (Neisser et al., 1996; Plomin & Rende, 1991; Rogers, Rowe, & May, 1994). The remaining half is clearly due to environment or to interactions between environment and heredity.

One useful way to conceptualize this interaction is with the concept of *reaction range*. The basic idea is that genes establish some range of possible reactions, some upper and lower boundary of functioning. Exactly where a child will fall within those boundaries will be determined by environment. Richard Weinberg (1989) estimates that the reaction range for IQ is about 20 to 25 points. That is, given some specific genetic heritage, each child's actual IQ test performance may vary as much as 20 or 25 points, depending on the richness or poverty of the environment in which he grows up. When we change the child's environment for the better, the child moves closer to the upper end of his reaction range. When we change the environment for the worse, the child's effective intellectual performance falls toward the lower end of his reaction range. Thus, even though intelligence as measured on an IQ test is highly heritable, the absolute score within the reaction range is determined by environment. But just what is it about family environments that seems to make a difference?

Specific Family Characteristics and IQ. When we watch the ways individual families interact with their infants or young children and then follow the children over time to see which ones later have high or low IQs, we can begin to get some sense of the kinds of specific family interactions that foster higher scores. At least five dimensions of family interaction or stimulation seem to make a difference. Families with higher-IQ children tend to do the following:

1. They provide an *interesting and complex physical environment* for the child, including play materials that are appropriate for the child's age and developmental level (Bradley et al., 1989; Pianta & Egeland, 1994).
2. They are *emotionally responsive* to and *involved* with their child. They respond warmly and contingently to the child's behavior, smiling when the child smiles, answering the child's questions, and in myriad ways reacting to the child's cues (Barnard et al., 1989; Lewis, 1993).
3. They *talk to their child* often, using language that is descriptively rich and accurate (Hart & Risley, 1995; Sigman et al., 1988). And when they play with or

interact with the child, they operate in what Vygotsky referred to as the *zone of proximal development* (described in Chapter 2), aiming their conversation, their questions, and their assistance at a level that is just above the level the child could manage on her own, thus helping the child to master new skills (e.g., Landry et al., 1996).

4. They *avoid excessive restrictiveness*, punitiveness, or control, instead giving the child room to explore, even opportunities to make mistakes (Bradley et al., 1989; Olson, Bates, & Kaskie, 1992). In a similar vein, they ask questions rather than giving commands (Hart & Risley, 1995).
5. They *expect* their child to do well and to develop rapidly. They emphasize and press for school achievement (Entwisle & Alexander, 1990).

You'll remember from Chapter 1 that there is a problem in research of this type. Because parents provide *both* the genes and the environment, we can't be sure that these environmental characteristics are really causally important. Perhaps these are simply the environmental features provided by brighter parents and it is the genes and not the environment that cause the higher IQs in their children. The way around this problem is to look at the link between environmental features and IQ in adopted children. Fortunately we have a few studies of this type, and they point to the same critical environmental features, although the relationships are somewhat weaker. That is, among adoptive families, those that behave in the ways listed above have adopted children who score somewhat higher on IQ tests (Plomin, Loehlin, & DeFries, 1985).

School Experience and Special Interventions. Home environments and family interactions are not the only sources of environmental influence. Many children also spend a very large amount of time in group care settings, including day care, special programs like Head Start, or regular preschools. How much effect do these environments have on the child's intellectual growth? I talked about some of the day-care effects in the last chapter, but I need to expand a bit.

On a theoretical level, this question is of interest because it may tell us something about early experience in general and about the resilience of children. Are the effects of an initially impoverished environment permanent, or can they be offset by an enriched experience, such as a special preschool? At a practical level, programs like Head Start are based squarely on the assumption that it *is* possible to modify the trajectory of a child's intellectual development, especially if you intervene early.

Attempts to test this assumption have led to a messy body of research. In particular, children are rarely assigned randomly to Head Start or non–Head Start groups, making interpretation difficult. Still, researchers have reached some agreement on the effects. Children enrolled in Head Start or other enriched preschool programs, compared with similar children without such preschool, normally show a gain of about 10 IQ points during the year of the Head Start experience. This IQ gain typically fades and then disappears within the first few years of school (Zigler & Styfco, 1993). But on other measures a clear residual effect can still be seen some years later. Children with Head Start or other quality preschool experience are less likely to be placed in special education classes, less likely to repeat a grade, and more likely to graduate from high school (Barnett, 1995; Darlington, 1991). They also have better health, better immunization rates, and better school adjustment than their peers (Zigler & Styfco, 1993). One very long-term longitudinal study even suggests that the impact may last well into adulthood. Young adults who had attended a particularly good experimental preschool program, the Perry Preschool Project in Milwaukee, had higher rates of high school graduation, lower rates of criminal behavior, lower rates of unemployment, and a lower probability of being on welfare than did their peers who had not attended such enriched preschools (Barnett, 1993).

Children who attend enrichment programs like this Head Start program typically do not show lasting gains in IQ, but they are more likely to succeed in school.

When the enrichment program is begun in infancy rather than at age 3 or 4, even IQ scores remain elevated after the intervention has ended. The best-designed and most meticulously reported of the infancy interventions is Craig Ramey's North Carolina study, called the Abecedarian project (Campbell & Ramey, 1994; Ramey, 1993; Ramey & Campbell, 1987). Infants from poverty-level families whose mothers had low IQs were randomly assigned either to a special day-care program or to a control group that received nutritional supplements and medical care but no special enriched day care. The special day-care program, which began when the infants were 6 to 12 weeks of age and lasted until they began kindergarten, involved very much the kinds of "optimum" stimulation I just described.

The average IQ scores of the children in each of these two groups from age 2 to age 12 are shown in Figure 7.3. You can see that the IQs of the children who had been enrolled in the special program were higher at every age. Fully 44 percent of the control group children had IQ scores classified as borderline or retarded (scores below 85), compared with only 12.8 percent of the children who had been in the special program. In addition, the enriched day-care group had significantly higher scores on both reading and mathematics tests at age 12 and were only half as likely to have repeated a grade (Ramey, 1992, 1993).

These results do *not* mean that all mental retardation could be "cured" by providing children with heavy doses of special education in infancy. What they do show is that the intellectual power of those children who begin life with few advantages can be significantly increased if richer stimulation is provided early in life.

CRITICAL THINKING

Considering the results of Ramey's study, would you be in favor of providing such enriched day care to all infants from high-risk or poverty-level families? What are the arguments, pro and con?

Racial Differences in IQ

So far I have sidestepped an extremely difficult set of questions, namely racial differences in IQ or cognitive power. Debates about such differences were reenergized by the publication of a highly controversial book, *The Bell Curve*, in which Richard Herrnstein and Charles Murray (1994) reviewed and analyzed the evidence. Because these issues have powerful personal and political ramifications and can easily be blown

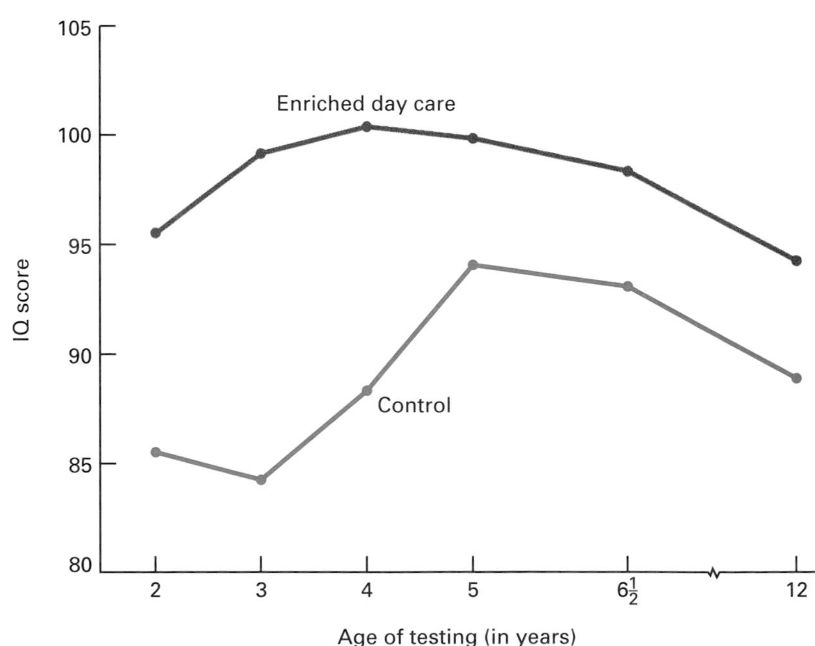

FIGURE 7.3 In Ramey's study, children from poverty-level families were randomly assigned in infancy to an experimental group with special day care or to a control group, with the intervention lasting until age 5. At kindergarten, both groups entered public school. The difference in IQ between the experimental and control groups remained statistically significant even at age 12, seven years after the intervention had ended. (*Source:* Ramey & Campbell, 1987, Figure 3, p. 135, with additional data from Ramey, 1993, Figure 2, p. 29.)

out of proportion, I do not want to place too much emphasis on this topic. But you should have some idea of what we know, what we don't know, and how we are trying to explain such differences.

The evidence shows a number of racial differences in intellectual performance, including consistently higher performance on achievement tests—particularly math and science tests—by Chinese and Japanese children (Geary et al., 1993; Stevenson et al., 1990; Sue & Okazaki, 1990). But the basic finding that has been most troublesome for researchers and theorists (and that Herrnstein and Murray discuss at length) is that in the United States, black children consistently score lower than white children on measures of IQ. This difference, which is on the order of 12 IQ points, is *not* found on infant tests of intelligence or on measures of infant habituation rate (Fagan & Singer, 1983), but it becomes apparent by the time children are 2 or 3 years old (Brody, 1992; Peoples, Fagan, & Drotar, 1995). There is some indication that the size of the difference between black and white children has been declining in the past several decades and may now be less than 10 points (Neisser et al., 1996). But a noticeable difference persists.

Some scientists, including the authors of *The Bell Curve*, acknowledge that the environments of the two groups are, on average, substantially different. But they conclude that the IQ difference must nonetheless reflect—at least in part—basic genetic differences between the races (Jensen, 1980). Other scientists, even granting that IQ is highly heritable, point out that the 10- or 12-point difference falls well within the presumed reaction range of IQ. They emphasize that the environments in which black and white children are typically reared differ sufficiently to account for the average difference in score (Brody, 1992). Black children in the United States are more likely to be born with low birth weight, are more likely to suffer from subnutrition, are more likely to have high blood levels of lead, and are less likely to be read to or provided with a wide range of intellectual stimulation. And each of these environmental characteristics is known to be linked to lower IQ scores.

Some of the most convincing research supporting such an environmental explanation comes from Sandra Scarr and her colleagues (Scarr & Weinberg, 1983; Weinberg, Scarr, & Waldman, 1992). For example, she has found that black children adopted at an early age into white middle-class families scored only slightly less well on IQ tests than did white children adopted into the same families. Findings like these persuade me that the IQ difference we see primarily reflects the fact that the tests, and schools, are designed by the majority culture to promote a particular form of intellectual activity and that many black or other minority families rear their children in ways that do not promote or emphasize this particular set of skills.

In a similar vein, Harold Stevenson and others have argued that the differences between Asian and American children in performance on mathematics achievement tests result not from genetic differences in capacity, but from differences in cultural emphasis on the importance of academic achievement, number of hours spent on homework, and differences in the quality of the math instruction in the schools (Chang & Murray, 1995; Schneider et al., 1994; Stevenson & Lee, 1990; Stigler, Lee, & Stevenson, 1987).

The fact that we may be able to account for such racial differences in IQ or achievement test performance by appealing to the concept of reaction range and to cultural or subcultural variations does not make the differences disappear, nor does it make them trivial. But perhaps it puts such findings into a less explosive framework.

Critical Thinking

Some psychologists have argued that the reason blacks achieve lower IQ scores than whites is that the tests are systematically biased against blacks or other minority group members. What kind of research results would demonstrate such a bias? What kind would argue against it?

The Measurement of Intelligence: One More Look

One of the questions that students often ask at about this point is whether, given all the factors that can affect a test score, it is worth bothering with IQ tests at all. I think it is definitely worth it. Let me tell you why.

First of all, IQ tests are important tools for identifying children who have special school needs, including both gifted and retarded children. There are other methods for selecting children for special programs, such as teacher recommendations, but none of the alternatives is as reliable or valid as an IQ test for measuring that set of cognitive abilities that are demanded by school.

Second, IQ tests have been an invaluable research tool, providing us with a widely accepted measure of the effect of a variety of environmental variations. As just one example, Ramey used IQ scores as one critical measure of the success of his special day-care program. In the same way, physicians have used IQ scores as a way to demonstrate the detrimental effect of lead exposure on children's mental development. In this sense, the IQ test is a tool for detecting the effects of environmental variations, just as a thermometer is a tool for detecting variations in body temperature. And if you use the tool correctly, not expecting it to tell you more than it is designed to say, it can be extremely valuable.

Summary

1. Physical development is slower from 2 to 6 than in infancy, but is still steady. Motor skills continue to improve gradually, with marked improvement in large muscle skills (running, jumping, galloping) and slower advances in small muscle (fine motor) skills.
2. Preschool children average 4 to 6 acute illnesses each year, with such illnesses more common among children living under high stress.
3. Language development moves at a rapid pace between ages 2 and 4, beginning with simple two-word sentences, followed by a grammar explosion when grammatical inflections are added, followed by complex sentences. A variety of meanings is conveyed in even the simplest sentences.
4. From the earliest sentences, children's language is creative, including forms and combinations that the child has not heard but that follow apparent rules.
5. The development of word meanings (semantic development) follows a less-predictable course. Children appear to have many concepts or categories before they have words for them, but learning new words also creates new categories. The earliest words are typically highly specific and context-bound in meaning; later, children typically "overextend" their usage.
6. Some linguists have concluded that in determining word meanings, a child has built-in constraints or biases, such as the assumption that words refer to objects or actions but not both, or the principle of contrast.
7. Simple imitation or reinforcement theories of language development are not adequate to explain the phenomenon. More complex environmental theories, emphasizing the role of environmental richness or motherese, are more helpful but also not sufficient.
8. Innateness theorists assume the child is born with a set of "operating principles" that focus the child on relevant aspects of language input. Other theorists emphasize the child as a "little linguist" who constructs a language as he constructs all cognitive understandings.
9. Piaget marked the beginning of the preoperational period at about 18–24 months, at the point when the child begins to use mental symbols. Despite this advance, the preschool child still lacks many sophisticated cognitive characteristics. In Piaget's view, such children are still egocentric, lack understanding of conservation, and are generally captured by appearances.
10. Recent research on the cognitive functioning of preschoolers makes it clear that they are much less egocentric than Piaget thought. By age 4, they can distinguish between appearance and reality in a variety of tasks, and develop a surprisingly sophisticated theory of how minds work. They understand that other people's actions are based on thoughts and beliefs, not on "reality."
11. By age 4 or 5, children also understand some of the links between specific situations and other people's likely emotions.
12. Language development proceeds at varying speeds in different children, with faster development associated with linguistically richer environments.
13. Children also differ in cognitive power, as measured by standard intelligence tests. Scores on such tests are predictive of school performance and are at least moderately consistent over time.
14. Differences in IQ have been attributed to both heredity and environment. Twin and adoption studies make it clear that at least half the variation in IQ scores is due to genetic differences; the remainder, to environment and the interaction of heredity and environment.
15. Qualities of the environment that appear to make a difference include the complexity of stimulation, the responsiveness and involvement of parents, the relative lack of restrictiveness, and high expectations for the child's performance.
16. Children's IQs can be raised by providing specially stimulating environments, such as enriched day care or preschools.
17. Several kinds of racial differences in IQ or test performance have been found consistently. Such differences seem most appropriately attributed to environmental variation, rather than genetics.

Key Terms

conservation	inflections	metamemory	Stanford-Binet
egocentrism	intelligence quotient (IQ)	motherese	theory of mind
infant-directed speech	metacognition	overregularization	WISC-III

Suggested Readings

Flavell, J. H. (1992). Cognitive development: Past, present, and future. *Developmental Psychology*, 28, 998–1005.

This brief paper by one of the leading thinkers and researchers in the field of cognitive development gives you a quick tour of what Flavell thinks we now know, don't know, and are still arguing about. Flavell's 1985 book Cognitive Development, *cited in the references, is also a wonderful source.*

Goldstein, J. (Ed.). (1994). *Toys, play, and child development*. Cambridge, England: Cambridge University Press.

A collection of current papers on the role of play in children's development. Included is an interesting chapter on war toys and their effect.

Hakuta, K. (1986). *Mirror of language: The debate on bilingualism*. New York: Basic Books.

An elegant and comprehensible discussion of many of the issues about bilingualism and bilingual education I have discussed in the Real World *box on page 165.*

Neisser, U., Boodoo, G., Bouchard, T. J., Jr., Boykin, A. W., Brody, N., Ceci, S. J., Halpern, D. F., Loehlin, J. C., Perloff, R., Sternberg, R. J., & Urbina, S. (1996). Intelligence: Knowns and unknowns. *American Psychologist*, 51, 77–101.

A remarkable paper prepared as a collaborative effort by nearly all the leading experts on intelligence, designed in part as a response to The Bell Curve. *These scientists were asked by the American Psychological Association to prepare a summary of the basic, agreed-upon facts about intelligence and its measurement. The paper is dense, but it includes good explanations of most of the key concepts. It is a wonderful source for further study.*

Pinker, S. (1994). *The language instinct: How the mind creates language*. New York: William Morrow.

This splendid book, written by one of the most articulate and easy-to-understand linguists, lays out the argument for a built-in language instinct.

Shatz, M. (1994). *A toddler's life: Becoming a person*. New York: Oxford University Press.

Marilyn Shatz uses her grandson Ricky as an example throughout this engaging book, bringing in research as she goes along.

Shore, C. M. (1995). *Individual differences in language development*. Thousand Oaks, CA: Sage.

A small book summarizing what we know about individual differences in rate and style of language development, and the alternative explanations of those differences.

de Villiers, P. A., & de Villiers, J. G. (1992). Language development. In M. H. Bornstein & M. E. Lamb (Eds.), *Developmental psychology: An advanced textbook* (3rd ed.) (pp. 337–418). Hillsdale, NJ: Lawrence Erlbaum Associates.

A thorough and clear review of this subject, much easier to read than many current discussions or descriptions of language development, and touching on many of the issues I have raised here. Strongly recommended as a next source.

8 Social and Personality Development from 2 to 6

If you asked a random sample of adults to tell you the most important characteristics of children between the ages of 2 and 6, my hunch is that the first thing on the list would be the immense changes children make in their social abilities during these years. They go from being naysaying, oppositional toddlers during the famed "terrible twos" to being skilled playmates and interesting conversationalists by age 5 or 6. Certainly, the huge improvements in the child's language skills are a crucial ingredient in this transition. But the most obvious thing about 5-year-olds is how socially "grown up" they seem compared to toddlers.

Theoretical Perspectives

A number of theorists have tried their hand at describing or explaining this set of social/emotional changes. Both Freud and Erikson, whose theories you encountered briefly in Chapter 2, offered key insights, as have modern theorists such as Willard Hartup, who has focused on the role of relationships with peers as well as parents during these preschool years.

Freud and Erikson

If you go back and look at Table 2.1 (page 29), you'll see that Freud described two stages during these preschool years, each highlighting a different aspect of sexual sensitivity. The first of these, the *anal stage*, he thought was dominant between roughly ages 1 and 3, when the normal cephalocaudal developmental pattern leads to increased sensitivity in the anal region. This stage is significant particularly because it typically coincides with the parents' desire to toilet train the child.

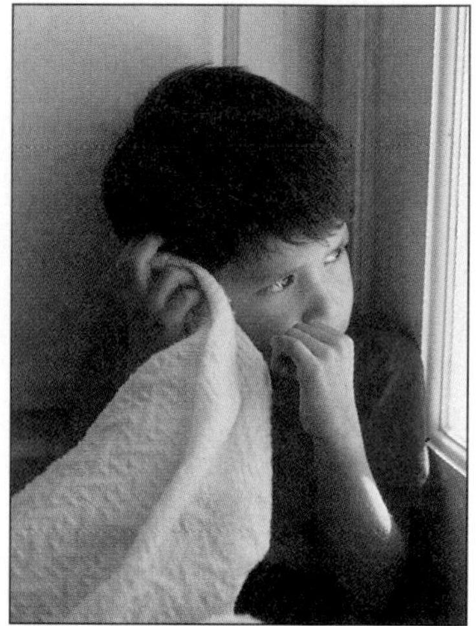

We don't know just what emotion this youngster is feeling, but it might well be shame. Three- and 4-year-olds experience a sense of shame when they fail to live up to others' expectations of them; they often show their shame by covering their face, averting their eyes, or collapsing the body inward (Mascolo & Fischer, 1995), all of which this boy shows to some degree.

The *phallic stage* occurs between ages 3 and 5, when Freud thought the genitals increased in sensitivity. It is during this stage that Freud thought the Oedipus conflict occurred, resulting in identification with the same-sex parent.

Erikson placed the emphasis somewhat differently. Both of the stages he listed within this period (recall from Table 2.2, p. 30) are triggered by new physical, cognitive, or social skills of the child rather than by changes in sexual sensitivity as Freud suggested. The stage Erikson called *autonomy versus shame and doubt*, for example, is centered around the toddler's new mobility and the accompanying desire for autonomy. The stage of *initiative versus guilt* is ushered in by new cognitive skills, particularly the preschooler's ability to plan, which accentuates his wish to take the initiative.

Both theorists seem to be saying that the key to this period is the balance between the child's emerging skills and desire for autonomy, and the parent's need to protect the child and control the child's behavior. Thus, the parent's task changes rather dramatically after the baby leaves infancy. In the early months of life, the key task for the parents is to provide enough warmth, predictability, and responsiveness to foster a secure attachment and to support basic physiological programming. But once the child becomes physically, linguistically, and cognitively more independent, the need to control becomes a central aspect of the parents' task. Too much control and the child will not have sufficient opportunity to explore; too little control and the child will become unmanageable and fail to learn the social skills he will need to get along with peers as well as adults.

Hartup's Perspective

Neither Freud nor Erikson talked much about the role of the child's peers in development, but in recent years a number of theorists such as Hartup have emphasized the vital significance of such encounters. He suggests that each child needs experience in two different kinds of relationships: *vertical* and *horizontal* (1989). A vertical relationship involves an attachment to someone who has greater social power or knowledge, such as a parent, a teacher, or even an older sibling. Such relationships are complementary rather than reciprocal. The bond may be extremely powerful in both directions, but the actual behaviors the two partners show toward one another are not the same. Horizontal relationships, in contrast, are reciprocal and egalitarian. The individuals involved, such as same-age peers, have equal social power and their behavior toward one another comes from the same repertoire.

Hartup's point is that these two kinds of relationships serve different functions for the child, and both are needed for the child to develop effective social skills. Vertical relationships are necessary to provide the child with protection and security. In these relationships the child creates her basic internal working models and learns fundamental social skills. But it is in horizontal relationships—in friendships and in peer groups—that the child practices her social behavior and acquires those social skills that can only be learned in a relationship between equals: cooperation, competition, and intimacy. Let me begin by talking about the vertical relationships—in particular, the core relationship between child and parent.

Relationships with Parents

Attachment

You'll remember from Chapter 6 that by 12 months of age, the baby has normally established a clear attachment to at least one caregiver. The infant displays this attachment in a wide variety of attachment behaviors, including smiling, crying, clinging, social referencing, and "safe base behavior." By age 2 or 3, the attachment appears no less strong but many of these attachment behaviors have become less continuously visible. Children this age are cognitively advanced enough to understand Mom if she explains why she is going away and that she will be back, so their anxiety at separation wanes. They can even use a photograph of their mother as a "safe base" for exploration in an unfamiliar situation (Passman & Longeway, 1982), which reflects the major cognitive advance of symbolic representation. Of course attachment behaviors have not completely disappeared. Three-year-olds still want to sit on Mom's or Dad's lap; they are still likely to seek some closeness when Mom returns from an absence. But in nonfearful or nonstressful situations, the preschool child is able to wander further and further from her safe base without apparent distress. She can also deal with her potential anxiety at separation by creating shared plans with the parents ("I'll be home after your naptime") (Crittenden, 1992).

An even broader change occurs at about age 4, when the child's attachment seems to change in quality. Bowlby described this new stage or level as a *goal-corrected partnership*. Just as the first attachment probably requires the baby to understand that his mother will continue to exist when she isn't there, so now the preschooler grasps that the *relationship* continues to exist even when the partners are apart.

Off she goes, into greater independence. Children this age, especially those with secure attachments, are far more confident about being at a distance from their safe base.

At about the same age, the child's internal model of attachment appears to generalize, a process I mentioned in Chapter 6. Bowlby argued that the child's model becomes less a property of each individual relationship, and more a property of relationships in some more general sense. Four- and 5-year-olds are thus more likely to apply their internal model to new relationships, including relationships with peers.

In sum, the preschooler's attachment to the parent(s) remains strong and central, but it changes in form in a number of significant ways as the child's cognitive abilities advance.

CRITICAL THINKING

What effect do you think the child's increasingly complex theory of mind has on the child's relationship with her parents?

Compliance and Defiance

At the same time, the 2-year-old's greater autonomy brings him into more and more situations in which the parents want one thing and the child another. Contrary to the popular image of the "terrible twos," 2-year-olds actually comply with parents' requests more often than not. They are more likely to comply with safety requests ("Don't touch that, it's hot!") or with prohibitions about care of objects ("Don't tear up the book"), than they are with requests to delay ("I can't talk to you now, I'm on the phone") or self-care, such as washing hands or going to bed when requested. But on the whole, children this age comply fairly readily (Gralinski & Kopp, 1993). When they resist, it is most likely to be passively, by simply not doing what is asked. Only a small percentage of the time does the child say "NO" or actively defy the parent (Kuczynski et al., 1987). Overt refusals become more common by age 3 or 4.

Many psychologists think it is important to make a distinction between a simple refusal or nay-saying ("I don't want to" or "No"), and defiance, in which the child's refusal is accompanied by anger, temper tantrums, or whining (e.g., Crockenberg & Litman, 1990). The former seems to be an important and healthy aspect of self-assertion and has been linked both to secure attachments and to greater maturity (Matas, Arend, & Sroufe, 1978). Defiance, on the other hand, has been linked to insecure attachment or to a history of abuse.

Direct defiance declines over the preschool years; we are less likely to see temper tantrums, whining, or equivalent outbursts in a 6-year-old than in a 2-year-old, in part because the child's cognitive and language skills have developed to the point where negotiation has become more possible. We can see the effects of these same cognitive changes in the child's relationships with peers as well.

Relationships with Peers

The child's family experience is undeniably a central influence shaping the child's emerging personality and social relationships, particularly in these early years when children still spend a good portion of their time with their parents and siblings. But over the years from 2 to 6, relationships with nonsibling peers become increasingly important.

Children first begin to show some positive interest in other infants as early as 6 months of age. If you place two babies that age on the floor facing each other, they will look at each other, touch, pull each other's hair, imitate each other's actions, and smile at one another. By 14 to 18 months, we begin to see two or more children playing together with toys—sometimes cooperating together, sometimes simply playing side by side with different toys (a pattern referred to as *parallel play*). Toddlers this age express interest in one another, gazing at or making noises at each other. But it isn't until around 18 months that we begin to see much coordinated play, such as when one toddler chases another, or one imitates the other's action with some toy.

By 3 or 4, children appear to prefer playing with peers to playing alone, and their play with one another is much more cooperative and coordinated. They build things together, play in the sandbox together, create pretend fantasies with each other. In all these interactions, we can also see both positive and negative behaviors, both aggression and altruism (Hartup, 1992).

Aggression

The most common definition of **aggression** is behavior with the apparent intent to injure another person or object (Feshbach, 1970). Every child shows at least some behavior of this type, but the form and frequency of aggression changes over the preschool years, as you can see in the summary in Table 8.1.

When 2- or 3-year-old children are upset or frustrated, they are most likely to throw things or hit each other. As their verbal skills improve, however, they shift away from such overt physical aggression toward greater use of verbal aggression, such as taunting or name calling, just as their defiance of their parents shifts from physical to verbal strategies.

The decline in physical aggression over these years also undoubtedly reflects the preschooler's declining egocentrism and increasing understanding of other children's thoughts and feelings. Yet another factor in the decline of physical aggression is the emergence of **dominance hierarchies.** As early as age 3 or 4, groups of children arrange themselves in well-understood *pecking orders* of leaders and followers (Strayer, 1980). They know who will win a fight and who will lose one, which children they dare attack and which ones they must submit to—knowledge that serves to reduce the actual amount of physical aggression.

CRITICAL THINKING

Think about the groups you belong to. Do they have clear dominance hierarchies? Now imagine a group of adults coming together for the first time. Within a few weeks a pecking order will have emerged. What determined that order? How does a dominant person establish such dominance?

A second change in the quality of aggression during the preschool years is a shift from primarily *instrumental* aggression to more *hostile* aggression. The latter is aimed at hurting another person or at gaining advantage; the former is aimed at gaining or damaging some object. So when 3-year-old Sarah pushes aside her playmate Lucetta in the sandbox and grabs Lucetta's bucket, she is showing instrumental aggression. When Sarah gets angry at Lucetta and calls her a dummy, she is displaying hostile aggression.

Where does aggression come from? Why is it so common among children? What triggers it or controls it? Psychologists have identified several key factors.

Frustration. One early group of American psychologists (Dollard et al., 1939) argued that aggression is always preceded by frustration and that frustration is always fol-

Table 8.1 Changes in the Form and Frequency of Aggression Between Ages 2 and 8

	2- to 4-Year-Olds	4- to 8-Year-Olds
Physical aggression	At its peak	Declines
Verbal aggression	Relatively rare at 2; increases as the child's verbal skill improves	Dominant form of aggression
Goal of aggression	Primarily "instrumental aggression," aimed at obtaining or damaging an object rather than directly hurting someone else	More "hostile aggression," aimed at hurting another person or another's feelings
Occasion for aggression	Most often after conflicts with parents	Most often after conflicts with peers

Source: Cummings et al., 1986; Goodenough, 1931; Hartup, 1974.

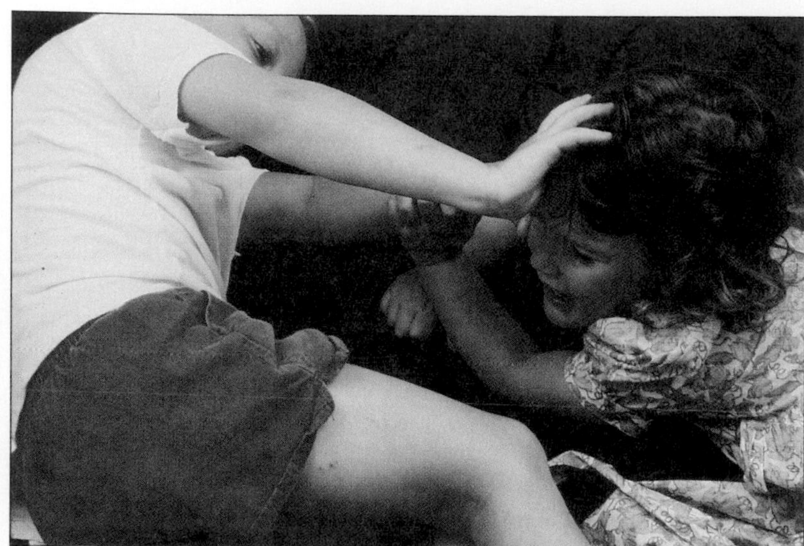

Six-year-old Christopher and his 4-year-old sister Helen may be less likely to get into this kind of a physical fight than was true a few years ago, but clearly this type of physical aggression does not totally disappear in the preschool years.

lowed by aggression. This *frustration-aggression hypothesis* turns out to be too broadly stated; all frustration does not lead to aggression, but frustration does make aggression more likely. Toddlers and preschoolers are often frustrated—because they cannot always do what they want, and because they cannot express their needs clearly—so they often express that frustration through aggression. As the child acquires greater ability to communicate, plan, and organize her activities, her frustration level declines and overt aggression drops.

Reinforcement and Modeling. When Sarah pushes Lucetta away and grabs her toy, Sarah is reinforced for her aggression because she gets the toy. This straightforward effect of reinforcement clearly plays a vital role in children's development of aggressive patterns of behavior. One good example is Gerald Patterson's work, which I described in Chapter 1 (e.g., Patterson et al., 1991). When parents give in to their young child's tantrums or aggression, they are reinforcing the very behavior they deplore, and they thereby help to establish a long-lasting pattern of aggression and defiance.

Modeling, too, plays a key role in children's learning of aggressive behaviors. Kids learn specific forms of aggression by watching other people perform them (e.g., Bandura, Ross, & Ross, 1961, 1963). As just one example, preschoolers today have learned special attack kicks from watching *Power Rangers*. Children also learn that aggression is an effective or approved way of solving problems by watching their parents and others behave aggressively. Indeed, parents who consistently use physical punishment with their children have kids who are *more* aggressive than are children whose parents do not model aggression in this way (Eron, Huesmann, & Zelli, 1991)—a point I will expand on later in the chapter. When children have many different aggressive models, especially if those aggressive models appear to be rewarded for their aggression, then we should not be surprised that the child learns similar patterns of aggressive behavior. Certainly many inner-city neighborhoods in the United States appear to fit such a pattern.

Prosocial Behavior

At the other end of the spectrum of peer relationships is a set of behaviors psychologists call **prosocial behavior:** "Intentional, voluntary behavior intended to benefit

Research Report

Siblings and Their Differences

The great majority of children grow up with brothers and sisters. In the preschool years, in fact, interactions with siblings may be a more important part of a child's social world than at any other age. Until recently, most psychological research on siblings focused on a single issue, the effect of birth order. Does it matter to the child's development if he is the oldest, the youngest, or in the middle? The typical finding from this early research was that first-borns were more likely to be strongly achievement-oriented and more anxious; later-born children were likely to be more sociable and more influenced by others' opinions. Recent studies of sibling relationships have turned away from this somewhat simplistic question toward several more interesting issues, including the nature of sibling relationships and the differences in parents' treatment of siblings.

Stories such as the tale of Cain and Abel might lead us to believe that rivalry or jealousy is the key ingredient of sibling relationships. But observations of preschoolers with their siblings point toward other ingredients. Toddlers and preschoolers help their brothers and sisters, imitate them, and share their toys. Judy Dunn (Dunn & Kendrick, 1982), in a detailed longitudinal study of a group of 40 families in England, observed that the older child often imitated a baby brother or sister; by the time the younger child was a year old, he or she began imitating the older sib, and from then on most of the imitation flowed in that direction, with the younger child copying the older one.

At the same time, brothers and sisters also hit one another, snatch toys, and threaten and insult each other. The older child in a pair of preschoolers is likely to be the leader and is therefore likely to show more of both aggressive and helpful behaviors (Abramovitch, Pepler, & Corter, 1982). For both members of the pair, however, the dominant feature seems to be ambivalence. Both supportive and negative behaviors are evident in about equal proportions. In Abramovitch's research, such ambivalence occurred whether the pair were close in age or further apart, and whether the older child was a boy or a girl. Naturally there are variations on this theme; some pairs show mostly antagonistic or rivalrous behaviors while some show mostly helpful and supportive behaviors. Most sibling pairs show both types of behavior.

One apparent cause of such variations in sibling relationships seems to be the extent to which parents treat their children differently. Some of the best evidence comes from several studies by Dunn (Dunn & McGuire, 1994) in both England and the United States. She has found that parents may express warmth and pride toward one child and scorn toward another, may be lenient toward one and strict with another. Here's an example from one of Dunn's observations, of 30-month-old Andy and his 14-month-old sister, Susie.

> Andy was a rather timid and sensitive child, cautious, unconfident, and compliant. . . . Susie was a striking contrast—assertive, determined, and a handful for her mother, who was nevertheless delighted by her boisterous daughter. In [one] observation of Andy and his sister, Susie persistently attempted to grab a forbidden object on a high kitchen counter, despite her mother's repeated prohibitions. Finally, she succeeded, and Andy overheard his mother make a warm, affectionate comment on Susie's action: "Susie, you *are* a determined little devil!" Andy, sadly, commented to his mother, "*I'm* not a determined little devil!" His mother replied, laughing, "No! What are you? A poor old boy!" (Dunn, 1992, p. 6)

Not only are such episodes common in family interactions, children are highly sensitive to such variations in treatment. Notice how Andy had monitored his mother's interaction with Susie, and then compared himself with his sister. Children this age are already aware of the emotional quality of exchanges between themselves and their parents, as well as the exchanges between their siblings and parents. Dunn finds that those who receive less affection and warmth from their mothers are likely to be more depressed, worried, or anxious than are their siblings. And the more differently the parents treat siblings, the greater the rivalry and hostility between the brothers and sisters (G. H. Brody et al., 1992). When both parents favor one child over the other, the less favored child is also more likely to show significant behavior problems in other settings, such as school (McGuire, Dunn, & Plomin, 1995; Stocker, 1995).

Of course parents treat children differently for many reasons, including the child's age. Susie's mother may be accepting of Susie's naughty behavior simply because the toddler is so young. Parents also respond to temperamental differences in the children. But whatever the cause, it now seems clear that such differences in treatment are an important ingredient in the child's emerging internal model of self, and contribute greatly to variations in behavior between children growing up in the same families.

another" (Eisenberg, 1992, p. 3). In everyday language, this is essentially what we mean by **altruism,** and it changes with age, just as other aspects of peer behavior change.

We first see such altruistic behaviors in children of about 2 or 3—at about the same time that they begin to show real interest in play with other children. They will offer to help another child who is hurt, offer a toy, or try to comfort another person (Marcus, 1986; Zahn-Waxler & Radke-Yarrow, 1982; Zahn-Waxler et al., 1992). As I pointed out in the last chapter, children this young have only a beginning understanding of the fact that others feel differently from themselves, but they obviously understand enough about the emotions of others to respond in supportive and sympathetic ways when they see other children or adults hurt or sad.

Past these early years, changes in prosocial behavior show a mixed pattern. Some kinds of prosocial behavior seem to increase with age. For example, if you give children an opportunity to donate some treat to another child who is described as needy, older children donate more than younger children do. Helpfulness, too, seems to increase with age up through adolescence. But not all prosocial behaviors show this pattern. Comforting another child, for example, seems to be more common among preschool and early elementary school children than at older ages (Eisenberg, 1992).

We also know that children vary a lot in the amount of such altruistic behavior they show, and that young children who show relatively more empathy and altruism are also those who regulate their own emotions well. They show positive emotions readily, and negative emotions less often (Eisenberg et al., 1996b). These variations among children's level of empathy or altruism seem to be related to specific kinds of child rearing. I've translated some of the research into concrete advice in the Real World box below.

The Real World

Rearing Helpful and Altruistic Children

If you wish to encourage your own children to be more generous or altruistic, here are some specific things you can do, based on the work of Eisenberg and others (1992):

1. *Create a loving and warm family climate.* This is especially effective if such warmth is combined with clear explanations.
2. *Explain why and give rules.* Clear rules about what to do as well as what *not* to do are important. Explaining the consequences of the child's action in terms of its effects on others is also good; for example: "If you hit Susan, it will hurt her." Equally important is stating *positive* rules or guidelines; for example: "It's always good to be helpful to other people," or "We should share what we have with people who don't have so much."
3. *Provide prosocial attributions.* Attribute your child's helpful or altruistic action to the child's own internal character: "You're such a helpful child!" or "You certainly do a lot of nice things for other people." This strategy begins to be effective with children at about age 7 or 8, at about the same time that they are beginning to develop global notions of self-esteem. In this way you may be able to affect the child's self-scheme, which in turn may result in a generalized, internalized pattern of altruistic behavior.
4. *Have children do helpful things.* Children can help cook, take care of pets, make toys to give away, teach younger siblings or tutor in school, and so forth. This can backfire, however, if the coercion required to get the child to do the helpful thing is too strong: The child may now attribute his "good" behavior to the coercion ("Mother made me do it"), rather than to some inner trait of his own ("I am a helpful/kind person"), and no future altruism is fostered.
5. *Model thoughtful and generous behavior.* Stating the rules clearly will do little good if your own behavior does not match what you say!

Friendships

Beginning at about age 18 months, toddlers also show early hints of playmate preferences or individual friendships. For example, Carollee Howes (1983, 1987) noted that many children this young showed consistent preferences for one or more playmates over a full-year period in a day-care center. Using a somewhat stricter definition of friendship—that the pair spend at least 30 percent of their time together—Robert Hinde and his co-workers (1985) found that only about 20 percent of a group of $3\frac{1}{2}$-year-olds showed signs of a stable friendship; but by age 4, half of these same children regularly played this often with one child.

To be sure, these early peer interactions are still quite primitive. Most of the time, toddlers ignore one another's bids for interaction, and when they play together it is mostly around common toys. Still, it is noteworthy that preschool friend pairs nonetheless show more mutual liking, more reciprocity, more extended interactions, more positive and less negative behavior, and more supportiveness in a novel situation than is true between nonfriend pairs at this same age, all signs that these relationships are more than merely passing fancies.

One of the really intriguing facts about such early friendships is that they are more likely between same-sex pairs, even among children as young as age 2 or 3. John Gottman (1986) reports that perhaps 65 percent of friendships in preschool children in the United States are with a same-sex peer. Social interactions with children other than the chosen friend(s) are also more likely to be with children of the same sex, beginning as early as age $2\frac{1}{2}$ or 3 (Maccoby, 1988, 1990; Maccoby & Jacklin, 1987). By school age, peer relationships are almost exclusively same-sex.

You can see the early development of this preference in Figure 8.1, which shows the results of a study of preschool play groups by La Frenière, Strayer, and Gauthier

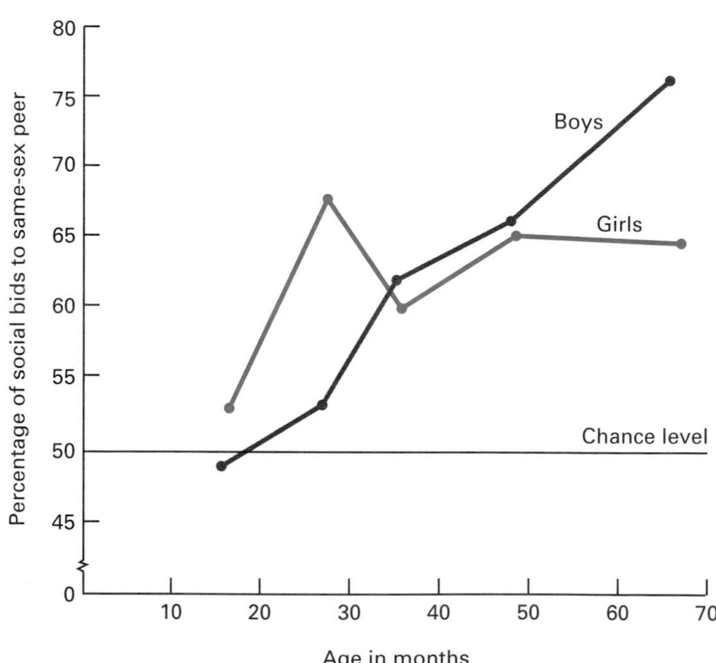

FIGURE 8.1 La Frenière and his colleagues counted how often preschool children played with same-sex or opposite-sex playmates. You can see that in this sample, children as young as $2\frac{1}{2}$ already showed at least some preference for same-sex playmates. (*Source:* La Frenière, Strayer, & Gauthier, 1984, Figure 1, p. 1961. Copyright by the Society for Research in Child Development, Inc.)

(1984). By age 3, about 60 percent of play groups were same-sex groupings and the rate rose from there.

CRITICAL THINKING

How many explanations can you think of for the fact that children begin to prefer to play with same-sex peers as early as age 3 or 4?

Sex Differences in Social Interactions. Not only are preschoolers' friendships and peer interactions increasingly sex-segregated, it is also becoming clear that boy-boy interactions and girl-girl interactions differ in quality, even in these early years. Eleanor Maccoby, one of the leading theorists in this area (1990), describes the girls' pattern as an *enabling style*. Enabling includes such behaviors as supporting the partner, expressing agreement, and making suggestions. All these behaviors tend to foster a greater equality and intimacy in the relationship and keep the interaction going. In contrast, boys are more likely to show what Maccoby calls a *constricting* or *restrictive* style. "A restrictive style is one that tends to derail the interaction—to inhibit the partner or cause the partner to withdraw, thus shortening the interaction or bringing it to an end" (1990, p. 517). Contradicting, interrupting, boasting, and other forms of self-display are all aspects of this style.

These two patterns begin to be visible in the preschool years. For example, Maccoby (1990) points out that beginning as early as age 3 or 4, boys and girls use quite different strategies in their attempts to influence each other's behavior. Girls generally ask questions or make requests; boys are much more likely to make demands or phrase things using imperatives ("Give me that!"). The really intriguing finding is that even at this early age, boys simply don't comply very much to the girls' style of influence attempt. So playing with boys yields little positive reinforcement for girls and they begin to avoid such interactions and band together.

Similar differences in relationship style are evident in older children and adults. Girls and women have more intimate relationships with their friends. And in pairs or groups, girls and women seem to focus their attention on actions that will keep the interaction going. Adult men are more likely to be task-oriented, women to be relationship-oriented. I'll have more to say about these differences in later chapters. For now I only want to point out that these subtle and profound differences seem to begin very early in childhood.

CRITICAL THINKING

Do your observations of adult relationships match the distinction Maccoby is making here? What do you think happens when one man and one woman interact in some nonromantic encounter? Is the resulting style some combination of enabling and constricting, or does one style dominate?

How might such differences arise so early? We are a long way from being able to answer that question. But we do know more and more about how a child figures out whether he is a boy or she is a girl—an understanding that is, in turn, part of the more general emergence of the preschool child's sense of self.

The Emergence of the Sense of Self

When we left the 18- to 24-month-old in Chapter 6, he was beginning to develop what Lewis calls the *objective self*. The toddler already understands himself to be an object in the world, with various properties. Between 2 and 6 the child certainly continues to define himself in this way. By the end of this period, a child can give you quite a full description of himself on a whole range of dimensions. Still, these early self-concepts remain highly concrete. For example, Susan Harter (1987, 1990; Harter & Pike, 1984) has found that children between 4 and 7 have clear notions of their own competence on a whole range of specific tasks, such as solving puzzles, counting, knowing a lot in school, climbing or skipping or jumping rope, or being able to make friends. But these separate aspects of the *self-scheme* or internal working model of the self have not yet coalesced into a global assessment of self-worth. For this reason, Harter argues that it is not appropriate to say of a preschooler that she has high or low self-esteem. She may have a high or low opinion of her ability to do some specific task or her ability to relate to others in specific situations, but high or low self-esteem in a more global sense does not seem to emerge until about age 7.

The self-concept of a preschool child is concrete in another way as well; he tends to focus on his own visible characteristics—whether he's a boy or girl, what he looks like, what or who he plays with, where he lives, what he is good or bad at doing—rather than on more enduring inner qualities. This pattern obviously parallels what we see in cognitive development at the same ages; it is in these same years that children's attention tends to be focused on the external appearance of objects rather than on their enduring properties.

The Social Self. Another facet of the child's emerging sense of self is an increasing awareness of herself as a player in the social game. By age 2, the toddler has already learned a variety of social "scripts"—routines of play or interaction with others in her world. Case (1991) points out that the toddler now begins to develop some implicit understanding of her own roles in these scripts. So she begins to think of herself as a "helper" in some situations, or as "the boss" when she is telling some other child what to do. You can see this clearly in children's sociodramatic play, as they begin to take explicit roles: "I'll be the daddy and you be the mommy," or "I'm the boss." As part of the same process, the preschool child also gradually understands her place in the network of family roles. She has sisters, brothers, father, mother, and so forth.

The Gender Concept and Sex Roles

One of the most fascinating aspects of the preschool child's emerging sense of self is the development of a sense of gender. The child has several related tasks. On the cognitive side, she must learn the nature of the gender category itself—that boyness or girlness is permanent and unchanged by such things as modifications in clothing or hair length. This understanding is usually called the **gender concept.** On the social side, she has to learn what behaviors go with being a boy or a girl. That is, she must learn the **sex role** appropriate for her gender.

The Development of the Gender Concept. How soon does a child figure out that she is a girl or he is a boy? It depends on what we mean by "figure out." There seem to be three steps. First comes **gender identity,** which is simply a child's ability to label his own sex correctly and to identify other people as men or women, boys or girls. By 9 to 12 months, babies already treat male and female faces as if they were different categories (Fagot & Leinbach, 1993). Within the next year, they begin to learn the verbal labels that go with these categories. By age 2, if you show them a set of pictures of a same-sex child and several opposite-sex children and ask "Which one

Through their pretend play, Lucy and Rachel, at age 3, are not only learning about how to interact with a peer, they are rehearsing various social scripts.

is you?," most children can correctly pick out the same-sex picture (Thompson, 1975). By $2\frac{1}{2}$ or 3, most children can correctly label and identify the sex of others as well (point out "which one is a girl" or "which one is a boy" in a set of pictures).

Accurate labeling, though, does not signify complete understanding. The second step is **gender stability,** which is the understanding that you stay the same gender throughout life. Researchers have measured this by asking children such questions as "When you were a little baby, were you a little girl or a little boy?" or "When you grow up will you be a mommy or a daddy?" Most children understand the stability aspect of gender by about age 4 (Slaby & Frey, 1975).

The final step is the development of true **gender constancy,** which is the recognition that someone stays the same gender even though he may appear to change by wearing different clothes or changing his hair length. For example, boys don't change into girls by wearing dresses. It may seem odd that a child who understands that he will stay the same gender throughout life (gender stability) can nonetheless be confused about the effect of changes in dress or appearance on gender. But numerous studies show this sequence, including studies of children growing up in other cultures, such as Kenya, Nepal, Belize, and Samoa (Munroe, Shimmin, & Munroe, 1984).

The underlying logic of this sequence may be a bit clearer if I draw a parallel between gender constancy and the concept of conservation. Conservation involves recognition that an object remains the same in some fundamental way even though it changes externally. Gender constancy is thus a kind of "conservation of gender," and is not typically understood until about 5 or 6, when other conservations are first grasped (Marcus & Overton, 1978).

In sum, children as young as 2 or $2\frac{1}{2}$ know their own sex and that of people around them, but they do not have a fully developed concept of gender until they are 5 or 6.

The Development of Sex-Role Concepts and Stereotypes. Figuring out your gender and understanding that it stays constant is only part of the story. Learning what goes with being a boy or a girl in a given culture is also a vital part of the child's task.

Researchers have studied this in two ways—by asking children what boys and girls (or men and women) like to do and what they are like (which is an inquiry about gender stereotypes), and by asking children if it is *okay* for boys to play with dolls or girls to climb trees or to do equivalent cross-sex things (an inquiry about roles).

In every culture, adults have clear sex-role stereotypes. Indeed, the content of those stereotypes is remarkably similar in cultures around the world. John Williams and Deborah Best (1990), who have studied gender stereotypes in 28 different countries, including non-Western countries such as Thailand, Pakistan, and Nigeria, find that the most clearly stereotyped traits are weakness, gentleness, appreciativeness, and soft-heartedness for women, and aggression, strength, cruelty, and coarseness for men. In most cultures, men are also seen as competent, skillful, assertive, and able to get things done, while women are seen as warm and expressive, tactful, quiet, gentle, aware of others' feelings, and lacking in competence, independence, and logic.

Studies of children show that these stereotyped ideas develop early. The 3-year-old daughter of a friend announced one day that mommies use the stove and daddies use the grill. Even 2-year-olds already associate certain tasks and possessions with men and women, such as vacuum cleaners and food with women and cars and tools with men. By age 3 or 4, children can assign occupations, toys, and activities to the stereotypic gender. (Another friend told me the story of a 4-year-old who came home from nursery school one day insisting that doctors were always men and nurses were always women—even though his own father was a nurse!) By age 5, children begin to associate certain personality traits with males or females, and such

As their gender concept develops, children change their views about whether it is all right for little boys to play with dolls.

knowledge is well developed by age 8 or 9 (Martin, 1993; Serbin, Powlishta, & Gulko, 1993).

Studies of children's ideas about how men and women (or boys and girls) ought to behave add an interesting further element. An early study by William Damon (1977) illustrates the point particularly nicely. He told a story to children aged 4 through 9 about a little boy named George who likes to play with dolls. George's parents tell him that only little girls play with dolls; little boys shouldn't. The children were then asked a batch of questions about this, such as "Why do people tell George not to play with dolls?" or "Is there a rule that boys shouldn't play with dolls?"

Four-year-olds in this study thought it was okay for George to play with dolls. There was no rule against it and he should do it if he wanted to. Six-year-olds, in contrast, thought it was *wrong* for George to play with dolls. By about age 9, children had differentiated between what boys and girls usually do, and what is "wrong." One boy said, for example, that breaking windows was wrong and bad, but that playing with dolls was not bad in the same way: "Breaking windows you're not supposed to do. And if you play with dolls, well you can, but boys usually don't."

What seems to be happening is that the 5- and 6-year-old, having figured out that gender is permanent, is searching for a *rule* about how boys and girls behave (Martin & Halverson, 1981). The child picks up information from watching adults, from TV, from listening to the labels that are attached to different activities (e.g., "Boys don't cry"). Initially children treat these as absolute, moral rules. Later they understand that these are social conventions, at which point sex role concepts become more flexible and stereotyping declines somewhat (Katz & Ksansnak, 1994). In a similar way, many kinds of fixed, biased ideas about other people—such as bias against obese children, against those who speak another language, or against those of other races—are at their peak in the early school years and then decline throughout the remaining years of childhood and adolescence (Doyle & Aboud, 1995; Powlishta et al., 1994).

The Development of Sex Role Behavior. The final element in the equation is the actual behavior children show with their own and with the opposite sex. The unexpected finding here is that children's *behavior* is sex-typed earlier than are their ideas about sex roles.

By 18 to 24 months, children begin to show some preference for sex-stereotyped toys, such as dolls for girls or trucks or building blocks for boys, which is some months *before* they can consistently identify their own gender (O'Brien, 1992). By age 3, children begin to show a preference for same-sex playmates and are much more sociable with playmates of the same sex—at a time when they do not yet have a concept of gender stability (Maccoby, 1988, 1990; Maccoby & Jacklin, 1987).

The other intriguing pattern is that children in early elementary school seem to begin to pay more attention to the behavior of same-sex than opposite-sex adults or playmates, and to play more with new toys that are labeled as being appropriate for their own sex (Bradbard et al., 1986; Ruble, Balaban, & Cooper, 1981). Overall, then, we see many signs that children are both aware of and affected by gender from very early, perhaps by age 1, certainly by age 2. Gender becomes a still more potent force in guiding behavior and attitudes at around age 5 or 6.

Critical Thinking

In Western cultures, it is far more common for young girls to be "tomboys" than it is for boys to show "girlish" behavior. Does this mean girls have a less clear gender concept? What do you think might be causing such a difference?

Explaining Sex Role Development. Theorists from most of the major traditions have tried their hand at explaining these patterns of development. Freud relied on the concept of identification to explain the child's adoption of appropriate sex-role behavior, but his theory founders on the fact that children begin to show clearly sex-typed behavior long before age 4 or 5, when Freud thought identification occurred.

Social learning theorists such as Bandura (1977a) and Mischel (1966, 1970) have naturally emphasized the role of parents in shaping children's sex-role behavior and attitudes. This notion has been far better supported by research than have Freud's ideas. Parents do seem to reinforce sex-typed activities in children as young as 18 months old, not only by buying different kinds of toys for boys and girls, but by responding more positively when their sons play with blocks or trucks, or when their daughters play with dolls (Fagot & Hagan, 1991; Lytton & Romney, 1991). Such differential reinforcement is particularly clear with boys, especially from fathers (Siegal, 1987). Some evidence also suggests that toddlers whose parents are more consistent in rewarding sex-typed toy choice or play behavior, and whose mothers favor traditional family sex roles, learn accurate gender labels earlier than do toddlers whose parents are less focused on the gender-appropriateness of the child's play (Fagot & Leinbach, 1989; Fagot, Leinbach, & O'Boyle, 1992)—findings clearly consistent with the predictions of social learning theory.

By age 2 or 3 we already see clear sex-role differences in children's toy choices. Left to their own devices, boys like this will select blocks or trucks to play with. Girls the same age are more likely to choose dolls, or tea sets, or dress-up clothes.

Still, helpful as it is, a social-learning explanation is probably not sufficient. In particular, parents differentially reinforce boy- versus girl-behavior less than you'd expect, and probably not enough to account for the very early and robust discrimination children seem to make on the basis of gender. Even children whose parents seem to treat their young sons and daughters in highly similar ways nonetheless learn gender labels and show same-sex playmate choices.

A third alternative, based strongly on Piagetian theory, is Lawrence Kohlberg's suggestion that the crucial aspect of the process is the child's understanding of the gender concept (1966; Kohlberg & Ullian, 1974). Once the child realizes that he is a boy or she is a girl forever, she or he becomes highly motivated to learn how to behave in the way that is expected or appropriate for that gender. Specifically, Kohlberg predicted that we should see systematic same-sex imitation only *after* the child has shown full gender constancy. Most studies designed to test this hypothesis have supported Kohlberg. Children do seem to become much more sensitive to same-sex models after they have understood gender constancy (Frey & Ruble, 1992). But Kohlberg's theory cannot handle the obvious fact that children show clear differential sex-role behavior, such as toy preferences, long before they have achieved full understanding of the gender concept.

The most fruitful current explanation is usually called **gender schema theory** (Martin, 1991; Martin & Halverson, 1981). Just as the self-concept can be thought of as a "scheme" or a "self-theory," so the child's understanding of gender can be seen in the same way. The gender schema begins to develop as soon as the child notices the differences between male and female, knows his own gender, and can label the two groups with some consistency—all of which happens by age 2 or 3. Perhaps because gender is clearly an either/or category, children seem to understand very early that this is a key distinction, so the category serves as a kind of magnet for new information. In Piaget's terms, once the child has established even a primitive gender scheme, a great many experiences are assimilated to it. Thus, as soon as this scheme begins to be formed, children may begin to show preference for same-sex playmates or for gender-stereotyped activities (Martin & Little, 1990).

Preschoolers first learn some broad distinctions about what kinds of activities or behavior go with each gender, both by observing other children and through the reinforcements they receive from parents. They also learn a few gender "scripts"—whole sequences of events that normally go with a given gender, such as "fixing dinner" or "building with tools" (Levy & Fivush, 1993)—just as they learn other social scripts at about this age. Then between ages 4 and 6 the child learns a more subtle and complex set of associations for his or her *own* gender—what children of his own gender like and don't like, how they play, how they talk, what kinds of people they associate with. Only at about age 8 to 10 does the child develop an equivalently complex view of the opposite gender (Martin, Wood, & Little, 1990).

The key difference between this theory and Kohlberg's is that for the initial gender schema to be formed, the child need not understand that gender is permanent. When gender constancy is understood at about 5 or 6, children develop a more elaborate rule or schema of "what people who are like me do" and treat this "rule" the same way they treat other rules—as absolutes. Later, the child's application of the "gender rule" becomes more flexible. She knows, for example, that most boys don't play with dolls, but that they *can* do so if they like.

The Development of Self-Control

Along with a self-concept, the preschooler must also develop another aspect of the self—self-control. I talked briefly about the control of emotion in the last chapter, but let me expand a bit.

Toddlers live in the here and now. When they want something, they want it immediately. When they are tired, they cry; when they are hungry, they insist on food. They are bad at waiting or at working toward distant goals, and find it hard to resist temptation. There is a joyous side to this same quality: Because they live in the moment, they see things with new eyes—the bug on a leaf, the color of a particular flower, the delight in a favored food. But to function as acceptable social beings they must learn self-control.

The process of acquiring such self-control is fundamentally one in which control shifts slowly from the parents to the child. With toddlers, parents provide most of the control through the use of prohibitions and requests. Over the years from 2 to 6, the child gradually internalizes the various standards and expectations and takes on more of the control task for herself.

Such internalization, and the accompanying improvement in self-control, is built on many earlier developments, especially the growth of language. As early as age 2, children use a kind of "private speech" to help control or monitor their own behavior. For example, when 2- or 3-year-olds play by themselves, they give themselves instructions, stop themselves with words, or describe what they are doing: "No, not there," "I put that there," or "put it" (Furrow, 1984). Such self-regulatory language has largely gone "underground" by age 9 or 10, but it can still be heard in older children—even in adults—when they are working on hard problems (Bivens & Berk, 1990).

Critical Thinking

Can you think of occasions when you use "private speech" of this kind? When you're working on a hard problem? When you're trying to figure out how to get some reluctant machine to work?

The child's improving language also makes it a great deal easier for parents to communicate clearly with their child, so they can explain rules for behavior—rules the child can then internalize. Internalization is also fostered by the same kinds of family interactions that foster secure attachments in the first year of life: parental warmth, sensitivity, responsiveness, and child-centered methods of control.

Individual Differences

So far I've been talking primarily about shared developmental patterns. But I am sure it is obvious to you that in the preschool years, children's relationships, social behavior, and personalities become even more divergent than was true among infants. Some toddlers and preschoolers are highly aggressive, defiant, difficult to manage (Campbell & Ewing, 1990; Patterson et al., 1991). Some are shy and retiring, while others are sociable and outgoing. These differences obviously have a variety of sources. Inborn temperament clearly plays some role, as does the security or insecurity of the child's first attachment, as you have already seen in Chapter 6. Yet another causal element seems to be the parents' style of child rearing—the way they deal with the need to discipline and control the child, the extent to which they show affection and warmth, the contingency of their responses.

Temperament Differences

As I mentioned in Chapter 6, variations in the child's temperament, such as "easiness" or "difficultness" or "inhibition" are reasonably stable over infancy, toddlerhood, and later ages. By preschool, we also begin to see a link between difficultness of temperament and both concurrent and future behavior problems: 3- or 4-year-olds with difficult temperament are more likely to show heightened aggressiveness, delinquency, or other forms of behavior problems in school, as teenagers, and as adults (Bates, 1989; Caspi et al., 1995; Chess & Thomas, 1984). It is important to understand, though, that this is a *probability* statement. The majority of preschoolers who are classed as having difficult temperaments do *not* develop later behavior problems, although the likelihood of such an outcome is greater. Probably the easiest way to think of it is that a difficult temperament creates a *vulnerability* in the child. If this vulnerable child has supportive and loving parents who are able to deal effectively with the child's difficultness, the trajectory is altered and the child does not develop broader social problems. But if the parents do not like the child or lack suitable child-rearing skills, or if the family is facing other stresses, the vulnerable, difficult child is highly likely to emerge from the preschool years with serious problems relating to others (Bates, 1989; Fish, Stifter, & Belsky, 1991).

If this tantrum by young Frank is part of a regular pattern of difficult behavior, then the chances are increased that he will later have behavior problems in elementary school or adolescence. But such an outcome is not inevitable. Many difficult children change their behavior sufficiently to allow them to get along well with their peers at later ages.

The Impact of the Family: Styles of Parenting

The research on temperament gives us but one of many illustrations of the importance of understanding the family's role in the child's emerging personality or social behavior. Psychologists have struggled over the years to identify the best ways of describing the many dimensions along which families may vary. At the moment, the most fruitful conceptualization is one offered by Diana Baumrind (1972), who focuses on four aspects of family functioning: (1) warmth or nurturance; (2) level of expectations, which she describes in terms of "maturity demands"; (3) clarity and consistency of rules; and (4) communication between parent and child.

Each of these four dimensions has been independently shown to be related to various child behaviors. Children with nurturant and warm parents, as opposed to those with more rejecting parents, are more securely attached in the first two years of life; have higher self-esteem; are more empathetic, more altruistic, more responsive to others' hurts or distress; have higher measured IQs in preschool and elementary school; do better in school; and are less likely to show delinquent behavior in adolescence or criminal behavior in adulthood (e.g., Maccoby, 1980; Maughan, Pickles, & Quinton, 1995; Simons, Robertson, & Downs, 1989). High levels of affection can even buffer the child against the negative effects of otherwise disadvantageous environments. Several studies of children and teens growing up in poor, tough neighborhoods show that the single ingredient that most clearly distinguishes the lives of those who do *not* become delinquent from those who do is a high level of maternal love (Glueck & Glueck, 1972; McCord, 1982). In contrast, parental hostility is linked to declining school performance and higher risk of delinquency (Melby & Conger, 1996).

The degree and clarity of the parents' control over the child is also significant. Parents with clear rules, consistently applied, have children who are much less likely to be defiant or noncompliant—a pattern you'll remember from Gerald Patterson's research (Figure 1.3, p. 14). Such children are also more competent and sure of themselves (Kurdek & Fine, 1994) and less aggressive (Patterson, 1980).

Equally important is the *form* of control the parent uses. The most optimal outcomes for the child occur when the parent is not overly restrictive, explains things to the child, and avoids the use of physical punishments such as spanking—a control strategy I've discussed in the Real World box on page 204.

We also find more optimal outcomes for children whose parents have high expectations, high "maturity demands" in Baumrind's language. Such children have

The Real World

To Spank or Not to Spank

In Sweden, there is a *law* against physical punishment of children (Palmérus & Scarr, 1995). In the United States, in contrast, nine out of ten parents of preschoolers say that they spank their children at least occasionally, most often in response to some aggressive act by the child (Holden, Coleman, & Schmidt, 1995); about half of parents of teenagers also report spanking their children (Straus, 1991a; Straus & Donnelly, 1993). Most of these parents think of spanking as an effective way of discipline. But I think they are wrong. Let me tell you why.

Note, please: I am not talking here about physical abuse, although certainly some parents do abuse their children by spanking excessively with a switch or a belt or fists. I'm talking about the ordinary kind of spanking that most people think of as normal and helpful: Two or three hard swats on the rear or (more likely with older children) a quick slap.

In the short term, spanking a child usually *does* get the child to stop the particular behavior you didn't like, and it seems to have a *temporary* effect of reducing the chance that the child will repeat the bad behavior. Since that's what you wanted, it may seem like a good strategy. But even in the short term there are some negative side effects. The child may have stopped misbehaving, but after a spanking he is likely to be crying, which may be almost as distressing as the original misbehavior. And crying is a behavior that spanking does not decrease: It is virtually impossible to get children to stop crying by spanking them! So you have exchanged one unpleasantness for another, and the second unpleasantness (crying) can't be dealt with by using the same form of punishment.

Another short-term side effect is that *you* are being negatively reinforced for spanking whenever the child stops misbehaving after you spank her. Thus, you are being "trained" to use spanking the next time, and a cycle is being built up.

In the longer term, the effects are clearly negative. First, when you spank, the child observes you using physical force or violence as a method of solving problems or getting people to do what you want. You thus serve as a model for a behavior you do *not* want your child to use with others. Second, by repeatedly pairing your presence with the unpleasant or painful event of spanking, you are undermining your own positive value for your child. Over time, this means that you are less able to use *any* kind of reinforcement effectively. Eventually even your praise or affection will be less powerful in influencing your child's behavior. That is a very high price to pay.

Third, spanking frequently carries a strong underlying emotional message—anger, rejection, irritation, dislike of the child. Even very young children read this emotional message quite clearly (Rohner, Kean, & Cournoyer, 1991). Spanking thus helps to create a family climate of rejection instead of warmth, with all the attendant negative consequences.

Finally, we have research evidence that children who are spanked—just like children who are abused—at later ages show higher levels of aggression and less popularity with their peers, lower self-esteem, more emotional instability, higher rates of depression and distress, and higher levels of delinquency and later criminality (Laub & Sampson, 1995; Rohner et al., 1991; Strassberg et al., 1994; Turner & Finkelhor, 1996). As adults, children who have been spanked are more likely to be depressed than are those who were never or rarely spanked (Straus, 1995), and have higher risks of various other types of adult problems, including problems holding a job, divorce or violence within a relationship, and criminality (Maughan et al., 1995). All these negative effects are especially clear if the physical punishment is harsh and erratic, but the risks for these poor outcomes are increased even with fairly mild levels of physical punishment.

I am *not* saying that you should never punish a child. I *am* saying that *physical punishment,* such as spanking, is not a good way to go about it. Yelling at the child is not a good alternative strategy, either. Strong *verbal* aggression by a parent toward a child is also linked to many poor outcomes in the child, including increased risk of delinquency and adult violence (Straus, 1991b). All in all, the bulk of the evidence is persuasive: Spanking and other forms of harsh discipline have negative consequences for children.

higher self-esteem, show more generosity and altruism toward others, and exhibit lower levels of aggression.

Finally, open and regular communication between parent and child has been linked to more positive outcomes. Listening to the child is as important as talking. Ideally, the parent needs to convey to the child that what the child has to say is *worth* listening to, that his ideas are important and should be considered in family decisions. Children from such families have been found to be more emotionally and socially mature (Baumrind, 1971; Bell & Bell, 1982).

While each of these characteristics of families may be significant individually, in fact they do not occur in isolation. They occur in combinations and patterns. Baumrind has identified three such patterns or styles:

- The **permissive parental style** is high in nurturance but low in maturity demands, control, and communication.
- The **authoritarian parental style** is high in control and maturity demands but low in nurturance and communication.
- The **authoritative parental style** is high in all four.

Eleanor Maccoby and John Martin (1983) have proposed a variation of Baumrind's category system, shown in Figure 8.2, that I find even more helpful. They categorize families on two dimensions, the degree of demand or control, and the amount of acceptance versus rejection. The intersection of these two dimensions creates four types, three of which correspond quite closely to Baumrind's authoritarian, authoritative, and permissive types. Maccoby and Martin's conceptualization adds a fourth type, the uninvolved or **neglecting parental style,** which current research tells us may be the most detrimental of the four. Let me talk briefly about each style.

The Authoritarian Type. Children growing up in authoritarian families—with high levels of demand and control but relatively low levels of warmth or responsiveness—do less well in school, have lower self-esteem, and are typically less skilled with peers than are children from other types of families. Some of these children appear subdued; others may show high aggressiveness or other indications of being out of control. Which of these two outcomes occurs may depend in part on how skillfully the parents use the various disciplinary techniques. Patterson finds that the "out of control" child is most likely to come from a family in which the parents are authoritarian by inclination but lack the skills to enforce the limits or rules they set.

These effects are not restricted to preschool-age children. In a series of large studies of high school students, including longitudinal studies of more than 6000 teens, Laurence Steinberg and Sanford Dornbusch and their co-workers (Dornbusch et al., 1987; Lamborn et al., 1991; Steinberg et al., 1995; Steinberg et al., 1992; Steinberg et al., 1994) have found that teenagers from authoritarian families have poorer grades in school and more negative self-concepts than do teenagers from authoritative families.

The Permissive Type. Children growing up with indulgent or permissive parents, too, show some negative outcomes. Steinberg and Dornbusch find that they do

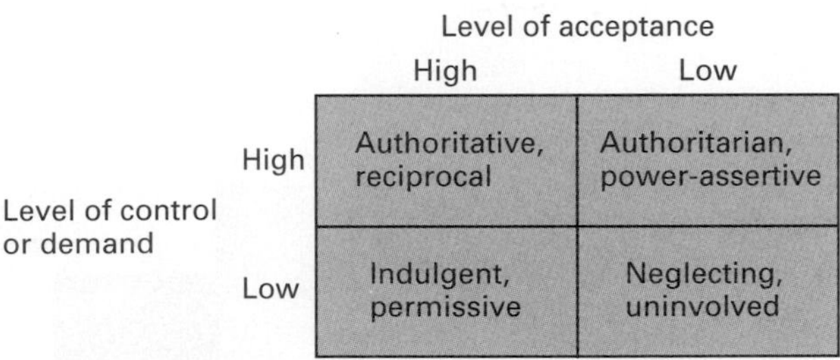

FIGURE 8.2 Maccoby and Martin expanded on Baumrind's categories in this two-dimensional category system. The new parental style described here is the neglecting type. (*Source:* Adapted from E. E. Maccoby & J. A. Martin, 1983. Socialization in the context of the family: Parent-child interaction. In E. M. Hetherington (Ed.), *Handbook of child psychology,* Figure 2, p. 39. New York: Wiley.)

slightly worse in school during adolescence, are likely to be both more aggressive—particularly if the parents are specifically permissive toward aggressiveness—and somewhat immature in their behavior with peers and in school. They are less likely to take responsibility and are less independent.

Critical Thinking

It is somewhat surprising that children reared in permissive families are *less* independent and take *less* responsibility. You might think that such children have been specifically encouraged and reinforced for independence and decision making. Can you think of any reason why this pattern of results might occur?

The Authoritative Type. The most consistently positive outcomes have been associated with an authoritative pattern in which the parents are high in both control and warmth, setting clear limits but also responding to the child's individual needs. Children reared in such families typically show higher self-esteem, are more independent but at the same time are more likely to comply with parental requests, and may show more altruistic behavior as well. They are self-confident and achievement-oriented in school and get better grades (e.g., Crockenberg & Litman, 1990; Dornbusch et al., 1987; Steinberg, Elmen, & Mounts, 1989).

The Neglecting Type. The most consistently negative outcomes are associated with the fourth pattern, the neglecting or uninvolved type. You may remember from the discussion of secure and insecure attachments in Chapter 6 that one of the family characteristics often found in children rated as insecure/avoidant is the "psychological unavailability" of the mother. The mother may be depressed or may be overwhelmed by other problems in her life and simply not have made any deep emotional connection with the child. Whatever the reason, such children continue to show disturbances in their relationships with peers and with adults for many years. At adolescence, for example, youngsters from neglecting families are more impulsive and antisocial, less competent with their peers, and much less achievement-oriented in school (Block, 1971; Lamborn et al., 1991; Pulkkinen, 1982).

Figure 8.3 illustrates these contrasting outcomes with data from the Steinberg and Dornbusch study of adolescents, showing variations in grade point average as a function of family style. In a longitudinal analysis, these same researchers have found that students who described their parents as most authoritative at the beginning of the study showed more *improvement* in academic competence and self-reliance and the smallest increases in psychological symptoms and delinquent behavior over the succeeding two years. So these effects persist.

But the system is more complex than this makes it sound. For example, authoritative parents are much more likely to be involved with their child's school, attending school functions and talking to teachers, and this involvement seems to play a crucial role in their children's better school performance. When an otherwise authoritative parent is *not* also more involved with the school, the academic outcomes for the student are not so clearly positive. Similarly, a teenager whose parent is highly involved with the school but is not authoritative shows less optimal outcomes. It is

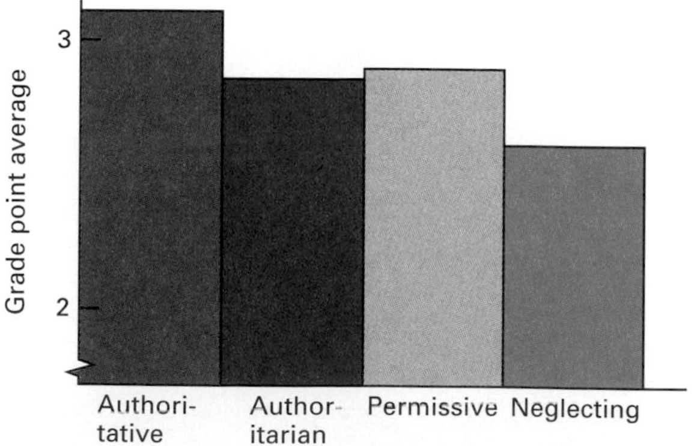

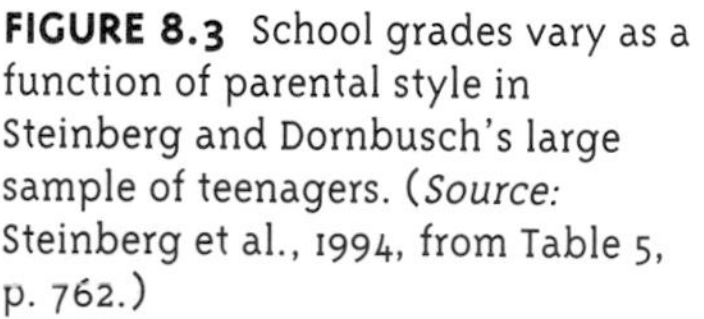
FIGURE 8.3 School grades vary as a function of parental style in Steinberg and Dornbusch's large sample of teenagers. (*Source:* Steinberg et al., 1994, from Table 5, p. 762.)

the combination of authoritativeness and school involvement that is associated with the best results (Steinberg et al., 1992).

Despite these additional complexities—and the complexities discussed in the Cultures and Contexts box below—we can draw several important conclusions from the research on family style. First, it seems clear that children are strongly affected by the family "climate" or style. Most likely, these effects persist well into adulthood. Second, many of us are accustomed to thinking about family styles as if permissive and authoritarian patterns were the only options. But research on the authoritative pattern shows clearly that one can be *both* affectionate and firm and that children respond to this combination in very positive ways.

Family Structure: Divorce and Other Variations

I cannot leave this discussion of family style and family functioning without at least some mention of the impact of variations in family structure. For those of us who live in cultures with high rates of divorce and single-parent families, this is an issue of profound practical importance.

Cultures and Contexts

Ethnic Differences in Styles of Parenting

It is important for us to know something about the incidence of the various styles of parenting among the major ethnic groups in our culture. If we were to find, for example, that the authoritative pattern is found only among white families, then we could not be sure whether the more positive outcomes associated with this style were simply the result of belonging to the majority culture, or whether they were really a consequence of the way the parents behaved. The best evidence on this point comes once again from the Dornbusch and Steinberg study of adolescents (Steinberg et al., 1991).

They have cross-sectional data from roughly 10,000 ninth- through twelfth-grade students, chosen so as to be representative of four different ethnic groups: white, black, Hispanic, and Asian. Each subject answered questions about the acceptance, control, and autonomy they received from their parents. When the adolescent described his family as above the average on all three dimensions, the family was classed as authoritative. The table below shows the percentages classed in this way in the four ethnic groups, broken down further by the social class and intactness of the family.

You can see that the authoritative pattern was most common among white families and least common among Asian Americans, but in each ethnic group, authoritative parenting was more common among the middle class and (with one exception) more common among intact families than in single-parent or stepparent families. Furthermore, these researchers find that some relationship between authoritative parenting and positive outcomes occurred in all ethnic groups. In all four groups, for example, teenagers from authoritative families showed more self-reliance and less delinquency than did those from nonauthoritative families. However, school grades were strongly linked to authoritative parental style for whites and Hispanics but only weakly for African Americans or Asian Americans. This last result raises a cautionary flag and points to a paradox that researchers are still exploring: Asian-Americans as a group do extremely well in school even though their parents are among the least authoritative. Perhaps the four categories of family style Maccoby and Martin (and Baumrind) suggest are at least partially ethnocentric, and do not capture all the significant aspects of family style in every culture. Nonetheless, this four-category system seems to be a highly heuristic first approximation.

Percentage of Authoritative Families

	Working Class		Middle Class	
Ethnic Group	**Intact***	**Not Intact***	**Intact**	**Not Intact**
White	17.2	11.5	25.0	17.6
Black	13.4	12.2	14.0	16.0
Hispanic	10.7	9.8	15.8	12.9
Asian	7.5	6.1	15.6	0.8

*"Intact" means the child is still living with both biological parents; "not intact" may mean single parent, stepfamily, or any family configuration other than both natural parents.

Source: Steinberg et al., 1991, from Table 1, p. 25 (*Journal of Research on Adolescence;* reprinted by permission of Lawrence Erlbaum Associates, Inc., and the author).

What may shock you is just how rare it is in the United States today for a youngster to spend her entire childhood and adolescence living with both natural parents. Donald Hernandez, in his remarkable book, *America's Children* (1993), estimates that only 40 to 45 percent of the children born in 1980—today's teenagers—will spend all their years up to age 18 living with both natural parents. Among African Americans, Hernandez estimates, this figure is only 20 percent, while among Euro-Americans it is about 55 percent.

You can get some feeling for the variety of family structures in which children live today from Figure 8.4, which shows the percentages of five different family types among white, African-American, and Hispanic 13-year-olds in the United States, based on a nationally representative sample of over 21,000 children studied by Valerie Lee and her colleagues (Lee et al., 1994). But even this chart doesn't begin to convey the diversity of family structures or the number of changes in family structure a child may experience over time. Divorced mothers, for example, may have live-in relationships with one or more men before a remarriage, or may have lived for a while with their own parents. And many children, especially children with never-married mothers, live in extended families with grandparents or other family members as well as a parent. All in all, the evidence makes it inescapably clear that the *majority* of children in the United States today experience at least two different family structures, often many more than that, in the course of their growing up. This is especially true of African Americans, but is increasingly true of other ethnic groups in our culture as well.

In other industrialized countries, single-parent families are less common, but they are on the rise everywhere. By the mid-1980s, the proportions ranged from less than 5 percent in Japan to about 15 percent in Australia, the United Kingdom, and Sweden, to nearly 25 percent in the United States (Burns, 1992). Because cultures are complex, knowledge gleaned about the impact of family structure on children's development in one country may not be valid elsewhere. But the issue is growing in importance in many parts of the world.

What do we know about the impact on children of being reared in such varied or varying family structures?

The broadest statement I can make is that, at least in U.S. studies, the optimum family structure for children is to have two natural parents. All other structures, including never-married mothers, divorced mothers or fathers who have not remarried, and stepfamilies, are frequently linked to less positive outcomes. Some examples:

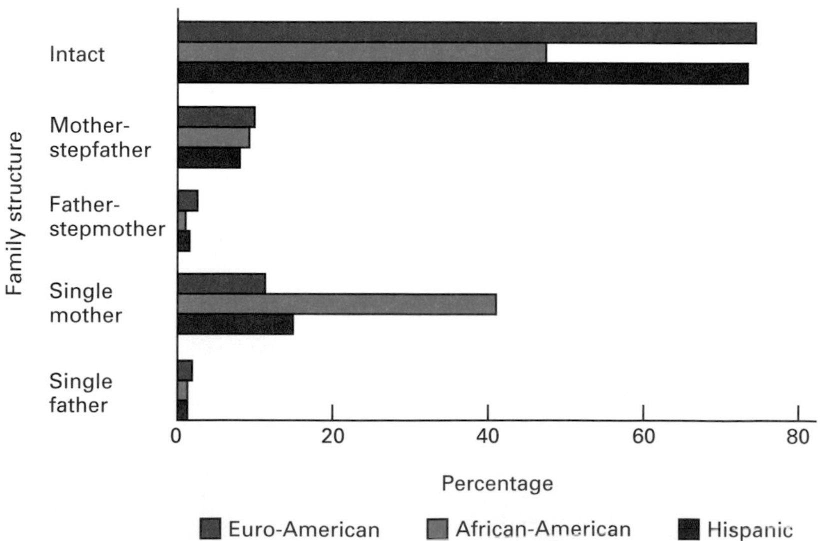

FIGURE 8.4 Variations in family structure among current U.S. 13-year-olds. (*Source:* V. E. Lee et al., 1994, from Table 2, p. 419.)

- Children growing up in single-parent families (whether the mother is divorced or never-married) are about twice as likely to drop out of high school, twice as likely to have a child before age 20, and less likely to have a steady job in their late teens or early 20s (McLanahan & Sandefur, 1994).
- In the first few years after a divorce, children typically show declines in school performance and show more aggressive, defiant, negative, or depressed behavior (Furstenberg & Cherlin, 1991; Hetherington & Clingempeel, 1992; Morrison & Cherlin, 1995). If they are adolescents, they are likely to show some increase in delinquent behavior (Kurtz & Tremblay, 1995).
- Negative effects of divorce may persist; those whose parents divorce have a higher risk of mental health problems in adulthood, although the majority of children of divorce do *not* show such problems (Chase-Lansdale, Cherlin, & Kiernan, 1995). Adults whose parents divorced are themselves more likely to divorce.
- Children living in stepparent families also have higher rates of delinquency and lower school grades than do those in intact families (Lee et al., 1994).

Many single parents manage to overcome the substantial obstacles and give their children the support and supervision they need. But on average, children of single parents have poorer life outcomes.

As a general rule, these negative effects are more pronounced for boys than for girls, although some research suggests that among adolescents, girls show equally or even greater negative effects (Amato, 1993; Hetherington, 1991a, 1991b). Age differences in the severity of the reaction, however, are typically not found. Specifically, although Freud's theory might lead us to expect larger effects for children in the Oedipal period, when the identification process would be disrupted by divorce, there is little indication that preschoolers are more severely affected than those of other ages.

Critical Thinking

If children in the Oedipal period do not show more negative reactions to their parents' divorce, what might this say about Freud's theory about this stage?

Ethnicity, incidentally, does *not* appear to be a causal factor here. Yes, a larger percentage of African-American children grow up in single-parent families. But the same negative outcomes occur in white single-parent families, and the same positive outcomes are found in two-parent minority families. For example, the school dropout rate for a white child from a single-parent family is higher than the dropout rate for a Hispanic or African-American child reared in a two-parent family (McLanahan & Sandefur, 1994).

How are we to understand all these various findings? My own reading of this growing body of evidence is that nonintact family structures have negative effects (or less positive effects) for three key reasons.

First, single parenthood or divorce reduces the financial and emotional resources available to support the child. With only one parent, the household typically has only one income and only one adult to respond to the child's emotional needs. An example: Data from the United States indicate that a woman's income drops an average of 40 to 50 percent after a divorce (Smock, 1993). Remarriage does indeed add a second adult to the family system, which alleviates these problems to some degree, but adds others.

Second, *any* family transition involves upheaval. This is true of the birth of a new sibling in an intact family. It is even more true of divorce or of remarriage. Both adults and children adapt slowly and with difficulty to the subtraction or addition of new adults to the family system (Hetherington & Stanley-Hagan, 1995). The period of maximum disruption appears to last several years, during which the parents often find it difficult to maintain good monitoring and control over their children. Parents can take specific actions to reduce this disruption (discussed in the Real World box, p. 210), but some disruption is unavoidable.

Finally and perhaps most importantly, single parenthood, divorce, and stepparenthood all increase the likelihood that the family climate or style will shift away from authoritative parenting toward less optimal forms. We see this in the first few years after a divorce when the custodial parent (usually the mother) is distracted or depressed and less able to manage warm control; we see it in stepfamilies as well, where rates of authoritative parenting are lower than in intact families.

The Real World

Softening the Effects of Divorce

Given the rate of divorce in our culture, a significant percentage of you reading these words will go through a divorce when you have children still living at home. You cannot eliminate all the short-term disruptive effects of such an event on your children, but here are some specific things you can do that are likely to soften or shorten the effects:

1. Try to keep the number of separate changes the child has to cope with to a minimum. If at all possible, keep the children in the same school or day-care setting, and the same house or apartment.
2. If your children are teenagers, consider having each child live with the parent of the same gender. The data are not totally consistent, but it looks as if this may be a less stressful arrangement (Lee et al., 1994). Alternatively, consider an arrangement in which the children spend roughly equal time with each parent. Some research suggests that this arrangement provides marginally better psychological support for the child than one in which the child lives entirely with one parent (Buchanan, Maccoby, & Dornbusch, 1992).
3. If your children live with you full time, help them stay in touch with the noncustodial parent. If you are the noncustodial parent, maintain as much contact as possible with your children, calling regularly, seeing them regularly, attending school functions, and so on. The evidence on this point is not as clear-cut as for some of the other items on this list; some studies show no special benefit to the child of continued regular contact with the noncustodial parent (Emery, 1988; King, 1994). The key for positive outcomes seems to be to maintain such contact with the absent parent without high levels of interspousal conflict.
4. Keep the conflict to a minimum. Most of all, try not to fight in front of the children. Open conflict has negative effects on children whether the parents are divorced or not (Amato, 1993; Coiro, 1995; Insabella, 1995). So divorce is not the only culprit. But divorce *combined* with open conflict between the adults has worse effects.
5. Whatever else you do, do not use the child as a go-between or talk disparagingly about your ex-spouse to your child. Children who feel caught in the middle between the two parents are more likely to show various kinds of negative symptoms, such as depression or behavior problems (Buchanan, Maccoby, & Dornbusch, 1991).
6. Maintain your own network of support, and use that network liberally. Stay in touch with friends, seek out others in the same situation, join a support group. In whatever way you can, nurture yourself and your own needs.

In the midst of your own emotional upheaval from a divorce, these are not easy prescriptions to follow. But if you are able to do so, your children will suffer less.

The key thing to understand is that authoritative child rearing is linked to low levels of disturbed behaviors and higher levels of psychological adjustment in the child, *no matter what family structure the child grows up in*. And authoritarian or neglecting parenting is linked to poor outcomes whether it is triggered by a divorce, a stressful remarriage, the father's loss of a job, or any other stress (Goldberg, 1990). Ultimately, it is this *process* within the family that is significant for the child. The likelihood of a nonoptimal family process is greater in single-parent families, but this does not mean that the probability is 100 percent. Many single parents are able to find the strength within themselves to maintain a supportive process with their children. After all, we know that three-quarters of children reared in single-parent or stepfamilies manage to finish high school, and roughly half of those high school graduates go on to at least some college (McLanahan & Sandefur, 1994). Similarly, the great majority of children reared by a single parent or in a stepfamily do not become delinquent or show significant behavior problems. Indeed, one recent study of inner-city African-American teenage boys suggests that those in single-parent households are no more likely to be delinquent than are those in two-parent households because in this sample, the single mothers actually had more supportive relationships with their sons than did many of the married or remarried mothers (Zimmerman, Salem, & Maton, 1995). It is thus clearly possible for single or divorced parents to surmount the extra problems. But we need to face up to the fact that such family systems are less stable and, on average, less supportive for children.

Summary

1. Freud and Erikson each described two stages of personality development during the preschool years, the anal and phallic in Freud's theory, and autonomy and initiative in Erikson's theory.
2. Both vertical relationships, such as with parents and teachers, and horizontal relationships with peers are highly important in these years. Only in play with peers can the child learn about reciprocal relationships, both cooperative and competitive.
3. The child's attachment to the parent(s) remains strong, but except in stressful situations, attachment behaviors become less visible as the child gets older.
4. Preschoolers show more refusals and defiance of parental influence attempts than do infants. Outright defiance, however, declines from 2 to 6.
5. Both these changes are clearly linked to the child's language and cognitive gains.
6. Play with peers is visible before age 2 and becomes increasingly central through the preschool years.
7. Physical aggression toward peers increases and then declines during these years, while verbal aggression increases among older preschoolers. Aggression is often linked to frustration, and is clearly affected by patterns of reinforcement and modeling.
8. Children as young as 2 also show altruistic behavior toward others, and this behavior seems to grow as the child's ability to take another's perspective increases.
9. Short-term friendships, mostly based on proximity, are evident in children in this age range. The majority of such pairs are same-sex.
10. As early as age 3 or 4, boys and girls show different patterns or styles of interaction with peers, a difference that continues well into adulthood.
11. The preschooler continues to define himself along a series of objective dimensions but does not yet have a global sense of self-esteem.
12. Children make major strides in self-control in the preschool years, as the parents gradually turn over the job of control to the child.
13. Between 2 and 6, most children move through a series of steps in their understanding of gender constancy, first labeling their own and others' gender, then understanding the stability of gender, and, finally, comprehending the constancy of gender at about age 5 or 6.
14. In these same years, children begin to learn what is "appropriate" behavior for their gender. By age 5 or 6, most children have developed fairly rigid rules about what boys or girls are supposed to do or be.
15. Neither Freud's nor Kohlberg's explanations of gender development has fared well. Social learning explanations are more persuasive, because parents do appear to do some differential reinforcement of sex-appropriate behavior. The most useful current theory is gender schema theory, which combines some elements of Piagetian and social learning models.
16. Children also differ widely in social behavior and personality. Temperament plays some role. Children with more difficult temperament are more likely to show later behavior problems or delinquency.
17. Parental styles are also significant. Authoritative parenting, combining high warmth, clear rules and communication, and high maturity demands, is associated with the most positive outcomes. Neglecting parenting is associated with the least positive. Two other patterns, each with specific effects, are the authoritarian and the permissive.
18. Family structure also affects children. In U.S. data, any family structure other than two biological parents is linked to more negative outcomes. Following a divorce, children typically show disrupted behavior for several years. Parental styles also change, becoming less authoritative.

Key Terms

aggression
altruism
authoritarian parental style
authoritative parental style
dominance hierarchy
gender concept
gender constancy
gender identity
gender schema theory
gender stability
neglecting parental style
permissive parental style
prosocial behavior
sex role

Suggested Readings

Dunn, J. (1993). *Young children's close relationships.* Newbury Park, CA: Sage.

A wonderful small book, written in a clear and engaging style by one of the experts on children's social relationships.

Eisenberg, N. (1992). *The caring child.* Cambridge, MA: Harvard University Press.

An excellent and thoughtful book on the origins of prosocial or altruistic behavior.

Furstenberg, F. F., Jr., & Cherlin, A. J. (1991). *Divided families: What happens to children when parents part.* Cambridge, MA: Harvard University Press.

A relatively brief current review of this important subject, aimed at lay readers and decision makers rather than at other psychologists.

Golombok, S., & Fivush, R. (1994). *Gender development.* Cambridge, England: Cambridge University Press.

A basic, up-to-date description of all facets of gender development.

Lickona, T. (1983). *Raising good children.* Toronto: Bantam Books.

One of the very best "how to" books for parents I have ever seen, with excellent concrete advice as well as theory. Lickona's emphasis is on many of the issues I raised in the Real World *box on rearing altruistic children.*

Maccoby, E. E. (1990). Gender and relationships: A developmental account. *American Psychologist, 45,* 513–520.

In this brief paper, Maccoby reviews the accumulating evidence suggesting that boys and girls show quite different styles of interaction, beginning in the preschool years.

McLanahan, S., & Sandefur, G. (1994). *Growing up with a single parent: What hurts, what helps.* Cambridge, MA: Harvard University Press.

A sobering book, based on a careful reading of five major national studies, several of them longitudinal in design. It is well worth a look, if only because it raises some crucial issues. It is also written in a not-too-technical style that I think you will find comprehensible.

Interlude 2

Summing Up Preschool Development

Basic Characteristics of the Preschool Period

The table on page 214 summarizes the changes in children's abilities and behavior between 2 and 6. The sense one gets of this period is that the child is making a slow but immensely important shift from dependent baby to independent child. The toddler and preschooler can now move around easily, can communicate more and more clearly, has a sense of herself as a separate person with specific qualities, and has the beginning cognitive and social skills that allow her to interact more fully and successfully with playmates. At the same time the child's thinking is *decentering,* becoming less egocentric and less tied to the outside appearances of things.

In the beginning, these newfound skills and new independence are not accompanied by much impulse control. Two-year-olds are pretty good at doing; they are lousy at *not* doing. If frustrated, they hit things, or wail, scream, or shout (isn't language wonderful?). A large part of the conflict parents experience with children at this age comes about because the parent *must* limit the child, not only for the child's own survival, but to help teach the child impulse control.

The preschool years also stand out as the period in which the seeds are sown for the child's—and perhaps the adult's—social skills and personality. The attachment process in infancy continues to be formative because it helps to shape the internal working model of social relationships the child creates. But in the years from 2 to 6, this early model is revised, consolidated, and established more firmly. The resultant interactive patterns tend to persist into elementary school and beyond. The 3-, 4-, or 5-year-old who develops the ability to share, to read others' cues well, to respond positively to others, and to control aggression and impulsiveness is likely to be a socially successful, popular 8-year-old. In contrast, the noncompliant, hostile preschooler is far more likely to become an unpopular, aggressive schoolchild (Campbell et al., 1991; Eisenberg et al., 1995; Patterson et al., 1991).

Central Processes

Many forces are at play in creating these changes, beginning with two immense cognitive advances in this period: the 18- or 24-month-old child's new ability to use symbols, and the rapid development of a more sophisticated theory of mind between ages 3 and 5.

Symbol Use

The development of symbol use is reflected in many different aspects of the child's life. We see it in the rapid surge of language development, in the child's approach to cognitive tasks, and in play, where the child now pretends, having an object *stand for* something else. The ability to use language more skillfully, in turn, affects social behavior in highly significant ways, such as the increasing use of verbal rather than physical aggression, and the use of negotiation with parents in place of tantrums or defiant behavior.

Theory of Mind

The emergence of the child's more sophisticated theory of mind has equally broad effects, especially in the social arena, where the child's newfound abilities to read and understand others' behaviors form the foundation for new levels of interactions with peers and parents. It is probably not accidental that individual friendships between children are first visible at about the time that they also show the sharp drop in egocentrism that occurs with the emergence of a representational theory of mind.

We also see the seminal role of cognitive changes in the growing importance of several basic schemes. Not only does the 2- or 3-year-old have a more and more generalized internal model of attachment, she also develops a self-scheme and a gender-scheme, each of which forms part of the foundation of both social behavior and personality.

A Summary of the Threads of Development During the Preschool Years

Aspect of Development	2	3	4	5	6
	Age in Years				
Physical development	Runs easily; climbs stairs one step at a time	Rides tricycle; draws	Climbs stairs one foot per step; kicks and throws large ball	Hops and skips; some ball games with more skill	Jumps rope; skips; may ride bike
Cognitive development	Symbol use; 2- and 3-step play sequences	Ability to take others' physical perspective; beginning theory of mind	More advanced theory of mind; understands false belief	Conservation of quantity	
Language development	2-word sentences	3- and 4-word sentences and grammatical markers	Continued improvement of inflections, past tense, plurals, passive sentences, and other language complexities		
Self/ personality development	Self-definition based on comparisons of size, age, gender			Self-definition based on physical properties or skills	
	Gender identity		Gender stability		Gender constancy
	Erikson's stage of autonomy vs. shame and doubt	Erikson's stage of initiative vs. guilt			
	Freud's anal stage		Freud's phallic stage		
Social development	Attachment behavior less and less overt, primarily shown under stress				
	Multistep turn-taking sequences in play with peers	Some altruism; beginning same-sex peer choice	Beginning signs of individual friendships	Negotiation, rather than defiance, more common with parents	
	Aggression primarily physical		Aggression more and more verbal		
				Sociodramatic play	Roles in play

Social Contacts

Important as these cognitive changes are, they are clearly not the only causal forces. Equally central is the child's play with peers, which is itself made possible by the new physical and cognitive skills we see in the 2-year-old. When children play together they expand each other's experience with objects and suggest new ways of pretending to one another, thus fostering still further cognitive growth. When two children disagree about how to explain something, or insist on their own different views, it enhances each child's awareness that there *are* other ways of thinking or playing, thus creating opportunities to learn about others' mental processes. Thus, social interactions are the arena in which much cognitive growth occurs, just as Vygotsky proposed. For example, in one recent study, Charles Lewis finds that children who have many siblings or who interact regularly with a variety of adult relatives show more rapid understanding of other people's thinking and acting than do children with fewer social partners (Lewis, Freeman, & Maridaki-Kassotaki, 1995). Similarly, Jenkins and Astington (1996) find that children from larger families show more rapid development of a representational theory of mind. Some new research also shows that children with secure attachments show a more rapid shift to understanding false belief and other aspects of a representational theory of mind than do children with insecure attachments (Charman, Redfern, & Fonagy, 1995; Steele, Holder, & Fonagy, 1995)—a result that points to the importance of the *quality* as well as the quantity of social interactions for the child's cognitive development.

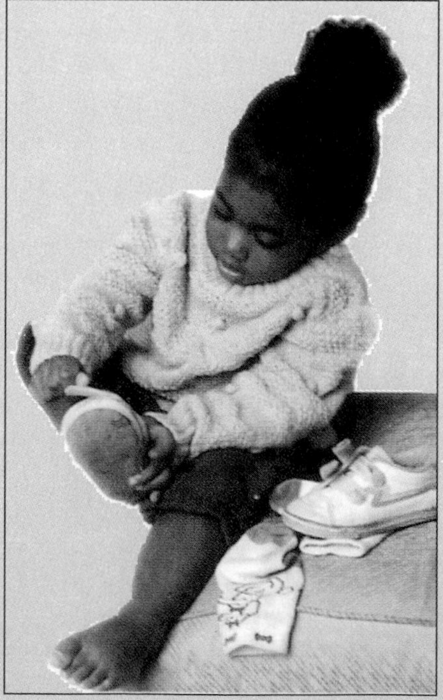

Play with other children also forms the foundation of the child's emerging gender schema. Noticing whether other people are boys or girls and what toys boys and girls play with is itself the first step in the long chain of sex-role learning.

Naturally enough, it is also in social interactions, especially those with parents, that the child's pattern of social behaviors are modified or reinforced. The parents' style of discipline becomes critical here. Gerald Patterson's work shows clearly that parents who lack the skills to control the toddler's impulsivity and demands for independence are likely to end up strengthening noncompliant and disruptive behavior, even if the parent's intention is the reverse (Patterson et al., 1991).

Influences on the Basic Processes

The family's ability to support the child's development in these years is affected not only by the skills and knowledge the parents bring to the process, but also by the amount of stress they are experiencing from outside forces and by the quality of support they have in their personal lives (Crockenberg & Litman, 1990). In particular, mothers who are experiencing high levels of stress are more likely to be punitive and negative toward their children, with resulting increases in the child's defiant and noncompliant behavior (Webster-Stratton, 1988). Maternal negativity, in turn, is implicated in the persistence of noncompliant behavior into elementary school. This link is clear, for example, in a longitudinal study of a group of such noncompliant children by Susan Campbell (Campbell & Ewing, 1990; Campbell et al., 1991). She finds that among a group of 3-year-olds who were labeled "hard-to-manage," those who improved by age 6 had mothers who had been less negative.

The mother's stress is obviously not the only factor in her level of negativity toward the child. Depressed mothers are also more likely to show such behavior (Conrad & Hammen, 1989), as are mothers from working-class or poverty-level families, who may well have experienced such negativity and harsh discipline in their own childhoods. But stress and lack of personal social support are both part of the equation. Thus, the preschooler, like children of every age, is affected by broader social forces outside the family as well as by the family interaction itself.

9 Physical and Cognitive Development from 6 to 12

The years of middle childhood, marked on one side by the beginning of schooling and on the other by the onset of puberty, are often passed over rather briefly, as if they were somehow insignificant. Far less research has been done on children in this age group than on either preschoolers or adolescents. Yet it is clear that major cognitive advances occur in these years, and that patterns and habits established during this time will affect not only adolescent experience, but also adulthood.

The beginning of formal schooling is itself a remarkable change. Even for children with many years of day-care or preschool experience, kindergarten or first grade represents a major change in expectations and level of demand; the child must now begin to learn all those specific competencies and roles that are part of his culture, including the three Rs. Erikson focused on precisely this aspect of the period, calling it the stage of *industry versus inferiority*.

Children all over the world start school at about the same age. Here you can see a Czech classroom and one in an aboriginal school in Australia.

Physical Changes

Perhaps one reason that middle childhood has been such a neglected area of study is that children's physical changes in this period are more subtle than at earlier ages. The growth patterns established in the late preschool years continue, with 2 to 3 inches and about 6 pounds added each year. Large muscle coordination continues to improve, so that children become more and more skillful at things like bike riding, and increase in both strength and speed. As just one example, 5-year-olds can jump about 34 inches in a standing broad jump, while 11-year-olds can jump an average of about 64 inches (Cratty, 1979).

Perhaps even more significant is the school-age child's increasingly good *fine* motor coordination, which makes writing possible, as well as the playing of most musical instruments, drawing, cutting, and many other skills.

Girls in this age range are still ahead of boys in their overall rate of maturation; they also have slightly more body fat and slightly less muscle tissue than do boys, a combination that makes boys slightly faster and stronger. Still, the sex differences in both strength and speed are small at this age and the distributions overlap a great deal. For example, the average 9-year-old boy can run 16.5 feet per second; a 10-year-old girl can run 17 feet per second (Cratty, 1979).

The Real World

Sports for Children

In the United States, and increasingly in other industrialized countries, children no longer play much in the street or in backyards; they play on organized teams and groups: soccer teams, Little League baseball, swimming clubs, and the like. Many children begin such programs when they are 6 or 7, often with great enthusiasm. But participation peaks by age 10 or 11 and then declines rapidly. Why?

Kids drop out of such programs because the emphasis on competition and winning is so great (Harvard Education Letter, 1992). Amateur coaches often have poor understanding of normal motor skills among 6- or 7-year-olds, so when they see a child who does not yet throw a ball skillfully or who kicks a ball awkwardly, they label this child as clumsy or uncoordinated. From then on, these perfectly normal kids get little playing time or encouragement. Only the stars—children with unusually good or early motor skill development—get maximum attention and exercise.

In fact, 6 or 7 is really too early for most children to be playing on full-sized playing fields or in competitive games (Kolata, 1992). It would be far better to wait until age 9 or 10—if then—for competitive games, and to have kids spend the earlier years learning and perfecting basic skills in activities that are fun regardless of your skill level and involve as much movement as possible. Among sports activities, soccer or swimming are particularly likely to meet these conditions, not only because everyone is likely to get at least some aerobic exercise, but also because the basic skills are within the abilities of 6- or 7-year-olds. Baseball, in contrast, is *not* a good sport for most kids this age because it requires real eye-hand coordination to hit or catch the ball, coordination that most 7-year-olds do not yet have. By age 10 or so, many children will be ready to play sports such as basketball, but many organized sports, such as tennis, are still difficult for the average child of this age.

If you want to encourage your children to be involved in sports, choose carefully. Let the child try several sports to see which one or ones he or she may enjoy, and be sure to select programs in which *all* children are given skill training and encouragement and in which competition is initially deemphasized. And don't push too fast or too hard. If you do, your child is likely to drop out of any type of organized sport by age 10 or 11, saying—as many do—that they feel inadequate, or that it isn't fun any more.

Another important set of physical changes beginning in these years are the hormone changes that eventually lead to puberty. Such hormone changes may begin as early as age 8 in girls, and at 9 or 10 for boys. Since it is not until adolescence that we see these hormone changes in full flower, I will save the description of puberty until Chapter 11, where I can describe the whole process in one connected discussion.

Health

The rate of illness in these years is slightly lower than what we see in preschool children. In the United States, the average elementary school youngster has 4 to 6 short-term illnesses each year, mostly colds and flu.

In contrast, the risk of injuries from accidents rises in this age range—cuts or broken limbs from active play, or injuries from fires, auto accidents, and the like. The annual rate of such injuries is about .4 per preschool child. Among elementary school boys, the rate is about .8 per child per year, and among girls about .6 (Schor, 1987)—illustrating the general point that boys are consistently at higher risk for almost all kinds of physical injuries.

Other Health Hazards: Obesity. Acute or chronic diseases are not the only health hazards for children. Aside from accidents, one of the most significant risks is obesity. Obesity is most often defined as a body weight 20 percent or more above the normal weight for height. By this definition, perhaps 15 percent of U.S. youngsters are obese, with the incidence rising steadily in the past 30 years (Centers for Disease Control, 1994e; Gortmaker et al., 1987). Equivalently high rates of obesity are common in other Western countries as well. For example, researchers in Italy found that 23.4 percent of a sample of 10-year-old boys and 12.7 percent of girls were obese (Maffeis et al., 1993).

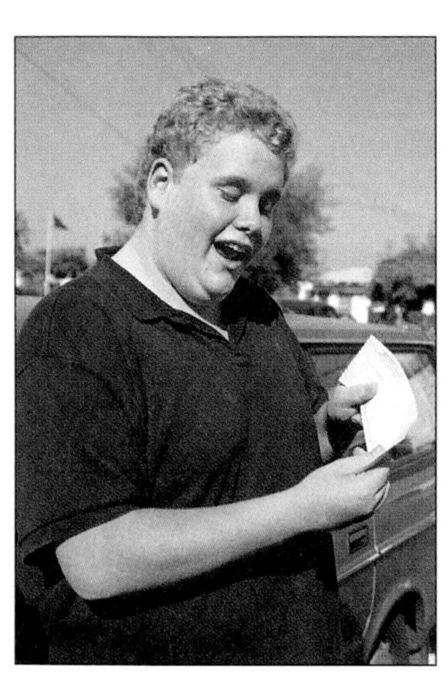

This overweight child not only has different kinds of encounters with his peers, he is also more likely to be fat as an adult, with accompanying increased health risks.

Obesity is *not* typically more common among poor children, although the incidence is unusually high in individual ethnic groups, including many Native American groups and—perhaps—inner-city blacks (Bandini & Dietz, 1992; Gilbert et al., 1992; Okamoto, Davidson, & Conner, 1993; Sherry et al., 1992).

Many, but not all, fat children continue to be overweight in adulthood. Only about a fifth of obese babies are still obese as adults, but half of those who are obese in elementary school are still obese as adults (Serdula et al., 1993). This does not mean, by the way, that all fat adults were fat children. More than half of obese adults were *not* fat as children. But being obese in childhood significantly increases the risk.

Obesity in childhood or adulthood appears to result from an interaction between a genetic predisposition and environmental factors that promote overeating or low levels of activity. Both twin and adoption studies show a clear genetic component. Adult identical twins have extremely similar adult weights even if they are reared apart, while fraternal twins differ much more in weight (Stunkard et al., 1990). Similarly, adopted children reared by obese parents are less likely to be obese than are the natural children of obese parents (Stunkard et al., 1986).

Whether a child with a genetic propensity to fatness will actually become obese, however, depends on "energy balance"—the balance between the calories taken in and the number expended by exercise. In particular, obese children typically choose more sedentary activities, or exercise somewhat less. For example, recent studies show a link between amount of TV watching and obesity, presumably because kids who watch a lot of TV simply have less time for active play (Dietz & Gortmaker, 1985).

Obesity obviously affects a child's social experiences during the school years, which may have effects detectable into adulthood. It also represents a significant long-term health problem. Among adults, the obese have shorter life expectancies and higher risk of heart disease and high blood pressure. At the same time, I should point out that *fear* of fatness may also become a significant problem for some children.

Serious eating disorders such as bulimia and anorexia—which I'll talk about in Chapter 11—don't become common until adolescence, but many school-age children, well aware of current cultural norms of thinness, are already dieting (Mellin, Irwin, & Scully, 1992). The balancing act required for the parents of an overweight child, then, is to try to help the child develop better eating and exercise habits without so emphasizing the importance of thinness that the child develops pathological patterns of dieting.

Language Development

By age 5 or 6, virtually all children have mastered the basic grammar and pronunciation of their native tongue. They can create remarkably complex sentences and have a vocabulary of perhaps 15,000 words. But anyone who has talked recently with a 6-year-old is well aware that the child still has a fair distance to go before reaching adultlike facility with language. During middle childhood, children learn such things as how to maintain the topic of conversation, how to create unambiguous sentences, and how to speak politely or persuasively (Anglin, 1993).

They also continue to add new vocabulary at a fairly astonishing rate of 5,000 to 10,000 words per year. This estimate comes from several recent, careful studies by Jeremy Anglin (1993, 1995), who estimates children's total vocabularies by testing them on a sample of words drawn at random from a large dictionary. Figure 9.1 shows Anglin's estimates for first, third, and fifth grade. Between third and fifth grades, Anglin finds that the largest gain occurs in knowledge of the type of words he calls *derived words*: words that have a basic root to which some prefix or suffix is added, such as happ*ily* or *un*wanted.

Anglin argues that at about age 8 or 9, the child shifts to a new level of understanding of the structure of language, figuring out relationships between whole categories of words, such as between adjectives and adverbs (*happy* and *happily*, *sad* and *sadly*), or between adjectives and nouns (*happy* and *happiness*), and the like. Having understood these relationships, the child can now understand and create a whole class of new words and his vocabulary thereby increases rapidly.

Cognitive Changes

Such an understanding of underlying patterns is just what Piaget also thought was new about these years of middle childhood. Piaget argued that this new quality of children's learning and understanding, which becomes apparent at about age 6 or 7, was as striking, and as significant, as the acquisition of symbol usage at age 2.

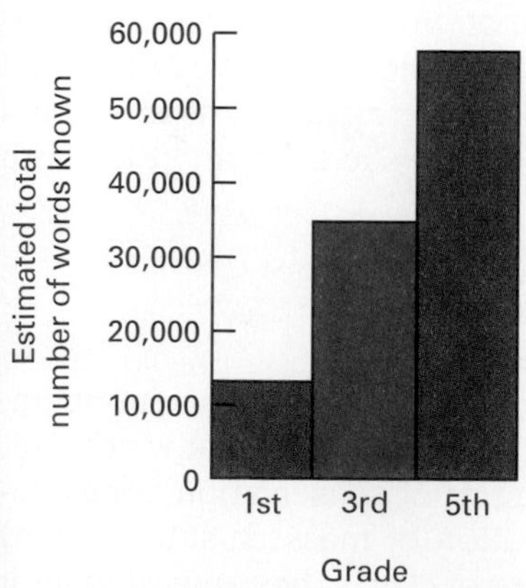

FIGURE 9.1 Anglin's estimates of the total vocabulary of first-, third-, and fifth-graders. (*Source:* Anglin, 1995, from Figure 6, p. 7.)

Piaget's View of Concrete Operations

The new skills we see at age 6 or 7 build on all the small changes we have already seen in the preschooler, but from Piaget's perspective a great leap forward occurs when the child discovers or develops a set of immensely powerful abstract general "rules" or "strategies" for examining and interacting with the world. Piaget calls this new set of skills *concrete operations*. By an "operation," Piaget means any of a set of powerful, abstract internal schemes such as reversibility, addition, subtraction, multiplication, division, and serial ordering. Each of these is a kind of internal rule about objects and their relationships. The child now understands the *rule* that adding makes something more and subtracting makes it less; she understands that objects can belong to more than one category at once and that categories have logical relationships.

Of all the operations, Piaget thought the most critical was *reversibility*—the understanding that both physical actions and mental operations can be reversed. The clay sausage in a conservation experiment can be made back into a ball; the water can be poured back into the shorter, fatter glass. This understanding of the basic reversibility of actions lies behind many of the gains made during this period. For example, if you possess the operation of reversibility, then knowing that A is larger than B also tells you that B is smaller than A. The ability to understand hierarchies of classes, such as Fido, spaniel, dog, and animal also rests on this ability to go backward as well as forward in thinking about relationships.

Piaget also proposed that during this third stage the child develops the ability to use **inductive logic.** She can go from her own experience to a general principle. For example, she can move from the observation that when you add another toy to a set and then count the set, it has one more than it did before, to a general principle that adding always makes it more.

Elementary school children are pretty good observational scientists, and will enjoy cataloging, counting species of trees or birds, or figuring out the nesting habits of guinea pigs. But they are not yet good at **deductive logic,** which requires starting with a general principle and then predicting some outcome or observation, like going from a theory to a hypothesis. For example, suppose I asked you to think of all the ways human relationships would be different if women were physically as strong as men. Coming up with answers to this problem requires deductive, not inductive, logic; the problem is hard because you must imagine things that you have not experienced. The concrete operations child is good at dealing with things she knows or can see and manipulate—that is, she is good with *concrete* things; she does not do well with manipulating ideas or possibilities. Piaget thought that deductive reasoning did not develop until the period of formal operations in junior high or high school.

CRITICAL THINKING

Try thinking about this question and watch yourself as you are thinking about it. Can you see how your deductive logic works? Can you think of everyday situations in which you use inductive or deductive logic?

Piaget did not say, by the way, that all these concrete operations skills popped out at the same moment, as if a light bulb had gone on in the child's head. He understood that it took the child some years to apply these new cognitive skills to all kinds of problems. But he did think that the shift to concrete operations involved a profound change in the *way* the child thinks, the strategies she uses, and the depth of understanding she can achieve.

Direct Tests of Piaget's Ideas

Researchers who have followed up on Piaget's descriptions of the concrete operational period have generally found that Piaget was right about the ages at which children first show various skills or understandings. Studies of conservation, for example, consistently show that children grasp conservation of mass or substance by about age 7. That is, they understand that the amount of clay is the same whether it is in a pancake or a ball or some other shape. They generally understand conservation of weight (that the two balls of clay weigh the same amount no matter their shape) at about age 8, but they understand conservation of volume (that an amount of water or clay takes up the same amount of *space* no matter its shape) only at about age 11.

Studies of classification skills show that at about age 7 or 8 the child first grasps the principle of **class inclusion,** that subordinate classes are *included in* larger, superordinate classes. Bananas are included in the class of fruit, and fruit is included in the class of food, and so forth. Preschool children understand that bananas are *also* fruit, but they do not yet fully understand the relationship between the classes.

A good illustration of all these changes comes from an early longitudinal study of concrete operations tasks by Carol Tomlinson-Keasey and her colleagues (Tomlinson-Keasey et al., 1979). They followed a group of 38 children from kindergarten through third grade, testing them with five traditional concrete operations tasks each year: conservation of mass, weight, and volume; class inclusion; and hierarchical classification. You can see from Figure 9.2 that the children got better at all five tasks over the three-year period, with a spurt between the end of kindergarten and the beginning of first grade (about the age Piaget thought that concrete operations really began), and another spurt during second grade.

New Themes: Memory and Strategy Development

Some researchers, rather than simply repeating Piaget's tasks, have tried to devise other ways to test the proposition that school-age children, compared to younger children, approach tasks in ways that are more general and are based on broader principles. In particular, the notion that older children consciously use *strategies* for solving problems or for remembering things has been the basis for a whole new look

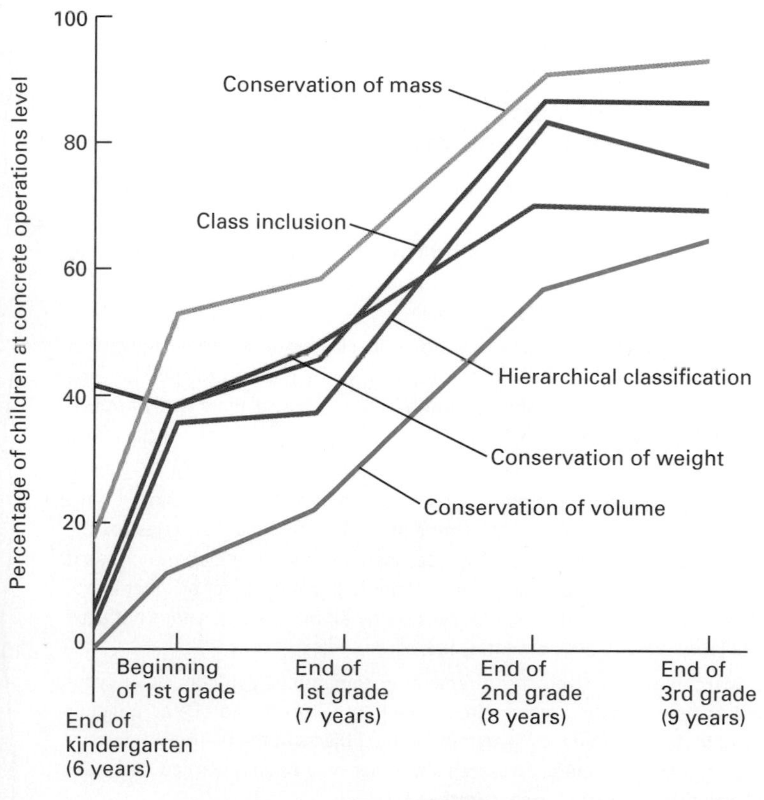

FIGURE 9.2 In this longitudinal study, children were given the same set of concrete operations tasks five times, beginning in kindergarten and ending in third grade. (*Source:* Tomlinson-Keasey et al., 1979, adapted from Table 2, p. 1158.)

at cognitive development. Work on memory and memory strategies is a particularly good example.

Critical Thinking

How would you go about remembering this list of things to do? Would you write down the list? What other strategies might you use?

Rehearsal Strategies. Suppose you need to run a set of errands: stop at the cleaners, buy some stamps, copy your IRS forms, and buy milk, bread, orange juice, carrots, lettuce, spaghetti, and spaghetti sauce at the grocery store. To remember such a list, you might use any one of several possible strategies, some of which I have listed (with examples) in Table 9.1. You could rehearse the list, you could organize the route in your mind, you could remember your menu for dinner when you get to the grocery store.

Do children do these things when they try to remember? One classic early study (Keeney, Cannizzo, & Flavell, 1967) indicated that school-age children did but younger children did not. Keeney showed children a row of seven cards with pictures on them and told them to try to remember all the pictures in the same order they were laid out. A space helmet placed over the child's head then kept the child from seeing the cards but allowed the experimenter to see if the child seemed to be rehearsing the list by muttering under his breath. Children under 5 almost never showed any rehearsal while 8- to 10-year-old children usually did. Interestingly, when 5-year-olds were *taught* to rehearse, they were able to do so and their memory scores improved. But when these same 5-year-olds were then given a new problem without being reminded to rehearse, they stopped rehearsing. That is, they could use the strategy if they were reminded, but they did not produce it spontaneously—a pattern described as a *production deficiency*.

More recent work suggests that preschool-age children can show some kinds of strategies in their remembering if the task is quite simple, such as the game of hide-and-seek (DeLoache, 1989). In one of Judy DeLoache's research techniques, the child

Table 9.1 Some Common Information Processing Strategies Involved in Remembering

- **Rehearsal.** Either mental or vocal repetition, or repetition of movement (as in learning to dance). May occur in children as young as 2 years under some conditions, and is common in older children and adults.
- **Clustering.** Grouping ideas or objects or words into clusters to help you remember them, such as "all animals," or "all the ingredients in the lasagna recipe," or "the chess pieces involved in the move called castling." This strategy is more easily applied in an area where you have experience or particular knowledge. Primitive clustering occurs in 2-year-olds.
- **Elaboration.** Finding shared meaning or a common referent for two or more things that need to be remembered. The helpful mnemonic for recalling the notes for the lines on the musical staff ("Every Good Boy Does Fine") is a kind of elaboration, as is associating the name of a person you have just met with some object or other word. This form of memory aid is not used spontaneously by all individuals, and is not used skillfully until fairly late in development, if then.
- **Systematic Searching.** When you try to remember something, you can "scan" your memory for the whole domain in which it might be found. Three- and 4-year-old children can begin to do this when they search for actual objects in the real world, but are not good at doing this in memory. So search strategies may be first learned in the external world and then applied to inner searches.

Source: Flavell, 1985.

watches the experimenter hide an attractive toy in some obvious place (e.g., behind a couch), and is then told that when a buzzer goes off, she can go and find the toy. While playing with other toys during the 4-minute delay interval, 2-year-olds often talked about the toy's hiding place, or pointed to or looked at the hiding place—all of which seem clearly to be early forms of mnemonic strategies.

These results and others like them tell us that no magic shift from nonstrategic to strategic behavior occurs at age 5 or 6 or 7. Children as young as 2 use primitive strategies. But school-age children seem to use strategies far more flexibly and efficiently, a quality of thinking that becomes increasingly evident in older schoolchildren (Bjorklund & Coyle, 1995). For example, when learning a list of words, 8-year-olds are more likely to practice the words one at a time ("cat, cat, cat") while still older children practice them in groups ("desk, lawn, sky, shirt, cat"). The 8-year-olds, tested again a year later, show signs of a shift toward the more efficient strategy (Guttentag, Ornstein, & Siemens, 1987).

Research Report

Memory and the Child as Witness

In England, a 7-year-old was able to provide the police with details of her experience after a sexual assault and was later able to identify her attacker in a lineup (Davies, 1993). In several famous cases in the United States, children as young as 3 have testified in court about physical or sexual abuse by nursery school teachers, testimony that has sometimes (but not always) led to convictions. Such testimony by children has raised a storm of controversy, centering on two main issues: (1) Can young children accurately remember faces or events and report on their experiences, even after a period of time has passed? (2) Are children more suggestible than adults about what they might have seen or experienced? Will they report what they have been told to say, what may have been suggested to them, or what they actually saw or felt? There is a lot we still don't know about this process, but a few conclusions have emerged from this growing body of research.

First, recall of specific events or the faces of people seen at a previous time does improve with age, but even preschoolers can recall action-related events with considerable accuracy. When experimenters have staged various crises or happenings, preschoolers and school-age children can describe what happened and can pick out a photo of the "culprit" almost as well as adults can. They report less detail than adults do, but they rarely report something that didn't actually occur (Baker-Ward, 1995; Baker-Ward et al., 1993; Ceci & Bruck, 1993; Davies, 1993). In one real-life study, Steward (1993) asked preschool children to describe their experiences on a recent visit to a medical clinic-visits that had been videotaped. The children reported only a quarter of the actual occasions when they had been touched on some part of their body by a medical person, but 94 percent of the reports they did give were accurate.

At the same time, younger children, particularly preschoolers, *are* more suggestible than older children or adults. To study this, researchers first show a film or tell a story to children and adults. Then, while asking questions about what the subject saw, the investigator injects some misleading question into the set—a question that assumes something that didn't really happen (e.g., "He was carrying a pipe wrench when he came into the room, wasn't he?"). Some days or weeks later, the subjects are again asked to describe what happened in the film or story. In this way you can check to see whether the inaccurate or misleading suggestion has been absorbed into the story. Young children are more affected than are older children or adults by such misleading suggestions (Leichtman & Ceci, 1995). Indeed, it is possible to mislead young children enough so that they will report inaccurately about specific physical events, such as having been kissed while being bathed or having been spanked (Bruck et al., 1995; Ceci & Bruck, 1993).

Thus, it *is* possible for an interviewer—psychologist, social worker, attorney, whomever—to nudge a child's testimony in one direction or another, unintentionally or intentionally. When the misinformation comes from parents, children are particularly likely to incorporate the parents' version into their own free recall (Ricci, Beal, & Dekle, 1995). Adult witnesses are *also* susceptible to suggestions of various kinds. So the difference here is one of degree and not of kind. From the legal point of view, this does not mean that children should not testify; it speaks only to the weight one might give their recollections and the care that should be used in framing questions.

Other Memory Strategies. Other strategies that help improve memory involve putting the items to be learned or remembered into some meaningful organization. When you mentally organize your grocery list with all the fruits and vegetables in one group and all the canned food in another, you are using this principle, called clustering or chunking.

Studies of clustering often involve having children or adults learn lists of words that have potential categories built into them. For example, I might ask you to remember this list of words: chair, spaghetti, lettuce, cat, desk, chocolate, duck, lion, table. I give you two minutes to try to memorize the list, using whatever method(s) you wish, making sure you understand that you don't have to remember them in the order I listed them, but in any order you like. I'm only interested in how many you can recall. Then I ask you to list the words for me. If you have used some kind of clustering technique, you are likely to list the same-category words together (*cat, duck,* and *lion*; *chair, desk, table*; and *spaghetti, chocolate, lettuce*).

School-age children do show this kind of internal organization when they recall things, while preschoolers do not. And within the school years, older children use this strategy more and more efficiently, using a few large categories rather than many smaller ones (Bjorklund & Muir, 1988).

In sum, we can see some primitive signs of memory strategies under optimum conditions as early as age 2 or 3, but with increasing age children use more and more powerful ways of helping themselves remember things. In the use of each strategy children also appear to shift from a period in which they don't use it at all, to a period in which they will use it if reminded or taught, to one in which they use it spontaneously. Finally, they use these strategies more and more skillfully, and generalize them to more and more situations. These are obviously changes in the *quality* of the child's strategies as well as the quantity.

Expertise

However . . . and this is a big however . . . all these apparent developmental changes may well turn out to be as much a function of expertise as they are of age. Piaget obviously thought that children apply broad forms of logic to most or all their experiences in any given stage. If that's true, then the amount of specific experience a child has had with some set of material shouldn't make a lot of difference. A child who understands hierarchical classification but who has never seen pictures of dinosaurs ought to be able to create classifications of dinosaurs about as well as could a child who had played a lot with dinosaur models.

These school-age chess players, unless they are rank novices, would remember a series of chess moves or an arrangement of chess pieces far better than I could, since they have expertise and I do not.

But in fact we now have a great deal of research showing that specific knowledge makes a huge difference. Children and adults who know a lot about some subject or some set of materials (dinosaurs, baseball cards, mathematics, or whatever) not only categorize information in that topic area in more complex and hierarchical ways, they are also better at remembering new information on that topic and better at applying more advanced forms of logic to material in that area. Furthermore, such expertise seems to generalize very little to other tasks (Ericsson & Crutcher, 1990). A child who is a devout soccer fan will be better than a nonfan at recalling lists of soccer words or the content of a story about soccer, but the two children are likely to be equally good at remembering random lists of words (Schneider & Bjorklund, 1992; Schneider et al., 1995).

Furthermore, the research on expertise tells us that even the typical age differences in strategy use or memory ability disappear when the younger group has more expertise than the older. For example, Michelene Chi, in her now-classic early study (1978), showed that expert chess players can remember the placement of chess pieces on a board much more quickly and accurately than can novice chess players, *even when the expert chess players are children and the novices are adults.* To paraphrase Flavell

(1985), expertise makes any of us look very smart, very cognitively advanced; lack of expertise makes us look very dumb.

Since young children are novices at almost everything, while older children are more expert at many things, perhaps the apparent age difference in the use of cognitive strategies is just the effect of the accumulation of more specific knowledge, and *not* the result of stagelike changes in fundamental cognitive structures.

CRITICAL THINKING

Think about your own areas of expertise and the areas about which you have little knowledge. Can you see any differences in the *way* you think about these different areas, in the form of logic you use, or the way you go about remembering?

Overview of the Thinking of the Schoolchild

When we look at what we know about the thinking of children between 6 and 12, we find a sort of paradox. On the one hand, there seems to be a genuine qualitative change in the form of the child's thinking, just as Piaget suggested. The 8-year-old, in contrast to a 4-year-old, approaches new tasks differently. He is more likely to attempt a more complex strategy, and if that strategy fails, he is more likely to try another one.

Yet it looks very much as if these new cognitive skills do not arise from any broad reorganization of schemes at about age 6 or 7, as Piaget proposed. Instead, the developmental process appears to be both gradual and heavily affected by the amount of experience the child has in a particular domain. The third major approach to cognitive development, the *information processing* approach, seems especially helpful in understanding just such a pattern of gradual qualitative change.

Information Processing: Another View of Cognitive Development

The information processing approach is not really a theory of cognitive development; it is an approach to studying thinking and remembering—a set of questions and some methods of analysis. The basic metaphor underlying this approach has been that of the human mind as computer. As with a computer, we can think of the "hardware" of cognition, such as the physiology of the brain, and the "software" of cognition, which would be the set of strategies or "programs" using the basic hardware. To understand thinking in general, we need to understand the processing capacity of the hardware and just what programs have to be "run" to perform any given task. What inputs (facts or data) are needed, what coding, decoding, remembering, or analyzing are required? To understand cognitive *development*, we need to discover whether the basic processing capacity of the system and/or the nature of the programs used change in any systematic way with age. Do children develop new types of processing (new programs)? Or do they simply learn to use basic programs on new material?

Changes in Processing Capacity. One obvious place to look for an explanation of developmental changes in cognitive skills is in the hardware itself. Any computer has physical limits on the number of different operations it can perform at one time or in a given space of time. As the brain and nervous system develop in the early years of life, with synapses formed and then pruned to remove redundancies, perhaps the capacity of the system increases.

One type of evidence consistent with this possibility is the finding that over the years of childhood, children are able to remember longer and longer lists of numbers, letters, or words—a pattern clear in Figure 9.3. Alternatively, these results might simply be yet another reflection of age differences in expertise, because older children naturally will have more experience with numbers, letters, or words. Thus, the memory-span data don't give us a clear-cut answer to the question of whether basic processing capacity increases with age.

But whether a change in basic capacity occurs or not, psychologists agree that processing *efficiency* increases steadily with age, a change that most developmentalists now see as the basis on which cognitive development occurs (Case, 1985; Halford et al., 1994; Kuhn, 1992).

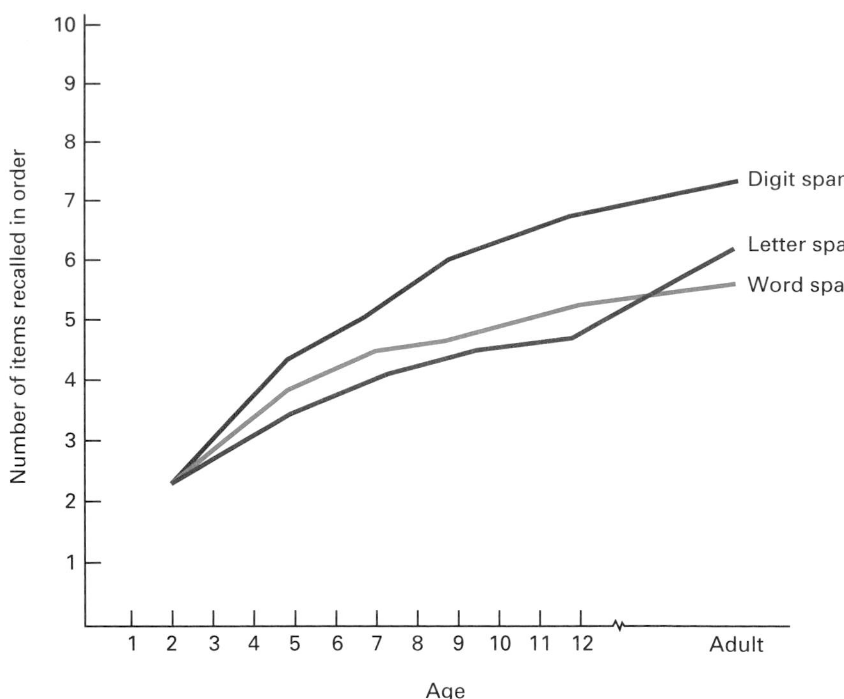

FIGURE 9.3 Psychologists have tried to measure basic memory capacity by asking subjects to listen to a list of numbers, letters, or words, and then to repeat back the list in order. This figure shows the number of such items children of various ages are able to remember and report accurately. (*Source:* Dempster, 1981, from Figures 1, 2, and 3, pp. 66, 67, 68.)

Processing Efficiency. The best evidence that cognitive processing becomes more efficient is that it gets steadily faster with age. Robert Kail (1991; Kail & Hall, 1994) has found virtually the same exponential increase with age in processing speed for a wide variety of tasks, including such perceptual-motor tasks as tapping, simple response time to a stimulus (like pressing a button when you hear a buzzer), and cognitive tasks such as mental addition. He has found virtually identical patterns of speed increases in studies in Korea as well as in the United States, which adds a useful bit of cross-cultural validity to the argument.

The most plausible explanation for this common pattern is that over time the physical system changes in some fundamental way that allows greater and greater speed of both response and mental processing. The most likely candidate for such a basic change is the "pruning" of synapses—a process I talked about in Chapter 4 (Hale, Fry, & Jessie, 1993). If pruning begins at about 18 months and then continues steadily throughout childhood, one effect could be to make the "wiring diagram" steadily more efficient and thus faster.

Greater efficiency in processing is also gained as a result of the child's acquisition of new strategies for solving problems or recalling information. Of course the new strategies themselves may appear because of increased underlying capacity or efficiency. But once present, these more powerful strategies make the whole system more efficient, much as we see in the behavior of experts at some task, who can perform that type of task with remarkable speed and directness.

Rules for Problem Solving. But how do these new strategies arise? Robert Siegler proposes that they emerge rather directly from experience—from repeated trial and error and experimentation (Siegler, 1994). Some of Siegler's own early work on the development of *rules* illustrates how the system may operate (Siegler, 1976, 1978,

FIGURE 9.4 This balance scale is similar to what Siegler used in his experiments.

1981). Siegler's approach was a kind of cross between Piagetian theory and information processing. He argued that cognitive development consists in acquiring a set of basic rules that are then applied to a broader and broader range of problems on the basis of experience. There are no stages, only sequences.

In one test of this approach, Siegler used a balance scale with a series of pegs on either side of the center, like the one in Figure 9.4. The child is asked to predict which way the balance will fall, depending on the location and number of discs placed on the pegs. A complete solution requires the child to take into account both the number of discs on each size, and the specific location of the discs.

Children do not develop such a complete solution immediately. Instead, Siegler predicts that four rules will develop, in order: Rule I is basically a "preoperational" rule, taking into account only one dimension, the number of weights. Children using this rule will predict that the side with more discs will go down, no matter which peg they are placed on. Rule II is a transitional rule. The child still judges on the basis of number except when the same number of weights appear on each side, and in that case takes distance from the fulcrum into account. Rule III is basically a concrete operational rule; the child tries to take both distance and weight into account simultaneously, except that when the information is conflicting (such as when the side with weights closer to the fulcrum has more weights), the child simply guesses. Rule IV involves the understanding of the actual formula for calculating the combined effect of weight and distance (distance × weight for each side).

Experience with a teeter-totter, like this boy is getting, may be one source of knowledge about how balance scales work.

Siegler has found that virtually all children perform on this and similar tasks as if they were following one or another of these rules, and that the rules seem to develop in the given order. Very young children behave as if they don't have a rule (they guess or behave randomly); when a rule develops, it is always Rule I that comes first. But progression from one rule to the next depends heavily on experience. If children are given practice with the balance scale so that they can make predictions and then check which way the balance actually falls, many show rapid shifts upward in the sequence of rules.

Thus, Siegler is attempting to describe a logical sequence children follow, not unlike the basic sequence of stages that Piaget describes, but Siegler shows that the specific step in this sequence that we see in a particular child depends not so much on age as on the child's specific experience with a given set of material. In Piaget's terminology, this is rather like saying that when accommodation of some scheme occurs, it always occurs in a particular sequence, but the rate with which the child moves through that sequence depends on experience.

Metacognition and Executive Processes. A third area in which information processing researchers have been active is in studying how children come to know what they know. If I asked you how you had tried to recall the list of nine items (chair, spaghetti, lettuce . . .) I listed earlier, I am sure you could describe your mental processes. You may even have consciously considered the various alternative strategies and then selected the best one. You could also tell me other things about the way your mind works, such as good ways to study particular subjects, or which kinds of tasks will be hardest, and why. These are all examples of metamemory or metacognition—knowing about remembering, or knowing about knowing. Such skills are part of a larger category that information processing theorists refer to as **executive processes:** planning what to do and considering alternative strategies.

Critical Thinking

Write down four good ways to study. In choosing one of these methods, does it matter what subject you are studying? How do you know all this? Do you think about it consciously when you are starting to study?

These skills are of particular interest because there is some suggestion that it may be precisely such metacognitive or executive skills that emerge (gradually) with age. Performance on a whole range of tasks will be better if the child can monitor her own performance or can recognize when a particular strategy is called for and when it is not. I pointed out in Chapter 7 that 4- and 5-year-old children do show some such monitoring, but it is rarely found earlier than that and it clearly improves fairly rapidly after school age. Such executive skills may well form the foundation of some of the age changes Piaget described.

A Summary of Developmental Changes in Information Processing

If I add up all the bits and pieces of evidence about information processing capacity and skills, I arrive at a set of tentative generalizations:

1. There may or may not be any increase in the basic processing capacity of the system (the hardware), but there clearly is an increase in the efficiency with which the hardware is used, resulting in steadily greater processing speed.
2. The sheer amount of specific knowledge the child has about any given task increases as the child experiments, explores, and studies things. This leads to more and more "expert" approaches to remembering and solving problems, which in turn improves the efficiency of the processing system.
3. Genuinely new strategies are acquired, probably in some kind of order. In particular, a school-age child seems to develop some "executive" or "metacognitive" abilities—she knows that she knows, and can *plan* a strategy for the first time.
4. Existing strategies are applied to more and more different domains, and more and more flexibly. If a child learned to rehearse on one kind of memory problem, the older child is more likely to try it on a new memory task; the younger child (particularly younger than 5 or 6) is not likely to generalize the strategy to the new task.
5. With increasing age, a wider range of different strategies can be applied to the same problem, so that if the first doesn't work, a backup or alternative strategy can be used. If you can't find your misplaced keys by retracing your steps, you try a backup, such as looking in your other purse or the pocket of your jacket, or searching each room of the house in turn. Young children do not do this; school-age children and adolescents do.

If this preschooler doesn't find what he's looking for on the first few tries, he will have trouble thinking of other possible places or ways to search. Elementary school children have more strategies and use them more flexibly.

Thus, some of the changes that Piaget observed and chronicled with such detail and richness seem to be the result simply of increased experience with tasks and problems, and increased speed and efficiency of processing (all quantitative changes, if you will). But there also seems to be a qualitative change in the complexity, generalizability, and flexibility of strategies used by the child.

Schooling and Its Impact

Although I started this chapter by pointing out that children all over the world begin school at age 6 or 7, thus far I have been talking about cognitive development as if it were entirely separate from the experience of schooling. But surely schooling itself must have some impact—on the child's thinking, on the child's skills, on the child's beliefs about his own skills.

Schooling and Cognitive Development

One question is whether some kind of school experience is itself necessary for the child to develop the full range of strategic abilities that we commonly see in children this age. Researchers have attempted to answer this question by studying children in societies or cultures in which schooling is not compulsory or is not universally available. By comparing similar groups of children, some of them in school and some of them not, it may be possible to discover the role that schooling plays in cognitive development.

A wide variety of such studies—in Mexico, Peru, Colombia, Liberia, Zambia, Nigeria, Uganda, Hong Kong, and many other countries—has led to the conclusion that school experiences are indeed *causally* linked to the emergence of some advanced cognitive skills. Children who do not attend schools not only do not learn some complex concepts and strategies, they are also not as good at generalizing a learned concept or principle to some new setting. So attending school helps children learn to think—precisely what it is intended to do.

A good example comes from Harold Stevenson's study of the Quechua Indian children of Peru (Stevenson & Chen, 1989; Stevenson et al., 1991). He and his associates tested 6- to 8-year-old children, some of whom had been in school for about 6 months and some who had not yet started school or who were living in an area where school was not available. Stevenson found that in both rural and urban areas, schooled children performed better on virtually all tasks, including a measure of seriation (putting things in serial order, such as by size or length) and a measure of concept formation. These differences remained even if the parents' level of education, the nutritional status of the child, and the amount of educational enrichment offered at home were taken into account. Only on measures of memory, such as the ability to repeat back a set of numbers that had been read to the child, were there no differences.

This does not mean that schooling is the only way for children to acquire complex forms of thinking. Specific experience in some area can also promote expertise. But schooling exposes children to many specific skills and types of knowledge, and appears to stimulate the development of more flexible generalized strategies for remembering and solving problems.

Adjusting to School

In the early years of schooling, the child faces a whole host of tasks. He must adapt to the rules of the classroom, he must get along with several dozen other children, and he must learn to read.

Learning to Read. Research on reading tells us that what affects a child's speed or ease of learning this crucial skill is not IQ but rather the child's specific understanding of the structure and sound of language. Especially significant are the child's ability to recognize individual letters and her awareness that spoken and written words are made up of individual sounds (Adams, 1990).

I already mentioned in Chapter 5 that very young babies pay attention to individual sounds, which linguists call *phonemes*. But the understanding that words are made up of strings of such sounds—referred to as *phonemic awareness*—seems to be more advanced, and is essential to reading.

Suppose you say to a child, "Tell me a word that starts the same as tap." To respond to such a request correctly, the child has to be able to identify which sound in the string of sounds comes first in the word *tap*. She must also be able to recognize this same sound in other words. You can get at this same skill in other ways, such as by asking children to recognize or produce rhyming words, or by reading them two words that differ in only one sound, such as *sing* and *sink*, and asking the child if the two words are the same or different. We now have abundant evidence that children who are more skilled at such tasks at age 3, 4, or 5 later learn to read much more easily (Bryant et al., 1990; Hansen & Bowey, 1994; Whitehurst, 1995). Furthermore, if you train preschoolers or kindergartners in phonemic awareness, their reading skills in first grade improve—a result that has been found in studies in Scandinavia and Germany as well as the United States (Schneider et al., 1995).

Cultures and Contexts

How Asian Teachers Teach Math and Science So Effectively

The way school subjects are taught may also make a major difference in children's intellectual development—a possibility that emerges especially clearly from comparisons of mathematics and science teaching in Asia and America. James Stigler and Harold Stevenson (Stevenson, 1994; Stigler & Stevenson, 1991) have observed such teaching in 120 classrooms in Japan, Taiwan, and the United States, and are convinced that Asian teachers have devised a particularly effective mode of presenting these subjects.

Japanese and Chinese teachers approach mathematics and science by crafting a series of "master lessons," each organized around a single theme or idea, and each involving specific forms of student participation. These lessons are like good stories, with a beginning, a middle, and an end. They frequently begin with a problem posed for the students. Here is one example from a fifth-grade class in Japan:

> The teacher walks in carrying a large paper bag full of clinking glass. . . . She begins to pull items out of the bag, placing them, one-by-one, on her desk. She removes a pitcher and a vase. A beer bottle evokes laughter and surprise. She soon has six containers lined up on her desk. . . . The teacher, looking thoughtfully at the containers, poses a question: "I wonder which one would hold the most water?" Hands go up, and the teacher calls on different students to give their guesses: "the pitcher," "the beer bottle," "the teapot." The teacher stands aside and ponders: "Some of you said one thing, others said something different. . . . There must be some way we can find out who is correct. How can we know who is correct?" (Stigler & Stevenson, 1991, p. 14)

The lesson continues as the students agree on a plan for determining which will hold the most. In such lessons, students are frequently divided into small groups, each assigned to work on part of the problem. These small groups then report back to the class as a whole. At the end of the lesson, the teacher reviews the original problem, and what they have learned. In this particular case, the children have learned something not only about measurement but about the process of hypothesis testing.

In U.S. classrooms, by contrast, it is extremely uncommon for teachers to spend 30 or 60 minutes on a single coherent math or science lesson involving the whole class of children and a single topic. Instead, they shift often from one topic to another during a single math or science "lesson." They might do a brief bit on addition, then talk about measurement, then about telling time, and back to addition. Asian teachers shift *activities* in order to provide variety, such as shifting from lecture format to small-group discussions; American teachers shift *topics* for the same apparent purpose.

Stigler and Stevenson also found striking differences in the amount of time teachers actually spend leading instruction for the whole class. In the United States classrooms they observed, this occurred only 49 percent of the time; group instruction occurred 74 percent of the time in Japan and 91 percent in Taiwan.

Stigler and Stevenson point out that the Asian style of teaching is not new to Western teachers. American educators frequently recommend precisely such techniques. "What the Japanese and Chinese examples demonstrate so compellingly is that when widely implemented, such practices can produce extraordinary outcomes" (Stigler & Stevenson, 1991, p. 45).

Where does such early language awareness come from? How does it happen that some 5- and 6-year-olds have extensive understanding of the way words are put together while others have little? The answer seems to be quite simple: exposure and expertise. For a child to learn about letters and sounds, he has to have had a great deal of exposure to language, both written and spoken. Such children are talked to a lot as infants, are read to regularly, are taught nursery rhymes, may have toy letters to play with, are told the sounds that go with each letter, or may be quite specifically taught the alphabet at an early age.

Of all the types of early experience that may contribute to such expertise, the most crucial seems to be the experience of being read to, regularly and in a fashion that invites the child's attention and response—a point I made in a Research Report in Chapter 7. Families that do not engage in such reading, or do not encourage other prereading experiences, have children who have far more difficulty learning to read once they begin school.

For those lacking such expertise at the start of school, the only solution is to try to build a parallel base of knowledge through many of the same kinds of experiences that more expert readers have had at home. This means that poor readers need a great deal of exposure to sound/letter combinations. But they also need to learn how to recognize patterns of letters in words. One need not—indeed must not—choose between those two hotly contesting educational systems, phonics and "whole word" training. Both are needed, along with instruction in syntax, so that the child will understand better what words *could* appear in certain places in sentences.

Marilyn Adams, who has analyzed all the evidence on early reading, also makes a persuasive case that the poor reader must have maximum possible success in oral reading, preferably with texts that are full of the sort of rhyme and repetition that will help to foster phonemic awareness and learning of language regularities. Programs with this emphasis, such as the Reading Recovery Program devised by Marie Clay (Clay, 1979), have been highly successful with poor readers, while more drill-like phonics programs have not (Hatcher, Hulme, & Ellis, 1994). In other words, poor readers seem to learn to read most easily through programs that to some degree mimic the naturally occurring home experiences of good readers: a great deal of reading, "play" with words, active questioning and experimentation.

Fitting In and Adapting. Whether a child comes to school ready to learn to read is clearly one of the key factors influencing her overall adjustment to school. But it is not the only factor. Parent involvement in the school also matters, as do some aspects of the child's temperament.

When parents come to parent-teacher conferences, attend school events, and get involved in supervising the child's homework, children are more strongly motivated, feel more competent, and adapt better to school. They learn to read more readily, get better grades through elementary school, and stay in school for more years (Brody, Stoneman, & Flor, 1995; Grolnick & Slowiaczek, 1994; Reynolds & Bezruczko, 1993). This effect of parent involvement has been found within groups of poor children as well as among the middle class, which tells us that the effect is not just a social class difference in disguise (e.g., Luster & McAdoo, 1996; Reynolds & Bezruczko, 1993).

It also matters whether the child's own personality or temperament matches the qualities valued and rewarded within the school setting. For example, Karl Alexander and his colleagues (Alexander, Entwisle, & Dauber, 1993) have found that children who are enthusiastic, interested in new things, cheerful, easygoing, and not restless do better in the early years of school than those who are more withdrawn or moody or high-strung.

What all this research indicates is that how a child starts out in the first few years of school has a highly significant effect on the rest of her school experience and success. To a considerable degree, "the rich get richer." Children who come to school with good skills clearly have an easier time. They quickly acquire more new skills and thereby adapt to later school demands more easily. Children who enter school with poor skills, or with less optimal temperamental qualities, learn less in the early years. Such a slow trajectory is not inevitable. Parent involvement can improve the chances of a less advantaged child, as can a particularly skillful kindergarten or first grade teacher (Pianta, Steinberg, & Rollins, 1995). But the key point is that the child does not enter school with a blank slate; she brings her history and her qualities with her.

Self-Judgments in School. The child's success at the various school tasks, in turn, affects his view of himself and his own abilities. Kindergarten and first-grade children seem to judge themselves and their abilities mostly on direct information of their own success or failure. They pay relatively little attention to how well others do at a particular task; in fact, the great majority will confidently tell you that they are the smartest kid in their class. But by third grade or so, children begin to compare themselves with others and judge themselves accordingly. They notice whether their classmates finish a test sooner than they did or whether someone else got a better grade or more corrections on her spelling paper.

Teachers' behavior shows a similar change: In the first few grades, teachers emphasize effort and work habits. But over succeeding years, they gradually begin to use more comparative judgments. By junior high, teachers compare children not only to each other but to fixed standards, other schools, and national norms (Stipek, 1992). These comparative processes are sometimes subtle, but they can be powerful. Robert Rosenthal, in his famous "Pygmalion in the classroom" studies, has shown that a teacher's belief about a given student's ability and potential has a small but significant effect on her behavior toward that student and on the student's eventual achievement (Rosenthal, 1994). When the teacher believes the student can achieve, the student does better.

The beliefs about their own abilities that students develop through these processes are usually quite accurate. Students who consistently do well in comparison to others come to believe that they are academically competent and that they are in control of academic outcomes. Interestingly, this seems to be less true of girls than of boys, at least in American culture. On average, girls get better school grades than boys do, but they have lower perceptions of their own ability. When they do well, they are more likely to attribute it to hard work than ability; when they do poorly, they see it as their own fault (Stipek & Gralinski, 1991).

Collectively, these experiences of success and failure mean that by seventh or eighth grade, most students have well-established ideas about their own academic skills and their ability to control the events around themselves.

Assessing Students' Progress: IQ and Achievement Tests in the Schools

One source of information children have about how well they are doing academically is their performance on various kinds of standardized tests. There are two basic types, IQ tests—which you read about in Chapter 7—and achievement tests.

IQ Tests in the Schools. You already know that IQ test scores are good predictors of school performance. It is for this reason that such tests are most often used within school systems as a method of selecting or identifying children who might benefit from special programs. Children whose speed of learning seems to be much faster or slower than normal may be given an IQ test to see whether they might be retarded or gifted. Similarly, a child who is having difficulty learning to read but is otherwise doing okay may be given a test like the WISC-III or other special tests designed to diagnose specific learning disabilities or brain damage. In each case, the pattern of scores on the test as a whole, or on individual subtests, is then used along with other data to decide whether the child should be in a special class.

Such uses of IQ tests are very close to what Binet envisioned nearly 100 years ago. Nonetheless, such diagnostic functions for IQ tests have been the subject of a good deal of debate, much of it heated.

Everyone agrees that schools must often diagnose or sort children into groups. Clearly, some children do require additional assistance. The arguments center on whether IQ tests ought to be used as the central basis for such sorting. There are several strong reasons usually given against such a use.

First, as I pointed out in Chapter 7, IQ tests do not measure all the facets of a child's functioning that may be relevant. For example, clinicians have found that some children with IQs below 70, who would be considered retarded if the score alone were used for classification, nonetheless have sufficient social skills to enable them to function well in a regular classroom. If we use only the IQ score, some retarded children would be incorrectly placed in special classes. Second, there is the problem of the self-fulfilling prophecy of an IQ test score. Because many parents and teachers still believe that IQ scores are a permanent feature of a child, once a child is labeled as "having" a particular IQ, that label tends to be difficult to remove later.

The most important negative argument is that tests may simply be biased in such a way that some subgroups of children are more likely to score high or low, even though their underlying ability is the same. For example, the tests may contain items that are not equally accessible to minorities and whites; taking such tests and doing well may also require certain test-taking skills, motivations, or attitudes less common among some minority children, especially African-American children (Kaplan, 1985; Reynolds & Brown, 1984).

In response to these arguments, most major tests have been revised to eliminate all obvious types of bias. Yet a troubling fact remains: When IQ tests are used for diagnosis in schools, proportionately more minority than white children continue to be diagnosed as retarded or slow. This fact has led to a number of lawsuits, including *Larry P. v. Riles*, a case in which a group of parents of black children sued the California school system for bias. The parents argued that there was no underlying difference in basic ability between black and white children, so if differences in test scores led to larger numbers of black children being assigned to special classes, the tests must clearly be biased.

The school system argued that IQ tests don't measure underlying capacity or ability, but only a child's existing repertoire of basic intellectual skills. In the terms I used in Chapter 7, this is like saying that an IQ test cannot tell you what the upper limit of some child's intellectual "reaction range" may be; all it can tell you is where the child is now functioning within that range. By school age, the child's level of functioning has already been affected by such environmental factors as prenatal care, diet, health, and family stability—all of which tend to be less optimal among African Americans. Thus, the test may accurately reflect a child's current abilities and be a proper basis for assigning the child to a special program, even though that child might have a greater underlying capacity or competence that could have been expressed under more ideal life circumstances.

In this particular case, the judge originally ruled in favor of the parents and prohibited the use of standardized IQ test scores for placement in special classes in California. Other legal decisions, including subsequent rulings in the California case, have gone the other way (Elliott, 1988). So the legal question is not settled, although there are places in the United States in which the use of IQ tests for diagnosis and placement of African-American or other minority children is forbidden. One unintended consequence of this is that since placement decisions must still be made, they are now being made based on evidence that may be even more culturally biased, such as less-standardized tests or teacher evaluations.

I have no quick or easy solution to this dilemma. It is certainly true that schools in the United States reflect the dominant middle-class Euro-American culture, with all its values and assumptions. But it is also true that succeeding in these schools is essential if the child is to acquire the basic skills needed to cope with the complexities of life in an industrialized country. For a host of reasons, including poorer prenatal care, greater poverty, and different familial patterns, more African-American children appear to *need* special classes in order to acquire the skills they lack. Yet I am well aware that placing a child in a special class may create a self-fulfilling prophecy. Expectations are typically lower in such classes, so the children—who were already learning more slowly—are challenged still less and so proceed even more slowly. Yet to offer no special help to children who come to school lacking the skills needed to succeed there seems equally unacceptable to me. In the end, I conclude that IQ tests are more reliable and valid than the alternatives. I would not want a single IQ test used as the sole basis for a placement decision, especially early in elementary

CRITICAL THINKING

Do you agree with me? Why or why not?

school when IQ test scores are still relatively variable. I would want to take into account the level of stress in the child's life at the time the test was given. But it seems foolish to me to throw out the tests altogether.

Achievement Tests. The second major type of test used in schools is an **achievement test,** a type of exam with which nearly all of you have doubtless had personal experience. Achievement tests are designed to assess *specific* information learned in school, using items like those in Table 9.2. The child taking an achievement test doesn't end up with an IQ score, but his performance is still compared to that of other children in the same grade across the country.

How are these tests different from an IQ test? The designers of IQ tests thought they were measuring the child's basic capacity, her underlying **competence.** An achievement test, in contrast, is intended to measure what the child has actually learned (her **performance**). This is an important distinction. Each of us presumably has some upper limit of ability—what we could do under ideal conditions, when we are maximally motivated, well, and rested. But since everyday conditions are rarely ideal, we typically perform below our hypothetical ability.

The authors of the famous IQ tests believed that by standardizing the procedures for administering and scoring the tests they could come close to measuring competence. But because we can never be sure that we are assessing any ability under the best of all possible circumstances, we are *always* measuring performance at the time the test is taken. What this means in practical terms is that the distinction between IQ tests and achievement tests is one of degree rather than of kind. IQ tests include items that are designed to tap fairly fundamental intellectual processes like comparison and analysis; the achievement tests call for specific infor-

Table 9.2 Some Sample Items from a Fourth-Grade Achievement Test

Vocabulary
jolly old man
1. angry
2. fat
3. merry
4. sorry

Language Expression
Who wants ____ books?
1. that
2. these
3. them
4. this

Mathematics
What does the "3" in 13 stand for?
1. 3 ones
2. 13 ones
3. 3 tens
4. 13 tens

Reference Skills
Which of these words would be first in ABC order?
1. pair
2. point
3. paint
4. polish

Spelling
Jason took the *cleanest* glass.
right ____ wrong ____

Mathematics computation

79	149	62
+ 14	− 87	× 3

Source: From Comprehensive Tests of Basic Skills, Form S. Reprinted by permission of the publisher, CTB/McGraw-Hill, Del Monte Research Park, Monterey, CA 93940.

In the United States, virtually all fourth-graders—like these in Austin, Texas—are given achievement tests, so as to allow schools to compare their students' performances against national norms.

mation the child has learned in school or elsewhere. College entrance tests, like the Scholastic Aptitude Tests (SATs, which many of you have taken recently) fall somewhere in between. They are designed to measure basic "developed abilities," such as the ability to reason with words, rather than just specific knowledge. But all three types of tests measure aspects of a child or young person's performance and not competence.

The use of achievement tests in schools has been almost as controversial as the use of IQ tests. I've explored some of the arguments and counterarguments in the Real World discussion on page 236.

School Quality

A very different set of questions about school experience has to do with variations in the quality of the schools themselves. Real estate agents have always touted a "good school district" as a reason for settling in one town or neighborhood rather than another. Now we have research to show that the real estate agents are right: Specific characteristics of schools and teachers do affect children's development.

Researchers interested in possible effects of good and poor schools have most often approached the problem by identifying unusually "effective" or "successful" schools (Good & Weinstein, 1986; Rutter, 1983). In this research, an effective school is defined as one in which pupils show one or more of the following characteristics at higher rates than you would predict, given the kind of families or neighborhoods the pupils come from: high scores on standardized tests, good school attendance, low rates of disruptive classroom behavior and delinquency, a high rate of later college attendance, and high self-esteem. Some schools seem to achieve these good outcomes year after year, so the effect is not just chance variation. When these successful schools are compared with others in similar neighborhoods that have less impressive track records, certain common themes emerge, summarized in Table 9.3 (p. 237)

What strikes me when I read this list is how much effective schools sound like authoritative parenting. Such schools have clear goals and rules, good control, good

The Real World

Achievement Tests in Schools

The major arguments for using achievement tests in schools are that they provide parents and taxpayers with a way of assessing the quality of their schools, and provide teachers with important information about the strengths and weaknesses of their class or individual students.

But do such tests actually serve any of these purposes well? Maybe not. For one thing, when schools know that they are being evaluated based on test scores, they have a strong incentive to "teach to the test" (Corbett & Wilson, 1989). For another, teachers report that even when they do not spend time teaching specific material that is likely to be tested, they do spend more time on the general subject matter covered by the tests, and therefore have less time for skills that are not included in most achievement tests, such as discussing ideas, solving problems inductively, writing, or creative activities (Darling-Hammond & Wise, 1985).

The failure of most standardized tests to tap the child's ability to draw inferences, apply information, or ask good questions seems especially troublesome, because these are all problem-solving skills that appear to have long-range significance for adult success.

Overall, it seems clear that achievement tests will be useful as measures of the quality of schools only if there is a good match between what the tests measure and our basic educational goals. If one of our goals is to teach children how to write, then the usual achievement tests are not helpful because they do not measure such a skill. But if our goal is to teach basic computational skills, an achievement test can be a good measure of how well we have succeeded.

A second argument against achievement tests is that they are not terribly helpful for teachers trying to design programs for individual children. Teachers report that they rarely use test scores as a basis for diagnosing a specific child's strengths and weaknesses. Most feel that a child's day-to-day classroom performance yields better diagnostic information than a one-shot test under high-stress conditions.

There is no easy solution to all this (Harvard Education Letter, 1988). We need better tests that tap more basic problem-solving skills rather than merely rote learning; we need other ways of judging whether our schools are meeting our social mandate. At the very least, you need to be a very skeptical reader of those annual "school report cards" that purport to tell us how well a given school or school district is performing its job.

communication, and high nurturance. The same seems to be true of effective teachers: It is the "authoritative" teachers whose pupils do best academically. Such teachers have clear goals, clear rules, effective management strategies, and personal and warm relationships with their pupils (Linney & Seidman, 1989). They also have high expectations for their students and make sure that virtually all the students in their classes complete the year's normal work (Mac Iver, Reuman, & Main, 1995).

But as with any system, the quality of the whole school is more than the sum of the quality of the teachers or classrooms. Each school also has an overall climate or ethos that affects its students. The most positive school climate occurs when the principal provides clear and strong leadership, is dedicated to effective teaching and provides concrete assistance for such teaching, and when goals are widely shared. In such schools parents also typically participate in school activities at a high rate. If you are making a decision about a city or a neighborhood in which to rear your children, these are the qualities to look for.

Individual Differences

I have already raised a number of issues of individual differences—differences in children's early reading ability, the use of IQ tests to identify students for special classes, and the like. But let me explore three other individual difference questions, all of which may have considerable practical relevance.

Table 9.3 Characteristics of Unusually Effective Schools

- **Qualities of Pupils.** Pupils represent a *mixture* of backgrounds or abilities but with a reasonably large concentration of pupils who come to school with good academic skills.
- **Goals of the School.** School leaders place strong emphasis on academic excellence, with high standards and high expectations.
- **Organization of Classrooms.** Classes are focused on specific academic learning. Daily activities are structured, with a high percentage of time in actual group instruction.
- **Homework.** Homework is assigned regularly, graded quickly.
- **Discipline.** Most discipline is handled within the classroom, with relatively little fall-back to "sending the child to the principal." In really effective schools, not much class time is actually spent in discipline because these teachers have very good control of the class.
- **Praise.** Pupils receive high doses of praise for good performance, or for meeting stated expectations.
- **Teacher Experience.** The school staff includes many teachers with extensive teaching experience, presumably because it takes time to learn effective class management and instruction strategies.
- **Building Surroundings.** The school building, even if it is old, is clean, attractive, and orderly.
- **School Leadership.** The school principal states his or her goals clearly and often, and back up his or her intentions with actions.
- **Responsibilities for Children.** Children are given real responsibilities—in individual classrooms and in the school as a whole.
- **Size.** As a general rule, smaller schools are more effective, in part because in such schools children feel more involved and are given more responsibility. This effect is particularly clear in studies of high schools.
- **Money.** Increasing the amount of money spent on schools (above the basic amount needed to provide a physically safe, clean environment, staffed with highly competent teachers) does not *automatically* improve quality, but if the added money is carefully spent, it can have positive effects. For example, reducing class size doesn't automatically result in better school performance, but if smaller classes are combined with new methods of instruction, it can be beneficial.

Sources: Linney & Seidman, 1989; Mosteller, 1995; Rutter, 1983; Sadowski, 1995; Stringfield, 1991.

Individual Differences in Information Processing

In my earlier discussion of information processing, I focused on the *developmental* aspects—those changes in processing capacity or efficiency or strategies that appear to be common across children. But information processing researchers have also turned their attention to questions of individual differences, asking what fundamental processes lie behind an individual's performance on an IQ test or other measure of cognitive skill. A few preliminary answers have emerged.

Speed of Information Processing. Given that increases in speed or efficiency of processing appear to be one of the underpinnings of age changes in cognitive skills, it makes sense to hypothesize that differences in speed may also underlie individual

One of the marks of successful schools is that they assign regular homework. And one of the characteristics of academically successful children is that their parents supervise their homework, as this Native American father is doing.

CRITICAL THINKING

One of the synonyms of "intelligent" is "quick." Do you think this reflects some basic assumption that speed of processing is a central ingredient of what we think of as intelligent behavior? Can one be very intelligent and slow?

differences in IQ. A number of different investigators have found just such a link: Subjects with faster reaction times or speed of performance on a variety of simple tasks also have higher IQ scores on standard tests (Vernon, 1987). We even have a few studies in which speed of processing has been directly linked to central nervous system functioning and to IQ. For example, it is now possible to measure the speed of conduction of impulses along individual nerves, such as nerves in the arm. Philip Vernon (1993; Vernon & Mori, 1992) has found that such a measure of neural speed correlates about .45 with IQ.

Most of this research has been done with adults, but a link between speed of reaction time and IQ has also been found in a few studies with children (Keating, List, & Merriman, 1985; Saccuzzo, Johnson, & Guertin, 1994). Furthermore, we have some pretty clear indications that such speed-of-processing differences may be built in at birth. In particular, recall the research I talked about in Chapter 5, linking speed of infant habituation and recognition memory with later IQ.

CRITICAL THINKING

One reason for so many children being identified as learning disabled is that school districts receive extra money to serve children given this label, but do not receive extra funds to teach "slow learners." If you were a state legislator, would you change the law? What are the pros and cons?

Learning Disabilities

Some children with normal IQs and essentially good adaptive functioning nonetheless have difficulty learning to read, write, or do arithmetic. The typical label for this problem is **learning disability (LD),** although you will also hear terms like *dyslexia* (literally "nonreading") or *minimal brain damage*. The official definition of this problem includes the presumption that the difficulty arises from some kind of central nervous system dysfunction or damage.

How common such learning disabilities may be is still a matter of considerable dispute. Sylvia Farnham-Diggory (1992), one of the leading experts in the field, argues that up to 80 percent of all children classified by school systems as learning disabled are misclassified. She claims that only about 5 out of every 1000 children has a genuine neurologically based learning disability. The remainder who are so classified are more appropriately called slow learners, or they suffer from some other difficulty, perhaps temporary emotional distress, poor teaching, or whatever.

Practically speaking, however, the term *learning disability* is used very broadly within school systems (at least within the United States) to label a grab-bag of children who have unexpected or otherwise unexplainable difficulty with schoolwork, particularly reading. Nearly 5 percent of all children in the United States are currently labeled in this way (Farnham-Diggory, 1992).

Explanations of the problem are just as uncertain as are definitions. One difficulty is that children labeled as learning disabled rarely show any signs of major brain damage on any standard neurological tests. So if a neurological problem is the explanation, it must be a subtle one. A number of current researchers have suggested that a large number of small abnormalities may develop in the brain during prenatal life, such as some irregularity of neuron arrangement, or clumps of immature brain cells, or scars or congenital tumors. The growing brain compensates for these problems by "rewiring" around the problem areas. These rewirings, in turn, may scramble normal information processing procedures just enough to make reading or calculation or some other specific task very difficult (Farnham-Diggory, 1992).

Alternatively, some experts argue that there may not be any underlying neurological problem at all. Instead, children with learning disabilities (especially *reading* disabilities) may simply have a more general problem with understanding the sound and structure of language, a point that is entirely consistent with what I have already said about the basic processes of learning to read.

These disagreements about both definition and explanation are (understandably) reflected in confusion at the practical level. Children are labeled "learning disabled" and assigned to special classes, but whether an individual child will be helped by a particular type of intervention program will depend on whether that specific program is (1) any good, and (2) happens to match his or her type of disability or problem. Remediation does seem to be possible, but it is *not* simple, and a program that works well for one child may not work at all for another. Of course this is not good news for parents whose child may be having difficulty with some aspect of schooling, whose only recourse is trial and error and eternal vigilance. But it reflects the disordered state of our knowledge, despite thousands of research studies and diligent effort by many creative people.

School can be a discouraging and frustrating place for a child with a learning disability.

Sex Differences in Cognitive Skills

Comparisons of total IQ test scores for boys and girls do *not* reveal consistent differences. It is only when we break down the total score into several separate skills that some patterns of sex differences emerge. On average, studies in the United States show that girls do slightly better on verbal tasks and at arithmetic computation, and that boys do slightly better at numerical reasoning. For example, on the math portion of the Scholastic Aptitude Tests (SATs), the average score for boys is consistently higher than the average score for girls. Many of these differences have been getting smaller in recent years, although this is not true for the SAT mathematics score difference, which has persisted over the past three decades among students in the United States (Brody, 1992; Byrnes & Takahira, 1993; Jacklin, 1989).

Two other differences are also found regularly. More boys than girls are found among children who test as gifted in mathematics (Benbow, 1988; Lubinski & Benbow, 1992). And on tests of spatial visualization, like the ones illustrated in Figure 9.5, boys have higher average scores. On measures of mental rotation (illustrated by item *c* in the figure) the sex difference is quite large and becomes larger with age (Voyer, Voyer, & Bryden, 1995).

I want to point out that even on tests of mental rotation, the two distributions overlap. That is, many girls and women are good at this type of task, and many boys and men are not, although the average difference is quite large.

Where might such differences come from? The explanatory options should be familiar by now. Biological influences have been most often argued in the case of sex differences in spatial abilities, where there may be both genetic differences and—more speculatively—differences in brain functioning resulting from prenatal variations in hormones (Newcombe & Baenninger, 1989).

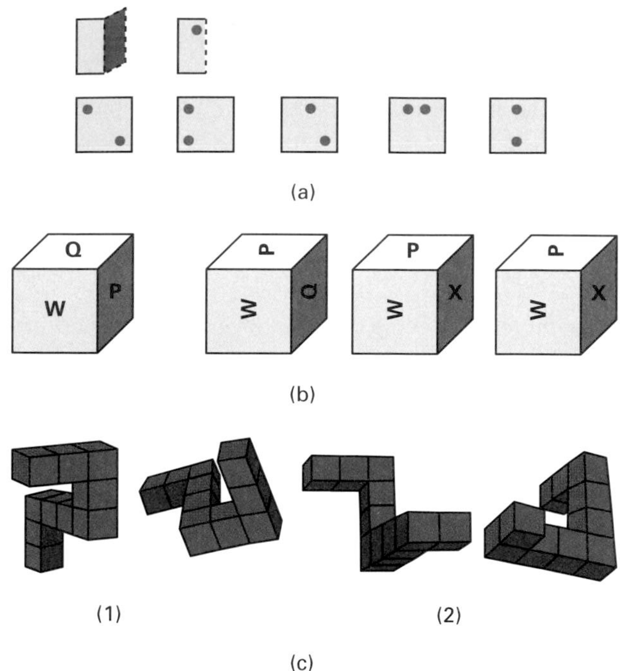

FIGURE 9.5 All three of these items test aspects of spatial visualization. Item *a* represents folded paper. A hole is punched through all the thicknesses. Which figure shows what the paper would look like when it is unfolded? In *b*, you must figure out which of the three cubes on the right could be a different view of the cube on the left. Item *c* is a measure of mental rotation. In each pair, would the two figures be the same if they were appropriately rotated? (*Source:* Halpern, 1986, Figure 3.1, page 50, and Figure 3.2, p. 52.)

In contrast, environmental explanations have been prominent in discussions of the sex differences in mathematical or verbal reasoning. Especially in the case of mathematics we have considerable evidence that girls' and boys' skills are systematically shaped by a series of environmental factors:

- Boys take more math courses than girls do. When the amount of math exposure is held constant, the sex difference becomes much smaller.
- Parental attitudes about mathematics are markedly different for boys and girls. Parents are more likely to attribute a daughter's success in mathematics to effort or good teaching; poor performance by a girl is attributed to lack of ability. In contrast, parents attribute a boy's success to ability and his failure to lack of application (Holloway & Hess, 1985; Parsons, Adler, & Daczala, 1982).
- Girls and boys have different experiences in math classes. In elementary school, teachers pay more attention to boys during math instruction (and more attention to girls during reading instruction), and in high school, math teachers direct more of their questions and comments to boys, even when girls are outspoken in class.

The cumulative effect of these differences in expectation and treatment show up in high school, when sex differences on standardized math tests usually become evident. In part, then, the sex differences in math achievement test scores appear to be perpetuated by subtle family and school influences on children's attitudes. Whether these differences can explain the greater percentage of boys than girls who show real giftedness in mathematics is not so clear. One possibility is that because tests of mathematical ability involve at least some items that require mental rotation ability, very high scores on such tests are less likely for girls. Indeed, one recent study (Casey et al., 1995) shows that when mental rotation ability is subtracted out, the sex difference in SAT math scores among high-ability groups disappears. Still, this issue, like many of the issues I have touched on in this chapter, remains hotly debated.

Summary

1. The period of middle childhood has been studied less than other age periods, but is nonetheless highly significant for the child's development.
2. Physical development from 6 to 12 is steady and slow. The onset of puberty brings a whole host of hormonal changes.
3. Illnesses are less common during this period than at earlier ages but continue to be fairly regular. Other health problems include accidents and obesity.
4. Obesity, increasing in frequency in Western countries, appears to be caused by hereditary tendencies plus some combination of too little energy expenditure and too many calories taken in.
5. During the school years, children learn a great deal about the conversational customs of language; they also add many thousands of new words to their vocabularies.
6. Piaget proposed a major change in the child's thinking at about age 6, when powerful "operations" such as reversibility, addition, or multiple classification were understood. The child also learns to use inductive logic, but does not yet use deductive logic.
7. Recent research on this period confirms many of Piaget's descriptions of sequences of development but calls into question Piaget's basic concept of stages.
8. Studies of expertise also point to a more important role than Piaget believed of specific task experience in the sophistication of the child's thinking.
9. Information processing theorists have searched for the basic building blocks of cognition, both the "hardware" and the "software."
10. Most theorists conclude that there are no age-related changes in the capacity of the hardware, but there are clearly improvements in speed and efficiency.
11. One form of increased efficiency is the greater and greater use of various types of processing strategies with age, including strategies for remembering. Preschoolers use some strategies, but school-age children use them far more and more flexibly.
12. At school age, most children also develop some "executive skills"—the ability to monitor their own cognitive processes and thus to plan their mental activity.
13. School has a significant effect in fostering this shift to a more abstract or strategic form of thinking. Children who lack school experience show fewer such skills.
14. The best single predictor of the child's ease of learning to read in first and second grade is the child's "phonemic awareness," an awareness fostered by being read to, by rhyming, by extensive exposure to language.
15. The child's adaptation to the school setting is affected by cognitive readiness, parental involvement, and the child's temperament.
16. One of the main effects of school experience is to shape a child's sense of self-efficacy. By adolescence, children have a clearly developed idea of their comparative skills and abilities.
17. Children's intellectual or school performance is assessed with both IQ tests and achievement tests. Both must be understood as measures of performance, not competence. Both are controversial.
18. Children's intellectual and social development is affected by the quality of the schools they attend. Successful or effective schools have many of the same qualities we see in "authoritative" families: clear rules, good control, good communication, and high warmth.
19. Studies of individual differences in information processing suggest that variations in IQ are linked both to speed of basic neural processing, and to flexibility and generality of strategy use.
20. Roughly 5 percent of the school population in the United States is labeled as learning disabled. There is still considerable dispute about how to identify genuine learning disability, and many childern may be misclassified.
21. There are no sex differences in overall IQ, but boys typically do better at tasks involving spatial visualization and on tests of advanced mathematical ability. Girls do somewhat better on verbal tasks. There is as yet no clear agreement on how to explain such differences.

Key Terms

achievement test
competence
executive processes
learning disability (LD)
class inclusion
deductive logic
inductive logic
performance

Suggested Readings

Adams, M. J. (1990). *Beginning to read: Thinking and learning about print.* Cambridge, MA: The MIT Press.

This is a wonderful book about reading. It is easy to read, complete, thoughtful, and up-to-date. If you are planning a career as a teacher, especially if you expect to teach early elementary school grades, you should go right out and buy a copy.

Collins, W. A. (Ed.) (1984). *Development during middle childhood: The years from six to twelve.* Washington, D.C.: National Academy Press.

This book covers the exact age range I described in this chapter and will discuss in the next. It includes chapters on most aspects of the child's functioning, including physical development, health, and cognitive change.

Farnham-Diggory, S. (1992). *The learning-disabled child.* Cambridge, MA: Harvard University Press.

This revision of an excellent book will give you an up-to-date source, pitched at the level of the lay reader.

Social and Personality Development from 6 to 12

10

At age 8, Roger was prone to emotional outbursts, insisted on his own way when he played with other children, and bullied weaker children on the playground. At 13 he was arrested for shoplifting; at 17 he dropped out of school. As an adult, he had a hard time finding and keeping a job and his marriage lasted only a few years. His wife claimed that she couldn't deal with his temper.

David, in contrast, was very shy at age 8. He rarely joined groups of other children when they were playing, although he would join in if asked or urged. He had a few friends in school but was mostly a loner. He went to college, but had a very hard time settling on a career and changed jobs frequently until his late 20s. His marriage has been stable, but he has been disappointed at his rate of progress in his job. His job supervisors say that David has a habit of withdrawing whenever they press him for something or when the stress level at work gets high, so they are reluctant to promote him.

Both cases are fictitious, but the links between these types of childhood social behaviors and adult outcomes are not. Certainly the cognitive changes I described in the last chapter play a central role in preparing the child for the demands of adolescence and adulthood. But relationships in middle childhood also play a significant part in shaping the life course.

Let me build a bridge between cognition and social relationships by beginning with a look at how children in this age range *understand* themselves and their relationships. Such understandings form part of the basis of the relationships themselves.

Children's Understanding of Self and Relationships

The Self-Concept at School Age

In Chapter 8, I pointed out that by age 5 or 6, most children define themselves along a number of different dimensions, such as size or gender. But these early self-descriptions are highly concrete, often quite situation-specific. Over the elementary school years we see a shift toward a more abstract, more comparative, more generalized self-definition. A 6-year-old might describe herself as "smart" or "dumb;" a 10-year-old is more likely to say that he is "smarter than most other kids," or "not as good at baseball as my friends" (Rosenberg, 1986; Ruble, 1987). In these same years, the child's self-concept also becomes gradually less focused on external characteristics and more on enduring internal qualities.

A number of these themes are illustrated in the results of an older study by Montemayor and Eisen of self-concepts in 9- to 18-year-olds (1977), each of whom was asked to give 20 answers to the question "Who am I?" The researchers found that the younger children were still using mostly surface qualities to describe themselves, as in this description by a 9-year-old:

> My name is Bruce C. I have brown eyes. I have brown hair. I have brown eyebrows. I am nine years old. I LOVE! Sports. I have seven people in my family. I have great! eye site. I have lots! of friends. I live on 1923 Pinecrest Dr. I am going on 10 in September. I'm a boy. I have a uncle that is almost 7 feet tall. My school is Pinecrest. My teacher is Mrs. V. I play Hockey! I'm almost the smartest boy in the class. I LOVE! food. I love fresh air. I LOVE school. (p. 317)

In contrast, look at the self-description of this 11-year-old girl in the sixth grade:

> My name is A. I'm a human being. I'm a girl. I'm a truthful person. I'm not very pretty. I do so-so in my studies. I'm a very good cellist. I'm a very good pianist. I'm a little bit tall for my age. I like several boys. I like several girls. I'm old-fashioned. I play tennis. I am a *very* good swimmer. I try to be helpful. I'm always ready to be friends with anybody. Mostly I'm good, but I lose my temper. I'm not well-liked by some girls and boys. I don't know if I'm liked by boys or not. (pp. 317–318)

This girl, like the other youngsters of this age in the Montemayor and Eisen study, describes her external qualities, but she also emphasizes her beliefs, the quality of her relationships, and her general personality traits. Thus, as the child moves through the concrete operations period, her self-definition becomes more complex, more comparative, less tied to external features, and more centered on feelings and ideas.

Critical Thinking

Before you go on and read any of the examples, take a moment and write down 20 answers to the "Who am I?" question yourself. Then after you have read the examples, go back and look at your own answers to the question again. What types of descriptions did you include?

Describing Other People

In these elementary school years, children's descriptions of others move through highly similar changes, from the concrete to the abstract, from the ephemeral to the stable. If you ask a 6- or 7-year-old to describe others, he will focus almost exclusively on external features—what the person looks like, where he lives, what he does. This description by a 7-year-old boy, taken from a study in England by Livesley & Bromley (1973), is typical:

> He is very tall. He has dark brown hair, he goes to our school. I don't think he has any brothers or sisters. He is in our class. Today he has a dark orange [sweater] and gray trousers and brown shoes. (p. 213)

When young children do use internal or evaluative terms to describe people, they are likely to use quite global terms, such as "nice" or "mean," "good" or "bad." Further, young children do not seem to see these qualities as lasting or general traits of the individual, applicable in all situations or over time (Rholes & Ruble, 1984). In other words, the 6- or 7-year-old has not yet developed a concept we might think of as "conservation of personality."

Then beginning at about age 7 or 8, a rather dramatic shift occurs in children's descriptions of others. The child begins to focus more on the inner traits or qualities of another person and to assume that those traits will be visible in many situations (Gnepp & Chilamkurti, 1988). Children this age still describe others' physical features, but now those descriptions are used as examples of more general points about internal qualities. You can see the change when you compare the 7-year-old's description with this (widely quoted) description by a nearly 10-year-old:

> He smells very much and is very nasty. He has no sense of humour and is very dull. He is always fighting and he is cruel. He does silly things and is very stupid. He has brown hair and cruel eyes. He is sulky and 11 years old and has lots of sisters. I think he is the most horrible boy in the class. He has a croaky voice and always chews his pencil and picks his teeth and I think he is disgusting. (Livesley & Bromley, 1973, p. 217)

This description still includes many external physical features but goes beyond such concrete surface qualities to the level of personality traits, such as lack of humor and cruelty.

I can illustrate these changes less anecdotally with some findings from a study by Carl Barenboim (1981). He asked 6-, 8-, and 10-year-olds to describe three people; a year later, he asked them to do the same thing again. This variation of a cohort-sequential research design gives Barenboim both longitudinal and cross-sectional information. Figure 10.1 shows the results for two of the categories Barenboim used in his analysis. A *behavioral comparison* was any description that involved comparing a child's behaviors or physical features with another child or with a norm. Examples would be "Billy runs a lot faster than Jason," or "She draws the best in our whole class." Statements that involved some internal personality trait he called *psychological constructs*, such as "Sarah is so kind," or "He's a real stubborn idiot!" You can see that behavioral comparisons peaked at around age 8 or 9 but that psychological constructs rose steadily throughout middle childhood.

If you asked 4- and 8-year-olds to describe this boy, their descriptions would probably be quite different. The younger children would describe his physical characteristics; the older children might focus on his feelings or more enduring characteristics.

Critical Thinking

Write down a description of your best friend. How does your description compare with the ones given by children? Can you define the difference in precise terms?

Understanding Friendships

A very similar developmental progression emerges when we ask children to describe or define various kinds of relationships. Let me use descriptions of friendships as an illustration.

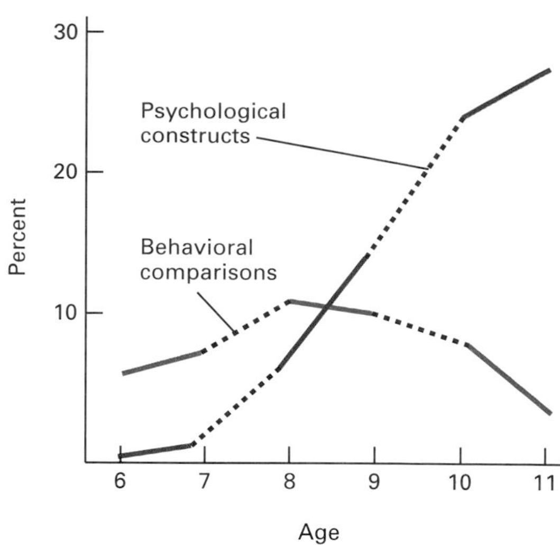

FIGURE 10.1 These data from Barenboim's study show the change in children's descriptions of their peers during the years of middle childhood. The heavy lines represent longitudinal data, the dashed lines cross-sectional comparisons. (*Source:* Barenboim, 1981, Figure 1, p. 134.)

Preschool children seem to understand friendships mostly in physical terms. If you ask a young child how people make friends, the answer is usually that they "play together" or spend time physically near each other (Damon, 1977, 1983; Selman, 1980). Children this age think of friendship as something that involves sharing toys or giving things to one another.

Robert Selman's research and extensive studies by Thomas Berndt (1983, 1986) show that in elementary school this early view of friendship gives way to one in which the key concept seems to be *reciprocal trust*. Friends are now seen as special people with desired qualities other than mere proximity, as people who are generous with one another, who help and trust one another.

Linking Cognition and Social Behavior

When we put all these various jigsaw pieces together, we find a picture of a child whose attention has shifted from externals to internals. Just as the schoolchild can understand conservation in part because he can set aside the *appearance* of change and focus on the underlying continuity, so the child of this same age looks beyond (or behind) physical appearance and searches for deeper consistencies that will help him to interpret both his own and other people's behavior.

Selman suggests another link between thinking and relationships in these years. The preschool child may have a theory of others' minds, but he does not yet understand that other people also read *his* mind. As I noted in Chapter 7, the 4-year-old may understand the statement "I know that you know," but he does not yet understand the next step in this potentially infinite regress: "I know that you know that I know." This reciprocal aspect of perspective taking seems to be grasped some time in the early elementary school years. Selman's point is that only when the child understands reciprocality of perspective do we see really reciprocal relationships between friends. Only then do qualities like fairness and trust become central to children's ideas of friendship.

Just what is cause and what is effect is not so obvious. We should not necessarily assume that the cognitive horse is pulling the relationship cart, although that is one possibility. It is also plausible that the child learns important lessons about the distinction between appearance and reality, and between external and internal qualities, in play with peers and interactions with parents and teachers. Whichever way the causality runs, the central point is that children's relationships with others both reflect and shape their *understanding* of themselves and of relationships. With that in mind, let's look at the relationships themselves.

Relationships

Relationships with Parents

Among elementary school children, as among preschoolers, visible attachment behaviors such as clinging or crying appear only in stressful situations, such as perhaps the first day of school, illness or upheaval in the family, or the death of a pet. Because fewer experiences are new and potentially stressful to the 7- or 8-year-old than to the preschooler, we see much less obvious safe-base behavior, and less open affection from child to parent (Maccoby, 1984).

But it would be a great mistake to assume that the attachment has weakened. Schoolchildren continue to use their parents as a safe base; they continue to rely on their presence, support, and affection (Buhrmester, 1992); and they continue to be strongly influenced by their parents' judgments. What does change is the agenda of issues between parent and child. Parents of preschoolers are most concerned with teaching the child some level of physical independence and controlling the child's behavior. They worry about toilet training, temper tantrums, defiance, and fights with siblings. Occasions requiring discipline are common. When the child reaches elementary school, disciplinary encounters decline. The agenda now includes such issues as whether the child will do regular chores, the standards for the child's

CRITICAL THINKING

Seven- and 8-year-olds often seem to actively reject public displays of affection from their parents, squirming away from hugs or refusing kisses—especially in front of peers. Do you have any guesses about how to explain such behavior?

Research Report

Sibling Relationships in Middle Childhood

When psychologists talk about families, we most often talk about "parents" and "children" and the relationships between the two. But what about brothers' and sisters' relationships to each other? We know relatively little about the quality of such sibling relationships in middle childhood, but we have a few pieces of information.

First of all, as a general rule, sibling relationships do seem to be less central to children's lives in this age range than are relationships with either friends or parents (Buhrmester, 1992). Elementary school–age children are less likely to turn to a sibling for affection than they are to parents, and are less likely to turn to a brother or sister for companionship or intimacy than they are to a friend.

But while this is true in general, sibling relationships vary enormously. On the basis of direct studies of young children as well as retrospective reports by young adults about their sibling relationships when they were at school age, researchers have identified several patterns or styles of sibling relationship: (1) A *caregiver* relationship, in which one sibling serves as a kind of quasi-parent for the other, a pattern that seems to be more common between an older sister and younger brother than in any other combination; (2) a *buddy* relationship, in which both members of the pair try to be like one another and take pleasure in being together; (3) a *critical* or conflictual relationship, which includes attempts by one sibling to dominate the other, teasing, and quarrelling; (4) a *rival* relationship, which contains many of the same elements as a critical relationship but is also low in any form of friendliness or support; and (5) a *casual* relationship, in which the siblings have relatively little to do with one another (Murphy, 1993; Stewart, Beilfuss, & Verbrugge, 1995).

Rivalrous or critical relationships seem to be more common when siblings are close together in age (four or fewer years apart) (Buhrmester & Furman, 1990); friendly and intimate relationships appear to be somewhat more common in pairs of sisters (Buhrmester & Furman, 1990), while rivalry seems to be highest in boy-boy pairs (Stewart et al., 1995).

Do you recognize your own middle-childhood sibling relationships in these categories? Has your relationship with your brothers and sisters changed in the years since you were in elementary school?

school performance, and the level of independence that will be allowed (Maccoby, 1984). Is it okay for Joe to stop off at his friend's house after school without asking ahead of time? How far from home may Diana ride her bike? In many non-Western cultures, parents must also now begin to teach children quite specific tasks, such as agricultural work and care of younger children or animals, all of which may be necessary for the survival of the family.

When we look at the various ways parents try to accomplish all these tasks, we see the same parental styles that are evident among parents of preschoolers: authoritarian, authoritative, permissive, and neglecting. And in this age range, as at the earlier ages, it is clear that the authoritative style is by far the best for fostering and supporting the child's emerging competence.

Baumrind (1991) has provided illustrative data in a recent analysis of her small longitudinal sample. She classified each parent's style of interaction on the basis of extensive interviews and direct observation when the children were preschoolers. When the children were 9 she measured their level of social competence. Those rated "optimally competent" were seen as both assertive and responsible in their relationships; those rated "partially competent" typically lacked one of these skills; those rated incompetent showed neither. You can see in Table 10.1 that the children from authoritative families were nearly all rated as fully competent, while those from neglecting families were most often rated as incompetent.

Relationships with Peers

The biggest shift in relationships in the years of middle childhood is the increasing centrality of the peer group. The vertical relationships with parents or teachers obviously don't disappear, but playing with other kids is what 7-, 8-, 9-, or 10-year old children prefer. Such activities—along with watching TV—take up virtually all children's time when they are not in school, eating, or sleeping (Timmer, Eccles, & O'Brien, 1985).

Shared play interests continue to form the major basis of these school-age peer relationships. Furthermore, kids this age *define* play groups in terms of common activities, rather than in terms of common attitudes or values. You can see this pattern in Figure 10.2, which shows the results of a study by Susan O'Brien and Karen Bierman (1988). They asked fifth-, eighth-, and eleventh-grade subjects to tell them about the different groups of kids that hang around together at their school, and then to say how they could tell that a particular bunch of kids was "a group." For the fifth-

Table 10.1 Social Competence in 9-Year-Olds as a Function of Parental Style

	Percentage of Children Rated		
Parental Style	**Competent**	**Partially Competent**	**Incompetent**
Authoritative	85	15	0
Authoritarian	30	57	13
Permissive	8	67	25
Neglecting	0	47	53

Source: Baumrind, 1991, adapted from Table 5.1, p. 129.

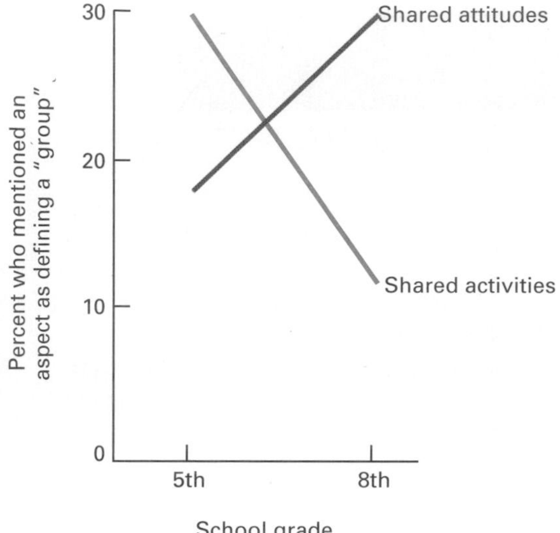

FIGURE 10.2 O'Brien and Bierman's results illustrate the change between elementary and high school in children's ideas about what defines "a group" of peers. (*Source:* O'Brien & Bierman, 1988, Table 1, p. 1363.)

graders, the single best criterion of "a group" was that the kids did things together. For eighth-graders, shared attitudes and common appearance became much more important—yet another example of the broad shift from concrete to abstract views of relationships.

Gender Segregation. Beyond the centrality of shared activities, the most striking thing about peer group interactions in the elementary school years is how gender-segregated they are, a pattern that seems to occur in every culture in the world (Cairns & Cairns, 1994; Harkness & Super, 1985) and that is frequently visible in children as young as 3 or 4. Boys play with boys and girls play with girls, each in their own areas and at their own kinds of games. There are some ritualized "boundary violations" between these separate territories, such as chasing games (e.g., "You can't catch me, nyah nyah," followed by chasing accompanied by screaming by the girls) (Thorne, 1986). But on the whole, girls and boys between the ages of 6 and 12 actively avoid interacting with one another and show strong favoritism toward their own gender and negative stereotyping of the opposite gender (Powlishta, 1995). Given a forced choice between playing with a child of the opposite gender or a child of a different race, researchers have found that elementary school–age children will make the cross-race choice rather than the cross-gender choice (Maccoby & Jacklin, 1987).

In middle childhood, boys play with boys, girls play with girls. In fact, children's play groups are more sex-segregated at this age than at any other.

Friendships. This pattern is even more pronounced when we look at friendships. By age 7, gender segregation in friendships is almost total. Parents in one U.S. study reported that about a quarter of the friendships of their 5- or 6-year-olds but *none* of the friendships of their 7- and 8-year-olds were cross-sex (Gottman, 1986).

School-age children spend more time with their friends than do preschoolers, and they gradually develop a larger collection of individual friendships. Second-graders name about four friends each, while seventh-graders name about seven (Reisman & Shorr, 1978). In these same years, friendships also become more stable—more likely to endure for a year or longer (Cairns & Cairns, 1994). But at either age, children's behavior within friendships is quite different from what they display with strangers. Children are more open and more supportive with chums, smiling, looking, laughing, and touching one another more than with nonfriends; they talk

Critical Thinking

Do you still have any friends from your elementary school years? If not, why do you think those early friendships did not survive? If yes, what do you think differentiates an early friendship that survives from one that does not?

Cultures and Contexts

Gender Segregation in Other Cultures

Many of the statements I make about "children's development" are based exclusively on research done in the United States or other Western industrialized countries. It is always appropriate to ask whether the same developmental changes, the same behavioral patterns, would appear in children reared in very different environments. In the case of gender segregation, the answer seems quite clear: What we observe on U.S. school playgrounds is true all over the world.

A good example is an observational study of children in a Kipsigis settlement in rural Kenya (Harkness & Super, 1985). This particular settlement consists of 54 households engaged in traditional hoe agriculture and cattle raising. Women care for the children, cook, and carry firewood and water. Men are in charge of the cows, plow the fields when needed, maintain the dwellings, and participate in the political business of the community.

For this study, observers went to the settlement at different times of the day to record the gender of each child's companions. They found little sex segregation among children younger than 6, but clear separation for children between 6 and 9. In this age group, two-thirds of boys' and three-quarters of girls' companions were of the same gender. The differences were even larger when they looked at the sex of the child to which each youngster addressed his or her specific bids for attention: 72 percent of boys' and 84 percent of girls' bids were made to another child of the same gender.

These numbers reflect somewhat less sex segregation than we commonly observe in the United States. But what impresses me is that even this much sex segregation exists in a culture in which children spend a good deal of their time in their own compound, with only siblings and half-siblings available as playmates.

This is not to say that context or culture have no effect. They clearly do. The Kipsigis encourage certain kinds of sex-segregation by assigning somewhat different tasks to boys and girls. And in Western countries, children attending "progressive" schools in which equality of sex roles is a specific philosophy show less sex-segregation in their play than is true in more traditional schools (Maccoby & Jacklin, 1987). But even in progressive schools, the majority of contacts are still with children of the same gender. All in all, it seems to be the case universally that when children this age are free to choose their playmates, they strongly prefer playmates of the same sex.

more with friends and cooperate and help one another more. Pairs of friends are also more successful than are nonfriends in solving problems or performing some task together. Yet school-age children are also more critical of friends and have more conflicts with them (Hartup, 1996); they are more polite with strangers. At the same time, when such conflicts with friends occur, children are more concerned about resolving them than is true of disagreements among nonfriends. Thus, friendships represent an arena in which children can learn how to manage conflicts (Newcomb & Bagwell, 1995).

Girls' and boys' friendships also differ in quality in intriguing ways. Waldrop and Halverson (1975) refer to boys' relationships as *extensive* and to girls' relationships as *intensive*. Boys' friendship groups are larger and more accepting of newcomers than are girls'. They play more outdoors and roam over a larger area in their play. Girlfriends are more likely to play in pairs or in smaller, more exclusive groups, and they spend more playtime indoors or near home or school (Benenson, 1994; Gottman, 1986).

At the level of actual interaction we also see sex differences, a point I made in Chapter 8 as well. Boys' groups and boys' friendships appear to be focused more on competition and dominance than are girls' friendships (Maccoby, 1995). In fact, among school-age boys, we see *higher* levels of competition between pairs of friends than between strangers, the opposite of what we see among girls. Friendships between girls also include more agreement, more compliance, and more self-disclosure than is true for boys. For example, Leaper (1991) finds that "controlling" speech—a category that includes rejecting comments, ordering, manipulating, challenging, defiance, refutation, or resistance of other's attempts to control—is twice as common among pairs of 7- and 8-year-old male friends as among pairs of female friends. Among the 4- and 5-year-olds in this study there were no sex differences in controlling speech.

None of this should obscure the fact that the interactions of male and female friendship pairs have a great many characteristics in common. For example, collaborative and cooperative exchanges are the most common forms of communication in both boys' and girls' friendships in these years. Nor should we necessarily conclude that boys' friendships are less important to them than are girls'. Nevertheless, it seems clear that there are differences in form and style that may well have enduring implications for the patterns of friendship over the full life span.

Why do you think it is that among boys, competition is such a strong feature of friendship interactions? Do you think this is true in every culture?

Patterns of Aggression. I pointed out in Chapter 8 that physical aggression declines over the preschool years, while verbal aggression increases. In the years of middle childhood and adolescence, physical aggression becomes still less common as children learn the cultural rules about when and how much it is acceptable to display anger or aggression. In most cultures, this means that anger is more and more disguised and aggression more and more controlled with increasing age (Underwood, Coie, & Herbsman, 1992).

One interesting exception to this general pattern is that in all-boy pairs or groups, at least in U.S. studies, physical aggression seems to remain both relatively high and constant over the years of childhood. Indeed, at every age, boys show more physical aggression and more assertiveness than do girls, both within friendship pairs and in general (Fabes, Knight, & Higgins, 1995). Table 10.2 gives some highly representative data from a very large, careful survey in Canada (Offord, Boyle, & Racine, 1991) in which teachers completed checklists describing each child's behavior. It is clear that boys are described as far more aggressive on nearly any measure of physical aggressiveness.

Results like these have been so clear and so consistent that most psychologists concluded that boys are simply "more aggressive" in every possible way. But that may turn out to be wrong. Instead, it begins to look as if girls simply express their aggressiveness in a different way, using what has recently been labeled **relational aggression,** instead of either physical aggression or nasty words. Physical aggression hurts others through physical damage or threat of such damage; relational aggression is aimed at damaging the other person's self-esteem or peer relationships, such as by ostracism or threats of ostracism ("I won't invite you to my birthday party if you

Table 10.2 Percentage of Boys and Girls Aged 4 to 11 Rated by Their Teachers as Displaying Each Type of Aggressive Behavior

Behavior	Boys	Girls
Mean to others	21.8	9.6
Physically attacks people	18.1	4.4
Gets in many fights	30.9	9.8
Destroys own things	10.7	2.1
Destroys others' things	10.6	4.4
Threatens to hurt people	13.1	4.0

Source: Offord, Boyle, & Racine, 1991, from Table 2.3, p. 39.

do that"), cruel gossiping, or facial expressions of disdain. Children experience such indirect aggression as genuinely hurtful and they are likely to shun other kids who use this form of aggression a lot, just as they tend to reject peers who are physically aggressive (Casas & Mosher, 1995; Cowan & Underwood, 1995; Crick & Grotpeter, 1995).

Girls are much more likely to use relational aggression than are boys, especially toward other girls, a difference that begins as early as the preschool years and becomes very marked by the fourth or fifth grade. For example, in one recent study of nearly 500 children in the third through sixth grades, Nicki Crick found that 17.4 percent of the girls but only 2 percent of the boys were high in relational aggression—almost precisely the reverse of what we see for physical aggression (Crick & Grotpeter, 1995). Whether this difference in the form of aggression has some hormonal/biological basis or is trained at an early age, or both, we do not know. We do know that higher rates of physical aggression in males have been observed in every human society and in all varieties of primates. And we know that a least some link exists between rates of physical aggression and testosterone levels (e.g., Susman et al., 1987, particularly at adolescence and later ages. But where the apparent propensity toward relational aggression comes from among girls is still an open question.

Individual Differences

I've spent most of this chapter talking about common developmental patterns. But if we are to understand development, we must understand the individual pathways as well as the common ones. Sex differences represent one form of differential pathway. We also need to look at more individual variations, of which the two most important and pervasive in this age range appear to be variations in self-esteem and in popularity.

Hitting a home run will only raise this girl's self-esteem if she places a high value on being good at sports or at baseball specifically.

Self-Esteem

Thus far I have talked about the self-concept as if there were few values attached to the categories by which we define ourselves. But the self-concept obviously contains an evaluative aspect as well. Note, for example, the differences in tone in the answers to the "Who am I?" question that I have already quoted. The 9-year-old makes a lot of positive statements about himself while the 11-year-old gives a more mixed self-evaluation.

These evaluative judgments have several interesting features. First of all, over the years of elementary school and high school, children's evaluations of their own abilities become increasingly differentiated, with quite separate judgments about skills in academics or athletics, physical appearance, peer social acceptance, friendships, romantic appeal, and relationships with parents (Harter, 1990).

Paradoxically, however, it is at school age—around age 7—that children first develop a *global* self-evaluation. Seven- and 8-year-olds (but not younger children) readily answer questions about how well they like themselves as people, how happy they are, or how well they like the way they are leading their lives. It is this global evaluation of one's own worth that is usually referred to as **self-esteem,** and this global evaluation is *not* merely the sum of all the separate assessments the child makes about his skills in different areas.

Instead, as Susan Harter's extremely interesting research on self-esteem tells us, each child's level of self-esteem is a product of two internal assessments or judgments (Harter, 1987; 1990). First, each child experiences some degree of discrepancy between what he would like to be (or thinks he *ought* to be) and what he thinks he is. When that discrepancy is low, the child's self-esteem is generally high. When the discrepancy is high—when the child sees himself as failing to live up to his *own* goals or values—self-esteem will be much lower.

The standards are not the same for every child. Some value academic skills highly; others value sports skills or having good friends. The key to self-esteem, Harter proposes, is the amount of discrepancy between what the child desires and what the child thinks he has achieved. Thus, a child who values sports prowess but who isn't big enough or coordinated enough to be good at sports will have lower self-esteem than will an equally small or uncoordinated child who does not value sports skill so highly. Similarly, being good at something, like singing or playing chess, won't raise a child's self-esteem unless the child values that particular skill.

The second major influence on a child's self-esteem, according to Harter, is the overall sense of support the child feels from the important people around her, particularly parents and peers. Children who feel that other people generally like them the way they are have higher self-esteem scores than do children who report less overall support.

Both these factors are clear in the results of Harter's own research. She asked third-, fourth-, fifth-, and sixth-graders how important it was to them to do well in each of five domains, and how well they thought they actually did in each. The total discrepancy between these sets of judgments constituted the discrepancy score. Remember that a high discrepancy score indicates that the child didn't feel he was doing well in areas that mattered to him. The social support score was based on children's replies to a set of questions about whether they thought others (parents and peers) liked them as they were, treated them as a person, or felt that they were important. Figure 10.3 shows the results for the third- and fourth-graders; the findings for the fifth- and sixth-graders are virtually identical, and both sets of data support Harter's hypothesis, as does other research, including studies of African-American youth (Luster & McAdoo, 1995). Note that a low discrepancy score alone does not protect a child completely from low self-esteem if she lacks sufficient social support. Similarly, a loving and accepting family and peer group does not guarantee high self-esteem if the youngster does not feel she is living up to her own standards.

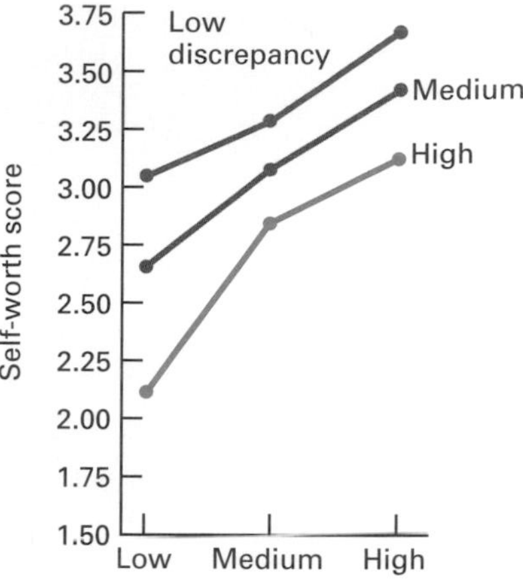

FIGURE 10.3 For these third- and fourth-graders in Harter's studies, self-esteem was about equally influenced by the amount of support the child saw herself as receiving from parents and peers, and by the degree of discrepancy between the value the child placed on various domains and the skill she saw herself having in each of those domains. (*Source:* Harter, 1987, Figure 9.2, p. 227.)

Critical Thinking

Think about the following somewhat paradoxical proposition: If Harter's model of self-esteem is correct, then our self-esteem is most vulnerable in the area in which we may appear (and feel) the most competent. Does this fit with your experience?

A particularly deadly combination occurs when the child perceives that the parents' support is *contingent* on good performance in some area—getting good grades, making the first-string football team, winning the audition to play with the school orchestra, being popular with other kids. Then if the child does not measure up to the standard, he experiences both an increased discrepancy between ideal and achievement, and a loss of support from the parents.

Consistency of Self-Esteem over Time. How stable are these self-judgments? Is a third-grader with low self-esteem doomed to feel less than worthy for the rest of his life? A number of longitudinal studies of elementary school–age children and teenagers show that global self-esteem is quite stable in the short term but somewhat less so over periods of several years. The correlation between two self-esteem scores obtained a few months apart is generally about .60. Over several years, this correlation drops to something more like .40 (Alsaker & Olweus, 1992; Block & Robins, 1993). So it is true that a child with high self-esteem at age 8 or 9 is more likely to have high self-esteem at age 10 or 11. But it is also true that a good deal of variation occurs around that stability.

Consequences of Variations in Self-Esteem. Harter and others have found that the child's level of self-esteem is *strongly* negatively correlated with depression in both middle childhood and adolescence. That is, the lower the self-esteem score, the more depressed the child describes himself to be. The correlations in several of Harter's studies range from −.67 to −.80—remarkably high for research of this type (Harter, 1987; Renouf & Harter, 1990). Bear in mind, though, that this is still correlational evidence. These findings don't prove a causal connection between low self-esteem and depression. More persuasive is Harter's finding from her longitudinal studies that when a child's self-esteem score rises or falls, her depression score drops or rises accordingly.

Origins of Differences in Self-Esteem. Where do differences in self-esteem come from? There are at least three sources. First, of course, a child's own direct experience with success or failure in various arenas plays an obvious role. I pointed out in the last chapter that children in elementary school become aware of their relative academic successes; they gain equally direct comparative information when they play sports, take clarinet lessons, or try out for the school play.

Second, the value a child attaches to some skill or quality is obviously affected fairly directly by peers' and parents' attitudes and values. For example, peer (and general cultural) standards for appearance establish benchmarks for all children and teens. A child who is "too tall" or "too fat" or deviates in some other way from the accepted norms is likely to feel a sense of inadequacy. Similarly, the degree of emphasis parents place on the child's performing well in some domain—whether it is school, athletics, or playing chess—is an important element in forming the child's aspirations in each area.

Finally, labels and judgments from others play a highly significant role. To a very considerable extent, we come to think of ourselves as others think of us (Cole, 1991). Children who are repeatedly told that they are "smart," "a good athlete," or "pretty" are likely to have higher self-esteem than are children who are told that they are "dumb," "clumsy," or "a late bloomer." A child who brings home a report card with C's and B's on it and hears the parent say, "That's fine, honey. We don't expect you to get all A's," draws conclusions both about the parents' expectations and about their judgments of her abilities.

From all these sources, the child fashions her ideas (her internal model) about what she should be and what she is. Like the child's internal model of attachment, a child's self-scheme is not fixed in stone. It is responsive to changes in others' judgments as well as to changes in the child's own experience of success or failure. But once created, the model does tend to persist, both because the child will tend to choose experiences that will confirm and support her self-scheme, and because the social environment—including the parents' evaluations of the child—tends to be at least moderately consistent.

Popularity and Rejection

In a similar way, a child's degree of rejection by peers tends to be consistent over the years of middle childhood and into adolescence. Rejected children tend to stay rejected; if they move out of this category, it is rare for them to move all the way to a high level of acceptance (Asher, 1990).

Psychologists who study popularity in children have concluded that it is important to distinguish between several subgroups of unpopular children. The most frequently studied are those children who are overtly *rejected* by peers. If you ask children to list peers they would *not* like to play with, or if you observe which children are avoided on the playground, you can get a measure of rejection of this type. A second type has come to be called *neglected*. Children in this category are reasonably well liked but lack individual friends and are rarely chosen as most preferred by their peers. Neglect seems to be much less stable over time than is rejection, but children who are neglected nonetheless seem to share certain qualities. Interestingly, such children often do quite well in school (Wentzel & Asher, 1995), but they are more prone to depression and loneliness than are accepted children (Cillessen et al., 1992; Rubin et al., 1991). Where might such differences in popularity or peer acceptance come from?

Critical Thinking

One reasonable hypothesis might be that neglected children would be more likely to have had insecure attachments as infants. Can you think of refinements of this hypothesis? And how could you test it?

Qualities of Rejected and Popular Children. Some of the characteristics that differentiate popular and unpopular children are things outside a child's control. In particular, attractive children and physically larger children are more likely to be popular—perhaps merely a continuation of the preference for attractive faces that Langlois detected in young infants and that I described in Chapter 5. The most crucial ingredient, though, is not how the child looks but how the child behaves.

Popular children behave in positive, supporting, nonpunitive, and nonaggressive ways toward most other children. They explain things, take their playmates' wishes into consideration, take turns in conversation, and are able to regulate the expression of their strong emotions. Rejected children are aggressive, disruptive, uncooperative, and often unable to control the expression of their strong feelings (Eisenberg et al., 1995; Pettit et al., 1996). They interrupt their play partners more often and fail to take turns in a systematic way.

This child might be classed as neglected rather than rejected. The long-term prognosis for such children is better than for rejected children, but they are more likely to be depressed in childhood and adolescence—as this boy seems to be.

These conclusions emerge from a variety of types of research, including at least a few cross-cultural studies. For example, aggression and disruptive behavior are linked to rejection and unpopularity among Chinese children, just as they are among American children (Chen, Rubin, & Li, 1995; Chen, Rubin, & Sun, 1992). Among the best sources of evidence are studies involving direct observation of groups of previously unacquainted children who spend several sessions playing with one another and then pick their favorite playmates from among the group (e.g., Coie & Kupersmidt, 1983; Dodge, 1983; Shantz, 1986). In these studies, children who are most consistently positive and supportive during the play sessions are those who end up being chosen as leaders or as friends. Those who consistently participate in conflicts are most often rejected.

Rejected children also seem to have quite different internal working models of relationships and of aggression from those of popular children. In a series of studies, Kenneth Dodge (Dodge et al., 1990; Dodge & Feldman, 1990; Dodge & Frame, 1982; Quiggle et al., 1992) has shown that aggressive/rejected children are much more likely to see aggression as a useful way to solve problems. They are also much more likely to interpret someone else's behavior as hostile or attacking than is true for less aggressive or more popular children. Given an ambiguous event, such as being hit in the back with a kickball, aggressive or rejected children—especially boys—are much more likely to assume that the ball was thrown on purpose, and they retaliate. Of course such retaliation, in turn, is likely to elicit hostility from others, so their expectation that other people are hostile to them is further confirmed.

This body of research can also be linked to Gerald Patterson's work, whose model I described in Chapter 1. Patterson is persuaded that a child's excess aggressiveness can be traced originally to ineffective parental control. But once the child's aggressiveness is well established, the child displays this same behavior with peers, is rejected by those peers, and is then driven more and more toward the only set of peers who will accept him, usually other aggressive or delinquent youngsters. These antisocial kids are not friendless, but their friends are almost always other kids with similar antisocial patterns, and these friendships tend to be fairly transitory and focused on mutual coercion (Dishion, Andrews, & Crosby, 1995).

The seriousness of this set of connected problems is amply demonstrated by a growing body of research showing that the combination of aggression and rejection by one's peers in elementary school is one of the very few aspects of childhood functioning that consistently predicts behavior problems or emotional disturbances later in childhood, adolescence, and adulthood—a set of results I've discussed in the Across Development box.

Happily, not all rejected children remain rejected; not all develop serious behavior problems or delinquency. And not all aggressive children are rejected. Recent research gives us a few hints about what may differentiate among these several subgroups. For example, some aggressive children also show fairly high levels of altruistic or prosocial behavior, and this mixture of qualities carries a much more positive prognosis than does aggression unleavened by helpfulness (Coie & Cillessen, 1993; Newcomb, Bukowski, & Pattee, 1993). Distinctions like these may help us not only to refine our predictions but to design better intervention programs for rejected/aggressive children.

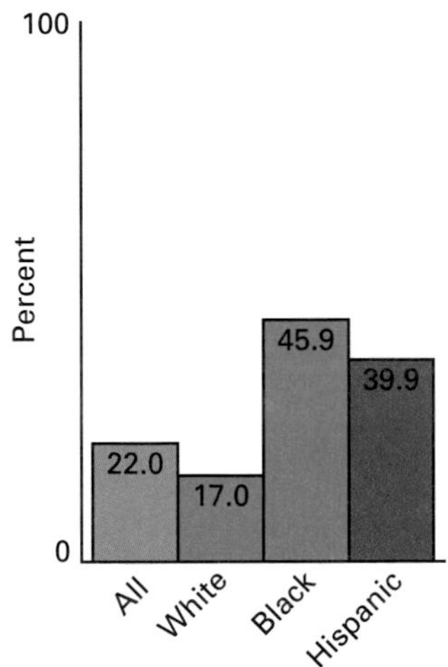

FIGURE 10.4 The percentage of children under age 18 living in poverty in the United States in 1992. (*Source:* U.S. Bureau of the Census, 1994, Table 728, p. 475.)

The Role of the Larger Society

As at earlier ages, the daily life of the school-age child is shaped not just by the hours she spends in school or playing with pals. She is also affected by her family's economic circumstances, by the neighborhood she lives in, by the television programs she watches. Within the family, the pattern of interaction between parent and child is also affected by many of these same forces, as well as by the quality of the parent's job, the amount of emotional support the parents have from family or friends, and many other factors I've talked about in earlier chapters. Let me talk about two of these components of the larger culture that seem especially important in these elementary school years: the effects of poverty, and the effects of television.

The Effects of Poverty

Figure 10.4 shows the most recent U.S. national data, from 1993, on the percentage of children who live below the poverty line—defined in 1993 as an income for a family of 4 of $14,763 per year or less. *Proportionately more children in the United States live in poverty than in any other industrialized country in the world.* By way of specific contrast, the poverty rate for children in Canada is roughly 9 percent; in Sweden it is 2 percent.

Figure 10.4 also makes clear that poverty is unequally distributed across ethnic groups in the United States. It is also unequally distributed across family structures: Children reared by single mothers are far more likely to be living in poverty. Roughly 60 percent of black and Hispanic children, and 40 percent of white children reared by single mothers in the United States live in poverty (Zill & Nord, 1994). Many of these mothers have jobs, but the jobs pay too little to lift the family out of poverty.

Across Development

Long-Term Consequences of Childhood Aggression and Peer Rejection

A growing body of research points to significant links between rejection by one's peers in elementary school—particularly rejection that is related to excessive aggressiveness—and behavior problems or emotional disturbances in adolescence and adulthood. Let me give you a sampling of the findings.

- Leonard Eron, in a 22-year longitudinal study, has found that a high level of aggressiveness toward peers at age 8 is related to various forms of aggressiveness at age 30, including "criminal behavior, number of moving traffic violations, convictions for driving while intoxicated, aggressiveness toward spouses, how severely the subjects punished their own children" (Eron, 1987, p. 439).
- In the Concordia Project in French Canada, Lisa Serbin (Serbin et al., 1991) has studied several thousand children who were initially identified by their peers in Grade 1, 4, or 7 as either highly aggressive, withdrawn, or both. A large comparison group of nonaggressive and nonwithdrawn children was also studied. Both aggressive girls and aggressive boys later showed poorer school achievement in high school. In adulthood, 45.5 percent of the aggressive but only 10.8 percent of the nonaggressive men had appeared in court. For women, the ratio was about 2 to 1 (3.8 percent versus 1.8 percent).
- Farrington (1991) has studied a group of 400 working-class boys in England, beginning when they were 8 and continuing into their 30s. Those who were rated by their teachers as most aggressive at age 8, 10, and 12 were more likely to describe themselves at 32 as getting into fights, carrying a weapon, or fighting police officers. They were also twice as likely as were less aggressive children to commit a violent offense (20.4 percent versus 9.8 percent), twice as likely to be unemployed, more likely to hit their wives, and half again as likely to have a drunk-driving conviction.
- John Coie and his colleagues (Coie et al., 1995) have followed a group of over a thousand children from the third to the tenth grade. Among the boys, those who were both aggressive and rejected in third grade were far more likely to show delinquency or other behavior problems in high school than were any other group of boys. Among girls, aggressiveness but not peer rejection was linked to later behavior problems.
- You may also remember a related study that I described in Chapter 1 (Figure 1.2, p. 11). Caspi and his colleagues (Caspi et al., 1987) found that boys in the Berkeley/Oakland longitudinal studies who were classed as "explosive" or ill-tempered in elementary school were more ill-tempered as adults, had lower levels of occupational success, and were more likely to divorce. Among women the relationships were less striking, but the spouses and children of women who had been ill-tempered girls perceived them as less adequate and more ill-tempered parents. They also tended to "marry down" in social class. Thus, both groups have adult lives we might reasonably describe as less successful.

We could explain such a link between early aggression or unpopularity and later behavior problems in any of several ways. The simplest explanation is that problems with peers arise out of high levels of aggression and that such aggression simply persists as the individual's primary mode of interaction. It is also possible that a failure to develop friendships itself causes problems that later become more general. Or it could signify a seriously warped internal working model of relationships, or all the above.

Whatever the explanation, the point to remember is that such deviant behavior does tend to persist and may have profound effects on an individual's entire life pattern. I will say yet again that this does not mean that it is impossible to deflect an individual from such a pathway, or that individuals may not be resilient enough to recover from early patterns of deviance. None of these studies shows perfect continuity; all speak only of increased risks or increased probabilities. But it would be foolish to think that life begins all over again at age 20 with entirely new choices and a clean slate. Instead, we carry the traces of our childhood forward with us through our lives, in the form of established behavior patterns and powerful internal working models.

The Effects of Poverty on Families and Children. Among many other things, poverty reduces options for parents. They may not be able to afford prenatal care, so their children are more likely to be born with some sort of disability. When the mother works, she is likely to have fewer choices of affordable child care. Such children spend more time in poor-quality care and shift more from one care arrangement to another. Poor families also live in smaller and less-adequate housing, often in decaying neighborhoods with high rates of violence, and many such families move frequently, which means their children change schools often. The parents are less likely to feel they have adequate social support, and the children often lack a stable group of playmates (Dodge, Pettit, & Bates, 1994). Overall, poverty environments are more chaotic, more highly stressed, with fewer psychological and social resources (Brooks-Gunn, 1995; McLoyd & Wilson, 1991).

Mothers and fathers living in poverty also treat their children quite differently than do parents in working-class or middle-class families in the United States. They talk to them less, provide fewer age-appropriate toys, spend less time with them in intellectually stimulating activities, explain things less often and less fully, are less warm, and are stricter and more physical in their discipline (Dodge et al., 1994; Sampson & Laub, 1994). In the terms I introduced in Chapter 8, poor parents are more likely to be either neglecting or authoritarian and less likely to be authoritative.

Some of this pattern of parental behavior is undoubtedly a response to the extraordinary stresses and special demands of the poverty environment—a point buttressed by the repeated observation that those parents living in poverty who nonetheless feel they have enough social support are much less likely to be harshly punitive or unsupportive toward their children (Hashima & Amato, 1994; Taylor & Roberts, 1995). To some extent, the stricter discipline and emphasis on obedience we see in poor parents may be thought of as a logical response to the realities of life in a very poor neighborhood.

Some of the differences in child-rearing patterns between poor and nonpoor parents may also result from straightforward modeling of the way these same parents were reared; some may be a product of ignorance of children's needs. Poor parents with relatively more education, for example, typically talk to their children more, are more responsive, and provide more intellectual stimulation than do equally poor parents with lower levels of education (Kelley, Sanches-Hucles, & Walker, 1993). But whatever the cause, nearly all children reared in poverty experience both different physical conditions and quite different interactions with their parents.

Not surprisingly, such children turn out differently. Children from poverty environments have higher rates of birth defects and early disabilities, they recover less well from early problems, and they are more often ill and undernourished throughout their childhood years (Klerman, 1991). Typically, they also have lower IQs and move through the sequences of cognitive development more slowly (Brooks-Gunn, 1995). They come to school less ready to learn to read and thereafter they do consistently less well in school and are less likely to go on to college (Huston, 1994). As adults, they are more likely to be poor, thus continuing the cycle through another generation. All these effects are greater for those children who have lived continuously in poverty than for children who have experienced some mixture of poverty and greater affluence (Bolger et al., 1995; Duncan, Brooks-Gunn, & Klebanov, 1994).

The Special Case of Inner-City Poverty. These negative effects are also exacerbated for children growing up in poverty-ravaged urban neighborhoods. They are exposed to street gangs and street violence, to drug pushers, to overcrowded homes and abuse. Whole communities have become like war zones.

In the United States, almost 13 million children live in such urban poverty (Garbarino, Kostelny, & Dubrow, 1991). More than 1.5 million live in public housing developments, including some settings with the highest crime rates in the country.

Surveys in a number of large cities indicate that nearly half of inner-city elementary and high school students have witnessed at least one violent crime in the past year (Osofsky, 1995). Guns are common in schools as well as on the streets. In a 1993 national survey by the Centers for Disease Control, 22.1 percent of high school students reported that they had carried a weapon (gun, knife, or club) sometime in the previous 30 days; 7.9 percent had carried a gun (Kann et al., 1995).

A growing body of evidence shows that the effect of living in such a concentrated pocket of poverty is to intensify all the ill effects of family poverty (Klebanov et al., 1995; Kupersmidt et al., 1995). When the whole neighborhood is poor, parents have fewer other resources to rely on and children have more violent and fewer supportive adult models; rates of child abuse rise, as do rates of aggression and delinquency in the children (Coulton et al., 1995). When the whole neighborhood also lacks what sociologist William Wilson calls *connectedness* and *stability*—when the adults do not collaborate to monitor the children and do not provide practical or emotional support to one another—the effects are still worse (Wilson, 1995).

Many children living in such neighborhoods show all the symptoms of posttraumatic stress disorder (Garbarino et al., 1992), including sleep disturbances, irritability, inability to concentrate, angry outbursts, and hypervigilance. Many experience flashbacks or intrusive memories of traumatic events. And because they are likely to have missed out on many of the forms of intellectual stimulation and consistent family support that would allow them to succeed in school, they have high rates of behavior problems and academic failures. Less than half of urban poor children

CRITICAL THINKING

Are you shocked by such statistics? What do you think we ought to do about it?

When you look at scenes of urban poverty like this, you can see why some refer to them as "war zones."

The Real World

Children in Danger

I cannot leave the subject of urban poverty—so common now in America—without quoting some of James Garbarino's eloquent words.

> What is truly needed in America's urban war zones is restoration of a safe environment where children can have a childhood, and where parents can exert less energy on protecting children from random gunfire and more on helping children to grow. No one can eliminate all risk from the lives of families. But America does have the resources to make a real childhood a real possibility even for the children of the urban poor. But sometimes the war close to home is the most difficult to see. (Garbarino et al., 1991, p. 148)

graduate from high school (Garbarino et al., 1991). The reasons for such school failures are complex but there is little doubt that the chronic stress experienced by poor children is one highly significant component.

The Role of Stress and Protective Factors. Arnold Sameroff and his colleagues have argued that the effects of various different kinds of stresses accumulate. A child may be able to handle one or two, but as the stresses and risks pile up, the probability that a child will thrive intellectually, emotionally, or socially declines steadily (Sameroff et al., 1987). For a child growing up in poverty, perhaps especially urban poverty, the chances of experiencing multiple separate types of stress are very high indeed.

At the same time, studies of resilient and vulnerable children (Easterbrooks, Davidson, & Chazan, 1993; Furstenberg & Hughes, 1995; Garmezy & Masten, 1991; Masten et al., 1990; Winfield, 1995) suggest that certain characteristics or circumstances may help to protect some children from the detrimental effects of repeated stresses and upheavals. Here are some of the key protective factors:

- High IQ in the child
- Competent adult parenting, such as an authoritative style (good supervision and monitoring of the child seems especially important)
- Effective schools
- A secure initial attachment of the child to the parent
- A strong community help network, including friends, family, or neighbors

For example, in a major longitudinal study in Kauai, Hawaii, Emmy Werner (Werner & Smith, 1992) has found that a subset of those children reared in poverty nonetheless became competent, able, autonomous adults. The families of these resilient children were clearly more authoritative, more cohesive, and more loving than were the equivalently poor families whose children had worse outcomes. Similarly, studies of boys reared in high-crime inner-city neighborhoods show that high intelligence and at least a minimum level of family cohesion increase a boy's chance of creating a successful adult life pattern (Long & Vaillant, 1984; McCord, 1982; Sampson & Laub, 1994). Boys reared in poverty-level families in which the parents have strong antisocial tendencies, high use of alcohol, or low IQ are much less likely to develop the competence needed to bootstrap themselves out of their difficult circumstances.

Thus, the outcome depends on some joint effect of the number of stresses the child must cope with and the range of competencies or advantages the child brings to the situation. Poverty does not guarantee bad outcomes, but it stacks the deck against most children. As Judith Musick puts it, these environments are "densely layered with risk" (1994, p. 1).

Television and Its Effects

Another major influence on children, particularly in industrialized countries, is television. Ninety-eight percent of American homes have a television set. Children between the ages of 2 and 11 spend an average of about 22 hours a week watching TV, adolescents a bit less (American Psychological Association, 1993; Fabrikant, 1996). This number has declined in the past decade, dropping from more than 26 hours a week in 1984, but it is still the case that "by the time American children are 18 years old, they have spent more time watching television than in any other activity except sleep" (Huston et al., 1990). In the United States, high levels of viewing are more common among African-American children than among whites or Hispanics, and more common in families in which the parents are less well educated (Anderson et al., 1986).

Viewing rates are not as high in most other countries, but TV ownership is above 50 percent of households in Latin America and in most of Eastern and Western Europe, so this is not an exclusively American phenomenon (Comstock, 1991).

I can give you only a few tidbits from the vast amount of research designed to detect any effects such viewing may have on children and on adults. Still, a taste is better than no meal at all.

In the United States, children between 6 and 12 spend more time watching TV than they do playing.

Positive Educational Effects. Programs specifically designed to be educational or to teach children positive values do indeed have demonstrable positive effects. This

Research Report

Family Viewing Patterns

The mythical "average child" in the United States watches three to four hours of TV a day. But such averages obviously disguise very large variations among families in both viewing patterns and attitudes about television. To a considerable extent, parents control their children's TV viewing through explicit rules and through attitudes—an example of the way in which broad cultural forces interact with individual family styles. Nearly half of families have consistent rules about the specific programs or types of program a child may view. About 40 percent restrict the number of hours a child can watch, while another 40 percent encourage the child's viewing at least some of the time (Comstock, 1991).

Michelle St. Peters (St. Peters et al., 1991) found that she could classify families into one of four types, on the basis of the degree of regulation and degree of encouragement of TV viewing parents imposed: *Laissez-faire* parents had few regulations but did not specifically encourage viewing; *restrictive* parents had high regulations and little encouragement; *promotive* parents had few regulations and high levels of encouragement for TV viewing; and *selective* parents had high regulations but encouraged some types of viewing.

In a 2-year longitudinal study of 5-year-olds and their parents, St. Peters found that children in restrictive families watched the least TV (11.9 hours per week). When they watched, it was most likely to be entertainment or educational programs aimed specifically at children (such as *Sesame Street, Mr. Rogers Neighborhood,* or Walt Disney). The heaviest viewers were children with parents classed as promotive, who watched an average of 21.1 hours per week. They watched not only children's programs but also adult comedy, drama, game shows, and action adventure. Both laissez-faire families (16.7 hours) and selective families (19.2 hours) watched an intermediate number of hours each week.

The key point here is that families create the conditions for children's viewing and thus for what children learn from TV. Parents not only establish a degree of regulation, they may also watch with the child and interpret what the child sees. A family that wishes to do so can take advantage of the beneficial things TV has to offer and minimize exposure to programs with aggressive, violent, or sexist content. The difficulty for many families, however, is that such a planned approach to TV may mean that the parents will have to give up their own favorite programs.

is particularly clear among preschoolers, for whom most such programming is largely designed. For example, children who watch *Sesame Street* more regularly develop larger vocabularies than do children who do not watch or watch less often (Rice et al., 1990). Moreover, those who watch programs that emphasize sharing, kindness, and helpfulness, such as *Mr. Rogers' Neighborhood*, *Sesame Street*, or even *Lassie*, show more kind and helpful behavior (Murray, 1980). Results like these show that, as Huston and Wright say, "Television can be an ally, not an enemy, for parents. Parents can use television programs for their children's benefit just as they use books and toys" (1994, p. 80).

CRITICAL THINKING

How many different explanations can you think of for the relationship between amount of TV watching and school performance? What kind of data would you need to check the plausibility of each of your explanations?

Negative Effects of TV on Cognitive Skills. However, among elementary and high school students, heavy TV viewing is associated with *lower* scores on achievement tests, including measures of such basic skills as reading, arithmetic, and writing. This is particularly clear in the results of an enormous study in California that included more than 500,000 sixth- and twelfth-graders (California Achievement Program, 1980). The researchers found that the more hours the students watched TV, the lower their scores on standardized tests. This relationship was actually *stronger* among children from well-educated families, so this result is not an artifact of working-class or low-education families watching more TV. However, among children with limited English fluency, high levels of viewing were associated with somewhat higher school achievement. Thus, television can help to teach children things they did not already know (including language), but among children with basic skills at the start of school, TV viewing time appears to have a negative effect on school performance.

Television and Aggression. By far the largest body of research has focused on the potential impact of TV on children's aggressiveness. On U.S. television, the level of violence is remarkably high and has remained high over the past two decades, despite many congressional investigations and cries of alarm. In prime-time programs, a violent act occurs 5 or 6 times per hour; on Saturday morning cartoons, the rate is 20 to 25 times per hour. The highest rates of violence are generally found in programs broadcast between 6:00 and 9:00 in the morning, and between 2:00 and 5:00 in the afternoon—both times when young children are likely to be watching (Donnerstein, Slaby, & Eron, 1994). Cable TV, now available in roughly 60 percent of homes in the United States, adds to this diet of violence. The violence portrayed on these various programs is typically shown as a successful way of solving problems, and it is frequently rewarded: People who are violent get what they want.

Does the viewing of such a barrage of violence *cause* higher rates of aggression or violence in children? Demonstrating such a causal link is a bit like demonstrating a causal connection between smoking and lung cancer. Unequivocal findings would require an experimental design—a strategy ruled out for obvious ethical reasons. One cannot assign some people randomly to smoke for 30 years, nor assign some children to watch years of violent TV while others watch none. But we have three other types of research evidence that all point strongly toward the existence of a causal link.

First, we do have a few genuinely experimental studies in which one group of children is exposed to a few episodes of moderately aggressive TV while others watch neutral programs. Collectively, these studies show a significant short-term increase in aggression among those who watched the aggressive programs (Paik & Comstock, 1994). In a recent example of this type of study, Chris Boyatzis (1995) found that early elementary school–age children who were randomly assigned to watch episodes of a recently popular (and highly violent) children's program, *The Mighty Morphin Power Rangers*, showed seven times as many aggressive acts during subsequent free play with peers as did comparable children who had not just viewed the violent program.

A second type of research involves comparing levels of aggression among children who vary in the amount of TV they watch in their everyday lives. The almost universal finding is that those who watch more TV are more aggressive than their low–TV-watching peers. Of course this leaves us with a problem of interpretation. In particular, children who already behave aggressively may *choose* to watch more TV and more violent TV. And families in which TV is watched a great deal may also be more likely to use patterns of discipline that will foster aggressiveness in the child. One partial solution to this dilemma is to study children longitudinally, as Leonard Eron did in a 22-year study of aggressiveness from age 8 to age 30 (Eron, 1987).

Eron found that the best predictor of a young man's aggressiveness at age 19 was the violence of television programs he watched when he was 8. When Eron interviewed the men again when they were 30, he found that those who had had higher rates of TV viewing at age 8 were much more likely to have a record of serious criminal behavior in adulthood, a set of results shown in Figure 10.5. The pattern is the same for women, by the way, but the level of criminal offenses is far lower, just as the level of aggression is lower among girls in childhood.

The results shown in the figure, of course, are still a form of correlation. They don't prove that the TV viewing contributed in any causal way to the later criminality, because those children who chose to watch a lot of violent TV at age 8 may already have been the most violent children. Indeed, Eron found just such a pattern: 8-year-old boys who watched a lot of violent television were already more aggressive with their peers, indicating that aggressive boys choose to watch more violent TV. However, the longitudinal design allows Eron to tease out some additional patterns. In particular, he finds that among the *already* aggressive 8-year-olds, those who watched the most TV were more delinquent or aggressive as teenagers and as adults (Eron, 1987; Huesmann, Lagerspetz, & Eron, 1984).

Shorter-term longitudinal studies in Poland, Finland, Israel, and Australia show similar links between TV viewing and later increased aggression among children (Eron et al., 1991). Collectively, the evidence suggests that the causality runs both ways: "Aggressive children prefer violent television, and the violence on television causes them to be more aggressive" (Eron, 1987, p. 438).

The newest type of evidence comes from epidemiologist Brandon Centerwall (1989, 1992), who argued that we might think of societal violence as an epidemic disease and use exactly the same strategies to study it that an epidemiologist would use in trying to trace the causal factors in any other epidemic. One such strategy is to examine the conditions surrounding the emergence of a particular disease in a se-

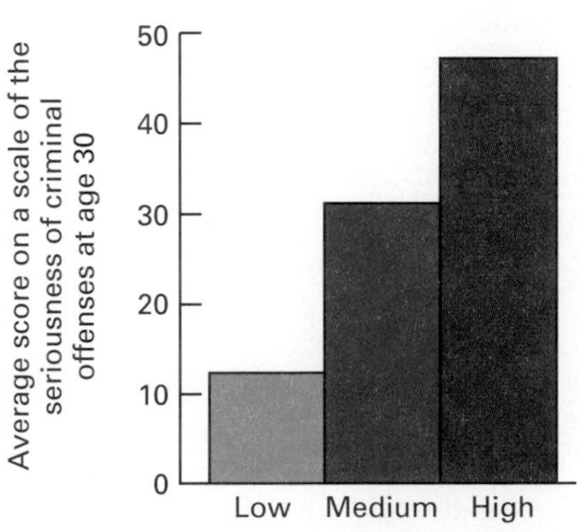

FIGURE 10.5 Eron finds a strong relationship between the amount of TV a group of boys watched when they were 8 and the average severity of criminal offenses they had committed by the age of 30. However, this finding alone does not prove there is a causal link between TV and later violence. (*Source:* Eron, 1987, Figure 3, p. 440.)

ries of different countries, to see whether it is possible to identify common antecedents. In his study of societal violence, Centerwall looked at changes in the homicide rates in Canada as a whole, and among whites in the United States and South Africa, as a function of the time since television was introduced into each country.

Television was introduced in both the United States and Canada in about 1950; in South Africa, widespread TV was available only about 25 years later. In each of these three countries, the homicide rate began to rise rapidly 10 to 15 years after TV viewing became widespread. That is, as soon as the first generation of children who had grown up watching TV became adults, homicide rates soared.

Naturally, this is *also* correlational evidence. You might well argue that other changes in these three societies could have caused a rise in violence in those particular years. To try to rule out such alternative explanations, Centerwall checked out a number of the more obvious possibilities, such as changes in the age distribution of the populations (since young people are more violent), in urbanization, economic conditions, alcohol consumption, civil unrest, or in the availability of firearms. He found that the pattern of changes on each of these dimensions in the three countries did *not* match the shifts in the homicide rates. Only the introduction of TV was temporally linked to the rise in violence.

Virtually all psychologists, after reviewing the combined evidence, would agree with Eron's testimony before a Senate committee:

> There can no longer be any doubt that heavy exposure to televised violence is one of the causes of aggressive behavior, crime and violence in society. The evidence comes from both the laboratory and real-life studies. Television violence affects youngsters of all ages, of both genders, at all socioeconomic levels and all levels of intelligence. The effect is not limited to children who are already disposed to being aggressive and is not restricted to this country. (Eron, 1992, p. S8539)

Other evidence suggests that repeated viewing of TV violence leads to emotional desensitization toward violence, to a belief that aggression is a good way to solve problems, and to a reduction in prosocial behavior (Donnerstein et al., 1994). Violent television is clearly not the only, or even the major, cause of aggressiveness among children or adults. But it is a significant influence, both individually and at the broader cultural level.

For parents, the clear message from all the research on TV is that television is an educational medium. Children learn from what they watch—vocabulary words, helpful behaviors, dietary preferences, and aggressive behaviors and attitudes. The overall content of television—violence and all—may indeed reflect general cultural values. But an individual family can pick and choose among the various cultural messages by controlling what the child watches on TV.

Critical Thinking

Given all that you have now read about television and children's development, how could you as a parent maximize the benefits and limit the negative effects? Would you be willing to give up having a television altogether if you thought that was necessary for your child's optimum development?

Summary

1. Patterns of relationships established in elementary school may have greater impact on adolescent and adult life than do cognitive changes in these same years.
2. In middle childhood, the self-concept becomes more abstract, more comparative, more generalized.
3. Similar changes occur in children's descriptions of others and in their understanding of relationships such as friendships. Friendships are increasingly seen as reciprocal relationships in which generosity and trust are important elements.
4. These changes parallel the cognitive changes we see in the same years, particularly the child's reduced reliance on appearances.
5. Relationships with parents become less overtly affectionate, with fewer attachment behaviors, in middle

childhood. The strength of the attachment, however, appears to persist.

6. Peer relationships become increasingly central. Gender segregation of peer group activities is at its peak in these years, and appears in every culture.
7. Individual friendships also become more common and more enduring; they are almost entirely sex-segregated. Boys' and girls' friendships appear to differ in quite specific ways. Boys' relationships are more extensive and more "restrictive," with higher levels of competition and aggression; girls' relationships are more intensive and enabling, with more compliance and agreement.
8. Physical aggression declines, while verbal insults and taunts increase. Boys show markedly higher levels of physical and direct verbal aggression, and higher rates of conduct disorders, but girls show higher rates of "relational aggression."
9. Self-esteem appears to be shaped by two factors: The degree of discrepancy a child experiences between goals and achievements, and the degree of perceived social support from peers and parents.
10. Low self-esteem is strongly associated with depression in children this age.
11. Socially rejected children are most strongly characterized by high levels of aggression or bullying and low levels of agreement and helpfulness. Aggressive/rejected children are much more likely to show behavior problems in adolescence and a variety of disturbances in adulthood.
12. Rejected children are more likely to interpret others' behavior as threatening or hostile. Thus, they have different internal models of relationship.
13. A large fraction of children in the United States grow up in poverty. Such children, especially those experiencing persistent urban poverty, are markedly disadvantaged in many ways, including having less access to medical care and more exposure to multiple stresses. They do worse in school and drop out of school at far higher rates.
14. Some protective factors, including a secure attachment, higher IQ, authoritative parenting, and effective schools, can counterbalance poverty effects for some children.
15. The average American child watches 4 hours of television per day. Preschoolers can learn vocabulary, politeness, and other skills. Among schoolchildren, the more TV watched, the lower the grades.
16. Experts agree that watching violence on TV also increases the level of personal aggression or violence shown by a child.

Key Terms

relational aggression   self-esteem

Suggested Readings

Asher, S. R., & Coie, J. D. (Eds.) (1990). *Peer rejection in childhood.* Cambridge: Cambridge University Press.

This edited volume contains papers by all the leading researchers on this important subject. The papers are aimed at an audience of fellow psychologists, so the technical level is fairly high. Still, it is a wonderful next source if you are interested in this subject.

Eron, L. D., Gentry, J. H., & Schlegel, P. (Eds.) (1994). *Reason to hope: A psychological perspective on violence and youth.* Washington, DC: American Psychological Association.

The chapter on the effect of TV on violence is a good current review of this material. The book also includes many other fascinating chapters.

Garbarino, J., Dubrow, N., Kostelny, K., & Pardo, C. (1992). *Children in danger: Coping with the consequences of community violence.* San Francisco: Jossey-Bass.

A striking, frightening book about children growing up in "war zones," including areas of urban poverty in the United States, as well as in literal war zones in other countries.

Huston, A. C. (Ed.) (1991). *Children in poverty: Child development and public policy.* Cambridge: Cambridge University Press.

An excellent collection of papers on all aspects of poverty.

Kozol, J. (1995). *Amazing Grace.* New York: Crown Publishing.

A deeply affecting book about children growing up in one of the most concentrated pockets of poverty in the United States, the South Bronx. It will astonish you—and make you weep.

Interlude 3

Summing Up Middle Childhood Development

Basic Characteristics of Middle Childhood

You can see from the table, which summarizes the changes and continuities of middle childhood, that many of the changes in this period are gradual ones: greater and greater physical skill, less and less reliance on appearance and more and more attention to underlying qualities and attributes, greater and greater role of peers. The one interval during these years in which there seems to be a more rapid change is right at the beginning of middle childhood, at the point of transition from the preschooler to the schoolchild. And of course at the other end of this age range, puberty causes another set of rapid changes.

The Transition Between 5 and 7

Some kind of a transition into middle childhood has been noted in a great many cultures. There seems to be widespread recognition that a 6-year-old is somehow qualitatively different from a 5-year-old: more responsible, more able to understand complex ideas. Among the Kipsigis of Kenya, for example, the age of 6 is said to be the first point at which the child has *ng'omnotet,* translated as "intelligence" (Harkness & Super, 1985). The fact that schooling begins at this age seems to reflect an implicit or explicit recognition of this fundamental shift.

Psychologists who have studied development across this transition have pointed to a whole series of changes.

- Cognitively, we see a shift to what Piaget calls concrete operational thinking. The child now understands conservation problems, seriation, and class inclusion. More generally, the child seems to pay less attention to surface properties of objects and more to underlying continuities and patterns. We see this not only in children's understanding of physical objects but in their understanding of others, of relationships, and of themselves. In studies of information processing, we see a parallel rapid increase in the child's use of executive strategies.
- In the self-concept, we first see a global judgment of self-worth at about age 7 or 8.
- In peer relationships, gender segregation becomes virtually complete by age 6 or 7, especially in individual friendships.

The apparent confluence of these changes is impressive and seems to provide some support for the existence of a Piaget-like stage. On the surface, at least, it looks as if some kind of change in the basic structure of the child's thinking has occurred that is reflected in all aspects of the child's functioning. But impressive as these changes are, it is not so clear that what is going on here is a rapid, pervasive, structural change to a whole new way of thinking and relating. Children don't make this shift all at once in every area of their thinking or relationships. For example, while the shift from a concrete to a more abstract self-concept may become noticeable at 6 or 7, it occurs quite gradually and is still going on at age 11 and 12. Similarly, a child may grasp conservation of quantity at age 5 or 6, but typically does not understand conservation of weight until several years later.

Furthermore, expertise, or the lack of it, strongly affects the pattern of the child's cognitive progress. Thus, while I think most psychologists would agree that a set of important changes normally emerge together at about this age, most would also agree that there is no rapid or abrupt reorganization of the child's whole mode of operating.

A Summary of the Threads of Development During Middle Childhood

Aspect of Development	Age in Years: 6	7	8	9	10	11	12
Physical development	Jumps rope; skips; may ride bike	Rides two-wheeled bike	Rides bike well Uses pencil well	Puberty begins for some girls		Puberty begins for some boys	
Cognitive development	Gender constancy; various concrete operations skills, including some conservation, class inclusion, various memory strategies, executive processes (metacognition)		Inductive logic: better and better use of concrete operations skills: conservation of weight			Conservation of volume	
Self/personality development	Concept of self increasingly more abstract, less tied to appearance; descriptions of others increasingly focused on internal, enduring qualities						
		Global sense of self-worth Friendship based on reciprocal trust					
	Gender segregation in play and friendship almost total						
	Enduring friendships appear, continue throughout these years						

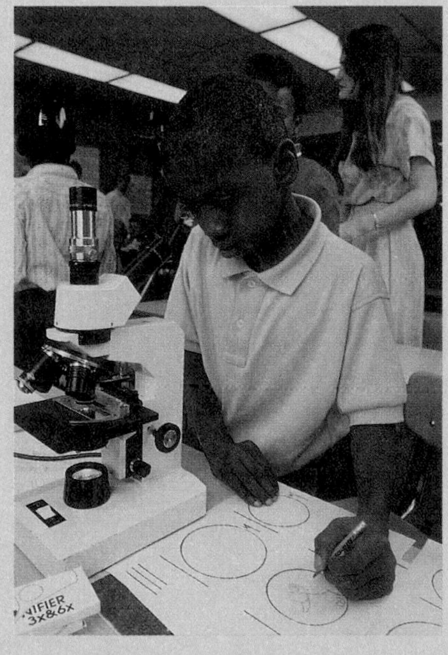

Central Processes

In trying to account for the developmental shifts we see during middle childhood, my bias has been to see the cognitive changes as most central, the necessary but not sufficient condition for the alterations in relationships and in the self-scheme during this period. A good illustration is the emergence of a global sense of self-worth, which seems to require not only a tendency to look beyond or behind surface characteristics, but also the use of inductive logic. The child appears to arrive at a global sense of self-worth by some summative, inductive process.

Similarly, the quality of the child's relationships with peers and parents seems to rest, in part, on a basic cognitive understanding of reciprocity and perspective taking. The child now understands that others read him as much as he reads them. Children of 7 or 8 will now say of their friends that they "trust each other," something you would be very unlikely to hear from a 5-year-old.

Such a cognitive bias dominated theories and research on middle childhood for many decades, largely as a result of the powerful influence of Piaget's theory. This imbalance has begun to be redressed in recent years, as the central importance of the peer group and the child's social experience have been better understood. There are two aspects to this revision of thinking. First, we have reawakened to the (obvious) fact that a great deal of the experience on which the child's cognitive progress is based occurs in social interactions, particularly in play with other children. Second, we have realized that social relationships make a unique set of demands, both cognitive and interactive, and have unique consequences for the child's social and emotional functioning. It is in these elementary school years, for example, that patterns of peer rejection or acceptance are consolidated, with reverberations through adolescence and into adult life.

People, as objects of thought, are simply not the same as rocks, beakers of water, or balls of clay. Among many other things, people behave *intentionally,* and they can reveal or conceal information about themselves. Further, unlike relationships with objects, relationships with people are mutual and reciprocal. Other people talk back, respond to your distress, offer things, get angry.

Children also have to learn social scripts, those special rules that apply to social interactions, such as politeness rules, or rules about when you can and cannot speak, about when you should or should not display emotions, or about power or dominance hierarchies. Such scripts change with age, so at each new age the child must learn a new set of roles, a new set of rules about what she may and may not do. To be sure, these changes in the scripts are partly in *response* to the child's growing cognitive sophistication. But they also reflect changes in the child's role in the social system. One obvious example is the set of changes when children start school. The script associated with the role of "student" is simply quite different from the one connected with the role of "little kid." School classrooms are more tightly organized than are preschools or day-care centers, expectations for obedience are higher, and many new drills and routines must be learned. These changes are bound to affect the child's pattern of thinking.

Just what role physical change plays in this collection of developments I do not know. Clearly physical changes *are* going on. Girls, in particular, begin the early steps of puberty during elementary school. But we simply don't know whether the rate of physical development in these years is connected in any way to the rate of the child's progress through the sequence of cognitive or social understandings. There has been virtually no research linking the first row in the summary table with any of the other rows. We do have data showing that bigger, more coordinated, early-developing children are likely to have slightly faster cognitive development and be somewhat more popular with peers, but this is clearly only one piece of the puzzle. Obviously, this is an area in which we need far more knowledge.

Influences on the Basic Processes: The Role of Culture

Most of what I have said about middle childhood—and about other ages as well—is almost entirely based on research on children growing up in Western cultures. I've tried to balance the scales a bit as I've gone along, but we must still ask, again and again, whether the patterns we see are specific to particular cultures or whether they reflect underlying developmental processes common to all children everywhere.

In the case of middle childhood, there are some obvious differences in the experiences of children in Western cultures versus those growing up in parts of the world where families live by subsistence agriculture, and schooling is not a dominant force in children's lives (Weisner, 1984). In many such cultures, children of 6 or 7 are thought of as "intelligent" and responsible, and are given almost adultlike roles. They are highly likely to be given the task of caring for younger siblings and to begin their apprenticeship in the skills they will need as adults, such as agricultural skills or animal husbandry, learning alongside the adult. In some West African and Polynesian cultures, it is also common for children this age to be sent out to foster care, perhaps with relatives, or to apprentice with a skilled tradesperson.

Children growing up in such cultures obviously have a very different set of social tasks to learn in the middle childhood years. They do not need to learn how to relate to or make friends with strangers. Instead, from an early age they need to learn their place in an existing network of roles and relationships. For the Western child, the roles are less prescribed and the choices for adult life are far more varied.

Yet the differences in the lives of Western and non-Western children should not obscure the very real similarities. In all cultures, children this age develop individual friendships, segregate their play groups by gender, develop the cognitive underpinnings of reciprocity, learn the beginnings of what Piaget calls concrete operations, and acquire some of the basic skills that will be required for adult life. These are not trivial similarities. They speak to the power of the common process of development, even in the midst of obvious variation in experience.

Physical and Cognitive Development in Adolescence

Most of us use the word *adolescence* as if the term applied to a fairly precise set of years, such as the teenage years, or the time that starts with junior high school, or the years from 12 to 20. But in fact, the relevant age range is fairly fuzzy around the edges. If we mean to include the physical process of puberty within the years of adolescence then we need to think of adolescence as beginning before age 12, especially for girls, some of whom begin puberty at 8 or 9. And on the other end, it is not clear that it is still appropriate to refer to a young man of 18 with a job and a wife and child as an adolescent.

It makes more sense to think of adolescence as the period that lies psychologically and culturally between childhood and adulthood rather than as a specific age range. It is the period of transition in which the child changes physically, mentally, and emotionally into an adult. The timing of this transition differs from one society to another and from one individual to another within a culture. But every child must cross through such a transitional period to achieve adult status. In most industrial-

Cultures and Contexts

Adolescent Initiation Rituals

So important is the change in status from child to adult that many societies have marked this passage with some kind of rite or ritual. Such rituals vary enormously in content but certain practices are especially common (Cohen, 1964).

One such practice, more common for boys than for girls, is the separation of the child from the family, referred to by anthropologists as *extrusion.* The child may spend the day with his family but sleep elsewhere, or he may live in a separate dwelling with other boys or with relatives. For example, among the Kurtatchi of Melanesia, boys go through an extrusion ceremony at about age 9 or 10, after which they sleep in a special hut used by boys and unmarried men (Cohen, 1964). This practice obviously symbolizes the separation of the child from the birth family, marking a coming-of-age. But it also emphasizes that the child "belongs" not just to the family but to the larger group of kin or societal/tribal members.

A related theme is the accentuation of differences between females and males. In many cultures, for example, nudity taboos begin only at adolescence. In other societies, adolescents are forbidden to speak to any opposite-sex siblings, a taboo that may extend until one of the siblings marries (Cohen, 1964). This practice seems to have at least two purposes. First and most obviously, it strengthens the incest taboo that is so important to avoid inbreeding. Second, it signifies the beginning of the time in life when males and females have quite different life patterns. Girls and boys have begun to learn gender-appropriate tasks long before adolescence, but at adolescence they take up their distinct roles far more completely.

These two patterns may form the backdrop for the initiation ritual itself, which is usually brief and fairly intense, often including considerable drama and pageantry. During this time—usually in groups and separately for each sex—youth are indoctrinated by the elders into the customary practices of their tribe or society. They may learn the history and songs of their people as well as special religious rituals or practices, such as the learning of Hebrew as preparation for the Bar Mitzva or Bat Mitzva in the Jewish tradition.

Physical mutilation or trials of endurance also play a part in the initiation in some cases. Boys may be circumcised or cut so as to create certain patterns of scars, or they may be sent out into the wilderness to undergo spiritual purification or to prove their manhood by achieving some feat. This is less common in girls' initiation rituals, but physical trials or mutilation do occur, such as the removal of the clitoris, whipping, or scarification.

Among the Hopi, for example, both boys and girls go through specific rituals in which they are taught the religious ceremonies of the kachina cult and are whipped. After these ceremonies, they may participate fully in the adult religious practices.

In modern U.S. culture, as in most other Western cultures, we have no universally shared initiation rites, but there are still many changes of status and a few experiences that have some properties in common with traditional adolescent *initiation rituals.* For example, we do not deliberately separate adolescents from family or from adults, but we do send adolescents to a new level of school, thus effectively segregating them from all but their peers. Boot camp, for those who enter the military, is a more obvious parallel because the recruits are sent to a separate location and undergo various physical trials before they are accepted. Until relatively recent times, it was also common for adolescent boys and girls in our culture to attend separate schools. Even within coeducational schools, physical education classes were sex-segregated until very recently, as were such traditional gender-stereotyped classes as home economics and shop.

Various other changes in legal standing also mark the passage to adult status in modern Western cultures. In the United States, for example, young people can have a driver's license at 16 and can see R-rated movies at 17. At 18, they can vote, marry, and enter the military without parental consent, and they can be tried in adult rather than juvenile court for any legal offense.

These various remnants of older initiation patterns are considerably less condensed in modern society than are traditional initiation rites. One result of this is that the passage into adult status is much fuzzier for young people in most industrialized countries. Perhaps this is one reason why adolescents in our society often create their own separation and distinctness, such as by wearing unusual or even outlandish clothing or hairstyles.

ized cultures, this transitional stage is quite lengthy, lasting from perhaps 12 to 18 or 20.

Because the physical and emotional changes that are part of this transition are so striking, the period of adolescence has acquired a reputation as being full of *Sturm und Drang* (storm and stress). Such a description considerably exaggerates the degree of emotional upheaval most adolescents experience. But the *importance* of the process is difficult to exaggerate, beginning with the remarkable physical changes of puberty.

CRITICAL THINKING

What do you think are some of the consequences of the lack of clear initiation rituals and of the relatively long period of adolescence in modern Western societies? How might our culture be different if we did have shared initiation rites?

Physical Changes

The many body changes associated with puberty are largely controlled by hormones, which play a central role in the physical drama of adolescence.

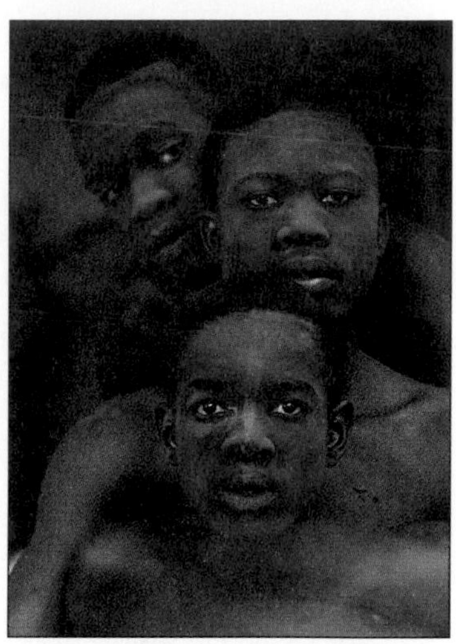

In the initiation rite of the Kota tribe of the Congo, boys' faces are painted blue to make them appear ghostlike, to symbolize the phantom of their now-departed childhood.

Hormones

Hormones, which are secretions of the various **endocrine glands** in the body, govern pubertal growth and physical changes in several ways, summarized in Table 11.1. Of all the endocrine glands, the most critical is the **pituitary gland,** because it provides the trigger for release of hormones from other glands. For example, the thyroid gland secretes thyroxine only when it has received a signal to do so in the form of a specific thyroid-stimulating hormone secreted by the pituitary.

Of course hormones play a central role in growth and development at earlier ages as well. Thyroid hormone (thyroxine) is present from about the fourth month of gestation, and appears to be involved in stimulating normal brain development prenatally. The pituitary also secretes growth hormone as early as 10 weeks after conception, thus helping to stimulate the very rapid growth of cells and organs of the body. And as I mentioned in Chapter 3, testosterone is produced prenatally in the testes of the developing male and influences both the development of male genitals and some aspects of brain development.

After birth, the rate of growth is governed largely by thyroid hormone and pituitary growth hormone. Thyroid hormone is secreted in greater quantities for the first two years of life and then falls to a lower level and remains steady until adolescence (Tanner, 1978). Secretions from the testes and ovaries, as well as adrenal androgen, are also at very low levels in the early years of childhood. This changes at age 7 or 8, when adrenal androgen begins to be secreted—the first signal of the changes of puberty (Shonkoff, 1984).

Following this first step there is a complex sequence of hormone changes, beginning with a signal from the hypothalamus, a small structure in the brain that plays a vital role in regulating a variety of behaviors, including eating, drinking, and sexuality. In the pubertal process, the thalamus signals to the pituitary gland, which then begins secreting increased levels of **gonadotrophic hormones** (2 in males, 3 in females). These in turn stimulate the development of the glands in the testes and ovaries that then begin to secrete more hormones—testosterone in boys and a form of **estrogen** called *estradiol* in girls. Over the course of puberty, the levels of testosterone increase 18-fold in boys, while levels of estradiol increase 8-fold in girls (Biro et al., 1995; Nottelmann et al., 1987).

At the same time, the pituitary also secretes three other hormones that interact with the specific sex hormones and affect growth: adrenal androgen, thyroid stimulating hormone, and general growth hormone. Adrenal androgen, which is chemically very similar to testosterone, plays a particularly important role for girls, triggering the growth spurt and affecting pubic hair development. Thus, it takes a "male" hormone to produce the growth spurt in girls. For boys, adrenal androgen is less significant, presumably because they already have male hormone in the form of testosterone floating about in their bloodstream.

Table 11.1 Major Hormones Involved in Physical Growth and Development

Gland	Hormone(s) Secreted	Aspects of Growth Influenced
Thyroid	Thyroxine	Normal brain development and overall rate of growth
Adrenal	Adrenal androgen	Some changes at puberty, particularly the development of secondary sex characteristics in girls
Testes (in boys)	Testosterone	Crucial in the formation of male genitals prenatally; also triggers the sequence of primary and secondary sex characteristic changes at puberty in the male
Ovaries (in girls)	Estrogen (Estradiol)	Development of the menstrual cycle and breasts in girls; has less to do with other secondary sex characteristics than testosterone does for boys
Pituitary	Growth hormone, activating hormones	Rate of physical maturation; signals other glands to secrete

It is somewhat misleading, by the way, to talk about "male" and "female" hormones. Both males and females have at least some of each (estrogen or estradiol, and testosterone or androgen); the difference is essentially in the relative proportion of the two.

All these hormonal changes are reflected in two sets of body changes: the well-known changes in sex organs, and a much broader set of changes in muscles, fat, bones, and body organs.

Height, Shape, Muscles, and Fat

Height. One of the most striking physical changes of adolescence is in height. You'll remember from earlier chapters that in infancy, the baby gains in height very rapidly, adding 10 to 12 inches in length in the first year. The toddler and elementary school–age child grow much more slowly. The third phase begins with the dramatic adolescent growth spurt, triggered by the big increases in growth hormones. During this phase, the child may add 3 to 6 inches a year for several years. After the growth spurt, in the fourth phase, the teenager again adds height and weight slowly until his or her final adult size is reached. You can see the shape of the growth curve in Figure 11.1.

Shape. At the same time, because the different parts of the child's body do not grow to full adult size at the same pace, the shape and proportions of the adolescent's body go through a series of changes. A teenager's hands and feet grow to full adult size earliest, followed by the arms and legs, with the trunk usually the slowest part to grow. (In fact, a good signal for a parent that a child's puberty is beginning is a rapid increase in the child's shoe size.) Because of this asymmetry in the body parts, we often think of an adolescent as "awkward" or uncoordinated. Interestingly, research does not bear out such an impression. Robert Malina, who has done extensive research on physical development, has found no point in the adolescent growth process at which teenagers become consistently less coordinated or less skillful at physical tasks (Malina, 1990).

Children's heads and faces also change in childhood and adolescence. During the elementary school years, the size and shape of a child's jaw change when the permanent teeth come in. In adolescence both jaws grow forward and the forehead becomes more prominent. This set of changes often gives teenagers' faces (espe-

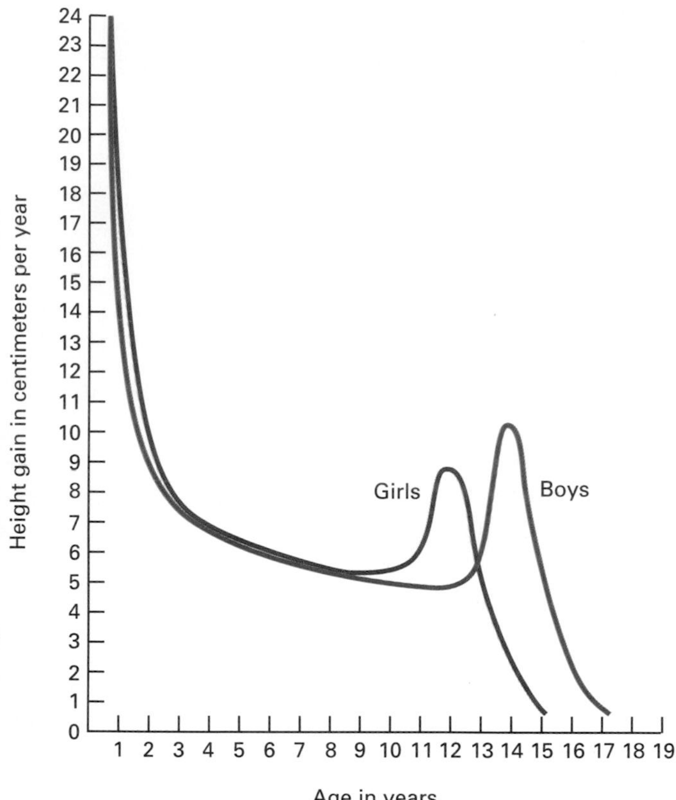

FIGURE 11.1 These curves show the gain in height for each year from birth through adolescence, with the adolescent growth spurt easily identifiable. (*Sources:* Malina, 1990; Tanner, 1978, p. 14.)

cially boys') an angular, bony appearance, quite unlike their earlier look—as you can see in the set of pictures in Figure 11.2.

Muscles. Muscle fibers, like bone tissues, also go through a growth spurt at adolescence, becoming thicker and denser, so that adolescents become quite a lot stronger in just a few years. Both boys and girls show this increase in strength, but the increase is much greater in boys. For example, in a cross-sectional study in Canada involving 2673 children and teenagers, Smoll and Schutz (1990) measured strength by having each child hang from a bar, with eyes level with the bar, for as long as possible. Between age 9 and age 17, boys increased the average length of their bar hang by 160 percent, while girls increased only 37 percent. By age 17, the boys in this study were three times as strong as the girls. This substantial difference in strength reflects the underlying sex difference in muscle tissue that is accentuated at adolescence: Among adult men, about 40 percent of total body mass is muscle, compared to only about 24 percent in adult women.

Such a sex difference in muscle mass (and accompanying strength) seems to be largely a result of hormone differences. But sex differences in exercise patterns or activity may also be involved. For example, the sex difference in *leg* strength is much less than in arm strength, a pattern that makes sense if we assume that all teenagers walk and use their legs a similar amount but that boys use their arm muscles in various sports activities more than girls do (Tanner, Hughes, & Whitehouse, 1981). Still, there does seem to be a basic hormonal difference as well, because we know that very fit girls and women are still not as strong as very fit boys and men.

Fat. Another major component of the body is fat, most of which is stored immediately under the skin. This *subcutaneous fat* is first laid down beginning at about 34

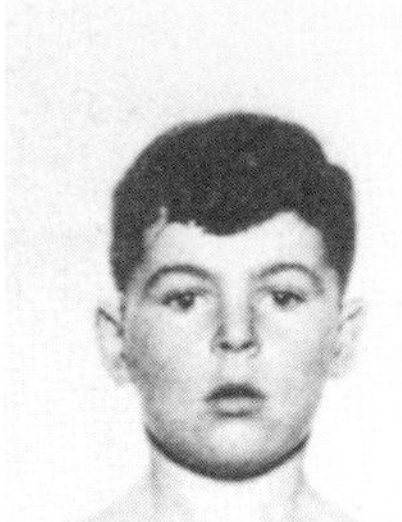
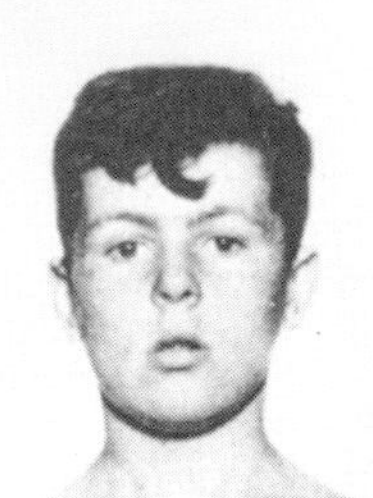
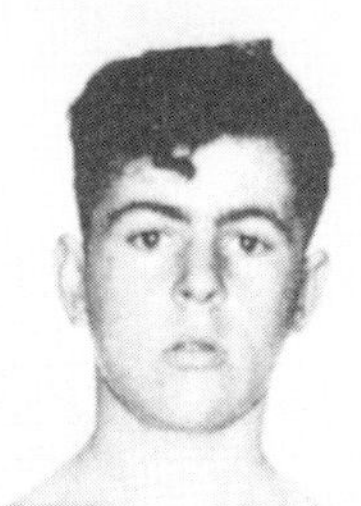
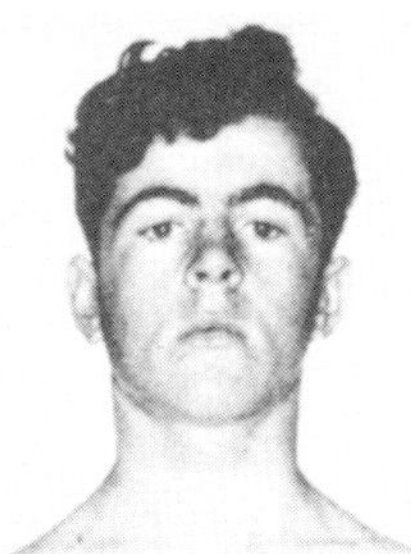

FIGURE 11.2 These photos of the same boy before, during, and after puberty show the striking changes in the jaws and forehead that dramatically alter appearance in many teenage boys. The same changes occur in girls' faces, but are not as dramatic. (Reprinted by permission of the publisher from *Fetus into Man by* J. M. Tanner, Cambridge, Mass.: Harvard University Press, copyright © 1978, 1989 by J. M. Tanner.)

weeks prenatally and has an early peak at about 9 months after birth. The thickness of this layer of fat then declines until about age 6 or 7, then rises until adolescence.

Here, too, there is a sex difference. From birth, girls have slightly more fat tissue than boys do, and this discrepancy becomes gradually more marked during childhood and adolescence. The size of the difference is illustrated nicely in the results of the same Canadian study (Smoll & Schutz, 1990). Between age 13 and age 17, the percentage of body weight made up of fat rose from 21.8 to 24 percent among girls in this study but dropped from 16.1 to 14.0 percent among boys. So, during and after puberty, proportions of fat rise among girls and decline among boys, while the proportion of weight that is muscle rises in boys and declines in girls.

Other Body Changes. Puberty also brings important changes in other body organs. In particular, the heart and lungs increase considerably in size and the heart rate drops. Both of these changes are more marked for boys than for girls—another of the factors that increases the capacity for sustained effort by boys relative to girls. Before about age 12, boys and girls have similar physical strength, speed, and endurance, although even at these earlier ages, when there is a difference it favors the boys because of their lower levels of body fat. After puberty, boys have a clear advantage in all three (Smoll & Schutz, 1990).

CRITICAL THINKING

Assume that you are a member of a local school board, faced with a decision about whether to have teenage boys and girls play on the same competitive teams, such as volleyball, soccer, or baseball. Given all that I have said about sex differences in physical characteristics at puberty, how would you decide? Why?

Development of Sexual Maturity

The hormone changes of puberty also trigger the development of full sexual maturity, including changes in *primary sex characteristics*, such as the testes and penis in the male, and the ovaries, uterus, and vagina in the female; and changes in *secondary sex characteristics*, such as breast development in girls, changing voice pitch and beard growth in boys, and the growth of body hair in both sexes.

Each of these physical developments occurs in a defined sequence, customarily divided into five stages following a system originally suggested by J. M. Tanner (1978). Stage 1 always describes the preadolescent stage, stage 2 the first signs of pubertal change, stages 3 and 4 the intermediate steps, and stage 5 the final adult characteristic.

Sexual Development in Girls. Studies of preteens and teens in both Europe and North America (Malina, 1990) show that in girls, the various sequential changes are interlocked in a particular pattern, shown schematically in the upper part of Figure 11.3. The first steps are typically the early changes in breasts and pubic hair, followed by the peak of the growth spurt and by stage 4 of both breast and pubic hair development. Only then does first menstruation occur, an event called **menarche** (pronounced men-ARE-kee). Menarche typically occurs two years after the beginning of other visible changes and is succeeded only by the final stages of breast and pubic hair development. Among girls in industrialized countries today, menarche occurs,

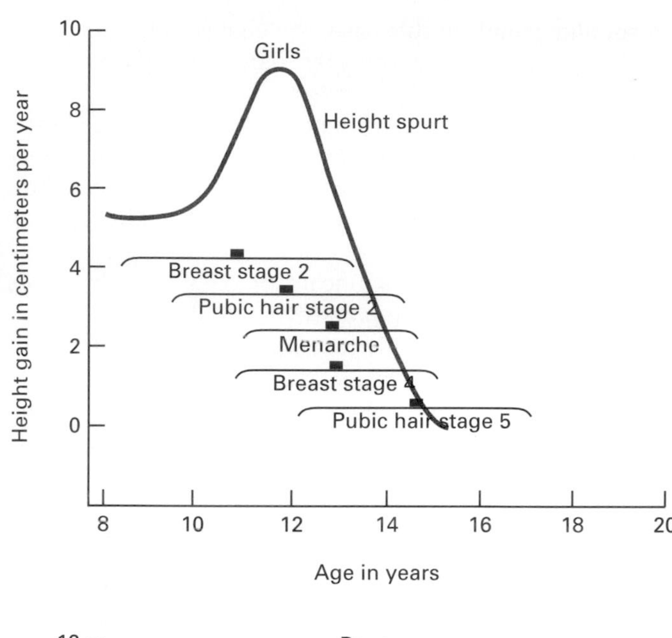

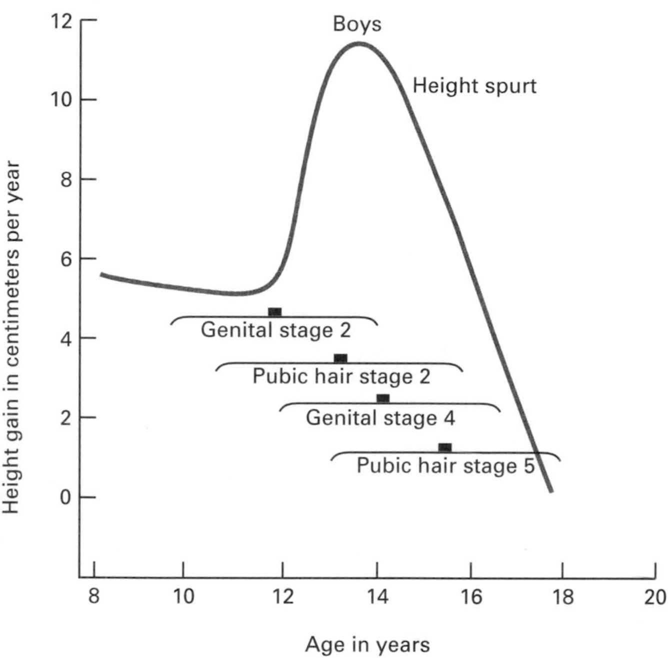

FIGURE 11.3 The typical sequence of pubertal development for girls (upper figure) and boys (lower figure). The colored curved line shows the *gains* in height at various ages; the box on each black line represents the average attainment of that change, while the line shows the range of normal times. Note the *wide* range of normality for all of these changes. Also note how late in the sequence menarche occurs for girls, and that girls are about two years ahead of boys. (*Sources:* Biro et al., 1995; Chumlea, 1982; Garn, 1980; Malina, 1990; Tanner, 1978.)

on average, between age 12½ and 13½; 95 percent of all girls experience this event between the ages of 11 and 15 (Malina, 1990).

Interestingly, the timing of menarche has changed rather dramatically over the past 100 years. In 1840, the average age of menarche in Western industrialized countries was roughly 17; the average has dropped steadily since that time at a rate of about 4 months per decade among European populations (Roche, 1979), an example of what psychologists call a **secular trend.** In this case, the change has been most likely caused by significant changes in lifestyle and diet, particularly increases in protein intake.

Menarche does not signal full sexual maturity. It is possible to conceive shortly after menarche, but irregularity is the norm for some time. In as many as three-quarters of the cycles in the first year, and half the cycles in the second and third years after menarche, no ovum is produced (Vihko & Apter, 1980). Full adult fertility thus develops over a period of years.

This initial menstrual irregularity has some significant practical consequences for sexually active teenagers. For one thing, such irregularity no doubt contributes to the widespread (but false) assumption among early-teenage girls that they cannot get pregnant because they are "too young." At the same time, menstrual irregularity makes any form of rhythm contraception unreliable, even among teenagers who have enough basic reproductive knowledge to realize that the time of ovulation is normally the time of greatest fertility—knowledge that is not widespread.

Sexual Development in Boys. In boys, as in girls, the peak of the growth spurt typically comes fairly late in the sequence, as you can see in the bottom part of Figure 11.3. Malina's data suggest that on average a boy completes stages 2, 3, and 4 of genital development and stages 2 and 3 of pubic hair development before the growth peak is reached (Malina, 1990). The development of a beard and the lowering of the voice typically occur near the end of the sequence. Precisely when in this sequence the boy begins to produce viable sperm is very difficult to determine, although current evidence places this event some time between ages 12 and 14, usually *before* the boy has reached the peak of the growth spurt (Brooks-Gunn & Reiter, 1990).

Two things are particularly interesting about these sequences. First, while boys begin the early stages of pubertal change only a short time later than do girls, the growth spurt comes about two years later in boys. Most of you remember that period in late elementary school or junior high when the girls were suddenly taller than the boys. (Do I remember that time! I *towered* over everyone.)

A second intriguing thing is that while the order of development seems to be highly consistent *within* each sequence (such as breast development or pubic hair development), there is quite a lot of variability *across* sequences. I've shown the normative or average pattern in Figure 11.3, but individual teenagers often deviate from the norm. For instance, a girl might move through several stages of pubic hair development before the first clear breast changes, or experience menarche much earlier in the sequence than normal. It is important to keep this variation in mind if you are trying to make a prediction about an individual teenager.

Early-developing girls, like this fifth-grader who is already developing breasts, report much less positive adolescent experiences and more depression than do on-time or later-developing girls.

Early Versus Late Pubertal Development

Yet another form of variation in the pattern of puberty is the *timing* of the entire process. In any random sample of 12- and 13-year-olds, you will find some who are already at stage 5, and others still at stage 1 in the steps of sexual maturation. What is the psychological effect of such variation on the child who is very early, or very late?

The cumulative body of research on this question points to an interesting and complex hypothesis that once again underlines the importance of internal models. The general idea is that each young child or teenager has an internal model about the "normal" or "right" timing for puberty (Faust, 1983; Lerner, 1987; Petersen, 1987). Each girl has an internal model about the "right age" to develop breasts or begin menstruation; each boy has an internal model or image about when it is right to begin to grow a beard or to reach adult size. According to this hypothesis, it is the discrepancy between an adolescent's expectation and what actually happens that determines the psychological effect, just as it is the discrepancy between goals and achievements that determines self-esteem. Those whose development occurs outside the desired or expected range are likely to think less well of themselves, to be less happy with their bodies and with the process of puberty, perhaps have fewer friends, or experience other signs of distress.

In American culture today, most young people seem to share the expectation that pubertal changes will happen sometime between age 12 and 14; anything earlier is seen as "too soon," anything later is thought of as late. If you compare these expectations to the actual average timing of pubertal changes, you'll see that such a norm includes girls who are average in development and boys who are *early*. So we should expect that these two groups—normal-developing girls and early-developing boys—should have the best psychological functioning. Early-maturing boys may have an added advantage because they are more likely to be of the *mesomorphic* body type, with wide shoulders and a large amount of muscle. This body type is consistently preferred at all ages, and because boys with this body type tend to be good at sports, the early-developing boy should be particularly advantaged.

Figure 11.4 shows the specific predictions graphically. Because of the twin advantages of having puberty fall within the "normative" time and having a more mesomorphic body type, early-developing boys should be best off, followed by average boys and girls. The least well off should be late-developing boys and early-developing girls, both of whom are "off time."

Research in the United States generally confirms these predictions. Girls who are early developers (before 11 or 12 for major body changes) show consistently more negative body images, such as thinking themselves too fat. Such girls are also more likely to get into trouble in school and at home, are more likely to get involved with misbehaving peer groups, and are more likely to be depressed (Alsaker, 1995; Rierdan & Koff, 1993; Silbereisen & Kracke, 1993). Very late development in girls also appears to be somewhat negative, but the effect of lateness is not so striking for girls as it is for boys.

Among boys, as Figure 11.4 predicts, the relationship is essentially linear. The earlier the boy's development, the more positive his body image, the better he does in school, the less trouble he gets into, and the more friends he has (Duke et al., 1982).

In nearly all these studies, earliness or lateness has been defined in terms of the actual physical changes. The results are even clearer when researchers have instead asked teenagers about their internal model of earliness or lateness. For example, Rierdan, Koff, and Stubbs (1989) found that the negativeness of a girl's menarcheal experience was predicted by her *subjective* sense of earliness; those who perceived

Critical Thinking

Do you remember your own puberty as very early, early, on time, or late? Do you think that perception had any effect on your overall experience of adolescence?

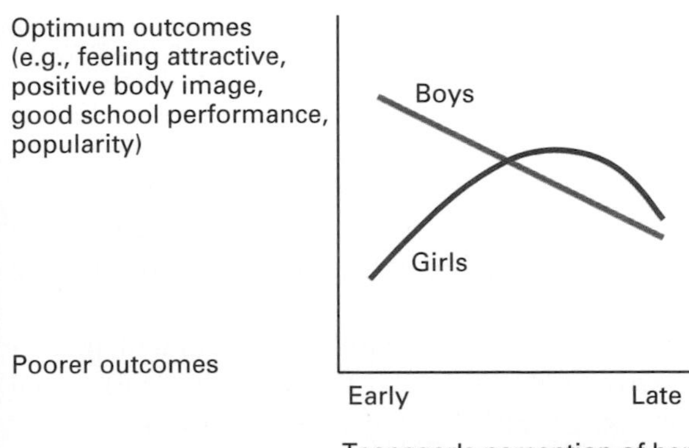

FIGURE 11.4 According to this model of the effects of early and late puberty, the best position for girls is to be "on time," while for boys the best position is to be "early." For both sexes, however, it is the *perception* of earliness or lateness, and not the actual timing, that is thought to be critical. (*Source:* Adapted from Tobin-Richards, Boxer, & Petersen, 1983, p. 137.)

themselves as early reported a more negative experience. But such a negative experience was *not* related to the actual age of her menarche.

This link between the internal model and the outcome is especially vivid in a study of ballet dancers by Jeanne Brooks-Gunn (Brooks-Gunn, 1987; Brooks-Gunn & Warren, 1985). She studied 14- to 18-year-old girls, some of whom were serious ballet dancers studying at a national ballet company school. In this group, a very lean, almost prepubescent body is highly desirable. Brooks-Gunn therefore expected that among dancers, those who were very late in pubertal development would actually have a better image of themselves than those who were on time. And that is exactly what she found. Among the nondancers, menarche at the biologically average time was associated with a better body image than was late menarche, but exactly the reverse was true for the dancers.

Thus, it seems to be the discrepancy or mismatch between the desired or expected pattern and a youngster's actual pattern that is critical, not the absolute age of pubertal development. Because the majority of young people in any given culture share similar expectations, we can see common effects of early or late development. But to predict the effect of early or late development in any individual teenager, we would need to know more about her or his internal model.

Adolescent Sexuality and Pregnancy

The many physical changes of puberty mean that the young person is stronger, faster, and better-coordinated than before. These changes also obviously make mature sexual behavior possible. What do we know about the choices teenagers make about their sexual activity?

As is usually the case, what I can tell you about this is almost entirely specific to the United States and to other industrialized countries. It is good to keep in mind that the whole question of adolescent sexuality is a central issue for those of us in such cultures in large part because we have created such a long delay between physical sexual maturity and social maturity: Young people are physically mature at 13 or 14 but they are not financially independent or fully trained until age 20 or later. In cultures in which 12- or 14-year-olds are considered ready to take on adult tasks and responsibilities, to marry, and to bear children, adolescent sexuality is handled very differently. In the United States, where teen pregnancy has become extremely common, it is perceived as a significant problem.

Adolescent sexual activity has increased fairly dramatically in the United States since the late 1950s (Miller, Christopherson, & King, 1993). By 1993, roughly half of teens reported they had had intercourse at least once (Kann et al., 1995). Figure 11.5 shows the most current findings from a 1993 national survey by the Centers for Disease Control. You can see that the percentage increases steadily with age and that at every age, more boys than girls report sexual activity—although this difference is far smaller now than it was a decade ago.

At every age, we find consistent ethnic differences in sexual activity. In the same survey, 79.7 percent of black high school students reported at least one experience of intercourse, compared to 56.0 percent of Hispanics and 48.4 percent of whites.

Although sexual activity is somewhat correlated with the amount of testosterone in the blood among boys (Halpern et al., 1993; Udry & Campbell, 1994), social factors are much better predictors of teen sexual activity than hormones. Those who begin sexual activity early are more likely to live in poor neighborhoods in which young people have little monitoring by adults; they come from poorer families or from families in which sexual activity is condoned and dating rules are lax; they are more likely to use alcohol. Among girls, those who are sexually active are also more likely to have had early menarche, to have low interest in school, and to have a history of sexual abuse (Billy, Brewster, & Grady, 1994; Hovell et al., 1994; Small & Luster, 1994). In general, these same factors predict sexual activity among whites, blacks, and Hispanics. And in every group, the greater the number of these risk fac-

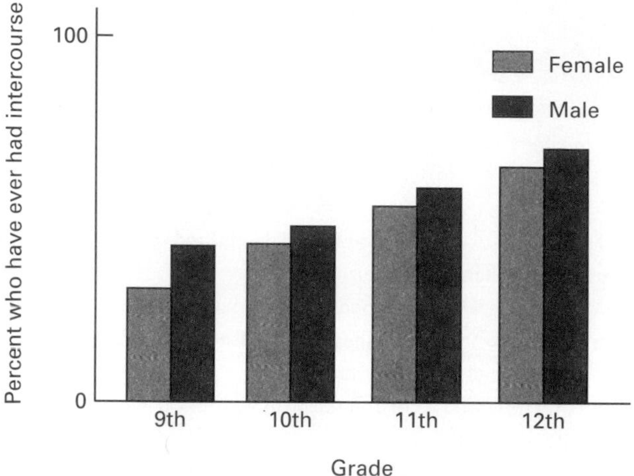

FIGURE 11.5 These data are from a nationally representative sample of 16,296 high school students interviewed in 1993 by the Centers for Disease Control. (*Source:* Kann et al., 1995, from Table 20, p. 47.)

tors present in the life of an individual teenager, the greater the likelihood that he or she will be sexually active.

Despite their high levels of sexual activity, teenagers know remarkably little about physiology and reproduction. At best, only about half of white and a quarter of black teenagers can describe the time of greatest fertility in the menstrual cycle (Freeman & Rickels, 1993; Morrison, 1985). Despite increases in contraceptive use in recent years, less than half of teenage girls use any type of contraceptives the first time they have intercourse; even fewer regularly use effective methods, such as condoms or the pill. Contraceptive use is even less likely among Hispanics than among Anglos (Fennelly, 1993), and in all groups is least likely among younger girls (Luster & Small, 1994). In contrast, contraceptive use is widespread in several European countries (e.g., Sweden and the Netherlands), in which such use is culturally acceptable and contraceptive information is readily available (Jones et al., 1986).

Teenage Pregnancy. Given these facts, we shouldn't be surprised that the rate of teenage pregnancy is higher in the United States than in any other developed Western country (Ambuel, 1995). In the Netherlands, for example, the pregnancy rate for girls between the ages of 15 and 19 is 14 per 1000 girls per year. In the United States it is 111 pregnancies per 1000 girls per year, of which four-fifths are unintended (Henshaw, 1993). The pregnancy rate is about four times higher among African-American teen girls than among whites; Hispanic Americans fall in between (Centers for Disease Control, 1993b). Sandra Hofferth estimates that fully 44 percent of all teenage girls in the United States will be pregnant at least once before the age of 20 (Hofferth, 1987a). About half of these pregnancies are carried to term.

Critical Thinking

How many different reasons can you think of why teenagers would *not* use contraceptives? Which of those explanations might account for the lower use of contraception among Hispanic Americans?

Let me try to put these fairly astonishing numbers into some kind of context. Birth rates have actually dropped among the entire U.S. population since the 1960s and early 1970s, *including among teenagers*. Indeed, the proportion of all births in the United States that are teenage births has declined steadily since 1975. What has increased since the 1960s is the rate of births to *nonmarried* teens. In 1991, of all girls under 18 who gave birth in the United States, 75 percent were unmarried; among black girls, the rate was 95 percent (U.S. Bureau of the Census, 1994). Thus, it is not that more and more teenagers are bearing children, but that more and more pregnant teenage girls are choosing to rear their children without marrying.

Whether one sees this as a worrisome trend or not depends not only on one's religious or moral beliefs but also on evidence about the long-term consequences

The Real World

Which Teenage Girls Get Pregnant?

Whether a girl becomes pregnant during her teenage years depends on many of the same factors that predict sexual activity in general, including family background, educational aspirations, timing of sexual activity, and subcultural attitudes. A girl's history of peer relationships in elementary school also is predictive (Underwood, Kupersmidt, & Coie, 1996). The likelihood of pregnancy is *higher*

- The younger a girl is when she becomes sexually active;
- Among girls from poor families, from single-parent families, or from families with relatively uneducated parents;
- Among girls whose mothers became sexually active early and who bore their first child early;
- Among girls who were rejected by their peers in elementary school, especially if they were high in aggressiveness (Underwood et al., 1996).

The likelihood of pregnancy is *reduced*

- Among girls who do well in school and have strong educational aspirations—such girls are more likely to use contraception if they are sexually active;
- Among girls with more stable and committed relationships with their sexual partners;
- Among girls who have good communication about contraception with their mothers and whose mothers support the use of contraception;
- Among girls who were popular with their peers in elementary school.

Black and Hispanic teenagers are more likely than are Anglos to become pregnant, but for different reasons. Blacks are more likely to be sexually active, while Hispanics, who have lower rates of sexual activity, are less likely to use contraception than are Anglos.

The riskiest time for teen pregnancy is in the first year or so after a girl has become sexually active. It is during these early months that girls are least likely to seek out contraceptive information or to use contraception consistently.

Teenage sexual activity is not more common in the United States than in most other Western industrialized countries, but teen pregnancy is. Girls like this one who give birth during their teens are more likely to have problems in adulthood, including lower income, less education, and higher risk of divorce, although many teenage moms manage to surmount these problems.

of adolescent childbearing for the adult lives of the girls involved and for the lives of the children they bear. The bulk of that evidence points to negative consequences for the teenage mothers, although it has been difficult to sort out which effects are due to early childbearing itself and which might be due to self-selection or the impact of poverty. Most studies indicate that teenage childbearing—whether the woman was married or unmarried—is associated with a larger total number of children, more closely spaced children, fewer years of total education throughout adult life, lower levels of occupational success, lower income in adulthood, and higher likelihood of divorce in adult life. These relationships are found among African-American, Hispanic, and Anglo teens, so these negative outcomes are not just ethnic differences in disguise (Astone, 1993; Hofferth, 1987b; Moore et al., 1993).

The picture is not entirely bleak. More than half of girls who become pregnant before age 18 nonetheless manage to complete high school by the time they are in their early 20s (Upchurch, 1993). And many of those who struggle economically in their early adult years manage to recover in their 30s and 40s, especially if they were able to complete at least high school (Upchurch, 1993; Werner & Smith, 1992). Despite these findings, though, it is still true that teenage mothers as a group are disadvantaged. For black inner-city girls in particular, the chances of moving out of poverty in adulthood seem to be far better for those who delay childbearing into their 20s than for those who bear children in adolescence (Freeman & Rickels, 1993).

For the children of these teenage mothers, the news is not good. These children are simply far more likely to grow up in poverty, with all the accompanying negative consequences for the child's optimum development (Osofsky et al., 1993).

Health

Adolescents have fewer acute illnesses than do infants, toddlers, or school-age children, but teenagers in every culture appear to have what Jeffrey Arnett (1995) describes as a heightened level of sensation seeking and recklessness, leading to markedly increased rates of accidents and injuries in this age range. The form this recklessness takes, and the extent to which it is allowed expression, varies from one culture and one historical time to the next. In the United States at this time, the cultural mores allow—perhaps even encourage—a wide variety of risky behaviors. Adolescents drive faster, tailgate more often, and use seat belts less than adults (Arnett, 1992; Centers for Disease Control, 1994d). Rates of drunk driving are also high among adolescents, although arrests for driving while intoxicated are actually at their peak among those in their middle 20s (U.S. Bureau of the Census, 1994).

Not surprisingly, such high-risk behaviors lead to a variety of problems, especially for teenage males, in whom the tendency toward sensation seeking and risk taking is especially marked. Auto accidents, homicide, and suicide are the leading causes of death among teenage boys (U.S. Bureau of the Census, 1995).

High-risk sexual behavior among teens (such as multiple partners and unprotected sex) is also common, resulting not only in high rates of pregnancy but also high rates of sexually transmitted diseases. Four percent of adolescents in the United States contract such a disease each year, a rate that has been rising in the past decade, especially for syphilis (Panel on High Risk Youth, 1993). And AIDS is now the fastest-growing cause of death among adolescents and young adults. There are roughly 8,000 reported cases of AIDS among U.S. teens and young adults (aged 13 to 29); an additional 36,000 are likely infected with HIV, based on estimates from the Centers for Disease Control. Those teens at greatest risk for infection are runaways, those with homosexual experiences, those engaged in prostitution, and intravenous drug users. But the disease has begun to spread beyond these risk groups within the adolescent population in the United States (Panel on High Risk Youth, 1993).

One of the risky behaviors many teenagers experiment with is smoking, although in U.S. culture white and Hispanic youth are much more likely to smoke than are African-American teens.

Alcohol and Drug Use

Another major type of risk-taking behavior among teenagers is alcohol and drug use. National data suggest that many types of teenage drug use declined in the United States over the past several decades, reaching a low point in 1992. For example, 23 percent of teenagers in 1974 reported that they had used marijuana, compared to only 11.7 percent in 1992 (U.S. Bureau of the Census, 1995). Since 1992, however, illegal drug use has risen rather rapidly. In 1995, 35 percent of high school seniors said they had used marijuana at least once (Wren, 1996). Alcohol use is also high and rising in these teen years. In 1992, 80 percent of high school students said they had tried alcohol at least once in their lives, nearly half (48 percent) had had at least one drink in the past month, and 30 percent reported that they had engaged in binge drinking (usually defined as 5 or more drinks on a single occasion) at least once in the last month (Centers for Disease Control, 1994d). Alcohol use is highest among teens where "racial or ethnic minorities live in circumscribed, impoverished areas such as ghettos, barrios, and Indian reservations" (Mitchell et al., 1996, p. 152).

Risky Behavior in Context

These various risky behaviors appear to be unusually common in adolescence because they help many teenagers to meet important psychological and social goals, including peer acceptance or respect, establishing autonomy from parents and from other authority figures, coping with anxiety or fear of failure, and affirming maturity. Richard Jessor (1992) argues that these are absolutely normal, central goals of adolescence. So when some risky behavior, such as smoking, drinking, or early sexual activity, helps individual teenagers to meet those goals, such behaviors will be hard to

The Real World

How To Get Your Teenager to Stop Smoking, or Not to Start

Nearly half of eighth-graders think that smoking a pack or two of cigarettes a day carries no great risk. By senior year, only about 30 percent still believe this, but by then many have a well-established smoking habit. In fact, nearly all first tobacco use occurs before high school graduation; most of those who do not smoke in high school never develop the habit, while most of the 3 million adolescents who do smoke become addicted and are unable to quit, even when they try (Centers for Disease Control, 1994c). Ethnic groups differ widely in tobacco use. Less than 5 percent of African-American high school seniors smoke daily, compared to about 12 percent of Hispanics and more than 20 percent of whites (Hilts, 1995).

The health risks linked to smoking are well established. What is not well established is how to prevent young people from taking up this habit. Among young blacks, family and peer pressure *against* smoking appears to be the crucial factor. Among white teens, there appears to be some pressure toward smoking, at least in some subgroups. So how can a parent change this? Reminding young people of the long-term health risks turns out not to be an especially effective strategy, at least not in isolation. Several other strategies are much more successful.

- *Stop Smoking Yourself.* If you are a smoker but want your children *not* to smoke, the first step is for you to quit. The data are clear: Children of parents who smoke are more likely to smoke themselves—a pattern that is especially clear for mothers and daughters (Kandel & Wu, 1995).
- *Emphasize the Bad Breath.* Tell them about all the negative *social* consequences of smoking. Their breath will smell bad, their teeth will turn yellow, their hair and clothes will smell like smoke all the time, and their ability to do well in athletics may be impaired. Tell them that teenagers themselves say that they find smokers less attractive.
- *Encourage Your Schools to Adopt Antismoking Programs.* All these messages are more effective if they come from other teenagers rather than from Mom and Dad, so lobby the local high school to organize systematic school-based prevention programs, with teens as models. Such programs work, especially if they are reinforced by community efforts and parent participation. Lobby your school board to adopt a complete ban on smoking on the school premises. In schools that allow smoking, 25 percent more of the students become smokers than in schools that forbid it on the schoolgrounds.
- *Focus on the Manipulation.* Remind your child that the cigarette companies are trying to manipulate them through their advertising. You may want to get them to look at specific ads and talk about the particular forms of manipulation involved.
- *Pay Attention to Your Child's Friends.* Teenagers whose friends smoke are more likely to take up the habit. You need to start paying attention to this *very* early—certainly by junior high school, when you may still have enough influence over the child's choice of friends to help steer the child toward a different crowd of kids.

change *unless* alternative ways of meeting these same goals are available or encouraged.

Jessor's argument also implies that those teenagers who will be most likely to show high-risk behaviors are those who enter adolescence with few social skills and hence few alternative avenues for meeting their social and personal goals. And that is indeed what researchers have found. Those teens who show high rates of reckless behaviors are likely to have had poor school records, early rejection by peers, neglect at home, or some combination of these early problems (Robins & McEvoy, 1990). By default, such children or teens are drawn to peers who share their patterns and their internal models of the world.

Bulimia and Anorexia

Two eating disorders, bulimia and anorexia nervosa, are also growing health problems among adolescents—although in this case mostly among girls. What we are learning about the causes of these disorders underlines both the impact of cultural values and the importance of the child's internal working models.

Bulimia (sometimes called *bulimia nervosa*) involves an intense concern about weight combined with binge eating followed by purging, either through self-induced vomiting, excessive use of laxatives, or excessive exercise (Attie, Brooks-Gunn, & Petersen, 1990). Alternating periods of restrained and binge eating are common among individuals in all weight groups. Only when binge eating occurs as often as twice a week and is combined with repeated episodes of some kind of purging is the syndrome properly called bulimia. Bulimics are ordinarily not exceptionally thin, but they are obsessed with their weight, feel intense shame about their abnormal behavior, and often experience significant depression. The physical consequences include marked tooth decay (from repeated vomiting), stomach irritation, lowered body temperature, disturbances of body chemistry, and loss of hair (Palla & Litt, 1988).

The incidence of bulimia appears to have been increasing in recent decades in many Western countries, particularly among adolescent girls, but firm numbers have been hard to establish. Current estimates are that from 1.0 to 2.8 percent of adolescent girls and young adult women show the full syndrome of bulimia; as many as 20 percent of girls in Western industrialized countries show at least some bulimic behaviors, such as occasional purging (Attie & Brooks-Gunn, 1995; Graber et al., 1994). In contrast, bulimic disorders are unheard of in countries where food is scarce.

When this anorexic 15-year-old looks at herself in the mirror, chances are she sees herself as "too fat," despite her obvious emaciation.

Anorexia nervosa is less common but potentially more deadly. It is characterized by extreme dieting, intense fear of gaining weight, and obsessive exercise. In girls or women (who are by far the most common sufferers) the weight loss eventually produces a variety of physical symptoms associated with starvation: sleep disturbance, cessation of menstruation, insensitivity to pain, loss of hair on the head, low blood pressure, a variety of cardiovascular problems, and reduced body temperature. Anorexics' body image is so distorted that they can look in the mirror at a skeletally thin body and remain convinced that they are "too fat." Ten to 15 percent of anorexics literally starve themselves to death; others die because of some type of cardiovascular dysfunction (Deter & Herzog, 1994).

Perhaps 1 girl out of every 500 in Western countries is anorexic (Graber et al., 1994); the rate is considerably higher among subgroups who are under pressure to maintain extreme thinness, such as ballet dancers and high-performance athletes in sports in which thinness is highly valued, such as gymnastics (Stoutjesdyk & Jevne, 1993).

The causes of both these eating disorders are unknown. Some theorists have proposed biological causes, such as some kind of brain dysfunction in the case of bulimics, who often show abnormal brain waves. Others argue for a psychoanalytic explanation, such as perhaps a fear of growing up. The most promising explanation, in my view, lies in the discrepancy between the young person's internal image of a desirable body and her (or his) perception of her own body. Both syndromes seem to be increasing in frequency because of the currently intense emphasis in many Western countries on a very slender, almost prepubescent body shape as the ideal for girls. Because this is an extremely difficult body shape to achieve and maintain, a great many girls feel that their bodies do not measure up to their ideal. Furthermore, from very early in life, girls (much more than boys) are taught both explicitly and implicitly that it matters whether they are pretty or attractive and that thinness is one of the critical variables in attractiveness. Current research, for example, shows that roughly three-quarters of teenage girls have dieted or are dieting. If you look only at chronic dieters (those who have dieted at least ten times in the past year), the figures are lower, but still striking, as you can see in Figure 11.6. These numbers come from a questionnaire study of all junior high and high school students in Minnesota in 1987 and 1988—a total of more than 36,000 teenagers (Story et al., 1991). You can

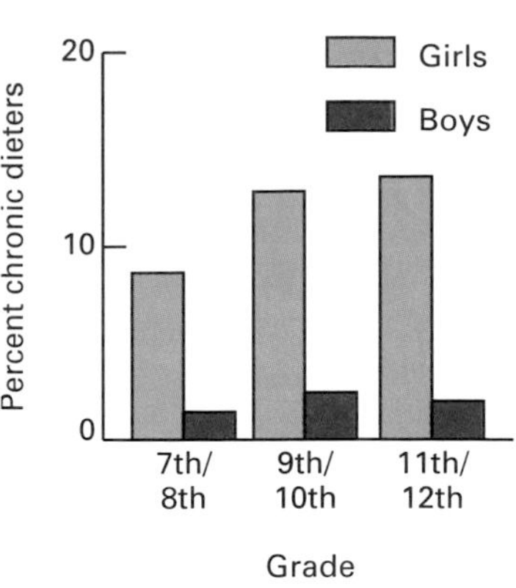

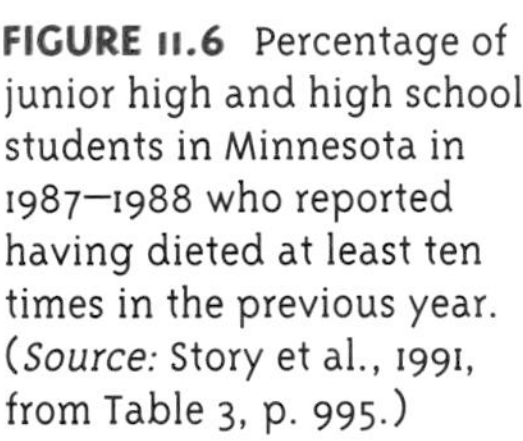

FIGURE 11.6 Percentage of junior high and high school students in Minnesota in 1987–1988 who reported having dieted at least ten times in the previous year. (*Source:* Story et al., 1991, from Table 3, p. 995.)

see that chronic dieting is far less common among boys than among girls. Such dieting was also less common among black than among Hispanic and white girls.

Both anorexia and bulimia seem to develop in adolescence, and not before that, precisely because one of the effects of puberty is to increase the amount of fat in the girl's body. This is particularly true of early-developing girls, who characteristically acquire and retain higher fat levels than do later-maturing girls. Indeed, early-developing girls are nearly twice as likely to have an eating disorder as are normal- or late-developing girls (Graber et al., 1994; Killen et al., 1992). Thus, an early-developing girl who deeply believes that thinness is essential for beauty and that beauty is essential for happiness, especially if she sees her own body as failing to meet her internalized standard, seems at particularly high risk for developing bulimia or anorexia (Attie & Brooks-Gunn, 1989; Rolls, Fedoroff, & Guthrie, 1991; Striegel-Moore, Silberstein, & Rodin, 1986).

CRITICAL THINKING

If you had the power to change our culture in such a way that the rate of bulimia and anorexia would go way down, what changes would you want to make? Why and how?

Research like this certainly points to the centrality of cognitive processes in every facet of the child's development—in health, in self-esteem, in social behavior. Those cognitive processes appear to go through yet another significant shift at adolescence.

Cognitive Development

Ask an 8-year-old what she wants to be when she grows up and she is likely to give you a very specific answer like "a firefighter," "a veterinarian," or "an artist." Ask a 15-year-old the same question and you are likely to get a quite different answer, such as: "Well, I'm thinking about several things. I know I want to go to college, but I don't know where, and I'm not sure what I want to study. Maybe science." The teenager's response is typically more future-oriented, more thoughtful, and more questioning. Such a change might merely reflect the fact that the adolescent is much closer to significant life decisions and so is more aware of their complexity. But it could also reflect an underlying change in the kind of thinking that has become possible. Piaget proposed just such a major shift at adolescence, to what he called *formal operations*.

Piaget's View of Formal Operational Thought

Piaget's observations led him to conclude that this new level of thinking emerged fairly rapidly in early adolescence, between roughly ages 12 and 16. It has a number of key elements.

From the Actual to the Possible. One of the first steps in the process is for the child to extend her concrete operational reasoning abilities to objects and situations

Research Report

An Australian Study Illustrating Sex Differences in Body Image Among Adolescents

Susan Paxton's study of Australian high school students illustrates that the preoccupation with thinness among teenage girls is not restricted to the United States and shows what such a preoccupation can do to girls' body images (Paxton et al., 1991).

A total of 562 teenagers in grades 7 through 11 reported on their current weight and height, and their judgment of that weight as underweight, good weight, or overweight. They also responded to questions about the effect being thinner might have on their lives and described their weight-control behaviors, including dieting and exercise.

Paxton reports that among teenagers who were actually *normal* in weight for their height, 30.1 percent of the girls but only 6.8 percent of the boys described themselves as overweight. Thus, many girls *perceive* themselves as too fat when they are actually normal. Furthermore, the majority of girls thought that being thinner would make them happier; a few even thought that being thinner would make them more intelligent. Boys, in contrast, thought that being thinner would actually have some negative effects.

Not surprisingly, these differences in the perception of thinness were reflected in dieting behavior in this sample. Twenty-three percent of the girls reported that they went on a crash diet at least occasionally; 4 percent said they did so once or twice a week. The comparable percentages for boys were 9 and 1 percent, respectively. More girls than boys also reported taking diet pills, using laxatives, and vomiting, although the rates were low for both sexes.

that she has not seen or experienced firsthand or that she cannot see or manipulate directly. Instead of thinking only about real things and actual occurrences, as the younger child can do, she can think about possible occurrences. This skill is obviously essential if the teenager is to think about the future systematically. The preschool child plays "dress up" by putting on real grown-up clothes. The teenager *thinks* about options and possibilities, imagining herself going or not going to college, marrying or not marrying, having children or not. She can imagine future consequences of actions she might take now, so that some kind of long-term planning becomes possible (Lewis, 1981).

Systematic Problem Solving. Another important feature of formal operations is the ability to search systematically and methodically for the answer to a problem. To study this, Piaget and his colleague Barbel Inhelder (Inhelder & Piaget, 1958) presented adolescents with complex tasks, mostly drawn from the physical sciences. In one of these tasks, subjects were given varying lengths of string and a set of objects of various weights that could be tied to the strings to make a swinging pendulum. They were shown how to start the pendulum by pushing the weight with differing amounts of force, and by holding the weight at different heights. The subject's task was to figure out which one or combination of length of string, weight of object, force of push, or height of push determine the "period" of the pendulum, which is the amount of time for one swing. (In case you have forgotten your high school physics, the answer is that only the length of the string affects the period of the pendulum.)

If you give this task to a concrete operational child, she will usually try out many different combinations of length, weight, force, and height in an inefficient way. She might try a heavy weight on a long string, and then a light weight on a short string. Because both string length and weight have changed, the child cannot draw a clear conclusion about either factor.

Critical Thinking

Can you think of any real-life examples of tasks that demand this sort of systematic problem solving?

High school science classes like this chemistry class may be one of the first places where adolescents are required to use deductive logic—a skill Piaget did not think was present until the period of formal operations.

In contrast, an adolescent using a formal operations approach is likely to be more organized, attempting to vary just one of the four factors at a time. She may try a heavy object with a short string, then with a medium string, then with a long one. After that, she might try a light object with the three lengths of string. Of course not all adolescents (or all adults, for that matter) are quite this methodical in their approach. But a significant difference in the overall strategy used by 10-year-olds and 15-year-olds marks the shift from concrete to formal operations.

Logic. Another facet of this shift is the appearance of deductive logic in the teenager's repertoire of skills. I mentioned in Chapter 9 that the concrete operational child is able to use inductive reasoning, which involves arriving at a conclusion or a rule based on a lot of individual experiences. The more difficult kind of reasoning, deductive reasoning, involves if → then relationships: "If all people are equal, then you and I must be equal." Children as young as 4 or 5 can understand some such relationships if the premises given are factually true. But only at adolescence are young people able to understand and use the basic *logical* relationship (e.g., Ward & Overton, 1990).

A great deal of the logic of science is of this deductive type. We begin with a theory and propose, "If this theory is correct, then I should observe such and such." In doing this, we are going well beyond our observations. We are conceiving things that we have never seen that *ought* to be true or observable. We can think of this change as part of a general decentering process that began much earlier in cognitive development. The preoperational child gradually moves away from his egocentrism and comes to be able to take the physical or emotional perspective of others. During formal operations, the child takes another step by freeing himself even from his reliance upon specific experiences.

Direct Tests of Piaget's Ideas

Edith Neimark summarizes the accumulated information succinctly:

> An enormous amount of evidence from an assortment of tasks shows that adolescents and adults are capable of feats of reasoning not attained under normal circumstances by [younger] children, and that these abilities develop fairly rapidly during the ages of about 11 to 15. (1982, p. 493)

Furthermore, many of the qualities of adolescent thought Piaget identified do seem to emerge during this period. Adolescents, much more than school-age children, operate with possibilities in addition to reality and they are more likely to use deductive logic. As Flavell puts it (1985, p. 98), the thinking of the school-age child "hugs the ground of . . . empirical reality," while the teenager is more likely to soar into the realm of speculation and possibility.

Some research illustrations would probably make the change clearer. In an early cross-sectional study, Susan Martorano (1977) tested 20 girls at each of four grades (sixth, eighth, tenth, and twelfth) on ten different tasks that required one or more of what Piaget called formal operations skills. Indeed, many of the tasks she used were those Piaget himself had devised. Results from two of these tasks are given in Figure 11.7. The pendulum problem is one I just described; the "balance" problem requires a youngster to predict whether or not two varying weights, hung at varying distances on either side of a scale, will balance—a task similar to the balance scale problem Siegler used (recall Figure 9.4). To solve this problem using formal operations the teenager must consider both weight and distance simultaneously. You can see in the figure that older students generally did better, with the biggest improvement in scores between eighth and tenth grades (between ages 13 and 15).

In a more practical vein, Catherine Lewis (1981) has shown that these new cognitive abilities alter the ways teenagers go about making decisions. Lewis asked eighth-, tenth-, and twelfth-grade students to respond to a set of dilemmas that in-

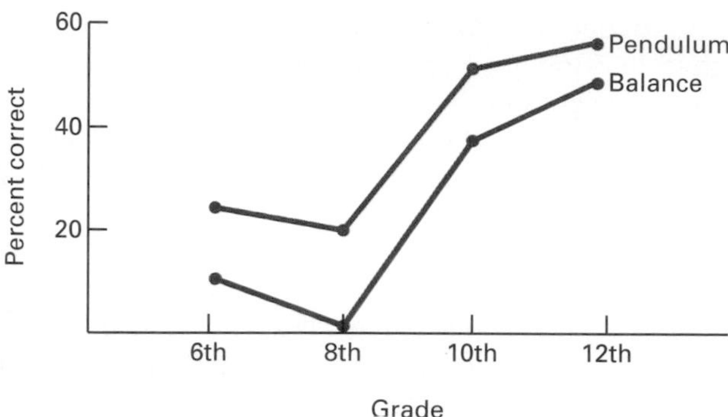

FIGURE 11.7 These are the results from two of the ten different formal operational tasks used in Martorano's cross-sectional study. (*Source:* Martorano, 1977, p. 670. Copyright by the American Psychological Association.)

volved a person facing a difficult decision, such as whether or not to have an operation to remove a facial disfigurement. Forty-two percent of the twelfth-graders but only 11 percent of the eighth-graders mentioned future possibilities in their answers to these dilemmas.

In answer to the cosmetic surgery dilemma, for example, a twelfth-grader said:

> Well, you have to look into the different things . . . that might be more important later on in your life. You should think about, will it have any effect on your future and with, maybe, the people you meet. (p. 541)

An eighth-grader, in response to the same dilemma, said:

> The different things I would think about in getting the operation is like if the girls turn you down on a date, or the money, or the kids teasing you at school. (p. 542)

The eighth-grader, as is characteristic of her age group, is focused on the here and now, on concrete things. The teenager is considering things that *might* happen in the future.

But note that even among the twelfth-graders in Lewis's study, nearly three-fifths did not show this type of future orientation. And take another look at Figure 11.7: Only about 50 to 60 percent of twelfth-graders solved the two formal operations problems, and Martorano found that only 2 of the 20 twelfth-grade subjects used formal operations logic on all ten problems.

These findings reflect a common pattern in research on adolescent thinking: By no means all teenagers (or adults) use these more abstract forms of logic and thought. Only about 50 to 60 percent of 18- to 20-year-olds in Western countries seem to use formal operations at all, let alone consistently (Keating, 1980). In non-Western countries the rates are even lower.

Why Doesn't Every Teenager Use Formal Operations? There are several possible explanations. One is that expertise is once again the crucial element. That is, most of us have some formal operational ability but we can apply it only to topics or tasks with which we are highly familiar. For example, I use formal operations reasoning about psychology because it is an area I know well. But I am a lot less skillful at applying the same kind of reasoning to fixing my car—about which I know next to nothing. Willis Overton and his colleagues (Overton et al., 1987) have found considerable support for this possibility in their research. They found that as many as 90 percent of adolescents could solve quite complex logic problems if the problems were stated using familiar content, while only half could solve the identical logical problem when it was stated in abstract language.

Critical Thinking

What was the last major decision you had to make? Think for a minute about how you went about it. What factors did you consider? Did you think about future consequences or only about the here and now?

Another possibility is that most of our everyday experiences and tasks do not require formal operations. Inductive reasoning or other simpler forms of logic are quite sufficient most of the time. So we get into a cognitive rut, applying our most usual mode of thinking to new problems as well. We can kick our thinking up a notch under some circumstances, especially if someone reminds us that it would be useful to do so, but we simply don't rehearse formal operations very much.

The fact that formal operations thinking is found more often among young people or adults in Western cultures may be interpreted in the same way. Industrialized cultures include high levels of technology and complex lifestyles. They may therefore demand more formal operational thought. By this argument, all nonretarded teenagers and adults are thought to have the *capacity* for formal logic, but only those of us whose lives demand its development will actually acquire it.

The Development of Moral Reasoning

Another aspect of cognitive development that interested Piaget and has continued to fascinate researchers is the child's reasoning about moral questions. How does a child decide what is good or bad, right or wrong, in his own and other people's behavior? You make such decisions often in your ordinary life: Should you give the store clerk back the excess change she handed you? Should you turn in a classmate you see cheating on an exam? How bad is it to lie in a job interview? Does your judgment change if you know that the person desperately needs the job to support his handicapped child?

Children younger than adolescents clearly make such judgments as well. But because several key changes in moral reasoning appear to coincide with adolescence or with the emergence of formal operations reasoning, this is a good place to introduce you to this very intriguing body of theory and research.

Lawrence Kohlberg's Theory. Piaget was the first to offer a description of the development of moral reasoning (Piaget, 1932), but the theorist whose work has had the most powerful impact has been Lawrence Kohlberg (e.g., Colby et al., 1983; Kohlberg, 1976, 1981). Building on and revising Piaget's ideas, Kohlberg pioneered the practice of assessing moral reasoning by presenting a subject with a series of dilemmas in story form, each of which highlighted a specific moral issue, such as the value of human life. One of the most famous is the dilemma of Heinz:

> In Europe, a woman was near death from a special kind of cancer. There was one drug that the doctors thought might save her. It was a form of radium that a druggist in the same town had recently discovered. The drug was expensive to make, but the druggist was charging ten times what the drug cost him to make. He paid $200 for the radium and charged $2000 for a small dose of the drug. The sick woman's husband, Heinz, went to everyone he knew to borrow the money, but he could only get together about $1000. . . . He told the druggist that his wife was dying, and asked him to sell it cheaper or let him pay later. But the druggist said, "No, I discovered the drug and I'm going to make money from it." So Heinz got desperate and broke into the man's store to steal the drug for his wife. (Kohlberg & Elfenbein, 1975, p. 621)

After hearing this story, the child or young person is asked a series of questions, e.g., Should Heinz have stolen the drug? What if Heinz didn't love his wife—would that change anything? Should Heinz steal the drug if the person dying was a stranger?

On the basis of answers to dilemmas like this one, Kohlberg concluded that there were three main levels of moral reasoning, with two substages within each level, as summarized in Table 11.2.

At level I, **preconventional morality,** the child's judgments are based on sources of authority who are close by and physically superior to himself—usually the

Table 11.2 Kohlberg's Stages of Moral Development

Level I: Preconventional Morality

- **Stage 1: Punishment and Obedience Orientation.** The child decides what is wrong on the basis of what is punished. Obedience is valued for its own sake, but the child obeys because the adults have superior power.
- **Stage 2: Individualism, Instrumental Purpose, and Exchange.** The child follows rules when it is in his immediate interest. What is good is what brings pleasant results.

Level II: Conventional Morality

- **Stage 3: Mutual Interpersonal Expectations, Relationships, and Interpersonal Conformity.** Moral actions are those that live up to the expectations of the family or other significant group. "Being good" becomes important for its own sake.
- **Stage 4: Social System and Conscience (Law and Order).** Moral actions are those so defined by larger social groups or the society as a whole. One should fulfill duties one has agreed to and uphold laws except in extreme cases.

Level III: Principled or Postconventional Morality

- **Stage 5: Social Contract or Utility and Individual Rights.** This stage involves acting so as to achieve the "greatest good for the greatest number." The teenager or adult is aware that most values are relative and laws are changeable, although rules should be upheld in order to preserve the social order. Still, there are some basic nonrelative values, such as the importance of each person's life and liberty.
- **Stage 6: Universal Ethical Principles.** The adult develops and follows self-chosen ethical principles in determining what is right. These ethical principles are part of an articulated, integrated, carefully thought-out and consistently followed system of values and principles.

Sources: After Kohlberg, 1976; Lickona, 1978.

parents. Just as his descriptions of others at this same stage are largely external, so the standards the child uses to judge rightness or wrongness are external rather than internal. In particular, it is the outcome or consequence of his actions that determines the rightness or wrongness of those actions.

In stage 1 of this level—the *punishment and obedience orientation*—the child relies on the physical consequences of some action to decide whether it is right or wrong. If he is punished, the behavior was wrong; if he is not punished, it was right. He is obedient to adults because they are bigger and stronger.

In stage 2—*individualism, instrumental purpose, and exchange*—the child begins to operate on the principle that you should do things that are rewarded and avoid things that are punished. For this reason, the stage is sometimes called a position of *naive hedonism*. If it feels good, or brings pleasant results, it is good. Some beginning of concern for other people is apparent during this phase, but only if that concern can be expressed as something that benefits the child himself as well. So he can enter into agreements like "If you help me, I'll help you."

As illustration, here are some responses to variations of the Heinz dilemma, drawn from studies of children and teenagers in a number of different cultures, all of which would be rated as stage 2:

> He should steal the food for his wife because if she dies he'll have to pay for the funeral, and that costs a lot. [Taiwan]
>
> [He should steal the drug because] he should protect the life of his wife so he doesn't have to stay alone in life. [Puerto Rico] (Snarey, 1985, p. 221)

At the next major level, **conventional morality,** children shift from judgments based on external consequences and personal gain to judgments based on rules or norms of a group to which the child belongs, whether that group is the family, the peer group, a church, or the nation. What the chosen reference group defines as right or good *is* right or good in the child's view, and the child internalizes these norms to a considerable extent.

Stage 3 (the first stage of level II) is the stage of *mutual interpersonal expectations, relationships, and interpersonal conformity* (sometimes also called the *Good Boy/Nice Girl* stage). Children at this stage believe that good behavior is what pleases other people. They value trust, loyalty, respect, gratitude, and maintenance of mutual relationships. Andy, a boy Kohlberg interviewed who was at stage 3, said:

> I try to do things for my parents, they've always done things for you. I try to do everything my mother says, I try to please her. Like she wants me to be a doctor and I want to, too, and she's helping me get up there. (Kohlberg, 1964, p. 401)

Another mark of this third stage is that the child begins to make judgments based on intentions as well as on outward behavior. If someone "didn't mean to do it" their wrongdoing is seen as less serious than if they did it "on purpose."

Stage 4, the second stage of the conventional level, shows the child turning to larger social groups for her norms. Kohlberg labeled this the stage of *social system and conscience*. It is also sometimes called the *law-and-order orientation*. People reasoning at this stage focus on doing their duty, respecting authority, following rules and laws. The emphasis is less on what is pleasing to particular people (as in stage 3) and more on adhering to a complex set of regulations. However, the regulations themselves are not questioned.

The transition to level III, **principled morality** (also called *postconventional moral reasoning*), is marked by several changes, the most important of which is a shift in the source of authority. At level I children see authority as totally outside themselves; at level II, the judgments or rules of external authorities are internalized, but they are not questioned or analyzed; at level III, a new kind of personal authority emerges in which individual choices are made, with individual judgments based on self-chosen principles.

Critical Thinking

Imagine a society in which everyone handled moral issues at Kohlberg's stage 3. Now think about one in which everyone operated at stage 5. How would those two societies be likely to differ?

In stage 5 at this level, called the *social contract* orientation by Kohlberg, we see the beginning of such self-chosen principles. Rules, laws, and regulations are not seen as irrelevant; they are important ways of ensuring fairness. But people operating at this level also see times when the rules, laws, and regulations need to be ignored or changed. The American system of government is based on moral reasoning of this kind. Citizens are of course expected to obey the laws, but they are also encouraged to try to change laws they think are wrong or immoral.

In his original writing about moral development, Kohlberg also included a sixth stage, the *universal ethical principles* orientation. People who reason in this way assume personal responsibility for their own actions, based upon fundamental and universal principles such as justice and basic respect for persons. Kohlberg eventually concluded that such people are quite rare, but they do represent the logical end point to the sequence of stages.

In all this, it is important to understand that what determines the stage or level of a person's moral judgment is not the specific moral choice but the *form of reasoning* used to justify that choice. For example, a choice either that Heinz should steal the drug or that he should not could be justified with logic at any given stage. I've already given you some examples of a stage 2 justification for Heinz's stealing the drug; here's a stage 5 justification of the same choice, drawn from a study in India:

> [What if Heinz was stealing to save the life of his pet animal instead of his wife?] If Heinz saves an animal's life his action will be commendable. The right use of the drug is to administer it to the needy. There is some difference, of course—human life is more evolved and hence of greater importance in the scheme of nature—but an animal's life is not altogether bereft of importance. (Snarey, 1985, p. 223, drawn originally from Vasudev, 1983, p. 7)

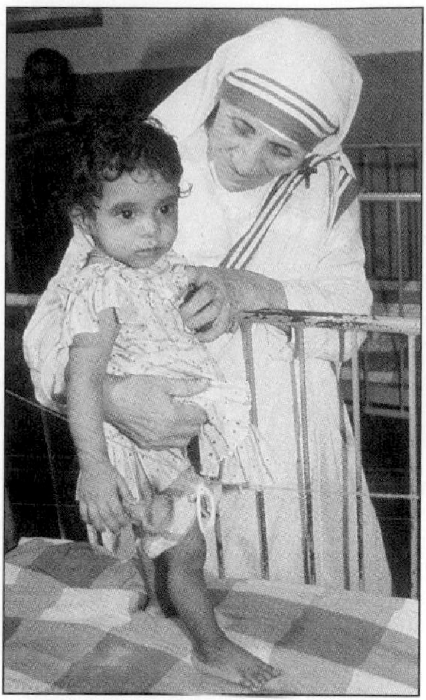

Kohlberg thought that there were at least a few people, perhaps like Mother Teresa, whose moral reasoning was based on universal ethical principles.

If you compare this answer to the ones I quoted before, you can see that the form of reasoning is different, even though the action being justified is precisely the same.

Kohlberg argued that this sequence of reasoning is both universal and hierarchically organized. That is, each stage follows and grows from the preceding one and has some internal consistency. Individuals should not move "down" the sequence, but only "upward" along the stages, if they move at all. Kohlberg did *not* suggest that all individuals eventually progress through all six stages, or even that each stage is tied to specific ages. But he insisted that the order is invariant and universal. Let me take a brief critical look at these claims.

Age and Moral Reasoning. Kohlberg's own findings, confirmed by many other researchers (e.g., Walker, de Vries, & Trevethan, 1987) show that preconventional reasoning (stages 1 and 2) is dominant in elementary school, with stage 2 reasoning still evident among many early adolescents. Conventional reasoning (stages 3 and 4) emerges as important in middle adolescence and remains the most common form of moral reasoning in adulthood. Postconventional reasoning (stages 5 and 6) is relatively rare, even in adulthood. For example, among men in their 40s and 50s who have been part of the Berkeley longitudinal study, only 13 percent were rated as using stage 5 moral reasoning (Gibson, 1990). You can see the whole pattern of age changes in Figure 11.8, which shows the results from Kohlberg's own longitudinal study of 58 boys, first interviewed when they were 10, and subsequently followed for more than 20 years (Colby et al., 1983).

Sequence of Stages. The evidence also seems fairly strong that the stages follow one another in the sequence Kohlberg proposed. Long-term longitudinal studies of

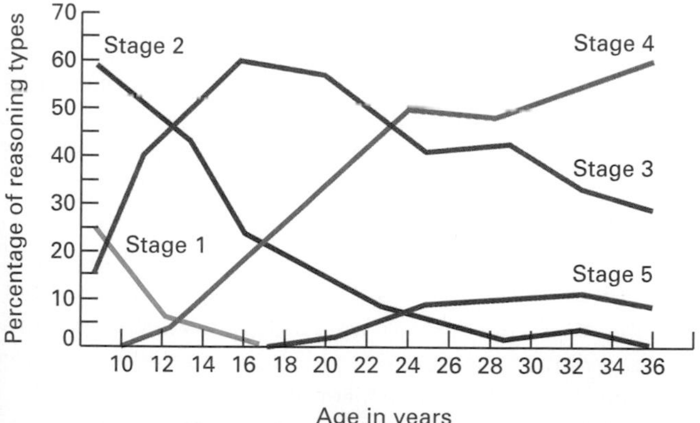

FIGURE 11.8 These findings are from Colby and Kohlberg's long-term longitudinal study of a group of boys who were asked about Kohlberg's moral dilemmas every few years from age 10 through early adulthood. As they got older the stage or level of their answers changed, with conventional reasoning appearing fairly widely at high school age. Postconventional or principled reasoning, though, was not very common at any age. (*Source:* Colby et al., 1983, Figure 1, p. 46. © The Society for Research in Child Development.)

teenagers and young adults in the United States (Colby et al., 1983; Walker, 1989), in Israel (Snarey, Reimer, & Kohlberg, 1985), and in Turkey (Nisan & Kohlberg, 1982) show that changes in subjects' reasoning nearly always occur in the hypothesized order. Subjects do not skip stages, and movement down the sequence rather than up occurs only about 5 to 7 percent of the time.

Universality. Variations of Kohlberg's dilemmas have been used with children in a wide range of countries, including both Western and non-Western, industrialized and nonindustrialized (Snarey, 1985). In every culture, researchers find higher stages of reasoning among older than younger children, but cultures differ in the highest level of reasoning observed. In complex urban societies (both Western and non-Western), stage 5 is typically the highest stage observed, while in those cultures Snarey calls "folk" societies, stage 4 is typically the highest. Collectively, this evidence seems to provide quite strong support for the universality of Kohlberg's stage sequence.

Moral Development: A Critique. Kohlberg's theory has withstood a barrage of research and commentary remarkably well. There does appear to be a clear set of stages in the development of moral reasoning, and these stages seem to be universal. Still, the theory has not emerged unscathed. For example, some psychologists are troubled by the fact that so few teenagers or adults seem to reason at the postconventional level (stages 5 or 6). The effective range of variation is from stage 2 to stage 4, which is not nearly so interesting or impressive as is the full range of stages (Shweder, Mahapatra, & Miller, 1987).

Other, highly vocal critics have pointed out that Kohlberg is really not talking about all aspects of "moral reasoning." Instead, as Kohlberg himself acknowledged in his later writings (Kohlberg, Levine, & Hewer, 1983), he is talking about the development of reasoning about *justice and fairness*. We might also want to know about other ethical bases than justice, such as an ethic based on concern for others. In this category, the best-known critic has been Carol Gilligan.

Gilligan's Ethic of Caring. Gilligan (1982; Gilligan & Wiggins, 1987) argues that there are at least two distinct "moral orientations": justice and care. Each has its own central injunction: not to treat others unfairly (justice), and not to turn away from someone in need (caring). Boys and girls learn both of these injunctions, but Gilligan has hypothesized that girls are more likely to operate from an orientation of caring or connection, while boys are more likely to operate from an orientation of justice or fairness. Because of these differences, they tend to perceive moral dilemmas quite differently.

Given the emerging evidence on sex differences in styles of interaction and in friendship patterns, which I talked about in both Chapters 8 and 10, Gilligan's hypothesis makes some sense. Perhaps girls, focused more on intimacy in their relationships, judge moral dilemmas by different criteria. But in fact, research on moral dilemmas has not shown that boys are more likely to use justice reasoning or that girls more often use care reasoning. Several studies of adults do show such a pattern (e.g., Lyons, 1983; Wark & Krebs, 1996), but studies of children generally have not (Jadack et al., 1995; Smetana, Killen, & Turiel, 1991; Walker et al., 1987).

Gilligan's arguments have often been quoted in the popular press as if they were already proven, when in fact the empirical base is really quite weak. Gilligan herself has done no systematic studies of children's (or adults') care reasoning. Yet despite these weaknesses, I am not ready to discard all her underlying points, primarily because the questions she is asking seem to me to fit so well with the newer research on sex differences in styles of relationship. The fact that we typically find no differences between boys and girls in their tendencies to use care versus justice orientations does not mean that males and females are completely alike in the assumptions they bring to relationships or to moral judgments. This seems to me to be clearly an area in which we need to learn more.

Moral Judgment and Behavior. Kohlberg's theory has also sometimes been criticized on the grounds that moral behavior does not always match the level of moral reasoning. Kohlberg never said that there should be a one-to-one correspondence between the two. Reasoning at stage 4 (conventional reasoning) does not mean that you will never cheat or always be kind to your mother. Still, the form of reasoning a young person typically applies to moral problems should have at least *some* connection with real-life choices.

One such connection proposed by Kohlberg is that the higher the level of reasoning a young person shows, the stronger the link to behavior ought to become. Thus, young people reasoning at stage 4 or stage 5 should be more likely to follow their own rules or reasoning than should children reasoning at lower levels. For example, Kohlberg and Candee (1984) studied students involved in some of the precursors to the Vietnam War protests at Berkeley in the late 1960s. They interviewed and tested the moral judgment levels of a group that had participated at a sit-in in the university administration building, plus a group randomly chosen from the campus population. Of those who thought it was morally right to hold a sit-in, nearly three-quarters of those reasoning at stages 4 or 5 actually participated, compared with only about a quarter of those reasoning at stage 3. Thus, the higher the stage of reasoning, the more consistent the behavior was with the reasoning.

CRITICAL THINKING

Do you think that a person's stage or level of moral reasoning has any impact on political behavior, such as voting or political party affiliation? Can you generate a hypothesis about such a link and figure out how you might test that hypothesis?

In other studies, Kohlberg and others have asked whether a link exists between stage of moral reasoning and the probability of making some "moral choice," such as not cheating. For example, Kohlberg (1975) found that only 15 percent of students reasoning at the principled level (stage 5) cheated when they were given an opportunity, while 55 percent of conventional level and 70 percent of preconventional students cheated.

Other researchers have explored the connections between moral reasoning and moral behavior by comparing the levels of moral reasoning of delinquents and nondelinquents. The repeated finding is that delinquents (male or female) have lower levels of moral reasoning than do nondelinquents, even when the two groups are carefully matched for levels of education, social class, and IQ (Smetana, 1990). In one recent study, for example, Virginia Gregg and her colleagues (1994) found that only 20 percent of a group of incarcerated male and female delinquents were reasoning at stage 3 or higher, while 59 percent of a carefully matched comparison group of nondelinquents were reasoning at this level. Like younger children who act out more in school, delinquents are most likely to use highly hedonistic reasoning, scored at Kohlberg's stage 2 (Richards et al., 1992).

Yet despite this abundant evidence of a link between moral reasoning and behavior, no one has found the correspondence to be perfect. After all, in Kohlberg's studies, 15 percent of the principled moral reasoners did cheat, and a quarter of stage 4 and stage 5 reasoners who thought it morally right to participate in a sit-in did not do so. As Kohlberg said, "One can reason in terms of principles and not live up to those principles" (Kohlberg, 1975, p. 672).

What else besides level of reasoning might matter? We don't have all the answers to that question yet, but some influences are clear. For one thing, even though you might think it morally right to take some action in a given situation, you may not see that action as morally *necessary* or obligatory. I might be able to make a good argument for the moral acceptability of a sit-in protest, but still not see it as my *own* duty or responsibility to participate.

A second significant element is the cost to the person of doing something helpful (or of refraining from doing something morally "wrong," like cheating). If helping someone else has little cost in time, money, or effort, then most children and adults will help, regardless of their overall level of moral reasoning. But when there is some cost associated with the more "moral" choice, then level of moral reasoning becomes more significant. This suggests the more general principle that moral reasoning becomes a factor in moral behavior only when something about the situation

The Real World

Applying Kohlberg's Theory to Education

A lot of what I have said about Kohlberg's theory may seem pretty abstract to you. In Kohlberg's own view, though, there were many potential practical implications for education. The question that interested him was whether children or young people could be taught higher stages of moral reasoning, and if so, whether such a change in moral reasoning would change their behavior in school.

We know from early research by Elliot Turiel (1966) that, at least under some conditions, exposing young people to moral arguments one step above their own level of reasoning can lead to an increase in their level of moral judgment. Young people who attend college also continue to show increases in moral stage scores, while those who quit school after high school typically show no further increase (Rest & Thoma, 1985). Because arguments about moral and philosophical issues in class and over coffee (or a few beers) in the wee small hours of the night are one of the hallmarks of the college experience for many young people, perhaps it is the discussion—the exposure to other people's ideas, other people's logic—that makes a difference.

If that's true, what would happen if high school students were given systematic opportunities to explore moral dilemmas? Would that change them, too? Apparently it can.

One educational application has involved the creation of special discussion classes in which moral dilemmas similar to those Kohlberg devised are presented and argued. In the process, the teacher attempts to model higher levels of reasoning. Other programs are broader-based, involving not just discussion but also cross-age teaching (to encourage nurturance and caring), empathy training, cooperation games, volunteer service work, and the like. The dozens of studies on the effectiveness of programs of this kind show that on average, the programs succeed in shifting young people's moral reasoning upward an average of about a half a stage (Schaefli, Rest, & Thoma, 1985). The largest effects are generally found in programs focusing exclusively on discussions of moral dilemmas, but broader-based programs work too. Courses lasting longer than three or four weeks seem to work better than very short programs, and the effects are generally larger with older students—college students and even post-college-age adults. Among high school students, we see some impact but it is not as large.

An even broader-based educational application, designed to change students' moral behavior as much as their moral reasoning, has been the development of the so-called *just community*. These experimental schools, typically set up as a "school within a school," operate as a kind of laboratory for moral education (Higgins, 1991; Kohlberg & Higgins, 1987).

Kohlberg insisted that the crucial feature of these just communities must be complete democracy: Each teacher and student has one vote, and community issues and problems have to be discussed in open forum. Rules are typically created and discussed at weekly communitywide meetings. In this way, students become *responsible* for the rules and for one another.

In experimental schools following this model, Kohlberg and his co-workers found that as students' level of Kohlbergian moral reasoning shifted upward, so did their reasoning about responsibility and caring. The link between moral reasoning and moral behavior was strengthened as well. For example, stealing and other petty crime virtually disappeared in one school after the students had repeatedly discussed the problem and arrived—painfully—at a solution that emphasized the fact that stealing damaged the whole community, and thus the whole community had to be responsible. For example, after one stealing episode the group agreed that if the stolen money had not been returned (anonymously) by a specified date, each community member would be assessed 15 cents to make up the victim's loss (Higgins, 1991).

This effect of just communities makes sense when you think about the factors that seem to affect moral behavior. In these schools, two elements are added that would tend to support more moral behavior: a sense of personal responsibility, and a group norm of higher moral reasoning and caring.

Among teenagers, the emotional impact of the group pressure may be especially significant, in addition to whatever effect there may be from exposure to more mature arguments. If you find yourself in the minority in some argument about a moral issue, the "social disequilibrium" you feel may help to make you more open to other arguments and thus to change your view. Certainly in experimental schools like those studied by Kohlberg, this additional emotional impact is no doubt part of the process (Haan, 1985).

Classes in moral education have not proven to be the "quick fix" that many educators hoped for. The gains in moral reasoning are not huge and may not be reflected in increases in moral behavior in the school unless an effort is made to alter the overall moral atmosphere of the entire school. But these programs do show that provocative and helpful applications of some of the abstract developmental theories are possible.

heightens the sense of moral conflict, such as when a cost is involved, or when the individual feels personally responsible.

Finally, competing motives or ethics are often at work as well, such as the pressure of a peer group, or motives for self-protection or self-reward. In early adolescence, when the impact of the peer group is particularly strong, we might expect an especially strong group effect on moral actions. So kids this age may be most susceptible to group decisions to go joy-riding or to sneak beer into a party, even when their own moral standards would argue against such behavior.

Thus, moral *behavior* results from a complex of influences, of which the level of moral reasoning is only one element.

Schooling During the Adolescent Years

I cannot end this chapter on cognitive development in adolescence without saying a further word about the impact of school experiences. Such experiences are clearly formative in middle childhood, as you'll recall from Chapter 9. School is no less a central force in the lives of adolescents. But the effect is different for the two age groups. In middle childhood, school experience is focused on learning a whole set of basic skills and specific knowledge—how to read, how to do mathematics, how to write. In adolescence, while additional specific knowledge is obviously conveyed in school, and while schooling may contribute to the development of formal operational thought, the school setting serves a host of other functions in adolescence. Not only is it an arena in which teenagers can practice new social skills, it is also the setting in which society attempts to shape young people's attitudes and behaviors to prepare them for adult life. High schools teach driver's education, "family life" education including sexuality, home economics, civics, current affairs; guidance counselors help the teenager decide about college or about future job options; organized sports programs offer opportunities for nonacademic success (or failure).

Despite this very broad range of educational roles played by the high school, most researchers have focused on academic success or school completion as measures of the impact of schooling. So let me say a word or two about the two ends of the continuum, those who achieve academic success, and those who drop out of school.

Those Who Achieve

The best single predictor of a student's academic performance in high school is IQ, and this is true for every ethnic and social class group in U.S. society. Both adolescent IQ and school grades also predict adult job success to at least some degree (Barrett & Depinet, 1991). A myriad of studies of military jobs, for example, show correlations in the range of .45 to .55 between scores on IQ-like tests and the recruits' later proficiency and success at a wide range of jobs (Ree & Earles, 1992). Outside of the military, the same general relationship holds, although education plays a key intervening role. Students with higher IQ or better grades in high school tend to go on to more years of additional education, and this is as true among children reared in poverty as it is among the middle class (Barrett & Depinet, 1991). Those extra years of education, in turn, have a powerful effect on the career path a young person enters in early adulthood (Rosenbaum, 1984).

These relationships exist not just because brighter kids have an easier time with schoolwork, but also because the cumulative effect of success over many years of schooling fosters a greater sense of self-efficacy in these intellectually more able students. Those who achieve, especially those who achieve despite poverty backgrounds or other daunting obstacles, also are more likely to have parents who have high aspirations for them (Brooks-Gunn, Guo, & Furstenberg, 1993) or an authoritative family style—a point you will recall from the data given in Figure 8.3 (page 206). So as always, the effect of the family and the effect of the school interact.

The best single predictor of achievement in high school is a student's IQ or earlier school success. But family interactive style makes a difference too.

Those Who Drop Out

At the other end of the continuum are those who drop out of school before completing high school—a rarer occurrence than you might guess. Almost three-quarters of young adults in the United States receive a high school diploma, and another 12 percent receive a General Equivalency Diploma (GED) at some later age. Only about 15 percent of current young adults fail to graduate from high school (McLanahan & Sandefur, 1994). Among students in the most recent high school classes, the rate is even lower. For example, among those students who entered high school in 1988, only 11 percent had failed to graduate by 1993. Hispanics had the highest dropout rates in this group at 32 percent, compared with 16 percent for African Americans and 10 percent for Anglos (*New York Times*, 1994b).

Despite these ethnic differences, social class is a better predictor of school completion than is ethnicity. Kids growing up in poor families—especially poor families with a single parent—are considerably more likely to drop out of high school than are those from more economically advantaged or intact families. When you hold social class constant, dropout rates among blacks, whites, and Hispanics differ very little (Entwisle, 1990). But because minority youth in the United States are so much more likely to come from poor families or from families that do not provide psychological support for academic achievement, they are also more likely to drop out of school. When a teenager's peer group also puts a low value on achievement, as is true in many black and Hispanic teen groups in the United States, the risk of dropping out is even stronger (Takei & Dubas, 1993).

Teenagers who drop out of school list many reasons for such a decision, including not liking school, poor grades, being suspended, and needing to find work to support a family. For girls there are additional factors. They most often say that they dropped out because they planned to marry, were pregnant, or felt that school was simply not for them (Center for Educational Statistics, 1987). Some of these same factors appear when we try to *predict* which kids will drop out. For example, in their longitudinal study of more than 500 children, Robert and Beverly Cairns (1994) found two strong predictors of subsequent dropout: whether the teenager had a history of low academic success, often including repeating a grade, and whether there was a pattern of aggressive behavior. More than 80 percent of boys and about 50 percent of girls who had shown *both* characteristics in seventh grade later dropped out of school before completing high school. For girls in this study, giving birth or getting married were also strongly linked to dropping out—although it was also true that early pregnancy was more likely among girls who had a history of poor school performance or high levels of aggression. So it is unclear what is cause and what is effect here.

Yet another factor for some adolescents is their perception that a high school diploma won't buy them much extra in the job world. Some of the young men in the Cairns study, for example, were already working part time at jobs that paid above the minimum wage and saw no rationale for staying in school when they could earn more by working full time. Here are two voices:

> [School] was boring, I felt like I knew all I had to know. . . . I was going to go back, . . . but I figure I was making $6 an hour and nothing in school, so . . ." (Chuck)

> I just hate it. I said well if I could go to school 8 hours a day, I could get me a job 8 hours a day, 5 days a week. I said I'm going to school 40 hours a week and I said I'm not getting paid for it and I said well I'm gonna go get me a job and get paid. (Amy) (Cairns & Cairns, 1994, pp. 180, 181)

Yet in the long term, teens who use such a rationale for dropping out of high school are wrong. Unemployment is higher among high school dropouts than in any other education group, and dropouts who do manage to find jobs earn lower wages than do those with a high school diploma. In 1984, for example, the average yearly income of young men (aged 25–44) with some high school education was $15,684, compared to $21,851 for those who had graduated from high school and $33,319 for those who had graduated from college (Crystal, Shae, & Krishnaswami, 1992). The difference between these two groups may be smaller today than it was in 1984; a man or woman with a high school diploma can no longer count on finding well-paying skilled industrial jobs, as was the case even a decade ago. But a high school education still offers distinct advantages. Those who drop out enter a very different—and far less optimal—life trajectory.

Summary

1. Adolescence is defined not only as a time of pubertal change, but as the transitional period between childhood and full adult role adoption.
2. Because of the importance of this transition, it is marked by rites and rituals in many cultures—although not in most modern Western countries.
3. The physical changes of adolescence are triggered by a complex set of hormonal changes, beginning at about age 8 or 9. Very large increases in gonadotrophic hormones, including estrogen and testosterone, are central to the process.
4. Effects are seen in a rapid growth spurt in height, and an increase in muscle mass and in fat. Boys add more muscle, and girls more fat.
5. In girls, mature sexuality is achieved in a set of changes beginning as early as age 8 or 9. Menarche occurs relatively late in the sequence.
6. Sexual maturity is later in boys, with the growth spurt occurring a year or more after the start of genital changes.
7. Variations in the rate of pubertal development have some psychological effects. In general, children whose

physical development is markedly earlier or later than they expect or desire show more negative effects than do those whose development is "on time."

8. Sexual activity among teens has increased in recent decades in the United States. Roughly half of all U.S. high school students are sexually active, and one in ten teenage girls becomes pregnant each year.

9. Long-term consequences for girls who bear children during adolescence are generally negative, although a minority of such girls are able to overcome their early disadvantages.

10. Adolescents have fewer acute illnesses than younger children but more deaths from accidents, particularly automobile accidents. In general, they show higher rates of various kinds of risky behavior, including unprotected sex, drug use, fast driving, and the like.

11. Alcohol and drug use among U.S. teenagers, after declining for several decades, are now on the rise. Those most likely to use or abuse drugs are those who also show other forms of deviant or problem behavior, including poor school achievement.

12. Eating disorders such as bulimia and anorexia are more common among teenage girls. Both appear to be a response to a major discrepancy between culturally defined body ideals and girls' perceptions of their own bodies.

13. Piaget proposed a fourth major level of cognitive development in adolescence, formal operational thought. It is characterized by the ability to apply basic operations to ideas and possibilities, in addition to actual objects.

14. Deductive logic and systematic problem solving are also part of formal operational thought.

15. Researchers have found clear evidence of such advanced forms of thinking in at least some adolescents. But formal operational thinking is not universal, nor is it consistently used even by those who possess the ability.

16. Another facet of adolescent thinking is the development of new levels of moral reasoning. Kohlberg proposed six stages of such reasoning, organized into three levels.

17. Preconventional moral reasoning includes reliance on external authority: What is punished is bad, and what feels good is good.

18. Conventional morality is based on rules and norms provided by outside groups, the family, church, or society. This is the dominant form of moral reasoning among teenagers and adults.

19. Principled or postconventional morality is based on self-chosen principles. Only about 15 percent of adults reason at this level.

20. Research evidence suggests that these levels and stages do develop in a specified order, and that they are found in this same sequence in all cultures studied so far.

21. Kohlberg's model has been criticized on the grounds that it deals only with reasoning about justice and fairness. Gilligan suggests that people may also reason based on caring and connection, and that girls are more likely to use the latter model. Research does not support Gilligan on this point.

22. Moral reasoning is not perfectly correlated with moral behavior. Moral behavior is also affected by the degree of responsibility the individual feels and the cost associated with behaving morally.

23. The school environment is one of the most formative in the adolescent's experience. Those who succeed academically in high school are those with higher IQ, and/or from authoritative families. Those who drop out are more likely to be poor, or to be doing poorly in school.

Key Terms

anorexia nervosa
bulimia
conventional morality
endocrine glands
estrogen
gonadotrophic hormones
menarche
pituitary gland
preconventional morality
principled morality
secular trend

Suggested Readings

Gullotta, T. P., Adams, G. R., & Montemayor, R. (Eds.) (1993). *Adolescent sexuality*. Newbury Park, CA: Sage.

A first-rate volume of papers on all aspects of this important subject. Of particular interest are a paper by Dyk reviewing information on physical changes at adolescence and one by Miller et al. on sexual behavior in adolescents.

Kurtines, W. M., & Gewirtz, J. L. (Eds.) (1991). *Handbook of moral behavior and development*. Hillsdale, NJ: Lawrence Erlbaum Associates.

This is a massive three-volume work, prepared as a commemoration of the work of Lawrence Kohlberg. *Volume* 1 *deals with theory, Volume* 2 *with research, and Volume* 3 *with application. If this area intrigues you, there is no more complete source.*

Malina, R. M. (1990). Physical growth and performance during the transitional years (9–16). In R. Montemayor, G. R. Adams, & T. P. Gullotta (Eds.), *From childhood to adolescence: A transitional period?* (pp. 41–62). Newbury Park, CA: Sage.

To some extent Malina has picked up where Tanner has left off, providing us with updated information on normal physical growth. This particular paper focuses on puberty.

Millstein, S. G., Petersen, A. C., & Nightingale, E. O. (Eds.) (1993). *Promoting the health of adolescents. New directions for the twenty-first century*. New York: Oxford University Press.

An excellent new volume covering all aspects of the important question of how we can promote better health and health habits in adolescence.

Steinberg, L. & Levine, A. (1990). *You and your adolescent: A parent's guide for ages 10 to 20*. New York: Harper & Row.

This absolutely first-class book is clearly intended for parents, so it is not overly technical. But because Steinberg is one of the most innovative researchers studying adolescence, it is strongly based on research.

Tanner, J. M. (1978). *Fetus into man: Physical growth from conception to maturity*. Cambridge, MA: Harvard University Press.

A detailed but very thorough and remarkably understandable small book that covers all but the most current information about physical growth.

12 Social and Personality Development in Adolescence

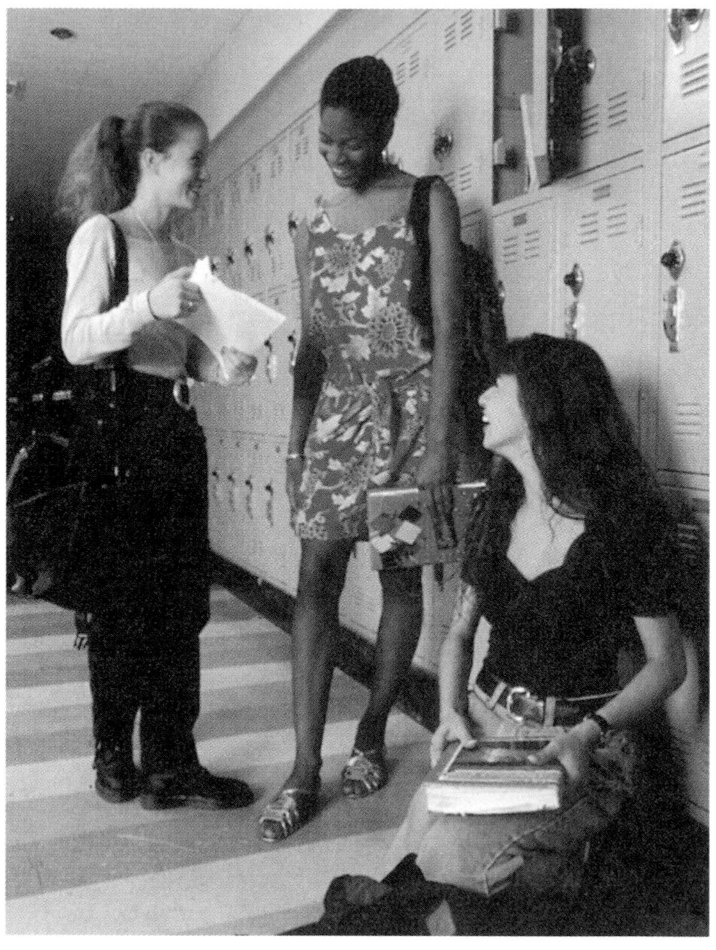

In my own memories of adolescence, the physical changes loom large. Certainly the fact that I grew 6 inches the year I was 12, towering over absolutely everyone, was a highly important event. I recall very vividly that I had little notion how long my arms and legs were during this period, and regularly hit people as I was making grand gestures; I recall my mother's despair at keeping me in clothes that fit; I know that this experience colored all my relationships and deeply affected my self-concept.

Significant as these physical changes were, my memories of those years are equally colored by another set of adolescent tasks: gaining some independence from my family, figuring out who I was and what I could or should do with my life, discovering some of the mysteries of relationships with that other species, *boys*. It is these tasks of independence, identity, and relationship that are the central story of this chapter.

Understanding the Self and Relationships

Let me begin, as I did in Chapter 10, by looking at the cognitive aspect of these tasks. How does the child's understanding of himself and his relationships change at adolescence?

The Self-Concept

Through the elementary school years, the child's self-concept becomes less and less tied to outer qualities, more and more focused on enduring internal characteristics. This trend continues in adolescence, with self-definitions becoming more and more abstract. You may remember the replies of a 9-year-old and an 11-year-old to the question "Who am I?" in Montemayor and Eisen's study, quoted in Chapter 10 (page 244). Here's a 17-year-old's answer to the same question:

> I am a human being. I am a girl, I am an individual. I don't know who I am. I am a Pisces. I am a moody person. I am an indecisive person. I am an ambitious person. I am a very curious person. I am not an individual. I am a loner. I am an American (God help me). I am a Democrat. I am a liberal person. I am a radical. I am a conservative. I am a pseudoliberal. I am an atheist. I am not a classifiable person (i.e., I don't want to be). (Montemayor & Eisen, 1977, p. 318)

Clearly, this girl's self-concept is even less tied to her physical characteristics or even her abilities than are those of the younger children. She is describing abstract traits or ideology.

You can see the change very graphically in Figure 12.1, based on the answers of all 262 subjects in the Montemayor and Eisen study. Each of the subjects' answers to

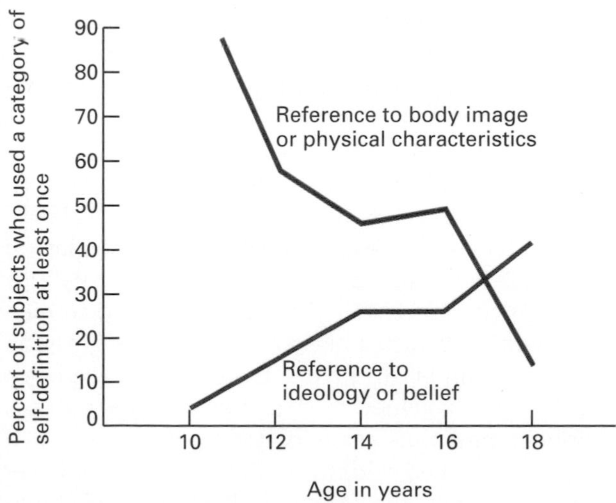

FIGURE 12.1 As they get older, children and adolescents define themselves less and less by what they look like and more and more by what they believe or feel. (*Source:* Montemayor & Eisen, 1977, from Table 1, p. 316.)

the "Who am I?" question was placed in one or more specific categories, such as references to physical properties ("I am tall," "I have blue eyes"), or references to ideology ("I am a Democrat," "I believe in God," etc.). As you can see, appearance was a highly salient dimension in the preteen and early teen years but became less dominant in late adolescence, at a time when ideology and belief became more salient. By late adolescence, most teenagers think of themselves in terms of enduring traits, beliefs, personal philosophy, and moral standards (Damon & Hart, 1988).

At the same time, the adolescent's self-concept becomes more differentiated as the teenager comes to see herself somewhat differently in each of several roles: as a student, with friends, with parents, and in romantic relationships (Harter & Monsour, 1992). Self-concepts also become more flexible in the sense that categories are held less rigidly. One example of this is the greater flexibility adolescents show in their views about what is acceptable behavior for people of their gender.

Sex Role Concepts in Adolescence. Seven- and 8-year-olds appear to treat gender categories as if they were fixed rules. Adolescents, by contrast, understand that these are social conventions, so sex-role concepts become more flexible (Katz & Ksansnak, 1994). Teenagers have largely abandoned the automatic assumption that whatever their own gender does is better or preferable (Powlishta et al., 1994). Indeed, a significant minority of teenagers and youths begin to define themselves as having both masculine and feminine traits.

In the early days of research on masculinity and femininity, psychologists conceived of these two qualities as opposite ends of a single continuum. A person could be masculine *or* feminine, but couldn't be both. But work by Sandra Bem (1974) and Janet Spence and Robert Helmreich (1978) has shown that masculinity and femininity should be thought of as independent dimensions or aspects. A person can be high or low on either or both. Indeed, if we categorize people as high or low on each of these two dimensions, based on each individual's self-description, we end up with four basic sex-role types, called *masculine, feminine, androgynous,* and *undifferentiated*. The masculine and feminine types are the traditional combinations in which a person sees himself or herself as high in one quality and low in the other. A "masculine" teenager or adult, by this conceptualization, is thus one who perceives himself (or herself) as having many traditional masculine qualities and few traditional feminine qualities. A feminine teenager or adult shows the reverse pattern. In contrast, androgynous individuals see themselves as having *both* masculine and feminine traits; undifferentiated individuals describe themselves as lacking both.

Critical Thinking

Make yourself a 2 × 2 grid to show these four types. Why does this conceptualization of masculinity and femininity radically alter the way we think about these qualities, compared with a conceptualization of the two qualities as opposite ends of the same continuum?

Several studies show that roughly 25–35 percent of U.S. high school students define themselves as androgynous (e.g., Lamke, 1982a; Rose & Montemayor, 1994). More girls than boys seem to show this pattern and more girls fall into the masculine category than boys in the feminine group.

More striking is the finding that either an androgynous or a masculine sex-role self-concept is associated with higher self-esteem among *both* boys and girls (Burnett, Anderson, & Heppner, 1995; Lamke, 1982a, 1982b; Rose & Montemayor, 1994). This finding makes sense if we assume the existence of a kind of "masculine bias" in American and other Western societies, such that traditionally masculine qualities like independence and competitiveness are more valued by both men and women than are many traditionally female qualities. If such a bias exists—and there is good reason to think that it does (e.g., Broverman et al., 1970)—then the teenage boy's task is simpler than the teenage girl's. He can achieve high self-esteem and success with his peers by adopting a traditional masculine sex-role. But a girl who adopts a traditional gender role is adopting a less-valued role, with attendant risks of lower self-esteem and a reduced sense of competence (Massad, 1981; Rose & Montemayor, 1994).

Findings like these suggest the possibility that while the creation of rigid rules or schemas for sex roles is a normal—even essential—process in young children, a blurring of those rules may be an important process in adolescence, particularly for girls, for whom a more masculine or androgynous self-concept is associated with more positive outcomes.

Teenage boys like these may have an easier time achieving high self-esteem because both boys and girls seem to place a higher value on certain traditionally "masculine" qualities than on traditionally "feminine" qualities.

Identity in Adolescence

A somewhat different way to look at adolescent self-concept is through the lens of Erikson's theory. In this model, the central task or dilemma of adolescence is that of *identity versus role confusion*. Erikson argued that the child's early sense of identity comes partly unglued in early adolescence because of the combination of rapid body growth and the sexual changes of puberty. He referred to this period as one in which the adolescent's mind is in a kind of *moratorium* between childhood and adulthood. The old identity will no longer suffice; a new identity must be forged, one that must serve to place the young person among the myriad roles of adult life—occupational roles, sexual roles, religious roles. Confusion about all these role choices is inevitable. Erikson put it this way:

> In general it is primarily the inability to settle on an occupational identity which disturbs young people. To keep themselves together they temporarily overidentify, to the point of apparent complete loss of identity, with the heroes of cliques and crowds. . . . They become remarkably clannish, intolerant, and cruel in their exclusion of others who are "different," in skin color or cultural background . . . and often in entirely petty aspects of dress and gesture arbitrarily selected as *the* signs of an in-grouper or out-grouper. It is important to understand . . . such intolerance as the necessary *defense against a sense of identity confusion*, which is unavoidable at [this] time of life." (1980a, pp. 97–98)

The teenage clique or group thus forms a base of security from which the young person can move toward a unique solution of the identity process. Ultimately, each teenager must achieve an integrated view of himself, including his own pattern of beliefs, occupational goals, and relationships.

Nearly all the current work on the formation of adolescent identity has been based on James Marcia's descriptions of *identity statuses* (Marcia, 1966, 1980), which are rooted in Erikson's general conceptions of the adolescent identity process. Following one of Erikson's ideas, Marcia argues that adolescent identity formation has two key parts: a *crisis* and a *commitment*. By a "crisis" Marcia means a period of decision-making when old values and old choices are reexamined. This may occur as a sort of upheaval—the classic notion of a crisis—or it may occur gradually. The outcome of the reevaluation is a commitment to some specific role, some particular ideology.

If you put these two elements together, as in Figure 12.2, you can see that four different "identity statuses" are possible.

- **Identity achievement:** The person has been through a crisis and reached a commitment to ideological or occupational goals.
- **Moratorium:** A crisis is in progress, but no commitment has yet been made.
- **Foreclosure:** A commitment has been made without having gone through a crisis. No reassessment of old positions has been made. Instead the young person has simply accepted a parentally or culturally defined commitment.
- **Identity Diffusion:** The young person is not in the midst of a crisis (although there may have been one in the past) and no commitment has been made. Diffusion may thus represent either an early stage in the process (before a crisis), or a failure to reach a commitment after a crisis.

Whether every young person goes through some kind of identity crisis I cannot tell you, since there have been no longitudinal studies covering all the relevant

Critical Thinking

The implication in Marcia's formulation is that the foreclosure status is less developmentally mature—that one must go through a crisis in order to achieve a mature identity. Does this make sense to you?

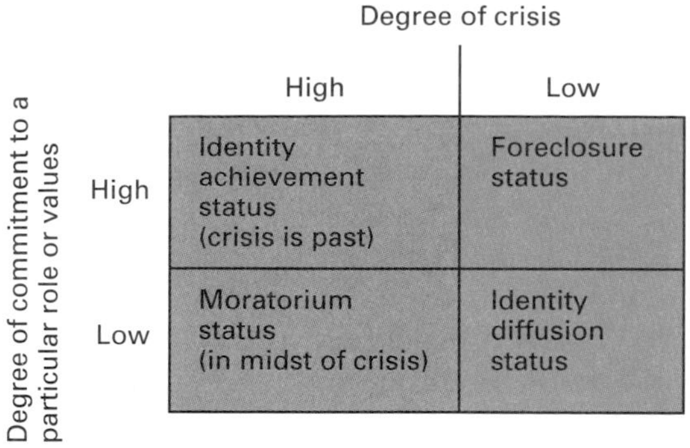

Degree of crisis

Degree of commitment to a particular role or values	High	Low
High	Identity achievement status (crisis is past)	Foreclosure status
Low	Moratorium status (in midst of crisis)	Identity diffusion status

FIGURE 12.2 The four identity statuses proposed by Marcia, based on Erikson's theory. For a fully achieved identity, the young person must both have examined her values or goals and have reached a firm commitment. (*Source:* Marcia, 1980.)

years. Cross-sectional studies of the years of adolescence and early adulthood, however, suggest that the whole process of identity formation may occur later than Erikson thought, when it occurs at all. In one combined analysis of 8 separate cross-sectional studies, Alan Waterman (1985) found that the identity achievement status occurred most often in college, not during the high school years. Among these subjects, the moratorium status was relatively uncommon except in the early years of college. So if most young people are going through an identity crisis, the crisis is occurring fairly late in adolescence and not lasting terribly long. What's more, about a third of the young people at every age were in the foreclosure status, which may indicate that many young people simply do not go through a crisis at all, but follow well-defined grooves.

As a further caveat, I should point out that all the subjects in the studies Waterman analyzed were either in college or in college-preparatory high school programs. This may give a false impression of the process of identity formation for young people who do not go to college, who do not have the luxury of a long period of questioning but must work out some kind of personal identity while still in their teens.

The whole conception of an adolescent identity crisis has also been strongly influenced by current cultural assumptions in Western societies, in which full adult status is postponed for almost a decade after puberty. In such cultures, young people do not normally or necessarily adopt the same roles or occupations as their parents. Indeed, they are encouraged to choose for themselves. In such a cultural system, adolescents are faced with what may be a bewildering array of options, a pattern that might well foster the sort of identity crisis Erikson described. In less-industrialized cultures, especially those with clear initiation rites of the type I described in Chapter 11, there may well be a shift in identity from that of child to that of adult, but without a crisis of any kind.

Ethnic Identity

Minority teenagers, especially those of color in a predominantly white culture, face another task in creating an identity in adolescence: They must develop an ethnic or racial identity, including self-identification as a member of some specific group, commitment to that group and its values and attitudes, and some positive (or negative) attitudes about the group to which they belong.

Jean Phinney (1990; Phinney & Rosenthal, 1992) has proposed that in adolescence, the development of a complete ethnic identity moves through three rough stages. The first stage is an "unexamined ethnic identity," equivalent to what Marcia calls a foreclosed status. For some subgroups in U.S. society, such as African

Americans and Native Americans, this unexamined identity typically includes the negative images and stereotypes common in the wider culture. Indeed, it may be especially at adolescence, with the advent of the cognitive ability to reflect and interpret, that the young person becomes keenly aware of the way in which his own group is perceived by the majority. As Spencer and Dornbusch (1990) put it, "The young African-American may learn as a child that black is beautiful but conclude as an adolescent that white is powerful" (p. 131).

Many minority teenagers initially prefer the dominant white culture, or wish they had been born into the majority. An African-American journalist, Sylvester Monroe, who grew up in an urban housing project, clearly describes this initial negative feeling:

> If you were black, you didn't quite measure up. . . . For a black kid there was a certain amount of self-doubt. It came at you indirectly. You didn't see any black people on television, you didn't see any black people doing certain things. . . . You don't think it out but you say, "Well, it must mean that white people are better than we are. Smarter, brighter—whatever." (Spencer & Dornbusch, 1990, pp. 131–132)

Not all minority teenagers arrive at such negative views of their own group. Individual youngsters may have very positive ethnic images, conveyed by parents or others around the child. Phinney's point is that this initial ethnic identity is not arrived at independently but comes from outside sources.

The second stage is the "ethnic identity search," parallel to the crisis in Marcia's analysis of ego identity. This search is typically triggered by some experience that makes ethnicity salient—perhaps an example of blatant prejudice or merely the widening experience of high school. At this point the young person begins to compare her own ethnic group with others, to try to arrive at her *own* judgments.

This exploration stage is eventually followed by a resolution of the conflicts and contradictions—analogous to Marcia's status of identity achievement. This is often a difficult process. For example, some African-American adolescents who wish to try to compete in and succeed in the dominant culture may experience ostracism from their black friends, who accuse them of "acting white" and betraying their blackness. Latinos often report similar experiences. Some resolve this by keeping their own ethnic group at arm's length; others deal with it by creating essentially two identities, as expressed by one young Chicano interviewed by Phinney:

> Being invited to someone's house, I have to change my ways of how I act at home, because of culture differences. I would have to follow what they do. . . . I am used to it now, switching off between the two. It is not difficult. (Phinney & Rosenthal, 1992, p. 160)

Still others resolve the dilemma by wholeheartedly choosing their own ethnic group's patterns and values, even when that choice may limit their access to the larger culture.

In both cross-sectional and longitudinal studies, Phinney has found that African-American teens and young adults do indeed move through these steps or stages toward a clear ethnic identity. Furthermore, research shows that African-American, Asian-American, and Mexican-American teens and college students who have reached the second or third stage in this process—those who are searching for or who have reached a clear identity—have higher self-esteem and better psychological adjustment than do those who are still in the "unexamined" stage (Phinney, 1990). In contrast, among Caucasian students, ethnic identity has essentially no relationship to self-esteem or adjustment.

This stagelike model may be a decent beginning description of the process of ethnic identity formation. But let us not lose sight of the fact that the details and the content of the ethnic identity will differ markedly from one subgroup to another.

Those groups that encounter more overt prejudice will have a different road to follow than will those who may be more easily assimilated; those whose own ethnic culture espouses values that are close to those of the dominant culture will have less difficulty resolving the contradictions than will those whose subculture is at greater variance with the majority. Whatever the specifics, young people of color and those from clearly defined ethnic groups have an important additional identity task in their adolescent years.

Self-Esteem

Self-esteem also shows interesting shifts during the teenage years. The overall trend is a steady rise in esteem through the years of adolescence; the average 19- or 20-year-old has a considerably more positive sense of her global self-worth than she did at age 8 or 11 (Harter, 1990; Wigfield et al., 1991). But there is an interesting glitch in this pattern: At the very beginning of adolescence, self-esteem very often drops rather abruptly. In one study, Edward Seidman and his colleagues (Seidman et al., 1994) followed a group of nearly 600 Latino, black, and white youngsters over the two years from sixth grade to junior high. Seidman found a significant average drop in self-esteem over that period, a decline that occurred in each of the three ethnic groups.

This decline seems to be linked not so much to age as to changing schools at the same time as puberty (Harter, 1990). Researchers have noted it especially among students who shift to junior high school at seventh grade (Wigfield et al., 1991). When the transition process is more gradual, as for children in a middle school that includes fifth through eighth grades, we see no parallel drop in self-esteem in early adolescence.

Summary of Developmental Changes in the Self-Concept

Let me combine the bits of information I have given in several chapters, and sum up this developmental progression. The infant or toddler develops first a primitive sense of her own separateness, followed quickly by an understanding of her own constancy and of herself as an actor or agent in the world. By 18 to 24 months, most children achieve self-awareness; they grasp the fact that they are also *objects* in the world. At that point, children begin to define themselves in terms of their physical properties (age, size, gender), and their activities and skills. Over the period of concrete and formal operations (from age 6 through adolescence), the content of the child's self-concept becomes gradually more abstract, less and less tied to outward physical qualities, more based on the assumption of enduring inner qualities. During late adolescence, the whole self-concept also appears to undergo a kind of reorganization, with a new future-oriented sexual, occupational, and ideological identity created.

As a final point, I want to emphasize once again that a child's self-concept, including her level of self-esteem, appears to be a highly significant mediating concept. Once such a "theory" of the self is well established—once a global judgment of one's own self-worth is created—it reverberates throughout a child's behavior. Among other things, each child systematically chooses experiences and environments that are consistent with her beliefs about herself. A child who believes that she can't do long division will behave quite differently in the classroom from the child whose self-concept includes the idea "I am good at math." A child who believes she can't make friends makes different choices than one who sees herself as having many friends. These beliefs are pervasive, many develop early, and although they are somewhat responsive to changing circumstances, they also act as self-fulfilling prophecies and thus help to shape the trajectory of the person's life throughout adulthood.

Critical Thinking

Can you think of examples of how your own self-concept affects your choices and your behavior?

Concepts of Relationships

In parallel fashion, the teenager's understanding of others, and of relationships, becomes more and more abstract, less and less tied to externals. For example, teenagers' descriptions of other people contain more comparisons of one trait with another or one person with another, more recognition of inconsistencies and exceptions, more shadings of gray than we hear in descriptions given by younger children (Shantz, 1983). As illustration, here's a description by a 15-year-old:

> Andy is very modest. He is even shyer than I am when near strangers and yet is very talkative with people he knows and likes. He always seems good tempered and I have never seen him in a bad temper. He tends to degrade other people's achievements, and yet never praises his own. He does not seem to voice his opinions to anyone. He easily gets nervous. (Livesley & Bromley, 1973, p. 221)

We see similar changes in children's descriptions of friendships, which become more qualified, more shaded. Damon's research suggests that in late adolescence, young people understand that even very close friendships cannot fill every need and that friendships are not static: They change, grow, or dissolve, as each member of the pair changes. A really good friendship, then, is one that *adapts* to these changes. At this age, young people say things about friendship like "trust is the ability to let go as well as to hang on" (Selman, 1980, p. 141).

In an intriguing series of interviews, Robert Selman (1980) has also studied friendships by asking children and adolescents how they settle disagreements or arguments with friends. Table 12.1 lists some of the answers given by children of various ages, illustrating the kind of progression I have been describing.

Table 12.1 Comments by Children of Various Ages About How to Solve Disagreements or Arguments Between Friends

- "Go away from her and come back later when you're not fighting." (age 5)
- "Punch her out." (age 5)
- "Around our way the guy who started it just says he's sorry." (age 8)
- "Well if you say something and don't really mean it, then you have to mean it when you take it back." (age 8½)
- "Sometimes you got to get away for a while. Calm down a bit so you won't be so angry. Then get back and try to talk it out." (age 14)
- "If you just settle up after a fight that is no good. You gotta really feel that you'd be happy the way things went if you were in your friend's shoes. You can just settle up with someone who is not a friend, but that's not what friendship is really about." (age 15½)
- "Well, you could talk it out, but it usually fades itself out. It usually takes care of itself. You don't have to explain everything. You do certain things and each of you knows what it means. But if not, then talk it out." (age 16)

Source: Selman, 1980, pp. 107–113.

Critical Thinking

Can you recognize your own thinking in these comments? How would you describe your ways of settling arguments with your friends?

Relationships

All these cognitive changes in the child's understanding of herself and her relationships form an important part of the foundation of the child's actual relationships, although the causality clearly runs both ways: Relationships affect the child's thinking just as much as the changes in the child's understanding affect her relationships. In adolescence, the key relationships continue to be with parents and with peers.

Relationships with Parents

Teenagers have two, apparently contradictory, tasks in their relationships with their parents: to establish autonomy from them, and also to maintain their sense of relatedness with them. The push for autonomy shows itself in increases in conflict between parent and adolescent; the maintenance of connection is seen in the continued strong attachment of child to parent.

While it is true that discord rises in many families when children reach puberty, it is a myth that parents and teenagers are constantly in conflict.

Increases in Conflict. The rise in conflict between parents and their teenagers has been documented by a number of researchers (e.g., Flannery, Montemayor, & Eberly, 1994; Laursen, 1995; Steinberg, 1988). In the great majority of families, it seems to consist of an increase in mild bickering or conflicts over everyday issues like chores or personal rights—for example, whether the adolescent should be allowed to wear a bizarre hairstyle or black clothes held together with safety pins, or whether and when the teen should be required to do family chores. Teenagers and their parents also interrupt each other more often and become more impatient with one another.

This increase in discord is widely found, but we need to be careful not to assume that it signifies a major disruption of the quality of the parent-child relationships. Laurence Steinberg, one of the key researchers in this area, estimates that only 5 to 10 percent of the families studied in the United States experience a substantial or pervasive deterioration in the quality of parent-child relationship in these years of early adolescence—a fact that flies in the face of the usual assumption that adolescence is a time of inevitable storm and stress (Steinberg, 1990).

But if the rise in conflict doesn't signify that the relationship is falling apart, what does it mean? Steinberg and others have suggested that the temporary discord, far from being a negative event, may instead be developmentally healthy and necessary—a part of the process of individuation and separation. We see the same kind of increase in conflict among primates, especially between adult males and newly adolescent males. The young males begin to make competitive gestures and may be driven off into a brief period of independent life before returning to the troop. Among humans, we have accumulating evidence that the increase in family conflict is linked with the hormonal changes of puberty, rather than age, which would lend further support to the argument that this is a normal and even necessary process.

For example, Steinberg (1988) followed a group of teenagers over a one-year period, assessing their stage of puberty and the quality of their relationship with their parents at the beginning and end of the year. He found that as the early pubertal stages began, family closeness declined, parent-child conflict rose, and autonomy in the child went up. Other researchers (e.g., Inoff-Germain et al., 1988) have taken this a step further by measuring actual hormone levels and showing links between the rise of the various hormones of puberty and the rise in aloofness toward or conflict with parents. Among girls, conflict seems to rise after menarche (Holmbeck & Hill, 1991).

The pattern of causes is obviously complex. Hormonal changes may be causally linked to increases in assertiveness, perhaps especially among boys. But parents' reactions to pubertal changes may also be highly important parts of the mix. Visible pubertal changes, including menarche, change parents' expectations for the child and increase their concern about guiding and controlling the adolescent to help her avoid the shoals of too much independence.

In fact, adolescence may actually be more stressful to *parents* than to the young people themselves (Gecas & Seff, 1990). Almost two-thirds of parents perceive their children's adolescence as the most difficult stage of parenting, because of both loss of control over the adolescent and fear for the adolescent's safety.

In the midst of the increased conflict, and perhaps partially as a result of it, the overall level of the teenager's autonomy within the family increases steadily throughout the adolescent years. Parents give the youngster more and more room to make independent choices and to participate in family decision making. Steinberg argues that this "distancing" is an essential part of the adolescent development process.

Attachment to Parents. Paradoxically, despite this distancing and temporarily heightened family conflict, teenagers' underlying emotional attachment to their parents remains strong. Results from a study by Mary Levitt and her colleagues (1993) illustrate the point.

Levitt interviewed African-American, Hispanic-American, and Anglo children aged 7, 10, and 14. Each child was shown a drawing with a set of concentric circles and was asked to place in the middle circle those "people who are the most close and important to you—people you love the most and who love you the most." In the next circle outward from the middle, children were asked to place the names of "people who are not quite as close but who are still important—people you really love or like, but not quite as much as the people in the first circle." A third, outermost circle contained names of somewhat more distant members of this personal "convoy." The interviewer then asked about the kind of support each listed person provided to the subject.

Critical Thinking

You might find it interesting to complete such a "personal convoy" map for your own relationships. Are your parents in the center circle? Friends? Partner?

Levitt found that for all three ethnic groups, at all three ages, parents and other close family members were by far the most likely to be placed in the inner circle. Even 14-year-olds rarely placed friends in this position. So the parents remain central. At the same time, it is clear from Levitt's results that peers become increasingly important as providers of support, as you can see in Figure 12.3, which shows the total amount of support the children and adolescents described from each source. Friends clearly provided more support among the 14-year-olds than among the younger children, a pattern that occurred in all three ethnic groups.

A recent large study in the Netherlands (van Wel, 1994) suggests that the teenager's bond with his parents may weaken somewhat in the middle of adolescence (ages 15 and 16) and then recover. But virtually all the current researchers who

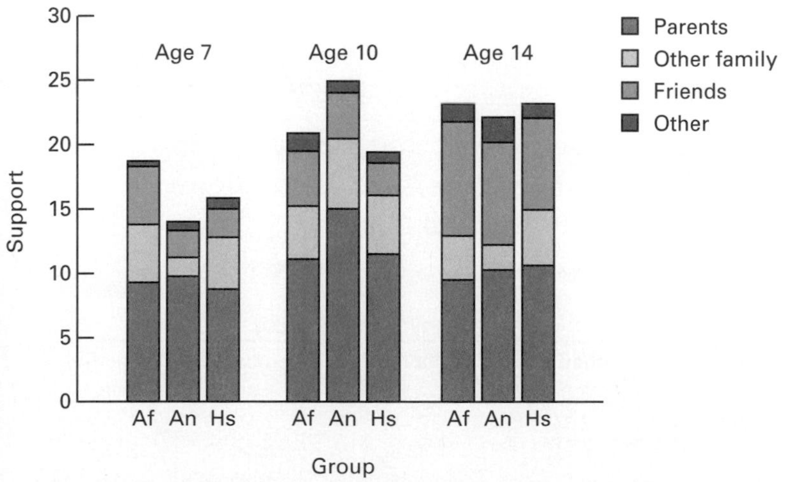

FIGURE 12.3 African-American (Af), Anglo-American (An), and Hispanic-American (Hs) children and teens were asked about the amount and type of support they received from various members of their "social convoy." Note that for teens, friends become more significant sources of support, but parents do not become *less* important. (*Source*: Levitt, Guacci-Franco, & Levitt, 1993, Figure 2, p. 815.)

have explored this question find that a teenager's sense of well-being or happiness is more strongly correlated with the quality of his attachment to his parents than with the quality of his attachments to his peers (e.g., Greenberg, Siegel, & Leitch, 1983; Raja, McGee, & Stanton, 1992). Thus, even while the teenager is becoming more autonomous, the parents are needed to provide a highly important psychological safe base.

Variations in Family Relationships

During these adolescent years, as at all earlier times, some parents are better than others at creating such a safe base. I already talked at length in Chapter 8 about differences in family interactive style and their effects on children and teenagers. Among adolescents, as among younger children, authoritative parenting is consistently associated with more positive outcomes. I mentioned in Chapter 11 that teenagers whose parents use an authoritative style do better in school than do those whose parents use authoritarian or other styles. The same benefit of authoritative parenting is also found when we look at aspects of emotional and mental health.

Table 12.2 shows one set of results from the very large multiethnic study by Dornbusch and his colleagues (Lamborn et al., 1991). Roughly 10,000 high school students, in Wisconsin and California, reported on their family patterns and answered a set of questions about each of several aspects of their own behavior and feelings, using a 4-point scale where 1 always means a low amount, and 4 always means the highest amount. The numbers entered in the table are the average scores on these 4-point scales. When you look at the numbers, it is clear that the outcomes were best for the students who described their families as authoritative and least good for those from neglectful families.

Family Structure. Family structure, too, continues to be an important factor in the teenager's life. But in adolescence we see an interesting exception to the typical pattern of effects. You'll remember from Chapter 8 that boys are usually more negatively affected than girls by parental divorce or remarriage. Among adolescents, it is girls who show more distress, both in families in which the girl lives with her still-single mother, and in stepparent families (Amato, 1993; Hetherington & Clingempeel, 1992). Adolescent girls, but apparently not preschool or elementary school–age girls, have more trouble interacting with the new stepfather than do their brothers, and treat him more as an intruder. They are resistant, critical, and sulky, and try to

Table 12.2 Average Scores on Various Measures of Adolescent Behavior for Teenagers from Families with Different Styles of Discipline and Control

	Style of Parenting			
Outcome Measure	**Authoritative**	**Authoritarian**	**Permissive**	**Neglectful**
Self-reliance	3.09_a	2.96_b	3.03_a	2.98_b
Psychological symptoms	2.36_a	2.46_a	2.43_a	2.65_b
School misconduct	2.16_a	3.26_b	2.38_c	2.43_c
Drug use	1.41_a	1.38_a	1.69_b	1.68_b

Note: Each number represents the average score on a 4-point scale, where 1 always indicates a low amount of the particular behavior, and 4 means the maximum amount. In each row, any pair of numbers with different subscripts are significantly different from one another.

Source: Lamborn et al., 1991, Table 9 and Table 10, pp. 1060 and 1061.

Chances are the daughter in this stepfamily is more likely to be upset and disturbed by her mother's remarriage and late baby than is her brother.

avoid contact with him, despite the obvious effort of many stepfathers to be thoughtful and nonauthoritarian. Girls in this situation are also likely to become depressed, and are more likely than boys in stepfamilies to get involved with drugs.

Why this pattern occurs is not so obvious. The daughter may feel displaced from a special or more responsible position in the family system that she held after her parents' divorce and before the mother's remarriage; she may feel disturbed by the mother's romantic and clearly sexual involvement with the stepfather. In contrast, the teenage boy may have more to gain by the addition of the stepfather because he acquires a male role model. Whatever the explanation, findings like these remind us once again that family systems are astonishingly complex. Simple categories like "intact" and "stepparent" families will need to give way, ultimately, to more fine-grained analyses that take into account not only the child's age and gender, but family style, the history and sequence of family structures, the presence of other relatives in the system, and so forth.

Relationships with Peers

At the same time, there is no gainsaying the fact that peer relationships become far more significant at adolescence than they have been at any earlier stage, and perhaps than they will be at any later time in life. Teenagers spend more than half their waking hours with other teenagers and less than 5 percent of their time with either parent. Their friendships are also increasingly intimate, in the sense that adolescent friends share more and more of their inner feelings and secrets, and are more knowledgeable about each other's feelings. Loyalty and faithfulness become more valued characteristics of friendship. These friendships are also more likely to endure for a year or longer. In one longitudinal study, Robert and Beverly Cairns found that only about 20 percent of friendships among fourth-graders lasted as long as a year, while about 40 percent of friendships formed by these same youngsters when they were tenth-graders were long-lasting (1994).

Beyond these changes in individual relationships, the *function* of the peer group changes in adolescence. In elementary school, peer groups are mostly the setting for mutual play and for all the learning about relationships and the natural world that is part of such play. But the teenager uses the peer group in another way. He is struggling to make a slow transition from the protected life of the family to the independent life of adulthood; the peer group becomes the *vehicle* for that transition. As Erikson pointed out, clannishness and intense conformity to the group is a normal—even an essential—part of the process. Such conformity seems to peak at about age 13 or 14 (at about the same time that we see a drop in self-esteem) and then wanes as the teenager begins to arrive at a sense of identity that is more independent of the peer group.

However, while it is very clear that peers do indeed put pressure on each other to conform to peer group behavior standards, it is also true that peer group pressures are less potent and less negative than popular cultural stereotypes might lead you to believe (Berndt, 1992). For one thing, let us remember that adolescents *choose* their friends and their crowd. And they are likely to choose to associate with a group that shares their values, attitudes, and behaviors. If the discrepancy between their own ideas and those of their friends becomes too great, teens are more likely to move toward a more compatible group of friends than to be persuaded to shift toward the first group's values or behaviors. Furthermore, teenagers report that when explicit peer pressure is exerted, it is likely to be pressure toward positive activities, such as school involvement, and *away* from misconduct. Only in "druggie-tough" crowds does there seem to be explicit pressure toward misconduct or lawbreaking, and here the motive may be as much a desire to prove "I'm as tough as you are" as it is explicit pressure from peers (Berndt & Keefe, 1995b; Brown, Dolcini, & Leventhal, 1995). Thus, while Erikson appears to be quite correct in saying that peers are a major force in shaping a child's identity development in adolescence, peer influence is neither monolithic nor uniformly negative.

Changes in Peer Group Structure in Adolescence. The structure of the peer group also changes over the years of adolescence. The classic, widely quoted early study is Dunphy's observation of the formation, dissolution, and interaction of teenage groups in a high school in Sydney, Australia, between 1958 and 1960 (Dunphy, 1963). Dunphy identified two important subvarieties of groups. The first type, which he called a **clique,** is made up of four to six young people who appear to be strongly attached to one another. Cliques have strong cohesiveness and high levels of intimate sharing. In the early years of adolescence, these cliques are almost entirely same-sex groups—a residual of the preadolescent pattern. Gradually, however, the cliques

Research Report

Are African-American Adolescents More Susceptible to Peer Influence?

One assumption made by a great many adults, including many social scientists, is that African-American youth, more than any other group, are likely to be strongly peer-oriented and to be more vulnerable to peer pressure. One typical argument is that because black teenagers more often live in single-parent families, they are more likely to depend on peers for affiliation and support. Several recent studies call this assumption into question.

Peggy Giordano and her colleagues (Giordano, Cernkovich, & DeMaris, 1993) studied a group of 942 teenagers, chosen as a representative sample of all adolescents living in Toledo, Ohio. Half the group was black; the remainder was mostly non-Hispanic whites. These teens were asked a wide variety of questions about their friendships and their relationships with peers, such as:

> How important is it to you to do things your friends approve of?
>
> How important is it to you to have a group of friends to hang around with?

They were also asked about family intimacy (e.g., "I'm closer to my parents than a lot of kids my age are") and about parental supervision and control.

In this sample, African-American adolescents reported significantly *more* family intimacy, *more* parental supervision and control, *less* need for peer approval, and *less* peer pressure than did white teens.

Similarly, Vicki Mack (Mack et al., 1995), in a study of nearly 1000 teens in Detroit, found that the African-American youth described *lower* levels of compliance to friends and *higher* scores on measures of the importance of their relationship with their parents. These two studies certainly raise questions about widespread cultural assumptions.

combine into larger sets Dunphy called **crowds,** which include both males and females. Finally, the crowd breaks down again into heterosexual cliques and then into loose associations of couples. In Dunphy's study, the period of the fully developed crowd was roughly between ages 13 and 15—the very years when we see the greatest conformity to peer pressure.

Bradford Brown and others of the current generation of adolescence researchers have changed Dunphy's labels somewhat (1990; Brown, Mory, & Kinney, 1994). Brown uses the word *crowd* to refer to the "reputation-based" group with which a young person is identified, either by choice or by peer designation. In U.S. schools these groups have labels like *jocks, brains, nerds, dweebs, punks, druggies, toughs, normals, populars, preppies,* and *loners*. Studies in American junior high and high schools make it clear that teenagers can readily identify and have quite stereotypic—even caricatured—descriptions of each of the major crowds in their school (e.g., "The partyers goof off a lot more than the jocks do, but they don't come to school stoned like the burnouts do"). Each of these descriptions serves as what Brown calls an "identity prototype" (Brown et al., 1994, p. 133): Labeling others and labeling oneself as belonging to one or more of these groups helps to create or reinforce the adolescent's own identity. Such labeling also helps the adolescent identify potential friends or foes. Thus, membership in one crowd or another channels each adolescent toward particular activities and particular relationships.

CRITICAL THINKING

Think back to your own high school. Can you draw some kind of diagram or map to describe the organization of crowds and cliques? Were those crowds or cliques more or less important in the last few years of high school than they had been earlier?

Within any given school, these various crowds are organized into a fairly clear, widely understood pecking order. In U.S. schools, the groups labeled as some variant of "jocks," "populars," or "normals" are typically at the top of the heap, with "brains" somewhere in the middle and "druggies," "loners," and "nerds" at the bottom (Brown et al., 1994).

Through the years of junior high and high school, the social system of crowds becomes increasingly differentiated, with more and more distinct groups. For example, in one midwestern school system, Kinney found that junior high students labeled only two major crowds, one small high-status group (called *trendies* in this school) and the great mass of lower-status students, called *dweebs* (Kinney, 1993). A few years later the same students named five distinct crowds, three with comparatively high social status and two low-status groups (*grits* and *punkers*). By late high school, these same students identified seven or eight crowds, but by this age the crowds seem to be less significant in the social organization of the peer group; mutual friendships and dating pairs are more central (Urberg et al., 1995).

From one kind of clique to another.

Within (and sometimes across) these crowds, adolescents create smaller friendship groups Brown calls *cliques*—a usage that is very similar to Dunphy's meaning for the same term. These groups, as Dunphy observed, are almost entirely same-sex in early adolescence; by late adolescence they have become mixed in gender, often composed of groups of dating couples.

Whatever specific clique or crowd a teenager may identify with, theorists agree that the peer group performs the highly important function of helping the teenager shift from friendships to "partner" social relationships. The 13- or 14-year-old can begin to try out her new relationship skills in the wider group of the crowd or clique; only after some confidence is developed do we see the beginnings of dating and of more committed pair relationships. For the great majority of teens, of course, this is a shift from unisexual to heterosexual relationships; for the small subgroup of homosexual teens—discussed in the Real World box on page 314—the underlying need is similar but the process is necessarily different.

Heterosexual Relationships in Adolescence

Of all the changes in social relationships in adolescence, perhaps the most profound is this shift from the total dominance of same-sex friendships to heterosexual relationships. These new relationships are clearly part of the preparation for assuming a

The Real World

Homosexuality Among Adolescents

For the great majority of teens, the progression of peer relationships moves from unisexual to heterosexual groups and then to heterosexual pairs. For the subgroup of homosexual teens, the process is different.

In a recent study of nearly 35,000 youths in Minnesota public schools, Remafedi (Remafedi et al., 1992) found that less than 1 percent of the adolescent boys and only 0.4 percent of the girls *defined* themselves as homosexual, but a much larger number said they were "unsure" of their sexual orientation, and 2 to 6 percent reported that they were attracted to others of the same sex. These figures are generally consistent with the newest and most comprehensive data on U.S. adults (Laumann et al., 1994): 2 to 3 percent of adults say they think of themselves as homosexual or bisexual; roughly twice that many say they are attracted to those of the same sex.

Recent evidence has greatly strengthened the hypothesis that homosexuality has a biological basis (Gladue, 1994; Pillard & Bailey, 1995). For example, several new twin studies show that when one identical twin is homosexual, the probability that the other will also be homosexual is 50 to 60 percent, while this "concordance rate" is only about 20 percent for fraternal twins and only about 11 percent among pairs of biologically unrelated boys adopted into the same families (Bailey & Pillard, 1991; Bailey et al., 1993; Whitam, Diamond, & Martin, 1993). More direct comparisons of gene patterning and brain architecture of homosexual and heterosexual men also points to the possibility (not yet firmly established) that homosexual behavior may be hard-wired (e.g., Hamer et al., 1993; LeVay, 1991).

Additional studies suggest that prenatal hormone patterns may also be causally involved in homosexuality. For example, women whose mothers took the drug diethylstilbestrol (DES, a synthetic estrogen) during pregnancy are more likely to be homosexual as adults than are women who did not have such DES exposure (Meyer-Bahlburg et al., 1995).

Finally, there is accumulating information showing that boys who show strong cross-sex-typed behavior in early childhood are highly likely to show homosexual preferences when they reach adolescence (Bailey & Zucker, 1995), findings that are consistent with the hypothesis that homosexuality is built in by the time of birth.

Such biological evidence does not mean that environment plays no role in homosexuality. No behavior is entirely controlled by either nature or nurture, as I have said many times. At the very least, we know that when one of a pair of identical twins is homosexual, 40 or 50 percent of the time the other twin will *not* share the same sexual orientation. Something beyond biology must be at work, although we do not yet know what environmental factors may be involved.

Whatever the cause, homosexual teenagers are a minority who face high levels of prejudice and stereotyping. Many are verbally attacked or ridiculed; as many as a third are physically assaulted by their peers (Remafedi, Farrow, & Deisher, 1991; Savin-Williams, 1994). For these and other reasons, these young people are at high risk for a variety of problems. In Remafedi's Minneapolis study, for example, four-fifths of homosexual teens showed deteriorating school performance and more than a quarter dropped out of high school (Remafedi, 1987a). They must also cope with the decision about whether to "come out" about their homosexuality. Those who do come out are far more likely to tell peers than parents, although telling peers carries some risk: In his Minneapolis study, Remafedi found that 41 percent of homosexual male youths had lost a friend over the issue (Remafedi, 1987b). Some research suggests that as many as two-thirds of homosexual youth have not told their parents (Rotheram-Borus, Rosario, & Koopman, 1991).

There is obviously much that we do not know about homosexual adolescents. But it is a reasonable hypothesis that the years of adolescence may be particularly stressful for this subgroup. Like ethnic-minority youth, homosexual teens have an additional task facing them in forming a clear identity.

full adult sexual identity. Physical sexuality is part of that role, but so are the skills of personal intimacy with the opposite sex, including flirting, communicating, and reading the form of social cues used by the other gender.

In Western societies, these skills are learned first in larger crowds or cliques and then in dating pairs (Zani, 1993). Studies of U.S. adolescents in the 1980s suggest that dating begins most typically at 15 or 16, as you can see from Table 12.3, which shows results from a representative sample of Detroit teenagers (Thornton, 1990). More than half of both boys and girls in this same study had become sexually active

Table 12.3 Age at First Date Among U.S. Adolescents

Age	Males	Females
13 or younger	21.2%	8.6%
14	17.9%	16.2%
15	21.2%	33.6%
16	29.5%	29.3%
17–18	7.2%	10.0%

Source: Thornton, 1990, Table 1, pp. 246–247.

by the time they were 18, following the same kind of steady increase with age you saw in Figure 11.5 (page 279).

You'll also recall from Chapter 11 that heterosexual behavior varies across ethnic groups within American society. African-American teens begin dating and sexual experimentation earlier than do Anglos or Hispanics. Early dating and early sexual activity are also more common among the poor of every ethnic group and among those who experience relatively early puberty. Religious teachings and individual attitudes about the appropriate age for dating and sexual behavior also make a difference, as does family structure. Girls from divorced or remarried families, for example, report earlier dating and higher levels of sexual experience than do girls from intact families, and those with strong religious identity report later dating and lower levels of sexuality (Bingham, Miller, & Adams, 1990; Miller & Moore, 1990). But for every group, these are years of experimentation with presexual and sexual relationships.

Individual Differences

These shared developmental patterns are obviously a central part of the story of adolescence. Yet young people's experience of these years clearly varies widely. Most generally, young people vary in personality, just as infants and young children differ in temperament, and these variations affect the adolescent's experience and her behavior.

Personality in Adolescence

You'll recall from Chapter 6 that most psychologists today think of personality as being built on the matrix or substrate of the child's inborn temperament. But just how should we describe personality? What are the key dimensions on which personalities differ? Over the years, researchers and theorists have disagreed vehemently on how many such dimensions there might be, how they should be measured, or even whether there were any stable personality traits at all. But in the past decade, somewhat to the surprise of many psychologists, researchers in this disputatious field have reached consensus that adult personality can be adequately described as a set of variations along five major dimensions, often referred to as the **Big Five,** described in Table 12.4: **extraversion, agreeableness, conscientiousness, neuroticism,** and **openness/intellect** (Digman, 1990; McCrae & John, 1992). To link up this list with the key temperament dimensions I described in Chapter 6, I've suggested

Table 12.4 **The "Big Five" Personality Traits**

Trait	Qualities of Individual High in That Trait	Possible Temperament Components
Extraversion	Active, assertive, energetic, enthusiastic, outgoing, talkative	High activity level; sociability; positive emotionality
Agreeableness	Affectionate, forgiving, generous, kind, sympathetic, trusting	Perhaps high approach/ positive emotionality; perhaps effortful control
Conscientiousness	Efficient, organized, prudent, reliable, responsible, thorough	Effortful control/task persistence
Neuroticism (also called emotional instability)	Anxious, self-pitying, tense, touchy, unstable, worrying	Negative emotionality; irritability
Openness/Intellect	Artistic, curious, imaginative, insightful, original, wide interests	Approach; low inhibition

Sources: McCrae & Costa, 1990; John et al., 1994, Table 1, p. 161; Ahadi & Rothbart, 1994.

some of the possible connections in the table—although these links are still quite speculative (e.g., Ahadi & Rothbart, 1994; Digman, 1994).

CRITICAL THINKING

How would you rate your own personality on each of the Big Five?

These Big Five dimensions have now been found in studies of adults in a variety of countries, including some non-Western cultures (Bond, Nakazato, & Shiraishi, 1975; Borkenau & Ostendorf, 1990). We also have good evidence that these five are stable traits; among adults, scores on these five dimensions have been shown to be stable over periods as long as a decade or two—a point I'll come back to in Chapter 14.

New research suggests that these same five dimensions also describe teenagers' personalities. For example, Cornelis van Lieshout and Gerbert Haselager, in a large study of children and adolescents in the Netherlands (1994), found that the five clearest dimensions characterizing their young subjects matched the Big Five very well. In this sample, agreeableness and emotional instability were the clearest dimensions, followed by conscientiousness, extraversion, and openness.

Similar results have come from a study in the United States by Oliver John and his colleagues (John et al., 1994), who studied a group of 350 ethnically diverse 12- and 13-year-old boys drawn at random from the Pittsburgh public school system. Like the Dutch researchers, John found strong evidence that the five-factor model captures the personality variations among these early teen boys. John's study is also helpful as a test of the five-factor model because he has information on other aspects of the boys' behavior, such as their school success or delinquent behavior. By comparing the personality profiles of boys who differ in some specified behavior, he can check to see whether the personality patterns differ in ways that make theoretical and conceptual sense. For example, Figure 12.4 contrasts the personality profiles of boys who reported delinquent activity versus boys who reported none. As John predicted, delinquent boys were markedly lower than nondelinquent boys in both conscientiousness and agreeableness. John also found that boys higher in conscientiousness did slightly better in school, just as you would expect.

These early results are impressive and point to the usefulness of the five-factor model in describing child and adolescent personality.

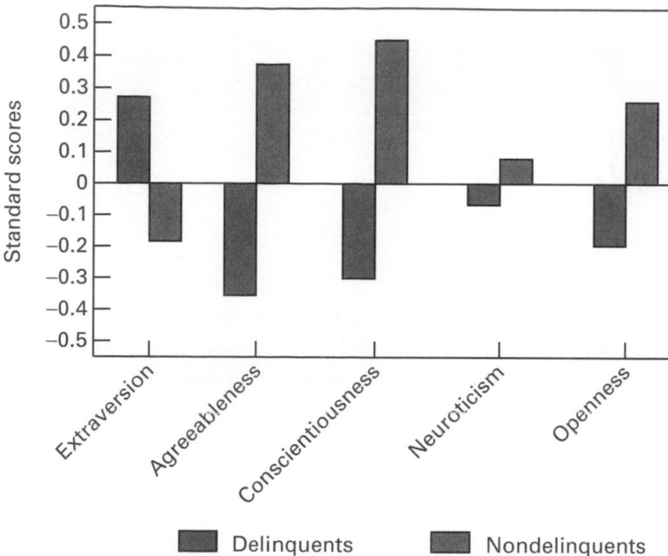

FIGURE 12.4 Delinquent 12-year-olds have quite different personality profiles than do nondelinquents of the same age—a set of results that helps to validate the usefulness of the Big Five personality traits as a description of adolescent personality. (*Source:* John et al., 1994, Figure 1, p. 167.)

Two Common Problems: Depression and Delinquency

Adolescents also differ in the extent to which they experience two of the most common psychological/social problems of this age period: depression and delinquency. Delinquency gets more press, but depression is an equally significant problem among teens.

Depression. For many years, psychiatrists took the position that significant depression could not occur in children or adolescents. But we now have abundant evidence that depression is actually quite common in adolescence and occurs at least occasionally among younger children. Perhaps 10 percent of preadolescent children and 30 to 40 percent of adolescents experience significant short-term depressed mood (Compas, Hinden, & Gerhardt, 1995; Petersen et al., 1993). When such a depressed mood lasts six months or longer and is accompanied by other symptoms such as disturbances of sleeping or eating and difficulty concentrating, it is usually referred to as **clinical depression** or a *depressive disorder.* Recent epidemiological studies tell us that at any given time, 1 to 2 percent of preadolescents and 5 to 8 percent of adolescents are in the midst of such an enduring depression. Perhaps twice that many will experience a serious depression at some time in their adolescent years (Compas, Ey, & Grant, 1993; Merikangas & Angst, 1995). These are not trivial states of unhappiness. A significant portion of depressed teens say they think about suicide. In one longitudinal study of youth growing up in a working-class neighborhood in the United States, a fifth of those who had had a serious depression by age 18 had also attempted suicide (Reinherz et al., 1993).

This teenager seems to be going through the common experience of the "blues" or depressed mood. As many as 10 or 15 percent of teenagers experience a more protracted and serious episode of depression at some time during adolescence.

Interestingly, among preadolescents, boys appear to be slightly more likely than girls to be unhappy or depressed, but beginning at about age 13, girls are twice as likely to report high or chronic levels of depression, a sex difference that exists throughout adulthood and that has been found in a number of industrialized countries and among African Americans, Hispanic Americans, and Anglo Americans (Nolen-Hoeksema & Girgus, 1994; Petersen et al., 1993; Roberts & Sobhan, 1992).

Where do such depressions come from, and why do girls have more of them? The search for the developmental pathways leading to later depression begins with the clear finding that children growing up with depressed parents are much more

The Real World

Adolescent Suicide and Its Prevention

You'll recall from Chapter 10 that Susan Harter documents a pathway from low self-esteem to depression. In some young people, that same pathway includes another step, namely thoughts of suicide (Harter, Marold, & Whitesell, 1992). In some, sadly, such thoughts lead to action. Suicide is very uncommon in children before adolescence. Even among children between 10 and 14, less than 1 child in 100,000 in the United States commits suicide each year. But among those between 15 and 19, the rate is considerably higher, and rising. In a recent survey by the U.S. Centers for Disease Control (Kann et al., 1995), an astonishing 24.1 percent of high school students reported that they had thought seriously about suicide some time during the previous year; 19 percent had made a suicide plan, and 8.6 percent had implemented at least part of that plan.

The likelihood of a completed suicide is almost five times as high among adolescent boys as among girls, and nearly twice as high among whites as among nonwhites *except* for Native American youth, who attempt and commit suicide at higher rates than any other group (Centers for Disease Control, 1994a). The rate among Native Americans is 26.3 per 100,000 per year, compared with about 20 per 100,000 among white teen males. In contrast, suicide *attempts* are estimated to be three times more common in girls than in boys (Garland & Zigler, 1993). Girls, more often than boys, use less "successful" methods, such as self-poisoning.

It is obviously very difficult to uncover the contributing factors in successful or completed suicides, because the crucial individual is no longer available to be interviewed. Researchers and clinicians are forced to rely on secondhand reports by parents or others about the mental state of the suicide before the act—reports that are bound to be at least partially invalid, because in many cases the parents or friends had no suspicion that a suicide attempt was imminent. Nonetheless, it does seem clear that some kind of significant psychopathology is virtually a universal ingredient, including but not restricted to depression. Behavior problems such as aggression are also common in the histories of completed suicides, as is a family history of psychiatric disorder or suicide, or a pattern of drug or alcohol abuse (Garland & Zigler, 1993).

But these factors alone are not enough to explain suicidal behavior. After all, many teenagers (or adults) display one or more of these risk factors, and very few actually commit suicide. David Shaffer (Shaffer et al., 1988) suggests at least three other important elements:

1. Some *Triggering Stressful Event.* Studies of suicides suggest that among adolescents, this triggering event is often a disciplinary crisis with the parents, or some rejection or humiliation, such as breaking up with a girlfriend or boyfriend, or failure in a valued activity.
2. *An Altered Mental State,* which might be an attitude of hopelessness, reduced inhibitions from alcohol consumption, or rage (Swedo et al., 1991). Among girls, in particular, the sense of hopelessness seems to be common: a feeling that the world is against them *and that they can't do anything about it.*
3. *An Opportunity*—a loaded gun available in the house, a bottle of sleeping pills in the parents' medicine cabinet, or the like.

Attempts to prevent teen suicide have not been notably successful. Despite the fact that most suicides and suicide attempters have displayed significantly deviant behavior for some time before the event, most do not find their way to mental health clinics or other professionals, and increasing the availability of such clinics or of hot lines or crisis phones has not proven effective in reducing suicide rates.

Other prevention efforts have focused on education, such as providing training to teachers or to teenagers on how to identify students who are at risk for suicide, in the hope that vulnerable individuals might be reached before they attempt suicide. Special training in coping abilities has also been offered to students, so that teenagers might be able to find a nonlethal solution to their problems. Unfortunately, most such programs appear to be ineffective in changing student attitudes or knowledge (Shaffer et al., 1991).

These discouraging results are not likely to change until we know a great deal more about the developmental pathways that lead to this particular form of psychopathology. What makes one teenager particularly vulnerable and another able to resist the temptation? What combination of stressful circumstances is most likely to trigger a suicide attempt, and how do those stressful circumstances interact with the teenager's personal resources? Only when we can answer questions of this kind will we be on the road to understanding teenage suicide.

likely to develop depression themselves than are those growing up with nondepressed parents (Merikangas & Angst, 1995). Of course this could indicate a genetic factor at work here, a possibility supported by at least a few studies of twins and adopted children (Petersen et al., 1993). Or we could understand this link between parental and child depression in terms of the changes in the parent-child interaction that are caused by the parent's depression.

I mentioned in Chapter 6 that depressed mothers are much more likely than are nondepressed mothers to have children who are insecurely attached. In particular, their behavior with their children is often so nonresponsive that it seems to foster in the children a kind of helpless resignation. Such a sense of helplessness has been found to be strongly related to depression in both adults and adolescents (Dodge, 1990).

Of course not all children of depressed parents are themselves depressed. About 60 percent show no abnormality at all. Whether a child moves along a pathway toward depression or not seems to be in large part a function of the number of other stresses that are present in the family life, such as an illness, family arguments, work stress, loss of income, job loss, or marital separation.

The detrimental role of stress in the emergence of depression is just as clear among children whose parent or parents are not depressed. Any combination of stresses—such as the parents' divorce, the death of a parent or another loved person, the father's loss of job, a move, or a change of schools—increases the likelihood of depression in the child (Compas et al., 1993). Indeed, the role of such individual life stresses may help to explain the sex differences in depression among adolescents. Anne Petersen (Petersen, Sarigiani, & Kennedy, 1991) has proposed that girls are more likely to experience simultaneous stressful experiences in adolescence, such as pubertal changes combined with a shift in schools. In her own longitudinal study, Petersen found that depression was *not* more common among girls than among boys when both groups had encountered equal levels of life stress or simultaneous stressful experiences.

Susan Nolen-Hoeksema agrees with Petersen that one of the keys is that teenage girls face more stresses than do teenage boys (1994; Nolen-Hoeksema & Girgus, 1994). But she also argues that girls respond to their "down" moods quite differently than do boys. Girls (and women) are more likely to *ruminate* about their sadness or distress, a coping strategy that actually accentuates the depression ("What does it mean that I feel this way?" "I just don't feel like doing anything"), producing longer-lasting depressive episodes. Boys (and men), on the other hand, are more likely to use distraction to deal with their blue moods—exercising, playing a game, or working—a coping strategy that tends to reduce depression.

Critical Thinking

Can you think of any other possible explanations of the higher rates of depression among teenage girls than teenage boys? What sort of study would you have to do to test your hypotheses?

You'll remember from Chapter 10 that low self-esteem is also part of the equation. Susan Harter's studies tell us that a young person who feels she (or he) does not measure up to her (or his) own standards is much more likely to show symptoms of a clinical depression. The fact that depression increases markedly in adolescence makes good sense from this point of view. We know that in adolescence, children are much more likely to define themselves and others in *comparative* terms—to judge against some standard, or to see themselves as "less than" or "more than" some other person. We also know that at adolescence, appearance becomes highly salient and that a great many teenagers are convinced that they do not live up to the culturally defined appearance standards. Self-esteem thus drops in early adolescence and depression rises. Girls in current Western cultures seem especially vulnerable to this process, because the increase in body fat that is typical for girls in adolescence runs counter to the desired slim body type.

All this research has taken us a fair distance in our efforts to understand both the rise in depression in adolescence and the marked gender difference in rates of depression. But teenagers still vary widely in their responses to what appear to be the same levels of stress. Not every teenager who faces multiple stresses, fails to live up to some standard, is inclined to ruminate rather than use distraction, or is temperamentally shy ends up being clinically depressed. These are all risk factors, but even with these risk factors, some are more vulnerable than others.

Juvenile Delinquency. Delinquency is a subvariety of what psychologists call *conduct disorders*, a pattern that includes high levels of aggression, argumentativeness, bullying, disobedience, high irritability, and threatening and loud behavior. Delinquency is defined more narrowly to include only intentional lawbreaking, although a great many teenagers who break laws also show other aspects of a conduct disorder, so the two categories overlap a great deal (American Psychiatric Association, 1994).

It is extremely difficult to estimate how many teenagers engage in delinquent behavior. One window on the problem is to look at the number of arrests—although arrest rates are arguably only the tip of the iceberg. More than two million juveniles were arrested in the United States in 1993, which is almost 7 percent of all youngsters between ages 10 and 17. Among those aged 15 to 17, the arrest rate is roughly 10 percent (U.S. Bureau of the Census, 1995)—a higher rate than we see for any other age group across the entire life span. Many of these arrests are for relatively minor infractions, but about a third are for serious crimes, including murder, burglary, rape, and arson.

When adolescents themselves describe their own law-breaking, they report even higher rates. Four-fifths of U.S. youngsters between ages 11 and 17 say that they have been delinquent at some time or another. One-third admit truancy and disor-

Some, but by no means all, delinquents are also members of identifiable street gangs; many who identify with a gang in one year do not remain in such gangs. But gang members show some of the most pervasive and persistent forms of delinquency, drug-taking, and violence (e.g., Esbensen & Huizinga, 1993).

derly conduct, and a fifth say they have committed criminal acts, most often physical assaults or thefts (Dryfoos, 1990). Terrie Moffitt (1993) reports similar figures from a large New Zealand sample, among whom 93 percent of males acknowledged some form of delinquent activity by age 18.

Just as conduct disorders are much more common among preschool and elementary school–age boys than girls, delinquent acts and arrests are far more common among teenage males than females. Among those actually arrested, the ratio is more than 4:1; in self-reports the ratios vary, but the more physically violent the act, the more common it is among boys.

Most psychologists who study delinquent behavior now agree that there are at least two important subvarieties of delinquents, distinguished by the age at which the delinquent behavior (or a broader conduct disorder) begins. *Childhood-onset* disorders are more serious, with high levels of persisting aggression and high likelihood

Research Report

Delinquency Among Girls

When we use the term *delinquent,* most of us think immediately of teenage boys. But although the incidence of delinquency or criminality in girls is much lower, it is not zero. Girls are much less likely to be involved in forms of delinquency that involve violence, just as girls are consistently less physically aggressive at every age. But girls do get involved in delinquent behaviors such as shoplifting or the use of illegal drugs (Zoccolillo, 1993).

A study in New Zealand by Avshalom Caspi and his colleagues (Caspi et al., 1993) provides some interesting insights into the possible origins of such delinquent behavior. The sample of students involved in this study included all the children born in one town in one year (1972–1973), a group of more than 1000. The children were tested and assessed repeatedly, at ages 3, 5, 7, 9, 11, 13, and 15. In one analysis, Caspi looked at rates of delinquency among the girls as a function of the earliness or lateness of their menarche, and of whether they went to an all-girls or a mixed-sex high school. Caspi's hypothesis was that girls who attended a mixed-sex secondary school would be more likely to be involved in delinquent activities because they would have more rule-breaking models (delinquent boys) among their peers. He also expected to find that girls with early puberty would be more likely to become delinquent, especially in mixed-sex schools.

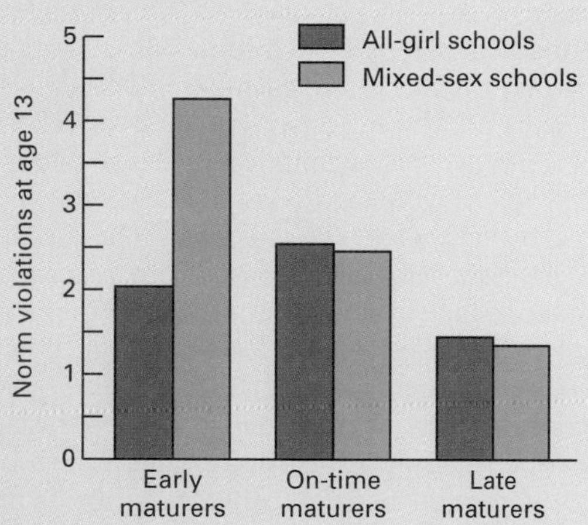

These hypotheses were generally confirmed, although there were some interesting wrinkles. At age 13, the girls were asked to report on "norm violations," which included a variety of mild delinquent acts, such as breaking windows, stealing from schoolmates, getting drunk, swearing loudly in public, or making prank telephone calls. As you can see in the figure, such norm violations were most common among early-maturing girls attending coed schools. Further analysis shows that this difference is almost entirely contributed by a small group of girls who had had a history of high levels of aggression earlier in childhood *and* who had early puberty. Early-maturing girls in coed schools who had no such history of early problems showed no heightened rate of delinquency.

To make it still more complicated, Caspi found that at age 15, early-developing girls in coed schools continued to have high rates of delinquency, but at this age the highest rate of delinquency was found among *on-time–puberty* girls attending coed schools. Puberty, whether early or on-time, thus seems to increase the likelihood that vulnerable girls will get involved with antisocial peers. But this is only true of girls in coed schools.

I find this study fascinating not only because it points to the complex relationships between physical maturation and social relationships, but also because it offers an interesting argument in favor of all-girls schools . . . .

of adult criminality. *Adolescent-onset* problems are typically milder and more transitory, apparently more a reflection of peer group processes or testing the limits of authority than a deeply ingrained behavior problem.

The developmental pathway for early-onset conduct disorders or delinquency is one you are familiar with by now from all I have said about Patterson's research on aggressive children. In early life, these are children who throw tantrums and defy parents; indeed, they may also develop insecure attachments (Greenberg, Speltz, & DeKlyen, 1993). Once the defiance appears, if the parents are not up to the task of controlling the child, the child's behavior worsens to overt aggression toward others, who then reject the child, which aggravates the problem, pushing the seriously aggressive child in the direction of other children with similar problems, who then become the child's only supportive peer group (Shaw, Kennan, & Vondra, 1994). By adolescence, these youngsters are firmly established in delinquent or antisocial behavior, with friends drawn almost exclusively from among other delinquent teens (Tremblay et al., 1995). They are also highly likely to display a whole cluster of other problem behavior, including drug and alcohol use, truancy or dropping out of school, and early and risky sexual behavior, including multiple sexual partners (Dishion, French, & Patterson, 1995).

For young people whose delinquency appears first in adolescence, the pathway is different. These seem to be primarily young people whose parents provide insufficient monitoring, whose individual friendships are not very supportive or intimate, and who are drawn to a clique or crowd that includes some teens who are experimenting with drugs or mild lawbreaking. After a period of months of hanging out with such a group of peers, this particular subgroup of previously nondelinquent kids show some increase in risky or antisocial behaviors, such as increased drug-taking (Berndt & Keefe, 1995a; Dishion et al., 1995; Steinberg, Fletcher, & Darling, 1994). But parents continue to have an important role in this process: When parents *do* provide good monitoring and emotional support for their teenager, the adolescent is unlikely to get involved in delinquent acts or drug use even if she hangs around with a tougher crowd or has a close friend who engages in such behavior (Brown & Huang, 1995; Mounts & Steinberg, 1995).

Thus adolescent-onset delinquency reflects a type of peer pressure, a finding that confirms the assumption by many adults that kids would be okay if they just didn't fall in with "bad companions." But let us be very careful about making too broad a claim about the effect of adolescent peer groups in seducing young people into delinquency. First, as I have already said, among *early*-onset delinquents there is no "seduction" into bad behavior; the teenager who is already deviant chooses to hang out with other deviant kids. Collectively, these kids then reinforce one another's delinquent behavior. Second, the majority of initially nondelinquent teens become involved with *non*delinquent peer groups, which continue to reinforce *non*delinquency. Only a subgroup is "lured" into significant delinquency or misbehavior by contact with "bad companions," and kids in this subgroup are already subtly different before they hit adolescence. Their early behavior is not overtly deviant, as is the case with the early-onset delinquents, but they seem to lack the kind of skills in friendship-making that would help to buffer them from the effects of peer pressure (Berndt & Keefe, 1995a). And very often they have parents who do not provide adequate supervision or monitoring. So it is only the minority whose behavior is negatively influenced by a crowd that encourages and reinforces disruptive or risky behavior.

Pathways and Trajectories

One way to conceptualize these variations among teens is in terms of "pathways" through adolescence. Bruce Compas and his colleagues (Compas et al., 1995) have provided a very useful visual model to describe such pathways, shown in Figure 12.5. Path 1 in this model describes the young person who sails through adolescence with

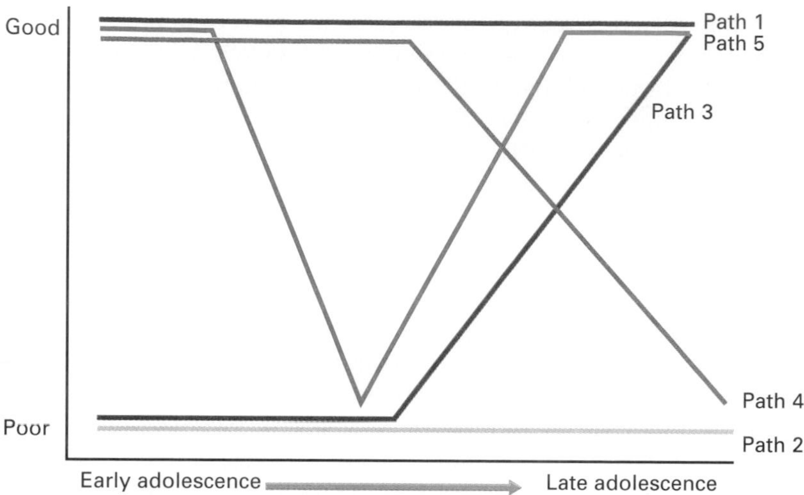

FIGURE 12.5 Five paths through adolescence. The majority of teens follow paths 1 and 2; a smaller number shows significant change during the adolescent years. (*Source:* Compas, Hinden, & Gerhardt, 1995, Figure 1, p. 272.)

little depression or delinquency, with supportive friendships and decent academic success. These youths most often come from low-risk environments. On the other end of the continuum is path 2, which describes a consistently *poor* adaptation. This group includes the early-onset delinquents as well as some young people who enter adolescence with poor self-esteem and relatively high levels of depression, and who tend to persist in those patterns.

The remaining three paths all involve change of some type during adolescence. Path 3 describes a turnaround or recovery from some previous negative pattern. This might happen because of a new relationship with a particularly attentive and helpful teacher; for some, military service in the late teens provides a kind of "recovery" experience (Elder, 1986). Path 4 is the reverse—a decline in functioning during adolescence that is not presaged by problems at earlier ages and that seems to persist. Such loss of competency or adequate functioning may occur because of some major upheaval in the child's family; in some cases it can be triggered by genetic effects that do not "turn on" until adolescence, such as some forms of schizophrenia (Rutter & Rutter, 1993). Finally, path 5 describes a pattern of temporary deviance, often reflecting short-term experimentation with risk-taking behaviors or delinquent acts that is not embedded in a broader pattern of deviance (Moffitt, 1993)—precisely the group I was just talking about.

I cannot tell you how many teenagers follow each of these five paths. Answering such a question obviously requires large-scale, long-term longitudinal studies, of which we have very few. What we do know is that the stable pathways (paths 1 and 2) are more common than the unstable ones. Thus, although adolescence is a time of change for virtually all teens—changes in body, form of thinking, identity, and social relationships—the majority of young people respond to the special demands of this period of life in a way that is consistent with their earlier patterns. Competent and secure young people are not typically thrown off course by adolescence. When we see deviant behavior in adolescence, it nearly always has roots in earlier developmental periods.

The Impact of the Larger Society

All the changes of adolescence occur against the backdrop of the larger culture or society in which the teenager lives. Adolescents in most Western countries continue to watch several hours of television a day; cultural values and specific habits and attitudes are all communicated through this medium. The broad economic climate also affects families, in turn affecting teenagers. For example, high school students in families that experience significant new economic hardships are more likely to be depressed, to use drugs, or be delinquent than are youngsters from less economically pressed families (Lempers & Clark-Lempers, 1990).

For many youngsters in the United States, however, a new point of contact with the larger culture is added during adolescence: a job.

Joining the Work World

In earlier historical eras (and in many cultures around the world today), teenagers already fulfilled normal adult work responsibilities. They worked in the mines and in the fields, herded animals, and fished. Child labor laws changed this picture drastically in the nineteenth century in most industrialized countries. Today, adolescents are in school for many hours each day and are not available for adult work. Yet increasingly, adolescents have jobs. In the United States, teenage employment rates have risen steadily since the 1950s. Today, roughly three-fifths of all high school juniors have some kind of formal part-time job during at least part of the school year and the great majority of students have had at least some work experience before they graduate (Bachman & Schulenberg, 1993).

For some, work is an economic necessity. Others work to earn money for college or to support their favorite hobbies or habits—a car, pizza with friends, or whatever. Parents are often very supportive of such work on the grounds that it "builds character" and teaches young people about "real life." Here's one parental voice:

> Let's face it . . . sometime in life, someone is going to tell you what to do. . . . I think work is the only place to learn to deal with it. . . . Parents can give you a little discipline, but it isn't accepted. . . . You can't learn that in school, because there is another so-called tyrant, the teacher. But then they get . . . a boss, and you get out there and learn it. (Greenberger & Steinberg, 1986, p. 39)

Most teenage jobs are in low-level, low-responsibility, low-paying jobs like this one. Rather than teaching character and good work habits, as many parents suppose, such part-time work is linked to poorer school performance and higher delinquency and drug use.

But are parents right about such beneficial effects of work? Does it really teach responsibility and reliability? Maybe, but maybe not. Results of several decades of research on students in the United States give us mixed answers.

The Pessimistic View. On the pessimistic side we find several major studies suggesting that the more hours adolescents work, the more *negative* the consequences are. In the largest single study, Jerald Bachman and John Schulenberg (1993) accumulated information from more than 70,000 students, seniors in the graduating classes of 1985 through 1989. Subjects were drawn each year from both private and public schools in every state in the country. Roughly four-fifths of the students worked at least a few hours per week, most of them for pay. Nearly half of the boys (46.5 percent) and more than a third of the girls (38.4 percent) worked more than 20 hours per week.

Bachman and Schulenberg found that the more hours a student worked, the more he (or she) used drugs (alcohol, cigarettes, marijuana, cocaine), the more aggression he showed toward peers, the more arguments he had with parents, the less sleep he got, the less often he ate breakfast, the less exercise he had, and the less satisfied he was with life. An impressive list of negatives, isn't it?

The second major piece of pessimistic evidence comes from a study with which you are very familiar by now—the Steinberg and Dornbusch study of Wisconsin and California teens (1991; Steinberg, Fegley, & Dornbusch, 1993). They have employment information from 5300 of their sample of ninth- to twelfth-graders, data collected in 1987 and 1988. Like Bachman and Schulenberg, they find that work has a variety of negative effects on teenagers, including lower school grades and weaker commitment to school.

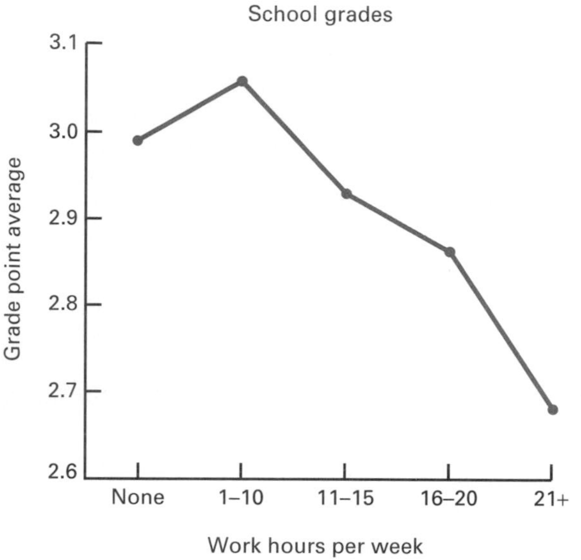

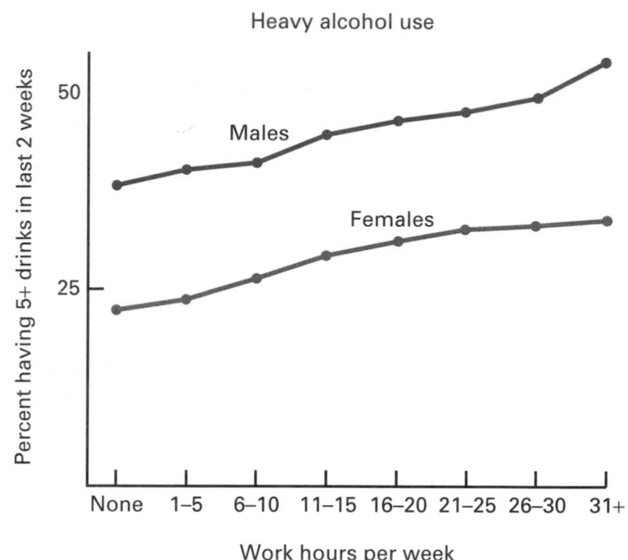

FIGURE 12.6 Evidence for the negative effect of teenage employment: Data on the left come from Steinberg and Dornbusch's study; data on the right come from Bachman and Schulenberg. (*Sources:* Steinberg & Dornbusch, 1991, from Figure 1, p. 308; Bachman & Schulenberg, 1993, from Figure 1, p. 226.)

Figure 12.6 gives one finding from each of these studies, so you can see the size of the effects. I should note, by the way, that Steinberg and Dornbusch found essentially the same pattern of results for all the ethnic groups in their study, and for students from every economic level. So this is a widespread and significant effect.

At this point, some of you are undoubtedly thinking that results like those in Figure 12.6 may not mean that working during the high school years *causes* bad effects. Instead, the findings might reflect self-selection: Those students who are least interested in school and who already hang out with others who smoke or drink more may be the same ones who choose to work more. In fact, Bachman and Schulenberg's data are consistent with such an interpretation. They find that those high school seniors who are getting the best grades and who are planning to go on to college are least likely to work. But that is still correlational evidence and doesn't solve the problem. Steinberg and his colleagues are able to help unravel these two factors because they have longitudinal data. They found that those who later worked 20 hours a week had indeed been less involved with or committed to school in earlier years, which illustrates the effect of self-selection. But these same students became even *more* withdrawn from school and showed not only increases in drug use and delinquency but a *decline* in self-reliance after they began working.

The Optimistic View. A quite different answer to the question of the impact of teenage employment comes from a recent study by Jeylan Mortimer and her colleagues (1995), who have studied a group of more than 1000 students from Minnesota, following them from ninth through twelfth grades. She finds that over these years, teenagers work more and more hours and their work becomes somewhat more complex. She also finds no correlation between the number of hours students work and their school grades or risk for problem behavior—with the exception of alcohol use, which is higher among those students who work more. What mattered more than work per se, in this group of young people, was the quality of work they were doing. Students who had positive work experiences developed increased feelings of competence and efficacy; those students who saw themselves gaining useful skills through their work also seemed to develop that constellation of work-related values and attitudes that most adults mean when they say that work "builds character."

Critical Thinking

What was your own work experience as a teenager? What lessons do you think you learned from that work, if any? In light of your own experience and the data from these studies, would you want your own children to work when they are teenagers?

It is not clear how we should add up the results of these several studies. One possible resolution is suggested by Kristelle Miller (Miller & Pedersen-Randall, 1995), who finds that only work on weekdays, and *not* weekend work, has a detrimental effect on high school students' grades. This suggests the hypothesis that work is academically detrimental to the extent that it distracts young people from academic tasks. Even Mortimer's findings are consistent with this. In her study, the employed eleventh- and twelfth-graders often said that the time on the job made it hard to get homework done and meant they often came to school tired. On the other hand, Mortimer is probably right that the quality of work is a critical ingredient in the equation. Low-skilled work that affords little opportunity for independence and little chance to learn long-term job skills is much more likely to be associated with poor outcomes than is complex, skilled work.

Collectively, these findings are a good illustration of why it is so very difficult to arrive at clear social policy recommendations. At the very least, however, this mixture of results should make parents think twice before they (we) encourage teenagers to work 15 or 20 hours a week.

Summary

1. Self-definitions become increasingly abstract at adolescence, with more emphasis on enduring, internal qualities and ideology.
2. Teenagers also increasingly define themselves in terms that include both masculine and feminine traits. When both are high, the individual is described as androgynous. High levels of androgyny are associated with higher self-esteem in both male and female adolescents.
3. Erikson emphasized that adolescents must go through a crisis and a redefinition of the self. Many adolescents clearly do so, but we do not know whether all do.
4. Young people of color or those in clearly identifiable minority groups have the additional task in adolescence of forming an ethnic identity, a process that appears to have several steps analogous to Marcia's model of identity formation.
5. Self-esteem drops somewhat at the beginning of adolescence, and then rises steadily through the teen years.
6. Concepts of relationships also undergo change, becoming more flexible, more shaded. Friendships are increasingly seen as adaptive and changeable.
7. Adolescent-parent interactions typically become somewhat more conflicted in early adolescence, possibly linked to the physical changes of puberty. But the attachment to parents remains strong.
8. Authoritative family interactions continue to be the optimal pattern at adolescence. Teenagers in such families are more self-reliant, use fewer drugs, and have higher self-esteem than do those in neglecting or authoritative families.
9. The parents' remarriage during the child's adolescence appears to have a more negative effect for girls than for boys.
10. Peer relationships become increasingly important, both quantitatively and qualitatively. Theorists emphasize that peers serve an important function as a bridge between the dependence of childhood and the independence of adulthood.
11. Reputation-based groups, called "crowds" by current researchers, are an important part of adolescent social relationships, particularly in the early high school years. Smaller groups of friends, called "cliques," are also present and gradually shift from same-sex to mixed-sex to dating pairs.
12. Susceptibility to peer group pressure appears to be at its peak at about age 13 or 14, but peer pressure is as often away from deviant behavior as toward it, and individual teens vary considerably in their susceptibility to such pressure.
13. On average in Western cultures, dating begins at about age 15, but there is wide variability.
14. Researchers studying adult personality have agreed on a set of five dimensions (the Big Five) that capture most of the variation among individuals: extraversion, agreeableness, conscientiousness, neuroticism, and openness/intellect.
15. Recent research suggests that the same five dimensions may give us an accurate picture of variations in adolescent personality as well.
16. Rates of depression increase sharply at adolescence, and are higher among girls than boys. Depressed teens are more likely to come from families with at least one depressed parent, but there are other pathways, including poor peer acceptance in elementary school, low self-esteem, and high levels of life change or stress at adolescence.
17. Delinquent acts also increase at adolescence, especially among boys. Early-onset delinquency and adolescent-onset delinquency have quite different causes and patterns.

18. Part-time employment by teenagers has become very common. Most—but not all—researchers find that such work is associated with lower school performance and higher rates of delinquent behavior. An exception may exist when the specific work is interesting and provides real skill training.

Key Terms

agreeableness
Big Five
clinical depression
clique
conscientiousness
crowd
extraversion
foreclosure
identity achievement
identity diffusion
moratorium
neuroticism
openness/intellect

Suggested Readings

Adams, G. R., Gullotta, T. P., Montemayor, R. (Eds.) (1992). *Adolescent identity formation*. Newbury Park, CA: Sage.

One of a series of excellent books on facets of adolescence edited by these same three psychologists. It includes a discussion of the Erikson/Marcia view of identity by Waterman, as well as Phinney's paper on ethnic identity.

Crockett, L. J., & Crouter, A. C. (Eds.) (1995). *Pathways through adolescence*. Mahwah, NJ: Lawrence Erlbaum Associates.

Another excellent collection of papers on adolescence, written by many of the current leading researchers.

Eron, L. D., Gentry, J. H., & Schlegel, P. (Eds.) (1994). *Reason to hope: A psychological perspective on violence and youth*. Washington, DC: American Psychological Association.

A comprehensive discussion of what we know about the causes, consequences, and possible cures of youth violence.

Montemayor, R., Adams, R. G., & Gullotta (Eds.) (1994). *Personal relationships during adolescence*. Thousand Oaks, CA: Sage.

A first-rate collection of papers, including an especially fascinating discussion of teen crowds by Bradford Brown.

Petersen, A. C., Compas, B. C., Brooks-Gunn, J., Stemmler, M., Ey, S., & Grant, K. E. (1993). Depression in adolescence. *American Psychologist, 48*, 155–68.

A brief, fairly dense review of the most current information on this important subject.

Interlude 4

Summing Up Adolescent Development

Basic Characteristics of Adolescence

A number of experts on adolescence argue that it makes sense to divide the period of years from 12 to about 20 into two subperiods, one beginning at 11 or 12, the other perhaps at 16 or 17, a categorization I have followed in the summary table. Some label these as *adolescence* and *youth* (Keniston, 1970), others as *early* and *late* adolescence (e.g., Brooks-Gunn, 1988). However we label them, there are distinct differences.

Early adolescence is, almost by definition, a time of transition, in which significant change occurs in virtually every aspect of the child's functioning. Late adolescence is more a time of consolidation, when the young person establishes a cohesive new identity, with clearer goals and role commitments. Norma Haan (1981a), borrowing Piaget's concepts, suggests that early adolescence is dominated by assimilation, while late adolescence is primarily a time of accommodation.

The 12- or 13-year-old is assimilating an enormous amount of new physical, social, and intellectual experiences. While all this absorption is going on, but before it is digested, the young person is in a more or less perpetual state of disequilibrium. Old patterns, old schemes, no longer work very well, but new ones have not yet been established. It is during this early period that the peer group is so centrally important. Ultimately, the 16- or 17- or 18-year-old begins to make the needed accommodations, pulls the threads together and establishes a new identity, new patterns of social relationships, new goals and roles.

Early Adolescence

In some ways the early years of adolescence have a lot in common with the early years of toddlerhood. Two-year-olds are famous for their negativism and for their constant push for more independence. At the same time they are struggling to learn a vast array of new skills. Teenagers show many of these same qualities, albeit at much more abstract levels. Many of them go through a period of negativism right at the beginning of the pubertal changes, particularly with parents. And many of the conflicts with parents center on issues of independence—they want to come and go when they please, listen to the music they prefer at maximum volume, and wear the clothing and hairstyles that are "in."

As with the negativism of the 2-year-old, it is easy to overstate the depth or breadth of the conflict between young teenagers and their parents. It is important to keep in mind that we are not talking here about major turmoil, but only a temporary increase in disagreements or disputes. The depiction of adolescence as full of *Sturm und Drang* is as much an exaggeration as is the phrase *terrible twos.* But both ages are characterized by a new push for independence that is inevitably accompanied by more confrontations with parents over limits.

While this push for independence is going on, the young adolescent is also facing a whole new set of demands and skills to be learned—new social skills, new and more complex school tasks, and the need to form an adult identity. The sharp increases in the rate of depression (especially among girls) and the drop in self-esteem we see at the beginning of adolescence seem to be linked to this surplus of new demands and changes. A number of investigators have found that those adolescents who have the greatest number of simultaneous changes at the beginning of puberty—changing to junior high school, moving to a new town or new house, perhaps a parental separation or divorce—also show the greatest loss in self-esteem, the largest rise in problem behavior, and the biggest drop in grade point average (Simmons, Burgeson, & Reef, 1988). Young adolescents who can cope with these changes one at a time, as when the youngster remains in the same school through eighth or ninth grade before shifting to junior or senior high school, show fewer symptoms of stress.

Facing major stressful demands, the 2-year-old uses Mom (or some other central attachment figure) as a safe base for exploring the world, returning for reassurance when fearful. Young adolescents seem to do the same with the family, using it as a safe base from which to explore the rest of the world, including the world of peer relationships. Parents

A Summary of the Threads of Development During Early and Late Adolescence

Aspect of Development	Age in Years: 12	13	14	15	16	17	18	19+
	Early Adolescence				Late Adolescence (Youth)			
Physical development	Major pubertal change begins for boys		Boys' height spurt				Puberty completed for boys	
	Girls' height spurt	Average age of menarche			Puberty completed for girls			
Cognitive development	Beginning formal operations: systematic analysis; some deductive logic				Consolidated formal operations (for some)			
	Kohlberg's stage 3 ("good boy, nice girl" orientation) continues to dominate							
				Kohlberg's stage 4 ("law and order") for a few				
		Descriptions of self and others begin to include exceptions, comparisons, special conditions; deeper personality traits						
Personality and social development	Self-esteem declines	Self-esteem begins to rise and continues to rise for remainder of adolescence						
	Rate of depression rises sharply and remains high						Clear identity achievement for perhaps half	
	Erikson's stage of identity vs. role diffusion							
	Parent-child conflict peaks at beginning of puberty		Maximum impact of peer group pressure	Normal time for first dating				

of young adolescents must try to find a difficult balance between providing the needed security, often in the form of clear rules and limits, and still allowing independence—just as the parent of a 2-year-old must walk the fine line between allowing exploration and keeping the child safe. Among teenagers, as among toddlers, the most confident and successful are those whose families manage this balancing act well.

Still a third way in which theorists have likened the young teenager to the 2-year-old is in egocentrism. David Elkind (1967) suggested some years ago that egocentrism rises in adolescence. This new egocentrism, according to Elkind, has two facets: (1) The belief that "others in our immediate vicinity are as concerned with our thoughts and behavior as we ourselves are" (Elkind & Bowen, 1979, p. 38), which Elkind describes as having an *imaginary audience;* and (2) the possession of a *personal fable,* a tendency to consider their own ideas and feelings unique and singularly important. This is typically accompanied by a sense of invulnerability—a feeling that may lie behind the adolescent's apparent attraction to high-risk behavior, such as unprotected sex, drugs, drinking, high-speed driving, and the like (Arnett, 1995).

Elkind's own research (Elkind &

Bowen, 1979) shows that preoccupation with others' views of the self (imaginary audience behavior) peaks at about age 13 to 14. Teenagers this age are most likely to say that if they went to a party where they did not know most of the kids, they would wonder *a lot* about what the other kids were thinking of them. They also report that they worry a lot when someone is watching them work, and feel desperately embarrassed if they discover a grease spot on their clothes, or have newly erupted pimples. Of course younger children and adults may also worry about these things, but they seem to be much less disturbed or immobilized by these worries than are 13- and 14-year-olds—an age when the dominance of the peer crowd or clique is at its peak.

Drawing a parallel between the early adolescent and the toddler makes sense in that both age groups face the task of establishing a separate identity. The toddler must separate herself from the symbiotic relationship with Mom or central caregiver. She must figure out not only that she is separate but that she has abilities and qualities. Physical maturation also allows her new levels of independent exploration. The young adolescent must separate himself from his family, and from his identity as a child, and begin to form a new identity as an adult. This, too, is accompanied by major maturational changes that make possible new levels and kinds of independence.

Late Adolescence

To carry the basic analogy further, late adolescence is more like the preschool years. Major changes have been weathered and a new balance has been achieved. The physical upheavals of puberty are mostly complete, the family system has changed to allow the young person more independence and freedom, and the beginnings of a new identity have been created. This period is not without its strains. For most young people, a clear identity is not achieved until college age, if then, so the identity-formation process continues. And the task of forming emotionally intimate sexual or presexual partnerships is a key task of late adolescence. Nonetheless, I think Haan is correct about this later period being more one of accommodation than assimilation. At the very least we know that it is accompanied by rising levels of self-esteem and declining levels of family confrontation or conflict.

Central Processes and Their Connections

In other interludes, I have suggested that changes in one or another of the facets of development may be central to the constellation of transformations we see at a given age. In infancy, underlying physiological change along with the creation of a first central attachment appear to have such key causal roles; in the preschool years, cognitive changes seem especially dominant, while among school-age children, both cognitive and social changes appear to be formative. In adolescence, *every* domain shows significant change. At this point, we simply do not have the research data to clarify the basic causal connections among the transformations in these various areas. Still, we have *some* information about linkages.

The Role of Puberty

The most obvious place to begin is with puberty itself. Puberty not only defines the beginning of early adolescence, it clearly affects all other facets of the young person's development, either directly or indirectly.

Direct effects might be seen in several ways. Most clearly, the surges of pubertal hormones stimulate sexual interest while they also trigger body changes that make adult sexuality and fertility possible. These changes seem inescapably causally linked to the gradual shift (for the great majority of teens) from same-sex peer groupings to heterosexual crowds and finally to heterosexual pair relationships.

Hormones and Family Relationships. Hormone changes may also be directly implicated in the increases in confrontation or conflict between parents and children, and the rise in various kinds of aggressive or delinquent behavior. Steinberg's research suggests such a direct link because he finds pubertal stage and not age to be the critical variable in predicting the level of adolescent-parent conflict. Other investigators have found that in girls, the rise in estradiol at the beginning of puberty is associated with increases in verbal aggression and a loss of impulse control, while in boys, increases in testosterone are correlated with increases in irritability and impatience (Paikoff & Brooks-Gunn, 1990). But many studies find no such connection (e.g., Coe, Hayashi, & Levine, 1988), which has led most theorists to conclude that the connections between pubertal hormones and changes in adolescent social behavior are considerably more complicated than we had first imagined.

One of the complications is that the physical changes of puberty have highly significant indirect effects as well. When the child's body grows and becomes more like that of an adult, the parents begin to treat the child differently and the child begins to see himself as a soon-to-be-adult. Both of these changes may be linked to the brief rise in parent-adolescent confrontation and may help to trigger some of the searching self-examinations that are part of this period of life.

The adolescent's pubertal changes also require other adaptations from the parents that change the family dynamics. It can be very confusing to parents to deal with a young teenager who seems, simultaneously, to demand both more independence, authority, and power, and more nurturance and guidance. What is more, the presence of a sexually charged pubescent teen may reawaken the parents' own unresolved adolescent issues, just when they are themselves facing a sense of physical decline in their 40s or 50s. Then, too, teenagers may stay up late, severely restricting private time for parents. Perhaps, then, it is not surprising that many parents (particularly fathers) report that marital satisfaction is at its lowest ebb during their children's adolescence (Glenn, 1990). Taking all this together, you can see why it is so difficult to sort out the direct and the indirect effects of pubertal hormone changes on social behavior.

Puberty and Cognitive Change. Physiological changes may also play some role in the shift to formal operations. We have some indication, for example, that a second major synaptic and dendritic "pruning" occurs at adolescence. At the same time, any link between formal operational thinking and pubertal change cannot be inevitable, because we know that all adolescents experience puberty but not all make the transition to formal operations. The best guess at the moment is that neurological or hormonal changes at adolescence may be *necessary* for further cognitive gains, but they cannot be *sufficient* conditions for such developments.

The Role of Cognitive Changes

An equally attractive possibility to many theorists has been the proposition that it is the cognitive changes that are central. The cognitive shift from concrete to formal operations obviously does not cause pubertal changes, but cognitive development may be central to many of the other changes we see at adolescence, including changes in the self-concept, the process of identity formation, increases in level of moral reasoning, and changes in peer relationship.

There is ample evidence, for example, that the greater abstractness of the child's self-concept and of her descriptions of others are intimately connected to the broader changes in cognitive functioning (Harter, 1990). The emergence of concrete operations at 7 or 8 is reflected in the child's use of trait labels to describe herself and others; the emergence of formal operations is reflected in self-descriptions that focus more and more on interior states, and descriptions of others that are both flexible and based on subtle inferences from behavior.

A somewhat broader proposal about connections between cognitive and other changes at adolescence comes from Kohlberg (1973, 1976). He hypothesized that the child first moves to a new level of logical thought, then applies this new kind of logic to relationships as well as objects, and only then applies this thinking to moral problems. More specifically, Kohlberg argued that at least some formal operations and at least some mutual perspective taking in relationships are necessary (but not sufficient) for the emergence of conventional moral reasoning. Full formal operations and still more abstract social understanding may be required for postconventional reasoning.

The research examining such a sequential development is scant, but it supports Kohlberg's hypothesis. Lawrence Walker (1980) found that among a group of fourth- to seventh-graders he had tested on all three dimensions (concrete and formal operations, social understanding, and moral reasoning), half to two-thirds were reasoning at the same level across the different domains, which makes the whole thing look unexpectedly stagelike. When a child was ahead in one progression, the sequence was always that the child developed logical thinking first, then more advanced social understanding, and then the parallel moral judgments. Thus, a young person still using concrete operations is unlikely to use postconventional moral reasoning. But the coherence is not automatic. The basic cognitive understanding makes advances in social and moral reasoning *possible,* but does not guarantee them. Experience in relationships, and with moral dilemmas, is necessary too.

One moral of this (if you will excuse the pun) is that just because a young person or adult shows signs of formal operations does *not* necessarily mean that he or she will show sensitive, empathetic, and forgiving attitudes toward friends or family. It's a point worth keeping in mind. . . .

Some ability to use formal operations may also be necessary but not sufficient for the formation of a clear identity. One of the characteristics of formal operations thinking is the ability to imagine possibilities that you have never experienced and to manipulate ideas in your head. These new skills may help to foster the broad questioning of old ways, old values, and old patterns that are a central part of the identity-formation process. Several studies show that among high school and college students, those in Marcia's identity achievement or moratorium statuses are much more likely also to be using formal operations reasoning than are those in the diffusion or foreclosure statuses (e.g., Leadbeater & Dionne, 1981; Rowe & Marcia, 1980). In Rowe and Marcia's study, the *only* individuals who showed full identity achievement were those who were also using full formal operations. But the converse was not true. That is, there were a number of subjects who used formal operations but who had not yet established a clear identity. Thus, formal operations thinking may *enable* the young person to rethink many aspects of his life, but it does not guarantee that he will do so.

Overall, we are left with the impression that both the physical changes of puberty and the potential cognitive changes of formal operations are central to the phenomena of adolescence, but the connections between them and their impact on social behavior are still largely a mystery. I know it is frustrating to have me keep saying that we don't know, but that's an accurate statement of our current knowledge.

Influences on the Basic Processes

I do not have space enough to detail all the many factors that will influence the teenager's experience of adolescence.

Many I have already mentioned, including such cultural variations as the presence or absence of initiation rites, the timing of the child's pubertal development, and the degree of personal or familial stress.

But one more general point is worth repeating: Adolescence, like every other developmental period, does not begin with a clean slate. The individual youngster's own temperamental qualities, behavioral habits, and internal models of interaction, established in earlier years of childhood, obviously have a profound effect on the experience of adolescence. Examples are easy to find.

- Sroufe's longitudinal study, which I described in Chapter 6 (Sroufe, 1989), shows that those who had been rated as having a secure attachment in infancy were more self-confident and more socially competent with peers at the beginning of adolescence.
- Delinquency and heightened aggressiveness in adolescence are most often presaged by earlier behavior problems, and by inadequate family control as early as the years of toddlerhood (Dishion, French, & Patterson, 1995). Even those delinquents who show such antisocial behavior for the first time as teenagers enter adolescence with different qualities, including poorer-quality friendships (Berndt & Keefe, 1995a).
- Depression in adolescents is more likely among those who enter adolescence with lower self-esteem (Harter, 1987).

Avshalom Caspi and Terrie Moffitt (1991) make the more general point that *any* major life crisis or transition, including adolescence, has the effect of *accentuating* earlier personality or behavioral patterns rather than creating new ones. This is not unlike the observation that the child's attachment to the parent is only revealed when the child is under stress. As one example of the more general process, Caspi and Moffitt point out that girls with very early puberty, on average, have higher rates of psychological problems than do those with normal-time puberty. But closer analysis reveals that it is only the early-puberty girls who already had social problems before puberty whose pubertal experience and adolescence is more negative. Very early puberty does not increase psychological problems for girls who were psychologically healthier to begin with.

I think this is an important point for understanding the various transitions of adult life as well as adolescence. Not only do we carry ourselves with us as we move through the roles and demands of adult life, but existing patterns may be most highly visible when we are under stress. This does not mean that we never change or learn new and more effective ways of responding. But we must never lose sight of the fact that by adolescence, and certainly by adulthood, our internal working models and our repertoire of coping behaviors are already established, creating a bias in the system. Another way of putting it is that while change is possible, continuity is the default option.

Physical and Cognitive Development in Early Adulthood 13

Because I started college when I was a bit younger than normal and finished my Ph.D. quite early, for most of my 20s and 30s I was "off time." When I took my first academic position as an assistant professor, I was younger than most of the graduate students, and for the succeeding 10 years I was often the youngest person—and frequently the only woman—in groups of professional colleagues. I came to think of myself as a "young Turk." So it was a particular shock as my 40s approached to realize that I was nearing what I thought of as middle age.

Critical Thinking

When you think about adult life, do you mentally divide it into segments of some kind? Where are the break points in your own mind? When does "middle age" start? When does "old age" begin? Do you think that your expectations or definitions are likely to have any effect on how you interpret the experiences in your life?

No doubt each of us has our own definition of a "young adult," or of "middle age" or "old age." These definitions not only change over historical time, they may differ from one subgroup to another. Even social scientists have not reached clear agreement on how we should divide up the years of adulthood. Physical and cognitive change in adulthood is more gradual and *far* more variable from one individual to the next than is true in childhood. So it is not so obvious how we ought to divide up the years. Most gerontologists today mark a major dividing line at about 60 or 65, the age at which most adults in industrialized countries retire from paid work (although as you'll recall from Chapter 2, it is now customary to subdivide this group of elders still further into the *young old*, 60 to 75; the *old old*, 75 to 85; and the *oldest old*, 85 and up). But dividing at 60 or 65 still leaves us with a huge block of years from 20 to 60. How should we divide up this span? The most commonly used dividing point is at about 40 or 45, a choice justified on any of several grounds.

- It divides the adult years into three roughly equal parts: early adulthood from 20 to 40, middle adulthood from 40 to about 65, and late adulthood from 65 until death.
- It reflects a set of role changes that often (but not always) occur in the early 40s, when children begin to leave home and careers typically reach their peak.
- It reflects the fact that optimum physical and cognitive functioning, clearly present in one's 20s and 30s, begins to wane in some noticeable and measurable ways in the 40s and 50s. The slope of change may be very gradual, but it is clearly moving downward after age 40. This results not only in an increase in disease and disability rates, but also in an increased *awareness* of physical decline in one's 40s.

For all these reasons, I will follow this common usage and define "young adulthood" as the period from 20 to 40. But you should remember, always, that this is an arbitrary division. Adulthood, far more than childhood, is marked by *wide* variability in the timing of many defining events and by very gradual change in many key physical and mental abilities.

It's hard to define a clear demarcation point between "early adulthood" and "middle adulthood" because the physical and mental changes are so gradual; even at 30, adults may find that it takes a bit more work to get into or stay in shape than it did at 20.

Maturation and Aging

Another way in which the study of adults differs from the study of children has to do with the role of maturation and the other forms of shared change I talked about in Chapter 1. For one thing, when we study children's development, we are looking at increases, at improvements. When we study adults, especially when we study their physical and cognitive functioning, we begin to ask questions about loss of function or decline. Can we use the same theoretical models, the same ways of thinking and analyzing, to study decline that we use to study increases?

Answers to such questions are influenced by just how one defines development. A child's development has clear direction and order. The baby goes from sitting to crawling to walking; the adolescent moves through the steps of pubertal change; the child moves cognitively from concrete to abstract, from egocentric to relational. We can also agree that physical maturation forms the substrate of many of these developmental changes. But we have much less agreement about whether changes over the adult years can or should be described as *development* in the same sense.

Certainly there are widely (but not universally) shared role changes in adult life, many of which occur in early adulthood. But is there any direction, any pattern, to the changes we see in adults that we might reasonably think of as development? Do people get smarter, wiser, more stable, or slower as they age? And in all this, what role does maturation play?

On the face of it, it seems obvious that there are shared, inevitable physical changes in adulthood, normally referred to as *aging*, all of which seem self-evidently maturational in nature. I look at myself in the mirror and can readily see such changes. My hair has been white since my middle 30s, so that seems not so strikingly different to me. But my middle-50s face now has many more lines and a bit of droop here and there. Many of us past the age of 40 believe we can detect similar changes in our thinking: It seems to take longer to remember names; learning new things seems to take more time and effort.

Physiologists and psychologists do not dispute these observations; there *is* a biological clock and it clearly ticks more and more loudly as one moves through adult life. But recent research is beginning to tell us that some of what we have attributed to inevitable physical aging may have other causes, including disease and disuse. At the heart of the question is a methodological dilemma.

How Do We Study Physical Aging? Suppose we want to know something about changes in heart or lung function over the years of adulthood. What happens to blood pressure, or aerobic capacity, or the heart's ability to pump blood? Do these systems change in inevitable ways as we get older?

Data from cross-sectional studies seem to answer "yes" to this question. Such research shows that the older the adult, the less efficient the heart and the lower the capacity for taking in and transmitting oxygen. But such comparisons have a built-in difficulty: We also know that older adults are more likely to suffer from heart *disease*. So each succeeding age group in random cross-sectional samples will have a larger and larger proportion of subjects who suffer from heart disease (e.g., Christensen et al., 1992). So how much of the "change" in heart function we see in cross-sectional comparisons is really "aging," and how much is simply the presence of more disease?

Longitudinal research will not help in this case. If we started with a random group of 20-year-olds and measured their heart and lung function every 10 years for 60 years, it would still be the case that at each succeeding testing point a larger percentage of the subjects would be suffering from heart disease.

We know that heart disease itself is *not* a normal part of aging, because not everyone shows this disease process. So if we want to get some sense of the basic, underlying, inevitable aging process, uncomplicated by disease (called **primary aging** by most developmentalists [Birren & Schroots, 1996]), we need to study adults who are disease-free.

Secondary aging, in contrast, is the product of environmental influences, health habits, or disease, and is neither inevitable nor shared by all adults. Indeed, some aspects of secondary aging may be reversible. The growing body of research on healthy adults suggests that primary aging is both slower and later than many of us had supposed. And some changes we thought were part of primary aging may turn out to be secondary aging.

I am not trying to create a picture of rosy optimism. The sands do indeed fall through the hourglass; death does come to us all. But it is important to try to sort out which changes are primary and which are secondary, if only because secondary aging processes are often preventable. The distinction is important even when we look at physical and cognitive functioning in early adulthood, when performance is at its peak by any measure. The newer research points to the possibility that the advantage enjoyed by young adults may be smaller than we had thought. With that background in mind, let's look at some of the evidence.

Physical Functioning

By early adulthood, physical growth is largely complete and the body is clearly at its peak. Young adults perform better than do the middle-aged or old on virtually every physical measure. The adult in her 20s and 30s has more muscle tissue; maximum calcium in her bones; more brain mass; better eyesight, hearing, and sense of smell; greater oxygen capacity; and a more efficient immune system. She is stronger, faster, and better able to recover from exercise or to adapt to changing conditions such as alterations in temperature or light levels.

After this early peak, we see a gradual decline on almost every measure of physical functioning through the years of adulthood. I'll be talking about a number of these individual changes in more detail in Chapters 15 and 17, when I talk about the physical status of middle-aged and older adults. But to give you a sense of the overall shape and sweep of the differences, I've summarized them in Table 13.1.

Table 13.1 A Summary of Age Changes in Physical Functioning

Body Function	Age at Which Change Begins to Be Clear or Measurable	Nature of Change
Vision	Mid-40s	Lens of eye thickens and loses accommodative power, resulting in poorer near vision and more sensitivity to glare.
Hearing	50 or 60	Loss of ability to hear very high and very low tones.
Smell	About 40	Decline in ability to detect and discriminate among different smells.
Taste	None	No apparent loss in taste discrimination ability.
Muscles	About 50	Loss of muscle tissue, particularly in "fast twitch" fibers used for bursts of strength or speed.
Bones	Mid-30s; accelerated by menopause in women	Loss of calcium in the bones, called *osteoporosis.* Also wear and tear on bone joints, called *osteoarthritis,* more marked after about 60.
Heart and lungs	35 or 40	Most functions (such as aerobic capacity or cardiac output) do not show age changes *at rest,* but do show age changes during work or exercise.
Nervous system	Probably gradual throughout adulthood	Some loss (but not clear how much) of neurons in the brain; gradual reduction of density of dendrites; gradual decline of total brain volume and weight.
Immune system	Adolescence	Loss in size of thymus; reduction in number and maturity of T cells. Not clear how much of this change is due to stress and how much is primary aging.
Reproductive system	Mid-30s for women; about 40 for men.	Women: increased reproductive risk and lowered fertility, followed by menopause. Men: gradual decline in viable sperm beginning about age 40; very gradual decline in testosterone from early adulthood.
Cellular elasticity	Gradual	Gradual loss in most cells, including skin, muscle, tendon, and blood vessel cells. Faster deterioration in cells exposed to sunlight.
Height	40	Compression of disks in the spine, with resulting loss of height of 1 to 2 inches by age 80.
Weight	Nonlinear pattern	In U.S. studies, maximum weight in middle adulthood and then gradual decline in old age.
Skin	40	Increase in wrinkliness, due to loss of elasticity; oil-secreting glands become less efficient.
Hair	About 50	Becomes thinner and may gray.

Sources: Bartoshuk & Weiffenbach, 1990; Blatter et al., 1995; Braveman, 1987; Briggs, 1990; Brock, Guralnik, & Brody, 1990; Doty et al., 1984; Fiatarone & Evans, 1993; Fozard, 1990; Fozard, Metter, & Brant, 1990; Gray et al., 1991; Hallfrisch et al., 1990; Hayflick, 1994; Ivy et al., 1992; Kallman, Plato, & Tobin, 1990; Kline & Scialfa, 1996; Kozma, Stones, & Hannah, 1991; Lakatta, 1990; Lim et al., 1992; McFalls, 1990; Miller, 1990; Mundy, 1994; Scheibel, 1992, 1996; Shock et al., 1984; Weisse, 1992.

Bodies are at their peak in very early adulthood. These Texas college men are probably in better physical shape at this age, in their late teens or early 20s, than they will be at any later time in their lives.

Most of the summary statements in the table are based on both longitudinal and cross-sectional data; many are now based on studies that have controlled for the health of the subjects. So we can be reasonably confident that most of the age changes listed reflect *primary* aging and not secondary aging.

In the center column of the table I've suggested the age at which the degree of loss or decline reaches the point where the slowing or change becomes fairly readily apparent. Virtually all these changes begin in the period I'm calling early adulthood. But the early losses or declines are not typically noticeable in everyday physical functioning during these early years *except* when a person is attempting to operate at the absolute edge of physical ability. Among top athletes, for example, the very small losses of speed and strength that occur in the late 20s and 30s are highly significant, often dropping 25-year-olds or 30-year-olds out of the group of elite athletes—as you can see from the data reported in the Real World box. More ordinary folks, though, typically notice little or no drop in everyday physical functioning until middle age.

Another way to think of this is in terms of a balance between physical *demand* and physical *capacity*—what Alan Welford (1993) refers to as the *gerontological balance sheet*. In early adulthood almost all of us have ample physical capacity to meet the physical demands we encounter in everyday life. We can read the fine print in the telephone book without bifocals; we can carry heavy boxes or furniture when we move; our immune systems are strong enough to fight off most illnesses, and we recover quickly from sickness. As we move into middle adulthood, the balance sheet changes; we find more and more arenas in which our physical capacities no longer quite meet the demands. Let me give you a couple of more detailed examples.

Heart and Lungs. The most common measure of overall aerobic fitness is **maximum oxygen uptake (VO_2 max),** which reflects the ability of the body to take in and transport oxygen to various body organs. When this is measured at rest we find only minimal decrements associated with age. But when we measure VO_2 max during exercise (such as during a treadmill test) it shows a systematic decline with age of about 1 percent per year beginning at about age 35 or 40 (Goldberg, Dengel, & Hagberg, 1996). I've given some typical results from both cross-sectional and longitudi-

The Real World

Age and Peak Sports Performance

One of the most obvious ways to test the principle that human bodies are at their physical peak in early adulthood is to look at sports performances. Olympic athletes or other top world performers in any sport are pushing their bodies to the limit of their abilities in some area. If early adulthood is really the peak, we should find that most world-record-holders and top performers are in their 20s or perhaps early 30s. Another strategy to get at the same question is to look at the average performance of top athletes in each of several age groups, including those in "masters" age categories. Both types of analysis lead inescapably to the same conclusion: Athletic performance peaks early in life, although this varies somewhat from sport to another.

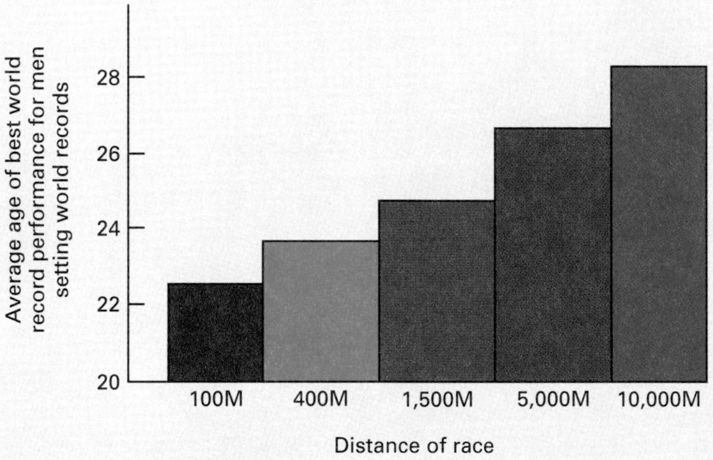

Swimmers, for example, reach their peak very early—at about age 17 for women and about 19 for men. Golfers peak the latest, at about age 31 (Ericsson, 1990; Schulz & Curnow, 1988; Stones & Kozma, 1996). Runners fall in between, with top performances in the early or middle 20s, although the longer the distance, the later the peak. You can see that pattern in the figure, which represents the average age at which each of a series of top male athletes ran his fastest time.

Cross-sectional comparisons of the top performances of competitors of different ages lead to the same conclusion. For example, Germany holds national swimming championships each year, giving awards to the top performers in each 5-year age range from 25 through 70. The best times drop steadily with age (Ericsson, 1990).

At the same time, it is also true that older athletes can perform far better than many of us may have supposed. World records for performers 35 and older (called "master" athletes) have been dropping steadily over the past several decades; in many sports, present-day 50-year-olds are performing at higher levels than did Olympic athletes of 100 years ago. The human body, at any age, is more responsive to training than researchers even a decade ago had presumed. But it is still true that for those who achieve and maintain a high level of fitness throughout adult life, peak performance will come in early adulthood (Stones & Kozma, 1996).

nal studies of women in Figure 13.1. Similar results are found with men (Kozma et al., 1991; Lakatta, 1990). Notice the slight decline in the years of early adulthood, followed by a somewhat more rapid drop in the middle years, a pattern that is highly typical of data on physical changes over adulthood.

Similarly, under resting conditions the quantity of blood flow from the heart (called cardiac output) does not decline with age, but under exercise or work conditions it declines significantly, dropping 30 to 40 percent between age 25 and 65 (Lakatta, 1990; Rossman, 1980).

One exception to the general statement that heart and lungs do not change with age under resting conditions is found in measurements of blood pressure. You know that when your blood pressure is tested you are given two numbers. The higher number represents systolic pressure, which is the force of the blood when your heart is contracting. On this measure we see age differences even under resting conditions. Systolic pressure is lowest in adults in their 20s and 30s and then rises steadily with age, apparently as a result of loss of elasticity in the blood vessels, a reflection of a much more general loss of elasticity in tissues in all parts of the body (the cause of those wrinkles I see in my mirror).

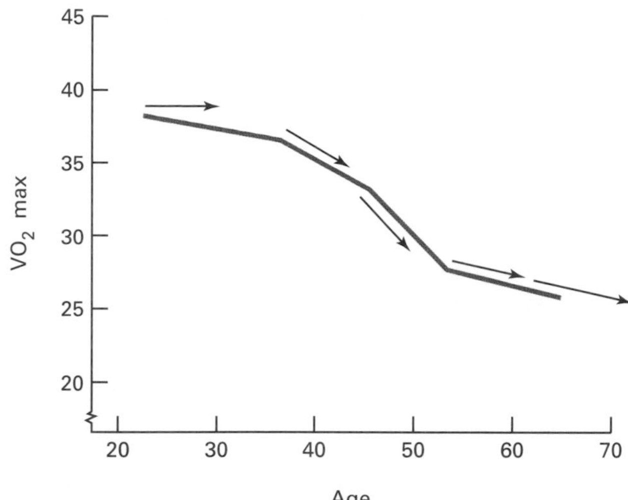

FIGURE 13.1 The continuous line shows VO_2 max averages for cross-sectional comparisons; the arrows show changes on the same measure for groups of women studied longitudinally. The two sets of findings match remarkably. Note that the largest drop was between ages 40 and 50. (*Source:* Plowman, Drinkwater, & Horvath, 1979, Figure 1, p. 514.)

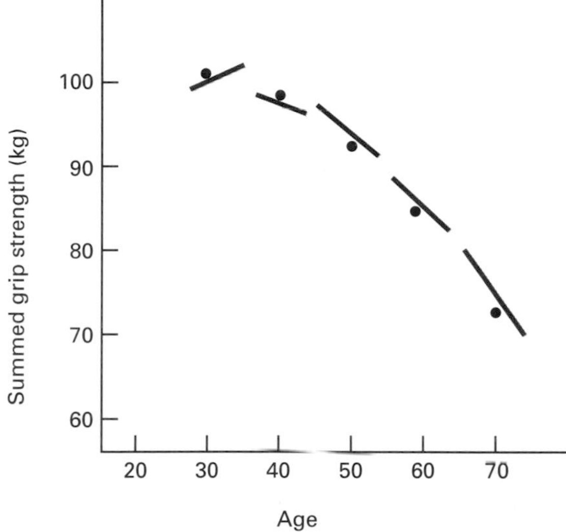

FIGURE 13.2 These data, from the Baltimore Longitudinal Study of Aging, show both cross-sectional (the dots) and longitudinal data (the lines) for grip strength among men. Once again, there is striking agreement between the two sets of information. (*Source:* Kallman et al., 1990, Figure 2, p. M84.)

Because we know that all these aspects of cardiovascular functioning can be improved with exercise, it is likely that some of these losses with age are secondary rather than primary aging, resulting from an increasingly sedentary lifestyle among older adults (Goldberg et al., 1996)—a possibility I'll be coming back to in Chapters 15 and 17.

Strength and Speed. The collective effect of the changes in muscles and cardiovascular fitness is a general loss of strength and speed with age—not just in top athletes, but in all of us. Figure 13.2 shows both cross-sectional and nine-year longitudinal changes in grip strength in a group of men who participated in the Baltimore

Longitudinal Studies of Aging (Kallman et al., 1990). Clearly, strength was at its peak in the 20s and early 30s and then declined steadily. Once again I need to point out that such a difference might be the result of the fact that younger adults are more physically active, or more likely to be engaged in activities or jobs that demand strength. Arguing against this conclusion, however, are studies of physically active older adults, who also show loss of muscle strength (e.g., Phillips et al., 1992).

The accompanying gradual loss of speed seems to be one of the most central and pervasive aspects of primary aging, visible in virtually every aspect of bodily function (Birren & Fisher, 1995; Earles & Salthouse, 1995; Salthouse, 1993). As you get older, your eyes adapt more slowly to changes in light level; it takes longer to warm up after you have been very cold, or to cool off after you have been hot; your reaction time to sudden events slows, so you don't respond quite as quickly to a swerving car. On intellectual tasks, too, we see a gradual slowdown over the years of adulthood. For example, it takes a 45-year-old a fraction of a second longer to remember someone's name than it does a 20-year-old.

This pervasive slowing appears to be the result of very gradual changes at the neuronal level, particularly the loss of dendrites and a slowing of the "firing rate" of nerves. In early adulthood, the nervous system is so redundant—with so many alternative pathways for every signal—that the dendritic loss has relatively little practical effect on behavior. But over the full sweep of the adult years, the loss of speed becomes very noticeable.

Reproductive Capacity. I pointed out in Chapter 3 that the risk of miscarriage and other complications of pregnancy is higher in a woman's 30s than in her 20s. An equivalent change occurs in fertility—the ability to conceive—which is at its highest in late teens and early 20s and drops steadily thereafter (McFalls, 1990; Mosher, 1987; Mosher & Pratt, 1987). Infertility is typically defined as the inability to conceive after one or more years of unprotected intercourse. Using this definition, one large U.S. study (McFalls, 1990) found that only 7 percent of women ages 20 to 24 were infertile, compared with 15 percent of those between 30 and 34, and 28 percent of those between 35 and 39. This does not mean, by the way, that 28 percent of women in their late 30s will be totally unable to conceive; it means that rapid conception is more likely in the early 20s, and that a significant minority of women who postpone childbearing into their late 30s or 40s will not conceive.

The reasons for this decline with age in women's fertility are multiple, including increased problems with ovulation, endometriosis, and a higher probability of having contracted at least one sexually transmitted disease (STD) because of more years of potential exposure (Garner, 1995). STDs increase the risk of pelvic inflammatory disease, which frequently results in a blockage of the fallopian tubes and thus prevents conception.

Among men, fertility does not follow the same pattern. We do not have much research, but it appears that a man's capacity to impregnate does not change over the years of early adulthood. Male fertility declines somewhat after age 40, but (as I'll describe in detail in Chapter 15) there is no equivalent of menopause among men, who may be able to impregnate well into late life. When men in early adulthood have infertility problems—and a significant minority do—it is because they consistently produce an insufficient number of viable sperm, not because they have lost fertility that they once had. In couples experiencing problems conceiving, the problem is as likely to be with the man as the woman (Davajan & Israel, 1991). About half of those couples who seek medical help with infertility problems are eventually able to conceive by means of such methods as artificial insemination, drugs to stimulate ovulation, and *in vitro* fertilization (Stanton & Danoff-Burg, 1995).

Immune System Functioning. All of us have become a great deal more aware of the importance of the immune system, having seen in AIDS patients what happens when this crucial body system no longer functions normally. The two key organs in the immune system are the thymus gland and the bone marrow. Between them, they create two types of cells, B cells and T cells, each of which plays a distinct role. B cells fight against external threats by producing antibodies against such disease organisms as viruses or bacteria; T cells defend against essentially internal threats, such as transplanted tissue, cancer cells, and viruses that live within the body's cells (such as the AIDS virus) (Kiecolt-Glaser & Glaser, 1995). It is T cells that are most deficient in someone with AIDS, and it is T cells that decline most in number and efficiency with age (Miller, 1996).

Changes in the thymus gland appear to be central to the aging process. This gland is largest in adolescence and declines dramatically thereafter in both size and mass. By age 45 or 50, the thymus has only about 5 to 10 percent of the cellular mass it had at puberty (Braveman, 1987; Hausman & Weksler, 1985). This smaller, less functional thymus is less able to turn the immature T cells produced by the bone marrow into fully "adult" cells. As a result, both of the basic protective mechanisms work less efficiently. Adults produce fewer antibodies than do children or teenagers. And T cells partially lose the ability to "recognize" a foreign cell, so that some disease cells (cancer cells, for example) may not be fought. Thus, one of the key physical changes over the years of adulthood is an increasing susceptibility to disease.

Critical Thinking

If an increase in the risk of disease is a normal part of aging, then why does it still make sense to study normal aging by studying only *healthy* adults?

But it is not entirely clear whether this is primary or secondary aging. These changes in the immune system are found in healthy adults, which makes it look like primary aging. But we also have growing evidence that the functioning of the immune system is highly responsive to psychological stress and depression (Maier, Watkins, & Fleshner, 1994; Weisse, 1992). College students, for example, show lower levels of one variety of T cells ("natural killer" T cells) during exam periods than at other times (Glaser et al., 1992). And adults who have recently been widowed show a sharp drop in immune system functioning (Irwin & Pike, 1993). Chronic stress, too, has an effect on the immune system (Kiecolt-Glaser et al., 1991), initially stimulating an increase in immune efficiency, followed by a drop.

Next time you study for exams, remember that the stress of exam time reduces the efficiency of your immune system, so you are more likely to catch a cold. Take care.

Collectively, this research points to the possibility that life experiences that demand high levels of change or adaptation will affect immune system functioning. Over a period of years and many stresses, the immune system becomes less and less efficient. It may well be that the immune system changes with age in basic ways *irrespective* of the level of stress. But it is also possible that what we think of as normal aging of the immune system is a response to cumulative stress. If so, then we might expect those adults who have encountered higher levels of stress to have higher rates of disease and shorter life expectancies. That is, they should "age" faster—an expectation borne out by research on disease and death rates, to which we now turn.

Physical Health and Disease

When we look directly at age differences in health and death rates, the research follows the expected pattern. Most obviously, the older you are, the higher the likelihood that you will die in any given year. In the United States, slightly fewer than 2 young adults out of every thousand die each year; for those between ages 65 and 75, the rate is 15 times higher: 27 out of every thousand (U.S. Bureau of the Census, 1995). Table 13.2 lists the leading causes of death for adults between 25 and 44 as of 1992 (the most recent year for which we have complete data). You can see that young men die at more than twice the rate of young women, mostly from violent causes (homicide, suicide, and accidents). When young men die of disease, it is most likely AIDS, which is actually the single leading cause of death for men in this age range in the United States today. The rate of death from AIDS has increased significantly for young women in recent years, to the point that by 1994 it was the third-leading cause of death for women in this age range (Hilts, 1996), but the rate is far higher for men, especially black men. For young women in this age group, the leading cause of death is cancer, which rises in frequency in the late 30s for both men and women.

Table 13.2 Rates of Death per 100,000 Population Aged 25 to 44 in the United States in 1992

	Women		Men	
	Age 25–34	**Age 35–44**	**Age 25–34**	**Age 35–44**
Total death rate	70.0	143.0	200.0	325.0
Accidents	14.4	13.8	50.6	46.7
Suicide	5.0	6.6	24.0	23.7
Homicide	7.1	4.9	27.5	17.6
Heart disease	5.4	16.1	10.7	47.8
Cancer	12.9	46.5	12.1	38.1
AIDS	7.5*		52.5*	

*The Census Bureau does not provide AIDS data separately for these two age groups, but only for the age range 25–44.

Source: U.S. Bureau of the Census, 1995, Tables 127, 128, 130, 131, 132.

Rates of chronic illness or disability are also low in early adulthood, then rise steadily through the middle and late adult years, a pattern that is especially clear in a set of survey data analyzed by James House and his colleagues (House, Kessler, & Herzog, 1990; House et al., 1992). This nationally representative U.S. sample of 3617 adults was asked a variety of questions about their health and level of physical disability. Figure 13.3 shows the average number of chronic conditions (e.g., arthritis, lung disease, high blood pressure, heart trouble, diabetes, cancer) as a function of age, computed separately for four different social class groups.

Clearly, young adults have many fewer chronic problems than do older persons. No big surprise. But the figure also shows that health varies markedly from one social class to another. Among adults aged 35 to 44, for example, those who are in the lowest social class group report almost four times as many chronic conditions as do those in the highest social class group (defined as those with 16 or more years of education and an income of $20,000 or more in 1986 dollars). Equivalent social class differences in adult health, rate of disability, or longevity have been found in many other industrialized counties, such as Sweden (Thorslund & Lundberg, 1994) and England (Eames, Ben-Schlomo, & Marmot, 1993), and they occur *within* ethnic groups in the United States as well as overall. That is, among blacks, among Hispanics, and among Asian Americans, better-educated adults or those with higher incomes have longer life expectancies and better health (Guralnik et al., 1993) than do those with less education.

What might cause such social class differences? House and his colleagues looked at several possibilities, among them health habits, such as drinking and smoking, and life stresses, including both chronic stresses like financial troubles and life changes such as losing a job, a divorce, moving, or the like. They found, as have others (e.g., James, Keenan, & Browning, 1992), that working-class adults—black and white—had poorer health habits and higher levels of stress. When these differences are subtracted statistically, the social class differences apparent in Figure 13.3 become considerably smaller, although they do not disappear altogether (House et al., 1992). In particular, upper-class adults continue to have a clear health advantage, even when health habits and stress have been accounted for.

CRITICAL THINKING

What other explanations can you think of for the health advantage of the upper and middle classes? Can you think of a way to test your hypotheses?

These data, then, not only substantiate what you already knew—that the risk of disease or disability rises with age—they also provide support for the hypothesis

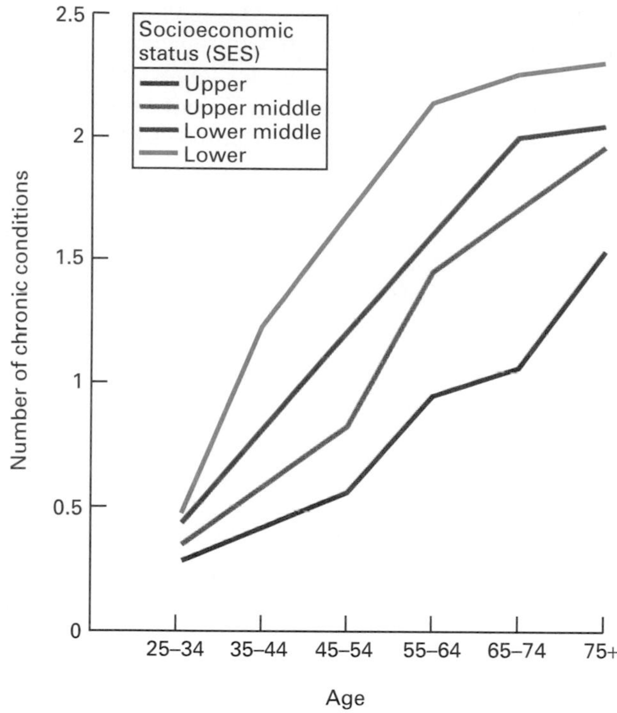

FIGURE 13.3 As people get older, they are more and more likely to experience some kind of chronic illness, but this change is earlier and larger among poor and working-class adults. (*Source:* House et al., 1990, Figure 1, p. 396.)

that cumulative stress may be one of the causal factors, because adults with lower levels of chronic stress "age" more slowly.

Exceptions to the General Pattern. There are several important exceptions to the general rule that young adults have fewer diseases and disabilities. First of all, young adults are about twice as likely as are those over 65 to suffer from acute illnesses—short-term illnesses such as colds, the flu, infections, and intestinal upsets. It is only chronic illnesses that are less common in young adults.

A second exception is that drug and alcohol abuse and sexually transmitted diseases are more common among young adults than at any other period of adulthood. Alcoholism and significant drug addiction peak between 18 and about 40, after which they decline gradually. The rates are higher for men than for women, but the age pattern is very similar in both genders (Anthony & Aboraya, 1992). One large study in the United States finds a rate of alcohol abuse or dependence of about 6 percent among those in young adulthood, compared with 4 percent in middle adulthood and 1.8 percent for those over 65 (Regier et al., 1988). Binge drinking (usually defined as five or more drinks on one occasion) is also particularly common among college students in the United States. A recent survey of over 17,000 students on 140 college campuses (Wechsler et al., 1994) indicated that almost half (44 percent) of students were binge drinkers; 19 percent were frequent binge drinkers. Although most binge drinkers do not think of themselves as having a problem with alcohol, they clearly do display a variety of problem behaviors, including substantially higher rates of unprotected sex, physical injury, driving while intoxicated, and trouble with the police.

Sexually transmitted diseases (SDTs), including syphilis, gonorrhea, chlamydia, herpes, and AIDS, are also contracted at far higher rates among the young, with the highest rates among those 20 to 24 (Fogel, 1995)—a group that is much more likely to show those specific high-risk behaviors linked to SDTs: multiple sexual partners, sex without adequate protection, and frequent drug or alcohol use. Rates of infection are generally higher in men than in women, but women often develop more severe and lasting symptoms, including increased risks of cervical cancer, reduced fertility, and possible transmission of the disease to children during pregnancy or childbirth. For most adults STDs remain one of the taboo topics; many sexually active adults are unwilling to insist on the use of condoms; many do not seek medical attention when they develop symptoms or do not inform their partners of potential problems. But the risks are considerable, especially with the increase in drug-resistant strains of gonorrhea and syphilis and the spread of AIDS into the heterosexual population. So take note: Safe sex practices—including knowledge of your *partner's* sexual history—are worth the effort.

Mental Health

Another exception to the pattern of optimal health in young adulthood is found in studies of age differences in mental health problems. Studies in a number of developed countries show that the risk of virtually every kind of emotional disturbance is *higher* between the ages of 25 and 44 than in middle age (Kessler et al., 1992; Regier et al., 1988). In the case of depression there *may* be a rise again in old age, although this point is in dispute, as you'll see further in Chapter 17. But everyone agrees that rates of depression and anxiety are higher in early adulthood than in middle age. Thus, paradoxically, the time of life in which we experience our peak of physical and intellectual functioning is also the time in which we may be most prone to depression or other forms of emotional distress.

Why might this be so? The most plausible explanation—one I'll expand on in the next chapter—is that early adulthood is the period in which adults have both the highest expectations and the highest level of both role conflict and role strain. These are the years when each of us must learn a series of huge new roles (spouse, parent, worker); these are the years when we must address Erikson's task of intimacy, creating new loving relationships. If we fall short of our expectations, loneliness and depression are common outcomes.

Cognitive Functioning

As with most aspects of physical functioning, intellectual processes are at their peak in early adulthood. Indeed, it now looks as if the intellectual peak lasts longer than many early researchers had thought, and that the rate of decline is quite slow. Current research also makes it clear that the rate and pattern of cognitive decline varies widely, differences that appear to be caused by a variety of environmental and lifestyle factors, as well as heredity. Let's begin with some of the basic findings.

IQ

Early studies of age changes in IQ, relying on cross-sectional evidence, showed a peak at about age 30 and a steady decline thereafter. But as you'll remember from the discussion of cross-sectional research in Chapter 1, such studies confound age and cohort. So if older subjects differ in some systematic way from younger ones, such as amount of education, we can't tell how much of the apparent decline in IQ reflects real primary aging, and how much of it is an artifact of cohort differences. Longitudinal studies solve part of this problem by following the same cohort over time. And these studies give us a much more optimistic picture of the timing and degree of cognitive decline over the adult years.

The best single source of evidence is a remarkable 35-year cross-sequential study by Werner Schaie, referred to as the Seattle Longitudinal Study (1983b, 1989a, 1993, 1994, 1996; Schaie & Hertzog, 1983). Schaie began in 1956 with a set of cross-sectional samples, 7 years apart in age, covering the ages from 25 to 67. A subset of the subjects in each age group was then followed over 35 years with retestings every 7 years. In 1963, another set of cross-sectional samples, covering the same age

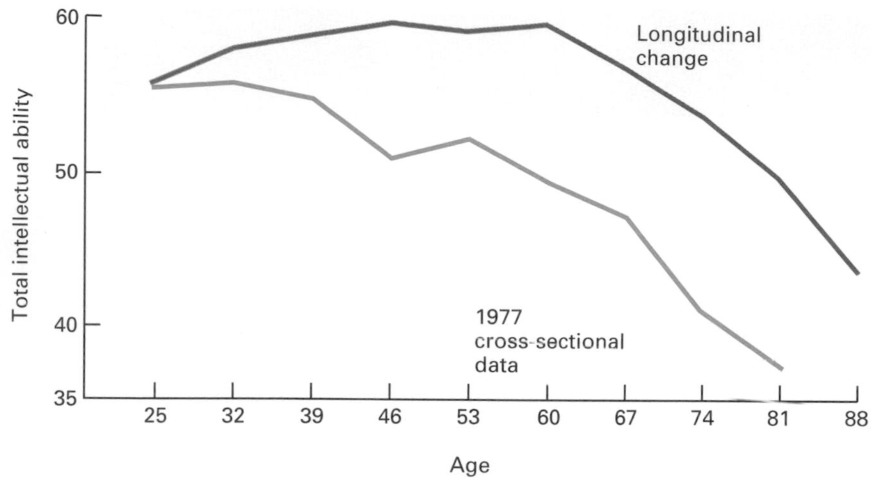

FIGURE 13.4 These results from the Seattle Longitudinal Study show both cross-sectional and longitudinal data for a measure of overall intellectual skill (average score = 50). (*Source:* Schaie, 1983b, Tables 4.5 and 4.9, pp. 89 and 100.)

ranges, was tested, and a subset of these was retested 7, 14, 21, and 28 years later. Further samples were added in 1970, 1977, 1984, and 1991. This remarkable data-collection process enables Schaie to look at IQ changes over 7-, 14-, 21-, and 28-year intervals for several sets of subjects, each from a slightly different cohort. Figure 13.4 shows one set of cross-sectional comparisons in 1977 as well as 14-year longitudinal results smoothed over the whole age range. The test involved in this case is a measure of global intelligence on which the average score is set at 50 points (equivalent to an IQ of 100 on most other tests).

You can see that the cross-sectional comparisons show a steady drop in IQ. But the longitudinal evidence suggests that overall intelligence test scores actually rise in early adulthood and then remain quite constant until perhaps age 60, when they begin to decline. Since this pattern has also been found by other researchers (e.g., Sands, Terry, & Meredith, 1989; Siegler, 1983) we have good support for the temptingly optimistic view that intellectual ability remains essentially stable through most of adulthood. But when we look a bit deeper, we find a few wrinkles.

The first wrinkle becomes clear as soon as we look at subscores instead of total IQ scores. Theorists have suggested several ways to subdivide intellectual tasks, of which perhaps the most influential has been Raymond Cattell and John Horn's distinction between crystallized and fluid intelligence (Cattell, 1963; Horn, 1982; Horn & Donaldson, 1980). **Crystallized intelligence** depends heavily on education and experience. It consists of the set of skills and bits of knowledge that we each learn as part of growing up in any given culture, such as vocabulary, the ability to read and understand the newspaper, the ability to evaluate experience, and technical skills you may learn for your job or your life (balancing a checkbook, using a computer, making change, finding the mayonnaise in the grocery store). **Fluid intelligence,** in contrast, involves more "basic" abilities that depend more on the efficient functioning of the central nervous system and less on specific experience. A common measure of this is a "letter series test" in which you are given a series of letters (like A C F J O) and must figure out what letter should go next. This demands abstract reasoning rather than reasoning about known or everyday events. Most tests of memory are also part of fluid intelligence, as are many tests measuring response speed and those measuring more difficult or abstract kinds of mathematics. Schaie's results, and the results of many other investigators, suggest that adults *maintain* crystallized abilities throughout early and middle adulthood, but that fluid abilities decline fairly

Research Report

Continuities in IQ Scores in Adulthood

In the main part of the chapter I have talked about *changes* in IQ over the years of adulthood. But it is also interesting to ask about continuities. Does each person's IQ score tend to stay in roughly the same range? That is, is a high-IQ teenager still likely to be among those with the highest IQ scores in young adulthood or middle age?

The answer is clearly yes. The correlations between IQ scores at different ages in adulthood, even ages decades apart, are normally extremely high. For example, in the Berkeley/Oakland longitudinal studies, the correlation between IQ scores at age 17 and in middle age was .83 for males and .77 for females (Eichorn, Hunt, & Honzik, 1981). A recent study of Canadian army veterans, tested first when they were in their early 20s and then again in their early 60s, yields similar results: a correlation of .78 between verbal IQ scores at the two time points (Gold et al., 1995). Over shorter intervals the correlations are even higher. Christopher Hertzog and Warner Schaie, using data from the Seattle Longitudinal Study, have found that over seven-year intervals the correlations range from .89 to .96 (Hertzog & Schaie, 1986).

These are very strong relationships. But these results do not mean that a person's IQ never changes after adolescence. In the Berkeley sample, for example, 11 percent of the subjects gained as many as 13 IQ points between age 17 and their middle 40s, while another 11 percent decreased as many as 6 points. The decliners included a disproportionate number of heavy drinkers and those who had experienced some debilitative illness. Those whose IQs had increased substantially were likely to have married someone with an IQ at least 10 points higher than their own IQ had been in late adolescence (Eichorn, Hunt, & Honzik, 1981), a pattern also found among the subjects in the Seattle Longitudinal Study (Schaie, 1994).

Overall then, IQ scores at the start of adulthood are highly predictive of IQ scores at later ages, although psychologically significant individual changes can and do occur.

steadily over adulthood, beginning at perhaps age 35 or 40 (Horn & Donaldson, 1980; Schaie, 1994).

Do results like these mean we have to revise the generally optimistic conclusion based on longitudinal studies of total IQ? On the face of it, yes: On some kinds of tests, adults appear to show some decline beginning as early as their 40s. But Schaie notes that even the decline in fluid test skills, while *statistically* significant, may not represent psychologically significant loss until at least late middle age. Schaie concludes:

> At the risk of possible overgeneralization, it is my general conclusion that reliably replicable age changes in psychometric abilities of more than trivial magnitude cannot be demonstrated prior to age 60, but that reliable decrement can be shown to have occurred for all abilities by age 74. (Schaie, 1983b, p. 127)

Optimism rises again. But again, there are wrinkles. Paul Baltes (Baltes, Dittmann-Kohli, & Dixon, 1984, 1986) makes the point that psychologically or functionally relevant decrements may show up in middle age or earlier when adults are faced with highly complex or difficult tasks—tasks that stretch the individual's skills to the limit—just as significant decrements in physical skill show up in early adulthood among top athletes. One of the ironies, then, is that adults whose occupations require them to function regularly at these intellectually more taxing levels are likely to become aware of some subtle decline in intellectual skills earlier in adulthood than do those whose life circumstances make less stringent intellectual demands, even though these same highly trained individuals may continue to function at a very high absolute level of skill throughout their early and middle years.

So where does this leave us in answering the question about intellectual maintenance or decline over adulthood? My reading of the evidence is much like Schaie's: In early adulthood intellectual abilities show essentially no decline except at the very top levels of intellectual demand. In middle adulthood, though, we see declines on fluid abilities—those tasks that are thought to represent the efficiency of the basic physiological process (Salthouse, 1991). Indeed, the rate of decline on measures of fluid intelligence closely matches the rate of decline in total brain size, suggesting a possible direct link (Bigler et al., 1995).

Memory

The pattern of results from studies of memory ability generally follow the pattern for fluid abilities: maintenance of memory skill during early adulthood, some decline during middle adulthood, and greater decline in late adulthood.

For example, measures of short-term memory—recalling something for only a short time, such as a phone number you've just looked up in the phone book and then call immediately—generally show a drop with age, as you've already seen in Figure 1.4 (p. 16). Age differences are still larger when we look at measures of long-term memory—items you have intended to store in your mind for longer periods, or permanently, such as when you try to memorize someone's phone number, learn a poem or vocabulary words in a new language, or the like. Both the process of getting memories into this long-term storage (a process called *encoding* by memory theorists) and the process of retrieving them again seem to be impaired among older adults as compared with young adults (Salthouse, 1991). With age we become both slower and less efficient in our memory processes—a set of findings I'll have much more to say about in Chapter 17.

Changes in Cognitive Structure

Schaie is not the only optimist among theorists who look at adult thinking. A number of post-Piagetian theorists are also quite upbeat in their view of adult cognition. Collectively, these theorists argue that Piaget's concept of formal operations simply doesn't capture many of the kinds of thinking that adults are called upon to do. They propose, instead, that new structures or new stages of thinking occur in adulthood. One such theorist is Gisela Labouvie-Vief (1980, 1990), who argues that formal operations thinking is highly adaptive in early adulthood when the young person has some need to explore or examine many options. But once each of us has made our initial choices we no longer have much need for formal operations; instead, we need thinking skills that are *specialized* and *pragmatic*. Each of us learns how to solve the problems associated with the particular social roles he occupies, or the particular job he holds. In the process, we trade off the deductive thoroughness of formal operations for contextual validity. In Labouvie-Vief's view, this trade-off does not reflect a regression or a loss, but rather a necessary structural change.

Labouvie-Vief also makes the point that many young adults begin to turn away from a purely logical, analytic approach, toward a more open, perhaps deeper mode of understanding that deals with myth and metaphor, with paradox instead of certainty. Michael Basseches (1984, 1989) calls this new adult type of thinking **dialectical thought.** He suggests that while formal thought "involves the effort to find fundamental fixed realities—basic elements and immutable laws—[dialectical thought] attempts to describe fundamental processes of change and the dynamic relationships through which this change occurs" (1984, p. 24). According to this view, adults do not give up their ability to use formal reasoning. Instead, they acquire a new ability to deal with the fuzzier problems that make up the majority of the problems of adulthood—problems that do not have a single solution, or in which some critical

CRITICAL THINKING

List four personal problems you have had to solve in the past six months. What kind of logic or thought process did you use to solve each one? Did your mode of thinking vary as a function of the nature of the problem?

What kind of thinking might this young couple be using as they struggle to balance their finances? Dialectic? Pragmatic? Concrete or formal operations?

pieces of information may be missing. Choosing what type of refrigerator to buy might be a decision aided by formal operational thought. But it is not so clear that such forms of logic will be helpful in making a decision about whether to adopt a child, or whether to place your aging parent in a nursing home. Basseches argues that such problems demand a different kind of thinking—not a "higher" kind of thinking, but a different one.

Still a third model of "postformal" thinking comes from Patricia Arlin (1975, 1989, 1990), who argues that Piaget's stage of formal operations is a stage of *problem solving*. Some adults, so Arlin proposes, develop a further stage characterized by *problem finding*. This new mode, which includes much of what we normally call *creativity*, is optimal for dealing with problems that have no clear solution, or that have multiple solutions. A person operating at this stage is able to generate many possible solutions to ill-defined problems, and to see old problems in new ways. Arlin argues that problem finding is a clear stage following formal operations, but that it is achieved by only a small number of adults, such as those involved in advanced science or arts.

Many of these new theories of postformal thought are intriguing, but they remain highly speculative, with little empirical evidence to back them up. More generally, psychologists do not yet agree on whether these new types of thinking represent "higher" forms of thought, built on the stages Piaget describes, or whether it is more appropriate simply to describe them as a "different" form of thinking that may or may not emerge in adulthood. What I think is important about this work is the emphasis on the fact that the normal problems of adult life, with their inconsistencies and complexities, cannot always be addressed fruitfully using formal operations logic. It seems entirely plausible that adults will be pushed toward more pragmatic, relativistic forms of thinking, using formal operational thinking only occasionally, if at all. Labouvie-Vief's point, which I think is correct, is that we should not think of this change as a *loss* or a deterioration, but rather as a reasonable adaptation to a different set of cognitive tasks.

A Model of Physical and Cognitive Aging

Many of the various bits and pieces of information I've given you about both physical and cognitive changes in adulthood can be fruitfully combined in a single model, suggested by Nancy Denney (1982, 1984) and shown in Figure 13.5. Denney proposed that changes with age on nearly any measure of physical or cognitive functioning

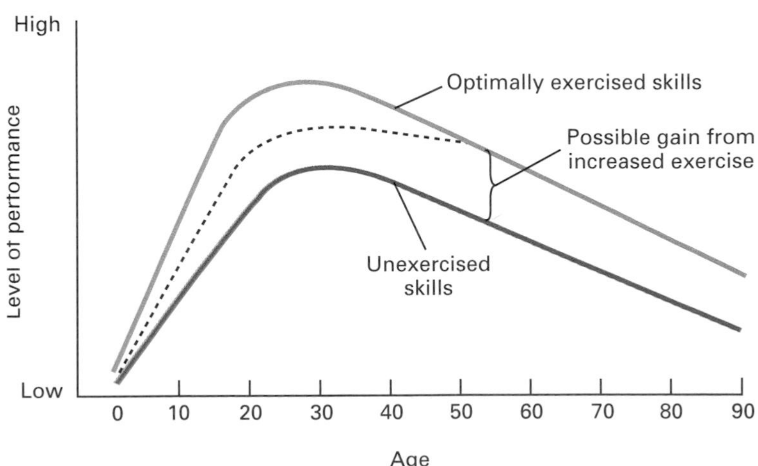

FIGURE 13.5 Denney's model suggests both a basic decay curve and a fairly large gap between actual level of performance on exercised and unexercised abilities. (*Source:* Denney, 1982, 1984).

follow a typical curve, like the green and blue curves shown in the figure. But she also argued that the height of the curve varies, depending on the amount an individual "exercises" some ability or skill. She used the word *exercise* very broadly to refer not only to physical exercise but also to mental exercise and to the extent some specific task may have been performed before. *Unexercised* abilities will generally have a lower peak level of performance; *exercised* abilities will generally have a higher peak. Many laboratory tests of memory, for example, such as memorizing lists of names, would tap unexercised abilities. Everyday memory tasks, such as recalling details from a newspaper column, would tap much more exercised abilities. The distinction is obviously somewhat similar to the distinction between crystallized and fluid abilities. Most crystallized abilities are at least moderately exercised, while many fluid abilities are relatively unexercised. But Denney was making a more general point: Among crystallized abilities or among fluid abilities, those that are more fully exercised will have a higher peak.

The gap between the curve for unexercised abilities and the curve for maximally exercised abilities represents the degree of *improvement* that would be possible for any given skill. Any skill that is not fully exercised can be improved, even in old age, if the individual begins to exercise that ability. There is clear evidence, for example, that aerobic capacity (VO_2 max) can be increased at any age if subjects begin a program of physical exercise (e.g., Blumenthal et al., 1991; Buchner et al., 1992). Nonetheless, in Denney's model, the maximum level you will be able to achieve, even with optimum exercise, will decline with age, just as performance of top athletes declines, even with optimum training regimens. One implication of this is that when you are young, you can get away with physical sloth or poor study habits and still perform well; as you get older, this becomes less and less true because you are fighting against the basic decay curve of aging.

The dashed line in the figure represents a hypothetical curve for a skill that is less than optimally exercised but still used fairly regularly. Many verbal skills would fall into this category, as would problem-solving skills. Because skills like these are demanded in a great many jobs, they are well exercised in our 20s and 30s and are well maintained, creating a flat-topped curve similar to what Schaie finds for vocabulary and other exercised or crystallized abilities. But if Denney is correct, then at some point even optimum exercise will no longer maintain these abilities at that same level, and some decline will be found—just as Schaie reports.

Critical Thinking

Suppose a blue-collar worker who had never been past high school decides, at age 40, to go to college. She goes to school for four years, gets a degree in English literature, and becomes a high school teacher. What line on Denney's curve might you predict for this person's score on a vocabulary test?

This model does not handle all the facts. In particular, Denney's model does not easily handle the wide degree of variation from one individual to the next in the pattern of maintenance or decline over age, variation revealed clearly in Schaie's longitudinal study (Schaie, 1990). But what Denny's model does do is to emphasize —correctly I think—that there *is* some kind of underlying decay curve. Early adulthood is the period of maximum potential in nearly every physical and intellectual arena, a time of greatest ease of performance. Those in middle adulthood may perform as well or better than the average young adult in arenas in which they maintain a high level of exercise. However, with increasing age, this high level of function requires more and more effort, until eventually a point is reached at which even maximum effort will no longer maintain peak function.

Individual Differences

One possible source of the individual variations in both physical and cognitive aging is the set of health habits followed in early and middle adulthood. When you are 25 or 30, it may seem that you can get away with any kind of neglect or abuse of your body. But it ain't so.

Health Habits and Their Long-Term Effects

The best evidence for the long-term effects of various health practices comes from a major longitudinal epidemiological study in a single county of California, the

Alameda County Study (Berkman & Breslow, 1983; Breslow & Breslow, 1993; Kaplan, 1992). The study began in 1965, when a random sample of all residents of the county, a total of 6928 subjects, completed an extensive questionnaire about many aspects of their lives, including their health habits and their health and disability. These subjects were contacted again in 1974 and 1983, when they again described their health and disability. The researchers also monitored death records and were able to specify the time of death of each of the subjects who died between 1965 and 1983. They could then link health practices reported in 1965 to later death, disease, or disability.

The researchers initially identified seven health practices that they thought might be critical: physical exercise, smoking, drinking, over- or undereating, snacking, eating breakfast, and regular sleep. Table 13.3 lists the optimum behavior for each of these habits, as defined in this study.

Data from the first 9 years of the Alameda study show that five of these seven practices were independently related to the risk of death. Only snacking and breakfast eating were unrelated to mortality. (Thank heavens—now I can eat those pretzels between meals!) When the five strong predictors were combined in the 1974 data, the researchers found the pattern shown in Figure 13.6. In every age group, those with poorer health habits had a higher risk of mortality. Not surprisingly, these health habits were also related to disease and disability rates over the 18 years of the study. Those who described poorer health habits in 1965 were more likely to report disability or disease symptoms in 1974 and in 1983 (Breslow & Breslow, 1993; Guralnik & Kaplan, 1989; Strawbridge et al., 1993).

The Alameda study is not the only one to show these connections between health habits and mortality. For example, a 20-year longitudinal study in Sweden confirms the link between physical exercise and lower risk of death (Lissner et al., 1996), and JoAnn Manson's analysis of the results of the Nurses Health Study (Manson et al., 1995) replicates the connection between weight and longevity. The Nurses Health Study is a huge longitudinal study of over 115,000 nurses first interviewed in 1976, when they were all between 30 and 55 years old. In their analysis of the data, Manson and her colleagues have looked at the link between the women's weight at the start of the study and risk of death over the succeeding 16 years. They found that the lower the woman's initial body-mass index (a measure of weight relative to height), the lower her likelihood of death. Indeed this study suggests that the ideal

Table 13.3 Optimum Health Practices as Defined in the Alameda County Study

- Usually sleep seven or eight hours per night.
- Eat breakfast almost every day.
- Eat between meals once in a while, rarely, or never.
- For men, weigh between 5 percent under and 20 percent over desirable weight for height; for women, weigh not more than 10 percent over desirable weight for height.
- Participate often in at least two or three of the following: swimming, walking, sports, gardening, fishing, or hunting.
- Never smoke cigarettes.
- Have no more than 4 drinks at a time; have no more than 16 drinks per month.*

*Note that the listed good health practice with regard to alcohol is not that the person never drinks but that the individual does not drink to excess. Numerous studies, including the Alameda study, suggest that a moderate amount of alcohol intake, on the order of one glass of wine per day, is associated with *better* health and longer life than is complete abstinence (e.g., Guralnik & Kaplan, 1989).

Source: Adapted from Berkman & Breslow, 1983.

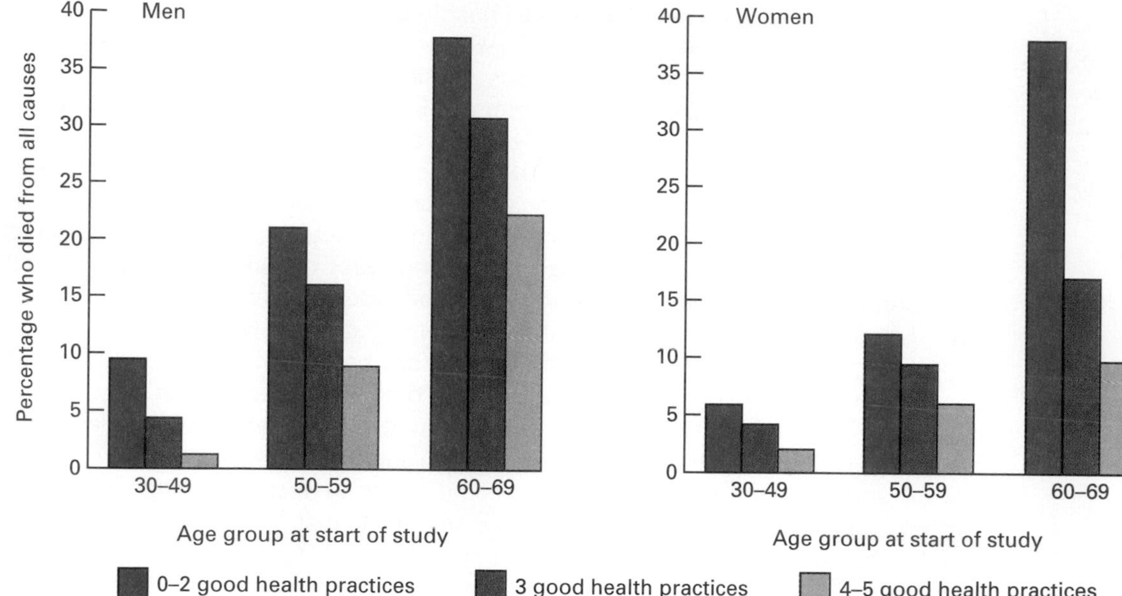

FIGURE 13.6 Health practices reported in 1965 predicted death rates over the next nine years in every age group for both men and women. (*Source:* Berkman and Breslow, 1983, Figure 3-9, p. 97).

weight is even thinner than the optimum level as defined in the Alameda study. Manson found that among women who did not smoke, the lowest risks occurred among those who had initially weighed *less* than the "desirable weight" listed in life insurance tables; those whose weight had been at or no more than 20 percent above the "desirable weight" had *slightly* elevated risks, while the risks rose more markedly for those who weighed more than 20 percent above the life insurance table levels.

Manson's data raise some disturbing issues, not the least of which is the possibility that findings like these—which have been widely publicized—may increase the risk of various types of eating disorders by strengthening the current cultural ideal of extreme slenderness. So it is important to emphasize that the increase in mortality risk Manson found for those at or slightly above the desirable weight is quite small. You do not have to be model-thin to live a long life, although being very thin increases your chances slightly. From a personal perspective I found this to be an important point: My own weight falls within the "desirable weight" range for my height; to shift into Manson's lowest weight category—the group with the lowest mortality risk—I would have to weigh 30 pounds less than I now do. Even when I ran 40 miles a week I didn't weigh 30 pounds less! Clearly, thoughtful personal choices are involved here: What risks am I willing to take, and what price am I willing to pay to reduce those risks? But the science seems clear: Very slender adults live longer and have fewer later health problems.

For maximum long-term benefit, healthy lifestyle choices are best made in early adulthood and then followed consistently. But few young adults do this. Indeed, the young have the least healthy lifestyle. Data from the U.S. National Center for Health Statistics (U.S. Bureau of the Census, 1989) show that young adults have the highest rates of such poor health habits as skipping breakfast, drinking to excess, and smoking. In contrast, obesity is most common among those 45–64, while the tendency to get too little sleep (six hours or less) is equally common at all ages.

Of course one of the reasons the young follow a riskier health path is that they have a difficult time seeing, or accepting, a link between their current behavior and such long-term outcomes as decreased life span, heart disease three decades later, or disability in old age. Human decision making is not completely rational. Among other things, we tend to be more optimistic about our own situation than is warranted by the facts: We might assume that although other people become addicted

CRITICAL THINKING

Think about your own less-than-ideal health habits. What rationalizations do you use to justify them to yourself?

to drugs or cigarettes, we will be able to handle it, or we say "it hasn't happened to me yet" (Jeffrey, 1989). We also tend to make decisions based on immediate rewards rather than on potential longer-term gains, so the immediate pleasure of overeating, alcohol, or smoking is likely to overwhelm any information we have about the long-term risks. But for those of you who are still young adults and whose health habits are less than optimal, remember that there is no free lunch. Not only is it difficult to break well-established habits, the effect of poor habits seems to be cumulative. In particular, poor health habits in early adulthood may set into motion or hasten the development of specific diseases, such as heart disease or cancer. There may be no symptoms during the years from 20 to 40, but the process has begun.

For example, the effect of a high cholesterol diet—a health habit that the Alameda researchers did not include in their study because its importance was not so well known in 1965—appears to add up over time. Research on heart disease also suggests cumulative effects of smoking. Fortunately, it is also true that if you quit smoking, the risk eventually drops down to the same level as that of a person who never smoked. And a radical lowering of fat levels in your diet may reverse the process of cholesterol buildup in the blood vessels (Ornish, 1990). So there is a payoff for changing your health habits, even in your 20s and 30s.

Other Personal Factors that Affect Health and Cognition

I've already mentioned one other factor that may affect health at any age: stress. Stress significantly reduces the efficiency of the immune system in the short term,

The Real World

Changing Your Health Habits Now

New epidemiological data on the various diseases of adulthood make it very clear that many risk factors are largely within your control. Certainly you can't control your heredity, and we know that heredity plays a role in a great many aspects of health and illness—including risks of some kinds of heart disease and cancer. But you *can* make choices about health habits. And if you develop good habits while you are young, not only will it be easier to maintain those habits, but you will reap benefits over many years. Here's my list of the most important choices you could make, based on all the research I've read.

- *Stop Smoking.* If you smoke now, stop. If you don't smoke, don't start.
- *Exercise, Exercise, Exercise.* Take the stairs instead of the elevator; walk to the grocery store or on other errands; ride a bike to work; get *at least* 20 to 30 minutes of vigorous exercise of some kind at least three times a week; more than that is better.
- *Eat a Lower-Fat Diet.* High fat in the diet has been linked to increased risks of both cancer and heart disease, as well as to overweight. The level currently recommended by the American Heart Association is 30 percent of calories from fat—well below the average American diet. But there is good evidence that a level of 15 or 20 percent of calories from fat would be even better. Achieving this level means eating lots less meat and dairy products and a lot more vegetables, fruits, grains, and beans. Goodbye fast foods!
- *Get Enough Calcium.* This is especially important for women, who lose more calcium from their bones than do men, especially after menopause. And once the calcium is lost, it is very hard—perhaps impossible—to regain it. So here is one place where *prevention* is critical. Weight-bearing exercise helps to retain calcium, but taking calcium supplements from early adulthood is also a good idea.

I know that doing all these things is not easy. On many mornings I can hardly bear the thought of getting out of bed at 5:45 so that I can walk my 3 miles before I eat breakfast; there are days when I drive the car six blocks to the store because I don't have time to walk; and there are days when I find a high-fat, high-calorie brownie irresistible. But I do try to do all these things and wish I had started doing them when I was 25. Most of you still have the chance to make these healthier choices at a young age. So think about them.

Cultures and Contexts

Health Habits in Blacks, Whites, and Hispanics in the United States

National survey data from 1990 (U.S. Bureau of the Census, 1995) indicate that no one of the three major ethnic groups in the United States has consistently better or worse health habits, although there are some minor variations. Whites are more likely to drink to excess; blacks are most likely to be 20 percent or more overweight and slightly more likely to smoke; both blacks and Hispanics exercise less regularly.

Social class or level of education may be a better predictor of health habits than ethnicity. For example, results from a study of 2030 adults living in a single county in North Carolina (James et al., 1992) show that adults with high school education or less reported poorer health and poorer health habits than did those with more than high school. Minority status may add to health risk, but social class or education is a significant variable across the board.

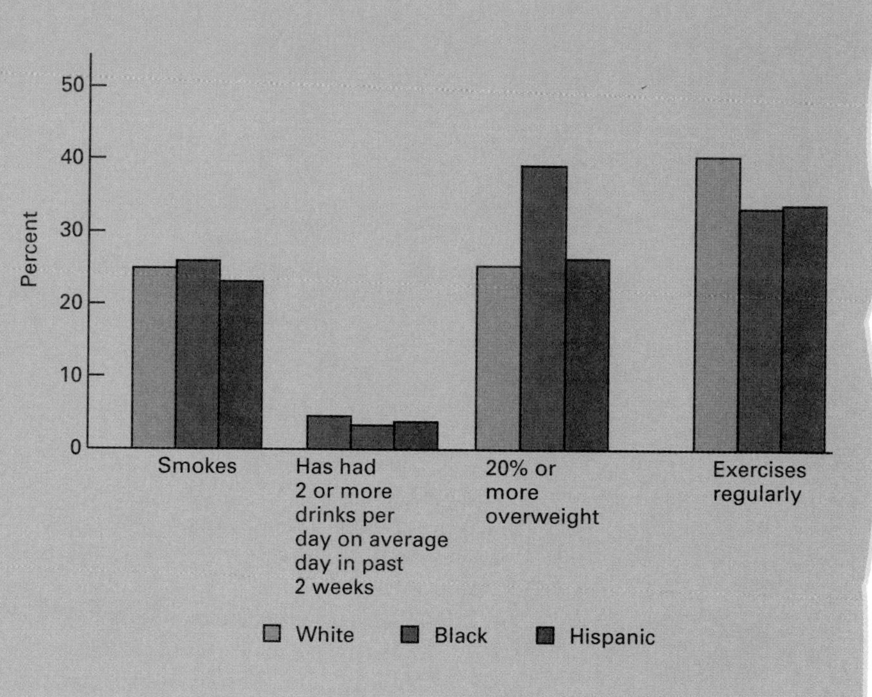

which increases the risk of disease. Fortunately, there are also protective factors—elements that may reduce the risk of disease and increase a person's sense of happiness or well-being. High on this list are social support and a sense of personal control.

Social Support. We now have abundant research showing that adults with adequate social support have lower risk of disease, death, and depression than do adults with weaker social networks or less supportive relationships (e.g., Berkman, 1985; Berkman & Breslow, 1983; Cohen, 1991).

Social support has been defined and measured in myriad ways (Cohen, Kessler, & Gordon, 1995). In early studies it was typically defined in terms of such objective criteria as marital status and frequency of reported contact with friends and relatives. Recent studies suggest that subjective measures may be more powerful; a person's *perception* of the adequacy of her social contacts and emotional support is more strongly related to physical and emotional health than are most objective measures (Feld & George, 1994; Sarason, Sarason, & Pierce, 1990). This greater potency of the subjective sense of support is entirely consistent with what I have been saying about the significance of internal models in shaping behavior and attitudes. It is not the objective amount of contact with others that is important, but how that contact is understood or interpreted. In fact Barbara Sarason and her colleagues (Sarason et

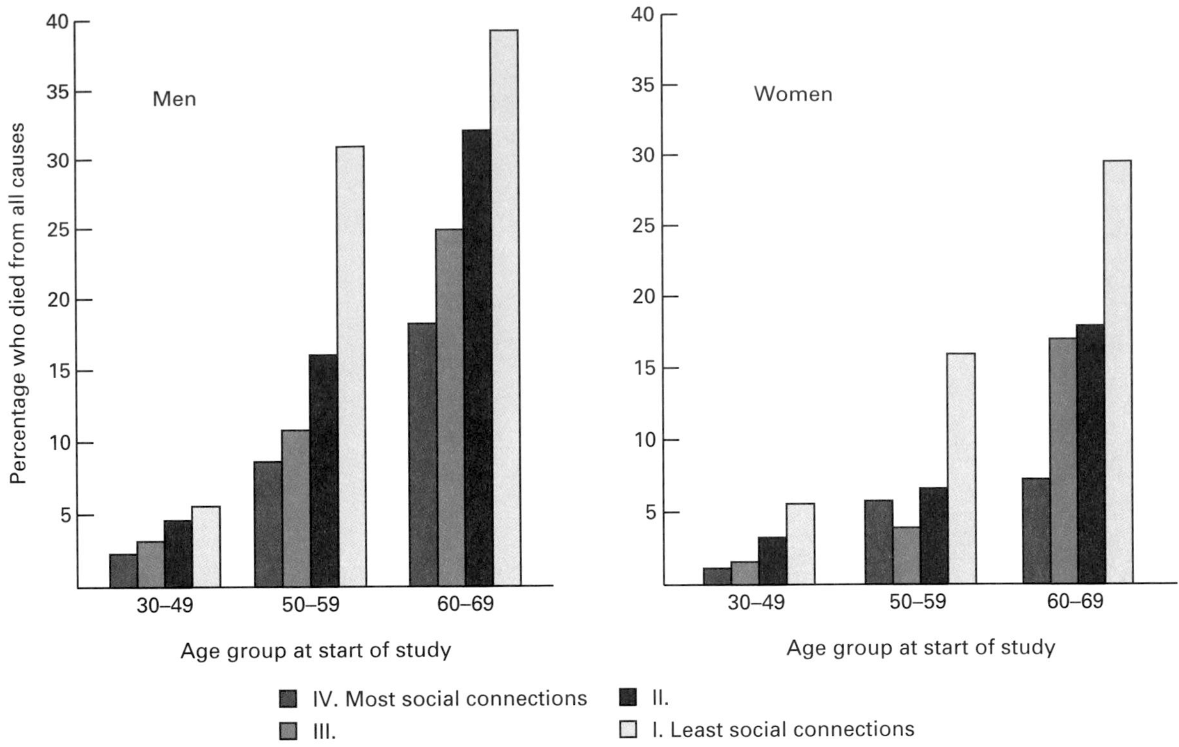

FIGURE 13.7 The extensiveness of a person's social network is predictive of the risk of death over the next decade, an example of the potency of the impact of social support on health. (*Source:* Berkman & Breslow, 1983, Figure 4-3, p. 130.)

al., 1990) propose a specific link between attachment and the sense of support, suggesting that the tendency to perceive support as being "out there" and "sufficient" is related to the security of a person's basic attachment. The more secure the attachment, the greater our "sense of social support" is likely to be.

The link between social support and health can again be illustrated with some of the findings from the Alameda study, shown in Figure 13.7. In this case, the social network index reflects an objective measurement: number of contacts with friends and relatives, marital status, church and group membership. But even using this less-than-perfect measure of support, the relationship is vividly clear. Similar patterns have been found in other countries, including Sweden (Orth-Gomér, Rosengren, & Wilhelmsen, 1993) and Japan (Sugisawa, Liang, & Liu, 1994), so this link between social contact and physical hardiness is not restricted to the United States, or to Western cultures.

Of course it is possible that social support is not the crucial variable here. Perhaps people with low social support are different in other ways that are significant for health, such as health habits or social class. Berkman (1985) checked out these possibilities in the Alameda data and found that the link between support and risk of death persisted even when initial physical health status, social class, smoking, alcohol consumption, level of physical activity, weight, race, and life satisfaction were taken into account.

This beneficial effect of social support is particularly clear when an individual is under high stress. That is, the negative effect of stress on health and happiness is smaller for those individuals with adequate social support than for those whose social support is weak. This pattern of results is usually described as the *buffering* effect of social support.

An excellent example comes from research on depression among women in England by George Brown and Tirril Harris (Brown, 1989, 1993; Brown & Harris, 1978). They initially studied 419 women who ranged in age from 18 to 65, gathering informa-

Table 13.4 Percentage of Women in the Brown and Harris Study Experiencing Significant Depression Following Major Stress

	Confidant		
	Husband or Boyfriend	Other Family Member	No Close Confidant
At least one severe stress within past year	10%	26%	41%
No severe stress in past year	1%	3%	4%

Source: Brown & Harris, 1978, adapted from Table 1, p. 177.

tion about the number of severe stressful events each woman had experienced in the past year (such as the death of someone close, a divorce or failed relationship, or the equivalent), about whether they were currently depressed, and about who—if anyone—served as an intimate confidant. Table 13.4 shows the relationship among these several variables. You can see that the likelihood of depression was far greater among women who have recently experienced a major stress. But within that group, depression was also linked to the source and degree of social support the woman had. Women who had a close confidant, especially if that confidant was her husband or boyfriend, were much less likely to become depressed under stress. That is, the social support of their partner or other confidant *buffered* them against the negative effects of the stress.

Whether any age differences exist in the strength of these relationships is not so clear. Examples of the buffering effect of social support can be found in studies of adults of every age group. But I could make an argument that social support may be especially critical in young adulthood. According to Erikson and others, the early years of adult life are focused on the task of creating satisfying intimate relationships with both a marital or cohabiting partner and with friends. We also have evidence that the *lack* of such intimacy is especially disturbing in these early years. More young adults describe themselves as lonely, for example, than is true of any other age group (Peplau et al., 1982), which may be a major contributing factor to the high rate of depression among young adults. Given the centrality of this issue in early adulthood, one might hypothesize that a social support measure would be more strongly related to health in this age group than at other ages. So far as I know, there is no study that tests this possibility, but it is a hypothesis worth exploring.

A Sense of Control. Another personal characteristic that affects physical and mental health is an individual's level of what Judith Rodin calls *perceived control* (1990). The sense of control has been described in varying language, and with varying emphases, by several important theorists. Albert Bandura (1977b; 1982c; 1986) talks about it in terms of **self-efficacy,** the belief in one's ability to perform some action or to control one's behavior or environment, to reach some goal or make something happen. Such a belief is one aspect of what I have called the internal model of the self, and is affected by one's whole history of experience with mastering tasks and overcoming obstacles.

Rotter (1966) expresses another aspect of the same broad idea in his concept of **locus of control.** He differentiates between *internal* and *external* locus of control orientations. An individual with an internal orientation believes that things happen to him because of what he himself has done; those with an external locus believe that they have no control over what happens to them, that control lies in others or in the system. Several studies in Finland suggest that adults become somewhat more external in their orientation with age, since they feel less able to control health and their children as they get older (Nurmi, Pulliainen, & Salmela-Aro, 1992). But at any age individuals vary widely in their tendency toward an internal or external sense of control.

Yet a third version of this same general idea comes from the work of Martin Seligman (1991), who differentiates between positions of *optimism* and *helplessness*. The pessimist, who feels helpless, believes that misfortune will last a long time, will undermine everything, and is his own fault. The optimist believes that setbacks are temporary and usually caused by circumstances. He is convinced that there is always some solution and that he will be able to work things out. Confronted by defeat, he sees it as a challenge and tries harder, whereas the pessimist gives up.

All these theorists propose that the basic sense of control/efficacy/optimism arises in childhood and adolescence, as a result of our early experiences of effectiveness and success or failure and frustration.

Research on the links between a sense of control and health show that those with a more helpless attitude or with a low sense of self-efficacy are more likely to become depressed or physically ill (Seligman, 1991; Syme, 1990; *New York Times*, 1994). The most striking demonstration of this connection is from the 35-year Grant study of a group of Harvard men who were first interviewed in their freshman year, in 1938–1940. Researchers were able to use interview material from a contact with these men when they were 25 to assess their degree of pessimism. Their later physical health from age 30 to 60 was then rated by physicians who examined the subjects every five years. Pessimism was not related to health at 30, 35, or 40, but at every assessment from 45 to 60, those who had had a more pessimistic approach at age 25 had significantly poorer health, and this was true even if physical and mental health at age 25 was controlled statistically (Peterson, Seligman, & Vaillant, 1988).

Pessimism or a lack of control may thus reflect a basic personality characteristic that affects both the choices adults make and their interpretation of experience. A person's sense of control is also clearly influenced by specific circumstances. Epidemiologist Leonard Syme (1990) points to research in both Sweden and the United States showing that the rate of heart disease is unusually high among workers whose job has a high level of demand but low discretion and latitude. That is, when the stress is high but your ability to make choices and control the situation is low, disease rates go up. Because the jobs held by many working-class and lower-class adults are likely to be of this type, while jobs held by the highest social class group are likely to allow more personal control, perhaps the concept of perceived control can help to explain the large social class differences in disease rates you saw in Figure 13.3.

Finally, it is also possible to show that experimentally increasing someone's sense of control improves his health, even improving immune function—a rare case in which we have both cross-sectional, longitudinal, and experimental evidence on the same point (Welch & West, 1995). In the earliest and best-known study of this kind, Judith Rodin and Ellen Langer (1977) found that mortality rates of nursing home residents were lower among those who had been given control over even quite simple aspects of their daily lives, such as whether to have scrambled eggs or omelettes for breakfast or whether to sign up to attend a movie.

It seems quite likely that children growing up in poverty-level families, or in circumstances in which they rarely have much control over their lives, may be more likely to develop a low sense of self-efficacy and little optimism. These psychological processes and enduring personality characteristics, in turn, affect roles, relationships, and physical health.

Summary

1. Although it is an arbitrary division, we can segment the adult years into three main periods, with young adulthood constituting the years from 20 to about 40.
2. It is important to distinguish between *primary aging* and *secondary aging*. The former refers to unavoidable, universal, maturationally based changes with age; the latter describes changes resulting from specific experience, disease, or environment. Research on physical changes over the adult years has not always been designed to make this distinction clear.

3. Nonetheless, it is clear that between 20 and 40, adults are at their peak both physically and cognitively. In these years a person has more muscle tissue, more calcium in the bones, more brain mass, better sensory acuity, greater aerobic capacity, and a more efficient immune system.
4. On most measures of physical functioning, however, some gradual decline nonetheless begins in the late 20s or 30s, although these changes may not accumulate sufficiently to be functionally noticeable until several decades later, *except* for those individuals attempting to function at the absolute upper edge of efficiency.
5. Studies of heart and lung function show no age change under resting conditions, but performance declines with age when tests are given during or after exercise.
6. A number of these changes contribute to a loss of speed with age—speed in neural functioning, response time to some stimulus, and movement speed.
7. Changes in the immune system may be especially critical in accounting for what we think of as the aging process, because they mean we become increasingly susceptible to disease as we get older.
8. Increases in disease and disability with age are earlier and larger for lower-class than upper-class adults, even when health habits and stress levels are taken into account.
9. In contrast, mental health is *worse* in early adulthood than in middle adulthood; young adults are more likely to be depressed, anxious, or lonely than are the middle-aged.
10. Measures of cognitive skill, like physical skill, show declines with age, but the decline is quite late for well-exercised abilities (crystallized abilities) like vocabulary, everyday memory problems, and normal problem solving. A measurable decline occurs earlier for so-called fluid abilities.
11. There *may* also be a change in cognitive structure in adult life, with several varieties of postformal operational stages suggested by theorists.
12. Exercise of either physical or cognitive abilities can improve performance at any age, although if Denney's model is correct, then the upper limit declines with increasing age.
13. The rate of physical and cognitive loss varies widely across individuals. Some of this difference seems to be explained by varying health habits. Adults with good health habits have lower risk of death and disease at any age.
14. Social support and a sense of personal control also affect the rate of disease and death, especially in the face of stress.

Key Terms

crystallized intelligence
dialectical thought
fluid intelligence
locus of control
maximum oxygen uptake (VO_2 max)
primary aging
secondary aging
self-efficacy

Suggested Readings

Adler, N. E., Boyce, T., Chesney, M. A., Cohen, S., Folkman, S., Kahn, R. L., & Syme, S. L. (1994). Socioeconomic status and health: The challenge of the gradient. *American Psychologist, 49*, 15–24.

A brief review of the data showing that poor adults (and children) have poorer health and shorter life expectancy than those from higher social classes. The alternative explanations are explored.

Hayflick, L. (1994). *How and why we age*. New York: Ballantine Books.

An excellent summary, written for a lay audience, of the facts and theories of physical aging. The book focuses more on middle age and old age than on early adulthood, but it covers many of the items I listed in Table 13.1.

Schaie, K. W. (1993). The Seattle Longitudinal Studies of adult intelligence. *Current Directions in Psychological Science, 2*, 171–175.

A brief current description of the major findings from Schaie's immense longitudinal study.

Seligman, M. E. P. (1991). *Learned optimism*. New York: Alfred A. Knopf.

A very readable description of Seligman's influential theory of optimism and learned helplessness, written for the lay reader. A wide-ranging and thought-provoking book.

Salthouse, T. A. (1991). *Theoretical perspectives on cognitive aging*. Hillsdale, NJ: Lawrence Erlbaum Associates.

An extremely detailed analysis of all the evidence on cognitive changes from early to late adulthood. This book is not for the casual reader, but is an excellent source of further references on virtually any aspect of this complex subject.

Schneider, E. L., & Rowe, J. W. (Eds.) (1996). *Handbook of the biology of aging*, 4th ed. San Diego, CA: Academic Press.

A compendium of technical papers describing current knowledge about various facets of biological aging, including changes in the brain, the circulatory system, and the immune systems.

14 Social and Personality Development in Early Adulthood

If you had glanced over the table of contents of this book before you began reading, I'd lay odds that it was this chapter that caught your eye. Nearly every one of you reading this text is a young adult, and while you may find the subtle biological changes I described in the last chapter somewhat interesting, it is the social and psychological stuff of your current life that is compelling. In early adulthood, each of us takes our place in our society. For nearly all of us, this means acquiring, learning, and performing the three roles central to adult life: worker, spouse, and parent.

The details of timing and content of these roles obviously differ from one culture to another, and from one cohort to another. In rural subsistence cultures, work and marriage come much earlier than in most industrialized cultures. And in our own society, there has been quite a lot of variability from one cohort to the next in the typical age for marriage or bearing children. For example, the median age for first marriage among women in the United States rose from 20.6 in 1970 to 23.7 in 1988—a very large change in a short span of years (U.S. Bureau of the Census, 1995). But regardless of such changes in the cultural norms, it is still true that in early adulthood we must each turn outward from our preoccupation with self-definition and take on a series of roles that involve intricate relationships with other people.

Leaving Home

One accompaniment, or precursor, of this role-acquisition process is leaving home. Of course, some young people (more often young women) leave home at the time of marriage and have no intervening period of independent or semi-independent living. Increasingly, however, young men and women in developed countries move through a transitional phase, living apart from their family but not yet married or cohabiting (Thornton, Young-DeMarco, & Goldscheider, 1993). College provides precisely this kind of transitional phase for large numbers of young people; others leave home to set up independent households, a pattern especially common among young adults who are working full time.

Attachment to Parents

Leaving home is more than just setting up a separate residence. It also involves a highly significant psychological emancipation process in which the young person distances himself emotionally from his parents to at least some degree. In essence, the young adult must transfer his most central attachment from the parent(s) to one or more peers. As Robert Weiss puts it:

> If children are eventually to form their own households, their bonds of attachment to the parents must become attenuated and eventually end. Otherwise, independent living would be emotionally troubling. The relinquishing of attachment to parents appears to be of central importance among the individuation-achieving processes of late adolescence and early adulthood. (1986, p. 100)

Critical Thinking

Do you buy Weiss's argument? How might you go about trying to determine whether adults are still attached to their parents, as attachment has been defined by Ainsworth (discussed in Chapter 6)?

Many theorists dispute Weiss's contention that the attachment to the parent is fully given up in adult life (e.g., Cicirelli, 1991). The great majority of adults maintain regular contact with their parents throughout their lives and experience deep grief at their parents' deaths. When we are under great stress, we may also long to have our

The moment of leaving home is not necessarily easy, but every young person must come to it eventually, whether it is to go off to college, to set up an independent household, or to marry.

parents there to comfort us—all signs that some form of attachment continues to exist. But we clearly pull back from this bond in early adulthood, a necessary step if the relationship to an intimate partner is to become the central attachment of one's emotional life. As Corinne Nydegger puts it, "The task [of the young adult] is to attain emotional emancipation from the parents, while remaining engaged as a son or daughter" (Nydegger, 1991, p. 102).

Such an emancipation occurs for most adults in their early 20s. If you ask children and adults questions like, "Who is the person you don't like to be away from?" or "Who is the person you know will always be there for you," children and teenagers most often list their parents, while adults most often name their spouse and almost never mention their parents (Hazan et al., 1991).

Let me say again that I am not trying to propose here that parents become unimportant to adult life. Indeed, four out of every five adults in a recent national sample said that their relationship with their parents is emotionally close (Lawton, Silverstein, & Bengtson, 1994). Relationships with mothers are closer than those with fathers (Rossi, 1989); when the parents are divorced, the relationship tends to be less close, especially with a divorced father (Cooney, 1994; Webster & Herzog, 1995). Even with these variations, it is still true that the adult child/parent relationship is affectionate and significant for most adults. But in early adulthood, the parent-child relationship ceases to be the *central* attachment for most of us.

Interestingly, it begins to look as if securely attached young people have an easier time making this transition than do those with anxious, ambivalent attachments. Among college students, for example, one study shows that those who are still "absorbed" by their relationship with their parents and with their need to become independent experienced greater stress and more physical and psychological symptoms than do those with a more secure relationship to their parents (Zirkel & Cantor, 1990). So just as an infant with a secure attachment feels more comfortable physically moving away from the parent and exploring new territory, the young adult with a secure attachment finds it easier to move away from the parent psychologically, and to shift her central attachment from parent to peer.

Finding a Partner

You'll remember that Erikson lists *intimacy versus isolation* as the key task of early adulthood, where intimacy is defined as "the ability to fuse your identity with someone else's without fear that you're going to lose something yourself" (Erikson, in Evans, 1969). This new level of intimacy can be and is expressed in a range of relationships, including friendships. But its most central expression is in a relationship with partner or mate—a single individual with whom we can find or create an intimate, secure attachment. That core relationship then forms the secure base from which each adult can move out into the adult world; it also obviously creates the nuclear family in which the next generation of children will be reared. An individual who fails to create such an intimate relationship will lack that secure base and will experience a sense of isolation or loneliness. Indeed, you may remember from the last chapter that loneliness is at its peak in the earliest years of adulthood, years when so many young people are betwixt and between, having turned partly away from family, but not yet found an intimate partnership.

You may have noticed that I have consistently used the word *partner* rather than spouse. I have done so quite deliberately, because I want to include homosexual and cohabiting heterosexual partnerships as well as marital partners in this discussion. We know far less about the former two groups than about married couples, but the available research suggests that many of the same processes are involved in all three types of relationship.

The Process of Choosing

What attracts us to one person and not another? Why do some pairs break up, while others continue to the point of commitment? We have a lot more heat than light on these questions—an enormous amount of research but not many clear answers.

One psychological approach has been to describe mate selection as a series of "filters" or steps (Cate & Lloyd, 1992). Bernard Murstein, for example (1970, 1976, 1986) suggests that when you meet a prospective partner you first check for the degree of match on basic "external" characteristics, such as appearance, manners, or apparent social class. If this first hurdle is passed, you then check for a match on attitudes and beliefs, such as politics or religion. Finally, if you are still interested in one another, the degree of "role fit" becomes an issue: Do your prospective partner's expectations fit with your needs or inclinations? Is there sexual compatibility, or agreement on gender roles? The research suggests that all these elements are important, but the sequence is probably not nearly as rigid as Murstein suggested. All three facets may be part of your reaction from the very beginning.

CRITICAL THINKING

Does Murstein's model make sense to you? When you meet someone new, do you have a sort of mental checklist? What's on that list?

Sociologists, in contrast, have focused more on external qualities, and here the findings are clear: The strongest single element in attraction and mate selection is similarity. We are drawn to those like ourselves—in age, education, social class, ethnic group membership, religion, attitudes, interests, and temperament. Sociologists describe this as a process of *assortive mating* or *homogamy*. Further, partnerships based on homogamy are much more likely to endure than are those in which the partners differ markedly (Murstein, 1986).

In addition to the process of assortive mating, choosing a partner appears to involve some kind of exchange process. Each of us has certain assets to offer to a potential mate. Exchange theorists (Edwards, 1969) argue that we each try for the best bargain, the best exchange, we can manage. According to this model, women frequently exchange their sexual and domestic services for the economic support offered by a man (Schoen & Wooldredge, 1989). In choosing a partner, this means that women are likely to be more concerned with the job prospects or economic status of a potential mate, while men are more focused on attractiveness. Survey data from the United States provide some support for this view (South, 1991). A national sample of over 2000 unmarried adults were asked to indicate how willing they would be to marry someone with various characteristics, such as someone who was not good looking, someone younger than themselves, someone with less or more education than themselves, and someone who earns more or less than themselves.

In this survey, white, black, and Hispanic men were all less willing than were women to marry someone who was not good looking, but more willing to marry someone with less education or lower income. Overall, women seem to aim to "marry up" economically or socially and are very concerned about the future economic prospects of a potential mate, while men are less concerned about such questions and more willing to marry "down" on any trait except attractiveness.

Social scientists have not done very well at devising theories to explain lovely moments of romance like this one.

Creating a Relationship

All that sounds as if choosing a partner is a pretty cold-blooded, rational process. But let us not forget the powerful role of sexual attraction and love, and the equally profound role of personality and attachment patterns in shaping both our choice of mate, and the pattern of relationship we create with that partner.

The Role of Attachment. In particular, the role of internal working models of attachment in partner selection and relationship formation has been the focus of a whole burst of research in the past few years (e.g., Crowell & Waters, 1995; Feeney, 1994; Fuller & Fincham, 1995; Hazan & Shaver, 1987; Owens et al., 1995; Rothbard &

Shaver, 1994). I find this new work fascinating because it helps to connect the often separate research on child and adult development. It also underlines yet again the importance of internal working models in shaping our behavior.

The basic argument is that each of us tends to recreate in our partnership relationships the pattern we carry in our internal model of attachment. That does not mean that the security of the very first attachment in infancy is invariably carried forward, unaltered. In the Across Development box in Chapter 6 (p. 140), I pointed out that change in these internal models clearly can occur. In particular, some adults with insecure attachment histories are able to analyze and accept their childhood relationships and create a new internal model. But whether a young adult's internal model is the product of redefinition or unchanged early assumptions, it will still affect her expectations for a partner, the sort of partner she chooses, the way she will behave with her partner, and the stability of the relationship.

Adults' attachment models have been measured in several different ways. The simplest method is one devised by Cindy Hazan and Phillip Shaver (1987) who ask each of their subjects to choose one of the three descriptions of relationships given in Table 14.1. In a sample of over 600 adults, of varying ages, they found 56 percent described themselves as secure (option 1), 25 percent chose option 2 (avoidant), and 19 percent chose option 3 (anxious or ambivalent), remarkably similar to the incidence of these three types in children.

A more in-depth method of measuring attachment is Mary Main's Adult Attachment Interview, described briefly in the box in Chapter 6. The two ways of measuring attachment security do not always yield identical results, but the research using both methods suggests strong parallels with the findings from research on children's attachment patterns.

The new research tells us that adults do indeed tend to create similar internal models of their attachment to their parents and their attachment to a prospective spouse. For example, Gretchen Owens and her colleagues (1995) found that nearly two-thirds of her sample of about-to-be-married young people scored in the same attachment category (secure, dismissing, or preoccupied) when they described their love relationship as when they described their relationship with their parents.

Other researchers have found that those adults with secure attachment models are inclined to trust others, to see their partner as their friend as well as lover, to

Table 14.1 Attachment Descriptions Used by Hazan and Shaver in Their Research

Which of the following best describes your feelings?

1. I find it relatively easy to get close to others and am comfortable depending on them and having them depend on me. I don't often worry about being abandoned or about someone getting too close to me.
2. I am somewhat uncomfortable being close to others; I find it difficult to trust them completely, difficult to allow myself to depend on them. I am nervous when anyone gets too close, and often, love partners want me to be more intimate than I feel comfortable being.
3. I find that others are reluctant to get as close as I would like. I often worry that my partner doesn't really love me or won't want to stay with me. I want to merge completely with another person, and this desire sometimes scares people away.

Source: Hazan & Shaver, 1987, Table 2, p. 515.

show little jealousy and little anxiety about whether their affection will be or is reciprocated. They give more support to their partners in tense or anxious situations and seek comfort from their partner more easily. Adults with a preoccupied attachment model (roughly equivalent to the anxious attachment of an infant) are unsure of themselves in relationships, anxious about whether their feelings are reciprocated, and jealous and preoccupied with their relationship. Those with a dismissing or detached internal model are less happy in their relationships, less trusting, avoid closeness, disclose little about themselves, and are less accepting of the other person. In a tense or anxious situation, they seek less support and provide less reassurance. Perhaps, expecting rejection, they hold back from commitment.

Just what role attachment models may play in relationship stability or satisfaction is not yet clear from the evidence we have. Some studies suggest that any pair including an insecurely attached individual is likely to be less stable and satisfying than are pairs in which both partners are securely attached (Berman, Marcus, & Berman, 1994; Feeney, 1994). But at least one longitudinal study, covering a period of four years, indicates that only those pairs with an avoidant man or an ambivalent woman are less stable (Kirkpatrick & Hazan, 1994). It seems highly likely that these internal models are linked in important ways with relationship processes and success, but we don't yet understand precisely how it works.

The Role of Love. A different approach to understanding the process of adult mating and bonding comes primarily from social psychologists, who have tried to understand the differences among various types of adult relationships. The most compelling of these theories comes from Robert Sternberg (1987), who argues that love has three key components: (1) *intimacy*, which includes feelings that promote closeness and connectedness; (2) *passion*, which includes a feeling of intense longing for union with the other person, including sexual union; and (3) *commitment* to a particular other, often over a long period of time. When these three components are combined in all possible ways, you end up with the eight subvarieties of love listed in Table 14.2.

Table 14.2 Sternberg's Eight Varieties of Love

Variety	Characteristics
Nonlove	None of the three components is present. Describes most casual relationships or acquaintanceships.
Liking	Intimacy without passion or commitment. Many friendships are in this category.
Infatuation	Passion without intimacy or commitment.
Empty love	Commitment without passion or intimacy. Describes some stagnant long-term marriages, or "friendships" that have gone on for years but have lost mutual involvement and mutual attraction.
Romantic love	Passion and intimacy without commitment. May be characteristic of the early stages of a relationship.
Companionate love	Intimacy and commitment without passion. May describe some long-term committed friendships, or relationships with parents or other kin, or with a partner with whom passion has waned.
Fatuous love	Passion and commitment without intimacy, as in a whirlwind courtship; the commitment is based on passion rather than on intimacy, though intimacy may come later.
Consummate love	All three components are present.

Source: Sternberg, 1987.

Critical Thinking

Think about your own current and previous relationships. How would you classify each of them in Sternberg's system?

Sternberg's approach is clearly much broader than models based on the concept of attachment. He is attempting to describe and understand the full range of adult relationships, not just those that involve attachment. But both theories make it clear that we need to understand the *quality* of particular relationships, including both the quality of the attachment models the adults bring to a relationship, and the degree of intimacy, passion, and commitment they invest. At this point it is not yet clear which of these two approaches will turn out to be the most fruitful. But both of them take us important steps forward in our attempt to understand the formation and functioning of partnerships in young adulthood and beyond.

Partnerships over Time

Greater understanding also requires us to study partnerships over time. Do relationships typically shift from one of Sternberg's categories of love to another? Do securely attached partners show different kinds of change over time than do insecurely attached pairs?

We have surprisingly little information relevant to such questions. Part of the problem is that cross-sectional studies, which might otherwise be a way to get some sense of marital changes over time, suffer in this case from a major methodological problem: If we compare 5-year marriages with 15-year marriages, the older group necessarily includes only enduring marriages. Couples who divorce between the fifth and fifteenth year are omitted from the studies. Thus, we may end up knowing something about the characteristics of *lasting* marriages/partnerships, but not about relationships in more general terms. Furthermore, duration of marriage is normally confounded with age. A 20-year marriage is typically a marriage between adults in their 40s, and we could not be sure that observed characteristics of the relationship were the result of changes in relationships in general, or of being fortysomething. To avoid this particular difficulty, we would need to study marriages that began at various ages, following each pair over time. No one has done such a study, or even anything close to it. The best information we have comes from a small set of longitudinal studies that cover only the first few years of marriage. Still, these few studies reveal some interesting changes in the actual interactions between partners in the early years.

The best single piece of research I know of is by Ted Huston and his colleagues (Huston & Chorost, 1994; Huston, McHale, & Crouter, 1986; MacDermid, Huston, & McHale, 1990), who studied 168 couples in their first marriages. Each partner was interviewed at length within the first three months of the marriage, and then again after one year. In addition, in the weeks surrounding each of these time points, each couple was called nine different times and asked to describe in detail what they had done over the previous 24 hours. Thus, Huston has information not only about feelings and attitudes but about actual activities. He found that over the first year there was a decrease in satisfaction with both the quantity and the quality of interaction. These couples reported lower levels of love after one year, and that was true whether they had had a child or not. Furthermore, their activities had changed. In the early months they spent a lot more time in joint leisure activities; after one year, when they did things together it was more likely to be on "instrumental tasks" (grocery shopping, errands, housework, and the like). They also talked to each other less. Perhaps most importantly, the husbands and wives both described a sizable drop in the frequency of positive interactions, a pattern you can see in the results shown in Figure 14.1. In Sternberg's terms, there was a decline in the intimacy aspect of love as well as in the passionate aspect.

Such a decline in pleasing behaviors, accompanied by a drop in marital satisfaction, is entirely consistent with the results of new research on the causes of stable and unstable, satisfying and unsatisfying marriages.

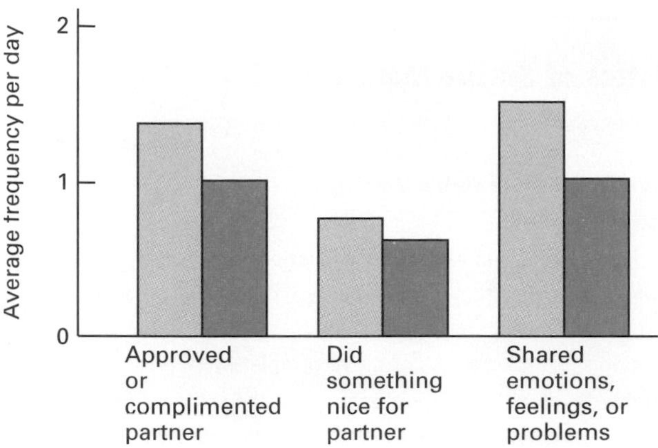

FIGURE 14.1 Most couples become less satisfied with their marriages in their first year together. The reason for such a decline is clear when you look at actual interactions, which become much less positive and supportive. (*Source:* Huston et al., 1986, from Table 7.4, p. 124.)

Good and Bad Marriages

Most of the rest of what we know about partnerships in the years of early adulthood comes from studies of the causes of divorce. By current estimates, between 50 and 60 percent of all first marriages in the United States will end in divorce (Gottman, 1994a), so this is clearly a vitally important subject. I've summarized some of the main conclusions from this very large body of research in Table 14.3, and you'll want to read the list carefully.

Two points stand out for me when I read this list. First, many powerful influences on marital success exist before a marriage even begins. Each partner brings to the relationship certain skills, resources, and traits that affect the emerging partnership system. Couples with better resources—more education, better ability to solve problems, better health (including low rates of alcoholism), and greater self-esteem—are more able to weather the storms and stresses of marriage. The personality characteristics of the partners seem to be especially important. For example, Kelly and Conley (1987), in a remarkable longitudinal study of 300 couples who were engaged in 1930 and studied until 1980, found that the single best predictor of divorce was a high level of the personality trait of neuroticism in either partner (a trait you'll recall as one of the "Big Five" personality traits listed in Table 12.4, p. 316). And among those couples in this study who remained married, those in which one or both partners was high in neuroticism had the lowest marital satisfaction.

But a marriage or partnership is more than the sum of the qualities or assets of the two individuals. Equally important for the success of marriage is the quality of the actual interactions that develop between the couple. And in those interactions, the most crucial feature seems to be simply the relative proportion of "nice" to "nasty" everyday encounters. John Gottman, whose research in this area is especially impressive, has found that those couples who eventually divorce can be identified years ahead of time by looking at the pattern of these positive and negative exchanges. When negative items—criticism, complaints, "yes-but" statements, put-downs, or the like—exceed the positive by too much, divorce becomes far more likely (Gottman, 1994a). As Gottman says, "One can think of each partner in a marriage having a built-in meter that measures the totality of accumulated negativity in this interaction" (1994a, p. 333). Gottman proposes that once the level of this meter

Table 14.3 Characteristics of Stable Marriages

Personal Characteristics of Individuals in More Stable Marriages

- They married between ages 20 and 30.
- They come from high-social-class families and have more education.
- Their parents display(ed) lower levels of conflict in their own marriage, and were less likely to have divorced.
- They have greater communication skill and greater cognitive complexity.
- They are more likely to be highly involved in religion or to be of the same religious background.
- They have higher levels of self-esteem.
- They have better overall mental health, lower levels of depression, and lower levels of the personality trait called "neuroticism" (recall Table 12.4, p. 316).
- They are more likely to have a secure internal working model of attachment.

Qualities of the Interaction of Couples in Stable Marriages

- They have more positive than negative interactions.
- They have high agreement on roles (including gender roles) and high satisfaction with the way the spouse is filling his or her roles.
- They are roughly matched on levels of self-disclosure (high, medium, or low in both partners).
- They have better conflict-resolution strategies, with low levels of both criticism and problem avoidance.
- They are more symmetrical in their skill at reading each other's signals. In dissatisfied marriages, the husband appears to "read" the wife less well than she reads him.
- They like each other and consider their spouse their best friend.
- They spend more leisure time together.

Sources: Cate & Lloyd, 1992; Davidson, Balswick, & Halverson, 1983; Filsinger & Thoma, 1988; Gottman, 1994a; Gottman, 1994b; Halford, Hahlweg, & Dunne, 1990; Heaton & Pratt, 1990; Hill, 1988; Karney & Bradbury, 1995; Kitson, 1992; Kitson, Babri, & Roach, 1985; Larson & Holman, 1994; Schafer & Keith, 1984; Wilson & Filsinger, 1986.

gets above some threshold, the partner's perception of the marriage "flips" from positive to negative. The accumulation of negativity may be gradual, but the *feeling*, the perception, switches rapidly, and the individual then considers separation or divorce.

Gottman does not propose that all good marriages are alike, or that all bad marriages are the same. He has identified three quite different types of stable or enduring marriages (Gottman, 1994b):

- *Validating*: Disagreements rarely escalate in these marriages. The partners express mutual respect even when they disagree, and listen well to one another.
- *Volatile*: These couples squabble a lot, disagree, don't listen to each other very well when they argue. But they still have more positive than negative encounters, showing high levels of laughter and affection.
- *Avoidant*. These pairs, whom Gottman also calls "conflict minimizers," don't try to persuade each other, they simply agree to disagree, without apparent rancor, a pattern sometimes described as "devitalized."

Equivalently, Gottman finds several types of unsuccessful marriages:

- *Hostile/engaged*. Like volatile couples, these pairs have frequent hot arguments, but they lack the balancing effect of humor and affection.

Critical Thinking

Think about your most recent unsuccessful relationship—a dating relationship that did not last, a marriage that ended in divorce. Was there a point in the relationship when the ratio of negative to positive encounters became so high that it spiraled out of control? Was the change gradual?

The Real World

Cohabitation and Its Effect on Subsequent Marriage

In the 1970s and 1980s, the average age at first marriage in the United States began to rise rapidly, and the number of young people listed as "never married" rose in tandem. For example, in 1970, only about 10 percent of women aged 25–29 had never married; by 1990 this number had tripled (U.S. Bureau of the Census, 1995). Such numbers might mean that young adults are simply more reluctant to marry today, perhaps because they want to establish careers before they marry. The alternative possibility, supported by the research, is that young people are forming committed partnerships just as early and as often, but many more are choosing to cohabit instead of marry (Bumpass & Sweet, 1989; Bumpass, Sweet, & Cherlin, 1991).

In the United States, as in most Western industrialized countries, rates of cohabitation have quadrupled since 1970. In a large U.S. survey in 1988, Bumpass and Sweet (1989) found that nearly half of all adults in their early 30s had cohabited at least once—a number that has doubtless risen since then. Sixty percent of these cohabitations result in marriage.

In effect, cohabitation is becoming a common step in the process of courtship and marriage, although this is more true in some subgroups than in others. You may think that cohabitation is largely a behavior of college students, but the data say otherwise. While more than a quarter of college students have cohabited before marriage, the rate is much higher among those with *less* education. Bumpass and his colleagues argue that this results because lower-education adults are less likely to have the economic resources to marry. Racial differences in cohabitation also run partially counter to stereotypic expectations: If you control for education, blacks are *less* likely to cohabit than are non-Hispanic whites. Hispanics have the lowest rates of the three groups (Bumpass & Sweet, 1989).

Most couples who live together conceive of cohabitation as a final "filter," a sort of "test" before marriage. Can we really get along together? Are we sexually compatible? In Sternberg's terms, it is a test of the commitment element of love. The assumption is that relationships that pass this test will end in marriage and that such marriages will be more satisfying and more durable. Interestingly, the great bulk of the evidence shows exactly the opposite.

Studies in the United States, Canada, and European countries such as Sweden all show that those who cohabit before marriage are *less* satisfied with their subsequent marriages and *more* likely to divorce than are those who marry without cohabiting (DeMaris & Rao, 1992; Hall & Zhao, 1995; Thomson & Colella, 1992). The most likely explanation of this surprising set of findings is not that cohabiting somehow spoils people for marriage but that adults who choose to live together before marriage are systematically different in key ways from those who reject such an option. DeMaris and Leslie (1984), for example, found that cohabitors are less traditional in gender roles, less likely to attend church, and less likely to agree that one should stick with a marriage no matter how bad it is, while noncohabitors are much more traditional in attitudes. Thus, the difference in marital stability between cohabitors and noncohabitors is a matter of self-selection, not some causal processes attributable to cohabitation itself. Such an explanation is further strengthened by the finding that the negative correlates of cohabitation have become smaller and smaller in recent cohorts, and have disappeared altogether in the cohort born between 1953 and 1957 (Schoen, 1992). Because cohabitation has become more and more common in these recent generations, self-selection is a less powerful factor, and the apparent negative effect vanishes.

Collectively, the data do not tell us that cohabitation somehow spoils people for later marriage. But neither do they suggest that cohabitation makes later marriage better, as most cohabitors believe.

- *Hostile/detached.* These couples fight regularly, but they rarely look at each other, the arguments tend to be brief, and they also lack affection and support.

In both unsuccessful types, the ratio of negative to positive encounters gets out of balance, and they spiral downward toward dissolution.

What is the direction of causality in all this? Do couples become unhappy because they are more negative, or more negative because they are already unhappy? Both may happen, but it looks as if the more common route is that couples become unhappy because they are negative. The best indication of this comes from studies of therapeutic interventions with unhappy couples: Couples who are trained to increase their rate of positive interactions typically show increases in their marital satisfaction (e.g., O'Leary & Smith, 1991).

As a final point, I am struck by the parallel between the qualities of a successful marriage and the qualities of a secure attachment. Adults in good marriages have a high level of the same kind of responsiveness to the other's signals that we see between securely attached infants and their parents. Satisfied partners take turns, read each other's cues, and respond positively. Whatever internal model of attachment an individual may bring to a marriage, the ability of the partners to create such a mutually interlocking and supportive interactive system seems to be critical in the survival of the marriage.

Social Networks: Friendships and Kin Relationships

Creating a partnership may be the most central task of the stage of intimacy, but it is certainly not the only reflection of that basic process. In early adult life, each of us creates what Toni Antonucci (1990, 1994b) calls a **convoy** of relationships, a "protective layer . . . of family and friends, who surround the individual and help in the successful negotiation of life's challenges" (Antonucci & Akiyama, 1987a, p. 519). The convoy includes family members, a partner if you have one, and friends.

Relationships with Family Members

Parents remain significant parts of the convoy for virtually all adults. Although our attachment to our parents may be attenuated, most of us still see or talk to our parents regularly. A good illustration comes from an older study by Jeffrey Leigh (1982).

Research Report

Homosexual Partnerships

Contrary to current cultural myths, long-term, committed partnerships are common among homosexuals. Estimates vary, but perhaps 70 percent of lesbians are in committed relationships, in most cases living together, most often monogamously. Among gay men, the percentages are somewhat lower: Between 40 and 60 percent are in long-term committed relationships, but only about a fifth of these relationships are monogamous (compared to roughly three-quarters of heterosexual partnerships) (Blumstein & Schwartz, 1983; Kurdek, 1995b).

Letitia Peplau, who has been one of the most active researchers in this area, also reports that homosexuals are as likely as heterosexuals to be satisfied with their partner relationships. What does differentiate the two types of partnerships is the nature of the power relation within the couple. Homosexual couples are more egalitarian than heterosexual couples, with less-sharp role prescriptions. It is quite uncommon for homosexual couples to have one partner occupy a "male" role and the other a "female" role. Instead, power and tasks are more equally divided. Again, however, this is more true of lesbian couples—among whom equality of roles is frequently a strong philosophical ideal—than for gay males (Kurdek, 1995a). Among male homosexual couples, the man who earns more money is likely to have greater power within the relationship (Blumstein & Schwartz, 1983).

Some of the same factors that affect the success of marriages seem to be important in the endurance of gay partnerships. As in marriages, gay couples experience a drop in their relationship satisfaction in the early months of their partnership (Kurdek & Schmitt, 1986); they argue over similar things (Kurdek, 1994); and, like marriages, gay relationships are more likely to last if the two partners share similar backgrounds and are equally committed to the relationship (Peplau, 1991). Although we have little research to support this, I assume that the interactional patterns that characterize lasting marriages would also typify lasting homosexual pairings.

All this means that gay partnerships are far more like heterosexual relationships than they are different. The urge to form a single, central committed attachment in early adult life is present in all of us, gay or straight.

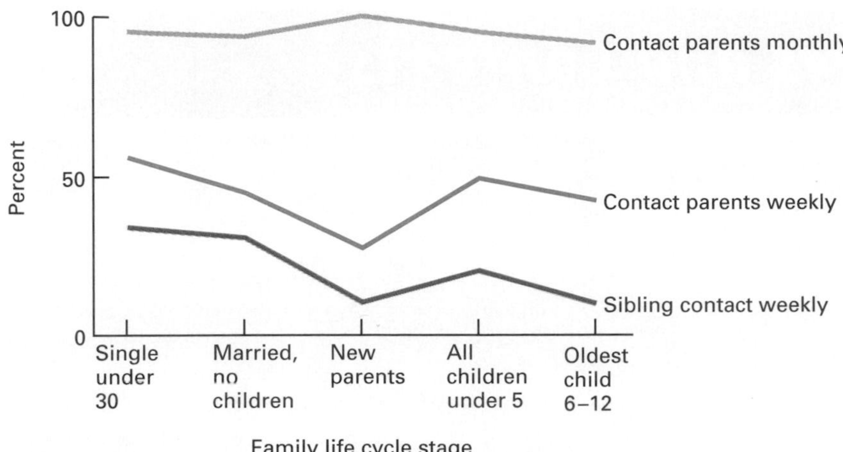

FIGURE 14.2 Despite the process of physical and emotional emancipation that occurs in young adulthood, virtually all adults are in contact with their parents at least monthly. (*Source:* Leigh, 1982, from Table 2, p. 202.)

He interviewed a total of about 1300 adults who varied in their stage in the traditional family life cycle. Each adult reported how frequently he or she saw, spoke with, or wrote to parents, brothers and sisters, cousins, and other family members. Figure 14.2 shows the percentage of the various groups of young-adult respondents who said they had at least monthly contact with their parents, the percentage who had weekly contact with parents, and the percentage who had weekly contact with their siblings. Clearly, some contact is the norm and frequent contact is common.

Not surprisingly, the amount and kind of contact an adult has with kin is strongly influenced by proximity. Adults who live within two hours of their parents and siblings see them far more often than is true of those who live at longer distance. But long distance does not prevent a parent or sibling being part of an individual adult's convoy. These relationships can provide support in times of need, even if physical contact is infrequent.

Friendships

Friends, too, can be important members of a convoy. We choose our friends as we choose our partner, from among those we see as like ourselves in education, social class, interests, family background, or family life cycle stage. Cross-sex friendships are more common among adults than they are among 10-year-olds, but they are still outnumbered by same-sex friendships. Young adults' friends are also overwhelmingly drawn from their own age group. Beyond this basic filter of similarity, close friendship seems to rest on mutual openness and personal disclosure.

Because of the centrality of the task of intimacy in early adulthood, most researchers and theorists assume that young adults have more friends than do middle-aged or older adults. We have some hints of support for this idea, but it has been a difficult assumption to test properly. We lack longitudinal data, and we lack clear agreement on definitions of friendship, which makes combining data across studies very difficult.

My best guess at the moment, based primarily on the work of Laura Carstensen and her colleagues (1992, 1995), is that the number of close and intimate friendships remains essentially constant over adult life, but that the number of more casual acquaintances or "liking" relationships peaks in early adulthood. But this hypothesis remains speculative; we simply do not have good information about constancy or change in friendship patterns over the years of adulthood.

Cultures and Contexts

Kin Relationships in Black and Hispanic Families

You may well wonder whether the description of young-adult kin relationships I've given you is equally valid for all subgroups or subcultures. In fact it is not. In the United States, both black and Hispanic family relationships differ from those in the "Anglo" culture.

Hispanic Kin Relationships

Among Hispanics, particularly among Mexican Americans, the convoy is strongly dominated by family ties, a pattern strengthened by the fact that Hispanic families typically choose to live nearer to one another than is true of Anglos. Given a choice, many non-Hispanics move *away* from kin networks in early adulthood while Hispanics move *toward* them (Vega, 1990). In the Hispanic culture, extensive kin networks are the rule rather than the exception, with frequent visiting and exchange not only between parents, children, and siblings, but with grandparents, cousins, aunts, and uncles (Keefe, 1984). These frequent contacts are not only perceived as enjoyable, they are seen as vital signs of the closeness of kin relationships. It is not enough to write or talk on the phone; to maintain close ties you need to see and touch your relatives and friends. Among Hispanics, an individual's self-esteem may also be more strongly related to the valuation given by the kin group. William Madsen describes the difference this way:

> When an Anglo fails, he thinks first of how this failure will affect him and his status in society. When a Chicano fails, his first evaluation of the failure is in terms of what it will do to his family and how it will affect his relationship to other family members. (Madsen, 1969, p. 224)

This pattern appears to be stronger in first-generation immigrants, who rely almost exclusively on family members for emotional support and problem solving. Second-generation immigrants seem to have more extensive nonkin networks. But in both generations, the extended family clearly plays a more central role in the daily life of Hispanics than it does in the Anglo culture.

Black Kin Relationships

The same is true of African Americans, although the reasons are somewhat different. A whole set of demographic differences distinguishes today between black and white families in the United States, contributing to markedly different kin contacts. For one thing, young adult blacks are much less likely to marry than are whites, a pattern resulting in part from the marked decline in employment among black men in the 1980s. Welfare rules have also contributed to this lower rate of marriage, as has the high rate of death from violence among young African-American males (Burgess, 1995). Many African-American couples live in cohabiting relationships, but many others live in multigeneration households with their parents, grandparents, or other relatives. The National Survey of Black Americans, a nationally representative sample studied in 1980, showed that 21.8 percent of all black families were of this extended type. Among black familes headed by a young adult the rate was 50 percent, most of these consisting of two generations of adult women and one or more children (Hatchett, Cochran, & Jackson, 1991). Over the period of young adulthood, 60 percent of black women live in such a household at least for a period of time, compared to only about 30 percent of white women (Beck & Beck, 1989). As a result, relationships between parents and adult children seem to be particularly central to young adult convoys in African-American culture, especially the relationship between mothers and their adult daughters.

Frequent and supportive kin and other network contact is also a significant part of the daily life of most black adults who do not live in extended family households (Hatchett & Jackson, 1993). In one large national survey of black Americans (Taylor, 1986), 37 percent reported that they had contact with family members nearly every day. African Americans also are more likely to form what have been called pseudo-kin networks or "fictive" kin relationships—close familylike relationships with neighborhoods or peers, in which a wide variety of aid is exchanged (Taylor et al., 1990).

Sex Differences in Early Adult Friendships. Much less speculative is the information about sex differences in friendship patterns. As in childhood, there are very striking sex differences in both the number and quality of friendships in the convoy. Women have more close friends, and their friendships are more intimate, with more self-disclosure and more exchange of emotional support. Young men's friendships, like those of boys and older men, are more competitive. Male friends are less likely to agree with each other or to ask for or provide emotional support to one another (Dindia & Allen, 1992; Maccoby, 1990). Adult women friends talk to one another; adult men friends do things together.

Whether one sees the female pattern, or the male pattern, as "better" or "worse" obviously depends on one's gender and point of view. Theorists continue to argue the point (Antonucci, 1994a). Most research shows men to be less satisfied with their friendships than are women (although they are equally satisfied with their family relationships), and women clearly gain in quite specific ways from the buffering effect of their social network. But men also gain from their style of relationship. Women's style, for example, sometimes has the effect of burdening them too much with emotional obligations, while men are more able to focus on their work (Antonucci, 1994a). Setting aside these value judgments, the important point remains: Men and women, boys and girls, appear to create different kinds of relationships and this difference permeates our culture.

Another facet of this same difference is that women most often fill the role of "kin-keeper" (Moen, 1996). They write the letters, make the phone calls, arrange the gatherings of family and friends. It is my daughter-in-law and not my son who writes to say thank you for gifts, and who calls to tell me how my grandson is doing. In later stages of adult life, it is also the women who are likely to take on the role of caring for aging parents—a pattern I'll have much more to say about in Chapter 16.

Taken together, all this means that women have a much larger "relationship role" than do men. In virtually all cultures it is part of the female role to be responsible for maintaining the emotional aspects of relationships, with a spouse, with friends, with family, and—of course—with children.

Critical Thinking

Make a list of all your own friends and rate each relationship on intimacy on a 5-point scale, where 5 is the most intimate and 1 is not at all intimate. What is the average score? Are your friendships with women more intimate than your friendships with men? What do you do with your friends? Does your experience match the research findings?

Parenthood

The second major new role acquired in early adulthood is that of parent. In the United States, nine out of every ten adults will become a parent, most in their 20s or 30s. For most, the role of parent brings profound satisfaction, a greater sense of purpose and self-worth, and a feeling of being grown up. It may also bring a sense of shared joy between husband and wife (Umberson & Gove, 1989). In one large study, 80 percent of the parents sampled said their lives had been changed for the better by the arrival of children (Hoffman & Manis, 1978). Yet it is also true that the birth of the first child signals a whole series of changes in adult lives, particularly in sex roles and in marital relationships, and not all these changes are without strain.

Changes in Sex Roles

One change is an intensification of traditional sex roles that seems to be triggered by the birth of the first child. Anthropologist David Gutmann refers to this as the **parental imperative** (1975). Because human children are remarkably vulnerable and slow-growing, they require a long period of both physical and emotional support.

Gutmann argues that as a species, we are "wired" to divide up those two responsibilities in particular ways, with mothers taking on the task of emotional support and fathers taking on the role of physical support and protection. According to Gutmann, even couples with an egalitarian philosophy will move toward a more traditional division of roles after the birth of the first child. Women, he argues, will be more and more oriented toward "hearth," while the man faces outward toward the world, figurative spear in hand. One man interviewed by Daniels and Weingarten (1988) illustrates the point:

> The baby's coming was a good thing, because it drove home to me that I had to have a better job. And I knew I'd need an education to get one. I transferred to the evening shift so I could go to college during the day. The hours were hard, I was under a lot of pressure, and I missed my family, but it was something I had to do. (p. 38)

Gutmann's own anthropological research among the Navaho, the Maya, and the Druze generally supports his claim, as does recent research in the United States. For example, Carolyn Cowan and her associates (1991) found that after the birth of a first child, a woman assumes more responsibility for both child care and household tasks than either partner had predicted before the child was born. Not every study supports Gutmann's hypothesis (e.g., Cunningham & Antill, 1984), but his proposal raises some intriguing issues, especially in light of the assumptions by many women that complete equality of roles within marriage is possible.

Parenthood and Happiness

More firmly established is the effect of the arrival of the first child on marital (or partnership) satisfaction. The general pattern is that such satisfaction is at its peak before the birth of the first child, after which it drops and remains at a lower level until the last child leaves home. Norvall Glenn (1990), in a review of all the research on this point, concludes that this curvilinear pattern "is about as close to being certain as anything ever is in the social sciences" (p. 853). Figure 14.3 illustrates the pattern,

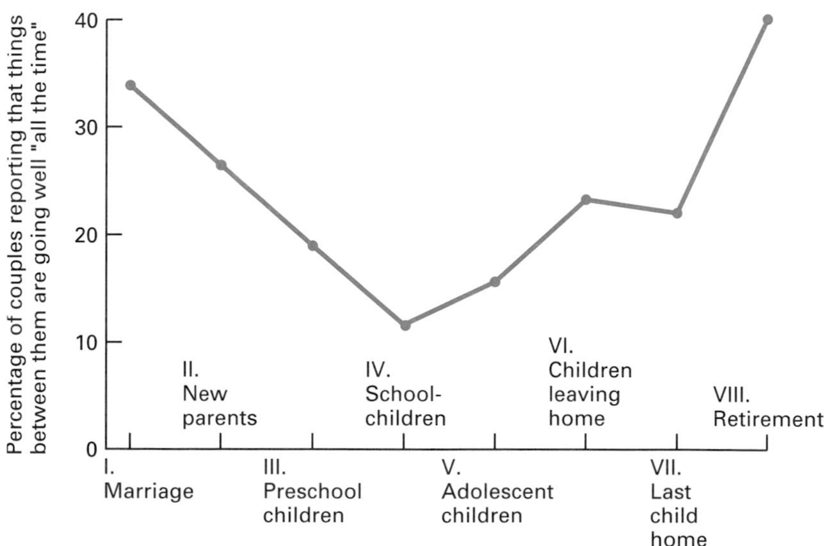

FIGURE 14.3 This pattern of change in marital satisfaction over the stages of the family life cycle is one of the best-documented findings in family sociology research. (*Source:* Rollins & Feldman, 1970, Tables 2 & 3, p. 24. Copyright 1970 by the National Council on Family Relations, 3989 Central Ave. NE, Suite 550, Minneapolis, MN 55421.)

based on results from an early and widely quoted study by Rollins and Feldman (1970). The best-documented portion of this curvilinear pattern is the drop in marital satisfaction after the birth of the first child, for which we have both longitudinal and cross-sectional evidence.

You've already seen in Figure 14.1 that, on average, *all* marriages decline in positive exchanges over the first year, whether children are born during that interval or not. Other research tells us that the advent of a child adds further role conflicts and role strains. Recall that role conflict exists when a person is attempting to fill two or more roles that are physically or psychologically incompatible with each other. New parents discover that the roles of parent and spouse are at least partially incompatible. There aren't enough hours in a day, and the hours that the child demands are usually subtracted from the hours spent with the partner. New parents report that they now have much less time for one another—for conversation, for sex, for simple affection, or even routine chores done together (e.g., Belsky, Lang, & Rovine, 1985).

Many new parents also experience considerable role strain—that sense that you do not know how to fill the role you find yourself in. And this sense of strain is exacerbated by anything that increases family stress, such as economic hardship, pressure from work, or a baby with a difficult temperament (Sirignano & Lachman, 1985).

These parents are doubtless delighted with the arrival of their baby, who was only a few weeks old when this photo was taken. But they may also feel a bit overwhelmed by this new role.

The Role of Worker

Adding to the stress is the fact that a large percentage of young adults are simultaneously filling a third time-consuming and relatively new role, that of worker. Young people take on this role in part to support themselves economically. But that is not the only reason for the centrality of this role. Satisfying work also seems to be an important ingredient in happiness or life satisfaction, for both men and women (Tait, Padgett, & Baldwin, 1989).

Virtually all men take on the role of worker, as do the majority of women in today's younger cohorts, although women still are likely to work for fewer years of their adult life. Current estimates are that women born in 1980 will spend nearly 30 years working outside the home, compared with only 12 years for the cohort born in 1940. But the average for men in both these cohorts is more like 40 years (Spenner, 1988), so there is still a sex difference in work-role experience. We also know far more about the work experiences of men than of women. So if it seems in the next few pages as if I keep saying "he" when I talk about workers, it is not because only men work, but because men have been the focus of most of the research.

Before we look at what we know about career steps and sequences in early adulthood, let me back up a step. How do young people choose an occupation?

Choosing an Occupation

As you might imagine, a plethora of factors influences a young person's choice of job or career: gender, ethnic group, intelligence, school performance, personality and self-concept, family background and values, and education.

Family Influences. The general rule is that young people tend to choose occupations at the same general social class level as their parents—although this is less true today than it was a decade or two ago (Biblarz, Bengtson, & Bucur, 1996). In part this effect operates through the medium of education: Middle-class families are more likely to encourage their children to go on for further education past high school; such added education, in turn, makes it more likely that the young person will qualify for middle-class jobs, for which a college education is frequently a required credential.

Families also influence job choices through their value systems. In particular, parents who value academic and professional achievement are far more likely to have children who attend college and choose professional-level jobs. This effect is not just social class difference in disguise. Among working-class families, it is those who place the strongest emphasis on their children's achievements whose children are most likely to move up into middle-class jobs (Gustafson & Magnusson, 1991).

Education and Intelligence. Education and intelligence also interact very strongly to influence not just the specific job a young person will choose, but also career success over the long haul. I mentioned some of these links in Chapter 11, but let me reiterate. The higher your intelligence, the more years of education you are likely to complete; the more education you have, the higher the rung of the career ladder on which you enter the job market; the higher the rung of entry, the further you are likely to go up the career ladder over your lifetime (Brody, 1992; Kamo et al., 1991).

Intelligence has direct effects on job choice and job success as well. Brighter students are more likely to choose technical or professional careers. And highly intelligent workers are more likely to advance, even if they enter the system on a lower rung of the career ladder (e.g., Dreher & Bretz, 1991).

Gender. Specific job choice is also strongly affected by gender. Despite the women's movement, and despite the vast increase in the proportion of women working, it is still true that sex-role definitions designate some jobs as "women's jobs" and some as "men's jobs" (Reskin, 1993). Stereotypically male jobs are more varied, more technical, and higher in both status and income (e.g., doctor, business executive, carpenter). Women's jobs are concentrated in service occupations, typically lower in status and lower-paid (e.g., teacher, nurse, secretary). One-third of all working women occupy clerical jobs; another quarter are in health care, teaching, or domestic service.

Children learn these cultural definitions of "appropriate" jobs for men and women in their early years, just as they learn all the other aspects of sex roles. So it is not surprising that most young women and men choose jobs that fit these sex-role designations. Cross-sex job choices are much more common among young people who see themselves as androgynous, or whose parents hold unconventional occupations. For instance, young women who choose traditionally masculine careers are more likely to have a mother who has had a long-term work commitment, and are more likely to define themselves either as androgynous or masculine (Betz & Fitzgerald, 1987; Fitzpatrick & Silverman, 1989).

Personality. A fourth important influence on job choice is the young person's personality. John Holland, whose work has been the most influential in this area (1973, 1992), proposes six basic personality types, summarized in Table 14.4. Holland's basic hypothesis is that each of us tends to choose, and be most successful at, an occupation that matches our personality.

Research in non-Western as well as Western cultures, and with African Americans, Hispanics, and Native Americans as well as whites in the United States, has generally supported Holland's proposal (e.g., Kahn et al., 1990; Tracey & Rounds, 1993; Upperman & Church, 1995). Ministers, for example, generally score highest on the social scale, engineers highest on the investigative scale, car salespersons on the enterprising scale, and career army men highest on the realistic scale.

People whose personality matches their job are also more likely to be satisfied with their work, although interestingly, job *success* is only very weakly related to personality/job match (Assouline & Meir, 1987). It is obviously quite possible to succeed at a job that is a poor match for your personality, but you're likely to be less happy with such a job in the long run.

Jobs over Time

Once the job or career has been chosen, what kinds of experiences do young adults have in their work life? Do they become more or less satisfied with their work over

Table 14.4 **Holland's Personality/Work Types**

Type	Personality and Work Preferences
Realistic	Aggressive, masculine, physically strong, often with low verbal or interpersonal skills; prefer mechanical activities and tool use, choosing jobs like mechanic, electrician, or surveyor.
Investigative	Oriented toward thinking (particularly abstract thinking), organizing, and planning; prefer ambiguous, challenging tasks, but are generally low in social skills; are often scientists or engineers.
Artistic	Asocial; prefer unstructured, highly individual activity; are often artists.
Social	Similar to extraverts (see Table 12.4, p. 316); humanistic, sociable, and need attention; avoid intellectual activity and dislike highly ordered activity; prefer to work with people and choose service jobs like nursing, education, and social work.
Enterprising	Highly verbal and dominating; enjoy organizing and directing others; are persuasive and high in leadership, often choosing careers in sales.
Conventional	Prefer structured activities and subordinate role; like clear guidelines and see themselves as accurate and precise; may choose occupations such as bookkeeping or filing.

Source: Holland, 1973, 1992.

time? Are there clear career steps that we might think of as stages or shared steps on the ladder?

Job Satisfaction. Many studies show that job satisfaction is at its *lowest* in early adulthood and rises steadily until retirement, a pattern that has been found in repeated surveys among both male and female respondents (Glenn & Weaver, 1985).

We know this is not just a cohort effect because similar findings have been reported over many years of research, and we know that it is not entirely culture-specific since it has been found in many industrialized countries. But what might cause it? Some research (e.g., Bedeian, Ferris, & Kacmar, 1992) points to the possibility that what we have here is the effect of time-in-job rather than age. Older workers are likely to have had their jobs longer, which may contribute to several sources of satisfaction, including better pay, more job security, and more authority. But there may also be some genuine age effects at work, too. The jobs young people hold are likely to be dirtier, physically harder, and less complex and interesting (Spenner, 1988).

One other possible explanation for the pattern of increasing job satisfaction with age is self-selection. By middle age, many workers have tried and discarded several jobs and have arrived at an occupation that suits them (White & Spector, 1987).

Critical Thinking

Before you read further, see if you can think of several different reasons why job satisfaction might increase with age.

This young construction worker may be reasonably satisfied with his job, but chances are his satisfaction will rise over the next decades as he acquires more responsibility and authority.

Career Ladders. Within any given career path, workers also tend to move from step to step up some sort of job sequence or career ladder. In academic jobs, the sequence is from instructor to assistant professor to associate and then full professor. In an automobile plant the ladder may go from assembly-line worker to foreman to general foreman to superintendent and on up. In the corporate world, there may be many rungs in a clear management ladder.

What kind of progress up such a ladder do young adults typically make? To answer such a question properly, of course, we need longitudinal studies. We do not have many of these, but fortunately we have a few, including a 20-year study of AT&T managers (Bray & Howard, 1983) and a 15-year study by James Rosenbaum (1984) of workers in a large manufacturing company.

This research suggests several generalizations about the developmental progression of work careers in early adulthood. First, college education makes a very large difference, as I already pointed out. Even with intellectual ability controlled, those with a college education advance further and faster.

Second, *early* promotion is associated with greater advancement over the long haul. In the particular company Rosenbaum studied, 83 percent of those who were promoted within the first year eventually got as far as lower management, while only 33 percent of those who were first promoted after three years of employment got that far.

Third, and perhaps most important, most work advancement occurs early in a career path, after which a plateau is reached. Rosenbaum's results make the point clearly. Company policy in the company he studied was that all workers—whether they had a college degree or not—should enter at the submanagement level. The first upward step was to the job of foreman, with lower management the second possible step. Figure 14.4 shows the percentages of workers who made these career moves at each age. Both steps obviously occurred early; by age 40, virtually all the promotions that were going to occur had already happened. The same pattern occurs in other career paths as well, such as those of accountants and academics (Spenner, 1988), so this is not unique to business career ladders.

Such a pattern *may* be unique, however, to adults who enter a profession in their 20s and stay in it through most of their adult lives. We have a least a few hints from research with women—whose work histories are frequently much less stable than this—that time-in-career rather than age may be the critical variable for the timing of promotions. There may be a window of 10 or 15 years between the time you enter a profession and the time you reach a plateau. If you begin in your 20s you are likely to have peaked by your mid-30s. But if you begin when you are 40 you may still have 15 years in which to advance.

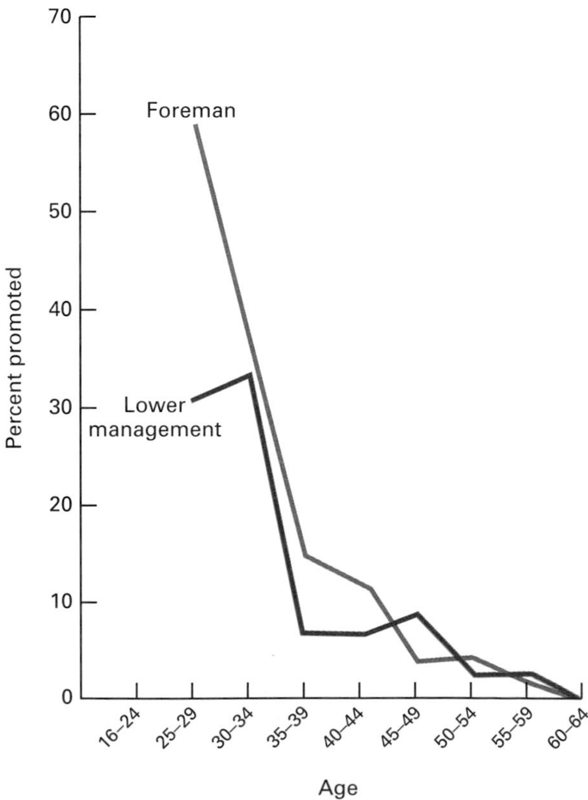

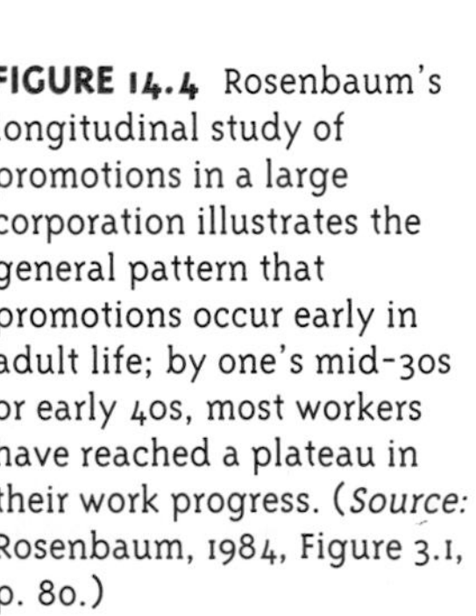
FIGURE 14.4 Rosenbaum's longitudinal study of promotions in a large corporation illustrates the general pattern that promotions occur early in adult life; by one's mid-30s or early 40s, most workers have reached a plateau in their work progress. (*Source:* Rosenbaum, 1984, Figure 3.1, p. 80.)

Another View of Work Sequences. Another way to describe the work experience of young adults is in terms of a series of stages, a model proposed originally by Donald Super (Super, 1971, 1986). First comes the **trial stage,** roughly between the ages of 18 and 25, more or less equivalent to the first phase of the young adult period proposed by Daniel Levinson (recall Figure 2.2, p. 46). In this stage the young person must decide on a job or career, searching for a fit between his interests and personality and the jobs available. The whole process involves a good deal of trial and error as well as luck and chance. Perhaps because many of the jobs available to those in this age range are not terribly challenging, and because many young adults have not yet found the right fit, job changes are at their peak during this period.

Next comes the **establishment stage** (also called the *stabilization* stage), roughly from age 25 to 45. Having chosen an occupation, the young person must learn the ropes and begin to move through the early steps in some career ladder as he masters the needed skills, perhaps with a mentor's help. In this period, the worker also focuses on fulfilling whatever aspirations or goals he may have set for himself. In Levinson's terms, he tries to fulfill his Dream. The young scientist pushes himself to win a Nobel prize; the young attorney bucks for partner; the young business executive tries to move as far up the ladder as he can; the young blue-collar worker may strive for job stability or promotion to foreman. It is in these years that most promotions do in fact occur, although it is also in these years that the job plateau is reached.

Women are working in larger and larger numbers, but fewer than a third work continuously during the early adult years.

Women's Work Patterns

Some of what I have said about work patterns is as true for women as it is for men. Women's work satisfaction goes up with age (and with job tenure), just as men's does, for example. But women's work experience in early adulthood differs from men's in one strikingly important respect: It is far less likely to be continuous. This difference, in turn, has a wide range of repercussions for women's work roles.

In 1994 in the United States, three-quarters of all women between the ages of 20 and 64 were in the labor force at least part time (U.S. Bureau of the Census, 1995). The rate is lower among Hispanic women and about equal for blacks and whites. But in every ethnic group, the more education a woman has, the more likely she is to work. Among women with at least four years of college, 80.8 percent are in the labor force (U.S. Bureau of the Census, 1995).

Nonetheless, most women do not work continuously over the years of early adulthood. Studies of several different cohorts of women in the United States suggest that only a fifth to a quarter of women are continuously employed throughout early adult life (Moen, 1985; Sørensen, 1983; U.S. Bureau of the Census, 1984). Continuous work is more common among women who choose traditionally "male" careers, among those with no children, and among those strongly philosophically committed to women's careers (Betz, 1984; Sørensen, 1983). But the great majority of women move in and out of the work force at least once, often many times.

Women's work patterns are obviously changing rapidly; it is quite possible that a larger percent of current cohorts of 20- and 30-year-old women will work continuously through early and middle adulthood. But here is one fragment of recent data that suggests otherwise: Francine Blau and Marianne Ferber (1991) asked a group of 1988 college business school seniors what their expectations were for their future earnings, work plans, and family plans. The 227 young women who responded, all part of today's cohort of twentysomethings, expected to work full time for 29.1 years, compared with 37.7 years for their male classmates. To be sure, these young women anticipated working more years than their own mothers had worked. But it is interesting that even in this highly educated group of current young women, most of whom have a strong commitment to a career, the average expectation includes some time out to bear and rear children. So although the cultural climate has changed drastically with regard to women's work patterns, it has not changed totally and is unlikely to do so.

Cultures and Contexts

Job Patterns for U.S. Women of Different Ethnic Groups

A fascinating study by Teresa Amott and Julie Matthaei (1991) shows that the work and family experiences of women of color in the United States are powerfully affected by the specific history and cultural values of their ethnic group. The figure below gives one of their findings, reflecting the variations in work experience for nine different ethnic groups. For comparison purposes, the pattern of jobs for European-American men is also given. For this analysis, jobs were classified into four categories by status, as follows:

Level 1: Managerial and professional, supervisory, owners of businesses or farms
Level 2: Technologists, precision production, crafts, repair persons, transportation
Level 3: Health technicians, sales, clerical, machine operators, assemblers, inspectors
Level 4: Service, cleaners, helpers, unskilled laborers

The figure makes clear that Asian-American women have caught up to and now exceed European-American women in their access to higher-level occupations. This seems to have occurred primarily through education. Asian families have always placed a high value on *male* education; in the past decades this value has been extended to female education, with the result that Asian woman have access to more upper-level jobs that have high educational entrance requirements.

The group that has lagged most in both occupational involvement and success are Chicanas, not only because of the immigration pattern over many decades, which placed many Chicanos/as in low-paying agricultural jobs, but also because their culture has had a strong emphasis on the importance of family life and the woman's central place in that life.

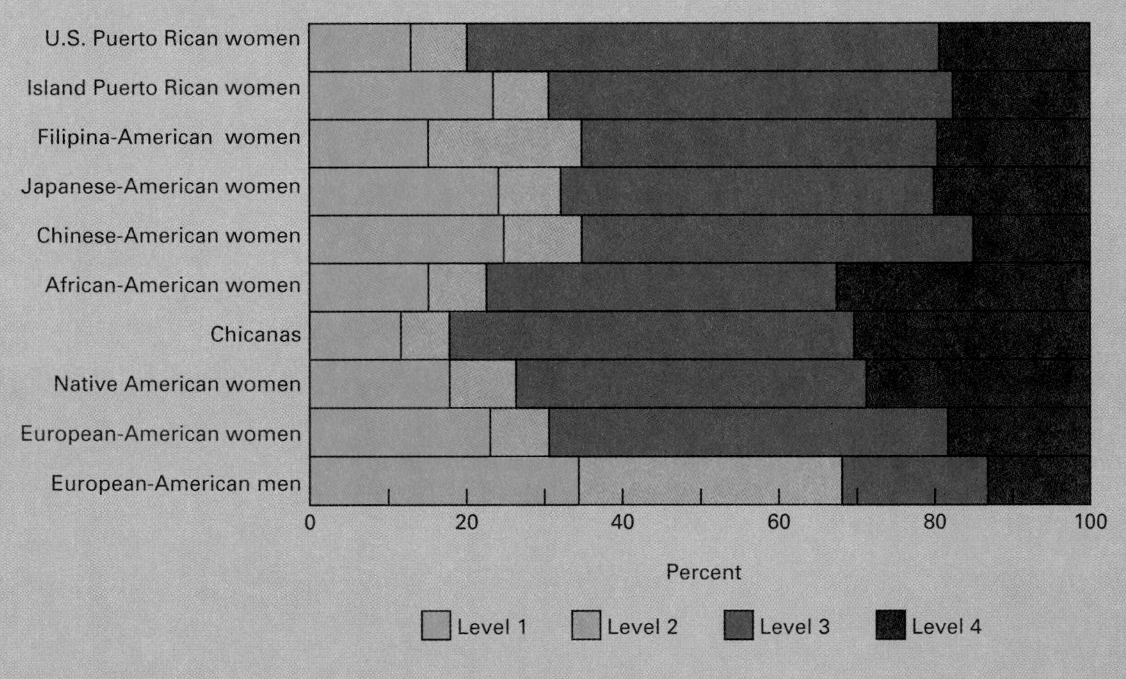

One way we might think of a woman's years out of the workforce is simply as an additional "stage" in the normal trial/establishment sequence, a stage we might call "in-and-out." For some women, this stage comes first, before they begin any kind of paid work. For others, it comes during or after the trial stage; for still others, it comes in the midst of the establishment period, as a hiatus from an established career. To compare the promotion history of women and men, we would have to subtract this in-and-out period from women's history, and compare only the years spent in continuous work. Unfortunately, no one has done that kind of research, so we cannot be sure whether women's work pathways would follow the same patterns as men's. But we do have some indication that the discontinuous aspect of women's work patterns affects their job success and work achievement.

For example, women who work continuously have higher salaries and achieve higher levels in their jobs than do those who have moved in and out of employment (Betz, 1984; Van Velsor & O'Rand, 1984). Among women who have not worked continuously, those who have had several short bursts of work during their in-and-out stage do better economically than those who were unemployed for a single long stretch, even when the total months or years of employment are the same in the two groups (Gwartney-Gibbs, 1988). Very likely these short bursts of work allow the woman to keep up her work skills, especially if she works at the same type of job each time she reenters the labor market. Part-time work also seems to serve some of the same function. Clearly, some strategies can help a woman maximize her work success while still allowing her to spend some period with her family, but it takes a good deal of thought and planning.

CRITICAL THINKING

For young women only: What plans do you now have to combine work and family? Might your planning, or your thinking, change as a result of what you have just read?

Combining Work and Family Roles

This point raises the more general question of how individuals, and couples, manage to combine the roles of worker and parent, or worker and spouse. It is an interesting testimony to our cultural patterns that we think it quite uncomplicated for a man to be worker, parent, and spouse, but we think it is problematical for a woman to be all three. Women do in fact *feel* more role conflict among these three roles than men do (Higgins, Duxbury, & Lee, 1994), for several clear reasons.

The most obvious reason is that if you add up the hours spent in family work (child care, cleaning, cooking, shopping, etc.) and in paid employment, employed women are working more hours a week than are their husbands or partners. Women do considerably more of the family tasks than men do, even when both partners work full time. Figure 14.5 gives a particularly clear depiction of this difference, based on data from Panel Study of Income Dynamics, a study of over 5000 families (Rexroat & Shehan, 1987). Among childless couples, labor is almost evenly distributed; but when children are young, women are simply putting in more hours. Among other things, this pattern provides further evidence for Gutmann's notion of the *parental imperative*. Sex roles become more traditional after the birth of a child.

The data shown in the figure were collected in 1976, and you may think that things have changed a lot since then—that men are doing much more housework now, especially if their wives work. And they are. In particular, men with working wives are doing more *child care* now than they used to (Higgins et al., 1994). But if you include all forms of housework—child care, cooking, cleaning, running errands, and so forth—wives still do roughly twice as much housework as husbands, even when both work full time (Blair & Johnson, 1992). Black and Hispanic men appear to spend slightly more time in household labor than do Anglo men, but the range of variation is not huge (Shelton & John, 1993). Thus, although the gap is decreasing, there is still a large difference between the size of the family role filled by women and by men.

Women also feel more conflict between family and work roles because of the way sex roles are defined in most cultures. The woman's role is to be relationship-oriented, to care for, to nurture. To the extent that a woman has internalized that role expectation—and most of us have—she will define herself, and judge herself, more by how well she performs such caring roles than by how well she performs on the job. Joseph Pleck argues that this means that the boundaries between work and family roles are therefore "asymmetrically permeable" for the two sexes (Pleck, 1977). That is, for a woman, family roles spill over into her work life. She not only takes time

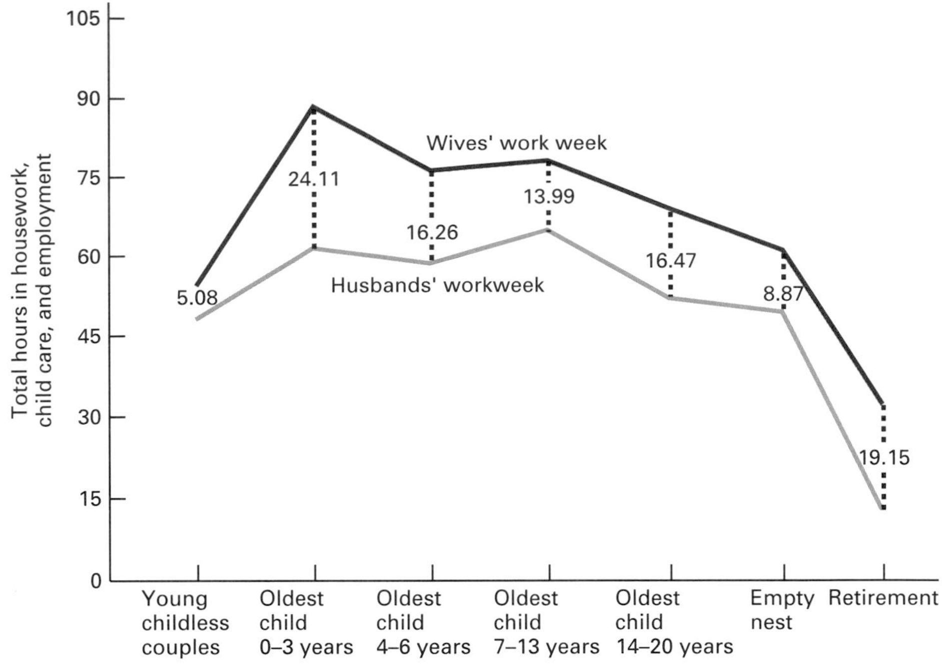

FIGURE 14.5 When both partners work full time, women still do more housework and child care, so that their total work week is many hours longer—contributing significantly to women's greater sense of role conflict between work and family roles. Note that the gap is greatest right after the birth of the first child—perhaps a time when the man is most likely to be intensely committed to his career. (*Source:* Rexroat & Shehan, 1987, Fig. 1, p. 746.)

off from her job when children are born, she stays home with the sick child, takes time off to go to a teacher's conference or a PTA meeting, and thinks about her family tasks during her workday. These simultaneous, competing demands are the very definition of role conflict.

For men, work and family roles are more sequential than simultaneous. Men are workers during the day, husbands and fathers when they come home. Women are mothers and wives all day, even when they work. If the two roles conflict for men, it is more likely to be the work role that spills over into family life than the other way around.

Not all the intersections of family and work roles are problematic for women. For example, working women have more power in their marriages or partnerships than do nonworking women (e.g., Blumstein & Schwartz, 1983; Spitze, 1988). The more equal the earnings of the partners, the more equality exists in decision making and in household work. But it remains true that the most striking single fact about work and family roles in this age of high women's employment is that women, more than men, struggle to resolve the conflict between the two. It is also clear that this conflict is vastly greater during early adulthood, when children are young and needing constant care, than it is in middle or later adult life. In many respects it is this maximally complex intersection of spousal, parental, and work roles that is the defining feature of early adult life in complex industrialized societies.

Personality in Early Adulthood

Perhaps because of the mutual impact of these several major roles, we also see some very interesting shared changes in personality qualities over the years of early adulthood. That is not to say that we all become alike. On the contrary, basic tem-

The Real World

Strategies for Coping with Family/Work Conflict

Are you overwhelmed by the many competing demands of work and family? Are there some days when you despair? I cannot offer you a magic formula for eliminating such conflict or distress, but I can tell you about some strategies that help. I'm going to phrase this as advice to women, because it is women who experience the greatest role conflict. But men can certainly profit from the same points.

The most helpful strategy overall is something psychologists call *cognitive restructuring*—recasting or reframing the situation for yourself in a way that identifies the positive elements. It includes things like reminding yourself that you have good reasons to have made the choice to have both a job and a family, or recalling other times when you have coped successfully with similar problems (Paden & Buehler, 1995).

A related kind of restructuring involves redefining family roles. In several older studies, Douglas Hall (1972, 1975) found that women who find ways to redistribute basic household tasks to other family members (husband and children), or who simply give up doing some tasks, experienced less stress and conflict. You might want to make a list of all the household chores you do and that your partner does and go over the list jointly, eliminating whatever items you can, and reassigning the others. Men *can* clean toilets; clutter can be dealt with less frequently (or, heaven forbid, not at all), meals can perhaps be simpler. Depending on economic resources, help can also be hired.

You can also redefine your concept of sex roles themselves. Where is it written that only women can stay home with a sick child? It is probably written in your internal model of yourself or in your gender schema. Many women find it difficult to give up such tasks, even when they cause severe role conflict, because such nurturing is part of their image of themselves. As one woman, whose husband was very involved in the care of their infant, said:

> I love seeing the closeness between him and the baby, especially since I didn't have that with my father, but if he does well at his work *and* his relationship with the baby, what's my special contribution? (Cowan & Cowan, 1987, p. 168)

It may be worth your while to try to discover whether the current division of labor in your own household exists because of resistance to participation by husband or children, or because of your own inner resistance to changing your view of yourself and your basic contribution to the family unit.

Finally, you may find it helpful to take a class in time management. Research tells us that good planning can in fact reduce the sense of strain you feel (Paden & Buehler, 1995). I am sure you have already been given lots of advice about how to organize things better. Easier said than done! But there actually are techniques that help, many of which are taught in workshops and classes in most cities.

What does *not* work is simply trying harder to do it all yourself. Women who continue to try to perform all three roles at a high level report maximum strain and stress. Something has to give, whether it is your standards for housework or your sense of your female role. And even then, combining all these roles is inherently full of opportunities for conflict. At best, the balance is delicate. At worst it is overwhelming.

perament or personality traits show strong continuity over this 20-year period. But overlaid on top of that continuity is a set of shared changes.

Personality Continuity

In Chapter 12 I introduced you to the Big Five personality dimensions: neuroticism, extraversion, openness, agreeableness, and conscientiousness. Research by Robert McCrae and Paul Costa, who have been leading figures in this area (e.g., Costa & McCrae, 1980b, 1994a, 1994b, McCrae & Costa, 1987, 1994), makes it clear that all five of these traits are highly consistent over relatively long periods in adulthood. The data in Table 14.5, drawn from the Baltimore Longitudinal Study of Aging (Costa & McCrae, 1988), are typical. This study involved a large number of men and women, aged 21 to 76 at the beginning, who were tested twice, six years apart. What is shown in the table is the correlation between the scores on each of the Big Five dimensions across those six years. These are very high correlations, indicating strong stability. Other research, covering periods up to 30 years (e.g., Finn, 1986; Helson & Moane,

Table 14.5 Correlations Between Measurements of the "Big Five" Personality Traits over Six Years

Neuroticism	.83
Extraversion	.82
Openness	.83
Agreeableness	.63
Conscientiousness	.79

Source: Adapted from Costa & McCrae, 1988, Table 4.

1987), confirms this general level of consistency, although the correlations drop slightly as the period of time lengthens.

Interestingly, Costa and McCrae find that adults in their 20s show the *least* individual consistency in personality, as if the final personality were not yet formed at this age (Costa & McCrae, 1994a). Still, even in these early adult years the basic five personality dispositions are at least moderately consistent.

All this means that we take ourselves along on our journey through adult life. We approach the new roles of early adulthood in ways that reflect our basic personality traits. In particular, individuals high in neuroticism seem to have an especially difficult time with many of life's tasks. They are consistently higher on measures of maladjustment or unhappiness, less satisfied with their lives (McCrae & Costa, 1990), and more likely to divorce, as you have already seen in the results from Kelly and Conley's longitudinal study.

CRITICAL THINKING

Can you think of other possible effects of these personality traits on a young adult's experience with the roles I've been talking about here? Which personality traits would you expect to be associated with greater marital stability? Which might predict good physical health?

Adults high in neuroticism also deal less well with stress. Faced with a significant life change, they are more likely to describe it (and experience it) as a crisis, and to show enduring consequences. For example, in one of his studies of the effect of the Great Depression, Elder (Liker & Elder, 1983) found that irritable men (presumably high in neuroticism) became more and more irritable under severe economic stress. Less neurotic men showed initially negative reactions to such stress and then bounced back. You may also remember from Chapter 1 (Figure 1.2, p. 11) the description of Elder's study of explosive and ill-tempered boys. These youngsters carried this trait with them into adult life and, as a consequence, were less successful in both work and family roles. In contrast, adults high in extraversion are consistently more satisfied with their lives.

Personality Change

At the same time there appears to be an interesting set of shared *changes* in personality in early adulthood—although this point has been a matter of considerable dispute. For many years, McCrae and Costa insisted that there was no essential change in personality over the years of adulthood. Recently, however, they have concluded that there are some systematic changes between adolescence and midlife: Young adults show small but consistent declines in neuroticism and extraversion, and slight but consistent increases in agreeableness and conscientiousness—all changes that sound as if a general "maturing" were taking place.

A somewhat different slant on personality change in early adulthood comes from a number of important longitudinal studies, each of which used more in-depth methods of measuring personality and covered a larger number of years of adult life than Costa and McCrae have studied. Between age 20 and age 40, these researchers find increases in a cluster of characteristics that includes confidence, self-esteem, independence, and achievement orientation.

The best single set of data comes from the Berkeley/Oakland longitudinal sample, a study I have talked about several times. You'll recall that several hundred subjects were studied from childhood into their 50s and 60s (Haan, 1981b; Haan, Millsap, & Hartka, 1986). Personality characteristics were measured with an unusual technique, called a *Q-sort*—a clever system for converting essentially qualitative or descriptive information into quantitative data. A Q-sort consists of a set of words or phrases that might describe an individual, such as "satisfied with self," "bullies others," or "socially poised." A skilled rater, using all the information available about each subject at a given age (interview material, observations or comments by other psychologists who have observed the subject, test results) sorts this set of words or phrases into nine separate piles. Pile 1 contains the statements *least* characteristic of the individual and pile 9 contains those that are the most. As an added feature, the rater is required to create a normal distribution across the nine piles; only a very few items are allowed in the most extreme piles (1 and 9) and the large bulk must be placed in the middle piles. This method is not unique to the Berkeley studies; among other things, a Q-sort strategy is now widely used as an alternative to the Strange Situation to measure the security of a child's attachment. What is important for you to remember about this technique is that it reflects the *relative weight* or *relative visibility* of a characteristic at a given time in the life span rather than the absolute level of some quality.

Figure 14.6 shows the pattern of change with age in a cluster of Q-sort items relating to aspects of assertiveness versus submissiveness. Figure 1.1 in Chapter 1 (page 5) showed the changes in another cluster, self-confidence versus the sense of being victimized. You ought to go back and look at that figure again. You'll see that both assertiveness and self-confidence rose in early adulthood among these subjects, especially between ages 30 and 40. In the same years there was also an increase in a cluster Haan calls "cognitively committed," which includes aspects of ambition, valuing independence, and valuing intellect.

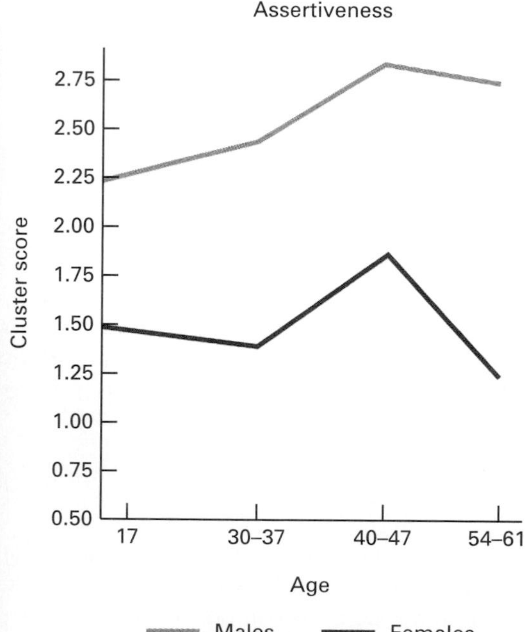

FIGURE 14.6 Scores for the assertiveness cluster of Q-sort items in the Berkeley/Oakland longitudinal studies. (*Source:* Haan, Millsap, & Hartka, 1986, Figure 2, p. 228.)

Other researchers report similar changes. In a study of women graduates of Mills College, Ravenna Helson found few shared personality changes between 21 and 27 (a time when personality appears to be more in flux), but between 27 and 43 the women increased in dominance, confidence, and independence (Helson et al., 1984, 1987; Helson & Stewart, 1994; Wink & Helson, 1993). The AT&T managers studied by Bray and Howard (1983) also showed a decline in dependency and an increase in the need for autonomy over the 20 years of the study, covering the ages from roughly 20 to 40, a pattern replicated with a very different sample by Stevens and Truss (1985).

Findings like these suggest the possibility that in early adulthood personality shifts toward greater autonomy, greater achievement striving, and greater self-confidence and personal assertiveness. The young adult not only becomes physically independent of her family, she becomes increasingly psychologically independent as well. And as she masters the various roles of early adult life, she becomes more confident, more able to assert her individuality.

Other theorists have talked about the underlying change in early adulthood in terms of a shift from an external to an internal definition of oneself (e.g., Loevinger, 1976, 1984). In our 20s, we each struggle to learn all the culturally defined and demanded roles. In that sense, we allow ourselves to be defined by external criteria. But these roles are not always a good fit, so eventually we begin to push at the edges, to find our own individuality.

Daniel Levinson (1978) used the term *detribalization* to describe this change. By the end of early adulthood, he said, the adult

> becomes more critical of the tribe—the particular groups, institutions and traditions that have the greatest significance for him, the social matrix to which he is most attached. He is less dependent upon tribal rewards, more questioning of tribal values. (p. 242)

This set of changes is not at all in conflict with the underlying consistency in basic personality traits described by McCrae and Costa. An extraverted 20-year-old will still be an extraverted 40-year-old, even though at 40 she is *also* more independent and self-confident than she was. As I see it, a basic set of *developmental* changes is overlaid on consistent personality traits. The way in which each of us handles the tasks of early adult life will be affected by our personality or temperament; an individual high in neuroticism will respond differently than will someone with a less prickly approach to life. But all of us are affected by the shared tasks of early adulthood—by the need to become independent of family and to learn a large set of new role skills.

Individual Differences

If the acquisition of the "big three" roles in early adulthood—marriage, parenthood, and work—are central to the rhythm and shape of this period of life, then we have to ask what happens to people who do not adopt all three roles, or who do not adopt them at the normative times. How do adults who do not marry (or cohabit) or those who do not have children differ from those who adopt these roles?

Those Who Do Not Marry

Marriage or long-term cohabitation brings certain advantages. Married young adults are happier, healthier, live longer, and have lower rates of a variety of psychiatric problems (Coombs, 1991; Glenn & Weaver, 1988; Lee, Seccombe, & Shehan, 1991; Ross, 1995; Sorlie, Backlund, & Keller, 1995) than do adults without committed partners. Linda Waite, in her 1995 presidential address to the Population Association of America (1995) concludes that "being unmarried is more dangerous than being overweight, having cancer or cigarette smoking and—for men—more dangerous than heart disease" (p. 2).

In this culture at least, men generally benefit more from marriage than do women on these measures of physical and mental health. That is, married men are generally the healthiest and live the longest, while unmarried men are collectively the worst off. The two groups of women fall in between, with married women at a slight advantage over the unmarried. But unmarried women are considerably healthier and happier than are unmarried men.

One possible explanation of this pattern is that some sort of self-selection is occurring. People who are healthy and happy are simply more likely to marry. Logical as it may sound, researchers have found little support for this explanation (Coombs, 1991; Waite, 1995). A second alternative is that married adults follow better health practices. For example, Dutch researchers (Joung et al., 1995) find that married adults are less likely to smoke or drink to excess, and more likely to exercise than are unmarried adults.

Still a third explanation relies on the concept of social support. The argument is that married adults are less vulnerable to both disease and emotional distress because they are buffered by the support from their central attachment to their partner. Married men derive particular benefits precisely because men are less likely to have close confidants outside of marriage, and because wives, more than husbands, provide emotional warmth and support to their spouse.

If this argument is correct, then as a more general rule we ought to find that those adults whose spouses in fact provide higher levels of support should be specially benefited by marriage, while those whose spouses are less supportive should show fewer advantages in health and happiness. Equally, if this is the correct explanation, we should find that among single adults, those who have no partner or close confidant should be particularly badly off. Both of these hypotheses have been supported by research.

Figure 14.7 illustrates the point with data from a large U.S. national sample surveyed in 1990. Catherine Ross (1995) argued that it is not marital status per se that is the causal factor, but rather the quality of the relationship. Unmarried respondents were asked whether they were living with a partner, or whether they had a partner who lived in a separate household. And each respondent who was in a relationship (whether married or not) was asked to say how happy that relationship was. Figure 14.7 shows the level of depression among those without a partner, and among those

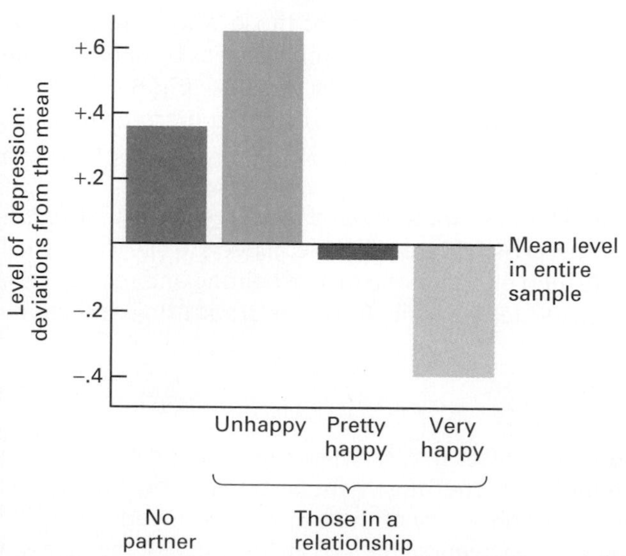

FIGURE 14.7 These findings support the argument that it is not marriage per se that creates a benefit in health and happiness, but rather the social and emotional support that a marriage can provide. (*Source:* Ross, 1995, adaptation of Figure 2, p. 138.)

in unhappy or happy relationships. Clearly, those whose relationship is very happy were the least likely to report symptoms of depression, while those without a partner *or* those with unhappy partnerships were most likely to be depressed.

I hasten to add that this does not mean that all single adults are lonely and unhappy. The differences I've described are averages and there are many exceptions. Many adults are single by preference; many have found alternative sources of support. Never-married women, for example, are more likely to maintain very close contact with their parents, perhaps retaining that central attachment in a less attenuated form (e.g., Allen & Pickett, 1987). They are also more likely than are their married peers to have full-time, continuous careers and to be more successful and better paid as a result (Sørensen, 1983). Still, there is no doubt that being unmarried changes the shape of early adulthood in significant ways and carries certain psychological risks.

Those Who Do Not Have Children

Having no children also affects the shape of adult life, both within marriages and in work patterns. Without the presence of children, marital satisfaction fluctuates less over time. As is true of all marriages, childless couples are likely to experience some drop in satisfaction in the first months and years of marriage (as you've seen in Figure 14.1). But over the whole range of years of adult life the curve is much flatter than the one shown in Figure 14.3 (Houseknecht, 1987; Somers, 1993). In their 20s and 30s, childless couples consistently report higher cohesion in their marriages than do couples with children.

Another difference is in the role of worker, especially for women. Childless married women, like unmarried women, are much more likely to have full-time continuous careers and to be more committed to the goal of career success than are women with children (Houseknecht, 1987).

Overall, then, childlessness has the expected effects on the way young adults distribute their energy among the main roles. At a deeper level, however, childlessness may demand a different kind of adaptation. One very interesting analysis comes from a 40-year longitudinal study of a group of inner-city but nondelinquent boys who had originally served as a comparison group for a study of delinquent youth (Snarey et al., 1987). Of the 343 married men still part of this sample in their late 40s, 29 had fathered no child. Snarey and his colleagues found that the way a man had earlier responded to this childlessness was predictive of his psychological health at age 47. At that age, each man was rated on his degree of what Erikson calls generativity. A man was considered to be generative if he had taken responsibility for the growth and well-being of other adults through some kind of mentoring or other teaching or supervising. Among those with no children, those who were rated as most generative were likely to have responded to their childlessness by finding some kind of substitute child to nurture. They adopted a child, became "Big Brothers," or got involved with the rearing of someone else's child, such as a niece or nephew. Those childless men rated as nongenerative were more likely to have chosen a pet as a child substitute.

Critical Thinking

Do these results mean that every adult has to have some nurturing experience with children to achieve maturity or optimum mental health at later ages? What other explanations can you think of?

This is only a single study, and I do not want to build too large a speculative edifice on top of it. But it raises the possibility that some aspects of psychological growth in early adulthood may depend either on the task of bearing and rearing children, or on some reasonable substitute that calls forth one's nurturing and caring qualities—just as Erikson proposed.

The Effect of Timing

Finally, let me say just a bit about the effect that variations in timing may have on a person's experience of early adulthood. The most general point is that being "off time" or out of sequence in the adoption of any of the major roles of early adult life seems to exact some price. You've already encountered one example of this general principle in Chapter 11, where I described the evidence about the long-term life histories of those who have their first child in their teens. Very early marriage (under age 20) is also linked to higher risks of later divorce.

Even the sequence in which you add key roles seems to make a difference. Dennis Hogan (1981), in an analysis of 1973 Census Bureau data on over 35,000 men, found the lowest divorce rates among those who had followed the normative sequence: finishing school, then finding a job, and then getting married. The highest divorce rates were for those who married first, even when that marriage was fairly late and even among men with high levels of education.

Norms obviously differ from one culture to another, and from one cohort to another. The "on-time" age for marriage is now much older in the United States than it was even a decade ago, and there is no surety that the "ideal" sequence Hogan identified would still be the optimal sequence today. The point is not that the major roles of early adulthood are best acquired in a fixed order, but that they are easier to learn and succeed at if they are acquired in the *accustomed* order and at the accustomed time. Any time you experience some life event or acquire or lose some social role at a time that is not typical for your generation, your risk for depression or distress is heightened.

Summary

1. The central tasks of young adult life are the acquisition and learning of three major new roles: partner/spouse, parent, and worker.
2. The process begins with leaving home, which involves both physical and emotional separation from parents. Some theorists think young people must severely attenuate their basic attachment to the parent.
3. The new central attachment becomes the one with one's partner, who may then serve as a safe base for ventures out into the world of work.
4. Choices of partner are most heavily influenced by similarity.
5. Increasingly, an attachment model is being used to describe adult relationships. At the least we know that internal models of attachment are related to the quality of relationships we create and the assumptions we make about others.
6. Sternberg's model of love is also influential. He posits three elements: intimacy, passion, and commitment. These three may be combined to produce eight varieties of love.
7. Committed partnerships—marriage or long-term cohabitation—tend to decline in quality in the first year as the rate of positive interactions drops.
8. Enduring relationships, compared with those that end in divorce or separation, are found among those who enter the relationship with good resources (education, problem-solving ability, etc.), and among those who create positive communication strategies. Good marriages look like secure attachments; poor or failing marriages look like insecure attachments.
9. Each adult also creates a convoy of relationships, including family and friends as well as partner. Young adults' relationships with their parents tend to be steady and supportive, even if less central than they were at earlier ages.
10. Young adults *may* have more friends than do older adults, but the number of intimate friendships remains about the same across adult life. Women's friendships are generally more intimate and more emotionally supportive.
11. Parenthood brings both joy and the stress of a new role to learn. On average, marital satisfaction declines after the birth of the first child and remains low for most of early adulthood. At the same time, sex roles generally become more traditional within the partnership, a process Gutmann calls the "parental imperative."
12. The specific job or career an adult chooses is affected by his or her education, intelligence, family background and resources, family values, personality, and gender. The majority of adults choose jobs that fit the cultural norms for their social class and gender. More intelligent young people, and those with more education, are more upwardly mobile.
13. Adults also tend to choose and be happier in jobs that fit their particular personality.
14. Job satisfaction rises steadily throughout early adulthood, in part because young-adult jobs are less well paid, more repetitive, less creative, and less powerful.
15. Within any given occupation or career, job advancement tends to occur fairly early in adult life, with promotions occurring by age 35 or 40.
16. We can think of the work role as having two stages in early adulthood: a trial stage in which alternative pathways are explored, and an establishment stage in which the career path is established.
17. For most women, an additional "in-and-out" stage occurs, in which family responsibilities alternate with out-of-home work periods. The more continuous a woman's work history, the more successful she is likely to be at her job.

18. When both partners work, the family responsibilities are not equally divided: Women continue to perform more of this work and feel more role conflict.

19. All five of the "Big Five" personality dimensions show strong stability through adulthood.

20. Personality also changes in some shared ways. Between ages 30 and 40, young adults become more independent, more confident, more assertive, more oriented toward achievement, more individualistic, and less governed by social rules.

21. These patterns differ somewhat in men and women who do not adopt one or more of the key roles, such as those who do not marry or those without children. Unmarried adults are, on average, less happy and more prone to illness. Married childless adults do not experience the same degree of decline in marital quality as do those with children.

22. The timing and sequencing of the several major young adult roles are also important. Any significant deviation from the normative timing and sequence exacts a price.

Key Terms

convoy | establishment stage | parental imperative | trial stage

Suggested Readings

Betz, N. E. & Fitzgerald, L. F. (1987). *The career psychology of women.* Orlando, FL: Academic Press.

Although it is no longer completely current, this is still one of the most splendidly detailed, thorough books on the subject.

Blieszner, R., & Adams, R. G. (1992). *Adult friendship.* Newbury Park, CA: Sage.

One of a series of small books published by Sage that explore aspects of personal relationships.

Cate, R. M., & Lloyd, S. A. (1992). *Courtship.* Newbury Park, CA: Sage.

Another book in the Sage series. This one offers a good review of our knowledge and ignorance about the courtship process.

Gottman, J. M. (1994b). *Why marriages succeed or fail.* New York: Simon & Schuster.

An absolutely wonderful book, aimed at a lay audience, written by one of the most thorough and thoughtful researchers to study marriage success and failure. The book has a number of quizzes you can take to identify your own relationship style and specific suggestions about how to improve your own partnership.

Heatherton, T. F., & Weinberger, J. L. (Eds.) (1994). *Can personality change?* Washington, DC: American Psychological Association.

Included in this book is a paper by Costa and McCrae, presenting the evidence for stability of personality in adulthood, and by Ravenna Helson and Abigail Stewart, arguing for personality change.

Karen, R. (1994). *Becoming attached.* New York: Warner Books.

Another wonderful new book written for the general reader.

Interlude 5

Summing Up Early Adult Development

Basic Characteristics of Early Adulthood

In our youth-oriented and youth-admiring culture, many of us think of young adulthood as the easiest or best years of life. Physically, that is certainly true. The body is at its peak in the years from 20 to 40. Any aspect of mental functioning that is based on physiological speed or efficiency is also at its peak, as is clear in the summary table. But socially and emotionally these years are probably more stressful and more difficult than any other part of adulthood.

These are the years in which more separate roles must be learned than at any other age, and in which there are likely to be more separate life changes than in any other era. Demographer Ronald Rindfuss (1991) refers to the years from 20 to 30 as "demographically dense" because there is more action in these years—more marriages, divorces, geographical moves, births, school leavings, and periods of unemployment—than at any other time of life.

Adults themselves place many of the tasks of this age high on their list of important events of their lives. If you ask older adults to think back over their entire adult life and identify the most important events, they list more events in early adulthood as significant (Martin & Smyer, 1990). The evidence makes it very clear that this intense concentration of major tasks carries some emotional price: Loneliness and depression are higher in these years than any other.

Because the prescriptions about the several key adult roles come from outside ourselves, this is also the time in our adult lives when we are most defined by external criteria. Not only do we measure ourselves against such criteria ("Am I a good mother?" "Am I going to get the promotion?"), we identify ourselves in terms of the roles we occupy.

In the language of Jane Loevinger's theory, this is a *conformist* stance, characterized not only by external sources of authority but also by a tendency to think in "us-them," stereotyped ways about others and about one's own emotional life. Evidence from the longitudinal studies I described in Chapter 14 suggests that this way of understanding ourselves,

so characteristic of the first part of early adulthood, gives way in our late 30s or early 40s to what Loevinger calls the *self-aware level,* and eventually to the *conscientious stage*—both perhaps aspects of what Levinson calls "detribalization." Having learned the key roles, we begin to free ourselves from their constraints; we figure out how to fulfill our various duties and still express our own individuality.

Of course I cannot say that young adults in every culture will necessarily become more self-confident, assertive, and independent by the time they are 40. We simply don't have the research to back up such an assertion. But it looks as if this may be a common thread, perhaps a basic part of the normal progress of adult life. Why might this be true?

Several possibilities occur to me. One is that over the years of young adulthood, many of us discover that following the rules, doing what you are "supposed to do," does not necessarily bring reward. You don't always get the promotion you worked so hard for; you may not find a mate, even though you have done all the "right" things. Having children may not bring consistent satisfaction or joy, as you may have expected. Inevitable disillusionments like these may lead many individuals to question the rules, to doubt the eternal correctness of role prescriptions.

Another push toward questioning comes from the expertise that many adults develop in their work roles. We may pursue a job or career because it is part of what is expected of us, but in the process we may discover our own talents and capacities. Such a discovery increases our self-confidence and may turn us more toward an inward and away from an outward definition of self. In the process, we may also become aware of those parts of ourselves that our collective roles do not allow us to express, and search for ways to express those parts.

This individualization process may begin in early adulthood and be in full

A Summary of the Threads of Development in Early Adulthood

Aspect of Development	Age in Years: 20	25	30	35	40
Physical development	Peak function on virtually all measures; maximum health; best time for childbearing; athletic performance at its peak in most sports.			Very gradual decline on most measures, detectable primarily when performing at peak.	
Cognitive development	Maximum performance on any mental task requiring speed; maximum memory ability on most measures.		*Increasing* IQ and improving performance on any "crystallized" intelligence test, such as vocabulary or problem solving.		
Social and personality development	Erikson's stage of Intimacy versus Isolation; dominant in 20s, still central in 30s.				
	Typical timing for the acquisition of three major new roles: spouse, parent, and worker.				
		Maximum sense of role conflict among these roles.			
Work	Trial stage: searching for right work.		Establishment stage: time of most promotions; plateau usually reached by 40.		
Partnership	Searching for partner.	Finding partner and marriage.	Decline in marital satisfaction after birth of first child and throughout rest of young adulthood.		
Personality	Peak time for definition of self in terms of the roles occupied.		Increasing self-confidence, assertiveness, independence; detribalization; greater individualization.		
	Continuity throughout this period on five major personality characteristics: neuroticism, extraversion, openness to experience, conscientiousness, and agreeableness.				
Emotional health	Highest levels of depression and loneliness in one's 20s.				

bloom by age 40. But it is still true that the years of early adulthood are more dominated by the social clock, by the demands and strictures of the central social roles, than will be true at any other time in adult life.

Central Processes

When asked about the keys to successful adult life, Freud is reported to have said "love and work." Freud was clearly correct. We know that those adults who are satisfied with their work and their relationships are also satisfied with their lives in general. But it begins to look as if love is the more important of the two. For instance, the single most significant predictor of a person's overall life satisfaction at any adult age is each person's reported happiness in marriage and family relationships (Campbell, 1981; Glenn & Weaver, 1981; Sears, 1977). Work satisfaction, though significant, is apparently not as central as satisfaction in love.

The centrality of love relationships is also underlined in the new work on internal models of attachment. Hazan and Shaver (1990), in an extremely interesting extension of attachment theory, have proposed that we can think of the relationship of love and work in adulthood in the same way that Bowlby and Ainsworth think of attachment and exploration in a young child. Bowlby believed that both the tendency to become attached and the tendency to explore are innate. Of the two, however, attachment is the more central; the exploration system can operate optimally only if the attachment system is not aroused. When the child has a secure attachment, the attachment figure can be used as a safe base for exploration. But if the child is anxious about the attachment, that anxiety dominates and the child explores less freely.

Among adults, so Hazan and Shaver argue, work is the equivalent of exploration. It is the major source of a sense of competence, just as is true of a child's exploration. And like the child's exploration, adult work is best accomplished when the adult has a safe emotional base from which to move outward into the world.

Hazan and Shaver have found support for this thesis in their preliminary research. They asked their adult subjects both about the quality of their basic sense of attachment (using the descriptions listed in Table 14.1) and about many facets of their work experience. In a sample of several hundred adults ranging in age from 18 to 79, they found clear differences among the three attachment types:

Securely attached adults were less worried about work failure and less likely to feel unappreciated. They did not let work demands interfere with their relationships or health, and enjoyed their vacations.

Anxiously attached adults, lacking the safe base of a secure relationship, continued to be preoccupied with attachment issues and thus had little energy left to focus on work tasks. They described themselves as worried about their job performance, "prefer to work with others but feel underappreciated and fear rejection for poor performance. They are also easily distracted, have trouble completing projects, and tend to slack off after receiving praise" (p. 277).

Avoidant subjects liked to work alone and seemed most inclined to become "workaholics," seldom taking vacations and not enjoying them when they took them. They used work to avoid social life, friends, and intimate relationships.

These parallels between the attachment system and work behaviors and feelings are striking. They suggest that one's approach to work is deeply affected by the strengths or deficiencies of one's internal model of attachment or relationships. This single study, of course, does not prove the basic hypothesis that love is more central than work. Ultimately, we will need longitudinal studies in which young people's attachment security and work attitudes are assessed at regular intervals throughout adult life. Only in this way can we figure out whether early adulthood attachment status predicts later job attitudes or success, rather than the reverse. But my hunch is that Hazan and Shaver are entirely correct about the relative roles of love and work in adult life. Certainly their view is consistent with Erikson's theory, with his emphasis on *intimacy* as the central task of young adulthood.

Influences on the Basic Processes

Each of us brings to the tasks of adult life certain advantages and disadvantages. High on the list would be each individual's history of secure or insecure attachment carried forward from childhood. Research tells us, for example, that adults who lost a parent in childhood—to death or divorce—are at greater risk for a variety of problems, including depression, separation, or divorce themselves, and poorer physical health (Amato & Keith, 1991; Harris, Brown, & Bifulco, 1990). More directly, we now have at least fragmentary evidence that adults who describe their early childhood relationships with parents as rejecting or ambivalent (who are thus more often insecurely attached) have more trouble establishing secure adult relationships. If Hazan and Shaver are correct, they may have more troubled work experiences as well.

Family Social Class

Attachment history is clearly not the only element in this equation. Other aspects of family background also have powerful effects. Most clearly, children growing up in poverty or working-class families are likely to complete fewer years of schooling, a difference with long-term repercussions for adult occupational experiences.

Bear in mind, though, that this is a *probability* statement. Lower education, and thus less successful work histories, are more *likely* for this subgroup, but they are not inevitable. It is possible for young people to escape from the constrictions and deprivations of a disorderly or poverty-stricken childhood, a fact clearly shown in the results from one of the long-term longitudinal studies I described in Chapter 14. As part of an investigation of delinquency and its roots and consequences, several hundred non-delinquent boys from inner city, multi-problem families were studied as a comparison group (Glueck & Glueck, 1968; Snarey, et al., 1987). When these non-delinquent teens were followed into middle age, most of them turned out to be stable, with decent incomes (Long & Vaillant, 1984). Yet it was also true that the more disadvantaged the man's family had been—the more disorganized, the more dependent on social agencies, the more neglecting or abusing—the more likely it was that the man would remain in the lower class as an adult. Those who worked their way out of the lowest social class levels were those whose families were poor but more stable and well organized. These researchers did not use Baumrind's system of categorizing families, but one might guess that an authoritative early family history would be most likely to support a move out of poverty. Thus the underclass does not invariably perpetuate itself in each new generation; there are avenues or pathways for change. But a disorderly or deprived family background is like starting adulthood with at least one strike against you.

Personality

Another significant predictor of the ability to master the various tasks of early adult life is the individual's personality. A high level of neuroticism seems to be especially detrimental. Indeed, it is possible that some of the differences Hazan and Shaver (and others) have ascribed to internal models of attachment are really basic personality variance in disguise. The anxiously attached person, for example, may also be someone who scores high on measures of neuroticism. Similar arguments made about the link between temperament and attachment security in infancy have not been well supported; many temperamentally "difficult" infants establish secure attachments, although there is some sign that an insecure attachment is somewhat more likely for such difficult babies. What we need now, in studies of adults, is separate measure-

ment of attachment security and personality traits. Are there adults who are high in neuroticism but secure in attachment? Do such adults have a different pattern of adult experiences than other highly neurotic adults? My own sense is that these two ways of looking at individual differences in adults—in terms of attachment security, and in terms of basic personality traits —overlap somewhat but not fully. Each is independently significant. But that's an empirical question yet to be answered.

Personal Choices

The pathway through early adulthood is also affected by a set of personal choices each of us makes, including such things as health practices and choices about the timing of key roles. The effects of health practices may be largely invisible in early adulthood, as I pointed out in Chapter 13. But the health chickens come home to roost later in adult life, in the form of higher rates of disease and disability for those with poor early health habits.

The effects of variation in timing, in contrast, may already be visible in early adulthood. The sequence and timing of marriage, parenthood, and work experiences create what various authors have called *pathways, trajectories,* or *anchor points* of adult life (Elder, 1991; Hagestad, 1990; O'Rand, 1990). One example is obviously the woman who works before marriage or childbearing, who will have higher lifetime earnings than will a woman who marries and has her children before she moves into the labor force. Similarly, delaying childbearing into one's 30s has a ripple effect on all subsequent family life stages. For one thing, it increases the likelihood of being "squeezed" in middle adulthood, with one's children still needing support at the same time as one acquires responsibility for aging parents.

Being "off time" in the sense of bucking the norm also has its price, as I have pointed out before. Why might this be true? One possibility is that "off timeness" operates through yet another internal model, what Mildred Seltzer and Lillian Troll call the *expected life history.* When asked, most young adults have no difficulty writing their own projected life story. Each of us carries around a model for the "normal" or "expectable" sequence of events in our lives, or the goals we expect to reach at particular ages. It is a road map for our future. "I will finish school, then marry, then have three children, then go to work. By the time I'm 50, my kids will have left home and I'll be able to really focus on my career." Or "I don't want to marry until I'm about 30 because I'm determined to be the youngest partner in my law firm before then."

These expectations have their origins both in specific family patterns and in the social role expectations of a given cohort in a particular culture. When they work out, expectations can help each of us anticipate potentially stressful events and thus reduce their negative impact precisely because we have prepared ahead of time. A perfect example is retirement, which looks like a major upheaval but which rarely has any negative effects, presumably because it is something anticipated and planned.

When our adult life does *not* follow our expectations, however, Seltzer and Troll argue that there is a psychological price to be paid. In my generation, college women expected to marry soon after they finished college. It was certainly what I expected, and when it didn't happen that way it required a major readjustment of my thinking—and some pain, I might add. Not to marry at 21 or 22 was to be "off time," to break an expected mold. It carried the message of failed femininity.

The negative effect of being off time may also be observable for a much simpler reason: In a given culture, some sequences may simply be objectively more difficult. For example, women who are widowed when they are still in their 30s have a considerably harder time adjusting to the loss than do women widowed in their 60s or 70s (Ball, 1976–1977). This *could* result because early widowhood is a deviation from the expected life history. But the greater adaptational difficulty of young widows may occur because the younger woman is more likely to have young children to support and may not have adequate economic resources.

Whether we think of the process in terms of yet another impact of internal models or as a function of more objective stresses associated with certain timing or sequences, the significant point is that the choices we make and the chance events we are dealt in our early adult life may shape our experiences for many decades.

An optimist may think of young adulthood as a time of opportunity; a pessimist may see it as a time of struggle. What is objectively true is that in these years we are physically more energetic, quicker, and stronger than at any other time in our lives—capacities that are needed if we are to master the complex tasks we are asked to learn and perform in these years.

Physical and Cognitive Development in Middle Adulthood

15

The great baseball player Satchel Paige, who was still pitching in the major leagues at age 62, once said, "Age is mind over matter. If you don't mind, it doesn't matter." It's a nice summary of the physical changes of the middle years. Yes, there are changes. Memory does get less efficient in some situations in midlife; vision and hearing get worse; we slow down slightly and become somewhat weaker. But what is surprising in all

CRITICAL THINKING

Why do you think there is such a widespread belief in our culture that significant physical decline begins in middle adulthood? What would it take to change this belief?

this is that among adults who are otherwise healthy the amount of loss is far less than folklore would have us believe. For healthy adults, the changes are small enough so that if you don't mind, it really doesn't matter.

Life Expectancy

Those adults who have survived to the age of 40 can expect to live a good many more years. The technical term is **life expectancy,** which refers to the average number of years remaining for a person of a given age. Figure 15.1, which gives information about life expectancy at age 40 in the United States, illustrates three important points: Women live longer than men, whites live longer than blacks, and life expectancy has increased dramatically in the past few decades. The Census Bureau has not regularly reported equivalent information separately for Hispanics, but current estimates are that the life expectancy for this subgroup is only slightly below that of whites.

Life expectancy, by the way, is not the same as **life span.** The latter phrase refers to the upper boundary, the maximum number of years any member of a given species could expect to live. The life span of humans—the upper boundary—seems to be about 110 years. At this point in human history, average life expectancy is a good deal less than the life span. But given the steadily rising life expectancy, shown clearly in Figure 15.1 (a pattern found in all industrialized countries), some physicians and physiologists have argued that the great majority of adults will ultimately be able to live to the full potential life span.

All this is encouraging news for those entering middle adulthood; the majority of 40-year-olds (in industrialized countries, at least) are only at the midpoint of their lives. What kind of changes in their bodies can these 40-year-olds expect over the succeeding 25 years?

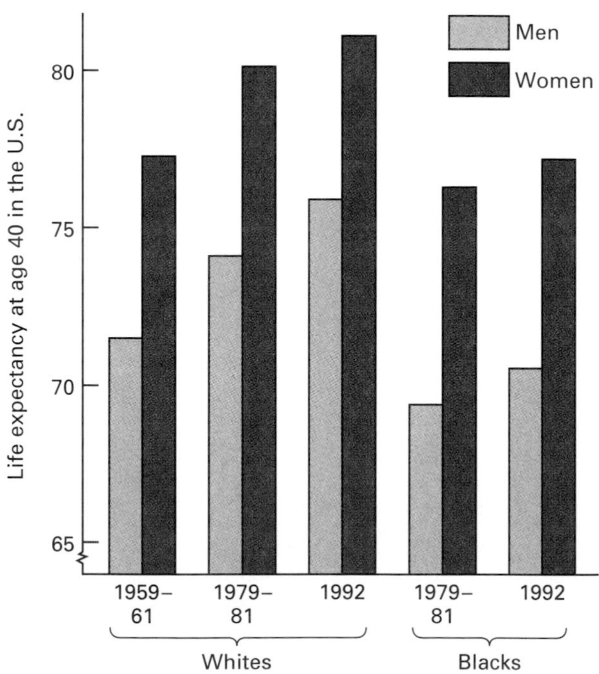

FIGURE 15.1 Life expectancy at age 40 in the United States over the past decades, for women and men, blacks and whites. (*Sources:* U.S. Bureau of the Census, 1990, Table 104, p. 73; U.S. Bureau of the Census, 1995, Table 115, p. 86.)

Research Report

Why Do Women Live Longer Than Men?

Women do not have an advantage over men in every culture, or in every era. Whenever or wherever rates of death in pregnancy and childbirth are very high, women's life expectancies are typically the same or lower than men's. But where maternal mortality has been reduced, women begin to show quite large advantages in longevity (Verbrugge & Wingard, 1987). Both biological and social explanations have been offered to account for this difference.

The most convincing biological argument is that women may be physically less vulnerable to some or all diseases. I pointed out in Chapters 3 and 4 that boys are more vulnerable to a host of problems prenatally and in the first year of life. Differences in longevity among middle-aged and older adults may simply reflect the same variation in basic vulnerability. Men are more likely to inherit sex-linked recessive diseases, they may be more vulnerable to fragile X syndrome, and their relative lack of estrogen may make them more vulnerable to heart disease. The difference in heart disease risk is especially striking. In the United States, between ages 45 and 54, 233 men out of every 100,000 die of heart disease, compared with only 81 women (U.S. Bureau of the Census, 1995). Past menopause, when women's estrogen levels decline, this difference in rates of heart disease diminishes, although it does not disappear totally even in late old age.

A variety of social factors also contributes to the greater life expectancy in women (Verbrugge, 1984, 1989; Verbrugge & Wingard, 1987). First, women's work exposes them to fewer environmental hazards. This may become less true over the next few cohorts, as we see greater equality in occupational opportunity. But among current middle-aged and elderly cohorts it is clearly the case that more men have been exposed to such hazards as asbestos, smoke, and chemicals of various kinds. Physically dangerous jobs, such as those of police officer, firefighter, or logger, are also more frequently done by men.

Women also seek more health care. They are more likely to get regular checkups, even when they are feeling well, and seek help earlier in an illness than do men, which improves their chances of amelioration or cure (Verbrugge & Wingard, 1987). And they generally have better health habits, beginning early in adulthood. They take vitamins more often, and are less likely to smoke or to drink heavily. In the Alameda County study, which I mentioned often in Chapter 13, Berkman and Breslow (1983) found that women were more likely to be overweight, but less likely to drink or smoke heavily. Sex differences in smoking are much smaller now than they were when today's elderly were young. So we might expect that sex differences in death from such smoking-related diseases as lung cancer and heart disease will eventually decline.

When the life expectancies of men and women are compared after all these social factors have been controlled, the size of the sex difference is reduced, but it is not eliminated. In particular, sex differences in the risk of death from heart disease remain large even when health habits and occupation have been removed from the equation (Verbrugge & Wingard, 1987). Either this means that the social explanations are not sufficient, or that we do not yet know all the social factors that may be important. Women's more intimate social networks, for example, may buffer them more fully from the effects of stress. We don't yet know all the answers, but the question is fascinating—and the fact that women live longer has substantial practical ramifications, not the least of which is that women have a very high likelihood of being widowed, and thus living alone for some portion of their later years.

Changes in the Physical Body

For a quick overview of the common physical changes of middle age, go back and take another look at Table 13.1 (page 336), which summarizes most of the evidence. For many physical functions, change and/or decline occurs very gradually through the 40s and 50s. But for a few physical functions, change or decline is already substantial in the middle adult years—a set of changes I need to talk about in more detail.

Reproductive System

If you were asked to name a single significant physical change occurring in the years of middle adulthood, chances are you'd list menopause—especially if you're a woman. The more general term is **climacteric,** which refers to the loss of reproductive capacity over the years of middle or late adulthood in both men and women.

Male Climacteric. In men, the climacteric is extremely gradual, with a slow loss of reproductive capacity, although the rate of change varies widely from one man to the next, and there are documented cases of men in their 90s fathering children. On average, the quantity of viable sperm produced declines slightly, beginning perhaps at about age 40. The testes also shrink very gradually, and the volume of seminal fluid declines after about age 60.

The causal factor is most likely a very slow drop in testosterone levels, beginning in early adulthood and continuing well into old age. There has been some disagreement among researchers about whether such a decline actually occurs; some longitudinal studies among only healthy adults show no such decline (e.g., Harman & Tsitouras, 1980). But the weight of the evidence now seems to point to a small, very gradual, average decline in testosterone over the adult years, but with wide variation from one man to the next in normal hormone levels (Tsitouras & Bulat, 1995).

This decline in testosterone is implicated in the gradual loss of muscle tissue (and hence strength) that we see in these middle and later years, as well as in the increased risk of heart disease in middle and old age. It also appears to affect sexual function. In particular, in the middle years, the incidence of impotence begins to increase—although many things other than the slight decline in testosterone contribute to this change, including an increased incidence of poor health, especially heart disease, blood pressure medication (and other medications), alcoholism, and smoking.

The most complete information about impotence in midlife comes from a study in Boston involving 1290 men between 40 and 90 (Feldman et al., 1994). Each man completed a questionnaire about the frequency and duration of his erections, and rated himself as having no impotence, minimal, moderate, or complete impotence. You can see the main results in Figure 15.2. Those describing "minimal impotence" reported some problems achieving and/or maintaining an erection, although most of these men did still have active sex lives. Those describing themselves as moderately impotent had more significant difficulties but most also reported that they had intercourse at least occasionally. Clearly, both categories of impotence rise during the middle years, a finding replicated in other studies (Keil et al., 1992).

Menopause. Declines in key sex hormones are also clearly implicated in the set of changes we call **menopause** in women, which means literally the cessation of the menses. You'll remember from Chapter 11 that several forms of estrogen, secreted

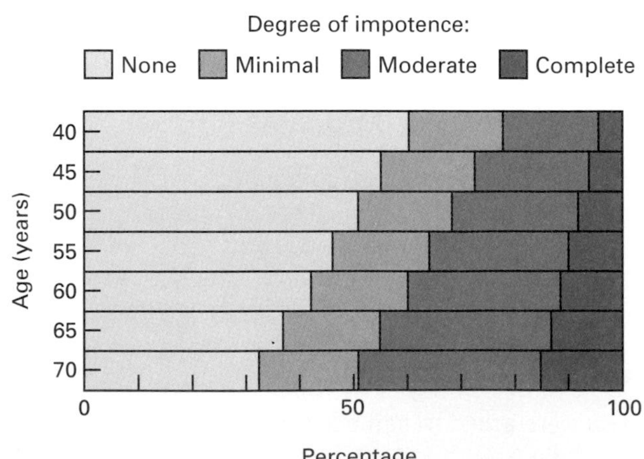

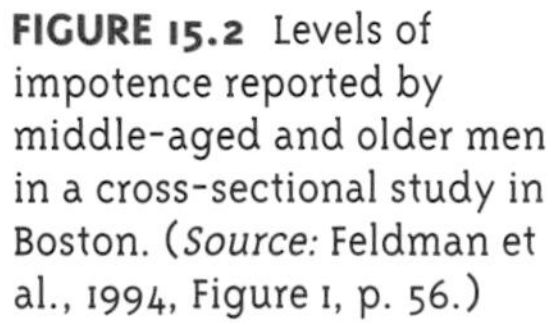
FIGURE 15.2 Levels of impotence reported by middle-aged and older men in a cross-sectional study in Boston. (*Source:* Feldman et al., 1994, Figure 1, p. 56.)

by the ovaries, increase rapidly during puberty, triggering the onset of menstruation as well as stimulating the development of breasts and secondary sex characteristics. In the adult woman, estrogen levels are high during the first 14 days of the menstrual cycle, stimulating the release of ova and the preparation of the uterus for possible implantation. Progesterone, which is secreted by the adrenal gland, rises during the second half of the menstrual cycle and stimulates the sloughing off of accumulated material in the uterus each month if no conception has occurred.

Estrogen levels begin to fluctuate and decline in the years just before menopause, producing irregularity in menstruation because the estrogen signal to the ovary to release an ovum is insufficient in some months. Eventually, estrogen and progesterone drop to a consistently low level and menstruation ceases. For example, estradiol and estrone, both subvarieties of estrogen, drop to about a quarter or less of their premenopausal levels. Progesterone decreases even more, from roughly 10,000 picograms per milliliter before menopause to roughly 200 after.

Menopause is said to occur when a woman has not menstruated for one year. The average age of menopause for both blacks and whites in the United States, and for women in other countries for which we have data, is roughly age 50; anything between age 40 and 60 is considered within the normal range (Bellantoni & Blackman, 1996). About 1 woman in 12 experiences menopause before the age of 40, referred to by physicians as *premature menopause* (Wich & Carnes, 1995).

The reduction in estrogen also has effects on genital and other tissue. The breasts become less firm, the genitals lose some tissue, the uterus shrinks somewhat in size, and the vagina becomes both shorter and smaller in diameter. The walls of the vagina also become somewhat thinner and less elastic, and produce less lubrication during intercourse (Weg, 1987; Wich & Carnes, 1995).

The other major physical symptom experienced by the majority of women in the period around menopause is the *hot flash* or *hot flush*, which involves a sensation of warmth in the upper body and head, an abrupt rise in skin temperature, increased heart rate, flushing, and usually visible sweating. The temperature of the skin can rise as much as 1 to 7 degrees in some parts of the body during a hot flash, although the core body temperature actually drops (Kronenberg, 1994). Hot flashes last, on average, about 3 minutes and may recur as seldom as daily or as often as 3 times per hour (Bellantoni & Blackman, 1996).

The causes of this very common phenomenon are not yet understood. No hormonal or neuroendocrinological substance is known to trigger a hot flash, although it must clearly be linked in some complex way to the drop in estrogen, since estrogen replacement therapy reduces or eliminates hot flashes—a point I've touched on in the Real World box.

Roughly three-quarters of women in the pre- or postmenopausal period report at least some hot flashes. Of those who have them, 85 percent will have them for more than a year; a third or more will have them for 5 years or more (Kletzky & Borenstein, 1987). They are certainly not fatal, but they can be socially disconcerting and may seriously disrupt one's sleep. If that sounds autobiographical, it is; I'm one of the minority with long-term, frequent hot flashes. My first experience with them was on a trip to China when I was 46, when I had such flashes perhaps 20 times each day. Our Chinese hosts kept commenting on how red my face was. True enough!

One other issue about the climacteric in women deserves some mention. It has been part of our folklore for a very long time that menopause involves major emotional upheaval as well as clear physical changes. Women were presumed to be emotionally volatile, angry, depressed, even shrewish during these midlife years. The available evidence allows us to put this idea to rest.

Four relevant, well-designed longitudinal studies exist, three in the United States and one in Sweden. None of them report any connection between menopausal status and a rise in depression or other psychological symptoms

The Real World

The Pros and Cons of Hormone Replacement Therapy

Most of the physical symptoms of the menopause—including hot flashes, thinning of the vaginal wall, and loss of vaginal lubrication—can be dramatically reduced by taking estrogen and progesterone. Because women readers may eventually have to decide whether to follow such a regimen, let me tell you a little about what we know and don't know.

Hormone replacement therapy has had a somewhat checkered history. In the 1950s and 1960s, estrogen therapy became extremely common. In some surveys, as many as half of all postmenopausal women in the United States reported using replacement estrogen, many of them over periods of 10 years or more (Stadel & Weiss, 1975). In the 1970s, however, new evidence showed that the risk of endometrial cancer (cancer of the lining of the uterus) increased three- to tenfold in women taking replacement estrogen (Nathanson & Lorenz, 1982). Not surprisingly, when this information became available the incidence of such therapy dropped dramatically.

The third act in this drama was the discovery that a combination of estrogen and progesterone, at quite low dosages, had the same benefits as estrogen alone and eliminated the increased risk of endometrial cancer. Furthermore, new studies also made clear that the use of replacement estrogen has two additional benefits: It reduces the risk of coronary heart disease by about half, and it significantly retards the bone loss of osteoporosis (Barrett-Connor & Bush, 1991; Ross et al., 1987). New research tells us that both these benefits occur with the newer estrogen-progesterone combinations as well as with estrogen alone (e.g., Cauley et al., 1995; Stampfer et al., 1991; The Working Group for the PEPI Trial, 1995).

This sounds almost too good to be true, doesn't it? Why shouldn't every postmenopausal woman be on a program of hormone replacements? There are two counterarguments. First, many women consider the process of aging, including the changes of menopause, to be natural physical processes with which they do not want to tinker. Second, although we have evidence that hormone replacement therapy is linked to slightly *lower* overall cancer risks (Posthuma, Westendorp, & Vandenbroucke, 1994), it is associated with somewhat *higher* rates of breast cancer and very slightly higher rates of ovarian cancer in some studies. When such increases are found—and they are *not* found in every study (e.g., Newcomb et al., 1995)—the increases are not huge. In the large Nurses Health Study (the same study from which I drew the information on the links between weight and mortality discussed in Chapter 13), researchers found that for every woman diagnosed with breast cancer who did *not* take replacement hormones, there were roughly 1.4 cancers diagnosed among women who use hormone therapy (Colditz et al., 1995). The equivalent contrast for ovarian cancers, drawn from another study (Rodriguez et al., 1995), is 1 to 1.15.

How can an individual woman add up these various benefits and risks? How do you weigh a halved risk of heart disease against a 40 percent increased risk of breast cancer? Ultimately, this is a decision you will have to make for yourself. Among other things, you should consider not only the overall risk of heart disease versus cancer (heart disease is actually the larger overall risk in the years of middle and late adulthood), but also your family history of cancer and heart disease. If you are at high risk for breast cancer, or if your family includes many people with early heart disease, such facts would certainly affect your decision.

My own decision was first to reject hormone replacement. I argued that menopause was a natural process, that millions of other women had survived hot flashes and so could I. But after four years of 10 to 30 flashes a day, and after the newer evidence on heart disease protection appeared, I changed my mind, especially given that my family has a long history of heart disease. At the same time, I also made a commitment to become more regular about physical exams, particularly mammograms. You will have to make your own choice, in light of the evidence available at the time you face the decision.

(Busch, Zonderman, & Costa, 1994; Hallstrom & Samuelsson, 1985; Matthews et al., 1990; McKinlay, McKinlay, & Brambilla, 1987). In the largest and most recent of these studies, a group of 3049 women aged 40 to 60 were followed over a ten-year period (Busch et al., 1994). The researchers divided these women into four groups, based on their initial menopausal status: pre-, in the midst of, and postmenopausal, with the latter group divided into those who had had surgical menopause (hysterectomy) and those with natural menopause. When the researchers compared these four groups cross-sectionally, they found essentially no differences in depression, well-being, or sleep disturbance. And those women whose menopausal status had changed over the ten years of the study showed no change in any of these characteristics linked to menopausal change. Similarly, Karen Matthews and her colleagues (Matthews et al., 1990), in a smaller but more detailed longitudinal study, found essentially no changes in psychological status over a 2½-year period surrounding menopause. Indeed, postmenopausal women in this study reported *lower* levels of stress than they had when they were premenopausal.

It is clear that a small minority of women experience significantly unpleasant physical symptoms associated with menopause—such as frequent hot flashes. Matthews estimates that perhaps only one in ten women experience some rise in depression or irritability as a result of these symptoms, while the remaining nine in ten do not. Thus, the myth of women's inevitable distress during menopause can be dispelled.

Sexual Activity. Despite all the changes in the reproductive system I've just described, the great majority of middle-aged adults remain sexually active, although the frequency of sex declines in these years. The best recent evidence supporting both of those statements is a large national study involving 3432 U.S. adults aged 18 to 59, each interviewed in depth about all aspects of sexual practices (Laumann et al., 1994; Michael et al., 1994). Table 15.1 gives the frequency of sex in the past year reported by respondents of various ages in this study. Take note, though: These figures include everyone in each age group, not just those who are married or cohabiting. This means that the percentages shown in the table reflect not only age changes, but also changes in the likelihood of having a regular partner. Young adults are more likely to be unmarried or unpartnered, which helps explain why 15 percent of the youngest group have had no sex at all in the past year. Still, even with this confounding factor, it is clear the rate of sexual activity drops through the period of middle adulthood.

It is unlikely that this decline during midlife is due wholly or even largely to drops in sex hormone levels; women do not experience major estrogen declines until their late 40s, but the decline in sexual activity begins much sooner. And the drop in testosterone among men is so gradual and slight during these years that it cannot be the full explanation. An alternative explanation is that the demands of other roles

CRITICAL THINKING

Can you think of any other explanations for the gradual decline in frequency of sexual activity during the middle adult years?

Table 15.1 Sexual Activity in Young and Middle Adulthood

	Frequency of Sex in the Past 12 Months				
Age and Gender	Not at All	A Few Times per Year	A Few Times per Month	2 or 3 Times a Week	4 or More Times a Week
Men					
18–24	15%	21%	24%	28%	12%
25–29	7%	15%	31%	36%	11%
30–39	8%	15%	37%	33%	6%
40–49	9%	18%	40%	27%	6%
50–59	11%	22%	43%	20%	3%
Women					
18–24	11%	16%	32%	29%	12%
25–29	5%	10%	38%	37%	10%
30–39	9%	16%	36%	33%	6%
40–49	15%	16%	44%	20%	5%
50–59	30%	22%	35%	12%	2%

Source: Michael et al., 1994, Table 8, p. 116.

are simply so complex that middle-aged adults find it hard to find time for sex. (The day I wrote this paragraph, I had tea with a 42-year-old friend who was feeling overwhelmed by the combination of a house being remodeled around her, two teenage children, Christmas soon to arrive, and two part-time jobs. When I described the topic of my writing that day, she laughed and said that her husband, just the night before, had asked rather wistfully if they couldn't please make a date. He hardly saw her any more. She apparently replied, "It'll have to wait till after Christmas.")

Bones

Another change that begins to be quite large in middle adulthood is a loss of calcium from the bones, resulting in reduced bone mass and more brittle and porous bones. Collectively, this process is called **osteoporosis.** It is clear from Figure 15.3, which shows the age changes graphically, that the bone loss begins at about age 30 for both men and women, but in women the process is accelerated by menopause. The major consequence of this loss of bone density is a significantly increased risk of fractures, beginning as early as age 50 for women, much later for men. In the United States, it is estimated that almost one in four women will experience a hip fracture before the age of 80 (Lindsay, 1985). Among older women—and men—such fractures can be a major cause of disability and reduced activity, so this is not a trivial change.

Any weight-bearing exercise will help prevent osteoporosis, but walking seems to be especially beneficial.

In women, it is clear that bone loss is linked quite directly to estrogen levels. We know that estrogen falls dramatically after menopause, and it is the timing of menopause rather than age that signals the increase in rate of bone loss. We also know that the rate of bone loss drops to premenopausal levels among women who take replacement estrogen (Duursma et al., 1991), all of which makes the link quite clear.

While the overall pattern of bone loss seems to be a part of primary aging, the amount of such loss nonetheless varies quite a lot from one individual to another. I've listed the known risk factors in Table 15.2.

Aside from taking replacement hormones, you can help prevent osteoporosis by either or both of two strategies. First, you can make sure that you get enough calcium during early adulthood, so that your peak level of bone mass is as robust as possible. Second, throughout adult life you can get regular exercise, particularly weight-bearing exercise such as walking or strength training. In one study, postmenopausal women who began a program of walking, jogging, or stair climbing for an hour, three times a week, showed an *increase* in bone mineral content of 5.2 percent within nine months, compared with a loss of 1.4 percent in the nonexercising comparison group (Dalsky et al., 1988). But this benefit faded if the exercise was not maintained. In another study, a group of middle-aged or older women were randomly assigned to a strength-training program twice a week for a year. They showed

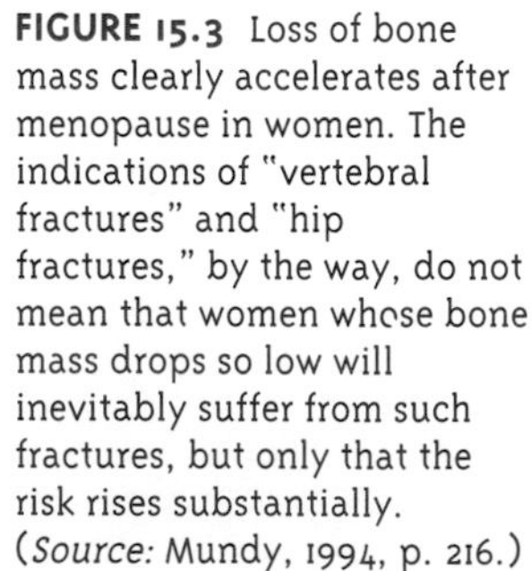

FIGURE 15.3 Loss of bone mass clearly accelerates after menopause in women. The indications of "vertebral fractures" and "hip fractures," by the way, do not mean that women whose bone mass drops so low will inevitably suffer from such fractures, but only that the risk rises substantially. (*Source:* Mundy, 1994, p. 216.)

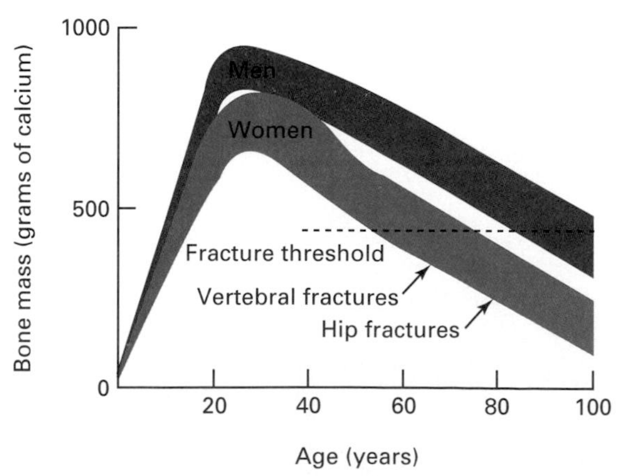

Table 15.2 Risk Factors for Osteoporosis

- *Race:* Whites are at higher risk than other races.
- *Gender:* Women have considerably higher risk than males.
- *Weight:* Those who are light for their height are at higher risk.
- *Timing of Climacteric:* Women with early menopause and those who have had their ovaries removed are at higher risk, presumably because their estrogen levels decline at earlier ages.
- *Family History:* Those with a family history of osteoporosis are at higher risk.
- *Diet:* A diet low in calcium during adolescence and early adulthood results in lower peak levels of bone mass, and hence greater risk of falling below critical levels later. Whether there is any benefit in increasing intake of calcium postmenopausally remains in debate. Diets high in either caffeine (especially black coffee) or alcohol are also linked to higher risk.
- *Exercise:* Those with a sedentary lifestyle are at higher risk. Prolonged immobility, such as bed rest, also increases rate of bone loss. Increasing exercise reduces the rate of bone loss.

Sources: Dalsky et al., 1988; Duursma et al., 1991; Gambert et al., 1995; Goldberg & Hagberg, 1990; Gordon & Vaughan, 1986; Lindsay, 1985; Morrison et al., 1994; Smith, 1982.

a gain in bone density over the year, while a control group without such weight training showed a loss (Nelson et al., 1994).

Vision and Hearing

One of the most noticeable physical changes occurring in the middle years is a loss of visual acuity. Most of us will need reading glasses or bifocals by the time we are 45 or 50. Two changes in the eyes, collectively called **presbyopia,** are involved. First, the lens of the eye thickens. In a process that begins in childhood but produces noticeable effects only in middle adulthood, layer after layer of slightly pigmented material is added to the lens. Because light coming into the eye must pass through this thickened, slightly yellowed material, the total light reaching the retina drops, which reduces a person's overall sensitivity, particularly to short-wave length colors such as blue, blue-green, and violet (Fozard, 1990).

Because of this thickening, it is also harder and harder for the muscles surrounding the eye to change the shape of the lens to adjust the focus. In a young eye, the

By age 45 or 50, nearly everyone will need to use glasses, especially for reading.

shape of the lens can be readily adjusted for each distance, so no matter how near or far away some object may be, the light rays passing through the eye converge on the retina in the back of the eye, giving a sharp image. But as the thickening increases, elasticity of the lens declines and it is no longer possible to make these fine adjustments. Many images becomes blurry. In particular, the ability to focus clearly on near objects deteriorates rapidly in the 40s and early 50s. As a result, middle-aged adults often hold books and other items further and further away, because only in that way can they get a clear image. Finally, of course, they cannot read the print at the distance at which they can focus, and they are driven to wearing reading glasses or bifocals. These same changes also affect the ability to adapt quickly to variations in levels of light or glare, such as passing headlights when driving at night or in the rain. So driving and equivalent activities may become more stressful. All in all, these changes in the eyes, which appear to be a genuine part of primary aging, require both physical and psychological adjustment.

The equivalent process in hearing is called **presbycusis.** The auditory nerves and the structures of the inner ear gradually degenerate as a result of basic wear and tear, resulting primarily in losses in the ability to hear high- and very-low-frequency sounds. But these changes do not accumulate to the level of significant hearing loss until somewhat later than what we see for presbyopia. Hearing loss is quite slow until about age 50, and only a small percentage of middle-aged adults require hearing aids (Fozard, 1990). After age 50 or 55, however, the rate of hearing loss accelerates. Such a pattern of loss does appear to be an aspect of primary aging. But some secondary aging processes are involved as well. In particular, the amount of hearing loss is considerably greater in adults who work or live in very noisy environments (Baltes, Reese, & Nesselroade, 1977)—or who listen regularly to very loud music. Rock musicians, I understand, suffer from very early presbycusis.

CRITICAL THINKING

If you were in charge of public health programs and wanted to convince young adults that they should not listen to loud music over earphones because of risks of early and extensive hearing loss, how would you go about persuading them? What arguments do you think would work?

Changes in Health

Another way to look at changes in the physical body over these middle years is to look at health. What kinds of diseases and disabilities do we see in middle-aged adults? If they die, what do they die of?

Illness and Disability

The number of truly healthy adults declines in midlife. Perhaps half of adults between 40 and 65 have either some diagnosed disease or disability or a significant but undiagnosed problem, such as the early stages of heart disease. Young adults may have more *acute* illnesses, as I mentioned in Chapter 13, but middle-aged adults have

Table 15.3 Age Differences in Rate of Common Chronic Illnesses in the United States in 1989

	Age Group		
Rate per 100 Population	**25–44**	**45–64**	**65+**
Heart conditions	3.6	11.9	23.2
High blood pressure	5.6	22.9	38.4
Arthritis	4.9	25.4	43.7
Diabetes	1.1	5.8	9.0

Source: U.S. Bureau of the Census, 1992, from Table 195, p. 126.

more chronic diseases and disabilities. You can see the difference in Table 15.3, which shows rates by age for selected chronic problems in the United States in 1989, the most recent year in which the Census Bureau reports the figures in this way (U.S. Bureau of the Census, 1992).

The same story emerges when we look at the behavioral effects of disease or disability. If you ask adults about their ability to perform various normal daily activities, you find that about a quarter of adults between 45 and 64 say they have at least some minor limitation in their daily activity, such as trouble lifting heavy objects. But very few have so much disability that they are unable to care for themselves physically (Verbrugge, 1984). After age 65, significant activity limitation becomes much more common.

Deaths. The causes of death also change in middle adulthood, especially for men. You'll recall that among young men in the United States today, AIDS and violence (accidents, homicide, and suicide) are the leading causes of death. In middle age, as you can see in Table 15.4, heart disease and cancer become the most common killers, although AIDS remains a major cause of death among men in their 40s. Among both young adult and middle-aged women, however, cancer is the leading killer.

Several other points are also suggested by the data shown in this table. First, the death rate roughly triples between the 45–54 decade and the 55–64 decade. Second, women have much lower death rates than men—yet another reflection of the basic sex difference in life expectancy I already noted. But what is not evident in either Table 15.3 or 15.4 is a fascinating paradox: Women live longer, but they have *more* diseases and disabilities. Women are more likely to describe their health as poor, they have more chronic conditions such as arthritis, and have more limitations in their daily activities. Such differences have been found in every country in which the pattern has been studied, including Third World countries (Rahman et al., 1994).

This difference is already present in early adulthood, and grows larger over age. By old age, women are substantially more likely to be chronically ill (Guralnik et al., 1993; Kunkel & Applebaum, 1992). In early adulthood, this gender difference in disease rate can be largely attributed to health problems associated with childbearing. At later ages, the difference cannot be explained in this same way.

How is it possible that men die younger but are healthier while they are alive? Lois Verbrugge, the leading researcher exploring such questions (Verbrugge, 1989), suggests that the apparent paradox can be resolved if we consider the specific dis-

Table 15.4 Leading Causes of Death for Middle-Aged Men and Women in the United States in 1992

Rank	Men	Women
	Age 45 to 54	
1	Heart disease (174)	Cancer (147)
2	Cancer (154)	Heart disease (58)
3	Accidents (41)	Cerebrovascular diseases (19)
	Age 55 to 64	
1	Cancer (513)	Cancer (370)
2	Heart disease (504)	Heart disease (205)
3	Chronic obstructive pulmonary diseases (56)	Chronic obstructive pulmonary diseases (41)

Note: The number in parentheses is the number of deaths by that cause in 1992, per 100,000 population in that age range.
Source: U.S. Bureau of the Census, 1995, Table 128, p. 95.

eases from which men and women suffer, and the diseases they die from. It's obvious from Table 15.4 that the primary killer diseases are cancer and heart disease, and men contract these diseases *earlier* in their lives. Because both these diseases often act quickly, men are less likely to have prolonged periods of disability before their deaths.

CRITICAL THINKING

What evidence could I muster to support a claim that "women are tougher than men?" What counterarguments could you offer?

Women die of these same diseases, but they contract them later, and live longer once they contract them, possibly because they seek treatment sooner. At the same time, women are also much more likely to suffer from *non*fatal chronic diseases, particularly arthritis, a disease that may be linked to the greater bone loss women experience following menopause. The net effect of these two patterns is that women are likely to spend many more years of adulthood with some kind of disability.

Before I leave this rather depressing subject of death and disease, let me say a bit more about the two leading causes of death in this age range: heart disease and cancer.

Coronary Heart Disease

The term **coronary heart disease** (often abbreviated **CHD**) covers a variety of physical problems, but the key change is in the arteries. In individuals suffering from CHD, the arteries become clogged with fibrous and calcified tissue, a process called *atherosclerosis*. Eventually, key arteries may become completely blocked, producing what laypeople call a *heart attack* if the blockage is in the coronary arteries, or a *stroke* if the blockage is in the brain. Atherosclerosis is *not* a normal part of aging. It is a disease, increasingly common with age, but not inevitable.

The rate of CHD has been dropping rapidly in the United States and in most other industrialized countries in recent years. Between 1973 and 1987, for example, it declined 42 percent among those under age 55, and declined by a third for those aged 55 to 84 (Davis, Dinse, & Hoel, 1994)—a fairly startling decline that has contributed greatly to the increased life expectancy among today's adults. Yet CHD remains the leading cause of death among adults over 55 in the United States and throughout the developed world.

Our best information about who is at risk for CHD comes from a number of very long-term epidemiological studies, such as the Framingham study or the Nurses Health Study, in which the health and habits of large numbers of individuals have been tracked over time. In the Framingham study, 5209 adults were first studied in 1948, when they were aged 30 to 59. Their health (and mortality) has since been assessed repeatedly (e.g., Anderson, Castelli, & Levy, 1987; Dawber, Kannel, & Lyell, 1963; Garrison et al., 1993; Kannel & Gordon, 1980), which makes it possible to identify those characteristics that predict subsequent CHD. The left side of Table 15.5 lists the well-established risk factors emerging from the Framingham and equivalent studies, along with a few others that are more speculative.

Because lists like these have appeared in numerous popular magazines and newspapers, there's not likely to be much that is news here. But let me make several points. First, the great majority of us are high on at least one of these risk factors. The Centers for Disease Control (1994f) found that of over 91,000 adults they interviewed in 1992, only 12.6 percent of men and 17.9 percent of women in the 35- to 49-year-old age range were low on all six of the controllable risks for CHD (smoking, weight, inactivity, blood pressure, cholesterol, and diabetes). In the 50- to 64-year-old group, these numbers are even lower—9.4 percent for men and 11.6 percent for women. So although rates of both smoking and high cholesterol have declined since the significance of these two risk factors became widely publicized, most Americans could still do a much better job at reducing their heart disease risks.

Second, it is important to understand that these risks are cumulative in the same way that the health habits investigated in the Alameda County study seem to be cumulative: The more high-risk behaviors or characteristics you have, the higher your risk of heart disease. Furthermore, the effect is not just additive. For example,

Table 15.5 **Risk Factors for Heart Disease and Cancer**

Risk	Heart Disease	Cancer
Smoking	Major risk; the more you smoke, the greater the risk. Quitting smoking reduces the risk.	Substantially increases the risk for lung cancer; also implicated in pancreatic cancer.
Blood pressure	Systolic pressure above 140 or diastolic pressure above 90 linked to higher risk; the higher the BP the higher the risk.	No known risk.
Weight	Some increased risk with any weight above the norm listed in traditional weight-for-height tables; risk is larger with weight 20% or more above the recommended amount.	Higher weight is linked to increased risk of several cancers, including breast cancer, but the effect is smaller than for heart disease.
Cholesterol	Clear risk for total cholesterol of 200 or more; an elevated level of low-density lipoproteins appears to be the culprit.	No known risk.
Inactivity	Inactive adults have roughly twice the risk.	Inactivity is associated in some studies with higher rates of colon cancer.
Diet	High-fat diet increases the risk; high-fiber, low-fat diet, or a diet rich in antioxidants such as vitamin E, vitamin C, or beta carotene may decrease the risk.	Results are still unclear; high-fat (especially high-saturated-fat) diet is linked to increased risks of some cancers in some studies, not in others; high-fiber diets appear to be protective for some cancers in some studies.
Alcohol	Moderate intake of alcohol, especially wine, linked to *lower* CHD risk than either abstinence or large intake.	No known link.
Heredity	7 to 10 times the risk for those with first-degree relatives with CHD; those who inherit a particular variant of the apolipoprotein E gene (apoE 4) are up to twice as likely to have CHD.	Some genetic component with nearly every cancer.

Sources: Centers for Disease Control, 1994f; Gaziano & Hennekens, 1995; Hunter et al., 1996; Lee et al., 1993; Manson et al., 1995; Morris, Kritchevsky, & Davis, 1994; Rich-Edwards et al., 1995; Risch et al., 1994; Rose, 1993; Stampfer et al., 1993; Willett et al., 1992, 1995; Woodward & Tunstall-Pedoe, 1995.

high cholesterol is three times more serious in a heavy smoker than in a nonsmoker (Tunstall-Pedoe & Smith, 1990).

Cancer

The second great killer disease of middle (and old) age (in industrialized countries, at least) is cancer. In middle-aged men, the likelihood of dying of these two diseases is about equal; among middle-aged women, in contrast, cancer is considerably more likely than heart disease, as you have already seen in Table 15.4.

Like heart disease, cancer does not strike in a totally random fashion. Indeed, as you can see in the right-hand side of Table 15.5, some of the same risk factors are involved in both. The most controversial item on the list is diet, particularly the role of dietary fat as a potential risk factor. The evidence linking high dietary fat and heart disease is increasingly clear; the data on dietary fat and cancer continue to be very confusing. Some experts estimate that as many as 35 percent of all cancer deaths can be attributed to diet (Bal & Foerster, 1991); others conclude that the effect is weak at best (e.g., Howe, 1994). This is clearly an area of active research. We can only hope that clearer conclusions—and thus clearer advice —will eventually emerge.

What I can say, as I have said before, is that most of the risk factors listed in Table 15.4 are at least partially under your own control. It helps to have established good health habits in early adulthood, but it is also clear from the research that improving your health habits in middle age can reduce your risks of either cancer or heart disease.

Research Report

Type A Behavior and Coronary Heart Disease

If you read the popular literature on heart disease, you'll know that I have left out of Table 15.5 one of the most-discussed potential risk factors, usually called **Type A behavior** or the **Type A personality.** I've left it out quite deliberately, because there is a good deal of dispute about just how risky this behavior pattern really is.

The Type A personality pattern was first described by two cardiologists, Meyer Friedman and Ray Rosenman (1974; Rosenman & Friedman, 1983). They were struck by the apparent consistency with which patients who suffered from heart disease shared several other characteristics, including competitive achievement striving, a sense of time urgency, and hostility or aggressiveness. These people, whom they named Type A, were perpetually comparing themselves to others, always wanting to win. They scheduled their lives tightly, timed themselves in routine activities, and often tried to do such tasks faster each day. They had frequent conflicts with their co-workers and family. Type B people, in contrast, were thought to be less hurried, more laid back, less competitive, and less hostile.

Early research by Friedman and Rosenman suggested that Type A behavior was linked to heightened levels of cholesterol, and hence to heightened risk of CHD, even among people who did not suffer from observable heart disease. Contradictory results from more extensive studies since then, however, have forced some modifications in the original hypothesis (e.g., Booth-Kewley & Friedman, 1987; Matthews, 1988; Miller et al., 1991; O'Connor et al., 1995).

For one thing, not all facets of the Type A personality, as originally described, seem to be equally significant for CHD. The most consistent link has been found between CHD and hostility, with hard-driving competitiveness showing weaker links. Time pressure is not consistently related to CHD at all (Friedman, Hawley, & Tucker, 1994; Miller et al., 1996; Siegel, 1992).

What is more, among individuals who are *already* at high risk of CHD—because of smoking, high blood pressure, or the like—having information about levels of hostility does not add to the accuracy of your prediction about heart disease. That is, if two adults each have high blood pressure and high cholesterol, they are both equally at risk of heart disease, even if one of them also displays high levels of hostility and the other does not. It is only among people who do *not* show other risk factors that measures of hostility add helpful information to the prediction. The effect is fairly small, but in large samples of low-risk adults, those who are hostile and competitive are slightly more likely to develop CHD than are those who are more easygoing.

I think that most people who have analyzed this research would now agree that *some* kind of connection exists between personality and CHD. What is less clear is just which aspect(s) of personality are most strongly predictive. Some research suggests that measures of neuroticism or depression may be even better risk predictors than hostility (Booth-Kewley & Friedman, 1987; Cramer, 1991). So stay tuned. This story is not over yet.

Mental Health

I mentioned in Chapter 13 that most types of emotional disturbance are considerably more common in early adulthood than in the middle years of adult life. Let me give you only one concrete example. Regier and his colleagues (Regier et al., 1988) interviewed 18,571 adults, from five different parts of the United States, about their psychological symptoms over the previous month. The researchers then identified those subjects whose replies were consistent with standard diagnostic criteria for various forms of psychiatric or emotional disorders, such as substance abuse, depression, anxiety, and the like. In this survey, 3 percent of those aged 25 to 44 were classed as suffering from a major depressive episode, compared with 2 percent among those between 45 and 64. The rate dropped further, to 0.7 percent, in those over 65. The pattern is essentially the same for both women and men, although the rates are higher for women at every age.

These findings raise questions about the existence of that widely discussed event, a "midlife crisis."

Midlife Crisis: Fact or Fallacy?

The concept of a midlife crisis was not invented by popular writers out of whole cloth. It has been part of several major theories of adult development, including Carl

Cultures and Contexts

Typical Diets and Cancer Rates Around the World

Aside from animal studies, which demonstrate a clear causal link between high-fat diets and cancer rates (e.g., Weisburger & Wynder, 1991), some of the strongest evidence for a link between diet and cancer comes from cross-national comparisons. For example, the typical Japanese diet contains only about 15 percent fat, while the typical United States diet is closer to 40 percent fat. Cancer (and CHD) is much less frequent in Japan. The possibility of a causal link between the two is further strengthened by the observation that in those areas in Japan in which Western dietary habits have been most adopted, cancer rates have risen to nearer Western levels (Weisburger & Wynder, 1991).

Comparisons of diet and cancer rates in many nations show similar patterns. This is especially clear in results from a study of United Nations data by Hugo Kesteloot and his colleagues (Kesteloot, Lesaffre, & Joossens, 1991). They have obtained two kinds of information for each of 36 countries: (1) the death rates from each of several types of cancer, and (2) the estimated per-person intake of fat from dairy products or lard. Only dairy and lard fat are included because these are the major sources of saturated fats, thought to be more strongly implicated in disease. Note that the unit of analysis for this study is a *country* and not an individual. The figure below shows the relationship between deaths from rectal cancer and fat consumption, one of the clearest connections. In this case the correlation between the two is .64.

The equivalent correlations for other types of cancer were .60 for breast cancer in women; .70 for prostate cancer in men; .43 for colon cancer in men and .47 in women. For all cancers combined, the correlations were .58 in men and .65 in women. The correlations between national fat intake and deaths from *heart disease* were also significant: .55 for men and .35 for women.

The relationship among dietary fat, other risk factors, and cancer is obviously complex, and we have much yet to learn. For one thing, the typical diets in these various countries differ widely in a great many other ways besides fat intake, any one of which might be involved in cancer rates. But cross-national comparisons of this type have generated highly useful hypotheses.

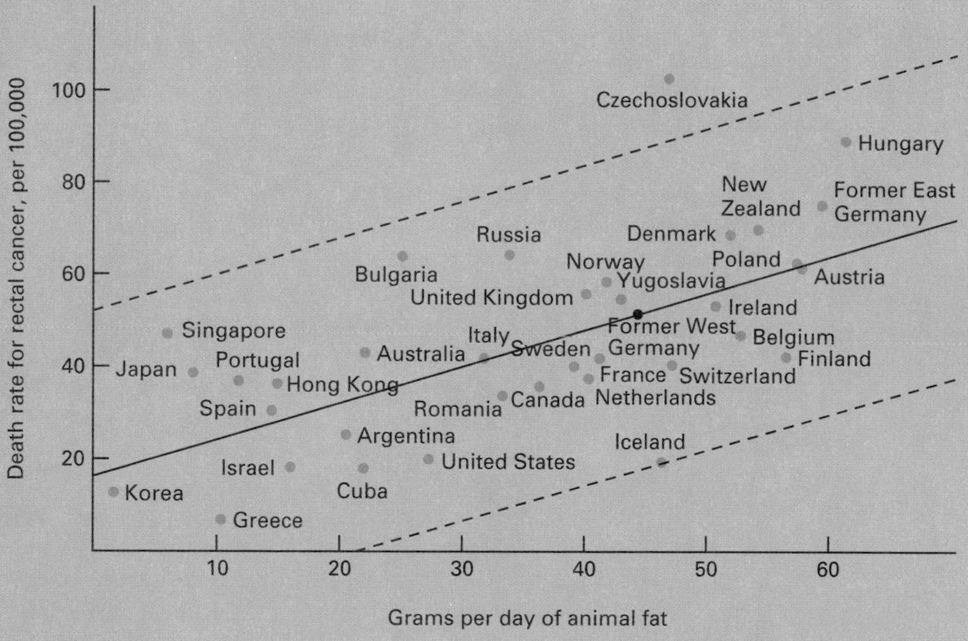

Jung's and Levinson's. Levinson argued that each person must confront a constellation of tasks at midlife that virtually guarantee a crisis of some kind: the awareness of one's own mortality, recognition of new physical limitations and health risks, and major changes in most roles. Dealing with all these tasks, according to Levinson, is highly likely to exceed an adult's ability to cope, thus creating a crisis.

When researchers look at the relevant research evidence, they often come to diametrically opposite conclusions. David Chiriboga concludes that "there is mounting evidence from research studies that serious mid-life problems are actually experienced by only 2 percent to 5 percent of middle agers" (1989, p. 117). Lois Tamir, reading the same evidence, concludes that midlife is a time of important psychological transition marked with "deep-seated self-doubts or confusion" (1989, p. 161).

CRITICAL THINKING

If you wanted to design the absolutely best study on midlife crisis, what would you need to do? What kind of sample, research design, and measures would you need to include?

My own conclusion is far more like Chiriboga's than like Tamir's. We do have evidence that the rate of depression peaks among women in the late 30s and early 40s (Anthony & Aboraya, 1992). But even at the peak the rate is only about 4.5 percent—hardly evidence for a universal crisis. I'm also impressed by results of several studies by personality researchers Paul Costa & Robert McCrae (1980a; McCrae & Costa, 1984). They devised a midlife crisis scale, including items about inner turmoil, marital or job dissatisfaction, and a sense of failing power. They then compared the responses of over 500 men in a cross-sectional study of subjects ranging in age from 35 to 70. They could find no age at which scores were significantly high. Others who have devised midlife crisis scales have arrived at the same conclusion (e.g., Farrell & Rosenberg, 1981), as have those who have studied responses to stress (e.g., Pearlin, 1975). Epidemiological studies also do not show any clear rise or peak in midlife for such likely signs of crisis as divorce, alcoholism, or depression in men (Hunter & Sundel, 1989).

Of course, it is possible that some kind of crisis is common in midlife but that it occurs at a different age for each person. That would mean that there would be no *single* age with a peak of problems, and could explain Costa & McCrae's results. But studies like Regier's are hard to explain away so easily, because they are contrasting adults by decade rather than by individual year. If a crisis were more common in midlife than in early adulthood, we ought to see some sign of it in increased rates of depression or anxiety during the 40s, or the 50s, compared to the 20s. But we simply do not find that.

The only subgroup of adults who seem to be quite likely to experience a midlife crisis are well-educated middle-class white men. Even among men in this group, though, a "crisis" is by no means universal at midlife. It may well reflect the experiences of quite specific cohorts studied so far by researchers.

Longitudinal studies do not lend much comfort to midlife crisis advocates, either. Norma Haan, for example, could find no indication that any kind of crisis was common at midlife among the subjects included in the Berkeley/Oakland longitudinal study (Haan, 1981b).

Only for one subgroup is there any confirming evidence: white men from the middle class, especially those with professional occupations. Lois Tamir (1982), in a national sample of about a thousand men who ranged in age from 25 to 69, found that college-educated men in the 45–49 age range reported more drinking problems, more prescription drug use (such as sleeping pills or tranquilizers), less reported "zest," and more "psychological immobilization."

Whether this pattern is characteristic only of a particular cohort we cannot tell from this one study. But even if this result were common in a number of cohorts, it would not begin to persuade me that a crisis is a necessary, or even a very common, experience of the middle years of adulthood. Certainly there are stresses and tasks that are unique to this period. But there is little sign that these stresses and tasks are more likely to overwhelm an adult's coping resources at this age than at any other (Gallagher, 1993).

Cognitive Functioning

In Chapter 13 I described the basic shape of cognitive changes in the middle years, contrasting it with what happens in early adulthood. If you'll go back and look at Figure 13.4 (page 345), and at Denney's model (Figure 13.5, page 348), you'll remember that in middle adulthood, most of us maintain or even gain in skill on any task that is highly practiced or based on specific learning. So our vocabularies get better and we generally maintain our problem-solving ability. On tasks that demand speed or that require underused or unpracticed skills, such as a timed arithmetic test or an ability to deal with three-dimensional spatial representations, declines are somewhat larger during the middle adult years. In particular, our mental processes get steadily slower as we age (Salthouse, 1991). Still, even in these domains the absolute size of the loss is quite small for most adults in this age range.

Figure 15.4 gives two results from the Baltimore Longitudinal Study of Aging that illustrate the point (Giambra et al., 1995). The left side of the figure shows longitudinal change in vocabulary scores for a group of 1163 men. Each point on the line shows the amount of *change* in vocabulary over the preceding six to nine years for men of that age group. For example, the men in the 52- to 57-year-old age group had increased slightly in vocabulary since the first testing six to nine years earlier. Declines occurred only for the 64–69 age group, and even this decline is quite slight.

The right half of the figure shows a similar analysis of change in scores on a measure of memory called the Benton Visual Retention Test. On this test, the subject is given a geometric design to look at for ten seconds and then must try to reproduce that design on paper immediately. The data shown represent the change in the number of errors the subjects made on this task over the same six- to nine-year period. Here you can see that declines begin among the 46- to 51-year-olds, although the amount of decline remains low until the 64–69 age range, after which it accelerates rapidly. This pattern—of maintenance or very gradual loss in middle adulthood, accelerating only after age 65 or so—is so common in research of this type that Werner Schaie, of Seattle Longitudinal Study fame, says (as you'll recall from Chapter 13),

> It is my general conclusion that reliably replicable age changes in psychometric abilities of more than trivial magnitude cannot be demonstrated prior to age 60, but that reliable decrement can be shown to have occurred for all abilities by age 74. (Schaie, 1983b, p. 127)

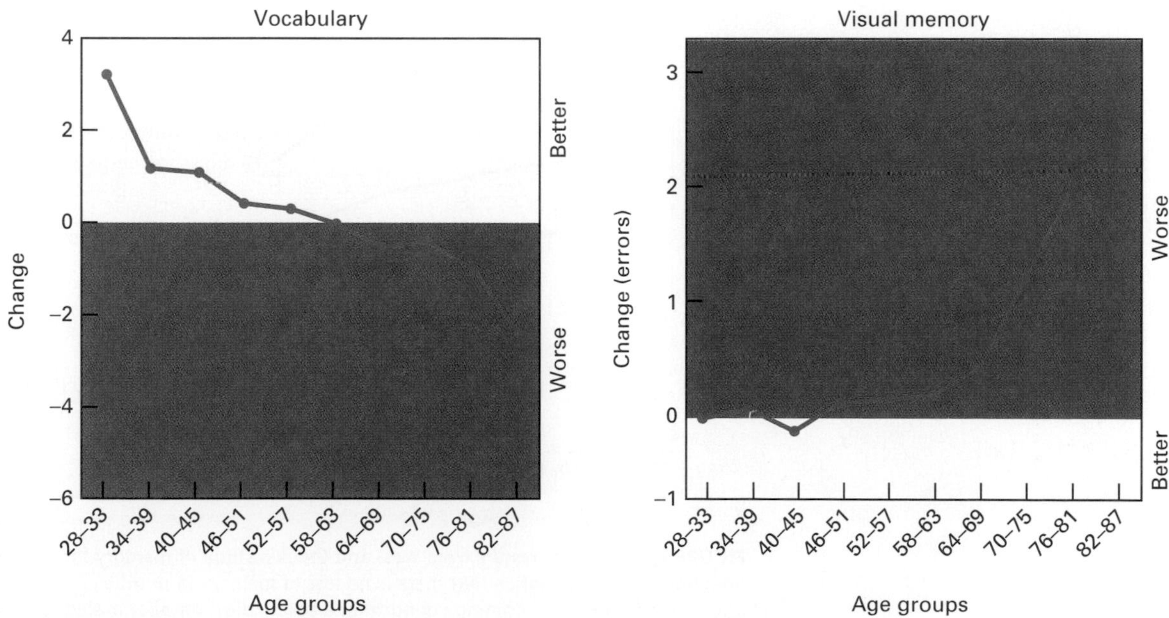

FIGURE 15.4 Each point on either graph shows the amount of *change* (improvement or decrement) since the previous testing six to nine years previously, for groups of men studied longitudinally. The left side shows changes in vocabulary scores; the right side shows changes on a measure of immediate memory. (*Source:* Giambra et al., 1995, adaptation of Figure 3, p. 131, and Figure 4, p. 132.)

More on Memory

Figure 15.4 already suggests that this same kind of general statement applies to measures of memory as much as to other tests of cognitive functioning. But let me expand a bit. In general, when an adult is dealing with familiar material, memory ability remains stable or declines only very slightly in middle adulthood. A somewhat larger decline occurs for less familiar material, or when a memory must be retained over an interval, or when there is some distraction. A good illustration of a number of these points comes from a study by Robin West and Thomas Crook (1990), who used a variant of a familiar, everyday task: remembering telephone numbers. Subjects sat in front of a computer screen, on which a series of seven-digit or ten-digit telephone numbers appeared, one at a time. The subject said each number as it appeared, the number then disappeared from the screen, and the subject had to dial the number she had just seen on a push-button phone attached to the computer. On some trials, the subjects got a busy signal when they first dialed and then had to dial the number over again. Figure 15.5 shows the relationship between age and the correct recall of the phone numbers under these four conditions.

Notice that there is essentially no decline with age in immediate recall of a normal seven-digit telephone number. This is the equivalent of what you do when you look a number up in the phone book, say it to yourself as you read it, and then dial it immediately. When the length of the number increases to the ten-digit length we use for long-distance numbers, however, you can see a decline with age, beginning at about age 60. And with even a brief delay, the decline occurs earlier.

The telephone number task is an example of a measure of *primary* or *short-term memory*—where some item is to be held in memory for perhaps 30 seconds. *Secondary* or *long-term* memory refers to recall over longer periods, from minutes to years. Do we find the same kinds of changes with age in long-term memory? On the whole, yes. Both the process of getting information into longer-term storage (a process called *encoding*), and the process of getting it out when you need it (*retrieval*) become gradually less efficient and speedy with age, but most of the drop occurs after age 60 rather than at midlife, much as Schaie finds with measure of overall cognitive skill. We see this pattern when subjects are asked to put names to familiar faces (a

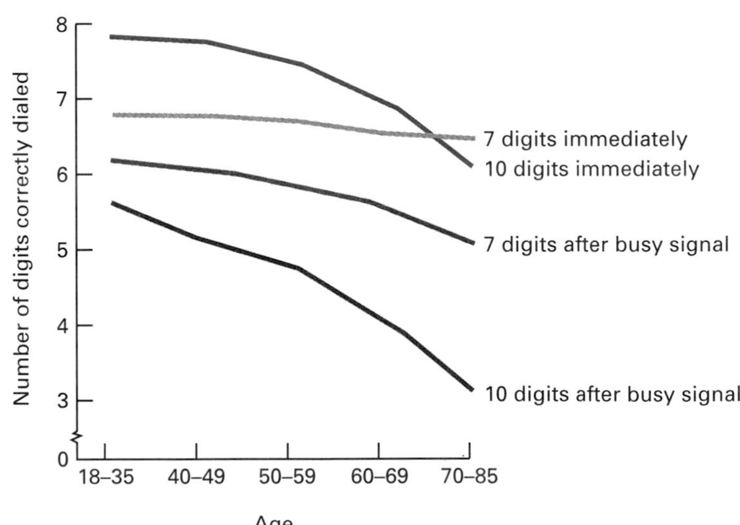

FIGURE 15.5 In these results from West and Crook's study of memory for telephone numbers, notice that there is no loss of memory in middle adulthood for the most common condition: a seven-digit number dialed immediately. But if the number of digits increases, or if you have to remember the number a bit longer, some decline in memory begins around age 50 or 60. (*Source:* West & Crook, 1990, from Table 3, page 524.)

retrieval task), or to learn lists of words and remember them several days later (an encoding task) (Salthouse, 1991).

The literature on memory change with age also offers a few tidbits in support of Labouvie-Vief's view that what happens to cognition in adulthood is not (only) decline but change in emphasis or structure. Labouvie-Vief (1990), as you may recall from Chapter 13, suggests that in adulthood we tend to shift away from the logical or formal-operational approach that dominates in adolescence and at college age, to a more pragmatic approach aimed at solving everyday problems. In memory, this might be reflected in a decline in memory for surface detail, but a compensatory memory for themes or meaning. A study by Cynthia Adams (1991) yields some confirmation.

Remembering what you read in a newspaper is no more difficult in middle age than in early adulthood, but middle-aged adults may focus less on details and more on basic themes.

Adams asked adults of various ages to read a story and then to recall it, in writing, immediately afterward. Younger adults were more likely to report specific events or actions in the story, while the middle-aged adults recalled more of the psychological motivations of the characters and offered more interpretations of the story in their recall. What this may mean is that the encoding process changes as we get older. We may simply not attempt to encode detail, but may store broader or more summary information.

Yet even if we assume that the type of information encoded changes from early to middle adulthood, it is still not clear how we should explain such a change. It could mean "loss in the service of growth," as Labouvie-Vief suggests. Or it could indicate "decline with compensation"—that is, we might aim for essence rather than detail because that has proven the most informative, or because the gradual loss in the efficiency and speed of memory processes has pushed us that way.

Using Intellectual Skills: Creative Productivity at Midlife

A somewhat different question about cognitive functioning in the middle years of adulthood—one that may have more direct relevance for our work life—has to do with creativity or productivity. Are middle-aged business executives as good (or better) at problem solving in their work? Are middle-aged scientists as creative as young ones?

Early research by Lehman (1953), which has been widely quoted, suggested that peak creativity, like peak physical functioning, occurs in early adulthood. Lehman identified a series of major scientific discoveries of the past several hundred years and asked how old each scientist was at the time of that discovery. Most were quite young, especially in science and mathematics. The classic example is Einstein, who was 26 when he developed the special theory of relativity.

These are interesting patterns, but this seems to me to be a backwards way to go at the question. The alternative is to study scientists or other problem-solvers over their whole working lives and see whether the ordinary (non-Einsteinian) person is more productive and creative in early or middle adult life. Dean Simonton (1991) has moved a step in this direction by looking at the lifetime creativity and productivity of thousands of notable scientists from the nineteenth and earlier centuries. He identified the age at which these individuals (nearly all men) published their first significant work, their best work, and their last work. In every scientific discipline represented in this unusual sample, the average age for the person's best work was right around age 40. But the curve is quite flat at the top. Most of these people were still publishing significant, even outstanding research through their 40s and into their 50s. In fact, Simonton proposes that the reason the best work is done at about 40 is not that the mind works better at that age, but that productivity is at its highest at that time. Chance alone would suggest that the best work will come during the time when the most work is being done.

Lifetime creative output of modern-day scientists follows a similar pattern. Mathematicians, psychologists, physicists, and other scientists born in this century

Dr. Rosalyn Yalow, who won the Nobel Prize for Medicine in 1977, continued to be highly productive and to do high-quality work throughout her middle-adult years—a pattern common among scientists.

have consistently shown their maximum productivity (usually measured by the number of papers published in a single year) when they were about age 40. But when you look at research quality, such as by counting the number of times each research paper is cited by peers, you find that quality remains high through age 50 or even 60 (Horner, Rushton, & Vernon, 1986; Simonton, 1988).

Among musicians or other artists, peak creativity may occur later, or be maintained far longer. In a second study, Simonton (1989) asked judges to rate the aesthetic qualities of musical compositions by the 172 composers whose works are most often performed. Late-in-life works ("swan songs") were most likely to be evaluated as masterpieces by the judges.

It is also possible to approach the question of age and creativity or professional effectiveness experimentally. Siegfried Streufert and his colleagues (Streufert et al., 1990) have done this in a particularly interesting study—a study that has the added advantage of focusing on business executives, which broadens our scope beyond the perhaps-atypical realm of academic careers. Streufert created sets of four-person decision-making teams, made up of midlevel managers from state and federal government and private industry. On 15 of the teams, the participants were all between ages 28 and 35. Members of another 15 teams were middle-aged (aged 45 to 55), and another 15 included only older adults (aged 65 to 75). Each team was given a wonderfully complex simulated task: They were asked to manage an imaginary developing country called Shamba. They were given packets of information about Shamba ahead of time, and could request additional information during their group work, via a computer—which was of course programmed so as to make the experience of the different groups as much alike as possible, although the participants did not know that. Every group faced a crisis in Shamba at about the same time in their work; the computer later specified a particular resolution of that crisis, no matter what solutions the group had proposed.

CRITICAL THINKING

If creativity, productivity, and ability to deal with complex problems all decline past the years of midlife, does this mean that our political leaders should all be younger than 65? Why or why not?

Streufert recorded all the questions, suggestions, and plans generated by each group, from which he created a series of measures of activity rate, speed, depth, diversity, and strategic excellence of each group's performance. The young groups and the middle-aged groups differed significantly on only 3 out of the 16 measures: The younger groups did more things (made more decisions and took more actions); they asked for more additional information (often excessively, to the point of overload); they suggested a greater diversity of actions. Middle-aged teams asked for just about the right amount of information—not too much to overload the system, but enough to make good decisions —and used the information effectively. On most of the measures the researchers devised, such as assessments of the use of strategy, planning, handling emergencies, and using the information they obtained, there were no differences between the young and middle-aged. In contrast, the oldest groups performed less well by virtually every measure. Their interactions tended to be task-oriented but diffuse.

Although this is only a single study, cross-sectional rather than longitudinal in design, it points in the same direction as does the literature on age and scientific productivity. Middle-aged adults appear to retain their ability to do high-level productive work and problem solving.

Individual Differences

You've already encountered a good deal of information about individual differences in this chapter, especially in the discussion of risk factors and health habits associated with heart disease and cancer. Other information suggests that many of the same characteristics that are linked to increased or decreased risk of these two diseases are also linked to the rate of change or maintenance of overall health and intellectual skill in the middle years.

One example comes from Schaie's analysis of data from the Seattle Longitudinal Study (1983b). He has found that those subjects who have some kind of cardiovascular disease—either CHD or high blood pressure—show earlier and larger declines on intellectual tests than do those who are disease free. Other researchers have found similar linkages. Even adults whose blood pressure is controlled by medication seem to show earlier declines (Sands & Meredith, 1992; Schultz et al., 1986). Schaie cautions us about taking these findings too far. The size of the effect is quite small and it may operate indirectly rather than directly. For example, adults with cardiovascular disease may become physically less active as a response to their disease. The lower level of activity, in turn, may affect the rate of intellectual decline.

Exercise and Health

This raises the possibility that exercise may be one of the critical factors in determining an individual adult's overall physical health and cognitive performance during these years. A growing amount of information confirms such an effect.

One particularly large and well-designed study by Lee and his colleagues (Lee, Hsieh, & Paffenbarger, 1995) involves 17,321 Harvard alumni who had been students between 1916 and 1950. In 1962 or 1966, when the men were in their 30s, 40s, or 50s, each man provided detailed information about his daily levels of physical activity. The researchers then tracked all these men until 1988 to identify who had died and of what cause. The measures of physical activity were quite detailed. Each man reported how many blocks he normally walked each day, how often he climbed stairs, the amount of time per week he normally engaged in various sports, and so on. All the answers were then converted into estimates of calories expended per week in physical activity. For example, walking 1 mile on level ground uses roughly 100 calories; climbing one flight of stairs uses about 17. The link between the level of physical activity and death rates over the succeeding 25 years is shown clearly in Figure 15.6: The more exercise a man reported in his 30s, 40s, or 50s, the lower his mortality risk over the next 25 years.

Lee and his colleagues were careful to exclude from the study any man who was already known to suffer from heart disease or other disease at the onset of the study, in the 1960s. Furthermore, it turned out that the groups that differed in level of energy expenditure did *not* differ in age, smoking, hypertension, weight, or family history of early death, which makes the effect of exercise even clearer. To be sure, because the level of exercise was each man's own choice, there may have been other differences that separated the various exercise groups that could account for the different death rates. But the pattern, which has been replicated in other groups of both men and women (e.g., Blair et al., 1995; Lissner et al., 1996), is so substantial

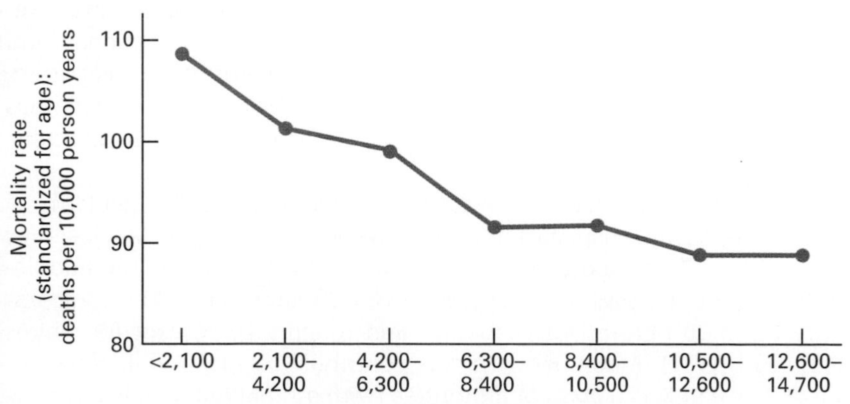

FIGURE 15.6 Results from the Harvard Alumni Study show clearly that those who are more physically active in middle adulthood have lower risk of mortality over the next decades. (*Source:* Lee et al., 1995, adapted from data from Table 2, p. 1181.)

and striking that alternative explanations are hard to come by. By far the most likely alternative is that a causal connection really exists between health/longevity and level of physical activity.

Physical exercise also seems to help maintain cognitive abilities in these same years, very likely because it helps to maintain cardiovascular fitness (e.g., Clarkson-Smith & Hartley, 1989; Rogers, Meyer, & Mortel, 1990). Among physically healthy middle-aged and older adults, those who are more physically active—doing gardening, heavy housework, or aerobic exercise such as walking, running, or swimming—have higher scores on tests of reasoning, reaction time, and short-term memory.

CRITICAL THINKING

Before you read any further, figure out the flaw in this research strategy.

Of course, studies like these have the same potentially major flaw that exists in the Lee study of Harvard alumni: They compare people who *choose* to be active with those who choose not to be, and those who exercise are likely to be different in other ways from those who do not. In most of these studies, the researchers have been careful to match the two groups as well as possible on variables they thought might make a difference, including physical health and education level, but the basic methodological problem remains.

A better test would be to assign some people randomly to an exercise program and some to a nonexercise control, and then see whether the two groups differ in their cognitive functioning after a period of exercise. The results of the small number of studies of this type have been quite mixed. Everyone finds that exercise increases measures of physical functioning, such as VO_2 max, even in very aged adults. Some—but not all—also show that exercise improves thinking (Hawkins, Kramer, & Capaldi, 1992; Hill, Storandt, & Malley, 1993), while others do not (e.g., Buchner et al., 1992; Emery & Gatz, 1990; Madden et al., 1989). In most cases, the experimental exercise program lasts only a few months, and that may not be sufficient to make any difference in mental functioning. Were I making a bet at this point, based on the fragmentary evidence we now have, I'd bet that long-term exercise has some effect on cognitive performance but that it isn't a very large effect. Still, because we already know that exercise is linked to lower levels of disease and greater longevity, prudence alone would argue for building it into your life.

Social Class and Ethnic Differences in Health

In my enthusiasm for preventive actions such as exercise, I should not forget to reemphasize the large importance for midlife health and mental ability of those ubiquitous demographic variables, social class and ethnicity. If you go back and look at Figure 13.3 (page 342), you'll see that social class is a more significant predictor of variations in health in middle age than at any other time of adult life. Virtually all young adults are healthy, while most older adults have some chronic problems or restrictions in daily activities. It is in the middle of adulthood that occupational level and education are most predictive of health. Figure 13.3 does not break this pattern down by race, but separate research suggests that the same link between social class and health is found among Hispanic Americans and African Americans (Chatters, 1991; James et al., 1992; Markides & Lee, 1991).

Ethnic status itself is also linked both to overall health and to the incidence of specific diseases. Blacks and Hispanics not only have shorter life expectancies, they have poorer overall health than do whites in the United States. Among the middle-aged, nearly 40 percent of blacks describe their health as fair or poor. The comparable figures are 28 to 30 percent for Hispanics and roughly 20 percent for whites (Markides & Mindel, 1987). A number of factors contribute to such a difference, including the lower overall social class of minorities (with all that entails), less access to health care, greater stress, and perhaps poorer health habits.

CRITICAL THINKING

Aside from differences in timeliness of medical care, what other explanations can you think of for higher cancer rates in African Americans? How could you test your hypotheses?

There are also differences in incidence of specific diseases, not all to the disadvantage of minorities. Hispanic men, for example, have lower rates of both heart disease and cancer than do white men. Hispanic women, regrettably, do not have this same advantage (Markides & Mindel, 1987). Black men show the reverse pattern:

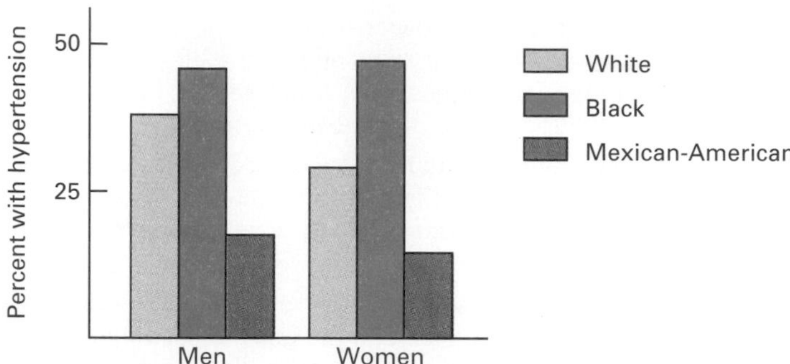

FIGURE 15.7 Combined data from two large national studies illustrate the standard finding of higher rates of hypertension among blacks, and lower rates among Hispanics. (*Source:* Sorel, Ragland, & Syme, 1991, from Table 3, p. 375.)

They are *more* likely to die of heart disease than are white men. In addition, blacks have higher rates of two other significant diseases: cancer and high blood pressure. Blacks have higher incidence of most types of cancer, including breast, uterine, prostate, and stomach cancers, and have poorer survival rates once cancer is diagnosed, perhaps because they receive medical care later in the illness (Blakeslee, 1994; Chatters, 1991; Jackson & Perry, 1989). In the United States, 55.5 percent of white cancer patients survive at least five years; in blacks the comparable figure is 40.4 percent (U.S. Bureau of the Census, 1995).

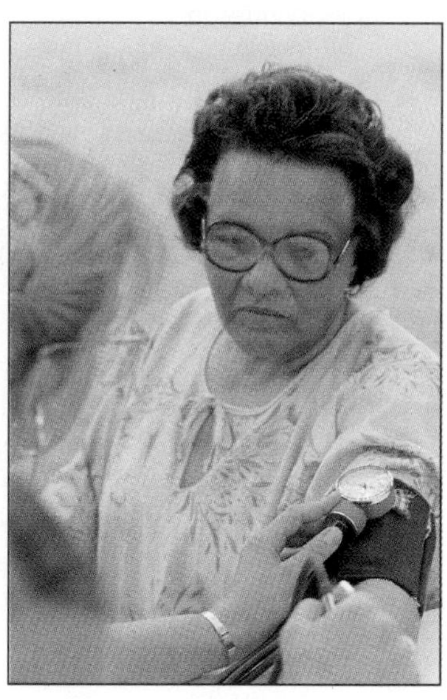

Physicians and epidemiologists have not yet uncovered the reason for the higher rates of hypertension among blacks in the United States.

Blacks are also more likely than whites to suffer from high blood pressure, more properly called **hypertension,** most often defined as a systolic pressure above 140, or a *diastolic* pressure (the lower number you are given) above 90. Figure 15.7 shows the combined findings from two large national surveys in the United States of adults between age 25 and 65 (Sorel, Ragland, & Syme, 1991). You can see that blacks have higher rates than whites and that this difference is considerably larger among women than among men. You can also see that among Mexican Americans, rates of hypertension are markedly *lower* than in either of the other two groups. This is an especially important piece of information. It suggests that poverty alone cannot be the explanation of higher rates of hypertension among blacks, because Mexican Americans also have high rates of poverty.

Physicians and epidemiologists have not yet reached agreement on the cause of African Americans' higher levels of hypertension. Blacks in Africa do not have the same unusually high rates, which argues against one kind of genetic explanation. Another possibility is that hypertension rates may be linked to weight differences. Williams (1992) reports that in one set of national survey data, the race difference in hypertension among women could be entirely explained as a function of higher rates of obesity in blacks. But in the national survey data shown in Figure 15.7, the racial differences remain even when body mass is taken into account. Clearly we need to know a good deal more about the unique health problems of blacks, Hispanics, and other minority groups, as well as their causes, if we are to design effective heath care programs for adults of all ages.

Summary

1. Most adults believe that significant physical and mental decline begins in the years of middle adulthood, although in fact the changes are fairly small and gradual.
2. At age 40, U.S. adults can expect to live an additional 35 to 40 years, and this figure has been increasing steadily; human life span, in contrast, is likely to remain at about 110.
3. Many physical functions show small changes in the 40s, 50s, and 60s; a few show significant changes.
4. The loss of reproductive capacity, called the climacteric in both men and women, occurs very gradually in men, but rapidly in women. In men, levels of testosterone decline very gradually, and they gradually produce fewer viable sperm and a smaller quantity of

seminal fluid. Because of these changes, and for other health-related causes, rates of impotence rise in the middle years.

5. Menopause typically occurs at about age 50, as a result of a series of hormone changes, including rapid declines in both estrogen and progesterone. The most common accompanying physical symptom is the hot flash. Contrary to folklore, however, no increase in psychological symptoms typically accompanies menopause.
6. The great majority of middle-aged adults remain sexually active, but the frequency of such activity declines over these years.
7. Bone mass declines significantly beginning at about age 30, with accelerated decline in women at menopause, linked to declines in estrogen. Faster bone loss occurs in women with early menopause, who are underweight, exercise little, and have low-calcium diets.
8. Added layers to the lens of the eye, with accompanying loss of elasticity, reduces visual acuity noticeably in one's 40s or 50s. Hearing loss is more gradual.
9. The rate of illness and death rises noticeably in middle adulthood. Young adults have more acute illnesses; middle-aged adults have more chronic illnesses. Women have significantly more illnesses than men, even though they die at later ages.
10. The two major causes of death in middle adulthood are cancer and heart disease. Death rates for both these diseases are higher among men.
11. Coronary heart disease is not a normal part of aging; it is a disease, for which there are known risk factors, including smoking, high blood pressure, high blood cholesterol, obesity, and high-fat diet.
12. Cancer, too, has known risk factors, including smoking, high-fat diet, obesity, and an inactive lifestyle. The role of a high-fat diet has been controversial, but most evidence supports its causal contribution.
13. Middle-aged adults have lower rates of emotional disturbances of virtually every kind than do young adults. There is little evidence of any widespread "midlife crisis."
14. Cognitive skills are generally retained well in the middle-adult years, although the general slowing that appears to be part of primary aging affects cognitive skills that require speed, as well as unexercised abilities.
15. Some loss of memory speed and skill occurs, but on most measures the loss is quite small until fairly late in the middle years.
16. Creative productivity also appears to remain high during middle adulthood, at least for adults in challenging jobs, on whom most of this research has been done.
17. The importance of exercise is a continuing theme in research on both physical and cognitive functioning in middle adulthood. Adults who maintain high levels of exercise are healthier and retain their physical and (probably) their mental abilities better than do those who are more sedentary.
18. On all measures of both physical and mental functioning, working-class or poverty-level adults show poorer maintenance or more decline.
19. Members of most U.S. minority groups have poorer patterns of health and longevity, although each group shows a different profile of problems: for example, blacks have higher levels of hypertension, while Hispanics and Native Americans have higher rates of diabetes.

Key Terms

climacteric
coronary heart disease (CHD)
hypertension
life expectancy
life span
menopause
osteoporosis
presbycusis
presbyopia
Type A behavior
Type A personality

Suggested Readings

Adler, N. E., Boyce, T., Chesney, M. A., Cohen, S., Folkman, S., Kahn, R. L., & Syme, S. L. (1994). Socioeconomic status and health: The challenge of the gradient. *American Psychologist*, 49, 15–24.

A brief review of the data showing that poor adults (and children) have less good health and shorter life expectancy than those from higher social classes. The alternative explanations are explored.

Blair, S. N., Kohl, H. W., Gordon, N. F., & Paffenbarger, R. S., Jr. (1992). How much physical activity is good for health? *Annual Review of Public Health*, 13, 99–126.

This is an especially good review of the research on the link between health and exercise.

Cutler, W. B., & Garcia, C. (1993). *Menopause: A guide for women and those who love them*. New York: W. W. Norton.

A revised, up-to-date version of a basic reference book. It includes information on hormone replacement therapy, among other things.

Salthouse, T. A. (1991). *Theoretical perspectives on cognitive aging*. Hillsdale, NJ: Erlbaum.

Not easy, but a remarkably complete source of information about virtually every aspect of cognitive aging.

Social and Personality Development in Middle Adulthood

16

When I look at social and personality development in these middle years of adult life, what is most striking is how much less tightly the garment of social roles now fits. In the metaphor I have been using all along, the social clock is ticking much less loudly. Many of the same roles that dominate early adult life continue, of course. Most middle-aged adults are married, parents, and workers. But by age 40 or 50, these roles have changed in important ways. Children begin to leave home, which dramatically alters and reduces the intensity of the role of parent; job promotions have usually topped out, so workers have less need to learn new work skills (although this may be less true for today's middle-aged cohorts who face corporate downsizing and the need for retraining). And when both parenting and working are less demanding, partners can find more time for one another.

Collectively, these changes mean that many people find their middle adult years to be less stressful and happier than the first 20 years of adult life. I am aware as I write those words that I have a vested interest in their truth; I am 56, still within the range of years I have defined as middle adulthood. But vested interest or no, both the data and my own experience support the proposition that these are in many ways the optimum years of adult life.

At the same time, a third truth about this time is that individuals' experiences are far more variable than was the case earlier. In young adulthood, many life changes are *normative*. The timing may vary, but nearly everyone marries, has children, and begins some kind of job in their early adult years. In middle adulthood, few role changes or other experiences are normative in the same powerful way. Children leave home, but this is typically a very gradual process, varying widely in timing. And in today's uncertain economic climate, some young people who initially leave their parents' home later return, making the "launching" process far more complex for some families than for others. In these years of middle age we also begin to see increasingly large differences in health, a pattern you've already seen in Chapter 15. We can also see wider variations in what we might think of as psychological growth. Some adults begin to show a kind of "mellowing" in late midlife, while others do not.

To illustrate all these points, let me look at some of the same roles and relationships I described in Chapter 14.

Partnerships

Several lines of evidence suggest that, on average, marital satisfaction rises in midlife, reaching higher levels than at any time since very early marriage, a pattern you've already seen in Figure 14.3 (page 372). The most likely explanation of this pattern is simply that role overload declines as the children begin to leave home, leaving husbands and wives with more time to spend together.

A similar pattern emerges if you ask not about satisfaction, but about marital problems. Joseph Veroff and his colleagues (Veroff, Douvan, & Kulka, 1981) have evidence on this point from two national cross-sectional samples, one set studied in 1957 and one in 1976, together creating a cross-sequential study. You can see in the left side of Figure 16.1 that older adults in both surveys were less likely to describe problems with their marriage—although it is interesting that in 1957, every age group reported fewer problems than was true in 1976.

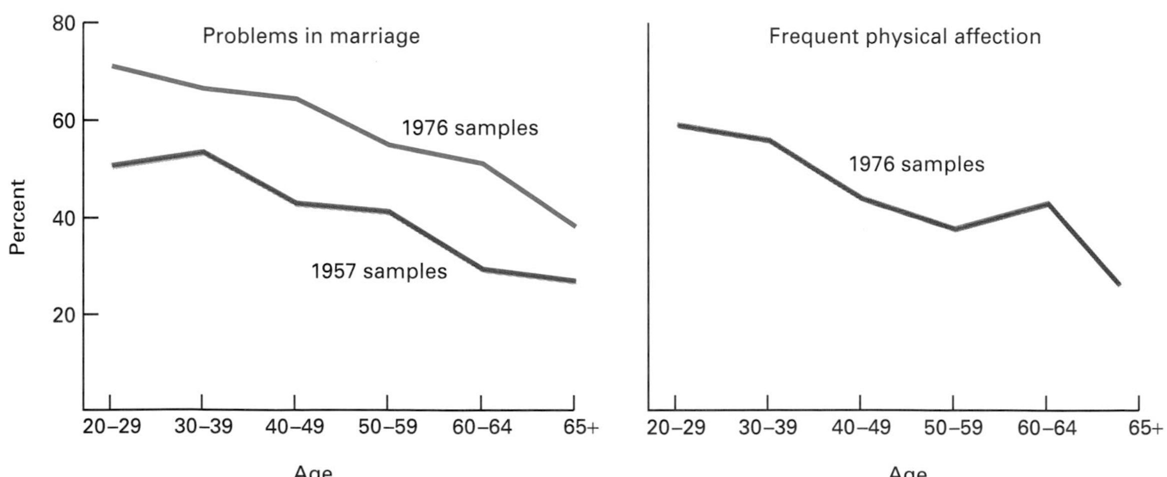

FIGURE 16.1 Both problems and affection appear to decline in marriages over time, judging from these cross-sectional comparisons. Some have interpreted this pattern as indicating that marriages become more "devitalized" or "empty" with time; others see it as a sign of more companionable marriages in midlife. (*Source:* Veroff et al., 1981, Table 4.20, p. 183, and Table 4.21, p. 185.)

Of course results like this could mean that over time, the more troubled marriages end in divorce. As these poor relationships are weeded out of the pool of marriages, it is not surprising that older couples report fewer problems. Alternatively, it could be that marital satisfaction rises with age because problems have truly declined.

The other side of the same coin, however, is that middle-aged marriages may also involve fewer positive interactions: fewer episodes of physical affection, fewer episodes of self-disclosure or encouragement. Another set of results from Veroff's study illustrates the point. In 1976 they added a question about the frequency of physical affection between partners. Data on the right half of Figure 16.1 show that the percentage of individuals who reported high rates of such affection with their spouse went down with age.

A remarkably similar pattern emerged from another cross-sectional study, by Clifford Swensen and his colleagues (Swensen, Eskew, & Kohlhepp, 1981), one of my favorite pieces of research in this area. Swensen interviewed 776 adults spanning the family life cycle stages from newlyweds to postretirement couples, using two scales to describe each person's marriage. A "love scale" measured expressions of affection, self-disclosure, moral support and encouragement, material support, and toleration of the less pleasant aspects of the other person. A "marital problems scale" assessed the level of problems in six separate areas: child rearing and home labor, personal care and appearance (e.g., "Does your partner leave more mess than you like?"), money management, problem solving and decision making, relationships with relatives and in-laws, and expressions of affection. Figure 16.2 shows the results.

Critical Thinking

Can you think of any kind of research design that would get around the problem of the confounding of age and length of marriage in studies on changes in marital quality with age? How could we discover whether the increase in marital satisfaction at midlife is really related to "midlifeness," rather than to long marriages?

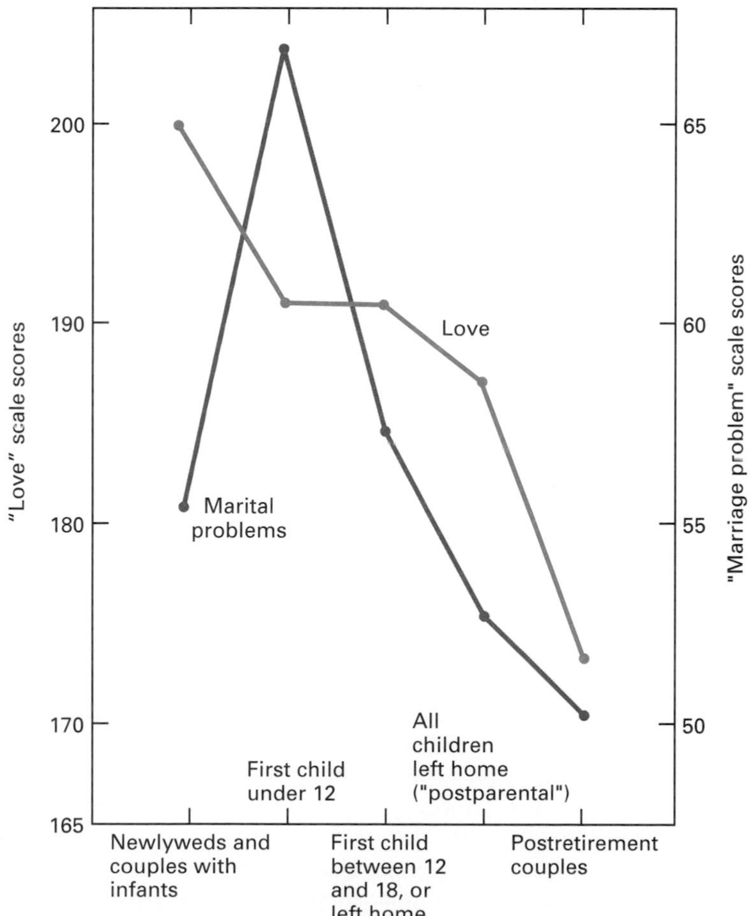

FIGURE 16.2 This set of findings suggests that the greater marital satisfaction couples report in middle adulthood comes about mostly because the rate of problems has dropped, rather than the rate of affection increasing. (*Source:* Swensen et al., 1981, Figure 1, p. 848.)

In these marriages, expressions of love were lower in each succeeding family life stage group, while marital problems peaked among those with young children at home. If overall marital satisfaction is some kind of net difference between love and problems, then you can see that the life stage in which the couple has young children at home would involve the least satisfaction. Couples in this group report high problems and relatively low expressions of love. Midlife couples, in contrast, appear to have a balance tilted toward satisfaction. But they may do so not because expressions of love are particularly high, but because problems are lower.

Some observers have described these middle-aged marriages as *devitalized*—in Sternberg's terms, characterized by *empty love*. But it is also possible that many marriages in this period represent what Sternberg would call *companionate love*, with intimacy and commitment, but without much passion. Whatever label we apply, it seems clear that the underlying attachment between the partners remains strong. Partners of this age turn to one another in times of stress and grieve when the spouse dies—both strong indications of a basic attachment. But it may be accurate to say that overt attachment behaviors in the absence of stress become less frequent, just as we see in young children, whose attachment remains powerful but is less visible.

Let me caution yet again that all this is highly speculative, based as it is on cross-sectional data. The few longitudinal studies we have involve very small numbers of subjects and suffer from the usual confounding of age and length of marriage. One such study of a group of 17 couples followed for 40 years does point to the possibility of a period of "empty love" somewhere in early middle age, with a shift toward a deeper or more intimate relationship in late middle age. But this curvilinear pattern described only 7 of the 17 couples. Five more had marriages that had been consistently high in love and affection over 40 years; three were neutral at every time point, and two were mostly negative. We have no way of knowing how typical of enduring marriages these 17 couples may be. But the results suggest that there are many pathways through the marriage relationship. On average, marital satisfaction may rise and fall in a particular pattern. But that does not describe every marriage. There is no developmental necessity for either a rise in satisfaction or for a devitalization of marriage in the middle years. Nonetheless, it is true that as a group, middle-aged adults describe themselves as being more satisfied with their marriages than do young adults.

Parents and Children

When I talked about the relationship between young adults and their families in Chapter 14, I was talking almost entirely about connections up the chain of family generations—the relationship with one's own middle-aged parents. When we look at family relationships in middle age, we have to look in both directions: down the generational chain to relationships with now-grown children, and up the chain to relationships with now-aging parents.

One of the striking effects of increased life expectancy in developed countries is that we are likely to spend many more years with both upward and downward family relationships. For example, in 1800, a woman in the United States could expect both her parents to be dead by the time she was 37 (Watkins, Menken, & Bongaarts, 1987). In the late 1980s, the average woman could expect to have one parent still living until she was in her late 50s (Bumpass & Aquilino, 1995), and this pattern will only become stronger as life expectancy increases still further.

Each of the positions in a family's generational chain has certain role prescriptions (Hagestad, 1986, 1990), and we expect to move in an orderly way through those roles. In middle adulthood, for current cohorts at least, the family role involves not only maximum amounts of assistance given in both directions in the generational chain, but also the maximum responsibility for maintaining affectional bonds, producing what is sometimes called the midlife "squeeze," or the "sandwich generation."

Critical Thinking

To bring this fact home to you even more clearly, you might want to make some inquiries in your own family. Find out how old your parents each were when their last living parent died (if, indeed, that has yet occurred). And how old were your *grandparents* when they became the oldest in the lineage? Can you go back one more step in the lineage?

Such a squeeze is illustrated in the results of interviews with over 13,000 adults in the 1987–1988 National Survey of Families and Households. Among many other things, each respondent was asked about the amount of help of various kinds—financial, child care, household assistance, and so forth—given to and received from both adult children and aging parents (Bumpass & Aquilino, 1995). The results, shown in Figure 16.3, make it clear that those between ages 40 and 65 give more than they receive in both directions in the family lineage—to adult children and to aging parents—a pattern confirmed in a variety of other studies, in Canada as well as the United States (e.g., Gallagher, 1994; Hirdes & Strain, 1995).

Whether most middle-aged adults experience this combination of responsibilities as a burden is not clear from the available information (Bengtson, Rosenthal, & Burton, 1996). Doubtless some do and some do not, depending on the degree of infirmity of the aging parents, the nature of the relationship the middle-aged adult has with those aging parents, and the degree of help required by the young adult children. A 50-year-old whose divorced daughter has returned with young grandchildren to live at home, or who has a parent living nearby who is suffering from the early stages of Alzheimer's, is far more likely to experience major role strain than is someone of the same age who occasionally babysits with grandchildren and helps out her aging parents by doing occasional shopping, snow shoveling, or housecleaning. But on average, it is clear that the middle adult years are likely to be a time when more help is given than is received.

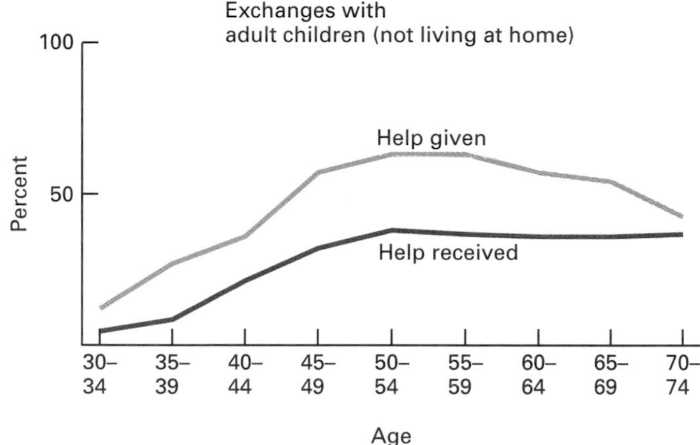

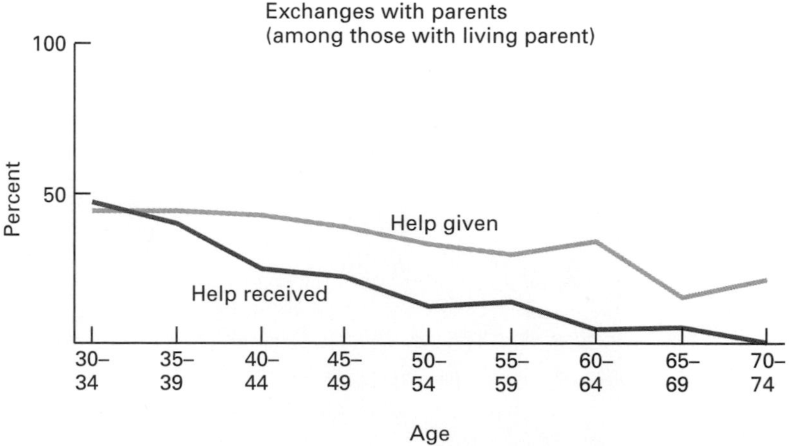

FIGURE 16.3 The midlife "squeeze," or "sandwich generation," is illustrated by these data from a national survey of adults. Middle-aged adults give more help than they receive to both their adult children and their own parents. (*Source:* Bumpass & Aquilino, 1995, data from Tables 11, 12, 25, and 26.)

A quite different look at patterns of family interaction among middle-aged adults can be gleaned from sociologist Gunhild Hagestad's fascinating three-generation family study (1984). She was interested not so much in patterns of aid, but in attempts to influence other generations in the family. Middle-aged adults in this sample of 148 families typically spent more effort trying to influence their children than their parents, but both examples occurred fairly regularly. Their most successful influences on their aging parents came in the form of practical advice about where to live or how to manage the household and money. Attempts to change their parents' views about social issues, or to comment on family dynamics, largely fell on deaf ears.

Influence attempts toward their young adult children were aimed mostly at shaping the child's transition into all the key adult roles. So they talked about educational choices, work, money, and personal lifestyle.

Influence attempts did not radiate exclusively from the middle generation. Both the young adult children and the aging grandparents in this study tried to influence the middle-aged parent generation, with varying success. Hagestad found that parents, whatever their age, kept trying to influence their children, and that children, whatever their age, continued to resist such influence and advice. Advice in the other direction, from child to parent, was much more likely to be successful. Only about a third of the influence attempts from parents to children were effective, while about 70 percent of the influence attempts in the other direction were positively received.

CRITICAL THINKING

What is the conversational glue that holds your own family together? Do the male lineage chains talk about different things than the females?

Hagestad also found that each family seemed to have a particular agenda or set of themes that cropped up again and again in their descriptions of interactions across the generations. Some families spent a lot of time talking about money; others never mentioned this subject. Some focused on family dynamics or on health issues. Themes like this are particularly clear if you look at all-male or all-female lineages. In more than half the families Hagestad studied, the three generations of women regularly talked about some aspect of interpersonal relationships—particularly family dynamics—while such a theme never appeared in the male lineages. Grandfathers, fathers, and grown sons were more likely to talk about work, education, or money with one another. Other studies of multigeneration families, both in the United States and in Germany, confirm these same patterns. When women family members have conflicts, it is most likely to be over how members of the family ought to relate to one another. When fathers, sons, and grandsons have conflicts, they are likely to be about nonfamily issues, such as politics or social issues (e.g., Hagestad, 1985; Lehr, 1982).

I am particularly fond of Hagestad's research because it gives us a glimpse into the complex workings of family relationships across several generations. But we can gain still further understanding of family relationships for middle-aged adults by

Three generations of adults in the same family, like this grandfather, son, and grown grandson, are now the rule rather than the exception. Probably these three men have certain subjects they talk about regularly, a shared agenda of their relationship.

looking separately at specific relationships either down or up the generational chain. Research on the "empty nest," on grandparenthood, and on care of aging parents begins to give us a picture of this sandwich generation.

The Departure of the Children: The "Empty Nest"

The timing of the "empty nest" stage in the family life cycle obviously depends on a person's (or couple's) age when the last child was born. Women born between 1940 and 1949 in the United States—those now in their 40s and 50s—had their last child, on average, when they were about age 26. If we assume that this last child will have left home by the time he or she is 24 or 25, then women in this cohort will be roughly 50 when the last child leaves. Because men are typically somewhat older at marriage, they will be 53 to 55 when the last child leaves. Obviously, those who delay childbearing will push this empty nest stage to a later age—a pattern more and more typical of today's young adults.

Hagestad's work reinforces the obvious fact that the role of parent does not cease when the child leaves home. Support and advice continue to be expected and offered. But the content of the parental role in this "postparental" phase is clearly quite different from what it was when the children were still at home. On a day-to-day basis, the child is not there to be fed or cleaned up after. As a result, adults have much more time for their spousal roles, a change that undoubtedly contributes to the higher reported marital satisfaction in this stage of family life. Interestingly (and quite sensibly), there also seems to be some sign of a weakening of the "parental imperative." Go back and look again at Figure 14.5. You can see that in this postparental phase, husbands and wives are much more equal in their total work/family contributions than was true at earlier phases.

But wait a minute. Isn't the "empty nest" supposed to be a *more* stressful time rather than less, especially for women? Folklore (in Western cultures) would have it that some, even most, women will be depressed or upset at this time because they are losing the central role of mother. Of course it is possible that such a pattern exists in some cultures, but it seems not to be true of U.S. culture, at least not for the great majority of middle-aged women.

Once the kids are grown and gone, many couples find it easier to spend time together—perhaps one of the reasons that marital satisfaction generally rises in middle age.

Suicide rates do go up for women in midlife, but the rise begins between 31 and 40, when children are still at home, and then drops for those women over 50, which is when the empty nest typically occurs. Similarly, the blip on the curve of depression among midlife women appears in the late 30s and early 40s, before the children have left home. Alcohol abuse also declines in women in their 40s and 50s (U.S. Bureau of the Census, 1984).

More to the point, when women are specifically asked about positive and negative transitions in their lives, those who list the departure of the last child as significant are more likely to describe this event as positive than negative. In one study of 60 women between the ages of 45 and 60, Rochelle Harris and her colleagues (Harris et al., 1986) found that only a third of the women described any significant transition point when the last child left home. Of these, 25 percent reported that the transition involved a distinct "mellowing," increased marital satisfaction, or increased inner stability; 17 percent reported that the transition involved an adjustment to the departure of the children.

Those few women who do experience some distress in this role transition appear to be those whose sense of self-identity has been heavily invested in the role of mother. In contrast, women in this age range who are in the labor force are much more likely to experience the empty nest as positive.

The "Cluttered Nest": When Adult Children Do Not Leave Home. Interestingly, the *failure* of young adult children to leave home, or their return to the family home after a period of independence, may be more stressful for middle-aged parents than is the emptying of the nest. In these days of economic uncertainty, young adult children are leaving home later, and more are returning home—after a divorce, after losing a job, or some equivalent. In 1994, 12 percent of young adults between 25 and 34 were living with their parents, compared with only 8 percent in 1970 (U.S. Bureau of the Census, 1995).

We have relatively little research on such families, but the limited evidence suggests that such "cluttered nests" may be stressful for a number of reasons. First, such a living arrangement violates the parents' (and doubtless the young adults') expectations. Parents *expect* their children to stay launched once they have left home, and most expect their children to be launched well before age 25. When they return, it creates what Leonard Pearlin calls an *unscheduled* role change (Pearlin, 1980), a concept similar to the notion of being "off time." And as with off-time life changes, unscheduled changes are linked to increased stress.

Second, when the young adult returns (or remains for an extended period), family roles must be renegotiated. Parents complain about their young adult children's late hours, about unpredictable comings and goings, and about lack of help with household chores. Young adults may feel that they are being "treated like children," and they struggle with the issue of privacy (Clemens & Axelson, 1985).

Despite these potential stresses, current research suggests that more than half of parents with adult coresident children manage to work out good systems for handling the potential stresses, and say they are satisfied with the arrangement (Aquilino & Supple, 1991). In fact, some parents enjoy greater social support from their coresident children than from their children who live away from home (Umberson, 1992). But there is little doubt that such an arrangement brings a new set of tasks and roles, and that in many families it is linked to somewhat higher stress.

Grandparenthood

The role that most adults add in middle adulthood is that of grandparent. In the United States, about a third of adults become a grandparent by their late 40s and half of women become grandmothers by their early 50s (Bumpass & Aquilino, 1995). As the average age of childbearing has risen in recent cohorts, the timing of grandparenthood may shift to a slightly later age, but such a shift would not change the basic fact that the acquisition of this role is a middle adulthood experience—indeed, one could argue that it is one of the few normative experiences of middle adulthood.

Most grandparents see or talk to their grandchildren regularly. They may write, call, or visit as often as every couple of weeks, and most describe their relationships as warm and loving. At the same time, the role of grandparent has few fixed prescriptions. Unlike parenthood, which clearly involves full-time responsibility, there are many ways to be a grandparent. Which pattern a given adult follows will depend on proximity, gender, ethnic group, and personal preference.

Several studies suggest that African-American and Hispanic grandparents have closer and more frequent contact with their grandchildren than Anglos do (Bengtson, 1985; Kivett, 1991). And among all ethnic groups, the role of grandmother is likely to be both broader and more intimate than that of grandfather (Hagestad, 1985).

But style differences also cut across these ethnic and gender patterns. Andrew Cherlin and Frank Furstenberg (1986), who interviewed a nationally representative sample of over 500 grandparents, identified three basic styles.

1. Remote Relationships. These grandparents, who represented 29 percent of the total group Cherlin and Furstenberg studied, see their grandchildren relatively infrequently and have little direct influence over their grandchildren's lives. The most common reason for this remoteness is physical distance, but some grandparents live nearby and are still emotionally detached. One grandmother interviewed by Cherlin and Furstenberg, when asked what it has meant to her to be a grandmother, said—in a formal, distant voice—

> Well, I'm grateful that I've lived long enough to see the children. And I'm grateful that my children are carrying out the principles, the goals, the ideals that I wanted to put into them. And I hope that my grandchildren put it into their children. You know, to lead the good life, be educated, and to continue your education long after you get out of school. (p. 54)

2. The Companionate Relationship. In sharp contrast is this statement by another woman in the same study:

> When you have grandchildren, you have more love to spare. Because the discipline goes to the parents and whoever's in charge. But you just have extra love and you will tend to spoil them a little bit. And you know, you give. (p. 55)

Grandparents with this kind of attitude—the most common of all the patterns, at 55 percent—create very warm, pleasurable relationships with their grandchildren. Yet these grandparents also say that they are glad they no longer have the day-to-day responsibility. They can love the grandchildren and then send them home.

Young Rosa seems delighted with her grandfather, with whom she seems to have what what Cherlin and Furstenberg would call a "companionate" relationship.

3. The Involved Relationship. The third and least common type (16 percent) includes grandparents who are much more actively involved in the rearing of their grandchildren. Some of them live in three-generation households with one or more children and grandchildren; some have nearly full-time care of the grandchildren. But involved relationships also occur in some cases in which the grandparent has no daily responsibility for the grandchild's care but creates an unusually close link.

Within American society, this type of involved grandparent care is far more common among African Americans than either Hispanics or Anglos. Twelve percent of black children in 1991 were being reared by or with a head-of-household grandparent, compared with 3.7 for Anglos and 5.6 for Hispanics. Full-time grandparent care is especially likely when the daughter is unmarried. In such cases, grandmothers frequently take on child-care responsibilities so that the daughter can continue in school, or hold down a job. That such assistance is indeed helpful is indicated by the fact that teenage mothers who have such help from their own mothers complete more years of education and have more successful work careers in adulthood (Taylor et al., 1990).

In Cherlin and Furstenberg's study, grandmothers more often fell into the companionate category, as did younger grandparents of both sexes. In contrast, grandparents over 65 are more likely to have a remote relationship, sometimes because their health is no longer good or because they find the heightened level of activity around young children more difficult to tolerate.

Critical Thinking

Think of a design for a study to check the hypothesis that health differences can explain most of the age differences in styles of grandparenting.

The role of grandparent obviously brings many middle-aged and older adults a good deal of pleasure and satisfaction. What is more interesting to me, though, is the repeated finding that an adult's overall life satisfaction is affected very little by the quality of relationships with grandchildren. Grandparents who see their grandchildren more often do not describe themselves as happier than those who see them less often (Palmore, 1981). This does not mean that grandparents are displeased with the role. It means instead that for most adults in middle age, grandparenthood is not central to their lives, to their sense of self, or to their overall morale. In this, it is quite unlike the roles of spouse and parent, new roles in early adulthood that have highly significant effects on overall happiness or life satisfaction.

Caring for an Aging Parent

Another role that may be added at midlife, and that does have a powerful effect on overall life satisfaction, is that of major caregiver to one's aging parents. The great majority of adults, in virtually every culture, feel a strong sense of filial responsibility. Should their parents need assistance, they will endeavor to provide it (Ogawa & Retherford, 1993; Wolfson et al., 1993). But just how many adults actually take on this role is surprisingly unclear, despite the many articles in the recent popular press that have painted a bleak picture of the "woman in the middle," who is depicted as inevitably taking on a burdensome role of caring for elders.

Much of the information we have comes from studies of elderly adults who are asked about the kind and amount of care they receive from their children. But this does not tell us what we need to know about the typical experience of the middle-aged adult. For example, we know that among the elderly in the United States who have an adult child, 18 percent actually live with one of those children (Crimmins & Ingegneri, 1990; Hoyert, 1991). But because most elders have more than one child, it is not true that 18 percent of middle-aged children have a parent living with them. Nor is it true that all those home-sharing elders are disabled or in need of regular care. So this strategy will not tell us how many of the middle-aged are providing regular or extensive care to an elder parent.

Better information comes from a small number of cross-sectional studies in which representative samples of middle-aged adults have been asked how much and what kind of assistance they provide to their parents (e.g., Rosenthal, Matthews, & Marshall, 1989; Spitze & Logan, 1990). In one such study, Spitze and Logan interviewed 1200 middle-aged adults in upstate New York. Figure 16.4 shows that in this sample, only about 11 percent of adults between 40 and 65 were providing as much as three hours per week of assistance to an older parent—a relatively low level of care.

Combining this information with evidence from other similar research (Scharlach & Fredricksen, 1994), we can estimate that something between 10 and 15 percent of middle-aged adults are providing some kind of regular care for an older parent at any given time. But let's be careful about what this number means.

First of all, studies like these give us only a slice of time, not longitudinal information. So we do not know what percentage of adults will take on such a caregiving role at *some time* in their lives. Several researchers have tried to make such an estimate, but they have used quite widely varying definitions of "providing care." Christine Himes (1994), who used a very broad definition (anyone who said that they had provided any kind of care for a non-coresident seriously ill or disabled relative in the

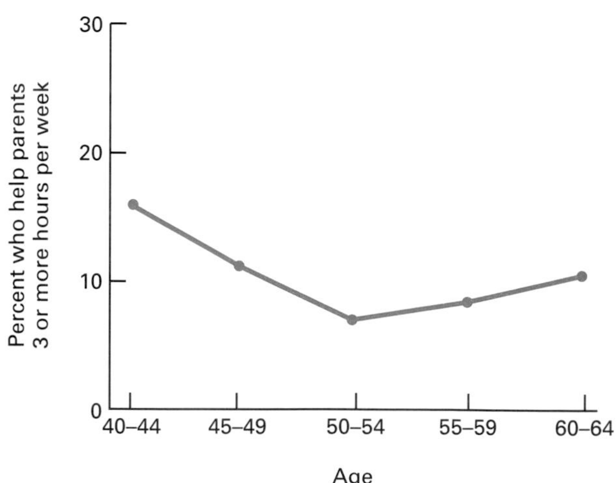

FIGURE 16.4 These cross-sectional data indicate that relatively few middle-aged adults are involved in extensive caregiving for one or both parents at any one time. But such evidence does not tell us what percentage of adults will fill such a role at *some time* in their lives. (*Source:* Spitze & Logan, 1990, from Table 2, p. 189.)

past year), calculates that roughly 40 percent of women now aged 45 to 49 will be involved in at least some minimal caregiving in their lifetime, about half of them before the age of 55. Using longitudinal data and a much stricter definition of care, Julie Robison and her colleagues (Robison, Moen, & Dempster-McClain, 1995) find that about a quarter of the women in their sample provided significant levels of care to their own parents or parents-in-law at some time in their middle years. Furthermore, Robison finds that the likelihood of such a role has risen steadily from one cohort to the next in this century. Only 17 percent of the women in their sample who had been born between 1905 and 1917 ever were major caregivers to a parent, while a third of those in the cohort born from 1927 to 1934 had taken on such a role. As life expectancy continues to rise, the likelihood of caring for an aging parent will rise still further. But even with such increases, it seems clear that while the role of caregiver to an aging parent is a *common* midlife role, it is not a *normative* experience, even for those in current cohorts.

The Effects of Caregiving on the Caregiver. Just what impact does such caregiving have on the middle-aged adult? In the past decade, there have been hundreds of studies exploring the impact on the caregiver of tending to the daily needs of a

The Real World

Who Helps When An Elder Becomes Frail or Disabled?

Faced with an aging parent who needs some kind of regular assistance, who takes on the task, and why? The simple answer is that women do—daughters and daughters-in-law. Daughters are two to four times as likely as sons to provide such assistance (Dwyer & Coward, 1991; Lee, Dwyer, & Coward, 1993). The more complex answer is that families negotiate the caregiving task along a number of dimensions, including competing demands and availability of resources. Within a group of siblings, the one most likely to take on the task of caregiving is the one who has no children still at home, is not working, not married, and lives closest to the aging parent (Brody et al., 1994; Stoller, Forster, & Duniho, 1992). The child with the strongest attachment to the parent is also most likely to provide help, although this effect is often overridden by proximity and time availability (Whitbeck, Simons, & Conger, 1991).

Most of these factors, in today's society, combine to make a daughter or daughter-in-law the most likely candidate for the role of caregiver. In today's middle-aged cohorts, women are more likely to be unemployed and less likely to be married because both widowed and divorced women are less likely to remarry than are widowed or divorced men.

But it makes a difference whether the frail elder is a mother or a father. Daughters are four times as likely as their brothers to help an older mother, but only 40 percent more likely than are sons to help a frail father (Lee, Dwyer, & Coward, 1993). Because women (mothers) live longer than men and are thus more likely to require help, this tendency for children to provide relatively more help to the same-sex parent means that women will end up with a much higher probability of providing such care.

Another factor that increases daughters' involvement in parental care is simple proximity. Perhaps because of their greater emotional closeness to their parents, or their socialization toward the role of kin-keeping, daughters are more likely to live near their parents. And parents, when they approach their later years, are more likely to move to be close to a daughter than to a son.

Yet sons are quite often involved in the care of an elder. If a son is unmarried, he is more likely to take on the caregiving role than is his married sister (Stoller et al., 1992). And if both son and daughter are involved, the two often divide the responsibilities, with sons providing more financial assistance or instrumental support (mowing the lawn, repairs, perhaps shopping) and daughters more often providing help with actual physical activities of daily living, such as dressing, cleaning, or cooking.

But despite these complexities, it is still inescapable that women are far more likely than are men to take on the role of caregiver to an aging parent, just as women are more likely to take on the role of caregiver within a marriage and with children. Whether this will change in the next few decades, as many more middle-aged women enter or remain in the labor force, we will have to wait and see. But my hunch is that, just as the balance of housework has not changed much in response to radical changes in women's work patterns, caregiving patterns are not likely to change rapidly either.

parent (or spouse) who is disabled, frail, or demented. In the large majority of studies, the recipient of care has been diagnosed with Alzheimer's disease or some other dementia. Such individuals gradually lose their ability to perform ordinary daily tasks, may ultimately be unable to dress or feed themselves, and may not recognize their caregivers. Providing care for such an individual, especially if the caregiver is also trying to meet the needs of her (or his) own job and family, may drain both energy and finances.

Not surprisingly, such a demanding role takes its toll. The cumulative evidence indicates that such caregivers are more depressed and have lower marital satisfaction than is true for matched comparison groups of similar age and social class (Hoyert & Seltzer, 1992; Jutras & Lavoie, 1995; Schulz, Visintainer, & Williamson, 1990)—although one recent study comparing black and white caregivers finds heightened depression only for white caregivers (Haley et al., 1995), an interesting finding that needs to be replicated. Some research also suggests that those who care for demented or frail elders are more often ill themselves, or that they have some reduced efficiency of immune system function (Dura & Kiecolt-Glaser, 1991; Hoyert & Seltzer, 1992; Kiecolt-Glaser et al., 1987). Collectively, these effects usually go by the name of *caregiver burden*.

Let me be careful about these statements, as I have tried to be with earlier generalizations. For one thing, many of the studies involve subjects who were recruited from among support groups of families with Alzheimer's patients. It is reasonable to suppose that those who join such support groups may be those for whom caregiving is especially burdensome. Second, although scores on standard scales of depression do indeed rise among those taking on the caregiving role, few of these adults show all the symptoms of a full-scale clinical depression. Third, we know much less about the amount of burden experienced by those who provide relatively low levels of assistance, such as three hours per week or less. On the face of it, there seem more than a few orders of magnitude difference between daily care of a demented elder and occasional lawn mowing or shopping assistance. Finally, it is clear that certain factors can significantly mitigate the feeling of burden, even for those with major caregiving responsibilities. Those who have good support networks (including a supportive spouse), as well as other caregivers who can share the burden, experience fewer negative consequences (E. M. Brody et al., 1992; Pearlin et al., 1996; Schulz & Williamson, 1991).

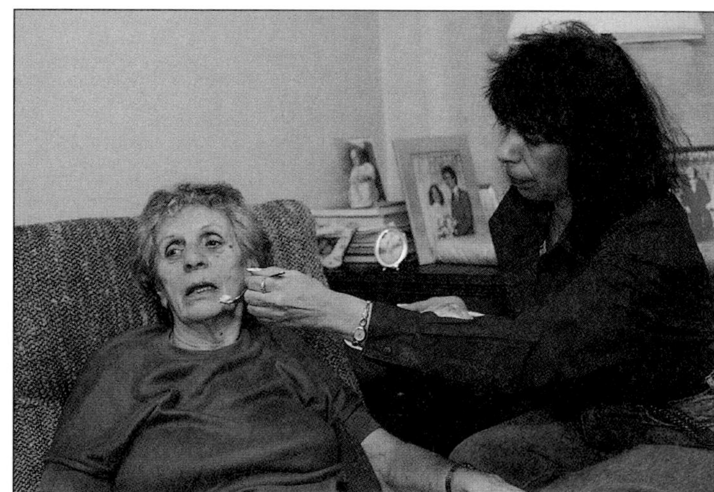

Daughters, far more than sons, are likely to take on the role of significant caregiver for a disabled or demented parent, as this daughter has done for her mother, suffering from Alzheimer's disease.

I am not trying to minimize the enormity of the task that may be involved for an individual middle-aged son or daughter (or elderly spouse) caring full time for a demented or extremely frail elder. There are clearly costs, sometimes very great costs. But such a burden is *not* a normal part of the experience of current cohorts of middle-aged adults.

For the majority of middle-life adults, the pattern is far less extreme, and far more positive. We give more assistance to our parents than we did at earlier ages, but we also continue to see them regularly for ceremonial and celebratory occasions and continue to feel affection as well as filial responsibility. Our parents are also important *symbolically*, because so long as they are alive, they occupy the niche of "elder" in the family lineage. When they are gone, each generation moves up a notch in the sequence of family generations, and those in the middle generation must come to terms with the fact that they are now "next in line" for death.

Friends

The scant research on friendships in middle adulthood suggests that the total number of friendships is lower in these years than is true in young adulthood. For example, in one small study, Mary Levitt and her associates (Levitt, Weber, & Guacci, 1993) interviewed three generations of women in each of 53 families, some Anglos and some Hispanic. Each woman was asked to describe her close relationships, using the same "concentric circles" measure of the relationship convoy you saw in Figure 12.3. Figure 16.5 shows the proportion of those listed who were close family, other family, and friends, for the young adult and middle-aged generations, for each of the two cultures. Among both the Anglos and the Hispanic families, the young adult women included more friends in their convoy than did their middle-aged mothers.

At the same time, we have other bits of research suggesting that midlife friendships are as intimate and close as is true at earlier ages. Laura Carstensen has analyzed information from the files of 50 subjects who were part of the now-familiar Berkeley longitudinal studies, who had been interviewed or tested repeatedly from

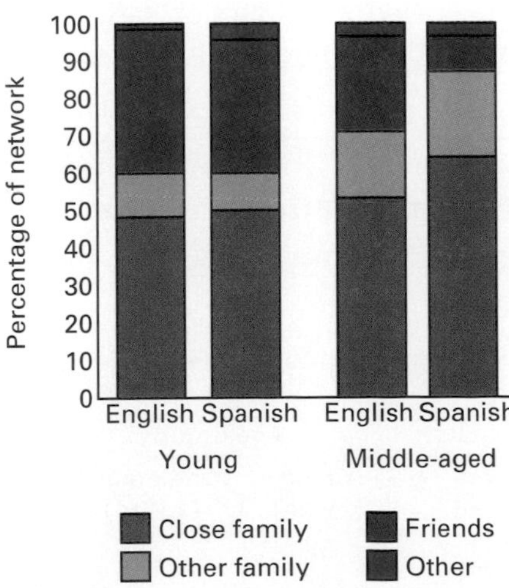

FIGURE 16.5 Levitt asked middle-aged women and their young-adult daughters to list all the members of their key relationship "convoy." Among both Anglos and Hispanics in this sample, the young women listed more friends in their convoy than did their mothers. (*Source:* Levitt et al., 1993, adapted from Figure 1, p. 325.)

adolescence through age 50 (1992). Among other things, she rated the relationship each subject described with a best friend: the frequency of their interaction, their reported closeness, and their reported satisfaction with this relationship. Carstensen found that the frequency of interaction with a best friend dropped between age 17 and age 50, but that the closeness of the best-friend relationship remained high.

Carstensen's general model, which she calls "socioemotional selectivity theory," is that over adulthood, we each selectively reduce our social interactions, narrowing our focus to fewer relationships in an effort to maximize social and emotional gains and minimize social and emotional risks. But at the same time, she argues, the retained relationships become closer. So we have fewer friendships, but the ones we have are more intimate; we may see our friends less often, but the relationships nonetheless become deeper over time. This hypothesis makes sense to me, but we have as yet little data to test it.

Work

The story of work in midlife contains two paradoxes. First, work satisfaction is at its peak in these years, despite the fact that most adults receive few work promotions in middle age. Second, the quality of work performance remains high, despite the gradual slowing of mental and physical processes I've already described.

Work Satisfaction

Despite the plateau in work achievement that occurs for most adults in these middle years, job satisfaction is typically at its peak, as is a sense of power or clout in the job. Lois Tamir (1982) suggests two explanations for this apparent paradox. On the one hand, many men have achieved genuine success and status by midlife and are quite reasonably satisfied. Alternatively, middle-aged men may become resigned to the idea that they are unlikely to be promoted further and so convince themselves that they have achieved sufficient status, or they change their expectations or their work values.

Tamir's cross-sectional study of a nationally representative sample of men offers some evidence consistent with the second of these explanations, as you can see in Table 16.1. Among young adult men in this study (aged 25 to 39), job satisfaction was linked to various measures of personal satisfaction, while among the middle-

Table 16.1 Job Satisfaction and Life Satisfaction in Different Age Groups of Men

Correlation Between Job Satisfaction and . . .	Age Group: Young (25–39)	Age Group: Middle-Aged (40–49)
Overall life satisfaction	.31*	.04
Zest	.43*	.09
Self-esteem	.26*	−.02

*This correlation is significant at the .001 level, which means that if there were really no link between the two variables, such a correlation would occur by chance only once in every 1000 samples of this size.

Source: Tamir, 1982, Tables 4.14, 4.15, and 4.16, pp. 91–92.

aged it was not. Middle-aged men, in other words, have begun to disengage from their work as a primary source of personal fulfillment or satisfaction, even while they are likely to be more pleased with the work itself.

Whether the same is true of women workers at midlife is not so clear. For those women who begin to work steadily only in their 30s or 40s, the middle adult years may be the time of most rapid work advancement rather than a time of maintenance of previous gains. For such women, we might expect that work satisfaction would play the same role in overall life satisfaction as it does for young adult men.

Interestingly, though, a shift to full-time employment when the nest is finally empty is not a very common pattern for women, at least in current cohorts. Ten-year longitudinal data from the Michigan Panel Study of Income Dynamics (Moen, 1991) suggest that most current middle-aged and "young old" women began paid employment while their children were still at home. Few began work for the first time after the last child left home. When women did return to full-time work only in middle adulthood, the most likely reasons were divorce or widowhood, not the final departure of children.

All this suggests that the work lives of middle adult women continue to be far more variable than is true of men of the same age. We are almost entirely lacking in any knowledge of the psychological effect of work on women in this age group. We know they are more satisfied with their work than are younger women, but we do not know whether they have a greater sense of authority or clout in their jobs at this age. We know that middle-aged women who work have somewhat higher life satisfaction than women who don't (e.g., Betz & Fitzgerald, 1987). But we do not know whether the same pattern of relationship between work satisfaction and life satisfaction that Tamir observed in men would hold for women as well. My own guess is that among women who have worked continuously, the pattern might be the same. But I doubt that that is true for women whose work history is more variable.

Job Performance

In the great majority of occupations, job performance remains high throughout the middle years of adulthood (McEvoy & Cascio, 1989). The few exceptions are those occupations in which physical strength or speedy reaction time are critical elements, such as longshoremen, air traffic controllers, truck drivers, professional athletes, and the like. In these jobs, performance begins to decline at midlife or earlier, just as you would expect (Sparrow & Davies, 1988). In fact, many adults in such occupations change jobs at midlife in anticipation of, or because of, such declines. But in the great majority of occupations, including most occupations that demand high levels of cognitive skill, performance remains at essentially the same level throughout middle adulthood (Salthouse & Maurer, 1996).

Paul and Margaret Baltes (1990a) argue that maintaining high productivity or job performance is possible because adults, faced with small but noticeable erosions of cognitive or physical skill, engage in a process the Balteses call "selective optimization with compensation." Three subprocesses are involved:

- *Selection*, which involves narrowing one's range of activities, such as by focusing on only the most central tasks, delegating more responsibilities to others, or giving up or reducing peripheral job activities;
- *Optimization*, which involves deliberate "exercise" of crucial abilities—such as by added training, or polishing rusty skills—so as to remain as close to maximum skill as possible; and
- *Compensation*, which involves pragmatic strategies for overcoming specific obstacles, such as getting stronger glasses or hearing aids, or devising ways to reduce memory loads with systematic list-making; it may also involve carefully emphasizing one's strengths and minimizing weaknesses when talking to co-workers or bosses.

Joseph Abraham and Robert Hansson (1995) have now tested this model in a study of 224 working adults aged 40 to 69. They measured each of the three aspects of the proposed compensatory process as well as job competence, and found that the link between the use of selection, optimization, and compensation on the one hand and the quality of work performance on the other got stronger and stronger with increasing age. That is, the older the worker, the more it mattered whether he or she used helpful compensatory practices. In the older groups (primarily those in their 50s and early 60s), those who used the most selection, optimization, and compensation had the highest work performance. But among the younger workers in this sample (those in their early 40s), the same relationship did not hold. This is obviously only one study, but the results provide some support for the idea that job performance remains high during middle age at least in part because adults take deliberate compensatory actions.

Preparation for Retirement

Many middle-aged adults also begin to prepare for retirement in various ways, often as early as 15 years before their anticipated retirement date. One aspect of such preparation is a gradual reduction in workload. For example, Figure 16.6 shows the hours worked per year for men and women in a random national sample of 1339 adults (Herzog, House, & Morgan, 1991). You can see that the percentage of men and women working very long hours (2500 hours per year or more, which averages out to 48 hours a week) drops among those aged 55 to 64.

CRITICAL THINKING

I have interpreted Figure 16.6 as meaning that in middle adulthood, there is a kind of winding down of involvement with work. Are there other possible interpretations or explanations of these data?

As they get nearer to the normative time for retirement, middle-aged adults also increase both formal and informal preparations (Evans, Ekerdt, & Bossé, 1985). They talk to their spouse or with friends or co-workers about retirement options, and read more articles in the popular press. A minority also take part in such formal preparations as attending financial planning seminars, asking the Social Security Administration how much income they can expect at retirement age, investigating their pension plan at work in more detail, or seeking professional retirement planning guidance.

Such preparations are more likely among workers who are looking forward to retirement, who are dissatisfied with their work, or have a retired friend (Evans et al., 1985). Those who dread retirement do the least planning, but even in this group, the incidence of informal planning increases as the time of retirement approaches.

If we combine all these pieces of information about work patterns in middle adulthood, the picture is of a gradual reduction in the centrality of the work role in

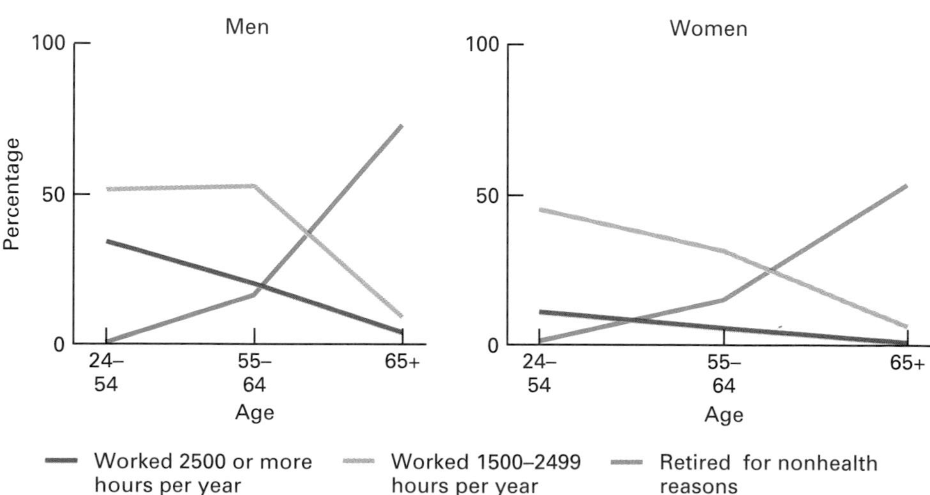

FIGURE 16.6 Most of us think of 65 as "retirement age," but in fact many adults begin a gradual process of reduction in the intensity of work well before that age. (*Source:* Herzog et al., 1991, Table 1, p. 205.)

an adult's life. This seems to be true both literally and psychologically. The number of hours worked tends to go down (although I wish someone would tell that to my 60+ work-hours-per-week professor husband, who works more hours at age 58 than he did ten years ago), and thoughts about retirement rise. Perhaps more centrally, satisfaction with one's work becomes less critical for feelings of happiness or well-being than was true in the earlier decades of adult life. Like family roles, then, for the majority of adults the work role becomes less intense in middle age.

Personality

Suggestions of such a lowering of intensity also appear in research on personality in the middle adult years. Most observers agree that over the years from 40 to 65 adults shift away from the achievement striving, independence, assertiveness, and individualism that we see peaking at about midlife. But personality theorists have not agreed on just how to characterize the direction of change. Let me describe five different views of the process.

Interiority. Bernice Neugarten (1977) proposed that the shift is toward what she called *interiority*. She believed that in old age, adults turn away from their preoccupation with the outer world and become much more focused on interior processes—on reminiscence, on understanding their own life. In support of this hypothesis is the finding from several cross-sectional studies that introversion increases slightly over the adult years (Costa et al., 1986; Leon et al., 1979). On the other side of the scale is research by Carol Ryff (1984; Ryff & Heincke, 1983). She could find no indication of an increase in interiority in late middle age or among older subjects, either in the subjects' descriptions of their current selves or in their recollections of themselves at earlier ages.

Generativity to Ego Integrity. Erikson's theory offers another model. The primary stage of middle adulthood in Erikson's theory is *generativity versus stagnation*; the potential strength to be gained is that of *care*. It involves primarily an interest in establishing and guiding the next generation, of passing on the flame in some fashion. It is expressed not only in bearing or rearing one's own children, but in more symbolic ways through teaching, serving as mentor, or taking on leadership roles in various civic, religious, or charitable organizations. Merely having children is not enough to develop or express generativity in Erikson's terms. The optimum expression of generativity requires a turning outward from preoccupation with self, a kind of psychological expansion toward caring for others. Those individuals who fail to develop generativity often suffer from a "pervading sense of stagnation and personal impoverishment" (Erikson, 1963, p. 267), and begin to indulge themselves "as if they were their own one and only child" (p. 267).

Erikson thought that bearing and rearing children was one way to develop the quality of generativity, but it is not the only way or the only expression of that quality. Generativity can also be expressed through teaching (as here), mentoring, or civic activities.

The final stage of adulthood, according to Erikson, is *ego integrity versus despair*. Erikson was quite indefinite about just when this task begins, but in most modern writings the timing is set at some time around age 60—at the end of the period I have been calling middle adulthood. Thus, in trying to understand personality change in the middle adult years, we might look for some kind of subtle shift from generativity toward ego integrity. The task of achieving ego integrity, according to Erikson, is not unlike Neugarten's notion of interiority. To succeed at this task, the individual must come to terms with what she has done with her life, to find meaning in her choices, and to accept the "inalterability of the past" (Erikson et al., 1986, p. 56). If Erikson's view is correct, we might see signs of a shift toward such a reflective attitude in very late middle age.

There are hints of changes of this kind, but the findings are much less clear than is the case for the set of changes I described in early adult life. One hint comes from the Berkeley/Oakland longitudinal studies. If you go back and look at Figure 14.6, and at the parallel figure from Chapter 1 (Figure 1.1), you'll see that while self-confidence continues to rise through the 50s, assertiveness peaked in the 40s and then dropped. In that same study, a measure of outgoingness also peaked in the 40s among women, and then dropped, as did the measure the Berkeley researchers call *cognitively committed*, which includes aspects of ambition, valuing independence, and valuing intellect. In this sample then, we see signs of a sea change around age 50, after which assertiveness, ambition, and outgoingness seem to decline. Whether these changes continue into later decades we cannot tell from this study, because the sample has not yet been studied at ages beyond about 55.

Flexibility and Tenacity. Another intriguing set of findings that cast the personality changes of this era in somewhat different terms comes from research in Germany by Jochen Brandtstädter (Brandtstädter & Baltes-Götz, 1990; Brandtstädter & Greve, 1994). He has tested several thousand adults, using measures of two personality traits or qualities that he calls *tenacious goal pursuit* and *flexible goal adjustment*. An individual high in tenacious goal pursuit is one who would agree with statements like these (Brandtstädter & Baltes-Götz, 1990, p. 216):

> The harder a goal is to achieve, the more desirable it often appears to me.
>
> Even if everything seems hopeless, I still look for a way to master the situation.

Someone high in flexible goal adjustment would agree with the following (pp. 215–216):

> In general, I'm not upset very long about an opportunity passed up.
>
> I can adapt quite easily to changes in a situation.
>
> I usually recognize quite easily my own limitations.

Figure 16.7 shows cross-sectional differences on both these measures in Brandtstädter's large German sample. Tenacious goal pursuit went down in middle adulthood, while flexible goal adjustment rose, suggesting a kind of "mellowing" of personality in the middle years.

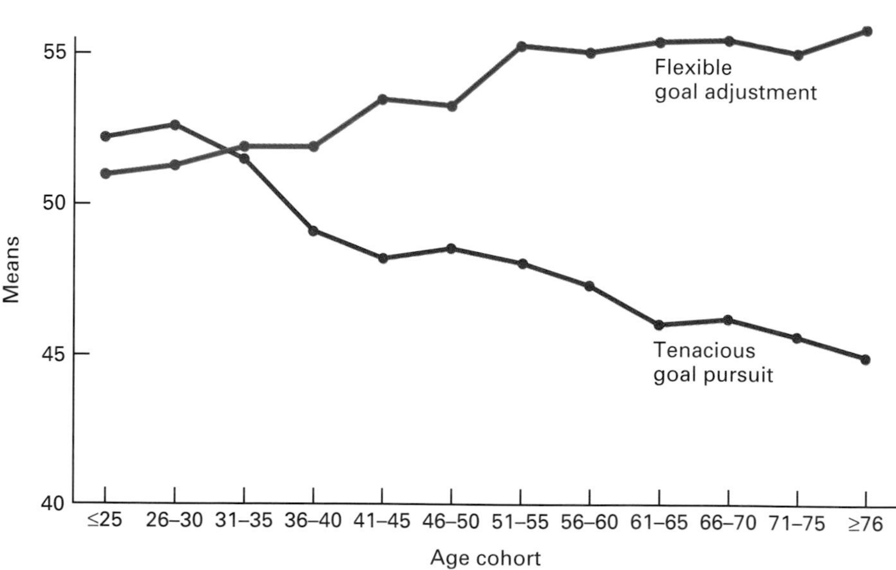

FIGURE 16.7 These cross-sectional data from a large study in Germany suggest a kind of "mellowing" of personality in middle adulthood, with an increase in flexibility and a decline in tenacious pursuit of goals. (*Source:* Brandtstädter & Greve, 1994, Figure 3, p. 67.)

Maturity of Defense Mechanisms. Still another way to look at personality change in these middle years is to focus on defense mechanisms. In Chapter 2, I mentioned George Vaillant's general theoretical proposal that what happens with development is a gradual shift away from the most reality-distorting defense mechanisms. To test this notion, Vaillant divided the defenses into three types: (1) immature, such as projection, distortion, and denial; (2) neurotic, such as repression, intellectualization, and displacement; and (3) mature, such as suppression, humor, and altruism. He then analyzed the types of defenses used by 100 of the Harvard men in the Grant study at various ages. The results generally confirmed his expectations: These men used more and more mature defenses as they aged. By middle adulthood, mature defenses constituted about 40 percent of the total.

Similar results have emerged from several other longitudinal studies. Haan (1976) reports decreases with age in self-defensiveness, fantasizing, and projection among subjects in the Berkeley longitudinal study; Helson finds that the women in her longitudinal study of Mills College graduates showed consistent increases in such "coping" skills as objectivity and intellectuality, and decreases in the use of denial and primitive defenses (Helson & Moane, 1987; Helson & Wink, 1992).

All these studies show gradual changes in the maturity of defenses, beginning in early adulthood. So this is not a process unique to middle age. Still, by middle adulthood, many adults have become considerably better at handling anxieties and stresses without resorting to the most reality-distorting forms of defense.

Sex-Role Crossover. A fifth view of personality change in middle adulthood comes from anthropologist David Gutmann, whose ideas you have already met in the concept of the parental imperative. His studies of many cultures led him to conclude that sex roles change again in late middle age. At that time, Gutmann argues, men's and women's roles "cross over," with men beginning to express more feminine qualities and women expressing more masculine qualities. Women become more assertive, men more passive. He says:

> Paradoxically, these gender reversals are most evident in those culture areas that also sponsor the fierce machismo of younger men, for example, rural Mexico and the American Southwest. Thus, as Indian women age, they can enter the ritual dances that are closed to younger women. By the same token, without feeling shame or censure, older Indian men can join the ranks of the women. (1987, p. 95)

There are many other examples. Older Iroquois women become "manly-hearted" and can hold religious and political office for the first time in their lives. Japanese women over 60, Gutmann reports, acquire a whole range of freedoms, including implicit permission to make bawdy jokes in mixed company; older women in Lebanese villages become similarly bawdy, aggressive, and controlling toward males.

There appears to be kernel of truth in Gutmann's view of these changes, but more systematic studies suggest that it is better to describe the change as an *expansion* of gender roles (or perhaps a blurring) rather than as a crossover. Gutmann's model implies that men and women trade places in some sense, and there is little evidence to support this (Huyck, 1994). But *androgyny* does seem to increase in middle age, at least among some groups (e.g., Nash & Feldman, 1981; Vaillant, 1977). Perhaps because of the gradual hormone changes I described in the last chapter, perhaps because pressure toward traditional role divisions declines after the children leave home, perhaps for other reasons associated with deeper personality changes, both men and women at midlife can begin to express the unexpressed or underexpressed parts of themselves. For some men, this means an increased expression of compassion; for some women this means increased assertiveness or autonomy.

Adding Up the Changes. These various views of personality change in the middle years of adulthood do not paint a single coherent picture, even though they all point to *some* kind of change in personality past midlife. The adult in her 50s or 60s seems less intense, less preoccupied with achieving specific goals, perhaps slightly more introverted, perhaps more willing or able to adapt to circumstances, and more able (or willing) to express all facets of herself.

But by no means all the evidence fits with even this very general description. For example, Schaie and Willis (1991) find that adults in their 60s become *less* flexible in their attitudes and their thinking. And of course we should not forget all the evidence showing that many personality traits are highly consistent over middle adulthood, including the Big Five traits McCrae and Costa have identified.

There are several possible reasons why the findings should be so difficult to add up. First, we have really very little research on personality change in the years of middle adulthood. Longitudinal studies, for example, tend to begin either in early adulthood or at age 60 or so, and rarely cover the middle-adult years.

In addition, individual variability seems to be higher in middle adulthood (and higher still in old age) than is true in early adulthood (Nelson & Dannefer, 1992). Perhaps because of the power of the central roles, young adults are much more likely to march to the same drummer; by middle adulthood, there are many different beats. Pathways and trajectories have diverged. Most adults this age are healthy, but some are not; some have achieved their work goals, while others have not. Some achieve generativity and move toward grappling with the task of integrity. Some have given up immature defense mechanisms while others have not. In Loevinger's terms, some shift from the conformist stance of early adulthood to a more individualistic stance. Some later move on to a stage she calls *autonomous*, in which the individual moves from a preoccupation with self toward greater humanitarian concern. All these variations mean *shared* patterns of personality change are much less likely in these years. There may be an underlying pathway described by a shift toward lessened achievement strivings, less intensity, more introversion, and more mature defenses. But even if the path itself is shared—a point on which not all observers or theorists would agree—not all adults will move the same distance along it, which makes it far more difficult to detect the direction of change. What we need now is a more subtle look at personality continuity and change in these middle years, one that takes into account the wider degree of variability and the different levels of growth or development.

Individual Differences

A look at individual differences in adult life experiences may give us one kind of window on the variability of middle adult patterns. The pathway an adult follows, or the degree of movement along any one pathway, is affected by a whole range of factors, including individual family history and personality as well as the stresses and crises each person has had to cope with.

We all deal with some stresses, including the daily hassles of working with annoying co-workers, a long commute, racial or ethnic or gender prejudice that may be directed our way, an in-law we simply can't bear, or whatever. By midlife, many of us have also encountered specific crises, such as a divorce, poor health, early widowhood, losing a job, or moving. What are the effects of such crises on adult life patterns?

One effect you have already read about: High levels of stress, whether from chronic hassles or specific crises, are associated with poorer immune function and poorer health. But many significant crises have an impact on other areas of the adult's life as well. Let me say just a bit more about two particularly common such crises, divorce and unemployment.

Across Development

Predictions of Psychological Adjustment at Midlife from Earlier Measures of Personality and Family Background

Can we tell what kind of middle adulthood a person is likely to have, based on what we know about his childhood, adolescence, or early adult life? To answer this question we obviously need long-term longitudinal data, of which we have very little. But we have some fragments of information, from both the Berkeley/Oakland study and the Grant study of Harvard men.

In both studies, middle-age psychological health was judged by comparing each subject with an ideal of some kind. In the Berkeley study, a Q-sort pattern was established that defined an ideally healthy middle-aged adult as warm, compassionate, dependable, responsible, insightful, productive, candid, and calm. Each subject's own descriptive Q-sort was then compared to the ideal.

In the Grant study, George Vaillant (1975; Vaillant & Vaillant, 1990) identified specific behaviors or accomplishments he considered signs of adjustment, including enjoyment of one's job, stable marriage, steady advance in career, low level of illness, regular vacation, and low use of alcohol or other drugs. Each man in this study was then judged on these standards.

In the Berkeley study, those who were closer to the ideal of psychological health at 40 and 50 had grown up with more open-minded, intellectually competent parents who had stable marriages and used more reasonable and consistent types of control with their children. Their mothers were warm, pleasant, poised, and nondefensive. As teenagers, these better-adjusted adults were more adept in their relationships with both peers and adults (Hightower, 1990; Livson & Peskin, 1981; Peskin & Livson, 1981).

Similarly, men in the Grant study who were better adjusted at midlife had come from warmer families and had better relationships with both their fathers and mothers in childhood than had less-well-adjusted middle-aged men. Collectively, these findings suggest the not-so-surprising conclusion that those who start out well are likely to continue along that path. And "starting well" seems to include the components of warmth from parents and good social skills. But none of these links between childhood and adulthood is incredibly strong. Many adults start well but do not look so put together at 45 or 50; many came from unstable or difficult childhoods but nonetheless look healthy at middle age.

One possible explanation for such discontinuities comes from yet another analysis of the Berkeley data, this time by Florine Livson (1976, 1981). She began by identifying a group of adults who had all been rated as high in overall psychological health when they were 50. Because all these subjects had also been rated on the same scale when they were 40, Livson was able to identify two subsets: those who were rated as psychologically healthy or mature at *both* 40 and 50 (called "stable"), and those who had been rated as less integrated or optimal in functioning at 40, but who had got it together by the time they were 50 (called "improvers"). She then asked whether these two groups had different histories.

What she found was that those men and women who had shown stable patterns of psychological health in middle age were those whose temperament or personality as teenagers and young adults happened to be a good match for the prevailing sex roles and societal norms of their era. The stable women had been extroverted as teenagers, moved happily into the roles of wife and mother, and had little ambition for a career outside the home—a pattern that fit well with the expectations for women of this cohort. The stable men were achievement-oriented and fairly conformist. They moved into adulthood, taking on the various roles, feeling comfortable with the expectations that they achieve and support their families.

In contrast, those who looked less healthy at 40 but good at 50 had been teenagers and young adults who did not fit easily into the roles assigned them. These improver men had been unconventional teenagers, often with artistic interests, often emotionally more expressive than the norm. They had tried to fit themselves into the norms for their culture, but by 40 they were unhappy. At that stage they kicked over the traces to at least some extent, and allowed some of their humor and creativity to flower. Similarly, the improver women had been more intellectual as teenagers (not so acceptable for girls of that generation), but had married at the usual time. By 40, they were irritable, thin-skinned, unhappy. When their children left home, they went back to school or found jobs they liked, and by 50 they had found avenues to express themselves more fully.

This analysis suggests that the *match* between the demands or expectations of a particular era and an individual's own temperament or interests may play a major role in shaping adult personality or psychological health. Those who fit easily into the niche assigned to them will move more comfortably through the early decades of adult life. Those who do not match well—either because they lack certain skills or because of basic temperament—will struggle far more. Some will not succeed in that struggle, perhaps turning to drugs or alcohol, becoming depressed, or moving through a series of unsuccessful relationships. Others, though, like the "improvers" Livson identified, will respond to the struggle with personal growth and will eventually find ways to express their own qualities. This may be particularly possible in middle age, when "detribalization" becomes acceptable and when the roles fit more loosely. For some, then, middle age offers an opportunity for individual expression that may not be so apparent in early adult life.

Divorce

Fifty to 60 percent of new marriages in the United States today will end in divorce; roughly 70 percent of those divorced adults will eventually remarry, and more than half of those remarried couples will divorce a second time (Gottman, 1994a). In Chapter 8 I talked about the substantial effects divorce has on children. Certainly it is no less disruptive for adults, and it may have significant consequences for the patterning or sequencing of adult roles.

Psychological Effects. At a psychological level, divorce is clearly a major stressor. It is associated with increases in both physical and emotional illness. Recently separated or divorced adults have more automobile accidents, are more likely to commit suicide, lose more days at work because of illness, and are more likely to become depressed (Bloom, White, & Asher, 1979; Menaghan & Lieberman, 1986; Stack, 1992a, 1992b; Stack & Wasserman, 1993). They also report strong feelings of failure and a loss of self-esteem, as well as loneliness (Chase-Lansdale & Hetherington, 1990).

One particularly good illustration of the impact of divorce on depression comes from Elizabeth Menaghan and Morton Lieberman's panel study (1986) of a group of Chicago adults first interviewed in 1972 and reinterviewed four years later. Of these subjects, 758 were married to the same spouse at both times, while 32 had been married at the first interview but were subsequently divorced. The married and the subsequently divorced had *not* differed significantly on a measure of depression when they were first interviewed, but the divorced were significantly more depressed after the divorce—a pattern shown in Figure 16.8. These negative effects are strongest in the first months after the separation or divorce, much as we see the most substantial effects for children during the first 12 to 24 months (Chase-Lansdale & Hetherington, 1990; Kitson, 1992).

Longer-term effects vary far more. Some adults seem to grow from the experience and show better psychological functioning five or ten years later than they had shown before the divorce. Others seem to be worse off psychologically, even ten years later (Wallerstein, 1986). It looks as if those who remarry are likely to be happier than those who remain single—yet another bit of evidence supporting the general conclusion that marriage (or a stable partnership) is linked to better mental and physical health. Yet for those whose second marriage ends in divorce, the negative consequences can be substantial (Spanier & Furstenberg, 1987). At the moment, the most we can say is that adults are highly heterogeneous in their responses to divorce. And we know very little about the factors that might predict good or poor long-term reactions, except that those adults with adequate social support are less disrupted in the short term (Chase-Lansdale & Hetherington, 1990).

CRITICAL THINKING

Another possible explanation of all these findings is that people who are already more depressed or unhealthy are more likely to divorce. What kind of evidence would you have to have to rule out this explanation?

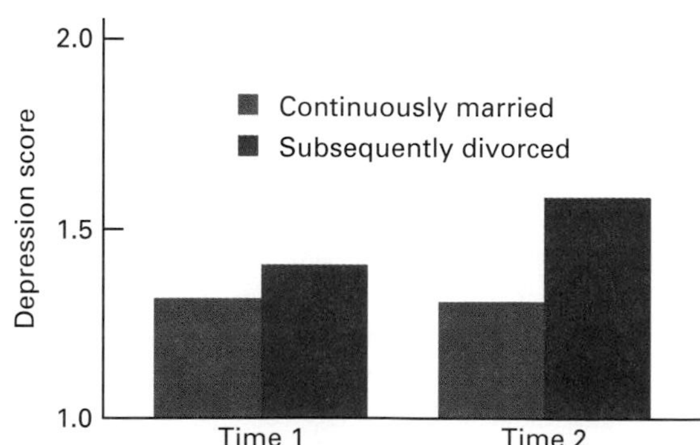

FIGURE 16.8 A clear example of the negative effect of divorce, based on longitudinal data. (*Source:* Menaghan & Lieberman, 1986, from Table 1, p. 323.)

Economic Effects. The psychological effects of divorce are often significantly exacerbated by serious economic effects, particularly for women. Because most men have had continuous work histories, they commonly leave a marriage with far greater earning power than do women. Women not only typically lack high earning capacity, they also usually retain custody of any children, with attendant costs. Several longitudinal studies in both the United States and European countries show that divorced men generally improve in their economic position, while divorced women are strongly adversely affected, with an average decline of 40 to 50 percent of household income (e.g., Morgan, 1991; Smock, 1993). Furthermore, this negative economic effect does not disappear quickly, if at all. The most reliable means of economic recovery for divorced women is remarriage, which brings most women back to near or above predivorce levels. For those women who do not remarry, however, the economic effects tend to persist.

Such a long-term economic loss from divorce is especially likely for working-class women or those with relatively low levels of education. Women who were earning above-average incomes before their divorce are more likely to recover financially, even if they do not remarry (Holden & Smock, 1991).

I do not want to minimize the stressful effects of this kind of economic hardship on divorcing women, but I find it very interesting that, despite their relative lack of economic stress, divorced men nonetheless seem to show more psychological symptoms than do divorced women. The difference may be linked to women's more intimate and extensive social support networks, which they use to very good effect in the aftermath of a divorce.

Age Differences in the Effects of Divorce. In the United States today, roughly half of all divorces occur within the first seven years of marriage, so the majority of divorces actually occur during early adulthood rather than middle adulthood (Uhlenberg, Cooney, & Boyd, 1990). Only about a quarter occur when the couple is over the age of 40. But divorce among middle-aged and older adults appears to be more emotionally disruptive than it is for younger adults (Bloom et al., 1979). This is precisely the opposite of what we see for widowhood, which is psychologically much more difficult if it occurs early in life. Both these patterns, of course, are consistent with the notion that being "off time" for any kind of life change or transition is more stressful. Divorce is not easy at any time, but among young adults in today's cohorts it is at least fairly common, and is thus "on time."

The economic impact of divorce may also be more severe during the middle adult years—at least for women—although we have no data that I know of to test this hypothesis. Certainly many middle-aged women in current cohorts have little or no work experience. After a divorce, such women—often called "displaced homemakers"—have very poor job prospects. They also have lower chances of remarriage than is true of younger women (Cherlin, 1992a). Younger divorced women in current cohorts, in contrast, may have better job skills but are more likely to have young children to rear, which considerably exacerbates their economic problems. Thus, the source of the economic problem may vary in different age groups, but the size of the problem may well be comparable.

Life Pathways. For many adults, divorce also affects the sequence and timing of family roles. Even though some divorced women have further children in a subsequent marriage, the average number of years of childbearing for divorced women is only slightly larger than what we see in women who remain married (Norton, 1983). In some cases, however, the total number of years of child *rearing* may be significantly larger for the divorced, especially for divorced men who remarry younger women with young children. One effect of this is to reduce the number of years a man (or woman) may have between the departure of the last child and the time when elder parents may need economic or physical assistance.

Divorce also brings a whole new set of roles. For a custodial parent, divorce means taking on those parenting roles previously filled by the now departed spouse. A divorced woman is also likely to take on a greatly expanded job role. And both men and women, custodial parent or not, must now deal with all the chores the spouse used to attend to, whatever they may have been in their relationship—fixing the leak in the roof, doing the grocery shopping, or taking clothes to the cleaners.

Remarriage frequently brings the remarkably complex role of stepparent. If several sets of children are involved, there may be stages added to the standard family role cycle. A women with children in elementary school may now find herself suddenly also the parent of teenagers, which demands different skills. Each of these changes seems to be accompanied by a new period of adaptation, often with considerable upheaval. If we think about this in Levinson's theoretical language, this means divorced/remarried adults have fewer opportunities to create stable life structures and have more periods of transition or crisis. Thus, divorce changes the *rhythm* of adult life, for good or ill.

Unemployment

Involuntary unemployment has effects that are remarkably similar to those of divorce. Adults who have been laid off from work or who are on extended strikes show heightened levels of anxiety and depression and higher risk of physical illness in the months after the job loss (Kessler, Turner, & House, 1988; Liem & Liem, 1988; Price, 1992). Such effects are not unique to workers in the United States. Equivalent results have been found in studies in England, Denmark, and in other Western developed countries (e.g., Iversen & Sabroe, 1988; Warr, Jackson, & Banks, 1988). You can see an example of this effect in Figure 16.9, which shows results from a study comparing 146 unemployed and 184 employed men and women in Michigan during the middle 1980s (Kessler et al., 1988). Interestingly, just as remarriage alleviates many of the stresses associated with divorce, reemployment seems to restore health, emotional stability, and the sense of well-being quite rapidly.

The causal chain linking unemployment and emotional or physical distress is both direct and indirect. The financial strain of job loss is itself a major contributor to the heightened levels of anxiety and depression. When job loss occurs without significant financial strain—such as when the spouse continues to work at a well-paying job, or the family has other resources—the negative effects of job loss is only about half as great (Kessler et al., 1988). We can also see indirect effects of job loss through changes in family relationships and from loss of self-esteem. Most strikingly, marital relationships deteriorate rapidly after one or the other spouse has

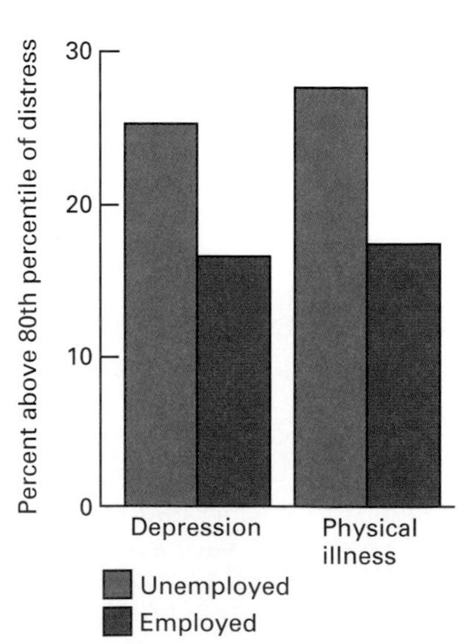

FIGURE 16.9 Adults who are involuntarily unemployed report more distress on nearly every measure, including both depression and physical illness, as in this study in Michigan. (*Source:* Kessler et al., 1988, from Table 2, p. 74.)

been laid off. The number of hostile or negative interactions increases and the number of warm and supportive interactions declines, which means that the crucial ratio of positive to negative spirals downward. Separation and divorce become much more common as a result (Conger, Patterson, & Ge, 1995; Crouter & McHale, 1993; Elder & Caspi, 1988; McLoyd et al., 1994).

You may wonder whether self-selection isn't at work here. You may remember from Caspi and Elder's research, which I mentioned in Chapter 1 (Caspi & Elder, 1988; Caspi et al., 1987, 1988), that ill-tempered children are more likely to change jobs often as adults. They may also be laid off more often, and thus be overrepresented in the ranks of the unemployed. But we know that this cannot be the whole story, because we see the same pattern of distress and discord in situations in which everyone employed in a single factory has been laid off, with no selection for the personality of the worker (e.g., Iversen & Sabroe, 1988). Longitudinal studies also show that even those who were psychologically very stable and healthy before becoming unemployed show increases in problems after being laid off (Warr et al., 1988).

Age Differences. These negative effects of unemployment are seen in both young and middle-aged adults, but those between 30 and 60 seem to show the largest effects—the greatest increases in physical illness and the biggest drops in mental health (Warr et al., 1988). This pattern makes some sense in terms of the stages of men's work lives I talked about in Chapter 14. During the trial stage, young adults between 18 and 29 may interpret periods of unemployment as a normal part of the trial-and-error process of finding the right job. But in the stabilization stage, workers may interpret job loss quite differently—either as a sign of personal failure, or as an unrecoverable loss of security. Younger workers are also more likely to be unmarried, with fewer economic responsibilities, and they may be able to return to live with their parents during their unemployed period. So for them, the stress is less pronounced.

Racial Differences. The dynamics of job loss appear to be much the same for workers of every racial group. For example, black unemployed, like other unemployed groups, show higher rates of distress and illness and lower levels of life satisfaction (Bowman, 1991). But in the United States and in most European countries, unemployment is considerably more common among blacks than whites. Vonnie McLoyd, who has studied the effects of black unemployment, says,

> Even in the best of times, the official unemployment rate of black workers typically is twice that of white workers. Blacks' increased vulnerability to unemployment is attributable to several factors, including lesser education, lesser skill training, less job seniority, fewer transportable job skills, and institutional barriers. (1990, p. 316)

What is more, recent structural changes in the U.S. economy have made this problem worse, because there has been heavy job loss in manufacturing and other blue-

In December of 1991, General Motors announced that over 74,000 employees would be laid off over the next few years. These men, who have just heard that they may lose their jobs, are likely to exhibit many symptoms of stress over the months to come.

collar job sectors in which black men are most likely to be employed. Black women, more often employed in the service sector, have been less severely affected by these recent changes. These two changes, in combination, have the effect of increasing still further the number of black families headed by women.

The magnitude of the effect of unemployment may also be larger for blacks than whites because it is so often accompanied by a lack of any sense of personal control over the situation. When jobs become increasingly scarce, even hard work and diligence will not necessarily pay off in reemployment. A sense of victimization is a common result, as is increased ill health and depression. Because many blacks, confronted with chronic racism or chronic urban poverty, are already functioning at very high levels of stress, unemployment increases the risks proportionately more.

The Role of Social Support. As with all types of stress, the effects of unemployment can be partially buffered by having adequate social support (Vinokur & van Ryn, 1993). The irony, of course, is that one of the effects of unemployment is to weaken the marital relationship, which may be the central source of social support for many men.

The Effects of Timing

The pattern of effects of both divorce and unemployment fits the general principle that being "off time" or atypical in your life trajectory has specific psychological costs. Divorce and unemployment are both more stressful for middle-aged adults because both stresses are less common, less "normative," in this age group.

There are other midlife examples of this same principle. If your children do not leave the nest by the time they are 25 or so, you are likely to feel extra strain, even a sense of failure (Hagestad, 1986); those who become grandparents unusually early or unusually late seem to be less comfortable with the role (Burton & Bengtson, 1985; Troll, 1985); those whose parents die early find themselves unexpectedly thrust into the role of family "elders" before they are ready for that designation. As one 40-year-old man whose parents had both just died said, "I'm too young to be next in line!" (Hagestad, 1986).

All these are examples in which the person's life does not follow the pattern of the "expected life history." We may not be consciously aware of this set of expectations, this internal model of the "normal" or "expected" adult life, but we seem to be significantly and negatively affected by any violations of the anticipated pattern.

Are All Crises Negative?

In Chinese, the characters that form the word "crisis" mean both danger and opportunity (Levinson, 1990). Mindful of this point, perhaps we ought to look to see whether crisis also has a less negative side. Indeed many theories of adult development have as one of their cornerstone concepts the notion that stress or crisis can be transformative rather than (or in addition to) being disruptive. Erikson's theory has some of this element, as does Carl Jung's. Morton Lieberman and Harvey Peskin (1992) suggest several examples:

> The envy of youth in middle age may mobilize untapped resources of caring . . . ; the keener awareness of death in middle age may permit a more equanimous attitude toward one's mortality, a lessening of strivings for perfection, and a new realization of creative potential . . . ; the death of a loved parent may help free the survivor to become more his or her own person. (p. 132)

Whether some kind of stress or crisis is *required* for psychological growth is another matter, although some such link makes a certain amount of sense. Just as it is pain that usually tells us that something is wrong with our physical body, so unhappiness or anguish may be necessary to get our attention, to tell us that we need to change in some way. Marriages may become deeper and more intimate if the couple has been through difficult times and learned how to communicate better; early widow-

Critical Thinking

Can you think of any examples in your own life, times when you have learned something constructive, or grown in some fashion, because of a crisis? Can you also think of an opposite example—instances in which you have experienced a crisis or a major life change that led to distress or suffering, but that did not seem to bring any redeeming growth?

Cultures and Contexts

Very Early Grandparenthood in Black Families

The impact of being "off time" is vividly illustrated in a study by Linda Burton and Vern Bengtson (1985) of a group of 41 black families in Los Angeles, each of which included a new mother, a grandmother, and a great-grandmother. Each generation was divided into those who were "early" and those who were "on time" for being in that particular role. For the grandmothers, being on time was defined as becoming a grandmother between 42 and 57; early grandmothers had all acquired the role before they were 38, several of them in their 20s. The large majority of these grandmothers had at least a high school education; few were on welfare. So these are mostly working-class or middle-class families.

What is striking is how different the experience of grandmotherhood was for those who were early as opposed to those who were on time. Early grandmothers reported far more strain and distress. In part this occurs because these young grandmothers are still in early adulthood themselves, with all that that signifies about role conflict and role overload. Many of these early grandmothers still had their own young children at home to rear. They were distressed to have the role of grandparent added to the list, especially if they expected to have to take on some of the task of rearing this grandchild.

But the off-timeness itself also seems to be disturbing. These women associate grandparenthood with being "old," and they do not want to feel old.

> I could break my daughter's neck for having this baby. I just got a new boyfriend. Now he will think I'm too old. It was bad enough being a mother so young—now a grandmother too! (Burton & Bengtson, 1985, p. 61)

So speaks a 28-year-old grandmother. Another who became a grandmother at 27 said, "I'm too young to be a grandmother. You made this baby, you take care of it" (p. 61). Many of these very early grandmothers did end up helping to rear their new grandchildren, but clearly they were less than thrilled by this task. In contrast, women in this study who became grandmothers at the normative time were much more willing to participate in the new child's care, and much more pleased about becoming grandmothers.

Many confounding factors are clearly involved here. Very early grandmothers must, of necessity, have been early mothers themselves, so they are a different group to begin with. But these results are consistent with what else we know about the impact of being on time or off time in major life transitions.

hood may force a young woman to develop her own skills in a way she would not have done otherwise.

Some longitudinal researchers have found a few hints of such positive effects of stress. Glen Elder, for example, notes that many teenagers whose families suffered severe economic hardship during the Great Depression of the 1930s were *more* successful as adults than were their peers whose families had had an easier time financially (Elder, 1979). And Norma Haan, in her analysis of the results of the Berkeley/Oakland study, has found that adults who were physically ill more often in their early adult years were rated as more empathetic and more tolerant of ambiguity in late middle age (Haan, 1982).

I am not at all trying to downplay the stressful effects of major life changes or crises. Psychological pain and suffering do not invariably (or even often) lead to personal growth; more often they lead to depression, illness, or other manifestations of distress. But I do want to raise the possibility that pain or crisis or stress may be necessary—although not sufficient—for some kinds of psychological growth, just as the oyster creates a pearl only if a grain of sand is inside the shell. At the very least, I find this a comforting hypothesis because it suggests that there is always something to be gained from every painful experience. I would find life a good deal more discouraging if I did not believe that such growth is possible.

Summary

1. By a number of measures, the years of middle adulthood are less stressful and happier than early adulthood.

2. Marital satisfaction is typically higher at midlife than earlier. This appears to be due primarily to a drop in problems and negative encounters.

3. Middle-aged adults have significant family interactions both up and down the generational chain, creating a "generational squeeze" or "sandwich generation." Middle adults provide more assistance in both directions and attempt to influence both preceding and succeeding generations.
4. Individual families appear to have particular sets of topics or activities that serve as conversational glue between the generations.
5. There is little sign that middle-aged parents experience negative reactions at the time of the "empty nest," when the last child leaves home. On the contrary, the reduction in role demands may contribute to the rise in life satisfaction at this age.
6. Most adults become grandparents in middle age. The majority have warm, affectionate relationships with their grandchildren, although there are also many remote relationships. A minority of grandparents are involved in day-to-day care of grandchildren.
7. Only a minority of middle-aged adults seem to take on the role of significant caregiver for an aging parent. Those who do, particularly if the parent suffers from some form of dementia, report considerable burden and suffer increased depression.
8. Women are two to four times as likely as men to fill the role of caregiver to a frail elder.
9. Friendships appear to be somewhat less numerous in middle adulthood, although they appear to be as intimate and central to the individual.
10. Work satisfaction is at its peak in middle adulthood, and work productivity remains high. But the centrality of the work role appears to wane somewhat, and work satisfaction is less clearly linked to overall life satisfaction than at earlier ages.
11. Middle-aged adults prepare for retirement in several ways, not only by specific planning but also by reducing the number of hours they work.
12. Many different models of personality change in middle adulthood have been proposed, but none has been strongly supported. Personality changes during middle adulthood are less clearly shared than are changes seen in early adulthood. There are some signs of "mellowing," a lowering of intensity and striving, but middle-aged adults vary more in personality traits than is true at earlier ages.
13. Variations in experiences of life changes and crises may account for some of the variation in personality patterns. Divorce, for example, increases emotional distress and physical illness, and may permanently alter the role path and the financial status of an adult, particularly divorced women.
14. Job loss also brings increased risk of emotional distress and physical illness, both directly via loss of economic security, and indirectly via deterioration of marital relationships and loss of self-esteem.
15. The negative impact of both divorce and job loss appears to be larger among middle-aged adults than among young adults. For both types of crisis, negative consequences are mitigated for those adults with adequate social support.
16. Any role change or crisis that is off-time, that deviates from normative expectations for that cohort or that culture, is associated with higher levels of stress, including very early grandparenthood, early death of one's parents, and late departure of grown children from the home.
17. Some theorists argue that crises may lead to growth as well as to distress. Indeed, crisis or significant life change may be necessary for psychological growth to occur. This remains an open question.

Suggested Readings

Cherlin, A. J., & Furstenberg, F. F., Jr. (1986). *The new American grandparent*. New York: Basic Books.

A nicely written book, aimed at the lay reader rather than fellow psychologists, that describes the authors' own and others' research on grandparents.

Cherlin, A. J. (1992). *Marriage, divorce, remarriage*. Cambridge, MA: Harvard University Press.

This is a wonderful update of a fine book, written in a very clear and interesting style.

Hagestad, G. O. (1984). The continuous bond: A dynamic, multigenerational perspective on parent-child relations between adults. In M. Perlmutter (Ed.), *Minnesota symposia on child psychology*, Vol. 17 (pp. 129–158). Hillsdale, NJ: Lawrence Erlbaum Associates.

All Hagestad's papers are excellent; if you are interested in family interactions and cross-generational relations you might profitably read any of her papers listed in the bibliography at the end of the book. This one is particularly good.

Vaillant, G. E. (1977). *Adaptation to life: How the best and brightest came of age*. Boston: Little, Brown.

This is a fascinating report of the lives of 100 of the men included in the Grant study of Harvard men. At the time this book was written, the men had been followed into early middle age. Vaillant gives many intriguing case studies, which will give you a feel for the wide variations in adult pathways.

Weiss, R. S. (1990). *Staying the course: The emotional and social lives of men who do well at work*. New York: The Free Press.

The men described in this book are a particular subset, namely those who have achieved well in demanding careers. But because many of you aim to be such men, or will marry such men, you will find this book fascinating.

Interlude 6

Summing Up Middle Adult Development

Basic Characteristics of the Middle Adult Period

I've summarized the changes seen in these middle adult years in the table on page 445, but in this case the summary does not capture the most interesting aspects of this age period. What strikes me most about this period is how full of paradoxes it seems.

The most obvious paradox lies in the juxtaposition of high levels of marital and work satisfaction with a growing awareness of physical decline. A second lies in the fact that the tight grip of family and work roles loosens considerably in these years, but that this is also a time when many of us acquire several new roles over which we have little personal control. We enter the postparental stage when the last child leaves home; we become grandparents when our children have children; we take on the task of caring for aging parents only if they become too ill or disabled to care for themselves. While we may have some influence over the process of our children leaving home, we have little or no influence over the timing of grandchildren or over our parents' health or disability.

The easing of the demands of such central roles as parent and worker is also part of another paradox, because this change creates an increased sense of choice. We have more options about how to fill individual roles and fewer clear rules about how we must behave. Yet at the same time, middle adults also seem to feel some decline in their sense of personal control. For example, Brandtstädter (Brandtstädter & Baltes-Götz, 1990) has both longitudinal and cross-sectional data from his study in Germany showing that between age 40 and age 60, adults increasingly feel that their ability to achieve their goals is affected by conditions beyond their control. But Brandtstädter also found that these same adults increased between ages 40 and 60 in the sense that their ability to reach personal goals depends on their own actions. Thus, middle-aged adults have *both* an increased sense of choice *and* an increased awareness that uncontrollable forces are at work, such as a potential decline in their own health or in the health of their parents.

It may seem impossible that both these things could be simultaneously true, but if you think about specific examples it makes perfectly good sense. As I move through my 40s and 50s, I may understand more and more that maintaining good friendships requires effort on my part, but also realize that I have no control over the timing of the death of my friends; I may become increasingly aware that my day-to-day health is affected by whether I exercise and watch my diet, and still have a growing awareness of the extent to which I have no control over basic disease processes.

Central Processes

What obviously lies behind these apparent paradoxes is a set of changes in the centrality of the biological and social clocks in this middle adult period. In early adulthood, the social clock is positively deafening while the biological clock is all but inaudible. In middle adulthood, the two are far more balanced in their effects: The social clock becomes less and the biological clock more significant. The weakening of the social clock gives rise to that increased sense of choice and personal control, while the ascendancy of the biological clock contributes to the sense of loss of control.

The Biological Clock

It is certainly during these years that the first signs of aging become visible to most of us. We may need to wear glasses for the first time; hair begins to turn white; skin becomes more noticeably wrinkled; it becomes harder to climb several flights of stairs and harder to regain fitness after losing it. I pointed out repeatedly in Chapter 15 that most of these changes are quite gradual, with wide individual variability in timing. But it is impossible to move through the middle adult years without awareness of *some* physical decline or deterioration.

David Karp (1988) has documented the growing awareness of this change in a wonderfully evocative series of interviews with men and women in their 50s. This is by no means a random sample. All 72 subjects were white; all worked in professional occupations. We simply don't know whether working-class or minority adults in this culture (let alone adults in other cultures) would describe their experiences in the same terms. Still, this study gives us a rare in-depth view of the experiences of middle-aged adults, for whom, as Karp says, "the fact of aging seems to be one of life's great surprises" (p. 729).

The surprise is sprung from both the body and the culture. The body messages include all the many manifestations of slowing down. One of the men Karp interviewed said:

> I'm getting more creakiness. I'm snoring at night. I can still appreciate

A Summary of the Threads of Development During Middle Adulthood					
Aspect of Development	**Age in Years**				
	40	**45**	**50**	**55**	**65**
Physical development	Many types of physical changes become visible between 40 and 50, including vision changes, decline in aerobic capacity, skin changes, slowing of nervous system and hence reaction time.		Menopause in women. Increased bone loss. Increased loss of muscle tissue.		Increased rate of hearing loss.
Cognitive development	IQ increases to about age 50 or 55, then shows very gradual decline. Earlier loss on less practiced skills, e.g., spatial visualization.				
	Little change in memory until fairly late in this period, although there is some loss of speed of recall.				
Personality development	Erikson's stage of generativity.				
				Erikson's stage of ego integrity versus despair.	
		Some signs of "mellowing" after the peak of individuality, assertiveness, and confidence at 40–45.			
Roles and Relationships		Empty nest: last child leaves home.			
		Grandparent role acquired by most adults.			
			May take on role as caregiver of aging parent.		
	Work roles become less prominent; gradual decline in hours worked; preparation for retirement.				
		Heightened marital satisfaction.			

beauty in a woman certainly, but you know, the testosterone is not quite there. I've also been noticing it with my kid over the last few years. My kid was playing baseball and I wasn't getting down for the ground balls as much. We'd go down to the field and I'd say, "John, instead of those ground balls, why don't you hit me some fly balls." And I wouldn't go out so far because it was harder for me to throw the balls in. I noticed those changes. (p. 730)

The cultural messages may be more subtle, but they are potent. Younger adults begin to treat you as an "older person," which may mean that you get either more respect or less, depending on the circumstances. Or you may find yourself eligible for various programs for "senior citizens." As just one example, I was quite shocked to be invited to join the American Association of Retired Persons when I turned 50: "Wait just a minute! I'm not retired yet."

Generational reminders also come from the increasing infirmity or death of one's own parents. One of Karp's subjects said, "As I see my father becoming physically impaired I know it's going to happen to me eventually" (p. 731).

There are also generational reminders from now adult children, and from young people encountered at work. Most of us in this age range have become aware that young people seem much younger than they used to! Yet the paradox remains, because virtually all Karp's subjects said that they still *felt* young on the inside. The inner picture of ourselves we have at 40 or 50 or 60 does not yet include the gray hair, the wrinkles, the slower body. So adults in this age period experience repeated moments of shock, when the body reminders and the cultural and generational reminders jog their awareness yet again that they are indeed aging.

The Social Clock

At the same time, adults in middle age frequently feel a sense of being at the height of their powers, of having learned the ropes and now being able to make things happen. One of Karp's subjects put it this way: "I'm more seeing myself as not just a beginner . . . but as having arrived" (p. 729). Others talk of an increased sense of the value of accumulated experience, even wisdom. Many talk of seeing their life in a more holistic way, from a larger perspective—perhaps a beginning of the process Erikson calls ego integrity.

This increased sense of knowledge, wisdom, and perspective seems to be one of the fruits of having learned the roles of early adulthood, and then of having found one's own individuality through the process Levinson calls detribalization. But a greater sense of control and choice also emerges because at least some of the dominant roles of early adulthood have become considerably less demanding. In particular, the role of parent, which consumes an enormous amount of time and energy for perhaps 20 years, now becomes far more occasional and part time. Inevitably, this means that middle-aged adults have more time and energy for other roles, including the role of spouse or partner. The gradual reduction in the dominance of the work role over these same years also means that adults have more time and energy for other roles, perhaps including involvement in community activities, or with friends. Many middle-aged adults reap the benefits of these changes in the form of increased marital and work satisfaction.

Influences on the Basic Processes

The extent to which any given adult will experience middle adulthood in these ways is obviously affected by a whole host of things, three of which seem particularly significant: health, the timing of family and work events, and the existence of crises and unanticipated life changes.

Health

Probably the biggest single factor influencing the individual experience of middle adulthood is health. Most adults are still quite healthy in these years. But for the minority who experience significant ill health in their 50s and 60s, the recognition of physical aging is far more profound, and the sense of choice and control is far less apparent. Among the Harvard men in the Grant study, for example, the two events that were most likely to shift a man in midlife from good to poor psychological adjustment were either a significant deterioration of health or alcoholism (Vaillant & Vaillant, 1990).

Similarly, those who retire in their 50s and 60s are most likely to do so because of ill health. Such adults may find themselves in straitened financial circumstances, without fully adequate pensions. And certainly their sense of control and choice is much lower than what we see in an individual who can select the timing of her or his retirement. Not surprisingly, adults who retire early because of ill health also enjoy their retirement far less and are more likely to be depressed (Palmore et al., 1985).

The Timing of Family and Work Roles

Another highly significant influence on the experience of middle adulthood is the precise timing of various family or work events, most potently the timing of childbearing. There are both cohort and individual differences in such timing. For example, women born in 1920 in the United States gave birth to their last child at the average age of about 31. For such women, the postparental period began at roughly age 55. Because these same women had a life expectancy of about 73 years, they could expect to live only about 18 years after their last child left home. In contrast, the average woman born in 1950, now in middle adulthood, had her last child at the age of 25 and could expect to live to the age of about 80, which gives a net increase of 13 postparental years, half of which are in middle adulthood.

The same logic obviously applies to individuals. Those who bear their children late are reducing their postparental years, and thus delaying the point in their lives at which the social clock becomes less dominant. These are not trivial differences, and they contribute greatly to the wide degree of variability in adults' experience of middle adulthood.

The timing of various work experiences, such as promotions, doubtless affects the shape of middle adulthood as well, although we have less direct evidence here. Someone who is still moving up an occupational ladder in her (or his) 40s and 50s may continue to place the work role in a central position in her life far more than is true of someone whose career topped out at 35. Bray and Howard's study of AT&T managers (1983), for example, shows that those men who had moved furthest up the corporate hierarchy were more satisfied with their jobs in their 40s and 50s than were those who stopped advancing at an earlier age. Interestingly, however, they were not more satisfied with their lives overall, and were not better adjusted.

Findings like these underline yet again the wide variability among middle-aged adults in their experience of these years. Many pathways can lead to life satisfaction in middle age. For some, satisfaction continues to be found through work. Many more adults seem to find it in their partnership, or in other family and personal relationships.

Crises

Middle adulthood, like early adulthood, is also shaped by the various unanticipated life changes and crises each adult must

confront. The years from 40 to 65 are very different for a divorced woman with few job skills than for a woman of the same age in an intact marriage who has a successful career. They are different for a man who is laid off from his steady job at age 50 and who cannot readily find other work than they are for a man who experiences no interruption in employment. Economic differences are not the only effects of such variations, although they may be substantial. Those who have experienced many crises, many losses, are more likely to experience episodes of ill health, and are less likely to feel that they have control over their own choices and opportunities. And of course both ill health and a sense of helplessness have widespread repercussions in many other areas of life.

Yet it may well be how an adult copes with such crises, rather than the crises themselves, that is most significant in shaping the experience of middle adulthood. In Vaillant's study of the Harvard men who participated in the Grant Study, for example, one of the best predictors of good health and emotional adjustment at age 65 was the *lack* of use of mood-altering drugs (such as tranquilizers) or alcohol at age 45 (Vaillant & Vaillant, 1990). Another good predictor was the maturity of the defense mechanisms the men had used at 45. Those who looked worst at 65 were those who had been most likely to deal with middle-aged crises by denial or repression, while those who were well-adjusted and healthy at 65 had used less reality-distorting defenses. The 45-year-olds who had turned to drugs or alcohol, and those who used less mature forms of defense, had not actually faced any more crises than had the more mature men. But they had dealt with those crises and strains quite differently.

So what determines how an individual deals with crisis or life strains? One obvious answer is personality. McCrae and Costa have some evidence that adults who are high in neuroticism are more likely to react to crises in self-defeating ways. And you've already seen Caspi's data, from the Berkeley/Oakland studies, showing that childhood or adolescent personality patterns such as shyness or ill-temper predict a number of aspects of the adult life course. I also mentioned in the Across Development box in Chapter 16 that both Vaillant and the Berkeley researchers have found that those adults who look healthiest and most psychologically mature at age 40 or 50 are those who came from warmer families, and who had higher self-esteem in adolescence and early adulthood.

But personality is not destiny. All the relevant correlations are comparatively small, so many adults who begin with several strikes against them nonetheless respond well to the normal crises of adult life, moving into and through middle adulthood with grace and growth. And many adults who appear to have everything going for them nonetheless falter in the face of normal (or extraordinary) crises, beginning a downward spiral, often including alcohol or drugs or depression. As yet we know painfully little about what may cause such variations. But I think this is one of the crucial questions if we are to understand either middle adulthood or the whole of adult life.

Physical and Mental Changes in Late Adulthood

17

We turn now, finally, to the seventh of the "seven ages of man," the time of old age. Shakespeare had a dim view of this final stage of the life span. In *As You Like It,* he described it as "second childishness, and mere oblivion, sans [without] teeth, sans eyes, sans taste, sans everything." This is certainly no longer an accurate

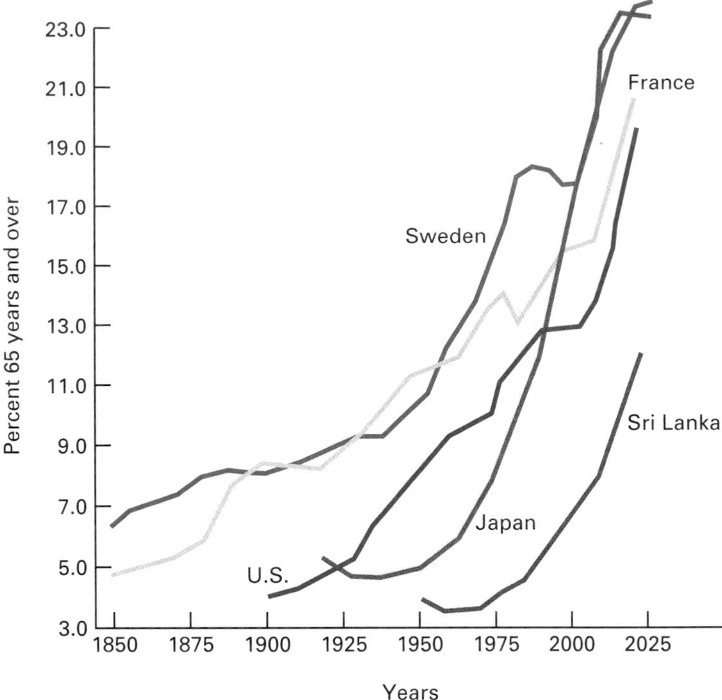

FIGURE 17.1 The rapid recent rise in the percentage of older adults in the population is not restricted to the United States. (*Source:* Myers, 1990, Figure 2-2, p. 27.)

One effect of the "graying" of the population is an increase in political power for the elderly, through organizations like the Gray Panthers or the American Association of Retired Persons, which is already one of the largest and most politically powerful lobbying groups in the country.

description of the years of old age in many parts of the world. But most lifespan theorists do at least agree with Shakespeare that old age is the seventh stage.

One of the most striking demographic changes in the past few decades, ranking right up there with the massive increase in women's labor force participation, has been the rapid graying of the population of the world. The rather astonishing numbers are given in Figure 17.1, which shows the percentage of the population that is age 65 or older in each of several countries, projected up to the year 2025. This change has been more pronounced in developed countries, but some increase has occurred in every part of the world (Myers, 1990). The increase in life expectancy obviously plays a significant role in this change. Another major contributor is the existence of the exceptionally large baby boom cohorts, born after World War II and now just starting to hit 50. As they begin to turn 65, in the year 2010, they will greatly swell the ranks of the elderly. By 2040, when most of the baby boomers will have died, the rate of expansion of the elderly population will drop sharply.

This demographic change will have a variety of effects, both obvious and subtle, on the culture of every country affected by it. Pension plans, including Social Security, will be severely strained; health care spending will rise dramatically; nursing homes and other health care delivery systems will come under increasing pressure. We will also undoubtedly see changes in the style or form of advertising on television and elsewhere as ads are increasingly aimed at the elderly. Within families, longer-lived elders and smaller families may mean that a larger and larger percentage of middle-aged adults will need to take on the role of caregiver for a frail elder. Every segment of society will have to adjust in some fashion to this remarkable change in the age distribution of the population.

Critical Thinking

Can you think of other effects on society that this increase in the proportion of elders will have?

Subgroups of the Elderly

It would be a mistake, though, to think of the "elderly" as a single group. You'll recall that gerontologists these days divide the later years into the *young old* (60–75), the *old old* (75–85) and the *oldest old* (85 and up). The oldest old are the fastest-growing segment of the population in the United States at present. These three subgroups differ significantly in their risk of significant disability or ill health. In addition, a number of measures of physical and mental functioning show a more rapid decline among the old old than among the young old, including total IQ, hearing loss, and aerobic capacity.

Yet I do not want to overemphasize the distinction among these three age groups. If psychologists and gerontologists have learned anything in the past few decades of research, it is that the process of aging is highly individual. Some adults at 65 are already disabled; others are still full of vim and vigor at 85 or older. Perhaps it would be better, in fact, to distinguish between healthy and unhealthy elderly. Still, frailty is far more likely in an individual over the age of 75 than in one between 65 and 75, and among the oldest old it is the norm. The distinction between young old and old old may also help us to keep in mind that aging is not something that happens rapidly at age 65. But it is equally important to keep in mind that the needs and abilities of elders in each age group vary enormously.

Life Expectancy

Let's begin with the most basic information: How much longer can a person of 65 expect to live? You've already seen some basic figures on life expectancy at age 40 in Figure 15.1. Table 17.1 tells you how many more years a person of 65, 75, 85, or 95 can expect to live. The table also shows the average number of years of *active life expectancy*, which is defined as the number of additional years without a disability that would interfere with a person's ability to take care of her own daily needs. For comparison purposes, I've also shown life expectancy at 65 and 75 for Japanese adults (Liu et al., 1995).

Several things are clear from these data. First of all, note that Japanese adults live longer than U.S. adults—a useful piece of information to help us avoid the typical ethnocentric view that the United States has the best health and the best health

***Table 17.1* Life Expectancy and Active Life Expectancy for Adults over 65 in the United States and Japan**

	U.S. Women		U.S. Men		Japanese Adults
At Age	Total Life Expectancy	Active Life Expectancy	Total Life Expectancy	Active Life Expectancy	Total Life Expectancy
65	18.6*	13.6	14.4*	11.9	18.9
75	11.7	7.0	9.0	6.4	11.2
85	6.4	2.3	5.2	2.6	—
95	3.7	0.4	3.2	0.6	—

*The 1992 numbers, which are the most recently available Census Bureau figures, are 19.2 years for women and 15.4 years for men aged 65 (U.S. Bureau of the Census, 1995). But the Census Bureau does not yet provide 1992 data for 75-, 85-, or 95-year-olds.

Source: U.S. data: Manton & Stallard, 1991, Table 4, p. S179. Japanese data: Liu et al., 1995, Table 6, p. S391.

The Real World

Institutionalization Among Older Adults

Table 17.1 tells us that the average older adult will spend at least a few years with some kind of disability. How often does disability mean nursing home care? There are several answers to that question, depending on what statistics you look at.

One frequently quoted statistic is that only 5.1 percent of all adults over 65 in the United States are in any kind of institutional care (Pynoos & Golant, 1996). More women are in nursing homes than men, and among the oldest old, 24.5 percent are in nursing homes. Still, these numbers may be lower than you would have guessed.

A second important piece of information is the estimate that the average 65-year-old U.S. man can expect to spend about five months in such an institution before he dies. The average woman can expect to spend 16 to 17 months (Manton, Stallard, & Liu, 1993). But neither of these statistical approaches tells us what is perhaps the most important piece of information: What is the probability that any given 65-year-old will spend time in a nursing home or other institution? In the United States, that probability is about 40 percent (Belgrave, Wykle, & Choi, 1993; Kane & Kane, 1990). That is, roughly 40 percent of current older adults can expect to spend at least some time in a nursing home before death. If we put these several pieces of data together, it looks as if some kind of institutional care is common but by no means universal in the years of late adulthood, and that such care is most often fairly brief. Only a quarter of those over 65 can expect to spend as long as a year in a nursing home.

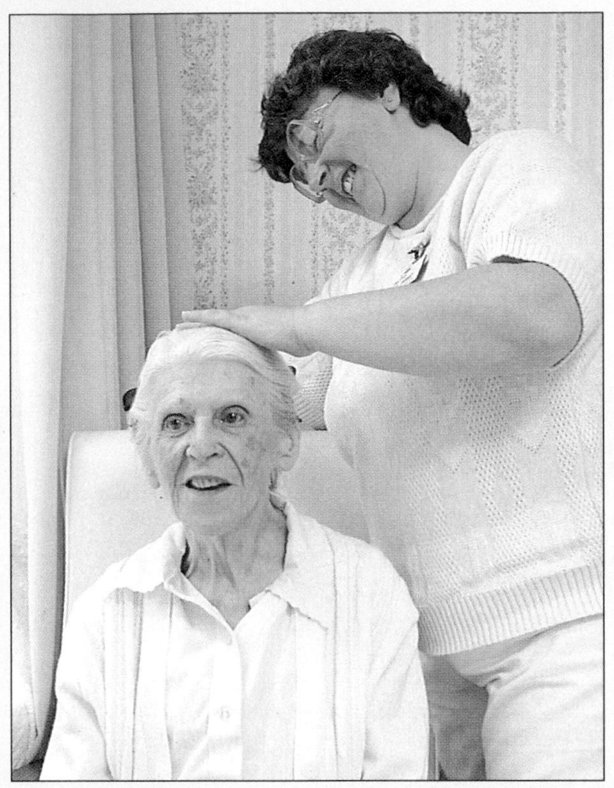

When we look at the actual experiences of those in nursing homes, we find both rosy and gloomy pictures. It is true that placement in a nursing home is often followed by death within a relatively short space of time. But it is *not* true that nursing home care necessarily *shortens* a person's life over what it might have been in home care or some other setting. Only when an older adult has been *involuntarily* moved to an institution (or to any other living situation) is there evidence that the move itself is a causal factor in rapid decline and death. Involuntarily institutionalized elders show much higher death rates in the ensuing months and years than do equivalently disabled elders who remain at home (Lawton, 1985, 1990), although even this effect is not inevitable. When the institution itself is one with high levels of warmth, individuation, and opportunity for choice and control, even an involuntary move need not accelerate the process of physical or mental decline (Fields, 1992).

The moral of the story is that it would be wise for each of us to plan ahead for our own older years, so that should some kind of institutional care become necessary—as it well might—we will have maximum say in the matter.

care in the world. Second, the U.S. data show, once again, that women live longer than men. This difference gets slightly smaller with increasing age but does not disappear. Finally, these numbers illustrate yet again a point I made in Chapter 15: Women may live longer, but they are more often disabled. A woman of 65 can expect to spend roughly twice as many years with some kind of disability as will a man. Still, three-quarters of her remaining time is likely to be free of such disability, so the picture is not as gloomy as it may look at first.

Physical Changes in Specific Body Systems

I have already sketched the overall pattern of change and decline in various body systems during adulthood in Chapters 13 and 15, so you know that some loss of function begins at age 30 or 40 for virtually all body systems and then continues gradually through the remainder of life—a pattern very like the general shape of the curve Denney proposed in her overall model of cognitive and physical change in adulthood (Figure 13.5, page 348). A few of these gradual changes result in significant loss of function during middle adulthood, such as in vision and, for women, in bone mass. But most such changes do not lead to noticeable or significant *functional* loss until past 65. Let me talk about a few of the more important losses in more detail.

Changes in the Brain

If you look back at Table 13.1, you'll see four main changes in the brain during the adult years: a reduction of brain weight, a loss of gray matter, a loss of density in the dendrites, and slower synaptic speed.

The most central of these changes is the loss of dendritic density. You'll remember from Chapter 4 that during the first few years after birth, dendrites are "pruned," with redundant or unused pathways eliminated. The loss of dendrites in middle and late adulthood does not seem to be pruning of this same type. Rather, there appears to be a real loss of useful dendritic connections. Figure 17.2 illustrates the change.

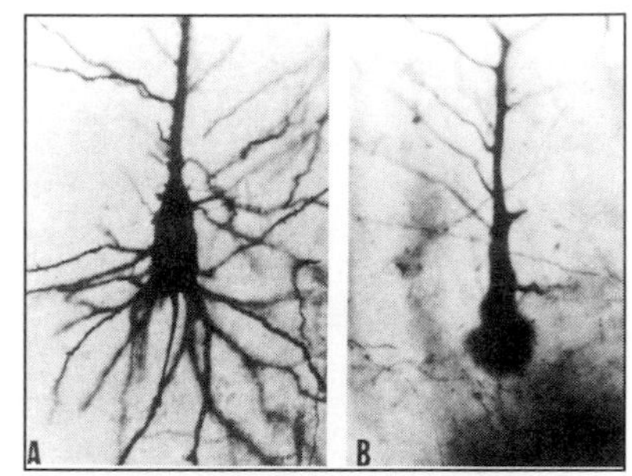

FIGURE 17.2 Changes in the density of dendrites with age are clear in these photos of a neuron from a normal mature adult (a) and in a normal 80-year-old (b). (*Source:* Scheibel, 1992, Figure 5, p. 160.)

This dendritic loss is apparently not equally distributed over the brain. In some brain regions there may actually be continued increases in dendritic density in old age (Scheibel, 1992). But there is little doubt that overall, the synaptic structure of the brain becomes less dense and less efficient. The reduction of total brain weight and the specific loss of gray matter both appear to be consequences of this reduced density of dendrites (Lim et al., 1992).

Dendritic loss also results in a gradual slowing of synaptic speed, with consequent slowing of reaction time in many everyday tasks. Neural pathways are redundant enough that it is nearly always possible to find some route from neuron A to neuron B, or from neuron A to some muscle cell. But with the increasing loss of dendrites, the shortest route may be lost, so reaction time increases. David Morgan (1992) refers to this process as a loss of "synaptic plasticity."

One final change in the nervous system, about which there is a good deal of dispute among physiologists, is the loss of neurons themselves. For many years the standard statement in texts was that 100,000 neurons were lost every day in adult life. It now appears that this conclusion, like many such conclusions about primary aging, was based on cross-sectional comparisons that included many older adults with specific pathologic conditions, such as Alzheimer's disease, that are known to affect brain composition and functioning. Researchers have not yet reached a consensus on just how much loss occurs among healthy aging adults (e.g., Finch, 1986; Ivy et al., 1992; Scheibel, 1996), but most agree 100,000 neurons lost per day is a considerable overestimation. Note, too, that even if there really were a daily loss of 100,000 neurons, the number of neurons in the brain is so vast that the proportion lost over a lifetime would be very small. Current estimates are that the brain has perhaps one *trillion* neurons (Morgan, 1992). A loss of 100,000 per day, even if it began at birth and lasted for a lifespan of 100 years, would only be about 4 billion neurons, leaving the vast majority still intact.

The key point is that the number of neurons and dendrites is so huge that enormous redundancies are built into the system. It is only when significant interconnectivity is lost, which occurs as dendrites shrink in number, that "computational power" declines and symptoms of old age appear (Scheibel, 1992, p. 168).

Changes in the Senses

Vision. I talked about the basic processes of presbyopia in Chapter 15, changes that continue in late adulthood. But vision in old age is also affected by a variety of other body changes. For example, blood flow to the eye decreases (perhaps a side effect of atherosclerosis), which results in an enlarged "blind spot" on the retina and thus a reduced field of vision. The pupil does not widen or narrow as much or as quickly either, which means that the older adult has more difficulty seeing at night and responding to rapid changes in brightness, such as glare (Kline & Scialfa, 1996). And a significant minority of older adults suffer from diseases of the eye, such as cataracts or glaucoma, that further diminish visual acuity and adaptability. For example, among U.S. adults under age 65, only about 2 percent suffer from cataracts; for those over 75, the rate is roughly ten times as high (U.S. Bureau of the Census, 1995). Collectively, these changes mean that many more older adults must adapt to significant impairments of vision.

Hearing. You'll recall from Chapter 15 that wear and tear on the auditory system results in some hearing loss (presbycusis) beginning in middle adulthood, but these gradual losses don't typically add up to functionally significant loss until late adulthood. National statistics in the United States suggest that about 14 percent of middle-aged adults have some "hearing impairment," while for those over 65 this rate more than doubles (U.S. Bureau of the Census, 1995). Table 17.2 breaks this down further for the young old and the old old, showing the steady rise in hearing problems. The table also shows that auditory problems, unlike many other disabilities of old age, are more likely to be experienced by men than by women. This sex difference is normally attributed to differential exposure to noise, because more men, at least in current cohorts of older adults in developed countries, have worked in environments with high levels of noise.

A third or more of older adults have some significant hearing loss. Whether this loss interferes with daily living depends on how severe it is and how well the individual can compensate. This man appears to be handling the problem well with the use of a hearing aid.

Late adult hearing difficulties have several components:

- *Loss of ability to hear high-frequency sounds.* Both cross-sectional and longitudinal studies suggest that, for the range of sounds in normal human speech (between 500 and 2000 hertz), the loss after age 60 is such that a given sound has to be about one to two decibels louder each year for the individual to report that he hears it (Fozard, 1990; Kline & Scialfa, 1996).
- *Difficulties in word discrimination.* Even when the sound is loud enough, older adults have more difficulty identifying individual words they have just heard (Schieber, 1992).

Table 17.2 Percentage of Older Adults with Hearing Impairments

	Those with Hearing Impairment			Those Who Use Hearing Aids		
Age	**Total**	**Male**	**Female**	**Total**	**Male**	**Female**
65–74	23.2	30.3	17.7	5.7	7.0	4.7
75–84	34.3	43.2	29.5	10.7	13.6	8.9
85+	51.4	—*	—*	19.0	—*	—*

*No separate gender data are provided for this age group.

Source: U.S. Bureau of the Census, 1990, Table 192, p. 119.

- *Problems hearing under noise conditions.* The loss of ability to discriminate individual words is even greater in noisy conditions. So large group gatherings become increasingly difficult for older adults.
- *Tinnitus*, a persistent ringing in the ears, also increases in incidence with age, although this problem appears to be independent of the other changes just described. Roughly 10 percent of adults over 65 experience this problem (U.S. Bureau of the Census, 1995), which *may* be caused by exposure to noise, although that is not well established.

Even mild hearing loss can pose communication problems in some situations. Those with such problems may also be perceived by others as disoriented or suffering from poor memory, especially if the person with the hearing loss is unwilling to admit the problem and ask for a repeat of some comment or instruction. Nonetheless, it is not the case that the older adult with a hearing impairment is necessarily socially isolated or unhappy. Mild and moderate hearing loss, even if uncorrected with a hearing aid, is simply not correlated with measures of general social, emotional, or psychological health among elderly adults. It is only when the loss is severe that we see an increase in social or psychological problems, including heightened rates of depression (Corso, 1987; Schieber, 1992).

CRITICAL THINKING

How do you think a hearing impairment is likely to affect the life of an older adult? Aside from wearing a hearing aid, how could a person with a moderate impairment adapt his life so as to reduce the impact of the disability?

Presbycusis and the other changes in hearing seem to result from gradual degeneration of virtually every part of the auditory system. Older adults secrete more ear wax, which may block the ear canal; the bones of the middle ear become calcified and less elastic; the cochlear membranes of the inner ear become less flexible and less responsive; and the nerve pathways to the brain show some degenerations (Schieber, 1992), apparently as part of the more general changes in the nervous system.

Smell and Taste. The ability to taste the four basic flavors (salty, bitter, sweet, and sour) does not seem to decline over the years of adulthood. Taste receptor cells (taste buds) have short lives and are constantly replaced (Bornstein, 1992). But other changes in the taste system affect older adults, such as the secretion of somewhat less saliva, producing a sensation of "wooly mouth" for some. Many elders also report that flavors seem blander than in earlier years, leading them to prefer more intense concentrations of flavors such as sweetness (de Graaf, Polet, & van Staveren, 1994). But it may well be that this perception of flavor blandness results more from a loss of the sense of smell than from loss of taste.

The sense of smell clearly deteriorates in old age. The best information comes from a cross-sectional study by Richard Doty and his colleagues (Doty et al., 1984), who tested nearly 2000 children and adults on their ability to identify 40 different smells—everything from pizza to gasoline. You can see in Figure 17.3 that young and middle-aged adults had equally good scores on this smell identification test, but that scores declined rapidly after age 60.

Interestingly, just as is true of hearing loss, the loss of the sense of smell seems to have an environmental component. Specifically, both men and women who worked in factories (where, presumably, they were exposed to more pollutants) show much greater losses of smell in old age than do those who worked in offices (Corwin, Loury, & Gilbert, 1995).

These changes in taste and smell can reduce many pleasures in life. But they can also have practical health consequences. Smell enhances the pleasure of food, so as smell becomes less acute, elders are less motivated to prepare tasty food. In some cases, this can result in subnutrition or significant dietary imbalances.

Changes in Sleep Patterns

Another primary aging pattern is a shift in sleep patterns in old age, which occurs among both healthy and less healthy elders. Adults older than 65 typically wake up

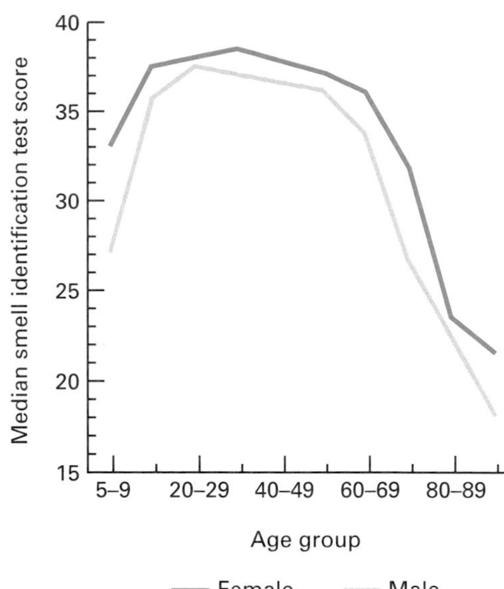

FIGURE 17.3 Doty's data show a very rapid drop in late adulthood in the ability to identify smells. (*Source:* Doty et al., 1984.)

more frequently in the night and show decreases in rapid eye movement (REM) sleep—the lighter sleep state in which dreaming occurs. Older adults are also more likely to wake early in the morning and go to bed early at night. They become "morning people" instead of "night people" (Hoch et al., 1992; Richardson, 1990). And because their night sleep is more often interrupted, older adults also nap more during the day in order to accumulate the needed amount of sleep.

CRITICAL THINKING

How would your life be different if you needed at least one nap a day to stay functional?

Health and Disability

All the physical changes I have described, here and in Chapters 13 and 15, and all the bad health habits that come home to roost contribute to a major increase in health problems and disabilities in the years after age 65. Older adults themselves are well aware of such changes. For example, if you ask adults to rate their own health as excellent, very good, good, fair, or poor, you find that with increasing age, more rate their health as poor and fewer rate it as excellent. In one such study of a nationally representative sample, Verbrugge (1989) found that 52.3 percent of those aged 45 to 64 rated their health as excellent or very good compared with only 35.2 percent of those over 65. Such self-ratings turn out to be remarkably accurate; each of us, in some sense, "knows" how our body is doing. Researchers have repeatedly found that those who rate their own health as "poor" are indeed more likely to die or to become more disabled over the succeeding few years than are those who rate their health as excellent (Idler & Kasl, 1995; Schoenfeld et al., 1994).

CRITICAL THINKING

What are some of the implications for *society* of the fact that older women live more years with disability than do men?

Ill health can manifest itself in several ways. For some (more often men) it means the rapid onset and rapid progress of some fatal disease, such as cancer or a fatal heart attack. Death from pneumonia, which becomes increasingly common in old age, also generally follows this rapid pattern. Many such individuals have few symptoms and little or no period of disability before the onset of disease. Others (more often women) have a number of symptoms of disease for a longer period of time, often accompanied by various minor or major physical disabilities. Because I have already talked about both cancer and heart disease in Chapter 15, let me focus my attention here on the second pattern, particularly on physical disabilities such as arthritis, and on the various dementias, including Alzheimer's disease, which frequently involve long periods of mental disability.

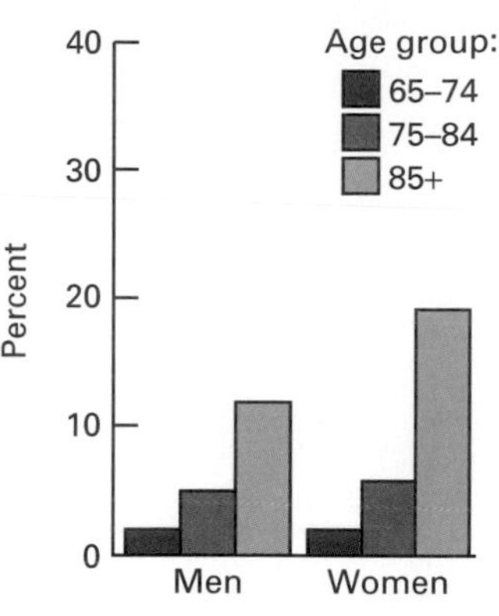

FIGURE 17.4 Percentage of the young old, the old old, and the oldest old who have difficulty performing one specific self-help task, in this case doing light housework. (*Source:* Guralnik & Simonsick, 1993, from Figure 2, p. 5.)

Physical Disabilities

Gerontologists generally define **disability** as a limitation in an individual's ability to perform certain socially defined roles and tasks (Jette, 1996), particularly self-help tasks and other chores of daily living. This is most often measured by asking each subject about her ability to perform both basic and more complex self-care activities, including bathing, dressing, walking a short distance, shifting from a bed to a chair, using the toilet, eating, preparing meals, shopping for personal items, doing light housework, and so on. You can get some sense of how many older adults have difficulty performing such tasks from Table 17.3, which reflects responses to two large surveys, one in the United States and one in Canada (Kunkel & Applebaum, 1992). Figure 17.4 adds to the picture by illustrating the age changes in the rate of problems older adults have performing one specific task, namely doing light housework.

Clearly, the incidence of such disabilities rises with age. But equally clearly, disability is not universal among older adults, even among the oldest old. Roughly half of those over 85 report at least *some* level of difficulty performing some basic daily life activities (Jette, 1996). But this means that half of these oldest old do not have such problems. To be sure, these surveys generally exclude adults who are living in institutions, the vast majority of whom are severely disabled according to the usual definition. And of course many of those with significant disability die before age 85, leaving only the healthiest still surviving among the oldest old. Still, it is important to understand that among the oldest old who live outside of nursing homes, the level of disability is nowhere near 100 percent. Even more encouraging is the finding that the rate of disability among the old old and the oldest old has been declining slowly but steadily in the past few decades in the United States (Kolata, 1996), perhaps because of better health care or better health habits.

The physical problems or diseases that are most likely to contribute to some functional disability are arthritis and cardiovascular problems, including both

Table 17.3 Percentages of Older Adults with Disabilities

Disability Category	Age Group	Men	Women
Little or none	65–74	90.9	89.0
	75–84	82.7	77.1
	85+	58.3	80.2
Moderate	65–74	5.1	6.3
	75–84	9.1	12.1
	85+	19.9	21.8
Severe	65–74	4.0	4.6
	75–84	8.2	10.8
	85+	21.7	31.7

Source: Kunkel & Applebaum, 1992, from Table 3, p. S257.

Table 17.4 Percentages of Older Americans Who Suffered from Major Chronic Illnesses in 1993

	Age 65–74		Age 75+	
Condition	**Men**	**Women**	**Men**	**Women**
Arthritis	37.4	53.3	46.7	58.3
Hypertension	32.3	35.9	30.4	38.8
Heart disease	34.7	22.4	37.6	33.3

Source: U.S. Bureau of the Census, 1995, from Table 215, p. 141.

chronic forms of heart disease and hypertension. Table 17.4 gives the incidence of these problems in the United States in 1993 (U.S. Bureau of the Census, 1995).

Not everyone with these problems is disabled. But the risk of some kind of functional disability is two to three times higher among those who suffer from these diseases than among those elders who do not (Verbrugge, Lepkowski, & Konkol, 1991). Because women are considerably more likely to have some level of arthritis, they are also more often disabled in the various movements and tasks necessary for independent life (Brock et al., 1990). When we put these bits together with the fact that women are more likely to be widowed and thus to lack a partner who could assist with these daily living tasks, it should not be surprising that more women than men live with their children or in nursing homes.

Mental Disabilities: Alzheimer's Disease and Other Dementias

Another major disease symptom that is found more often among those over 65 is **dementia,** a term used for any global deterioration of intellectual functions, including loss of memory, judgment, social functioning, and control of emotions. When it occurs in an older adult, it is usually called *senile dementia*.

Strictly speaking, dementia is a symptom and not a disease. The two most frequent causes are **Alzheimer's disease (AD)** and multiple small strokes (called *multi-infarct dementia*), but it can also be caused by depression, metabolic disturbances, drug intoxication, Parkinson's disease, hypothyroidism, multiple blows to the head (as among boxers), a single head trauma, some kinds of tumors, vitamin B_{12} deficiency, advanced stages of AIDS, anemia, or alcohol abuse (Anthony & Aboraya, 1992). I give you this list not because I expect you to memorize it, but to make it clear that Alzheimer's disease is not the only cause of dementia, and that many of the other causes are treatable, including depression. Indeed, roughly 10 percent of all patients who are evaluated for dementia turn out to have some reversible problem. So when an older person shows signs of dementia, it is critical to arrange for a careful differential diagnosis. Such a diagnosis will soon be made easier by the promised availability of a new test that will, for the first time, allow positive diagnosis of Alzheimer's disease. But this test is not yet available, so the diagnosis must still be made by ruling out the other alternatives.

Characteristics of Alzheimer's Disease. Dementia of the Alzheimer's type is caused by a specific set of changes in brain structure, including a kind of atrophying or shrinkage in certain areas of the brain (Small et al., 1995), as well as a kind of tangling of dendritic fibers within nerve cell bodies, illustrated in Figure 17.5. *All* aging adults appear to have some of these neurofibrillary tangles, but the number of them is vastly higher among those with Alzheimer's disease. The effect is to short-circuit many of the neural pathways, making memory and other everyday activities increasingly difficult.

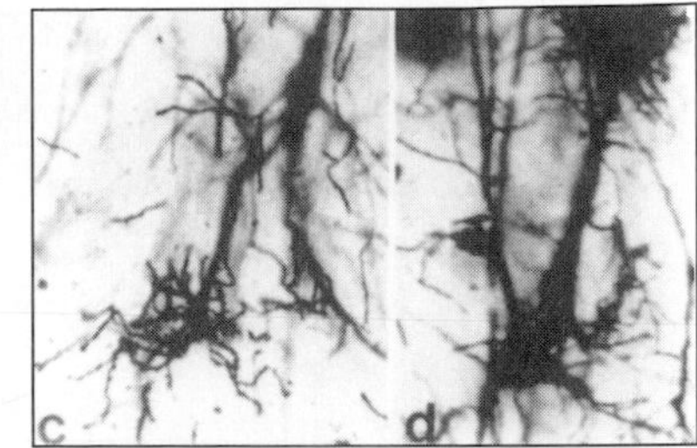

FIGURE 17.5 Compare these neurons, from a patient who died of Alzheimer's disease, with the normal aging neuron shown in Figure 17.2. (*Source:* Scheibel, 1992, figure 6, p. 162.)

The early stages of Alzheimer's disease usually move very slowly, beginning with subtle memory difficulties, repetitions in conversations, and disorientation in unfamiliar settings. Then memory for recent events begins to go. Memory for distant events or for well-rehearsed daily routines is often retained until late in the illness, presumably because these memories can be accessed through many alternative neural pathways. Eventually, however, an individual with Alzheimer's disease may fail to recognize family members, may be unable to remember the names of common objects or how to perform such routine activities as tooth brushing or dressing. Some patients also show angry outbursts, others an increased level of dependency and clinginess to family or friends (Raskind & Peskind, 1992).

Incidence of Alzheimer's and Other Dementias. Evidence from studies around the world (including research in China, Sweden, France, Great Britain, Italy, the United States, Canada, and Japan) is converging on the conclusion that something between 2 and 8 percent of all adults over age 65 show significant symptoms of dementia, and that 2 to 5 percent have Alzheimer's disease (Corrada, Brookmeyer, & Kawas, 1995; Rockwood & Stadnyk, 1994). Experts also agree that the rate of dementia, including Alzheimer's disease, rises rapidly through the 70s and 80s. For example, a large, careful study in Canada shows a rate of 11.1 percent in adults over 75 and 26.0 percent among those over 85 (Rockwood & Stadnyk, 1994). When mild as well as moderate and severe forms of dementia are counted, as has been done in several widely publicized U.S. studies, the numbers are even higher. In one of these U.S. studies, Evans and his colleagues in Boston estimated that 15 percent of all those over 65 and as many as 47 percent of those over 85 suffer from some level of dementia of the Alzheimer's type (Evans et al., 1989; Hebert et al., 1995).

CRITICAL THINKING

Think for a minute about the practical implications of these different estimates. What differences would it make to society if the real rate of dementia among those over 65 were 15 percent rather than 5 percent?

Causes of Alzheimer's Disease. We do not yet know what causes dementias of this type, although genetic researchers have now found three separate genes that appear to be implicated. The most common of these genetic indicators is a gene on chromosome 19 that controls a protein called Apolipoprotein E (abbreviated ApoE). When this protein degenerates, neurofibrillary tangling increases. It turns out that there are four different variants of the ApoE gene, one of which, ApoE4, is linked to Alzheimer's disease. Everyone has a gene for one of the four variants of the ApoE gene. Those who have ApoE1, ApoE2, or ApoE3 have no increased risk of this disease, but those who carry the gene for ApoE4 are at considerably increased risk. Adults who have *two* copies of the gene (one copy from the mother, one from the father) have as much as a 90 percent risk of developing Alzheimer's disease by the age of 80 compared with those having any other ApoE variant. Those who have only one copy of the ApoE4 gene have about three times the normal risk of Alzheimer's, but not nearly as high as those with two copies of the gene (Rose, 1995).

What is particularly fascinating about ApoE4 is that its presence is *also* implicated in heart disease. Those with two copies of the relevant gene have a 30 to 50 percent increased risk of heart disease. In fact, physicians have recently begun to use the blood test for ApoE4 as a screening strategy for identifying adults who are at special risk for atherosclerosis (Kolata, 1995). Such a link obviously raises a whole host of fascinating questions for researchers and may eventually give us important clues to the specific causes and treatment of Alzheimer's.

CRITICAL THINKING

Here's a question for you to mull over: The test for detecting ApoE4 is a fairly simple blood test. Would you want to have this test done, given what you have just read? That is, would you want to know whether you are at high risk for Alzheimer's? Why or why not?

Cultures and Contexts

Ethnic Group Differences in Health and Disability in Late Adulthood in the United States

All the figures I have given you on health and disability in the aged are average numbers for the entire U.S. population. It is important to ask whether these figures are equally valid for all minority groups. You will not be surprised to know that they are not. Yet it is not the case that all minority groups are disadvantaged; each minority group has a different pattern of death and disability. Before I give you some of the details, I need to emphasize that in most cases we cannot sort out the differential roles of ethnicity and social class. Those minority groups that show the highest rates of disability and the shortest life expectancy are generally also those with higher percentages of older adults living in poverty, and both factors undoubtedly affect the pattern we see.

By some accounts, the least healthy group of elders appears to be Native Americans. Indeed, some authors contend that "the elder American Indian may be the most significantly deprived individual in the country" (Stanford & Du Bois, 1992), although we have little national data to support this assertion. One fact we do have is that Native Americans have the shortest life expectancy of any minority group in the United States, although this picture has been improving in recent decades (Markides & Black, 1996). Native American elders are also more likely than are other groups to suffer from several potentially disabling diseases, most notably diabetes and alcoholism. In many tribes, 20 percent of the middle-aged and elderly have been diagnosed with diabetes, linked to high rates of obesity as well as genetic propensity (Markides & Mindel, 1987). As Markides and Mindel conclude,

> Despite the lack of adequate data on such indicators as self-rated health, restriction of activity, and bed-disability days, there is little doubt that Native Americans are disadvantaged on all such variables. These disadvantages are no doubt related to physically demanding labor, poor nutrition, unsanitary living conditions, as well as poor access to adequate medical care. (p. 90)

African-American elders are also disadvantaged in health, as you already know from earlier chapters. Blacks have shorter life expectancies, higher rates of disability, and higher rates of certain diseases, such as hypertension and cancer (Blakeslee, 1994; Chatters, 1991; Jackson & Perry, 1989; Sorlie et al., 1995). A relative disadvantage continues in elderly blacks, but the size of the disadvantage diminishes somewhat. One sign of this is that among those who reach the age of 75, life expectancy is *longer* among blacks than whites, a crossover effect that is particularly clear for elderly black women (Johnson, Gibson, & Luckey, 1990). Similarly, while more older blacks describe their health as fair or poor than is true for older whites, the difference is smaller than in middle adulthood. But these facts do not mean that blacks are getting healthier as they age. Instead, this pattern of findings seems to be another illustration of one of the classic pitfalls of cross-sectional comparisons: Only those blacks who are relatively healthier survive to late adulthood.

In contrast to the story for both Native Americans and African Americans, the health of elderly Hispanic Americans and Asian Americans appears to be equal to or better than that of majority whites. For example, Hispanic 65-year-olds have

Mental Health

I have been careful to talk about Alzheimer's disease and other dementias as a separate category apart from the discussion of mental health in old age. The great majority of cases of dementia are caused by physical *diseases* and do not properly belong in the category of psychological disorders or emotional disturbances. Depression, which is a psychological disorder, can cause some symptoms of dementia, but most depressed individuals do not exhibit significant dementia.

Just how common the various forms of psychological disorders may be in late adulthood is a matter of some dispute. For some disorders, such as schizophrenia, or alcohol or drug abuse, the data are clear: Older adults have lower rates of problems than any other age group. Where we are still uncertain is in the case of depression.

The earliest studies of age differences in depression suggested that older adults were at higher risk for such disorders than any other age group, contributing to a slightly longer life expectancies than do non-Hispanic whites. Part of this difference appears to be due to a lower rate of heart disease and hypertension among Hispanics, particularly Hispanic men. They also have fewer limitations of activity due to chronic conditions. The other side of the coin is that elderly Hispanics are more likely to die from infectious diseases, flu, pneumonia, or diabetes than are other groups. The difference in rates of diabetes are particularly large: Two to five times more Mexican Americans suffer from this disease than the general U.S. population, a difference not entirely explainable by obesity patterns (Bassford, 1995). As yet we know very little about the role social class or education may play in these patterns, although we have a few hints that the close kin networks in Hispanic families may serve as a protective, buffering factor for both mental and physical health among all members of this minority, whether elderly or not (Stanford & Du Bois, 1992).

Elderly Asian Americans, particularly those of Chinese and Japanese ancestry, appear to have the best health and mortality pattern of any U.S. group, although this conclusion is based on relatively little data. We do know that Asian Americans have longer life expectancies, but this pattern is largely carried by Japanese Americans and Chinese Americans, both well-acculturated groups with high levels of education and social class. More recent Asian immigrant groups do not enjoy the same advantage. We know far less about the day-to-day health status of elderly Asians, although at least a few studies of inner-city Asians, such as those in Chinatowns in San Francisco or Los Angeles, suggest that elders in these settings may have considerably poorer health and higher rates of disability than is typical for Asians in other areas (Markides & Mindel, 1987).

What general conclusions can we draw from these various profiles of health in different ethnic groups? First, it is simply not yet clear how much of these variations is due to social class differences or to overt or subtle forms of discrimination. An alternative form of explanation is that there may be ethnic differences in genetic propensities for particular diseases, such as diabetes, coronary heart disease, hypertension, or cancer. For example, recent research suggests that a particular enzyme, if present in the blood, can help detoxify one of the carcinogens in nicotine. Blacks appear to be less likely to have this enzyme, or they have it in lower quantities (Blakeslee, 1994), and thus blacks who smoke are more likely to develop lung cancer. But genetic differences cannot explain all the black/white differences. For example, blacks in Africa do not have the same high rate of hypertension as is found among African Americans (Sorel et al., 1991).

Finally, we know far too little about the impact of specific cultural patterns on health among the elderly. What role does family structure or social support play? Is it the case that the supportive family systems typically created by Hispanics and the extended family patterns created by blacks provide a buffering effect of some kind? And what role does acculturation play? Among Hispanics, there are hints that those who are *most* acculturated have the highest rates of depression and other emotional disturbance (Stanford & Du Bois, 1992). Is this widely true, and is it true in other groups? We have more questions than answers.

widespread cultural stereotype of the inevitably depressed elder. This view slowly gave way in the face of newer epidemiological studies that suggested the exact opposite—that late adulthood was a time of particularly *low* incidence of depression and other emotional disturbances (e.g., Regier et al., 1988). Now this rosier conclusion, too, is being called into question because of several careful recent studies that suggest a U-shaped curve, with high rates of depression in both young adulthood and among the old old and the oldest old.

A particularly good example is Ronald Kessler's analysis of a large cross-sectional U.S. sample (Kessler et al., 1992). Kessler argued that one of the problems in many of the earlier studies was that all adults 65 and older were lumped into a single group. This disguises any rise in symptoms or problems that might occur in late old age. When he uses a finer-grained age analysis he finds a rise, beginning at age 70 or 75, in the number of adults who report sad, lonely, or blue feelings, as you can see in Figure 17.6.

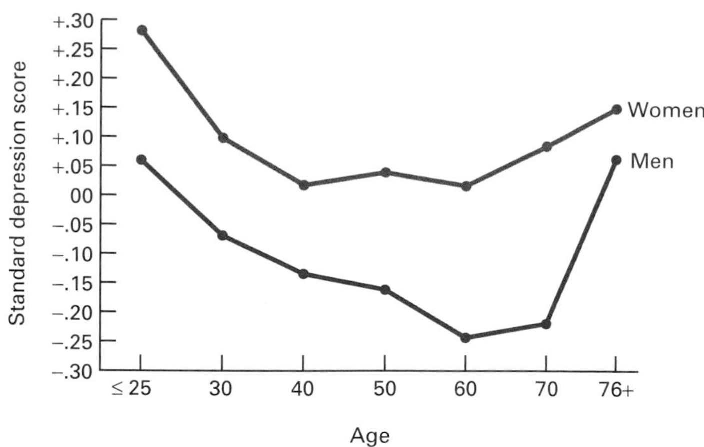

FIGURE 17.6 Self-reported depressive feelings among adults of various ages, drawn from a large, nationally representative cross-sectional sample interviewed in 1987–1988 in the National Survey of Families and Households. (*Source:* Kessler et al., 1992, from Figures 1 and 2, page 123. Copyright © 1992 by the American Psychological Association. Adapted with permission.)

Kessler's study also avoids another pitfall that has troubled interpretation of much of the other research on this question. Standard questionnaire assessments of depression include many questions about physical symptoms commonly accompanying depression, such as loss of appetite, sleep disturbances, and a lack of energy. Older adults are more likely to report such symptoms even when their mood is positive, so they are more likely to wind up with higher scores on these standardized depression scales. Thus, when total scores from such instruments are used to compare "depression" at various ages, the meaning of any rise in late adulthood is unclear. Kessler avoided this problem by dividing the usual depression measure into two parts, a set of questions about depressed mood and a set about physical symptoms. Figure 17.6 shows the results only for the former, which makes the results considerably more persuasive.

Yet before you are totally convinced, let me add several important caveats. First, this curvilinear pattern of results has not been found by everyone. For example, in one of the rare longitudinal studies, Joy Newmann and her associates (Newmann, Engel, & Jensen, 1991) studied a group of 251 women for over five years. These women, who were between 51 and 92 years at the start of the study, *declined* in reported depressive affect over time, but increased in something Newmann calls a "depletion syndrome," which is primarily characterized by a loss of physical energy. Clearly we need more longitudinal data to understand more fully just what is happening to depressive feelings in late adulthood.

A second caveat is that it is important to distinguish between depressed *mood* and a full-fledged *clinical depression*. The latter, as defined by the Diagnostic and Statistical Manual of the American Psychiatric Association, involves problems of longer duration that are sufficiently severe to interfere with a person's ability to carry out normal activities, or lead to self-medication, or precipitate a visit to a physician. The available evidence suggests that clinical depression is, if anything, *less* common among older adults than among younger adults, while depressed mood (the "blues") rises somewhat in frequency in late old age (Gatz, Kasl-Godley, & Karel, 1996).

The causes of such depressed mood in the elderly are not difficult to identify: inadequate social support, inadequate income, emotional loss such as bereavement, and nagging health problems. For example, in Dan Blazer's study of 4,000 adults aged 65 and older, 13.4 percent of those with incomes below $5,000 had high scores on a depression scale, compared with only 5.5 percent of those with incomes over

$15,000 (Blazer et al., 1991). Blazer and his colleagues argue that age itself is not the causal variable at work here. The risk factors for depression are essentially the same at every age, including poor health and lack of social support. To the extent that these risk factors are more likely to be present among the old old, depression rates will rise. When these risk factors are addressed or held constant, the rate of depression is actually lower among the elderly than among other age groups.

I know that this mix of contradictory research findings is confusing, so let me underline the one point I want you to carry away with you from the research on mental health in old age: Increased depression is not at all an inevitable aspect of old age. Depression is no more a necessary part of "normal aging" than is heart disease. Even in the face of poor health, bereavement, or economic difficulties, the majority of older adults do not become depressed or anxious.

The Effects of Physical Changes and Disease on Behavior

All the changes in the physical body that become more measurable in the years of late adulthood may be interesting to physicians and physiologists, but for most of us they become important only when they affect our daily lives. I've described a number of such effects as I've gone along, such as the increased level of physical disabilities or problems with understanding conversations in crowded or noisy conditions. But let me just say another word or two about the kinds of behavioral changes that may be troubling to those in late adulthood.

General Slowing

The biggest single effect is a general sense of slowing down, a process I talked about in Chapter 13. Dendritic loss at the neural level clearly contributes substantially to this general slowing, but other factors are also involved, including arthritic changes in the joints and loss of elasticity in the muscles. Writing things down takes longer (Schaie & Willis, 1991), tying your shoes takes longer, adapting to changes in temperature or changes in light conditions takes longer. Even tasks that involve words, which otherwise tend to decline very little with age, nonetheless are done more slowly (Lima, Hale, & Myerson, 1991; Madden, 1992).

This older man has obviously chosen a very sporty car and doubtless thinks of himself as still a skillful driver. But it is nonetheless true that many of the physical changes associated with aging will make it harder for him to respond quickly, to see clearly in glare, and to adapt rapidly to changing driving conditions.

One of the arenas in which such changes add up to really significant differences in functioning is in a complex motor activity like driving. Young adults have more auto accidents than any other age group, primarily because they drive too fast. But older adults have more accidents *per mile driven* (Bianchi, 1993). Of course, other physical changes beyond general slowing contribute to driving problems in old age. The changes in the eyes mean that older adults have more trouble reading signs at night and adjusting to the glare of oncoming headlights. But the general slowing of reaction time affects your ability to switch attention from one thing to the next, or to react quickly and appropriately when a vehicle appears unexpectedly on the periphery. Older adults also say they have more trouble judging their own speed, and that the instrument panel is too dim (Kline et al., 1992). Overall, it becomes harder and harder for older drivers to respond appropriately to rapidly changing conditions.

Critical Thinking

Do you think that there should be an upper age limit for driver's licenses? Why or why not?

Balance, Dexterity, and Stamina

The various physical changes associated with aging also combine to produce a reduction in stamina, dexterity, and balance. The loss of stamina clearly arises in large part from the changes in the cardiovascular system, as well as from changes in muscles. Dexterity is lost primarily as a result of arthritic changes in the joints.

Another significant change, one with particularly clear practical ramifications, is a gradual loss of balance (Guralnik et al., 1994; Simoneau & Liebowitz, 1996). Older adults, who may be quite mobile in their home environments, are likely to have greater difficulty handling an uneven sidewalk or adapting their bodies to a swaying bus. Such situations require the ability to adjust rapidly to changing body cues and the muscular strength to maintain body position, both of which decline in old age. So older adults fall more often. About one-quarter of the young old and more than a third of the old old report a fall in the previous year (Hornbrook, Stevens, & Wingfield, 1994). Because of osteoporosis, such falls more often result in fractures in old age, often a very serious health complication for an older adult.

Sexual Activity

Another behavior that is affected by the cumulative physical changes of aging is sexual behavior. You've already seen in Chapter 15 that the frequency of sexual activity declines gradually in middle adulthood. This trend continues in late adulthood, as you can see in Figure 17.7, which is based on data from both cross-sectional and longitudinal studies. The cross-sectional data come from a nationally representative sample of 807 adults interviewed in the late 1980s (Marsiglio & Donnelly, 1991). The longitudinal data are from the Duke longitudinal studies (Palmore, 1981), in which several hundred adults were interviewed on two occasions, six years apart. Figure 17.7 shows the results for only those subjects in both studies who were married and thus had an available sexual partner. Notice how similar the findings are from these two sources, despite the fact that the data in the two studies were collected twenty years apart and that one study used a random sample while the other did not.

These data, as well as other studies (e.g., Call, Sprecher, & Schwartz, 1995), tell us that by age 70, only about half of *married* adults are still sexually active. Among those who are, frequency of intercourse also declines. Those 75 and older who are still sexually active report having intercourse 3 to 4 times a month, compared with about 7 times per month for those in their 50s.

The decline in sexual activity in late adulthood doubtless has many causes. The continuing decline in testosterone levels among men clearly plays some role. Overall health also plays an increasingly large role. For example, blood pressure medication sometimes produces impotence as a side effect; chronic pain may affect sexual desire. There may also be some effect of social definitions that portray old age as an essentially asexual period of life.

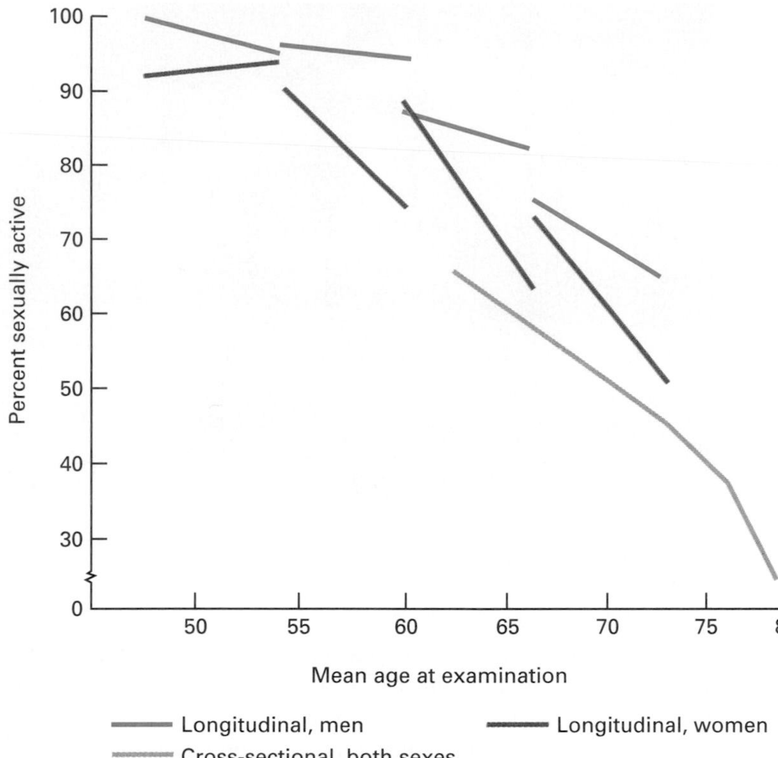

FIGURE 17.7 Each of the longitudinal lines in this figure represents a group of adults interviewed twice, six years apart. The cross-sectional data reflect interview responses of 807 adults of different ages interviewed only once. Both sets of information show a steady decline in late adulthood in the number of people, of those with an available sexual partner, who report that they had had sexual intercourse in the past month. But the number does not drop to zero, even among the old old. (*Sources:* Marsiglio & Donnelly, 1991, data from Table 2, p. S341; Palmore, 1981, Figure 6-3, p. 87.)

What is striking to me, though, is not so much that sexual activity declines as that many older adults, despite the physical changes, nonetheless continue to find pleasure in sexual activity. The more general point is that while many everyday activities may become more difficult in late adulthood, most adults nonetheless find ways to adapt with inventiveness and some grace.

Theories of Aging

Why do all these changes occur as we age? What are the basic causes of aging? Current theorists agree that the most likely explanation lies in basic cellular processes, which appear to change with age in specific ways that reduce the efficiency of cellular functioning. A number of theoretical variations on this theme have been proposed.

Repair of Genetic Material. One explanation focuses on the cell's ability to repair breaks in DNA. Some breaks in DNA strands are a common daily event, resulting from some unknown metabolic processes. Because the organism is apparently unable to repair all the damage, over time the accumulation of unrepaired breaks results in loss of cellular function, and the organism ages (Tice & Setlow, 1985).

Cross-Linking. A related theory focuses on another cellular process called **cross-linking,** which occurs more often in cell proteins in older than in younger adults. Cross-linking occurs when undesirable bonds form between proteins or fats. In skin

The effects of physical aging are clear here. But what causes all the changes we see?

and in connective tissue, for example, two proteins called collagen and elastin form cross-linkages, either between molecules or within a given protein molecule. The resulting molecules cannot assume the correct shape for proper function, producing various effects such as wrinkling of the skin and arterial rigidity. An equivalent process, by the way, occurs in old rubber, as on older windshield wipers, which explains why they become stiffer over time.

Free Radicals. A third type of cellular process that may contribute to aging relates to the body's ability to deal with free radicals. Free radicals, which are molecules or atoms that possess an unpaired electron, are a normal by-product of body metabolism, as well as a response to diet, sunlight, X-rays, or air pollution. These molecules, especially the subgroup called oxygen free radicals, enter into many potentially damaging chemical reactions, resulting in irreparable molecular damage that accumulates with age. For example, oxidation reactions caused by free radicals can damage cell membranes, thereby reducing the cell's protection against toxins and carcinogens. Oxygen free radicals are also implicated in the body's reaction to cholesterol: Oxidation helps to transform some types of cholesterol into a form that latches onto artery walls, narrowing them and increasing the risk of heart attack and stroke (Brody, 1994).

Research on diet variations points to the possibility that some foods, especially foods high in fat, promote the formation of oxygen free radicals, while others, referred to as *antioxidants*, inhibit it or produce chemical processes that help the body defend against free radicals. Foods high in vitamins C and E and beta carotene (vitamin A) all belong in the latter group (Ornish, 1993). Several large epidemiological studies show that people who eat diets higher in antioxidants or who take regular supplements of vitamin E or beta carotene live somewhat longer and have lower rates of heart disease (Blumberg, 1996). Not all studies show this effect, however (e.g., The Alpha-Tocopherol Beta Carotene Cancer Prevention Study Group, 1994), so although the dietary evidence provides growing support for the free radical theory of the aging process, the jury is still out.

A quite different line of evidence on this same theory comes from the work of William Orr and Rajindar Sohal (1994), who genetically engineered a group of fruit flies in a way that enhanced their built-in capacity to defend against free radicals. These altered flies lived roughly one-third longer than did normal fruit flies—a result that raises the possibility that we might eventually be able to alter the genetic limit of lifespan via genetic engineering.

Genetic Limits

The notion of genetic limits has been an important aspect of a somewhat different theory of aging. This approach centers around the observation that each species has a characteristic maximum life span. For humans this seems to be about 110 or 120 years; for turtles, it is far longer, and for chickens, far less. This persuaded biologists like Leonard Hayflick (1977, 1987) that there may be some genetic process that limits life span. Hayflick bolstered this argument with his observation—since replicated in many laboratories throughout the world—that embryo cells placed in nutrient solution would divide only a fixed number of times, after which the cell colony would degenerate. Human embryo cells will double about 50 times; those from the Galapagos tortoise double roughly 100 times, while a chicken cell will double only about 25 times. Furthermore, cells taken from human adults will double only about 20 times, as if they had already "used up" some of their genetic capacity. The theoretical proposal that emerges from such observations is that each species has some **Hayflick limit,** after which cells simply no longer have any capacity to replicate themselves accurately (Norwood, Smith, & Stein, 1990).

Hayflick's argument has been strengthened by the recent discovery that each chromosome in the human body (and presumably in other species, too) has, at its tip, a string of repetitive DNA called *telomeres* (Angier, 1992; Campisi, Dimri, & Hara, 1996). Among other functions, telomeres appear to serve as a kind of timekeeping mechanism for the organism. Researchers have found that the number of telomeres is reduced slightly each time a cell divides, so that the number remaining in a 70-year-old is much lower than what is found in a child. This raises the possibility that there may be a crucial minimum number of telomeres; when the total falls below that number, then disease or death comes fairly quickly.

What all these theoretical approaches have in common is the assumption that aging results from the gradual accumulation of errors or changes in cellular functioning. Such errors could result from the operation of some kind of internal genetic clock, or from simple multiplication of normal imperfections, such as cross-linkages or nonrepair of DNA. What we see as aging is the product of all these factors.

Cognitive Changes

If middle adulthood is the period in which adults maintain most of their cognitive abilities, late adulthood is the period in which those abilities decline more noticeably. Among the young old (65 to 75), these changes are still fairly small, and on a few measures, such as vocabulary knowledge, the young old show little or no average decline. But the old old and the oldest old show average declines on virtually all measures of intellectual skill, with the largest declines on any measure that involves speed or unexercised abilities (Cunningham & Haman, 1992; Giambra et al., 1995). Recall Schaie's comment, quoted in Chapter 15, that "reliable decrement can be shown to have occurred for all abilities by age 74" (Schaie, 1983b, p. 127). By the 80s, the declines are substantial on most abilities (Schaie, 1993).

Memory

One area in which we see such late adulthood changes is in memory, although the degree of loss varies depending on the familiarity of the material and the length of time it must be remembered. If your own long-term memory is working, you'll recall the West and Crook study I described in Chapter 15, in which adults were asked to remember a telephone number displayed briefly on a computer screen, and then to

This French baker has little trouble remembering the recipe for bread he's been baking all his life. But he might find it takes longer to memorize a new recipe than it did when he was 25.

dial the number from memory. Scores on this kind of simple short-term (or *primary*) memory task shows relatively little decline even in late late adulthood, except that when the task is made more difficult by adding a delay or requiring some kind of processing, older adults show more loss.

The losses are considerably larger on *secondary* memory tasks, both in encoding and retrieval. The encoding side of this—the input process—would include such things as trying to memorize a phone number, learn a song or poem by heart, or memorizing a list of items to buy at the grocery store. The retrieval or output side would include problems like remembering someone's name, remembering the grocery list when you get to the store, recalling whether you were supposed to meet your friend Mary for lunch on Tuesday or Wednesday, remembering the name of the street on which the doctor's office is located, or the like.

Encoding Processes. The older adult has very much the same kind of difficulty in encoding as we see in preschool children—a failure to use efficient strategies for remembering new information. Given a list of items to memorize, older adults are less likely to use such efficient strategies as chunking the items into logical groupings or even basic rehearsal, although older adults—again like young children—can and do use such strategies when they are reminded to do so (Sugar & McDowd, 1992). This suggests the possibility that at least part of the apparent decline in memory skills in old age may reflect disuse rather than loss of ability. Older adults, in fact, are much more likely to use such external aids as list-making to help them remember things, so they may be simply out of practice in the use of many kinds of internal memory strategies. Still, this can't be the whole explanation because even with such reminders, younger adults normally outperform older adults on memory tasks.

Retrieval. Retrieval also becomes less efficient with age. Perhaps most noticeably, retrieval become *slower* (Craik, 1994; Madden, 1992). But more than just speed seems to be involved here. Older adults generally do about as well as (although slower than) younger adults on tasks demanding *recognition*, but much less well on tasks demanding *recall*. If you give a subject a list of words to learn, for example, and ask him later to tell you merely whether particular words were in the list, an older adult can do that quite well. But if you ask him to recall as many of the words as possible, he has more difficulty (Labouvie-Vief & Schell, 1982). In general, memories become less accessible as we get older. Findings like these reinforce the impression of many older adults that they often "know" things that they cannot readily or quickly bring to mind. If they are given a hint, or reminded of the item at some later time, the memory comes back.

Familiar and Unfamiliar Material. One common argument from those who take a more optimistic view of cognitive aging is that older adults may be able to remember just as well as younger adults but that they are simply less motivated to memorize lists of unrelated words given to them by researchers in a laboratory. If we tested adults with memory for more ordinary things, perhaps we would find no age differences.

It's a comforting thought, but it turns out to be mostly wrong. On virtually all "everyday" tasks, such as remembering the main points of a story or a newspaper article; recalling movies, conversations, grocery lists, or recipes; recalling the information from a medicine label; remembering whether some action has been performed ("Did I turn off the stove before I left the house?"); remembering where you heard something (called *source memory*); or remembering to do something in the future, such as taking medication once a day, older adults recall less well than younger adults (Brown, Jones, & Davis, 1995; Light, 1991; Mäntylä, 1994; Maylor, 1993; Salthouse, 1991; Verhaeghen & Marcoen, 1993; Verhaeghen, Marcoen, & Goossens, 1993). We even see a decline on highly familiar items crucial to everyday functioning in a person's occupation or avocation. For example, older recreational pilots make more errors than do younger ones in recalling instructions given to them by air-traffic controllers (Taylor et al., 1994).

Only in a few limited types of everyday tasks does the age difference in memory performance get smaller or disappear. For example, older adults appear to be equally good at remembering items of experience that were highly salient at the time, such as whether they voted in an election four years earlier (Herzog & Rogers, 1989).

These few exceptions aside, the weight of the accumulating evidence is quite clear: Memory ability declines with age for everyday memory tasks as well as on traditional laboratory tasks. Such a decline is also found in the few longitudinal studies of memory, particularly after age 70 (Arenberg, 1983; Hultsch et al., 1992; Zelinski, Gilewski, & Schaie, 1993).

Let me hasten to say that this rather negative set of summary statements does *not* mean that older adults cannot remember things. They can and do. And the same basic rules seem to apply to memory processes among older as among younger adults. For both groups, for example, recognition is easier than recall, and speed makes tasks more difficult. But older adults do all these things less readily and less efficiently than do young adults.

Preliminary Explanations. How do we account for these changes in memory? What underlying process might be involved? The biggest change appears to be in the speed of the whole memory process. It takes longer to register some new piece of information, longer to encode it, longer to retrieve it. Some of the clearest evidence of the important role of speed in memory decline in old age comes from an extensive series of studies by Timothy Salthouse (e.g., Salthouse, 1991, 1993, 1996). He has tested both basic reaction speed and memory or other cognitive skills in adults of various ages, and finds that a very large portion of the age decline in memory can be accounted for simply by slower reaction times in older adults. Salthouse is convinced that the loss of speed is at the level of the central nervous system and not at some more peripheral level. So the physiological changes in neurons I described earlier, and the accompanying loss of nerve conductance speed, may be the root cause of the changes in memory. Salthouse offers a nice metaphor:

> The functioning of working memory might be analogous to someone trying to juggle items inside a room with a fairly low ceiling. Under conditions such as these, where the presence of a ceiling limits the height of the tosses and gravity serves to ensure that all items drop at the same rate, the primary limit on the number of items that can be kept active is the speed of catching and tossing . . . the items. (Salthouse, 1992, p. 77)

If the older adult catches and tosses more slowly, then she can catch and toss fewer items at once, which means that we ought to see a decline on any task that demands even moderate levels of **working memory**—a phrase used to describe the process of simultaneously holding some information in mind and using that information to solve some problem, learn something new, or make some decision (Craik & Jennings, 1992). The more any given cognitive task makes demands on working memory, the larger the decline with age we see.

I think that virtually all the experts would now agree with Salthouse that loss of speed is a key aspect of the process. But most would also agree that speed is not the entire explanation. There appear to be other losses as well, such as a loss in the capacity to maintain attention or to divide attention among several items, or a loss in the capacity of working memory itself. A computer analogy might help here. Those of you who work with computers know that it is important to distinguish between the amount of memory capacity on the hard disk (equivalent to long-term memory) and the random access memory (RAM), which is the basic working memory capacity of the machine at any moment. When you call out a specific program, such as a word processing program, you load it into the RAM space. If your computer has a relatively small RAM space, or if you try to use several programs simultaneously so that both are held in working memory, you will see little signs on your screen that tell you there isn't enough memory to do what you want to do. This is not a question of speed, but of simple capacity. It begins to look as if there may be some loss of "RAM" space as we get older, in addition to the loss of speed—although that conclusion is still highly tentative.

Problem Solving

"Problem solving" refers to the complex set of processes you use to figure out a solution to some dilemma. If your furnace suddenly stops functioning, you try to solve the problem by thinking up possible explanations and possible solutions. Changes in such activity with age follow a pattern very similar to what we see with memory: Ability clearly declines over the years of late adulthood, although the degree of decline varies somewhat from one type of problem to another.

Laboratory tasks used to study this ability are varied, but a typical one involves asking a subject to figure out what combination of button pushing will turn on a light. On such tasks, younger adults do quite a lot better than older adults, using more optimal strategies and arriving at solutions sooner. This age difference appears even if the subjects are encouraged to take notes and keep track of the combinations they have already tried. Older adults under such conditions take fewer and apparently less effective notes (Kluwe, 1986)—a particularly interesting result because it suggests that the compensatory processes used by older adults, like note taking, are not fully effective.

You might well argue, as some researchers have, that these are pretty artificial tasks. How do elderly adults do on more familiar or more practically relevant problems? Nancy Denney approached this issue by asking a group of older adults to help her identify a set of real-life problems that older adults might typically face. Here's one problem on a topic suggested by the elders:

Critical Thinking

How many solutions to this problem can you think of?

> Let's say that a 67-year-old man's doctor has told him to take it easy because of a heart condition. It's summertime and the man's yard needs to be mowed but the man cannot afford to pay someone to mow the lawn. What should he do? (Denney & Pearce, 1989, p. 439)

Denney then posed ten such problems to groups of adults of various ages from 20 to 79, and counted the number of safe and effective solutions proposed by each subject. On this task—intentionally biased to favor the older subjects—adults between 30 and 50 had the best scores, while those over 50 did least well (Denney & Pearce, 1989; Denney, Tozier, & Schlotthauer, 1992). Other research suggests that older adults are as good as younger adults at *recognizing* a good problem solution when they hear one (Light, 1992), but they are less good at thinking up possible solutions, even when the problems to be solved are clearly practically relevant.

These senior citizens in Texas, lobbying their legislators, are demonstrating one form of problem solving. But research tells us that older adults on average are likely to think of fewer and less varied solutions to everyday problems.

Longitudinal studies, although few in number, suggest that the drop in problem-solving skill occurs later than age 50. For instance, data from the Baltimore Longitudinal Study points to age 70 as the age at which problem-solving ability begins to decline (Arenberg, 1974; Arenberg & Robertson-Tchabo, 1977), a pattern that is highly consistent with Schaie's data on IQ and other general cognitive skills. Rainer Kluwe, after reviewing the data, concludes that in older adults, "the solution search, given well-defined problems, is not very well organized, it is inefficient, redundant, and finally not very successful" (1986, p. 519). Yet the fact that older adults solve problems more slowly or less efficiently does not signify incompetence. Sherry Willis points out that the great majority of older adults cope effectively with most everyday problems—buying groceries, managing their finances, reading bus schedules, planning their lives (Willis, 1996).

Two More Optimistic Views

The somewhat pessimistic, albeit realistic appraisal of the evidence on cognitive decline in old age I have just given can be balanced with two other sets of information, one suggesting that training can have a significant effect and the other emphasizing the compensating effect of wisdom.

Training Effects. An extensive body of research now shows that with appropriate training, older adults can significantly improve their performance on a variety of cognitive tasks, including memory tests and IQ-like tests (Baltes & Kliegl, 1992; Dittmann-Kohli et al., 1991; Kliegl, Smith, & Baltes, 1989, 1990; Verhaeghen et al., 1992). There is even one longitudinal study, involving some of the older subjects in the Seattle Longitudinal Study, showing that among adults in their 70s, the effects of such training persist over periods as long as 6 years (Willis & Nesselroade, 1990).

But—and this is a big *but*—these training gains do not bring the older adult's performance up to that of a young adult. When both older and younger adults are given the same kind of training, the most common result is that the age difference gets larger rather than smaller.

A study by Reinhold Kliegl and his colleagues in Germany is typical (Baltes & Kliegl, 1992; Kliegl et al., 1990). Kliegl tested 18 young college students and 19 older adults, with the two groups roughly equivalent in tested intelligence. The older adults, all physically healthy, ranged in age from 65 to 80, with an average age of 71.7 years. The task used was a traditional laboratory memory task in which the subject is presented with a list of 30 words to remember, each presented for some fixed length of time, with the time ranging from 20 seconds per word down to 1 second per word. When the whole list has been presented, the subject must try to write down as many of the words as possible.

After a pretest, each subject in Kliegl's study was given extensive training on a mnemonic strategy called the Method of Loci. In this method, you first memorize some sequence of images, such as buildings along your route to work, or a set of streets that occur in sequence. You create vivid images for each item in this series, and then you hook each item in the word list to one of the sequence of images—the first word to the first image, the second word to the second image, and so on. In Kliegl's study, the subjects were first given a set of pictures of 30 familiar buildings in Berlin and asked to memorize this set, in sequence, with a vivid mental image for each one. Only when every subject could repeat back this sequence in 90 seconds did they begin to use this sequence as an aid in remembering lists of words. In training sessions, each subject attempted to use the method. Then, after learning each list, the experimenter asked the subject what images he or she had used and suggested possible improvements. These training sessions were interspersed with test sessions to check on the subject's progress. Figure 17.8 shows the results for those tests in which the subjects were given the words at 5-second intervals.

You can see that the older adults showed some improvement after training, but younger adults benefited *more* from training than did the older adults. Other results from this study show that on the very hardest trials—when the words to be memorized were presented every second—the oldest adults showed no improvement at all after training, while the younger subjects did improve. This suggests that the encoding process simply takes longer for the older adult—longer to create the mental image, and longer to link that image up with the word in the list.

In general, the fact that the younger adults benefited more from training than did the elders argues against the proposal that declines in cognitive skill in late adulthood represent simply lack of regular practice. In these experiments, subjects were given *lots* of practice, but the practice didn't help the older adults as much as it helped the younger ones.

If we relate these findings to Denney's overall model, shown in Figure 13.5 (page 348), we might conclude that Denney has underestimated the degree to which the

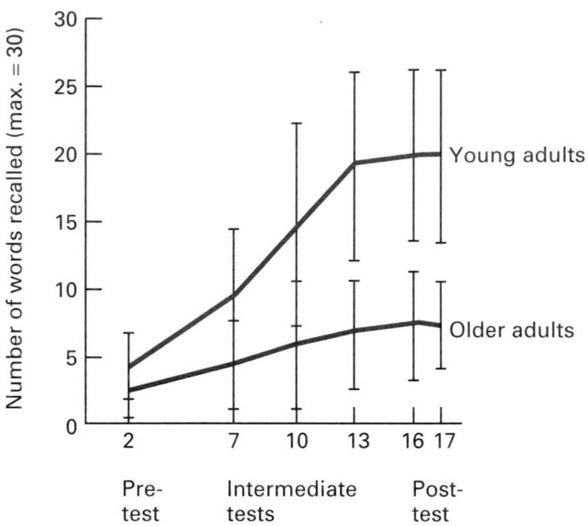

FIGURE 17.8 These fascinating results from Kliegl's study show that older adults can indeed improve their memory performance after training, but they don't gain as much as do younger adults, suggesting that the "reserve capacity" is smaller in old age than in young adulthood. (*Source:* Kliegl et al., 1990, adapted from Figure 2, p. 899.)

unpracticed and the practiced ability lines converge in later adulthood. The difference between these two lines, which a number of authors refer to as *reserve capacity* (e.g., Baltes & Baltes, 1990a), appears to be smaller in older adulthood than in the young. But even the oldest adults have *some* reserve capacity that can be mobilized. This is true for measures of physical functioning, such as VO_2 max (maximum oxygen uptake), which improves with exercise even among the very old, and for measures of cognitive performance, which improve with practice at every age.

Wisdom. Theorists who study cognition in older adults have also recently begun to ask whether elders might have some advantages over the young because of their accumulation of knowledge and skills. In other words, older adults might be more *wise*. Researchers in this area have not yet agreed on a common definition of wisdom, but most authors emphasize that it goes beyond mere accumulations of facts. It reflects understanding of "universal truths" or basic laws or patterns; it is knowledge that is blended with values and meaning systems; it is knowledge based on the understanding that clarity is not always possible, that unpredictability and uncertainty are part of life (Baltes & Smith, 1990; Baltes, Smith, & Staudinger, 1992; Baltes et al., 1995; Csikszentmihalyi & Rathunde, 1990; Sternberg, 1990a). A wise person, then, will have unusual insight into life problems and unusually good judgment or advice to offer.

Critical Thinking

Make a list of the people you think of as wise. How old are they? Is old age necessary for wisdom? If not, how do you think wisdom is acquired?

Virtually all theorists who have written about wisdom assume that if wisdom exists, it is more likely to be found in the middle-aged and the elderly. As yet, however, we have almost no empirical evidence. Paul Baltes (Baltes & Smith, 1990; Baltes et al., 1992, 1995) has some limited evidence indicating that older adults are *as good* as are younger adults on one task intended to measure wisdom, in which the subject is asked to evaluate the lessons or meaning to be gained from one person's life. And Lucinda Orwoll (Orwoll & Perlmutter, 1990) has found that those older adults singled out by their peers as more wise are indeed different from "average" elders: They are more likely to be rated as high in what Erikson calls ego integrity and are more likely to show concern for humanity as a whole. But neither of these pieces of evidence tells us that older adults, as a group, are able to compensate for their loss of speed and mental efficiency by a gain in wisdom. Still, this line of theory and research does point to renewed interest on the part of psychologists in aspects of cognitive functioning that cannot be readily measured by standard IQ or memory tests, and on which older adults *might* have some advantage.

Individual Differences

The single best word to describe individual variations in patterns of physical and mental change in old age is *huge*. Some adults are already displaying significant disability and significant cognitive losses by their 50s and 60s; others seem to keep all their mental marbles, and most of their physical vigor, well into their 70s and 80s—even 90s. As an illustration, take a look at the data in Figure 17.9, which shows the scores on a measure of vocabulary knowledge (a crystallized skill) for four individual subjects in Schaie's Seattle Longitudinal Study, each tested five times over 28 years (Schaie, 1989b). The degree of variability is striking and makes one wonder how meaningful it is to talk about patterns of shared, "normal" aging of cognitive functioning.

Schaie doesn't tell us much about these individuals, but he does give a few broad brush strokes. Subject A is a woman who has been a homemaker all her adult life; her husband is still alive and in good health. Subject B, in contrast, is a woman who worked as a teacher for a good portion of her life. After she turned 60 she was divorced, retired, and began to experience significant health problems. Subject C is a man with a high school education who did clerical work most of his life. He showed essentially no change until his 70s, and again poor health may be implicated in this decline, since the final testing, at age 83, was only a year before his death. Finally, subject D is a man with a grade school education who had worked in a white-collar job. When he retired, his score on this test actually increased; it has gone down only at the latest assessment, at a time when he had recently become a widower and was experiencing health problems.

Sherry Willis found equally high levels of variability in a seven-year longitudinal study of 102 older adults, first tested when they were between ages 62 and 86. Over the ensuing seven years, when most of the subjects shifted from being "young old" to being "old old," 62 percent of the group showed either stability or actual improvement in competence on everyday intellectual tasks (Willis et al., 1992), while the remaining 38 percent showed decline.

There have been two approaches to attempting to understand these variations. The first of these, labeled with the rather depressing name of the **terminal drop hypothesis,** centers on the suggestion that all adults retain excellent function until a

One of the favored few who maintains high levels of functioning throughout late adulthood, Bess Whitehead Scott of Austin, Texas, seems fit as a fiddle on her hundredth birthday.

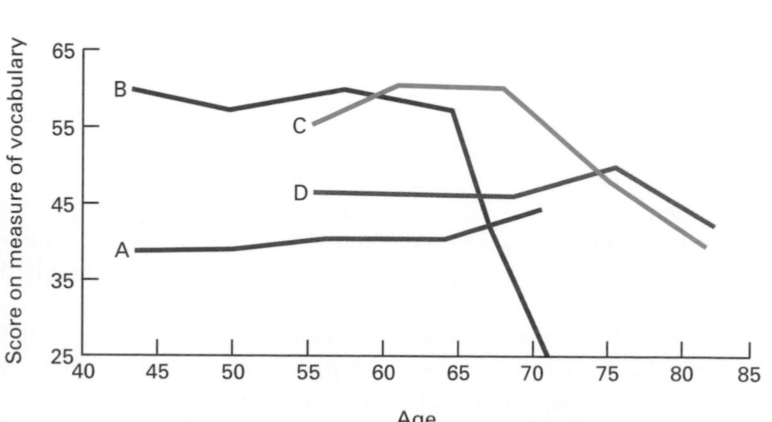

FIGURE 17.9 Patterns of maintenance or change on a vocabulary test over 28 years for four individual subjects in the Seattle Longitudinal Study. No one of these subjects' performances matches the average pattern of change on this measure. The variations *may* be linked to health differences, but we don't know enough yet to be sure. (*Source*: Schaie, 1989b, Figures 5.13 and 5.14, pp. 82–83).

period a few years before death, at which time they drop rather precipitously in physical and mental functioning. The second approach involves a search for individual characteristics, such as family heredity and lifestyle, that may predict differences in rate or pattern of aging.

Terminal Drop

Kleemeier (1962) first proposed the idea of terminal drop to describe a pattern of rapid decline in cognitive functioning during the final years of life. He suggested that intellectual skill is maintained virtually unchanged until five to seven years before death, at which time it drops rapidly. When we compare groups of individuals cross-sectionally, or when we follow individuals longitudinally, each successive age group contains more and more individuals who are in this period of terminal drop, and thus the average score will tend to go down. But if Kleemeier is right, then the average pattern doesn't tell us anything about the individual pattern. The only way to test Kleemeier's hypothesis is to track backward from death for individuals for whom we have regular data at previous ages. This has now been done with data from several longitudinal studies in several countries, including the United States and Germany (Berg, 1996; Birren & Schroots, 1996).

In one typical study, Palmore and Cleveland (1976) analyzed data from the Duke longitudinal studies, examining the pattern of earlier test scores for 178 deceased men. They found no indication of terminal drop for their many measures of physical functioning, all of which showed gradual decline. But they did find a pattern of terminal drop for total IQ, which tended to remain stable until a few years before each man's death.

Equivalent studies of other longitudinal samples (e.g., Johansson & Berg, 1989; Siegler, McCarty, & Logue, 1982; White & Cunningham, 1988) suggest that the terminal drop pattern is most likely to occur on measures of well-exercised (crystallized) abilities. But on measures of most physical changes, and for most measures of unexercised (fluid) cognitive abilities, the decline appears to be gradual for each person. Yet it is still true that this decline begins much earlier in some individuals than in others. Available explanations of such differences focus on both heredity and on lifestyle variations.

Heredity

Some general tendency to "live long and prosper" (to quote Mr. Spock from *Star Trek*) is clearly inherited. Identical twins are more similar in length of life than are fraternal twins, and adults whose parents and grandparents are long-lived are also more likely to have long lives (Plomin & McClearn, 1990). The amount of illness prior to death also seems to be linked to genetic patterns. In the Swedish twin studies, for example, identical twins have more similar rates of illness than do fraternal twins (Pedersen & Harris, 1990). Similarly, Vaillant, studying the Harvard men in the Grant study sample, has found a small but significant correlation between the longevity of each man's parents and grandparents and his own health at age 65. Only about a quarter of those whose oldest grandparent had lived past 90 had any kind of chronic illness at age 65, compared with nearly 70 percent of those whose oldest grandparent had died at 78 or younger (Vaillant, 1991).

Just what it is that might be inherited is not entirely clear. One possibility is that different individuals may have slightly different "Hayflick limits," or there may be variations in the basic rate of physical maturation. Whatever the explanation, I want to emphasize that the effect of heredity on longevity, or on health in late life, does not appear to be enormous. If your grandparents all died when they were in their 60s or 70s this need not mean that you will die early or necessarily be troubled with chronic problems. But there is some connection.

Lifestyle and Health

What is likely to be far more important for your experience of late adulthood is your health, along with all the lifestyle factors I have talked about in earlier chapters, including health habits, mental and physical exercise, and adequacy of social support.

Health. The single largest factor determining the trajectory of an adult's physical or mental status over the years past 65 is health. Those who are already suffering from one or more chronic diseases at 65 show far more rapid declines than do those who begin late adulthood with no disease symptoms. In part, of course, this is an expression of disease processes themselves. Cardiovascular disease results, among other things, in restricted blood flow to many organs, including the brain, with predictable effects on an adult's ability to learn or remember. Analyses from the Seattle Longitudinal Study show that adults with this disease show earlier declines on all mental abilities (Schaie, 1996). And of course those suffering from the early stages of Alzheimer's disease or another disease that causes dementia will experience far more rapid declines in mental abilities than will those free of such disease.

Ill health also has an indirect effect through its influence on health habits, particularly exercise. Those who have disabilities that prevent them from exercising regularly are likely to show earlier or more rapid decline in many physical and mental functions because of that secondary lack of exercise.

Health Habits. Health habits also have direct effects, even among those who are not disabled. The same health habits that were important predictors of longevity and health in early adulthood continue to be significant predictors among the elderly. For example, a 17-year follow-up of those subjects in the Alameda County epidemiological study who had been 60 or over at the start of the study shows that smoking, low levels of physical activity, and too low or too high weight are linked to increased risk of death over the succeeding 17 years (Kaplan, 1992). Many other large epidemiological studies confirm such connections (e.g., Brody, 1996; Paffenbarger et al., 1987).

Even among older adults living in poverty, whose general risk of poor health is high, individual health habits are related to illness. James Lubben (Lubben, Weiler, & Chi, 1989) has studied the incidence of hospitalization among a group of California elders, all Medicaid recipients, all with incomes of $550 a month or less in 1982. Hospital use in the following year was significantly higher among those who smoked and those who engaged in physical activity less than once a week, even after controlling for the initial level of health in these various groups.

Physical Exercise. Perhaps the most crucial variable is physical exercise, which has been clearly linked not only to greater longevity but also to lower rates of diseases such as heart disease, cancer, osteoporosis, diabetes, gastrointestinal problems, and arthritis (Brody, 1995; Deeg, Kardaun, & Fozard, 1996). Good evidence on this point comes from a longitudinal study of nearly 7000 subjects who were all age 70 or older when they were first tested in 1984 (Wolinsky, Stump, & Clark, 1995). They were then retested every two years until 1990. Those who reported that they had had a regular exercise routine or had walked a mile or more at least once a week in 1984 maintained better physical functioning over the succeeding years, were less likely to die, and were less likely to be in a nursing home by 1990. These predictions held even when the variations in health in 1984 were factored out—that is, it isn't just that healthy adults are more likely to exercise, but that exercise keeps people healthier.

This same point is underlined by a few studies in which older adults have been assigned randomly to exercise and nonexercise groups (e.g., Blumenthal et al.,

There are many ways to maintain physical fitness in old age. In China, you often see the elderly practicing Tai Chi in the early morning. In the United States, adults have many choices, including the synchronized swimming chosen by these women (aged 73–83) in a retirement community in Pennsylvania.

1991). In these studies, too, those who exercised have better scores on various measures of physical functioning.

Physical exercise also seems to help maintain higher levels of cognitive performance among the elderly (Albert et al., 1995). Studies with rats, for example, show that older rats who exercise regularly on treadmills have higher levels of a nerve growth factor that keeps neurons healthy (Cotman & Neeper, 1996). Studies of humans, naturally enough, provide less direct evidence, but nonetheless point in the same direction. One particularly clear study comes from Robert Rogers and his colleagues (Rogers et al., 1990), who followed a group of 85 men from age 65 through age 69. All were well educated and in good health at the start of the study, with no symptoms of heart disease or dementia. In the succeeding four years, a third of the men chose to continue working, mostly at fairly high-level jobs. Another third retired but remained physically active, while the remaining group retired and became physically (and mentally) inactive. The inactive subjects showed progressive declines on a measure of blood flow to the brain and performed significantly lower than either the active retired or the still-working men on a battery of cognitive tests—a set of results shown in Figure 17.10.

If anything, physical exercise seems to be even more important in the later years than at earlier ages. When you are young, you can get away with being sedentary: Your body will still run efficiently even if you neglect it. But with increasing age, optimum function rests to a surprising degree on maintaining at least a moderate level of physical activity. Some authors have suggested that as much as half of the decline in various aspects of physical (and perhaps cognitive) functioning in old age could be prevented through improved lifestyle, particularly exercise. Yet less than a fifth of older adults in the United States exercise regularly (McAuley, 1993; Wolinsky et al., 1995). People give many reasons for not exercising, including poor health, arthritic pain, time demands from an ailing spouse, culturally based assumptions about what is appropriate behavior for older persons, embarrassment about exposing an aging

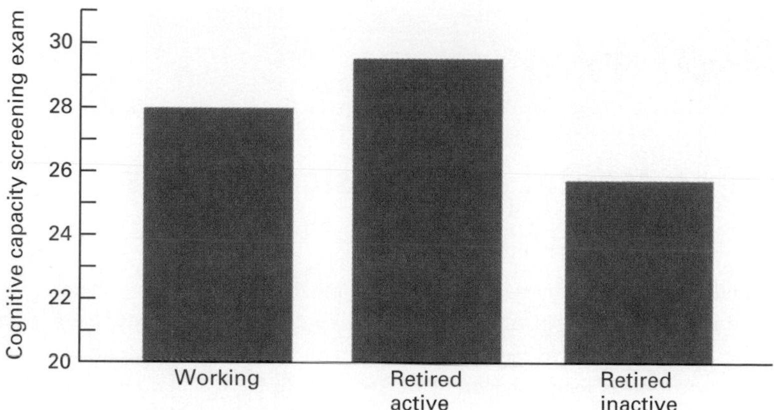

FIGURE 17.10 In this longitudinal study of healthy men, those who became inactive after they retired performed significantly more poorly on tests of mental ability four years later. (*Source:* Rogers et al., 1990, Figure 2, p. 126.)

body to others in an exercise program, lack of available facilities, lack of transportation to suitable fitness sites, fears of various kinds, and plain lethargy.

Mental Exercise. The effects of mental exercise on cognitive functioning among the elderly have been harder to pin down, but several pieces of evidence suggest that "mental fitness" may be as important as physical fitness. Studies with rats, for example, show that older rats placed in very rich, interesting environments show actual *growth* of brain tissue, while rats placed in neutral or boring environments show a decline of brain mass (Cotman & Neeper, 1996). Neurophysiologists involved in this animal research are convinced that something analogous occurs among humans as well, namely that those older adults who seek out and maintain involvement in complex mental activities can delay, or even reverse, the normal decline in brain mass that is part of primary aging. Correlational evidence supports this argument. For example, those older subjects in the Duke longitudinal studies who reported participating in many intellectual activities at the start of the study (such as reading, playing games, or doing hobbies) increased in verbal skills over the following six-year period, while those who were less active showed a decline (Busse & Wang, 1971).

In another study, researchers found that older adults who played bridge regularly had higher scores on tests of both memory and reasoning than did non–bridge players. The two groups did not differ in education, health, exercise levels, or life satisfaction, or on other measures of physical or cognitive functioning that have less obvious relationship to bridge playing, such as reaction time or vocabulary size (Clarkson-Smith & Hartley, 1990). Only on cognitive skills that one might reasonably expect to be sharpened by regular bridge playing was a difference observable. Thus, the effects of intellectual exercise may be quite specific. Memorizing things helps maintain your memory, tasks that demand reasoning help maintain those skills, reading helps maintain your vocabulary, and the like.

The difficulties inherent in this research are obvious, most particularly a serious self-selection problem. People who choose to remain mentally active are doubtless different to begin with from those who choose not to. And teasing out the unique effect of mental activity from the role of education, social class, and health is clearly very difficult. But I think some real effect exists here, some—perhaps significant—enhancement or better maintenance of intellectual skills that comes from an "engaged" and intellectually active lifestyle (Gold et al., 1995).

Social Support. Finally, the adequacy of social support affects both physical and cognitive functioning in old age, just as it does at earlier points in the life span. Two

The Real World

Practical Advice for Maintaining Mental and Physical Fitness in Old Age

After reading everything I have said in the chapters on adulthood, you could probably write this list as well as I can. But let me restate the obvious and tell you how I have tried to implement my own advice.

1. *Establish good health habits early.* Don't wait until you are old to change your health habits. Make changes now, whatever your age. Stop smoking (or don't start); eat a lower-fat diet, particularly one low in cholesterol; keep your weight within 20 percent of the guidelines for your height and build; get enough sleep. These have not all been easy for me to implement. I quit smoking when I was 30, and my weight has always been within about 20 percent of norms (although it *does* fluctuate more than I would like and I am tired of worrying about it!). Because I am a vegetarian, my diet is fairly low in cholesterol naturally, but I have recently increased my efforts to cut down on fat intake. Sleep is the hardest item on this list for me; there are not enough hours in the day.

2. *Exercise your body regularly.* This could be listed under health habits, but it is so important that it is worth listing separately. Begin now, whatever age you are. You don't have to become a long-distance runner or a champion swimmer. You only need to do some aerobic exercise for at least a half hour three times a week. Walking regularly is the easiest way to accomplish this goal, especially if you get into the habit of walking instead of driving to local appointments or to nearby stores. I can no longer jog because my feet won't tolerate it, so I walk 3 miles every morning, and then I walk for most errands that are within a range of about 20 minutes. It adds up to about 25 to 30 miles of walking a week.

3. *Exercise your mind regularly.* Don't stop with your formal education. Keep learning new things. Learn a new language; memorize poetry; learn to play a mentally challenging game like chess or bridge and play it regularly; read the newspaper every day; do crossword puzzles. Challenge your mind, and do so in as wide a variety of ways as you can. Many of these things have been regular parts of my adult life, but there is always room for more. I worked hard to learn a new language (German) when I was 53, and though it was harder than it might have been at 23, it was very gratifying. I can now talk to my in-laws!

4. *Stay in touch with friends and family.* If you do not maintain your social "convoy," it won't be there when you need it, whether the need occurs in old age or at some earlier point. Maintenance of the convoy requires not only that you take time to gather with friends and relatives, it also means taking time to respond to *others'* times of need. I have a large group of women friends I see as often as I can. One friend, who lives nearby, and I have created a tradition of the "hug visit"—a 2-minute visit, when one of us is out running errands, just for a quick hug. With others, who live further away, I make a special effort to get together at least once a year.

5. *Find ways to reduce or control chronic stress.* Bookstore shelves are full of books about stress management. If you are chronically stressed, you may want to look at one or more of those. My own specific advice is to take time each day, even if it is only 5 minutes, for "centering" yourself. This might be through prayer, or meditation, or simply sitting quietly and breathing deeply. My own routine includes several such moments during the day—and when I do not leave time for them, I notice the difference in my level of tension.

6. *Take vacations.* Longer breaks also seem to be important. Vaillant has consistently included an item about vacations in his measure of optimum psychosocial functioning, a measure he finds to be linked to a variety of aspects of health. I try for two 10-day interludes a year, but I confess that I do not always manage that much.

examples come from studies I have already mentioned: In both the Alameda study and in Lubben's study of poor elderly in California, those elders who were more socially isolated at the start of the study had a higher risk of illness or death in the subsequent years than did those with more adequate social networks, independent of their health status or health habits.

I cannot emphasize enough just how large the differences are in the quality of both physical and intellectual functioning among those over 65. Even among the old old and the oldest old there are enormous differences. Every longitudinal study of the elderly has found at least a few subjects who show no decline at all in their mental abilities. What all this suggests is the intriguing possibility that decline may be the typical, but not the *invariable* accompaniment of aging. If that is true, it holds out the hope that by understanding the causes of good or poor maintenance of skills in the last years of life, we may be able to increase greatly the number of adults who are able to keep all their mental (and physical) marbles until very near death. That is a hope well worth vigorous research pursuit.

Summary

1. The percentage of the population above 65 has been increasing rapidly in the past decades, and will continue to increase into the next century.
2. In the United States, a woman of 65 can expect to live an average of another 19 years, while a man can expect 15 more years. More of those years will include disability for women than for men.
3. Changes in the brain associated with aging include most centrally a loss of dendritic density in neurons, which has the effect of slowing reaction time for almost all tasks.
4. Further changes in the eyes mean that older adults have more difficulty adapting to darkness and light, especially glare.
5. Loss of hearing is more common and more noticeable after 65 than at earlier ages; it includes loss of hearing for high sounds, some loss of ability to discriminate words, and greater difficulty hearing under noise conditions.
6. Taste discrimination remains largely unchanged with age, but smell discrimination declines substantially in late adulthood.
7. Older adults also show different sleep patterns: less REM sleep, earlier waking, and more frequent waking in the night.
8. The rate of physical disability also increases in late adulthood, but at every age there are at least some adults who have no restriction in activity. Arthritis, hypertension, and heart disease are the most likely causes of disability.
9. Dementia is rare before late adulthood, becoming steadily more common with advancing age and affecting 15 percent or more of those over 85. The most common cause is Alzheimer's disease.
10. Alzheimer's disease is characterized by specific forms of brain degeneration. The causes are not fully understood, but several specific genetic patterns clearly contribute, including the presence of a gene for ApoE4.
11. Most forms of emotional disturbance are less frequent in late adulthood. The exception is mild or moderate depression, which appears to rise in frequency past age 70 or 75. Serious clinical depression, however, appears not to be more common in old age.
12. The most noticeable effect of all the physical changes of aging on day-to-day behavior is a general slowing of all responses. Another effect is a general decline in dexterity, balance, and stamina.
13. Many older adults continue to be sexually active, although this becomes less common with increasing age.
14. There is as yet no widely accepted theory of the aging process. Current alternatives emphasize the possible existence of genetic limiting conditions and/or the cumulative effects of malfunction within cells.
15. On virtually all measures of cognitive functioning, reliable decrements are found after about age 70. On speeded or unexercised tasks significant loss occurs earlier.
16. This is reflected on most tests of memory, including tests of "familiar" or "everyday" memory problems. The difficulty occurs in both encoding and retrieval processes, and appears to reflect both the general slowing in the nervous system and perhaps a loss of working memory capacity.
17. Problem-solving skill shows a similar pattern; even on familiar material older adults appear to be less skillful at finding varied solutions.
18. Even in late adulthood, however, adults have "reserve capacity"—the ability to improve performance on any cognitive task with training, although younger adults have *more* reserve capacity.
19. Some authors suggest that older adults are more wise, but research on this question is in its infancy.
20. There are vast individual differences in the timing and pace of all the physical and mental changes described.
21. For some types of ability, skills may be retained at peak level until a few years from death (the terminal drop hypothesis). For others, the decline is more gradual.
22. The timing and rate of decline is affected by heredity, overall health, current and prior health habits (particularly physical and mental exercise), and availability of adequate social support. Skills that are not used regularly show more rapid decline. Thus, "use it or lose it."

Key Terms

Alzheimer's disease (AD)
cross-linking
dementia
disability
Hayflick limit
terminal drop hypothesis
working memory

Suggested Readings

Baltes, P. B. (1993). The aging mind: Potential and limits. *The Gerontologist, 33,* 580–594.

In this paper, Baltes offers a particularly optimistic view of cognitive aging.

Birren, J. E., & Schaie, K. W. (Eds.) (1996). *Handbook of the psychology of aging* (4th ed.). San Diego, CA: Academic Press.

A somewhat technical, detailed, highly current set of papers on a wide range of topics relating to physical and psychological aging. A very good source of current references.

Bond, J., & Coleman, P. (Eds.) (1990). *Aging in society: An introduction to social gerontology.* London: Sage Publications.

A very good general source on many aspects of aging, written primarily by British researchers, which means that it provides a welcome look at the process of aging in elders outside the United States.

Hayflick, L. (1994). *How and why we age.* New York: Ballantine Books.

In this excellent book aimed at a lay audience, Hayflick reviews what we know about the aging of various parts of the body, and considers evidence supporting or refuting the several existing theories of aging. He concludes that we still do not have the key to the puzzle.

Sternberg, R. J. (Ed.) (1990b). *Wisdom: Its nature, origins, and development.* Cambridge, England: Cambridge University Press.

The best single current source on this interesting subject, although far more theorizing than data is offered.

Social and Personality Development in Late Adulthood

18

It may seem that the physical and mental changes in late adulthood are so striking and so pervasive that they necessarily dominate any discussion of these final years of life. Certainly the biological clock *is* far louder in these years. But the changes in roles and relationships are perhaps just as striking. If early adulthood is the period when we add complex, time-consuming roles and middle adulthood is the period when those roles are redefined and renegotiated, then late adulthood is the time when many of them are shed.

Overall Changes in Roles

The role of worker is given up at retirement; the role of daughter or son is given up when the last parent dies; widowhood means giving up the role of spouse. Many smaller roles a person may have filled in religious or community organizations may also be given up in these later years in favor of younger people. An older adult may step down from the position as chair of the local United Way fund drive, or as head of the program committee for the garden club, or as member of a local school board or church committee.

CRITICAL THINKING

Can you think of other examples of "empty" roles occupied by older adults? Can you think of counterexamples—roles filled by older adults that are not empty, that have clear rules and expectations attached to them?

Moreover, as sociologist Irving Rosow has pointed out (1985), the roles that do remain in late adulthood have far less content, far fewer duties or expectations. For example, most older adults continue to occupy the role of parent, but this role is typically far less demanding in these late years. Unless you had your children very late or they have encountered unusual difficulties in getting established in their own lives, by the time you are 65 your last child is long since launched and fully independent. Similarly, in other arenas, elders may occupy roles that have titles, but fewer duties. A retired university professor, for instance, may have the title of *emeritus professor*, a position that carries a few benefits but essentially no obligations. In other organizations, an older individual may be given the title of "honorary chairman."

In a practical sense, this decline in role content means that for many older adults the routines of life are no longer structured by specific roles. But is this good or bad? Some, including Rosow, see this loss of role definition as carrying with it a significant risk of isolation or alienation. Other social scientists see distinct advantages to this "roleless" time in late life.

One such advantage is a greater "licence for eccentricity" (Bond & Coleman, 1990, p. 78). Because they do not have to fit into the sometimes tight confines of role expectations, older adults feel far freer to express their own individuality—in dress, language, and personal preferences. I think this change begins before age 65; the gradual assertion of just such individuality seems to be characteristic of middle adulthood as well. But certainly in late adulthood there is a kind of institutionalized acceptance of eccentricity. As Jenny Joseph's popular poem says,

> When I am old, I will wear purple
> with a red hat which doesn't go, and doesn't suit me.
> And I shall spend my pension on brandy and summer gloves
> and satin sandals, and say we've no money for butter

To see whether the optimistic or the pessimistic vision of role loss in late adulthood is more valid, we need to look at the changes in roles and relationships among older adults. One place to begin is with a look at demographic changes in household composition and patterns of assistance. In middle adulthood, the majority of adults still live with a spouse or partners. In late adulthood that becomes less and less common.

Living Arrangements

Figure 18.1 shows marital statuses for the young old and the old old in the United States in 1994. For comparison purposes, I've also given marital statuses for those in late middle age.

Several things ought to jump out at you immediately from this figure. First, the percentage of married adults clearly drops in late adulthood. But even more clearly, this change is vastly larger and more rapid for women than for men. Because men typically marry younger women, and because women live longer than men, the normal expectation for a man is that he will have a spouse or intimate partner until he dies. The normal expectation for a woman is that she will eventually be without such

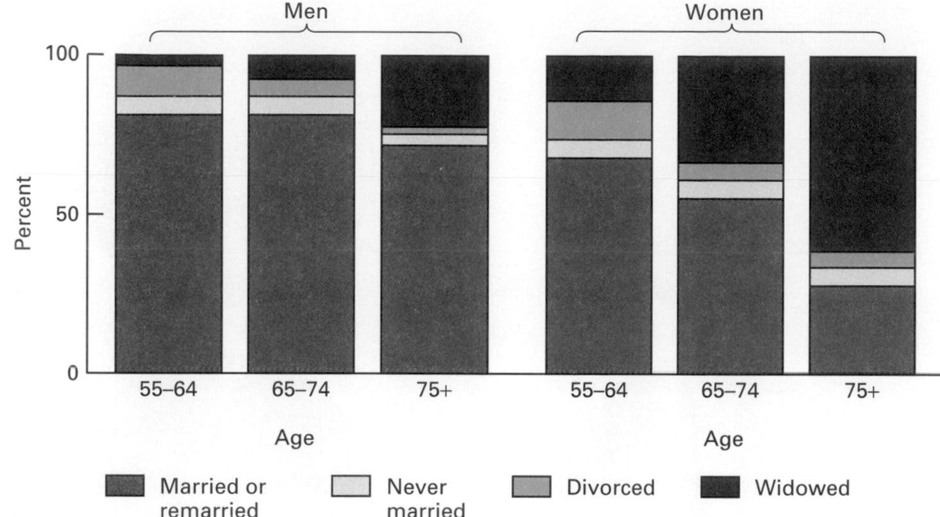

FIGURE 18.1 These data from the United States in 1994 show that among all elders, but most dramatically among older women, there is a decline in the likelihood of living with a spouse. (*Source:* U.S. Bureau of the Census, 1995, from Table 59, p. 55.)

a partner, often for many years. It is hard to exaggerate the importance of that difference for the experience of late adulthood for men and women.

This same difference is also clearly reflected in the second set of data, in Figure 18.2, which shows the living arrangements of noninstitutionalized U.S. elders. Seventy-five percent of men over 65 live with their spouses, compared with only 41 percent of women—a pattern matched in other industrialized countries.

In the United States and many other Western industrialized countries, living alone is the most common choice among unmarried elders, even among those whose health has declined. A particularly intriguing set of data comes from a study by Jacqueline Worobey and Ronald Angel (Worobey & Angel, 1990), who interviewed 2498 unmarried men and women over 70. Each of these subjects had been contacted twice, once in 1984 and once in 1986, so it was possible for Worobey and Angel to look at changes in living arrangements for those whose health stayed the same, improved, or declined. Of those who lived alone at the start of the study and whose health declined over the next two years, 81 percent of the men and 76 percent of the women still lived alone two years later.

That does not mean that health has no impact on living arrangements. It clearly does. In the United States, older adults with significant health problems are more likely to live with their children or with other relatives than are those who are more healthy (e.g., Choi, 1991; Stinner, Byun, & Paita, 1990). But most elders with mild or moderate disability or health problems do not live with relatives. Most appear to prefer to live alone and do so as long as possible—at least in our culture in current cohorts. In other cultures, the pattern is often quite different. In Japan, for example, only 7 percent of adults over 60 live alone, and only 29 percent live with a spouse only. Over half live with a child (Tsuya & Martin, 1992).

Other than health, the factors that affect the probability that a single older adult in the United States will live with a child or with other relatives include

- *Income*: Those with lower incomes are more likely to live with family, although this difference is not large (Choi, 1991). Many elders with marginal or below-poverty incomes live alone.
- *Ethnicity*: White elders are considerably more likely to live alone than are African-American, Hispanic, or Asian-American elderly—yet another manifestation of the broader ethnic differences in family living patterns I have al-

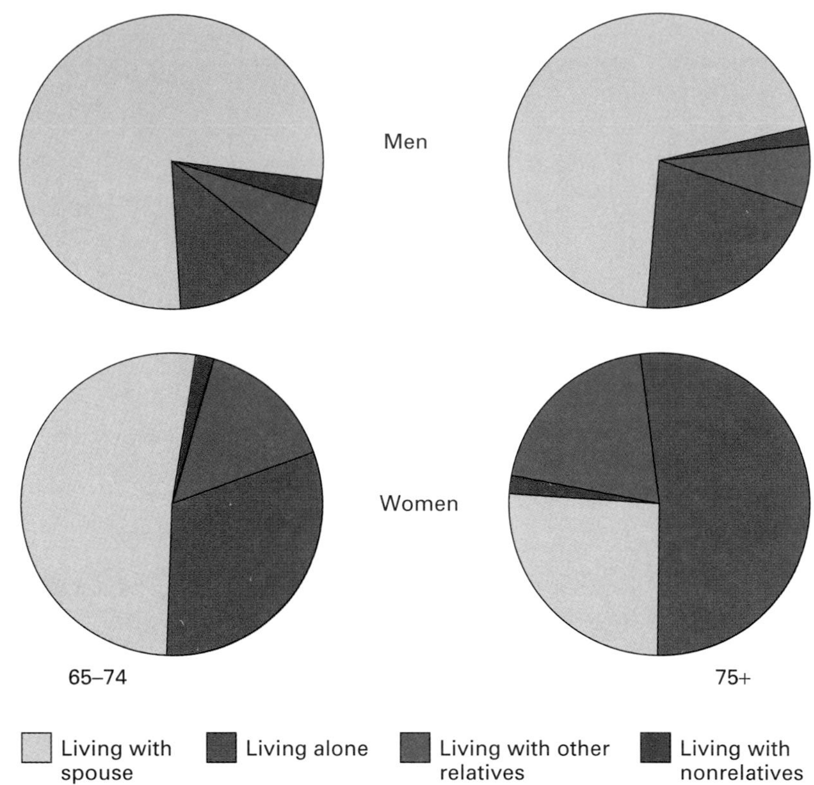

FIGURE 18.2 These U.S. data from 1994 describe the living arrangements of noninstitutionalized elders. You can see that for those elders who are not living with a spouse, living alone is the most common alternative, followed by living with relatives. Only a small percentage live with nonrelatives. (*Source:* U.S. Bureau of the Census, 1995, Table 62, p. 56.)

ready described. Data from the 1990 census show that only 9.8 percent of unmarried white adults over 60 lived with kin, compared with roughly 25 percent among blacks, Hispanics, and Asians (Himes, Hogan, & Eggebeen, 1996).

- *Number of daughters and sons:* The more children an elder has, the more likely he or she is to live with a child, but this is more true of daughters than of sons. That is, elders with more daughters are more likely to live with a child than are those with few daughters, but having more sons does not increase the likelihood (Soldo, Wolf, & Agree, 1990).

What do all these statistics suggest about the roles and relationships of older adults? First and foremost, of course, they point to a sharp divergence of experience between men and women in these later years. They also tell us that we will need to look beyond the spousal or partnership relationship if we are to understand the pattern of social interactions that are central to the aging individual. With so many unmarried elders, relationships with children and other family members may become more central. With so many elders living alone, relationships with friends may also become more significant.

Relationships

Partner Relationships

We have little information about partnerships in late adulthood that would change what I have already said about such relationships in midlife. Cross-sectional comparisons tell us that marital satisfaction is higher in these late years than when chil-

The Real World

Deciding on Nursing Home Care

In Chapter 17 I talked a bit about the numbers of older adults living in nursing homes and other institutions. Who are those institutionalized elders? And how do they and their families make the decision that this is the best form of care?

First of all, let me say that special institutions for the care of the elderly appear to be unique to industrialized countries, primarily those in the West. The norm in other parts of the world, particularly in strongly communal cultures, is for elders to be cared for by their families (Holmes & Holmes, 1995). Even in Western cultures, nursing home care is a relatively recent alternative and is clearly the alternative of last resort in the great majority of families (McAuley & Blieszner, 1985). Nursing home care is widely perceived as impersonal and lacking in dignity and personal control (e.g., Biedenharn & Normoyle, 1991).

The economics of nursing home care also make it unattractive for many older adults. Such care now costs $3000 and up per month, costs not covered by Medicare or most health insurance plans. A stay of as long as a year will exhaust the disposable assets of the majority of older adults. To be eligible for Medic*aid* coverage for such care, all disposable assets must first be used up, which may leave a surviving spouse in very difficult financial straits. Many states now have laws that permit certain assets, such as a home, to be transferred to a surviving spouse so that this asset need not be used up before the partner in the nursing home is eligible for Medicaid—a procedure that leaves the surviving spouse in somewhat better financial condition. But there may still be significant impoverishment.

In the face of such personal preferences and economic realities, family members make the decision for nursing home placement with great reluctance, only after all other options have been ruled out or exhausted. It is an immensely difficult decision, fraught with guilt and distress.

Not surprisingly, the likelihood of nursing home placement varies considerably from one subgroup to another. Studies in the United States, Canada, and European countries show that the most likely candidate for institutional care is an unmarried white woman over the age of 75 with no or few children (in particular, with no daughters), with significant disability or dementia, and with few economic resources (Carrière & Pelletier, 1995; Montgomery & Kosloski, 1994; Steinbach, 1992; Wolinsky et al., 1993). Married elders are about half as likely as unmarried ones to spend any time in a nursing home, and those with at least one daughter are about one-quarter as likely (Freedman, 1996). Nursing home care is especially likely if the elder is no longer able to use the toilet without help or feed herself, although even among those who are disabled to this extent, home care rather than institutional care is still the most common arrangement.

The problem for individual families is to try to balance the needs of everyone in the system: the need of the older adult for independence and control; the financial support available; the needs of younger family members who have lives of their own to lead. Susan Kushner Resnick's description of the family decision with and for her 90-year-old grandmother conveys the complexity and the distress:

> Nobody wanted to send her to the home, as it's called. After she broke her hip, she went there to recover, but she never got well enough to leave. The alternatives were worse than institutionalization. She could stay in her apartment only with 24-hour nursing care. The expense was the first deterrent; the second, her fear of the possibility that one night the nurse would call in sick and she would have to stay alone. We discussed sending her to her daughter's (my mother's) house, but since both of my parents work, she wouldn't have gotten constant care. Besides, the sandwich generation wasn't equipped for the strain of catering night and day to an elderly person. So it was decided. "I know I need to stay here," Nana told me, . . . "but I *hate* to break up my house." (*New York Times,* March 8, 1992, p. 22)

What often tips the balance, one way or the other, is whether any family member is able or willing to provide assistance, and whether other community services can help fill the service gap. In the case of Resnick's grandmother, sufficient support was not available. But for other families, Meals on Wheels, visiting nurses, adult day-care services, or the equivalent may make it possible for family members to continue to care for a frail or demented elder. An intermediate alternative, growing in availability, is some kind of "supportive housing," in which the older person has an individual apartment and thus lives independently, but has nursing and meal services available in the building or complex (Pynoos & Golant, 1996).

Certainly, if average nursing home care were of much higher quality than it now is, with built-in opportunities for personal control, challenging activities, and first-rate medical care, and if such care were covered by Medicare or other national health insurance, choosing such a care option might be less difficult. But until we reach that optimistic point, the choice of nursing home care—for oneself or for an aging parent—is likely to continue to be wrenching and painful.

Affection and mutual pleasure between married couples clearly does not disappear in old age. Frank and Palmina Canovi, married over 70 years, were both over 100 when this photo was taken.

dren are still at home or being launched. But this satisfaction may have a somewhat different basis in late adulthood than is true of the high marital satisfaction of the early years of marriage. Late adulthood marriages are less based on passion and mutual disclosure and more on loyalty, familiarity, and mutual investment in the relationship (Bengtson, Rosenthal, & Burton, 1990). In Sternberg's terms (recall Table 14.2, p. 363), they are more likely to reflect companionate love than romantic or even consummate love.

But this does not mean that late-life marriages are necessarily devitalized or neutral. That may well be true for some, but we have evidence to the contrary for many. You'll recall from Chapter 17 (Figure 17.7) that at least half of late-life couples are still sexually active. Collectively, older couples also report higher levels of pleasure and lower levels of conflict in their relationships than do middle-aged couples. When they do have conflicts, they resolve them in more affectionate and less negative ways (Carstensen, Gottman, & Levenson, 1995; Levenson, Carstensen, & Gottman, 1993). Older couples also spend more time with each other than with family or friends, and although much of this time is spent in passive activities or basic maintenance—watching TV, doing housework, running errands—it is also true that those married elders who spend more time with their spouses report that they are happier (e.g., Larson, Mannell, & Zuzanek, 1986).

Further evidence of the deep bond that continues to exist in late-life marriages is the remarkable degree of care and assistance older spouses give each other when one or the other is disabled or demented. Among married elders with some kind of disability, by far the largest source of assistance is the spouse, not children or friends. Many husbands and wives continue to care for severely ill or demented spouses over very long periods of time. And many elderly couples in which both spouses suffer from significant disabilities nonetheless continue to care for one another 'til death do them part. Late adult marriages may thus be less romantic or less emotionally intense than is true of the early years of marriage, but they are typically satisfying and highly committed.

It is the *loss* of the partnership/marriage relationship through the death of the spouse or partner that alters this pattern for so many older adults, as you have already seen in Figure 18.1. The gender difference in marital status among elders is further increased by a higher rate of *re*marriage for older men than for women, a pattern found both among the widowed and the divorced at every age. Twenty percent of single men over 65 remarry, compared with only 2 percent of women. Older unmarried men are also more likely to date, and more likely to cohabit (Bulcroft & Bulcroft, 1991).

Critical Thinking

How many different explanations can you think of for the fact that older single men are more likely to remarry than are women?

I will be talking about the grief and loss of widowhood in Chapter 19. Here I want only to reemphasize what I have said before about the impact of marriage (or other central partnership) on other aspects of physical and psychological functioning. Married older adults, like married adults of any age, have certain distinct advantages: They have higher life satisfaction, better health, and lower rates of institutionalization. Such differential advantages are generally greater for married older men than for married older women, again as is true among younger adults. This difference might be interpreted as indicating that marriage affords more benefits to men than to women. Or we might conclude that men rely more on their marriage relationship for social support and are thus more affected by its loss. Whatever the explanation, it seems clear that among older women, marital status is less strongly connected to health or life satisfaction, *except* that marital status is strongly connected to financial security among older women—a point I'll come back to in a moment.

At the risk of repeating myself, I want to emphasize yet again how profound is the difference between the normal experience of older men and women. Women *expect* to be widowed; men do not. Women expect to spend some time living alone; men do not. In fact it is quite possible that this difference in expectation plays some role in the differential impact of marital status on older men and women. We know that unexpected or unplanned life changes are generally more difficult to handle than are ex-

More older men than women are married not only because men tend to die before their wives, but because they are more likely to remarry if they are widowed, as this man is doing. As is typical, he is marrying a woman younger than himself, increasing the likelihood that she will be widowed in her turn.

pected or planned changes. Women may thus prepare psychologically for singleness, while men do not.

Relationships with Children and Other Kin

Folklore and popular press descriptions of late adulthood suggest that family, particularly children and grandchildren, form the core of the social life of older adults, perhaps especially those older adults who are widowed. There is some support for such a view, but also some curious nonconfirmations.

Older adults do describe their intergenerational bonds as strong and important; most report a significant sense of family solidarity and support (Bengtson et al., 1996). These bonds are reflected, among other things, in regular contact between elders and their kin. For example, in one very large national sample of over 11,000 adults aged 65 and older, 63 percent reported that they saw at least one of their children once a week or more often; another 16 percent saw a child one to three times a month, and only 20 percent saw their children as rarely as once a month or less (Crimmins & Ingegneri, 1990). Such regular contact is made easier by the fact that even in the United States, where distances are large and mobility has been high, three-quarters of elders live within an hour's travel of at least one of their children. Very similar figures are reported by researchers in other developed countries such as England (Jerrome, 1990), so this pattern is not unique to the United States.

Patterns of Aid. Part of the regular contact between elders and their children is, of course, aid given to and received from the elder person—a pattern I already described in Chapter 16. The great majority of the aid needed by older adults that cannot be provided by a spouse is provided by other family members, principally children. One representative set of numbers comes from the National Survey of Families and Households, a large national U.S. sample that included over 1500 adults over 65 who had at least one living child. In this group, 52 percent were receiving some household help, and 21 percent were receiving some financial help from at least one child (Hoyert, 1991).

Not surprisingly, the same factors that contribute to the likelihood of an elder living with a child also predict the amount of non-live-in help an older adult will receive from her children: Blacks and Hispanics are more likely to receive help than are whites, and those with lower incomes receive more help, as do those with more children. Unmarried older women receive the most help from their children.

Emotional Connections. But relationships between older parents and their children cannot be reduced simply to the exchange of aid. A great deal of the interaction is social as well as functional, and the great majority of older adults describe their relationships with their adult children in positive terms. Most see their children not only out of obligation or duty but because such contacts are pleasurable, and a very large percentage describe at least one child as a confidant (Connidis & Davies, 1992).

There are obviously exceptions—parent-child relationships that are distant, cold, or fraught with strain and difficulty. But in the main, elders describe their relationships with their children as being close and compatible.

Children and Life Satisfaction. The puzzle comes when we look at the correlation between an older adult's contacts with her children and her overall level of satisfaction with her life. Given the obvious centrality of relationships with children in the daily life of most elders, it seems entirely reasonable to assume that those who have more frequent contact with their offspring will report higher levels of happiness or life satisfaction. But this is *not* what researchers have found. Those who see their children more often, or report more positive interactions, do not describe themselves as happier or healthier overall than do those who have less frequent or less positive relationships with their children (e.g., Lee & Ishii-Kuntz, 1987; Lee & Shehan, 1989; Mullins & Mushel, 1992; Seccombe, 1987). For example, in one study of over 1000 elders in Florida, all of whom were participating in a home-delivered meal program, the amount of loneliness elders reported was *not* related to how often they saw their children or how emotionally close they were to their children (Mullins & Mushel, 1992). Far more important was the presence or absence of a set of friends.

I have found such results surprising, and thought at first that the pattern might be unique to the dominant white American culture, within which independence is such a valued trait. But similar results have been found in a study of elders in India (Venkatraman, 1995), and in at least one study among Mexican-American elders (Lawrence, Bennett, & Markides, 1992), both groups for whom familial contact is a strong cultural value. Indeed, in the Mexican-American study, those adults who had the most contact with their children had the highest levels of psychological *distress*, including depression. Even among those who were not physically dependent on their children, frequency of contact was not linked to satisfaction or to lower levels of depression. In all these studies, the adults reported regular contact with children and grandchildren and said they enjoyed it. But family interaction was not necessary for nor did it enhance their sense of well-being.

This older couple clearly get much pleasure from the company of their daughter and granddaughter. But research suggests that such family contact is not an essential ingredient in an older adult's overall morale.

The Real World

Elder Abuse

One extreme manifestation of conflict and strain between elders and their children is the existence of physical abuse of elders. Such abuse has received a great deal of media coverage in recent years, but in fact it is *not* especially common; current estimates are that only about 3 percent of U.S. elders are physically abused (Bengtson et al., 1996). Physical abuse is most likely to be directed at demented elders, twice as often by *spouses* as by children (Pillemer & Finkelhor, 1988).

Researchers have identified several risk factors for this form of abuse, including mental illness or alcoholism in the abuser, financial dependency of the abuser on the victim, social isolation, and external stresses (Pillemer & Suitor, 1990, 1992):

> A likely candidate for elder abuse is an elderly widow sharing her household with a dependent son who has a mental illness problem or a drug or alcohol dependency: the son is dependent for housing and money on the mother; the mother is too dependent on her son to kick him out, and too ashamed of the abuse to tell others about it. (Bengtson et al., 1996, p. 272)

Abuse is also more likely when the demented elder is physically violent, as well as in couples in which the husband has physically abused his wife throughout their adult lives and simply continues to do so in old age.

Other forms of elder abuse may be far more subtle, including financial exploitation or failure to provide needed aid. Certainly the existence of such destructive forms of interaction remind us that older adults' relationships with their kin are not all sweetness and light. But it is also important to bear in mind that these highly negative patterns are the exception rather than the rule. For most elders, relationships with children and other kin may be a mixed bag, but the scale most often balances toward the positive rather than the negative.

One possible explanation of this apparent paradox might be that combining results for married and unmarried elders in these correlations is confusing the issue. Married elders have each other and thus do not need their children's emotional support in order to feel satisfied. If that's true, we might expect to find that contact with children is critical for overall happiness or sense of well-being only for unmarried elders. But once again that's not what the research shows. The lack of connection between contact with children and well-being holds for older widows as well as for those with spouses still living.

Another possible explanation is that the relationship with one's children is still full of role prescriptions, even in old age. It may be friendly, but it is not chosen in the same way that a relationship with a friend is. With your friend, you may feel free to "be yourself," you may feel accepted as who you are. With your children, you may feel the need to live up to their demands and expectations.

Several small research studies support this possibility. For instance, Maria Talbott (1990) interviewed 55 older widows at some length about their relationships with their children. These women said many positive things about those relationships, but they described certain negatives as well. Some felt neglected by their children, some felt unappreciated, some were afraid of bothering or burdening their children.

In a rather different type of study, Reed Larson and his colleagues (Larson et al., 1986) asked a group of 92 older adults to wear pagers for a week. During the day, each subject was paged about once every two hours. When paged, the subject wrote down who he was with; what he was doing; and how happy, cheerful, friendly, sociable, alert, energetic, active, or excited he felt at that moment. Larson found that subjects described fewer positive emotions when they were paged while interacting with their children than while interacting with friends. These older adults also described quite different activities with the two groups. When with children, they were most likely to report doing housework; with friends they most often reported socializing or eating.

Critical Thinking

Think about the oldest generation in your family. How would you describe the family role that those aging parents (or grandparents) fill? What are the family's expectations? Can you detect potential sources of strain in this role?

Yet another possibility is that one of the potential negatives about relationships with children in late adulthood is that these relationships are not *reciprocal*, not balanced. For instance, several earlier studies by Linda Thompson and Alexis Walker (Thompson & Walker, 1984; Walker & Thompson, 1983) show greater attachment and affection between mothers and daughters when the relationship is perceived as equal in giving and receiving. To the extent that parent-child relationships in late adulthood become *less* reciprocal—as they typically do—the aging parent may experience those relationships as less satisfying and thus less contributory to high morale.

Finally, it is quite possible that in most of this research we have focused on the wrong aspect of family relationships in trying to understand their role in older adult lives. Just as other research on social support tells us that it is *satisfaction* with one's level of support rather than the objective amount of support that is linked to health, so it may well be that satisfaction with family contacts would be linked to overall satisfaction. The only study I know of that approached the question in this way does indeed show precisely this. Crohan and Antonucci (1989), in a study of 718 American adults aged 50 to 95, found that satisfaction with family relationships was correlated with overall life satisfaction, while *quantity* of contact with family was not.

Social scientists are still trying to unravel this particular skein of results. For now, the best I can tell you is that family relationships, while essential for many aspects of care and assistance for older adults, are full of ripples and eddies, demands and inequities, paradoxes as well as pleasures.

Research Report

Late-Life Relationships Among the Never-Married or Childless

Research on the experiences of never-married or married but childless elders adds further to the somewhat contradictory information about the potential importance or unimportance of relationships with children in late adulthood. Snippets of information point in quite opposite directions.

On the negative side, in the United States and other industrialized countries, widowed men without children are more prone to suicide, alcoholism, and accidental death, while widowed childless women are more likely to be institutionalized (Aldous & Klein, 1991). Childless widowed elders, both men and women, are also more likely to live alone and more likely to have low levels of contact with others. In one national survey in 1974 (Bachrach, 1980), a quarter of those over 65 who were childless and living alone reported having had no contact with any other person in the previous two days, compared with only 10 percent of those living alone who had at least one child. These statistics paint a rather bleak picture of the late years among childless adults.

On the other hand, several studies show that childless elderly are no less satisfied with their lives than are those with children (e.g., Connidis & McMullin, 1993; Glenn & McLanahan, 1981). Those who are still married find satisfaction within that relationship. One study even shows that marital satisfaction is higher among those elders without children than among those who have at least one child (Lee, 1988). And those who never married, perhaps especially never-married women, have often created rich networks of other relationships, with kin, with friends, with the children of kin or friends (Dykstra, 1995). One older never-married woman interviewed by Robert Rubinstein (Rubinstein et al., 1991) described such a network of friends:

> Family has had practically no meaning to me. Very little. My friends have been my family. And there are people out there in Michigan who really feel that I am a part of their family. We call each other up on the phone. They're concerned. (p. S275)

Some of the women in this study did express some concern about their ability to care for themselves in late old age without the support of children or grandchildren. But these women had found creative ways to fill their needs for companionship and social support, beyond or in place of traditional family ties.

These apparently contradictory findings are a good illustration of why it is so difficult to draw broad generalizations about "the elderly." There are obviously many pathways, each with potentially positive adaptations. Childless single men may be a particularly vulnerable subgroup precisely because they appear to find it more difficult to create alternative or compensatory relationships (Brubaker, 1990). But the lack of marriage, or children, is not at all an inevitable recipe for discontent in old age.

Siblings. I have not said much about sibling relationships between adults, primarily because brothers and sisters do not ordinarily loom large in adults' social networks. Most adults have at least one living sibling, and most report that they have at least moderately close relationships with their brothers and sisters. But few would place a brother or sister in the center circle of their social network (Cicirelli, 1982; Goetting, 1986). Most write or call occasionally and see one another on family occasions but are not exceptionally close. Faced with an important decision, few adults say that they would turn to a sibling for advice. A few small studies suggest that sibling relationships are closer among some ethnic groups, such as Italian Americans and African Americans (Gold, 1990; Johnson, 1982). But even in these groups the number of emotionally intimate sibling relationships appears to be fairly small.

Interestingly, though, it looks as if relationships with siblings may become more important in late adulthood (Bedford, 1989; Gold, 1989). Siblings seldom provide much practical assistance to one another in old age, but older siblings can and often do serve two other important functions. First, many elders see their siblings as a kind of "insurance policy" in old age, a source of support of last resort (Connidis, 1994). More generally, in these later years, siblings can provide a unique kind of emotional support for one another, based on shared reminiscences and companionship—what Deborah Gold calls *generational solidarity*. No one else knows all the old stories, all the family jokes, the names and history of former friends and neighbors. But it seems once again to be especially sisters who provide the most such helpful support. For example, Victor Cicirelli, in a small study of 83 older adults (1989), found that those who described themselves as close to a sister had the lowest levels of depression. Those with poor relationships with their sister(s) had the highest levels of depression, while the quality of relationships with brothers was unrelated to depression. Similarly, Shirley O'Bryant (1988) found that among recently widowed women, those who had a sister nearby adjusted far better to widowhood than did those lacking such sisterly support. The availability of brothers had no such beneficial effect in this study, and neither did contact with children—yet another example to reinforce the point I made earlier.

These findings point once again to the differential role of women as kin-keepers, as providers of emotional support. In late adulthood, sisters may sometimes take the place of a spouse as a close confidant.

Friends

Relationships with friends in later life are less ambivalent than are relationships with family, although they may be equally complex in other ways. The small amount of research we have is consistent with the hypothesis that the number of friendships may diminish gradually from age 65 onward (e.g., Blieszner & Adams, 1992; Levitt, Weber, & Guacci, 1993). Most close friends at this age are friends of long standing; as they die the network becomes smaller. Widowed adults may also lose contact with still-married friends.

Critical Thinking

Why might it be the case that most friends in late adulthood are friends of long standing? Are there social barriers to creating new friendships in old age? Are there psychological barriers?

At the same time, mounting evidence suggests that contact with friends—unlike contact with family members—has a significant impact on overall life satisfaction, on self-esteem, and on the amount of loneliness reported by older adults (Adams & Blieszner, 1989; Antonucci, 1990; Jerrome, 1990; Lee & Ishii-Kuntz, 1987; Lee & Shehan, 1989). This is particularly true of unmarried elders, but is at least somewhat true for those still married as well.

Friends meet different kinds of needs for older adults than do family members. For one thing, relationships with friends are likely to be more reciprocal or equitable, and we know that such equitable relationships are more valued and less stressful. Friends provide companionship, opportunities for laughter, sharing of activities. In one Canadian study, for example, friends were second only to spouses as sources of companionship among those over 65 (Connidis & Davies, 1992). And because friends generally come from the same cohort, they can also provide the same "generational

In late adulthood, friends seem to play a special role, perhaps because they share the same background and memories—like favorite old tunes.

solidarity" that elders may find with their siblings. Friends may also provide significant assistance with daily tasks, such as shopping or housework, although they typically provide less help of this kind than do family members.

Gender Differences in Friendships and in Network Structure. As at earlier ages, women and men appear to form different kinds of social networks, with men's friendships involving less disclosure and less intimacy than is true among women. A particularly helpful set of data to illustrate these differences comes from Toni Antonucci's national survey of network systems in adults aged 50 plus (Antonucci & Akiyama, 1987b). In order to make the two gender groups comparable, she included only men and women who were married and had at least one living child. Antonucci found no differences in the number of friends men and women identified, but she did find several other differences, which she summarizes:

> The differences between men and women in some ways are quite simple: men rely on their spouse; women rely on children and friends in addition to their spouse. (Antonucci & Akiyama, 1987b, p. 748)

It would be very helpful to have an equivalent set of data for unmarried older men and women with living children. Lacking a spouse, does a man turn more to his children, or perhaps to a sister? Or does he then extend his friendship network? Research on the impact of widowhood on men suggests indirectly that many men may do none of these. Widowed men appear to be at greater risk for a variety of health problems and emotional distress than are widowed women—indications that their social support systems are not sufficient to buffer them from this major stress. But it would be good to have more direct information about the role of friends among unmarried older adults.

Ethnic Group Differences: Social Networks Among African-American Elderly. Not only do older blacks appear to have somewhat warmer relationships with their siblings and higher rates of coresidence with their children, they also show two other creative patterns of social network use. They create strong relationships with fictive kin, a pattern I described in a Cultures and Contexts box in Chapter 14 (page 370). In African-American groups, friends often acquire a status like that of a close sibling, aunt, uncle, or grandparent. Among elders of all ethnic groups, such fictive kin may be important sources of both emotional and instrumental support (Mac Rae, 1992), but the pattern is particularly prevalent among African Americans (e.g., Johnson & Barer, 1990).

A second network pattern seen more among African-American elders than among white elders is the use of a church community as a significant source of social support. For example, among black older women in one large national sample, those who regularly participated in social events at a church were more likely to give and receive high levels of help from friends rather than from children (Hatch, 1991). Other research suggests that among black elders more than among whites, participation in church social activities is linked to higher levels of well-being (Bryant & Rakowski, 1992; Walls & Zarit, 1991). Given the fact that many more African-American elders than whites are unmarried, heads of households, or poor, both the use of fictive kin and the reliance on church support seem effective strategies for increasing overall social support.

Participation in church activities is more likely to be a central aspect of the support system for older African Americans than for other older groups in the United States.

An Overview of Relationships in Late Adulthood

Two things stand out for me in looking at relationship patterns in late adulthood. First of all, there is a great deal of continuity in relationships from earlier periods of life. Women continue to create more intimate networks and continue their role as kin keepers; men continue to rely primarily on their spouses as confidants. African Americans and other U.S. minorities continue to create more extended families and rely more on their families for a variety of assistance. This continuity exists at an individual level as well: Those who have many friends and extensive networks in early and middle adulthood are likely to continue to create such networks in old age (Hansson & Carpenter, 1994; McCrae & Costa, 1990), while those who are more solitary or introverted are likely to persist in that pattern.

The second thing that strikes me is that this continuity occurs despite significant attrition in the older adult's personal convoy. The majority of older women are widowed; both older men and women lose friends and siblings to death. Yet most older adults adapt to these changes remarkably well and continue to maintain active social contacts throughout the remainder of their lives. They see friends and family and continue to attend church or other organizations. The limiting condition for social activity in late adulthood is far more likely to be an elder's own physical disability than the death of partner or friends. This persistence of social contacts in old age speaks not only to the continuing importance of such interactions for adults' sense of connection and well-being, but also to the robust capacity for adaptation that remains in late life.

Work in Late Adulthood: The Process of Retirement

A similarly robust capacity for adaptation marks the transition from work to retirement. While this transition certainly does involve the loss of a major role, virtually all the folklore about the negative effects of this particular role loss turns out to be wrong, at least for current cohorts in developed countries. Our knowledge about the whole process has been greatly enhanced by the availability of a series of excellent longitudinal studies, each following a group of men or women from before retirement into the years past retirement. In a particularly helpful analysis, Erdman Palmore and his colleagues (Palmore et al., 1985) combined the results of seven such studies, yielding a sample of over 7000 adults, each interviewed at least twice, and often many more times than that. Although these data are not completely current, I will draw heavily on their findings because this is by far the most comprehensive set of longitudinal information available.

Critical Thinking

Before you read the section on retirement, think about your own attitudes toward this life change. Do you expect it to be positive and enjoyable, or do you anticipate it with dread or some anxiety? What do you think has shaped your attitudes?

The Timing of Retirement

One inaccurate piece of folklore is that 65 is the normal age of retirement. As recently as 1970 in the United States, 65 was indeed the most common age of retirement for men. But in recent decades, both in the United States and in most industrialized countries, the average age of retirement has been getting younger and younger. In many countries, 60 is now the pensionable age; in many others, 65 is the age at which a full pension may be received, but reduced pensions may be drawn at earlier ages, as is true in the United States (Inkeles & Usui, 1989).

In part because of these various early pension benefits, the age of retirement has dropped rapidly in many countries, as is apparent in Figure 18.3 (Kohli, 1994). Some European countries are trying to reverse this trend by gradually raising the age of eligibility for public pensions. A similar change has been proposed in the United States, and such public policy changes may affect individual retirement decisions in the future. But at this moment in the United States, the single most common age for men to retire is 62; only about 40 percent of men between ages 62 and 64 and a quarter of men between 65 and 69 are still in the workforce (Quadagno & Hardy, 1996). A similar shift toward earlier and earlier exit from the labor force has also occurred for women.

Reasons for Retirement

Results from Palmore's combined analysis, as well as other more recent data (e.g., Kohli, 1994; Quadagno & Hardy, 1996), point to a series of "pushes" and "pulls" that combine to influence each person's decision to retire.

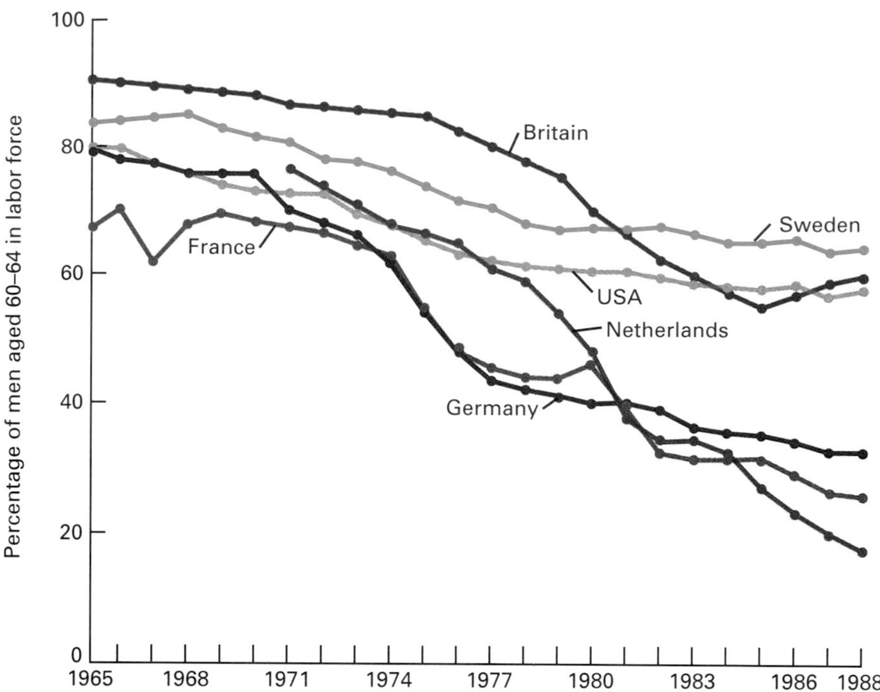

FIGURE 18.3 These data, which show the percentage of men aged 60 to 64 who were in the labor force in each year since 1965 in six different Western countries, clearly show the very substantial drop in retirement age over the past few decades. (*Source:* Kohli, 1994, Figure 4-2, p. 85.)

Age. Age itself is obviously an important ingredient in the equation because many occupations have widely shared retirement expectations. Internal models also play an important part. If a person's "expected life history" includes retirement at age 62 or 65, he or she is strongly inclined to retire at that age, regardless of other factors.

Health. A particularly strong push toward *early* retirement is poor health (Schulz, 1995). Poor health lowers the average age of retirement from one to three years (Sammartino, 1987), an effect seen among Hispanics and African Americans as well as among whites (Stanford et al., 1991), and in other countries than the United States (e.g., McDonald & Wanner, 1990). Indeed, the generally earlier ages of retirement among African-American men can be explained almost entirely by their higher rates of disability in their 50s and early 60s (Hayward, Friedman, & Chen, 1996).

However, among those who retire at 65 or later, health is a less powerful factor, presumably because most of those who retire later are in good health. Their retirement decision is affected by a variety of other factors, including the following:

Family Composition. Those who are still supporting minor children retire later than do those in the postparental stage. Thus, men and women who bear their children very late, those who acquire a second and younger family in a second marriage, and those rearing grandchildren are likely to continue to work until these children are launched.

Pension Programs. Equally important, both for early and for on-time retirement, is the availability of adequate financial support after retirement. Those who anticipate pension support in addition to Social Security, or who have personal savings to draw upon, retire earlier than do those who have no such financial backup.

Anticipated pension and health frequently work in opposite directions, because many working-class men and women who have worked in unskilled jobs can expect little supplementary retirement income *and* are in poor health. In general, working-class adults retire *earlier* than do middle and upper-class workers, responding to ill health and normative pressures, but a significant subset of poor or working-class adults continue working well past the normal retirement ages in order to supplement their incomes.

On the other end of the social class scale, health and pension adequacy work against one another in the opposite way. Adults in this group generally have both better health and better pensions. They also tend to have more interesting jobs. The three factors combine to produce somewhat later retirement for this more socially favored group.

Work Characteristics. This leads to the more general point that those who like their work and are highly work-committed, including many self-employed adults, retire later—often quite a lot later—than do those who are less gratified with their work. Those in challenging and interesting jobs are likely to postpone retirement until they are pushed by ill health or attracted by some special financial inducement. For them, availability of normal pension programs is less of an influence (Hayward & Hardy, 1985).

A quite different kind of work influence occurs in occupations or industries in which major "downsizing" of the work force has taken place in recent years. A great many workers, blue collar and white collar alike, have been pushed by their companies to accept early retirement, lured by special incentives (Hardy & Quadagno, 1995).

Women Versus Men. None of these influences on retirement decisions, except age, is as significant a factor among women as among men (Palmore et al., 1985). Women retire at about the same age as do men, but neither retirement benefits, health, nor job characteristics are helpful in predicting just when they will retire. The most frequently found predictor of retirement for a woman is whether her husband has retired (Weaver, 1994). A contrary force, tending to keep women in the labor force, is the lure of higher earnings that will augment the woman's future Social Security benefits—a factor that may be especially important in current cohorts of women nearing retirement, many of whom entered the labor force only in middle adulthood. But beyond these preliminary pieces of information, we really know very little about women's retirement decisions.

The Effects of Retirement

A particularly striking example of negative myths about retirement came to my attention several years ago: A one-page reprint of an article about retirement was handed

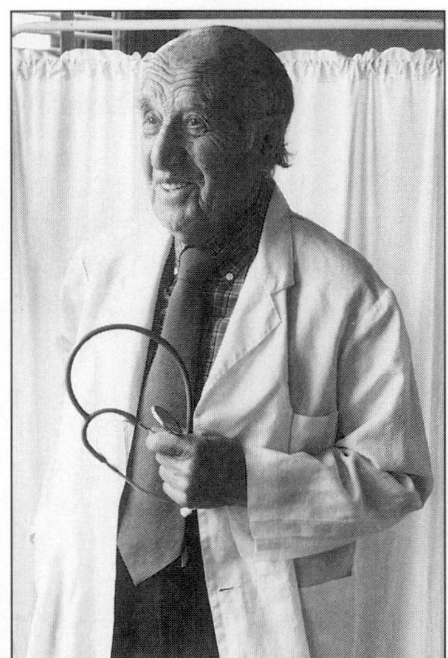

Some people never retire. Dr. Julius Manes, 87 when the photo was taken, worked as a physician until his death at 88. Anna Bobbitt Gardner was Director of the Academy of Musical Arts in Boston when she was 80.

Research Report

Choosing Not to Retire

The great majority of retirees have no desire to begin work again. When asked what they would do if they were offered a job in their geographical area, only 5 percent of a nationally representative sample of men aged 69 to 84 said they would take the job (Parnes & Sommers, 1994). Most say they have "had it" with work, or that their health would not permit it. But a significant number of adults nontheless do continue working past the normative retirement ages. This subgroup actually includes two types of people: (1) those who never retire from their previous line of work but continue to work at their normal occupation until they die, such as college professors who become emeritus professors and maintain an active research life into their 70s and 80s, or legislators like the late Congressman Claude Pepper of Florida, champion of causes of the elderly; and (2) those who retire from their regular occupation but then take what is sometimes called a *bridge job*—often part time, often in a totally new line of work. An analysis of the data from the Retirement History Study (Quinn & Burkhauser, 1990) suggests that as many as 20 percent of current American workers continue working past the typical retirement age following one or the other of these two patterns. Four to 5 percent continue working full time, even into their 70s and 80s (Herzog et al., 1991; Parnes & Sommers, 1994). Such individuals are often described as having "shunned" retirement.

We know almost nothing about women who choose not to retire, but we do know something about men who shun retirement. Some of them are men with very low education, poor retirement benefits, and thus very low incomes. These men continue working out of economic necessity. A larger fraction of the retirement shunners are highly educated, healthy, highly work-committed professionals, often with wives who are also still working (Parnes & Sommers, 1994). Many of them have been highly work-committed all their adult lives. For example, men in the National Longitudinal Surveys sample, a group that has been studied over 25 years, were asked in their 50s whether they would continue working if they suddenly found themselves with enough money to live comfortably. Those who said they would continue working no matter what are much more likely to shun retirement and to be still working in their 70s and 80s (Parnes & Sommers, 1994). These are men with a strong work commitment and a distaste for retirement. For them, work continues to provide more satisfaction than they expect retirement to offer.

Of course not all men (or women) who were highly work-committed in their 40s, 50s, and early 60s shun retirement. Many do stop work at the typical ages. One of the things that differentiates those who do and those who do not choose to stop paid work are their expectations about retirement itself. Highly work-committed men who expect retirement to be unpleasant are far more likely to keep on working. They may have few interests or hobbies outside their work. Equally work-committed men who anticipate retirement with more pleasure are more likely to stop work. Overall then, those who shun retirement do so either because of economic necessity, to ease themselves gradually into a nonworking state, or because they continue to find their work more satisfying than they expect retirement to be.

around among faculty at a large university. Among other things, it said, "There is no way to describe adequately the letdown many people feel when they retire from a responsible executive post." It went on to predict that faculty who retired would experience a desperate search for other sources of meaning in their lives, followed by depression and illness.

There may well be some self-fulfilling prophecy at work here. It is indeed true that a small fraction of adults adjust badly to retirement, and that such poor adjustment is more likely (but not inevitable) among highly work-committed adults. But as a general rule, gloomy expectations about negative effects of retirement are unfounded.

Effects on Income. One potentially significant change at retirement is in income, although what I can tell you about retirement income is highly culture-specific. Pension programs differ widely from one culture to another, so I simply can't give you a general picture. I will try to give you some cultural comparisons where possible, but most of what I will be talking about here is specific to the United States.

In the United States, retired adults have five potential sources of income: government pensions, such as Social Security; other pensions, such as those offered

Table 18.1 **Percentage of Household Income from Five Different Sources for Adults over Age 65 in the United States**

		Total Household Income				
Source of Income	**All Households**	**<$6,570**	**$6,571–$10,752**	**$10,753–$17,208**	**$17,209–$28,714**	**$28,715 and up**
Social Security	36%	79%	76%	59%	41%	18%
Other pensions	18%	3%	8%	16%	23%	20%
Earnings	18%	1%	3%	7%	12%	27%
Assets	25%	4%	9%	15%	21%	33%
Public assistance	8%	11%	3%	1%	0	0
Other	2%	2%	3%	3%	3%	2%

Source: Reno, 1993, Table 5, p. 33.

through an employer or military pensions; earnings from continued work; income from savings or other assets; and, for those living below the poverty line, public assistance beyond Social Security, including food stamps and Supplemental Security Income. You can see how these various sources contribute to household income for older adults in the United States in Table 18.1. These data are from 1990 but there is little reason to believe that the distribution of income sources has changed much since then. Social Security is clearly the largest single source of retirement income overall; for nearly half of older Americans it is the *only* source of income.

These numbers, though, do not tell us anything about the average level of income for older adults in comparison with their own incomes *before* retirement. Data from Palmore's combined analysis suggest that incomes decline roughly 25 percent after retirement. But this figure paints a misleadingly negative picture of the actual financial status of retired persons. In the United States, as in many developed countries, many retired adults own their own homes and thus have no mortgage payments; their children are launched; they are eligible for Medicare as well as for many special Senior Citizen benefits. When you adjust for all these factors, you find that, *on average*, retired adults in the United States, Australia, and most European countries have incomes that are 85 percent to 100 percent of preretirement levels (Smeeding, 1990). (The most striking exception to this statement, by the way, is Britain, where as many as 60 percent of elders have incomes at or near poverty levels [Walker, 1990].) For some, particularly some of the working poor, income may actually increase after retirement. A combination of Social Security and Supplemental Security Income (SSI) may be more than these individuals were able to earn in their working years (Palmore et al., 1985).

Critical Thinking

Compare your current budget to what you might anticipate when you are 65 or older. Where would your expenses be less? In what areas might your expenses rise in late adulthood?

Twenty years ago I could not have written such an upbeat summary. But significant improvements in Social Security benefits in the United States (and equivalent improvements in many other countries), including regular cost-of-living increases, have meant that in the past few decades the relative financial position of the elderly has improved more than that of any other age group in the population. For example, in 1970, 24.6 percent of all adults over 65 in the United States were living below the poverty line; in 1993, only 12.2 percent were at that low economic level. In contrast, 22.7 percent of children lived in poverty in 1993 (U.S. Bureau of the Census, 1995).

But such low rates of poverty among the elderly also give a false picture—in this case deceptively positive. A large percentage of older adults fall into a category Smeeding (1990) calls "'tweeners," those whose income is just above the poverty

Table 18.2 Incidence of Poverty for Various Subgroups of Older Adults in the United States in 1993

	All Adults over 65	Whites	Blacks	Hispanics
Total poverty rates	12.2%	10.7%	28.0%	21.4%
Men	7.9%	6.4%	23.2%	16.3%
Married men	5.7%	4.5%	18.0%	13.8%
Men living alone	13.9%	12.3%	26.8%	30.7%
Women	15.2%	13.7%	31.0%	25.3%
Married women	5.4%	4.3%	21.3%	10.6%
Women living alone	26.2%	24.4%	43.6%	46.7%

Source: U.S. Department of Commerce, Current Population Reports, Series P60-188, 1995, Table 8, pp. 22–25.

level. Roughly a fifth of all older couples and two-fifths of single elders are in this category. These adults are "not well off enough to be financially secure, while not poor enough to qualify for the means-tested elderly safety net" (Smeeding, 1990, p. 372). The fact that twice as many single as married elders fall in the "'tweener" group is one sign of a more pervasive difference. Table 18.2, which shows poverty rates for different subgroups of elders, makes the point even more clearly. Single elders have almost twice the chance of being poor as do married elders. Two other points are also very clear from the table. First, black and Hispanic elders have higher rates of poverty than do whites, and second, older women are more likely to be poor than are older men.

This "gendering of poverty" in old age flows from a whole string of differences in adult life experiences for men and women now in late life. In particular, current cohorts of older women are much less likely to have had paid employment, are less likely to have been involved in a private pension plan even if they did work, and worked at lower wages than did their male peers (Hardy & Hazelrigg, 1993). As a result, a very large percentage of older widows rely entirely on Social Security income. (In 1993, the average monthly Social Security payment to a widow was $630, which is only slightly above the poverty line.) Some of these gender differences in pension earnings will still exist for today's middle-aged and younger cohorts, and will thus continue to contribute to gender differences in economic conditions in old age for some time to come. But the gender differences in old-age poverty are likely to shrink at least somewhat in later generations.

In the face of these statistics, it is easy to become discouraged about the financial status of the elderly. But let us also not forget the more positive points with which I began this section: (1) Overall adequacy of income does *not* decline, on average, after retirement; and (2) elderly adults in the United States are better off financially today than they have ever been.

Effects on Health. The longitudinal studies tell us quite clearly that health simply does not change, for better or worse, *because of* retirement. When ill-health accompanies retirement, the causal sequence is nearly always that the individual retired because he or she was in poor health. Among those in good health at retirement age, retirement itself has little or no effect on health status over the succeeding years (Palmore et al., 1985). This clear set of research results is interesting because it sug-

Cultures and Contexts

Contrasting U.S. and German Public Pensions

Richard Burkhauser and his colleagues (Burkhauser, Duncan, & Hauser, 1994) have provided a fascinating comparison of public retirement benefits in the United States and Germany that can give us some insight into the ways social policies can affect individual experience. In particular, they focus on the rules regarding women's retirement benefits and the impact of such rules when the woman is widowed.

When a married woman in the United States retires (or reaches the official retirement age), she receives either her own worker's benefit from Social Security or half of her husband's entitlement, whichever is higher. Her husband, of course, also receives his entitlement. So while both are alive, the minimum household income is 150 percent of the husband's entitlement. When she is widowed, she receives either her own worker's benefit or 100 percent of her husband's, whichever is more. If she was receiving half her husband's benefit while he was alive, her total household income thus drops by one-third when he dies—from 150 to 100 percent of the husband's benefit. If the woman's own work benefits are as large as her husband's, the drop in household income when he dies is actually greater. In such a case, the couple would have had a minimum income of twice the husband's benefit (his full benefit plus her full benefit). After his death, she must get along on half that amount, namely her own benefit alone. (Of course, the same is true for a surviving male spouse; I emphasize the situation for women here because they are so much more likely to be the surviving spouse.) Burkhauser estimates that, in order to maintain the same standard of living, the surviving spouse needs an income that is 80 percent of the couple's previous income, so in the cases I'm describing, the spouse's death means a significant loss of living standards for the survivor.

In Germany, the situation differs. A widow who did not work and thus has no worker's benefit of her own is worse off than in the United States; she receives only 60 percent of her husband's benefit. But if she worked, she is usually better off, because by German rules, a retired woman continues to receive *both* her own worker's benefit and the 60 percent of her husband's benefit. Thus, in this system, the closer the wife's worker's benefit is to her husband's, the better off she will be after his death, which is the opposite of what happens under the U.S. system.

Neither the German nor the U.S. system provides the 80 percent of the prewidowed income that Burkhauser estimates is required to retain the same standard of living after widowhood as before. But the German system will work better and better with succeeding cohorts in which women have worked more and more, while the U.S. system will not.

gests that for the vast majority of adults, retirement is not a highly stressful life change.

Effects on Attitudes and Mental Health. Similarly, the bulk of the evidence suggests that retirement has essentially no impact on overall life satisfaction or subjective well-being. Longitudinal studies that have included measures of such attitudes show little difference in scores before and after retirement, and those recently retired show little sign of any increase in depression (Palmore et al., 1985). For most, retirement is not perceived as a stress at all.

If this retiring man is at all typical, he is under 65, has planned at least a little bit for his retirement, and will experience few stresses associated with the transition.

One set of data that makes this point particularly clearly comes from a study by Raymond Bossé and his colleagues (Bossé et al., 1991), who have studied a group of more than 1500 men over a period of years. In the most recent contact, the subjects were asked to indicate which of 31 possibly stressful life events they had experienced in the past year and to rate the overall stressfulness of each of these events. Retirement was ranked thirtieth out of 31 in overall stressfulness, below even such items as "move to a less desirable residence," or "decrease in responsibilities or hours at work or where you volunteer." Of those who had retired in the previous year, seven out of ten said that they found retirement either not at all or only a little stressful. Those men in the sample who were still working were almost twice as likely to list work problems as retired men were to list retirement problems.

The Real World

Moving South: Residential Mobility After Retirement

For many adults, retirement brings an increase in choices about where to live. When your job or your spouse's job no longer ties you to a specific place, you can choose to move to sunnier climes, or to live nearer to one of your children. Many of you may have the notion, as did I, that such a move is common among older adults. Somewhat to my surprise, I find that it is not (Burkhauser, Butrica, & Wasylenko, 1995; De Jong et al., 1995).

There *is* a small burst of residential moves right around retirement age, so it is clear that some older adults do indeed choose to take advantage of their greater freedom in this way. But this burst only brings the rate of moves to about 1 percent a year (Longino, 1990). Another burst of moves occurs roughly ten years later, beginning at about age 75.

Charles Longino (Jackson et al., 1991; Litwak & Longino, 1987; Longino, 1990; Longino et al., 1991), who has been one of the most diligent investigators of residential moves among the elderly, suggests that there are three types of move. The first, which he calls an *amenity* move, is the one most of us think of when we think of older adults changing residences. If an older adult makes such a move, it is almost always right around the time of retirement. Most typically, amenity moves are in a direction *away* from the older person's children, frequently to a warmer climate—Florida, California, and Arizona being the most popular destinations in the United States. In Canada, amenity moves are most often westward, particularly to British Columbia; in Britain, the equivalent move is to the seaside.

Those who make such amenity moves are likely to be still married, be relatively healthy, and have adequate or good retirement income (De Jong et al., 1995; Hazelrigg & Hardy, 1995). Often the relocating pair have vacationed in the new location; many have planned the move carefully over a number of years (e.g., Cuba & Longino, 1991). Most—but not all—report higher levels of life satisfaction or morale after such a move, although some move back to their home base because they find themselves too isolated from kin. These days, a growing number of older adults try to split the difference with a pattern of *seasonal migration,* spending winter months in sunnier areas and summer months at home, nearer to family. One survey of older residents of Minnesota shows that 9 percent follow such a pattern (Hogan & Steinnes, 1994).

The second type of move, which Longino calls *compensatory migration* or a *kinship migration,* occurs when the older adult—most often a widow living alone—has developed a sufficient level of chronic disability that she is having serious difficulty managing an independent household. When a move of this type occurs, it is nearly always a shift to be closer to a daughter, son, or some other relative who can provide regular assistance. In some cases this means moving in with that daughter or son, but often the move is to an apartment or house nearby, or into a special retirement community in which the individual lives independently but has supportive services available. My maternal grandparents spent the last several decades of their lives living in such a retirement community within a few miles of my mother's house.

The final type of migration in late adulthood is what Longino calls *institutional migration,* to nursing home care. Three of my four grandparents made such a move for the final few weeks of their lives, when their health had deteriorated to the point where they needed regular nursing care that no one in the family could provide for them.

Of course very few older adults actually move three times. Longino's point is that these are three very different kinds of moves, made by quite different subsets of the population of elderly, and at different times in the years of late adulthood. Amenity moves are usually early, kinship or compensatory moves are likely to occur in middle to late old age, while institutional moves are clearly late in life. Only the first of these reflects the increase in choices and options that may open up during the retirement years.

Critical Thinking

One of the other bits of folklore about retirement is that it is hard on wives, who must adjust to the full-time presence of a husband who previously was out of the house most of the day. How could you design a study that would tell you whether this is true or not?

Among the 30 percent of retired men in this study who did list some problems with retirement, poor health and poor family finances were the most likely causes. Those with marital problems were also likely to describe more daily hassles in their retirement life.

Other evidence suggests that those who respond least well to retirement are those who had the least control over the process. Those who are forced to retire by poor health, or those who took special early retirement offers ("golden handshakes") from their companies are likely to report lower satisfaction and higher levels of stress than do those who feel they had more control over the retirement decision (Hardy & Quadagno, 1995; Herzog et al., 1991). Retirement is also likely to be more stressful for those whose economic situation is poor, or for those who must simultaneously cope with both retirement and other major life changes, such as widowhood (Stull & Hatch, 1984). But for those whose retirement is anticipated and on-time, this role loss is not stressful.

If we look at an even broader pattern, what predicts life satisfaction in later adulthood is not whether a person has retired or not but whether he or she was satisfied with life in earlier adulthood. We take ourselves with us through the years; grumpy, negative young people tend to be grumpy, negative old people, and satisfied young adults find satisfactions in retirement as well. The consistency in this is quite striking and provides very good support for consistency or continuity theories of adulthood. Work does shape our daily lives for upwards of 40 years of our adulthood; but our happiness or unhappiness with life, our growth or stagnation, seems less a function of the specifics of the work experience than it is a function of the attitudes and qualities we bring to the process.

Personality Changes

If the personality changes of young adulthood can be described as "individuation," and those of middle adulthood (more tentatively) as "mellowing," how might we describe the changes of late adulthood? Does mellowing simply continue? Are there other changes? Several theorists have hypothesized specific forms of change, but there is little agreement and very little information. Still, you should at least be familiar with the alternative views.

Erikson's View of Integrity

Erikson thought that the task of achieving ego integrity began in middle adulthood but was most central in late adulthood. To achieve it, the older adult must come to terms with who she is and has been, how her life has been lived, the choices that she made, the opportunities gained and lost. It also involves coming to terms with death and accepting its imminence.

We have essentially no longitudinal or even cross-sectional data to tell us whether older adults are more likely than younger or middle-aged adults to achieve such self-acceptance. What we have instead are a few bits of information suggesting that those who have achieved it are less fearful of death and most likely to reminiscence happily about their lives.

In one such study, Maxine Walaskay (Walaskay, Whitbourne, & Nehrke, 1983–1984) used a method very like Marcia's Ego Identity Interview to classify older adults into one of four statuses:

- *Integrity achieved*: The individual is aware of her own aging, able to accept her own unique life as it was lived, and able to adjust to changes.
- *Despairing*: The person has come to a negative evaluation of her own life, does not accept it, sees life as "too short" to make up for mistakes.
- *Foreclosed*: The individual is content with her current life but resists any self-exploration, any assessment of the whole lifetime.
- *Dissonant*: The person is just beginning to try to resolve the integrity dilemma and is full of ambivalence.

When Walaskay classified a group of 40 older adults on the basis of her interviews and then also assessed their fear of death and their overall life satisfaction, she found that those in the achieved and foreclosed statuses were most satisfied with their lives and least anxious about death.

Such a study is suggestive, but barely more than that. Because the integrity and foreclosed statuses differed little in levels of either satisfaction or fear, it is not at all clear that acceptance of one's own life is a necessary ingredient for contentment with current life or even adaptation to old age. It would be useful to have more research of this kind, but I am not convinced that Erikson is correct that integrity versus despair is the most helpful conceptualization of the central personal task of old age.

Reminiscence and Life Review

One aspect of Erikson's theory has been the notion that reminiscence is a necessary, healthy part of achieving ego integrity, and thus an important part of old age. Some years ago, Robert Butler (1963) expanded on this idea, proposing that in old age, all of us go through a process he called a **life review,** in which there is a "progressive return to consciousness of past experience, and particularly, the resurgence of unresolved conflicts." Butler argued that in this final stage of life, as preparation for our now clearly impending death, we engage in an analytic and evaluative review of our earlier life. Echoing Erikson, Butler argued that such a review is a necessary part of achieving ego integrity in late life.

This has been an attractive hypothesis, widely influential among clinicians who work with the elderly, who have devised a wide variety of "life review" interventions for use with older adults. And indeed several studies show that a process of structured reminiscence may increase life satisfaction and self-esteem among older adults (Haight, 1988, 1992). However, the research evidence is generally weak and far from uniformly supportive of Butler's ideas. A number of investigators have found no beneficial effects of a life review process (Stevens-Ratchford, 1993; Wallace, 1992). More significantly, the research does not clearly show that reminiscence is actually more common in the elderly than among the middle-aged or any other age group. At this point, we are left with many unanswered questions: Is some form of reminiscence really more common among the elderly than at other ages? How much do elderly individuals vary in the amount of reminiscence they engage in? How much of reminiscence is really integrative or evaluative, rather than merely storytelling for amusement or information? Is reminiscence a necessary ingredient in achieving some form of integration in late life?

On the whole, I think there is good reason to doubt the validity of Butler's specific hypothesis. At the same time, it is clear that some kind of preparation for death is an inevitable, even central, part of life in these last years. While death certainly comes to some adults in their 30s, 40s, 50s, or 60s, most younger adults can continue to push the idea of death away. But in the years past 75 the imminence of death is inescapable and must be faced by each of us—a story I will turn to in the next chapter.

Disengagement Versus Activity

A related theoretical issue regarding personality changes in old age has been framed in terms of the contrast between **disengagement theory** and **activity theory.** The basic question is whether it is normal, necessary, or healthy for older adults to remain active as long as possible, or whether the more typical and healthy pattern is some kind of gradual turning inward.

The latter view is represented by *disengagement theory*, first proposed by Cumming and Henry (1961) to describe what they saw as a central psychological process of old age. As reformulated by Cumming (1975), the theory has three aspects:

- *Shrinkage of life space*: As we age, we interact with fewer and fewer others, fill fewer and fewer roles.
- *Increased individuality*: In the roles and relationships that remain, the older individual is less and less governed by strict rules or expectations.
- *Acceptance—even embrace—of these changes*: The healthy older adult actively disengages from roles and relationships, turning more and more inward and away from interactions with others.

The first two of these points seem largely beyond dispute. What has been controversial about disengagement theory is the third point. Cumming and Henry argued that the normal and healthy response to the shrinkage of roles and relationships is for the older adult to step back still further, to stop seeking new roles, to spend more time alone, to turn inward. In essence, they proposed a kind of personality change, not just a decline in involvement. The contrasting view, typically described as *activity theory*, says that exactly the opposite is true—that the psychologically and physically healthiest response to old age is to maintain the greatest possible level of activity and involvement in the greatest possible number of roles.

On this point, the research evidence provides a good deal more support for activity theory than disengagement theory. The common finding is that the most active older adults report slightly greater satisfaction with themselves or their lives, are healthiest, and have the highest morale (Adelmann, 1994; Bryant & Rakowski, 1992; George, 1996; Holahan, 1988; McIntosh & Danigelis, 1995; Palmore, 1981). The effect is not large but the direction of the effect is consistently positive: More social involvement is linked to better outcomes, even among those elders who suffer from disabilities such as arthritis, for whom active social participation may bring more pain than would inactivity (Zimmer, Hickey, & Searle, 1995).

On the other hand, we can find some support for disengagement theory in the observation that older adults seem to be more content with solitude than is true at earlier ages. Recall the point I made in Chapter 14 that older adults are *least* likely to describe themselves as lonely, while young adults are most likely. It is also true that every in-depth study of lifestyles of older adults identifies at least a few who lead contented, socially isolated lives, sometimes engaged in an all-consuming hobby (e.g., Maas & Kuypers, 1974; Rubinstein, 1986).

Clearly, then, it is possible to choose a highly disengaged lifestyle in late adulthood and to find satisfaction in it. But such disengagement is neither a normal part of old age for the majority, nor necessary for overall mental health in the later years. For most, some level of social involvement is both a sign, and probably a cause, of higher morale and lower levels of depression or other psychiatric symptoms. Roles and relationships may rule our lives less in late adulthood than at earlier ages, but they still seem to be essential ingredients for emotional balance, at least for most of us.

Each of these several approaches has been influential; none has been ultimately satisfactory as a description of late adult personality. As is the case with health and physical status in these same years, the clearest truth is probably that adults' ways

Some older adults are quite content with solitary lives, but they are most often people who have been introverted or solitary for most of their adult lives. Disengagement from social contacts is neither a typical nor an optimal choice for most elders.

of approaching and responding to old age vary immensely. There may be, at some deeper level, some kind of search for integrity, some kind of disengagement. But if so, we have not yet found the best way of capturing such a process in our theoretical or empirical sights.

Individual Differences

In recent years one of the guiding themes in the gerontology literature has been the concept of *successful aging* (e.g., Baltes & Baltes, 1990b), defined in terms of long life, good physical and mental health, good retention of mental abilities, social competence, a sense of personal control, and overall satisfaction with one's life. Researchers and theorists have begun to ask what characteristics of an individual might predict such good outcomes. I have already talked about the predictors of longevity and of physical and cognitive health in Chapter 17. Many of the same factors appear when we look at an outcome such as life satisfaction, as you can see from the list in Table 18.3.

Social support appears to be a critical ingredient in several of the patterns described in the table. For example, one of the reasons that adults with very low income or lower social class have lower overall satisfaction is that they have weaker social support networks. If you compare subgroups of middle- and lower-class adults who have equivalent social support, you find no differences in satisfaction (Murrell & Norris, 1991).

Table 18.3 Predictors of Happiness or Life Satisfaction in Older Adults

	Demographic Factors
Income/social class	Those who are very poor are less happy and satisfied, but among those with sufficient income, variations in wealth have little further effect. "Wealth, it seems, is like health: Its absence can breed misery, yet having it is no guarantee of happiness" (Myers & Diener, 1995, p. 13).
Education	More highly educated adults are slightly more satisfied, but the difference is small.
Gender	Men and women do not differ in overall satisfaction or happiness, despite the higher level of aches and pains and the larger number of widows among older women.
Marital status	Married adults consistently report higher life satisfaction.
Race/ethnicity	There appears to be no general tendency for blacks, Hispanics, or other minority groups to have lower (or higher) life satisfaction beyond the effect of poverty. Around the world, however, cultures differ widely in the likelihood that adults will describe themselves as very happy, with adults in collectivist cultures generally describing *lower* levels of happiness than those in individualistic cultures, perhaps because it is more acceptable to *express* personal happiness in individualistic cultures.
	Personal Qualities
Personality	Extraverted adults and those low in neuroticism are consistently more satisfied with their lives or happy, as are those with a strong sense of personal control and high self-esteem.
Social interaction	Those who have more contact with others, especially those with several intimate confidants, are more satisfied.
Health	Those with better self-perceived health are more satisfied. Indeed, self-perceived health is a better predictor than is health rated by a physician.
Religion	Those who describe themselves as more religious also describe themselves as more satisfied.
Negative life change	The more negative life changes an elder has recently had to deal with, the lower his life satisfaction is likely to be.

Sources: Antonucci, 1991; Diener, 1984; George, 1990; Gibson, 1986; Koenig et al., 1988; Levin et al., 1995; Markides & Mindel, 1987; Murrell & Norris, 1991; Myers & Diener, 1995; Willits & Crider, 1988.

We can also see the tracks of social support in the link between extraversion and life satisfaction: Extraverted adults tend to create larger and more intimate social networks (e.g., Krause, Liang, & Keith, 1990). Social support plays a similar role in the correlation between life changes and satisfaction. Those who have an adequate network are at least partially buffered from the worst effects of stressful life events.

A second thread running through the items in Table 18.3 is that old friend, a sense of control (Rodin, 1986), a characteristic I talked about in Chapter 13. For example, financial strain among the elderly appears to be linked to overall life satisfaction or depression primarily through the loss of any sense of control over one's life—a link found in studies in both Japan and the United States (Krause, Jay, & Liang, 1991). Even life events that seem objectively highly stressful may have little negative effect if the individual feels he has some choice. So an *involuntary* retirement or *involuntary* institutionalization has negative effects, while a planned and chosen retirement or move to a nursing home does not.

As a final point, let me emphasize yet again that what is critical in almost all cases is an individual's *perception* of her situation: Perceived adequacy of social support, perceived adequacy of income, and self-ratings of health are all better predictors of life satisfaction and morale than are any objective measures. This may mean that one adaptive response to the many losses and declines of late adulthood is to lower one's standards, to expect less and thus to be satisfied with less. When an older adult describes himself as being in "good health" he is unlikely to mean precisely the same thing that he meant when he was 25. But what seems to be critical for overall emotional balance, for a sense of satisfaction with one's life, is the degree of discrepancy between what one expects and what one has. Because such expectations are another example of internal models, we see yet again the importance of understanding such internal models if we are to understand any individual's course of development from birth to death.

Summary

1. Late adulthood is a time when many large and small roles are shed. Remaining roles also have less content. This may offer greater license for individuality and for choice.
2. One role that a great many older adults relinquish is that of spouse, occasioned by the death of husband or wife. This is especially true for older women, among whom the majority are widowed.
3. Among those elders who are not married, living alone is the most common living arrangement among elders in the United States, typically from preference. The minority who live with a child are most likely to be drawn from any of several subgroups: those with low income, minority elderly (especially African Americans), and those who have many daughters.
4. Spousal relationships in late adulthood are, on average, high in marital satisfaction, with strong loyalty and mutual affection. If one spouse is disabled, the healthier spouse is likely to provide care.
5. Married elders, as a group, are somewhat healthier and more satisfied with their lives than are single elders; this difference is larger among men than women.
6. The majority of elders have at least one living child, and most see their child(ren) regularly and with some pleasure. But (surprisingly) the amount of contact with children is *not* correlated with older adults' overall level of life satisfaction or morale.
7. There is some indication that relationships with siblings, particularly sisters, may become more significant in late adulthood than at earlier ages.
8. Degree of contact with friends *is* correlated with overall life satisfaction among older adults. Women in this age group continue to have larger social networks. Men rely more on their spouses for social support, while women rely on both friends and children.
9. Among African Americans, social networks often include fictive kin in central helping roles. Older blacks in the United States also rely on church groups for support and assistance more than is true of other groups.
10. The normative age of retirement is now closer to 62 than 65 in the United States and in most Western developed countries. Retirement earlier than the norm is most often caused by ill health. On-time retirement is affected by family responsibilities, adequacy of anticipated pension income, and satisfaction with one's job.
11. Income typically declines with retirement, but income *adequacy* does not decline so much. Improvements in

Social Security mean that elder adults are now better off financially than ever before, but 12 percent live in poverty and another quarter have near-poverty incomes. Among elders, women and minorities are most likely to live in poverty.

12. Retirement appears not to be a stressful life change for the great majority. It is not causally connected to any deterioration in physical or mental health. The minority who find it stressful are likely to be those who feel they have least control over the process.

13. No theory of personality change in late adulthood has been well supported by existing evidence. Erikson's concept of integrity and Butler's concept of life review have been influential, but research does not indicate that either process is prevalent or necessary.

14. The concept of disengagement has similarly been found wanting; high life satisfaction and good mental health are found most often among elders who disengage the *least*.

15. One aspect of "successful aging" is high life satisfaction, found most often among elders who are married, have adequate income, are somewhat extraverted in personality, feel they have good control over their lives, perceive their own health to be good, and are satisfied with the amount and quality of social interaction they have.

16. Adequacy of perceived social support and a sense of control appear to be especially crucial for happiness or high life satisfaction

Key Terms

activity theory

disengagement theory

life review

Suggested Readings

Binstock, R. H., & George, L. K. (Eds.) (1996). *Handbook of aging and the social sciences*, 4th ed. San Diego: Academic Press.

This is the latest edition of a handbook series that provides first-rate up-to-date summaries of research and theory on a whole range of subjects relevant to this chapter. The material is often dense, but this is a splendid source of current references.

Bond, J., & Coleman, P. (Eds.) (1990). *Aging in society*. London: Sage Publications.

I recommended this book in Chapter 17, and do so again here. It not only provides a very good review of research on retirement, living arrangements, intimate relationships, and many other topics, it also offers a non-U.S. perspective, because the authors are all British and rely on British research as well as studies in the United States and other countries.

Schulz, J. H. (1995). *The economics of aging*, 6th ed. Dover, MA: Auburn House.

Everything you ever wanted to know about the economic status of the elderly.

Interlude 7

Summing Up Late Adult Development

Key Characteristics of Late Adulthood

As usual, I've briefly summarized this age period in a table, which shows that there are some distinct differences among those called "young old," "old old," and "oldest old." Functionally significant decrements in many types of cognitive skills, for example, are not found until past age 75, and many physical measures show an accelerated rate of change at about the same time.

Yet despite the apparent clarity of the information in the table, this is an extremely difficult age period to talk about or to summarize. Depending on which facts you choose to emphasize, you can arrive at a fairly rosy description or a quite depressing one. Of late, social scientists have been tilting toward more optimistic statements, partly because newer research shows fewer inevitable declines. My own view is that the central fact about late adulthood is that *both* the optimistic and the pessimistic views are correct—for some people. Joseph Quinn makes the point very clearly:

> Never begin a sentence with "The elderly are . . ." or "The elderly do . . . ." No matter what you are discussing, some are, and some are not; some do, and some do not. The most important characteristics of the aged is their diversity. The average can be very deceptive, because it ignores the tremendous dispersion around it. Beware of the mean. (Quinn, 1987, p. 64)

Quinn is absolutely correct. There is enormous variability among older adults in physical and mental status, vigor, wisdom, satisfaction, zest, loneliness, and economic security. For those elders at the more positive ends of these various continua, late adulthood can be a time of choice and opportunity. Edwin Shneidman (1989), writing about the decade of one's 70s, seems to be describing this subgroup when he says:

> Consider that when one is a septuagenarian, one's parents are gone, children are grown, mandatory work is done; health is not too bad, and responsibilities are relatively light, with time, at long last, for focus on the self. These can be sunset years, golden years, an Indian Summer, a period of relatively mild weather for both soma and psyche in the late autumn or early winter of life, a decade of greater independence and increased opportunities for further self-development. (p. 684)

At the other end of the continuum are older adults who live below or close to poverty level, with significant physical ailments, for whom these last years are anything but an Indian summer.

No single summary statement can encompass this degree of diversity. Yet Quinn is also wrong, because there *are* some common patterns nonetheless. Yes, a small percentage of older adults retain excellent physical and mental functioning into late old age, but age *normally* brings a significant slowing of responses, wear and tear on the joints, higher rates of disease, and all the other physical changes I have described in detail. And no matter how unusually fit an older adult may be, he or she *cannot* run as fast as a fit 25-year-old.

All the emphasis on those adults who retain good fitness thus risks leaving the impression that for some people the sands do not fall through the hourglass. The fact that the biological clock does not tick equally loudly for all older adults cannot mask or disguise the fact that biological change/loss becomes more and more of an issue for everyone in these later years. As David Pendergast summarizes it,

> Aging is characterized by a progressive loss of the ability to adapt to stress. This ability to adapt to stress could be termed "functional reserve." With progressing age, the functional reserve falls below the level required for activities of daily living (ADLs) and may result in institutionalization. (Pendergast, Fisher, & Calkins, 1993, p. 61)

Thus, those who retain good function do so with greater effort and more care as they age. They more often operate nearer the limits of their reserve capacity than is true of younger adults. More "successful" older adults also cope by means of the various strategies I talked about in Chapter 16: "selective optimization with compensation" (Baltes & Baltes, 1990a). An older adult uses the strategy of "selection" when she gives up mountain climbing but walks regularly, or cuts down on the number of clubs or service groups she participates in, or rests up before a demanding activity. She uses "optimization" when she takes classes, reads the paper regularly, or maintains her levels of physical fitness with good diet and exercise. She uses "compensation" when she gets a hearing aid, organizes her activities so she has to drive

A Summary of the Threads of Development in Late Adulthood

Aspects of Development	Age in Years: "Young Old" 65	"Old Old" 75	85 "Oldest Old"	95
Physical development	Significant decline in hearing, speed of response; continued gradual decline on most physical measures. Incidence of disease and disability increased.	Accelerated decline on most physical measures, although there is wide individual variability even at this age.	Increased risk of disability and frailty.	
Cognitive development	On crystallized abilities generally little loss; gradual decline on many fluid abilities.	Reliably measurable decline on all cognitive measures, on average, but wide individual variability. Some indication of "terminal drop" for crystallized abilities.		
Personality development	No clear understanding of the process of personality change in late adulthood; Erikson suggests ego integrity as key task; Neugarten suggests interiority; Cumming and Henry suggest disengagement. None of these has strong empirical support.	Possible rise in incidence of depression past age 75.		
Social relationships and roles	Continued high rate of social involvement; degree of social involvement in general related to life satisfaction. Retirement for most working adults.	Some decline in social involvement for those whose physical disabilities make mobility more problematic.		

less often at night or when roads are crowded, or writes more lists rather than relying on internal memory systems.

The very fact that compensation is required to adjust well to old age is a crucial point. Yet it is also the case that a great many adults *do* compensate and adjust to their changing physical and social circumstances, often with inventiveness and humor. A personal example has made this very clear to me. My father, now 81, carries with him a fat notebook in which he keeps lists of things to do, items to buy, times of appointments, addresses, phone numbers. He refers to this notebook as his "brains," which always makes me laugh. If he momentarily loses track of this notebook, he asks, "Where are my brains?" Yet because of this highly successful compensatory device, he does not forget appointments, has frequently used phone numbers handy when he needs them, and is able to move efficiently through his days. He is frustrated by increasing problems remembering names; he walks slowly. But he *has* compensated successfully for many of his various limitations and disabilities so that he can still be active and do many of the things that matter to him.

Central Processes

The most central process in all of this is clearly the set of physical changes that makes up normal aging. These changes begin their slow march in young adulthood or even adolescence. But for most of us, it is only in late adulthood that the changes accumulate to the point that we need to compensate, or increase in rate so that we experience a rapid decline in some function. Recent research does tell us that at least some of the changes we had attributed to inevitable aging may be preventable or avoidable altogether—such as increases in cholesterol. But let us not swing too far in the other direction and conclude that there is no such thing as physical aging. Neurons lose dendrites; fewer mature T cells are produced by the immune system; damage to DNA in individual cells accumulates. Eventually, one or more body systems cannot continue to function, and we experience disease and ultimately death.

What makes this biological decline easier to deal with is the simultaneous change in the demands of many social roles. Older adults can adapt to physical or mental losses in part because they are less constrained by role expectations, including the role of parent and that of worker.

Of course it is not accidental that the weakening of the grip of social roles occurs at the time when the body is becoming less reliable. Young adults take on the burden of key social roles because they are physically fit to do so, because this is the optimum time for childbearing and childrearing, the time of greatest physical strength. This very same timing means that 30 or 40 years later, when late adulthood is reached, children will be grown and the younger generation(s) can take up the physical and mental burdens of work and intense family life.

Given the intertwining of these two sequences of change, it is easy to see how Cumming and Henry arrived at disengagement theory. They perceived a kind of harmony in the entire system: In old age, social obligations are gradually withdrawn and no new roles are offered. It makes some sense to assume that the older adult would naturally respond to this social loss by withdrawing still further. But while such symmetry may make conceptual sense, it turns out not to make psychological sense. Older adults may be freed of most role prescriptions, but they do not lose their desire for intimacy or for emotional support from others; they may be less likely to be lonely than are younger adults, but it is still true that those elders who lack supportive and intimate human relationships are at greater risk for illness and depression.

This observation leads us to the more general point that despite the physical changes of aging and the relative unimportance of the social clock in these later years, many of the same basic psychological processes that we see in teenagers, young adults, and middle-aged adults are still operative in old age. For example, life satisfaction is predicted by essentially the same factors at every age: adequate social support, a sense of control, low incidence of off-time or unplanned life changes, and adequate economic conditions. Among young adults, work satisfaction is a more significant ingredient in the equation, and among older adults, health rises to near the top of the list. But the common ingredients are notable.

Wallace Stegner made the point particularly well in his book *The Spectator Bird*—one of the best novels about aging I have ever read. One of the characters, a doctor in his early 80s, when asked whether he feels like an "old man," replies that he does not. He feels like a young man who has something wrong with him.

That inner sense that you are "the same" but that somehow your body has changed is a common sensation in middle and late adulthood. It becomes disconcerting to look in a mirror, not only because the physical changes themselves may be not so charming to see, but because of the sense of shock that the "older" person in the mirror is really you. Such a sense of dislocation between the physical changes and a less-changing inner self arises not only because we each take ourselves with us through adult life—our personality traits, our internal working models, our physical characteristics—but also because the same fundamental psychological processes are operative at every age. There are different shadings, to be sure. But we respond to stress in similar ways, regardless of age; we create attachments and use our central attachment figures in much the same ways, regardless of age.

Influences on the Basic Processes

I've made these points before, but let me state them yet again, if only for emphasis. The largest influences on the experiences of late adulthood are factors that begin far earlier in life.

In your 60s you may be able to choose when to retire; you can choose where you will live and how you will spend your time. But all those decisions will be heavily influenced by your health, and that in turn is strongly related to all the earlier health decisions you made (or did not make). To be sure, not everyone has a great deal of choice about early health decisions. A man or woman may spend many years working in an unhealthy environment—mining, or working with chemicals, asbestos, or the like—because that is the only work that is available to support the family. Many children and younger adults also do not have access to good health care or to a decent diet, deficits that will have repercussions at later ages. But whether we are talking about personal health choices like smoking or unavoidable health risks encountered earlier in life, it is clear that the chickens come home to roost in late life. And no single thing will affect the shape of late adulthood more than the individual's health. Those in robust health retain better intellectual abilities, they are able to maintain physical function better because they are more able to get adequate exercise, and they have more options for "optimization with compensation."

The timing of earlier roles also affects the shape of later adult life, especially for the young old. Those who had their children late are likely to have a quite different experience between 65

and 75 than will those whose childbearing was completed by age 25 or 30. The former group may find themselves working past normal retirement age because of financial needs of not yet launched children. And because such late-in-life children are more recently launched when the older adults reach a point at which they may need financial or other assistance, there is likely to be more conflict of roles.

A third early-established pattern that can affect the experience of late adulthood is the quality of intimate relationships—not only with a spouse or partner, but with friends. Those older adults who have a confidant weather the various stresses of aging more easily and buoyantly than do those who lack such a confidant. But confidants are not to be found hanging on trees, ready for plucking when you need them. They are created and nurtured over many years. Women seem to deal with the many changes of old age more easily than do men in no small part because they are more likely to have created a network of such intimate relationships throughout their lives.

There is at least one significant exception to the argument that the major influences on late adulthood are patterns established much earlier in life. Within the period of late adulthood, successful aging also depends very much on that wise old principle, *use it or lose it.* In almost every arena of life, retention of capacity in late adulthood depends on repeated use, on practice. This is far less true at earlier ages, when the body and the mind may operate well despite neglect and disuse. But in late adulthood, optimization depends on regular use. The mind remains sharp to the extent that we use it; the body retains function to the extent that we exercise it; social relationships remain supportive to the extent that we nurture them with regular contact. The habit of such use can certainly be established at earlier ages—all to the good. But even those who have neglected their bodies, their minds, and their relationships can change these patterns in late adulthood, and by so doing they can achieve a more "successful" aging.

In the end, successful aging does not mean cheating death, or necessarily living for more years. It does mean using the available years to the fullest extent. That this is possible is attested to by the minority of older adults who retain fitness and zest. I fully intend to become such a zestful, eccentric old lady.

Dying, Death, and Bereavement

19

The last dance"; "the end of the journey." These are among the many ways of describing death. We began our own journey in this book by studying the beginning of human life at conception; we must end it by talking about dying and death.

Death can come at any age, but for most of us in industrialized societies, death comes in late adulthood. Three-quarters of children born in the United States today can expect to die after age 65 (Marshall & Levy, 1990). So a good deal of what I will say about dying and death will concern older adults. But the story must begin earlier, with our understanding of and attitudes toward dying and death.

The Meaning of Death over the Life Span

As an adult, you understand that death is irreversible, that it comes to everyone, and that it means a cessation of all function. But how early do children understand these aspects of death?

Children's Understanding of Death

Results from a variety of studies suggest that preschool-age children typically understand none of these aspects of death. They believe that death can be reversed, for instance through prayer, magic, or wishful thinking; they believe that dead persons can still feel or breathe; and they believe that death can be avoided by at least some people, such as those who are clever or lucky, or members of their own family (Lansdown & Benjamin, 1985; Speece & Brent, 1984, 1992). At about school age, just at about the time Piaget described as the beginning of concrete operations, most children seem to understand both the permanence and universality of death.

You can hear this change clearly in children's own comments. In one study, children were told a story about two kids who used to go into a candy store kept by an old lady who had recently died (Lansdown & Benjamin, 1985). After they heard the story, the subjects were asked some questions about the old lady, and about what it meant that she was dead.

> A 5-year-old: "Someone came into the shop to kill her. She'll see them again and she'll die again. She can try to get up."
>
> A 7-year-old: "They never come alive again. You can't move because your heart has stopped. People wish you can come alive but you can't. Children can't die because they start at one and go to 100."
>
> A 9-year-old: "Their heart can't take it any longer and they die. Babies can die of cancer, kidney problems. Heaven is much nicer than down here." (Lansdown & Benjamin, 1985, p. 20)

The first of these children has not yet understood the permanence of death; the second has not understood the universality of it; the third seems to have grasped all three, although the excerpt given is not extensive enough to be conclusive.

These boys, comforting each other in front of their mother's grave, are likely to have far more developmentally mature concepts of death than would others their age who have not encountered death firsthand.

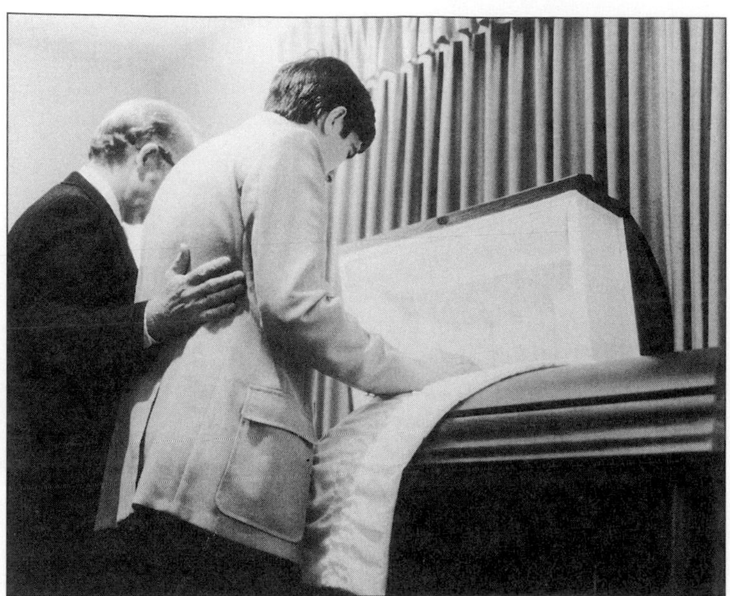

Death not only brings grief, it changes roles within families. This young man may well have to take on family responsibilities at an unusually early age.

Researchers have tried hard to connect the child's understanding of these aspects of the concept of death with the emergence of various facets of concrete operations. Some investigators have found that those children who understand conservation are also more likely to understand the permanence or universality of death. But not everyone has found such a link (Speece & Brent, 1984). Instead, as is true of so many other concepts in this age range, the child's specific experience seems to make a good deal of difference. Four- and 5-year-olds who have had direct experience with the death of a family member are more likely to have understood the permanence and loss of function associated with death than are those who have had no such personal experience (Stambrook & Parker, 1987).

The Meanings of Death in Adulthood

In adulthood, the concept of death goes well beyond the simple understanding of inevitability and universality. Most broadly, death has important social meaning. The death of any one person changes the roles and relationships of everyone else in that family. When an elder dies, everyone else in that particular lineage moves up one step in the generational system; if a middle-aged person dies, it may dislocate that same generational system by leaving no one in the "sandwich generation" to take on tasks of elder care; if a young adult or a child dies, the parents lose part of their role as parent. An individual's death also affects the roles of people beyond the family, such as by making room for younger adults in an organization to take on significant tasks. Retirement serves some of the same function because the older adult "steps aside" for the younger. But death brings many permanent changes in social systems.

Kalish (1985) lists four other meanings that death may have for adults:

Death as an Organizer of Time. At an individual level, the prospect of death may shape one's view of time. Bernice Neugarten proposes that in middle age, most individuals switch in the way they think of time, from "time since birth" to "time till death" (1968, 1977), a shift clearly reflected by this middle-aged subject:

CRITICAL THINKING

When you think of your own age, do you think of time since birth, or time till death, or both? If you think in terms of time till death, can you remember when you switched to this view, and why?

> Before I was 35, the future just stretched forth. There would be time to do and see and carry out all the plans I had. . . . Now I keep thinking, will I have time enough to finish off some of the things I want to do? (Neugarten, 1970, p. 78)

Such an "awareness of finitude"—to use Victor Marshall's phrase (1975)—is not a part of every middle-aged or older adult's view of death. Pat Keith (1981–1982), in a study of a group of adults aged 72 and older, found that only about half thought in terms of "time remaining." Interestingly, those who did think of death in these terms had less fear of death than did those who thought of their lives as "time lived." Other research confirms this: Those middle-aged and older adults who continue to be preoccupied with the past are more likely to be fearful and anxious about death (Pollack, 1979–1980).

Death as Punishment. Children are quite likely to think of death as punishment for being bad—a kind of ultimate stage 1 moral reasoning (see Table 11.2). But this view and its reverse (that long life is the reward for being good) are still common in adults. For example, Kalish and Reynolds (1976) found that 36 percent of adults in their study agreed with the statement that "most people who live to be 90 years old or older must have been morally good people." Such a view is strengthened by religious teachings that emphasize a link between sin and death.

Death as Transition. Many adults see death as a transition from one form of life to another, from physical life to some kind of immortality. In the United States, roughly 70 percent believe in some kind of life after death (Klenow & Bolin, 1989–1990). Such a belief is more common among women than men, and more common among Catholics and Protestants than among Jews, but there is no age difference. Twenty-year-olds are just as likely to report such a belief as are those over 60.

Death as Loss. The most pervasive meaning of death, for most adults, is that of loss. I do not mean here merely the understanding that body functions stop at death, but also the awareness that death means loss of relationships, loss of taste or smell, loss of pleasure. Death means I'll never taste another brownie, or hear another beautiful piece of music, or hold hands with my husband, or laugh, or cry.

Which of the many potential losses each person may fear or dread the most seems to change with age. Young adults are more concerned about loss of opportunity to experience things and about the loss of family relationships; older adults worry more about the loss of time to complete *inner* work. We can see such differences in the results of a study by Richard Kalish (Kalish & Reynolds, 1976), who interviewed roughly 400 adults, equally divided into four ethnic groups: African-American, Japanese-American, Mexican-American, and Anglo-American. Among many other questions, he asked, "If you were told that you had a terminal disease and six months to live, how would you want to spend your time until you died?"—a question you might want to think about for a moment yourself before you look at the results. Table 19.1 shows both the ethnic differences and the age differences in response to this question.

You can see that the only sizable ethnic difference was that Mexican Americans were the most likely to say that they would increase the time they spent with family or other loved ones. Age differences were more substantial. Younger adults were more likely to say they would seek out new experiences; older adults were considerably more likely to say they would turn inward—an interesting form of support for disengagement theory.

Fear and Anxiety About Death

If death is understood as punishment or loss, then it may be something to be feared. Fear of death may also include fear of the pain, suffering, or indignity that may be

Table 19.1 "What Would You Do If You Knew You Were to Die in Six Months?" Age and Ethnic Group Differences in Reply

	Ethnic Groups				Age Groups		
	Afr.-Amer.	Jap.-Amer.	Mex.-Amer.	Angl.-Amer.	20–39	40–59	60+
Make a marked change in lifestyle (e.g., travel, sex, experiences)	16	24	11	17	24	15	9
Center on inner life (e.g., read, contemplate, pray)	26	20	24	12	14	14	37
Focus concern on others; be with loved ones	14	15	38	23	29	25	12
Attempt to complete projects, tie up loose ends	6	8	13	6	11	10	3
No change in lifestyle	31	25	12	36	17	29	31

Source: Kalish & Reynolds, 1976, p. 205, item 037.

involved in the process of death itself, fear that one will not be able to cope well with such pain or suffering, fear of whatever punishment may come after death, and a fundamental fear of loss of the self.

Researchers have most often tried to measure such fears with some form of questionnaire. For example, David Lester asks subjects to indicate, on a five-point scale, how disturbed or anxious they are made by many aspects of death or dying, such as "the shortness of life" or "never thinking or experiencing anything again" or "your lack of control over the process of dying" (Lester, 1990). James Thorson and F. C. Powell, in a similar measure, include statements such as "I fear dying a painful death" or "Coffins make me anxious" or "I am worried about what happens to us after we die" (Thorson & Powell, 1992). On measures like these, researchers have quite consistently found that middle-aged adults show the greatest fear and older adults the least, with young adults falling somewhere in between (Gesser, Wong, & Reker, 1987–1988; Riley & Foner, 1968; Thorson & Powell, 1992). Older adults are more anxious about the process of *dying*, but have less fear of death itself.

The difference between the middle-aged and the aged is especially clear from a study by Vern Bengtson and his colleagues (Bengtson, Cuellar, & Ragan, 1977), who interviewed a sample of adults, aged 45 to 74, chosen to represent the population of the city of Los Angeles. Figure 19.1 shows the percentage of each age group who said they were very afraid or somewhat afraid of death. The fact that the shape of the curve is so remarkably similar for all three ethnic groups makes the results even more persuasive. And although these are cross-sectional results, similar patterns have emerged from cross-sectional comparisons done in the 1960s and the 1980s, which makes the conclusion that much more credible (e.g., Gesser et al., 1987–1988).

This peak of fear of death in the middle adult years is entirely consistent with the proposals of a number of theorists, including Levinson, that confronting the inevitability of one's own death is one of the major psychological tasks of middle age.

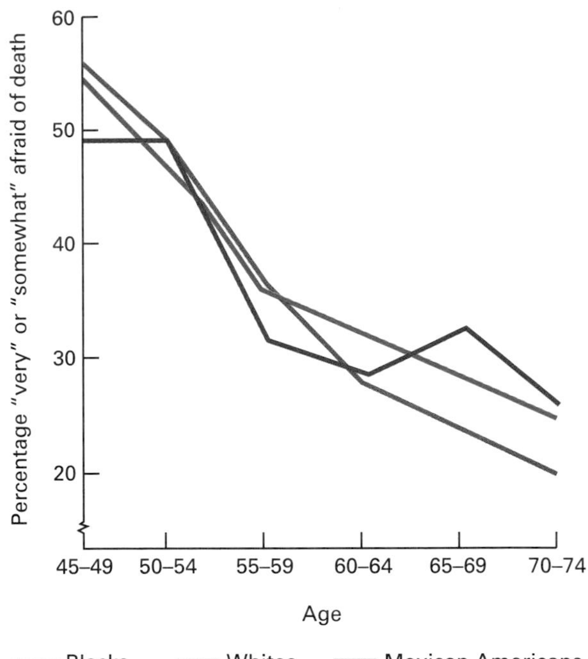

FIGURE 19.1 The remarkable similarity in the pattern of results for these three ethnic groups in southern California lends support to the generalization that older adults are less afraid of death than are the middle-aged. (*Source*: Bengtson et al., 1977, Figure 1, p. 80.)

Awareness of that inevitability is presumably triggered by all those signs of body aging that begin to be apparent in these middle years, as well as by the death of elderly parents. These events combine to break down our defenses against awareness of death and we become more consciously afraid.

Older adults do not become less *preoccupied* with death. On the contrary, the elderly think and talk more about death than do those at any other age. Death to the older person is highly salient. But it is apparently not as frightening as it was at middle life, perhaps because most individuals, having faced the inevitability, have come to terms with it. Older adults are more likely to fear the period of uncertainty *before* death than they are to fear death itself. They are anxious about where they may live, who will care for them, and whether they will be able to cope with the loss of control and independence that may be part of the last months or years of life (Marshall & Levy, 1990).

Critical Thinking

Is it possible that older adults are just as afraid of death as are the middle-aged, but that they simply deal with it differently? Can you think of any way you could study such a possibility?

Other Predictors of Fear of Death. Several characteristics other than age are also linked with fear of death, including religiosity and personality. The most typical finding is that adults who are deeply religious or who go to church regularly are less afraid of death than are those who describe themselves as less religious or who participate less regularly in religious activities (Kalish, 1985; Thorson & Powell, 1990). In some instances, however, researchers have found a curvilinear relationship, with both those who are deeply religious and those who are deeply irreligious describing less fear of death. Thus, the most fearful may be those who are uncertain about or uncommitted to any religious or philosophical tradition.

Among the Big Five personality traits, only neuroticism is linked to fear of death. A typical finding is Patricia Frazier and Deborah Foss-Goodman's (1988–1989) reported correlation of .41 between a measure of neuroticism and a measure of anxiety about death in a group of college students. Since neuroticism is generally characterized by greater fear or negative attitudes toward many aspects of life, we can see that to at least some extent, fear of death is a reflection of a more general trait.

More interesting, I think, is the link between feelings about death and one's sense of personal worth or competence. Adults who feel they have achieved the goals they set out to achieve, or who think of themselves as not too discrepant from the person they wanted to be, are less fearful of death than are those who are disappointed in themselves (Neimeyer & Chapman, 1980–1981). Adults who feel that their life has some purpose or meaning also appear to be less fearful of death (Durlak, 1972), as do those who feel some sense of personal competence (Pollack, 1979–1980). Such findings suggest the possibility that those adults who have successfully completed the major tasks of adult life, who have adequately fulfilled the demands of the roles they occupied, and who have developed inwardly are able to face death with greater equanimity. Those adults who have not been able to resolve the various tasks and dilemmas of adulthood face their late adult years more fearfully, more anxiously, even with what Erikson describes as despair. Fear of death may be merely one facet of such despair. If we think of fear of death in this way, then we might think of the whole of life as in some sense a preparation for death.

Preparation for Death

Preparation for death occurs on a number of other levels as well. At a practical level, a person can obtain life insurance or make out a will. Such preparations become more common as you move toward late adulthood and thus closer to the inevitability of death. For example, 61 percent of men between ages 18 and 24 have life insurance compared with 86 percent of men between 55 and 64 (U.S. Bureau of the Census, 1989). Far fewer people prepare for death by making out a will; only about 30 percent of adults in the United States have done so. But it is still true that older adults are more likely than younger ones to have taken this step. In Kalish and Reynolds' study (1976), only 10 percent of those aged 20 to 39 had made out a will, compared with 39 percent of those 60 and older. Similarly, older adults are more likely to have made arrangements for their own funeral or burial.

At a somewhat deeper level, adults may prepare for death through some process of reminiscence, such as the life review Butler suggested. I mentioned in the last chapter that we have little evidence that older adults typically or necessarily go through such a review process. But for some, such a review may be an important aspect of "writing the final chapter" or legitimizing one's life in some fashion (Marshall & Levy, 1990). Two of my grandparents, for instance, in their 80s wrote autobiographies for circulation within the family. I find the documents fascinating not only because they tell me more than I had known before about my grandparents' lives and about family history, but also because of the self-justification and self-explanations they contain. I know of no research that would tell me how common such explicit review may be, but such acts may form an important part of the preparation for death for at least some elders.

Deeper still, there may be unconscious changes that occur in the years just before death that we might think of as a type of preparation. I mentioned the physical and mental changes associated with the concept of "terminal drop" in Chapter 17. Research by Morton Lieberman has pointed to the possibility that there may be terminal psychological changes as well (Lieberman, 1965; Lieberman & Coplan, 1970).

Lieberman studied a group of older adults longitudinally, interviewing and testing each subject regularly over a period of three years. After the end of the testing, Lieberman kept track of the subjects and noted the time of their death. In this fashion he was able to identify one group of 40 subjects who had all died within one year after the end of the interviewing, and to compare them with another group of 40, matched to the early-death group by age, sex, and marital status, who had survived at least three years after the end of the testing. By comparing the psychological test scores of these two groups during the course of the three years of testing, Lieberman could detect changes that might take place near to death.

He found that those nearer to death not only showed terminal drop on tests of memory and learning, they also became less emotional, introspective, and aggressive or assertive; and more conventional, docile, dependent, and warm. In those near death, all these characteristics increased over the three years of interviewing, a pattern that did not occur among those the same age who were further from death. Thus, it was not that initially conventional, docile, dependent, unintrospective adults died sooner, but that these qualities became accentuated in those who were close to death.

CRITICAL THINKING

Given these findings, is it possible that Cumming and Henry were correct about disengagement being a natural process toward the end of life, but placed it too early and too sweepingly in the years of late adulthood?

This is only a single study. As always in such cases, we need to be careful about drawing sweeping conclusions from limited evidence. But the results are intriguing and suggestive. They paint a picture of a kind of psychological preparation for death—conscious or unconscious—in which the individual gives up tilting at windmills, becomes less active physically and psychologically. These near-death individuals do not necessarily become less involved with other people, but they do seem to show some kind of "disengagement" nonetheless.

The Process of Dying

Elizabeth Kübler-Ross (1969) drew very similar conclusions based on her work with terminally ill adults and children. In her early writings, she proposed that those who know they are dying move through a series of steps or stages, arriving finally at the stage she calls acceptance. This model of stages of dying has had many critics; even Kübler-Ross herself, in her later writings, no longer argues that dying moves through clear or sequential stages (Kübler-Ross, 1974). Instead, she now talks of emotional tasks rather than stages. But because her original ideas have been immensely influential and her terminology is still widely used, you need to have at least some familiarity with these concepts.

Kübler-Ross's Stages of Dying

Drawing on her observations of hundreds of dying patients, Kübler-Ross originally suggested five stages: denial, anger, bargaining, depression, and acceptance.

Denial. Many people, confronted with a terminal diagnosis, react with some variant of "Not me!," "It must be a mistake," "I'll get another opinion," or "I don't feel sick." All these are forms of denial, a psychological defense that may be highly useful in the early hours and days after such a diagnosis, since it helps to deal with the shock of knowing one is near death. Kübler-Ross thought that these extreme forms of denial faded within a few days, to be replaced by anger.

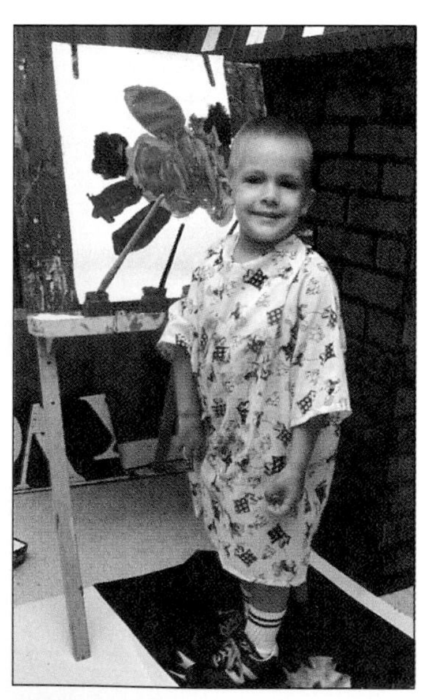

Children use some of the same defenses to deal with their own potential deaths as do adults. Young cancer patients, like this cheerful-looking child, may deny or bargain—for instance, "If I take my medicine I'll be able to go back to school in the fall."

Anger. Anger often expresses itself in thoughts like "It's not fair!" but it may also be expressed toward God, toward the doctor who should have done something sooner, toward nurses or family members. The anger seems to be a response not only toward the terminal diagnosis itself, but also to the sense of loss of control and helplessness that many patients feel in impersonal medical settings.

Bargaining. Stage three is an interesting new form of defense in which the patient tries to make "deals" with doctors, nurses, family, or God. "If I do everything you tell me, then I'll live till spring." Kübler-Ross gave a particularly compelling example of this: A patient with terminal cancer wanted to live long enough to attend the wedding of her eldest son. The hospital staff, to help her try to reach this goal, taught her self-hypnosis to deal with her pain and she was able to attend the wedding. Kübler-Ross goes on to describe: "I will never forget the moment when she returned to the hospital. She looked tired and somewhat exhausted and—before I could say hello—said, 'Now don't forget I have another son!'" (1969, p. 83).

Depression. Bargaining may be a successful defense for a while, but eventually—so Kübler-Ross thought—it breaks down in the face of all the signs of declining physical status. At this point the patient becomes depressed. Many dying persons sink into long-lasting despair. In Kübler-Ross's view, this depression or despair is a necessary preparation for the final step of acceptance. In order to reach acceptance, the dying person must grieve for all that will be lost with death.

Acceptance. When such grieving is finally done, the individual is ready to die. A particularly eloquent expression of acceptance comes from Stewart Alsop, a writer who kept a diary of the last years of his life, as he was dying of leukemia. In one of the very late entries in this journal he said: "A dying man needs to die as a sleepy man needs to sleep, and there comes a time when it is wrong, as well as useless, to resist" (Alsop, 1973, p. 299).

Criticisms and Alternative Views

Kübler-Ross's description has been (and still is) enormously influential. She has provided a common language for those who work with dying patients, and her highly compassionate descriptions have, without doubt, sensitized health care workers and families to the complexities of the process of dying. At some moments, what the patient needs is cheering up; at other moments he needs simply to be listened to; there are times to hold his hand quietly and times to provide encouragement or hope. Many new care programs for terminally ill patients, such as the hospice programs I'll describe in a moment, are clearly outgrowths of this greater sensitivity to the dying process.

These are all worthwhile changes. But Kübler-Ross's basic thesis—that the dying process necessarily involves these specific five stages, in this specific order—has been widely criticized, for several good reasons.

Methodological Problems. Kübler-Ross's hypothesized sequence was initially based on clinical observation of perhaps 200 patients, and she did not provide information about how frequently she talked to them or over how long a period she continued to assess them. She also did not report the ages of the patients she studied, although it is clear that many were middle-aged or young adults, for whom a terminal illness was obviously "off time." Nearly all were apparently cancer patients. Would the same processes hold for those dying of other diseases—diseases in which it is much less common to have a specific diagnosis or a short-term prognosis? Thus, Kübler-Ross's observations might be correct, but only for a small subset of dying individuals.

Critical Thinking

If you wanted to discover whether there really are widely shared stages in people's reactions to dying, what kind of study would you have to do? How might you study stages of dying in those who die from something other than a disease with a clear terminal diagnosis?

Culture Specificity. A related question has to do with whether reactions to dying are culture-specific or universal. Kübler-Ross wrote as if the five stages of dying were universal human processes. But most social scientists would now agree that reactions to dying are strongly culturally conditioned. For example, in some Native American cultures, tradition calls for death to be faced and accepted with composure. Because it is part of nature's cycle, it is not to be feared or fought (DeSpelder & Strickland, 1983). In such a culture, would we expect to find stages of denial, anger, and depression?

As another example, in Mexican culture, death is seen as a mirror of the person's life. Thus, your death, your way of dying, tells much about what kind of person you have been. And by contrast with the dominant U.S. culture, in which death is feared and thoughts of it repressed, in Mexican culture death is discussed frequently, even celebrated in a national feast day, the Day of the Dead (DeSpelder & Strickland, 1983). It seems inescapable that such cultural variations will affect an individual's reaction to his own impending death.

Are There Stages at All? The most potent criticism, however, centers on the issue of stages. Many clinicians and researchers who have attempted to study the process systematically have not found that all dying patients exhibit these five emotions at

Cultures and Contexts

The Good Death in Kaliai

It is important to be aware that our own cultural ways of dealing with death are not universal. So let me give you an example of a radically different set of death rituals, found among the Kaliai, a small Melanesian group in Papua New Guinea (Counts, 1976–1977). The Kaliai see death not as an end to life, but as a transition between different life states. Those who have passed through this transition become powerful superhuman beings—ordinarily invisible to the living person, but with their own forms and duties.

In Kaliai beliefs, all deaths are caused by some malevolent agent or cause—someone or something that the dying person has offended in some fashion, be it another living person who may kill directly or through sorcery, a ghost, or a superhuman being. No matter how careful a life one may lead, it is impossible to avoid giving offense to someone or something, so eventually death will come.

A "good death" is one in which the transition from human to superhuman has been done properly, which means that all social relationships have been brought into balance. In this cultural system, all social relationships involve exchanges of material goods through lending and gift giving. To die with these exchanges in balance, the individual must make preparations as death approaches, ensuring that he neither owes nor is owed anything. If a person dies unexpectedly, the family must complete this process, or the transition to the superhuman status—called *antu*—cannot be completed.

Any person who feels that he is near death moves from his house into a temporary shelter. At that point he does two things. He attempts to thwart death by all possible means, including appeasing whomever he thinks he may have offended and using whatever medicines or cures may be offered. And he begins to bring to closure all his social relationships, so that when death comes he is fully prepared. Family members gather during this dying process, all of them speculating at length about who the killer might be and what transgressions the victim might be guilty of. If the victim recovers, he or she simply resumes normal life; everyone assumes that the killer's feelings were somehow assuaged. If the victim dies, then the family members prepare the body for funeral rites, crying a grieving chant.

My purpose in describing this unusual cultural approach to death is not just to intrigue you with the range of human diversity, but to point out that in any culture, death customs flow naturally from beliefs about the causes and meaning of death. This is as true of our own cultures or subcultures as it is of the Kaliai. Those who believe in the possibility of miracle cures will be more likely to go to Lourdes; those who believe that death can be thwarted with proper medical care will react differently to a diagnosis of a serious illness than will someone who sees illness as God's choice or someone who believes in the law of karma. Each of us, and each culture or subculture collectively, has beliefs about death, dying, and the afterlife that will affect the way we approach our own deaths, as well as the way we react to the deaths of those close to us.

all, let alone in a specific order. Of the five, only some type of depression seems to be a common thread among Western patients, and neither acceptance nor disengagement appears to be a common end point of the process (Baugher et al., 1989–1990). Some patients display such acceptance while others remain as active and engaged as possible right up to the end. Edwin Shneidman (1980, 1983), a major theorist and clinician in the field of **thanatology** (the study of dying), puts it this way:

> I reject the notion that human beings, as they die, are somehow marched in lock step through a series of stages of the dying process. On the contrary, in working with dying persons, I see a wide panoply of human feelings and emotions, of various human needs, and a broad selection of psychological defenses and maneuvers—a few of these in some people, dozens in others—experienced in an impressive variety of ways. (1980, p. 110)

Instead of stages, Shneidman suggests we think of the dying process as having many "themes" that can appear, disappear, and reappear in the process of dealing with death in any one patient: terror ("I was really frightened"), pervasive uncertainty ("if there is a God . . ."), fantasies of being rescued ("somebody . . . that maybe could perform this miracle"), incredulity ("It's so far-fetched, so unreal. . . . It is a senseless death"), feelings of unfairness, a concern with reputation after death, the fight against pain, and so forth.

Another alternative is a "task-based" approach suggested by Charles Corr (1991–1992). In his view, coping with dying is like coping with any other problem or dilemma: You need to take care of certain specific tasks. He suggests four such tasks for the dying person:

1. Satisfying bodily needs and minimizing physical stress;
2. Maximizing psychological security, autonomy, and richness in living;
3. Sustaining and enhancing those interpersonal attachments significant to the dying person; and
4. Identifying, developing, or reaffirming sources of spiritual energy, and thereby fostering hope.

Corr is not denying the importance of the various emotional themes described by Shneidman. Rather, he is arguing that for health professionals who deal with dying individuals, it is more helpful to think in terms of the patient's tasks, because the dying person may need help in performing some or all of them.

Whichever model one uses, what is clear is that there are no lockstep stages, no common patterns that typify most or all reactions to impending death. Common themes exist, but they are blended together in quite different patterns by each of us as we face this last task.

Individual Adaptations to Potential Death

Such individual variations in response to impending death have themselves been the subject of a good deal of research interest in the past few decades. The question that researchers have begun to ask is whether specific variations in patients' emotional response to impending or probable death have any effect at all on the physical process of dying.

I should say at the outset that the great preponderance of research on individual variations or adaptations to dying involves studies of patients with terminal cancer. Not only is cancer a clear diagnosis, but also many forms of it progress quite rapidly, and the patient not only knows that she is terminally ill but roughly how long she has to live. Some other diseases, such as AIDS, have these same features, but most other diseases do not. Most particularly, heart disease, which along with cancer is the leading cause of death in middle and old age in industrialized countries, may exist for a long period, the patient may or may not know that she has significant heart disease, and the prognosis is highly variable. We simply do not know whether any of the conclusions drawn from studies of cancer patients can be applied to adults dying less rapidly or less predictably. Still, the research is quite fascinating.

The most influential single study in this area has been the work of Steven Greer and his colleagues (Greer, 1991; Greer, Morris, & Pettingale, 1979; Pettingale et al., 1985). They have followed a group of 62 women diagnosed in the 1970s with early stages of breast cancer. Three months after the original diagnosis, each woman was interviewed at some length and her reaction to the diagnosis and to her treatment was classed in one of five groups:

1. *Denial* (positive avoidance): Rejection of evidence about diagnosis; insistence that surgery was just precautionary.
2. *Fighting spirit*: An optimistic attitude, accompanied by a search for more information about the disease. These patients often see their disease as a challenge, and plan to fight it with every method available.
3. *Stoic acceptance* (fatalism): Acknowledgment of the diagnosis but without seeking any further information; ignoring the diagnosis and carrying on their normal life as much as possible.

4. *Helplessness/hopelessness*: Overwhelmed by diagnosis; see themselves as dying or gravely ill; devoid of hope.
5. *Anxious preoccupation*: This category had originally been included in the helplessness group, but was separated out later. It includes those whose response to the diagnosis was strong and persistent anxiety. If they seek information, they interpret it pessimistically; they monitor their body sensations carefully, interpreting each ache or pain as a possible recurrence.

Greer then checked on the survival rates of these five groups after 5, 10, and 15 years. Table 19.2 shows the 15-year results. Only 35 percent of those whose initial reaction had been either denial or fighting spirit had died of cancer 15 years later, compared with 76 percent of those whose initial reaction had been stoic acceptance, anxious preoccupation, or helplessness/hopelessness. Because the five groups had not differed initially in the stage of their disease or in their treatment, these results support the hypothesis that psychological responses contribute to disease progress—just as coping strategies more generally affect the likelihood of disease in the first place.

Similar results have emerged from studies of patients with melanoma (a form of skin cancer) as well as other cancers (Temoshok, 1987), and from several recent studies of AIDS patients (Reed et al., 1994; Solano et al., 1993). And at least one study of coronary bypass patients (Scheier et al., 1989) shows that those men who had had a more optimistic attitude before the surgery recovered more quickly in the six months after surgery and returned more fully to their presurgery pattern of life. In general, those who report less hostility, more stoic acceptance, more helplessness, and who fail to express negative feelings, die *sooner* (O'Leary, 1990). Those who struggle the most, who fight the hardest, who express their anger and hostility openly, and who also find some sources of joy in their lives, live longer. In some ways, the data suggest that "good patients"—those who are obedient and not too questioning, who don't yell at their doctors or make life difficult for those around them—are in fact likely to die sooner. Difficult patients, who question and challenge those around them, last longer.

Furthermore, a few studies now link these psychological differences to immune system functioning. A particular subset of immune cells thought to be an important defense against cancer, called NK cells, have been found to occur at lower rates among those patients who report *less* distress and who seem better adjusted to their

Table 19.2 Differences in 15-Year Outcomes Among Women Cancer Patients with Differing Psychological Responses to the Initial Diagnosis

	Outcome 15 Years Later			
Psychological Response 3 Months After Surgery	Alive and Well	Died from Cancer	Died from Other Causes	Total
Denial	5	5	0	10
Fighting spirit	4	2	4	10
Stoic acceptance	6	24	3	33
Anxious preoccupation	0	3	0	3
Hopelessness	1	5	0	6
Total	16	39	7	62

Source: Greer, 1991, from Table 1, p. 45.

illness (O'Leary, 1990). And among AIDS patients, one study shows that T-cell counts declined more rapidly among those who responded to their disease with repression (similar to the stoic acceptance or helplessness groups in the Greer study), while those showing fighting spirit had slower loss of T cells (Solano et al., 1993).

Despite the consistency of these results, two important cautions are nonetheless in order before we leap to the conclusion that a fighting spirit is the optimum response to any disease. First, some careful studies find *no* link between depression/stoic acceptance/helplessness and more rapid death from cancer (e.g., Cassileth, Walsh, & Lusk, 1988; Richardson et al., 1990).

Second, it is not clear that the same psychological response is necessarily optimum for every form of disease. Consider heart disease, for example. There is a certain irony in the fact that many of the qualities that appear to be optimal among cancer patients could be considered as reflections of a Type A (or perhaps A–) personality. Because the Type A personality constitutes a *risk* factor for heart disease, it is not so obvious that a "fighting spirit" response to a diagnosis of advanced heart disease would necessarily be the most desirable. This growing body of research does tell us, though, that connections exist between psychological defenses or ways of coping and physical functioning, even in the very last stages of life.

The Role of Social Support. Another important ingredient in an individual's response to imminent death is the amount of social support he or she may have available. Those with positive and supportive relationships describe lower levels of pain and less depression during their final months of illness (Carey, 1974; Hinton, 1975). Such well-supported patients also live longer. For example, heart attack patients who live alone are more likely to have a second attack than are those who live with someone else (Case et al., 1992), and those with significant levels of atherosclerosis live longer if they have a confidant than if they do not (Williams, 1992). The latter study involved a sample of African Americans, suggesting that the connection is not unique to Euro-American culture.

This link between social support and length of survival has also been found in *experimental* studies in which patients with equivalent diagnoses and equivalent medical care have been randomly assigned either to an experimental group in which subjects participate in regular support group sessions, or to a control group in which subjects have no such specially created support system. In one such study of a group of 86 women with metastatic breast cancer (that is, cancer that had spread beyond the original site), David Spiegel (Spiegel et al., 1989) found that the average length of survival was 36.6 months for those in the support group compared with 18.9 months in the control group. Thus, just as social support helps to buffer children and adults from some of the negative effects of many kinds of nonlethal stress, so it seems to perform a similar function for those facing death.

Critical Thinking

It is one thing to find that support groups extend life among those with terminal illnesses. It is another to explain why, or by what mechanism. What hypotheses can you generate about why social support works in this way?

Where Death Occurs: Hospitals and Hospices

In the United States and other industrialized countries, the great majority of adults die in hospitals, rather than at home or even in nursing homes. The exact pattern naturally varies a great deal as a function of such factors as age or type of disease. Among the old old, for example, death in a nursing home is quite common. Among younger adults, in contrast, hospital death is the norm. Similarly, adults with known progressive diseases, such as cancer or AIDS, are typically in and out of the hospital for months or years before death; at the other end of the continuum are many who are hospitalized with an acute problem, such as a heart attack or pneumonia, and die within a short space of time, having had no prior hospitalization. In between fall those who may have experienced several different types of care in the last weeks or months, including hospitalization, home health care, and nursing home care. Despite such diversity, it is still true that the majority of deaths, particularly among the

The Real World

Saying Goodbye

The Kaliai of New Guinea have ritualized systems for completing social relationships when death approaches. In most industrialized countries we have no such widely accepted rituals, but because the human need for closure and ritual is so strong, many adults nonetheless create some method of saying farewell.

A study in Australia, by Allan Kellehear and Terry Lewin (1988–1989), gives us a glimpse of the variety of goodbyes devised by the dying. They interviewed 90 terminally ill cancer patients, all of whom expected to die within one year or less. Most had known of their cancer diagnosis for at least a year prior to the interview, but had only recently been given a short-term prognosis. As part of the interview, each of these 90 people was asked if she (or he) had already said farewell to anyone, and to describe any plans she had for future farewells. To whom did she want to say goodbye, and how would those goodbyes be handled?

About a fifth of these people planned no farewells. Another three-fifths thought it was important to say goodbye, but wanted to put it off until very near the end so as to distress family and friends as little as possible. They hoped that there would then be time for a few final words with spouse, children, and close friends.

The remaining fifth began their farewells much earlier, and used many different avenues. Some planned special visits with family members or friends, to have "one last talk." Some wrote to friends or family, expressing in writing their feelings and their farewells. Some made special gifts. One woman sent photos and personal treasures to all her sisters; another made dolls to give to friends, family, and medical staff. In a particularly touching farewell gesture, another woman, who had two grown daughters but no grandchildren, knitted a set of baby clothes for each daughter, for the grandchildren she would never see.

Kellehear and Lewin make the important point that all these farewells are a kind of gift. They signal that the other person is worthy of a last goodbye. They may be a balancing of the relationship slate just as much as the balancing of physical gifts and obligations is among the Kaliai.

Farewells also may allow the dying person to disengage more readily when death comes closer, and to warn others that death is indeed approaching. It may thus help the living to begin a kind of anticipatory grieving, and in this way to prepare better for the loss.

elderly, are preceded by some weeks of hospitalization (Merrill & Mor, 1993; Shapiro, 1983).

In recent years, however, an alternative form of terminal care has become prominent—**hospice care.** The hospice movement was given a good deal of boost by Kübler-Ross's writings because she emphasized the importance of a "good death," or a "death with dignity," in which the patient and the patient's family have more control over the entire process. Many health care professionals, particularly in England and the United States, began to suggest that such a good death could be better achieved if the dying person were at home, or in a homelike setting in which contact with family and other friends would be part of the daily experience.

Hospice care emerged in England in the late 1960s, and in the United States in the early 1970s (Mor, 1987). By 1982, the idea had gained so much support in the United States that Congress was persuaded to add hospice care to the list of benefits paid for by Medicare. Today there are more than 1500 hospice programs in the United States, serving thousands of terminally ill patients and their families.

The philosophy that underlies this alternative setting or approach to the dying patient has several aspects (Bass, 1985):

1. Death should be viewed as normal, not to be avoided but to be faced and accepted.
2. The patient and family should be encouraged to prepare for the death by examining their feelings, planning for their later life, and talking openly about the death.

3. The family should be involved in the patient's care as much as is physically possible, not only because this gives the patient the emotional support of those who love her, but because it allows each family member to come to some resolution of her or his relationship with the dying person.
4. Control over the patient's care should be in the hands of the patient and the family. They decide what types of medical treatment they will ask for or accept; they decide whether the patient will remain at home or be hospitalized.
5. Medical care should be primarily palliative rather than curative. The emphasis is on controlling pain and maximizing comfort, not on invasive or life-prolonging measures.

Three somewhat different types of programs have been developed following these general guidelines. The most common types of hospice program are home-based programs in which one central family caregiver—most frequently the spouse—provides hour-to-hour care for the dying person with the support and assistance of specially trained nurses or other staff who visit regularly, provide medication, and help the family deal psychologically with the impending death. A second type is a special hospice center in which a small number of patients in the last stages of a terminal disease are cared for in a homelike setting. Finally, hospital-based hospice programs provide palliative care following the basic hospice philosophy, with daily involvement of family members in the patient's care, but within a hospital setting. It is interesting that these three options parallel so closely the basic birth options now available as well: home delivery, birthing centers, and hospital-based birthing rooms. The fourth choice, both at birth and at death, is traditional hospital care.

Research on Hospice Care. The choice of traditional hospital care versus hospice care is most often made on philosophical rather than medical grounds. But it is still worth asking how the two types of care compare medically or psychologically. Two large comparison studies suggest that the differences are small, although the results tilt slightly toward hospice care.

The National Hospice Study (Greer et al., 1986; Mor, Greer, & Kastenbaum, 1988) analyzed the experiences of 1754 terminally ill cancer patients treated in 40 different hospices and 14 conventional hospitals. Half the hospice programs were home-based, half hospital-based. The patients were not assigned randomly to hospice or conventional hospital care, but chose their own form of care. In comparing the two forms of care, the researchers looked at the patient's reported pain and satisfaction

This woman dying of cancer has chosen to stay at home during her last months, supported by regular visits from hospice nurses.

with care, and at the central caregiver's quality of life and satisfaction. What is remarkable is how few differences there were between the two. There were no differences in patients' reported pain, length of survival, or satisfaction with care. The major difference was that family members were most satisfied with hospital-based hospice care, while those with home-based hospice care reported the highest sense of burden.

In a smaller study, Robert Kane and his colleagues (Kane et al., 1985, 1984) assigned subjects randomly either to hospice or normal hospital care. The hospice care in this case was a combination of home-based and hospital-based. Most hospice patients remained at home but spent brief periods in the hospital's hospice ward, either when the family needed a break or when the patient's care become too complex to handle at home. As in the National Hospice Study, Kane found no differences between these two groups in reports of pain or length of survival. But he did find that patients in the hospice group were more consistently satisfied with the quality of care they received and with their degree of control over their own care. Similarly, the family members in the hospice group in Kane's study were more satisfied with their own involvement with the patient's care and had lower levels of anxiety than did family members of the hospital-treatment group.

CRITICAL THINKING

Given what you have just read and your own philosophical assumptions, do you think you would choose hospice care for your own death, or urge it on a spouse or parent in the last stages of a terminal illness? Why or why not?

Taken together, these two studies suggest that using purely physical yardsticks, such as control of pain or survival duration, these two types of terminal care do not differ in effectiveness. Where differences exist, it is on measures of attitudes or feelings. On some—but not all—such measures, those in hospice care and their families are slightly more satisfied. At the same time, both studies make it clear that home-based hospice care is a considerable burden, especially on the central caregiver, who may spend as much as 19 hours a day in physical care.

To my way of thinking, the most positive aspect of hospice care is that it offers a choice for the dying individual, just as the rise in the availability of birth centers has increased the choices for prospective parents. Because a sense of control appears to be an important ingredient in a person's satisfaction with life, having some control over the conditions of one's death is also likely to be an important ingredient in coping with this last of life's transitions.

Death Itself

Most of us use the word *death* as if it described a simple on/off phenomenon. You are either alive or dead. But in fact death is a process as well as a state, and physicians have different labels for different aspects of this process.

Clinical death describes the few minutes after the heart has stopped, when breathing has stopped and there is no evident brain function, but during which rescue is still possible. Heart attack patients are sometimes brought back from clinical death; presumably those who report *near-death experiences* were in a state of clinical death.

Brain death describes a state in which the person no longer has reflexes or any response to vigorous external stimuli, and no electrical activity in the brain. When the cortex, but not the brain stem, is affected, the patient may still be able to breathe without assistance and may survive for long periods in a vegetative state or on life support systems. When the brain stem is also dead, no body function can occur independently and the individual is said to be *legally* dead (Detchant, 1995). Brain death most often occurs only after a period of eight to ten minutes of clinical death, but there are cases in which brain death has occurred because of brain injury, as in an auto accident, when other body functions can still be maintained artificially. In such cases, other body organs, such as heart and kidneys, are briefly viable enough to be used for organ donation.

Finally, we may speak of **social death,** the point at which the person is treated like a corpse by others, for instance by preparing the body for death by closing the eyes or by signing a death certificate.

After Death: Rituals and Grieving

Once this point of social death is reached, family and friends, as well as the larger culture, must begin to deal with the loss. In virtually every culture, the immediate response is some kind of funeral ritual.

Ritual Mourning: Funerals and Ceremonies

When I was a teenager and a young adult, I thought funerals were largely empty gestures—a set of rituals that were dictated by the culture and had no function at all. What was the point, I thought, in coming together in this way just to put a dead body into the ground? As I have gotten older and have been through funerals for closer family members, I have come to understand that such rituals exist in every culture precisely because they serve many vital functions. As Marshall and Levy put it:

> Rituals provide a . . . means through which societies simultaneously seek to control the disruptiveness of death and to make it meaningful. . . . The funeral exists as a formal means to accomplish the work of completing a biography, managing grief, and building new social relationships after the death. (1990, pp. 246, 253)

Funerals help family members to manage their grief by giving them a specific set of roles to play. As with all roles, these include both expected and prohibited or discouraged behaviors. The content of these roles differs markedly from one culture to the next, but the clarity of the role in most cases provides a shape to the days or weeks immediately following the death of a loved person. In our culture, the rituals prescribe what one should wear, who should be called, who should be fed, what demeanor one should show, and far more. Depending on one's religious background, one may need to arrange to sit shiva, or gather friends and family for a wake, or arrange a memorial service. One may be expected to respond stoically or to wail and tear one's hair. But whatever the social rules, the grieving person has a role to fill that provides shape to the first numbing hours and days.

Friends and acquaintances, too, have guiding rules, at least for those first few days. They may bring food, write letters of condolence, offer help, and attend wakes and funerals.

Funerals and other rituals also bring family members together as no other occasion—with the possible exception of weddings—is likely to do. I was particularly struck

Each culture has its own funeral rituals. In Yugoslavia, where this photo was taken before the civil war, it was clearly the custom for mourners to wear black.

The Real World

Choosing Your Own Death

One element of having greater control over the process of dying might be the ability to choose the timing of that death—a highly controversial topic. When an individual dies by his own action or hand, we call it *suicide.* When he is assisted in his chosen death in some way, we call it *euthanasia.* Today, most physicians and medical ethicists distinguish between *active euthanasia* (also called *assisted suicide*), in which a physician or other individual hastens a patient's death (at the patient's request) by active means, such as the administration of a fatal dose of drugs; and *passive euthanasia,* in which a physician (or other person) hastens a death by *not* intervening with life support systems or medication that would prolong the life, or by *withdrawing* life support or other treatment that may be keeping a patient alive.

At the moment, our cultural response to the idea of passive euthanasia is massive ambivalence. An increasing number of adults have made out *living wills* specifying that life support systems or resuscitations *not* be used in case of their clinical death or near death. Such living wills essentially ask physicians to participate in a kind of passive euthanasia. It turns out that this request is often not followed, both because health care professionals who treat a patient on an emergency basis may not know of the living will and because many physicians find it extremely difficult to "give up," *not* to use the full armamentarium of treatments available to them to prolong a life. At the same time, many physicians, particularly those who have treated a patient over many years, are entirely comfortable with urging patients or family members to discontinue some life-prolonging treatment, thus hastening the patient's death.

Assisted suicide (or any other form of active euthanasia) is far less common and much more controversial—made more so in recent years in the United States by the actions of Dr. Jack Kevorkian, a physician who has defied laws and assisted a series of terminally ill or severely handicapped individuals to end their own lives. In the Netherlands, active euthanasia is technically illegal but has been sanctioned within the medical profession (and within the Dutch Reformed Church) for some years, so long as strict guidelines are followed. The patient must have repeatedly requested an end to suffering accompanying an incurable disease, and all other options must have been exhausted or refused by the patient. When these conditions have been met—and a great many requests for assisted death in Netherlands do *not* meet these conditions—the physician will not be prosecuted for administering drugs that will produce death (Nuland, 1993).

In the United States at present, the legal status of such a practice is tangled. Explicit attempts to legalize assisted suicide through voters' initiatives have been defeated in several states; one such referendum passed in Oregon, but its implementation has been delayed by court action (Alpers & Lo, 1995). Many other state legislatures enacted explicit bans against assisted suicide, but such bans were struck down on constitutional grounds by 1996 decisions in two federal appeals courts, deci-

by this at the funeral of my father's mother, who died about 10 years ago. Among those who came to the memorial service were several cousins I had not seen for at least 30 years. Not only was I quite unprepared for the strong sense of family connection I felt for and with these strangers, I found myself greatly drawn to one of the cousins I barely knew. We have since created a friendship that I expect to last for the rest of our lives.

In this way death rituals can strengthen family ties, clarify the new lines of influence or authority within a family, and pass on the flame in some way to the next generation. At the same time, death rituals are also designed to help the survivors understand the meaning of death itself, in part by emphasizing the meaning of the life of the person who has died. It is not accidental that most death rituals include testimonials, biographies, and witnessing. By telling the story of the person's life and describing that life's value and meaning, people can more readily accept the death. In a sense, a funeral is often like a "life review" and serves for the living some of the same purpose that Butler thought the life review served for the elderly person approaching death.

Finally, death rituals may give some transcendent meaning to death itself by placing it in some philosophical or religious context. In this way, they provide comfort to the bereaved by offering answers to that inevitable question, "Why?"

Critical Thinking

Think about the various funerals or equivalent death rituals you have attended. Do they seem to have served the purposes I've described? Do some forms of funeral seem to do a better job of meeting these needs than others?

sions that effectively make assisted suicide legal in the states governed by the particular district courts involved. These decisions will doubtless be appealed to the Supreme Court, so the ultimate legal status of this practice in the United States remains to be settled.

The only place in the world where such a practice is fully and explicitly legal is in one state of Australia (the Northern Territory), where a law took effect in 1996 officially sanctioning active euthanasia (Ryan & Kaye, 1996). The Northern Territory law sets strict conditions for active euthanasia similar to the Dutch guidelines, including a voluntary request by a patient who experiences severe and persisting suffering, and concurrence by at least two physicians.

Surveys of physicians and laypeople in the United States suggest that 50 to 60 percent of both groups favor either some form of legalization of assisted suicide or acceptance of the practice without a law (Bachman et al., 1996; Lee et al., 1996). Those who oppose such an acceptance of euthanasia offer several arguments. Many believe, on religious grounds, that it is not for human beings to choose the hour of their death. Others argue against active euthanasia on the grounds that it might be extremely difficult to set limits on the process, even with strict guidelines—a position often labeled "the slippery slope argument" (Twycross, 1996); we might come to the point where those who are infirm or severely disabled are subtly (or not so subtly) encouraged to end their own lives in order to remove the burden of their care; we might even reach a point where physicians administer fatal drugs without the patient's consent. A third argument against any form of active euthanasia is that modern pain management techniques allow even those with extremely painful terminal illnesses to be comfortable in the last days or weeks of their lives, so that it is not necessary to hasten death in order to avoid pain.

Those who take the opposite view note that modern medical technology has increasingly made it possible to prolong life well past the point at which death, in earlier decades, would naturally have occurred. The three judges in the New York Federal Appeals Court, in their decision against the New York State ban on assisted suicide, made this point: "What interest can the state possibly have in requiring the prolongation of a life that is all but ended?" (Bruni, 1996). More centrally, proponents of assisted suicide argue that each individual should have the right to decide for herself or himself how her or his life will end. Each of us should be able to say when we have had enough. And if a patient, having reached that point, is no longer physically able to take her own life, or does not have access to reliable means, she should be able to ask her physician to assist her.

This controversy is not going to go away soon; it will only grow as our technical ability to prolong life continues to increase. It is worth your while to consider your own views on this important issue.

Grieving

The ritual of a funeral, in whatever form it occurs, can provide a structure and comfort in the days immediately following a death. But what happens when that structure is gone? How do we each handle the sense of loss? Answering that question requires a look at the epidemiology of grief, as well as at individual variations in reaction to loss by death.

Epidemiology of Grieving: The Example of Widowhood. As a general rule, the most difficult death to recover from is that of a spouse. Being widowed is regularly listed as the most stressful single event on lists of negative life changes. Epidemiological studies support this generalization. In the year following bereavement, the incidence of depression rises substantially, while rates of death and disease rise slightly in the widowed (Reich, Zautra, & Guarnaccia, 1989; W. Stroebe & M. S. Stroebe, 1993). For example, in an enormous study in Finland, Kaprio and Koskenvuo (cited in W. Stroebe & M. S. Stroebe, 1986) examined the mortality rates for a group of 95,647 widowed persons over the five years following the spouse's death. They found that compared with the population at large, death rates among widows rose during the first six months after bereavement, after which the mortality risk returned to normal. We also know that immune system function declines in the first few months after a spouse's death, which doubtless contributes to the slightly higher rate of physical illness found among recent widows (Gallagher-Thompson et al., 1993; Irwin & Pike, 1993).

A very similar pattern is found for depression, which typically rises in the first six months after the spouse's death. For example, in one longitudinal study, Fran Norris and Stanley Murrell (1990) repeatedly interviewed a sample of 3000 adults, all age 55 or older at the beginning of the study. Forty-eight of these adults were widowed during the $2\frac{1}{2}$ years of the study, which allowed Norris and Murrell to look at depression and health status before and immediately after bereavement. They found no differences between the widowed and nonwidowed on physical health, but did find a rise in depression immediately following the loss, and then a decline by a year after bereavement, a set of results you can see in Figure 19.2.

Other research confirms that the first six months are the most difficult. Two years after widowhood, most studies show no differences between the widowed and nonwidowed on global measures of physical or mental health (e.g., McCrae & Costa, 1988).

These effects do vary somewhat by both age and gender, and by the suddenness or unexpectedness of the death. I pointed out in the Interlude summarizing young adulthood that younger widows, and those whose spouses died either suddenly or after a very short illness, show higher levels of problems than do those who are widowed "on time" or after a time of preparation (Ball, 1976–1977). I've also mentioned several times that widowhood is a more negative experience for men than for women. The risk of death from either natural causes or suicide in the months immediately after widowhood is significantly greater among men than among women (M. S. Stroebe & W. Stroebe, 1993), even when higher male death rates at most ages are taken into account. This difference is most often interpreted as yet another sign of the importance of social support. Because a man is more likely to have only his spouse as a close confidant, at her death he will more likely lack the buffering effect of social support from other sources.

Grief over the death of a child has similar effects, with bereaved parents reporting poorer health and depression for up to two years after the death (Arbuckle & De Vries, 1995).

Stages of Grief. Data like these tell us that widowhood or the loss of a parent or child is highly stressful for most people. But they do not tell us anything about the experience of grief on an individual level. Given the fondness of psychologists for stage theories of almost any process, you won't be surprised to find that a number of authors have proposed that grief proceeds in a number of stages, highly similar to

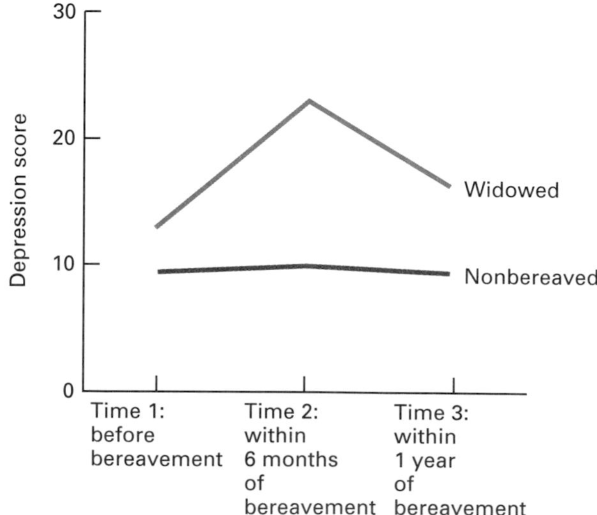

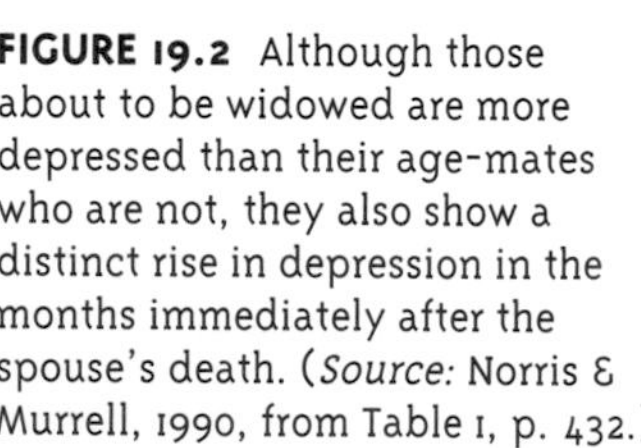
FIGURE 19.2 Although those about to be widowed are more depressed than their age-mates who are not, they also show a distinct rise in depression in the months immediately after the spouse's death. (*Source:* Norris & Murrell, 1990, from Table 1, p. 432.)

the stages of dying Kübler-Ross originally described. And as with the stages of dying, stage theories of grief have been widely criticized. It is nonetheless worth your while to have at least a passing knowledge of them, if only because—as with the stages of dying—they have affected the thinking of therapists, social workers, and others who work with the bereaved.

John Bowlby, whose work on attachment you already know, proposed four stages of grieving (1980). Catherine Sanders (1989) has proposed five stages, but as you can see in Table 19.3, the two systems overlap a great deal.

Some quotes from actual grieving individuals may give you a more complete taste of the experience. In the first period of shock or numbness, people say things like:

> "I feel so vague. I can't keep my mind on anything for very long." (p. 47)
>
> "I'm afraid I'm losing my mind. I can't seem to think clearly." (p. 48)
>
> "It was so strange. I was putting on my makeup, combing my hair, and all the time it was as if I were standing by the door watching myself go through these motions." (Sanders, 1989, p. 56).

In the stage of awareness of loss or yearning, when anger is a common ingredient, people say such things as "His boss should have known better than to ask him to work so hard." Bowlby also suggested that this period is equivalent to what we see in young children who have been temporarily separated from their closest attachment figure. They will literally search for this favored person, going from room to room. In adults who are widowed, some of the same searching goes on—sometimes physically, sometimes mentally.

In the stage of disorganization and despair, the restlessness of the previous period disappears and is replaced by a great lethargy. One 45-year-old whose child had just died described her feelings:

> I can't understand the way I feel. Up to now, I had been feeling restless. I couldn't sleep. I paced and ranted. Now, I have an opposite reaction. I sleep

Table 19.3 Stages of Grief Proposed by Bowlby and Sanders

Stage	Bowlby's Label	Sanders's Label	General Description
1	Numbness	Shock	Characteristic of the first few days, occasionally longer; disbelief, confusion, restlessness, feelings of unreality, a sense of helplessness.
2	Yearning	Awareness of loss	The bereaved person tries to recover the lost person; may actively search, or wander as if searching; may report that they see the dead person. Also full of anxiety and guilt, fear, frustration. May sleep poorly and weep often.
3	Disorganization and despair	Conservation/ withdrawal	Searching ceases and the loss is accepted, but acceptance of loss brings depression and despair, or a sense of helplessness. Often accompanied by great fatigue and a desire to sleep all the time.
4	Reorganization	Healing and renewal	Sanders sees two periods here; Bowlby only one. Both see this as the step in which the individual takes control again. Some forgetting occurs and some sense of hope emerges, along with increased energy, better health, better sleep patterns, and reduction of depression.

Sources: Bowlby, 1980; Sanders, 1989.

Studies of widows by Helena Lopata (1981, 1986) suggest that some "sanctification" of the deceased is almost universal, perhaps because by remembering their husband as saintly the widow is telling herself that she was worthy of the love of such a person.

> a lot. I feel fatigued and worn out. I don't even want to see the friends who have kept me going. I sit and stare, too exhausted to move. . . . Just when I thought I should be feeling better, I am feeling worse. (Sanders, 1989, p. 73)

> Bowlby and Sanders argue that these reactions are likely to occur at the loss of any person to whom we are attached, whether partner, parent, or child. The death of a friend, a grandchild, or someone who might be part of our convoy but not an intimate confidant is less likely to trigger this array of emotions (Murrell & Himmelfarb, 1989).

These descriptions of the grieving process are highly evocative. But as with the concept of stages of dying, we need to ask two important questions about these proposed stages of grieving: (1) Do they really occur in fixed stages? and (2) Does everyone feel all these feelings, in whatever sequence? The answer to both questions seems to be "no."

Alternative Views of the Grief Process. A growing set of "revisionist" views of grieving give a rather different picture than either Bowlby or Sanders offers. First, many researchers and theorists find that grieving simply does not occur in fixed stages, with everyone following the same pattern (Wortman & Silver, 1990). There may be common themes, such as anger, guilt, depression, or restlessness, but they may not appear in a fixed order.

One compromise suggestion I particularly like is a proposal from Selby Jacobs and his colleagues (Jacobs et al., 1987–1988) that each of the key themes in the grieving process may have a likely trajectory, such as the pattern shown in Figure 19.3. The basic idea, obviously, is that many themes are present at the same time, but that one or another may dominate, in an approximate sequence. Thus, we might well find that disbelief is highest immediately after the death, and that depression peaks some months later, which will make the process look stagelike, although in fact both elements are present throughout.

Jacobs does not argue that every bereaved person necessarily follows a pathway that looks like this. Some might move more quickly, others more slowly through

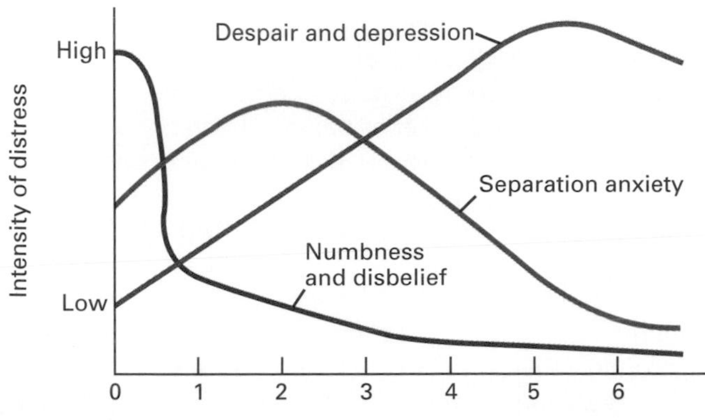

FIGURE 19.3 Jacobs offers this model as an alternative to strict stage theories of grieving. At any given moment, many different emotions or themes may be apparent, but each may have a particular common trajectory. (*Source:* Jacobs et al., 1987–1988, Figure 1, p. 43.)

these various themes. In contrast, other revisionist theorists and researchers contend that for some adults, grieving itself simply does not include all these elements. Camille Wortman and Roxane Silver (1989, 1990, 1992; Wortman, Silver, & Kessler, 1993) have amassed an impressive amount of evidence to support such a view.

Wortman and Silver dispute two points about the traditional view of grieving: that distress is an inevitable response to loss, and that *failure* to experience distress is a sign that the individual has not grieved "properly." The psychoanalytic view, represented in Bowlby's approach and dominant for many decades, holds that lack of overt distress must indicate significant repression or denial of painful feelings. Ultimately, according to this view, such denial or repression will have negative consequences. Bowlby argued that those who express their pain, who "allow themselves to grieve," are behaving in an ultimately healthy way.

If this formulation is correct, we should find that those widows or other grieving individuals who show the *most* distress immediately after the death should have the best long-term adjustment, while those who show the least immediate distress should display some kind of residual problem later on. But the data do not support this expectation. On the contrary, those who show the highest levels of distress immediately following a loss are very often the ones who are still depressed several years later, while those who show little distress immediately show no signs of delayed problems. Wortman and Silver (1990) conclude that there are at least four distinct patterns of grieving:

- *Normal*. Relatively great distress is felt immediately following the loss, with relatively rapid recovery.
- *Chronic*. Distress continues at a high level over several years.
- *Delayed*. Little distress is felt in the first few months, but the person feels high levels of distress some months or years later.
- *Absent*. No notable level of distress is felt either immediately or at any later time.

Contrary to the predictions of stage theories of grief, it turns out that the pattern of "absent" grief is remarkably common. In Wortman and Silver's own first study (Wortman & Silver, 1990), 26 percent of bereaved subjects showed essentially no distress either immediately after the death or several years later, a pattern confirmed in other research (Levy, Martinkowski, & Derby, 1994). The least common pattern is delayed grief. Only 1 to 5 percent of adults in current studies show such a response to loss, while as many as a third show chronic grief. Thus, we find little support for either aspect of the traditional view: High levels of distress are neither an inevitable nor a necessary aspect of the grieving process. Many adults seem to handle the death of a spouse, a child, or a parent without significant dislocation, although *on average* it remains true that widowed or other bereaved persons are higher in depression, lower in life satisfaction, and at greater risk for illness than are the nonbereaved.

As yet, we know relatively little about the characteristics of individuals who react to bereavement in these quite different ways, although Wortman and Silver's research (Wortman et al., 1993) gives us a few hints. In their studies, those widows who had had the *best* marriages were the ones who showed the most persistent grief reactions. More surprisingly, they found that those widows who had had the *strongest* sense of personal control, self-esteem, or mastery prior to the spouse's death had the *most* difficulty, as if the loss of the spouse had undermined this very sense of control. Research in Germany by Wolfgang and Margaret Stroebe (1993) suggests that neuroticism may be another important factor. In their study, those widows who were high in neuroticism before bereavement showed stronger and more persistent negative effects.

These are interesting findings, especially because some of them run against the grain of other research on coping with stress. It may well be that the death of a person to whom one is strongly attached is simply a different order of magnitude of stressful event, one for which many of the typical rules do not apply. It will be interesting to see, in the coming years, whether further research confirms these initial findings.

Overall, Wortman and Silver's views seem to me to be an important modification of the standard view of grief. Not only do they cause us to rethink old assumptions (always a valuable process in science), but they also point the way to potentially better understanding of individual variations in grief pathways. Obvious practical implications also flow from this perspective. To the extent that our cultural norm for grieving includes the expectations of heightened distress, "working through" the grief, and then getting on with your life, any bereaved person who does not follow this pattern is likely to be perceived as deviant. In particular, the person who shows little despair or depression may be accused of "not dealing" with her grief, or of not having loved the deceased person. Of course it *is* possible that such lower levels of distress are indicative of weaker attachments, but we have as yet little evidence to confirm (or reject) such a hypothesis. Meanwhile, Wortman and Silver's arguments should serve to make each of us more sensitive to the unique process of grieving we may see in friends or family members.

Those who seem deeply distressed or despairing may benefit from some kind of support group or therapy; certainly they are not likely to find it helpful or sensitive for you to urge them to get "back in the swim" right away. Those who express little obvious distress, on the other hand, may not be repressing but may be coping in other ways. They may not take kindly to your suggestion that they should "get it all out," or to "be sure to take time to grieve." As usual, the best way to be helpful to a person dealing with such a loss is to be highly attentive to the signals you are receiving, rather than imposing your own ideas of what is normal or expected.

Finally, let us not lose sight of the fact that loss can also lead to growth. Indeed, the majority of widows say not only that they have changed as a result of their husband's death, but that the change is in the direction of greater independence and greater skill (Wortman & Silver, 1990). Like all crises and all major life changes, bereavement can be an opportunity as well as, or instead of, a disabling experience. Which way we respond is likely to depend very heavily on the patterns we have established from early childhood: our temperament or personality, our internal working models of attachment and self, our intellectual skills, and the social network we have created. Ultimately, we respond to death—our own or someone else's—as we have responded to life.

Summary

1. Until about age 6 or 7, children do not understand that death is permanent, inevitable, and involves loss of function.
2. Among adults, death has many meanings: a signal for changes in familial roles; a punishment for failing to live a good life; a transition to another state, such as a life after death; and a loss of opportunity and relationships. Awareness of death may also serve as an organizer of time.
3. Fear of death appears to peak in midlife, after which it drops rather sharply. Older adults talk more about death but are less afraid.
4. Highly religious adults are typically less afraid of death, while those with high scores on a neuroticism scale are more fearful.
5. Many adults prepare for death in practical ways, such as by buying life insurance or writing a will. Reminiscence may also serve as some preparation. There are also some signs of deeper personality changes immediately before death, including more dependence and docility and less emotionality and assertiveness.
6. Kübler-Ross suggested five stages of dying: denial, anger, bargaining, depression, and acceptance. Research fails to support the hypothesis that all adults show all five or that they necessarily occur in this order. The most common ingredient is depression.
7. Research with cancer and AIDS patients suggests that those who are most docile and accepting, or most hopeless, in response to diagnosis and treatment have shorter life expectancies. Those who fight hardest, even in angry ways, live longer. Optimism, rather than pessimism, is also linked to better response to medical treatment.
8. Dying adults with better social support, either from family and friends or through specially created support groups, also live longer than those who lack such support.
9. The great majority of adults in industrialized countries die in hospitals. Hospice care for the dying, however, is becoming more common.
10. Hospice care emphasizes patient and family control of the process, and palliative rather than curative treatment. Some studies suggest that patients and families are slightly more satisfied with hospice than hospital care, but hospice care is also highly burdensome for the caregiver.
11. Funerals and other rituals after death serve important functions, including defining roles for the bereaved, bringing family together, and giving meaning to the deceased's life and death.
12. On average, bereaved individuals show heightened levels of sickness, death, and depression in the months immediately after the death of an attachment figure.
13. Theories of stages of grieving, such as Bowlby's, have not been widely supported by recent research. A significant number of bereaved adults show no heightened depression or problems, either immediately or later. Others show persistent problems even after many years.

Key Terms

brain death

clinical death

hospice care

social death

thanatology

Suggested Readings

Alsop, S. (1973) *Stay of execution: A sort of memoir*. New York: Lippincott.

A very personal, moving, and informative description of one man's journey from the beginning of his illness with leukemia until his death.

Feifel, H. (1990). Psychology and death: Meaningful rediscovery. *American Psychologist, 45*, 537–543.

A good brief review of many current themes in psychologists' current research on death and dying, along with an exploration of why it has taken so long for psychologists to begin to study this important subject.

Kübler-Ross, E. (1969). *On death and dying*. New York: Macmillan.

This was the original major book by Kübler-Ross that significantly changed the way many physicians and other health professionals viewed the dying process. It is full of case material, and reflects very well Kübler-Ross's great skill as a listener and clinician.

Nuland, S. B. (1993). *How we die*. New York: Alfred A. Knopf.

In this remarkable book, Nuland (who is a physician) considers many aspects of the process of dying and of dying itself, for patients with several types of diseases (heart disease, cancer, AIDS, Alzheimer's disease, and old age). Interweaving scientific information with case studies, he makes the process clear, touching, and very real. I highly recommend this book.

Schreiber, L. (1990). *Midstream*. New York: Viking.

Stewart Alsop's book gives a firsthand account of the time leading up to his own death; Le Anne Schreiber—a sportswriter of some renown—gives an equally moving secondhand account, in this instance the death of her mother from cancer, detailing both her own feelings and reactions and those of other family members.

Postlude

Another Look at the Basic Issues

In each of the interludes in this book, I have tried to suggest some of the key qualities or themes that characterize each age period in the years from birth to death. But even that summing up and analyzing process may have left you without a sense of the full sweep of development over all those years. So I want to close the circle of this book by returning, at least briefly, to some of the issues I raised in Chapters 1 and 2: continuity and change, individual differences and variability, and theories of development.

Continuity and Change

Continuity and change are the very warp and woof—the essential ingredients—of development. Certainly your experience of yourself and of your own development is made up of both. You feel yourself as the same person from moment to moment, from year to year, and at the same time you feel that you have changed. You are not the same at 25 or 45 as you were at 12. If you ask most middle-aged or older adults whether they would like to be 20 again, most laugh and say something like "Heavens, no!" They will then go on to tell you how much they have learned that they didn't know before and wouldn't want to do without. So both continuity and change exist simultaneously—one of the central truths about development.

Continuity

Among the many sources of continuity is inborn temperament. Certainly there is much about individual personality that is not genetically determined or even biologically influenced. But babies are born with certain response biases, certain patterns of reaction to events. Depending on how people respond to the baby, on what is reinforced and what is not, these initial biases may be strengthened or modified. By middle childhood—certainly by adolescence or adulthood—stable patterns have been established. These enduring personality patterns, in turn, affect the way each of us responds to the many events we encounter over our lifetime.

Those of us who have a more difficult temperament or who are high in neuroticism are likely to have a very different life course than others. Such people respond more negatively to almost any kind of stress, have more problems creating enduring relationships, and are less likely to be satisfied with their lives. In contrast, those high in extraversion or cheerfulness seem far more likely to create stable and satisfying relationships, recover more quickly from stressful experiences, and generally have higher morale.

In a similar way, internal models of the self, of gender, and of attachment tend to create continuity. Of course internal models are not independent of personality. A temperamentally "difficult" child is somewhat more likely to develop an insecure attachment to mother or father, creating a kind of double disadvantage for some children. But internal models are not merely another description of personality. I am talking here about an individual's *understanding,* the meaning he attaches to experiences, the expectations he may have about others, about relationships, and about the self. These are *cognitions* as well as feelings. And they appear to be immensely powerful.

Such constructed meaning systems are not fixed at some point in childhood, never to change. We have only to look at Mary Main's work on internal models of attachment in adults to see evidence for the possibility of change. If you go back and look at the Across Development box in Chapter 6 (p. 140) you'll see that the *secure-autonomous* category of adult attachment is sometimes found in adults who describe quite unloving or even abusive childhoods. They recognize that their childhood experiences were formative, but are able to be objective about them. We know far too little about how such a reassessment or transformation may have taken place. But it is important to recognize that such change *can* occur. Continuity may be the default option, but it is not invariable.

At the risk of overstating the case, I think the new emphasis on internal models is the single most significant theoretical advance in the field of developmental psychology in the past several decades. We have come to understand that environments do not "happen" to people, do not shape behavior in some automatic way, at any age. The intervening process is the individual's understanding of each experience. We obviously need to know a great deal more about how the basic internal models are formed and change, and how they affect choices and behavior. But I believe we are now on the right track. And when we figure out how to connect the new information on internal models with the even newer information on genetic influences and neuropsychology, we will *really* be on the right track.

Change

At the same time, development is also about change, both shared and individual.

Shared change, which has been the focus of most theories of development and a great deal of the research, is shaped throughout life by the twin processes I have referred to as the *biological clock* and the *social clock*. But these two influences are rarely balanced in their effect. In childhood, biological maturation plays an enormously powerful role. Indeed the whole rhythm of childhood is very much governed by such maturation: from physically helpless infant to more mature toddler, from nonverbal toddler to verbally fluent 4-year-old, from sexually immature to postpubescent adolescent. Of course experience makes a difference, and the child's own activity is critical in shaping the process of development. But beneath all the other formative processes, the biological clock is ticking away, loudly and in common form for virtually every child.

The social clock is not totally absent in these early years of life. There are some shared changes in social roles, such as the shift from preschool to school-age child, that have profound effects on the child's development. But the shared patterns of change we observe in children are far more a product of biological maturation, and of the fact that virtually all children experience similar early environments, than they are of clearly defined changes in social roles.

In early adulthood, the relative potency of these two influences reverses almost completely. Once fully past puberty, there begins a period of 20 or more years when the physical body operates at peak form. In these years the social clock defines the developmental hours, shaping the sequence of life changes that the great majority of us share: a change from single to married, from child to parent, from dependent to independent.

In middle adulthood, perhaps for the only time in the life span, these two major influences are in approximate balance. The internal biological changes we label as aging begin to be more apparent, while social definitions become less stringent or constricting. In very late adulthood, the biological processes again dominate. Notice that there is no single age period in which *both* biological and social clocks are extremely strong influences. Rather there is a kind of alternation, a predictable ebb and flow, creating one kind of shared rhythm of change over the life span.

Theories of Development

I am sure it is obvious to you by now that no one theory of development has adequately described this entire process over the whole life span. Stage theories have been highly attractive to many observers and researchers because they appear to create orderliness out of what might otherwise seem like confusing changes. But they have become less and less attractive because research fails to show strongly age-linked stages in a great many instances. Even in childhood, when stagelike changes seem especially likely, there are measurable variations in the timing of certain cognitive shifts as a function of specific experience or expertise. In adulthood, stage theories are even less well substantiated.

There are nonetheless two stagelike theoretical concepts that I think have merit. First, if development does not occur in stages, then it surely has *sequences*. Throughout development, we find strong evidence of shared sequences of development or experience. There is a sequence in children's understanding of the gender concept or conservation; there is a sequence in the emergence of moral reasoning; there is a family life cycle sequence that begins as soon as an adult becomes a parent for the first time; there is the sequence of generations within a family, as each of us moves from the young adult generation, to the "sandwich generation," to the status of elder within a given family; there are sequences in job experiences, and perhaps even in changes within partnership relationships.

It is probably true that only those sequences that are at least partially rooted in maturational change are *universally* experienced. But within any given culture or cohort, lifespan development proceeds along many common pathways.

A related concept that I think is enormously useful in understanding development, perhaps particularly adult development, is Levinson's notion of alternating periods of stable life structures and transition. I do not agree that the *content* of these alternating periods is anywhere near as fixed or universal as Levinson suggested. Not everyone has a midlife crisis or a transition at age 30. But the idea that there is an alternation of stability and transition seems to me to capture one aspect of the developmental process very well. Just as there is a basic rhythm created by the ebb and flow of the social and biological clocks, so there is a second basic rhythm created by the alternation of stability and change.

We can see this in children as well as adults. The transition of toddlerhood, for example, with its multiple adaptations (language, independent locomotion, establishment of a clear attachment) is followed by a period of several years in which both the child's behavior and the child's relationships with his parents are more predictable; the transition between ages 5 and 7, when the child begins school, is followed by several years in which the child and the family create a more stable life structure. Even among infants, change does not seem to occur at a continuous rate. There are times of rapid change and times of greater stability, such as the period from about 2 months to perhaps 6 months, and the period from about 8 months to perhaps 12 months.

In adulthood, the timing of the transitions and stable life structures may vary more from one individual to the next, depending on culture, on cohort, on the timing of marriage and childbearing, or on unique experiences. But a basic alternation between stability and transition seems to be a common thread in virtually all lives.

Many things may trigger a transition. In childhood and adolescence, physiological changes are at the root of some transitions, such as the obvious example of puberty. In adulthood, changes in health, or in the *awareness* of biological aging, may also be important. But role changes are more likely to provoke shifts out of a stable life structure in adulthood, as may unexpected or off-time life changes, such as the loss of a job.

In each of these transitions, I think there is an opportunity for growth, precisely because the transition may call the internal models into question or force you to face new issues. Puberty triggers a whole new set of questions about independence and autonomy; marriage forces each of us to deal with the habits and internal models we bring to relationships; middle age may cause you to question that most unexamined assumption, the feeling of invincibility or immortality. People living through crisis or transition sometimes say "I am beside myself." It is a revealing phrase, reflecting, perhaps, that sense of being momentarily outside of one's normal frame. There may well be pain involved, a sense of dislocation and loss, but there may also be an opportunity to *change* the frame, to reshape the internal models. In Piaget's terms, there is, in each such transition, an opportunity to *decenter,* to experience the world less and less egocentrically. Not everyone takes that opportunity. Many of us come to and through these points of transition without reexamining our assumptions or taking up the new tasks. But growth at some deeper level seems especially possible at these transitional points.

Jane Loevinger, whose theory I mentioned in Chapter 2 and elsewhere, argues for just such a *potential* sequence of changes, such as the shift that may occur from the typical conformist stance of young adulthood to what she calls the conscientious stage. Loevinger's basic proposition is that there is a pathway laid out, a growth sequence, but that not everyone moves the same distance along it. This is analogous to what we see in the development of moral reasoning, where there appears to be a sequence of understandings that everyone follows, but at somewhat different rates, and stopping at different points along the way.

If we combine the concept of sequences with Levinson's concept of alternations between stability and transition, we end up with something vaguely like a stage theory, but without the assumption that everyone will necessarily experience the transitions at the same time and without the idea that each transition will necessarily result in growth. For some, a transition results in depression, alcoholism, or perhaps even regression to earlier forms of coping. For others, the disequilibrium is followed by a return to the previous status quo. But there is an *opportunity* for change and growth at each turn of the spiral.

Individual Differences

These common patterns or rhythms should not and cannot disguise the other central fact about lifespan development, namely that there are enormous individual differences in timing and pathways. Such differences become especially visible during any period of the life span in which the biological clock is relatively unintrusive. Early in life, and in the very last years of life, the common ground is more apparent. But at every age there are wide variations, even in something so basic as the rate of maturation itself.

Here's one more example of the magnitude of the variation, to add to the many I have already given: Ronald Rindfuss (Rindfuss, Swicegood, & Rosenfeld, 1987) has studied a large sample of adults who graduated from high school in 1972. For the first eight years after graduation, he noted whether each of the nearly 14,000 subjects had passed into or out of specific role statuses, such as work, education, marriage, parenthood, or military service. There were 1100 different combinations of sequence and timing among the men in this study, and 1800 different combinations among the women. Virtually all these adults did indeed acquire one or more of these roles, but not in the same order or at the same age. When you compound such variations in timing and sequence with already existing variations in personality, internal models, education, and health, it is clear why sociologists and psychologists begin to talk of "fingerprints" or "trajectories" rather than "common paths."

If this is the case, then in what sense can we talk about "normal development" at all? I hope you will agree with me that it makes a good deal of sense to talk about common paths or normal development in *childhood.* In the first 12 to 15 years of life we see not only common maturational changes, we also see highly similar cultural responses to those maturational patterns. Babies are held and talked to; toddlers the world over are given more freedom; children in virtually all cultures begin schooling somewhere around age 6 or 7; rites of passage to adulthood are common themes of adolescent experience. The details vary, but there are clearly shared sequences and experiences.

But what about adulthood? Does it make sense to talk about "adult development" at all? As you will have gathered from what I have said already, I believe it does, but not with precisely the same meaning as when we say "child development." In adulthood, there is the much fainter but still present maturational timetable we call aging that provides a very rough common shape to adult experience. Key family and work roles also create a pattern that is widely shared, both within given cultures or cohorts, and across cultures. At a deeper level, there are also the shared rhythms of the balance between social and biological clocks, and the ebb and flow of transition and stability. Finally, there may be a common potential pathway of growth, of the kind Loevinger has described. These different rhythms are, at heart, what is meant by adult development. But upon that base, there is an almost infinite variety of life patterns.

A musical metaphor may make the point clearer. The basic shared rhythms are like the beat of a song, or the percussion part in a symphony. Every melody, every orchestration, must be built upon that beat, so every song, every symphony, will sound somewhat alike. But your song and mine will have different melodies. Whether the song is harmonious or disharmonious, whether new themes are introduced without dissonance or only with discord will depend on all the factors I have described throughout this book. But each of us will create a song, a life. May you enjoy writing your song as much as I have enjoyed creating mine.

Glossary

accommodation That part of the adaptation process by which a person modifies existing schemes to fit new experiences, or creates new schemes when old ones no longer handle the data.
achievement tests Tests designed to assess a child's learning of specific material taught in school, such as spelling or arithmetic computation, typically given to all children in designated grades.
activity theory As contrasted with disengagement theory, the theory that the normal and psychologically optimum pattern of behavior in old age is to remain socially and psychologically active rather than to withdraw.
affectional bond A "relatively long enduring tie in which the partner is important as a unique individual and is interchangeable with none other."
ageism A term used most generally to refer to any prejudice or discrimination against or in favor of a particular age group. More frequently refers to prejudice *against* older adults, a common feature of American culture.
age norms The set of expectations for the behavior of individuals of any given age group, such as teenagers or the elderly. Such norms are specific to a given culture or subculture, and may change from one cohort to another.
age strata Groupings by age within any given society, such as "toddlers," "teenagers," or "the elderly." Individuals in each stratum are expected to occupy certain roles and have certain privileges and responsibilities.
aggression Behavior with the apparent intent to injure some other person or object.
agreeableness One of the "Big Five" personality traits; characterized by trust, generosity, kindness, and sympathy.
alpha-fetoprotein test A prenatal diagnostic test frequently used to screen for the risk of neural tube defects. May also be used in combination with other tests to diagnose Down syndrome and other chromosomal anomalies.
altruism *See* **prosocial behavior**.
Alzheimer's disease (AD) The most common form of dementia, caused by specific changes in the brain—particularly a large increase in neurofibrillary tangles—and resulting in gradual and permanent loss of memory and other cognitive functions.
amniocentesis A medical test for genetic abnormalities in the embryo/fetus that may be done at about 15 weeks of gestation.
amnion The sac or bag, filled with liquid, in which the embryo/fetus floats during prenatal life.
anorexia nervosa A serious eating disorder characterized by extreme dieting, intense fear of gaining weight, and distorted body image.
Apgar score A rating system for newborns with a maximum of 10 points, based on assessment of heart and respiratory rates, muscle tone, response to stimulation, and color.
assimilation That part of the adaptation process that involves the "taking in" of new experiences or information into existing schemes. Experience is not taken in "as is," however, but is modified (or interpreted) somewhat so as to fit the preexisting schemes.
attachment An especially intense and central type of affectional bond in which the presence of the partner adds a special sense of security, a "safe base," for the individual; characteristic of the child's bond with the parent.
attachment behaviors The collection of (probably) instinctive behaviors of one person toward another that bring about or maintain proximity and caregiving, such as the smile of the young infant; behaviors that reflect an attachment.
authoritarian parental style One of the three styles of parenting described by Baumrind, characterized by high levels of control and maturity demands and low levels of nurturance and communication.
authoritative parental style One of the three styles of parenting described by Baumrind, characterized by high levels of control, nurturance, maturity demands, and communication.
axon The long appendage-like part of a neuron; the terminal fibers of the axon serve as transmitters in the synaptic connection with the dendrites of other neurons.
babbling The frequently repetitive vocalizing of consonant-vowel combinations by an infant, typically beginning at about 6 months of age.
Bayley Scales of Infant Development The best-known and most widely used test of infant "intelligence," revised most recently in 1993.
behavior genetics The study of the genetic basis of behavior, such as intelligence or personality.
being motives A class of motives suggested by Maslow. Includes the desire to discover and understand one's own and others' potential and to give love.
Big Five Five dimensions of personality variation found in studies of adults and widely perceived to describe the core facets of personality: extraversion, agreeableness, conscientiousness, neuroticism, and openness/intellect.

biological clock A phrase used to describe the fundamental sequence of biological changes that occur with age, beginning with conception and moving through old age.
brain death A state in which the person no longer has reflexes or any response to vigorous external stimuli, and no electrical activity in the brain; when the brain stem as well as the cortex is gone, the person is legally dead.
bulimia An eating disorder characterized by an intense concern about weight combined with binge eating followed by purging, either through self-induced vomiting, excessive use of laxatives, or excessive exercise.
cephalocaudal One of two basic patterns of physical development in infancy (the other is *proximodistal*), describing development that proceeds from the head downward.
cesarean section Delivery of the child through an incision in the mother's abdomen rather than vaginally.
chorion The outer layer of cells during the blastocyst stage of prenatal development, from which both the placenta and the umbilical cord are formed.
chorionic villus sampling A technique for prenatal genetic diagnosis that involves taking a sample of cells from the placenta. Can be performed earlier in the pregnancy than amniocentesis but carries slightly higher risks.
chromosome A string of DNA that contains signals and instructions for a wide variety of normal developmental processes and unique individual characteristics. Each human cell contains 46 chromosomes, arranged in 23 pairs.
classical conditioning One of three major types of learning. An automatic unconditioned response such as an emotion or a reflex comes to be triggered by a new cue, called the conditional stimulus (CS), after the CS has been paired several times with the original unconditional stimulus.
class inclusion The relationship between classes of objects, such that a subordinate class is included in a superordinate class, as bananas are part of the class "fruit."
climacteric The general term used to describe the period (in both men and women) in which reproductive capacity is lost during adulthood. *Menopause* is another word to describe the climacteric in women.
clinical death A period of a few minutes after the heart has stopped, when breathing has stopped and there is no evident brain function, but during which rescue is still possible.
clinical depression A combination of sad mood, sleep and eating disturbances, and difficulty concentrating, persisting for a period of several months or longer.
clique Defined by Dunphy as a group of six to eight friends with strong affectional bonds and high levels of group solidarity and loyalty; currently used by researchers to describe a self-chosen group of friends, in contrast to reputation-based crowds.
cohort A group of persons of approximately the same age who have shared the same pattern of historical experiences in childhood and adulthood.
collectivism A cultural perspective or belief system, contrasted with *individualism*, in which the emphasis is on collective rather than individual identity, and on group solidarity, decision making, duties, and obligations. Characteristic of most Asian, Hispanic, and African cultures.
competence The behavior of a person as it would be under ideal or perfect circumstances. It is not possible to measure competence directly.
concrete operational stage The stage of development between ages 6 and 12 proposed by Piaget, in which mental operations such as subtraction, reversibility, and multiple classification are acquired.
conditional stimulus In classical conditioning, the stimulus that, after being paired a number of times with an unconditional stimulus, comes to trigger the unconditioned response. For example, the sound of the mother's footsteps may become a conditional stimulus for the baby's turning his head as if to suck.
conscientiousness One of the "Big Five" personality traits, characterized by efficiency, organization, planfulness, and reliability.
conservation The concept that objects remain the same in fundamental ways, such as weight or number, even when there are external changes in shape or arrangement. Typically understood by children after age 5.
control group The group of subjects in an experiment that receives either no special treatment or some neutral treatment.
conventional morality The second level of moral judgment proposed by Kohlberg, in which the person's judgments are dominated by considerations of group values and laws.
convoy A term used by Antonucci to describe the set of individuals who make up a person's intimate social network, and who travel with the individual through the various stages of adulthood.
cooing An early stage during the prelinguistic period, from about 1 to 4 months of age, when vowel sounds are repeated, particularly the *uuu* sound.
coronary heart disease (CHD) A general term used by physicians to describe a set of disease processes in the heart and circulatory system, including most noticeably a narrowing of the arteries with plaque (atherosclerosis).
correlation A statistic used to describe the degree or strength of a relationship between two variables. It can range from +1.00 to –1.00. The closer it is to 1.00 the stronger the relationship being described.
cortex The convoluted gray portion of the brain that governs most complex thought, language, and memory.
critical period Any time period during development when the organism is especially responsive to and learns from a specific type of stimulation. The same stimulation at other points in development has little or no effect.

cross-cultural research Research involving in-depth study of non-Western cultures, or research involving comparisons of several cultures or subcultures.
cross-linking An exchange of DNA material between cells of different types, such as skin and connective tissue cells; results in a decrease in efficiency of cell protein.
cross-modal transfer The ability to transfer information gained through one sense to another sense at a later time; for example, identifying visually something you had previously explored only tactually.
cross-sectional design A form of research in which samples of subjects from several different age groups are studied at the same time.
crowd Defined by Dunphy as a larger and looser group of friends than a clique, normally made up of several cliques joined together; defined by current researchers as a reputation-based group, common in adolescent subculture, with widely agreed-upon characteristics (e.g., "brains," "jocks," or "druggies").
crystallized intelligence That aspect of intelligence that depends primarily on education and experience: knowledge and judgment acquired through experience.
culture A system of meanings and customs, shared by some identifiable group or subgroup, and transmitted from one generation of that group to the next.
deductive logic Reasoning from the general to the particular, from a rule to an expected instance, or from a theory to a hypothesis; characteristic of formal operational thought.
defense mechanisms Normal methods of dealing with anxiety proposed by Freud that are largely unconscious and at least somewhat distorting of reality. Includes such mechanisms as repression, intellectualization, projection, and suppression.
deficiency motives A class of motives proposed by Maslow including basic instincts or drives that involve correction of some imbalance or creation of homeostasis. Includes biological needs, need for safety, need for love and affection, and need for self-esteem.
dementia Any global deterioration of intellectual functions, including memory, judgment, social functioning, and control of emotions. A symptom and not a disease, caused by a wide variety of conditions, including most commonly Alzheimer's disease and multiple small strokes. When it occurs in older adults, it is usually called *senile dementia*.
dendrites The branchlike parts of a neuron that form one-half of a synaptic connections to other nerves. Dendrites develop rapidly in the final three prenatal months and the first year after birth.
deoxyribonucleic acid The chemical of which genes are composed; called DNA for short.
dependent variable The variable in an experiment that is expected to reflect manipulations of the independent variable; also called the *outcome variable*.
dialectical thought A proposed form of adult thought that involves recognition and acceptance of contradiction and paradox, and the seeking of synthesis.
disability A limitation in an individual's ability to perform certain socially defined roles and tasks, particularly self-help tasks and other tasks of daily living.
disengagement theory A theory proposed by Cumming and Henry, suggesting that the normal and psychologically healthy response to the loss of roles and role content in late adulthood is a gradual withdrawal or disengagement from social interactions, along with a kind of psychological withdrawal.
dominance hierarchy A set of dominance relationships in a group describing the rank order of "winners" and "losers" in competitive encounters; also called a "pecking order."
Down syndrome A genetic anomaly in which every cell contains three copies of chromosome 21 rather than two. Children born with this genetic pattern are usually mentally retarded and have characteristic physical features.
ego In Freudian theory, that portion of the personality that organizes, plans, and keeps the person in touch with reality. Language and thought are both ego functions.
egocentrism A cognitive state in which the individual (typically a child) sees the world only from his own perspective, without awareness that there are other perspectives.
embryo The name given to the organism during the period of prenatal development from about two to eight weeks after conception, beginning with implantation of the blastocyst into the uterine wall.
endocrine glands These glands—including the adrenals, the thyroid, the pituitary, the testes, and the ovaries—secrete hormones governing overall physical growth and sexual maturing.
equilibration The third part of the adaptation process as proposed by Piaget, involving a periodic restructuring of schemes into new structures.
establishment stage In Super's model of the stages of work life, the trial stage in one's 20s is followed by the establishment stage in one's 30s, during which a plateau of achievement is usually reached.
estrogen The female sex hormone secreted by the ovaries.
ethnography A detailed description of a single culture or context, based on extensive observation by a resident observer.
executive processes A proposed subset of information processes involving organizing and planning strategies. Similar in meaning to metacognition.
experiment A research strategy in which subjects are assigned randomly to experimental and control groups. The experimental group is then provided with some designated experience that is expected to alter behavior in some fashion.

experimental group The group (or groups) of subjects in an experiment that is given some special treatment intended to produce some hypothesized consequence.
expressive language The term used to describe the child's skill in speaking and communicating orally.
expressive style One of two styles of early language proposed by Nelson, characterized by low rates of noun-like terms and high use of personal-social words and phrases.
extinction A decrease and eventually the elimination of the strength of some response after nonreinforcement.
extraversion One of the "Big Five" personality traits, characterized by assertiveness, energy, enthusiasm, and outgoingness.
fallopian tube The tube between the ovary and the uterus down which the ovum travels and in which conception usually occurs.
family day care Nonparental care in which the child is cared for in someone else's home, usually with a small group of other children.
fetal alcohol syndrome (FAS) A pattern of physical and mental abnormalities, including mental retardation and minor physical anomalies, often found in children born to alcoholic mothers.
fetus The name given to the developing organism from about eight weeks after conception until birth.
fluid intelligence That aspect of intelligence reflecting fundamental biological processes and depending less on specific experience.
fontanels The "soft spots" in the skull present at birth. These disappear when the several bones of the skull grow together.
foreclosure One of four identity statuses proposed by Marcia, involving an ideological or occupational commitment without having gone through a reevaluation.
formal operational stage Piaget's name for the fourth and final major stage of cognitive development, occurring during adolescence, when the child becomes able to manipulate and organize ideas as well as objects.
gametes Sperm and ova. These cells, unlike all other cells of the body, contain only 23 chromosomes rather than 23 pairs.
gender concept The understanding of one's own gender, including the permanence and constancy of gender.
gender constancy The final step in developing a gender concept, in which the child understands that gender doesn't change even though there are external changes like clothing or hair length.
gender identity The first step in gender concept development, in which the child labels herself correctly and categorizes others correctly as male or female.
gender schema theory A theory to explain children's development of gender understanding, proposing that children create a basic schema beginning at age 18 months or younger with which they categorize people, objects, activities, and qualities by gender.
gender stability The second step in gender concept development, in which the child understands that a person's gender continues to be stable throughout the lifetime.
gene A uniquely coded segment of DNA in a chromosome that affects one or more specific body processes or developments.
genotype The pattern of characteristics and developmental sequences mapped in the genes of any specific individual. Will be modified by individual experience into the phenotype.
glial cells One of two major classes of cells making up the nervous system, glial cells provide the firmness and structure, the "glue," to hold the system together.
gonadotrophic hormones Hormones produced in the pituitary gland that stimulate the sex organs to develop.
habituation An automatic decrease in the intensity of a response to a repeated stimulus that enables the child or adult to ignore the familiar and focus attention on the novel.
Hayflick limit A theoretical upper limit on the life span for any given species, proposed by Leonard Hayflick.
holophrase A combination of a gesture with a single word that conveys a sentencelike meaning; often seen and heard in children between 12 and 18 months.
hospice care A relatively new pattern of care for terminally ill patients in which the majority of care is provided by family members, with control of care and care-setting in the hands of the patient and family. May be at home or in special wards or separate institutions.
hypertension Technical term for the disease of high blood pressure. Most often defined as a systolic pressure above 140, or a diastolic pressure above 90.
id In Freudian theory, the first, primitive portion of the personality; the storehouse of basic energy, continually pushing for immediate gratification.
identification The process of taking into oneself ("incorporating") the qualities and ideas of another person, which Freud thought was the result of the Oedipal crisis between the ages of 3 and 5. The child attempts to make himself like his parent of the same sex.
identity Term used in Erikson's theory to describe the gradually emerging sense of self, changing through a series of eight stages.
identity achievement One of four identity statuses proposed by Marcia, involving the successful resolution of an identity "crisis" and resulting in a new commitment.
identity diffusion One of four identity statuses proposed by Marcia, involving neither a current reevaluation nor a firm personal commitment.
inborn biases A phrase used to describe the entire collection of response tendencies already present in the newborn, including both shared response patterns and individual patterns, such as temperament.
independent variable A condition or event an experimenter varies in some systematic way in order to observe the impact of that variation on subjects' behavior.

individualism A cultural perspective or belief system, contrasted with *collectivism,* in which the emphasis is placed on the separateness and independence of individual development and behavior. Characteristic of most Western cultures.

inductive logic Reasoning from the particular to the general, from experience to broad rules. Characteristic of concrete operational thinking.

infant-directed speech The formal scientific term for "motherese," that special form of simplified, higher-pitched speech that adults use with infants and young children.

inflections The various grammatical "markers" contained in every language, such as (in English) the *s* for plurals or the *ed* for past tenses, auxiliary verbs such as *is,* and the equivalent.

information processing A phrase used to refer to a new, third approach to the study of intellectual development that focuses on changes with age and on individual differences in fundamental intellectual processes.

informed consent Agreement by a person to participate in a study or experiment, based on full disclosure of all possible risks and costs.

insecure attachment An internal working model of relationship in which the child does not as readily use the parent as a safe base and is not readily consoled by the parent if upset. Includes three subtypes of attachment: ambivalent, avoidant, and disorganized/disoriented.

intelligence quotient (IQ) Originally defined in terms of a child's mental age and chronological age, IQs are now computed by comparing a child's performance with that of other children of the same chronological age.

internal working model As applied to social relationships, cognitive construction, for which the earliest relationships may form the template, of the workings of relationships; for example, expectations of support or affection, trustworthiness, and so on.

intrinsic reinforcements Those inner sources of pleasure, pride, or satisfaction that serve to increase the likelihood that an individual will repeat the behavior that led to the feeling.

learning disability (LD) A term broadly used to describe any child with an unexpected or unexplained problem in learning to read, spell, or calculate. More precisely used to refer to a subgroup of such children who have some neurological dysfunction.

libido The term used by Freud to describe the pool of sexual energy in each individual.

life expectancy The average number of years a person of some designated age (e.g., at birth or at age 65) can expect still to live.

life review A process proposed by Butler as an essential ingredient in successful aging; reminiscence to examine and assess one's life.

life span The theoretical maximum number of years of life for a given species. Most gerontologists assume that even major new improvements in health care will not allow us to exceed this limit.

life structure A key concept in Levinson's theory: The "underlying pattern or design of a person's life at a given time," including roles, relationships, and behavior patterns.

locus of control A theoretical concept proposed by Rutter; individuals differ in their tendency to ascribe the causes and control of behavior to internal or external sources.

longitudinal design A research design in which the same subjects are observed or assessed repeatedly over a period of months or years.

low birth weight (LBW) A label given to any baby born below 2500 grams, including both those born too early (preterm) and those who are "small for date."

maturation The sequential unfolding of physical characteristics, governed by instructions contained in the genetic code and shared by all members of the species. Similar in meaning to the less-precise phrase *biological clock.*

maximum oxygen uptake (VO_2 max) The amount of oxygen that can be taken into the bloodstream and hence carried to all parts of the body. A major measure of aerobic fitness, VO_2 max decreases with age but can be increased again with exercise.

menarche Onset of menstruation.

menopause A term used to refer to the point in the female climacteric when menstruation completely ceases. More colloquially, the term is often used as a synonym for the entire climacteric period in women.

metacognition A general and rather loosely used term describing an individual's knowledge of his own thinking processes; knowing what you know, and how you go about learning or remembering.

metamemory A subcategory of metacognition; knowledge about your own memory processes.

modeling A term used by Bandura and others to describe observational learning.

moratorium One of four identity statuses proposed by Marcia, involving an ongoing reexamination but without a new commitment as yet.

motherese *See* **infant-directed speech**.

myelin Material making up an insulating sheath that develops around most axons. This sheath is not completely developed at birth.

myelinization The process by which myelin is added.

negative reinforcement The strengthening of a behavior because of the removal, cessation, or avoidance of an unpleasant stimulus.

neglecting parental style A fourth style of parenting characterized by low levels of nurturance, control, communication, and maturity demands.

neuron The second major class of cells in the nervous system, neurons are responsible for transmission and reception of nerve impulses.

neuroticism One of the "Big Five" personality traits, characterized by anxiety, self-pity, tenseness, and emotional instability.
objective self The second major step in the development of the self-concept; awareness of the self as an object with properties.
object permanence The understanding that an object continues to exist even when it is temporarily out of sight. More generally, the basic understanding that objects exist separate from one's own action on them.
observational learning Learning of motor skills, attitudes, or other behaviors through observing someone else perform them.
oldest old A term used increasingly by gerontologists to describe those over age 85.
old old A term now used fairly commonly by gerontologists to describe those over age 75, or those between 75 and 85.
openness/intellect One of the "Big Five" personality traits, characterized by curiosity, imagination, insight, originality, and wide interests.
operant conditioning That type of learning in which the probability of a person's performing some behavior is strengthened by positive or negative reinforcements.
operations Piaget's term for the new and powerful class of mental schemes he saw as developing between roughly ages 5 and 7, including reversibility, addition, and subtraction.
ossification The process of hardening by which soft tissue becomes bone.
osteoporosis Loss of bone mass with age, resulting in more brittle and porous bones.
overregularization The tendency on the part of children to make the language regular by creating regularized versions of irregular speech forms, such as past tenses or plurals—for example (in English), *beated* or *footses.*
ovum The gamete produced by a woman, which, if fertilized by a sperm from the male, forms the basis for the developing organism.
parental imperative Phrase used by David Gutmann to describe a possibly "wired-in" pattern of intensification of sex-role differentiation after the birth of the first child.
partial reinforcement Reinforcement of behavior on some schedule less frequent than every occasion.
performance The behavior shown by a person under actual circumstances. Even when we are interested in competence, all we can ever measure is performance.
permissive parental style One of the three styles of parenting described by Baumrind, characterized by high levels of nurturance and low levels of control, maturity demands, and communication.
personality The collection of individual, relatively enduring patterns of reacting to and interacting with others that distinguishes each child or adult; temperament is thought of as the emotional substrate of personality.
phenotype The expression of a particular set of genetic information in a specific environment; the observable result of the joint operation of genetic and environmental influences.
pituitary gland One of the endocrine glands. The pituitary gland plays a central role in controlling the rate of physical maturation and sexual maturing.
placenta An organ that develops during gestation between the fetus and the wall of the uterus. The placenta filters nutrients from the mother's blood, acting as liver, lungs, and kidneys for the fetus.
positive reinforcement The strengthening of a behavior by the presentation of some pleasurable or positive stimulus.
postpartum depression A period of depressed mood in a mother following the birth of her child.
preconventional morality The first level of morality proposed by Kohlberg, in which moral judgments are dominated by consideration of what will be punished and what feels good.
preoperational stage Piaget's term for the second major stage of cognitive development, from roughly ages 2 to 6, marked at the beginning by the ability to use symbols and later by the development of basic classification and logical abilities.
presbycusis Normal loss of hearing with aging, especially of high-frequency tones, resulting from basic wear and tear on the auditory system.
presbyopia Normal loss of visual acuity with aging, especially of ability to focus the eyes on near objects, resulting from build-up of layers on the lens and loss of elasticity.
primary aging A term often used to describe those aspects of physical change with age that are universally shared and inevitable, a result of some basic biological process rather than specific experience.
principled morality The third level of morality proposed by Kohlberg, in which considerations of justice, individual rights, and contracts dominate moral judgment.
prosocial behavior Intentional, voluntary behavior intended to benefit another.
proximodistal One of two basic patterns of physical development in infancy (the other is *cephalocaudal*), describing development that proceeds from the center outward, such as from the trunk to the limbs.
psychosexual stages The stages of personality development suggested by Freud, including the oral, anal, phallic, latency, and genital stages.
psychosocial stages The stages of personality development suggested by Erikson, including trust, autonomy, initiative, industry, identity, intimacy, generativity, and ego integrity.
punishment Unpleasant consequences, administered after some undesired behavior by a child or adult, with the intent of extinguishing the behavior.

receptive language A term used to describe the child's ability to understand (receive) language, as contrasted with his ability to express language.
referential style The second style of early language proposed by Nelson, characterized by emphasis on objects and their naming and description.
reflexes Automatic body reactions to specific stimulation, such as the knee jerk or the Moro reflex. Many reflexes remain among adults, but the newborn also has some "primitive" reflexes that disappear as the cortex is fully developed.
relational aggression A form of aggression aimed at damaging the other person's self-esteem or peer relationships, such as by ostracism or threats of ostracism, cruel gossiping, or facial expressions of disdain.
resilience A characteristic of an individual child or adult, product of both inborn and acquired characteristics, that enables the person to adapt successfully to the environment despite stress, threat, or challenging circumstances.
role A concept from sociology; the "job description" for some social position or status, such as teacher, employer, baseball manager, wife, man, or whatever. All individuals occupy multiple roles.
role conflict The experience of occupying two or more roles that are somewhat incompatible, either logistically or psychologically.
role strain The experience of occupying a role for which you are not properly equipped in either skills or personal qualities.
rubella A form of measles that, if contracted during the first few weeks of a pregnancy, is likely to have severe effects on the developing baby.
scheme Piaget's word for the basic actions of knowing, including both physical actions (sensorimotor schemes, such as looking or reaching) and mental actions, such as classifying or comparing or reversing. An experience is assimilated to a scheme, and the scheme is modified or created through accommodation.
secondary aging The part of the changes with age in physical functioning that is not inevitable but may result from widely shared environmental events, stress, or disease processes.
secular trend A pattern of change in some characteristic over several cohorts, such as systematic changes in the average timing of menarche or average height or weight.
secure attachment An internal working model of relationship in which the child uses the parent as a safe base and is readily consoled after separation, when fearful, or when otherwise stressed.
self-efficacy A theoretical concept proposed by Bandura; the belief in one's capacity to cause some intended event to occur, or to perform some task.
self-esteem A global judgment of self-worth; how well you like the person you perceive yourself to be.
sensitive period Similar to a *critical period,* except broader and less specific. A time in development when a particular type of stimulation is particularly important or effective.
sensorimotor stage Piaget's term for the first major stage of cognitive development, from birth to about 18 months, when the child moves from reflexive to voluntary action.
sequential design A family of research designs that involve multiple cross-sectional or multiple longitudinal studies, or a combination of the two.
sex role The set of behaviors, attitudes, rights, duties, and obligations that are part of the "role" of being a boy or a girl, a male or a female, in any given culture.
social clock The sequence of roles and expected social experiences that unfolds in common patterns over the life span within any given culture, such as moving from one school grade to the next, from school to independent life, or from work to retirement.
social death A phrase sometimes used to describe the point at which a deceased person is treated as a corpse by others, such as by closing the eyes or signing a death certificate.
social referencing Using another person's reaction to some situation as a basis for deciding on one's own reaction. A baby does this when she checks her parent's facial expression or body language before responding positively or negatively to something new.
Stanford-Binet The best-known American intelligence test. Developed by Louis Terman and his associates, it was based on the first tests by Binet and Simon.
states of consciousness Five main sleep/awake states identified in infants, from deep sleep to the active awake state.
Strange Situation A series of episodes used by Mary Ainsworth and others in studies of attachment. The child is observed with the mother, with a stranger, left alone, and when reunited with stranger and mother.
subjective self The first major step in the development of the self-concept; the initial awareness that "I exist" separate from others.
sudden infant death syndrome (SIDS) The unexpected death of an infant who otherwise appears healthy; also called *crib death.* The cause is unknown.
superego In Freudian theory, the "conscience" part of personality that develops as a result of the identification process. The superego contains the parental and societal values and attitudes incorporated by the child.
synapse The point of communication between two neurons, where nerve impulses are passed from one neuron to another by means of chemicals called neurotransmitters.
temperament A term sometimes used interchangeably with "personality," but best thought of as the emotional substrate of personality, at least partially genetically determined.
teratogen Any outside agent, such as a disease or a chemical, whose presence significantly increases the risk of deviations or abnormalities in prenatal development.
terminal drop hypothesis A theory that mental and physical functioning remains at a steady level during late adulthood until a point roughly five years from death, after which there is a rapid decline.

thanatology The technical term for the study of dying.
theory of mind A phrase used to describe one aspect of the thinking of 4- and 5-year-olds, when they show signs of understanding not only that other people think differently, but also something about the way others' minds work.
trial stage In Super's model of stages of work life, the period in one's 20s when various careers or jobs may be tried and/or needed skills acquired in some occupation.
Type A behavior Behavior of an individual with a Type A personality.
Type A personality A combination of competitiveness, a sense of time urgency, and hostility or aggressiveness; the latter quality has been linked to higher risk of coronary heart disease.
ultrasound A form of prenatal diagnosis in which high-frequency sound waves are used to provide a picture of the moving fetus. Ultrasound can be used to detect many physical deformities, such as neural tube defects, as well as multiple pregnancies and gestational age.
umbilical cord One of the support structures that develops during the embryonic period of prenatal development, connecting the embryo's or fetus's circulatory system to the placenta and through which nutrients are delivered and wastes removed.
unconditional stimulus In classical conditioning, the cue or signal that automatically triggers the unconditioned response. A touch on a baby's cheek, triggering head turning, is an unconditional stimulus.
unconditioned response In classical conditioning, the basic unlearned response that is triggered by the unconditional stimulus. A baby's turning of his head when touched on the cheek is an unconditioned response.
uterus The female organ in which the blastocyst implants itself and within which the embryo/fetus develops (popularly referred to as the womb).
vulnerability A characteristic of an individual child or adult, product of both inborn and acquired characteristics, that increases the likelihood that he or she will respond to stress in nonadaptive or pathological ways.
WISC-III The most recent revision of the Wechsler Intelligence Scale for Children, a well-known American IQ test that includes both verbal and performance (nonverbal) subtests.
working memory The process of simultaneously holding some information in mind and using that information to solve some problem, learn something new, or make some decision. Roughly analogous to Random Access Memory (RAM) on a computer.
young old Phrase now used by many gerontologists to describe those between roughly 60 and 75.
zone of proximal development As proposed by Vygotsky, the range of tasks or skills that is slightly too difficult for a child to do alone but that he can do successfully with guidance or "scaffolding" by an adult or a more experienced child.

References

Abraham, J. D., & Hansson, R. O. (1995). Successful aging at work: An applied study of selection, optimization, and compensation through impression management. *Journals of Gerontology: Psychological Sciences, 50B,* P94–P103.

Abramovitch, R., Pepler, D., & Corter, C. (1982). Patterns of sibling interaction among preschool-age children. In M. E. Lamb & B. Sutton-Smith (Eds.), *Sibling relationships: Their nature and significance across the lifespan* (pp. 61–86). Hillsdale, NJ: Erlbaum.

Abrams, E. J., Matheson, P. B., Thomas, P. A., Thea, D. M., Krasinski, K., Lambert, G., Shaffer, N., Bamji, M., Hutson, D., Grimm, K., Kaul, A., Bateman, D., Rogers, M., & New York City Perinatal HIV Transmission Collaborative Study Group (1995). Neonatal predictors of infection status and early death among 332 infants at risk of HIV-1 infection monitored prospectively from birth. *Pediatrics, 96,* 451–458.

Adams, C. (1991). Qualitative age differences in memory for text: A life-span developmental perspective. *Psychology and Aging, 6,* 323–336.

Adams, G. R., Gullotta, T. P., & Montemayor, R. (Eds.). (1992). *Adolescent identity formation.* Newbury Park, CA: Sage.

Adams, M. J. (1990). *Beginning to read: Thinking and learning about print.* Cambridge, MA: The MIT Press.

Adams, R. G., & Blieszner, R. (Eds.). (1989). *Older adult friendship.* Newbury Park, CA: Sage.

Adashek, J. A., Peaceman, A. M., Lopez-Zeno, J. A., Minogue, J. P., & Socol, M. L. (1993). Factors contributing to the increased cesarean birth rate in older parturient women. *American Journal of Obstetrics and Gynecology, 169,* 936–940.

Adelmann, P. K. (1994). Multiple roles and physical health among older adults: Gender and ethnic comparisons. *Research on Aging, 16,* 142–166.

Adesman, A. R. (1996). Fragile X syndrome. In A. J. Capute & P. J. Accardo (Eds.), *Developmental disabilities in infancy and childhood* (2nd ed.). Vol. II. *The spectrum of developmental disabilities* (pp. 255–269). Baltimore: Paul H. Brookes.

Adler, N. E., Boyce, T., Chesney, M. A., Cohen, S., Folkman, S., Kahn, R. L., & Syme, S. L. (1994). Socioeconomic status and health: The challenge of the gradient. *American Psychologist, 49,* 15–24.

Ahadi, S. A., & Rothbart, M. K. (1994). Temperament, development, and the big five. In C. F. Halverson, Jr., G. A. Kohnstamm, & R. P. Martin (Eds.), *The developing structure of temperament and personality from infancy to adulthood* (pp. 189–207). Hillsdale, NJ: Erlbaum.

Ahlsten, G., Cnattingius, S., & Lindmark, G. (1993). Cessation of smoking during pregnancy improves foetal growth and reduces infant morbidity in the neonatal period: A population-based prospective study. *Acta Paediatrica, 82,* 177–182.

Ainsworth, M. D. S. (1967). *Infancy in Uganda: Infant care and the growth of love.* Baltimore: Johns Hopkins University Press.

Ainsworth, M. D. S. (1972). Attachment and dependency: A comparison. In J. L. Gewirtz (Ed.), *Attachment and dependency* (pp. 97–138). Washington, DC: V. H. Winston.

Ainsworth, M. D. S. (1982). Attachment: Retrospect and prospect. In C. M. Parkes & J. Stevenson-Hinde (Eds.), *The place of attachment in human behavior* (pp. 3–30). New York: Basic Books.

Ainsworth, M. D. S. (1989). Attachments beyond infancy. *American Psychologist, 44,* 709–716.

Ainsworth, M. D. S., Blehar, M., Waters, E., & Wall, S. (1978). *Patterns of attachment.* Hillsdale, NJ: Erlbaum.

Ainsworth, M. D. S., & Marvin, R. S. (1995). On the shaping of attachment theory and research: An interview with Mary D. S. Ainsworth (Fall 1994). *Monographs of the Society for Research in Child Development, 60*(244, Nos. 2–3), 3–21.

Aksu-Koc, A. A., & Slobin, D. I. (1985). The acquisition of Turkish. In D. I. Slobin (Ed.), *The crosslinguistic study of language acquisition: Vol. 1. The data* (pp. 839–878). Hillsdale, NJ: Erlbaum.

Albert, M. S., Jones, K., Savage, C. R., Berkman, L., Seeman, T., Blazer, D., & Rowe, J. W. (1995). Predictors of cognitive change in older persons: MacArthur studies of successful aging. *Psychology and Aging, 10,* 578–589.

Aldous, J. (1996). *Family careers: Rethinking the developmental perspective.* Thousand Oaks, CA: Sage.

Aldous, J., & Klein, D. M. (1991). Sentiment and services: Models of intergenerational relationships in mid-life. *Journal of Marriage and the Family, 53,* 595–608.

Alexander, K. L., Entwisle, D. R., & Dauber, S. L. (1993). First-grade classroom behavior: Its short and long-term consequences for school performance. *Child Development, 64,* 801–814.

Allen, K. R., & Pickett, R. S. (1987). Forgotten streams in the family life course: Utilization of qualitative retrospective interviews in the analysis of lifelong single women's family careers. *Journal of Marriage and the Family, 49,* 517–526.

Allen, M. C. (1996). Preterm development. In A. J. Capute & P. J. Accardo (Eds.), *Developmental disabilities in infancy and childhood.* (2nd ed.) Vol. II. *The spectrum of developmental disabilities* (pp. 31–47). Baltimore: Paul H. Brookes.

Allen, M. C., Donohue, P. K., & Dusman, A. E. (1993). The limit of viability—neonatal outcome of infants born at 22 to 25 weeks' gestation. *New England Journal of Medicine, 329,* 1597–1601.

Alpers, A., & Lo, B. (1995). Physician-assisted suicide in Oregon: A bold experiment. *Journal of the American Medical Association, 274,* 483–487.

The Alpha-Tocopherol Beta Carotene Cancer Prevention Study Group (1994). The effect of vitamin E and beta carotene on the incidence of lung cancer and other cancers in male smokers. *New England Journal of Medicine, 330,* 1029–1035.

Alsaker, F. D. (1995). Timing of puberty and reactions to pubertal change. In M. Rutter (Ed.), *Psychosocial disturbances in young people: Challenges for prevention* (pp. 37–82). Cambridge, England: Cambridge University Press.

Alsaker, F. D., & Olweus, D. (1992). Stability of global self-evaluations in early adolescence: A cohort longitudinal study. *Journal of Research on Adolescence, 2,* 123–145.

Alsop, S. (1973). *Stay of execution.* New York: Lippincott.

Amador, M., Silva, L. C., & Valdes-Lazo, F. (1994). Breast-feeding trends in Cuba and the Americas. *Bulletin of the Pan American Health Organization, 28,* 220–227.

Amato, P. R. (1993). Children's adjustment to divorce: Theories, hypotheses, and empirical support. *Journal of Marriage and the Family, 55,* 23–38.

Amato, P. R., & Keith, B. (1991). Parental divorce and the well-being of children: A meta-analysis. *Psychological Bulletin, 110,* 26–46.

Ambert, A. (1994). An international perspective on parenting: Social change and social constructs. *Journal of Marriage and the Family, 56,* 529–543.

Ambuel, B. (1995). Adolescents, unintended pregnancy, and abortion: The struggle for a compassionate social policy. *Current Directions in Psychological Science, 4,* 1–5.

American Academy of Pediatrics Committee on Nutrition (1986). Prudent life-style for children: Dietary fat and cholesterol. *Pediatrics, 78,* 521–525.

American Psychiatric Association (1994). *Diagnostic and statistical manual of mental disorders* (4th ed.). Washington, DC: American Psychiatric Association.

American Psychological Association (1993). *Violence and youth: Psychology's response: Vol. 1. Summary report of the American Psychological Association Commission on Violence and Youth.* Washington, DC: American Psychological Association.

Amott, T., & Matthaei, J. (1991). *Race, gender, and work: A multicultural economic history of women in the United States.* Boston: South End Press.

Anderson, D. R., Lorch, E. P., Field, D. E., Collins, P. A., & Nathan, J. G. (1986). Television viewing at home: Age trends in visual attention and time with TV. *Child Development, 57,* 1024–1033.

Anderson, K. M., Castelli, W. P., & Levy, D. (1987). Cholesterol and mortality: 30 years of follow-up from the Framingham study. *Journal of the American Medical Association, 257,* 2176–2180.

Andersson, B. (1989). Effects of public day-care: A longitudinal study. *Child Development, 60,* 857–886.

Andersson, B. (1992). Effects of day-care on cognitive and socioemotional competence of thirteen-year-old Swedish schoolchildren. *Child Development, 63,* 20–36.

Angier, N. (June 9, 1992). Clue to longevity found at chromosome tip. *New York Times,* pp. B5, B9.

Anglin, J. M. (1993). Vocabulary development: A morphological analysis. *Monographs of the Society for Research in Child Development, 58* (Serial No. 238).

Anglin, J. M. (1995). *Word learning and the growth of potentially knowable vocabulary.* Paper presented at the biennial meetings of the Society for Research in Child Development, Indianapolis, March.

Anisfeld, E., Casper, V., Nozyce, M., & Cunningham, N. (1990). Does infant carrying promote attachment? An experimental study of the effects of increased physical contact on the development of attachment. *Child Development, 61,* 1617–1627.

Anisfeld, M. (1991). Neonatal imitation. *Developmental Review, 11,* 60–97.

Annunziato, P. W., & Frenkel, L. M. (1993). The epidemiology of pediatric HIV-1 infection. *Pediatric Annals, 22,* 401–405.

Anthony, J. C., & Aboraya, A. (1992). The epidemiology of selected mental disorders in later life. In J. E. Birren, R. B. Sloane, & G. D. Cohen (Eds.), *Handbook of mental health and aging* (2nd ed.) (pp. 28–73). San Diego, CA: Academic Press.

Antonucci, T. C. (1990). Social supports and social relationships. In R. H. Binstock & L. K. George (Eds.), *Handbook of aging and the social sciences* (3rd ed.) (pp. 205–226). San Diego, CA: Academic Press.

Antonucci, T. C. (1991). Attachment, social support, and coping with negative life events in mature adulthood. In E. M. Cummings, A. L. Greene, & K. H. Karraker (Eds.), *Life-span developmental psychology: Perspectives on stress and coping* (pp. 261–276). Hillsdale, NJ: Erlbaum.

Antonucci, T. C. (1994a). A life-span view of women's social relations. In B. F. Turner & L. E. Troll (Eds.), *Women growing older: Psychological perspectives* (pp. 239–269). Thousand Oaks, CA: Sage.

Antonucci, T. C. (1994b). Attachment in adulthood and aging. In M. B. Sperling & W. H. Berman (Eds.), *Attachment in adults: Clinical and developmental perspectives* (pp. 256–274). New York: Guilford Press.

Antonucci, T. C., & Akiyama, H. (1987a). Social networks in adult life and a preliminary examination of the convoy model. *Journal of Gerontology, 42,* 519–527.

Antonucci, T. C., & Akiyama, H. (1987b). An examination of sex differences in social support among older men and women. *Sex Roles, 17,* 737–749.

Apgar, V. A. (1953). A proposal for a new method of evaluation of the newborn infant. *Current Research in Anesthesia and Analgesia, 32,* 260–267.

Aquilino, W. S., & Supple, K. R. (1991). Parent-child relations and parent's satisfaction with living arrangements when adult children live at home. *Journal of Marriage and the Family, 53,* 13–27.

Arbuckle, N. W., & De Vries, B. (1995). The long-term effects of later life spousal and parental bereavement on personal functioning. *The Gerontologist, 35,* 637–647.

Arenberg, D. (1974). A longitudinal study of problem solving in adults. *Journal of Gerontology, 29,* 650–658.

Arenberg, D. (1983). Memory and learning do decline late in life. In J. E. Birren, J. M. A. Munnichs, H. Thomae, & M. Marios (Eds.), *Aging: A challenge to science and society: Vol. 3. Behavioral sciences and conclusions* (pp. 312–322). New York: Oxford University Press.

Arenberg, D., & Robertson-Tchabo, E. A. (1977). Learning and aging. In J. E. Birren & K. W. Schaie (Eds.), *Handbook of the psychology of aging* (pp. 441–449). New York: Van Nostrand Reinhold.

Arlin, P. K. (1975). Cognitive development in adulthood: A fifth stage? *Developmental Psychology, 11,* 602–606.

Arlin, P. K. (1989). Problem solving and problem finding in young artists and young scientists. In M. L. Commons, J. D. Sinnott, F. A. Richards, & C. Armon (Eds.), *Adult Development: Vol. 1. Comparisons and applications of developmental models* (pp. 197–216). New York: Praeger.

Arlin, P. K. (1990). Wisdom: The art of problem finding. In R. J. Sternberg (Ed.), *Wisdom. Its nature, origins, and development* (pp. 230–243). New York: Cambridge University Press.

Arn, P., Chen, H., Tuck-Muller, C. M., Mankinen, C., Wachtel, G., Li, S., Shen, C.-C., & Wachtel, S. S. (1994). SRVX, a sex reversing locus in Xp21.2→p22.11. *Human Genetics, 93,* 389–393.

Arnett, J. (1992). Reckless behavior in adolescence: A developmental perspective. *Developmental Review, 12,* 339–373.

Arnett, J. (1995). The young and the reckless: Adolescent reckless behavior. *Current Directions in Psychological Science, 4,* 67–71.

Asendorpf, J. B., Warkentin, V., & Baudonnière, P. (1996). Self-awareness and other-awareness. II: Mirror self-recognition, social contingency awareness, and synchronic imitation. *Developmental Psychology, 32,* 313–321.

Asher, S. R. (1990). Recent advances in the study of peer rejection. In S. R. Asher & J. D. Coie (Eds.), *Peer rejection in childhood* (pp. 3–16). Cambridge, England: Cambridge University Press.

Asher, S. R., & Coie, J. D. (Eds.). (1990). *Peer rejection in childhood.* Cambridge, England: Cambridge University Press.

Aslin, R. N. (1987). Visual and auditory development in infancy. In J. D. Osofsky (Ed.), *Handbook of infant development* (2nd ed.) (pp. 5–97). New York: Wiley-Interscience.

Assouline, M., & Meir, E. I. (1987). Meta-analysis of the relationship between congruence and well-being measures. *Journal of Vocational Behavior, 31,* 319–332.

Astington, J. W., & Gopnik, A. (1991). Theoretical explanations of children's understanding of the mind. In G. E. Butterworth, P. L. Harris, A. M. Leslie, & H. M. Wellman (Eds.), *Perspectives on the child's theory of mind* (pp. 7–31). New York: Oxford University Press.

Astington, J. W., & Jenkins, J. M. (1995). *Language and theory of mind: A theoretical review and a longitudinal study.* Paper presented at the biennial meetings of the Society for Research in Child Development, Indianapolis, March.

Astone, N. M. (1993). Are adolescent mothers just single mothers? *Journal of Research on Adolescence, 3,* 353–371.

Attie, I., & Brooks-Gunn, J. (1989). Development of eating problems in adolescent girls: A longitudinal study. *Developmental Psychology, 25,* 70–79.

Attie, I., & Brooks-Gunn, J. (1995). The development of eating regulation across the life span. In D. Cicchetti & D. J. Cohen (Eds.), *Developmental psychopathology: Vol. 2. Risk, disorder, and adaptation* (pp. 332–368). New York: Wiley.

Attie, I., Brooks-Gunn, J., & Petersen, A. (1990). A developmental perspective on eating disorders and eating problems. In M. Lewis & S. M. Miller (Eds.), *Handbook of developmental psychopathology* (pp. 409–420). New York: Plenum.

Avis, J., & Harris, P. L. (1991). Belief-desire reasoning among Baka children: Evidence for a universal conception of mind. *Child Development, 62,* 460–467.

Bachman, J. G., Alcser, K. H., Doukas, D. J., Lichtenstein, R. L., Corning, A. D., & Brody, H. (1996). Attitudes of Michigan physicians and the public toward legalizing physician-assisted suicide and voluntary euthanasia. *New England Journal of Medicine, 334,* 303–309.

Bachman, J. G., & Schulenberg, J. (1993). How part-time work intensity relates to drug use, problem behavior, time use, and satisfaction among high school seniors: Are these consequences or merely correlates? *Developmental Psychology, 29,* 220–235.

Bachrach, C. A. (1980). Childlessness and social isolation among the elderly. *Journal of Marriage and the Family, 42,* 627–638.

Bailey, J. M., & Pillard, R. C. (1991). A genetic study of male sexual orientation. *Archives of General Psychiatry, 48,* 1089–1096.

Bailey, J. M., Pillard, R. C., Neale, M. C., & Agyei, Y. (1993). Heritable factors influence sexual orientation in women. *Archives of General Psychiatry, 50,* 217–223.

Bailey, J. M., & Zucker, K. J. (1995). Childhood sex-typed behavior and sexual orientation: A conceptual analysis and quantitative review. *Developmental Psychology, 31,* 43–55.

Baillargeon, R. (1987). Object permanence in very young infants. *Developmental Psychology, 23,* 655–664.

Baillargeon, R. (1994). How do infants learn about the physical world? *Current Directions in Psychological Science, 3,* 133–140.

Baillargeon, R., & DeVos, J. (1991). Object permanence in young infants: Further evidence. *Child Development, 62,* 1227–1246.

Baillargeon, R., Spelke, E. S., & Wasserman, S. (1985). Object permanence in five-month-old infants. *Cognition, 20,* 191–208.

Baird, P. A., Sadovnick, A. D., & Yee, I. M. L. (1991). Maternal age and birth defects: A population study. *Lancet, 337,* 527–530.

Baker-Ward, L. (1995). *Children's reports of a minor medical emergency procedure.* Paper presented at the biennial meetings of the Society for Research in Child Development, Indianapolis, March.

Baker-Ward, L., Gordon, B. N., Ornstein, P. A., Larus, D. M., & Clubb, P. A. (1993). Young children's long-term retention of a pediatric examination. *Child Development, 64,* 1519–1533.

Bal, D., & Foerster, S. B. (1991). Changing the American diet. *Cancer, 67,* 2671–2680.

Balaban, M. T. (1995). Affective influences on startle in five-month-old infants: Reactions to facial expressions of emotion. *Child Development, 66,* 28–36.

Baldwin, D. A. (1995). *Understanding relations between constraints and a socio-pragmatic account of meaning acquisition.* Paper presented at the biennial meetings of the Society for Research in Child Development, Indianapolis, March.

Ball, J. F. (1976–1977). Widow's grief: The impact of age and mode of death. *Omega, 7,* 307–333.

Baltes, P. B. (1993). The aging mind: Potential and limits. *The Gerontologist, 33,* 580–594.

Baltes, P. B., & Baltes, M. M. (1990a). Psychological perspectives on successful aging: The model of selective optimization with compensation. In P. B. Baltes & M. M. Baltes (Eds.), *Successful aging* (pp. 1–34). Cambridge, England: Cambridge University Press.

Baltes, P. B., & Baltes, M. M. (Eds.). (1990b). *Successful aging.* Cambridge, England: Cambridge University Press.

Baltes, P. B., Dittmann-Kohli, F., & Dixon, R. A. (1984). New perspectives on the development of intelligence in adulthood: Toward a dual-process conception and a model of selective optimization with compensation. In P. B. Baltes & O. G. Brim, Jr. (Eds.), *Life-span development and behavior* (pp. 34–77). New York: Academic Press.

Baltes, P. B., Dittmann-Kohli, F., & Dixon, R. A. (1986). Multidisciplinary propositions on the development of intelligence during adulthood and old age. In A. B. Sørensen, F. E. Weinert, & L. R. Sherrod (Eds.), *Human development and the life course: Multidisciplinary perspectives* (pp. 467–508). Hillsdale, NJ: Erlbaum.

Baltes, P. B., & Kliegl, R. (1992). Further testing of limits of cognitive plasticity: Negative age differences in a mnemonic skill are robust. *Developmental Psychology, 28,* 121–125.

Baltes, P. B., Reese, H. W., & Nesselroade, J. R. (1977). *Life-span developmental psychology: Introduction to research methods.* Monterey, CA: Books/Cole.

Baltes, P. B., & Smith, J. (1990). Toward a psychology of wisdom and its ontogenesis. In R. J. Sternberg (Ed.), *Wisdom. Its nature, origins, and development* (pp. 87–120). Cambridge, England: Cambridge University Press.

Baltes, P. B., Smith, J., & Staudinger, U. M. (1992). Wisdom and successful aging. In T. B. Sonderegger (Ed.), *Nebraska Symposium on Motivation, 1991* (pp. 123–168). Lincoln: University of Nebraska Press.

Baltes, P. B., Staudinger, U. M., Maercker, A., & Smith, J. (1995). People nominated as wise: A comparative study of wisdom-related knowledge. *Psychology and Aging, 10,* 155–166.

Bamford, F. N., Bannister, R. P., Benjamin, C. M., Hillier, V. F., Ward, B. S., & Moore, W. M. O. (1990). Sleep in the first year of life. *Developmental Medicine and Child Neurology, 32,* 718–724.

Bandini, L. G., & Dietz, W. H. (1992). Myths about childhood obesity. *Pediatric Annals, 21,* 647–652.

Bandura, A. (1977a). *Social learning theory.* Englewood Cliffs, NJ: Prentice-Hall.

Bandura, A. (1977b). Self-efficacy: Toward a unifying theory of behavioral change. *Psychological Review, 84,* 91–125.

Bandura, A. (1982a). The self and mechanisms of agency. In J. Suls (Ed.), *Psychological perspectives on the self* (pp. 3–40). Hillsdale, NJ: Erlbaum.

Bandura, A. (1982b). The psychology of chance encounters and life paths. *American Psychologist, 37,* 747–755.

Bandura, A. (1982c). Self-efficacy mechanism in human agency. *American Psychologist, 37,* 122–147.

Bandura, A. (1986). *Social foundations of thought and action: A social cognitive theory.* Englewood Cliffs, NJ: Prentice-Hall.

Bandura, A. (1989). Social cognitive theory. *Annals of Child Development, 6,* 1–60.

Bandura, A., Ross, D., & Ross, S. A. (1961). Transmission of aggression through imitation of aggressive models. *Journal of Abnormal and Social Psychology, 63,* 575–582.

Bandura, A., Ross, D., & Ross, S. A. (1963). Imitation of film-mediated aggressive models. *Journal of Abnormal and Social Psychology, 66,* 3–11.

Bardoni, B., Zanaria, E., Guioli, S., Floridia, G., Worley, K. C., Tonini, G., Ferrante, E., Chiumello, G., McCabe, E. R. B., Fraccaro, M., Zuffardi, O., & Camerino, G. (1994). A dosage sensitive locus at chromosome Xp21 is involved in male to female sex reversal. *Nature Genetics, 7,* 497–501.

Barenboim, C. (1981). The development of person perception in childhood and adolescence: From behavioral comparisons to psychological constructs to psychological comparisons. *Child Development, 52,* 129–144.

Barnard, K. E., Hammond, M. A., Booth, C. L., Bee, H. L., Mitchell, S. K., & Spieker, S. J. (1989). Measurement and meaning of parent-child interaction. In J. J. Morrison, C. Lord, & D. P. Keating (Eds.), *Applied developmental psychology* (Vol. 3) (pp. 40–81). San Diego, CA: Academic Press.

Barnett, W. S. (1993). Benefit-cost analysis of preschool education: Findings from a 25-year follow-up. *American Journal of Orthopsychiatry, 63,* 500–508.

Barnett, W. S. (1995). Long-term effects of early childhood programs on cognitive and school outcomes. *The Future of Children, 5* (3), 25–50.

Barrett, G. V., & Depinet, R. L. (1991). A reconsideration of testing for competence rather than for intelligence. *American Psychologist, 46,* 1012–1024.

Barrett-Connor, E., & Bush, T. L. (1991). Estrogen and coronary heart disease in women. *Journal of the American Medical Association, 265,* 1861–1867.

Bartoshuk, L. M., & Weiffenbach, J. M. (1990). Chemical senses and aging. In E. L. Schneider & J. W. Rowe (Eds.), *Handbook of the biology of aging* (3rd ed.) (pp. 429–444). San Diego, CA: Academic Press.

Bass, D. M. (1985). The hospice ideology and success of hospice care. *Research on Aging, 7,* 307–328.

Basseches, M. (1984). *Dialectical thinking and adult development.* Norwood, NJ: Ablex.

Basseches, M. (1989). Dialectical thinking as an organized whole: Comments on Irwin and Kramer. In M. L. Commons, J. D. Sinnott, F. A. Richards, & C. Armon (Eds.), *Adult development: Vol. 1. Comparisons and applications of developmental models* (pp. 161–178). New York: Praeger.

Bassford, T. L. (1995). Health status of Hispanic elders. *Clinics in Geriatric Medicine, 11,* 25–38.

Bates, E. (1993). Commentary: Comprehension and production in early language development. *Monographs of the Society for Research in Child Development, 58* (3–4, Serial No. 233), 222–242.

Bates, E., Bretherton, I., Beeghly-Smith, M., & McNew, S. (1982). Social bases of language development: A reassessment. In H. W. Reese & L. P. Lipsitt (Eds.), *Advances in child development and behavior* (Vol. 16) (pp. 8–68). New York: Academic Press.

Bates, E., O'Connell, B., & Shore, C. (1987). Language and communication in infancy. In J. D. Osofsky (Ed.), *Handbook of infant development* (2nd ed.) (pp. 149–203). New York: Wiley.

Bates, J. E. (1989). Applications of temperament concepts. In G. A. Kohnstamm, J. E. Bates, & M. K. Rothbart (Eds.), *Temperament in childhood* (pp. 321–356). Chichester, England: Wiley.

Bates, J. E., Marvinney, D., Kelly, T., Dodge, K. A., Bennett, D. S., & Pettit, G. S. (1994). Child-care history and kindergarten adjustment. *Developmental Psychology, 30,* 690–700.

Baugher, R. J., Burger, C., Smith, R., & Wallston, K. (1989–1990). A comparison of terminally ill persons at various time periods to death. *Omega, 20,* 103–115.

Baumrind, D. (1971). Current patterns of parental authority. *Developmental Psychology Monograph, 4* (1, Part 2).

Baumrind, D. (1972). Socialization and instrumental competence in young children. In W. W. Hartup (Ed.), *The young child: Reviews of research* (Vol. 2) (pp. 202–224). Washington, DC: National Association for the Education of Young Children.

Baumrind, D. (1991). Effective parenting during the early adolescent transition. In P. A. Cowan & M. Hetherington (Eds.), *Family transitions* (pp. 111–163). Hillsdale, NJ: Erlbaum.

Baydar, N., & Brooks-Gunn, J. (1991). Effects of maternal employment and child-care arrangements on preschoolers' cognitive and behavioral outcomes: Evidence from the children of the National Longitudinal Survey of Youth. *Developmental Psychology, 27,* 932–945.

Baydar, N., Brooks-Gunn, J., & Furstenberg, F. F. (1993). Early warning signs of functional illiteracy: Predictors in childhood and adolescence. *Child Development, 64,* 815–829.

Bayley, N. (1969). *Bayley scales of infant development.* New York: Psychological Corporation.

Beck, R. W., & Beck, S. H. (1989). The incidence of extended households among middle-aged black and white women: Estimates from a 15-year panel study. *Journal of Family Issues, 10,* 147–168.

Beckwith, L., & Rodning, C. (1991). Intellectual functioning in children born preterm: Recent research. In L. Okagaki & R. J. Sternberg (Eds.), *Directors of development* (pp. 25–58). Hillsdale, NJ: Erlbaum.

Bedeian, A. G., Ferris, G. R., & Kacmar, K. M. (1992). Age, tenure, and job satisfaction: A tale of two perspectives. *Journal of Vocational Behavior, 40,* 33–48.

Bedford, V. H. (1989). Understanding the value of siblings in old age. *American Behavioral Scientist, 33,* 33–44.

Bee, H. L., Barnard, K. E., Eyres, S. J., Gray, C. A., Hammond, M. A., Spietz, A. L., Snyder, C., & Clark, B. (1982). Prediction of IQ and language skill from perinatal status, child performance, family characteristics, and mother-infant interaction. *Child Development, 53,* 1135–1156.

Belgrave, L. L., Wykle, M. L., & Choi, J. M. (1993). Health, double jeopardy, and culture: The use of institutionalization by African-Americans. *The Gerontologist, 33,* 379–385.

Bell, L. G., & Bell, D. C. (1982). Family climate and the role of the female adolescent: Determinants of adolescent functioning. *Family Relations, 31,* 519–527.

Bellantoni, M. F., & Blackman, M. R. (1996). Menopause and its consequences. In E. L. Schneider & J. W. Rowe (Eds.), *Handbook of the biology of aging* (4th ed.) (pp. 415–430). San Diego, CA: Academic Press.

Bellinger, D. C., Stiles, K. M., & Needleman, H. L. (1992). Low-level lead exposure, intelligence and academic achievement: A long-term follow-up study. *Pediatrics, 90,* 855–861.

Belsky, J. (1985). Prepared statement on the effects of day care. In Select Committee on Children, Youth, and Families, House of Representatives, 98th Congress, Second Session, *Improving child care services: What can be done?* Washington, DC: U.S. Government Printing Office.

Belsky, J. (1992). Consequences of child care for children's development: A deconstructionist view. In A. Booth (Ed.), *Child care in the 1990s: Trends and consequences* (pp. 83–94). Hillsdale, NJ: Erlbaum.

Belsky, J. (1993). Etiology of child maltreatment: A developmental-ecological analysis. *Psychological Bulletin, 114,* 413–434.

Belsky, J., Hsieh, K., & Crnic, K. (1996). Infant positive and negative emotionality: One dimension or two? *Developmental Psychology, 32,* 289–298.

Belsky, J., Lang, M. E., & Rovine, M. (1985). Stability and change in marriage across the transition to parenthood: A second study. *Journal of Marriage and the Family, 47,* 855–865.

Belsky, J., & Rovine, M. (1988). Nonmaternal care in the first year of life and the security of infant-parent attachment. *Child Development, 59,* 157–167.

Bem, S. L. (1974). The measurement of psychological androgyny. *Journal of Consulting and Clinical Psychology, 42,* 155–162.

Benbow, C. P. (1988). Sex differences in mathematical reasoning ability in intellectually talented preadolescents: Their nature, effects, and possible causes. *Behavioral and Brain Sciences, 11,* 169–232.

Bender, B. G., Harmon, R. J., Linden, M. G., & Robinson, A. (1995). Psychosocial adaptation of 39 adolescents with sex chromosome abnormalities. *Pediatrics, 96,* 302–308.

Bendersky, M., & Lewis, M. (1994). Environmental risk, biological risk, and developmental outcome. *Developmental Psychology, 30,* 484–494.

Benenson, J. F. (1994). Ages four to six years: Changes in the structures of play networks of girls and boys. *Merrill-Palmer Quarterly, 40,* 478–487.

Bengtson, V., Rosenthal, C., & Burton, L. (1990). Families and aging: Diversity and heterogeneity. In R. H. Binstock & L. K. George (Eds.), *Handbook of aging and the social sciences* (3rd ed.) (pp. 263–287). San Diego, CA: Academic Press.

Bengtson, V., Rosenthal, C., & Burton, L. (1996). Paradoxes of families and aging. In R. H. Binstock & L. K. George (Eds.), *Handbook of aging and the social sciences* (4th ed.) (pp. 253–282). San Diego, CA: Academic Press.

Bengtson, V. L. (1985). Diversity and symbolism in grandparent roles. In V. L. Bengtson & J. F. Robertson (Eds.), *Grandparenthood* (pp. 11–26). Beverly Hills, CA: Sage.

Bengtson, V. L., Cuellar, J. B., & Ragan, P. K. (1977). Stratum contrasts and similarities in attitudes toward death. *Journal of Gerontology, 32,* 76–88.

Benoit, D., & Parker, K. C. H. (1994). Stability and transmission of attachment across three generations. *Child Development, 65,* 1444–1456.

Berch, D. B., & Bender, B. G. (1987). Margins of sexuality. *Psychology Today, 21* (December), 54–57.

Berg, S. (1996). Aging, behavior, and terminal decline. In J. E. Birren & K. W. Schaie (Eds.), *Handbook of the psychology of aging* (4th ed.) (pp. 323–337). San Diego, CA: Academic Press.

Bergeman, C. S., Chipuer, H. M., Plomin, R., Pedersen, N. L., McClearn, G. E., Nesselroade, J. R., Costa, P. T., & McCrae, R. R. (1993). Genetic and environmental effects on openness to experience, agreeableness, and conscientiousness: An adoption/twin study. *Journal of Personality, 61,* 159–179.

Berkman, L. F. (1985). The relationship of social networks and social support to morbidity and mortality. In S. Coen & S. L. Syme (Eds.), *Social support and health* (pp. 241–262). Orlando, FL: Academic Press.

Berkman, L. F., & Breslow, L. (1983). *Health and ways of living: The Alameda County Study.* New York: Oxford University Press.

Berkowitz, G. S., Skovron, M. L., Lapinski, R. H., & Berkowitz, R. L. (1990). Delayed childbearing and the outcome of pregnancy. *New England Journal of Medicine, 322,* 659–664.

Berman, W. H., Marcus, L., & Berman, E. R. (1994). Attachment in marital relations. In M. B. Sperling & W. H. Berman (Eds.), *Attachment in adults: Clinical and developmental perspectives* (pp. 204–231). New York: Guilford Press.

Berndt, T. J. (1983). Social cognition, social behavior, and children's friendships. In E. T. Higgins, D. N. Ruble, & W. W. Hartup (Eds.), *Social cognition and social development: A sociocultural perspective* (pp. 158–192). Cambridge, England: Cambridge University Press.

Berndt, T. J. (1986). Children's comments about their friendships. In M. Perlmutter (Ed.), *Minnesota Symposia on Child Psychology* (Vol. 18) (pp. 189–212). Hillsdale, NJ: Erlbaum.

Berndt, T. J. (1992). Friendship and friends' influence in adolescence. *Current Directions in Psychological Science, 1,* 156–159.

Berndt, T. J., & Keefe, K. (1995a). Friends' influence on adolescents' adjustment to school. *Child Development, 66,* 1312–1329.

Berndt, T. J., & Keefe, K. (1995b). *Friends' influence on school adjustment: A motivational analysis.* Paper presented at the biennial meetings of the Society for Research in Child Development, Indianapolis, March.

Bertenthal, B. I., & Campos, J. J. (1987). New directions in the study of early experience. *Child Development, 58,* 560–567.

Bertenthal, B. I., Campos, J. J., & Kermoian, R. (1994). An epigenetic perspective on the development of self-produced locomotion and its consequences. *Current Directions in Psychological Science, 3,* 140–145.

Betancourt, H., & Lopez, S. R. (1993). The study of culture, ethnicity, and race in American psychology. *American Psychologist, 48,* 629–637.

Bettes, B. A. (1988). Maternal depression and motherese: Temporal and intonational features. *Child Development, 59,* 1089–1096.

Betz, E. L. (1984). A study of career patterns of women college graduates. *Journal of Vocational Behavior, 24,* 249–263.

Betz, N. E., & Fitzgerald, L. F. (1987). *The career psychology of women.* Orlando, FL: Academic Press.

Bhatt, R. S., & Rovee-Collier, C. (1996). Infants' forgetting of correlated attributes and object recognition. *Child Development, 67,* 172–187.

Bianchi, A. (1993, January–February). Older drivers: The good, the bad, and the iffy. *Harvard Magazine,* pp. 12–13.

Biblarz, T. J., Bengtson, V. L., & Bucur, A. (1996). Social mobility across three generations. *Journal of Marriage and the Family, 58,* 188–200.

Biedenharn, P. J., & Normoyle, J. B. (1991). Elderly community residents' reactions to the nursing home: An analysis of nursing home-related beliefs. *The Gerontologist, 31,* 107–115.

Bigler, E. D., Johnson, S. C., Jackson, C., & Blatter, D. D. (1995). Aging, brain size, and IQ. *Intelligence, 21,* 109–119.

Billy, J. O. G., Brewster, K. L., & Grady, W. R. (1994). Contextual effects on the sexual behavior of adolescent women. *Journal of Marriage and the Family, 56,* 387–404.

Binet, A., & Simon, T. (1905). Méthodes nouvelles pour le diagnostic du niveau intellectuel des anormaux [New methods for diagnosing the intellectual level of the abnormal]. *L'Anée Psychologique, 11,* 191–244.

Bingham, C. R., Miller, B. C., & Adams, G. R. (1990). Correlates of age at first sexual intercourse in a national sample of young women. *Journal of Adolescent Research, 5,* 18–33.

Binstock, R. H., & George, L. K. (Eds.). (1996). *Handbook of aging and the social sciences* (4th ed.). San Diego, CA: Academic Press.

Biro, F. M., Lucky, A. W., Huster, G. A., & Morrison, J. A. (1995). Pubertal staging in boys. *Journal of Pediatrics, 127,* 100–102.

Birren, J. E., & Fisher, L. M. (1995). Aging and speed of behavior: Possible consequences for psychological functioning. *Annual Review of Psychology, 56,* 329–353.

Birren, J. E., & Schaie, K. W. (Eds.). (1996). *Handbook of the psychology of aging* (4th ed.). San Diego, CA: Academic Press.

Birren, J. E., & Schroots, J. J. F. (1996). History, concepts, and theory in the psychology of aging. In J. R. Birren & K. W. Schaie (Eds.), *Handbook of the psychology of aging* (4th ed.) (pp. 3–23). San Diego, CA: Academic Press.

Biswas, M. K., & Craigo, S. D. (1994). The course and conduct of normal labor and delivery. In A. H. DeCherney & M. L. Pernoll (Eds.), *Current obstetric and gynecologic diagnosis & treatment* (pp. 202–227). Norwalk, CT: Appleton & Lange.

Bivens, J. A., & Berk, L. E. (1990). A longitudinal study of the development of elementary school children's private speech. *Merrill-Palmer Quarterly, 36,* 443–463.

Bjorklund, D. F., & Coyle, T. R. (1995). *Utilization deficiencies, multiple strategy use, and memory development.* Paper presented at the biennial meetings of the Society for Research in Child Development, Indianapolis, March.

Bjorklund, D. F., & Muir, J. E. (1988). Remembering on their own: Children's development of free recall memory. In R. Vasta (Ed.), *Annals of child development* (Vol. 5) (pp. 79–124). Greenwich, CT: JAI Press.

Black, K. A., & McCartney, K. (1995). *Associations between adolescent attachment to parents and peer interactions.* Paper presented at the biennial meetings of the Society for Research in Child Development, Indianapolis, March.

Blackman, J. A. (1990). Update on AIDS, CMV, and herpes in young children: Health, developmental, and educational issues. In M. Wolraich & D. K. Routh (Eds.), *Advances in developmental and behavioral pediatrics* (Vol. 9) (pp. 33–58). London: Jessica Kingsley Publishers.

Blake, I. K. (1994). Language development and socialization in young African-American children. In P. M. Greenfield & R. R. Cocking (Eds.), *Cross-cultural roots of minority child development* (pp. 167–195). Hillsdale, NJ: Erlbaum.

Blair, S. L., & Johnson, M. P. (1992). Wives' perceptions of the fairness of the division of household labor: The intersection of housework and ideology. *Journal of Marriage and the Family, 54,* 570–581.

Blair, S. N., Kohl, H. W., III, Barlow, C. E., Paffenbarger, R. S., Gibbons, L. W., & Macera, C. A. (1995). Changes in physical fitness and all-cause mortality. *Journal of the American Medical Association, 273,* 1093–1098.

Blair, S. N., Kohl, H. W., Gordon, N. F., & Paffenbarger, R. S., Jr. (1992). How much physical activity is good for health? *Annual Review of Public Health, 13,* 99–126.

Blakeslee, S. (April 13, 1994). A genetic factor may help to explain variations in lung cancer rates. *New York Times,* p. B10.

Blatter, D. D., Bigler, E. D., Gale, S. D., Johnson, S. C., Anderson, C. V., Burnett, B. M., Parker, N., Kurth, S., & Horn, S. (1995). Quantitative volumetric analysis of brain MR: Normative database spanning five decades (16–65). *American Journal of Neuroradiology, 16,* 241–251.

Blau, F. D., & Ferber, M. A. (1991). Career plans and expectations of young women and men: The earnings gap and labor force participation. *The Journal of Human Resources, 26,* 581–607.

Blazer, D., Burchett, B., Service, C., & George, L. K. (1991). The association of age and depression among the elderly: An epidemiologic exploration. *Journals of Gerontology: Medical Sciences, 46,* M210–215.

Blieszner, R., & Adams, R. G. (1992). *Adult friendship.* Newbury Park, CA: Sage.

Block, J. (1971). *Lives through time.* Berkeley, CA: Bancroft.

Block, J., & Robins, R. W. (1993). A longitudinal study of consistency and change in self-esteem from early adolescence to early adulthood. *Child Development, 64,* 909–923.

Bloom, B. L., White, S. W., & Asher, S. J. (1979). Marital disruption as a stressful life event. In C. Levinger & O. C. Moles (Eds.), *Divorce and separation: Context, causes, and consequences* (pp. 184–200). New York: Basic Books.

Bloom, L. (1973). *One word at a time.* The Hague: Mouton.

Bloom, L. (1991). *Language development from two to three.* Cambridge, England: Cambridge University Press.

Bloom, L. (1993). *The transition from infancy to language: Acquiring the power of expression.* Cambridge, England: Cambridge University Press.

Blumberg, J. B. (1996). Status and functional impact of nutrition in older adults. In E. L. Schneider & J. W. Rowe (Eds.), *Handbook of the biology of aging* (4th ed.) (pp. 393–414). San Diego, CA: Academic Press.

Blumenthal, J. A., Emery, C. F., Madden, D. J., Schniebolk, S., Walsh-Riddle, M., George, L. K., McKee, D. C., Higginbotham, M. B., Cobb, R. R., & Coleman, R. E. (1991). Long-term effects of exercise on physiological functioning in older men and women. *Journals of Gerontology: Psychological Sciences, 46,* P352–361.

Blumstein, P., & Schwartz, P. (1983). *American couples.* New York: Morrow.

Bolger, K. E., Patterson, C. J., Thompson, W. W., & Kupersmidt, J. B. (1995). Psychosocial adjustment among children experiencing persistent and intermittent family economic hardship. *Child Development, 66,* 1107–1129.

Bond, J., & Coleman, P. (Eds.). (1990). *Aging in society.* London: Sage.

Bond, M. H., Nakazato, H., & Shiraishi, D. (1975). Universality and distinctiveness in dimensions of Japanese person perception. *Journal of Cross-Cultural Psychology, 6,* 346–357.

Booth, A. (Ed.). (1992). *Child care in the 1990s: Trends and consequences.* Hillsdale, NJ: Erlbaum.

Booth-Kewley, S., & Friedman, H. S. (1987). Psychological predictors of heart disease: A quantitative review. *Psychological Bulletin, 101,* 343–362.

Borkenau, P., & Ostendorf, F. (1990). Comparing exploratory and confirmatory factor analysis: A study on the five-factor model of personality. *Personality and Individual Differences, 11,* 515–524.

Bornstein, M. H. (1987). Sensitive periods in development: Definition, existence, utility, and meaning. In M. H. Bornstein (Ed.), *Sensitive periods in development: Interdisciplinary perspectives* (pp. 3—18). Hillsdale, NJ: Erlbaum.

Bornstein, M. H. (1992). Perception across the life span. In M. H. Bornstein & M. E. Lamb (Eds.), *Developmental psychology: An advanced textbook* (3rd ed.) (pp. 155–210). Hillsdale, NJ: Erlbaum.

Bornstein, M. H., Tal, J., & Tamis-LeMonda, C. S. (1991). Parenting in cross-cultural perspective: The United States, France, and Japan. In M. H. Bornstein (Ed.), *Cultural approaches to parenting* (pp. 69–90). Hillsdale, NJ: Erlbaum.

Bornstein, M. H., Tamis-LeMonda, C. S., Tal, J., Ludemann, P., Toda, S., Rahn, C. W., Pecheux, M., Azuma, H., & Vardi, D. (1992). Maternal responsiveness to infants in three societies: The United States, France, and Japan. *Child Development, 63,* 808–821.

Bossé, R., Aldwin, C. M., Levenson, M. R., & Workman-Daniels, K. (1991). How stressful is retirement? Findings from the normative aging study. *Journals of Gerontology: Psychological Sciences, 46,* P9–14.

Boston Women's Health Collective (1992). *The new our bodies, ourselves: A book by and for women.* New York: Simon & Schuster.

Botwinick, J., & Storandt, M. (1974). *Memory, related functions and age.* Springfield, IL: Charles C. Thomas.

Bouchard, T. J., Jr. (1984). Twins reared apart and together: What they tell us about human diversity. In S. Fox (Ed.), *The chemical and biological bases of individuality* New York: Plenum Press.

Bouchard, T. J., Jr., & McGue, M. (1981). Familial studies of intelligence: A review. *Science, 212,* 1055–1059.

Boukydis, C. F. Z., & Burgess, R. L. (1982). Adult physiological response to infant cries: Effects of temperament, parental status, and gender. *Child Development, 53,* 1291–1298.

Bowerman, M. (1985). Beyond communicative adequacy: From piecemeal knowledge to an integrated system in the child's acquisition of language. In K. E. Nelson (Ed.), *Children's language* (Vol. 5) (pp. 369–398). Hillsdale, NJ: Erlbaum.

Bowlby, J. (1969). *Attachment and loss: Vol. 1. Attachment.* New York: Basic Books.

Bowlby, J. (1973). *Attachment and loss: Vol. 2. Separation, anxiety, and anger.* New York: Basic Books.

Bowlby, J. (1980). *Attachment and loss: Vol. 3. Loss, sadness, and depression.* New York: Basic Books.

Bowlby, J. (1988a). Developmental psychiatry comes of age. *American Journal of Psychiatry, 145,* 1–10.

Bowlby, J. (1988b). *A secure base.* New York: Basic Books.

Bowman, P. J. (1991). Joblessness. In J. J. Jackson (Ed.), *Life in black America* (pp. 156–178). Newbury Park, CA: Sage.

Boyatzis, C. J., Matillo, G., Nesbitt, K., & Cathey, G. (1995). *Effects of "The Mighty Morphin Power Rangers" on children's aggression and prosocial behavior.* Paper presented at the biennial meetings of the Society for Research in Child Development, Indianapolis, March.

Bradbard, M. R., Martin, C. L., Endsley, R. C., & Halverson, C. F. (1986). Influence of sex stereotypes on children's exploration and memory: A competence versus performance distinction. *Developmental Psychology, 22,* 481–486.

Bradley, R. H., Caldwell, B. M., Rock, S. L., Barnard, K. E., Gray, C., Hammond, M. A., Mitchell, S., Siegel, L., Ramey, C. D., Gottfried, A. W., & Johnson, D. L. (1989). Home environment and cognitive development in the first 3 years of life: A collaborative study involving six sites and three ethnic groups in North America. *Developmental Psychology, 25,* 217–235.

Bradley, R. H., Whiteside, L., Mundfrom, D. J., Casey, P. H., Kelleher, K. J., & Pope, S. K. (1994). Early indications of resilience and their relation to experiences in the home environments of low birthweight, premature children living in poverty. *Child Development, 65,* 346–360.

Brandtstädter, J., & Baltes-Götz, B. (1990). Personal control over development and quality of life perspectives in adulthood. In P. Baltes & M. M. Baltes (Eds.), *Successful aging* (pp. 197–224). Cambridge, England: Cambridge University Press.

Brandtstädter, J., & Greve, W. (1994). The aging self: Stabilizing and protective processes. *Developmental Review, 14,* 52–80.

Braveman, N. S. (1987). Immunity and aging immunologic and behavioral perspectives. In M. W. Riley, J. D. Matarazzo, & A. Baum (Eds.), *Perspectives in behavioral medicine: The aging dimension* (pp. 94–124). Hillsdale, NJ: Erlbaum.

Bray, D. W., & Howard, A. (1983). The AT&T longitudinal studies of managers. In K. W. Schaie (Ed.), *Longitudinal studies of adult psychological development* (pp. 266–312). New York: Guilford Press.

Brazelton, T. B. (1984). *Neonatal Behavioral Assessment Scale.* Philadelphia: Lippincott.

Breitmayer, B. J., & Ramey, C. T. (1986). Biological nonoptimality and quality of postnatal environment as codeterminants of intellectual development. *Child Development, 57,* 1151–1165.

Breslau, N., DelDotto, J. E., Brown, G. G., Kumar, S., Ezhuthachan, S., Hufnagle, K. G., & Peterson, E. L. (1994). A gradient relationship between low birth weight and IQ at age 6 years. *Archives of Pediatric and Adolescent Medicine, 2148,* 377–383.

Breslow, L., & Breslow, N. (1993). Health practices and disability: Some evidence from Alameda County. *Preventive Medicine, 22,* 86–95.

Bretherton, I. (1991). Pouring new wine into old bottles: The social self as internal working model. In M. R. Gunnar & L. A. Sroufe (Eds.), *Minnesota Symposia on Child Development* (Vol. 23) (pp. 1–42). Hillsdale, NJ: Erlbaum.

Bretherton, I. (1992a). The origins of attachment theory: John Bowlby and Mary Ainsworth. *Developmental Psychology, 28,* 759–775.

Bretherton, I. (1992b). Attachment and bonding. In V. B. Van Hasselt & M. Hersen (Eds.), *Handbook of social development: A lifespan perspective* (pp. 133–155). New York: Plenum.

Briggs, R. (1990). Biological aging. In J. Bond & P. Coleman (Eds.), *Aging in society* (pp. 48–61). London: Sage.

Brock, D. B., Guralnik, J. M., & Brody, J. A. (1990). Demography and the epidemiology of aging in the United States. In E. L. Schneider & J. W. Rowe (Eds.), *Handbook of the biology of aging* (3rd ed.) (pp. 3–23). San Diego, CA: Academic Press.

Brody, E. M., Litvin, S. J., Albert, S. M., & Hoffman, C. J. (1994). Marital status of daughters and patterns of parent care. *Journals of Gerontology: Social Sciences, 49,* S95–103.

Brody, E. M., Litvin, S. J., Hoffman, C., & Kleban, M. H. (1992). Differential effects of daughters' marital status on their parent care experiences. *The Gerontologist, 32,* 58–67.

Brody, G. H., Stoneman, Z., & Flor, D. (1995). Linking family processes and academic competence among rural African American youths. *Journal of Marriage and the Family, 47,* 567–579.

Brody, G. H., Stoneman, Z., McCoy, J. K., & Forehand, R. (1992). Contemporaneous and longitudinal associations of sibling conflict with family relationship assessments and family discussions about sibling problems. *Child Development, 63,* 391–400.

Brody, J. E. (April 20, 1994). Making a strong case for antioxidants. *New York Times,* p. B9.

Brody, J. E. (October 4, 1995). Personal health. *New York Times,* p. B7.

Brody, J. E. (February 28, 1996). Good habits outweigh genes as key to a healthy old age. *New York Times,* p. B9.

Brody, N. (1992). *Intelligence* (2nd ed.). San Diego, CA: Academic Press.

Bronfenbrenner, U. (1979). *The ecology of human development.* Cambridge, MA: Harvard University Press.

Bronfenbrenner, U. (1989). Ecological systems theory. *Annals of Child Development, 6,* 187–249.

Brooks-Gunn, J. (1987). Pubertal processes and girls' psychological adaptation. In R. M. Lerner & T. T. Foch (Eds.), *Biological-psychosocial interactions in early adolescence* (pp. 123–154). Hillsdale, NJ: Erlbaum.

Brooks-Gunn, J. (1988). Commentary: Developmental issues in the transition to early adolescence. In M. R. Gunnar & W. A. Collins (Eds.), *Minnesota Symposia on Child Psychology* (Vol. 21) (pp. 189–208). Hillsdale, NJ: Erlbaum.

Brooks-Gunn, J. (1995). Children in families in communities: Risk and intervention in the Bronfenbrenner tradition. In P. Moen, G. H. Elder, Jr., & K. Lüscher (Eds.), *Examining lives in context: Perspectives on the ecology of human development* (pp. 467–519). Washington, DC: American Psychological Association.

Brooks-Gunn, J., Guo, G., & Furstenberg, F. F., Jr. (1993). Who drops out of and who continues beyond high school? A 20-year follow-up of black urban youth. *Journal of Research on Adolescence, 3,* 271–294.

Brooks-Gunn, J., & Matthews, W. S. (1979). *He and she: How children develop their sex-role identity.* Englewood Cliffs, NJ: Prentice-Hall.

Brooks-Gunn, J., & Reiter, E. O. (1990). The role of pubertal processes. In S. S. Feldman & G. R. Elliott (Eds.), *At the threshold: The developing adolescent* (pp. 16–53). Cambridge, MA: Harvard University Press.

Brooks-Gunn, J., & Warren, M. P. (1985). The effects of delayed menarche in different contexts: Dance and nondance students. *Journal of Youth and Adolescence, 13,* 285–300.

Broverman, I. K., Broverman, D., Clarkson, F. E., Rosenkrantz, P. S., & Vogel, S. R. (1970). Sex-role stereotypes and clinical judgments of mental health. *Journal of Consulting and Clinical Psychology, 34,* 1–7.

Brown, A. S., Jones, E. M., & Davis, T. L. (1995). Age differences in conversational source monitoring. *Psychology and Aging, 10,* 111–122.

Brown, B. B. (1990). Peer groups and peer cultures. In S. S. Feldman & G. R. Elliott (Eds.), *At the threshold: The developing adolescent* (pp. 171–196). Cambridge, MA: Harvard University Press.

Brown, B. B., Dolcini, M. M., & Leventhal, A. (1995). *The emergence of peer crowds: Friend or foe to adolescent health?* Paper presented at the biennial meetings of the Society for Research in Child Development, Indianapolis, March.

Brown, B. B., & Huang, B. (1995). Examining parenting practices in different peer contexts: Implications for adolescent trajectories. In L. J. Crockett & A. C. Crouter (Eds.), *Pathways through adolescence* (pp. 151–174). Mahwah, NJ: Erlbaum.

Brown, B. B., Mory, M. S., & Kinney, D. (1994). Casting adolescent crowds in a relational perspective: Caricature, channel, and context. In R. Montemayor, G. R. Adams, & T. P. Gullotta (Eds.), *Personal relationships during adolescence* (pp. 123–167). Thousand Oaks, CA: Sage.

Brown, G. W. (1989). Life events and measurement. In G. W. Brown & T. O. Harris (Eds.), *Life events and illness* (pp. 3–45). New York: Guilford Press.

Brown, G. W. (1993). Life events and affective disorder: Replications and limitations. *Psychosomatic Medicine, 55,* 248–259.

Brown, G. W., & Harris, T. (1978). *Social origins of depression.* New York: Free Press.

Brown, L., Karrison, T., & Cibils, L. A. (1994). Mode of delivery and perinatal results in breech presentation. *American Journal of Obstetrics and Gynecology, 171,* 28–34.

Brown, R. (1973). *A first language: The early stages.* Cambridge, MA: Harvard University Press.

Brown, R., & Hanlon, C. (1970). Derivational complexity and order of acquisition. In J. R. Hayes (Ed.), *Cognition and the development of language* (pp. 155–207). New York: Wiley.

Brownell, C. A. (1990). Peer social skills in toddlers: Competencies and constraints illustrated by same-age and mixed-age interaction. *Child Development, 61,* 836–848.

Brubaker, T. H. (1990). Families in later life: A burgeoning research area. *Journal of Marriage and the Family, 52,* 959–981.

Bruck, M., Ceci, S. J., Francoeur, E., & Barr, R. (1995). "I hardly cried when I got my shot!" Influencing children's reports about a visit to their pediatrician. *Child Development, 66,* 193–208.

Bruni, F. (April 3, 1996). A historic shift. Federal ruling allows doctors to prescribe drugs to end life. *New York Times,* pp. A1, C18.

Bryant, P. E., MacLean, M., Bradley, L. L., & Crossland, J. (1990). Rhyme and alliteration, phoneme detection, and learning to read. *Developmental Psychology, 26,* 429–438.

Bryant, S., & Rakowski, W. (1992). Predictors of mortality among elderly African-Americans. *Research on Aging, 14,* 50–67.

Buchanan, C. M., Maccoby, E. E., & Dornbusch, S. M. (1991). Caught between parents: Adolescents' experience in divorced homes. *Child Development, 62,* 1008–1029.

Buchanan, C. M., Maccoby, E. E., & Dornbusch, S. M. (1992). Adolescents and their families after divorce: Three residential arrangements compared. *Journal of Research on Adolescence, 2,* 261–292.

Buchner, D. M., Beresford, S. A. A., Larson, E. B., LaCroix, A. Z., & Wagner, E. H. (1992). Effects of physical activity on health status in older adults II: Intervention studies. *Annual Review of Public Health, 13,* 469–488.

Buehler, J. W., Kaunitz, A. M., Hogue, C. J. R., Hughes, J. M., Smith, J. C., & Rochat, R. W. (1986). Maternal mortality in women aged 35 years or older: United States. *Journal of the American Medical Association, 255,* 53–57.

Buhrmester, D. (1992). The developmental courses of sibling and peer relationships. In F. Boer & J. Dunn (Eds.), *Children's sibling relationships: Developmental and clinical issues.* Hillsdale, NJ: Erlbaum.

Buhrmester, D., & Furman, W. (1990). Perceptions of sibling relationships during middle childhood and adolescence. *Child Development, 61,* 1387–1398.

Bulcroft, R. A., & Bulcroft, K. A. (1991). The nature and functions of dating in later life. *Research on Aging, 13,* 244–260.

Bullock, M., & Lütkenhaus, P. (1990). Who am I? Self-understanding in toddlers. *Merrill-Palmer Quarterly, 36,* 217–238.

Bumpass, L. L., & Aquilino, W. S. (1995). *A social map of midlife: Family and work over the middle life course.* Report of the MacArthur Foundation research network on successful midlife development, Vero Beach, FL.

Bumpass, L. L., & Sweet, J. A. (1989). National estimates of cohabitation. *Demography, 26,* 615–625.

Bumpass, L. L., Sweet, J. A., & Cherlin, A. (1991). The role of cohabitation in declining rates of marriage. *Journal of Marriage and the Family, 53,* 913–927.

Burgess, N. J. (1995). Looking back, looking forward: African American families in sociohistorical perspective. In B. B. Ingoldsby & S. Smith (Eds.), *Families in multicultural perspective* (pp. 321–334). New York: Guilford Press.

Burkhauser, R. V., Butrica, B. A., & Wasylenko, M. J. (1995). Mobility patterns of older home owners. *Research on Aging, 17,* 363–384.

Burkhauser, R. V., Duncan, G. J., & Hauser, R. (1994). Sharing prosperity across the age distribution: A comparison of the United States and Germany in the 1980s. *The Gerontologist, 34,* 150–160.

Burnett, J. W., Anderson, W. P., & Heppner, P. P. (1995). Gender roles and self-esteem: A consideration of environmental factors. *Journal of Counseling and Development, 73,* 323–326.

Burns, A. (1992). Mother-headed families: An international perspective and the case of Australia. *Social Policy Report, Society for Research in Child Development, 6*(1), 1–22.

Burton, L. M., & Bengtson, V. L. (1985). Black grandmothers: Issues of timing and continuity of roles. In V. L. Bengtson & J. F. Robertson (Eds.), *Grandparenthood* (pp. 61–78). Beverly Hills, CA: Sage.

Busch, C. M., Zonderman, A. B., & Costa, P. T., Jr. (1994). Menopausal transition and psychological distress in a nationally representative sample: Is menopause associated with psychological distress? *Journal of Aging and Health, 6,* 209–228.

Buss, A. (1989). Temperaments as personality traits. In G. A. Kohnstamm, J. E. Bates, & M. K. Rothbart (Eds.), *Temperament in childhood* (pp. 49–58). Chichester, England: Wiley.

Buss, A. H., & Plomin, R. (1984). *Temperament: Early developing personality traits.* Hillsdale, NJ: Erlbaum.

Buss, A. H., & Plomin, R. (1986). The EAS approach to temperament. In R. Plomin & J. Dunn (Eds.), *The study of temperament: Changes, continuities and challenges* (pp. 67–80). Hillsdale, NJ: Erlbaum.

Busse, E. W., & Wang, H. S. (1971). *The multiple factors contributing to dementia in old age.* Proceedings of the Fifth World Congress of Psychiatry, Mexico City. (Reprinted in E. Palmore [Ed.], *Normal aging II* [pp. 151–159]. Durham, NC: Duke University Press, 1974.)

Butler, R. N. (1963). The life review: An interpretation of reminiscence in the aged. *Psychiatry, 256,* 65–76.

Byrnes, J. P., & Takahira, S. (1993). Explaining gender differences on SAT-Math items. *Developmental Psychology, 29,* 805–810.

Cairns, R. B., & Cairns, B. D. (1994). *Lifelines and risks: Pathways of youth in our time.* Cambridge, England: Cambridge University Press.

California Achievement Program (1980). *Student achievement in California schools: 1979–1980 annual report: Television and student achievement.* Sacramento: California State Department of Education.

Call, V., Sprecher, S., & Schwartz, P. (1995). The incidence and frequency of marital sex in a national sample. *Journal of Marriage and the Family, 57,* 639–652.

Campbell, A. (1981). *The sense of well-being in America.* New York: McGraw-Hill.

Campbell, D. W., & Eaton, W. O. (1995). *Sex differences in the activity level in the first year of life: A meta-analysis.* Paper presented at the biennial meetings of the Society for Research in Child Development, Indianapolis, March.

Campbell, F. A., & Ramey, C. T. (1994). Effects of early intervention on intellectual and academic achievement: A follow-up study of children from low-income families. *Child Development, 65,* 684–698.

Campbell, S. B., Cohn, J. F., Flanagan, C., Popper, S., & Meyers, T. (1992). Course and correlates of postpartum depression during the transition to parenthood. *Development and Psychopathology, 4,* 29–47.

Campbell, S. B., & Ewing, L. J. (1990). Follow-up of hard-to-manage preschoolers: Adjustment at age 9 and predictors of continuing symptoms. *Journal of Child Psychology and Psychiatry, 31,* 871–889.

Campbell, S. B., Pierce, E. W., March, C. L., & Ewing, L. J. (1991). Noncompliant behavior, overactivity, and family stress as predictors of negative maternal control with preschool children. *Development and Psychopathology, 3,* 175–190.

Campisi, J., Dimri, G., & Hara, E. (1996). Control of replicative senescence. In E. L. Schneider & J. W. Rowe (Eds.), *Handbook of the biology of aging* (4th ed.) (pp. 121–149). San Diego, CA: Academic Press.

Capron, C., & Duyme, M. (1989). Assessment of effects of socio-economic status on IQ in a full cross-fostering study. *Nature, 340,* 552–554.

Capute, A. J., Palmer, F. B., Shapiro, B. K., Wachtel, R. C., Ross, A., & Accardo, P. J. (1984). Primitive reflex profile: A quantification of primitive reflexes in infancy. *Developmental Medicine and Child Neurology, 26,* 375–383.

Carey, R. G. (1974). Living until death: A program of service and research for the terminally ill. *Hospital Progress.* (Reprinted in E. Kübler-Ross [Ed.], *Death. The final stage of growth.* Englewood Cliffs, NJ: Prentice-Hall, 1975.)

Carey, S., & Bartlett, E. (1978). Acquiring a single new word. *Papers and Reports on Child Language Development, 15,* 17–29.

Carlson, E. A., & Sroufe, L. A. (1995). Contribution of attachment theory to developmental psychopathology. In D. Cicchetti & D. J. Conen (Eds.), *Developmental psychopathology: Vol. 1. Theory and methods* (pp. 581–617). New York: Wiley.

Caron, A. J., & Caron, R. F. (1981). Processing of relational information as an index of infant risk. In S. Friedman & M. Sigman (Eds.), *Preterm birth and psychological development* (pp. 219–240). New York: Academic Press.

Carrière, Y., & Pelletier, L. (1995). Factors underlying the institutionalization of elderly persons in Canada. *Journals of Gerontology: Social Sciences, 50B,* S164–S172.

Carstensen, L. L. (1992). Social and emotional patterns in adulthood: Support for socioemotional selectivity theory. *Psychology and Aging, 7,* 331–338.

Carstensen, L. L. (1995). Evidence for a life-span theory of socioemotional selectivity. *Current Directions in Psychological Science, 4,* 151–156.

Carstensen, L. L., Gottman, J. M., & Levenson, R. W. (1995). Emotional behavior in long-term marriage. *Psychology and Aging, 10,* 149–149.

Carver, R. P. (1990). Intelligence and reading ability in grades 2–12. *Intelligence, 14,* 449–455.

Casas, J. F., & Mosher, M. (1995). *Relational and overt aggression in preschool: "You can't come to my birthday party unless . . ."* Paper presented at the biennial meetings of the Society for Research in Child Development, Indianapolis, March.

Case, R. (1985). *Intellectual development: Birth to adulthood.* New York: Academic Press.

Case, R. (1991). Stages in the development of the young child's first sense of self. *Developmental Review, 11,* 210–230.

Case, R. B., Moss, A. J., Case, N., McDermott, M., & Eberly, S. (1992). Living alone after myocardial infarction: Impact on prognosis. *Journal of the American Medical Association, 267,* 515–519.

Casey, M. B., Nuttall, R., Pezaris, E., & Benbow, C. P. (1995). Influence of spatial ability on gender differences in mathematics college entrance test scores across diverse samples. *Developmental Psychology, 31,* 697–705.

Caspi, A., Bem, D. J., & Elder, G. H., Jr. (1989). Continuities and consequences of interactional styles across the life course. *Journal of Personality, 57,* 375–406.

Caspi, A., & Elder, G. H., Jr. (1988). Childhood precursors of the life course: Early personality and life disorganization. In E. M. Hetherington, R. M. Lerner, & M. Perlmutter (Eds.), *Child development in life-span perspective* (pp. 115–142). Hillsdale, NJ: Erlbaum.

Caspi, A., Elder, G. H., Jr., & Bem, D. J. (1987). Moving against the world: Life-course patterns of explosive children. *Developmental Psychology, 23,* 308–313.

Caspi, A., Elder, G. H., Jr., & Bem, D. J. (1988). Moving away from the world: Life-course patterns of shy children. *Developmental Psychology, 24,* 824–831.

Caspi, A., Henry, B., McGee, R. O., Moffitt, T. E., & Silva, P. A. (1995). Temperamental origins of child and adolescent behavior problems: From age three to age fifteen. *Child Development, 66,* 55–68.

Caspi, A., Lynam, D., Moffitt, T. E., & Silva, P. A. (1993). Unraveling girls' delinquency: Biological, dispositional, and contextual contributions to adolescent misbehavior. *Developmental Psychology, 29,* 19–30.

Caspi, A., & Moffitt, T. E. (1991). Individual differences are accentuated during periods of social change: The sample case of girls at puberty. *Journal of Personality and Social Psychology, 61,* 157–168.

Cassidy, J., & Berlin, L. J. (1994). The insecure/ambivalent pattern of attachment: Theory and research. *Child Development, 65,* 971–991.

Cassileth, B. R., Walsh, W. P., & Lusk, E. J. (1988). Psychosocial correlates of cancer survival: A subsequent report 3 to 8 years after cancer diagnosis. *Journal of Clinical Oncology, 6,* 1753–1759.

Cate, R. M., & Lloyd, S. A. (1992). *Courtship.* Newbury Park, CA: Sage.

Cattell, R. B. (1963). Theory of fluid and crystallized intelligence: A critical experiment. *Journal of Educational Psychology, 54,* 1–22.

Caughy, M. O., DiPietro, J. A., & Strobino, D. M. (1994). Day-care participation as a protective factor in the cognitive development of low-income children. *Child Development, 65,* 457–471.

Cauley, J. A., Seeley, D. G., Ensrud, K., Ettinger, B., Black, D., & Cummings, S. R. (1995). Estrogen replacement therapy and fractures in older women. *Annals of Internal Medicine, 122,* 9–16.

Ceci, S. J., & Bruck, M. (1993). Suggestibility of the child witness: A historical review and synthesis. *Psychological Bulletin, 113,* 403–439.

Center for Educational Statistics (1987). *Who drops out of high school? From high school and beyond.* Washington, DC: Office of Educational Research and Improvement, U.S. Department of Education.

Centers for Disease Control (1992). Pregnancy risks determined from birth certificate data—United States, 1989. *Morbidity and Mortality Weekly Report, 41*(30), 556–563.

Centers for Disease Control (1993a). Rates of cesarean delivery—United States, 1991. *Journal of the American Medical Association, 269*(18), 2360.

Centers for Disease Control (1993b). Childbearing patterns among selected racial/ethnic minority groups—United States, 1990. *Morbidity and Mortality Weekly Reports, 42,* 399–403.

Centers for Disease Control (1994a). Programs for the prevention of suicide among adolescents and young adults. *Morbidity and Mortality Weekly Reports, 43*(RR-6, April 22), 3–7.

Centers for Disease Control (1994b). Recommendations of the U.S. Public Health Service task force on the use of zidovudine to reduce perinatal transmission of human immunodeficiency virus. *Morbidity and Mortality Weekly Report, 43*(August 5), 1–20.

Centers for Disease Control (1994c). Preventing tobacco use among young people. A report of the Surgeon General. Executive summary. *Morbidity and Mortality Weekly Report, 43*(RR-4), 2–10.

Centers for Disease Control (1994d). Health-risk behaviors among persons aged 12–21 years—United States, 1992. *Morbidity and Mortality Weekly Report, 43,* 231–235.

Centers for Disease Control (1994e). Prevalence of overweight among adolescents—United States, 1988–91. *Morbidity and Mortality Weekly Reports, 43,* 818–811.

Centers for Disease Control (1994f). Prevalence of adults with no known major risk factors for coronary heart disease—behavioral risk factor surveillance system, 1992. *Morbidity and Mortality Weekly Reports, 43,* 61–69.

Centerwall, B. S. (1989). Exposure to television as a cause of violence. In G. Comstock (Ed.), *Public communication and behavior* (pp. 1–58). San Diego, CA: Academic Press.

Centerwall, B. S. (1992). Television and violence. The scale of the problem and where to go from here. *Journal of the American Medical Association, 267*(22), 3059–3063.

Cernoch, J. M., & Porter, R. H. (1985). Recognition of maternal axillary odors by infants. *Child Development, 56,* 1593–1598.

Chang, L., & Murray, A. (1995). *Math performance of 5- and 6-year-olds in Taiwan and the U.S.: Maternal beliefs, expectations, and tutorial assistance.* Paper presented at the biennial meetings of the Society for Research in Child Development, Indianapolis, March.

Charman, T., Redfern, S., & Fonagy, P. (1995). *Individual differences in theory of mind acquisition: The role of attachment security.* Paper presented at the biennial meetings of the Society for Research in Child Development, Indianapolis, March.

Chase-Lansdale, P. L., Cherlin, A. J., & Kiernan, K. E. (1995). The long-term effects of parental divorce on the mental health of young adults: A developmental perspective. *Child Development, 66,* 1614–1634.

Chase-Lansdale, P. L., & Hetherington, E. M. (1990). The impact of divorce on life-span development: Short and long term effects. In P. B. Baltes, D. L. Featherman, & R. M. Lerner (Eds.), *Life-span development and behavior* (Vol. 10) (pp. 107–151). Hillsdale, NJ: Erlbaum.

Chatters, L. M. (1991). Physical health. In J. S. Jackson (Ed.), *Life in black America* (pp. 199–220). Newbury Park, CA: Sage.

Chen, X., Rubin, K. H., & Li, Z. (1995). Social functioning and adjustment in Chinese children: A longitudinal study. *Developmental Psychology, 31,* 531–539.

Chen, X., Rubin, K. H., & Sun, Y. (1992). Social reputation and peer relationships in Chinese and Canadian children: A cross-cultural study. *Child Development, 63,* 1336–1343.

Cherlin, A. J. (1992a). *Marriage, divorce, remarriage.* Cambridge, MA: Harvard University Press.

Cherlin, A. J. (1992b). Infant care and full-time employment. In A. Booth (Ed.), *Child care in the 1990s: Trends and consequences* (pp. 209–214). Hillsdale, NJ: Erlbaum.

Cherlin, A., & Furstenberg, F. F. (1986). *The new American grandparent.* New York: Basic Books.

Chess, S., & Thomas, A. (1984). *Origins and evolution of behavior disorders: Infancy to early adult life.* New York: Brunner/Mazel.

Chi, M. T. (1978). Knowledge structure and memory development. In R. S. Siegler (Ed.), *Children's thinking: What develops?* (pp. 73–96). Hillsdale, NJ: Erlbaum.

Chiriboga, D. A. (1989). Mental health at the midpoint: Crisis, challenge, or relief? In S. Hunter & M. Sundel (Eds.), *Midlife myths: Issues, findings, and practice implications* (pp. 116–144). Newbury Park, CA: Sage.

Chisholm, J. S. (1989). Biology, culture, and the development of temperament: A Navaho example. In J. K. Nugent, B. M. Lester, & T. B. Brazelton (Eds.), *The cultural context of infancy: Vol. 1. Biology, culture, and infant development* Norwood, NJ: Ablex.

Choi, N. G. (1991). Racial differences in the determinants of living arrangements of widowed and divorced elderly women. *The Gerontologist, 31,* 496–504.

Chomsky, N. (1965). *Aspects of a theory of syntax.* Cambridge, MA: MIT Press.

Chomsky, N. (1975). *Reflections on language.* New York: Pantheon.

Chomsky, N. (1986). *Knowledge of language: Its nature, origin, and use.* New York: Praeger.

Chomsky, N. (1988). *Language and problems of knowledge.* Cambridge, MA: MIT Press.

Christensen, K. J., Moye, J., Armson, R. R., & Kern, T. M. (1992). Health screening and random recruitment for cognitive aging research. *Psychology and Aging, 7,* 204–208.

Christophersen, E. R. (1989). Injury control. *American Psychologist, 44,* 237–241.

Chumlea, W. C. (1982). Physical growth in adolescence. In B. B. Wolman (Ed.), *Handbook of developmental psychology* (pp. 471–485). Englewood Cliffs, NJ: Prentice-Hall.

Cicchetti, D., & Barnett, D. (1991). Attachment organization in maltreated preschoolers. *Development and Psychopathology, 3,* 397–411.

Cicirelli, V. G. (1982). Sibling influence throughout the lifespan. In M. E. Lamb & B. Sutton-Smith (Eds.), *Sibling relationships* (pp. 267–304). Hillsdale, NJ: Erlbaum.

Cicirelli, V. G. (1989). Feelings of attachment to siblings and well-being in later life. *Psychology and Aging, 4,* 211–216.

Cicirelli, V. G. (1991). Attachment theory in old age: Protection of the attached figure. In K. Pillemer & K. McCargner (Eds.), *Parent-child relationships throughout life* (pp. 25–42). Hillsdale, NJ: Erlbaum.

Cillessen, A. H. N., van IJzendoorn, H. W., van Lieshout, C. F. M., & Hartup, W. W. (1992). Heterogeneity among peer-rejected boys: Subtypes and stabilities. *Child Development, 63,* 893–905.

Clark, E. V. (1975). Knowledge, context, and strategy in the acquisition of meaning. In D. P. Date (Ed.), *Georgetown University round table on language and linguistics.* Washington, DC: Georgetown University Press.

Clark, E. V. (1983). Meanings and concepts. In J. H. Flavell & E. M. Markman (Eds.), *Handbook of child psychology: Cognitive development* (Vol. 3) (pp. 787–840). New York: Wiley.

Clark, E. V. (1990). On the pragmatics of contrast. *Journal of Child Language, 41,* 417–431.

Clarke-Stewart, A. (1990). "The 'effects' of infant day care reconsidered" reconsidered: Risks for parents, children, and researchers. In N. Fox & G. G. Fein (Eds.), *Infant day care: The current debate* (pp. 61–86). Norwood, NJ: Ablex.

Clarke-Stewart, A. (1992). Consequences of child care for children's development. In A. Booth (Ed.), *Child care in the 1990s: Trends and consequences* (pp. 63–82). Hillsdale, NJ: Erlbaum.

Clarke-Stewart, K. A., Gruber, C. P., & Fitzgerald, L. M. (1994). *Children at home and in day care.* Hillsdale, NJ: Erlbaum.

Clarkson-Smith, L., & Hartley, A. A. (1989). Relationships between physical exercise and cognitive abilities in older adults. *Psychology and Aging, 4,* 183–189.

Clarkson-Smith, L., & Hartley, A. A. (1990). The game of bridge as an exercise in working memory and reasoning. *Journals of Gerontology: Psychological Sciences, 45,* P233–238.

Clay, M. M. (1979). *The early detection of reading difficulties.* Portsmouth, NH: Heinemann.

Clemens, A. W., & Axelson, L. J. (1985). The not-so-empty-nest: The return of the fledgling adult. *Family Relations, 34,* 259–264.

Cnattingius, S., Berendes, H. W., & Forman, M. R. (1993). Do delayed childbearers face increased risks of adverse pregnancy outcomes after the first birth? *Obstetrics and Gynecology, 81,* 512–516.

Coe, C., Hayashi, K. T., & Levine, S. (1988). Hormones and behavior at puberty: Activation or concatenation? In M. R. Gunnar & W. A. Collins (Eds.), *Development during the transition to adolescence: Minnesota Symposia on Child Psychology* (Vol. 21) (pp. 17–42). Hillsdale, NJ: Erlbaum.

Cohen, S. (1991). Social supports and physical health: Symptoms, health behaviors, and infectious disease. In E. M. Cummings, A. L. Greene, & K. H. Karraker (Eds.), *Life-span developmental psychology: Perspectives on stress and coping* (pp. 213–234). Hillsdale, NJ: Erlbaum.

Cohen, S., Kessler, R. C., & Gordon, L. U. (Eds.). (1995). *Measuring stress: A guide for health and social scientists.* New York: Oxford University Press.

Cohen, S., & Wills, T. A. (1985). Stress, social support, and the buffering hypothesis. *Psychological Bulletin, 98,* 310–357.

Cohen, Y. A. (1964). *The transition from childhood to adolescence.* Chicago: Aldine.

Cohn, D. A., Silver, D. H., Cowan, P. A., Cowan, C. P., & Pearson, J. L. (1991). *Working models of childhood attachment and marital relationships.* Paper presented at the biennial meetings of the Society for Research in Child Development, Seattle, April.

Coie, J., Terry, R., Lenox, K., Lochman, J., & Hyman, C. (1995). Childhood peer rejection and aggression as predictors of stable patterns of adolescent disorder. *Development and Psychopathology, 7,* 697–713.

Coie, J. D., & Cillessen, A. H. N. (1993). Peer rejection: Origins and effects on children's development. *Current Directions in Psychological Science, 2,* 89–92.

Coie, J. D., & Kupersmidt, J. B. (1983). A behavioral analysis of emerging social status in boys groups. *Child Development, 54,* 1400–1416.

Coiro, M. J. (1995). *Child behavior problems as a function of marital conflict and parenting.* Paper presented at the biennial meetings of the Society for Research in Child Development, Indianapolis, March.

Colby, A., Kohlberg, L., Gibbs, J., & Lieberman, M. (1983). A longitudinal study of moral judgment. *Monographs of the Society for Research in Child Development, 48*(1–2, Serial No. 200).

Colditz, G. A., Hankinson, S. E., Hunter, D. J., Willett, W. C., Manson, J. E., Stampfer, M. J., Hennekens, C., Rosner, B., & Speizer, F. E. (1995). The use of estrogens and progestins and the risk of breast cancer in postmenopausal women. *New England Journal of Medicine, 332,* 1589–1593.

Cole, D. A. (1991). Change in self-perceived competence as a function of peer and teacher evaluation. *Developmental Psychology, 27,* 682–688.

Cole, M. (1992). Culture in development. In M. H. Bornstein & M. E. Lamb (Eds.), *Developmental psychology: An advanced textbook* (pp. 731–789). Hillsdale, NJ: Erlbaum.

Collaer, M. L., & Hines, M. (1995). Human behavioral sex differences: A role for gonadal hormones during early development? *Psychological Bulletin, 118,* 55–107.

Collet, J. P., Burtin, P., Gillet, J., Bossard, N., Ducruet, T., & Durr, F. (1994). Risk of infectious diseases in children attending different types of day-care setting. Epicreche Research Group. *Respiration, 61,* 16–19.

Collins, W. A. (Ed.). (1984). *Development during middle childhood: The years from six to twelve.* Washington, DC: National Academy Press.

Colombo, J. (1993). *Infant cognition: Predicting later intellectual functioning.* Newbury Park, CA: Sage.

Colton, M., Buss, K., Mangelsdorf, S., Brooks, C., Sorenson, D., Stansbury, K., Harris, M., & Gunnar, M. (1992). *Relations between toddler coping strategies, temperament, attachment and adrenocortical stress responses.* Poster presented at the 8th International Conference on Infant Studies, Miami.

Committee on Infectious Diseases (1996). Recommended childhood immunization schedule. *Pediatrics, 97,* 143–146.

Compas, B. E., Ey, S., & Grant, K. E. (1993). Taxonomy, assessment, and diagnosis of depression during adolescence. *Psychological Bulletin, 114,* 323–344.

Compas, B. E., Hinden, B. R., & Gerhardt, C. A. (1995). Adolescent development: Pathways and processes of risk and resilience. *Annual Review of Psychology, 46,* 265–293.

Comstock, G. (1991). *Television and the American child.* San Diego, CA: Academic Press.

Conger, R. D., Patterson, G. R., & Ge, X. (1995). It takes two to replicate: A mediational model for the impact of parents' stress on adolescent adjustment. *Child Development, 66,* 80–97.

Connidis, I. A. (1994). Sibling support in older age. *Journals of Gerontology: Social Sciences, 49,* S309—317.

Connidis, I. A., & Davies, L. (1992). Confidants and companions: Choices in later life. *Journals of Gerontology: Social Sciences, 47,* S115–122.

Connidis, I. A., & McMullin, J. A. (1993). To have or have not: Parent status and the subjective well-being of older men and women. *The Gerontologist, 33,* 630–636.

Connolly, K., & Dalgleish, M. (1989). The emergence of a tool-using skill in infancy. *Developmental Psychology, 25,* 894–912.

Conrad, M., & Hammen, C. (1989). Role of maternal depression in perceptions of child maladjustment. *Journal of Consulting and Clinical Psychology, 57,* 663–667.

Coombs, R. H. (1991). Marital status and personal well-being: A literature review. *Family Relations, 40,* 97–102.

Cooney, T. M. (1994). Young adults' relations with parents: The influence of recent parental divorce. *Journal of Marriage and the Family, 56,* 45–56.

Cooper, R. P., & Aslin, R. N. (1994). Developmental differences in infant attention to the spectral properties of infant-directed speech. *Child Development, 65,* 1663–1677.

Corbet, A., Long, W., Schumacher, R., Gerdes, J., & Cotton, R. (1995). Double-blind developmental evaluation at 1-year corrected age of 597 premature infants with birth weights from 500 to 1350 grams enrolled in three placebo-controlled trials of prophylactic synthetic surfactant. *Journal of Pediatrics, 126,* S5–12.

Corbett, H. D., & Wilson, B. (1989). Two state minimum competency testing programs and their effects on curriculum and instruction. In R. Stake (Ed.), *Effects of changes in assessment policy: Vol. 1. Advances in program evaluation.* Greenwich, CT: JAI Press.

Corr, C. A. (1991–92). A task-based approach to coping with dying. *Omega, 24,* 81–94.

Corrada, M., Brookmeyer, R., & Kawas, C. (1995). Sources of variability in prevalence rates of Alzheimer's disease. *International Journal of Epidemiology, 24,* 1000–1005.

Corso, J. F. (1987). Sensory-perceptual processes and aging. In K. W. Schaie (Ed.), *Annual Review of Gerontology and Geriatrics* (Vol. 7) (pp. 29–56). New York: Springer.

Corwin, J., Loury, M., & Gilbert, A. N. (1995). Workplace, age, and sex as mediators of olfactory function: Data from the National Geographic smell survey. *Journals of Gerontology: Psychological Sciences, 50B,* P179–186.

Cossette, L., Malcuit, G., & Pomerleau, A. (1991). Sex differences in motor activity during early infancy. *Infant Behavior and Development, 14,* 175–186.

Costa, P. T., Jr., & McCrae, R. R. (1980a). Still stable after all these years: Personality as a key to some issues in adulthood and old age. In P. B. Baltes & O. G. Brim, Jr. (Eds.), *Life-span development and behavior* (pp. 65–102). New York: Academic Press.

Costa, P. T., & McCrae, R. R. (1980b). Influence of extraversion and neuroticism on subjective well-being: Happy and unhappy people. *Journal of Personality and Social Psychology, 38,* 668–678.

Costa, P. T., Jr., & McCrae, R. R. (1988). Personality in adulthood: A six-year longitudinal study of self-reports and spouse ratings on the NEO personality inventory. *Journal of Personality and Social Psychology, 54,* 853–863.

Costa, P. T., Jr., & McCrae, R. R. (1994a). Set like plaster? Evidence for the stability of adult personality. In T. F. Hetherton & J. L. Weinberger (Eds.), *Can personality change?* (pp. 21–40). Washington, DC: American Psychological Association.

Costa, P. T., Jr., & McCrae, R. R. (1994b). Stability and change in personality from adolescence through adulthood. In C. F. Halverson, Jr., G. A. Kohnstamm, & R. P. Martin (Eds.), *The developing structure of temperament and personality from infancy to adulthood* (pp. 139–150). Hillsdale, NJ: Erlbaum.

Costa, P. T., Jr., McCrae, R. R., Zonderman, A. B., Barbano, H. E., Lebowitz, B., & Larson, D. M. (1986). Cross-sectional studies of personality in a national sample: 2. Stability in neuroticism, extraversion, and openness. *Psychology and Aging, 1,* 144–149.

Cotman, C. W., & Neeper, S. (1996). Activity-dependent plasticity and the aging brain. In E. L. Schneider & J. W. Rowe (Eds.), *Handbook of the biology of aging* (4th ed.) (pp. 284–299). San Diego, CA: Academic Press.

Coulton, C. J., Korbin, J. E., Su, M., & Chow, J. (1995). Community level factors and child maltreatment rates. *Child Development, 66,* 1262–1276.

Counts, D. R. (1976–77). The good death in Kaliai: Preparation for death in western New Britain. *Omega, 7,* 367–372.

Cowan, B. R., & Underwood, M. K. (1995). *Sugar and spice and everything nice? A developmental investigation of social aggression among girls.* Paper presented at the biennial meetings of the Society for Research in Child Development, Indianapolis, March.

Cowan, C. P., & Cowan, P. A. (1987). Men's involvement in parenthood: Identifying the antecedents and understanding the barriers. In P. W. Berman & F. A. Pedersen (Eds.), *Men's transitions to parenthood: Longitudinal studies of early family experience* (pp. 145–174). Hillsdale, NJ: Erlbaum.

Cowan, C. P., Cowan, P. A., Heming, G., & Miller, N. B. (1991). Becoming a family: Marriage, parenting, and child development. In P. A. Cowan & M. Hetherington (Eds.), *Family transitions* (pp. 79–109). Hillsdale, NJ: Erlbaum.

Craik, F. I. M. (1994). Memory changes in normal aging. *Current Directions in Psychological Science, 3,* 155–158.

Craik, F. I. M., & Jennings, J. M. (1992). Human memory. In F. I. M. Craik & T. A. Salthouse (Eds.), *The handbook of aging and cognition* (pp. 51–110). Hillsdale, NJ: Erlbaum.

Crain-Thoreson, C., & Dale, P. S. (1995). *Parent vs. staff storybook reading as an intervention for language delay.* Paper presented at the biennial meetings of the Society for Research in Child Development, Indianapolis, March.

Cramer, D. (1991). Type A behavior pattern, extraversion, neuroticism and psychological distress. *British Journal of Medical Psychology, 64,* 73–83.

Cratty, B. (1979). *Perceptual and motor development in infants and children* (2nd ed.). Englewood Cliffs, NJ: Prentice-Hall.

Crick, N. R., & Grotpeter, J. K. (1995). Relational aggression, gender, and social-psychological adjustment. *Child Development, 66,* 710–722.

Crimmins, E. M., & Ingegneri, D. G. (1990). Interaction and living arrangements of older parents and their children. *Research on Aging, 12,* 3–35.

Crittenden, P. M. (1992). Quality of attachment in the preschool years. *Development and Psychopathology, 4,* 209–241.

Crittenden, P. M., Partridge, M. F., & Claussen, A. H. (1991). Family patterns of relationship in normative and dysfunctional families. *Development and Psychopathology, 3,* 491–512.

Crnic, K. A., Greenberg, M. T., Ragozin, A. S., Robinson, N. M., & Basham, R. B. (1983). Effects of stress and social support on mothers and premature and full-term infants. *Child Development, 54,* 209–217.

Crockenberg, S., & Litman, C. (1990). Autonomy as competence in 2-year-olds: Maternal correlates of child defiance, compliance, and self-assertion. *Developmental Psychology, 26,* 961–971.

Crockenberg, S. B. (1981). Infant irritability, mother responsiveness, and social support influences on the security of infant-mother attachment. *Child Development, 52,* 857–865.

Crockett, L. J., & Crouter, A. C. (Eds.). (1995). *Pathways through adolescence.* Mahwah, NJ: Erlbaum.

Crohan, S. E., & Antonucci, T. C. (1989). Friends as a source of social support in old age. In R. G. Adams & R. Blieszner (Eds.), *Older adult friendship* (pp. 129–146). Newbury Park, CA: Sage.

Cromer, R. F. (1991). *Language and thought in normal and handicapped children.* Oxford, England: Blackwell.

Crouter, A. C., & McHale, S. M. (1993). Familial economic circumstances: Implications for adjustment and development in early adolescence. In R. M. Lerner (Ed.), *Early adolescence. Perspectives on research, policy, and intervention* (pp. 71–91). Hillsdale, NJ: Erlbaum.

Crowell, J. A., & Feldman, S. S. (1988). Mothers' internal models of relationships and children's behavioral and developmental status: A study of mother-child interaction. *Child Development, 50,* 1273–1285.

Crowell, J. A., & Feldman, S. S. (1991). Mothers' working models of attachment relationships and mother and child behavior during separation and reunion. *Developmental Psychology, 27,* 597–605.

Crowell, J. A., & Waters, E. (1995). *Is the parent-child relationship prototype of later love relationships? Studies of attachment and working models of attachment.* Paper presented at the biennial meetings of the Society for Research in Child Development, Indianapolis, March.

Crystal, S., Shae, D., & Krishnaswami, S. (1992). Educational attainment, occupational history, and stratification: Determinants of later-life economic outcomes. *Journals of Gerontology: Social Sciences, 47,* S213–221.

Csikszentmihalyi, M., & Rathunde, K. (1990). The psychology of wisdom: An evolutionary interpretation. In R. Sternberg (Ed.), *Wisdom: Its nature, origins, and development* (pp. 25–51). Cambridge, England: Cambridge University Press.

Cuba, L., & Longino, C. F., Jr. (1991). Regional retirement migration: The case of Cape Cod. *Journals of Gerontology: Social Sciences, 46,* S33–42.

Cumming, E. (1975). Engagement with an old theory. *International Journal of Aging and Human Development, 6,* 187–191.

Cumming, E., & Henry, W. E. (1961). *Growing old.* New York: Basic Books.

Cummings, E. M., & Davies, P. T. (1994). Maternal depression and child development. *Journal of Child Psychology and Psychiatry, 35,* 73–112.

Cummings, E. M., Hollenbeck, B., Iannotti, R., Radke-Yarrow, M., & Zahn-Waxler, C. (1986). Early organization of altruism and aggression: Developmental patterns and individual differences. In C. Zahn-Waxler, E. M. Cummings, & R. Iannotti (Eds.), *Altruism and aggression* (pp. 165–188). Cambridge, England: Cambridge University Press.

Cunningham, A. S., Jelliffe, D. B., & Jelliffe, E. F. P. (1991). Breastfeeding and health in the 1980s: A global epidemiologic review. *Journal of Pediatrics, 118,* 659–666.

Cunningham, J. D., & Antill, J. K. (1984). Changes in masculinity and femininity across the family life cycle: A reexamination. *Developmental Psychology, 20,* 1135–1141.

Cunningham, W. R., & Haman, K. L. (1992). Intellectual functioning in relation to mental health. In J. E. Birren, R. B. Sloane, & G. D. Cohen (Eds.), *Handbook of mental health and aging* (2nd ed.) (pp. 340–355). San Diego, CA: Academic Press.

Cutler, W. B., & Garcia, C. (1993). *Menopause: A guide for women and those who love them.* New York: Norton.

Dalsky, G. P., Stocke, K. S., Ehsani, A. A., Slatopolsky, E., Waldon, C. L., & Birge, S. J. (1988). Weight-bearing exercise training and lumbar bone mineral content in postmenopausal women. *Annals of Internal Medicine, 108,* 824–828.

D'Alton, M. E., & DeCherney, A. H. (1993). Prenatal diagnosis. *New England Journal of Medicine, 328,* 114–118.

Daly, L. E., Kirke, P. N., Molloy, A., Weir, D. G., & Scott, J. M. (1995). Folate levels and neural tube defects: Implications for prevention. *Journal of the American Medical Association, 274,* 1698–1702.

Damon, W. (1977). *The social world of the child.* San Francisco: Jossey-Bass.

Damon, W. (1983). The nature of social-cognitive change in the developing child. In W. F. Overton (Ed.), *The relationship between social and cognitive development* (pp. 103–142). Hillsdale, NJ: Erlbaum.

Damon, W., & Hart, D. (1988). *Self understanding in childhood and adolescence.* New York: Cambridge University Press.

Daniels, P., & Weingarten, K. (1988). The fatherhood clock: The timing of parenthood in men's lives. In P. Bronstein & C. P. Cowan (Eds.), *Fatherhood today: Men's changing role in the family* (pp. 36–52). New York: Wiley-Interscience.

Dannefer, D. (1984a). Adult development and social theory: A paradigmatic reappraisal. *American Sociological Review, 49,* 100–116.

Dannefer, D. (1984b). The role of the social in life-span developmental psychology, past and future: Rejoinder to Baltes and Nesselroade. *American Sociological Review, 49,* 847–850.

Dannefer, D. (1988). What's in a name? An account of the neglect of variability in the study of aging. In J. E. Birren & V. L. Bengtson (Eds.), *Emergent theories of aging* (pp. 356–384). New York: Springer.

Darling-Hammond, L., & Wise, A. E. (1985). Beyond standardization: State standards and school improvement. *Elementary School Journal,* January, 315–336.

Darlington, R. B. (1991). The long-term effects of model preschool programs. In L. Okagaki & R. J. Sternberg (Eds.), *Directors of development* (pp. 203–215). Hillsdale, NJ: Erlbaum.

Davajan, V., & Israel, R. (1991). Diagnosis and medical treatment of infertility. In A. L. Stanton & C. Dunkel-Schetter (Eds.), *Infertility: Perspectives from stress and coping research* (pp. 17–28). New York: Plenum.

Davidson, B., Balswick, J., & Halverson, C. (1983). Affective self-disclosure and marital adjustment: A test of equity theory. *Journal of Marriage and the Family, 45,* 93–103.

Davies, G. M. (1993). Children's memory for other people: An integrative review. In C. A. Nelson (Ed.), *The Minnesota Symposia on Child Psychology* (Vol. 26) (pp. 123–157). Hillsdale, NJ: Erlbaum.

Davis, D. L., Dinse, G. E., & Hoel, D. G. (1994). Decreasing cardiovascular disease and increasing cancer among whites in the United States from 1973 through 1987. *Journal of the American Medical Association, 271,* 431–437.

Davis, S. F., Byers, R. H., Jr., Lindegren, M. L., Caldwell, M. B., Karon, J. M., & Gwinn, M. (1995). Prevalence and incidence of vertically acquired HIV infection in the United States. *Journal of the American Medical Association, 274,* 952–955.

Davis, T. L. (1995). Gender differences in masking negative emotions: Ability or motivation? *Developmental Psychology, 31,* 660–667.

Dawber, T. R., Kannel, W. B., & Lyell, L. P. (1963). An approach to longitudinal studies in a community: The Framingham study. *Annals of the New York Academy of Science, 107,* 539–556.

Dawson, D. A. (1991). Family structure and children's health and well-being: Data from the 1988 National Health Interview Survey on child health. *Journal of Marriage and the Family, 53,* 573–584.

DeCasper, A. J., & Fifer, W. P. (1980). Of human bonding: Newborns prefer their mothers' voices. *Science, 208,* 1174–1176.

DeCasper, A. J., Lecaneut, J., Busnel, M., Granier-Deferre, C., & Maugeais, R. (1994). Fetal reactions to recurrent maternal speech. *Infant Behavior and Development, 17,* 159–164.

DeCasper, A. J., & Spence, M. J. (1986). Prenatal maternal speech influences newborns' perception of speech sounds. *Infant Behavior and Development, 9,* 133–150.

de Chateau, P. (1980). Effects of hospital practices on synchrony in the development of the infant-parent relationship. In P. M. Taylor (Ed.), *Parent-infant relationships* (pp. 137–168). New York: Grune & Stratton.

Deeg, D. J. H., Kardaun, W. P. F., & Fozard, J. L. (1996). Health, behavior, and aging. In J. E. Birren & K. W. Schaie (Eds.), *Handbook of the psychology of aging* (4th ed.) (pp. 129–149). San Diego, CA: Academic Press.

de Graaf, C., Polet, P., & van Staveren, W. A. (1994). Sensory perception and pleasantness of food flavors in elderly subjects. *Journals of Gerontology: Psychological Sciences, 49,* P93–99.

de Haan, M., Luciana, M., Maslone, S. M., Matheny, L. S., & Richards, M. L. M. (1994). Development, plasticity, and risk: Commentary on Huttenlocher, Pollit and Gorman, and Gottesman and Goldsmith. In C. A. Nelson (Ed.), *The Minnesota Symposia on Child Psychology* (Vol. 27) (pp. 161–178). Hillsdale, NJ: Erlbaum.

De Jong, G. F., Wilmoth, J. M., Angel, J. L., & Cornwell, G. T. (1995). Motives and the geographic mobility of very old Americans. *Journals of Gerontology: Social Sciences, 50B,* S395–404.

DeLoache, J. S. (1989). The development of representation in young children. In H. W. Reese (Ed.), *Advances in child development and behavior* (Vol. 22) (pp. 2–37). San Diego, CA: Academic Press.

DeLoache, J. S. (1995). Early understanding and use of symbols: The model model. *Current Directions in Psychological Science, 4,* 109–113.

DeMaris, A., & Leslie, G. R. (1984). Cohabitation with the future spouse: Its influence upon marital satisfaction and communication. *Journal of Marriage and the Family, 46,* 77–84.

DeMaris, A., & Rao, K. V. (1992). Premarital cohabitation and subsequent marital stability in the United States: A reassessment. *Journal of Marriage and the Family, 54,* 178–190.

DeMeis, D. K., Hock, E., & McBride, S. L. (1986). The balance of employment and motherhood: Longitudinal study of mothers' feelings about separation from their first-born infants. *Developmental Psychology, 22,* 627–632.

Dempster, F. N. (1981). Memory span: Sources of individual and developmental differences. *Psychological Bulletin, 89,* 63–100.

Denney, N. W. (1982). Aging and cognitive changes. In B. B. Wolman (Ed.), *Handbook of developmental psychology* (pp. 807–827). Englewood Cliffs, NJ: Prentice-Hall.

Denney, N. W. (1984). Model of cognitive development across the life span. *Developmental Review, 4,* 171–191.

Denney, N. W., & Pearce, K. A. (1989). A developmental study of practical problem solving in adults. *Psychology and Aging, 4,* 438–442.

Denney, N. W., Tozier, T. L., & Schlotthauer, C. A. (1992). The effect of instructions on age differences in practical problem solving. *Journals of Gerontology: Psychological Sciences, 47,* P142–145.

Dennis, W. (1960). Causes of retardation among institutional children: Iran. *Journal of Genetic Psychology, 96,* 47–59.

Den Ouden, L., Rijken, M., Brand, R., Verloove-Vanhorick, S. P., & Ruys, J. H. (1991). Is it correct to correct? Developmental milestones in 555 "normal" preterm infants compared with term infants. *Journal of Pediatrics, 118,* 399—404.

DeSpelder, L. A., & Strickland, A. L. (1983). *The last dance: Encountering death and dying.* Palo Alto, CA: Mayfield.

Detchant, Lord Walton of (1995). Dilemmas of life and death: Part one. *Journal of the Royal Society of Medicine, 88*(311–315).

Deter, H., & Herzog, W. (1994). Anorexia nervosa in a long-term perspective: Results of the Heidelberg-Mannheim study. *Psychosomatic Medicine, 56,* 20–27.

de Villiers, P. A., & de Villiers, J. G. (1992). Language development. In M. H. Bornstein & M. E. Lamb (Eds.), *Developmental psychology: An advanced textbook* (3rd ed.) (pp. 337–418). Hillsdale, NJ: Erlbaum.

The Diagram Group (1977). *Child's body.* New York: Paddington.

Diamond, A. (1991). Neuropsychological insights into the meaning of object concept development. In S. Carey & R. Gelman (Eds.), *The epigenesis of mind: Essays on biology and cognition* (pp. 67–110). Hillsdale, NJ: Erlbaum.

Diener, E. (1984). Subjective well-being. *Psychological Bulletin, 95,* 542–575.

Dietz, W. H., & Gortmaker, S. L. (1985). Do we fatten our children at the television set? Obesity and television viewing in children and adolescents. *Pediatrics, 75,* 807–812.

Digman, J. M. (1990). Personality structure: Emergence of the five-factor model. *Annual Review of Psychology, 41,* 417–440.

Digman, J. M. (1994). Child personality and temperament: Does the five-factor model embrace both domains? In C. F. Halverson, Jr., G. A. Kohnstamm, & R. P. Martin (Eds.), *The developing structure of temperament and personality from infancy to adulthood* (pp. 323–338). Hillsdale, NJ: Erlbaum.

Dindia, K., & Allen, M. (1992). Sex differences in self-disclosure: A meta-analysis. *Psychological Bulletin, 112,* 106–124.

Dishion, T. J., Andrews, D. W., & Crosby, L. (1995). Antisocial boys and their friends in early adolescence: Relationship characteristics, quality, and interactional process. *Child Development, 66,* 139–151.

Dishion, T. J., Capaldi, D., Spracklen, K. M., & Li, F. (1995). Peer ecology of male adolescent drug use. *Development and Psychopathology, 7,* 803–824.

Dishion, T. J., French, D. C., & Patterson, G. R. (1995). The development and ecology of antisocial behavior. In D. Cicchetti & D. J. Cohen (Eds.), *Developmental psychopathology: Vol. 2. Risk, disorder, and adaptation* (pp. 421–471). New York: Wiley.

Dishion, T. J., Patterson, G. R., Stoolmiller, M., & Skinner, M. L. (1991). Family, school, and behavioral antecedents to early adolescent involvement with antisocial peers. *Developmental Psychology, 27,* 172–180.

Dittmann-Kohli, F., Lachman, M. E., Kliegl, R., & Baltes, P. B. (1991). Effects of cognitive training and testing on intellectual efficacy beliefs in elderly adults. *The Journals of Gerontology: Psychological Sciences, 46,* P162–164.

Dockett, S., & Smith, I. (1995). *Children's theories of mind and their involvement in complex shared pretense.* Paper presented at the biennial meetings of the Society for Research in Child Development, Indianapolis, March.

Dodge, K. A. (1983). Behavioral antecedents of peer social status. *Child Development, 54,* 1386–1399.

Dodge, K. A. (1990). Developmental psychopathology in children of depressed mothers. *Developmental Psychology, 26,* 3–6.

Dodge, K. A., Coie, J. D., Pettit, G. S., & Price, J. M. (1990). Peer status and aggression in boys groups: Developmental and contextual analysis. *Child Development, 61,* 1289–1309.

Dodge, K. A., & Feldman, E. (1990). Issues in social cognition and sociometric status. In S. R. Asher & J. D. Coie (Eds.), *Peer rejection in childhood* (pp. 119–155). Cambridge, England: Cambridge University Press.

Dodge, K. A., & Frame, C. L. (1982). Social cognitive biases and deficits in aggressive boys. *Child Development, 53,* 620–635.

Dodge, K. A., Pettit, G. S., & Bates, J. E. (1994). Socialization mediators of the relation between socioeconomic status and child conduct problems. *Child Development, 65,* 649–665.

Dollard, J., Doob, L. W., Miller, N. E., Mowrer, O. H., & Sears, R. R. (1939). *Frustration and aggression.* New Haven, CT: Yale University Press.

Donnerstein, E., Slaby, R. G., & Eron, L. D. (1994). The mass media and youth aggression. In L. D. Eron, J. H. Gentry, & P. Schlegel (Eds.), *Reason to hope: A psychosocial perspective on violence and youth* (pp. 219–250). Washington, DC: American Psychological Association.

Dornbusch, S. M., Ritter, P. L., Liederman, P. H., Roberts, D. F., & Fraleigh, M. J. (1987). The relation of parenting style to adolescent school performance. *Child Development, 58,* 1244–1257.

Doty, R. L., Shaman, P., Appelbaum, S. L., Bigerson, R., Sikorski, L., & Rosenberg, L. (1984). Smell identification ability: Changes with age. *Science, 226,* 1441–1443.

Doyle, A. B., & Aboud, F. E. (1995). A longitudinal study of white children's racial prejudice as a social-cognitive development. *Merrill-Palmer Quarterly, 41,* 209–228.

Dreher, G. F., & Bretz, R. D., Jr. (1991). Cognitive ability and career attainment: Moderating effects of early career success. *Journal of Applied Psychology, 76,* 392–397.

Dryfoos, J. (1990). *Adolescents at risk: Prevalence and prevention.* New York: Oxford University Press.

Duke, P. M., Carlsmith, J. M., Jennings, D., Martin, J. A., Dornbusch, S. M., Gross, R. T., & Siegel-Gorelick, B. (1982). Educational correlates of early and late sexual maturation in adolescence. *Journal of Pediatrics, 100,* 633–637.

Duncan, G. J., Brooks-Gunn, J., & Klebanov, P. K. (1994). Economic deprivation and early childhood development. *Child Development, 65,* 296–318.

Duncan, G. J., & Morgan, J. N. (1985). The panel study of income dynamics. In G. H. Elder, Jr. (Ed.), *Life course dynamics: Trajectories and transitions, 1968–1980* (pp. 50–74). Ithaca, NY: Cornell University Press.

Duncan, R. M. (1995). Piaget and Vygotsky revisited: Dialogue or assimilation? *Developmental Review, 15,* 458–472.

Dunn, J. (1992). Siblings and development. *Current Directions in Psychological Science, 1,* 6–9.

Dunn, J. (1993). *Young children's close relationships.* Newbury Park, CA: Sage.

Dunn, J. (1994). Experience and understanding of emotions, relationships, and membership in a particular culture. In P. Ekman & R. J. Davidson (Eds.), *The nature of emotion: Fundamental questions* (pp. 352–355). New York: Oxford University Press.

Dunn, J., & Kendrick, C. (1982). Siblings and their mothers: Developing relationships within the family. In M. E. Lamb & B. Sutton-Smith (Eds.), *Sibling relationships: Their nature and significance across the lifespan* (pp. 39–60). Hillsdale, NJ: Erlbaum.

Dunn, J., & McGuire, S. (1994). Young children's nonshared experiences: A summary of studies in Cambridge and Colorado. In E. M. Hetherington, D. Reiss, & R. Plomin (Eds.), *Separate social worlds of siblings: The impact of nonshared environment on development* (pp. 111–128). Hillsdale, NJ: Erlbaum.

Dunn, T. R., & Merriam, S. B. (1995). Levinson's age thirty transition: Does it exist? *Journal of Adult Development, 2,* 113–124.

Dunphy, D. C. (1963). The social structure of urban adolescent peer groups. *Sociometry, 26,* 230–246.

Dura, J. R., & Kiecolt-Glaser, J. K. (1991). Family transitions, stress, and health. In P. A. Cowan & M. Hetherington (Eds.), *Family transitions* (pp. 59–76). Hillsdale, NJ: Erlbaum.

Durlak, J. A. (1972). Relationship between attitudes toward life and death among elderly women. *Developmental Psychology, 8,* 146.

Duursma, S. A., Raymakers, J. A., Boereboom, F. T. J., & Scheven, B. A. A. (1991). Estrogen and bone metabolism. *Obstetrical and Gynecological Survey, 47,* 38–44.

Duvall, E. M. (1962). *Family development.* New York: Lippincott.

Dwyer, J. W., & Coward, R. T. (1991). A multivariate comparison of the involvement of adult sons versus daughters in the care of impaired parents. *Journals of Gerontology: Social Sciences, 56,* S259–269.

Dykens, E. M., Hodapp, R. M., & Leckman, J. F. (1994). *Behavior and development in Fragile X syndrome.* Thousand Oaks, CA: Sage.

Dykstra, P. A. (1995). Loneliness among the never and formerly married: The importance of supportive friendships and a desire for independence. *Journals of Gerontology: Social Sciences, 50B,* S321–329.

Eames, M., Ben-Schlomo, Y., & Marmot, M. G. (1993). Social deprivation and premature mortality: Regional comparison across England. *British Medical Journal, 307,* 1097–1102.

Earles, J. L., & Salthouse, T. A. (1995). Interrelations of age, health, and speed. *Journals of Gerontology: Psychological Sciences, 50B,* P33–41.

Easterbrooks, M. A., Davidson, C. E., & Chazan, R. (1993). Psychosocial risk, attachment, and behavior problems among school-aged children. *Development and Psychopathology, 5,* 389–402.

Edwards, J. N. (1969). Familial behavior as social exchange. *Journal of Marriage and the Family, 31,* 518–526.

Eichorn, D. H., Clausen, J. A., Haan, N., Honzik, M. P., & Mussen, P. H. (Eds.). (1981). *Present and past in middle life.* New York: Academic Press.

Eichorn, D. H., Hunt, J. V., & Honzik, M. P. (1981). Experience, personality, and IQ: Adolescence to middle age. In D. H. Eichorn, J. A. Clausen, N. Haan, M. P. Honzik, & P. H. Mussen (Eds.), *Present and past in middle life* (pp. 89–116). New York: Academic Press.

Eisenberg, N. (1992). *The caring child.* Cambridge, MA: Harvard University Press.

Eisenberg, N., Fabes, R. A., Guthrie, I. K., Murphy, B. C., Maszk, P., Holmgren, R., & Suh, K. (1996a). The relations of regulation and emotionality to problem behavior in elementary school children. *Development and Psychopathology, 8,* 141–162.

Eisenberg, N., Fabes, R. A., Murphy, B., Karbon, M., Smith, M., & Maszk, P. (1996b). The relations of children's dispositional empathy-related responding to their emotionality, regulation, and social functioning. *Developmental Psychology, 32,* 195–209.

Eisenberg, N., Fabes, R. A., Murphy, B., Maszk, P., Smith, M., & Karbon, M. (1995). The role of emotionality and regulation in children's social functioning: A longitudinal study. *Child Development, 66,* 1360–1384.

Elder, G. H., Jr. (1974). *Children of the Great Depression.* Chicago: University of Chicago Press.

Elder, G. H., Jr. (1978). Family history and the life course. In T. Hareven (Eds.), *Transitions: The family and the life course in historical perspective* (pp. 17–64). New York: Academic Press.

Elder, G. H., Jr. (1979). Historical change in life patterns and personality. In P. B. Baltes & J. O. G. Brim (Eds.), *Life-span development and behavior* (Vol. 2) (pp. 117–159). New York: Academic Press.

Elder, G. H., Jr. (1986). Military times and turning points in men's lives. *Developmental Psychology, 22,* 233–245.

Elder, G. H., Jr. (1991). Family transitions, cycles, and social change. In P. Cowan & M. Hetherington (Eds.), *Family transitions* (pp. 31–58). Hillsdale, NJ: Erlbaum.

Elder, G. H., Jr., & Caspi, A. (1988). Economic stress in lives: Developmental perspectives. *Journal of Social Issues, 44,* 25–45.

Elder, G. H., Jr., Liker, J. K., & Cross, C. E. (1984). Parent-child behavior in the Great Depression: Life course and intergenerational influences. In P. B. Baltes & O. G. Brim, Jr. (Eds.), *Life-span development and behavior* (Vol 6) (pp. 111–159). New York: Academic Press.

Elkind, D. (1967). Egocentrism in adolescence. *Child Development, 38,* 1025–1034.

Elkind, D., & Bowen, R. (1979). Imaginary audience behavior in children and adolescents. *Developmental Psychology, 15,* 38–44.

Elliott, R. (1988). Tests, abilities, race, and conflict. *Intelligence, 12,* 333–350.

Emde, R. N., Plomin, R., Robinson, J., Corley, R., DeFries, J., Fulker, D. W., Reznick, J. S., Campos, J., Kagan, J., & Zahn-Waxler, C. (1992). Temperament, emotion, and cognition at fourteen months: The MacArthur longitudinal twin study. *Child Development, 63,* 1437–1455.

Emery, C. F., & Gatz, M. (1990). Psychological and cognitive effects of an exercise program for community-residing older adults. *The Gerontologist, 30,* 184–192.

Emery, R. E. (1988). *Marriage, divorce, and children's adjustment.* Newbury Park, CA: Sage.

Entwisle, D. R. (1990). Schools and the adolescent. In S. S. Feldman & G. R. Elliott (Eds.), *At the threshold: The developing adolescent* (pp. 197–224). Cambridge, MA: Harvard University Press.

Entwisle, D. R., & Alexander, K. L. (1990). Beginning school math competence: Minority and majority comparisons. *Child Development, 61,* 454–471.

Entwisle, D. R., & Doering, S. G. (1981). *The first birth.* Baltimore, MD: Johns Hopkins University Press.

Epstein, S. (1991). Cognitive-experiential self theory: Implications for developmental psychology. In M. R. Gunnar & L. A. Sroufe (Eds.), *The Minnesota Symposia on Child Development* (Vol. 23) (pp. 79–123). Hillsdale, NJ: Erlbaum.

Ericsson, K. A. (1990). Peak performance and age: An examination of peak performance in sports. In P. Baltes & M. M. Baltes (Eds.), *Successful aging* (pp. 164–196). Cambridge, MA: Cambridge University Press.

Ericsson, K. A., & Crutcher, R. J. (1990). The nature of exceptional performance. In P. B. Baltes, D. L. Featherman, & R. M. Lerner (Eds.), *Life-span development and behavior* (Vol. 10) (pp. 188–218). Hillsdale, NJ: Erlbaum.

Erikson, E. H. (1950). *Childhood and society.* New York: Norton.

Erikson, E. H. (1959). *Identity and the life cycle.* New York: Norton (reissued, 1980).

Erikson, E. H. (1963). *Childhood and society* (2nd ed.). New York: Norton.

Erikson, E. H. (1964). *Insight and responsibility.* New York: Norton.

Erikson, E. H. (1974). *Dimensions of a new identity: The 1973 Jefferson lectures in the humanities.* New York: Norton.

Erikson, E. H. (1980a). *Identity and the life cycle.* New York: Norton (originally published 1959).

Erikson, E. H. (1980b). Themes of adulthood in the Freud-Jung correspondence. In N. J. Smelser & E. H. Erikson (Eds.), *Themes of work and love in adulthood* (pp. 43–76). Cambridge, MA: Harvard University Press.

Erikson, E. H. (1982). *The life cycle completed.* New York: Norton.

Erikson, E. H., Erikson, J. M., & Kivnick, H. Q. (1986). *Vital involvement in old age.* New York: Norton.

Eron, L. D. (1987). The development of aggressive behavior from the perspective of a developing behaviorism. *American Psychologist, 42,* 435–442.

Eron, L. D. (1992). Testimony before the Senate Committee on Governmental Affairs. *Congressional Record, 88*(June 18), S8538–8539.

Eron, L. D., Gentry, J. H., & Schlegel, P. (Eds.). (1994). *Reason to hope: A psychosocial perspective on violence and youth.* Washington, DC: American Psychological Association.

Eron, L. D., Huesmann, L. R., & Zelli, A. (1991). The role of parental variables in the learning of aggression. In D. J. Pepler & K. H. Rubin (Eds.), *The development and treatment of childhood aggression* (pp. 169–188). Hillsdale, NJ: Erlbaum.

Esbensen, F.-A., & Huizinga, D. (1993). Gangs, drugs, and delinquency in a survey of urban youth. *Criminology, 31,* 565–586.

Eskes, T. K. A. B. (1992). Home deliveries in the Netherlands—perinatal mortality and morbidity. *International Journal of Gynecology and Obstetrics, 38,* 161–169.

Espinosa, M. P., Sigman, M. D., Neumann, C. G., Bwibo, N. O., & McDonald, M. A. (1992). Playground behaviors of school-age children in relation to nutrition, schooling, and family characteristics. *Developmental Psychology, 28,* 1188–1195.

Evans, D. A., Funkenstein, H. H., Albert, M. S., Scherr, P. A., Cook, N. R., Chown, M. J., Hebert, L. E., Hennekens, C. H., & Taylor, J. O. (1989). Prevalence of Alzheimer's disease in a community population of older persons. *Journal of the American Medical Association, 262,* 2551–2556.

Evans, L., Ekerdt, D. J., & Bossé, R. (1985). Proximity to retirement and anticipatory involvement: Findings from the Normative Aging Study. *Journal of Gerontology, 40,* 368–374.

Evans, R. I. (1969). *Dialogue with Erik Erikson.* New York: Dutton.

Fabes, R. A., Knight, G. P., & Higgins, D. A. (1995). *Gender differences in aggression: A meta-analytic reexamination of time and age effects.* Paper presented at the biennial meetings of the Society for Research in Child Development, Indianapolis, March.

Fabrikant, G. (April 8, 1996). The young and restless audience: Computers and videos cut into children's time for watching TV and ads. *New York Times,* p. C1.

Fagan, J. F., III. (1992). Intelligence: A theoretical viewpoint. *Current Directories in Psychological Science, 1,* 82–86.

Fagan, J. F., & Singer, L. T. (1983). Infant recognition memory as a measure of intelligence. In L. P. Lipsett (Ed.), *Advances in infancy research* (Vol. 2) (pp. 31–78). Norwood, NJ: Ablex.

Fagard, J., & Jacquet, A. (1989). Onset of bimanual coordination and symmetry versus asymmetry of movement. *Infant Behavior and Development, 12,* 229–235.

Fagot, B. I., & Hagan, R. (1991). Observations of parent reactions to sex-stereotyped behaviors: Age and sex effects. *Child Development, 62,* 617–628.

Fagot, B. I., & Leinbach, M. D. (1989). The young child's gender schema: Environmental input, internal organization. *Child Development, 60,* 663–672.

Fagot, B. I., & Leinbach, M. D. (1993). Gender-role development in young children: From discrimination to labeling. *Developmental Review, 13,* 205–224.

Fagot, B. I., Leinbach, M. D., & O'Boyle, C. (1992). Gender labeling, gender stereotyping, and parenting behaviors. *Developmental Psychology, 28,* 225–230.

Famularo, R., Stone, K., Barnum, R., & Whatron, R. (1986). Alcoholism and severe child maltreatment. *American Journal of Orthopsychiatry, 56,* 481–485.

Farnham-Diggory, S. (1992). *The learning-disabled child.* Cambridge, MA: Harvard University Press.

Farrar, M. J. (1992). Negative evidence and grammatical morpheme acquisition. *Developmental Psychology, 28,* 90–98.

Farrell, M. P., & Rosenberg, S. D. (1981). *Men at midlife.* Boston: Auburn House.

Farrington, D. P. (1991). Childhood aggression and adult violence: Early precursors and later life outcomes. In D. J. Pepler & K. H. Rubin (Eds.), *The development and treatment of childhood aggression* (pp. 5–30). Hillsdale, NJ: Erlbaum.

Farver, J. M., Kim, Y. K., & Lee, Y. (1995). Cultural differences in Korean- and Anglo-American preschoolers' social interaction and play behaviors. *Child Development, 66,* 1088–1099.

Faust, M. S. (1983). Alternative constructions of adolescent growth. In J. Brooks-Gunn & A. C. Petersen (Eds.), *Girls at puberty: Biological and psychosocial perspectives* (pp. 105–126). New York: Plenum.

Feeney, J. A. (1994). Attachment style, communication patterns, and satisfaction across the life cycle of marriage. *Personal Relationships, 1,* 333–348.

Feifel, H. (1990). Psychology and death. Meaningful rediscovery. *American Psychologist, 45,* 537–543.

Feld, S., & George, L. K. (1994). Moderating effects of prior social resources on the hospitalizations of elders who become widowed. *Aging and Health, 6,* 275–295.

Feldman, H. A., Goldstein, I., Hatzichristou, D. G., Krane, R. J., & McKinlay, J. B. (1994). Impotence and its medical and psychosocial correlates: Results of the Massachusetts male aging study. *The Journal of Urology, 151,* 54–61.

Fennelly, K. (1993). Sexual activity and childbearing among Hispanic adolescents in the United States. In R. M. Lerner (Ed.), *Early adolescence: Perspectives on research, policy, and intervention* (pp. 335–352). Hillsdale, NJ: Erlbaum.

Fenson, L., Dale, P. S., Reznick, J. S., Bates, E., Thal, D. J., & Pethick, S. J. (1994). Variability in early communicative development. *Monographs of the Society for Research in Child Development, 59*(5, Serial No. 242).

Fergusson, D. M., Horwood, L. J., & Lynskey, M. T. (1993). Maternal smoking before and after pregnancy: Effects on behavioral outcomes in middle childhood. *Pediatrics, 92,* 815–822.

Fernald, A., & Kuhl, P. (1987). Acoustic determinants of infant preference for motherese speech. *Infant Behavior and Development, 10,* 279–293.

Feshbach, S. (1970). Aggression. In P. H. Mussen (Ed.), *Carmichael's manual of child psychology* (Vol. 2, 3rd ed.) (pp. 159–260). New York: Wiley.

Fiatarone, M. A., & Evans, W. J. (1993). The etiology and reversibility of muscle dysfunction in the aged. *The Journals of Gerontology, 48*(Special Issue), 77–83.

Field, T. (1990). *Infancy.* Cambridge, MA: Harvard University Press.

Field, T. (1995). Psychologically depressed parents. In M. H. Bornstein (Ed.), *Handbook of parenting: Vol. 4. Applied and practical parenting* (pp. 85–99). Mahwah, NJ: Erlbaum.

Field, T., Healy, B., Goldstein, S., Perry, S., Bendell, D., Schanberg, S., Zimmerman, E. A., & Duhn, C. (1988). Infants of depressed mothers show "depressed" behavior even with nondepressed adults. *Child Development, 59,* 1569–1579.

Field, T. M. (1977). Effects of early separation, interactive deficits, and experimental manipulations on infant-mother face-to-face interaction. *Child Development, 48,* 763–771.

Field, T. M. (1978). Interaction behaviors of primary versus secondary caretaker fathers. *Developmental Psychology, 14,* 183–185.

Field, T. M. (1991). Quality infant day-care and grade school behavior and performance. *Child Development, 62,* 863–870.

Field, T. M., De Stefano, L., & Koewler, J. H. I. (1982). Fantasy play of toddlers and preschoolers. *Developmental Psychology, 18,* 503–508.

Fields, R. B. (1992). Psychosocial response to environment change. In V. B. Van Hasselt & M. Hersen (Eds.), *Handbook of social development: A lifespan perspective* (pp. 503–544). New York: Plenum.

Fields, S. A., & Wall, E. M. (1993). Obstetric analgesia and anesthesia. *Primary Care, 20,* 705–712.

Filsinger, E. E., & Thoma, S. J. (1988). Behavioral antecedents of relationship stability and adjustment: A five-year longitudinal study. *Journal of Marriage and the Family, 50,* 785–795.

Finch, C. E. (1986). Issues in the analysis of interrelationships between the individual and the environment during aging. In A. B. Sørensen, F. E. Weinert, & L. R. Sherrod (Eds.), *Human development and the life course: Multidisciplinary perspectives* (pp. 17–30). Hillsdale, NJ: Erlbaum.

Finn, S. E. (1986). Stability of personality self-ratings over 30 years: Evidence for an age/cohort interaction. *Journal of Personality and Social Psychology, 50,* 813–818.

Fischer, K. W., & Bidell, T. (1991). Constraining nativist inferences about cognitive capacities. In S. Carey & R. Gelman (Eds.), *The epigenesis of mind: Essays on biology and cognition* (pp. 199–236). Hillsdale, NJ: Erlbaum.

Fish, M., Stifter, C. A., & Belsky, J. (1991). Conditions of continuity and discontinuity in infant negative emotionality: Newborn to five months. *Child Development, 62,* 1525–1537.

Fitzpatrick, J. L., & Silverman, T. (1989). Women's selection of careers in engineering: Do traditional-nontraditional differences still exist? *Journal of Vocational Behavior, 34,* 266–278.

Flannery, D. J., Montemayor, R., & Eberly, M. B. (1994). The influence of parent negative emotional expression on adolescents' perceptions of their relationships with their parents. *Personal Relationships, 1,* 259–274.

Flavell, J. H. (1985). *Cognitive development* (2nd ed.). Englewood Cliffs, NJ: Prentice-Hall.

Flavell, J. H. (1986). The development of children's knowledge about the appearance-reality distinction. *American Psychologist, 41,* 418–425.

Flavell, J. H. (1992). Cognitive development: Past, present, and future. *Developmental Psychology, 28,* 998–1005.

Flavell, J. H. (1993). Young children's understanding of thinking and consciousness. *Current Directions in Psychological Science, 2,* 40–43.

Flavell, J. H., Everett, B. A., Croft, K., & Flavell, E. R. (1981). Young children's knowledge about visual perception: Further evidence for the Level 1–Level 2 distinction. *Developmental Psychology, 17,* 99–103.

Flavell, J. H., Green, F. L., & Flavell, E. R. (1989). Young children's ability to differentiate appearance-reality and level 2 perspectives in the tactile modality. *Child Development, 60,* 201–213.

Flavell, J. H., Green, F. L., & Flavell, E. R. (1990). Developmental changes in young children's knowledge about the mind. *Cognitive Development, 5,* 1–27.

Flavell, J. H., Green, F. L., Wahl, K. E., & Flavell, E. R. (1987). The effects of question clarification and memory aids on young children's performance on appearance-reality tasks. *Cognitive Development, 2,* 127–144.

Flavell, J. H., Zhang, X.-D., Zou, H., Dong, Q., & Qi, S. (1983). A comparison of the appearance-reality distinction in the People's Republic of China and the United States. *Cognitive Psychology, 15,* 459–466.

Fleming, A. S., Ruble, D. L., Flett, G. L., & Schaul, D. L. (1988). Postpartum adjustment in first-time mothers: Relations between mood, maternal attitudes, and mother-infant interactions. *Developmental Psychology, 24,* 71–81.

Floyd, R. L., Rimer, B. K., Giovino, G. A., Mullen, P. D., & Sullivan, S. E. (1993). A review of smoking in pregnancy: Effects on pregnancy outcomes and cessation efforts. *Annual Review of Public Health, 14,* 379–411.

Fogel, C. I. (1995). Sexually transmitted diseases. In C. I. Fogel & N. F. Woods (Eds.), *Women's health care* (pp. 571–610). Thousand Oaks, CA: Sage.

Folk, K. F., & Yi, Y. (1994). Piecing together child care with multiple arrangements: Crazy quilt or preferred pattern for employed parents of preschool children? *Journal of Marriage and the Family, 56,* 669–680.

Folven, R. J., & Bonvillian, J. D. (1991). The transition from nonreferential to referential language in children acquiring American Sign Language. *Developmental Psychology, 27,* 806–816.

Fox, N. A., Kimmerly, N. L., & Schafer, W. D. (1991). Attachment to mother/attachment to father: A meta-analysis. *Child Development, 62,* 210–225.

Fozard, J. L. (1990). Vision and hearing in aging. In J. E. Birren & K. W. Schaie (Eds.), *Handbook of the psychology of aging* (3rd ed.) (pp. 150–171). San Diego, CA: Academic Press.

Fozard, J. L., Metter, E. J., & Brant, L. J. (1990). Next steps in describing aging and disease in longitudinal studies. *Journals of Gerontology: Psychological Sciences, 45,* P116–127.

Fraiberg, S. (1974). Blind infants and their mothers: An examination of the sign system. In M. Lewis & L. A. Rosenblum (Eds.), *The effect of the infant on its caregiver* (pp. 215–232). New York: Wiley.

Fraiberg, S. (1975). The development of human attachments in infants blind from birth. *Merrill-Palmer Quarterly, 21,* 315–334.

Francis, P. L., Self, P. A., & Horowitz, F. D. (1987). The behavioral assessment of the neonate: An overview. In J. D. Osofsky (Ed.), *Handbook of infant development* (2nd ed.) (pp. 723–779). New York: Wiley-Interscience.

Fraser, A. M., Brockert, J. E., & Ward, R. H. (1995). Association of young maternal age with adverse reproductive outcomes. *New England Journal of Medicine, 332,* 1113–1117.

Frazier, P. H., & Foss-Goodman, D. (1988–89). Death anxiety and personality: Are they truly related? *Omega, 19,* 265–274.

Freedman, D. G. (1979). Ethnic differences in babies. *Human Nature, 2,* 36–43.

Freedman, V. A. (1996). Family structure and the risk of nursing home admission. *Journals of Gerontology: Social Sciences, 51B,* S61–69.

Freeman, E. W., & Rickels, K. (1993). *Early childbearing: Perspectives of black adolescents on pregnancy, abortion, and contraception.* Newbury Park, CA: Sage.

Freud, S. (1905). *The basic writings of Sigmund Freud* (A. A. Brill, Trans.). New York: Random House.

Freud, S. (1920). *A general introduction to psychoanalysis* (J. Rivière, Trans.). New York: Washington Square Press.

Frey, K. S., & Ruble, D. N. (1992). Gender constancy and the "cost" of sex-typed behavior: A test of the conflict hypothesis. *Developmental Psychology, 28,* 714–721.

Friedman, H. S., Hawley, P. H., & Tucker, J. S. (1994). Personality, health, and longevity. *Current Directions in Psychological Science, 3,* 37–41.

Friedman, M., & Rosenman, R. H. (1974). *Type A behavior and your heart.* New York: Knopf.

Fu, Y., Pizzuti, A., Fenwick, R. G., Jr., King, J., Rajnarayan, S., Dune, P. W., Dubel, J., Nasser, G. A., Ashizawa, T., de Jong, P., Wieringa, B., Korneluk, R., Perryman, M. B., Epstein, H. F., & Caskey, C. T. (1992). An unstable triplet repeat in a gene related to myotonic muscular dystrophy. *Science, 225,* 1256–1258.

Fuller, T. L., & Fincham, F. D. (1995). Attachment style in married couples: Relation to current marital functioning, stability over time, and method of assessment. *Personal Relationships, 2,* 17–34.

Furrow, D. (1984). Social and private speech at two years. *Child Development, 55,* 355–362.

Furstenberg, F. F., Jr., & Cherlin, A. J. (1991). *Divided families: What happens to children when parents part.* Cambridge, MA: Harvard University Press.

Furstenberg, F. F., Jr., & Hughes, M. E. (1995). Social capital and successful development among at-risk youth. *Journal of Marriage and the Family, 57,* 580–592.

Gallagher, S. K. (1994). Doing their share: Comparing patterns of help given by older and younger adults. *Journal of Marriage and the Family, 56,* 567–578.

Gallagher, W. (1993, May). Midlife myths. *The Atlantic Monthly,* pp. 51–68.

Gallagher-Thompson, D., Futterman, A., Farberow, N., Thompson, L. W., & Peterson, J. (1993). The impact of spousal bereavement on older widows and widowers. In M. S. Stroebe, W. Stroebe, & R. O. Hansson (Eds.), *Handbook of bereavement: Theory, research, and intervention* (pp. 227–239). Cambridge, England: Cambridge University Press.

Gambert, S. R., Schultz, B. M., & Hamdy, R. C. (1995). Osteoporosis: Clinical features, prevention, and treatment. *Endocrinology and Metabolism Clinics of North America, 24,* 317–371.

Garbarino, J., Dubrow, N., Kostelny, K., & Pardo, C. (1992). *Children in danger: Coping with the consequences of community violence:* San Francisco: Jossey-Bass.

Garbarino, J., Kostelny, K., & Dubrow, N. (1991). *No place to be a child: Growing up in a war zone.* Lexington, MA: Lexington Books.

Garbarino, J., & Sherman, D. (1980). High-risk neighborhoods and high-risk families: The human ecology of child maltreatment. *Child Development, 51,* 188–198.

Gardner, D., Harris, P. L., Ohmoto, M., & Hamasaki, T. (1988). Japanese children's understanding of the distinction between real and apparent emotion. *International Journal of Behavioral Development, 11,* 203–218.

Gardner, H. (1983). *Frames of mind: The theory of multiple intelligence.* New York: Basic Books.

Garland, A. F., & Zigler, E. (1993). Adolescent suicide prevention: Current research and social policy implications. *American Psychologist, 48,* 169–182.

Garmezy, N. (1993). Vulnerability and resilience. In D. C. Funder, R. D. Parke, C. Tomlinson-Keasey, & K. Widaman (Eds.), *Studying lives through time: Personality and development* (pp. 377–398). Washington, DC: American Psychological Association.

Garmezy, N., & Masten, A. S. (1991). The protective role of competence indicators in children at risk. In E. M. Cummings, A. L. Green, & K. H. Karraker (Eds.), *Life-span developmental psychology: Perspectives on stress and coping* (pp. 151–174). Hillsdale, NJ: Erlbaum.

Garmezy, N., & Rutter, M. (Eds.). (1983). *Stress, coping, and development in children.* New York: McGraw-Hill.

Garn, S. M. (1980). Continuities and change in maturational timing. In O. G. Brim, Jr. & J. Kagan (Eds.), *Constancy and change in human development* (pp. 113–162). Cambridge, MA: Harvard University Press.

Garner, C. (1995). Infertility. In C. I. Fogel & N. F. Woods (Eds.), *Women's health care* (pp. 611–628). Thousand Oaks, CA: Sage.

Garrison, R. J., Gold, R. S., Wilson, P. W. F., & Kannel, W. B. (1993). Educational attainment and coronary heart disease risk: The Framingham offspring study. *Preventive Medicine, 22,* 54–64.

Gatz, M., Kasl-Godley, J. E., & Karel, M. J. (1996). Aging and mental disorders. In J. E. Birren & K. W. Schaie (Eds.), *Handbook of the psychology of aging* (4th ed.) (pp. 365–381). San Diego, CA: Academic Press.

Gaziano, J. M., & Hennekens, C. H. (1995). Dietary fat and risk of prostate cancer. *Journal of the National Cancer Institute, 87,* 1427–1428.

Geary, D. C., Bow-Thomas, C. C., Fan, L., & Siegler, R. S. (1993). Even before formal instruction, Chinese children outperform American children in mental addition. *Cognitive Development, 8,* 517–529.

Gecas, V., & Seff, M. A. (1990). Families and adolescents: A review of the 1980s. *Journal of Marriage and the Family, 52,* 941–958.

Gelman, R. (1972). Logical capacity of very young children: Number invariance rules. *Child Development, 43,* 75–90.

Genesee, F. (1993). Bilingual language development in preschool children. In D. Bishop & K. Mogford (Eds.), *Language development in exceptional circumstances* (pp. 62–79). Hove, UK: Erlbaum.

Gentner, D. (1982). Why nouns are learned before verbs: Linguistic relativity versus natural partitioning. In S. A. Kuczaj, II (Ed.), *Language development: Vol. 2. Language, thought, and culture* (pp. 301–334). Hillsdale, NJ: Erlbaum.

George, L. K. (1990). Social structure, social processes, and social-psychological states. In R. H. Binstock & L. K. George (Eds.), *Handbook of aging and the social sciences* (3rd ed.) (pp. 186–204). San Diego, CA: Academic Press.

George, L. K. (1993). Sociological perspectives on life transitions. *Annual Review of Sociology, 19,* 353–373.

George, L. K. (1996). Social factors and illness. In R. H. Binstock & L. K. George (Eds.), *Handbook of aging and the social sciences* (4th ed.) (pp. 229–252). San Diego, CA: Academic Press.

Georgieff, M. K. (1994). Nutritional deficiencies as developmental risk factors: Commentary on Pollitt and Gorman. In C. A. Nelson (Ed.), *The Minnesota Symposia on Child Development* (Vol. 27) (pp. 145–159). Hillsdale, NJ: Erlbaum.

Gesell, A. (1925). *The mental growth of the preschool child.* New York: Macmillan.

Gesser, G., Wong, P. T. P., & Reker, G. T. (1987–88). Death attitudes across the life-span: The development and validation of the death attitude profile (DAP). *Omega, 18,* 113–128.

Giambra, L. M., Arenberg, D., Zonderman, A. B., Kawas, C., & Costa, P. T., Jr. (1995). Adult life span changes in immediate visual memory and verbal intelligence. *Psychology and Aging, 10,* 123–139.

Gibson, D. M. (1986). Interaction and well-being in old age: Is it quantity or quality that counts? *International Journal of Aging and Human Development, 24,* 29–40.

Gibson, D. R. (1990). Relation of socioeconomic status to logical and sociomoral judgment of middle-aged men. *Psychology and Aging, 5,* 510–513.

Gilbert, T. J., Percy, C. A., Sugarman, J. R., Benson, L., & Percy, C. (1992). Obesity among Navajo adolescents: Relationship to dietary intake and blood pressure. *American Journal of Diseases of Children, 146,* 289–295.

Gilligan, C. (1982). *In a different voice: Psychological theory and women's development.* Cambridge, MA: Harvard University Press.

Gilligan, C., & Wiggins, G. (1987). The origins of morality in early childhood relationships. In J. Kagan & S. Lamb (Eds.), *The emergence of morality in young children* (pp. 277–307). Chicago: University of Chicago Press.

Gilman, E. A., Cheng, K. K., Winter, H. R., & Scragg, R. (1995). Trends in rates and seasonal distribution of sudden infant deaths in England and Wales, 1988–1992. *British Medical Journal, 30,* 631–632.

Giordano, P. C., Cernkovich, S. A., & DeMaris, A. (1993). The family and peer relations of black adolescents. *Journal of Marriage and the Family, 55,* 277–287.

Gladue, B. A. (1994). The biopsychology of sexual orientation. *Current Directions in Psychological Science, 3,* 150–154.

Glaser, R., Kiecolt-Glaser, J. K., Bonneau, R. H., Malarkey, W., Kennedy, S., & Hughes, J. (1992). Stress-induced modulation of the immune response to recombinant hepatitis B vaccine. *Psychosomatic Medicine, 54,* 22–29.

Gleitman, L. R., & Gleitman, H. (1992). A picture is worth a thousand words, but that's the problem: The role of syntax in vocabulary acquisition. *Current Directions in Psychological Science, 1,* 31–35.

Glenn, N. D. (1990). Quantitative research on marital quality in the 1980s: A critical review. *Journal of Marriage and the Family, 52,* 818–831.

Glenn, N. D., & McLanahan, S. (1981). The effects of offspring on the psychological well-being of older adults. *Journal of Marriage and the Family, 43,* 409–421.

Glenn, N. D., & Weaver, C. N. (1981). The contribution of marital happiness to global happiness. *Journal of Marriage and the Family, 43,* 161–168.

Glenn, N. D., & Weaver, C. N. (1985). Age, cohort, and reported job satisfaction in the United States. In A. S. Blau (Ed.), *Current perspectives on aging and the life cycle. A research annual: Vol. 1. Work, retirement and social policy* (pp. 89–110). Greenwich, CT: Jai Press.

Glenn, N. D., & Weaver, C. N. (1988). The changing relationship of marital status to reported happiness. *Journal of Marriage and the Family, 50,* 317–324.

Glueck, S., & Glueck, E. (1968). *Delinquents and nondelinquents in perspective.* Cambridge, MA: Harvard University Press.

Glueck, S., & Glueck, E. (1972). *Identification of pre-delinquents: Validation studies and some suggested uses of Glueck Table.* New York: Intercontinental Medical Book Corp.

Gnepp, J., & Chilamkurti, C. (1988). Children's use of personality attributions to predict other people's emotional and behavioral reactions. *Child Development, 50,* 743–754.

Goetting, A. (1986). The developmental tasks of siblingship over the life cycle. *Journal of Marriage and the Family, 48,* 703–714.

Gold, D. P., Andres, D., Etezadi, J., Arbuckle, T., Schwartzman, A., & Chaikelson, J. (1995). Structural equation model of intellectual change and continuity and predictors of intelligence in older men. *Psychology and Aging, 10,* 294–303.

Gold, D. T. (1989). Generational solidarity. *American Behavioral Scientist, 33,* 19–32.

Gold, D. T. (1990). Late-life sibling relationships: Does race affect typological distribution? *The Gerontologist, 30,* 741–748.

Goldberg, A. P., Dengel, D. R., & Hagberg, J. M. (1996). Exercise physiology and aging. In E. L. Schneider & J. W. Rowe (Eds.), *Handbook of the biology of aging* (4th ed.) (pp. 331–354). San Diego, CA: Academic Press.

Goldberg, A. P., & Hagberg, J. M. (1990). Physical exercise in the elderly. In E. R. Schneider & J. W. Rowe (Eds.), *Handbook of the biology of aging* (3rd ed.) (pp. 407–428). San Diego, CA: Academic Press.

Goldberg, S. (1972). Infant care and growth in urban Zambia. *Human Development, 15,* 77–89.

Goldberg, W. A. (1990). Marital quality, parental personality, and spousal agreement about perceptions and expectations for children. *Merrill-Palmer Quarterly, 36,* 531–556.

Goldfield, B. A., & Reznick, J. S. (1990). Early lexical acquisition: Rate, content, and the vocabulary spurt. *Journal of Child Language, 17,* 171–183.

Goldsmith, H. H., Buss, K. A., & Lemery, K. S. (1995). *Toddler and childhood temperament: Expanded content, stronger genetic evidence, new evidence for the importance of environment.* Paper presented at the biennial meetings of the Society for Research in Child Development, Indianapolis, March.

Goldstein, J. H. (Ed.). (1994). *Toys, play, and child development.* Cambridge, England: Cambridge University Press.

Golinkoff, R. M., Mervis, C. B., & Hirsh-Pasek, K. (1994). Early object labels: The case for lexical principles. *Journal of Child Language, 21,* 125–155.

Golombok, S., & Fivush, R. (1994). *Gender development.* Cambridge, England: Cambridge University Press.

Good, T. L., & Weinstein, R. S. (1986). Schools make a difference: Evidence, criticisms, and new directions. *American Psychologist, 41,* 1090–1097.

Goodenough, F. L. (1931). *Anger in young children.* Minneapolis: University of Minnesota Press.

Goodsitt, J. V., Morse, P. A., Ver Hoeve, J. N., & Cowan, N. (1984). Infant speech recognition in multisyllabic contexts. *Child Development, 55,* 903–910.

Gopnik, A., & Astington, J. W. (1988). Children's understanding of representational change and its relation to the understanding of false belief and the appearance-reality distinction. *Child Development, 59,* 26–37.

Gopnik, A., & Meltzoff, A. (1987). The development of categorization in the second year and its relation to other cognitive and linguistic developments. *Child Development, 58,* 1523–1531.

Gopnik, A., & Meltzoff, A. N. (1992). Categorization and naming: Basic-level sorting in eighteen-month-olds and its relation to language. *Child Development, 63,* 1091–1103.

Gopnik, A., & Wellman, H. M. (1994). The theory theory. In L. A. Hirschfeld & S. A. Gelman (Eds.), *Mapping the mind* (pp. 257–293). Cambridge, England: Cambridge University Press.

Gordon, G. S., & Vaughan, C. (1986). Calcium and osteoporosis. *Journal of Nutrition, 116,* 319–322.

Gortmaker, S. L., Dietz, W. H., Sobol, A. M., & Welher, C. A. (1987). Increasing pediatric obesity in the United States. *American Journal of the Diseases of Children, 141,* 535–540.

Gottesman, I. I., & Goldsmith, H. H. (1994). Developmental psychopathology of antisocial behavior: Inserting genes into its ontogenesis and epigenesis. In C. A. Nelson (Ed.), *The Minnesota Symposia on Child Psychology* (Vol. 27) (pp. 69–104). Hillsdale, NJ: Erlbaum.

Gottman, J. M. (1986). The world of coordinated play: Same- and cross-sex friendship in young children. In J. M. Gottman & J. G. Parker (Eds.), *Conversations of friends: Speculations on affective development* (pp. 139–191). Cambridge, England: Cambridge University Press.

Gottman, J. M. (1994a). *What predicts divorce? The relationship between marital processes and marital outcomes.* Hillsdale, NJ: Erlbaum.

Gottman, J. M. (1994b). *Why marriages succeed or fail.* New York: Simon & Schuster.

Graber, J. A., Brooks-Gunn, J., Paikoff, R. L., & Warren, M. P. (1994). Prediction of eating problems: An 8-year study of adolescent girls. *Developmental Psychology, 30,* 823–834.

Gralinski, J. H., & Kopp, C. B. (1993). Everyday rules for behavior: Mothers' requests to young children. *Developmental Psychology, 29,* 573–584.

Gray, A., Berlin, J. A., McKinlay, J. B., & Longcope, C. (1991). An examination of research design effects on the association of testosterone and male aging: Results of a meta-analysis. *Journal of Clinical Epidemiology, 44,* 671–684.

Greenberg, J., & Kuczaj, S. A., II (1982). Towards a theory of substantive word-meaning acquisition. In S. A. Kuczaj, II (Ed.), *Language development: Vol. 1. Syntax and semantics* (pp. 275–312). Hillsdale, NJ: Erlbaum.

Greenberg, M. T., Siegel, J. M., & Leitch, C. J. (1983). The nature and importance of attachment relationships to parents and peers during adolescence. *Journal of Youth and Adolescence, 12,* 373–386.

Greenberg, M. T., Speltz, M. L., & DeKlyen, M. (1993). The role of attachment in the early development of disruptive behavior problems. *Development and Psychopathology, 5,* 191–213.

Greenberger, E., & Goldberg, W. A. (1989). Work, parenting, and the socialization of children. *Developmental Psychology, 25,* 22–35.

Greenberger, E., & Steinberg, L. (1986). *When teenagers work: The psychological and social costs of adolescent employment.* New York: Basic Books.

Greenfield, P. M. (1994). Independence and interdependence as developmental scripts: Implications for theory, research, and practice. In P. M. Greenfield & R. R. Cocking (Eds.), *Cross-cultural roots of minority child development* (pp. 1–37). Hillsdale, NJ: Erlbaum.

Greenough, W. T. (1991). Experience as a component of normal development: Evolutionary considerations. *Developmental Psychology, 27,* 11–27.

Greenough, W. T., Black, J. E., & Wallace, C. S. (1987). Experience and brain development. *Child Development, 58,* 539–559.

Greer, D. S., Mor, V., Morris, J. N., Sherwood, S., Kidder, D., & Birnbaum, H. (1986). An alternative in terminal care: Results of the National Hospice Study. *Journal of Chronic Diseases, 39,* 9–26.

Greer, S. (1991). Psychological response to cancer and survival. *Psychological Medicine, 21,* 43–49.

Greer, S., Morris, T., & Pettingale, K. W. (1979). Psychological response to breast cancer: Effect on outcome. *Lancet,* 785–787.

Gregg, V., Gibbs, J. C., & Basinger, K. S. (1994). Patterns of developmental delay in moral judgment by male and female delinquents. *Merrill-Palmer Quarterly, 40,* 538–553.

Griffith, D. R., Azuma, S. D., & Chasnoff, I. J. (1994). Three-year outcome of children exposed prenatally to drugs. *Journal of the American Academy of Child and Adolescent Psychiatry, 33,* 20–27.

Grolnick, W. S., & Slowiaczek, M. L. (1994). Parents' involvement in children's schooling: A multidimensional conceptualization and motivational model. *Child Development, 65,* 237–252.

Grossmann, K., Grossmann, K. E., Spangler, G., Suess, G., & Unzner, L. (1985). Maternal sensitivity and newborns' orientation responses as related to quality of attachment in northern Germany. *Monographs of the Society of Research in Child Development, 50*(1–2, Serial No. 209), 233–256.

Grusec, J. E. (1992). Social learning theory and developmental psychology: The legacies of Robert Sears and Albert Bandura. *Developmental Psychology, 28,* 776–786.

Guerin, D. W., & Gottfried, A. W. (1994a). Temperamental consequences of infant difficultness. *Infant Behavior and Development, 17,* 413–421.

Guerin, D. W., & Gottfried, A. W. (1994b). Developmental stability and change in parent reports of temperament: A ten-year longitudinal investigation from infancy through preadolescence. *Merrill-Palmer Quarterly, 40,* 334–355.

Gullotta, T. P., Adams, G. R., & Montemayor, R. (Eds.). (1993). *Adolescent sexuality.* Newbury Park, CA: Sage.

Gunnar, M. R. (1994). Psychoendocrine studies of temperament and stress in early childhood: Expanding current models. In J. E. Bates & T. D. Wachs (Eds.), *Temperament: Individual differences at the interface of biology and behavior* (pp. 175–198). Washington, DC: American Psychological Association.

Guo, S. F. (1993). Postpartum depression. *Chung-Hua Fu Chan Ko Tsa Chi, 28,* 532–533, 569.

Guralnik, J. M., & Kaplan, G. A. (1989). Predictors of healthy aging: Prospective evidence from the Alameda County Study. *American Journal of Public Health, 79,* 703–708.

Guralnik, J. M., Land, K. C., Blazer, D., Fillenbaum, G. G., & Branch, L. G. (1993). Educational status and active life expectancy among older blacks and whites. *New England Journal of Medicine, 329,* 110–116.

Guralnick, J. M., & Paul-Brown, D. (1984). Communicative adjustments during behavior-request episodes among children at different developmental levels. *Child Development, 55,* 911–919.

Guralnik, J. M., & Simonsick, E. M. (1993). Physical disability in older Americans. *The Journals of Gerontology, 48*(Special Issue), 3–10.

Guralnik, J. M., Simonsick, E. M., Ferrucci, L., Glynn, R. J., Berkman, L. F., Blazer, D. G., Scherr, P. A., & Wallace, R. B. (1994). A short physical performance battery assessing lower extremity function: Association with self-reported disability and prediction of mortality and nursing home admission. *Journals of Gerontology: Medical Sciences, 49,* M85–94.

Gustafson, S. B., & Magnusson, D. (1991). *Female life careers: A pattern approach.* Hillsdale, NJ: Erlbaum.

Gutmann, D. (1975). Parenthood: A key to the comparative study of the life cycle. In N. Datan & L. H. Ginsberg (Eds.), *Life-span developmental psychology: Normative life crises* (pp. 167–184). New York: Academic Press.

Gutmann, D. (1987). *Reclaimed powers: Toward a new psychology of men and women in later life.* New York: Basic Books.

Guttentag, R. E., Ornstein, P. A., & Siemens, L. (1987). Children's spontaneous rehearsal: Transitions in strategy acquisition. *Cognitive Development, 2,* 307–326.

Guyer, B., Strobino, D. M., Ventura, S. J., & Singh, G. K. (1995). Annual summary of vital statistics—1994. *Pediatrics, 96,* 1029–1039.

Gwartney-Gibbs, P. A. (1988). Women's work experience and the "rusty skills" hypothesis: A reconceptualization and reevaluation of the evidence. In B. A. Gutek, A. H. Stromberg, & L. Larwood (Eds.), *Women and work: An annual review* (Vol. 3) (pp. 169–188). Newbury Park, CA: Sage.

Gzesh, S. M., & Surber, C. F. (1985). Visual perspective-taking skills in children. *Child Development, 56,* 1204–1213.

Haan, N. (1976). ". . . Change and sameness . . ." reconsidered. *International Journal of Aging and Human Development, 7,* 59–65.

Haan, N. (1981a). Adolescents and young adults as producers of their own development. In R. M. Lerner & N. A. Busch-Rossnagel (Eds.), *Individuals as producers of their own development* (pp. 155–182). New York: Academic Press.

Haan, N. (1981b). Common dimensions of personality development: Early adolescence to middle life. In D. H. Eichorn, J. A. Clausen, N. Haan, M. P. Honzik, & P. H. Mussen (Eds.), *Present and past in middle life* (pp. 117–153). New York: Academic Press.

Haan, N. (1982). The assessment of coping, defense, and stress. In L. Goldberger & S. Breznitz (Eds.), *Handbook of stress: Theoretical and clinical aspects* (pp. 254–269). New York: Free Press.

Haan, N. (1985). Processes of moral development: Cognitive or social disequilibrium? *Developmental Psychology, 21,* 996–1006.

Haan, N., Millsap, R., & Hartka, E. (1986). As time goes by: Change and stability in personality over fifty years. *Psychology and Aging, 1,* 220–232.

Hack, M., Taylor, C. B. H., Klein, N., Eiben, R., Schatschneider, C., & Mercuri-Minich, N. (1994). School-age outcomes in children with birth weights under 750 g. *New England Journal of Medicine, 331,* 753–759.

Hagestad, G. O. (1984). The continuous bond: A dynamic, multigenerational perspective on parent-child relations between adults. In M. Perlmutter (Ed.), *Minnesota Symposia on Child Psychology* (pp. 129–158). Hillsdale, NJ: Erlbaum.

Hagestad, G. O. (1985). Continuity and connectedness. In V. L. Bengtson (Ed.), *Grandparenthood* (pp. 31–38). Beverly Hills, CA: Sage.

Hagestad, G. O. (1986). Dimensions of time and the family. *American Behavioral Scientist, 29,* 679–694.

Hagestad, G. O. (1990). Social perspectives on the life course. In R. H. Binstock & L. K. George (Eds.), *Handbook of aging and the social sciences* (3rd ed.) (pp. 151–168). San Diego, CA: Academic Press.

Haier, R. J., Chueh, D., Touchette, P., Lott, I., Buchsbaum, M. S., MacMillan, D., Sandman, C., LaCasse, L., & Sosa, E. (1995). Brain size and cerebral glucose metabolic rate in nonspecific mental retardation and Down syndrome. *Intelligence, 20,* 191–210.

Haight, B. K. (1988). The therapeutic role of a structured life review process in homebound elderly subjects. *Journals of Gerontology: Psychological Sciences, 43,* P40–44.

Haight, B. K. (1992). Long-term effects of a structured life review process. *Journals of Gerontology: Psychological Sciences, 47,* P312–315.

Haith, M. M. (1980). *Rules that babies look by.* Hillsdale, NJ: Erlbaum.

Haith, M. M. (1990). Progress in the understanding of sensory and perceptual processes in early infancy. *Merrill-Palmer Quarterly, 36,* 1–26.

Hakuta, K. (1986). *Mirror on language: The debate on bilingualism.* New York: Basic Books.

Hakuta, K., & Garcia, E. E. (1989). Bilingualism and education. *American Psychologist, 44,* 374–379.

Hale, S., Fry, A. F., & Jessie, K. A. (1993). Effects of practice on speed of information processing in children and adults: Age sensitivity and age invariance. *Developmental Psychology, 29,* 880–892.

Haley, W. E., West, C. A. C., Wadley, V. G., Ford, G. R., White, F. A., Barrett, J. J., Harrell, L. E., & Roth, D. L. (1995). Psychological, social, and health impact of caregiving: A comparison of black and white dementia family caregivers and noncaregivers. *Psychology and Aging, 10,* 540–552.

Halford, G. S., Maybery, M. T., O'Hare, A. W., & Grant, P. (1994). The development of memory and processing capacity. *Child Development, 65,* 1338–1356.

Halford, W. K., Hahlweg, K., & Dunne, M. (1990). The cross-cultural consistency of marital communication associated with marital distress. *Journal of Marriage and the Family, 52,* 487–500.

Hall, D. R., & Zhao, J. Z. (1995). Cohabitation and divorce in Canada: Testing the selectivity hypothesis. *Journal of Marriage and the Family, 57,* 421–427.

Hall, D. T. (1972). A model of coping with role conflict: The role behavior of college educated women. *Administrative Science Quarterly, 17,* 471–486.

Hall, D. T. (1975). Pressures from work, self, and home in the life stages of married women. *Journal of Vocational Behavior, 6,* 121–132.

Hallfrisch, J., Muller, D., Drinkwater, D., Tobin, J., & Adres, R. (1990). Continuing diet trends in men: The Baltimore Longitudinal Study of Aging. *Journals of Gerontology: Medical Sciences, 45,* M186–191.

Hallstrom, T., & Samuelsson, S. (1985). Mental health in the climacteric: The longitudinal study of women in Gothenberg. *Acta Obstetrics Gynecology Scandanavia, 130*(Suppl), 13–18.

Halpern, C. T., Udry, J. R., Campbell, B., & Suchindran, C. (1993). Testosterone and pubertal development as predictors of sexual activity: A panel analysis of adolescent males. *Psychosomatic Medicine, 55,* 436–447.

Halpern, D. F. (1986). *Sex differences in cognitive abilities.* Hillsdale, NJ: Erlbaum.

Hamer, D. H., Hu, S., Magnuson, V. L., Hu, N., & Pattatucci, A. M. (1993). A linkage between DNA markers on the X chromosome and male sexual orientation. *Science, 261,* 321–327.

Hamilton, C. E. (1995). *Continuity and discontinuity of attachment from infancy through adolescence.* Paper presented at the biennial meetings of the Society for Research in Child Development, Indianapolis, March.

Hanna, E., & Meltzoff, A. N. (1993). Peer imitation by toddlers in laboratory, home, and day-care contexts: Implications for social learning and memory. *Developmental Psychology, 29,* 701–710.

Hansen, J., & Bowey, J. A. (1994). Phonological analysis skills, verbal working memory, and reading ability in second-grade children. *Child Development, 65,* 938–950.

Hansson, R. O., & Carpenter, B. N. (1994). *Relationships in old age: Coping with the challenge of transition.* New York: Guilford Press.

Hardy, M. A., & Hazelrigg, L. E. (1993). The gender of poverty in an aging population. *Research on Aging, 15,* 243–278.

Hardy, M. A., & Quadagno, J. (1995). Satisfaction with early retirement: Making choices in the auto industry. *Journals of Gerontology: Social Sciences, 50B,* S217–228.

Harkness, S., & Super, C. M. (1985). The cultural context of gender segregation in children's peer groups. *Child Development, 56,* 219–224.

Harman, S. M., & Tsitouras, P. D. (1980). Reproductive hormones in aging men: I. Measurement of sex steroids, basal luteinizing hormone, and Leydig cell response to human chorionic gonadotropin. *Journal of Clinical Endocrinology and Metabolism, 51,* 35–40.

Harris, B., Lovett, L., Newcombe, R. G., Read, G. F., Walker, R., & Riad-Fahmy, D. (1994). Maternity blues and major endocrine changes: Cardiff puerperal mood and hormone study II. *British Medical Journal, 308,* 949–953.

Harris, M. (1992). *Language experience and early language development: From input to uptake.* Hove, England: Erlbaum.

Harris, P. L. (1989). *Children and emotion: The development of psychological understanding.* Oxford: Blackwell.

Harris, R. L., Ellicott, A. M., & Holmes, D. S. (1986). The timing of psychosocial transitions and changes in women's lives: An examination of women aged 45 to 60. *Journal of Personality and Social Psychology, 51,* 409–416.

Harris, T., Brown, G. W., & Bifulco, A. (1990). Loss of parent in childhood and adult psychiatric disorder: A tentative overall model. *Development and Psychopathology, 2,* 311–328.

Hart, B., & Risley, T. R. (1995). *Meaningful differences in the everyday experience of young American children.* Baltimore: Paul H. Brookes.

Harter, S. (1987). The determinations and mediational role of global self-worth in children. In N. Eisenberg (Ed.), *Contemporary topics in developmental psychology* (pp. 219–242). New York: Wiley-Interscience.

Harter, S. (1990). Processes underlying adolescent self-concept formation. In R. Montemayor, G. R. Adams, & T. P. Gullotta (Eds.), *From childhood to adolescence: A transitional period?* (pp. 205–239). Newbury Park, CA: Sage.

Harter, S., Marold, D. B., & Whitesell, N. R. (1992). Model of psychosocial risk factors leading to suicidal ideation in young adolescents. *Development and Psychopathology, 4,* 167–188.

Harter, S., & Monsour, A. (1992). Developmental analysis of conflict caused by opposing attributes in the adolescent self-portrait. *Developmental Psychology, 28,* 251–260.

Harter, S., & Pike, R. (1984). The Pictorial Perceived Competence Scale for Young Children. *Child Development, 55,* 1969–1982.

Hartup, W. W. (1974). Aggression in childhood: Developmental perspectives. *American Psychologist, 29,* 336–341.

Hartup, W. W. (1989). Social relationships and their developmental significance. *American Psychologist, 44,* 120–126.

Hartup, W. W. (1992). Peer relations in early and middle childhood. In V. B. Van Hasselt & M. Hersen (Eds.), *Handbook of social development: A lifespan perspective* (pp. 257–281). New York: Plenum.

Hartup, W. W. (1996). The company they keep: Friendships and their developmental significance. *Child Development, 67,* 1–13.

Hartup, W. W., & van Lieshout, C. F. M. (1995). Personality development in social context. *Annual Review of Psychology, 46,* 655–687.

Harvard Education Letter (1988). Testing: Is there a right answer? September/October, 1–4.

Harvard Education Letter (1992). Youth sports: Kids are the losers. July/August, 1–3.

Hashima, P. Y., & Amato, P. R. (1994). Poverty, social support, and parental behavior. *Child Development, 65,* 394–403.

Hatch, L. R. (1991). Informal support patterns of older African-American and white women. *Research on Aging, 13,* 144–170.

Hatcher, P. J., Hulme, C., & Ellis, A. W. (1994). Ameliorating early reading failure by integrating the teaching of reading and phonological skills: The phonological linkage hypothesis. *Child Development, 65,* 41–57.

Hatchett, S. J., Cochran, D. L., & Jackson, J. S. (1991). Family life. In J. S. Jackson (Ed.), *Life in black America.* Newbury Park, CA: Sage.

Hatchett, S. J., & Jackson, J. S. (1993). African American extended kin systems: An assessment. In H. P. McAdoo (Ed.), *Family ethnicity: Strength in diversity* (pp. 90–108). Newbury Park, CA: Sage.

Hausman, P. B., & Weksler, M. E. (1985). Changes in the immune response with age. In C. E. Finch & E. L. Schneider (Eds.), *Handbook of the biology of aging* (2nd ed.) (pp. 414–432). New York: Van Nostrand Reinhold.

Haviland, J. M., & Lelwica, M. (1987). The induced affect response: 10-week-old infants' responses to three emotional expressions. *Developmental Psychology, 23,* 97–104.

Hawkins, H. L., Kramer, A. F., & Capaldi, D. (1992). Aging, exercise, and attention. *Psychology and Aging, 7,* 643–653.

Hawley, T. L., & Disney, E. R. (1992). Crack's children: The consequences of maternal cocaine abuse. *Social Policy Report. Society for Research in Child Development, 6*(4), 1–22.

Hayflick, L. (1977). The cellular basis for biological aging. In C. E. Finch & L. Hayflick (Eds.), *Handbook of the biology of aging* (pp. 159–186). New York: Van Nostrand Reinhold.

Hayflick, L. (1987). Origins of longevity. In H. R. Warner, R. N. Butler, R. L. Sprott, & E. L. Schneider (Eds.), *Aging: Vol. 31. Modern biological theories of aging* (pp. 21–34). New York: Raven Press.

Hayflick, L. (1994). *How and why we age.* New York: Ballantine Books.

Hayne, H., & Rovee-Collier, C. (1995). The organization of reactivated memory in infancy. *Child Development, 66,* 893–906.

Hayward, M. D., Friedman, S., & Chen, H. (1996). Race inequities in men's retirement. *Journals of Gerontology: Social Sciences, 51B,* S1–10.

Hayward, M. D., & Hardy, M. A. (1985). Early retirement processes among older men: Occupational differences. *Research on Aging, 7,* 491–518.

Hazan, C., Hutt, M., Sturgeon, J., & Bricker, T. (1991). *The process of relinquishing parents as attachment figures.* Paper presented at the biennial meetings of the Society for Research in Child Development, Seattle, April.

Hazan, C., & Shaver, P. (1987). Romantic love conceptualized as an attachment process. *Journal of Personality and Social Psychology, 52,* 511–524.

Hazan, C., & Shaver, P. (1990). Love and work: An attachment-theoretical perspective. *Journal of Personality and Social Psychology, 59,* 270–280.

Hazelrigg, L. E., & Hardy, M. A. (1995). Older adult migration to the sunbelt: Assessing income and related characteristics of recent migrants. *Research on Aging, 17,* 109–234.

Heagarty, M. C. (1991). America's lost children: Whose responsibility? *Journal of Pediatrics, 118,* 8–10.

Heaton, T. B., & Pratt, E. L. (1990). The effects of religious homogamy on marital satisfaction and stability. *Journal of Family Issues, 11,* 191–207.

Hebert, L. E., Scherr, P. A., Beckett, L. A., Albert, M. S., Pilgrim, D. M., Chown, M. J., Funkenstein, H. H., & Evans, D. A. (1995). Age-specific incidence of Alzheimer's disease in a community population. *Journal of the American Medical Association, 273,* 1354–1359.

Helson, R., Mitchell, V., & Moane, G. (1984). Personality and patterns of adherence and nonadherence to the social clock. *Journal of Personality and Social Psychology, 46,* 1079–1096.

Helson, R., & Moane, G. (1987). Personality change in women from college to midlife. *Journal of Personality and Social Psychology, 53,* 176–186.

Helson, R., & Stewart, A. (1994). Personality change in adulthood. In T. F. Hetherton & J. L. Weinberger (Eds.), *Can personality change?* (pp. 210–225). Washington, DC: American Psychological Association.

Helson, R., & Wink, P. (1992). Personality change in women from the early 40s to the early 50s. *Psychology and Aging, 7,* 46–55.

Heneborn, W. J., & Cogan, R. (1975). The effect of husband participation on reported pain and the probability of medication during labour and birth. *Journal of Psychosomatic Research, 19,* 215–222.

Henshaw, S. K. (1993). Teenage abortion, birth and pregnancy statistics by state, 1988. *Family Planning Perspectives, 25,* 122–126.

Hernandez, D. (1993). *America's Children.* New York: Russell Sage Foundation.

Herrnstein, R. J., & Murray, C. (1994). *The bell curve: Intelligence and class structure in American life.* New York: Free Press.

Hertzog, C., & Schaie, K. W. (1986). Stability and change in adult intelligence: 1. Analysis of longitudinal covariance structures. *Psychology and Aging, 1,* 159–171.

Herzog, A. R., House, J. S., & Morgan, J. N. (1991). Relation of work and retirement to health and well-being in older age. *Psychology and Aging, 6,* 202–211.

Herzog, A. R., & Rogers, W. L. (1989). Age differences in memory performance and memory ratings as measured in a sample survey. *Psychology and Aging, 4,* 173–182.

Hess, E. H. (1972). "Imprinting" in a natural laboratory. *Scientific American, 227,* 24–31.

Hetherington, E. M. (1989). Coping with family transitions: Winners, losers, and survivors. *Child Development, 60,* 1–14.

Hetherington, E. M. (1991a). The role of individual differences and family relationships in children's coping with divorce and remarriage. In P. A. Cowen & M. Hetherington (Eds.), *Family transitions* (pp. 165–194). Hillsdale, NJ: Erlbaum.

Hetherington, E. M. (1991b). Presidential address: Families, lies, and videotapes. *Journal of Research on Adolescence, 1,* 323–348.

Hetherington, E. M., & Clingempeel, W. G. (1992). Coping with marital transitions: A family systems perspective. *Monographs of the Society for Research in Child Development, 57*(2–3, Serial No. 227).

Hetherington, E. M., & Stanley-Hagan, M. M. (1995). Parenting in divorced and remarried families. In M. H. Bornstein (Ed.), *Handbook of parenting: Vol. 3. Status and social conditions of parenting* (pp. 233–254). Mahwah, NJ: Erlbaum.

Hetherton, T. F., & Weinberger, J. L. (Eds.). (1994). *Can personality change?* Washington, DC: American Psychological Association.

Hickey, C. A., Cliver, S. P., Goldenberg, R. L., Kohatsu, J., & Hoffman, H. J. (1993). Prenatal weight gain, term birth weight, and fetal growth retardation among high-risk multiparous black and white women. *Obstetrics and Gynecology, 81,* 529–535.

Higgins, A. (1991). The just community approach to moral education: Evolution of the idea and recent findings. In W. M. Kurtines & J. L. Gewirtz (Eds.), *Handbook of moral behavior and development: Vol. 3. Application* (pp. 111–141). Hillsdale, NJ: Erlbaum.

Higgins, C., Duxbury, L., & Lee, C. (1994). Impact of life-cycle stage and gender on the ability to balance work and family responsibilities. *Family Relations, 43,* 144–150.

Hightower, E. (1990). Adolescent interpersonal and familial precursors of positive mental health at midlife. *Journal of Youth and Adolescence, 19,* 257–275.

Hill, M. S. (1988). Marital stability and spouses' shared time: A multidisciplinary hypothesis. *Journal of Family Relations, 9,* 427–451.

Hill, R. D., Storandt, M., & Malley, M. (1993). The impact of long-term exercise training on psychological function in older adults. *Journals of Gerontology: Psychological Sciences, 48,* P12–17.

Hilts, P. J. (1995). Black teen-agers are turning away from smoking, but whites puff on. *New York Times,* April 19, p. B7.

Hilts, P. J. (1996). AIDS death rate rising in 25–44 age group. *New York Times,* February 16, p. A10.

Himes, C. L. (1994). Parental caregiving by adult women. *Research on Aging, 16,* 191–211.

Himes, C. L., Hogan, D. P., & Eggebeen, D. J. (1996). Living arrangements of minority elders. *Journals of Gerontology: Social Sciences, 51B,* S42–48.

Hinde, R. A., Titmus, G., Easton, D., & Tamplin, A. (1985). Incidence of "friendship" and behavior toward strong associates versus nonassociates in preschoolers. *Child Development, 56,* 234–245.

Hinton, J. (1975). The influence of previous personality on reactions to having terminal cancer. *Omega, 6,* 95–111.

Hirdes, J. P., & Strain, L. A. (1995). The balance of exchange in instrumental support with network members outside the household. *Journals of Gerontology: Social Sciences, 50B,* S134–142.

Hirsch, H. V. B., & Tieman, S. B. (1987). Perceptual development and experience-dependent changes in cat visual cortex. In M. H. Bornstein (Ed.), *Sensitive periods in development: Interdisciplinary perspectives* (pp. 39–80). Hillsdale, NJ: Erlbaum.

Hirsh-Pasek, K., Trieman, R., & Schneiderman, M. (1984). Brown and Hanlon revisited: Mothers' sensitivity to ungrammatical forms. *Journal of Child Language, 11,* 81–88.

Hoch, C. C., Buysse, D. J., Monk, T. H., & Reynolds, C. F. I. (1992). Sleep disorders and aging. In J. E. Birren, R. B. Sloane, & G. D. Cohen (Eds.), *Handbook of mental health and aging* (2nd ed.) (pp. 557–582). San Diego, CA: Academic Press.

Hofferth, S. L. (1987a). Teenage pregnancy and its resolution. In S. L. Hofferth & C. D. Hayes (Eds.), *Risking the future: Adolescent sexuality, pregnancy, and childbearing. Working papers* (pp. 78–92). Washington, DC: National Academy Press.

Hofferth, S. L. (1987b). Social and economic consequences of teenage childbearing. In S. L. Hofferth & C. D. Hayes (Eds.), *Risking the future: Adolescent sexuality, pregnancy, and childbearing. Working papers* (pp. 123–144). Washington, DC: National Academy Press.

Hofferth, S. L., Boisjoly, J., & Duncan, G. (1995). *Does children's school attainment benefit from parental access to social capital?* Paper presented at the biennial meetings of the Society for Research in Child Development, Indianapolis, March.

Hoffman, H. J., & Hillman, L. S. (1992). Epidemiology of the sudden infant death syndrome: Maternal, neonatal, and postneonatal risk factors. *Clinics in Perinatology, 19*(4), 717–737.

Hoffman, L. W., & Manis, J. D. (1978). Influences of children on marital interaction and parental satisfactions and dissatisfactions. In R. M. Lerner & G. B. Spanier (Eds.), *Child influences on marital and family interaction* (pp. 165–213). New York: Academic Press.

Hogan, D. P. (1981). *Transitions and social change: The early lives of American men.* New York: Academic Press.

Hogan, T. D., & Steinnes, D. N. (1994). Toward an understanding of elderly seasonal migration using origin-based household data. *Research on Aging, 16,* 463–475.

Hogue, C. J. R., & Hargraves, M. A. (1993). Class, race, and infant mortality in the United States. *American Journal of Public Health, 83,* 9–12.

Holahan, C. K. (1988). Relation of life goals at age 70 to activity participation and health and psychological well-being among Terman's gifted men and women. *Psychology and Aging, 3,* 286–291.

Holden, C. (1987). Genes and behavior: A twin legacy. *Psychology Today, 21*(9), 18–19.

Holden, G. W., Coleman, S. M., & Schmidt, K. L. (1995). Why 3-year-old children get spanked: Parent and child determinants as reported by college-educated mothers. *Merrill-Palmer Quarterly, 41,* 431–452.

Holden, K. C., & Smock, P. J. (1991). The economic costs of marital dissolution: Why do women bear a disproportionate cost? *Annual Review of Sociology, 17,* 51–78.

Holland, J. L. (1973). *Making vocational choices: A theory of careers.* Englewood Cliffs, NJ: Prentice-Hall.

Holland, J. L. (1992). *Making vocational choices: A theory of vocational personalities and work environments* (2nd ed.). Odessa, FL: Psychological Assessment Resources.

Holloway, S. D., & Hess, R. D. (1985). Mothers' and teachers' attributions about children's mathematics performance. In I. E. Sigel (Ed.), *Parental belief systems: The psychological consequences for children* (pp. 177–200). Hillsdale, NJ: Erlbaum.

Holmbeck, G. N., & Hill, J. P. (1991). Conflictive engagement, positive affect, and menarche in families with seventh-grade girls. *Child Development, 62,* 1030–1048.

Holmes, E. R., & Holmes, L. D. (1995). *Other cultures, elder years* (2nd ed.). Thousand Oaks, CA: Sage.

Honzik, M. P. (1986). The role of the family in the development of mental abilities: A 50-year study. In N. Datan, A. L. Greene, & H. W. Reese (Eds.), *Life-span developmental psychology: Intergenerational relations* (pp. 185–210). Hillsdale, NJ: Erlbaum.

Hopkins, J., Marcus, M., & Campbell, S. B. (1984). Postpartum depression: A critical review. *Psychological Bulletin, 95,* 498–515.

Horn, J. L. (1982). The aging of human abilities. In B. B. Wolman (Ed.), *Handbook of developmental psychology* (pp. 847–870). Englewood Cliffs, NJ: Prentice-Hall.

Horn, J. L., & Donaldson, G. (1980). Cognitive development in adulthood. In O. G. Brim, Jr. & J. Kagan (Eds.), *Constancy and change in human development* (pp. 415–529). Cambridge, MA: Harvard University Press.

Hornbrook, M. C., Stevens, V. J., & Wingfield, D. J. (1994). Preventing falls among community-dwelling older persons: Results from a randomized trial. *The Gerontologist, 34,* 16–23.

Horner, K. W., Rushton, J. P., & Vernon, P. A. (1986). Relation between aging and research productivity of academic psychologists. *Psychology and Aging, 1,* 319–324.

Horowitz, F. D. (1987). *Exploring developmental theories: Toward a structural/behavioral model of development.* Hillsdale, NJ: Erlbaum.

Horowitz, F. D. (1990). Developmental models of individual differences. In J. Colombo & J. Fagen (Eds.), *Individual differences in infancy: Reliability, stability, prediction* (pp. 3–18). Hillsdale, NJ: Erlbaum.

House, J. A., Kessler, R. C., & Herzog, A. R. (1990). Age, socioeconomic status, and health. *The Milbank Quarterly, 68,* 383–411.

House, J. S., Kessler, R. C., Herzog, A. R., Mero, R. P., Kinney, A. M., & Breslow, M. J. (1992). Social stratification, age, and health. In K. W. Schaie, D. Blazer, & J. M. House (Eds.), *Aging, health behaviors, and health outcomes* (pp. 1–32). Hillsdale, NJ: Erlbaum.

Houseknecht, S. K. (1987). Voluntary childlessness. In M. B. Sussman & S. K. Steinmetz (Eds.), *Handbook of marriage and the family* (pp. 369–395). New York: Plenum.

Hovell, M., Sipan, C., Blumberg, E., Atkins, C., Hofstetter, C. R., & Kreitner, S. (1994). Family influences on Latino and Anglo adolescents' sexual behavior. *Journal of Marriage and the Family, 56,* 973–986.

Howe, G. R. (1994). Dietary fat and breast cancer risks: An epidemiologic perspective. *Cancer, 74*(3 Suppl.), 1078–1084.

Howes, C. (1983). Patterns of friendship. *Child Development, 54,* 1041–1053.

Howes, C. (1987). Social competence with peers in young children: Developmental sequences. *Developmental Review, 7,* 252–272.

Howes, C., & Matheson, C. C. (1992). Sequences in the development of competent play with peers: Social and pretend play. *Developmental Psychology, 28,* 961–974.

Howes, C., Phillips, D. A., & Whitebook, M. (1992). Thresholds of quality: Implications for the social development of children in center-based child care. *Child Development, 63,* 449–460.

Hoyert, D. L. (1991). Financial and household exchanges between generations. *Research on Aging, 13,* 205–225.

Hoyert, D. L., & Seltzer, M. M. (1992). Factors related to the well-being and life activities of family caregivers. *Family Relations, 41,* 74–81.

Hubbard, F. O. A., & van IJzendoorn, M. H. (1987). Maternal unresponsiveness and infant crying. A critical replication of the Bell & Ainsworth study. In L. W. C. Tavecchio & M. H. v. IJzendoorn (Eds.), *Attachment in social networks* (pp. 339–378). Amsterdam: Elsevier North-Holland.

Huesmann, L. R., Lagerspetz, K., & Eron, L. D. (1984). Intervening variables in the television violence-aggression relation: Evidence from two countries. *Developmental Psychology, 20,* 746–775.

Hultsch, D. F., Hertzog, C., Small, B. J., McDonald-Miszczak, L., & Dixon, R. A. (1992). Short-term longitudinal change in cognitive performance in later life. *Psychology and Aging, 7,* 571–584.

Hunter, D. J., Spiegelman, D., Adami, H., Beeson, L., van den Brandt, P. A., Folsom, A. R., Fraser, G. E., Goldbohm, A., Graham, S., Howe, G. R., Kushi, L. H., Marshall, J. R., McDermott, A., Miller, A. B., Speizer, F. E., Wolk, A., Yuan, S., & Willett, W. (1996). Cohort studies of fat intake and the risk of breast cancer—a pooled analysis. *New England Journal of Medicine, 334,* 356–361.

Hunter, S., & Sundel, M. (1989). *Midlife myths: Issues, findings, and practice implications.* Newbury Park, CA: Sage.

Huntington, L., Hans, S. L., & Zeskind, P. S. (1990). The relations among cry characteristics, demographic variables, and developmental test scores in infants prenatally exposed to methadone. *Infant Behavior and Development, 13,* 533–538.

Hurwitz, E., Gunn, W. J., Pinsky, P. F., & Schonberger, L. B. (1991). Risk of respiratory illness associated with day-care attendance: A nationwide study. *Pediatrics, 87,* 62–69.

Huston, A. C. (Ed.). (1991). *Children in poverty: Child development and public policy.* Cambridge, England: Cambridge University Press.

Huston, A. C. (1994). Children in poverty: Designing research to affect policy. *Social Policy Report, Society for Research in Child Development, 8*(2), 1–12.

Huston, A. C., & Wright, J. C. (1994). Educating children with television: The forms of the medium. In D. Zillmann, J. Bryant, & A. C. Huston (Eds.), *Media, children, and the family: Social scientific, psychodynamic, and clinical perspectives* (pp. 73–84). Hillsdale, NJ: Erlbaum.

Huston, A. C., Wright, J. C., Rice, M. L., Kerkman, D., & St. Peters, M. (1990). Development of television viewing patterns in early childhood: A longitudinal investigation. *Developmental Psychology, 26,* 409–420.

Huston, T. L., & Chorost, A. F. (1994). Behavioral buffers on the effect of negativity on marital satisfaction: A longitudinal study. *Personal Relationships, 1,* 223–239.

Huston, T. L., McHale, S. M., & Crouter, A. C. (1986). When the honeymoon's over: Changes in the marriage relationship over the first year. In R. Gilmour & S. Duck (Eds.), *The emerging field of personal relationships* (pp. 109–132). Hillsdale, NJ: Erlbaum.

Hutt, S. J., Lenard, H. G., & Prechtl, H. F. R. (1969). Psychophysiological studies in newborn infants. In L. P. Lipsitt & H. W. Reese (Eds.), *Advances in child development and behavior* (Vol. 4) (pp. 128–173). New York: Academic Press.

Huttenlocher, J. (1995). *Children's language in relation to input.* Paper presented at the biennial meetings of the Society for Research in Child Development, Indianapolis, March.

Huttenlocher, P. R. (1994). Synaptogenesis, synapse elimination, and neural plasticity in human cerebral cortex. In C. A. Nelson (Ed.), *The Minnesota Symposia on Child Psychology* (Vol. 27) (pp. 35–54). Hillsdale, NJ: Erlbaum.

Huyck, M. H. (1994). The relevance of psychodynamic theories for understanding gender among older women. In B. F. Turner & L. E. Troll (Eds.), *Women growing older: Psychological perspectives* (pp. 202–238). Thousand Oaks, CA: Sage.

Idler, E. L., & Kasl, S. V. (1995). Self-ratings of health: Do they also predict change in functional ability? *Journals of Gerontology: Social Sciences, 50B,* S344–353.

Ingram, D. (1981). Early patterns of grammatical development. In R. E. Stark (Ed.), *Language behavior in infancy and early childhood* (pp. 327–358). New York: Elsevier North-Holland.

Inhelder, B., & Piaget, J. (1958). *The growth of logical thinking from childhood to adolescence.* New York: Basic Books.

Inkeles, A., & Usui, C. (1989). Retirement patterns in cross-national perspective. In D. I. Kertzer & K. W. Schaie (Eds.), *Age structuring in comparative perspective* (pp. 227–262). Hillsdale, NJ: Erlbaum.

Inoff-Germain, G., Arnold, G. S., Nottelmann, E. D., Susman, E. J., Cutler, G. B., Jr., & Chrousos, G. P. (1988). Relations between hormone levels and observational measures of aggressive behavior of young adolescents in family interactions. *Developmental Psychology, 24,* 129–139.

Insabella, G. M. (1995). *Varying levels of exposure to marital conflict: Prediction of adolescent adjustment across intact families and stepfamilies.* Paper presented at the biennial meetings of the Society for Research in Child Development, Indianapolis, March.

Irwin, M., & Pike, J. (1993). Bereavement, depressive symptoms, and immune function. In M. S. Stroebe, W. Stroebe, & R. O. Hansson (Eds.), *Handbook of bereavement: Theory, research, and intervention* (pp. 160–171). Cambridge, England: Cambridge University Press.

Isabella, R. A. (1995). The origins of infant-mother attachment: Maternal behavior and infant development. *Annals of Child Development, 10,* 57–81.

Isabella, R. A., Belsky, J., & von Eye, A. (1989). Origins of infant-mother attachment: An examination of interactional synchrony during the infant's first year. *Developmental Psychology, 25,* 12–21.

Istvan, J. (1986). Stress, anxiety, and birth outcomes. A critical review of the evidence. *Psychological Bulletin, 100,* 331–348.

Iversen, L., & Sabroe, S. (1988). Psychological well-being among unemployed and employed people after a company closedown: A longitudinal study. *Journal of Social Issues, 44,* 141–152.

Ivy, G. O., MacLeod, C. M., Petit, T. L., & Marcus, E. J. (1992). A physiological framework for perceptual and cognitive changes in aging. In F. I. M. Craik & T. A. Salthouse (Eds.), *The handbook of aging and cognition* (pp. 273–314). Hillsdale, NJ: Erlbaum.

Izard, C. E., Fantauzzo, C. A., Castle, J. M., Haynes, O. M., Rayias, M. F., & Putnam, P. H. (1995). The ontogeny and significance of infants' facial expressions in the first 9 months of life. *Developmental Psychology, 31,* 997–1013.

Izard, C. E., & Harris, P. (1995). Emotional development and developmental psychopathology. In D. Cicchetti & D. J. Cohen (Eds.), *Developmental psychopathology: Vol. 1. Theory and methods* (pp. 467–503). New York: Wiley.

Izard, C. E., & Malatesta, C. Z. (1987). Perspectives on emotional development I: Differential emotions theory of early emotional development. In J. D. Osofsky (Ed.), *Handbook of infant development* (2nd ed.) (pp. 494–554). New York: Wiley-Interscience.

Jacklin, C. N. (1989). Female and male: Issues of gender. *American Psychologist, 44,* 127–133.

Jackson, D. J., Longino, C. F., Jr. , Zimmerman, R. S., & Bradsher, J. E. (1991). Environmental adjustments to declining functional ability: Residential mobility and living arrangements. *Research on Aging, 13,* 289–309.

Jackson, J. J., & Perry, C. (1989). Physical health conditions of middle-aged and aged blacks. In K. S. Markides (Ed.), *Aging and health* (pp. 111–176). Newbury Park, CA: Sage.

Jackson, J. S., & Antonucci, T. C. (1994). Survey methodology in life-span human development research. In S. H. Cohen & H. W. Reese (Eds.), *Life-span developmental psychology: Methodological contributions* (pp. 65–94). Hillsdale, NJ: Erlbaum.

Jacobs, S. C., Kosten, T. R., Kasl, S. V., Ostfeld, A. M., Berkman, L., & Charpentier, P. (1987–1988). Attachment theory and multiple dimensions of grief. *Omega, 18,* 41–52.

Jacobson, S. W., & Frye, K. F. (1991). Effect of maternal social support on attachment: Experimental evidence. *Child Development, 62,* 572–582.

Jadack, R. A., Hyde, J. S., Moore, C. F., & Keller, M. L. (1995). Moral reasoning about sexually transmitted diseases. *Child Development, 66,* 167–177.

James, S. A., Keenan, N. L., & Browning, S. (1992). Socioeconomic status, health behaviors, and health status among blacks. In K. W. Schaie, D. Blazer, & J. M. House (Eds.), *Aging, health behaviors, and health outcomes* (pp. 39–57). Hillsdale, NJ: Erlbaum.

Jeffrey, R. W. (1989). Risk behaviors and health. Contrasting individual and population perspectives. *American Psychologist, 44,* 1194–1202.

Jenkins, J. M., & Astington, J. W. (1996). Cognitive factors and family structure associated with theory of mind development in young children. *Developmental Psychology, 32,* 70–78.

Jensen, A. R. (1980). *Bias in mental testing.* New York: Free Press.

Jerrome, D. (1990). Intimate relationships. In J. Bond & P. Coleman (Eds.), *Aging in society* (pp. 181–208). London: Sage.

Jessor, R. (1992). Risk behavior in adolescence: A psychosocial framework for understanding and action. *Developmental Review, 12,* 374–390.

Jette, A. M. (1996). Disability trends and transitions. In R. H. Binstock & L. K. George (Eds.), *Handbook of aging and the social sciences* (4th ed.) (pp. 94–116). San Diego, CA: Academic Press.

Johansson, B., & Berg, S. (1989). The robustness of the terminal decline phenomenon: Longitudinal data from the digit-span memory test. *Journals of Gerontology: Psychological Sciences, 44,* P184–186.

John, O. P., Caspi, A., Robins, R. W., Moffitt, T. E., & Stouthamer-Loeber, M. (1994). The "little five": Exploring the nomological network of the five-factor model of personality in adolescent boys. *Child Development, 65,* 160–178.

Johnson, C. L. (1982). Sibling solidarity: Its origin and functioning in Italian-American families. *Journal of Marriage and the Family, 44,* 155–167.

Johnson, C. L., & Barer, B. M. (1990). Families and networks among older inner-city blacks. *The Gerontologist, 30,* 726–733.

Johnson, H. R., Gibson, R. C., & Luckey, I. (1990). Health and social characteristics. Implications for services. In Z. Harel, E. A. McKinney, & M. Williams (Eds.), *Black aged* (pp. 131–145). Newbury Park, CA: Sage.

Johnston, J. R. (1985). Cognitive prerequisites: The evidence from children learning English. In D. I. Slobin (Ed.), *The crosslinguistic study of language acquisition: Vol. 2. Theoretical issues* (pp. 961–1004). Hillsdale, NJ: Erlbaum.

Jones, E. F., Forrest, J. D., Goldman, N., Henshaw, S. K., Lincoln, R., Rosoff, J. L., Westoff, C. F., & Wulf, D. (1986). *Teenage pregnancy in industrialized countries.* New Haven, CT: Yale University Press.

Joshi, M. S., & MacLean, M. (1994). Indian and English children's understanding of the distinction between real and apparent emotion. *Child Development, 65,* 1372–1384.

Joung, I. M. A., Stronks, K., van de Mheen, H., & Mackenbach, J. P. (1995). Health behaviours explain part of the differences in self reported health associated with partner/marital status in The Netherlands. *Journal of Epidemiology and Community Health, 49,* 482–488.

Jutras, S., & Lavoie, J. (1995). Living with an impaired elderly person: The informal caregiver's physical and mental health. *Journal of Aging and Health, 7,* 46–73.

Kagan, J. (1994). *Galen's prophecy.* New York: Basic Books.

Kagan, J., Arcus, D., Snidman, N., Feng, W. Y., Hendler, J., & Greene, S. (1994). Reactivity in infants: A cross-national comparison. *Developmental Psychology, 30,* 342–345.

Kagan, J., Kearsley, R., & Zelazo, P. (1978). *Infancy: Its place in human development.* Cambridge, MA: Harvard University Press.

Kagan, J., Reznick, J. S., & Snidman, N. (1990). The temperamental qualities of inhibition and lack of inhibition. In M. Lewis & S. M. Miller (Eds.), *Handbook of developmental psychopathology* (pp. 219–226). New York: Plenum.

Kagan, J., Snidman, N., & Arcus, D. (1993). On the temperamental categories of inhibited and uninhibited children. In K. H. Rubin & J. B. Asendorpf (Eds.), *Social withdrawal, inhibition, and shyness in childhood* (pp. 19–28). Hillsdale, NJ: Erlbaum.

Kahn, S. B., Alvi, S., Shaukat, N., Hussain, M. A., & Baig, T. (1990). A study of the validity of Holland's theory in a non-Western culture. *Journal of Vocational Behavior, 36,* 132–146.

Kail, R. (1991b). Processing time declines exponentially during childhood and adolescence. *Developmental Psychology, 27,* 259–266.

Kail, R., & Hall, L. K. (1994). Processing speed, naming speed, and reading. *Developmental Psychology, 30,* 949–954.

Kalish, R. A. (1985). The social context of death and dying. In R. H. Binstock & E. Shanas (Eds.), *Handbook of aging and the social sciences* (2nd ed.) (pp. 149–170). New York: Van Nostrand Reinhold.

Kalish, R. A., & Reynolds, D. K. (1976). *Death and ethnicity: A psychocultural study.* Los Angeles: University of Southern California Press. (Reprinted 1981, Baywood Publishing Co, Farmingdale, NJ.)

Kallman, D. A., Plato, C. C., & Tobin, J. D. (1990). The role of muscle loss in the age-related decline of grip strength: Cross-sectional and longitudinal perspectives. *Journals of Gerontology: Medical Sciences, 45,* M82–88.

Kamo, Y., Ries, L. M., Farmer, Y. M., Nickinovich, D. G., & Borgatta, E. F. (1991). Status attainment revisited. The National Survey of Families and Households. *Research on Aging, 13,* 124–143.

Kandel, D. B., & Wu, P. (1995). The contributions of mothers and fathers to the intergenerational transmission of cigarette smoking in adolescence. *Journal of Research on Adolescence, 5,* 225–252.

Kane, R. L., & Kane, R. A. (1990). Health care for older people: Organizational and policy issues. In R. H. Binstock & L. K. George (Eds.), *Handbook of aging and the social sciences* (3rd ed.) (pp. 415–437). San Diego, CA: Academic Press.

Kane, R. L., Klein, S. J., Bernstein, L., Rothenberg, R., & Wales, J. (1985). Hospice role in alleviating the emotional stress of terminal patients and their families. *Medical Care, 23,* 189–197.

Kane, R. L., Wales, J., Bernstein, L., Leibowitz, A., & Kaplan, S. (1984). A randomized controlled trial of hospice care. *Lancet,* 890–894.

Kann, L., Warren, C. W., Harris, W. A., Collins, J. L., Douglas, K. A., Collins, M. E., Williams, B. I., Ross, J. G., & Kolbe, L. J. (1995). Youth risk behavior surveillance—United States, 1993. *Morbidity and Mortality Weekly Reports, 44*(SS 1), 1–55.

Kannel, W. B., & Gordon, T. (1980). Cardiovascular risk factors in the aged: The Framingham study. In S. G. Haynes & M. Feinleib (Eds.), *Second conference on the epidemiology of aging.* U.S. Department of Health and Human Services, NIH Publication No. 80–969 (pp. 65–89). Washington, DC: U.S. Government Printing Office.

Kaplan, G. A. (1992). Health and aging in the Alameda County study. In K. W. Schaie, D. Blazer, & J. M. House (Eds.), *Aging, health behaviors, and health outcomes* (pp. 69–88). Hillsdale, NJ: Erlbaum.

Kaplan, R. M. (1985). The controversy related to the use of psychological tests. In B. B. Wolman (Ed.), *Handbook of intelligence: Theories, measurements, and applications* (pp. 465–504). New York: Wiley.

Karen, R. (1994). *Becoming attached.* New York: Warner Books.

Karmiloff-Smith, A. (1991). Beyond modularity: Innate constraints and developmental change. In S. Carey & R. Gelman (Eds.), *The epigenesis of mind: Essays on biology and cognition* (pp. 171–197). Hillsdale, NJ: Erlbaum.

Karney, B. R., & Bradbury, T. N. (1995). The longitudinal course of marital quality and stability: A review of theory, method, and research. *Psychological Bulletin, 118,* 3–34.

Karp, D. A. (1988). A decade of reminders: Changing age consciousness between fifty and sixty years old. *The Gerontologist, 28,* 727–738.

Katz, P. A., & Ksansnak, K. R. (1994). Developmental aspects of gender role flexibility and traditionality in middle childhood and adolescence. *Developmental Psychology, 30,* 272–282.

Kaye, K. L., & Bower, T. G. R. (1994). Learning and intermodal transfer of information in newborns. *Psychological Science, 5,* 286–288.

Keating, D. P. (1980). Thinking processes in adolescence. In J. Adelson (Ed.), *Handbook of adolescent psychology* (pp. 211–246). New York: Wiley.

Keating, D. P., List, J. A., & Merriman, W. E. (1985). Cognitive processing and cognitive ability: Multivariate validity investigation. *Intelligence, 9,* 149–170

Keefe, S. E. (1984). Real and ideal extended familism among Mexican Americans and Anglo Americans: On the meaning of "close" family ties. *Human Organization, 43,* 65–70.

Keeney, T. J., Cannizzo, S. R., & Flavell, J. H. (1967). Spontaneous and induced verbal rehearsal in a recall task. *Child Development, 38,* 935–966.

Keil, J. E., Sutherland, S. E., Knapp, R. G., Waid, L. R., & Gazes, P. C. (1992). Self-reported sexual functioning in elderly blacks and whites. *Journal of Aging and Health, 4,* 112–125.

Keith, P. M. (1981–1982). Perception of time remaining and distance from death. *Omega, 12,* 307–318.

Kellehear, A., & Lewin, T. (1988–1989). Farewells by the dying: A sociological study. *Omega, 19,* 275–292.

Kelley, M. L., Sanches-Hucles, J., & Walker, R. R. (1993). Correlates of disciplinary practices in working- to middle-class African-American mothers. *Merrill-Palmer Quarterly, 39,* 252–264.

Kelly, E. L., & Conley, J. J. (1987). Personality and compatibility: A prospective analysis of marital stability and marital satisfaction. *Journal of Personality and Social Psychology, 52,* 27–40.

Kempe, A., Wise, P. H., Barkan, S. E., Sappenfield, W. M., Sachs, B., Gortmaker, S. L., Sobol, A. M., First, L. R., Pursley, D., Reinhart, H., Kotelchuck, M., Cole, F. S., Gunter, N., & Stockbauer, J. W. (1992). Clinical determinants of the racial disparity in very low birth weight. *New England Journal of Medicine, 327,* 969–973.

Keniston, K. (1970). Youth: A "new" stage in life. *American Scholar, 8*(Autumn), 631–654.

Kessler, R. C., Foster, C., Webster, P. S., & House, J. S. (1992). The relationship between age and depressive symptoms in two national surveys. *Psychology and Aging, 7,* 119–126.

Kessler, R. C., Turner, J. B., & House, J. S. (1988). Effects of unemployment on health in a community survey: Main, modifying, and mediating effects. *Journal of Social Issues, 44,* 69–85.

Kesteloot, H., Lesaffre, E., & Joossens, J. V. (1991). Dairy fat, saturated animal fat, and cancer risk. *Preventive Medicine, 20,* 226–236.

Kiecolt-Glaser, J. K., Dura, J. R., Speicher, C. E., Trask, O. J., & Glaser, R. (1991). Spousal caregivers of dementia victims: Longitudinal changes in immunity and health. *Psychosomatic Medicine, 54,* 345–362.

Kiecolt-Glaser, J. K., & Glaser, R. (1995). Measurement of immune response. In S. Cohen, R. C. Kessler, & L. U. Gordon (Eds.), *Measuring stress: A guide for health and social scientists* (pp. 213–229). New York: Oxford University Press.

Kiecolt-Glaser, J. K., Glaser, R., Suttleworth, E. E., Dyer, C. S., Ogrocki, P., & Speicher, C. E. (1987). Chronic stress and immunity in family caregivers of Alzheimer's disease patients. *Psychosomatic Medicine, 49,* 523–535.

Killen, J. D., Hayward, C., Litt, I., Hammer, L. D., Wilson, D. M., Miner, B., Taylor, B., Varady, A., & Shisslak, C. (1992). Is puberty a risk factor for eating disorders? *American Journal of Diseases of Childhood, 146,* 323–325.

Kilpatrick, S. J., & Laros, R. K. (1989). Characteristics of normal labor. *Obstetrics and Gynecology, 74,* 85–87.

Kim, U., Triandis, H. C., Kâgitçibasi, Ç., Choi, S., & Yoon, G. (Eds.). (1994). *Individualism and collectivism: Theory, method, and applications.* Thousand Oaks, CA: Sage.

King, V. (1994). Variation in the consequences of nonresident father involvement for children's well-being. *Journal of Marriage and the Family, 56,* 963–972.

Kinney, D. A. (1993). From "nerds" to "normals": Adolescent identity recovery within a changing social system. *Sociology of Education, 66,* 21–40.

Kirkpatrick, L. A., & Hazan, C. (1994). Attachment styles and close relationships: A four-year prospective study. *Personal Relationships, 1,* 123–142.

Kitson, G. C. (1992). *Portrait of divorce: Adjustment to marital breakdown.* New York: Guilford Press.

Kitson, G. C., Babri, K. B., & Roach, M. J. (1985). Who divorces and why. A review. *Journal of Family Issues, 6,* 255–293.

Kivett, V. R. (1991). Centrality of the grandfather role among older rural black and white men. *Journals of Gerontology: Social Sciences, 46,* S250–258.

Klaus, H. M., & Kennell, J. H. (1976). *Maternal-infant bonding.* St. Louis, MO: Mosby.

Klebanov, P. K., Brooks-Gunn, J., Hofferth, S., & Duncan, G. J. (1995). *Neighborhood resources, social support and maternal competence.* Paper presented at the biennial meetings of the Society for Research in Child Development, Indianapolis, March.

Kleemeier, R. W. (1962). Intellectual changes in the senium. *Proceedings of the Social Statistics Section of the American Statistics Association, 1,* 290–295.

Klenow, D. J., & Bolin, R. C. (1989–1990). Belief in an afterlife: A national survey. *Omega, 20,* 63–74.

Klerman, L. V. (1991). The health of poor children: Problems and programs. In A. C. Huston (Ed.), *Children in poverty: Child development and public policy* (pp. 136–157). Cambridge, England: Cambridge University Press.

Kletzky, O. A., & Borenstein, R. (1987). Vasomotor instability of the menopause. In D. R. Mishell, Jr. (Ed.), *Menopause: Physiology and pharmacology.* (pp. 53–66). Chicago: Year Book Medical Publishers.

Kliegl, R., Smith, J., & Baltes, P. B. (1989). Testing-the-limits and the study of adult age differences in cognitive plasticity of a mnemonic skill. *Developmental Psychology, 25,* 247–256.

Kliegl, R., Smith, J., & Baltes, P. B. (1990). On the locus and process of magnification of age differences during mnemonic training. *Developmental Psychology, 26,* 894–904.

Kline, D. W., Kline, T. J. B., Fozard, J. L., Kosnik, W., Schieber, F., & Sekuler, R. (1992). Vision, aging, and driving: The problem of older drivers. *Journals of Gerontology: Psychological Sciences, 47,* P27–34.

Kline, D. W., & Scialfa, C. T. (1996). Visual and auditory aging. In J. E. Birren & K. W. Schaie (Eds.), *Handbook of the psychology of aging* (4th ed.) (pp. 181–203). San Diego, CA: Academic Press.

Kline, M., Tschann, J. M., Johnston, J. R., & Wallerstein, J. S. (1989). Children's adjustment in joint and sole physical custody families. *Developmental Psychology, 25,* 430–438.

Klonoff-Cohen, H. D., Edelstein, S. L., Lefkowitz, E. S., Srinivasan, I. P., Kaegi, D., Chang, J. C., & Wiley, K. J. (1995). The effect of passive smoking and tobacco exposure through breast milk on sudden infant death syndrome. *Journal of the American Medical Association, 273,* 795–798.

Kluwe, R. H. (1986). Psychological research on problem-solving and aging. In A. B. SFrensen, F. E. Weinert, & L. R. Sherrod (Eds.), *Human development and the life course: Multidisciplinary perspectives* (pp. 509–534). Hillsdale, NJ: Erlbaum.

Koenig, H. G., Kvale, J. N., & Ferrell, C. (1988). Religion and well-being in later life. *The Gerontologist, 28,* 18–28.

Kohlberg, L. (1964). Development of moral character and moral ideology. In M. L. Hoffman & L. W. Hoffman (Eds.), *Review of child development research* (Vol. 1) (pp. 283–332). New York: Russell Sage Foundation.

Kohlberg, L. (1966). A cognitive-developmental analysis of children's sex-role concepts and attitudes. In E. E. Maccoby (Ed.), *The development of sex differences* (pp. 82–172). Stanford, CA: Stanford University Press.

Kohlberg, L. (1973). Continuities in childhood and adult moral development revisited. In P. B. Baltes & K. W. Schaie (Eds.), *Life-span developmental psychology: Personality and socialization* (pp. 180–204). New York: Academic Press.

Kohlberg, L. (1975) The cognitive-developmental approach to moral education. *Phi Delta Kappan,* June, 670–677.

Kohlberg, L. (1976). Moral stages and moralization: The cognitive-developmental approach. In T. Lickona (Ed.), *Moral development and behavior: Theory, research, and social issues* (pp. 31–53). New York: Holt.

Kohlberg, L. (1981). *Essays on moral development: Vol. 1. The philosophy of moral development.* New York: Harper & Row.

Kohlberg, L., & Candee, D. (1984). The relationship of moral judgment to moral action. In W. M. Kurtines & J. L. Gewirtz (Eds.), *Morality, moral behavior, and moral development* (pp. 52–73). New York: Wiley.

Kohlberg, L., & Elfenbein, D. (1975). The development of moral judgments concerning capital punishment. *American Journal of Orthopsychiatry, 54,* 614–640.

Kohlberg, L., & Higgins, A. (1987). School democracy and social interaction. In W. M. Kurtines & J. L. Gewirtz (Eds.), *Moral development through social interaction* (pp. 102–130). New York: Wiley-Interscience.

Kohlberg, L., Levine, C., & Hewer, A. (1983). *Moral stages: A current formulation and a response to critics.* Basel, Switzerland: S. Karger.

Kohlberg, L., & Ullian, D. Z. (1974). Stages in the development of psychosexual concepts and attitudes. In R. C. Friedman, R. M. Richart, & R. L. Vande Wiele (Eds.), *Sex differences in behavior* (pp. 209–222). New York: Wiley.

Kohli, M. (1994). Work and retirement: A comparative perspective. In M. W. Riley, R. L. Kahn, & A. Foner (Eds.), *Age and structural lag* (pp. 80–106). New York: Wiley-Interscience.

Kolata, G. (1992). A parents' guide to kids' sports. *New York Times Magazine,* April 26, pp. 12–15, 40, 44, 46.

Kolata, G. (1995). If tests hint Alzheimer's, should a patient be told? *New York Times,* October 24, pp. A1, B8.

Kolata, G. (1996). New era of robust elderly belies the fears of scientists. *New York Times,* February 27, pp. A1, B10.

Kopp, C. B. (1990). Risks in infancy: Appraising the research. *Merrill Palmer Quarterly, 36,* 117–140.

Korner, A. F., Hutchinson, C. A., Koperski, J. A., Kraemer, H. C., & Schneider, P. A. (1981). Stability of individual differences of neonatal motor and crying patterns. *Child Development, 52,* 83–90.

Kozma, A., Stones, M. J., & Hannah, T. E. (1991). Age, activity, and physical performance: An evaluation of performance models. *Psychology and Aging, 6,* 43–49.

Kozol, J. (1995). *Amazing grace.* New York: Crown.

Krause, N., Jay, G., & Liang, J. (1991). Financial strain and psychological well-being among the American and Japanese elderly. *Psychology and Aging, 6,* 170–181.

Krause, N., Liang, J., & Keith, V. (1990). Personality, social support, and psychological distress in later life. *Psychology and Aging, 5,* 315–326.

Krause, N., Liang, J., & Yatomi, N. (1989). Satisfaction with social support and depressive symptoms: A panel analysis. *Psychology and Aging, 4,* 88–97.

Kronenberg, F. (1994). Hot flashes: Phenomenology, quality of life, and search for treatment options. *Experimental Gerontology, 29,* 319–336.

Kübler-Ross, E. (1969). *On death and dying.* New York: Macmillan.

Kübler-Ross, E. (1974). *Questions and answers on death and dying.* New York: Macmillan.

Kuczaj, S. A., II (1977). The acquisition of regular and irregular past tense forms. *Journal of Verbal Learning and Verbal Behavior, 49,* 319–326.

Kuczaj, S. A., II (1978). Children's judgments of grammatical and ungrammatical irregular past tense verbs. *Child Development, 49,* 319–326.

Kuczynski, L., Kochanska, G., Radke-Yarrow, M., & Girnius-Brown, O. (1987). A developmental interpretation of young children's noncompliance. *Developmental Psychology, 23,* 799–806.

Kuhn, D. (1992). Cognitive development. In M. H. Bornstein & M. E. Lamb (Eds.), *Developmental psychology: An advanced textbook* (3rd ed.) (pp. 211–272). Hillsdale, NJ: Erlbaum.

Kunkel, S. R., & Applebaum, R. A. (1992). Estimating the prevalence of long-term disability for an aging society. *Journals of Gerontology: Social Sciences, 47,* S253–260.

Kupersmidt, J. B., Griesler, P. C., DeRosier, M. E., Patterson, C. J., & Davis, P. W. (1995). Childhood aggression and peer relations in the context of family and neighborhood factors. *Child Development, 66,* 360–375.

Kurdek, L. A. (1994). Areas of conflict for gay, lesbian, and heterosexual couples: What couples argue about influences relationship satisfaction. *Journal of Marriage and the Family, 56,* 923–934.

Kurdek, L. A. (1995a). Developmental changes in relationship quality in gay and lesbian cohabiting couples. *Developmental Psychology, 31,* 86–94.

Kurdek, L. A. (1995b). Lesbian and gay couples. In A. R. D'Augelli & C. J. Patterson (Eds.), *Lesbian, gay, and bisexual identities over the lifespan: Psychological perspectives* (pp. 243–261). New York: Oxford University Press.

Kurdek, L. A., & Fine, M. A. (1994). Family acceptance and family control as predictors of adjustment in young adolescents: Linear, curvilinear, or interactive effects? *Child Development, 65,* 1137–1146.

Kurdek, L. A., & Schmitt, J. P. (1986). Early development of relationship quality in heterosexual married, heterosexual cohabiting, gay, and lesbian couples. *Developmental Psychology, 22,* 305–309.

Kurtines, W. M., & Gewirtz, J. L. (Eds.). (1991). *Handbook of moral behavior and development: Vol. 1. Theory; Vol. 2, Research; Vol. 3. Application.* Hillsdale, NJ: Erlbaum.

Kurtz, L., & Tremblay, R. E. (1995). *The impact of family transition upon social, sexual, and delinquent behavior in adolescent boys: A nine year longitudinal study.* Paper presented at the biennial meetings of the Society for Research in Child Development, Indianapolis, March.

Labouvie-Vief, G. (1980). Beyond formal operations: Uses and limits of pure logic in life-span development. *Human Development, 23,* 141–161.

Labouvie-Vief, G. (1990). Modes of knowledge and the organization of development. In M. L. Commons, C. Armon, L. Kohlberg, F. A. Richards, T. A. Grotzer, & J. D. Sinnott (Eds.), *Adult development: Vol. 2. Models and methods in the study of adolescent and adult thought* (pp. 43–62). New York: Praeger.

Labouvie-Vief, G., & Schell, D. A. (1982). Learning and memory in later life. In B. B. Wolman (Ed.), *Handbook of developmental psychology* (pp. 828–846). Englewood Cliffs, NJ: Prentice-Hall.

La Freniere, P., Strayer, F. F., & Gauthier, R. (1984). The emergence of same-sex affiliative preferences among preschool peers: A developmental/ethological perspective. *Child Development, 55,* 1958–1965.

Lakatta, E. G. (1990). Heart and circulation. In E. L. Schneider & J. W. Rowe (Eds.), *Handbook of the biology of aging* (3rd ed.) (pp. 181–217). San Diego, CA: Academic Press.

Lamb, M. E. (1981). The development of father-infant relationships. In M. E. Lamb (Ed.), *The role of the father in child development* (2nd ed.) (pp. 459–488). New York: Wiley.

Lamb, M. E., Frodi, A. M., Hwang, C., Frodi, M., & Steinberg, J. (1982). Mother- and father-infant interaction involving play and holding in traditional and nontraditional Swedish families. *Developmental Psychology, 18,* 215–221.

Lamb, M. E., Sternberg, K. J., & Prodromidis, M. (1992). Nonmaternal care and the security of infant-mother attachment: A reanalysis of the data. *Infant Behavior and Development, 15,* 71–83.

Lamborn, S. D., Mounts, N. S., Steinberg, L., & Dornbusch, S. M. (1991). Patterns of competence and adjustment among adolescents from authoritative, authoritarian, indulgent, and neglectful families. *Child Development, 62,* 1049–1065.

Lamke, L. K. (1982a). Adjustment and sex-role orientation. *Journal of Youth and Adolescence, 11,* 247–259.

Lamke, L. K. (1982b). The impact of sex-role orientation on self-esteem in early adolescence. *Child Development, 53,* 1530–1535.

Landry, S. H., Garner, P. W., Swank, P. R., & Baldwin, C. D. (1996). Effects of maternal scaffolding during joint toy play with preterm and full-term infants. *Merrill-Palmer Quarterly, 42,* 177–199.

Langlois, J. H., Ritter, J. M., Casey, R. J., & Sawin, D. B. (1995). Infant attractiveness predicts maternal behaviors and attitudes. *Developmental Psychology, 31,* 464–472.

Langlois, J. H., Ritter, J. M., Roggman, L. A., & Vaughn, L. S. (1991). Facial diversity and infant preferences for attractive faces. *Developmental Psychology, 27,* 79–84.

Langlois, J. H., & Roggman, L. A. (1990). Attractive faces are only average. *Psychological Science, 1,* 115–121.

Langlois, J. H., Roggman, L. A., Casey, R. J., Ritter, J. M., Rieser-Danner, L. A., & Jenkins, V. Y. (1987). Infant preferences for attractive faces: Rudiments of a stereotype? *Developmental Psychology, 23,* 363–369.

Langlois, J. H., Roggman, L. A., & Musselman, L. (1994). What is average and what is not average about attractive faces? *Psychological Science, 5,* 214–220.

Langlois, J. H., Roggman, L. A., & Rieser-Danner, L. A. (1990). Infants' differential social responses to attractive and unattractive faces. *Developmental Psychology, 26,* 153–159.

Lansdown, R., & Benjamin, G. (1985). The development of the concept of death in children aged 5–9 years. *Child Care, Health and Development, 11,* 13–30.

La Pine, T. R., Jackson, J. C., & Bennett, F. C. (1995). Outcome of infants weighing less than 800 grams at birth: 15 years' experience. *Pediatrics, 96,* 479–483.

Larson, J. H., & Holman, T. B. (1994). Premarital predictors of marital quality and stability. *Family Relations, 43,* 223–237.

Larson, R., Mannell, R., & Zuzanek, J. (1986). Daily well-being of older adults with friends and family. *Psychology and Aging, 1,* 117–126.

Laub, J. H., & Sampson, R. J. (1995). The long-term effect of punitive discipline. In J. McCord (Ed.), *Coercion and punishment in long-term perspectives* (pp. 247–258). Cambridge, England: Cambridge University Press.

Laumann, E. O., Gagnon, J. H., Michael, R. T., & Michaels, S. (1994). *The social organization of sexuality: Sexual practices in the United States.* Chicago: University of Chicago Press.

Laursen, B. (1995). Conflict and social interaction in adolescent relationships. *Journal of Research on Adolescence, 5,* 55–70.

Lawrence, R. H., Bennett, J. M., & Markides, K. S. (1992). Perceived intergenerational solidarity and psychological distress among older Mexican Americans. *Journals of Gerontology: Social Sciences, 47,* S55–65.

Lawton, L., Silverstein, M., & Bengtson, V. (1994). Affection, social contact, and geographic distance between adult children and their parents. *Journal of Marriage and the Family, 56,* 57–68.

Lawton, M. P. (1985). Housing and living environments of older people. In R. H. Binstock & E. Shanas (Eds.), *Aging and the social sciences* (2nd ed.) (pp. 450–478). New York: Van Nostrand Reinhold.

Lawton, M. P. (1990). Residential environment and self-directedness among older people. *American Psychologist, 45,* 638–640.

Leadbeater, B. J., & Dionne, J. (1981). The adolescent's use of formal operational thinking in solving problems related to identity resolution. *Adolescence, 16,* 111–121.

Leaper, C. (1991). Influence and involvement in children's discourse: Age, gender, and partner effects. *Child Development, 62,* 797–811.

Lee, G. R. (1988a). Marital satisfaction in later life: The effects of nonmarital roles. *Journal of Marriage and the Family, 50,* 775–783.

Lee, G. R., Dwyer, J. W., & Coward, R. T. (1993). Gender differences in parent care: Demographic factors and same-gender preferences. *Journals of Gerontology: Social Sciences, 48,* S9–16.

Lee, G. R., & Ishii-Kuntz, M. (1987). Social interaction, loneliness, and emotional well-being among the elderly. *Research on Aging, 9,* 459–482.

Lee, G. R., Seccombe, K., & Shehan, C. L. (1991). Marital status and personal happiness: An analysis of trend data. *Journal of Marriage and the Family, 53,* 839–844.

Lee, G. R., & Shehan, C. L. (1989). Social relations and the self-esteem of older persons. *Research on Aging, 11,* 427–442.

Lee, I., Manson, J. E., Hennekens, C. H., & Paffenbarger, R. S., Jr. (1993). Body weight and mortality; A 27-year follow-up of middle-aged men. *Journal of the American Medical Association, 270,* 2823–2828.

Lee, I.-M., Hsieh, C., & Paffenbarger, R. S. (1995). Exercise intensity and longevity in men. *Journal of the American Medical Association, 273,* 1179–1184.

Lee, M. A., Nelson, H. D., Tilden, V. P., Ganzini, L., Schmidt, T. A., & Tolle, S. W. (1996). Legalizing assisted suicide—views of physicians in Oregon. *New England Journal of Medicine, 334,* 310–315.

Lee, V. E., Burkham, D. T., Zimiles, H., & Ladewski, B. (1994). Family structure and its effect on behavioral and emotional problems in young adolescents. *Journal of Research on Adolescence, 4,* 405–437.

Lehman, H. C. (1953). *Age and achievement.* Princeton, NJ: Princeton University Press.

Lehr, U. (1982). Hat die Grosfamilie heute noch eine Chance? [Does the extended family have a chance these days?]. *Der Deutsche Artz, 18 Sonderdruck.*

Leigh, G. K. (1982). Kinship interaction over the family life span. *Journal of Marriage and the Family, 44,* 197–208.

Leichtman, M. D., & Ceci, S. J. (1995). The effects of stereotypes and suggestions on preschoolers' reports. *Developmental Psychology, 31,* 568–578.

Lempers, J. D., & Clark-Lempers, D. (1990). Family economic stress, maternal and paternal support and adolescent distress. *Journal of Adolescence, 13,* 217–229.

Leon, G. R., Gillum, B., Gillum, R., & Gouze, M. (1979). Personality stability and change over a 30-year period—middle age to old age. *Journal of Consulting and Clinical Psychology, 47,* 517–524.

Lerner, R. M. (1986). *Concepts and theories of human development* (2nd ed.). New York: Random House.

Lerner, R. M. (1987). A life-span perspective for early adolescence. In R. M. Lerner & T. T. Foch (Eds.), *Biological-psychosocial interactions in early adolescence* (pp. 9–34). Hillsdale, NJ: Erlbaum.

Lester, B. M. (1987). Prediction of developmental outcome from acoustic cry analysis in term and preterm infants. *Pediatrics, 80,* 529–534.

Lester, B. M., Boukydis, C. F. Z., Garcia-Coll, C. T., Hole, W., & Peucker, M. (1992). Infantile colic: Acoustic cry characteristics, maternal perception of cry, and temperament. *Infant Behavior and Development, 15,* 15–26.

Lester, B. M., & Dreher, M. (1989). Effects of marijuana use during pregnancy on newborn cry. *Child Development, 60,* 765–771.

Lester, D. (1990). The Collett-Lester fear of death scale: The original version and a revision. *Death Studies, 14,* 451–468.

LeVay, S. (1991). A difference in hypothalamus structure between heterosexual and homosexual men. *Science, 253,* 1034–1037.

Leve, L. D., & Fagor, B. I. (1995). *The influence of attachment style and parenting behavior on children's prosocial behavior with peers.* Paper presented at the biennial meetings of the Society for Research in Child Development, Indianapolis, March.

Levenson, R. W., Carstensen, L. L., & Gottman, J. M. (1993). Long-term marriage: Age, gender, and satisfaction. *Psychology and Aging, 8,* 301–313.

Levin, J. S., Chatters, L. M., & Taylor, R. J. (1995). Religious effects on health status and life satisfaction among black Americans. *Journals of Gerontology: Social Sciences, 50B,* S154–163.

Levinson, D. J. (1978). *The seasons of a man's life.* New York: Knopf.

Levinson, D. J. (1980). Toward a conception of the adult life course. In N. J. Smelser & E. H. Erikson (Eds.), *Themes of work and love in adulthood* (pp. 265–290). Cambridge, MA: Harvard University Press.

Levinson, D. J. (1986). A conception of adult development. *American Psychologist, 41,* 3–13.

Levinson, D. J. (1990). A theory of life structure development in adulthood. In C. N. Alexander & E. J. Langer (Eds.), *Higher stages of human development* (pp. 35–54). New York: Oxford University Press.

Levinson, D. J. (1996). *The seasons of a woman's life.* New York: Knopf.

Levitt, M. J., Guacci-Franco, N., & Levitt, J. L. (1993). Convoys of social support in childhood and early adolescence: Structure and function. *Developmental Psychology, 29,* 811–818.

Levitt, M. J., Weber, R. A., & Guacci, N. (1993). Convoys of social support: An intergenerational analysis. *Psychology and Aging, 8,* 323–326.

Levy, G. D., & Fivush, R. (1993). Scripts and gender: A new approach for examining gender-role development. *Developmental Review, 13,* 126–146.

Levy, L. H., Martinkowski, K. S., & Derby, J. F. (1994). Differences in patterns of adaptation in conjugal bereavement: Their sources and potential significance. *Omega, 29,* 71–87.

Lewis, C. C. (1981). How adolescents approach decisions: Changes over grades seven to twelve and policy implications. *Child Development, 52,* 538–544.

Lewis, C. N., Freeman, N. H., & Maridaki-Kassotaki, K. (1995). *The social basis of theory of mind: Influences of siblings and, more importantly, interactions with adult kin.* Paper presented at the biennial meetings of the Society for Research in Child Development, Indianapolis, March.

Lewis, M. (1990). Social knowledge and social development. *Merrill-Palmer Quarterly, 36,* 93–116.

Lewis, M. (1991). Ways of knowing: Objective self-awareness of consciousness. *Developmental Review, 11,* 231–243.

Lewis, M., Allesandri, S. M., & Sullivan, M. W. (1992). Differences in shame and pride as a function of children's gender and task difficulty. *Child Development, 63,* 630–638.

Lewis, M., & Brooks, J. (1978). Self-knowledge and emotional development. In M. Lewis & L. A. Rosenblum (Eds.), *The development of affect* (pp. 205–226). New York: Plenum.

Lewis, M., & Sullivan, M. W. (1985). Infant intelligence and its assessment. In B. B. Wolman (Ed.), *Handbook of intelligence* (pp. 505–599). New York: Wiley-Interscience.

Lewis, M., Sullivan, M. W., Stanger, C., & Weiss, M. (1989). Self development and self-conscious emotions. *Child Development, 60,* 146–156.

Lewis, M. D. (1993). Early socioemotional predictors of cognitive competence at 4 years. *Developmental Psychology, 29,* 1036–1045.

Lewkowicz, D. J. (1994). Limitations on infants' response to rate-based auditory-visual relations. *Developmental Psychology, 30,* 880–892.

Lickona, T. (1978). Moral development and moral education. In J. M. Gallagher & J. J. A. Easley (Eds.), *Knowledge and development* (Vol. 2) (pp. 21–74). New York: Plenum.

Lickona, T. (1983). *Raising good children.* Toronto: Bantam Books.

Lieberman, M., Doyle, A., & Markiewicz, D. (1995). *Attachment to mother and father: Links to peer relations in children.* Paper presented at the biennial meetings of the Society for Research in Child Development, Indianapolis, March.

Lieberman, M. A. (1965). Psychological correlates of impending death: Some preliminary observations. *Journal of Gerontology, 20,* 182–190.

Lieberman, M. A., & Coplan, A. S. (1970). Distance from death as a variable in the study of aging. *Developmental Psychology, 2,* 71–84.

Lieberman, M. A., & Peskin, H. (1992). Adult life crises. In J. E. Birren, R. B. Sloane, & G. D. Cohen (Eds.), *Handbook of mental health and aging* (2nd ed.) (pp. 119–143). San Diego, CA: Academic Press.

Liem, R., & Liem, J. H. (1988). Psychological effects of unemployment on workers and their families. *Journal of Social Issues, 44,* 87–105.

Light, L. L. (1991). Memory and aging: Four hypotheses in search of data. *Annual Review of Psychology, 42,* 333–376.

Light, L. L. (1992). The organization of memory in old age. In F. I. M. Craik & T. A. Salthouse (Eds.), *The handbook of aging and cognition* (pp. 111–166). Hillsdale, NJ: Erlbaum.

Liker, J. K., & Elder, G. H., Jr. (1983). Economic hardship and marital relations in the 1930s. *American Sociological Review, 48,* 343–359.

Lillard, A. S., & Flavell, J. H. (1992). Young children's understanding of different mental states. *Developmental Psychology, 28,* 626–634.

Lim, K. O., Zipursky, R. B., Watts, M. C., & Pfefferbaum, A. (1992). Decreased gray matter in normal aging: An in vivo magnetic resonance study. *Journals of Gerontology: Biological Sciences, 47,* B26–30.

Lima, S. D., Hale, S., & Myerson, J. (1991). How general is general slowing? Evidence from the lexical domain. *Psychology and Aging, 6,* 416–425.

Lindberg, L. D. (1996). Women's decisions about breastfeeding and maternal employment. *Journal of Marriage and the Family, 58,* 239–251.

Lindsay, R. (1985). The aging skeleton. In M. R. Haug, A. B. Ford, & M. Sheafor (Eds.), *The physical and mental health of aged women* (pp. 65–82). New York: Springer.

Linney, J. A., & Seidman, E. (1989). The future of schooling. *American Psychologist, 44,* 336–340.

Lissner, L., Bengtsson, C., Björkelund, C., & Wedel, H. (1996). Physical activity levels and changes in relation to longevity: A prospective study of Swedish women. *American Journal of Epidemiology, 143,* 54–62.

Litwak, E., & Longino, C. F., Jr. (1987). Migration patterns among the elderly: A developmental perspective. *The Gerontologist, 27,* 266–272.

Liu, X., Liang, J., Muramatsu, N., & Sugisawa, H. (1995). Transitions in functional status and active life expectancy among older people in Japan. *Journals of Gerontology: Social Sciences, 50B,* S383–394.

Livesley, W. J., & Bromley, D. B. (1973). *Person perception in childhood and adolescence.* London: Wiley.

Livson, F. B. (1976). Patterns of personality development in middle-aged women: A longitudinal study. *International Journal of Aging and Human Development, 7,* 107–115.

Livson, F. B. (1981). Paths to psychological health in the middle years: Sex differences. In D. H. Eichorn, J. A. Clausen, N. Haan, M. P. Honzik, & P. H. Mussen (Eds.), *Present and past in middle life* (pp. 195–221). New York: Academic Press.

Livson, N., & Peskin, H. (1981). Psychological health at 40: Prediction from adolescent personality. In D. H. Eichorn, J. A. Clausen, N. Haan, M. P. Honzik, & P. H. Mussen (Eds.), *Present and past in middle life* (pp. 184–194). New York: Academic Press.

Lo, Y. D., Patel, P., Wainscoat, J. S., Sampietro, M., Gillmer, M. D. G., & Fleming, K. A. (1989). Prenatal sex determination by DNA amplification from maternal peripheral blood. *Lancet,* 1363–1365.

Loehlin, J. C. (1992). *Genes and environment in personality development.* Newbury Park, CA: Sage.

Loehlin, J. C., Horn, J. M., & Willerman, L. (1994). Differential inheritance of mental abilities in the Texas Adoption Project. *Intelligence, 19,* 325–336.

Loevinger, J. (1976). *Ego development.* San Francisco: Jossey-Bass.

Loevinger, J. (1984). On the self and predicting behavior. In R. A. Zucker, J. Aronoff, & A. I. Rabin (Eds.), *Personality and the prediction of behavior* (pp. 43–68). New York: Academic Press.

Long, J. V. F., & Vaillant, G. E. (1984). Natural history of male psychological health: Escape from the underclass. *American Journal of Psychiatry, 141,* 341–346.

Longino, C. F., Jr. (1990). Geographical distribution and migration. In R. H. Binstock & L. K. George (Eds.), *Handbook of aging and the social sciences* (3rd ed.) (pp. 45–63). San Diego, CA: Academic Press.

Longino, C. F., Jr., Jackson, D. J., Zimmerman, R. S., & Bradsher, J. E. (1991). The second move: Health and geographic mobility. *Journals of Gerontology: Social Sciences, 46,* S218–224.

Lopata, H. Z. (1981). Widowhood and husband sanctification. *Journal of Marriage and the Family, 43,* 439–450.

Lopata, H. Z. (1986). Time in anticipated future and events in memory. *American Behavioral Scientist, 29,* 695–709.

Lubben, J. E., Weiler, P. G., & Chi, I. (1989). Health practices of the elderly poor. *American Journal of Public Health, 79,* 731–734.

Lubinski, D., & Benbow, C. P. (1992). Gender differences in abilities and preferences among the gifted: Implications for the math-science pipeline. *Current Directions in Psychological Science, 1,* 61–66.

Luke, B., & Murtaugh, M. (1993). The racial disparity in very low birth weight. *New England Journal of Medicine, 328,* 285–286.

Lundh, W., & Gyllang, C. (1993). Use of the Edinburgh Postnatal Depression Scale in some Swedish child health care centres. *Scandinavian Journal of Caring Sciences, 7,* 149–154.

Luster, T., Boger, R., & Hannan, K. (1993). Infant affect and home environment. *Journal of Marriage and the Family, 55,* 651–661.

Luster, T., & McAdoo, H. (1996). Family and child influences on educational attainment: A secondary analysis of the High/Scope Perry Preschool data. *Developmental Psychology, 32,* 26–39.

Luster, T., & McAdoo, H. P. (1995). Factors related to self-esteem among African American youths: A secondary analysis of the High/Scope Perry Preschool data. *Journal of Research on Adolescence, 5,* 451–467.

Luster, T., & Small, S. A. (1994). Factors associated with sexual risk-taking behaviors among adolescents. *Journal of Marriage and the Family, 56,* 622–632.

Luthar, S. S., & Zigler, E. (1992). Intelligence and social competence among high-risk adolescents. *Development and Psychopathology, 4,* 287–299.

Lykken, D. T., McGue, M., Tellegen, A., & Bouchard, T. J., Jr. (1992). Emergenesis: Genetic traits that may not run in families. *American Psychologist, 47,* 1565–1577.

Lyon, T. D., & Flavell, J. H. (1994). Young children's understanding of "remember" and "forget." *Child Development, 65,* 1357–1371.

Lyons, N. P. (1983). Two perspectives: On self, relationships, and morality. *Harvard Educational Review, 53,* 125–145.

Lytton, H., & Romney, D. M. (1991). Parents' differential socialization of boys and girls: A meta-analysis. *Psychological Bulletin, 109,* 267–296.

Maas, H. S., & Kuypers, J. A. (1974). *From thirty to seventy.* San Francisco: Jossey-Bass.

Maccoby, E. E. (1980). *Social development: Psychological growth and the parent-child relationship.* New York: Harcourt Brace Jovanovich.

Maccoby, E. E. (1984). Middle childhood in the context of the family. In W. A. Collins (Ed.), *Development during middle childhood: The years from six to twelve* (pp. 184–239). Washington, DC: National Academy Press.

Maccoby, E. E. (1988). Gender as a social category. *Developmental Psychology, 24,* 755–765.

Maccoby, E. E. (1990). Gender and relationships: A developmental account. *American Psychologist, 45,* 513–520.

Maccoby, E. E. (1995). The two sexes and their social systems. In P. Moen, G. H. Elder, Jr., & K. Lüscher (Eds.), *Examining lives in context: Perspectives on the ecology of human development* (pp. 347–364). Washington, DC: American Psychological Association.

Maccoby, E. E., & Jacklin, C. N. (1987). Gender segregation in childhood. In H. W. Reese (Ed.), *Advances in child development and behavior* (Vol. 20) (pp. 239–288). Orlando, FL: Academic Press.

Maccoby, E. E., & Martin, J. A. (1983). Socialization in the context of the family: Parent-child interaction. In E. M. Hetherington (Ed.), *Handbook of child psychology: Socialization, personality, and social development* (Vol. 4) (pp. 1–102). New York: Wiley.

MacDermid, S. M., Huston, T. L., & McHale, S. M. (1990). Changes in marriage associated with the transition to parenthood: Individual differences as a function of sex-role attitudes and changes in the division of household labor. *Journal of Marriage and the Family, 52,* 475–486.

MacGowan, R. J., MacGowan, C. A., Serdula, M. K., Lane, J. M., Joesoef, R. M., & Cook, F. H. (1991). Breast-feeding among women attending Women, Infants, and Children clinics in Georgia, 1987. *Pediatrics, 87,* 361–366.

MacIver, D. J., Reuman, D. A., & Main, S. R. (1995). Social structuring of the school: Studying what is, illuminating what could be. *Annual Review of Psychology, 46,* 375–400.

Mack, V., Urberg, K., Lou, Q., & Tolson, J. (1995). *Ethnic, gender and age differences in parent and peer orientation during adolescence.* Paper presented at the biennial meetings of the Society for Research in Child Development, Indianapolis, March.

MacRae, H. (1992). Fictive kin as a component of the social networks of older people. *Research on Aging, 14,* 226–247.

Madden, D. J. (1992). Four to ten milliseconds per year: Age-related slowing of visual word identification. *Journals of Gerontology: Psychological Sciences, 47,* P59–68.

Madden, D. J., Blumenthal, J. A., Allen, P. A., & Emery, C. F. (1989). Improving aerobic capacity in healthy older adults does not necessarily lead to improved cognitive performance. *Psychology and Aging, 4,* 307–320.

Madsen, W. (1969). Mexican Americans and Anglo Americans: A comparative study of mental health in Texas. In S. C. Plog & R. B. Edgerton (Eds.), *Changing perspectives in mental illness* (pp. 217–247). New York: Holt, Rinehart and Winston.

Maeda, D. (1993). Japan. In E. B. Palmore (Ed.), *Developments and research on aging: An international handbook* (pp. 201–219). Westport, CT: Greenwood Press.

Maffeis, C., Schutz, Y., Piccoli, R., Gonfiantini, E., & Pinelli, L. (1993). Prevalence of obesity in children in north-east Italy. *International Journal of Obesity, 14,* 287–294.

Maier, S. F., Watkins, L. R., & Fleshner, M. (1994). The interface between behavior, brain, and immunity. *American Psychologist, 49,* 1004–1017.

Main, M., & Hesse, E. (1990). Parents' unresolved traumatic experiences are related to infant disorganized attachment status: Is frightened and/or frightening parental behavior the linking mechanism? In M. T. Greenberg, D. Cicchetti, & E. M. Cummings (Eds.), *Attachment in the preschool years: Theory, research, and intervention* (pp. 161–182). Chicago: University of Chicago Press.

Main, M., Kaplan, N., & Cassidy, J. (1985). Security in infancy, childhood, and adulthood: A move to the level of representation. *Monographs of the Society for Research in Child Development, 50* (Serial No. 209), 66–104.

Main, M., & Solomon, J. (1990). Procedures for identifying infants as disorganized/disoriented during the Ainsworth Strange Situation. In M. T. Greenberg, D. Cicchetti, & E. M. Cummings (Eds.), *Attachment in the preschool years: Theory, research, and intervention* (pp. 121–160). Chicago: University of Chicago Press.

Malina, R. M. (1982). Motor development in the early years. In S. G. Moore & C. R. Cooper (Eds.), *The young child: Reviews of research* (Vol. 3) (pp. 211–232). Washington, DC: National Association for the Education of Young Children.

Malina, R. M. (1990). Physical growth and performance during the transition years. In R. Montemayor, G. R. Adams, & T. P. Gullotta (Eds.), *From childhood to adolescence: A transitional period?* (pp. 41–62). Newbury Park, CA: Sage.

Malloy, M. H., & Hoffman, H. J. (1995). Prematurity, sudden infant death syndrome, and age of death. *Pediatrics, 96,* 464–471.

Manson, J. E., Willett, W. C., Stampfer, M. J., Colditz, G. A., Hunter, D. J., Hankinson, S. E., Hennekens, C. H., & Speizer, F. E. (1995). Body weight and mortality among women. *New England Journal of Medicine, 333,* 677–685.

Manton, K. G., & Stallard, E. (1991). Cross-sectional estimates of active life expectancy for the U.S. elderly and oldest-old populations. *Journals of Gerontology: Social Sciences, 46,* S170–182.

Manton, K. G., Stallard, E., & Liu, K. (1993). Forecasts of active life expectancy: Policy and fiscal implications. *The Journals of Gerontology, 48* (Special Issue), 11–26.

Mäntylä, T. (1994). Remembering to remember: Adult age differences in prospective memory. *Journals of Gerontology: Psychological Sciences, 49,* P276–282.

Marcia, J. E. (1966). Development and validation of ego identity status. *Journal of Personality and Social Psychology, 3,* 551–558.

Marcia, J. E. (1980). Identity in adolescence. In J. Adelson (Ed.), *Handbook of adolescent psychology* (pp. 159–187). New York: Wiley.

Marcus, D. E., & Overton, W. F. (1978). The development of cognitive gender constancy and sex role preferences. *Child Development, 49,* 434–444.

Marcus, G. F., Pinker, S., Ullman, M., Hollander, M., Rosen, T. J., & Fei, X. (1992). Overregularization in language acquisition. *Monographs of the Society for Research in Child Development, 57* (4, Serial No. 228).

Marcus, R. F. (1986). Naturalistic observation of cooperation, helping, and sharing and their association with empathy and affect. In C. Zahn-Waxler, E. M. Cummings, & R. Iannotti (Eds.), *Altruism and aggression: Biological and social origins* (pp. 256–279). Cambridge, England: Cambridge University Press.

Marean, G. C., Werner, L. A., & Kuhl, P. K. (1992). Vowel categorization by very young infants. *Developmental Psychology, 28,* 396–405.

Markides, K. S., & Black, S. A. (1996). Race, ethnicity, and aging: The impact of inequality. In R. H. Binstock & L. K. George (Eds.), *Handbook of aging and the social sciences* (4th ed.) (pp. 153–169). San Diego, CA: Academic Press.

Markides, K. S., & Lee, D. J. (1991). Predictors of health status in middle-aged and older Mexican Americans. *Journals of Gerontology: Social Sciences, 46,* S243–249.

Markides, K. S., & Mindel, C. H. (1987). *Aging and ethnicity.* Newbury Park, CA: Sage.

Markman, E. M. (1992). Constraints on word learning: Speculations about their nature, origins, and domain specificity. In M. R. Gunnar & M. Maratsos (Eds.), *Minnesota Symposia on Child Psychology* (Vol. 25) (pp. 59–101). Hillsdale, NJ: Erlbaum.

Marshall, V. W. (1975). Age and awareness of finitude in developmental gerontology. *Omega, 6,* 113–129.

Marshall, V. W. (1996). The state of theory in aging and the social sciences. In R. H. Binstock & L. K. George (Eds.), *Handbook of aging and the social sciences* (4th ed.) (pp. 12–30). San Diego, CA: Academic Press.

Marshall, V. W., & Levy, J. A. (1990). Aging and dying. In R. H. Binstock & L. K. George (Eds.), *Handbook of aging and the social sciences* (3rd ed.) (pp. 245–260). San Diego, CA: Academic Press.

Marsiglio, W., & Donnelly, D. (1991). Sexual relations in later life: A national study of married persons. *Journals of Gerontology: Social Sciences, 46,* S338–344.

Martin, C. L. (1991). The role of cognition in understanding gender effects. In H. W. Reese (Ed.), *Advances in child development and behavior* (Vol. 23) (pp. 113–150). San Diego, CA: Academic Press.

Martin, C. L. (1993). New directions for investigating children's gender knowledge. *Developmental Review, 13,* 184–204.

Martin, C. L., & Halverson, C. F., Jr. (1981). A schematic processing model of sex typing and stereotyping in children. *Child Development, 52,* 1119–1134.

Martin, C. L., & Little, J. K. (1990). The relation of gender understanding to children's sex-typed preferences and gender stereotypes. *Child Development, 61,* 1427–1439.

Martin, C. L., Wood, C. H., & Little, J. K. (1990). The development of gender stereotype components. *Child Development, 61,* 1891–1904.

Martin, P., & Smyer, M. A. (1990). The experience of micro- and macroevents: A life span analysis. *Research on Aging, 12,* 294–310.

Martin, R. P., Wisenbaker, J., & Huttunen, M. (1994). Review of factor analytic studies of temperament measures based on the Thomas-Chess structural model: Implications for the Big Five. In C. F. Halverson, Jr., G. A. Kohnstamm, & R. P. Martin (Eds.), *The developing structure of temperament and personality from infancy to adulthood* (pp. 157–172). Hillsdale, NJ: Erlbaum.

Martorano, S. C. (1977). A developmental analysis of performance on Piaget's formal operations tasks. *Developmental Psychology, 13,* 666–672.

Mascolo, M. F., & Fischer, K. W. (1995). Developmental transformations in appraisals for pride, shame, and guilt. In J. P. Tangney & K. W. Fischer (Eds.), *Self-conscious emotions: The psychology of shame, guilt, embarrassment, and pride* (pp. 64–113). New York: Guilford Press.

Maslow, A. H. (1968). *Toward a psychology of being* (2nd ed.). New York: Van Nostrand Reinhold.

Maslow, A. H. (1970a). *Religions, values, and peak-experiences.* New York: Viking. (Original work published 1964.)

Maslow, A. H. (1970b). *Motivation and personality* (2nd ed.). New York: Harper & Row.

Maslow, A. H. (1971). *The farther reaches of human nature.* New York: Viking.

Massad, C. M. (1981). Sex role identity and adjustment during adolescence. *Child Development, 52,* 1290–1298.

Masten, A. S., Best, K. M., & Garmezy, N. (1990). Resilience and development: Contributions from the study of children who overcome adversity. *Development and Psychopathology, 2,* 425–444.

Masur, E. F. (1995). Infants' early verbal imitation and their later lexical development. *Merrill-Palmer Quarterly, 41,* 286–306.

Matas, L., Arend, R. A., & Sroufe, L. A. (1978). Continuity of adaptation in the second year: The relationship between quality of attachment and latter competence. *Child Development, 49,* 547–556.

Mather, P. L., & Black, K. N. (1984). Heredity and environmental influences on preschool twins' language skills. *Developmental Psychology, 20,* 303–308.

Mathew, A., & Cook, M. (1990). The control of reaching movements by young infants. *Child Development, 61,* 1238–1257.

Matthews, K. A. (1988). Coronary heart disease and Type A behaviors: Update on and alternative to the Booth-Kewley and Friedman (1987) quantitative review. *Psychological Bulletin, 104,* 373–380.

Matthews, K. A., Wing, R. R., Kuller, L. H., Meilahn, E. N., Kelsey, S. F., Costello, E. J., & Caggiula, A. W. (1990). Influences of natural menopause on psychological characteristics and symptoms of middle-aged healthy women. *Journal of Consulting and Clinical Psychology, 58,* 345–351.

Maughan, B., Pickles, A., & Quinton, D. (1995). Parental hostility, childhood behavior, and adult social functioning. In J. McCord (Ed.), *Coercion and punishment in long-term perspectives* (pp. 34–58). Cambridge, England: Cambridge University Press.

Maurer, D., & Maurer, C. (1988). *The world of the newborn.* New York: Basic Books.

Maylor, E. A. (1993). Aging and forgetting in prospective and retrospective memory tasks. *Psychology and Aging, 8,* 420–428.

McAuley, E. (1993). Self-efficacy, physical activity, and aging. In J. R. Kelly (Ed.), *Activity and aging. Staying involved in late life* (pp. 187–205). Newbury Park, CA: Sage.

McAuley, W. J., & Blieszner, R. (1985). Selection of long-term care arrangements by older community residents. *The Gerontologist, 25,* 188–193.

McCall, R. B. (1993). Developmental functions for general mental performance. In D. K. Detterman (Ed.), *Current topics in human intelligence: Vol. 3. Individual differences and cognition* (pp. 3–30). Norwood, NJ: Ablex.

McCarthy, J., & Hardy, J. (1993). Age at first birth and birth outcomes. *Journal of Research on Adolescence, 3,* 374–392.

McCord, J. (1982). A longitudinal view of the relationship between parental absence and crime. In J. Gunn & D. P. Farrington (Eds.), *Abnormal offenders, delinquency, and the criminal justice system* (pp. 113–128). London: Wiley.

McCrae, R. R., & Costa, P. T., Jr. (1984). *Emerging lives, enduring dispositions: Personality in adulthood.* Boston: Little, Brown.

McCrae, R. R., & Costa, P. T., Jr. (1987). Validation of the five-factor model of personality across instruments and observers. *Journal of Personality and Social Psychology, 52,* 81–90.

McCrae, R. R., & Costa, P. T., Jr. (1988). Psychological resilience among widowed men and women: A 10-year follow-up of a national sample. *Journal of Social Issues, 44,* 129–142.

McCrae, R. R., & Costa, P. T., Jr. (1990). *Personality in adulthood.* New York: Guilford Press.

McCrae, R. R., & Costa, P. T., Jr. (1994). The stability of personality: Observations and evaluations. *Current Directions in Psychological Science, 3,* 173–175.

McCrae, R. R., & John, O. P. (1992). An introduction to the Five-Factor Model and its applications. *Journal of Personality, 60,* 175–215.

McCune, L. (1995). A normative study of representational play at the transition to language. *Developmental Psychology, 31,* 198–206.

McDonald, P. L., & Wanner, R. A. (1990). *Retirement in Canada.* Toronto: Butterworths.

McEvoy, G. M., & Cascio, W. F. (1989). Cumulative evidence of the relationship between employee age and job performance. *Journal of Applied Psychology, 74,* 11–17.

McFalls, J. A., Jr. (1990). The risks of reproductive impairment in the later years of childbearing. *Annual Review of Sociology, 16,* 491–519.

McGue, M. (1994). Why developmental psychology should find room for behavior genetics. In C. A. Nelson (Ed.), *The Minnesota Symposia on Child Development* (Vol. 27) (pp. 105–119). Hillsdale, NJ: Erlbaum.

McGuire, S., Dunn, J., & Plomin, R. (1995). Maternal differential treatment of siblings and children's behavioral problems: A longitudinal study. *Development and Psychopathology, 7,* 515–528.

McIntosh, B. R., & Danigelis, N. L. (1995). Race, gender, and the relevance of productive activity for elders' affect. *Journals of Gerontology: Social Sciences, 50B,* S229–239.

McKinlay, J. B., McKinlay, S. M., & Brambilla, D. J. (1987). Health status and utilization behavior associated with menopause. *American Journal of Epidemiology, 125,* 110–121.

McLanahan, S., & Sandefur, G. (1994). *Growing up with a single parent: What hurts, what helps.* Cambridge, MA: Harvard University Press.

McLaughlin, B. (1984). *Second-language acquisition in childhood: Vol. 1. Preschool children* (2nd ed.). Hillsdale, NJ: Erlbaum.

McLoyd, V. C. (1990). The impact of economic hardship on black families and children: Psychological distress, parenting, and socioemotional development. *Child Development, 61,* 311–346.

McLoyd, V. C., Jayaratne, T. E., Ceballo, R., & Borquez, J. (1994). Unemployment and work interruption among African American single mothers: Effects on parenting and adolescent socioemotional functioning. *Child Development, 65,* 562–589.

McLoyd, V., & Wilson, L. (1991). The strain of living poor: Parenting, social support, and child mental health. In A. C. Huston (Ed.), *Children in poverty: Child development and public policy* (pp. 105–135). Cambridge, England: Cambridge University Press.

Melby, J. N., & Conger, R. D. (1996). Parental behaviors and adolescent academic performance: A longitudinal analysis. *Journal of Research on Adolescence, 6,* 113–137.

Mellin, L. M., Irwin, C. E., & Scully, S. (1992). Prevalence of disordered eating in girls: A survey of middle-class children. *Journal of the American Dietetic Association, 92,* 851–853.

Melson, G. F., Ladd, G. W., & Hsu, H. (1993). Maternal support networks, maternal cognitions, and young children's social and cognitive development. *Child Development, 64,* 1401–1417.

Meltzoff, A. N. (1988). Infant imitation and memory: Nine-month-olds in immediate and deferred tasks. *Child Development, 59,* 217–225.

Meltzoff, A. N. (1995). Understanding the intentions of others: Re-enactment of intended acts by 18-month-old children. *Developmental Psychology, 31,* 838–850.

Menaghan, E. G., & Lieberman, M. A. (1986). Changes in depression following divorce: A panel study. *Journal of Marriage and the Family, 48,* 319–328.

Merikangas, K. R., & Angst, J. (1995). The challenge of depressive disorders in adolescence. In M. Rutter (Ed.), *Psychosocial disturbances in young people: Challenges for prevention* (pp. 131–165). Cambridge, England: Cambridge University Press.

Merrill, D. M., & Mor, V. (1993). Pathways to hospital death among the oldest old. *Journal of Aging and Health, 5,* 516–535.

Mervis, C. B., & Bertrand, J. (1994). Acquisition of the novel name—nameless category (N3C) principle. *Child Development, 65,* 1646–1662.

Mervis, C. B., Bertrand, J., Robinson, B. F., Armstrong, S. C., Klein, B. P., Turner, N. D., Baker, D. E., & Reinberg, J. (1995). *Early language development of children with Williams Syndrome.* Paper presented at the biennial meetings of the Society for Research in Child Development, Indianapolis, March.

Meyer-Bahlburg, H. F. L., Ehrhardt, A. A., Rosen, L. R., Gruen, R. S., Veridiano, N. P., Vann, F. H., & Neuwalder, H. F. (1995). Prenatal estrogens and the development of homosexual orientation. *Developmental Psychology, 31,* 12–21.

Michael, R. T., Gagnon, J. H., Laumann, E. O., & Kolata, G. (1994). *Sex in America.* Boston: Little, Brown.

Miller, B. C., Christopherson, C. R., & King, P. K. (1993). Sexual behavior in adolescence. In T. P. Gullotta, G. R. Adams, & R. Montemayor (Eds.), *Adolescent sexuality* (pp. 57–76). Newbury Park, CA: Sage.

Miller, B. C., & Moore, K. A. (1990). Adolescent sexual behavior, pregnancy, and parenting: Research through the 1980s. *Journal of Marriage and the Family, 52,* 1025–1044.

Miller, K. E., & Pedersen-Randall, P. (1995). *Work, farm work, academic achievement and friendship: A comparison of rural and urban 10th, 11th and 12th graders.* Paper presented at the biennial meetings of the Society for Research in Child Development, Indianapolis, March.

Miller, R. A. (1990). Aging and the immune response. In E. L. Schneider & J. W. Rowe (Eds.), *Handbook of the biology of aging* (3rd ed.) (pp. 157–180). San Diego, CA: Academic Press.

Miller, R. A. (1996). Aging and the immune response. In E. L. Schneider & J. W. Rowe (Eds.), *Handbook of the biology of aging* (4th ed.) (pp. 355–392). San Diego, CA: Academic Press.

Miller, T. Q., Smith, T. W., Turner, C. W., Guijarro, M. L., & Hallet, A. J. (1996). A meta-analytic review of research on hostility and physical health. *Psychological Bulletin, 119,* 322–348.

Miller, T. Q., Turner, C. W., Tindale, R. S., Posavac, E. J., & Dugoni, B. L. (1991). Reasons for the trend toward null findings in research on Type A behavior. *Psychological Bulletin, 110,* 469–495.

Millstein, S. G., Petersen, A. C., & Nightingale, E. O. (Eds.). (1993). *Promoting the health of adolescents: New directions for the twenty-first century.* New York: Oxford University Press.

Mischel, W. (1966). A social learning view of sex differences in behavior. In E. E. Maccoby (Ed.), *The development of sex differences* (pp. 56–81). Stanford, CA: Stanford University Press.

Mischel, W. (1970). Sex typing and socialization. In P. H. Mussen (Ed.), *Carmichael's manual of child psychology* (Vol. 2) (pp. 3–72). New York: Wiley.

Mitchell, C. M., O'Nell, T. D., Beals, J., Dick, R. W., Keane, E., & Manson, S. M. (1996). Dimensionality of alcohol use among American Indian adolescents: Latent structure, construct validity, and implications for developmental research. *Journal of Research on Adolescence, 6,* 151–180.

Mitchell, P. R., & Kent, R. D. (1990). Phonetic variation in multisyllable babbling. *Journal of Child Language, 17,* 247–265.

Moen, P. (1985). Continuities and discontinuities in women's labor force activity. In G. H. Elder, Jr. (Ed.), *Life course dynamics* (pp 113–155). Ithaca, NY: Cornell University Press.

Moen, P. (1991). Transitions in mid-life: Women's work and family roles in the 1970s. *Journal of Marriage and the Family, 53,* 135–150.

Moen, P. (1996). Gender, age, and the life course. In R. H. Binstock & L. K. George (Eds.), *Handbook of aging and the social sciences* (4th ed.) (pp. 171–187). San Diego, CA: Academic Press.

Moen, P., & Erickson, M. A. (1995). Linked lives: A transgenerational approach to resilience. In P. Moen, G. H. Elder, Jr., & K. Lüscher (Eds.), *Examining lives in context: Perspectives on the ecology of human development* (pp. 169–210). Washington, DC: American Psychological Association.

Moffitt, T. E. (1993). Adolescence-limited and life-course-persistent antisocial behavior; a developmental taxonomy. *Psychology Review, 100,* 674–701.

Montemayor, R., Adams, G. R., & Gullotta, T. P. (Eds.). (1994). *Personal relationships during adolescence.* Thousand Oaks, CA: Sage.

Montemayor, R., & Eisen, M. (1977). The development of self-conceptions from childhood to adolescence. *Developmental Psychology, 13,* 314–319.

Montgomery, R. J. V., & Kosloski, K. (1994). A longitudinal analysis of nursing home placement for dependent elders cared for by spouses vs adult children. *Journals of Gerontology: Social Sciences, 49,* S62–74.

Moon, C., & Fifer, W. P. (1990). Syllables as signals for 2-day-old infants. *Infant Behavior and Development, 13,* 377–390.

Moore, K. A., Myers, D. E., Morrison, D. R., Nord, C. W., Brown, B., & Edmonston, B. (1993). Age at first childbirth and later poverty. *Journal of Research on Adolescence, 3,* 393–422.

Moore, K. L., & Persaud, T. V. N. (1993). *The developing human: Clinically oriented embryology* (5th ed.). Philadelphia: Saunders.

Mor, V. (1987). *Hospice care systems: Structure, process, costs, and outcome.* New York: Springer.

Mor, V., Greer, D. S., & Kastenbaum, R. (Eds.). (1988). *The hospice experiment.* Baltimore, MD: Johns Hopkins University Press.

Morgan, D. G. (1992). Neurochemical changes with aging: Predisposition towards age-related mental disorders. In J. E. Birren, R. B. Sloane, & G. D. Cohen (Eds.), *Handbook of mental health and aging* (2nd ed.) (pp. 175–200). San Diego, CA: Academic Press.

Morgan, J. L. (1994). Converging measures of speech segmentation in preverbal infants. *Infant Behavior and Development, 17,* 389–403.

Morgan, J. L., Bonamo, K. M., & Travis, L. L. (1995). Negative evidence on negative evidence. *Developmental Psychology, 31,* 180–197.

Morgan, L. A. (1991). *After marriage ends: Economic consequences for midlife women.* Newbury Park, CA: Sage.

Morris, D. L., Kritchevsky, S. B., & Davis, C. E. (1994). Serum carotenoids and coronary heart disease. The Lipid Research Clinics Coronary Primary Prevention Trial and Follow-up Study. *Journal of the American Medical Association, 272,* 1439–1441.

Morrison, D. M. (1985). Adolescent contraceptive behavior: A review. *Psychological Bulletin, 98,* 538–568.

Morrison, D. R., & Cherlin, A. J. (1995). The divorce process and young children's well-being: A prospective analysis. *Journal of Marriage and the Family, 57,* 800–812.

Morrison, N. A., Qi, J. C., Tokita, A., Kelly, P. J., Crofts, L., Nguyen, T. V., Sambrook, P. N., & Eisman, J. A. (1994). Prediction of bone density from vitamin D receptor alleles. *Nature, 367,* 284–287.

Morse, P. A., & Cowan, N. (1982). Infant auditory and speech perception. In T. M. Field, A. Houston, H. C. Quay, L. Troll, & G. E. Finley (Eds.), *Review of human development* (pp. 32–61). New York: Wiley.

Mortimer, J. T., Finch, M. D., Dennehy, K., Lee, C., & Beebe, T. (1995). *Work experience in adolescence.* Paper presented at the biennial meetings of the Society for Research in Child Development, Indianapolis, March.

Mosher, W. D. (1987). Infertility: Why business is booming. *American Demography,* June, 42–43.

Mosher, W. D., & Pratt, W. F. (1987). *Fecundity, infertility, and reproductive health in the United States, 1982: Vital Health Statistics, Series 23, No. 14. National Center for Health Statistics, US Public Health Service.* Washington, DC: USGPO.

Mosteller, F. (1995). The Tennessee study of class size in the early school grades. *The Future of Children, 5*(2, Summer/Fall), 113–127.

Mounts, N. S., & Steinberg, L. (1995). An ecological analysis of peer influence on adolescent grade point average and drug use. *Developmental Psychology, 31,* 915–922.

Mullins, L. C., & Mushel, M. (1992). The existence and emotional closeness of relationships with children, friends, and spouses. The effect on loneliness among older persons. *Research on Aging, 14,* 448–470.

Mundy, G. R. (1994). Boning up on genes. *Nature, 367,* 216–217.

Munroe, R. H., Shimmin, H. S., & Munroe, R. L. (1984). Gender understanding and sex role preference in four cultures. *Developmental Psychology, 20,* 673–682.

Murphy, S. O. (1993). *The family context and the transition to siblinghood: Strategies parents use to influence sibling-infant relationships.* Paper presented at the biennial meetings of the Society for Research in Child Development, New Orleans, April.

Murray, J. L., & Bernfield, M. (1988). The differential effect of prenatal care on the incidence of low birth weight among blacks and whites in a prepaid health care plan. *New England Journal of Medicine, 319,* 1385–1391.

Murray, J. P. (1980). *Television and youth: 25 years of research and controversy.* Stanford, CA: The Boys Town Center for the Study of Youth Development.

Murrell, S. A., & Himmelfarb, S. (1989). Effects of attachment bereavement and pre-event conditions on subsequent depressive symptoms in older adults. *Psychology and Aging, 4,* 166–172.

Murrell, S. A., & Norris, F. H. (1991). Differential social support and life change as contributors to the social class-distress relationship in old age. *Psychology and Aging, 6,* 223–231.

Murstein, B. I. (1970). Stimulus-Value-Role: A theory of marital choice. *Journal of Marriage and the Family, 32,* 465–481.

Murstein, B. I. (1976). *Who will marry whom? Theories and research in marital choice.* New York: Springer.

Murstein, B. I. (1986). *Paths to marriage.* Beverly Hills, CA: Sage.

Musick, J. S. (1994). Capturing the childrearing context. *Society for Research in Child Development Newsletter,* Fall, 6–7.

Myers, B. J. (1987). Mother-infant bonding as a critical period. In M. H. Bornstein (Ed.), *Sensitive periods in development: Interdisciplinary perspectives* (pp. 223–246). Hillsdale, NJ: Erlbaum.

Myers, D. G., & Diener, E. (1995). Who is happy? *Psychological Science, 6,* 10–17.

Myers, G. C. (1990). Demography of aging. In R. H. Binstock & L. K. George (Eds.), *Handbook of aging and the social sciences* (3rd ed.) (pp. 19–44). San Diego, CA: Academic Press.

Nachmias, M. (1993). *Maternal personality relations with toddler's attachment classification, use of coping strategies, and adrenocortical stress response.* Paper presented at the biennial meetings of the Society for Research in Child Development, New Orleans, April.

Nash, S. C., & Feldman, S. S. (1981). Sex role and sex-related attributions: Constancy and change across the family life cycle. In M. E. Lamb & A. L. Brown (Eds.), *Advances in developmental psychology* (pp. 1–36). Hillsdale, NJ: Erlbaum.

Nathanson, C. A., & Lorenz, G. (1982). Women and health: The social dimensions of biomedical data. In J. Z. Giele (Ed.), *Women in the middle years* (pp. 37–88). New York: Wiley.

Needleman, H. L., Riess, J. A., Tobin, M. J., Biesecker, G. E., & Greenhouse, J. B. (1996). Bone lead levels and delinquent behavior. *Journal of the American Medical Association, 275,* 363–369.

Neimark, E. D. (1982). Adolescent thought: Transition to formal operations. In B. B. Wolman (Ed.), *Handbook of developmental psychology* (pp. 486–502). Englewood Cliffs, NJ: Prentice-Hall.

Neimeyer, R. A., & Chapman, K. M. (1980–81). Self/ideal discrepancy and fear of death: The test of an existential hypothesis. *Omega, 11,* 233–239.

Neisser, U., Boodoo, G., Bouchard, T. J., Jr., Boykin, A. W., Brody, N., Ceci, S. J., Halpern, D. F., Loehlin, J. C., Perloff, R., Sternberg, R. J., & Urbina, S. (1996). Intelligence: Knowns and unknowns. *American Psychologist, 51,* 77–101.

Nelson, C. A. (1987). The recognition of facial expression in the first two years of life: Mechanisms of development. *Child Development, 58,* 889–909.

Nelson, E. A., & Dannefer, D. (1992). Aged heterogeneity: Fact or fiction? The fate of diversity in gerontological research. *The Gerontologist, 32,* 17–23.

Nelson, K. (1973). Structure and strategy in learning to talk. *Monographs of the Society for Research in Child Development, 38*(Serial No. 149).

Nelson, K. (1977). Facilitating children's syntax acquisition. *Developmental Psychology, 13,* 101–107.

Nelson, M. E., Fiatarone, M. A., Morganti, C. M., Trice, I., Greenberg, R. A., & Evans, W. J. (1994). Effects of high-intensity strength training on multiple risk factors for osteoporotic fractures. *Journal of the American Medical Association, 272,* 1909–1914.

Neugarten, B. L. (1968). The awareness of middle age. In B. L. Neugarten (Ed.), *Middle age and aging* (pp. 93–98). Chicago: University of Chicago Press.

Neugarten, B. L. (1970). Dynamics of transition of middle age to old age. *Journal of Geriatric Psychiatry, 4,* 71–87.

Neugarten, B. L. (1977). Personality and aging. In J. E. Birren & K. W. Schaie (Eds.), *Handbook of the psychology of aging* (pp. 626–649). New York: Van Nostrand Reinhold.

Neugarten, B. L. (1979). Time, age, and the life cycle. *American Journal of Psychiatry, 136,* 887–894.

Neugarten, B. L., & Neugarten, D. A. (1987). The changing meanings of age. *Psychology Today, 21*(5), 29–33.

Newcomb, A. F., & Bagwell, C. L. (1995). Children's friendship relations: A meta-analytic review. *Psychological Bulletin, 117,* 306–347.

Newcomb, A. F., Bukowski, W. M., & Pattee, L. (1993). Children's peer relations: A meta-analytic review of popular, rejected, neglected, controversial, and average sociometric status. *Psychological Bulletin, 113,* 99–128.

Newcomb, P. A., Longnecker, M. P., Storer, B. E., Mittendorf, R., Baron, J., Clapp, R. W., Bogdan, G., & Willett, W. C. (1995). Long-term hormone replacement therapy and risk of breast cancer in postmenopausal women. *American Journal of Epidemiology, 142,* 788–795.

Newcombe, N. S., & Baenninger, M. (1989). Biological change and cognitive ability in adolescence. In G. R. Adams, R. Montemayor, & T. P. Gullotta (Eds.), *Biology of adolescent behavior and development* (pp. 168–194). Newbury Park, CA: Sage.

Newmann, J. P., Engel, R. J., & Jensen, J. E. (1991). Changes in depressive-symptom experiences among older women. *Psychology and Aging, 6,* 212–222.

New York Times (1994a). Optimism can mean life for heart patients and pessimism death, study says. *New York Times,* April 16, p. 12.

New York Times (1994b). Students cite pregnancies as a reason to drop out. *New York Times,* September 14, p. B7.

New York Times (1996). Guns are No. 2 cause of death among the young, data show. *New York Times,* April 9, p. A8.

Nightingale, E. O., & Goodman, M. (1990). *Before birth. Prenatal testing for genetic disease.* Cambridge, MA: Harvard University Press.

Nilsson, L. (1990). *A child is born.* New York: Delacorte Press.

Nisan, M., & Kohlberg, L. (1982). Universality and variation in moral judgment: A longitudinal and cross-sectional study in Turkey. *Child Development, 53,* 865–876.

Nolen-Hoeksema, S. (1994). An interactive model for the emergence of gender differences in depression in adolescence. *Journal of Research on Adolescence, 4,* 519–534.

Nolen-Hoeksema, S., & Girgus, J. S. (1994). The emergence of gender differences in depression during adolescence. *Psychological Bulletin, 115,* 424–443.

Norris, F. H., & Murrell, S. A. (1990). Social support, life events, and stress as modifiers of adjustment to bereavement by older adults. *Psychology and Aging, 5,* 429–436.

Norton, A. J. (1983). Family life cycle: 1980. *Journal of Marriage and the Family, 45,* 267–275.

Norwood, T. H., Smith, J. R., & Stein, G. H. (1990). Aging at the cellular level: The human fibroblastlike cell model. In E. R. Schneider & J. W. Rowe (Eds.), *Handbook of the biology of aging* (3rd ed.) (pp. 131–154). San Diego, CA: Academic Press.

Nottelmann, E. D., Susman, E. J., Blue, J. H., Inoff-Germain, G., Dorn, L. D., Loriaux, D. L., Cutler, G. B., Jr., & Chrousos, G. P. (1987). Gonadal and adrenal hormone correlates of adjustment in early adolescence. In R. M. Lerner & T. T. Foch (Eds.), *Biological-psychosocial interactions in early adolescence* (pp. 303–324). Hillsdale, NJ: Erlbaum.

Notzon, F. C., Cnattingius, S., PergsjF, P., Cole, S., Taffel, S., Irgens, L., & Dalveit, A. K. (1994). Cesarean section delivery in the 1980s: International comparison by indication. *American Journal of Obstetrics and Gynecology, 170,* 495–504.

Nowakowski, R. S. (1987). Basic concepts of CNS development. *Child Development, 58,* 568–595.

Nuland, S. B. (1993). *How we die.* New York: Knopf.

Nurmi, J., Pulliainen, H., & Salmela-Aro, K. (1992). Age differences in adults' control beliefs related to life goals and concerns. *Psychology and Aging, 7,* 194–196.

Nydegger, C. N. (1991). The development of paternal and filial maturity. In K. Pillemer & K. McCartney (Eds.), *Parent-child relations throughout life* (pp. 93–112). Hillsdale, NJ: Erlbaum.

O'Beirne, H., & Moore, C. (1995). *Attachment and sexual behavior in adolescence.* Paper presented at the biennial meetings of the Society for Research in Child Development, Indianapolis, March.

O'Brien, M. (1992). Gender identity and sex roles. In V. B. Van Hasselt & M. Hersen (Eds.), *Handbook of social development: A lifespan perspective* (pp. 325–345). New York: Plenum.

O'Brien, S. F., & Bierman, K. L. (1988). Conceptions and perceived influence of peer groups: Interviews with preadolescents and adolescents. *Child Development, 59,* 1360–1365.

O'Bryant, S. L. (1988). Sibling support and older widows' well-being. *Journal of Marriage and the Family, 50,* 173–183.

O'Connor, N. J., Manson, J. E., O'Connor, G. T., & Buring, J. E. (1995). Psychosocial risk factors and nonfatal myocardial infarction. *Circulation, 92,* 1458–1464.

O'Connor, S., Vietze, P. M., Sandler, H. M., Sherrod, K. B., & Altemeier, W. A. (1980). Quality of parenting and the mother-infant relationships following rooming-in. In P. M. Taylor (Ed.), *Parent-infant relationships* (pp. 349–368). New York: Grune & Stratton.

Offord, D. R., Boyle, M. H., & Racine, Y. A. (1991). The epidemiology of antisocial behavior in childhood and adolescence. In D. J. Pepler & K. H. Rubin (Eds.), *The development and treatment of childhood aggression* (pp. 31–54). Hillsdale, NJ: Erlbaum.

Ogawa, N., & Retherford, R. D. (1993). Care of the elderly in Japan: Changing norms and expectations. *Journal of Marriage and the Family, 55,* 585–597.

O'Hara, M. W., Schlechte, J. A., Lewis, D. A., & Varner, M. W. (1992). Controlled prospective study of postpartum mood disorders: Psychological, environmental, and hormonal variables. *Journal of Abnormal Psychology, 100,* 63–73.

Okamoto, E., Davidson, L. L., & Conner, D. R. (1993). High prevalence of overweight in inner-city schoolchildren. *American Journal of Diseases of Children, 147,* 155–159.

O'Leary, A. (1990). Stress, emotion, and human immune function. *Psychological Bulletin, 108,* 363–382.

O'Leary, K. D., & Smith, D. A. (1991). Marital interactions. *Annual Review of Psychology, 42,* 191–212.

Oller, D. K. (1981). Infant vocalizations: Exploration and reflectivity. In R. E. Stark (Ed.), *Language behavior in infancy and early childhood* (pp. 85–104). New York: Elsevier North-Holland.

Olshan, A. F., Baird, P. A., & Teschke, K. (1989). Paternal occupational exposures and the risk of Down syndrome. *American Journal of Human Genetics, 44,* 646–651.

Olson, H. C., Sampson, P. D., Barr, H., Streissguth, A. P., & Bookstein, F. L. (1992). Prenatal exposure to alcohol and school problems in late childhood: A longitudinal prospective study. *Development and Psychopathology, 4,* 341–359.

Olson, S. L., Bates, J. E., & Kaskie, B. (1992). Caregiver-infant interaction antecedents of children's school-age cognitive ability. *Merrill-Palmer Quarterly, 38,* 309–330.

O'Neill, D. K., Astington, J. W., & Flavell, J. H. (1992). Young children's understanding of the role that sensory experiences play in knowledge acquisition. *Child Development, 63,* 474–490.

O'Rand, A. M. (1990). Stratification and the life course. In R. H. Binstock & L. K. George (Eds.), *Handbook of aging and the social sciences* (3rd ed.) (pp. 130–148). San Diego, CA: Academic Press.

Ornish, D. (1990). *Dr. Dean Ornish's program for reversing heart disease.* New York: Random House.

Ornish, D. (1993). *Eat more, weigh less.* New York: HarperCollins.

Orr, W. C., & Sohal, R. S. (1994). Extension of life-span by overexpression of superoxide dismutase and catalase in *Drosophila melanogaster. Science, 263,* 1128–1130.

Orth-Gomér, K., Rosengren, A., & Wilhelmsen, L. (1993). Lack of social support and incidence of coronary heart disease in middle-aged Swedish men. *Psychosomatic Medicine, 55,* 37–43.

Orwoll, L., & Perlmutter, M. (1990). The study of wise persons: Integrating a personality perspective. In R. J. Sternberg (Ed.), *Wisdom: Its nature, origins, and development* (pp. 160–180). Cambridge, England: Cambridge University Press.

Osofsky, J. D. (1995). The effects of exposure to violence on young children. *American Psychologist, 50,* 782–788.

Osofsky, J. D., Hann, D. M., & Peebles, C. (1993). Adolescent parenthood: Risks and opportunities for mothers and infants. In C. H. Zeanah, Jr. (Ed.), *Handbook of infant mental health* (pp. 106–119). New York: Guilford Press.

Ostoja, E., McCrone, E., Lehn, L., Reed, T., & Sroufe, L. A. (1995). *Representations of close relationships in adolescence: Longitudinal antecedents from infancy through childhood.* Paper presented at the biennial meetings of the Society for Research in Child Development, Indianapolis, March.

Overton, W. F., Ward, S. L., Noveck, I. A., Black, J., & O'Brien, D. P. (1987). Form and content in the development of deductive reasoning. *Developmental Psychology, 23,* 22–30.

Owens, G., Crowell, J. A., Pan, H., Treboux, D., O'Connor, E., & Waters, E. (1995). The prototype hypothesis and the origins of attachment working models: Adult relationships with parents and romantic partners. *Monographs of the Society for Research in Child Development, 60*(244, No. 2–3), 216–233.

Paden, S. L., & Buehler, C. (1995). Coping with the dual-income lifestyle. *Journal of Marriage and the Family, 57,* 101–110.

Padilla, A. M., Lindholm, K. J., Chen, A., Duran, R., Hakuta, K., Lambert, W., & Tucker, G. R. (1991). The English-only movement: Myths, reality, and implications for psychology. *American Psychologist, 46,* 120–130.

Paffenbarger, R. S., Hyde, R. T., Wing, A. L., & Hsieh, C. (1987). Physical activity, all-cause mortality, and longevity of college alumni. *New England Journal of Medicine, 314,* 605–613.

Page, D. C., Mosher, R., Simpson, E. M., Fisher, E. M. C., Mardon, G., Pollack, J., McGillivray, B., de la Chapelle, A., & Brown, L. G. (1987). The sex-determining region of the human Y chromosome encodes a finger protein. *Cell, 51,* 1091–1104.

Paik, H., & Comstock, G. (1994). The effects of television violence on antisocial behavior: A meta-analysis. *Communication Research, 21,* 516–546.

Paikoff, R. L., & Brooks-Gunn, J. (1990). Physiological processes: What role do they play during the transition to adolescence? In R. Montemayor, G. R. Adams, & T. P. Gullotta (Eds.), *From childhood to adolescence: A transitional period?* (pp. 63–81). Newbury Park, CA: Sage.

Palkovitz, R. (1985). Fathers' birth attendance, early contact, and extended contact with their newborns: A critical review. *Child Development, 56,* 392–406.

Palla, B., & Litt, I. R. (1988). Medical complications of eating disorders in adolescents. *Pediatrics, 81,* 613–623.

Palmérus, K., & Scarr, S. (1995). *How parents discipline young children: Cultural comparisons and individual differences.* Paper presented at the biennial meetings of the Society for Research in Child Development, Indianapolis, March.

Palmore, E. (1981). *Social patterns in normal aging: Findings from the Duke Longitudinal Study.* Durham, NC: Duke University Press.

Palmore, E. B. (1990). *Ageism: Negative and positive.* New York: Springer.

Palmore, E. B., Burchett, B. M., Fillenbaum, G. G., George, L. K., & Wallman, L. M. (1985). *Retirement. Causes and consequences.* New York: Springer.

Palmore, E. B., & Cleveland, W. (1976). Aging, terminal decline, and terminal drop. *Journal of Gerontology, 31,* 76–81.

Panel on High Risk Youth. (1993). *Losing generations: Adolescents in high risk settings. Commission on Behavioral and Social Sciences and Education, National Research Council.* Washington, DC: National Academy Press.

Papousek, H., & Papousek, M. (1991). Innate and cultural guidance of infants' integrative competencies: China, the United States, and Germany. In M. H. Bornstein (Ed.), *Cultural approaches to parenting* (pp. 23–44). Hillsdale, NJ: Erlbaum.

Parke, R. D., & Tinsley, B. R. (1981). The father's role in infancy: Determinants of involvement in caregiving and play. In M. E. Lamb (Ed.), *The role of the father in child development* (2nd ed.) (pp. 429–458). New York: Wiley.

Parke, R. D., & Tinsley, B. R. (1984). Fatherhood: Historical and contemporary perspectives. In K. A. McCluskey & H. W. Reese (Eds.), *Life-span developmental psychology. Historical and generational effects* (pp. 203–248). Orlando, FL: Academic Press.

Parmelee, A. H., Jr. (1986). Children's illnesses: Their beneficial effects on behavioral development. *Child Development, 57,* 1–10.

Parmelee, A. H., Jr., Wenner, W. H., & Schulz, H. R. (1964). Infant sleep patterns from birth to 16 weeks of age. *Journal of Pediatrics, 65,* 576–582.

Parnes, H. S., & Sommers, D. G. (1994). Shunning retirement: Work experience of men in their seventies and early eighties. *Journals of Gerontology: Social Sciences, 49,* S117–124.

Parsons, J. E., Adler, T. F., & Daczala, C. M. (1982). Socialization of achievement attitudes and beliefs: Parental influences. *Child Development, 53,* 310–321.

Passman, R. H., & Longeway, K. P. (1982). The role of vision in maternal attachment: Giving 2-year-olds a photograph of their mother during separation. *Developmental Psychology, 18,* 530–533.

Patterson, G. R. (1980). Mothers: The unacknowledged victims. *Monographs of the Society for Research in Child Development, 45*(Serial No. 186).

Patterson, G. R., Capaldi, D., & Bank, L. (1991). An early starter model for predicting delinquency. In D. J. Pepler & K. H. Rubin (Eds.), *The development and treatment of childhood aggression* (pp. 139–168). Hillsdale, NJ: Erlbaum.

Patterson, G. R., DeBarsyshe, B. D., & Ramsey, E. (1989). A developmental perspective on antisocial behavior. *American Psychologist, 44,* 329–335.

Paxton, S. J., Wertheim, E. H., Gibbons, K., Szmukler, G. I., Hillier, L., & Petrovich, J. L. (1991). Body image satisfaction, dieting beliefs, and weight loss behaviors in adolescent girls and boys. *Journal of Youth and Adolescence, 20,* 361–379.

Pear, R. (1996). Immunization of children up sharply, U.S. reports. *New York Times,* April 11, p. A8.

Pearlin, L. (1975). Sex roles and depression. In N. Datan & L. H. Ginsberg (Eds.), *Life-span developmental psychology: Normative life crises* (pp. 191–208). New York: Academic Press.

Pearlin, L. I. (1980). Life strains and psychological distress among adults. In N. J. Smelser & E. H. Erikson (Eds.), *Themes of work and love in adulthood* (pp. 174–192). Cambridge, MA: Harvard University Press.

Pearlin, L. I., Aneshensel, C. S., Mullan, J., & Whitlatch, C. J. (1996). Caregiving and its social support. In R. H. Binstock & L. K. George (Eds.), *Handbook of aging and the social sciences* (4th ed.) (pp. 283–302). San Diego, CA: Academic Press.

Peckham, C. S. (1994). Human immunodeficiency virus infection and pregnancy. *Sexually Transmitted Diseases, 21*(No. 2 Supplement), S28–31.

Pedersen, N. L., & Harris, J. R. (1990). Developmental behavioral genetics and successful aging. In P. B. Baltes & M. M. Baltes (Eds.), *Successful aging* (pp. 359–380). Cambridge, England: Cambridge University Press.

Pedersen, N. L., Plomin, R., McClearn, G. E., & Friberg, L. (1988). Neuroticism, extraversion and related traits in adult twins reared apart and reared together. *Journal of Personality and Social Psychology, 55,* 950–957.

Pederson, D. R., & Moran, G. (1995). A categorical description of infant-mother relationships in the home and its relation to Q-sort measures of infant-mother interaction. *Monographs of the Society for Research in Child Development, 60*(244, Nos. 2–3), 111–132.

Pederson, D. R., Moran, G., Sitko, C., Campbell, K., Ghesquire, K., & Acton, H. (1990). Maternal sensitivity and the security of infant-mother attachment: A Q-sort study. *Child Development, 61,* 1974–1983.

Pedlow, R., Sanson, A., Prior, M., & Oberklaid, F. (1993). Stability of maternally reported temperament from infancy to 8 years. *Developmental Psychology, 29,* 998–1007.

Pegg, J. E., Werker, J. F., & McLeod, P. J. (1992). Preference for infant-directed over adult-directed speech: Evidence from 7-week-old infants. *Infant Behavior and Development, 15,* 325–345.

Peisner-Feinberg, E. S. (1995). *Developmental outcomes and the relationship to quality of child care experiences.* Paper presented at the biennial meetings of the Society for Research in Child Development, Indianapolis, March.

Pence, A. R. (Ed.). (1988). *Ecological research with children and families: From concepts to methodology.* New York: Teachers College Press.

Pendergast, D. R., Fisher, N. M., & Calkins, E. (1993). Cardiovascular, neuromuscular, and metabolic alterations with age leading to frailty. *The Journals of Gerontology, 48*(Special Issue), 61–67.

Peoples, C. E., Fagan, J. F., III, & Drotar, D. (1995). The influence of race on 3-year-old children's performance on the Stanford-Binet: Fourth edition. *Intelligence, 21,* 69–82.

Peplau, L. A. (1991). Lesbian and gay relationships. In J. C. Gonsiorek & J. D. Weinrich (Eds.), *Homosexuality: Research implications for public policy* (pp. 177–196). Newbury Park, CA: Sage.

Peplau, L. A., Bikson, T. K., Rook, K. S., & Goodchilds, J. D. (1982). Being old and living alone. In L. A. Peplau & D. Perlman (Eds.), *Loneliness* (pp. 327–350). New York: Wiley.

Perez-Escamilla, R. (1994). Breastfeeding in Africa and the Latin American and Caribbean region. The potential role of urbanization. *Journal of Tropical Pediatrics, 40,* 137–143.

Perner, J., & Wimmer, H. (1985). "John thinks that Mary thinks that . . .": Attribution of second-order beliefs by 5- to 10-year-old children. *Journal of Experimental Child Psychology, 39,* 437–471.

Peskin, H., & Livson, N. (1981). Uses of the past in adult psychological health. In D. H. Eichorn, J. A. Clausen, N. Haan, M. P. Honzik, & P. H. Mussen (Eds.), *Present and past in middle life* (pp. 158–194). New York: Academic Press.

Petersen, A. C. (1987). The nature of biological-psychosocial interactions: The sample case of early adolescence. In R. M. Lerner & T. T. Foch (Eds.), *Biological-psychosocial interactions in early adolescence* (pp. 35–62). Hillsdale, NJ: Erlbaum.

Petersen, A. C., Compas, B. E., Brooks-Gunn, J., Stemmler, M., Ey, S., & Grant, K. E. (1993). Depression in adolescence. *American Psychologist, 48,* 155–168.

Petersen, A. C., Sarigiani, P. A., & Kennedy, R. E. (1991). Adolescent depression: Why more girls? *Journal of Youth and Adolescence, 20,* 247–272.

Peterson, C., Seligman, M. E. P., & Vaillant, G. E. (1988). Pessimistic explanatory style is a risk factor for physical illness: A thirty-five-year longitudinal study. *Journal of Personality and Social Psychology, 55,* 23–27.

Peterson, C. C., & Siegal, M. (1995). Deafness, conversation and theory of mind. *Journal of Child Psychology and Psychiatry, 36,* 459–474.

Petitto, L. A. (1988). "Language" in the prelinguistic child. In F. S. Kessell (Ed.), *The development of language and language researchers: Essays in honor of Roger Brown* (pp. 187–222). Hillsdale, NJ: Erlbaum.

Pettingale, K. W., Morris, T., Greer, S., & Haybittle, J. L. (1985). Mental attitudes to cancer: An additional prognostic factor. *Lancet,* 85.

Pettit, G. S., Clawson, M. A., Dodge, K. A., & Bates, J. E. (1996). Stability and change in peer-rejected status: The role of child behavior, parenting, and family ecology. *Merrill-Palmer Quarterly, 42,* 295–318.

Phillips, S. K., Bruce, S. A., Newton, D., & Woledge, R. C. (1992). The weakness of old age is not due to failure of muscle activation. *Journals of Gerontology: Medical Sciences, 47,* M45–49.

Phinney, J. S. (1990). Ethnic identity in adolescents and adults: Review of research. *Psychological Bulletin, 108,* 499–514.

Phinney, J. S., & Rosenthal, D. A. (1992). Ethnic identity in adolescence: Process, context, and outcome. In G. R. Adams, T. P. Gullotta, & R. Montemayor (Eds.), *Adolescent identity formation* (pp. 145–172). Newbury Park, CA: Sage.

Piaget, J. (1932). *The moral judgment of the child.* New York: Macmillan.

Piaget, J. (1952). *The origins of intelligence in children.* New York: International Universities Press.

Piaget, J. (1954). *The construction of reality in the child.* New York: Basic Books. (Originally published 1937.)

Piaget, J. (1970). Piaget's theory. In P. H. Mussen (Ed.), *Carmichael's manual of child psychology* (Vol. 1, 3rd ed.) (pp. 703–732). New York: Wiley.

Piaget, J. (1977). *The development of thought: Equilibration of cognitive structures.* New York: Viking.

Piaget, J., & Inhelder, B. (1959). *La genèse des structures logiques élémentaires: Classifications et sériations [The origin of elementary logical structures: Classification and seriation].* Neuchâtel, Switzerland: Delachaux et Niestlé.

Piaget, J., & Inhelder, B. (1969). *The psychology of the child.* New York: Basic Books.

Pianta, R., Egeland, B., & Erickson, M. F. (1989). The antecedents of maltreatment: Results of the Mother-Child Interaction Research Project. In D. Cicchetti & V. Carlson (Eds.), *Child maltreatment* (pp. 203–253). Cambridge, England: Cambridge University Press.

Pianta, R. C., & Egeland, B. (1994). Predictors of instability in children's mental test performance at 24, 48, and 96 months. *Intelligence, 18,* 145–163.

Pianta, R. C., Steinberg, M. S., & Rollins, K. B. (1995). Teacher-child relationships and deflections in children's classroom adjustment. *Development and Psychopathology, 7,* 295–312.

Pickens, J. (1994). Perception of auditory-visual distance relations by 5-month-old infants. *Developmental Psychology, 30,* 537–544.

Pillard, R. C., & Bailey, J. M. (1995). A biologic perspective on sexual orientation. *The Psychiatric Clinics of North America, 18*(1), 71–84.

Pillemer, K., & Finkelhor, D. (1988). The prevalence of elder abuse: A random sample survey. *The Gerontologist, 28,* 51–58.

Pillemer, K., & Suitor, J. J. (1990). Prevention of elder abuse. In R. Ammerman & M. Hersen (Eds.), *Treatment of family violence: A sourcebook* (pp. 406–422). New York: Wiley.

Pillemer, K., & Suitor, J. J. (1992). Violence and violent feelings: What causes them among family caregivers? *Journals of Gerontology: Social Sciences, 47,* S165–172.

Pinker, S. (1987). The bootstrapping problem in language acquisition. In B. MacWhinney (Ed.), *Mechanisms of language acquisition* (pp. 399–442). Hillsdale, NJ: Erlbaum.

Pinker, S. (1994). *The language instinct: How the mind creates language.* New York: Morrow.

Pleck, J. (1977). The work-family role system. *Social Problems, 24,* 417–427.

Plomin, R., & DeFries, J. C. (1985). *Origins of individual differences in infancy: The Colorado Adoption Project.* Orlando, FL: Academic Press.

Plomin, R., Emde, R. N., Braungart, J. M., Campos, J., Corley, R., Fulker, D. W., Kagan, J., Reznick, J. S., Robinson, J., Zahn-Waxler, C., & DeFries, J. C. (1993). Genetic change and continuity from fourteen to twenty months: The MacArthur longitudinal twin study. *Child Development, 64,* 1354–1376.

Plomin, R., Loehlin, J. C., & DeFries, J. C. (1985). Genetic and environmental components of "environmental" influences. *Developmental Psychology, 21,* 391–402, 417–427.

Plomin, R., & McClearn, G. E. (1990). Human behavioral genetics of aging. In J. E. Birren & K. W. Schaie (Eds.), *Handbook of the psychology of aging* (3rd ed.) (pp. 67–79). San Diego, CA: Academic Press.

Plomin, R., & McClearn, G. E. (Eds.). (1993). *Nature, nurture & psychology.* Washington, DC: American Psychological Association.

Plomin, R., & Rende, R. (1991). Human behavioral genetics. *Annual Review of Psychology, 42,* 161–190.

Plowman, S. A., Drinkwater, B. L., & Horvath, S. M. (1979). Age and aerobic power in women: A longitudinal study. *Journal of Gerontology, 34,* 512–520.

Pober, B. R. (1996). Williams syndrome. In A. J. Capute & P. J. Acardo (Eds.), *Developmental disabilities in infancy and childhood* (2nd ed.). *Vol. II. The spectrum of developmental disabilities* (pp. 271–279). Baltimore, MD: Paul H. Brookes.

Polka, L., & Werker, J. F. (1994). Developmental changes in perception of nonnative vowel contrasts. *Journal of Experimental Psychology: Human Perception and Performance, 20,* 421–435.

Pollack, J. M. (1979–80). Correlates of death anxiety: A review of empirical studies. *Omega, 10,* 97–121.

Pollitt, E., & Gorman, K. S. (1994). Nutritional deficiencies as developmental risk factors. In C. A. Nelson (Ed.), *The Minnesota Symposia on Child Development* (Vol. 27) (pp. 121–144). Hillsdale, NJ: Erlbaum.

Ponsonby, A., Dwyer, T., Gibbons, L. E., Cochrane, J. A., & Wang, Y. (1993). Factors potentiating the risk of sudden infant death syndrome associated with the prone position. *New England Journal of Medicine, 329,* 377–382.

Posada, G., Gao, Y., Wu, F., Posada, R., Tascon, M., Schöelmerich, A., Sagi, A., Kondo-Ikemura, K., Haaland, W., & Synnevaag, B. (1995). The secure-base phenomenon across cultures: Children's behavior, mothers' preferences, and experts' concepts. *Monographs of the Society for Research in Child Development, 60*(244, Nos. 2–3), 27–48.

Posthuma, W. F. M., Westendorp, R. G. J., & Vandenbroucke, J. P. (1994). Cardioprotective effect of hormone replacement therapy in postmenopausal women: Is the evidence biased? *British Medical Journal, 308,* 1268–1269.

Poulson, C. L., Nunes, L. R. D., & Warren, S. F. (1989). Imitation in infancy: A critical review. In H. W. Reese (Ed.), *Advances in child development and behavior* (Vol. 22) (pp. 272–298). San Diego, CA: Academic Press.

Powlishta, K. K. (1995). Intergroup processes in childhood: Social categorization and sex role development. *Developmental Psychology, 31,* 781–788.

Powlishta, K. K., Serbin, L. A., Doyle, A., & White, D. R. (1994). Gender, ethnic, and body type biases: The generality of prejudice in childhood. *Developmental Psychologym 30,* 526–536.

Prechtl, H. F. R., & Beintema, D. J. (1964). *The neurological examination of the full-term newborn infant: Clinics in Developmental Medicine, 12.* London: Heinemann.

Prentice, A. (1994). Extended breast-feeding and growth in rural China. *Nutrition Reviews, 52,* 144–146.

Price, R. H. (1992). Psychosocial impact of job loss on individuals and families. *Current Directions in Psychological Science, 1,* 9–11.

Pulkkinen, L. (1982). Self-control and continuity from childhood to late adolescence. In P. Baltes & O. G. Brim, Jr. (Eds.), *Life span development and behavior* (Vol. 4) (pp. 64–107). New York: Academic Press.

Pye, C. (1986). Quiche Mayan speech to children. *Journal of Child Language, 13,* 85–100.

Pynoos, J., & Golant, S. (1996). Housing and living arrangements for the elderly. In R. H. Binstock & L. K. George (Eds.), *Handbook of aging and the social sciences* (4th ed.) (pp. 303–324). San Diego, CA: Academic Press.

Quadagno, J., & Hardy, M. A. (1996). Work and retirement. In R. H. Binstock & L. K. George (Eds.), *Handbook of aging and the social sciences* (4th ed.) (pp. 325–345). San Diego, CA: Academic Press.

Quiggle, N. L., Garber, J., Panak, W. F., & Dodge, K. A. (1992). Social information processing in aggressive and depressed children. *Child Development, 63,* 1305–1320.

Quinn, J. F. (1987). The economic status of the elderly: Beware of the mean. *The Review of Income and Wealth, 1,* 63–82.

Quinn, J. F., & Burkhauser, R. V. (1990). Work and retirement. In R. H. Binstock & L. K. George (Eds.), *Handbook of aging and the social sciences* (3rd ed.) (pp. 307–327). San Diego, CA: Academic Press.

Rahman, O., Strauss, J., Gertler, P., Ashley, D., & Fox, K. (1994). Gender differences in adult health: An international comparison. *The Gerontologist, 34,* 463–469.

Raja, S. N., McGee, R., & Stanton, W. R. (1992). Perceived attachments to parents and peers and psychological well-being in adolescence. *Journal of Youth and Adolescence, 21,* 471–485.

Ramey, C. T. (1992). High-risk children and IQ: Altering intergenerational patterns. *Intelligence, 16,* 239–256.

Ramey, C. T. (1993). A rejoinder to Spitz's critique of the Abecedarian experiment. *Intelligence, 17,* 25–30.

Ramey, C. T., & Campbell, F. A. (1987). The Carolina Abecedarian Project: An educational experiment concerning human malleability. In J. J. Gallagher & C. T. Ramey (Eds.), *The malleability of children* (pp. 127–140). Baltimore: Paul H. Brookes.

Raskind, M. A., & Peskind, E. R. (1992). Alzheimer's disease and other dementing disorders. In J. E. Birren, R. B. Sloane, & G. D. Cohen (Eds.), *Handbook of mental health and aging* (2nd ed.) (pp. 478–515). San Diego, CA: Academic Press.

Ree, M. J., & Earles, J. A. (1992). Intelligence is the best predictor of job performance. *Current Directions in Psychological Science, 1,* 86–89.

Reed, G. M., Kemeny, M. E., Taylor, S. E., Wang, H. J., & Visscher, B. R. (1994). Realistic acceptance as a predictor of decreased survival time in gay men with AIDS. *Health Psychology, 13,* 299–307.

Regier, D. A., Boyd, J. H., Burke, J. D., Rae, D. S., Myers, J. K., Kramer, M., Robins, L. N., George, L. K., Karno, M., & Locke, B. Z. (1988). One-month prevalence of mental disorders in the United States. *Archives of General Psychiatry, 45,* 977–986.

Reich, J. W., Zautra, A. J., & Guarnaccia, C. A. (1989). Effects of disability and bereavement on the mental health and recovery of older adults. *Psychology and Aging, 4,* 57–65.

Reinherz, H. Z., Giaconia, R. M., Pakiz, B., Silverman, A. B., Frost, A. K., & Lefkowitz, E. S. (1993). Psychosocial risks for major depression in late adolescence: A longitudinal community study. *Journal of the American Academy of Child and Adolescent Psychiatry, 32,* 1155–1163.

Reinke, B. J., Holmes, D. S., & Harris, R. L. (1985). The timing of psychosocial changes in women's lives: The years 25–45. *Journal of Personality and Social Psychology, 48,* 1353–1364.

Reisman, J. M., & Shorr, S. I. (1978). Friendship claims and expectations among children and adults. *Child Development, 49,* 913–916.

Remafedi, G. (1987a). Adolescent homosexuality: Psychosocial and medical implications. *Pediatrics, 79,* 331–337.

Remafedi, G. (1987b). Male homosexuality: The adolescent's perspective. *Pediatrics, 79,* 326–330.

Remafedi, G., Farrow, J. A., & Deisher, R. W. (1991). Risk factors for attempted suicide in gay and bisexual youth. *Pediatrics, 87,* 869–875.

Remafedi, G., Resnick, M., Blum, R., & Harris, L. (1992). Demography of sexual orientation in adolescents. *Pediatrics, 89,* 714–721.

Reno, V. P. (1993). The role of pensions in retirement income: Trends and questions. *Social Security Bulletin, 56,* 29–43.

Renouf, A. G., & Harter, S. (1990). Low self-worth and anger as components of the depressive experience in young adolescents. *Development and Psychopathology, 2,* 293–310.

Reskin, B. (1993). Sex segregation in the workplace. *Annual Review of Sociology, 19,* 241–270.

Rest, J. R., & Thoma, S. J. (1985). Relation of moral judgment development to formal education. *Developmental Psychology, 21,* 709–714.

Rexroat, C., & Shehan, C. (1987). The family life cycle and spouses' time in housework. *Journal of Marriage and the Family, 49,* 737–750.

Reynolds, A. J., & Bezruczko, N. (1993). School adjustment of children at risk through fourth grade. *Merrill-Palmer Quarterly, 39,* 457–480.

Reynolds, C. R., & Brown, R. T. (Eds.). (1984). *Perspectives on bias in mental testing.* New York: Plenum.

Rholes, W. S., & Ruble, D. N. (1984). Children's understanding of dispositional characteristics of others. *Child Development, 55,* 550–560.

Ricci, C. M., Beal, C. R., & Dekle, D. J. (1995). *The effect of parent versus unfamiliar interviewers on young witnesses' memory and identification accuracy.* Paper presented at the biennial meetings of the Society for Research in Child Development, Indianapolis, March.

Ricciuti, H. N. (1993). Nutrition and mental development. *Current Directions in Psychological Science, 2,* 43–46.

Rice, M. L., Huston, A. C., Truglio, R., & Wright, J. (1990). Words from "Sesame Street": Learning vocabulary while viewing. *Developmental Psychology, 26,* 421–428.

Rich-Edwards, J. W., Manson, J. E., Hennekens, C. H., & Buring, J. E. (1995). The primary prevention of coronary heart disease in women. *New England Journal of Medicine, 332,* 1758–1766.

Richards, H. C., Bear, G. G., Stewart, A. L., & Norman, A. D. (1992). Moral reasoning and classroom conduct: Evidence of a curvilinear relationship. *Merrill-Palmer Quarterly, 38,* 176–190.

Richardson, G. A., & Day, N. L. (1994). Detrimental effects of prenatal cocaine exposure: Illusion or reality? *Journal of the American Academy of Child and Adolescent Psychiatry, 33,* 28–34.

Richardson, G. S. (1990). Circadian rhythms and aging. In E. R. Scheider & J. W. Rowe (Eds.), *Handbook of the biology of aging* (3rd ed.) (pp. 275–305). San Diego, CA: Academic Press.

Richardson, J. L., Zarnegar, Z., Bisno, B., & Levine, A. (1990). Psychosocial status at initiation of cancer treatment and survival. *Journal of Psychosomatic Research, 34,* 189–201.

Rierdan, J., & Koff, E. (1993). Developmental variables in relation to depressive symptoms in adolescent girls. *Development and Psychopathology, 5,* 485–496.

Rierdan, J., Koff, E., & Stubbs, M. L. (1989). Timing of menarche, preparation, and initial menstrual experience: Replication and further analysis in a prospective study. *Journal of Youth and Adolescence, 18,* 413–426.

Riley, M. W. (1976). Age strata in social systems. In R. H. Binstock & E. Shanas (Eds.), *Handbook of aging and the social sciences* (pp. 189–217). New York: Van Nostrand Reinhold.

Riley, M. W. (1986). Overview and highlights of a sociological perspective. In A. B. SFrensen, F. E. Weinert, & L. R. Sherrod (Eds.), *Human development and the life course: Multidisciplinary perspectives* (pp. 153–176). Hillsdale, NJ: Erlbaum.

Riley, M. W., & Foner, A. (1968). *Aging and society: Vol. 1. An inventory of research findings.* New York: Russell Sage Foundation.

Rindfuss, R. R. (1991). The young adult years: Diversity, structural change, and fertility. *Demography, 28,* 493–512.

Rindfuss, R. R., Swicegood, C. G., & Rosenfeld, R. A. (1987). Disorder in the life course: How common and does it matter? *American Sociological Review, 52,* 785–801.

Risch, H. A., Jain, M., Marrett, L. D., & Howe, G. R. (1994). Dietary fat intake and risk of epithelial ovarian cancer. *Journal of the National Cancer Institute, 86,* 1409–1415.

Roberts, R. E., & Sobhan, M. (1992). Symptoms of depression in adolescence: A comparison of Anglo, African, and Hispanic Americans. *Journal of Youth and Adolescence, 21,* 639–651.

Robins, L. N., & McEvoy, L. (1990). Conduct problems as predictors of substance abuse. In L. N. Robins & M. Rutter (Eds.), *Straight and devious pathways from childhood to adulthood* (pp. 182–204). Cambridge, England: Cambridge University Press.

Robison, J., Moen, P., & Dempster-McClain, D. (1995). Women's caregiving: Changing profiles and pathways. *Journals of Gerontology: Social Sciences, 50B,* S362–373.

Roche, A. F. (1979). Secular trends in human growth, maturation, and development. *Monographs of the Society for Research in Child Development, 44*(3–4, Serial No. 179).

Rockwood, K., & Stadnyk, K. (1994). The prevalence of dementia in the elderly: A review. *Canadian Journal of Psychiatry, 29,* 253–257.

Rodin, J. (1986). Aging and health: Effects of the sense of control. *Science, 233,* 1271–1275.

Rodin, J. (1990). Control by any other name: Definitions, concepts, and processes. In J. Rodin, C. Schooler, & K. W. Schaie (Eds.), *Self-directedness: Cause and effects throughout the life course* (pp. 1–17). Hillsdale, NJ: Erlbaum.

Rodin, J., & Langer, E. J. (1977). Long-term effects of a control-relevant intervention with the institutionalized aged. *Journal of Personality and Social Psychology, 35,* 897–902.

Rodriguez, C., Calle, E. E., Coates, R. J., Miracle-McMahil, H. L., Thun, M. J., & Heath, C. W., Jr. (1995). Estrogen replacement therapy and fatal ovarian cancer. *American Journal of Epidemiology, 141,* 828–835.

Rogers, C. R. (1961). *On becoming a person.* Boston: Houghton Mifflin.

Rogers, J. L., Rowe, D. C., & May, K. (1994). DF analysis of NLSY IQ/Achievement data: Nonshared environmental influences. *Intelligence, 19,* 157–177.

Rogers, R. L., Meyer, J. S., & Mortel, K. F. (1990). After reaching retirement age physical activity sustains cerebral perfusion and cognition. *Journal of the American Geriatric Society, 38,* 123–128.

Roggman, L. A., Langlois, J. H., Hubbs-Tait, L., & Rieser-Danner, L. A. (1994). Infant day-care, attachment, and the "file drawer problem." *Child Development, 65,* 1429–1443.

Rogoff, B. (1990). *Apprenticeship in thinking: Cognitive development in social contexts.* New York: Oxford University Press.

Rohner, R. P., Kean, K. J., & Cournoyer, D. E. (1991). Effects of corporal punishment, perceived caretaker warmth, and cultural beliefs on the psychological adjustment of children in St. Kitts, West Indies. *Journal of Marriage and the Family, 53,* 681–693.

Rollins, B. C., & Feldman, H. (1970). Marital satisfaction over the family life cycle. *Journal of Marriage and the Family, 32,* 20–27.

Rolls, B. J., Fedoroff, I. C., & Guthrie, J. F. (1991). Gender differences in eating behavior and body weight regulation. *Health Psychology, 20,* 133–142.

Rooks, J. P., Weatherby, N. L., Ernst, E. K. M., Stapleton, S., Rosen, D., & Rosenfield, A. (1989). Outcomes of care in birth centers: The National Birth Center Study. *New England Journal of Medicine, 321,* 1804–1811.

Rose, A. J., & Montemayor, R. (1994). The relationship between gender role orientation and perceived self-competence in male and female adolescents. *Sex Roles, 31,* 579–595.

Rose, D. P. (1993). Diet, hormones, and cancer. *Annual Review of Public Health, 14,* 1–17.

Rose, R. J. (1995). Genes and human behavior. *Annual Review of Psychology, 56,* 625–654.

Rose, S. A., & Feldman, J. F. (1995). Prediction of IQ and specific cognitive abilities at 11 years from infancy measures. *Developmental Psychology, 31,* 685–696.

Rose, S. A., & Ruff, H. A. (1987). Cross-modal abilities in human infants. In J. D. Osofsky (Ed.), *Handbook of infant development* (2nd ed.) (pp. 318–362). New York: Wiley-Interscience.

Rosenbaum, J. E. (1984). *Career mobility in a corporate hierarchy.* New York: Academic Press.

Rosenberg, M. (1986). Self-concept from middle childhood through adolescence. In J. Suls & A. G. Greenwald (Eds.), *Psychological perspectives on the self* (Vol. 3) (pp. 107–136). Hillsdale, NJ: Erlbaum.

Rosenblith, J. F. (1992). *In the beginning* (2nd ed.). Thousand Oaks, CA: Sage.

Rosenman, R. H., & Friedman, M. (1983). Relationship of Type A behavior pattern to coronary heart disease. In H. Selye (Ed.), *Selye's guide to stress research* (Vol. 2) (pp. 47–106). New York: Scientific and Academic Editions.

Rosenthal, C. J., Matthews, S. H., & Marshall, V. W. (1989). Is parent care normative? The experiences of a sample of middle-aged women. *Research on Aging, 11,* 244–260.

Rosenthal, R. (1994). Interpersonal expectancy effects: A 30-year perspective. *Current Directions in Psychological Science, 3,* 176–179.

Rosow, I. (1985). Status and role change through the life cycle. In R. H. Binstock & E. Shanas (Eds.), *Handbook of aging and the social sciences* (2nd ed.) (pp. 62–93). New York: Van Nostrand Reinhold.

Ross, C. E. (1995). Reconceptualizing marital status as a continuum of social attachment. *Journal of Marriage and the Family, 57,* 129–140.

Ross, G., Kagan, J., Zelazo, P., & Kotelchuck, M. (1975). Separation protest in infants in home and laboratory. *Developmental Psychology, 11,* 256–257.

Ross, R. K., Paganini-Hill, A., Mack, T. M., & Henderson, B. E. (1987). Estrogen use and cardiovascular disease. In D. R. Mishell, Jr. (Ed.), *Menopause: Physiology and pharmacology* (pp. 209–224). Chicago: Year Book Medical Publishers.

Rossi, A. S. (1989). A life-course approach to gender, aging, and intergenerational relations. In K. W. Schaie & C. Schooler (Eds.), *Social structure and aging: Psychological processes* (pp. 207–236). Hillsdale, NJ: Erlbaum.

Rossman, I. (1980). Bodily changes with aging. In E. W. Busse & D. G. Blazer (Eds.), *Handbook of geriatric psychiatry* (pp. 125–146). New York: Van Nostrand Reinhold.

Rothbard, J. C., & Shaver, P. R. (1994). Continuity of attachment across the life span. In M. B. Sperling & W. H. Berman (Eds.), *Attachment in adults. Clinical and developmental perspectives* (pp. 31–71). New York: Guilford Press.

Rothbart, M. K., Derryberry, D., & Posner, M. I. (1994). A psychobiological approach to the development of temperament. In J. E. Bates & T. D. Wachs (Eds.), *Temperament. Individual differences at the interface of biology and behavior* (pp. 83–116). Washington, DC: American Psychological Association.

Rotheram-Borus, M. J., Rosario, M., & Koopman, C. (1991). Minority youths at high risk: Gay males and runaways. In M. E. Colten & S. Gore (Eds.), *Adolescent stress: Causes and consequences* (pp. 181–200). New York: Aldine de Gruyter.

Rothman, K. J., Moore, L. L., Singer, M. R., Nguyen, U. D. T., Mannino, S., & Milunsky, A. (1995). Teratogenicity of high Vitamin A intake. *New England Journal of Medicine, 333,* 1369–1373.

Rotter, J. B. (1966). Generalized expectancies for internal versus external control of reinforcement. *Psychological Monographs, 80*(1, Whole No. 609).

Rovee-Collier, C. (1986). The rise and fall of infant classical conditioning research: Its promise for the study of early development. In L. P. Lipsitt & C. Rovee-Collier (Eds.), *Advances in infancy research* (Vol. 4) (pp. 139–162). Norwood, NJ: Ablex.

Rovee-Collier, C. (1993). The capacity for long-term memory in infancy. *Current Directions in Psychological Science, 2,* 130–135.

Rovet, J., & Netley, C. (1983). The triple X chromosome syndrome in childhood: Recent empirical findings. *Child Development, 54,* 831–845.

Rowe, I., & Marcia, J. E. (1980). Ego identity status, formal operations, and moral development. *Journal of Youth and Adolescence, 9,* 87–99.

Rowe, J. W., Wang, S. Y., & Elahi, D. (1990). Design, conduct, and analysis of human aging research. In E. R. Schneider & J. W. Rowe (Eds.), *Handbook of the biology of aging* (3rd ed.) (pp. 63–71). San Diego, CA: Academic Press.

Rubin, K. H., Fein, G. G., & Vandenberg, B. (1983). Play. In E. M. Hetherington (Ed.), *Handbook of child psychology: Socialization, personality, and social development* (Vol. 4) (pp. 693–774). New York: Wiley.

Rubin, K. H., Hymel, S., Mills, R. S. L., & Rose-Krasnor, L. (1991). Conceptualizing different developmental pathways to and from social isolation in childhood. In D. Cicchetti & S. L. Toth (Eds.), *Internalizing and externalizing expressions of dysfunction: Rochester Symposium on Developmental Psychopathology* (Vol. 2) (pp. 91–122). Hillsdale, NJ: Erlbaum.

Rubinstein, R. L. (1986). *Singular paths: Old men living alone.* New York: Columbia University Press.

Rubinstein, R. L., Alexander, B. B., Goodman, M., & Luborsky, M. (1991). Key relationships of never married childless older women: A cultural analysis. *Journals of Gerontology: Social Sciences, 46,* S270–277.

Ruble, D. N. (1987). The acquisition of self-knowledge: A self-socialization perspective. In N. Eisenberg (Ed.), *Contemporary topics in developmental psychology* (pp. 243–270). New York: Wiley-Interscience.

Ruble, D. N., Balaban, T., & Cooper, J. (1981). Gender constancy and the effects of sex-typed televised toy commercials. *Child Development, 52,* 667–673.

Russell, G. (1982). Shared-caregiving families: An Australian study. In M. E. Lamb (Ed.), *Nontraditional families* (pp. 139–172). Hillsdale, NJ: Erlbaum.

Rutter, M. (1978). Early sources of security and competence. In J. S. Bruner & A. Garton (Eds.), *Human growth and development* (pp. 33–61). London: Oxford University Press.

Rutter, M. (1983). School effects on pupil progress: Research findings and policy implications. *Child Development, 54,* 1–29.

Rutter, M. (1987). Continuities and discontinuities from infancy. In J. D. Osofsky (Ed.), *Handbook of infant development* (2nd ed.) (pp. 1256–1296). New York: Wiley-Interscience.

Rutter, M., & Rutter, M. (1993). *Developing Minds: Challenge and continuity across the life span.* New York: Basic Books.

Ryan, A. S., Rush, D., Krieger, F. W., & Lewandowski, G. E. (1991). Recent declines in breast-feeding in the United States, 1984 through 1989. *Pediatrics, 88,* 719–727.

Ryan, C. J., & Kaye, M. (1996). Euthanasia in Australia—the Northern Territory Rights of the Terminally Ill Act. *New England Journal of Medicine, 334,* 326–328.

Ryff, C. (1984). Personality development from the inside: The subjective experience of change in adulthood and aging. In P. B. Baltes & O. G. Brim, Jr. (Eds.), *Life-span development and behavior* (pp. 244–281). Orlando, FL: Academic Press.

Ryff, C., & Heincke, S. G. (1983). The subjective organization of personality in adulthood and aging. *Journal of Personality and Social Psychology, 44,* 807–816.

Saccuzzo, D. P., Johnson, N. E., & Guertin, T. L. (1994). Information processing in gifted versus nongifted African American, Latino, Filipino, and White children: Speeded versus nonspeeded paradigms. *Intelligence, 19,* 219–243.

Sack, W. H., Mason, R., & Higgins, J. E. (1985). The single parent family and abusive child punishment. *American Journal of Orthopsychiatry, 55,* 252–259.

Sadowski, M. (1995). The numbers game yields simplistic answers on the link between spending and outcomes. *Harvard Education Letter, 11*(2), 1–4.

Sagi, A. (1990). Attachment theory and research from a cross-cultural perspective. *Human Development, 33,* 10–22.

Sagi, A., van IJzendoorn, M. H., & Koren-Karie, N. (1991). Primary appraisal of the Strange Situation: A cross-cultural analysis of preseparation episodes. *Developmental Psychology, 27,* 587–596.

St. James-Roberts, I., Bowyer, J., Varghese, S., & Sawdon, J. (1994). Infant crying patterns in Manila and London. *Child: Care, Health and Development, 20,* 323–337.

St. Peters, M., Fitch, M., Huston, A. C., Wright, J. C., & Eakins, D. J. (1991). Television and families: What do young children watch with their parents? *Child Development, 62,* 1409–1423.

Salthouse, T. A. (1991). *Theoretical perspectives on cognitive aging.* Hillsdale, NJ: Erlbaum.

Salthouse, T. A. (1992). *Mechanisms of age-cognition relations in adulthood.* Hillsdale, NJ: Erlbaum.

Salthouse, T. A. (1993). Speed mediation of adult age differences in cognition. *Developmental Psychology, 29,* 722–738.

Salthouse, T. A. (1996). General and specific speed mediation of adult age differences in memory. *Journals of Gerontology: Psychological Sciences, 51B,* P30–42.

Salthouse, T. A., & Maurer, T. J. (1996). Aging, job performance, and career development. In J. E. Birren & K. W. Schaie (Eds.), *Handbook of the psychology of aging* (4th ed.) (pp. 353–364). San Diego, CA: Academic Press.

Sameroff, A., Seifer, R., Barocas, R., Zax, M., & Greenspan, S. (1987). Intelligence quotient scores of 4-year-old children: Social-environmental risk factors. *Pediatrics, 79,* 343–350.

Sammartino, F. J. (1987). The effect of health on retirement. *Social Security Bulletin, 50(2),* 31–47.

Sampson, R. J., & Laub, J. H. (1994). Urban poverty and the family context of delinquency: A new look at structure and process in a classic study. *Child Development, 65,* 523–540.

Sanders, C. M. (1989). *Grief: The mourning after.* New York: Wiley-Interscience.

Sands, L. P., & Meredith, W. (1992). Blood pressure and intellectual functioning in late midlife. *Journals of Gerontology: Psychological Sciences, 47,* P81–84.

Sands, L. P., Terry, H., & Meredith, W. (1989). Change and stability in adult intellectual functioning assessed by Wechsler item responses. *Psychology and Aging, 4,* 79–87.

Sapir, E. (1929). The status of linguistics as a science. *Language, 5,* 207–214.

Sarason, B. R., Sarason, I. G., & Pierce, G. R. (1990). Traditional views of social support and their impact on assessment. In B. R. Sarason, I. G. Sarason, & G. R. Pierce (Eds.), *Social support: An interactional view* (pp. 9–25). New York: Wiley.

Savin-Williams, R. C. (1994). Verbal and physical abuse as stressors in the lives of lesbian, gay male, and bisexual youths: Associations with school problems, running away, substance abuse, prostitution, and suicide. *Journal of Consulting and Clinical Psychology, 62,* 261–269.

Scarr, S. (1992). Developmental theories for the 1990s: Development and individual differences. *Child Development, 63,* 1–19.

Scarr, S., & Eisenberg, M. (1993). Child care research: Issues, perspectives, and results. *Annual Review of Psychology, 44,* 613–644.

Scarr, S., & Kidd, K. K. (1983). Developmental behavior genetics. In M. M. Haith & J. J. Campos (Eds.), *Handbook of child psychology: Vol. 2. Infancy and developmental psychobiology* (pp. 345–434). New York: Wiley.

Scarr, S., & McCartney, K. (1983). How people make their own environments: A theory of genotype ® environment effects. *Child Development, 54,* 424–435.

Scarr, S., & Weinberg, R. A. (1983). The Minnesota adoption studies: Genetic differences and malleability. *Child Development, 54,* 260–267.

Scarr, S., Weinberg, R. A., & Waldman, I. D. (1993). IQ correlations in transracial adoptive families. *Intelligence, 17,* 541–555.

Schaeffer, D. L. (Ed.). (1971). *Sex differences in personality: Readings.* Pacific Grove, CA: Brooks/Cole.

Schaefli, A., Rest, J. R., & Thoma, S. J. (1985). Does moral education improve moral judgment? A meta-analysis of intervention studies using the Defining Issues Test. *Review of Educational Research, 55,* 319–352.

Schafer, R. B., & Keith, P. M. (1984). A causal analysis of the relationship between the self-concept and marital quality. *Journal of Marriage and the Family, 46,* 909–914.

Schaie, K. W. (1983a). What can we learn from the longitudinal study of adult psychological development? In K. W. Schaie (Ed.), *Longitudinal studies of adult psychological development* (pp. 1–19). New York: Guilford Press.

Schaie, K. W. (1983b). The Seattle longitudinal study: A 21-year exploration of psychometric intelligence in adulthood. In K. W. Schaie (Ed.), *Longitudinal studies of adult psychological development* (pp. 64–135). New York: Guilford Press.

Schaie, K. W. (1989a). The hazards of cognitive aging. *The Gerontologist, 29,* 484–493.

Schaie, K. W. (1989b). Individual differences in rate of cognitive change in adulthood. In V. L. Bengtson & K. W. Schaie (Eds.), *The course of later life: Research and reflections* (pp. 65–86). New York: Springer.

Schaie, K. W. (1990). Intellectual development in adulthood. In J. E. Birren & K. W. Schaie (Eds.), *Handbook of the psychology of aging* (3rd ed.) (pp. 291–309). San Diego, CA: Academic Press.

Schaie, K. W. (1993). The Seattle Longitudinal Studies of adult intelligence. *Current Directions in Psychological Science, 2,* 171–175.

Schaie, K. W. (1994a). The course of adult intellectual development. *American Psychologist, 49,* 304–313.

Schaie, K. W. (1994b). Developmental designs revisited. In S. H. Cohen & H. W. Reese (Eds.), *Life-span developmental psychology: Methodological contributions* (pp. 45–64). Hillsdale, NJ: Erlbaum.

Schaie, K. W. (1996). Intellectual development in adulthood. In J. E. Birren & K. W. Schaie (Eds.), *Handbook of the psychology of aging* (4th ed.) (pp. 266–286). San Diego, CA: Academic Press.

Schaie, K. W., & Hertzog, C. (1983). Fourteen-year cohort-sequential analyses of adult intellectual development. *Developmental Psychology, 19,* 531–543.

Schaie, K. W., & Willis, S. L. (1991). Adult personality and psychomotor performance: Cross-sectional and longitudinal analyses. *Journals of Gerontology: Psychological Sciences, 46,* P275–284.

Scharlach, A. E., & Fredricksen, K. I. (1994). Eldercare versus adult care. Does care recipient age make a difference? *Research on Aging, 16,* 43–68.

Scheibel, A. B. (1992). Structural changes in the aging brain. In J. E. Birren, R. B. Sloane, & G. D. Cohen (Eds.), *Handbook of mental health and aging* (2nd ed.) (pp. 147–174). San Diego, CA: Academic Press.

Scheibel, A. B. (1996). Structural and functional changes in the aging brain. In J. E. Birren & K. W. Schaie (Eds.), *Handbook of the psychology of aging* (4th ed.) (pp. 105–128). San Diego, CA: Academic Press.

Scheier, M. F., Matthews, K. A., Owens, J. F., Magovern, G. J., Lefebvre, S., Abbott, R. A., & Carver, C. S. (1989). Dispositional optimism and recovery from coronary artery bypass surgery: The beneficial effects on physical and psychological well-being. *Journal of Personality and Social Psychology, 57,* 1024–1040.

Schieber, F. (1992). Aging and the senses. In J. E. Birren, R. B. Sloane, & G. D. Cohen (Eds.), *Handbook of mental health and aging* (2nd ed.) (pp. 252–306). San Diego, CA: Academic Press.

Schneider, B., Hieshima, J. A., Lee, S., & Plank, S. (1994). East-Asian academic success in the United States: Family, school, and community explanations. In P. M. Greenfield & R. R. Cocking (Eds.), *Cross-cultural roots of minority child development* (pp. 323–350). Hillsdale, NJ: Erlbaum.

Schneider, E. L., & Rowe, J. W. (Eds.). (1996). *Handbook of the biology of aging* (4th ed.). San Diego, CA: Academic Press.

Schneider, M. L. (1992). The effect of mild stress during pregnancy on birthweight and neuromotor maturation in rhesus monkey infants (*Macaca mulatta*). *Infant Behavior and Development, 15,* 389–403.

Schneider, W., & Bjorklund, D. F. (1992). Expertise, aptitude, and strategic remembering. *Child Development, 63,* 461–473.

Schneider, W., Reimers, P., Roth, E., & Visé, M. (1995). *Short- and long-term effects of training phonological awareness in kindergarten: Evidence from two German studies.* Paper presented at the biennial meetings of the Society for Research in Child Development, Indianapolis, March.

Schoen, R. (1992). First unions and the stability of first marriages. *Journal of Marriage and the Family, 54,* 281–284.

Schoen, R., & Wooldredge, J. (1989). Marriage choices in North Carolina and Virginia, 1969–71 and 1979–81. *Journal of Marriage and the Family, 51,* 465–481.

Schoendorf, K. C., Hogue, C. J. R., Kleinman, J. C., & Rowley, D. (1992). Mortality among infants of black as compared with white college-educated parents. *New England Journal of Medicine, 326,* 1522–1526.

Schoendorf, K. C., & Kiely, J. L. (1992). Relationship of Sudden Infant Death Syndrome to maternal smoking during and after pregnancy. *Pediatrics, 90,* 905–908.

Schoenfeld, D. E., Malmrose, L. C., Blazer, D. G., Gold, D. T., & Seeman, T. E. (1994). Self-rated health and mortality in the high-functioning elderly—a closer look at healthy individuals: MacArthur field study of successful aging. *Journals of Gerontology: Medical Sciences, 49,* M109–115.

Schor, E. L. (1987). Unintentional injuries: Patterns within families. *American Journal of the Diseases of Children, 141,* 1280.

Schramm, W. F., Barnes, D. E., & Bakewell, J. M. (1987). Neonatal mortality in Missouri home births, 1978–84. *American Journal of Public Health, 77,* 930–935.

Schreiber, L. (1990). *Midstream.* New York: Viking.

Schultz, N. R., Jr., Elias, M. F., Robbins, M. A., Streeten, D. H. P., & Blakeman, N. (1986). A longitudinal comparison of hypertensives and normotensives on the Wechsler Adult Intelligence Scale: Initial findings. *Journal of Gerontology, 41,* 169–175.

Schulz, J. H. (1995). *The economics of aging* (6th ed.). Westport, CT: Auburn House.

Schulz, R., & Curnow, C. (1988). Peak performance and age among superathletes: Track and field, swimming, baseball, tennis, and golf. *Journals of Gerontology: Psychological Sciences, 43,* P113–120.

Schulz, R., Visintainer, P., & Williamson, G. M. (1990). Psychiatric and physical morbidity effects of caregiving. *Journals of Gerontology: Psychological Sciences, 45,* 181–191.

Schulz, R., & Williamson, G. M. (1991). A 2-year longitudinal study of depression among Alzheimer's caregivers. *Psychology and Aging, 6,* 569–578.

Schwartz, R. M., Anastasia, M. L., Scanlon, J. W., & Kellogg, R. J. (1994). Effect of surfactant on morbidity, mortality, and resource use in newborn infants weighing 500 to 1500 g. *New England Journal of Medicine, 330,* 1476–1480.

Sears, R. R. (1977). Sources of life satisfactions of the Terman gifted men. *American Psychologist, 32,* 119–128.

Seccombe, K. (1987). Children: Their impact on the elderly in declining health. *Research on Aging, 9,* 312–326.

Seidman, E., Allen, L., Aber, J. L., Mitchell, C., & Feinman, J. (1994). The impact of school transitions in early adolescence on the self-sytem and perceived social context of poor urban youth. *Child Development, 65,* 507–522.

Seifer, R., Schiller, M., Sameroff, A. J., Resnick, S., & Riordan, K. (1996). Attachment, maternal sensitivity, and infant temperament during the first year of life. *Developmental Psychology, 32,* 12–25.

Seitz, V. (1988). Methodology. In M. H. Bornstein & M. E. Lamb (Eds.), *Developmental psychology: An advanced textbook* (pp. 51–84). Hillsdale, NJ: Erlbaum.

Seligman, M. E. P. (1991). *Learned optimism.* New York: Knopf.

Selman, R. L. (1980). *The growth of interpersonal understanding.* New York: Academic Press.

Serbin, L., Moskowitz, D. S., Schwartzman, A. E., & Ledingham, J. E. (1991). Aggressive, withdrawn, and aggressive/withdrawn children in adolescence: Into the next generation. In D. J. Pepler & K. H. Rubin (Eds.), *The development and treatment of childhood aggression* (pp. 55–70). Hillsdale, NJ: Erlbaum.

Serbin, L. A., Powlishta, K. K., & Gulko, J. (1993). The development of sex typing in middle childhood. *Monographs of the Society for Research in Child Development, 58* (2, Serial No. 232).

Serdula, M. K., Ivery, D., Coates, R. J., Freedman, D. S., Williamson, D. F., & Byers, T. (1993). Do obese children become obese adults? A review of the literature. *Preventive Medicine, 22,* 167–177.

Shaffer, D., Garland, A., Gould, M., Fisher, P., & Trautman, P. (1988). Preventing teenage suicide: A critical review. *Journal of the American Academy of Child and Adolescent Psychiatry, 27,* 675–687.

Shaffer, D., Garland, A., Vieland, V., Underwood, M., & Busner, C. (1991). The impact of curriculum-based suicide prevention programs for teenagers. *Journal of the American Academy of Child and Adolescent Psychiatry, 30,* 588–596.

Shantz, C. U. (1983). Social cognition. In J. H. Flavell & E. M. Markman (Eds.), *Handbook of child psychology.* Vol. 3. *Cognitive development* (pp. 495–555). New York: Wiley.

Shantz, D. W. (1986). Conflict, aggression, and peer status: An observational study. *Child Development, 57,* 1322–1332.

Shapiro, E. (1983). Impending death and the use of hospitals by the elderly. *Journal of the American Geriatric Society, 31,* 348–351.

Shatz, M. (1994). *A toddler's life: Becoming a person.* New York: Oxford University Press.

Shaw, D. S., Kennan, K., & Vondra, J. I. (1994). Developmental precursors of externalizing behavior: Ages 1 to 3. *Developmental Psychology, 30,* 355–364.

Shelton, B. A., & John, D. (1993). Ethnicity, race, and difference: A comparison of White, Black, and Hispanic men's household labor time. In J. C. Hood (Ed.), *Men, work, and family* (pp. 131–150). Newbury Park, CA: Sage.

Sherry, B., Springer, D. A., Connell, F. A., & Garrett, S. M. (1992). Short, thin, or obese? Comparing growth indexes of children from high- and low-poverty areas. *Journal of the American Dietetic Association, 92,* 1092–1095.

Shneidman, E. S. (1980). *Voices of death.* New York: Harper & Row.

Shneidman, E. S. (1983). *Deaths of man.* New York: Jason Aronson.

Shneidman, E. S. (1989). The Indian summer of life: A preliminary study of septuagenarians. *American Psychologist, 44,* 684–694.

Shock, N. W., Greulich, R. C., Andres, R., Arenberg, D., Costa, P. T., Jr., Lakatta, E. G., & Tobin, J. D. (1984). *Normal human aging: The Baltimore Longitudinal Study of Aging.* NIH Publication No. 84–2450, U.S. Department of Health and Human Services, National Institute on Aging. Washington, DC: U.S. Government Printing Office.

Shonkoff, J. P. (1984). The biological substrate and physical health in middle childhood. In W. A. Collins (Ed.), *Development during middle childhood: The years from six to twelve* (pp. 24–69). Washington, DC: National Academy Press.

Shore, C. (1986). Combinatorial play, conceptual development, and early multiword speech. *Developmental Psychology, 22,* 184–190.

Shore, C. M. (1995). *Individual differences in language development.* Thousand Oaks, CA: Sage.

Shweder, R. A., Mahapatra, M., & Miller, J. G. (1987). Culture and moral development. In J. Kagan & S. Lamb (Eds.), *The emergence of morality in young children* (pp. 1–82). Chicago: University of Chicago Press.

Siegal, M. (1987). Are sons and daughters treated more differently by fathers than by mothers? *Developmental Review, 7,* 183–209.

Siegel, J. M. (1992). Anger and cardiovascular health. In H. S. Friedman (Ed.), *Hostility, coping and health* (pp. 49–64). Washington, DC: American Psychological Association.

Siegler, I. C. (1983). Psychological aspects of the Duke Longitudinal Studies. In K. W. Schaie (Ed.), *Longitudinal studies of adult psychological development* (pp. 136–190). New York: Guilford Press.

Siegler, I. C., McCarty, S. M., & Logue, P. E. (1982). Wechsler memory scale scores, selective attrition, and distance from death. *Journal of Gerontology, 37,* 176–181.

Siegler, R. S. (1976). Three aspects of cognitive development. *Cognitive Psychology, 8,* 431–520.

Siegler, R. S. (1978). The origins of scientific reasoning. In R. S. Siegler (Ed.), *Children's thinking: What develops?* (pp. 109–150). Hillsdale, NJ: Erlbaum.

Siegler, R. S. (1981). Developmental sequences within and between concepts. *Monographs of the Society for Research in Child Development, 46* (2, Serial No. 189).

Siegler, R. S. (1994). Cognitive variability: A key to understanding cognitive development. *Current Directions in Psychological Science, 3,* 1–5.

Sigman, M. (1995). Nutrition and child development: More food for thought. *Current Directions in Psychological Science, 4,* 52–55.

Sigman, M., Neumann, C., Carter, E., Cattle, D. J., D'Souza, S., & Bwibo, N. (1988). Home interactions and the development of Embu toddlers in Kenya. *Child Development, 59,* 1251–1261.

Silbereisen, R. K., & Kracke, B. (1993). Variations in maturational timing and adjustment in adolescence. In S. Jackson & H. Rodrigues-Tomé (Eds.), *Adolescence and its social worlds* (pp. 67–94). Hove, England: Erlbaum.

Simmons, R. G., Burgeson, R., & Reef, M. J. (1988). Cumulative change at entry to adolescence. In M. R. Gunnar & W. A. Collins (Eds.), *Minnesota Symposia on Child Psychology* (Vol. 21) (pp. 123–150). Hillsdale, NJ: Erlbaum.

Simoneau, G. G., & Liebowitz, H. W. (1996). Posture, gait, and falls. In J. E. Birren & K. W. Schaie (Eds.), *Handbook of the psychology of aging* (4th ed.) (pp. 204–217). San Diego, CA: Academic Press.

Simons, R. L., Robertson, J. F., & Downs, W. R. (1989). The nature of the association between parental rejection and delinquent behavior. *Journal of Youth and Adolescence, 18,* 297–309.

Simonton, D. K. (1988). Age and outstanding achievement: What do we know after a century of research? *Psychological Bulletin, 104,* 251–267.

Simonton, D. K. (1989). The swan-song phenomenon: Last-works effects for 172 classical composers. *Psychology and Aging, 4,* 42–47.

Simonton, D. K. (1991). Career landmarks in science: Individual differences and interdisciplinary contrasts. *Developmental Psychology, 27,* 119–130.

Singh, G. K., & Yu, S. M. (1995). Infant mortality in the United States: Trends, differentials, and projections, 1950 through 2010. *American Journal of Public Health, 85,* 957–964.

Sirignano, S. W., & Lachman, M. E. (1985). Personality change during the transition to parenthood: The role of perceived infant temperament. *Developmental Psychology, 21,* 558–567.

Skinner, B. F. (1953). *Science and human behavior.* New York: Macmillan.

Skinner, B. F. (1957). *Verbal behavior.* New York: Prentice-Hall.

Skinner, B. F. (1980). The experimental analysis of operant behavior: A history. In R. W. Riebes & K. Salzinger (Eds.), *Psychology: Theoretical-historical perspectives.* New York: Academic Press.

Slaby, R. G., & Frey, K. S. (1975). Development of gender constancy and selective attention to same-sex models. *Child Development, 46,* 849–856.

Slater, A. (1995). Individual differences in infancy and later IQ. *Journal of Child Psychology and Psychiatry, 36,* 69–112.

Slater, A. M., & Bremner, J. G. (Eds.). (1989). *Infant development.* Hillsdale, NJ: Erlbaum.

Slobin, D. I. (1985a). Introduction: Why study acquisition crosslinguistically? In D. I. Slobin (Ed.), *The crosslinguistic study of language acquisition: Vol. 1. The data* (pp. 3–24). Hillsdale, NJ: Erlbaum.

Slobin, D. I. (1985b). Crosslinguistic evidence for the language-making capacity. In D. I. Slobin (Ed.), *The crosslinguistic study of language acquisition: Vol. 2. Theoretical issues* (pp. 1157–1256). Hillsdale, NJ: Erlbaum.

Small, G. W., La Rue, A., Komo, S., Kaplan, A., & Mandelkern, M. A. (1995). Predictors of cognitive change in middle-aged and older adults with memory loss. *American Journal of Psychiatry, 152,* 1757–1764.

Small, S. A., & Luster, T. (1994). Adolescent sexual activity: An ecological, risk-factor approach. *Journal of Marriage and the Family, 56,* 181–192.

Smeeding, T. M. (1990). Economic status of the elderly. In R. H. Binstock & L. K. George (Eds.), *Handbook of aging and the social sciences* (3rd ed.) (pp. 362–381). San Diego, CA: Academic Press.

Smelser, N. J., & Erikson, E. H. (Eds.) (1980). *Themes of work and love in adulthood.* Cambridge, MA: Harvard University Press.

Smetana, J. G. (1990). Morality and conduct disorders. In M. Lewis & S. M. Miller (Eds.), *Handbook of developmental psychopathology* (pp. 157–180). New York: Plenum.

Smetana, J. G., Killen, M., & Turiel, E. (1991). Children's reasoning about interpersonal and moral conflicts. *Child Development, 62,* 629–644.

Smith, D. W. (1978). Prenatal life. In D. W. Smith, E. L. Bierman, & N. M. Robinson (Eds.), *The biologic ages of man* (2nd ed.) (pp. 42–62). Philadelphia: Saunders.

Smith, E. L. (1982). Exercise for prevention of osteoporosis: A review. *Physician and Sportsmedicine, 10,* 72–83.

Smock, P. J. (1993). The economic costs of marital disruption for young women over the past two decades. *Demography, 30,* 353–371.

Smoll, F. L., & Schutz, R. W. (1990). Quantifying gender differences in physical performance: A developmental perspective. *Developmental Psychology, 26,* 360–369.

Snarey, J., Son, L., Kuehne, V. S., Hauser, S., & Vaillant, G. (1987). The role of parenting in men's psychosocial development: A longitudinal study of early adulthood infertility and midlife generativity. *Developmental Psychology, 23,* 593–603.

Snarey, J. R. (1985). Cross-cultural universality of social-moral development: A critical review of Kohlbergian research. *Psychological Bulletin, 97,* 202–232.

Snarey, J. R., Reimer, J., & Kohlberg, L. (1985). Development of social-moral reasoning among kibbutz adolescents: A longitudinal cross-sectional study. *Developmental Psychology, 21,* 3–17.

Soken, N. H., & Pick, A. D. (1992). Intermodal perception of happy and angry expressive behaviors by seven-month-old infants. *Child Development, 63,* 787–795.

Solano, L., Costa, M., Salvati, S., Coda, R., Aiuti, F., Mezzaroma, I., & Bertini, M. (1993). Psychosocial factors and clinical evolution in HIV–1 infection: A longitudinal study. *Journal of Psychosomatic Research, 37,* 39–51.

Soldo, B. J., Wolf, D. A., & Agree, E. M. (1990). Family, households, and care arrangements of frail older women: A structural analysis. *Journals of Gerontology: Social Sciences, 45,* S238–249.

Somers, M. D. (1993). A comparison of voluntarily childfree adults and parents. *Journal of Marriage and the Family, 55,* 643–650.

Sophian, C. (1995). Representation and reasoning in early numerical development: Counting, conservation, and comparisons between sets. *Child Development, 66,* 559–577.

Sorel, J. E., Ragland, D. R., & Syme, S. L. (1991). Blood pressure in Mexican Americans, whites, and blacks. *American Journal of Epidemiology, 134,* 370–378.

Sørensen, A. (1983). Women's employment patterns after marriage. *Journal of Marriage and the Family, 45,* 311–321.

Sorlie, P. D., Backlund, E., & Keller, J. B. (1995). U.S. mortality by economic, demographic, and social characteristics: The National Longitudinal Mortality Study. *American Journal of Public Health, 85,* 949–956.

Sosa, R., Kennell, J. H., Klaus, M. H., Robertson, S., & Urrutia, J. (1980). The effect of a supportive companion on perinatal problems, length of labor and mother-infant interaction. *New England Journal of Medicine, 303,* 597–600.

South, S. J. (1991). Sociodemographic differentials in mate selection preferences. *Journal of Marriage and the Family, 53,* 928–940.

Spanier, G. B., & Furstenberg, F. F., Jr. (1987). Remarriage and reconstituted families. In M. B. Sussman & S. K. Steinmetz (Eds.), *Handbook of marriage and the family* (pp. 419–434). New York: Plenum.

Sparrow, P. R., & Davies, D. R. (1988). Effects of age, tenure, training, and job complexity on technical performance. *Psychology and Aging, 3,* 307–314.

Speece, M. W., & Brent, S. B. (1984). Children's understanding of death: A review of three components of a death concept. *Child Development, 55,* 1671–1686.

Speece, M. W., & Brent, S. B. (1992). The acquisition of a mature understanding of three components of the concept of death. *Death Studies, 16,* 211–229.

Spelke, E. S. (1991). Physical knowledge in infancy: Reflections on Piaget's theory. In S. Carey & R. Gelman (Eds.), *The epigenesis of mind. Essays on biology and cognition* (pp. 133–169). Hillsdale, NJ: Erlbaum.

Spelke, E. S., & Owsley, C. J. (1979). Intermodal exploration and knowledge in infancy. *Infant Behavior and Development, 2,* 13–27.

Spence, J. T., & Helmreich, R. L. (1978). *Masculinity and femininity.* Austin: University of Texas Press.

Spencer, M. B., & Dornbusch, S. M. (1990). Challenges in studying minority youth. In S. S. Feldman & G. R. Elliott (Eds.), *At the threshold: The developing adolescent* (pp. 123–146). Cambridge, MA: Harvard University Press.

Spenner, K. I. (1988). Occupations, work settings and the course of adult development: Tracing the implications of select historical changes. In P. B. Baltes, D. L. Featherman, & R. M. Lerner (Eds.), *Life-span development and behavior* (Vol. 9) (pp. 244–288). Hillsdale, NJ: Erlbaum.

Spiegel, D., Bloom, J. R., Kraemer, H. C., & Gottheil, E. (1989). Effect of psychosocial treatment on survival of patients with metastatic breast cancer. *Lancet* (October 14), 888–901.

Spieker, S. J., & Booth, C. L. (1988). Maternal antecedents of attachment quality. In J. Belsky & T. Nezworski (Eds.), *Clinical implications of attachment* (pp. 95–135). Hillsdale, NJ: Erlbaum.

Spiers, P. S., & Guntheroth, W. G. (1994). Recommendations to avoid the prone sleeping position and recent statistics for Sudden Infant Death Syndrome in the United States. *Archives of Pediatric and Adolescent Medicine, 148,* 141–146.

Spitze, G. (1988). Women's employment and family relations: A review. *Journal of Marriage and the Family, 50,* 595–618.

Spitze, G., & Logan, J. (1990). More evidence on women (and men) in the middle. *Research on Aging, 12,* 182–198.

Sroufe, L. A. (1988). The role of infant-caregiver attachment in development. In J. Belsky & T. Nezworski (Eds.), *Clinical implications of attachment* (pp. 18–40). Hillsdale, NJ: Erlbaum.

Sroufe, L. A. (1989). Pathways to adaptation and maladaptation: Psychopathology as developmental deviation. In D. Cicchetti (Ed.), *The emergence of a discipline: Rochester symposium on developmental psychopathology* (pp. 13–40). Hillsdale, NJ: Erlbaum.

Sroufe, L. A. (1990). A developmental perspective on day care. In N. Fox & G. G. Fein (Eds.), *Infant day care: The current debate* (pp. 51–60). Norwood, NJ: Ablex.

Sroufe, L. A., Carlson, E., & Schulman, S. (1993). Individuals in relationships: Development from infancy through adolescence. In D. C. Funder, R. D. Parke, C. Tomlinson-Keasey, & K. Widaman (Eds.), *Studying lives through time: Personality and development* (pp. 315–342). Washington, DC: American Psychological Association.

Sroufe, L. A., Egeland, B., & Kreutzer, T. (1990). The fate of early experience following developmental change: Longitudinal approaches to individual adaptation in childhood. *Child Development, 61,* 1363—1373.

Stack, S. (1992a). The effect of divorce on suicide in Japan: A time series analysis, 1950–1980. *Journal of Marriage and the Family, 54,* 327–334.

Stack, S. (1992b). The effect of divorce on suicide in Finland: A time series analysis. *Journal of Marriage and the Family, 54,* 636–642.

Stack, S., & Wasserman, I. (1993). Marital status, alcohol consumption, and suicide: An analysis of national data. *Journal of Marriage and the Family, 55,* 1018–1024.

Stadel, B. V., & Weiss, N. S. (1975). Characteristics of menopausal women: A survey of King and Pierce Counties in Washington, 1973–74. *American Journal of Epidemiology, 102,* 209–216.

Stambrook, M., & Parker, K. C. H. (1987). The development of the concept of death in childhood: A review of the literature. *Merrill-Palmer Quarterly, 33,* 133–158.

Stampfer, M. J., Colditz, G. A., Willett, W. C., Manson, J. E. Rosner, B., Speizer, F. E., & Hennekens, C. H. Postmenopausal estrogen therapy and cardiovascular disease: Ten-year follow-up from the Nurses' Health Study. *New England Journal of Medicine, 325,* 756–762.

Stampfer, M. J., Hennekins, C. H., Manson, J. E., Colditz, G. A., Rosner, B., & Willett, W. C. (1993). Vitamin E consumption and the risk of coronary disease in women. *New England Journal of Medicine, 328,* 1444–1449.

Stanford, E. P., Happersett, C. J., Morton, D. J., Molgaard, C. A., & Peddecord, K. M. (1991). Early retirement and functional impairment from a multiethnic perspective. *Research on Aging, 13,* 5–38.

Stanford, P., & Du Bois, B. C. (1992). Gender and ethnicity patterns. In J. E. Birren, R. B. Sloane, & G. D. Cohen (Eds.), *Handbook of mental health and aging* (2nd ed.) (pp. 99–119). San Diego, CA: Academic Press.

Stanton, A. L., & Danoff-Burg, S. (1995). Selected issues in women's reproductive health: Psychological perspectives. In A. L. Stanton & S. J. Gallant (Eds.), *The psychology of women's health* (pp. 216–305). Washington, DC: American Psychological Association.

Starfield, B. (1991). Childhood morbidity: Comparisons, clusters, and trends. *Pediatrics, 88,* 519–526.

Stattin, H., & Klackenberg-Larsson, I. (1993). Early language and intelligence development and their relationship to future criminal behavior. *Journal of Abnormal Psychology, 102,* 369–378.

Steele, H., Holder, J., & Fonagy, P. (1995). *Quality of attachment to mother at one year predicts belief-desire reasoning at five years.* Paper presented at the biennial meetings of the Society for Research in Child Development, Indianapolis, March.

Stein, Z., Susser, M., Saenger, G., & Morolla, F. (1975). *Famine and human development: The Dutch hunger winter of 1944–1945.* New York: Oxford University Press.

Steinbach, U. (1992). Social networks, institutionalization, and mortality among elderly people in the United States. *Journals of Gerontology: Social Sciences, 47,* S183–190.

Steinberg, L. (1988). Reciprocal relation between parent-child distance and pubertal maturation. *Developmental Psychology, 24,* 122–128.

Steinberg, L. (1990). Autonomy, conflict and harmony in the parent-adolescent relationship. In S. S. Feldman & G. R. Elliott (Eds.), *At the threshold: The developing adolescent* (pp. 255–276). Cambridge, MA: Harvard University Press.

Steinberg, L., Darling, N. E., Fletcher, A. C., Brown, B. B., & Dornbusch, S. M. (1995). Authoritative parenting and adolescent adjustment: An ecological journey. In P. Moen, G. H. Elder, Jr., & K. Lüscher (Eds.), *Examining lives in context: Perspectives on the ecology of human development* (pp. 423–466). Washington, DC: American Psychological Association.

Steinberg, L., & Dornbusch, S. M. (1991). Negative correlates of part-time employment during adolescence: Replication and elaboration. *Developmental Psychology, 27,* 304–313.

Steinberg, L., Elmen, J. D., & Mounts, N. S. (1989). Authoritative parenting, psychosocial maturity, and academic success among adolescents. *Child Development, 60,* 1424–1436.

Steinberg, L., Fegley, S., & Dornbusch, S. M. (1993). Negative impact of part-time work on adolescent adjustment: Evidence from a longitudinal study. *Developmental Psychology, 29,* 171–180.

Steinberg, L., Fletcher, A., & Darling, N. (1994). Parental monitoring and peer influences on adolescent substance use. *Pediatrics, 93,* 1060–1064.

Steinberg, L., Lamborn, S. D., Darling, N., Mounts, N. S., & Dornbusch, S. M. (1994). Over-time changes in adjustment and competence among adolescents from authoritative, authoritarian, indulgent, and neglectful families. *Child Development, 65,* 754–770.

Steinberg, L., Lamborn, S. D., Dornbusch, S. M., & Darling, N. (1992). Impact of parenting practices on adolescent achievement: Authoritative parenting, school involvement, and encouragement to succeed. *Child Development, 63,* 1266–1281.

Steinberg, L., & Levine, A. (1990). *You and your adolescent: A parent's guide for ages 10 to 20.* New York: Harper & Row.

Steinberg, L., Mounts, N. S., Lamborn, S. D., & Dornbusch, S. D. (1991). Authoritative parenting and adolescent adjustment across varied ecological niches. *Journal of Research on Adolescence, 1,* 19–36.

Stenchever, M. A. (1978). Labor and delivery. In D. W. Smith, E. L. Bierman, & N. M. Robinson (Eds.), *The biologic ages of man* (2nd ed.) (pp. 78–86). Philadelphia: Saunders.

Sternberg, R. J. (1987). Liking versus loving: A comparative evaluation of theories. *Psychological Bulletin, 102,* 331–345.

Sternberg, R. J. (1990a). Wisdom and its relations to intelligence and creativity. In R. J. Sternberg (Ed.), *Wisdom: Its nature, origins, and development* (pp. 142–159). Cambridge, England: Cambridge University Press.

Sternberg, R. J. (Ed.). (1990b). *Wisdom: Its nature, origins, and development.* Cambridge, England: Cambridge University Press.

Sternberg, R. J., & Wagner, R. K. (1993). The g-ocentric view of intelligence and job performance is wrong. *Current Directions in Psychological Science, 2,* 1–5.

Stevens, D. P., & Truss, C. V. (1985). Stability and change in adult personality over 12 and 20 years. *Developmental Psychology, 21,* 568–584.

Stevenson, H. (1994). Moving away from stereotypes and preconceptions: Students and their education in East Asia and the United States. In P. M. Greenfield & R. R. Cocking (Eds.), *Cross-cultural roots of minority child development* (pp. 315–322). Hillsdale, NJ: Erlbaum.

Stevenson, H. W., & Chen, C. (1989). Schooling and achievement: A study of Peruvian children. *International Journal of Educational Research, 13,* 883–894.

Stevenson, H. W., Chen, C., Lee, S., & Fuligni, A. J. (1991). Schooling, culture, and cognitive development. In L. Okagaki & R. J. Sternberg (Eds.), *Directors of development* (pp. 243–268). Hillsdale, NJ: Erlbaum.

Stevenson, H. W., & Lee, S. (1990). Contexts of achievement: A study of American, Chinese, and Japanese children. *Monographs of the Society for Research in Child Development, 55* (1–2, Serial No. 221).

Stevenson, H. W., Lee, S., Chen, C., Lummis, M., Stigler, J., Fan, L., & Ge, F. (1990). Mathematics achievement of children in China and the United States. *Child Development, 61,* 1053–1066.

Stevens-Ratchford, R. G. (1993). The effect of life review reminiscence activities on depression and self esteem in older adults. *American Journal of Occupational Therapy, 47,* 413–420.

Steward, M. S. (1993). Understanding children's memories of medical procedures: "He didn't touch me and it didn't hurt!" In C. A. Nelson (Ed.), *The Minnesota Symposia on Child Psychology* (Vol. 26) (pp. 171–225). Hillsdale, NJ: Erlbaum.

Stewart, J. F., Popkin, B. M., Guilkey, D. K., Akin, J. S., Adair, L., & Flieger, W. (1991). Influences on the extent of breast-feeding: A prospective study in the Philippines. *Demography, 28,* 181–199.

Stewart, R. B., Beilfuss, M. L., & Verbrugge, K. M. (1995). *That was then, this is now: An empirical typology of adult sibling relationships.* Paper presented at the biennial meetings of the Society for Research in Child Development, Indianapolis, March.

Stigler, J. W., Lee, S., & Stevenson, H. W. (1987). Mathematics classrooms in Japan, Taiwan, and the United States. *Child Development, 58,* 1272–1285.

Stigler, J. W., & Stevenson, H. W. (1991). How Asian teachers polish each lesson to perfection. *American Educator* (Spring), 12–20, 43–47.

Stinner, W. F., Byun, Y., & Paita, L. (1990). Disability and living arrangements among elderly American men. *Research on Aging, 12,* 339–363.

Stipek, D. (1992). The child at school. In M. H. Bornstein & M. E. Lamb (Eds.), *Developmental psychology: An advanced textbook* (3rd ed.) (pp. 579–625). Hillsdale, NJ: Erlbaum.

Stipek, D., & Gralinski, H. (1991). Gender differences in children's achievement-related beliefs and emotional responses to success and failure in math. *Journal of Educational Psychology, 83,* 361–371.

Stocker, C. M. (1995). Differences in mothers' and fathers' relationships with siblings: Links with children's behavior problems. *Development and Psychopathology, 7,* 499–513.

Stoller, E. P., Forster, L. E., & Duniho, T. S. (1992). Systems of parent care within sibling networks. *Research on Aging, 14,* 28–49.

Stones, M. J., & Kozma, A. (1996). Activity, exercise, and behavior. In J. E. Birren & K. W. Schaie (Eds.), *Handbook of the psychology of aging* (4th ed.) (pp. 338–352). San Diego, CA: Academic Press.

Story, M., Rosenwinkel, K., Himes, J. H., Resnick, M., Harris, L. J., & Blum, R. W. (1991). Demographic and risk factors associated with chronic dieting in adolescents. *American Journal of Diseases of Childhood, 145,* 994–998.

Stoutjesdyk, D., & Jevne, R. (1993). Eating disorders among high performance athletes. *Journal of Youth and Adolescence, 22,* 271–282.

Strassberg, Z., Dodge, K. A., Pettit, G. S., & Bates, J. E. (1994). Spanking in the home and children's subsequent aggression toward kindergarten peers. *Development and Psychopathology, 6,* 445–461.

Straus, M. A. (1991a). Discipline and deviance: Physical punishment of children and violence and other crime in adulthood. *Social Problems, 38,* 133–152.

Straus, M. (1991b). New theory and old canards about family violence research. *Social Problems, 38,* 180–194.

Straus, M. A. (1995). Corporal punishment of children and adult depression and suicidal ideation. In J. McCord (Ed.), *Coercion and punishment in long-term perspectives* (pp. 59–77). Cambridge, England: Cambridge University Press.

Straus, M. A., & Donnelly, D. A. (1993). Corporal punishment of adolescents by American parents. *Youth and Society, 24,* 419–442.

Strawbridge, W. J., Camacho, T. C., Cohen, R. D., & Kaplan, G. A. (1993). Gender differences in factors associated with change in physical functioning in old age: A 6-year longitudinal study. *The Gerontologist, 33,* 603–609.

Strayer, F. F. (1980). Social ecology of the preschool peer group. In A. Collins (Ed.), *Minnesota symposia on child psychology* (Vol. 13) (pp. 165–196). Hillsdale, NJ: Erlbaum.

Streissguth, A. P., Aase, J. M., Clarren, S. K., Randels, S. P., LaDue, R. A., & Smith, D. F. (1991). Fetal alcohol syndrome in adolescents and adults. *Journal of the American Medical Association, 265,* 1961–1967.

Streissguth, A. P., Barr, H. M., & Sampson, P. D. (1990). Moderate prenatal alcohol exposure: Effects on child IQ and learning problems at age 7½ years. *Alcoholism. Clinical and Experimental Research, 14,* 662–669.

Streissguth, A. P., Barr, H. M., Sampson, P. D., Darby, B. L., & Martin, D. C. (1989). IQ at age 4 in relation to maternal alcohol use and smoking during pregnancy. *Developmental Psychology, 25,* 3–11.

Streissguth, A. P., Bookstein, F. L., Sampson, P. D., & Barr, H. M. (1995). Attention: Prenatal alcohol and continuities of vigilance and attentional problems from 4 through 14 years. *Development and Psychopathology, 7,* 419–446.

Streissguth, A. P., Landesman-Dwyer, S., Martin, J. C., & Smith, D. W. (1980). Teratogenic effects of alcohol in humans and laboratory animals. *Science, 209,* 353–361.

Streissguth, A. P., Martin, D. C., Barr, H. M., Sandman, B. M., Kirchner, G. L., & Darby, B. L. (1984). Intrauterine alcohol and nicotine exposure: Attention and reaction time in 4-year-old children. *Developmental Psychology, 20,* 533–541.

Streissguth, A. P., Martin, D. C., Martin, J. C., & Barr, H. M. (1981). The Seattle longitudinal prospective study on alcohol and pregnancy. *Neurobehavioral Toxicology and Teratology, 3,* 223–233.

Streufert, S., Pogash, R., Piasecki, M., & Post, G. M. (1990). Age and management team performance. *Psychology and Aging, 5,* 551–559.

Striegel-Moore, R. H., Silberstein, L. R., & Rodin, J. (1986). Toward an understanding of risk factors for bulimia. *American Psychologist, 41,* 246–263.

Stringfield, S., & Teddlie, C. (1991). Observers as predictors of schools' multiyear outlier status on achievement tests. *The Elementary School Journal, 91,* 357–376.

Stroebe, M. S., & Stroebe, W. (1993). The mortality of bereavement: A review. In M. S. Stroebe, W. Stroebe, & R. O. Hansson (Eds.), *Handbook of bereavement: Theory, research, and intervention* (pp. 175–195). Cambridge, England: Cambridge University Press.

Stroebe, W., & Stroebe, M. S. (1986). Beyond marriage: The impact of partner loss on health. In R. Gilmour & S. Duck (Eds.), *The emerging field of personal relations* (pp. 203–224). Hillsdale, NJ: Erlbaum.

Stroebe, W., & Stroebe, M. S. (1993). Determinants of adjustment to bereavement in younger widows and widowers. In M. S. Stroebe, W. Stroebe, & R. O. Hansson (Eds.), *Handbook of bereavement. Theory, research, and intervention* (pp. 208–226). Cambridge, England: Cambridge University Press.

Stull, D. E., & Hatch, L. R. (1984). Unravelling the effects of multiple life changes. *Research on Aging, 6,* 560–571.

Stunkard, A. J., Harris, J. R., Pedersen, N. L., & McClearn, G. E. (1990). The body-mass index of twins who have been reared apart. *New England Journal of Medicine, 322,* 1483–1487.

Stunkard, A. J., Sorensen, T. I. A., Hanis, C., Teasdale, T. W., Chakraborty, R., Schull, W. J., & Schulsinger, F. (1986). An adoption study of human obesity. *New England Journal of Medicine, 314,* 193–198.

Sue, S., & Okazaki, S. (1990). Asian-American educational achievements: A phenomenon in search of an explanation. *American Psychologist, 45,* 913–920.

Sugar, J. A., & McDowd, J. M. (1992). Memory, learning, and attention. In J. E. Birren, R. B. Sloane, & G. D. Cohen (Eds.), *Handbook of mental health and aging* (2nd ed.) (pp. 307–339). San Diego, CA: Academic Press.

Sugisawa, H., Liang, J., & Liu, X. (1994). Social networks, social support, and mortality among older people in Japan. *Journals of Gerontology: Social Sciences, 49,* S3–13.

Sullivan, K., Zaitchik, D., & Tager-Flusberg, H. (1994). Preschoolers can attribute second-order beliefs. *Developmental Psychology, 30,* 395–402.

Super, D. E. (1971). A theory of vocational development. In H. J. Peters & J. C. Hansen (Eds.), *Vocational guidance and career development* (pp. 111–122). New York: Macmillan.

Super, D. E. (1986). Life career roles: Self-realization in work and leisure. In D. T. H. &. Associates (Eds.), *Career development in organizations* (pp. 95–119). San Francisco: Jossey-Bass.

Susman, E. J., Inoff-Germain, G., Nottelmann, E. D., Loriaux, D. L., Cutler, G. B., Jr., & Chrousos, G. P. (1987). Hormones, emotional dispositions, and aggressive attributes in young adolescents. *Child Development, 58,* 1114–1134.

Swedo, S. E., Rettew, D. C., Kuppenheimer, M., Lum, D., Dolan, S., & Goldberger, E. (1991). Can adolescent suicide attempters be distinguished from at-risk adolescents? *Pediatrics, 88,* 620–629.

Swensen, C. H., Eskew, R. W., & Kohlhepp, K. A. (1981). Stage of family life cycle, ego development, and the marriage relationship. *Journal of Marriage and the Family, 43,* 841–853.

Syme, S. L. (1990). Control and health: An epidemiological perspective. In J. Rodin, C. Schooler, & K. W. Schaie (Eds.), *Self directedness: Cause and effects throughout the life course* (pp. 213–229). Hillsdale, NJ: Erlbaum.

Taffel, S. M., Keppel, K. G., & Jones, G. K. (1993). Medical advice on maternal weight gain and actual weight gain. Results from the 1988 National Maternal and Infant Health Survey. *Annals of the New York Academy of Sciences, 678,* 293–305.

Tait, M., Padgett, M. Y., & Baldwin, T. T. (1989). Job and life satisfaction: A reevaluation of the strength of the relationship and gender effects as a function of the date of the study. *Journal of Applied Psychology, 74,* 502–507.

Takei, Y., & Dubas, J. S. (1993). Academic achievement among early adolescents: Social and cultural diversity. In R. M. Lerner (Ed.), *Early adolescence: Perspectives on research, policy, and intervention* (pp. 175–190). Hillsdale, NJ: Erlbaum.

Talbott, M. M. (1990). The negative side of the relationship between older widows and their adult children: The mother's perspective. *The Gerontologist, 30,* 595–603.

Tamir, L. M. (1982). *Men in their forties: The transition to middle age.* New York: Springer.

Tamir, L. M. (1989). Modern myths about men at midlife: An assessment. In S. Hunter & M. Sundel (Eds.), *Midlife myths: Issues, findings, and practice implications* (pp. 157–179). Newbury Park, CA: Sage.

Tanner, J. M. (1962). *Growth at adolescence* (2nd ed.). Oxford: Blackwell.

Tanner, J. M. (1978). *Fetus into man: Physical growth from conception to maturity.* Cambridge, MA: Harvard University Press.

Tanner, J. M., Hughes, P. C. R., & Whitehouse, R. H. (1981). Radiographically determined widths of bone, muscle and fat in the upper arm and calf from 3–18 years. *Annals of Human Biology, 8,* 495–517.

Taylor, J. A., & Danderson, M. (1995). A reexamination of the risk factors for the sudden infant death syndrome. *Journal of Pediatrics, 126,* 887–891.

Taylor, J. L., Yesavage, J. A., Morrow, D. G., Dolhert, N., Brooks, J. O. I., & Poon, L. W. (1994). The effects of information load and speech rate on younger and older aircraft pilots' ability to execute simulated air-traffic controller instructions. *Journals of Gerontology: Psychological Sciences, 49,* P191–200.

Taylor, M., Cartwright, B. S., & Carlson, S. M. (1993). A developmental investigation of children's imaginary companions. *Developmental Psychology, 29,* 276–285.

Taylor, R. D., Casten, R., & Flickinger, S. M. (1993). Influence of kinship social support on the parenting experiences and psychosocial adjustment of African-American adolescents. *Developmental Psychology, 29,* 382–388.

Taylor, R. D., & Roberts, D. (1995). Kinship support and maternal and adolescent well-being in economically disadvantaged African-American families. *Child Development, 66,* 1585–1597.

Taylor, R. J. (1986). Receipt of support from family among black Americans: Demographic and familial differences. *Journal of Marriage and the Family, 48,* 67–77.

Taylor, R. J., Chatters, L. M., Tucker, M. B., & Lewis, E. (1990). Developments in research on black families: A decade review. *Journal of Marriage and the Family, 52,* 993–1014.

Tellegen, A., Lykken, D. T., Bouchard, T. J., Jr., Wilcox, K. J., Segal, N. L., & Rich, S. (1988). Personality similarity in twins reared apart and together. *Journal of Personality and Social Psychology, 54,* 1031–1039.

Temoshok, L. (1987). Personality, coping style, emotion and cancer: Towards an integrative model. *Cancer Surveys, 6,* 545–567.

Terman, L. (1916). *The measurement of intelligence.* Boston: Houghton Mifflin.

Terman, L., & Merrill, M. A. (1937). *Measuring intelligence: A guide to the administration of the new revised Stanford-Binet tests.* Boston: Houghton Mifflin.

Tesman, J. R., & Hills, A. (1994). Developmental effects of lead exposure in children. *Social Policy Report, Society for Research in Child Development, 8*(3), 1–16.

Teti, D. M., Gelfand, D. M., Messinger, D. S., & Isabella, R. (1995). Maternal depression and the quality of early attachment: An examination of infants, preschoolers, and their mothers. *Developmental Psychology, 31,* 364–376.

Tew, M. (1985). Place of birth and perinatal mortality. *Journal of the Royal College of General Practitioners, 35,* 390–394.

Thal, D., & Bates, E. (1990). Continuity and variation in early language development. In J. Colombo & J. Fagen (Eds.), *Individual differences in infancy: Reliability, stability, prediction* (pp. 359–385). Hillsdale, NJ: Erlbaum.

Tharp, R. G., & Gallimore, R. (1988). *Rousing minds to life.* New York: Cambridge University Press.

Thelen, E. (1981). Rhythmical behavior in infancy: An ethological perspective. *Developmental Psychology, 17,* 237–257.

Thelen, E. (1989). The (re)discovery of motor development: Learning new things from an old field. *Developmental Psychology, 25,* 946–949.

Thelen, E. (1995). Motor development: A new synthesis. *American Psychologist, 50,* 79–95.

Thelen, E., & Adolph, K. E. (1992). Arnold L. Gesell: The paradox of nature and nurture. *Developmental Psychology, 28,* 368–380.

Thelen, E., & Ulrich, B. D. (1991). Hidden skills: A dynamic systems analysis of treadmill stepping during the first year. *Monographs of the Society for Research in Child Development, 56*(1, Serial No. 223).

Thomas, A., & Chess, S. (1977). *Temperament and development.* New York: Brunner/Mazel.

Thomas, R. M. (Ed.). (1990a). *The encyclopedia of human development and education: Theory, research, and studies.* Oxford, England: Pergamon Press.

Thomas, R. M. (1990b). Motor development. In R. M. Thomas (Ed.), *The encyclopedia of human development and education: Theory, research, and studies* (pp. 326–330). Oxford, England: Pergamon Press.

Thompson, L., & Walker, A. J. (1984). Mothers and daughters: Aid patterns and attachment. *Journal of Marriage and the Family, 46,* 313–322.

Thompson, S. K. (1975). Gender labels and early sex role development. *Child Development, 46,* 339–347.

Thomson, E., & Colella, U. (1992). Cohabitation and marital stability: Quality or commitment? *Journal of Marriage and the Family, 54,* 259–267.

Thorne, B. (1986). Girls and boys together . . . but mostly apart: Gender arrangements in elementary schools. In W. W. Hartup & Z. Rubin (Eds.), *Relationships and development* (pp. 167–184). Hillsdale, NJ: Erlbaum.

Thornton, A. (1990). The courtship process and adolescent sexuality. *Journal of Family Issues, 11,* 239–273.

Thornton, A., Young-DeMarco, L., & Goldscheider, F. (1993). Leaving the parental nest: The experience of a young white cohort in the 1980s. *Journal of Marriage and the Family, 55,* 216–229.

Thorslund, M., & Lundberg, O. (1994). Health and inequalities among the oldest old. *Journal of Aging and Health, 6,* 51–69.

Thorson, J. A., & Powell, F. C. (1990). Meanings of death and intrinsic religiosity. *Journal of Clinical Psychology, 46,* 379–390.

Thorson, J. A., & Powell, F. C. (1992). A revised death anxiety scale. *Death Studies, 16,* 507–521.

Tice, R. R., & Setlow, R. B. (1985). DNA repair and replication in aging organisms and cells. In C. E. Finch & E. L. Schneider (Eds.), *Handbook of the biology of aging* (2nd ed.) (pp. 173–224). New York: Van Nostrand Reinhold.

Timmer, S. G., Eccles, J., & O'Brien, K. (1985). How children use time. In F. T. Juster & F. P. Stafford (Eds.), *Time, goods, and well being* (pp. 353–369). Ann Arbor: Institute for Social Research, The University of Michigan.

Tobin-Richards, M. H., Boxer, A. M., & Petersen, A. C. (1983). The psychological significance of pubertal change: Sex differences in perceptions of self during early adolescence. In J. Brooks-Gunn & A. C. Petersen (Eds.), *Girls at puberty. Biological and psychosocial perspectives* (pp. 127–154). New York: Plenum.

Todd, R. D., Swarzenski, B., Rossi, P. G., & Visconti, P. (1995). Structural and functional development of the human brain. In D. Cicchetti & D. J. Cohen (Eds.), *Developmental psychopathology: Vol. 1. Theory and methods* (pp. 161–194). New York: Wiley.

Tomlinson-Keasey, C., Eisert, D. C., Kahle, L. R., Hardy-Brown, K., & Keasey, B. (1979). The structure of concrete operational thought. *Child Development, 50,* 1153–1163.

Tracey, T. J., & Rounds, J. (1993). Evaluating Holland's and Gati's vocational-interest models: A structural meta-analysis. *Psychological Bulletin, 113,* 229–246.

Trehub, S. E., & Rabinovitch, M. S. (1972). Auditory-linguistic sensitivity in early infancy. *Developmental Psychology, 6,* 74–77.

Tremblay, R. E., Masse, L. C., Vitaro, F., & Dobkin, P. L. (1995). The impact of friends' deviant behavior on early onset of delinquency: Longitudinal data from 6 to 13 years of age. *Development and Psychopathology, 7,* 649–667.

Troll, L. E. (1985). The contingencies of grandparenting. In V. L. Bengtson & J. F. Robertson (Eds.), *Grandparenthood* (pp. 135–150). Beverly Hills, CA: Sage.

Tronick, E. Z., Morelli, G. A., & Ivey, P. K. (1992). The Efe forager infant and toddler's pattern of social relationships: Multiple and simultaneous. *Developmental Psychology, 28,* 568–577.

Tsitouras, P. D., & Bulat, T. (1995). The aging male reproductive system. *Endocrinology and Metabolism Clinics of North America, 24,* 297–315.

Tsuya, N. O., & Martin, L. G. (1992). Living arrangements of elderly Japanese and attitudes toward inheritance. *Journals of Gerontology: Social Sciences, 47,* S45–54.

Tunstall-Pedoe, H., & Smith, W. C. S. (1990). Cholesterol as a risk factor for coronary heart disease. *British Medical Bulletin, 46,* 1075–1087.

Turiel, E. (1966). An experimental test of the sequentiality of developmental stages in the child's moral judgment. *Journal of Personality and Social Psychology, 3,* 611–618.

Turner, H. A., & Finkelhor, D. (1996). Corporal punishment as a stressor among youth. *Journal of Marriage and the Family, 58,* 155–166.

Twycross, R. G. (1996). Euthanasia: Going Dutch? *Journal of the Royal Society of Medicine, 89,* 61–63.

Udry, J. R., & Campbell, B. C. (1994). Getting started on sexual behavior. In A. S. Rossi (Ed.), *Sexuality across the life course* (pp. 187–208). Chicago: University of Chicago Press.

Uhlenberg, P., Cooney, T., & Boyd, R. (1990). Divorce for women after midlife. *Journals of Gerontology: Social Sciences, 45,* S3–11.

Umberson, D. (1992). Relationships between adult children and their parents: Psychological consequences for both generations. *Journal of Marriage and the Family, 54,* 664–674.

Umberson, D., & Gove, W. R. (1989). Parenthood and psychological well-being. Theory, measurement, and stage in the family life course. *Journal of Family Issues, 10,* 440–462.

Underwood, M. K., Coie, J. D., & Herbsman, C. R. (1992). Display rules for anger and aggression in school-age children. *Child Development, 63,* 366–380.

Underwood, M. K., Kupersmidt, J. B., & Coie, J. D. (1996). Childhood peer sociometric status and aggression as predictors of adolescent childbearing. *Journal of Research on Adolescence, 6,* 201–224.

Ungerer, J. A., & Sigman, M. (1984). The relation of play and sensorimotor behavior to language in the second year. *Child Development, 55,* 1448–1455.

U.S. Bureau of the Census (1984). *Statistical Abstract of the United States: 1985.* Washington, DC: U.S. Government Printing Office.

U.S. Bureau of the Census (1989). *Statistical Abstract of the United States: 1989.* Washington, DC: U.S. Government Printing Office.

U.S. Bureau of the Census (1990). *Statistical abstract of the United States, 1990.* Washington, DC: U.S. Government Printing Office.

U.S. Bureau of the Census (1992). *Statistical Abstract of the United States: 1992.* Washington, DC: U.S. Government Printing Office.

U.S. Bureau of the Census (1994). *Statistical abstract of the United States: 1994.* Washington, DC: U.S. Government Printing Office.

U.S. Bureau of the Census (1995). *Statistical Abstract of the United States: 1995.* Washington, DC: U.S. Government Printing Office.

U.S. Department of Commerce (1995). Income, poverty, and valuation of noncash benefits: 1993. *Current Population Reports*(Series P60–188).

Upchurch, D. M. (1993). Early schooling and childbearing experiences: Implications for post-secondary school attendance. *Journal of Research on Adolescence, 3,* 423–443.

Upperman, P. U., & Church, A. T. (1995). Investigating Holland's typological theory with army occupational specialties. *Journal of Vocational Behavior, 47,* 61–75.

Urban, J., Carlson, E., Egeland, B., & Sroufe, L. A. (1991). Patterns of individual adaptation across childhood. *Development and Psychopathology, 3,* 445–460.

Urberg, K. A., Degirmencioglu, S. M., Tolson, J. M., & Halliday Scher, K. (1995). The structure of adolescent peer networks. *Developmental Psychology, 31,* 540–547.

Vaillant, G. E. (1975). Natural history of male psychological health: III. Empirical dimensions of mental health. *Archives of General Psychiatry, 32,* 420–426.

Vaillant, G. E. (1977). *Adaptation to life: How the best and brightest came of age.* Boston: Little, Brown.

Vaillant, G. E. (1991). The association of ancestral longevity with successful aging. *Journals of Gerontology: Psychological Sciences, 46,* P292–298.

Vaillant, G. E., & Vaillant, C. O. (1990). Natural history of male psychological health: XII. A 45-year study of predictors of successful aging at age 65. *American Journal of Psychiatry, 147,* 31–37.

Valdez-Menchaca, M. C., & Whitehurst, G. J. (1992). Accelerating language development through picture book reading: A systematic extension to Mexican day care. *Developmental Psychology, 28,* 1106–1114.

Van de Perre, P., Simonen, A., Msellati, P., Hitimana, D., Vaira, D., Bazebagira, A., Van Goethem, C., Stevens, A., Karita, E., Sondag-Thull, D., Dabis, F., & Lepage, P. (1991). Postnatal transmission of human immunodeficiency virus type 1 from mother to infant. *New England Journal of Medicine, 325,* 593–598.

van den Boom, D. (1995). Do first-year intervention effects endure? Follow-up during toddlerhood of a sample of Dutch irritable infants. *Child Development, 66,* 1798–1816.

van den Boom, D. C. (1994). The influence of temperament and mothering on attachment and exploration: An experimental manipulation of sensitive responsiveness among lower-class mothers with irritable infants. *Child Development, 65,* 1457–1477.

van IJzendoorn, M. H. (1995). Adult attachment representations, parental responsiveness, and infant attachment: A meta-analysis on the predictive validity of the Adult Attachment Interview. *Psychological Bulletin, 117,* 387–403.

van IJzendoorn, M. H., Goldberg, S., Kroonenberg, P. M., & Frenkel, O. J. (1992). The relative effects of maternal and child problems on the quality of attachment: A meta-analysis of attachment in clinical samples. *Child Development, 63,* 840–858.

van IJzendoorn, M. H., & Kroonenberg, P. M. (1988). Cross-cultural patterns of attachment: A meta-analysis of the Strange Situation. *Child Development, 59,* 147–156.

van Lieshout, C. F. M., & Haselager, G. J. T. (1994). The big five personality factors in Q-sort descriptions of children and adolescents. In C. F. Halverson, Jr., G. A. Kohnstamm, & R. P. Martin (Eds.), *The developing structure of temperament and personality from infancy to adulthood* (pp. 293–318). Hillsdale, NJ: Erlbaum.

Van Velsor, E., & O'Rand, A. M. (1984). Family life cycle, work career patterns, and women's wages at midlife. *Journal of Marriage and the Family, 46,* 365–373.

van Wel, F. (1994). "I count my parents among my best friends": Youths' bonds with parents and friends in the Netherlands. *Journal of Marriage and the Family, 56,* 835–843.

Vasudev, J. (1983). A study of moral reasoning at different life stages in India. Unpublished manuscript, University of Pittsburgh.

Vega, W. A. (1990). Hispanic families in the 1980s: A decade of research. *Journal of Marriage and the Family, 52,* 1015–1024.

Venkatraman, M. M. (1995). A cross-cultural study of the subjective well-being of married elderly persons in the United States and India. *Journals of Gerontology: Social Sciences, 50B,* S35–44.

Verbrugge, L. M. (1984). A health profile of older women with comparisons to older men. *Research on Aging, 6,* 291–322.

Verbrugge, L. M. (1989). Gender, aging, and health. In K. S. Markides (Ed.), *Aging and health* (pp. 23–78). Newbury Park, CA: Sage.

Verbrugge, L. M., Lepkowski, J. M., & Konkol, L. L. (1991). Levels of disability among U.S. adults with arthritis. *Journals of Gerontology: Social Sciences, 46,* S71–83.

Verbrugge, L. M., & Wingard, D. L. (1987). Sex differentials in health and mortality. *Women and Health, 12,* 103–145.

Verhaeghen, P., & Marcoen, A. (1993). Memory aging as a general phenomenon: Episodic recall of older adults is a function of episodic recall of young adults. *Psychology and Aging, 8,* 380–388.

Verhaeghen, P., Marcoen, A., & Goossens, L. (1992). Improving memory performance in the aged through mnemonic training: A meta-analytic study. *Psychology and Aging, 7,* 242–251.

Verhaeghen, P., Marcoen, A., & Goossens, L. (1993). Facts and fiction about memory aging: A quantitative integration of research findings. *Journals of Gerontology: Psychological Sciences, 48,* P157–171.

Vernon, P. A. (Ed.). (1987). *Speed of information-processing and intelligence.* Norwood, NJ: Ablex.

Vernon, P. A. (1993). Intelligence and neural efficiency. In D. K. Detterman (Ed.), *Current topics in human intelligence: Vol. 3. Individual differences and cognition* (pp. 171–187). Norwood, NJ: Ablex.

Vernon, P. A., & Mori, M. (1992). Intelligence, reaction times, and peripheral nerve conduction velocity. *Intelligence, 16,* 273–288.

Veroff, J., Douvan, E., & Kulka, R. A. (1981). *The inner American: A self-portrait from 1957 to 1976.* New York: Basic Books.

Vihko, R., & Apter, D. (1980). The role of androgens in adolescent cycles. *Journal of Steroid Biochemistry, 12,* 369–373.

Vinokur, A. D., & van Ryn, M. (1993). Social support and undermining in close relationships: Their independent effects on the mental health of unemployed persons. *Journal of Personality and Social Psychology, 65,* 350–359.

Vorhees, C. F., & Mollnow, E. (1987). Behavioral teratogenesis: Long-term influences on behavior from early exposure to environmental agents. In J. D. Osofsky (Ed.), *Handbook of infant development* (2nd ed.) (pp. 913–971). New York: Wiley-Interscience.

Voyer, D., Voyer, S., & Bryden, M. P. (1995). Magnitude of sex differences in spatial abilities: A meta-analysis and consideration of critical variables. *Psychological Bulletin, 117,* 250–270.

Vuchinich, S., Bank, L., & Patterson, G. R. (1992). Parenting, peers, and the stability of antisocial behavior in preadolescent boys. *Developmental Psychology, 28,* 510–521.

Vygotsky, L. S. (1962). *Thought and language.* New York: Wiley.

Vygotsky, L. S. (1978). *Mind and society: The development of higher mental processes.* Cambridge, MA: Harvard University Press. (Original works published 1930, 1933, and 1935.)

Wachs, T. D., & Sigman, M. (1995). *Chronic mild undernutrition and children's development in Egypt and Kenya.* Paper presented at the biennial meetings of the Society for Research in Child Development, Indianapolis, March.

Wahlström, J. (1990). Gene map of mental retardation. *Journal of Mental Deficiency Research, 34,* 11–27.

Waite, L. J. (1995). *Does marriage matter?* Presidential address to the Population Association of America, Chicago.

Walaskay, M., Whitbourne, S. K., & Nehrke, M. F. (1983–1984). Construction and validation of an ego integrity status interview. *International Journal of Aging and Human Development, 18,* 61–72.

Wald, N. J., Cuckle, H. S., Densem, J. W., Nanchahal, K., Royston, P., Chard, T., Haddow, J. E., Knight, G. J., Palomaki, G. E., & Canick, J. A. (1988). Maternal serum screening for Down's syndrome in early pregnancy. *British Medical Journal, 297,* 883–887.

Walden, T. A. (1991). Infant social referencing. In J. Garber & K. A. Dodge (Eds.), *The development of emotion regulation and dysregulation* (pp. 69–88). Cambridge, England: Cambridge University Press.

Waldrop, M. F., & Halverson, C. F. (1975). Intensive and extensive peer behavior: Longitudinal and cross-sectional analysis. *Child Development, 46,* 19–26.

Walker, A. (1990). Poverty and inequality in old age. In J. Bond & P. Coleman (Eds.), *Aging in society* (pp. 229–249). London: Sage.

Walker, A. J., & Thompson, L. (1983). Intimacy and intergenerational aid and contact among mothers and daughters. *Journal of Marriage and the Family, 45,* 841–849.

Walker, H., Messinger, D., Fogel, A., & Karns, J. (1992). Social and communicative development in infancy. In V. B. V. Hasselt & M. Hersen (Eds.), *Handbook of social development: A lifespan perspective* (pp. 157–181). New York: Plenum.

Walker, L. J. (1980). Cognitive and perspective-taking prerequisites for moral development. *Child Development, 51,* 131–139.

Walker, L. J. (1989). A longitudinal study of moral reasoning. *Child Development, 60,* 157–160.

Walker, L. J., de Vries, B., & Trevethan, S. D. (1987). Moral stages and moral orientations in real-life and hypothetical dilemmas. *Child Development, 58,* 842–858.

Walker-Andrews, A. S., & Lennon, E. (1991). Infants' discrimination of vocal expressions: Contributions of auditory and visual information. *Infant Behavior and Development, 14,* 131–142.

Wallace, J. B. (1992). Reconsidering the life review: The social construction of talk about the past. *The Gerontologist, 32,* 120–125.

Wallerstein, J. S. (1986). Women after divorce: Preliminary report from a ten-year-follow-up. *American Journal of Orthopsychiatry, 56,* 65–77.

Walls, C. T., & Zarit, S. H. (1991). Informal support from black churches and the well-being of elderly blacks. *The Gerontologist, 31,* 490–495.

Walton, G. E., Bower, N. J. A., & Bower, T. G. R. (1992). Recognition of familiar faces by newborns. *Infant Behavior and Development, 15,* 265–269.

Ward, S. L., & Overton, W. F. (1990). Semantic familiarity, relevance, and the development of deductive reasoning. *Developmental Psychology, 26,* 488–493.

Wark, G. R., & Krebs, D. L. (1996). Gender and dilemma differences in real-life moral judgment. *Developmental Psychology, 32,* 220–230.

Warr, P., Jackson, P., & Banks, M. (1988). Unemployment and mental health: Some British studies. *Journal of Social Issues, 44,* 47–68.

Wartner, U. B., Grossman, K., Fremmer-Bombik, E., & Suess, G. (1994). Attachment patterns at age six in south Germany: Predictability from infancy and implications for preschool behavior. *Child Development, 65,* 1014–1027.

Waterman, A. S. (1985). Identity in the context of adolescent psychology. *New Directions for Child Development, 30,* 5–24.

Waters, E., Treboux, D., Crowell, J., Merrick, S., & Albersheim, L. (1995). *From the Strange Situation to the Adult Attachment Interview: A 20-year longitudinal study of attachment security in infancy and early adulthood.* Paper presented at the biennial meetings of the Society for Research in Child Development, Indianapolis, March.

Watkins, S. C., Menken, J. A., & Bongaarts, J. (1987). Demographic foundations of family change. *American Sociological Review, 52,* 346–358.

Waxman, S. R., & Kosowski, T. D. (1990). Nouns mark category relations: Toddlers' and preschoolers' word-learning biases. *Child Development, 61,* 1461–1473.

Weaver, D. A. (1994). The work and retirement decisions of older women: A literature review. *Social Security Bulletin, 57,* 3–24.

Webster, M. L., Thompson, J. M., Mitchell, E. A., & Werry, J. S. (1994). Postnatal depression in a community cohort. *Australian & New Zealand Journal of Psychiatry, 28,* 42–49.

Webster, P. S., & Herzog, A. R. (1995). Effects of parental divorce and memories of family problems on relationships between adult children and their parents. *Journals of Gerontology: Social Sciences, 50B,* S24–34.

Webster-Stratton, C. (1988). Mothers' and fathers' perceptions of child deviance: Roles of parent and child adjustment and child deviance. *Journal of Consulting and Clinical Psychology, 56,* 909–915.

Wechsler, D. (1939). *The measurement of adult intelligence.* Baltimore, MD: Williams & Wilkins.

Wechsler, D. (1974). *Manual for the Wechsler Intelligence Scale for Children—Revised.* New York: Psychological Corp.

Wechsler, H., Davenport, A., Dowdall, G., Moeykens, B., & Castillo, S. (1994). Health and behavioral consequences of binge drinking in college. *Journal of the American Medical Association, 272,* 1672–1677.

Weg, R. B. (1987). Sexuality in the menopause. In D. R. Mishell, Jr. (Ed.), *Menopause: Physiology and pharmacology* (pp. 127–138). Chicago: Year Book Medical Publishers.

Weinberg, R. A. (1989). Intelligence and IQ: Landmark issues and great debates. *American Psychologist, 44,* 98–104.

Weinberg, R. A., Scarr, S., & Waldman, I. D. (1992). The Minnesota transracial adoption study: A follow-up of IQ test performance. *Intelligence, 16,* 117–135.

Weisburger, J. H., & Wynder, E. L. (1991). Dietary fat intake and cancer. *Hematology/Oncology Clinics of North America, 5,* 7–23.

Weisner, T. S. (1984). Ecocultural niches of middle childhood: A cross-cultural perspective. In W. A. Collins (Ed.), *Development during middle childhood: The years from six to twelve* (pp. 335–369). Washington, DC: National Academy Press.

Weiss, R. S. (1986). Continuities and transformations in social relationships from childhood to adulthood. In W. W. Hartup & Z. Rubin (Eds.), *On relationships and development* (pp. 95–110). Hillsdale, NJ: Erlbaum.

Weiss, R. S. (1990). *Staying the course.* New York: Free Press.

Weisse, C. S. (1992). Depression and immunocompetence: A review of the literature. *Psychological Bulletin, 111,* 475–489.

Welch, D. C., & West, R. L. (1995). Self-efficacy and mastery: Its application to issues of environmental control, cognition, and aging. *Developmental Review, 15,* 150–171.

Welford, A. T. (1993). The gerontological balance sheet. In J. Cerella, J. Rybash, W. Hoyer, & M. L. Commons (Eds.), *Adult information processing: Limits on loss* (pp. 3–10). San Diego, CA: Academic Press.

Wellman, H. M. (1982). The foundations of knowledge: Concept development in the young child. In S. G. Moore & C. C. Cooper (Eds.), *The young child: Reviews of research* (Vol. 3) (pp. 115–134). Washington, DC: National Association for the Education of Young Children.

Wen, S. W., Goldenberg, R. L., Cutter, G. R., Hoffman, H. J., Cliver, S. P., Davis, R. O., & DuBard, M. D. (1990). Smoking, maternal age, fetal growth, and gestational age at delivery. *American Journal of Obstetrics and Gynecology, 162,* 53–58.

Wentzel, K. R., & Asher, S. R. (1995). The academic lives of neglected, rejected, popular, and controversial children. *Child Development, 66,* 754–763.

Werker, J. F., & Desjardins, R. N. (1995). Listening to speech in the 1st year of life: Experiential influences on phoneme perception. *Current Directions in Psychological Science, 4,* 76–81.

Werker, J. F., Pegg, J. E., & McLeod, P. J. (1994). A cross-language investigation of infant preference for infant-directed communication. *Infant Behavior and Development, 17,* 323–333.

Werker, J. F., & Tees, R. C. (1984). Cross-language speech perception: Evidence for perceptual reorganization during the first year of life. *Infant Behavior and Development, 7,* 49–63.

Werner, E. E. (1986). A longitudinal study of perinatal risk. In D. C. Farran & J. D. McKinney (Eds.), *Risk in intellectual and psychosocial development* (pp. 3–28). Orlando, FL: Academic Press.

Werner, E. E. (1995). Resilience in development. *Current Directions in Psychological Science, 4,* 81–85.

Werner, E. E., & Smith, R. S. (1992). *Overcoming the odds: High risk children from birth to adulthood.* Ithaca, NY: Cornell University Press.

West, R. L., & Crook, T. H. (1990). Age differences in everyday memory: Laboratory analogues of telephone number recall. *Psychology and Aging, 5,* 520–529.

Whitam, F. L., Diamond, M., & Martin, J. (1993). Homosexual orientation in twins: A report on 61 pairs and three triplet sets. *Archives of Sexual Behavior, 22,* 187–206.

Whitbeck, L. B., Simons, R. L., & Conger, R. D. (1991). The effects of early family relationships on contemporary relationships and assistance patterns between adult children and their parents. *Journals of Gerontology: Social Sciences, 46,* S330–337.

White, A. T., & Spector, P. E. (1987). An investigation of age-related factors in the age-job-satisfaction relationship. *Psychology and Aging, 2,* 261–265.

White, N., & Cunningham, W. R. (1988). Is terminal drop pervasive or specific? *Journals of Gerontology: Psychological Sciences, 43,* P141–144.

Whitehurst, G. J. (1995). *Levels of reading readiness and predictors of reading success among children from low-income families.* Paper presented at the biennial meetings of the Society for Research in Child Development, Indianapolis, March.

Whitehurst, G. J., Arnold, D. S., Epstein, J. N., Angell, A. L., Smith, M., & Fischel, J. E. (1994). A picture book reading intervention in day care and home for children from low-income families. *Developmental Psychology, 30,* 679–689.

Whitehurst, G. J., Falco, F. L., Lonigan, C. J., Fischel, J. E., DeBaryshe, B. D., Valdez-Menchaca, M. C., & Caulfield, M. (1988). Accelerating language development through picture book reading. *Developmental Psychology, 24,* 552–559.

Whitehurst, G. J., Fischel, J. E., Crone, D. A., & Nania, O. (1995). *First year outcomes of a clinical trial of an emergent literacy intervention in Head Start homes and classrooms.* Paper presented at the biennial meetings of the Society for Research in Child Development, Indianapolis, March.

Whiting, B. B., & Edwards, C. P. (1988). *Children of different worlds: The formation of social behavior.* Cambridge, MA: Harvard University Press.

Whitney, M. P., & Thoman, E. B. (1994). Sleep in premature and full-term infants from 24-hour home recordings. *Infant Behavior and Development, 17,* 223–234.

Wich, B. K., & Carnes, M. (1995). Menopause and the aging female reproductive system. *Endocrinology and Metabolism Clinics of North America, 24,* 273–295.

Wiesenfeld, A. R., Malatesta, C. Z., & DeLoach, L. L. (1981). Differential parental response to familiar and unfamiliar infant distress signals. *Infant Behavior and Development, 4,* 281–296.

Wigfield, A., Eccles, J. S., MacIver, D., Reuman, D. A., & Midgley, C. (1991). Transitions during early adolescence: Changes in children's domain-specific self-perceptions and general self-esteem across the transition to junior high school. *Developmental Psychology, 27,* 552–565.

Wilcox, A. J., Baird, D. D., Weinberg, C. R., Hornsby, P. P., & Herbst, A. L. (1995). Fertility in men exposed prenatally to diethylstilbestrol. *New England Journal of Medicine, 332,* 1411–4116.

Wilcox, A. J., Weinberg, C. R., O'Connor, J. F., Baird, D. D., Schlatterer, J. P., Canfield, R. E., Armstrong, E. G., & Nisula, B. C. (1988). Incidence of early loss of pregnancy. *New England Journal of Medicine, 319,* 189–194.

Willett, W. C., Hunter, D. J., Stampfer, M. J., Colditz, G., Manson, J. E., Spiegelman, D., Rosner, B., Hennekens, C. H., & Speizer, F. E. (1992). Dietary fat and fiber in relation to risk of breast cancer: An 8-year follow-up. *Journal of the American Medical Association, 268,* 2037–2044.

Willett, W. C., Manson, J. E., Stampfer, M. J., Colditz, G. A., Rosner, B., Speizer, F. E., & Hennekens, C. H. (1995). Weight, weight change, and coronary heart disease in women: Risk within the "normal" weight range. *Journal of the American Medical Association, 273,* 461–465.

Williams, D. R. (1992). Social structure and the health behaviors of blacks. In K. W. Schaie, D. Blazer, & J. S. House (Eds.), *Aging, health behaviors, and health outcomes* (pp. 59–64). Hillsdale, NJ: Erlbaum.

Williams, J. E., & Best, D. L. (1990). *Measuring sex stereotypes: A multination study* (rev. ed.). Newbury Park, CA: Sage.

Willig, A. (1985). Meta-analysis of studies on bilingual education. *Review of Educational Research, 55,* 269–317.

Willis, S. L. (1996). Everyday problem solving. In J. E. Birren & K. W. Schaie (Eds.), *Handbook of the psychology of aging* (4th ed.) (pp. 287–307). San Diego, CA: Academic Press.

Willis, S. L., Jay, G. M., Diehl, M., & Marsiske, M. (1992). Longitudinal change and prediction of everyday task competence in the elderly. *Research on Aging, 14,* 68–91.

Willis, S. L., & Nesselroade, C. S. (1990). Long-term effects of fluid ability training in old–old age. *Developmental Psychology, 26,* 905–910.

Willits, F. K., & Crider, D. M. (1988). Health rating and life satisfaction in the later middle years. *Journals of Gerontology: Social Sciences, 43,* S172–176.

Wilson, M. R., & Filsinger, E. E. (1986). Religiosity and marital adjustment: Multidimensional interrelationships. *Journal of Marriage and the Family, 48,* 147–151.

Wilson, W. J. (1995). Jobless ghettos and the social outcome of youngsters. In P. Moen, G. H. Elder, Jr., & K. Lüscher (Eds.), *Examining lives in context: Perspectives on the ecology of human development* (pp. 527–543). Washington, DC: American Psychological Association.

Winfield, L. F. (1995). The knowledge base on resilience in African-American adolescents. In L. J. Crockett & A. C. Crouter (Eds.), *Pathways through adolescence* (pp. 87–118). Mahwah, NJ: Erlbaum.

Wink, P., & Helson, R. (1993). Personality change in women and their partners. *Journal of Personality and Social Psychology, 65,* 597–605.

Wolfson, C., Handfield-Jones, R., Glass, K. C., McClaran, J., & Keyserlingk, E. (1993). Adult children's perceptions of their responsibility to provide care for dependent elderly parents. *The Gerontologist, 33,* 315–323.

Wolinsky, F. D., Calahan, C. M., Fitzgerald, J. F., & Johnson, R. J. (1993). Changes in functional status and the risks of subsequent nursing home placement and death. *Journals of Gerontology: Social Sciences, 48,* S93–101.

Wolinsky, F. D., Stump, T. E., & Clark, D. (1995). Antecedents and consequences of physical activity and exercise among older adults. *The Gerontologist, 35,* 451–462.

Woodward, M., & Tunstall-Pedoe, H. (1995). Alcohol consumption, diet, coronary risk factors, and prevalent coronary heart disease in men and women in the Scottish heart health study. *Journal of Epidemiology and Community Health, 49,* 354–362.

The Working Group for the PEPI Trial (1995). Effects of estrogen or estrogen/progestin regimens on heart disease risk factors in postmenopausal women: The Postmenopausal Estrogen/Progestin Interventions (PEPI) Trial. *Journal of the American Medical Association, 273,* 199–208.

World Health Organization (1981). *Contemporary patterns of breast-feeding: Report on the WHO collaborative study on breast-feeding.* Geneva: Author.

World Health Organization (1994). Expanded Programme on Immunization, Global Advisory Group: Part 1. *Weekly Epidemiological Record, 69*(January 28), 21–28.

Worobey, J. L., & Angel, R. J. (1990). Functional capacity and living arrangements of unmarried elderly persons. *Journals of Gerontology: Social Sciences, 45,* S95–101.

Wortman, C. B., & Silver, R. C. (1989). The myths of coping with loss. *Journal of Consulting and Clinical Psychology, 57,* 349–357.

Wortman, C. B., & Silver, R. C. (1990). Successful mastery of bereavement and widowhood: A life course perspective. In P. B. Baltes & M. M. Baltes (Eds.), *Successful aging: Perspectives from the behavioral sciences* (pp. 225–264). New York: Cambridge University Press.

Wortman, C. B., & Silver, R. C. (1992). Reconsidering assumptions about coping with loss: An overview of current research. In L. Montada, S. Filipp, & M. J. Lerner (Eds.), *Life crises and experiences of loss in adulthood* (pp. 341–365). Hillsdale, NJ: Erlbaum.

Wortman, C. B., Silver, R. C., & Kessler, R. C. (1993). The meaning of loss and adjustment to bereavement. In M. S. Stroebe, W. Stroebe, & R. O. Hansson (Eds.), *Handbook of bereavement* (pp. 349–366). Cambridge, England: Cambridge University Press.

Wren, C. S. (1996). Marijuana use by youths rebounding after decline. *New York Times,* February 20, p. A12.

Wright, L. (1995). Double mystery. *The New Yorker,* August 7, pp. 45–62.

Zahn-Waxler, C., & Radke-Yarrow, M. (1982). The development of altruism: Alternative research strategies. In N. Eisenberg (Ed.), *The development of prosocial behavior* (pp. 109–138). New York: Academic Press.

Zahn-Waxler, C., Radke-Yarrow, M., Wagner, E., & Chapman, M. (1992). Development of concern for others. *Developmental Psychology, 28,* 126–136.

Zani, B. (1993). Dating and interpersonal relationships in adolescence. In S. Jackson & H. Rodrigues-Tomé (Eds.), *Adolescence and its social worlds* (pp. 95–119). Hove, England: Erlbaum.

Zaslow, M. J., & Hayes, C. D. (1986). Sex differences in children's responses to psychosocial stress: Toward a cross-context analysis. In M. E. Lamb, A. L. Brown, & B. Rogoff (Eds.), *Advances in developmental psychology* (Vol. 4) (pp. 285–338). Hillsdale, NJ: Erlbaum.

Zelazo, N. A., Zelazo, P. R., Cohen, K. M., & Zelazo, P. D. (1993). Specificity of practice effects on elementary neuromotor patterns. *Developmental Psychology, 29,* 686–691.

Zelinski, E. M., Gilewski, M. J., & Schaie, K. W. (1993). Individual differences in cross-sectional and 3-year longitudinal memory performance across the adult life span. *Psychology and Aging, 8,* 176–186.

Zigler, E., & Hall, N. W. (1989). Physical child abuse in America: Past, present, and future. In D. Cicchetti & V. Carlson (Eds.), *Child maltreatment* (pp. 38–75). Cambridge, England: Cambridge University Press.

Zigler, E., & Hodapp, R. M. (1991). Behavioral functioning in individuals with mental retardation. *Annual Review of Psychology, 42,* 29–50.

Zigler, E., & Styfco, S. J. (1993). Using research and theory to justify and inform Head Start expansion. *Social Policy Report, Society for Research in Child Development, VII*(2), 1–21.

Zill, N., & Nord, C. W. (1994). *Running in place: How American families are faring in a changing economy and an individualistic society.* Washington, DC: Child Trends.

Zimmer, Z., Hickey, T., & Searle, M. S. (1995). Activity participation and well-being among older people with arthritis. *The Gerontologist, 35,* 463–471.

Zimmerman, M. A., Salem, D. A., & Maton, K. I. (1995). Family structure and psychosocial correlates among urban African-American adolescent males. *Child Development, 66,* 1598–1613.

Zirkel, S., & Cantor, N. (1990). Personal construal of life tasks: Those who struggle for independence. *Journal of Personality and Social Psychology, 58,* 172–185.

Zoccolillo, M. (1993). Gender and the development of conduct disorder. *Development and Psychopathology, 5,* 65–78.

Credits

Photos

Unless otherwise acknowledged, all photographs are the property of Addison Wesley Educational Publishers, Inc. Page abbreviations are as follows: **(t)** = top; **(c)** = center; **(b)** = bottom; **(l)** = left; **(r)** = right.

Chapter 1: 1 Michael Manheim/PNI **3 (t)** Jim Whitmer **3 (c)** Jim Whitmer **3 (b)** R. Barrera/TexaStock **4 (t)** Laura Dwight/PNI **4 (b)** J. Coletti/StockBoston **5** Laura Dwight **12** Bob Daemmrich **15** M. Ferguson/PhotoEdit **22** Laura Dwight

Chapter 2: 26 T. Freeman/PhotoEdit **27** M. Ferguson/PhotoEdit **29** Laura Dwight **31** T. Freeman/PhotoEdit **35** Laura Dwight **40** Laura Dwight **42 (l)** Don Smetzer/TSW **42 (r)** Elizabeth Crews/Image Works **44** C. Wolinsky/Stock, Boston

Chapter 3: 51 D. Young-Wolff/PhotoEdit **52** Francis Leroy, Biocosmos/SPL/Photo Researchers **59 (l, r)** Petit Format/Nestle/SS/Photo Researchers **61** Jose Carrillo/PhotoEdit **67 (all)** Anne P. Streissguth, S. Landesman-Dwyer, J. C. Martin, and D. W. Smith (1980). Teratogenic effects of alcohol in humans and laboratory animals. *Science,* 209, 353–361 **75 (l)** S.I.U./Peter Arnold, Inc. **75 (r)** S. van Rees/Petit Format/Photo Researchers **76** D. Young-Wolff/PhotoEdit **77** Stock, Boston

Chapter 4: 83 Bob Daemmrich/The Image Works **85 (t)** Elizabeth Crews/The Image Works **85 (b)** Amy Etra/PhotoEdit **93** Laura Dwight **96 (t, l)** Laura Dwight/PhotoEdit **96 (t, r)** Laura Dwight **96 (b, r)** Laura Dwight **97** Laura Dwight

Chapter 5: 103 Laura Dwight **105** Laura Dwight **108** Laura Dwight **109** From Carolyn Rovee-Collier, *Current Directions in Psychological Science,* 2(4), 130–135. 1993 **110** Laura Dwight **113** Laura Dwight **115 (l, r)** Goodman/Monkmeyer **118** T. M. Field, Social perception and responsivity in early infancy. In T. M. Field, A. Huston, H. C. Quay, L. Troll and G. E. Finley (Eds.), *Review of Human Development.* Copyright 1982 by John Wiley & Sons, NY, p. 26. **121** Laura Dwight **124** Laura Dwight

Chapter 6: 127 Laura Dwight **128** Laura Dwight **129** Laura Dwight **130** J. Myers/Stock, Boston **133** Laura Dwight **139** Paul Conklin **142** Laura Dwight **144** M. Ferguson/PhotoEdit **150** D. Young-Wolff/PhotoEdit

Interlude 1: 155 Patrick Donehue/PNI **156** Laura Dwight **157** S. Arms/The Image Works

Chapter 7: 159 M. Ferguson/PNI **161** T. Freeman/PhotoEdit **162** Laura Dwight **166** Roy Kirby/Stock, Boston **167** M. Vintoniv/Stock, Boston **173 (l)** Laura Dwight **173 (r)** Laura Dwight/PhotoEdit **174 (l)** Sam Falk/New York Times Pictures **174 (r)** Laura Dwight **180** Bob Daemmrich **183** Bob Daemmrich

Chapter 8: 188 Laura Dwight **189** D. Young-Wolff/PhotoEdit **190** M. Rogers/Stock, Boston **194** Laura Dwight **198** Laura Dwight **200** Elizabeth Crews **201** Laura Dwight **203** Laura Dwight **209** Gilles Peress/Magnum

Interlude 2: 213 M. Ferguson/PhotoEdit/PNI **214** Laura Dwight

Chapter 9: 216 Bob Daemmrich **217 (t)** Paul Conklin **217 (b)** R. Frerck/Tony Stone Images **218** MK Denny/PhotoEdit **224** M. Newman/PhotoEdit **227** Tony Freeman/PhotoEdit **228** Tony Freeman/PhotoEdit **235** Bob Daemmrich/Stock, Boston **238** Bob Daemmrich **239** Stephen Shames/Matrix

Chapter 10: 243 Tony Freeman/PhotoEdit **245** Tony Freeman/PhotoEdit **249** D. Young-Wolff/PhotoEdit **251** Tony Freeman/PhotoEdit **252** Kim Robbie/Stock Market **255** Bob Daemmrich/Image Works **259** George Malave/Stock, Boston **261** Tony Freeman/PhotoEdit

Interlude 3: 266 Elizabeth Crews **267** Bob Daemmrich/Image Works **268** Bob Daemmrich/Image Works

Chapter 11: 269 Bill Aron/PhotoEdit **271** Daniel Laine/Actuel **274** Tanner, 1962 **276** Bob Daemmrich/Image Works **280** Gale Zucker/Stock, Boston **281** M. Newmann/PhotoEdit **283** Wm. Thompson/Picture Cube **286** Catalyst **291** J. C. Francolon/Gamma-Liaison **296** B. E. Barnes/Stock, Boston

Chapter 12: 300 M. Newman/PhotoEdit **303** M. Newman/PhotoEdit **308** B. E. Barnes/Stock, Boston **311** Phil Borden/PhotoEdit **313 (t)** Bob Daemmrich **313 (b)** Laura Dwight **317** Don Smetzer/Tony Stone Images **320** J. P. Laffont/Sygma **324** Cameramann International, Ltd.

Interlude 4: 328 Bill Aron/PhotoEdit **329** Laura Dwight **330** Bob Daemmrich/Image Works

Chapter 13: 333 Courtesy Helen Bee **334** Robert Brenner/PhotoEdit **337** J. Moore/Image Works **341** Tom Levy/PNI **348** C. Gupton/Tony Stone Images

Chapter 14: 358 Dan Bosler/Tony Stone Images **359** Tony Freeman/PhotoEdit **361** Myrleen Ferguson/PhotoEdit **371** King Features **373** Myrleen Ferguson/PhotoEdit **375** Yoav/PNI **377** D. Young-Wolff/PhotoEdit

Interlude 5: 389 Madeline Oton-Tarpey **391** Myrleen Ferguson/PhotoEdit

Chapter 15: 393 Myrleen Cate/PhotoEdit **400** Bob Daemmrich **401** Tony Freeman/PhotoEdit **408** Robert Brenner/PhotoEdit **411** Elizabeth Crews **412** Photoreporters, Inc. **415** Bob Daemmrich

Chapter 16: 417 Chad Ehlers/Tony Stone Images **422** Tony Freeman/PhotoEdit **423** SuperStock **425** Laura Dwight **428** Robert Brenner/PhotoEdit **433** Dana White/PhotoEdit **441** Ft. Worth Star Telegram/Joyce Marshall/Sipa Press

Interlude 6: 446 Tony Stone Images **447** SuperStock

Chapter 17: 449 Bob Daemmrich **450** Elizabeth Zuckerman/PhotoEdit **452** John Coletti/Tony Stone Images **453 (l, r)** Scheibel, 1992, Fig. 5, p. 160; in J. E. Birren, R. B. Sloane, and G. D. Cohen(Eds.), *Handbook of Mental Health and Aging,* 2nd ed., Academic Press, San Diego, CA, pp.147–174. Used with permission. **455** M. Richards/PhotoEdit **466** Alan Oddie/PhotoEdit **468** MK Denny/PhotoEdit **470** Bob Daemmrich **473** Bob Daemmrich **476 (l)** Suzanne Murphy **476 (r)** AP/The Intelligencer-Journal, Joan Decker

Chapter 18: 481 Bill Aron/PhotoEdit **486** Paul Boyer **487** Rhoda Sidney/PhotoEdit **492 (t)** Andras Dancs/Tony Stone Images **492 (b)** Owen Franken/PNI **495 (l, r)** Jamie Cope **499** Alan Oddie/PhotoEdit **503** Judy Canty/Stock, Boston

Interlude 7: 509 (l) Merritt Vincent/PhotoEdit **509 (r)** Frank Fournier

Chapter 19: 511 Tony Freeman/PhotoEdit **512** M. C. Walker/Picture Cube **513** H. Armstrong Roberts **518** Peter Southwick/PNI **525** William Thompson/Picture Cube **527** Alexandra Boulet/Sipa Press **532** Robert Brenner/PhotoEdit

Extracts, Figures, and Tables

Chapter 1: 5 Figure 1.1: From "As Time Goes By: Change and Stability in Personality over Fifty Years," by N. Haan, R. Millsap, and E. Hartka, from *Psychology and Aging,* 1, pp. 220–232. Copyright © 1986 by the American Psychological Association. Reprinted by permission. **14** Figure 1.3: From "A Developmental Perspective on Antisocial Behavior," by G. R. Patterson, B. D. DeBarshyshe, and E. Ramsey, in *American Psychologist,* 44. Copyright © 1989 by the American Psychological Association. Reprinted by permission.

Chapter 2: 46 Figure 2.2: From *The Seasons of a Man's Life* by Daniel J. Levinson et al. Copyright © 1978 by Daniel J. Levinson. Reprinted by permission of Alfred A. Knopf, Inc.

Chapter 5: 116 Figure 5.4: From *The Epigenesis of Mind* by Carey and Gelman. Reprinted by permission of Lawrence Erlbaum Associates, Inc., and the author. **119** Figure 5.6: Adaptation of Figure 2, "Listening to Speech in the First Year of Life: Experimental Influences on Phoneme Perception," by J. F. Werker and Renee N. Desjardins, in *Current Directions in Psychological Science,* Vol. 4, No. 3, 1995. Reprinted with the permission of Cambridge University Press.

Chapter 7: 182 Table 7.3: From "Assessment of Effects of Socio-Economic Status on IQ in a Full Cross-Fostering Study," by C. Capron and M. Duyme, in *Nature,* 340, pp. 552–554. Copyright © 1989. Reprinted by permission of Macmillan Magazines Limited and Laboratoire Genetique. **184** Figure 7.3: From *Educating All Students in the Mainstream of Regular Education* by James J. Gallagher and Craig T. Ramey. Reprinted by permission of Paul H. Brookes Publishing Co. and Craig T. Ramey.

Chapter 8: 207 From *Journal of Research on Adolescence.* Reprinted by permission of Lawrence Erlbaum Associates, Inc., and the author.

Chapter 9: 226 Figure 9.3: From "Memory Span: Sources of Individual and Development Differences," by F. N. Dempster, in *Psychological Bulletin,* 89, pp. 63–100. Copyright © 1981 by American Psychological Association. Reprinted by permission of American Psychological Association and F. N. Dempster. **240** Figure 9.5: From *Sex Differences in Cognitive Abilities,* 2nd edition, by D. F. Halpern. Reprinted by permission of Lawrence Erlbaum Associates, Inc., and the author.

Chapter 10: 263 Figure 10.5: From "The Development of Aggressive Behavior from the Perspective of a Developing Behaviorism," by L. D. Eron, in *American Psychologist,* 42, pp. 435–442. Copyright © 1987 by the American Psychological Association. Reprinted by permission of the American Psychological Association and L. D. Eron.

Chapter 12: 309 Figure 12.3: From "Convoys of Social Support and Early Adolescence: Structure and Function," by M. J. Levitt et al., in *Developmental Psychology,* 29, pp. 811–818. Copyright © 1993 by the American Psychological Association. Reprinted with permission. **316** Table 12.4: Adapted from *Child Development* by O. P. John et al., pp. 161 and 167, 1994. Reprinted by permission of Society for Research in Child Development. **317** Figure 12.4: Adapted from *Child Development* by O. P. John et al., pp. 161 and 167, 1994. Reprinted by permission of Society for Research in Child Development. **323** Figure 12.5: From "Adolescent Development: Pathways and Processes of Risk and Resilience," by B. E. Compas et al. Reproduced, with permission, from *Annual Review of Psychology,* Volume 46, © 1995 by Annual Reviews, Inc. **325** Figure 12.6: From "Negative Correlates of Part-Time Employment During Adolescence: Replication and Elaboration," by L. Steinberg and S. M. Dornbusch, in *Developmental Psychology,* 27, pp. 304–313. Copyright © 1991 by the American Psychological Association. Reprinted by permission of the American Psychological Association and Laurence Steinberg.

Chapter 13: 335 Table 13.4: Adapted with the permission of The Free Press, a division of Simon & Schuster and Tavistock Publications, from *Social Origins of Depression* by George W. Brown and Tirrill Harris. Copyright © 1978 by George W. Brown and Tirrill Harris. **351** Figure 13.6: From *Health and Ways of Living: The Alameda County Study* by Lisa Berkman and Lester Breslow. Copyright © 1983 by Lisa Berkman and Lester Breslow. Used by permission of Oxford University Press, Inc.

Chapter 14: 362 Table 14.1: From "Romantic Love Conceptualized as an Attachment Process," by C. Hazan and P. Shaver, in *Journal of Personality and Social Psychology,* 52, pp. 511–524. Copyright © 1987 by the American Psychological Association. Reprinted by permission of the American Psychological Association and the author. **372** Figure 14.3: From "Marital Satisfaction over the Family Life Cycle," by Boyd C. Rollins and Harold Feldman, in *Journal of Marriage and the Family,* 32:1, pp. 20–28. Copyright by the National Council on Family Relations, 3989 Central Avenue NE, Suite 550, Minneapolis, MN 55421. Reprinted by permission. **376** Figure 14.4: From Figure 3.1, p. 80, in *Career Mobility in a Corporate Hierarchy* by J. E. Rosenbaum. Reprinted by permission of Academic Press, Inc., and the author. **380** Figure 14.5: From "The Family Life Cycle and Spouses' Time in Housework," by Cynthia Rexroat and Constance Shehan, in *Journal of Marriage and the Family,* 49:4, pp. 737–750. Copyright by the National Council on Family Relations, 3989 Central Avenue NE, Suite 550, Minneapolis, MN 55421. Reprinted by permission. **385** Figure 14.7: From "Reconceptualizing Marital Status as a Continuum of Social Attachment," by Catherine E. Ross, in *Journal of Marriage and the Family,* 57:1, pp. 129–140, 1995. Copyright © 1995 by the National Council on Family Relations, 3989 Central Avenue NE, Suite 550, Minneapolis, MN 55421. Reprinted by permission.

Chapter 15: 396 Figure 15.2: From "Impotence and Its Medical Psychosocial Correlates: Results of the Massachusetts Male Aging Study," by H. A. Feldman et al., in *Journal of Urology,* 151, pp. 54–61, 1994. Reprinted by permission of Williams & Wilkins. 399 Table 15.1: From *Sex in America* by Robert T. Michael et al. Copyright © 1994 by CSG Enterprises, Inc., Edward O. Laumann, Robert T. Michael, and Gina Kolata. By permission of Little, Brown and Company. **400** Figure 15.3: From "Osteoporosis: Boning Up on Genes," by G. R. Mundy, in *Nature* magazine, 367, pp. 216–217. Copyright © 1994. Reprinted by permission of Macmillan Magazines Limited and the author. **407** From "Dairy Fat, Saturated Animal Fat, and Cancer Risk," by H. Kesteloot et al., from *Preventive Medicine,* 20, pp. 226–236, Figure 1, p. 229. Reprinted by permission of Academic Press, Inc., and the author. **409** Figure 15.4: From "Adult Life Span Changes in Immediate Visual Memory and Verbal Intelligence," by L. M. Giambra et al., in *Psychology and Aging,* 10, pp. 123–139. Copyright © 1995 by the American Psychological Association. Adapted with permission.

Chapter 16: 420 Figure 16.2: From "Stages of Family Life Cycle, Ego Development, and the Marriage Relationship," by Clifford H. Swensen et al., in *Journal of Marriage and the Family,* 43:4, pp. 841–853. Copyright by the National Council on Family Relations, 3989 Central Avenue NE, Suite 550, Minneapolis, MN 55421. Reprinted by permission. **429** Figure 16.5: From "Convoys of Social Support: An Intergenerational Analysis," by M. J. Levitt et al., in *Psychology and Aging,* 8, pp. 323–326. Copyright © 1993 by the American Psychological Association. Adapted with permission. **434** Figure 16.7: From "The Aging Self: Stabilizing and Protective Processes," by J. Brandstadter and W. Greve, in *Developmental Review,* 14, pp. 52–82, 1994. Reprinted by permission of Academic Press, Inc., and the author. **438** Figure 16.8: From Figure 12.8 in *The Journey of Adulthood,* 3rd edition, by Helen Bee. Copyright © 1996. Reprinted by permission of Prentice-Hall, Inc.

Chapter 17: 450 Figure 17.1: From Figure 2.2, p. 26, of "Demography of Aging" by George C. Myers, in *Handbook of Aging and the Social Sciences,* 3rd edition, edited by R. H. Binstock and L. K. George. Reprinted by permission of Academic Press, Inc., and the author. **456** Figure 17.3: From "Smell Identification Ability: Changes with Age" by R. L. Doty, in *Science,* Volume 226, p. 1441. Copyright © 1994 American Association for the Advancement of Science. Reprinted by permission of AAAS and the author. **457** Table 17.3: Adapted from "Estimating the Prevalence of Long-Term Disability for an Aging Society," by S. R. Kunkel and R. A. Applebaum, in *Journal of Gerontology: Social Sciences,* 47, pp. S253–S260, 1992. Reprinted by permission of the Gerontological Society of America. **457** Figure 17.4: From "Physical Disabilities in Older Americans," by J. M. Guralnik et al., in *Journal of Gerontology,* 48 (special issue), pp. 3–10, 1993. Reprinted by permission of the Gerontological Society of America. **462** Figure 17.6: From "The Relationship Between Age and Depressive Symptoms in Two National Surveys," by R. C. Kessler et al., in *Psychology and Aging,* 7, pp. 119–126. Copyright © 1992 by the American Psychological Association. Adapted with permission. **465** Figure 17.7: From E. Palmore, *Social Patterns in Normal Aging: Findings from a Duke Longitudinal Study,* Fig. 6.3, p. 87. Copyright 1981, Duke University Press. Reprinted with permission. **472** Figure 17.8: From "On the Locus and Process of Magnification of Age Differences During Mnemonic Training," by R. Kliegl, J. Smith, and P. B. Baltes, in *Developmental Psychology,* 26, pp. 894–904. Copyright © 1990 by the American Psychological Association. Reprinted by permission of the American Psychological Association and Reinhold Kliegl. **477** Figure 17.10: From "After Reaching Retirement Age Physical Activity Sustains Cerebral Perfusion and Cognition," by Robert L. Rogers, Ph.D., John S. Meyer, M.D., and Karl F. Mortel, Ph.D., in *Journal of the American Geriatric Society,* 38, pp. 123–128, 1990. Reprinted with permission of the American Geriatric Society.

Chapter 18: 485 Excerpt from "Moving On," by Susan Kushner Resnick, in *New York Times,* March 8, 1992. Copyright © 1992 by the New York Times Co. Reprinted by permission. **494** Figure 18.3: From *Age and Structural Lag* by M. W. Riley et al. Copyright © 1994. Reprinted by permission of John Wiley & Sons, Inc.

Chapter 19: 516 Figure 19.1: From *The Course of Later Life* by Bengtson & Schaie. Copyright 1989. Used by permission of Springer Publishing Company, Inc., New York 10012. **522** Table 19.2: Adaptation of Table 1, "Psychological Response to Cancer and Survival," by S. Greer, in *Psychological Medicine,* Vol. 21, 1991. Reprinted with the permission of Cambridge University Press. **533** Figure 19.3: From "Attachment Theory and Multiple Dimensions of Grief," by Selby C. Jacobs, M.D., et al., in *Omega, Journal of Death and Dying,* Vol. 18(1), Figure 1, p. 43. Reprinted by permission of Baywood Publishing Company, Inc., and the author.

Author Index

Note: Italicized page numbers indicate citations in tables and figures.

Subject Index

Note: Italicized page numbers indicate material in tables and figures.